Finding Lost Time and Getting Your Stride Back

The black hole of time—we've all encountered it. You don't know where the day went, you're not sure where the week disappeared to, and you don't have the slightest clue why you didn't get that project completed.

For several days or even a week, jot down what you're doing. You can focus on only the work portion of your day or you can track your personal time too. Use a piece of paper, a calendar, or any word processor, just make sure you're logging your activities. Include the things you do as you do them, and don't leave out things like opening e-mail or gossiping with co-workers. Each time you change activities, drop in an entry and note the time. It might even be a plus to note what your energy level is at various times throughout the day.

Analyze the log. How long have you spent on various tasks? You might be surprised at the results for how often you open and respond to e-mail or deal with interruptions. Now take a look at your energy log. Are there portions of the day where you consistently feel most energetic?

Your activity log can help prove that your time really isn't disappearing into the black hole—and it can help you to take a look at how you might be able to restructure your tasks and activities to work in tandem with your peak energy level. You could find that the time you thought was pulling a disappearing act is simply a low-energy time when you've chosen to wander the halls as a solution.

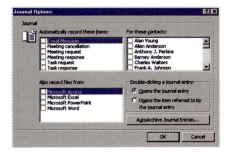

Electronically Track Your Activities

Outlook Journal can help you keep track of your activities. It can automatically record such things as e-mail messages you send and receive, and meeting or task requests. The Journal can even keep track of each time you work with an Office document. You also can use the Journal to manually record activities you want to track.

Stop Losing Notes

Do you find yourself fumbling through piles of notes? Are you constantly losing notes because the stickiness has long-since dried up? Save yourself the headache and lost time…just create an electronic note! Use Outlook Notes to jot down reminders and phone numbers.

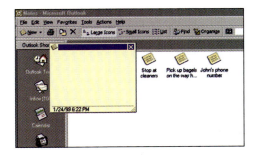

GETTING IN CONTROL

Creating a To-Do List to Live By

Short- and long-term plans are inherent to human nature. We account for the things we want or need to do. To-do lists are dynamic, changing and re-creating themselves as your day-to-day tasks come and go. But what about your long-term goals, do you add page after page to your list to include them? Of course! It's the best way to help them become a reality! Often, you'll find that as you complete your daily tasks, you might uncover a skill or solution that takes you one step closer to achieving a long-term goal.

The Long and Short of Tasks

Anyone who has had more than a few things to keep track of has made a list, crossed things off, and rewritten the list again and again. Outlook Tasks help you reign in your to-do's and keep an eye on your long-term plans—all without having to rewrite a thing.

List everything you need, plan, or hope to do. Assign priorities to your tasks—are they high, medium, low—and assign dates to as many as you can. Don't worry about limiting the tasks you include for fear your list will be too long. Outlook lets you choose how much information you want your list to display about your tasks at hand. And, when you feel like you're getting nowhere, you can view the Completed Tasks list to see that you actually have accomplished something!

Mistakes People Make with their Time

- Giving others access to your time too frequently.
- Spending time on things that aren't really a priority.
- Permitting too many interruptions.
- Refusing to ask for help.
- Underestimating the amount of time tasks or activities consume.

Staying on Task

OK, now you have your to-do list. Are there things on it that you really could delegate to others and allow yourself to stay focused on the important things? With Outlook, you can delegate a task to someone else—electronically ask them if you're connected through e-mail, or, if you aren't connected, manually note who is responsible in the task details.

A plus to being connected through e-mail with others is that when you offer a task to someone, you can request a report when the task is complete. Then, if the person accepts the task, an automatic report is sent to you when that person marks the task as complete. Yet another way to save yourself some time!

Managing Your Time

Time is a crucial commodity—there's a finite quantity to divide between your professional and personal life. Far too often, time spent on family, friends, or relaxation suffers the consequences of our increasingly busy lives. When it feels like you're running around in circles trying to please everyone, you need to take a timeout!

Using a calendar to organize your meetings, appointments, and tasks gives you a definite advantage. Staying on top of your day and your tasks is what will help you find time for yourself.

Using Outlook Calendar

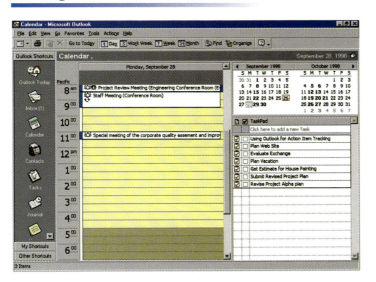

The Outlook Calendar deals with three principal types of activities: appointments, meetings, and events. Any of these activities can be one-time or recurring—don't worry, Calendar tracks them both and can even give you reminders 5 minutes to two days ahead of time.

Tasks are strongly related to your calendar, but Outlook deals with them separately. This is because tasks usually, but not necessarily, have a start date and a due date; they aren't associated with specific times on specific days. But when they are, Calendar helps you to keep track of them.

When you use Outlook in a corporate setting, you often have the ability to schedule people and resources, as do others when you share your own calendar, making meeting planning a much easier chore.

Time Management Tickler

Do you want to eliminate that clutter you call an in-box? Setting up a tickler file can help you keep your in-box under control and allow you to focus on your tasks when they are a priority. File folders or an accordion envelope arranged by numbers one through 31 will allow you to file your paperwork on the day when you need to take action. You can also use this same method when organizing electronic files.

It's a Small World After All

With the advances we've seen in technology, the world's getting even smaller. One commonly held belief is that we are all connected to one another—the six degrees of separation theory. Between everyone that I know, and everyone that they know, and so on for six rings worth of people, I am connected to you (give or take a few rings of people). With newsgroups, online communities, and online chat, people who once might never have met are finding themselves connected to various parts of the world. In recent times, Rolodexes and stacks of business cards were the norm. Today, all sorts of electronic gadgets are available to help you track who you know and what you know about them.

Getting Your Ducks in a Row with Outlook Contacts

We've been told, "It's all in who you know." Let Outlook Contacts help you keep track of exactly who it is that you know and what you want to remember about them.

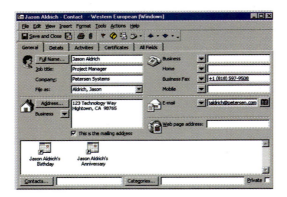

Entering your contacts in Outlook gives you a number of advantages. Contacts is the hub when it comes to Outlook—it gets used for things like addressing e-mail messages, addressing conventional mail, placing phone calls, sending faxes, arranging meetings, and assigning tasks. It towers above that little black book of yours, doesn't it?

Business Cards Hit a New Level

vCards are electronic business cards that use an industry-standard format recognized by Outlook and by several other e-mail clients. You can save information about the author of incoming messages directly to a vCard.

Automating Mailings

When you use Outlook Contacts to house all of your addresses, you can export data files. These files can be used with word processing software to perform mail merges.

How to End Your Workday Feeling Better

- Work on only one task at a time.
- Tackle your daily issues in descending order of importance.
- Avoid putting anything new on the day's to-do list late in the day.
- Take breaks throughout the day, even if only for a few minutes.
- Give yourself credit for what you achieved during the day.

Communicating with Your World

Moving at a snail's pace is a thing of the past. Today we can communicate with someone on the other side of the world in mere seconds. E-mail and the Internet have become a much-improved version of the Pony Express. You can send mail, files, pictures, sound clips—keep your colleagues or family apprised of your every move if you so desire.

Making the Most of Your E-mail World

Electronic communications can be great, when they don't bury you alive! Don't worry, Outlook can help.

Follow the Rules

Guess what…You get to choose the rules for once! A rule in this case is a set of conditions, actions, and exceptions that controls how Outlook processes and organizes messages. Some rules work on messages you receive; other rules work on messages you send.

For example, you can create a rule that forwards all messages you receive from a specific person to someone else. Or, you can create a rule that moves messages you receive from a specific person into a certain folder.

To create basic rules, choose Organize in the Inbox Information viewer's toolbar. To create more sophisticated rules, use Outlook's Rules Wizard to do things like perform an action when a message arrives, automatically delete messages that satisfy certain conditions, or notify you when recipients read certain messages.

Filtering Out the Junk

If you use Outlook to receive Internet e-mail, you probably receive a lot of junk mail that you'd rather not have to bother with. Outlook contains a built-in filter you can turn on to ignore messages containing certain words and phrases in the subject or body. If you don't turn the filter on, messages containing these words and phrases are handled normally.

You can determine how you want Outlook to handle junk mail. Maybe you want it to color or move the mail to a specific folder. It's as easy as making selections from a drop-down list. You should change the color of junk mail for a few days, then you'll see which type of messages Outlook detects. After that, if you're satisfied, you might prefer to have Outlook automatically send junk mail to a Junk E-mail folder that Outlook empties as trash.

Collecting Votes

Have you worked on a project where you needed a group of people to vote on something? Now Outlook can help you automate it. When you receive responses to a message containing voting buttons, those responses appear as usual in your Inbox Information viewer. The message header contains the name of the respondent in the From column and the name of the voting button he or she selected in the Subject column. With what you learned about rules, you can have these responses automatically collected in a folder of its own—and Outlook can even tally the responses.

Saving Time with Keyboard Shortcuts

While Outlook is menu-driven, there are a number of keyboard shortcuts you can also use.

E-mail Shortcuts

New mail message	Ctrl+N
Go to Inbox	Ctrl+Shift+I
Go to Outbox	Ctrl+Shift+O
Reply to mail message	Ctrl+R
Reply all to mail message	Ctrl+Shift+R
Mark as read	Ctrl+Q
Flag for follow-up	Ctrl+Shift+G

Calendar Shortcuts

New appointment	Ctrl+Shift+A
New meeting request	Ctrl+Shift+Q
New task	Ctrl+Shift+K
New task request	Ctrl+Shift+U
View 1 day	Alt+1
View 2 days through 9 days	Alt+*key for number of days*
View 10 days	Alt+0
Switch to weeks view	Alt+HYPHEN SIGN
Switch to month view	Alt+EQUAL SIGN

Contact Shortcuts

New contact	Ctrl+Shift+C
New distribution list	Ctrl+Shift+L
Display Address Book	Ctrl+Shift+B

Other Shortcuts

New folder	Ctrl+Shift+E
Microsoft Outlook Help	F1
Display ScreenTip for active item	Shift+F1
Move between Calendar, TaskPad, and Folder List	Ctrl+TAB or F6
New journal entry	Ctrl+Shift+J
New note	Ctrl+Shift+N
New Office document	Ctrl+Shift+H
Go to folder	Ctrl+Y
Synchronize all folders	F9
Advanced Find	Ctrl+Shift+F
Macros	Alt+F8
Visual Basic Editor	Alt+F11
Cancel current operation	ESC
Turn on editing in a field	F2
Switch case (with text selected)	Shift+F3
Save	Ctrl+S or Shift+F12
Close selected Outlook window	Shift+F4

64.27

Special Edition
Using
Microsoft®
Outlook®
2000

Written by Gordon Padwick

with Helen Feddema

A Division of Macmillan Computer Publishing, USA
201 W. 103rd Street
Indianapolis, Indiana 46290

CONTENTS AT A GLANCE

SPECIAL EDITION USING MICROSOFT® OUTLOOK® 2000

International Standard Book Number: 0-7897-1909-6

Library of Congress Catalog Card Number: 98-87795

Printed in the United States of America

First Printing: May 1999

01 00 99 4 3 2 1

TRADEMARKS

WARNING AND DISCLAIMER

Executive Editor
Mark Taber

Acquisitions Editor
Randi Roger

Development Editors
Laura Bulcher
Fran Hatton

Technical Editors
Diane Poremsky
Ken Slovak

Managing Editor
Lisa Wilson

Project Editor
Rebecca Mounts

Copy Editor
Howard Jones

Indexer
Heather Goens

Proofreaders
Benjamin Berg
Kim Cofer

Software Development Specialist
Todd Pfeffer

Interior Design
Ruth Harvey

Cover Design
Dan Armstrong
Ruth Harvey

Layout Technicians
Brandon Allen
Stacey DeRome
Heather Miller
Timothy Osborn
Staci Somers

TABLE OF CONTENTS

ABOUT THE AUTHORS

Gordon Padwick is a consultant who specializes in Microsoft Office applications and Visual Basic. In addition to training and supporting Office users, Gordon develops custom applications based on the Office suite. He has been working with computers for more years than he cares to remember in engineering, management, support, and marketing positions, and has been using Windows since Microsoft introduced the first version some twelve years ago.

Gordon has authored and contributed to many books about Windows and other PC-based applications, including *Special Edition Using Microsoft Office 97 Professional*, *Microsoft Office 97 User Manual*, *Special Edition Using Microsoft Outlook 97*, *Building Integrated Office Applications*, *Using Microsoft Outlook 98*, *Platinum Edition Using Microsoft Office 97*, and *Platinum Edition Using Microsoft Office 2000*.

He is a graduate of London University, has completed postgraduate studies in computer science and communications, and is a Senior Member of the Institute of Electrical and Electronics Engineers. Gordon currently lives in southern California.

Helen Feddema has a B.S. in philosophy from Columbia and an M.T.S. in theological studies from Harvard Divinity School. She was an Access 1.0 beta tester and has worked as a developer of Microsoft Office applications, concentrating on Access, Word, and Outlook.

Helen has been a co-author of or contributor to more than ten books since 1992 including Que's *Special Edition Using Microsoft Outlook 97* and *Special Edition Using Microsoft Project 98*. She also has been a regular contributor to Pinnacle's *Smart Access* and *Office Developer* journals, *Woody's Underground Office* newsletter, *PC Magazine's Undocumented Office* and the *MS Office and VBA Journal*. As well, Helen recently contributed articles to *Smart Access*, and *Woody's Office Watch* e-zine.

She is an MVP on the WOPR Lounge, a threaded discussion group devoted to Microsoft Office. And, Helen's Web page (www.ulster.net/~hfeddema) features a large selection of code samples concentrated on connecting Access, Outlook, Word, and Excel. She lives in the mid-Hudson area of New York state, with three cats and three computers.

About the Technical Editors

Diane Poremsky is a computer consultant specializing in Outlook, Office, FrontPage, and Windows 98 training and troubleshooting. She also designs custom applications for Word and Excel using VBA. Diane has been using and programming computers for nearly 20 years. She is currently living in East Tennessee with her husband and their five teenagers.

Ken Slovak is a consultant who specializes in Outlook, programming, and instrumentation systems engineering. He is a Microsoft Outlook MVP (Most Valuable Professional), a designation conferred on him by Microsoft in recognition of his support work for Outlook.

Prior to becoming a consultant, Ken was chief engineer for an industrial instrumentation manufacturing company and has been working with computers for more than 20 years. He has designed numerous instrumentation systems and developed applications and embedded system software in many computer languages, including C, assembly languages, Basic, Visual Basic, Access, and FoxPro. He has written many technical and operating manuals and has also developed technical and sales literature for numerous computerized systems. Ken currently resides in central Florida.

DEDICATION

To Kathy, my wife, inspiration, and best friend.—Gordon Padwick

ACKNOWLEDGMENTS

from Gordon Padwick

Writing the acknowledgments page for a new book is one of my favorite tasks—for two reasons. It's the last thing to be written for the book, so I can heave a huge sigh of relief that the project is almost complete. Also, it's my opportunity to look back over the last few months and gratefully remember the many people who have willingly helped me write the book.

My special thanks go to co-author **Helen Feddema** for writing the five chapters about developing Outlook-based applications. Many readers will recognize Helen's name as that of the Microsoft Access expert who also contributed to my first Outlook book. If you intend to use Outlook as a development environment, you couldn't have a more knowledgeable person than Helen to guide you.

My thanks also go to **Vince Averello**, a name you'll instantly recognize if you frequent Internet newsgroups that discuss Microsoft Office. When I had run out of time to complete this book, Vince willingly jumped in at the last minute to complete the appendixes.

Readers of this book owe a big vote of thanks to the two technical editors, **Diane Poremsky** and **Ken Slovak**. They carefully checked and corrected everything I'd written and made many detailed suggestions for additional material. I offer my personal thanks to Diane and Ken; I prefer to think of them as technical advisors, rather than as technical editors.

I also offer my thanks to many people at Microsoft: To the people who conceived and developed Outlook, and to others who've answered my many questions.

Thank you, **Jill Byus**, Acquisitions Editor, for originally inviting me to work on this book. Special thanks to **Randi Roger** who took over from Jill as the Acquisitions Editor while I was writing this book. Randi's other name, from an author's perspective, is "guardian angel."

Fran Hatton and **Laura Bulcher**, two more of my guardian angels, have made major contributions to this book as Development Editors. Thank you, Fran and Laura, for helping me organize and clarify the book.

My thanks also go to the many people in Macmillan Computer Publishing, whose names I don't know, who have performed the miracle of converting my original text into a book in an amazingly short period of time.

The many illustrations of what you can expect to see on your screen were captured with Collage Complete. Thank you, **Nancy** and **Neil Rosenburg** of Inner Media, for providing Collage Complete—it has to be the most bug-free and user-friendly application I've ever worked with.

As always, I want to acknowledge my gratitude to my wife, **Kathy**, for her support and patience while I've been writing this book. She's been willing to put up with me spending most my evenings and weekends pounding away at my computer. Her encouragement has made it possible for me to write this book.

TELL US WHAT YOU THINK!

As the reader of this book, *you* are our most important critic and commentator. We value your opinion and want to know what we're doing right, what we could do better, what areas you'd like to see us publish in, and any other words of wisdom you're willing to pass our way.

You can fax, email, or write me directly to let me know what you did or didn't like about this book—as well as what we can do to make our books stronger.

Please note that I cannot help you with technical problems related to the topic of this book, and that due to the high volume of mail I receive, I might not be able to reply to every message.

When you write, please be sure to include this book's title and author as well as your name and phone or fax number. I will carefully review your comments and share them with the author and editors who worked on the book.

Fax: 317-581-4666

Email: office_que@mcp.com

Mail: John Pierce
           Publisher
           Que
           201 West 103rd Street
           Indianapolis, IN 46290 USA

INTRODUCTION

In this chapter

Outlook hit the scene a little over two years ago as a new component in Microsoft's Office 97 suite. At that time, Que asked me to write a couple of chapters about Outlook for the book *Special Edition Using Microsoft Office 97*. I soon realized that Outlook deserved a book of its own, so I proposed that project to Que. Out of that came my first Outlook book *Special Edition Using Microsoft Outlook 97*. Very soon after that book was published, Microsoft released Outlook 98, a much improved version of Outlook. So, I was back at the keyboard, pounding out *Using Microsoft Outlook 98*. Now, I'm back at it again, writing about Outlook 2000.

It has been my good fortune to work with Outlook since before Outlook 97 was released. I have seen Outlook develop from pre-birth (the early Outlook 97 betas) through childhood (released Outlook 97), adolescence (Outlook 98), and now into the beginning of maturity (Outlook 2000). This book is my attempt to provide a comprehensive, up-to-date account of Outlook 2000 so that you can take advantage of as much of what Outlook has to offer as helps you be productive.

UNDERSTANDING OUTLOOK'S SCOPE

It's not easy to write about Outlook because it can be different things to different people. For example, you can choose to use Outlook only as a Personal Information Manager (PIM)—it's one of the best available—to keep track of your calendar, contacts, and tasks. Microsoft calls this *No E-mail* Outlook.

Going a step beyond that, you can use Outlook to send and receive Internet e-mail. Don't be misled by Microsoft's term *Internet Mail Only (IMO)* to describe this type of Outlook installation; it can also be used as a PIM as well as to send and receive faxes, to access Web sites, and to participate in Internet newsgroups.

Then, there's what I like to think of as full-blown Outlook. Microsoft calls this *Corporate and Workgroup (C/W)* because, in addition PIM and IMO capabilities, you can use this Outlook installation within a corporation or workgroup to send and receive e-mail by way of such messaging systems as Microsoft Exchange Server, Microsoft Mail, Lotus cc:Mail, Lotus Notes, and more.

IMO and C/W Outlook both provide extensive information sharing and collaboration capabilities. IMO Outlook makes use of the Internet, or an intranet, for this purpose; C/W Outlook can also use the Internet or an intranet, but is at its most powerful when it acts as a client for Microsoft Exchange Server.

The earlier chapters of this book describe how you can use Outlook more or less as it comes out of the box, without any customization. However, you can customize Outlook in many ways to suit your specific needs and preferences. At a simple, interactive level, you can do such things as modifying menus and toolbars, and creating additional toolbars. At a slightly more advanced level, you can set up Outlook to be your primary desktop environment instead of the normal Windows desktop.

Developers can use Outlook's programmability to create specialized applications that employ Outlook's built-in capabilities and interact with other Office and Office-compatible applications. For example, if Outlook's ability to manage tasks doesn't do all that you need, you can integrate Outlook with Microsoft Team Manager so that team managers and members can plan and keep track of tasks on a project-wide basis.

If you're new to Outlook, you should initially learn how to use it without much customization. When you're comfortable with Outlook at that level, take the time to explore; learn how you can, quite easily in many cases, customize Outlook so that it exactly satisfies your needs. You can, for example, modify Outlook's forms (the screens you use to input and display Outlook information) into customized forms.

Microsoft and other organizations have developed many add-ins and add-ons for Outlook, some available at no charge, some available as shareware for a small amount, and some available as commercial applications. You might well find that some of these provide the extended Outlook capabilities you need, so you don't have to develop your own.

WHAT'S NEW IN OUTLOOK 2000

Let me start by saying what isn't new in Outlook 2000. Outlook 2000 uses the same formats for storing data as Outlook 97 or Outlook 98. If you've been using a previous version of Outlook, you can switch to Outlook 2000 without modifying data formats. In most cases, you can share data between people who are using the three Outlook versions.

The list of enhancements in Outlook 2000 is much too long to list in detail here, so I'll just highlight a few of them. Many of Outlook 2000's enhancements are shared with other applications in the Office 2000 suite.

One of the first enhancements you'll notice if you previously have been using Outlook 97 is Outlook Today—a window into your current mail, calendar, and tasks—that first appeared in Outlook 98. You can configure Outlook so that Outlook Today always appears when you start Outlook.

In general, you'll notice that Outlook 2000 starts and shuts down faster than the previous versions. Opening and closing individual screens is also faster.

Outlook 2000's menus and toolbars have been simplified. Many of the symbols in toolbars have been replaced by words, making them easier to identify.

The use of pop-up ScreenTips has been greatly extended to make it easier to understand what you're seeing.

Outlook 98 enhanced the support for Internet standards in Outlook 97. Outlook 2000 contains even more enhancements to this support.

In common with other Office 2000 applications, Outlook 2000 includes enhanced Web page support. You can, for example, publish your personal or team calendar as a Web page.

In Outlook 97 and 98, you had to use a Personal Address Book if you wanted to create distribution lists. In Outlook 2000, you can create distribution lists within your Contacts folder, using items in that folder.

Contact Activity Tracking is also new in Outlook 2000. This provides an easy way to keep track of activities of all kinds on a contact-by-contact basis.

The Outlook Bar in Outlook 2000 can contain shortcuts to any file, folder, or Web page. If you choose a shortcut to a Web page, Outlook displays that page in the Information viewer.

A significant enhancement in Outlook 2000 from a developer's perspective is compatibility with Visual Basic for Applications (VBA), in common with other Office 2000 applications. While Outlook still uses Visual Basic Scripting Edition (VBS) for customizing forms, VBA is now available for integrating Outlook with other Office applications.

WHO SHOULD READ THIS BOOK

This book is for almost everyone who uses, or plans to use, Outlook 2000. If you use Outlook much as it comes out of the box, you'll find many answers to problems that arise from time to time. At the other extreme, if you use Outlook as a development environment you'll find information you need that either isn't available elsewhere or is difficult to mind. The vast majority of Outlook users who fit somewhere between these extremes will find this book to be an indispensable resource that they frequently refer to.

The many detailed examples of the exact steps necessary to achieve what you want to do will make it easy to explore Outlook capabilities you haven't worked with before.

HOW THIS BOOK IS ORGANIZED

The book contains eight major parts, each containing several chapters.

PART I: OUTLOOK BASICS

The two chapters (Chapters 1 and 2) in this part provide a description of how Outlook works and help you understand Outlook's three service options, No E-mail, Internet Mail Only (IMO), and Corporate and Workgroup (C/W).

PART II: SENDING AND RECEIVING E-MAIL AND FAXES

This part contains chapters that deal separately with IMO and C/W Outlook to explain how you can use Outlook to send and receive Internet e-mail, and also to send and receive faxes. Although the end result is the same, the two Outlook service options have significant differences. You probably need to read only the chapters that refer to the service option you're using.

Chapters 3 and 4 cover IMO Outlook. Chapters 5, 6, and 7 cover IMO Outlook. Chapter 8 contains information about both service options.

PART III: USING OUTLOOK AS A PERSONAL INFORMATION MANAGER

This part contains separate chapters that describe how to manage specific types of personal information:

- Chapter 9—Contacts (people and organizations)
- Chapter 10—Calendar (appointments, events, and meetings)
- Chapter 11—Tasks (tasks you create for yourself, tasks you create for other people, and tasks other people create for you)
- Chapter 12—Journal (keeping a record of your daily activities)
- Chapter 13—Notes (usually temporary information)

In addition, Chapter 14 explains how you can share information with other people; Chapter 15 describes how to organize the folders in which Outlook saves information. Chapter 16 contains information about managing your computer environment.

PART IV: MANAGING OUTLOOK

This part contains seven chapters that cover various aspects of managing Outlook on your computer, as well as managing the information that Outlook saves. Most of the information in these chapters applies to all service options.

- Chapter 17—"Using Outlook Templates." By becoming familiar with Outlook templates you can save yourself a lot of time.
- Chapter 18—"Finding and Organizing Outlook Items." What other reason for saving information is there than you subsequently need to find it? Learn in this chapter about Outlook's powerful tools for retrieving information.
- Chapter 19—"Importing and Exporting Outlook Items." You can import information saved in many formats into Outlook, and export information from Outlook in many formats.
- Chapter 20—"Compacting Folders and Archiving Outlook Items." If you don't learn and use the techniques described in this chapter, the space Outlook occupies may soon fill your hard disk.
- Chapter 21—"Using Categories and Entry Types." You should get into the habit of assigning categories to all Outlook items so that you can subsequently group items by category. Entry types allow you to extend the use of Outlook's Journal.
- Chapter 22—"Creating and Using Rules." Rules are primarily used to automate the way Outlook handles e-mail you send and receive.
- Chapter 23—"Managing Outlook for a Workgroup." In this chapter you'll learn how to manage Outlook in a way that simplifies information sharing within a workgroup.

PART V: USING OUTLOOK AS A CLIENT FOR EXCHANGER SERVER, MICROSOFT MAIL, AND CC:MAIL

Separate chapters in this part cover using Outlook as a client for certain e-mail servers.

- Chapters 24 through 28 describe how to set up and use Outlook as a client for Microsoft Exchange Server.
- Chapters 29 and 30 describe setting up and using Outlook as a client for a Microsoft Mail postoffice.
- Chapters 31 and 32 describe setting up and using Outlook as a client for Lotus cc:Mail.

PART VI: CUSTOMIZING OUTLOOK

The many ways you can customize Outlook interactively (without programming) are described in this part.

- Chapter 33—"Customizing the Outlook Bar." You can modify Outlook's default Outlook Bar so that it contains shortcut buttons to Outlook folders, Windows, files, and Web pages.
- Chapter 34—"Customizing Command Bars." You can customize Outlook's menu bar, menus, and toolbars to suit your needs.
- Chapter 35—"Setting Outlook's Options." This chapter explains what you can do by making choices in the various tabs of the Options dialog box.
- Chapter 36—"Customizing Outlook Today." Here, you learn about some simple changes you can make to the Outlook Today window. The chapter contains an introduction to working with HTML code to customize Outlook Today.
- Chapter 37—"Customizing the Folder List." You're not limited to Outlook's ten standard folders. This chapter explains how to create and organize your own folders.
- Chapter 38—"Creating Views and Print Styles." Learn how to modify the information views that come with Outlook and how to create your own. Also learn how to take control over how Outlook prints information.

PART VII: SECURITY CONSIDERATIONS

This part contains a single chapter (Chapter 39) that provides information about keeping your Outlook information secure. In addition to basic security issues, the chapter provides information about obtaining and using a certificate (Digital ID) to authenticate and encrypt your Internet and intranet e-mail.

PART VIII: DEVELOPING OUTLOOK-BASED APPLICATIONS

This part is for people who want to use Outlook as a development environment.

- Chapter 40—"Creating and Using Custom Forms." Learn how to create new forms based on Outlook's standard forms.
- Chapter 41—"Creating and Using Custom Fields." You're not limited to Outlook's standard fields. This chapter describes how to create new fields.
- Chapter 42—"Enhancing Outlook Forms with Visual Basic Script Code." You can use Visual Basic Script to change and enhance Outlook's standard forms and custom forms.
- Chapter 43—"Creating Application-wide Outlook Visual Basic for Applications Code." New in Outlook 2000, you can use Visual Basic for Applications to create integrated applications based on Outlook.

PART IX: APPENDIXES

The book contains eight appendices:

- Appendix A—"Installing Outlook." You'll probably initially install Outlook as a component of Office 2000. This appendix describes how you can modify the initial installation.
- Appendix B—"Using the Office 2000 Resource Kit." The Microsoft Office 2000 Resource Kit contains a lot of information about Outlook and other Office 2000 applications. This appendix draws your attention to information of interest to Outlook users and developers.
- Appendix C—"Outlook's Files, Folders, Fields, and Registry Keys." Here, you'll find lists of many of the places where Outlook saves information and settings.
- Appendix D—"Outlook's Symbols." Outlook uses symbols to identify information about items. Many of these symbols are listed in this appendix.
- Appendix E—"Outlook Resources." There's a wealth of information and add-on capabilities available for Outlook. Some of these are listed in this appendix.
- Appendix F—"Working with the Windows Registry." Many of Outlook's settings are saved in the Windows registry. This appendix shows you how to access and change these settings.
- Appendix G—"Outlook Shortcut Keys." Most of this book explains how to use your mouse to perform operations in Outlook. The shortcut keys listed here can help you to work faster with Outlook.
- Appendix H—"Outlook Fields and Equivalent Properties." A list of Outlook fields and the related object model properties.

GLOSSARY

The Glossary contains definitions of acronyms and terms used in Outlook and related subjects.

CONVENTIONS USED IN THIS BOOK

The special conventions used throughout this book are designed to help you get the most from the book as well as Outlook 2000.

SERVICE OPTION DISTINCTIONS

This book contains information that applies, in many cases, to whichever Outlook service option you're using. The paragraphs and sections that apply only to specific service options are marked by icons.

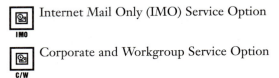

Internet Mail Only (IMO) Service Option

Corporate and Workgroup Service Option

TEXT CONVENTIONS

Different typefaces are used to convey various things throughout the book. They include the following:

Type	Meaning
Italic	A new term or phrase when it is initially defined. An italic term followed by a page number refers you to the page where that term is first defined.
<u>Underline</u>	Menu and dialog box options with letters that appear underlined onscreen indicate shortcut keys (hotkeys).
`Monospace`	Web addresses, information that you type, or onscreen messages.
Initial Caps	Menus, dialog box names, dialog box elements, and commands.

In this book, key combinations are represented with a plus sign. If the action you need to take is to press the Ctrl key and the S key simultaneously, the text tells you to enter Ctrl+S.

SPECIAL ELEMENTS

Throughout this book, you'll find Tips, Notes, Cautions, Cross References, and Troubleshooting Tips. These elements provide a variety of information, ranging from warnings you shouldn't miss to ancillary information that will enrich your Office experience, but isn't required reading.

"SIGNATURE" TIPS

Tip #1001 from	Tips point out special features, quirks, or software tricks that you might not necessarily know.

NOTES

Note	Notes highlight things that you should be aware of. If your time is at a premium, you can skip these notes. Generally, you'll find that they uncover extra information that sheds additional light on a topic.

CAUTIONS

Caution	Cautions are the hazard lights of this book and could save you precious hours in lost work—not to mention any associated headaches or ulcers.

TROUBLESHOOTING

At the end of most chapters, you'll encounter a "Troubleshooting" section. This is where you'll learn how to solve or avoid common problems you might typically face with Outlook 2000.

CROSS-REFERENCES

Cross-references will direct you to other locations in this book (or possibly even other books in the Que family) that will provide supplemental or supporting information. They look like:

→ If Microsoft Exchange Server isn't listed, you'll have to add that information service to your profile. **See** "Adding the Exchange Server Information Service to a Profile," **p. 665**.

AUTHOR'S FINAL COMMENT

As I always do in the books I write, I invite readers to send me their suggestions, comments, and questions. Send e-mail to me at `gpadwick@earthlink.net`.

I value all messages I receive and have, so far, been able to respond personally to each of them. While it's gratifying when people tell me they've found one of my books useful (some do), I also appreciate comments and questions that prompt me to think about things I've previously missed (many do that).

I hope you enjoy and benefit from this book.

Gordon Padwick

OUTLOOK BASICS

CHAPTER 1

HOW OUTLOOK WORKS

In this chapter

by Gordon Padwick

PUTTING OUTLOOK INTO PERSPECTIVE

This chapter puts Outlook 2000 into perspective and provides an overall understanding of what Outlook is, how it works, and what you can do with it. The chapter also contains information about how you can start Outlook in various ways.

INTRODUCING THE OUTLOOK FAMILY

This book is primarily about Microsoft Outlook 2000 (subsequently referred to in this book as Outlook), one of the applications included in the various versions of Microsoft Office 2000. Outlook is also supplied with Microsoft Exchange Server.

One of the significant differences you'll notice in Outlook 2000, if you've used previous versions of Outlook, is its high degree of integration with the Internet.

With Outlook, you can

- Send and receive e-mail and faxes
- Maintain information about the people and organizations with whom you are in contact
- Keep a calendar of your appointments, events, and meetings
- Keep track of your to-do list
- Maintain a journal of your activities
- Save miscellaneous notes
- Directly access Web pages

You can also use Outlook as an enhanced version of Windows Explorer. Outlook is tightly integrated with Internet Explorer so that you can access Internet sites and Internet newsgroups from within Outlook.

Outlook is the primary client for Microsoft *Exchange Server*. Although you can use Outlook on standalone computers and on computers that use messaging systems other than Exchange, the Exchange environment offers sophisticated collaboration facilities. With Outlook as a client for Exchange, you can benefit from such capabilities as group scheduling and public folders.

Although Microsoft offers Outlook primarily to satisfy the needs of business users, it's an excellent *Personal Information Manager* (PIM) that you can use at home as well as at the office. Why pay extra for a PIM when Outlook comes as part of the Office 2000 package?

Microsoft also offers *Outlook Express*, which you get when you install Internet Explorer, Windows 98, and Office 2000 for Macintosh. It is intended to satisfy home users. You can use Outlook Express to send and receive Internet e-mail, to maintain an address book, and to communicate with Internet newsgroups. Outlook uses facilities within Outlook Express to provide access to newsgroups.

Then there's *Outlook Web Access*, which Microsoft offers to people who use Exchange Server as an *information store*, but who don't have Outlook. With Outlook Web Access, you can use your Web browser to gain secure access to your e-mail and calendar you maintain on Exchange, and also to use group scheduling and have access to public folders. Outlook Web Access is mentioned here only to complete the coverage of the Outlook family of products; it isn't covered in detail elsewhere in this book.

Windows *CE Pocket Outlook*, which runs on Windows CE–based palmtop computers, is yet another member of the Outlook family. You can synchronize Outlook data between a palmtop computer running Pocket Outlook and a desktop or laptop computer running Outlook. While Pocket Outlook doesn't have all the capabilities of Outlook, it provides what you need for personal information management.

OUTLOOK AND OUTLOOK TODAY

Outlook is the name of the application that this book is about. Outlook Today is the name of an Outlook window that displays a summary of the information stored in Outlook that's relevant to today and the next few days.

Most people configure Outlook so that the Outlook Today window, such as that shown in Figure 1.1, is displayed each time Outlook starts.

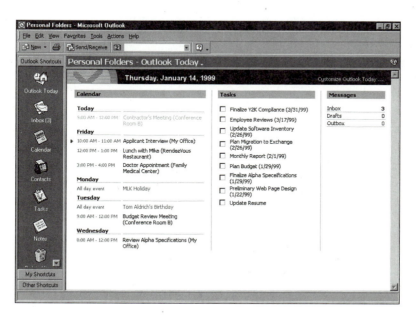

Figure 1.1
The Outlook Today window shows a summary of your current activities.

Tip #1 from

Gordon Padwick

If you don't see the Outlook Today window when you start Outlook, choose Outlook Today in the column of icons (the Outlook Bar) at the left side of the Outlook window. If you still don't see the Outlook Today window, choose View, Show Folder Home Page. Show Folder Home Page is only available in the menu when you've selected Outlook Today in the Outlook Bar.

→ For information about configuring Outlook so that the Outlook Today window appears each time you start Outlook, **see** "Other Options" **p. 880**.

The top of the Outlook Today window displays today's date, based, of course, on the date in your computer's internal clock.

The left side of the Outlook Today window shows a list of items on your calendar for today and the next few days. You can click any item on the list to see details about that item, as shown in Figure 1.2.

Figure 1.2
Outlook displays the details of a typical calendar item. Click the Close button (marked with an X) at the right end of the title bar to return to the Outlook Today window.

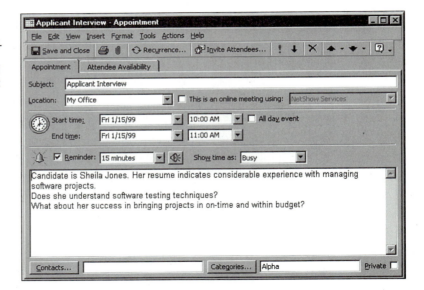

You can use the vertical scroll bar at the right side of the Outlook Today window to scroll down to items that aren't initially shown in the window.

Tip #2 from

Gordon Padwick

You can delete an appointment, event, or meeting from within Outlook Today. As you'll learn in Chapter 10, "Managing Calendars," you can use Outlook to create recurring appointments, events, and meetings. If the calendar item you delete from Outlook Today is recurring, you'll delete the entire recurring sequence, not just the item displayed in Outlook Today. Outlook Today doesn't tell you that a Calendar item is recurring, so be very careful about deleting calendar items in this way.

The center section of the Outlook Today window contains a list of your current tasks with the date each task is due. You can click any task to see the details of that task.

The top right side of the Outlook Today window shows how many unread messages are in your Inbox folder, how many drafts of messages are in your Drafts folder, and how many messages are waiting to be sent in your Outbox folder. You can click Messages to open your Inbox folder and start reading your messages.

The extreme left of the Outlook Today window contains the Outlook Bar, a set of shortcut icons you can click to go directly into parts of Outlook. After you do so, you see an *Information viewer* that displays specific types of Outlook items. Each of those viewers contains the same Outlook Bar. Click Outlook Today in an Information viewer to return to the Outlook Today window.

That's a quick explanation of the Outlook Today window as it appears after you first install Outlook. You can make some changes to the window by clicking Customize Outlook Today, to the right of the date at the top of the window.

→ For detailed information about customizing Outlook today, **see** "Customizing Outlook Today," **p. 899**.

You don't have to use the default Outlook Today window, nor are you limited to the choices made available when you click Options. The Outlook Today window is, in fact, defined by *Hypertext Markup Language* (HTML) code that you can customize.

HOW OUTLOOK SAVES INFORMATION

As an Outlook user, you need to have a basic understanding of how Outlook saves information. If your job is to support Outlook users and, perhaps, to develop applications based on Outlook, you need to have a detailed understanding of this subject.

As Chapter 2, "Understanding Outlook's Service Options," describes in detail, Outlook has three personalities (service options). You choose which of these personalities you initially want to use when you install Outlook. You can choose:

- No E-mail—Choose this if you want to use Outlook as a Personal Information Manager, with no capability to send and receive e-mail and faxes.

- Internet Mail Only (IMO)—Choose this if you want to use Outlook as a Personal Information Manager, to send and receive Internet e-mail, and to send and receive faxes.

- Corporate or Workgroup (C/W)—Choose this if you want to use Outlook as a Personal Information Manager, to send and receive e-mail by way of various mail servers (including Internet mail servers), to send and receive faxes, and to use Outlook as a client for Microsoft Exchange Server.

The No E-mail and Internet Mail Only service options save information in a file—your Personal Folders file—on your local hard disk. The Corporate or Workgroup Outlook service option can save your information in a Personal Folders file on your hard disk or, if you're using Outlook as a client for Exchange Server, it can save the information in a store within Exchange Server.

→ To find out about using Exchange Server **see** "Exchange Server Overview," **p. 657**.

Whether you're using a Personal Folders file on your local disk or a store in Exchange Server, that storage location contains what Outlook calls *folders*. There's a separate folder for each type of information that Outlook saves.

Note

A folder is space on a disk that contains items of information. You're probably used to thinking of folders as spaces on disks that contain files—you can use Windows Explorer to see these folders. In Outlook and Exchange, a folder is space that contains information items—you can't see these folders in Windows Explorer but you can, of course, see them in Outlook. Outlook folders are contained within files, and are similar to tables in a database.

YOUR PERSONAL FOLDERS FILE

The file Outlook uses to save items of information on your local hard drive is known as your Personal Folders file. This file can have any name you choose, but always has the file name extension .pst. If you choose to save Outlook items on your hard drive, Outlook provides one Personal Folders file and saves all Outlook items in that file. You can create additional Personal Folders files. When you're using Outlook, you designate one Personal Folders file to be the default file in which all Outlook items are saved.

A Personal Folders file contains certain default folders. You can add any number of other folders and subfolders to a Personal Folders file.

The default folders in a Personal Folders file are listed in Table 1.1. The same folders are normally available in an Exchange store.

TABLE 1.1   DEFAULT FOLDERS IN A PERSONAL FOLDERS FILE

Folder Name	Contents
Calendar	Appointments, events, and meetings
Contacts	People and organizations
Deleted Items	Items deleted from other folders
Drafts	Messages not ready to be sent
Inbox	Messages received
Journal	Activities

Folder Name	Contents
Notes	Miscellaneous information
Outbox	Messages waiting to be sent
Sent Items	Messages sent
Tasks	Personal tasks, tasks assigned to other people, and tasks received from other people

Each item of information within a folder is appropriately called an *item*. Each appointment, event, meeting, contact, received message, sent message, and so on is an Outlook item.

FIELDS WITHIN AN ITEM

Each Outlook item contains units of information. A *Contact* item, for example, contains a contact's first name, middle name, last name, and much more. In fact, a Contact item can contain more than one hundred separate pieces of information about a contact. Each of these units of information is saved in a *field*. When you create a new Contact item, you can provide information for whatever fields are appropriate.

Outlook provides space for certain standard fields for each type of item. If you need to, you can create custom fields for additional information.

→ For information about custom fields, **see** "Creating and Using Custom Fields," **p. 1093**.

SAVING OUTLOOK SETTINGS

As described previously, Outlook saves items of information in either a Personal Folders file or in the Exchange store. There's also a lot of information about how Outlook works—often referred to as Outlook's *settings*—that is saved. Most of this is saved in the Windows registry. If you're using Outlook to get your work done, you don't need to be concerned with the registry. Just let it do its job, and get on with your work. However, if you're supporting Outlook users, or have problems with how Outlook works on your computer, you may have to dig into the registry, at least somewhat.

Windows 95, Windows 98, and Windows NT all use a set of files, collectively known as the registry, to maintain information about your Windows configuration, how applications are set up to run under Windows, and information about people who use Windows. Many of the settings you establish in the Windows Control Panel are saved in the registry. Similarly, many of the settings you choose for Outlook (and other Office applications) when you choose Tools, Options are saved in the registry.

As far as possible, you should avoid making direct changes to the registry. However, for some purposes, the only way you can achieve what you need to do to is to batten down the hatches, grab the tiller, and steer into the storm. Various chapters in this book contain information about Outlook-related information in the registry.

→ To find out how to access the Windows registry, **see** "Working with the Windows Registry," **p. 1323**.

In addition to saving settings in the registry, Outlook saves certain information in other files on your hard disk. For example, if you make changes to Outlook's menus or toolbars, these changes are saved in a file called Outcmd.dat.

DISPLAYING ITEMS IN INFORMATION VIEWERS

Outlook keeps each type of item in a separate folder within your Personal Folders file or within your Exchange store. For example, all your Calendar items are kept in a Calendar folder, all your Contact items are kept in a Contact folder, and so on.

Note

When you first run Outlook after it's been installed, sample items are automatically installed in most Outlook folders. If you install Outlook 2000 on a computer on which Outlook 97 or Outlook 98 has been used, Outlook 2000 recognizes all previously created Outlook items.

Outlook displays the items in a folder in an *Information viewer*. By default, that Information viewer is appropriate for the type of items in a folder. For example, Calendar items in a Calendar folder are displayed in a Calendar Information viewer, such as that shown in Figure 1.3.

Figure 1.3
The Calendar Information viewer displays Calendar items. In addition to the monthly calendar shown here, Outlook can display weekly and daily calendars.

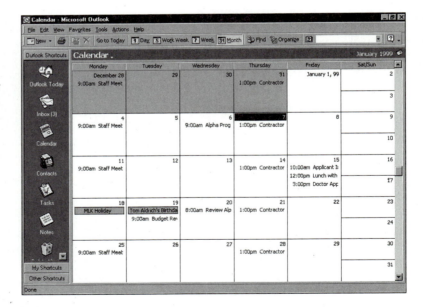

By default, Contact items are displayed in the Contacts Information viewer, which displays information about contacts much as information appears on index cards.

The way Outlook displays information in an Information viewer is referred to as a *view*. The view shown in Figure 1.3 is only one of several viewers you can choose to display Calendar items. In addition to the views supplied with Outlook, you can create your own custom views.

→ For information about creating custom views, **see** "Creating Views and Print Styles," **p. 943**.

An Information viewer displays only some of the information contained in Outlook items. To display detailed information about an item, double-click the item in the Information viewer. When you do so, the item is displayed in the form in which it was created. To return to the Information viewer from the form, click the Close button at the right end of the form's title bar.

USING THE OUTLOOK BAR

Each Information viewer contains the Outlook Bar at its left edge. You can click the shortcut icons in the Outlook Bar to select which Information viewer you want to see.

Tip #3 from

Gordon Crockett

If the Outlook Bar isn't displayed at the left side of an Information viewer, choose V̲iew, O̲utlook Bar.

The Outlook Bar contains three groups named Outlook Shortcuts, My Shortcuts, and Other Shortcuts. Only one group is displayed at a time. Click the name of a group to display the shortcut icons in that group.

Note

The Other Shortcut group in the Outlook Bar is present only if you have installed the Integrated File Management Outlook component.

OUTLOOK SHORTCUTS

The Outlook Shortcuts group in the Outlook Bar contains shortcut icons that provide access to most of Outlook's folders. The name of each shortcut identifies an Outlook folder and the name of the Information viewer used to display the contents of that folder. The shortcut icons in this group are listed in Table 1.2.

TABLE 1.2   SHORTCUTS IN THE OUTLOOK SHORTCUTS GROUP

Shortcut	Purpose
Outlook Today	Displays the Outlook Today window that summarizes your current activities.
Inbox	Displays the Inbox Information viewer that lists the headers of messages you've received and that are saved in the Inbox folder. The number in parentheses at the right of the icon name in the Outlook Bar is the number of messages in your Inbox folder that you haven't read.
Calendar	Displays the Calendar Information viewer that shows Calendar items saved in the Calendar folder.
Contacts	Displays the Contacts Information viewer that shows Contact items saved in the Contacts folder.
Tasks	Displays the Tasks Information viewer that shows Tasks items (personal tasks, tasks you've assigned to others, and tasks assigned to you) saved in the Tasks folder.
Notes	Displays the Notes Information viewer that shows Note items saved in the Notes folder.
Deleted Items	Displays the Deleted Items Information viewer that shows message headers or names of items you've deleted from other Outlook folders and are saved in the Deleted Items folder.

Depending on your monitor's resolution, you may not see all these icons. If some icons are hidden below the visible Outlook Bar group, click the button that's marked with a down-pointing triangle near the bottom of the group. Similarly, if some icons are hidden above the visible Outlook Bar group, click the button that's marked with an up-pointing triangle near the top of the group.

MY SHORTCUTS

The My Shortcuts group of the Outlook Bar contains five shortcut icons. These icons are listed in Table 1.3.

TABLE 1.3   SHORTCUTS IN THE MY SHORTCUTS GROUP

Shortcut	Purpose
Drafts	Displays the Drafts Information viewer that lists the headers of message drafts you haven't yet sent and are saved in the Drafts folder. The number in parentheses at the right of the icon name in the Outlook Bar is the number of drafts in the Drafts folder.
Outbox	Displays the Outbox Information viewer that lists headers of messages you've told Outlook to send, but are still in your Outbox folder waiting to be sent. The number in parentheses at the right of the icon name in the Outlook Bar is the number of messages waiting to be sent.
Sent Items	Displays the Sent Items Information viewer that lists headers of messages that Outlook has sent to your mail server.

Note

A number in parentheses at the right of the icon indicates the number of unread sent items, something that you don't normally see. However, if you use WinFax Pro to send and receive faxes, that application can automatically move sent faxes into the Sent Items folder, and classify them as unread.

Shortcut	Purpose
Journal	Displays the Journal Information viewer that shows Journal items saved in the Journal folder.
Outlook Update	If you have a connection to the Internet, or if Outlook is set up to automatically connect to the Internet, this shortcut accesses a Microsoft Web page that provides information about Outlook.

OTHER SHORTCUTS

If you have installed IMO Outlook, the Other Shortcuts group of the Outlook Bar is present only if you have also installed the Integrated File Management Outlook component. The shortcuts in this group provide the capability to use Outlook to manage Windows folders and files, but with some capabilities that aren't easily accessible within Windows Explorer.

If you have installed C/W Outlook, the Other Shortcuts group of the Outlook Bar is present only if you have installed the Integrated File Management Outlook component, or if you're using Outlook as a client for Exchange Server.

The shortcut icons you may see in the Other Shortcuts group of the Outlook Bar are listed in Table 1.4.

TABLE 1.4   SHORTCUTS IN THE OTHER SHORTCUTS GROUP

Shortcut	Purpose
My Computer	Displays your Windows environment. The information provided is similar to that provided when you choose My Computer from the Windows desktop. You can use this Information viewer to print lists of folders and files.
Personal	This shortcut is available if you're running Outlook under Windows NT. It displays a list of files in your Personal folder, the default folder in which applications running under Windows NT saves files.
My Documents	This shortcut is available if you're running Outlook under Windows 95 or Windows 98. It displays a list of files in your My Documents folder, the default folder in which applications running under Windows 95 or Windows 98 save files.
Favorites	Displays *uniform resource locators* (URLs), folders, and files in your Windows Favorites folder.
Public Folders	If you're using C/W Outlook as a client for Exchange Server, this Outlook Bar shortcut provides access to Exchange public folders.

CUSTOMIZING THE OUTLOOK BAR

The preceding sections have described the Outlook Bar as it appears after you first install Outlook. If you're using a computer on which someone has previously used Outlook, the Outlook Bar you see might be quite different. That's because you can customize the Outlook Bar to suit your personal needs. You can delete Outlook Bar groups, and delete shortcut icons within *groups*. You can also add shortcut icons to groups and create new groups. In addition to creating shortcuts to Outlook's folders, you can create shortcuts to files and folders within the Windows file system, as well as to Web sites. I mention this here only in case you're curious about why the Outlook Bar you see on your computer is different from what I've described.

→ For information about customizing the Outlook Bar, **see** "Customizing the Outlook Bar," **p. 799**.

USING FORMS TO CREATE AND DISPLAY OUTLOOK ITEMS

The preceding sections of this chapter provide an introduction to how you can see items of information that already exist in Outlook—items you or other people have created, or the sample items that are automatically installed when you first run Outlook. Now it's time to consider how you create Outlook items.

Outlook contains *forms* you use to create items; there is a separate form for each type of Outlook item. There's a form for creating Calendar items, a form for creating Contact items, a form for creating message items, and so on. Each of these forms is similar to a paper form. It contains boxes in which you enter information and lists from which you can choose information.

It doesn't matter what type of item you want to create; you proceed in much the same way. Let's suppose you want to record an appointment. One way you can do that is by entering information in the *Appointment form*.

To display the Appointment form:

1. With any Information viewer displayed, click the Calendar shortcut in the Outlook Bar to display the Calendar Information viewer.
2. Choose Actions, New Appointment to display the Untitled - Appointment form shown in Figure 1.4.

As you can see, this form contains various boxes in which you can enter information. Entering information into this form is fairly intuitive, so we won't go into details at this stage. You can find detailed information later in this book.

→ You can find detailed information about creating a one-time appointment later in this book. **See** "Creating a One-Time Appointment in the Calendar Information Viewer," **p. 358**.

InfoBar   Standard toolbar

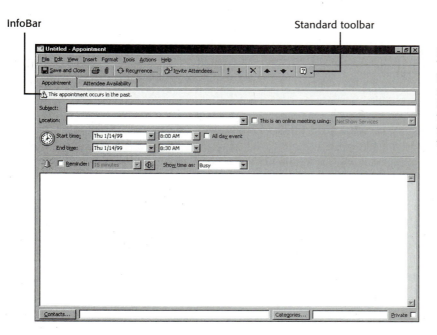

Figure 1.4
The form shown here
is maximized. You
may have to click the
Maximize button near
the right end of the
form's title bar to see
the entire form.

> **Note**
>
> In common with other Outlook forms, the Appointment form has an *InfoBar* near the top
> that provides important information about the contents of the form.

After you've entered information into the various boxes in the form, choose Save and Close
in the form's Standard toolbar to save the information as an Outlook item.

Having saved the information, you can open the appropriate Information viewer (the
Calendar Information viewer in this case) to display basic information about the item.
Double-click the item in the Information viewer to display the form that contains all the
information you originally entered in the form.

This short introduction to Outlook's forms refers only to the standard forms available after
you first install Outlook. You can modify these forms and create your own.

→ To find out how you can create custom forms, **see** "Creating and Using Custom Forms," **p. 1031**.

OUTLOOK'S COMMAND BARS

Office applications used to deal with menu bars and toolbars separately. Recently, though,
Microsoft has combined menu bars and toolbars, and the way you work with them, into the
single concept of *command bars*.

Outlook is similar to other Office applications. Each Information viewer and form has a
menu bar at the top and, under that, one or more toolbars.

The menu bar at the top of most Information viewers is almost identical, though the menu items available in each menu vary as appropriate for the type of item displayed by each viewer. Also, in some cases, menu items vary according to the actual view selected. The menu bars at the top of Outlook's forms contain menus appropriate to each form.

After you install Outlook, each Information viewer has one toolbar, the Standard toolbar, under the menu bar. To display an Advanced toolbar, choose View, move the pointer onto Toolbars, and choose Advanced to display a toolbar that contains additional Outlook icons. You can also choose View, Toolbars, Web to display a toolbar that contains Web-related icons.

> **Note**　　　The so-called "Advanced toolbar" is similar to the toolbar that was displayed in Outlook 97.

You can customize Outlook's menus by adding menus to, or deleting menus from, the menu bar. You can also create additional toolbars that contain buttons you choose, and add buttons to, or delete buttons from, the Standard, Advanced, and Web toolbars.

→ For information about creating and modifying menus and toolbars, **see** "Customizing Command Bars," **p. 815**.

CONTROLLING HOW OUTLOOK STARTS

After you install Outlook 2000, click the Microsoft Outlook icon on the Windows desktop to start Outlook. What you see depends on whether you have previously had a version of Outlook installed on your computer and, if so, whether it was Outlook 97 or Outlook 98.

If you haven't previously had a version of Outlook installed on your computer, within a few seconds the Outlook Today window, similar to that shown previously in Figure 1.1, is displayed.

If you've installed *C/W Outlook (page 54)*, this probably won't happen the first time you run Outlook. When you first start C/W Outlook, you'll probably see a Choose Profile dialog box similar to that shown in Figure 1.5.

Figure 1.5
The first time you run C/W Outlook, the Choose Profile dialog box usually opens, enabling you to select the profile you want to use.

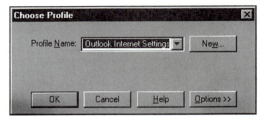

What you do at this point depends on whether you have used an earlier version of Outlook or Windows Messaging (previously known as Exchange Client) on the same computer you're now using for Outlook 2000. If you have, you already have one or more profiles tailored to your needs. Open the Profile <u>N</u>ame drop-down list in the Choose Profile dialog box, choose the *profile* you normally use, and choose OK to let the startup process continue.

Note

If your computer isn't connected to a network on which Exchange Server is running, you might see a message telling you that Your Microsoft Exchange Server is unavailable. Choose <u>W</u>ork Offline to continue the startup process.

If you haven't previously used Outlook or Windows Messaging, the only profile available is the one named Outlook Internet Settings (or perhaps another name), which is automatically created when you install Outlook.

Note

If you work in an organization that has a *local area network* (LAN), your LAN administrator can probably provide you with the profile you need. Otherwise you'll have to refer to Chapter 5, "Creating Profiles for Corporate/Workgroup Outlook" to find out how to create your own profile.

After you have Outlook running, you can specify which profile Outlook should automatically select each time it starts, and whether the Choose Profile dialog box should appear.

To set profile options:

1. Start Outlook and choose <u>T</u>ools, <u>O</u>ptions to open the Options dialog box.
2. Select the Mail Services tab shown in Figure 1.6.

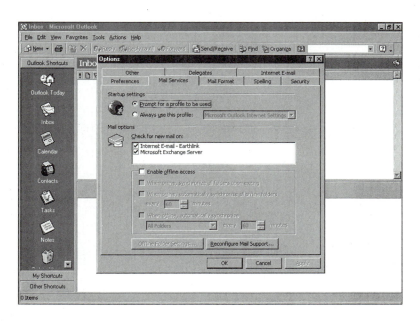

Figure 1.6
By default, Outlook proposes to prompt you for a profile each time it starts.

3. To have Outlook automatically select a specific profile and start without prompting you for a profile name, choose <u>A</u>lways <u>U</u>se This Profile. Then open the drop-down list of profile names, and select the one you want Outlook to use.

> **Note**
>
> If you've previously created profiles for Exchange Client, Outlook, or Windows Messaging, you can select one of those profiles. Otherwise, only the default profile that's created when you install Outlook is available.

4. Choose OK to close the dialog box.
5. Choose <u>F</u>ile, Exit and <u>L</u>og Off to close Outlook.

The next time you start Outlook, it will use the profile you just selected without asking you to choose one. You can, of course, go back to the Options dialog box at any time to select a different profile.

→ For information about creating profiles, **see** "Creating Profiles for Corporate/Workgroup Outlook," **p. 151**.

STARTING OUTLOOK FROM THE OFFICE SHORTCUT BAR

Instead of starting Outlook and then choosing what you want to do, you can create a new Outlook item by choosing a button in the Outlook shortcut bar. You can choose:

- New Message to open Outlook's Message form
- New Appointment to open Outlook's Appointment form
- New Task to open Outlook's Task form
- New Contact to open Outlook's Contact form
- New Note to open Outlook's Note form

> **Tip #4 from**
>
> To display the Office shortcut bar, in the Windows taskbar choose Start, move the pointer onto Programs, move the pointer onto Microsoft Office Tools, and then choose Microsoft Office Shortcut Bar.

You can also start Outlook by clicking the Outlook button in the Quick Launch section that appears next to the Start button in the Windows taskbar when you install Office 2000.

STARTING OUTLOOK AUTOMATICALLY WHEN YOU TURN ON YOUR COMPUTER

> **Tip #5 from**
>
> If you have sufficient system resources, it's a good idea to leave Outlook running while you work with other applications. By doing so, you'll always see Outlook's reminders at the time they're scheduled to appear. If Outlook isn't running, reminders don't appear until you start Outlook. You'll also have Outlook immediately available for making quick notes.

After you start using Outlook, you'll probably get into the habit of opening Outlook at the beginning of each day. It's convenient, then, for Outlook to open automatically when you turn on your computer.

To set Outlook to open automatically when you turn on your computer:

1. If Outlook is running, choose File, Exit and Log Off to close C/W Outlook, or choose File, Exit to close IMO Outlook.

2. Choose Start on the Windows taskbar, move the pointer onto Settings, and then choose Taskbar & Start Menu (Windows 95 and Windows 98) or Taskbar (Windows NT) to open the Taskbar Properties dialog box.

3. Choose the Start Menu Programs tab and then choose Add to display the Create Shortcut dialog box.

4. Choose Browse to display the Browse dialog box.

5. In the Look In drop-down list, select the disk drive (probably C:) that contains Outlook.

6. Navigate to the folder that contains Outlook (probably Program Files\Microsoft Office\Office). This folder is similar to that shown in Figure 1.7.

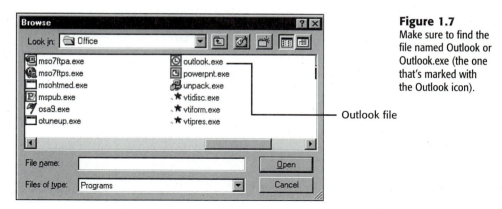

Figure 1.7
Make sure to find the file named Outlook or Outlook.exe (the one that's marked with the Outlook icon).

Outlook file

Note

Depending on how your computer is set up, executable files such as Outlook.exe may be displayed with or without the file name extension.

7. Double-click Outlook.exe or Outlook to return to the Create Shortcut dialog box shown in Figure 1.8.

8. Choose Next to display the Select Program Folder dialog box shown in Figure 1.9.

Figure 1.8
The Command Line box contains the complete path and filename of the file that runs to start Outlook.

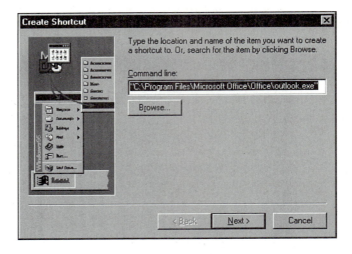

Figure 1.9
The folder named StartUp contains applications that run automatically when Windows starts.

StartUp folder —

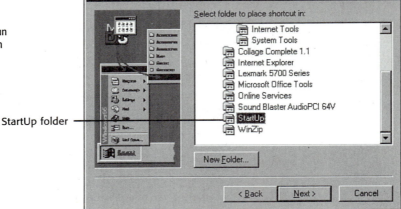

9. Select the StartUp folder (make sure you don't select Start Menu) and choose Next to display the Select a Title for the Program dialog box.

10. Enter a name, such as Outlook Startup, for the shortcut and then choose Finish to return to the Taskbar Properties dialog box. Choose OK to close the dialog box.

The next time you start Windows, Outlook will start automatically.

CHOOSING AN INFORMATION VIEWER TO DISPLAY WHEN OUTLOOK STARTS

By default, Outlook displays the Outlook Today window when it starts. You can choose to display one of Outlook's Information viewers instead, and you can make other choices about what happens when Outlook starts.

To select a default Information viewer:

1. Start Outlook, choose Tools, Options, and select the Other tab. Then choose Advanced Options to display the Advanced Options dialog box shown in Figure 1.10.

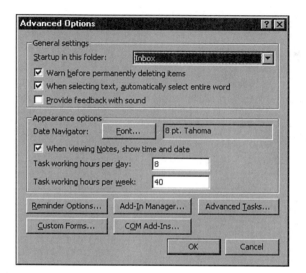

Figure 1.10
Use this dialog box to choose which Information viewer Outlook displays when it opens.

2. Open the Startup in This Folder drop-down list and select the Outlook folder that contains what you want Outlook to initially display.

3. Choose OK twice to close the dialog boxes.

After you've done this, when you next start Outlook, it will display the Information viewer you selected. To return to displaying Outlook Today at startup, you can repeat the preceding three steps.

You can also choose to display Outlook Today when Outlook starts from within the Outlook Today window:

1. Click the Outlook Today shortcut in the Outlook Bar to display the Outlook Today window.

2. Choose Customize Outlook Today at the top of the Outlook Today window to display the Outlook Today Options window shown in Figure 1.11.

3. Check the box labeled When Starting, Go Directly to Outlook Today if you want Outlook to open with Outlook Today displayed. This overrides any choice you may have previously made in the Options dialog box (as previously described).

4. Choose Save Changes.

Figure 1.11
You can select various Outlook Today options in this window.

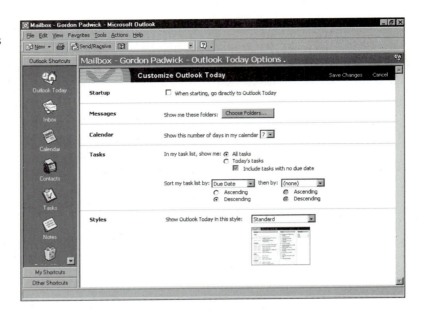

The other choices available in the Customize Outlook Today window are

- Messages—Select Choose Folders to open the Select Folder dialog box, in which you can check the names of message folders whose contents you want summarized in the Outlook Today window. By default, the window summarizes the contents of your Inbox, Drafts, and Outbox folders.

- Calendar—Select the number of days for which you want the Outlook Today window to list a summary of your appointments, events, and meetings. The default is five days.

- Tasks—Select the type of tasks you want listed in the Outlook Today window. The default is Outlook's simple list (your current tasks). You can also select how you want tasks to be sorted in the displayed list.

- Styles—Select the style in which you want Outlook Today to display information

After you've made any changes to the Outlook Today options, choose Save Changes to redisplay Outlook Today.

MAKING OTHER STARTUP CHOICES

Whether you start Outlook by clicking its icon on your Windows desktop, or have Outlook start automatically when you start Windows, Windows executes a command line to run the Outlook.exe program file. You saw an example of such a command line earlier in Figure 1.8.

To make Outlook behave in various ways when it starts, you have to modify the properties of an Outlook shortcut. One of these *properties (page 1094)* is the command line. By modifying a shortcut's properties you can

- Make Outlook always open in a maximized window
- Always have the opportunity to choose a profile before Outlook opens
- Make Outlook always open with a specific profile selected

Before continuing, you must have a clear understanding of the icons on your Windows desktop—not all of them are shortcuts. The next section gives you more information about creating shortcuts.

CREATING SHORTCUTS

We often think of all the icons on the Windows desktop as shortcuts because all of them seem to act as shortcuts. In fact, some of these icons represent programs or files themselves, although others represent shortcuts to those programs or files. Each icon that is truly a shortcut has a small square containing an up-and-to-the-right-pointing arrow (known as an overlay) in its bottom-left corner. Look closely at your desktop—you'll probably see that the Microsoft Outlook icon isn't a shortcut, whereas the Outlook Express icon is a shortcut.

Note

It's possible that shortcuts on your desktop don't have an overlay. The "Troubleshooting" section at the end of this chapter explains how you can hide and restore overlays.

Normally, whether an icon on your desktop is or isn't a shortcut is not a matter of concern. You just click an icon to start an application or open a file. When you want to work with Outlook command-line options, however, you have to be working with an Outlook shortcut, not with an icon that represents Outlook itself.

Because the Outlook installation process creates an icon on your desktop, rather than a shortcut, you have to create the shortcut yourself. Close Outlook if it's running, then follow these steps.

To create an Outlook startup shortcut:

1. From the Windows desktop, open Windows Explorer and navigate to the folder that contains Outlook.exe (probably C:\Program Files\Microsoft Office\Office).

2. Locate Outlook.exe (according to your setup, you may not see the file name extension—the file you're looking for in that case is named Outlook and its type is Application).

3. Select Outlook.exe (or Outlook), choose <u>F</u>ile, Create <u>S</u>hortcut. An item named Shortcut to Outlook.exe appears at the bottom of the list of files in the folder.

4. Drag Shortcut to Outlook.exe from Windows Explorer onto your desktop to create an icon on the desktop. This icon is a shortcut.

5. Close Windows Explorer and place the new icon wherever you want on the desktop.

6. While the shortcut is still open on your desktop, you may want to change its name from "Shortcut to Outlook.exe" to something more appropriate, such as "Outlook." Right-click the icon to display its context menu, then choose Rename. Now you can edit the displayed name. Press Enter to confirm the new name.

7. Click any unoccupied space on your desktop to deselect the shortcut.

Now you have an Outlook shortcut icon you can modify to contain command-line switches.

MODIFYING AN OUTLOOK SHORTCUT

To modify an existing Outlook shortcut, close Outlook and then right-click a Microsoft Outlook shortcut (not an icon that directly represents Outlook) on your Windows desktop to display the shortcut's context menu. Choose Properties in that menu and select the Shortcut tab to display the Shortcut to Outlook Properties dialog box shown in Figure 1.12.

Figure 1.12
You can control how Outlook starts by making choices in this dialog box.

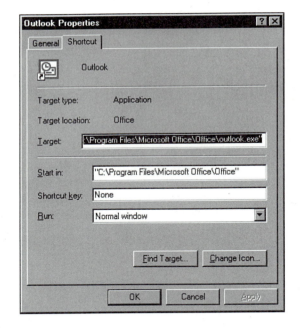

To choose several ways for Outlook to open, create several Outlook shortcuts on your Windows desktop and set different properties for each.

To create a copy of the Microsoft Outlook shortcut, right-click the shortcut and choose Copy from the context menu. Then right-click an empty space on the Windows desktop and choose Paste Shortcut from the context menu.

If you always want Outlook to be maximized when it starts, open the Run drop-down list box near the bottom of the Outlook Properties dialog box, and select Maximized.

You can make other changes to the way Outlook starts by appending a switch to the text in the Target box. By default, the text in this box contains the complete path of the program that starts Outlook—something like this:

```
"C:\Program Files\Microsoft Office\Office\outlook.exe"
```

You can add switches to this text. For example, if you want Outlook to open without displaying the Outlook Bar, place the insertion point at the right end of the text in the Target box, (after the double quotation mark) press the spacebar once, and then type /folder. Now the command line in the Run box looks something like this:

```
"C:\Program Files\Microsoft Office\Office\outlook.exe" /folder
```

Tip #6 from

Gordon Padwick

If the path includes long folder names (such as "Program Files" and "Microsoft Office"), the complete path name must be within quotation marks, as shown in this example.

Subsequently, when you start Outlook, it's displayed without the Outlook Bar—this might be the way you'd like to initially see Outlook Today.

Tip #7 from

Gordon Padwick

After you've opened Outlook without the Outlook Bar displayed, you can choose View, Outlook Bar to display the Outlook Bar.

Perhaps you normally run Outlook under one profile but occasionally want to use a different profile. As explained earlier in the "Controlling How Outlook Starts" section of this chapter, you can choose Tools, Options, and then select the Mail Services tab. In the Mail Services tab you can select a profile that Outlook will use when you click the normal Microsoft Outlook icon on the Windows desktop. That solves half of the problem: it allows you to select the profile you normally use, but doesn't allow you to occasionally choose another profile.

You can create an Outlook shortcut on your desktop and modify its properties so that when you double-click that shortcut, you are offered a choice of profiles, even though Outlook's options are set for it to open without showing that list.

To use a switch to cause Outlook to open the Choose Profile dialog box:

1. Create an Outlook shortcut on your Windows desktop, as explained earlier in this section.

2. Right-click that shortcut to display its context menu, then choose Properties to display the Shortcut to Outlook Properties dialog box. Select the Shortcut tab, shown previously in Figure 1.12.

3. Append a space and then the switch /profiles to the command line in the Run box, then choose OK to close the dialog box.

In addition to the two switches, /folder and /profiles, described in the preceding examples, there are several others you should know about. Table 1.5 contains a list of Outlook's command-line switches.

TABLE 1.5   OUTLOOK'S COMMAND-LINE SWITCHES

Command-Line Switch	Purpose
/a "file name"	Open the Outlook Message form with the specified file as an attachment
/c ipm.activity	Open the Outlook Journal Entry form
/c ipm.appointment	Open the Outlook Appointment form
/c ipm.contact	Open the Outlook Contact form
/c ipm.note	Open the Outlook Message form
/c ipm.post	Open the Outlook Discussion form
/c ipm.stickynote	Open the Outlook Note form
/c ipm.task	Open the Outlook Task form
/c "message class"	Create an item of the specified message class
/CheckClient	Prompt for the default manager of e-mail, news, and contacts
/CleanFreeBusy	Clean and regenerate free/busy information
/CleanReminders	Clean and regenerate reminders
/CleanSchedPlus	Delete all Schedule+ data from the server and allow the free/busy information in the Outlook calendar to be used by Schedule+ users
/CleanViews	Restore default views
/Folder	Hide the Outlook Bar (and also the folder list if that was displayed when you previously closed Outlook)
/NoPreview	Turn off the Preview pane and remove the option from the View menu
/Profiles	Offer a choice of profiles at startup (regardless of the setting in the Options dialog box)
/Profile "profile name"	Open using the specified profile (regardless of the setting in the Options dialog box)
/ResetFolders	Restore missing folders for the default delivery location
/ResetOutlookBar	Rebuild the Outlook Bar
/select "folder name"	Open with the contents of the specified Outlook folder displayed

The syntax for the /select switch when you're using C/W Outlook is

"<path\outlook.exe" /select "Outlook:<foldernams> /profile "profile name"

For IMO Outlook, the syntax is

"path\outlook.exe" /select "Outlook:<foldername>

For example, if the path for outlook.exe is

C:\Program Files\Microsoft Office\Office

your profile name is Jason Aldrich, and you want to open the Calendar folder, the format for C/W Outlook is

"C:\Program Files\Microsoft Office\Office\outlook.exe" /select "Outlook:Calendar" /profile "Jason Aldrich"

For IMO Outlook, the format is

"C:\Program Files\Microsoft Office\Office\outlook.exe" /select "Outlook:Calendar"

Note

There must be a space before each forward slash, but there must not be a space before each backslash, in these command lines.

You can append more than one switch to a command line.

Tip #8 from

Gordon Padwick

If you frequently open Outlook and go immediately to a particular folder or form, consider creating a shortcut on your Windows desktop for that purpose. You can create as many shortcuts as you need.

If you want to run Outlook regularly based on a command-line switch, create a shortcut on your Windows desktop as previously explained. However, if you want to use a command-line switch only occasionally, it's more convenient to start Outlook from the Run dialog box. The following example shows how you can use the /CleanViews switch to restore the default Outlook *views (page 944)*.

To start Outlook using a command-line switch from the Run dialog box:

1. Close Outlook if it's currently running.
2. Choose Start in the Windows taskbar, then choose <u>R</u>un in the start menu to display the Run dialog box.
3. In the Run dialog box, enter Outlook.exe /CleanViews.

You can use the same technique to start Outlook with any command-line switch.

SHUTTING DOWN OUTLOOK

To shut down IMO Outlook, choose <u>F</u>ile, E<u>x</u>it.

To shut down C/W Outlook, choose File, Exit and Log Off to ensure that all connections you may have established to mail servers and other Windows applications that Outlook has used are properly closed. If you choose File, Exit and have been using WordMail as your e-mail editor, or, if you're using C/W Outlook, you may leave instances of other applications running on your computer. To be on the safe side, always choose File, Exit and Log Off.

HAVING TWO OR MORE OUTLOOK WINDOWS VISIBLE

You may be one of those fortunate people who has a large monitor—17 inches or more. If that's the case, you can often speed your work by having two or more Outlook Windows visible at the same time. For example, it's often convenient to display your Inbox and Calendar simultaneously.

To display your Inbox and Calendar simultaneously:

1. Open Outlook as you normally do and choose Inbox in the Outlook Bar to display your Inbox Information viewer.

2. If your Outlook window is maximized, choose the Maximize/Restore button in the title bar and drag the borders of the window so that it occupies about half of your screen—make sure the Outlook Bar is visible.

3. Right-click Calendar in the Outlook Bar to display its context menu.

4. Choose Open in New Window to display the Calendar Information box in a separate window.

5. If the new window is maximized, choose the Maximize/Restore button in its title bar. Then position and size the window so that it occupies the remainder of the screen, as shown in Figure 1.13.

Figure 1.13
With two Outlook windows displayed, click either window to activate it. Alternatively, press Alt+Tab to switch from one window to the next.

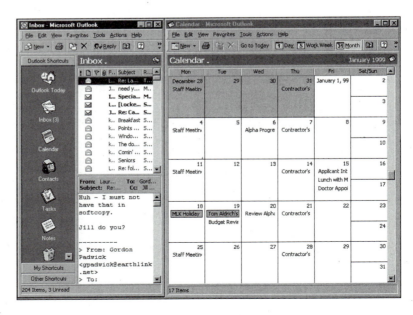

Now you can refer to your calendar while you read messages you've received. Instead of having the windows side by side on your screen, you can maximize them and press Alt+Tab to bring each window up in turn. You can display other Outlook Windows in the same way.

ACCESSING INTERNET EXPLORER FACILITIES FROM OUTLOOK

When you're working in Outlook and decide to use an Internet Explorer facility such as accessing newsgroups or Web sites, you can easily do so. For example, in Outlook you can:

- Choose View, move the pointer onto Go To, and choose News to access Outlook Express's capability of interacting with Internet newsgroups.

- Choose View, move the pointer onto Go To, and choose Web Browser to open Internet Explorer so you can access Web sites.

- Choose View, mover the pointer onto Go To, and choose Internet Call to call up NetMeeting and start an electronic conference.

This book is primarily about Outlook, rather than Internet Explorer, so we won't go into details here about using these facilities. For detailed information about these subjects, see *"Using Microsoft Internet Explorer 4.0,"* published by Que.

UNDERSTANDING PROTOCOLS

A *protocol* is a set of rules that control how computers communicate.

Outlook supports the major Internet messaging, directory, security, scheduling, and collaboration protocols. In addition C/W Outlook fully supports the *Messaging Application Programming Interface* (MAPI), which provides rich messaging, scheduling, and collaboration facilities when Outlook is used as a client for Exchange Server and other MAPI-compliant mail and collaboration servers.

Table 1.6 lists the Internet protocols supported by Outlook.

TABLE 1.6 INTERNET PROTOCOLS SUPPORTED BY OUTLOOK	
Protocol	**Description**
Hypertext Markup Language (HTML)	The standard format for information on the Web.
iCalendar	A means of sending and receiving free/busy calendar information over the Internet.
Internet Mail Access Protocol 4 (IMAP4)	A format for sending and receiving Internet e-mail messages that provides facilities beyond those in POP3 and SMTP.

continues

TABLE 1.6 CONTINUED

Protocol	Description
Lightweight Directory Access Protocol (LDAP)	Used to provide access to directories on the Internet.
Multipurpose Internet Mail Extensions (MIME)	An extension that allows binary attachments to e-mail messages.
Multipurpose Hypertext Markup Language (MHTML)	An extension of HTML that allows images to be embedded within e-mail messages.
Network News Transport Protocol (NNTP)	Used to post and retrieve newsgroup messages.
Post Office Protocol 3 (POP3)	The most widely used format for sending and receiving Internet e-mail.
Secure Multipurpose Internet Mail Extensions (S/MIME)	An extension that allows e-mail messages to be digitally signed and encrypted.
Simple Mail Transport Protocol (SMTP)	Another widely used format for sending and receiving Internet e-mail.
vCalendar	A means of sending and receiving calendars and schedules over the Internet.
vCard	A means of sending and receiving information (including pictures) about people over the Internet.

CHOOSING WINDOWS SETTINGS

To use Outlook properly, you should make sure that certain Windows settings are set correctly:

- Your monitor should have a resolution of 600 by 800 pixels or better in order to display Outlook's Information viewers and forms.

- Outlook depends on your computer's *real-time clock* (RTC) in order to properly date- and time-stamp items, so you must make sure the clock is set correctly.

- You should also make sure that Windows Regional Settings is correct, so that Outlook uses appropriate date and time formats. Having correct regional settings is particularly important if you use Outlook's calendar with two time zones.

Note

For detailed information on Windows settings, refer to a book such as "*Using Microsoft Windows 95*", "*Using Microsoft Windows 98,*" or "*Using Microsoft Windows NT Workstation 4.0,*" all published by Que.

GETTING HELP FOR OUTLOOK

Many sources of help are available to help you use Outlook. In addition to books such as this one, you can turn to the following sources:

- An experienced colleague
- The Office Assistant
- Outlook's online Help
- Internet Web sites and newsgroups

ASKING A COLLEAGUE

If you have a colleague who's an Outlook expert and has the time and patience to sit down with you in front of your computer, you're very fortunate. This one-on-one approach to problem-solving is usually the fastest way of getting answers to your questions.

The fact that you're reading this book, though, indicates that you are the Outlook expert in your organization, or intend to become the expert. If that's the case, you have to go else-where for help.

GETTING HELP FROM THE OFFICE ASSISTANT

When you first start Outlook, the Office Assistant appears on your screen as shown in Figure 1.14.

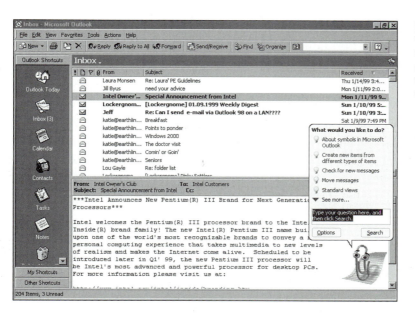

Figure 1.14
You can use the Office Assistant to choose what you want to do or to ask a question.

Tip #9 from

Gordon Padwick

If the Office Assistant isn't visible, choose Help, Show the Office Assistant. If only the Office Assistant icon appears (without the pane), click the icon to display the pane.

You can choose any of the items listed in the Office Assistant balloon. Alternatively, you can enter a question and then choose Search. As an example, if you enter the question "How do I send a message?" and choose Search, the Office Assistant responds by displaying a list of relevant topics, as shown in Figure 1.15.

Figure 1.15
These are examples of topics the Office Assistant offers in response to your question.

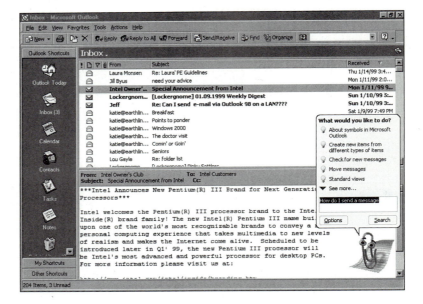

If you choose a topic, the Office Assistant opens a pane that provides detailed information about that topic. The Office Assistant displays more topics if you choose See More.

After you've started Outlook a few times, you might become weary of having the Office Assistant in front of you while you work. To hide the Office Assistant, choose Help, Hide the Office Assistant.

Choose Options in the Office Assistant pane to customize it. Outlook displays the dialog box shown in Figure 1.16.

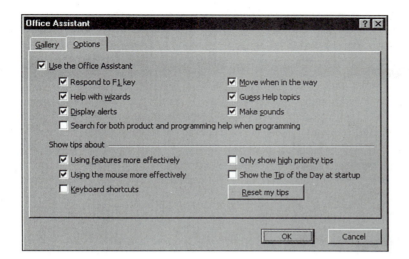

Figure 1.16
Use the Options tab
to specify how you
want the Office
Assistant to work.

Check the boxes in the Options tab to choose the Office Assistant facilities you want to use.

If you don't want to see the Office Assistant anymore, uncheck Use the Office Assistant.

Note

You can also select the Gallery tab to add a little variety to your life by choosing various animated icons to represent the Office Assistant. To conserve disk space, only the default Office Assistant is installed at the time you install Office 2000. When you choose an icon that isn't already installed, Outlook asks if you want to install it. If you choose Yes, you'll have to install the new icon from the Office 2000 CD-ROM or download it from your server.

If you right-click the Office Assistant, a context menu appears that contains these menu items:

- Hide—Choose this to temporarily hide the Office Assistant.
- Options—Choose this to display the Office Assistant dialog box with the Options tab selected, as shown previously in Figure 1.16.
- Choose Assistant—Choose this to display the Office Assistant dialog box with the Gallery tab selected.
- Animate—Start the Office Assistant performing some animation tricks—cute entertainment if you're bored!

Tip #10 from

Any changes you make to the way the Office Assistant behaves in Outlook affects all the Office Applications. Likewise, any change you make to the Office Assistant in another Office Application affects Outlook.

USING ONLINE HELP

Microsoft has revamped traditional online Help in all the Office 2000 applications, including Outlook.

Initially, when you choose Help, Microsoft Outlook Help, Outlook displays the Office Assistant. You can make a change that results in this command displaying Online Help. After you do so, you can choose Help, Show the Office Assistant to use the Office Assistant. To make this change, right-click the Office Assistant to display its context menu, then choose Options to display the dialog box previously shown in Figure 1.16. In that dialog box, uncheck Use the Office Assistant. Now you can directly access Online Help.

To use Online Help, disable the Office Assistant and then choose Help, Microsoft Outlook Help to display the Microsoft Outlook Help window shown in Figure 1.17.

Figure 1.17
Use this window to look up specific information topics.

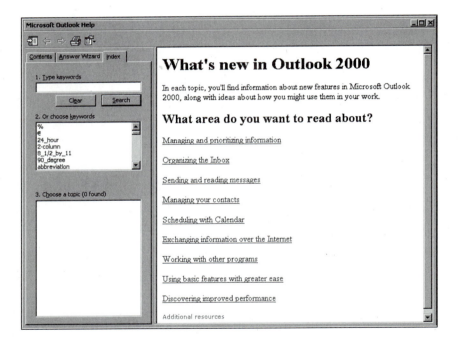

The Microsoft Outlook Help window has two panes. The left pane is where you select topics; the right pane shows information about the selected topic.

The left pane has three tabs:

- Select the Contents tab to select general areas of information. You can expand each area of information by clicking the + at the left of the information name. Then choose one of the listed subjects to see information about that subject in the right pane.

- Select the Answer Wizard tab if you want to ask a question in your own words. Enter your question into the What Would You Like to Do box and then choose Search. Outlook lists topics based on the words in your question. Select a topic to see information about that topic in the right pane.

- Select the Index tab to see an alphabetical list of major help topics. You can enter a keyword, or keywords, in the Type Keywords box and then choose Search to find corresponding topics. Alternatively, you can scroll down the list of topics. Double-click a topic to see subtopics in the Choose a Topic box. Select a subtopic to see details about it in the right pane.

WHAT'S THIS?

When you choose Help, What's This? (or press Shift+F1) a question mark is added to the pointer. Using this question mark pointer, point onto any menu item and click to get information about that item, or point onto any region of an Information viewer or form and click to get information about that region.

OFFICE ON THE WEB

When you choose Help, Office on the Web, Outlook opens Internet Explorer and opens a Web site in which you can obtain information about Office 2000 applications, including Outlook.

DETECT AND REPAIR

Choose Help, Detect and Repair to activate a utility that examines your Office installation and automatically corrects errors.

If it finds errors in your installation, is asks you to insert your Office 2000 disk into the drive. After you do that, the utility loads the correct files.

ABOUT MICROSOFT OUTLOOK

Choose Help, About Microsoft Outlook to display the dialog box shown in Figure 1.18

The top line in this dialog box shows the version and build numbers of Outlook that you have installed.

The second line contains "No E-mail" if you have installed Outlook's No E-mail service option. Otherwise, the line contains "Internet Mail Only" or "Corporate or Workgroup" to indicate which e-mail and *collaboration* option you have installed.

Figure 1.18
The About Microsoft
Outlook box displays
information about
your Outlook
installation.

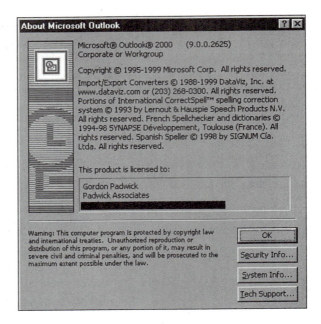

Choose one of the four buttons at the bottom-right of the dialog box:

- OK—Close the dialog box.
- Security Info—Displays information about the cipher strength available in the installed version of Outlook
- System Info—Displays information about your computer hardware and the installed operating system
- Tech Support—Displays information about resources for Outlook technical support

TROUBLESHOOTING

One of the troubles you may experience is that Windows and Windows applications on your computer may be somewhat, or very, different from what's described in this chapter. That's because Windows and many Windows applications are highly customizable. If you inherit a computer on which Outlook is already installed, you may find that Outlook looks quite different from the descriptions in this chapter.

Also, if you install Outlook on a computer that has previously had Outlook installed, what you see might be quite different from what you see in this book. That's because the Office 2000 installation procedure attempts to install Outlook (and other Office applications) in a manner that's as similar as possible to any previous installation.

Many of the settings for Windows and Windows applications are set by values in the Windows registry, some of which you can easily change from the *Control Panel*. However, there are many registry settings that can't be changed from the Control Panel. That's where Tweak UI, a utility supplied with Windows 98 (and also available for downloading from a Microsoft Web site) comes in very useful for fine-tuning the Windows user-interface.

INSTALLING TWEAK UI

You can easily install Tweak UI from your Windows 98 CD-ROM.

To install Tweak UI:

1. Close Outlook if it's running.
2. Insert your Windows 98 CD-ROM into the drive and open Windows Explorer.
3. Navigate to the folder Tools\Reskit\Powertoy on the Windows CD-ROM.
4. Right-click tweakiu.inf to display its context menu, then choose Install. After a few seconds, the installation is complete and an About Tweak UI information box is displayed.
5. Close the Tweak UI information box and close Windows Explorer.
6. Choose Start on the Windows taskbar, move the pointer onto Settings and choose Control Panel. Now you'll see an icon named Tweak UI on the control panel, as shown in Figure 1.19.

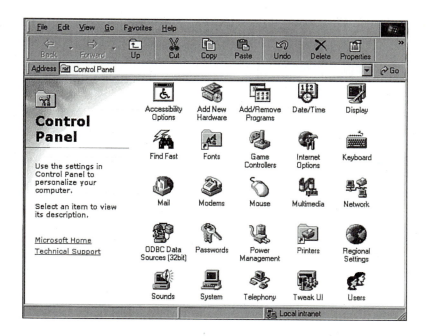

Figure 1.19
Use the Tweak UI button in the Control Panel to start Tweak UI.

USING TWEAK UI

After installing Tweak UI, double-click its icon in the Control Panel to start it. Tweak UI opens displaying the dialog box shown in Figure 1.20.

Figure 1.20
The Tweak UI dialog box has many tabs, each giving access to certain aspects of the Windows user interface.

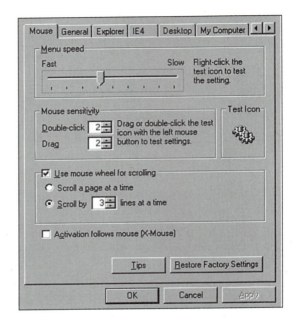

Many, but not all, Tweak UI's tabs contain a Restore Factory Settings button you can use to return the Windows user interface to its original state.

Only some of the Tweak UI tabs are visible at one time. You can use the buttons that contain left- and right-pointing arrows (at the right of the rightmost tab) to see other tabs.

The Tweak UI tabs are:

- Mouse
- General
- Explorer
- IE4
- Desktop
- My Computer
- Control Panel
- Network

- New
- Add/Remove
- Boot
- Repair
- Paranoia

It's a few minutes well-spent to open each of the tabs and gain an idea of what's there.

USING OTHER WAYS TO CUSTOMIZE OUTLOOK

This book contains a great deal of information about customizing Outlook, much of which is in Chapters 33 through 38. If Outlook isn't working the way you think it should, you'll probably find the answer to your problem in these chapters.

PART

I

CH

1

CHAPTER 2

UNDERSTANDING OUTLOOK'S SERVICE OPTIONS

In this chapter

by Gordon Padwick

Outlook contains many capabilities. You can use all of them, or just a few—it's up to you. You can install Outlook with only those capabilities you intend to use, so that Outlook doesn't clutter your disk with files you're not going to use. Also, by installing only what you're going to use, you'll minimize the time it takes to start and close Outlook.

OUTLOOK'S SERVICE OPTIONS

The major groups of Outlook's capabilities are known as service options. This chapter provides an insight into what those service options are. You'll find information about how to install service options in Appendix A, "Installing Outlook."

The following are the three available service options:

- No e-mail
- Internet mail only (IMO)
- Corporate or workgroup (C/W)

You have to choose one of these service options when you install Outlook. Only one service option can be enabled at a time, though you can switch from IMO to C/W and vice versa.

→ For information about changing from one service option to another, **see** "Switching to a Different Service Option, " **p. 1285**.

To find out which service option is installed on your computer, open Outlook and choose Help, About Microsoft Outlook. The second line of the About Microsoft Outlook dialog box contains "No E-mail" if you have the No E-mail option installed. Otherwise, the second line contains "Internet Mail Only," or "Corporate or Workgroup."

THE NO E-MAIL SERVICE OPTION

Outlook's No E-mail service option lets you use Outlook as a *Personal Information Manager* (PIM), *(page 14)* but provides no capability to send and receive e-mail and faxes. You might choose this service option if you don't use your computer for e-mail or for faxing, or if you're satisfied with other applications you have installed for e-mailing and faxing.

This service option uses a *Personal Folders file* in which you can save Calendar, Contact, Journal, Note, and Task items of information. You can share the information in this folder with other Outlook users in the same way that you can share other files. You can use Outlook's Import and Export Wizard to save specific types of Outlook items and items that satisfy certain criteria. You can also extract specific Outlook items by dragging them into a Windows folder.

→ For information about creating and using Outlook items, **see** "Managing Contacts," **p. 297**, "Managing Calendars," **p. 357**, "Managing Tasks," **p. 411**, "Keeping Your Journal," **p. 439**, "Using Outlook to Keep Notes," **p. 457** and "Importing and Exporting Outlook Items," **p. 565**.

INTERNET MAIL ONLY SERVICE OPTION

If you intend to use Outlook to send and receive Internet or intranet e-mail, but not e-mail using any other type of mail server, install Outlook's *Internet Mail Only* (IMO) service option. After you do so, you'll have all the capabilities of the No E-mail service option (described previously in this chapter), and the ability to send and receive e-mail by way of *Internet service providers* (ISPs) and also by way of your organization's intranets that use Internet protocols. This service option doesn't support servers that use the *Messaging Application Programming Interface* (MAPI) *(page 39)* standard.

PART

1

CH

2

Note

The last sentence of the preceding paragraph is generally true, but there is an exception. You can use Outlook's IMO service option to access e-mail on an Exchange server if that server has the *IMAP* service installed. In that case, you can create an IMAP account in IMO Outlook to access e-mail in an Exchange account.

After you've installed IMO Outlook, you can connect to any number of ISPs and intranets that use the POP3, SMTP, and IMAP *protocols (page 39)*. You can obtain a *digital signature* (certificate) and use it to authenticate messages you send and receive and, optionally, to encrypt and decrypt messages. In addition, you can access Internet-based directory services, including Bigfoot, Four11, Infospace, Infospace Business, SwitchBoard, VeriSign, and WhoWhere.

With IMO Outlook installed, you can use *Net Folders (page 453)* to share information with other people. You can publish most of your Outlook folders and give permission to specific people to access those folders. When the people to whom you have granted permission log on to the Internet, or on to an intranet, they see your published folders in the same way that they see their own Outlook folders.

Note

The term "folder publishing" is sometimes used to refer to Net Folders.

From within IMO Outlook, you can access Internet Explorer to access Web sites and Outlook Express to access *newsgroups*.

IMO Outlook also gives you the ability to send and receive faxes using the Symantec WinFax Starter Edition that's included with Office 2000. If you require more powerful faxing capabilities you can replace the WinFax Starter Edition with WinFax Pro version 9.0 (you have to purchase that from Symantec).

→ For detailed information about using IMO Outlook to send, receive, and share information, **see** "Understanding Protocols," **p. 39**, "Sending and Receiving E-mail with Internet Mail Only Outlook," **p. 59**, "Sending and Receiving Faxes with Internet Mail Only Outlook," **p. 127**, "Using Directory Services", **p. 349**, and "Outlook as a Sharing Tool," **p. 466**.

CORPORATE OR WORKGROUP SERVICE OPTION

Install the *Corporate or Workgroup* (C/W) Outlook service option if you intend to use Outlook as a client for Exchange Server or any other mail and collaboration server that is based on the *Messaging Application Programming Interface* (MAPI) *(page 39)* standard. This service option provides all the PIM capabilities described previously in this chapter, contains capabilities to send and receive Internet and intranet e-mail, use Internet Explorer to access Web sites, and use Outlook Express to participate in newsgroups. It also enables you to access all the mail and collaboration capabilities of MAPI-compliant servers. In short, C/W Outlook gives you everything Outlook has to offer.

The mail and collaboration capabilities available in C/W Outlook include access to:

- Internet and intranet e-mail, including Net Folders
- Mail and collaboration services in Exchange Server
- Faxing directly from your workstation or by way of Exchange Server
- Access to Microsoft Mail
- Use of all of Outlook's PIM capabilities with items saved either on your local hard drive or in the Exchange store
- Access to public folders on Exchange server
- The ability to work offline at a remote location and subsequently synchronize Outlook information with that on your server
- Access to Microsoft Mail, Lotus cc:Mail, and other MAPI-compliant mail servers
- Access to Lotus Notes (if you install an add-on available from Lotus)
- The ability to send messages to numeric and alphanumeric pagers (if you install an Outlook add-on available from various third-party suppliers)
- Access to address books created in other applications such as Corel WordPerfect

Don't install C/W Outlook unless you need its MAPI capabilities. Although C/W has enormous power, that power comes at a price:

- C/W Outlook occupies significantly more disk space than IMO Outlook
- C/W Outlook takes significantly longer to start up and shut down than IMO Outlook
- The way C/W Outlook sends and receives Internet e-mail is somewhat less convenient than the method used by IMO Outlook

→ For detailed information about using C/W Outlook to send, receive, and share information, **see** "Sending and Receiving E-mail with Corporate/Workgroup Outlook," **p. 167**, "Sending and Receiving Faxes with Corporate/Workgroup Outlook," **p. 233**, "Using Exchanger Server for E-mail," **p. 673**, "Working Remotely," **p. 729**, "Using Microsoft Mail for E-mail," **p. 775**, and "Using cc:Mail for E-mail," **p. 793**.

USING ADD-INS AND ADD-ONS

Microsoft supplies several additional capabilities, known as add-ins, with Outlook. These are not installed automatically when you install Outlook. If you want to use them, you must install them using Outlook's Add-in Manager.

Microsoft and other companies offer other additional capabilities, known as add-ons, that are not supplied with Outlook. Some of these are available at no charge. Others you must pay for, although trial versions are often available at no charge.

Appendix A contains information about installing add-ins and some add-ons. Appendix E, "Outlook Resources," contains information about sources of add-ons.

CONSIDER THIS

Choosing which Outlook service option to install is easy if you are one person at home, using Outlook for personal and (possibly) home office purposes. IMO Outlook is almost certainly what you need.

Choosing a service option for an enterprise is also easy. The enterprise already has, or plans to install, an e-mail system. Whether that system is Exchange, cc:Mail, Notes, or whatever, you need C/W Outlook to act as a client for the mail system.

The choice may not be so easy for a small office in which a few people work. IMO and C/W each has advantages and disadvantages in this situation:

- IMO Outlook has the advantage of simplicity. The disadvantages are that each user requires a modem and access to a phone line.

- If you require internal e-mail but no access to the Internet, C/W Outlook using Microsoft Mail for e-mail is a good solution because a separate server isn't required. If Internet access is required by some people, each of those people require a modem and access to a phone line.

- If most people require access to internal e-mail and to the Internet, or if you expect the office to grow to more than just a few people, a server-based LAN is the best choice. In this case each user needs to have C/W Outlook installed. One of the advantages of a server-based system, using Exchange as the mail server, is that one or more modems and phone lines can be shared by any number of people.

PART II

SENDING AND RECEIVING E-MAIL AND FAXES

CHAPTER 3

SENDING AND RECEIVING E-MAIL WITH INTERNET MAIL ONLY OUTLOOK

In this chapter

by Gordon Padwick

The material covered in this chapter applies specifically to *IMO Outlook (page 53)*. If you're using C/W Outlook, refer to Chapter 6, "Sending and Receiving Internet E-mail with Corporate/Workgroup Outlook," for information about sending and receiving Internet e-mail.

If you have an Internet e-mail account with an Internet service provider (ISP) you can use Outlook to exchange e-mail messages with anyone who also has an Internet e-mail account. You can also use Outlook to exchange e-mail messages by way of an *intranet* that uses Internet protocols. Outlook sends messages to your mail server, which routes those messages to recipients' mail servers. Messages addressed to you are delivered to your mail server, from which you can retrieve them.

Outlook saves copies of messages you send in the *Sent Items folder* within your Personal Folders file. Outlook saves messages you receive in the *Inbox folder* within your *Personal Folders file*.

Note

> The *folders (page 18)* named in the preceding paragraph are the folders that Outlook uses by default. You can set up Outlook to save copies of messages you send in folders other than Sent Items, and to save messages you receive in folders other than Inbox.

INSTALLING THE TCP/IP PROTOCOL

One of the common mistakes people make when they first try to connect to an ISP is not making sure that the *TCP/IP* protocol is installed on their computers. All Internet communication depends on the TCP/IP protocol, so you must have it installed in order to access Web sites, interact with newsgroups, or send and receive Internet e-mail. You don't need to understand TCP/IP; just make sure it's installed.

For information about installing TCP/IP under Windows 95, Windows 98, or Windows NT, see the Windows Help topic "Connecting to the Internet." If you follow the instructions carefully, you shouldn't have any problems. However, if you do have difficulty, your ISP's technical support people are there to help.

SETTING UP DIAL-UP NETWORKING

Outlook uses your computer's *modem* to connect to your ISP and to send information to, and receive information from, your mail server. The dial-up networking capability within Windows is used to place the phone call.

Note

> The information in the following paragraphs is based on the assumption you already have a modem properly installed in your computer. If that's not the case, install a modem before proceeding.

To verify that you have dial-up networking installed, open My Computer from your Windows desktop. One of the icons in the My Computer window should be Dial-Up Networking. If that icon isn't present, you must install dial-up networking in Windows. For information about doing that, look at the Dial-Up Networking topic in Windows Help.

Choose Dial-Up Networking in the My Computer window to open the Dial-Up Networking dialog box, such as that shown in Figure 3.1.

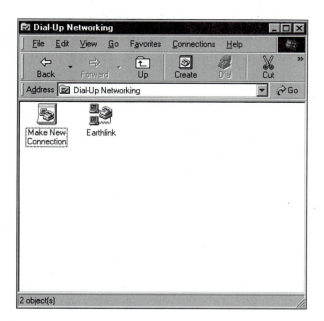

Figure 3.1
If you already have one or more dial-up connections, this dialog box contains icons representing them.

Note

The illustrations and procedures in this chapter are based on Outlook running under Windows 98. In some cases, there are differences between your screen and the figures if you're running Windows 95 or Windows NT.

To define a new dial-up connection:

1. In the Dial-Up Networking dialog box, double-click Make a New Connection to display the dialog box shown in Figure 3.2.

2. Replace "My Connection" in the Type a Name for the Computer You Are Dialing box with the name you want to use for the computer to which you will establish a dial-up connection. If you're creating a connection to an Internet service provider, you can use the ISP's name.

3. The Select a Device box contains the name of your modem driver. If you have more than one modem installed in your computer, open the drop-down list and select the appropriate driver.

Figure 3.2
This dialog box displays the name of the software driver that controls your modem.

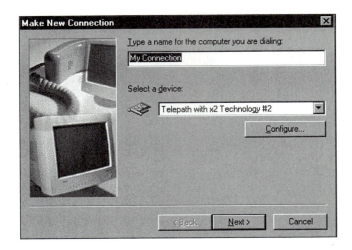

Note

After selecting a modem driver, you can choose Configure to configure the modem. If the modem is already working, this isn't necessary.

4. Choose Next > to display the next dialog box shown in Figure 3.3.

Figure 3.3
Use this dialog box to specify the phone number you want to call.

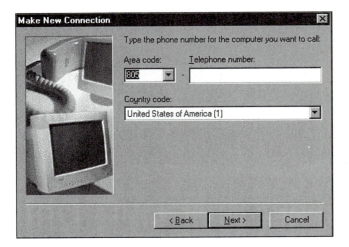

5. Enter the area code, telephone number, and country you want to call (your ISP's phone number), then choose Next > to display the final dialog box shown in Figure 3.4.

6. Choose Finish to return to the Dial-Up Networking dialog box, which now contains an icon representing the new dial-up connection.

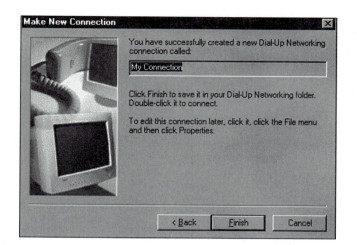

Figure 3.4
This dialog box confirms that you have created a new dial-up connection.

PART
II

CH
3

Note

Although the preceding steps provide a phone connection to an ISP, in most cases more is required to be able to log on to the Internet and on to mail servers provided by that ISP. For example, you may have to specify Internet Protocol (IP) addresses. The settings required are different for each ISP. Your ISP will provide detailed information about the required settings and how you must set up dial-up networking.

CREATING AN INTERNET ACCOUNT

First, you have to establish an account with an Internet service provider (*ISP*), then you have to create an Internet account within Outlook.

Establishing an account with an ISP usually involves choosing an ISP and then making a phone call to that ISP, or using your Web browser to connect to that ISP's Web site. Either way, you'll have to give the ISP your name, suggest a name for your account, provide a password, and agree to some way that the ISP will bill you (usually via a monthly charge to one of your credit cards). After you've done that, the ISP will provide whatever information is necessary for you to log on to your account.

CHOOSING AN INTERNET SERVICE PROVIDER

Don't choose your ISP lightly. Although you can change your ISP at any time, when you change your ISP, your Internet e-mail address changes.

You can choose from many ISPs, many of whom offer different services. Consider the following:

- Some ISPs have local access telephone numbers in many parts of the country, while others have local access numbers only for one city or region. If you're likely to want to connect to your ISP while traveling, choose an ISP that has local access numbers in the places you expect to visit.

- Some ISPs allow you to have more than one e-mail address for your account so that people who share the account can keep their e-mail separate. This is particularly useful for a small business or family. Not all ISPs offer this service.

- Some ISPs accommodate various types of connections, including high-speed modem, ISDN, and others. If you expect to become a frequent Internet user, choose an ISP that offers high-speed connections, even if you don't use those connections initially.

- Some ISPs offer free or low-cost disk space you can use to create your own Web site, others don't. If you anticipate having your own Web site, investigate the cost of it being hosted by the ISP before you make your choice.

- Most ISPs provide access to Internet newsgroups. If there are some newsgroups you need to use, make sure the ISP you choose provides access to them.

After you've evaluated ISPs based on these criteria, ask around to get the opinions of people who use the services you're interested in. What you need is an ISP that provides the services you require and that gives you fast access. Only people's experience can give you the information you need to make your choice.

CREATING AN OUTLOOK INTERNET ACCOUNT

After you signed up with an Internet service provider (ISP), your next step is to connect to that account from Outlook.

With IMO Outlook running, follow these steps.

Note   If you don't already have an e-mail account, the first time you start IMO Outlook, you're automatically led into the process of creating an Internet account. In that case, Step 1 in the following procedure occurs automatically.

To create an Outlook Internet account, start Outlook and proceed as follows:

1. Choose Tools, Accounts to open the dialog box shown in Figure 3.5.

2. Choose Add, Mail to open the first Internet Connection Wizard window, shown in Figure 3.6.

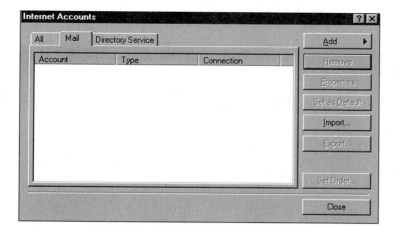

Figure 3.5
The Internet Accounts dialog box opens with the Mail tab selected. Any Internet accounts you already have set up are listed.

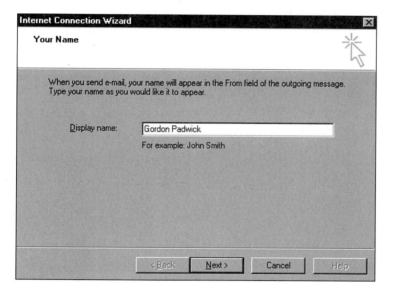

Figure 3.6
Use the first Internet Connection Wizard window to enter the name under which you intend to send messages.

3. Enter your name or pseudonym in the Display Name box, then choose Next > to open the second wizard window, shown in Figure 3.7.

4. Enter the Internet address your ISP provided in the E-mail Address box in this wizard window, then choose Next > to display the third wizard window, shown in Figure 3.8.

5. Open the drop-down list near the top of the wizard window and select either POP3 or IMAP according to the protocol your mail server uses for incoming mail.

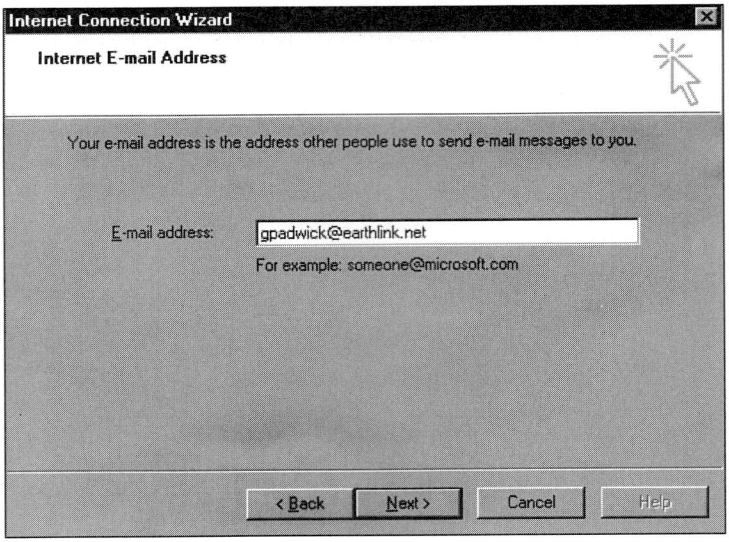

Figure 3.7
Use this wizard to enter your Internet address.

Figure 3.8
Use this wizard window to identify your incoming and outgoing mail servers.

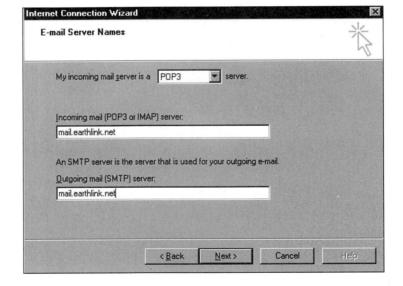

6. In the Incoming Mail (POP3 or IMAP) Server box, enter the name of that server.

7. In the Outgoing Mail (SMTP) Server box, enter the name of that server. The names of the incoming and outgoing mail servers may be the same or different. Choose Next > to display the fourth wizard window, shown in Figure 3.9.

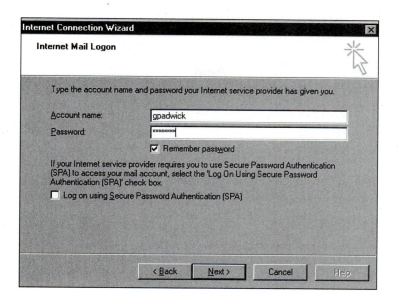

Figure 3.9
Use this wizard window to specify how you will log onto e-mail.

Note

Three ways exist to log on to e-mail. For everyday use when security isn't an issue, you can supply your e-mail account name and password in the Internet Connection Wizard. Subsequently, you don't have to provide your account name or password when you log on.

To gain more security, you can set up the account so that you have to enter a password in order to access e-mail. By doing so, you ensure that anyone who opens Outlook on your computer can't access your e-mail.

When security is an important issue, you should probably use a mail server that requires you to enter your account name and password each time you log on.

8. If you're not using a server that requires you to enter your account name when you log on, enter your account name in the Account Name box and enter your password in the Password box. If you want to be required to enter your password each time you log onto e-mail, uncheck the Remember Password box. If you are using a mail server that requires you to enter your name and password each time you log on, choose Log On Using Secure Password Authentication (SPA). Choose Next > to open the fifth wizard window, shown in Figure 3.10.

9. Choose Connect Using My Phone Line if that's what you will do, then choose Next > to open the sixth wizard window shown in Figure 3.11. If you are connecting to a local intranet, choose Connect Using My Local Area Network (LAN), then choose Next > to display the final wizard window shown in Figure 3.12. Otherwise choose I Will Establish My Internet Connection Manually, then choose Next > to display the final wizard window, shown in Figure 3.12.

Figure 3.10
Use this wizard window to specify how you will connect to your mail server.

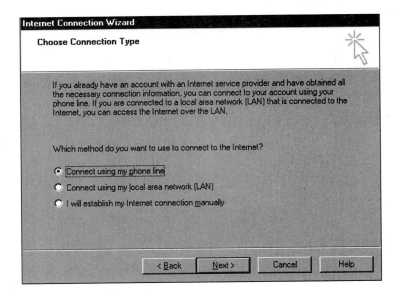

Figure 3.11
Use this wizard window to select a previously established dial-up connection or to create a new one.

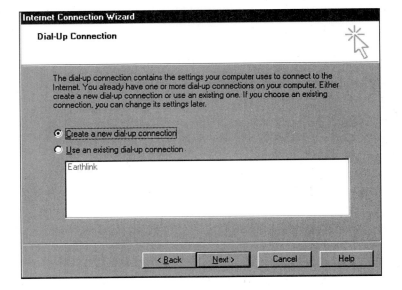

10. Choose Use an Existing Dial-up Connection, select one of the dial-up connections you previously established from those listed in this wizard window, then choose Next > to display the final wizard window, shown in Figure 3.12. If you haven't previously established a dial-up connection, choose Create a New Dial-up Connection and choose Next > to open the Internet Connection Wizard (described previously in this chapter).

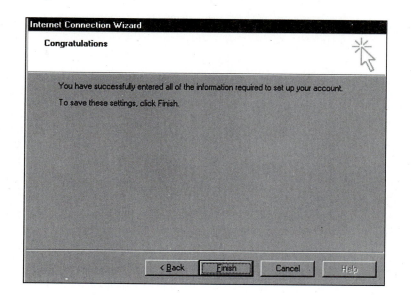

Figure 3.12
This wizard window
confirms that you
have finished setting
up a connection.

11. Choose <u>F</u>inish to close the wizard and return to the Internet Accounts dialog box in
    which the new account is listed.

You can repeat these steps to create additional Internet or intranet connections.

MANAGING INTERNET ACCOUNTS

You can use the Internet Accounts dialog box, shown previously in Figure 3.5, to manage
your Internet accounts.

ADDING AND REMOVING ACCOUNTS

As explained in the preceding section, choose <u>A</u>dd to create a new account.

To remove an account from the list, select that account, and then choose <u>R</u>emove. Outlook
displays a message asking you to confirm that you want to remove the selected account.

EXAMINING AND CHANGING AN ACCOUNT'S PROPERTIES

To examine or change an account's properties, select that account in the list and then
choose <u>P</u>roperties to open the four-tabbed dialog box shown in Figure 3.13 with the
General tab selected. Any changes you make within the four tabs are saved when you
choose OK.

The General tab contains some of the information you supplied when you used the Internet
Connection Wizard to create the account. You can edit this information and supply additional information.

Figure 3.13
The General tab of the Properties dialog box contains basic information about the selected account.

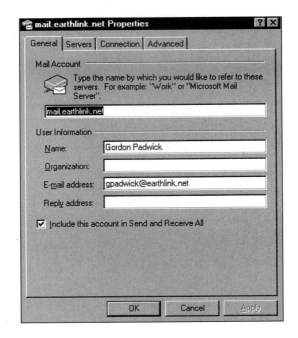

Some things to notice here are:

- You can enter the name of your organization.
- If you want people to reply to your messages using an e-mail address other than the one you use to send messages, you can enter that address in the Reply Address box. If you want people to reply to the e-mail address from which you sent the message, leave the Reply Address box empty.
- By default, the check box at the bottom of the tab is checked. By having this box checked, when you subsequently do a full Send and Receive, messages you've prepared for this account will be sent, and messages waiting for you in this account will be delivered to your Inbox. If this box is not checked, you have to separately send messages to, and receive messages from, this account.

The Servers tab, shown in Figure 3.14, contains more information you supplied in the Internet Connection Wizard.

The Connection tab, shown in Figure 3.15, contains information about the connection you specified in the Internet Connection Wizard.

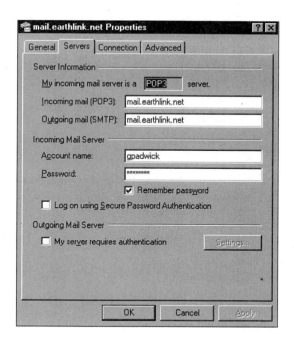

Figure 3.14
You can edit any information in this tab, with the exception that you can't change the incoming server type from POP3 to IMAP or vice versa.

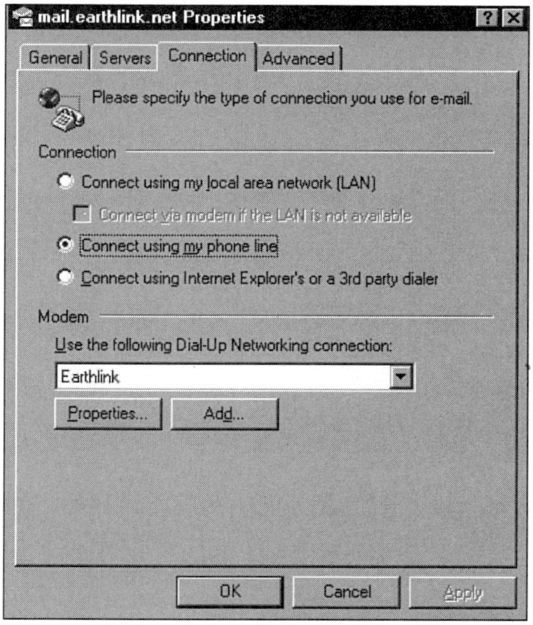

Figure 3.15
You can edit information in this tab, change the properties of your dial-up connection, and add a new dial-up connection.

The Advanced tab, shown in Figure 3.16, provides access to connection properties that were provided automatically when you used the Internet Connection Wizard to create a new connection.

Figure 3.16
Make changes in the Advanced tab only if the default settings give you problems.

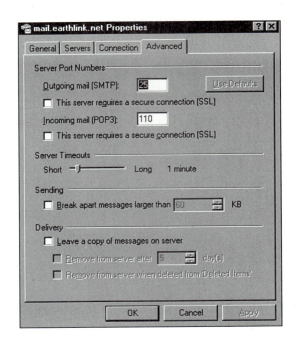

The Server Port Numbers section at the top contains information that's usually correct. Don't change the information in this section unless you have specific instructions from the server administrator to do so.

If you find that you're frequently disconnected from your mail server before the connection is completed, you may have to increase the time specified in the Server Timeouts section. In most cases the default value of one minute is adequate. If necessary, you can drag the pointer in this box to the right to increase the timeout, giving the server more time to process your request for service.

Some servers have a message size limit. To overcome that, you can set Outlook to break up long messages into several smaller ones. Check the Break Apart Messages Larger Than check box, and then enter the appropriate message size.

After you've downloaded a message waiting for you on a server, that message is normally automatically deleted from the server. You may be able to leave messages on your server after you've read them. Not all servers allow this; some that do limit the space you can use for this purpose and limit the period for which messages can be saved.

Tip #11 from

You can designate one computer as your main mail reader. When you read mail from other computers, leave that mail on the server. Allow the server to delete messages only when you read mail from your main computer. This ensures that all your mail is stored on one computer.

If you want to leave messages you've read on the server, check the Leave a Copy of Messages on the Server box. When you do so, the next two check boxes become enabled. If you leave these boxes unchecked, messages remain on the server as long as the server administrator permits. You can check the Remove from Server After box and specify a certain number of days. You can also check the Remove from Server when Deleted from "Deleted Items"; in that case, when you delete items from your *Deleted Items folder*, those items are also deleted from the server.

SELECTING A DEFAULT ACCOUNT

If you have two or more Internet accounts, you can make one account the default. Select that account in the Internet Accounts dialog box (shown previously in Figure 3.5), and choose Set as Default.

EXPORTING AND IMPORTING ACCOUNTS

After you've created an account, you can export that account to a file and subsequently import that account into Outlook running on another computer. This can be a time-saver if you set up accounts, say, on your office computer and want to have the same accounts on your home computer or a laptop you use while traveling.

To export an account to a file:

1. In the Internet Accounts dialog box, select the account you want to export.
2. Choose Export to display the dialog box shown in Figure 3.17.

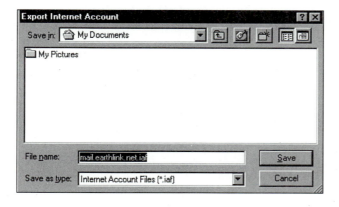

Figure 3.17
Use this dialog box to select the folder in which you want to save the account and to give the account a name.

3. Navigate to the folder in which you want to save the account file.
4. Outlook proposes to use the account name as the file name. You can replace the proposed name. Outlook automatically uses .iaf as the file name extension for saved accounts.
5. Choose Save to save the file.

Note

Don't be concerned if your account name includes a period. For example, if your account name is fastnet.net, the saved file could be fastnet.net.iaf. Windows 95, Windows 98, and Windows NT recognizes the characters after the last period in a file name as the extension; any preceding periods in the file name are part of the name itself.

To import a saved account:

1. In the Internet Accounts dialog box, choose Import to display the dialog box shown in Figure 3.18.

Figure 3.18
Use this dialog box to locate the account you want to import.

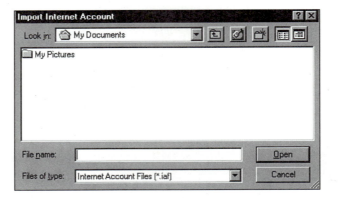

2. Navigate to the folder that contains the account you want to import and select the file that contains the account.

3. Choose Open to import the account. Outlook does not import the account if an account with the same name already exists.

Note

The Internet Accounts dialog box is also used to define directory services, as explained in Chapter 9, "Managing Contacts." The Set Order button is enabled only when you choose the Directory Service tab.

→ For information about using directory services to find e-mail addresses for people and organizations, **see** "Using Directory Services," **p. 349**.

LOGGING INTERNET MAIL CONNECTIONS

If you run into problems connecting with an Internet Mail Server (or an intranet server that uses Internet protocols) you may see the message "The connection to the server has failed." The problem may be in your mail server or TCP/IP settings.

*Detailed information about correcting these problems is beyond the scope of this book, but Microsoft offers some suggestions in a Knowledge Base article. **See** the Microsoft Knowledge Base article Q154578, Troubleshooting Problems Connecting to Mail Servers.*

If you encounter problems accessing Internet accounts, it's useful to able to log certain aspects of the connection. Outlook provides no direct way to do that, but you can activate logging by making changes to the *Windows registry (page 605)*.

Caution

> Always make a backup copy of the registry before making changes to it. See Appendix F, "Working with the Windows Registry," for information about backing up the registry and making changes to it.

To enable logging:

1. If Outlook is open, choose File, Exit to close it.

2. Choose Start on the Windows taskbar, and choose Run in the Start menu. Enter regedit in the Open box and choose OK to start the Registry Editor.

PART
II
CH
3

3. Using the method explained in Appendix F, access the key: HKEY_CURRENT_USER\Software\Microsoft\Office\9.0\Outlook\Options\Mail. The top of the Registry Editor window should show the selected registry key, as shown in Figure 3.19.

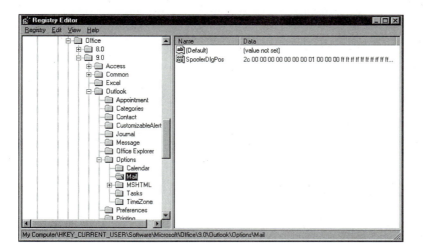

Figure 3.19
The Registry Editor window shows the original values in the selected key.

4. Choose Edit, move the pointer onto New, and choose DWORD Value. The value name New Value #1 is added to the list of value names in the Registry Editor's right pane.

5. Type in the word **Logging** to replace New Value #1 and press Enter.

6. With Logging selected, Choose Edit, Modify to open the Edit DWORD Value dialog box shown in Figure 3.20.

Figure 3.20
The new key initially contains the value 0 (zero).

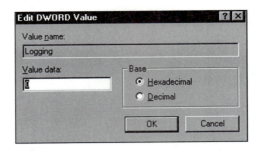

7. Enter 1 (the number one) in the Value Data box, then choose OK. The Registry Editor now shows the new key and its value, as shown in Figure 3.21.

8. Choose Registry, Exit to close the Registry Editor.

Figure 3.21
This is how the Registry Editor should look after you've added the new value.

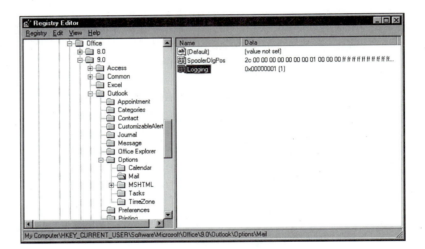

The next time you use Outlook to connect, or attempt to connect, to an Internet account, three files will be created in the Windows\Temp\Outlook Logging folder (Windows 95 or Windows 98) or in the WINNT\Temp\Outlook Logging folder (Windows NT):

- InetXP.txt—Logs the Internet session
- Pop3log.txt—Logs mail retrieval
- Smtplog.txt—Logs mail sending

 See Microsoft Knowledge Base articles Q155455 *How to Enable and Interpret the Smtp.log File* and Q155515 *How to Enable and Interpret the Pop3.log File* for information about interpreting data in the three logging files.

After you've finished troubleshooting, you can use the Registry Editor again to turn off logging by setting Logging to 0.

SAVING MESSAGES

When you first open Outlook, a Personal Folders file is automatically created. If you're the only user of your computer running Windows 95 or Windows 98, this file is created in your Windows folder and usually has the name Outlook.pst.

If you're using Outlook under Windows NT, this file is created in your Personal folder within your Windows profile and usually has the same name as your Windows logon name. For example, if your logon name is jaldrich, your Personal Folders file is probably C:\WINNT\Profiles\jaldrich\Personal\jaldrich.pst.

Outlook saves messages you receive in the Inbox folder within your Personal Folders file; it saves copies of messages you send in the Sent Items folder within your Personal Folders file (unless you designate other folders).

The creation and use of a Personal Folders file is automatic, something you normally don't have to be concerned with unless you want to password-protect it or, of course, something goes wrong.

PART

II

CH

3

PASSWORD PROTECTING YOUR PERSONAL FOLDERS FILE

You can protect all the Outlook items, including messages you send and receive, in your Personal Folders file by password-protecting that file.

To password-protect your Personal Folders file:

1. With any Outlook *Information viewer (page 17)* displayed, choose View, Folder List to display your folder list.

2. Right-click Outlook Today - [Personal Folders], then choose Properties for Personal Folders to display the dialog box shown in Figure 3.22.

3. Choose Advanced (near the bottom-right) to display the dialog box shown in Figure 3.23.

4. Choose Change Password to display the dialog box shown in Figure 3.24.

5. If you already have password-protected your Personal Folders file, enter the current password in the Old Password Box. Leave this box empty if you haven't previously password-protected your Personal Folders file.

6. Enter the new password into the New Password box, and enter the new password again into the Verify Password box.

7. Make sure the Save This Password in Your Password List box is unchecked, then choose OK three times to close the dialog boxes.

8. Choose File, Exit to close Outlook.

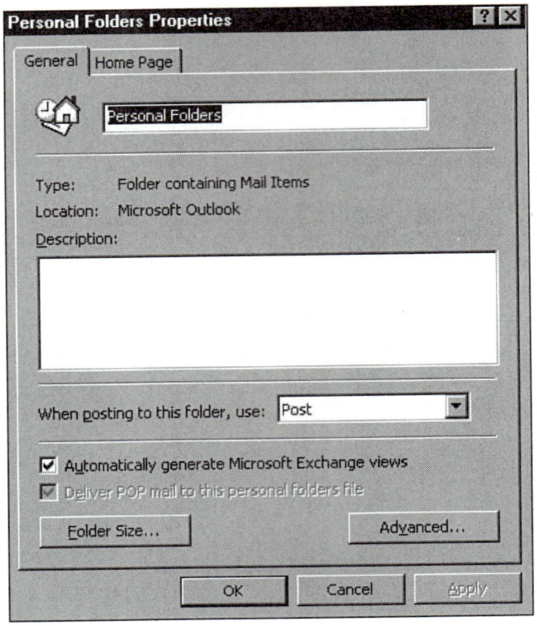

Figure 3.22
The Personal Folders
Properties dialog box
is displayed with the
General tab selected.

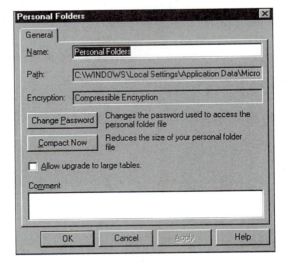

Figure 3.23
You can use the
Personal Folders dia-
log box for various
purposes, including
accessing the Change
Password dialog box.

Tip #12 from

This dialog box displays the complete path name of your Personal Folders file. Make a note
of that name—you might need it later if you run into problems.

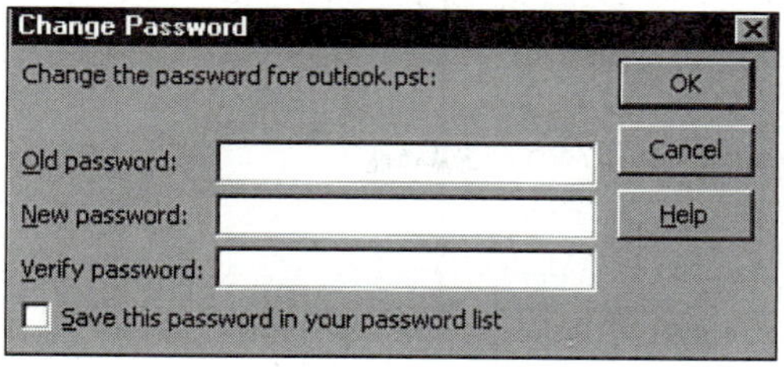

Figure 3.24
This dialog box is where you can change an existing password or create a new one.

The next time you open Outlook, you'll be asked to enter a password before Outlook will open.

Tip #13 from

To remove password protection, open the Change Password dialog box and enter the password in the Old Password box. Leave the New Password and Verify Password boxes empty, choose OK three times to close the dialog boxes, then close Outlook.

WHAT IF YOUR PERSONAL FOLDERS FILE BECOMES CORRUPTED?

If your Personal Folders file becomes corrupted (or if you move or rename it), you won't be able to access your Outlook folders and you may not even be able to open Outlook.

Caution

Don't rename your Personal Folders file or move it from one folder to another, unless you completely understand how to get Outlook back on track.

You may be able to solve these problems by following these steps:

To recreate your Personal Folders file:

1. If Outlook is running, choose File, Exit to close it.

2. From the Windows taskbar, choose Start, move the pointer onto Find, then choose Files and Folders to open the Find: All Files dialog box.

3. In the Named box, enter *.pst, in the Look In box, select My Computer, then choose Find Now. Windows searches your entire environment to look for any files that have .pst as their file name extensions.

4. Right-click the name of the Personal Folders file that's giving you problems to display its context menu. Choose Rename in the context menu, then replace the current name with a new name and press Enter. Close the Find dialog box.

5. Start Outlook. You'll see a message telling you that the old Personal Folders file can't be found. Choose OK to open the Create/Open Personal Folders File dialog box, which should now contain the new name you entered in the previous step. Select that name, and choose Open. Usually Outlook opens with your Personal Folders file available.

A Microsoft Knowledge Base article contains additional suggestions for dealing with corrupted Personal Folders files. **See** the Microsoft Knowledge Base article Q179743 Creating a New Personal Folder for an IMO Account.

SELECTING A MESSAGE FORMAT AND E-MAIL EDITOR

Outlook lets you choose three formats for sending messages. It also lets you create messages using two different editors. Outlook 2000 handles these capabilities more conveniently than did previous Outlook versions.

MESSAGE FORMAT CAPABILITIES

You can choose to send messages in HTML, Outlook Rich Text, or Plain Text formats. Table 3.1 compares these formats.

Note

Don't assume the people to whom you send e-mail messages will be able to receive your messages with all the formatting you create, nor that they will be able to open attachments to your messages. In some cases, you may have to send sample messages to ascertain whether the e-mail programs recipients use are capable of receiving what you send.

TABLE 3.1   MESSAGE FORMATS

Format	Description
HTML	The *Hypertext Markup Language* (HTML) format offers you the ability to quickly and easily create highly formatted pages that include horizontal lines, pictures, animated graphics, and multimedia files. You can also select a *stationery* that provides a background design for your messages. Use this format only if you know that the message recipients' use e-mail programs that can read HTML.
Outlook Rich Text	Outlook Rich Text is the standard Exchange format, so it's appropriate for C/W Outlook used as a client for Exchange. You can select fonts, font sizes, and font colors, and you can format paragraphs. You can embed objects, including pictures, within the text. Don't use this format to send messages that contain attachments to people who aren't using Outlook or Windows Messaging to receive e-mail. Instead of receiving the attachments you sent, recipients will see attachments called Winmail.dat that don't contain any meaningful information.
Plain Text	This format does what you'd expect: you can use it for unformatted text; you can attach files and Outlook items to Plain Text messages. Despite its limitations, this format is your best choice for general e-mail and for messages to newsgroups. Use this format for e-mail you send to people who aren't using Outlook or Windows Messaging as their e-mail program. You can, of course, use this format for messages to people who do use Outlook or Windows Messaging.

To be on the safe side, use Plain Text for Internet e-mail unless you really need the formatting capabilities of HTML. If you do use HTML, be prepared for the fact that some recipients may not receive your messages as you intended. An advantage of the Plain Text format is that it results in smaller files, something that's important for people who pay for Internet access by the minute, or pay long-distance phone charges.

As described subsequently in this chapter, you can use any of these mail formats to send messages that have attachments.

→ **See** a book about Internet Explorer, such as *Using Internet Explorer 4*, published by Que, for detailed information about HTML.

SELECTING A MESSAGE FORMAT

You can select a default message format, the format you expect to use for most of your messages, and you can select a format other than the default for specific messages (only if you're not using WordMail as your editor).

PART

II

CH

3

Tip #14 from	Unless you have a good reason for doing otherwise, select Plain Text as your default message format.

To select a default message format:

1. Choose Tools, Options and select the Mail Format tab shown in Figure 3.25.

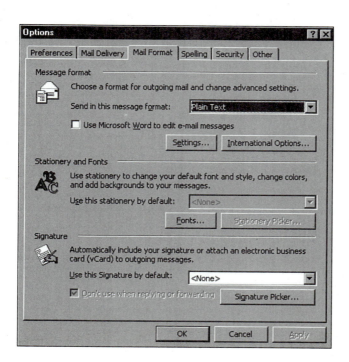

Figure 3.25
Use this dialog box to select a default mail format.

2. Open the Send in This Message Format drop-down list, and select HTML, Microsoft Outlook Rich Text, or Plain Text. Choose OK to close the dialog box.

Note

After you choose HTML, and have not checked Use Microsoft Word to Edit E-mail Messages, you can choose a default stationery.

Subsequently, when you create a message, Outlook will use the default format unless you choose a different format for that message.

When you reply to a message you've received, Outlook automatically uses the same message format as the message you received. Similarly, if you want to annotate a message you've received and then forward the message, Outlook uses the same format as the message you received.

Note

As described subsequently in this chapter, you can change the message format from the one Outlook automatically proposes.

→ **See** "Formatting a Message" **p. 92** later in this chapter for information about stationeries.
→ **See** "Mail Format Options," **p. 867** for complete information about the Options dialog box's Mail Format tab. To learn how to create a message, **see** "Creating a Message," **p. 84**.

SELECTING A MAIL EDITOR

A mail editor is a tool you use to create messages. No matter which mail format you select, you can use Outlook's native editor or WordMail as your editor. WordMail provides access to many of the components of Word 2000 and is available only if you have Word 2000 installed on your computer.

If you have Word 2000 installed on your computer, you have the choice of using Outlook's native editor or WordMail. The disadvantages of using WordMail are the slight delay incurred in loading Word the first time that you start editing in any Outlook session, not being able to use stationeries, and not being able to select message formats for individual messages. Another disadvantage of using WordMail is that recipients of your messages who aren't also using WordMail often see attachments as meaningless Winmail.dat files.

The advantages of using WordMail are that you can use Word's capabilities, such as justification and creating borders that aren't available in Outlook's native editor.

Note

Outlook doesn't let you use any editor or word processor other than WordMail or the Outlook native editor.

To select an e-mail editor, choose Tools, Options to open the Options dialog box and select the Mail Format tab, shown previously in Figure 3.25. Check Use Microsoft Word to Edit E-mail Messages if you want to use Word; leave the box unchecked if you want to use Outlook's native editor.

After you select WordMail as your editor and you start to create a new message with Plain Text selected as your message format, you'll have menus and toolbars similar to those available in Word at your disposal, as shown in Figure 3.26.

After you select Outlook's native editor and start to create a new message with Plain Text selected as your message format, the menus and toolbar shown in Figure 3.27 are available.

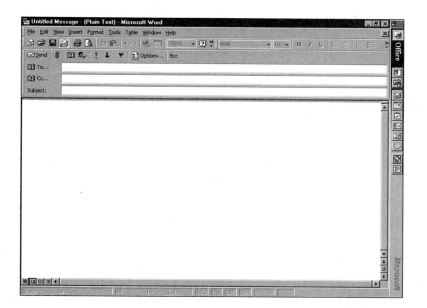

Figure 3.26
These are the menus and toolbars available when you use WordMail as your editor.

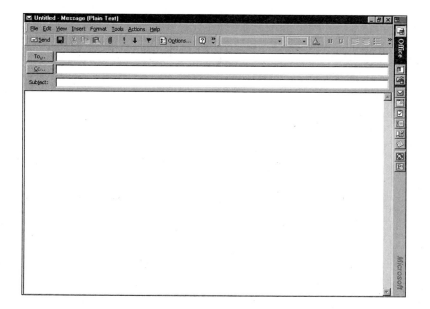

Figure 3.27
These are the menus and the toolbars available when you use Outlook's native editor.

CREATING A MESSAGE

This chapter is primarily about using Outlook to send and receive e-mail messages. However, within the Office environment, you don't necessarily need to open Outlook to send a message. You can send a message from within Word or one of the other Office applications.

SENDING A MESSAGE FROM WORD

In Word, or another Office application, you can create a document and send that document to an e-mail recipient. Here's how.

To create a message in Word and send it by e-mail:

1. Open Word and create the message.

2. Choose File, move the pointer onto Send To, and choose Mail Recipient. The Document form expands to show To, Cc, and Subject boxes at the top.

3. Choose To to open the Select Names dialog box, which displays a list of your contacts.

4. Select one or more people to whom you want to send the message, choose To-> to move the name or names into the Message Recipients list, then choose OK to return to the Document form in which the recipients names are displayed.

5. If appropriate, choose Cc to select the names of people to whom you want to copy the message.

6. Enter a subject of the message in the Subject box.

7. Choose Send a Copy in the form's toolbar to send the document as a message. When you do that, the document is placed in Outlook's Outbox, ready to be sent. The document is actually sent the next time you send messages from Outlook to your mail server.

> **Note**
>
> The preceding procedure referred specifically to sending a message from Word. You can use similar steps to send messages from other Office applications.

OPENING THE MESSAGE FORM

The following information assumes you're using Outlook's native editor and have selected Plain Text as your default message format, as described previously in this chapter.

To create a message, start by choosing Inbox in the Outlook Bar to display the Inbox Information viewer. Choose New at the left end of the Standard toolbar. The first time you make this choice, Outlook displays a dialog box that asks whether you would like to use Word as your e-mail editor. You can choose Yes or No. The remainder of this chapter assumes you choose No because you probably don't need Word's capabilities while you're creating e-mail messages.

Outlook displays a message form similar to that shown in Figure 3.27. Notice that the form's title bar reminds you which message format you have chosen as the default.

CHOOSING INTERNATIONAL OPTIONS

Something new in Outlook 2000 is the importance of International Options. In the Mail Format tab of the Options dialog box, shown previously in Figure 3.25, choose International Options to display the dialog box shown in Figure 3.28.

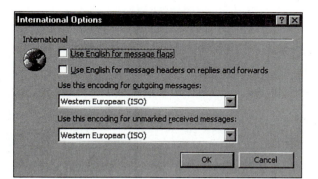

Figure 3.28
By default, Western European (ISO) encoding is selected for outgoing and unmarked received messages.

Note

"Encoding" refers to the relationship between the digital representations of characters in a message (or other file) and the way those characters appear on the screen or in print, and also the digital codes that are recorded by pressing keys on your keyboard. Encoding is controlled in the Windows environment by code pages, each of which contains a table of characters with a numeric index assigned to each character.

Normally, accept the defaults in this dialog box. You can open the Use This Encoding for Outgoing Messages and Use This Encoding the Unmarked Received Messages drop-down lists and select encoding other than the defaults.

Note

If you select encoding other than Western European (ISO), people who receive your messages using Outlook 97 or Outlook 98 will not be able to send replies to your messages.

If you use a non-English version of Outlook, you can check:

- Use English for Message Flags. After you do so, such flags as High Importance and Flag for Follow-up appear in English.
- Use English for Message Headers on Replies and Forwards. After you do so, the headers of message replies and forwarded messages use English for field name labels such as From, To, Sent, and Subject.

CHANGING THE MESSAGE FORMAT

If you want to use a message format other than your default, choose Format in the Message form's menu bar to display the menu shown in Figure 3.29. You can select an alternative format either before or after you've entered the message text.

Select HTML or Rich Text if you want to switch to either of those formats. The message form name in the form's title bar changes to show the new format you've selected.

After you've switched to HTML or Rich Text, or if you had chosen HTML or Rich Text as your default format, you can change to Plain Text. To do so, choose Format in the form's menu bar to see a menu that contains Plain Text as well as HTML or Rich Text. Choose Plain Text to switch to that format. When you do so, you'll see a message warning you about losing formatting. Choose Yes if you want to continue.

Changing from HTML to Rich Text, or vice versa, is a two-step process. First change from HTML (or Rich Text) to Plain Text. With the Plain Text format selected, choose Format in the form's menu bar to display a menu in which you can select HTML or Rich Text.

Figure 3.29
The Format menu contains your default format, Plain Text in this case, which is checked, and also HTML and Rich Text.

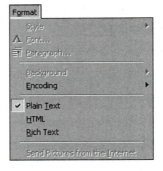

Note

When you change the message format in this way, the change affects only the current message. Subsequent messages use the default format. The only place to change the default format is to choose Tools, Options and select the Mail Format tab.

The remainder of this section assumes you're using the HTML message format, even though I recommend using Plain Text for most purposes. This is so that I can describe several capabilities offered by HTML that aren't available in Plain Text. You'll find minor differences if you're using the Plain Text or Rich Text formats.

You can also use the Message form's Format menu to change encoding from the default. Move the pointer onto Encoding and select from a list of available encoding formats. This is something you normally shouldn't have to do and, in fact, shouldn't do unless you understand the implications.

ADDRESSING THE MESSAGE

The blank message form shown previously in Figure 3.27 contains the message header consisting of the To, Cc, and Subject boxes. If you see only the To box, choose View, Message Header in the form's menu bar to display the complete message header.

Figure 3.30 shows a typical message form with recipient addresses, subject, and message text entered.

To address the message, enter one or more recipient e-mail addresses in the To box. You can do so in several ways, each of which is convenient in specific circumstances.

→ For detailed information about addressing a message, **see** "Managing Contacts," **p. 297**.

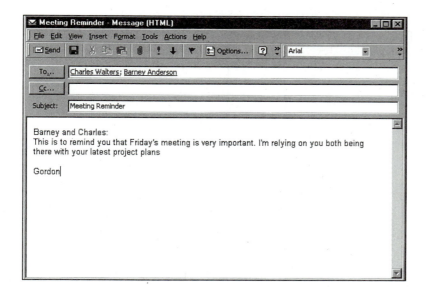

Figure 3.30
This message form is ready to send.

PART

II

CH

3

Note

The following sections make frequent reference to your Contact List. To use the information in these sections, you must already have Contact entries in your Address Book.

MANUALLY ENTERING AN E-MAIL ADDRESS

If you know recipients' e-mail addresses, you can enter those addresses in the To box, separating one address from the next with a semicolon. After you've completed entering addresses, press Tab to move to the next box. At that time, Outlook attempts to verify the e-mail addresses you entered by comparing them with information in your Address Book, a process referred to as *resolving* addresses.

When Outlook finds an address you've entered in the Address Book, Outlook replaces the address with the person's name and underlines that name. If Outlook doesn't find the e-mail address in your Address Book, but does recognize the address as being in acceptable Internet format, it simply underlines the address you entered. If Outlook doesn't recognize the address as being in Internet format, Outlook leaves the name as you entered it without underlining it.

If you enter several recipients' e-mail addresses, some of them may be in your Address Book, but not others. If that's the case, the To box contains a mixture of e-mail addresses and people's names.

ENTERING RECIPIENTS' NAMES

If you're sending a message to recipients whose names and e-mail addresses are in your Address Book, you can enter names instead of e-mail addresses. After you enter one or more names, separating one from the next with a semicolon, press Tab to move to the Cc box. At that time, Outlook looks for the names in your Address Book. If Outlook finds a name, Outlook underlines the name to indicate that it is acceptable.

To be sure the e-mail address is correct, right-click the person's name to display a context menu. Choose Properties in the context menu to display the dialog box shown in Figure 3.31.

Figure 3.31
The Summary tab in this dialog box shows the person's default e-mail address.

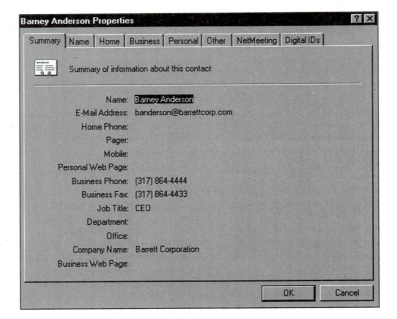

Barney Anderson Properties

Summary | Name | Home | Business | Personal | Other | NetMeeting | Digital IDs

Summary of information about this contact

Name:	Barney Anderson
E-Mail Address:	banderson@barrettcorp.com
Home Phone:	
Pager:	
Mobile:	
Personal Web Page:	
Business Phone:	(317) 864-4444
Business Fax:	(317) 864-4433
Job Title:	CEO
Department:	
Office:	
Company Name:	Barrett Corporation
Business Web Page:	

OK   Cancel

Caution

The fact that Outlook underlines a name in the To box on the Message form indicates only that the name exists in your Address Book, not that the Address Book contains an e-mail address for the *contact (page 298)*. That's why you should check a name's Properties to make sure an e-mail address is available.

ENTERING PARTIAL RECIPIENT NAMES

Instead of entering the complete names of recipients, you can enter partial names. For example, you could enter Frank and press Tab. Outlook searches your Address Book and, if it finds only one Frank, it displays that Frank's full name and underlines it. You should check the name's properties, as previously described, to ensure Outlook has chosen the correct e-mail address.

If there are two or more Franks in your address book and you haven't previously sent e-mail to either of them, Outlook places a squiggly red line under the name you entered to indicate that you have to make a decision. Right-click the name you entered and Outlook displays a list of all the Franks in your address book. Select the one to whom you want to send this message.

If there are two or more Franks in your address book and you have previously sent e-mail to any of them, Outlook assumes you want to send e-mail to the most recent Frank address you used and displays that person's name in the To box. To select a different Frank, right-click the name in the To box and then select the name you want to use.

SELECTING NAMES IN YOUR ADDRESS BOOK

Instead of entering recipients' names or e-mail addresses, you can select these names from your Address Book. In the Message form, choose To to display the contacts in your address book, as shown in Figure 3.32.

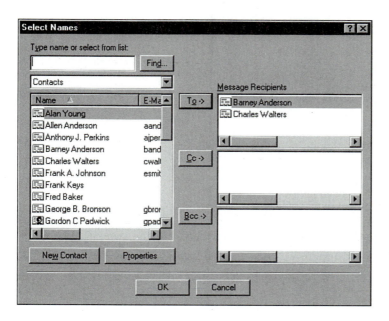

Figure 3.32
The Select Names dialog box shows the names in your Address Book. These names are listed at the left side of the dialog box.

You can use three methods to select recipients from the names in your Address Book.

One method is to scroll down the list of names, select the name of one recipient, then choose T<u>o</u>-> to copy that name into the <u>M</u>essage Recipients list at the right side of the dialog box. Choose OK to return to the Message form in which the name you selected is displayed in the To box.

Tip #15 from

Gordon Padwick

To designate more than one recipient, select the first, then hold down Ctrl while you select others. To select recipient names that are listed consecutively, select the first name and hold Shift while you select the last name.

Alternatively, you can repeatedly choose To on the message form to add names one at a time.

Instead of scrolling through the list, you can enter a person's name in the T<u>y</u>pe Name or Select from List box. When you do that, Outlook finds the first name in the list that matches what you enter.

A third alternative is to choose Fin<u>d</u>. When you do that, Outlook displays a dialog box in which you can enter a contact's name, e-mail address, address, or phone number, and then press <u>F</u>ind. If any of the information is stored in your address book, Outlook matches it to a contact.

After you've selected recipients, choose OK to return to the Message dialog box that now shows recipients' names in the To box.

SENDING CARBON COPIES AND BLIND CARBON COPIES OF MESSAGES

A traditional business practice is to send messages *to* people whom you expect to take some action as a result of the message, and to send *carbon copies* (cc) to people who should know about the message but aren't expected to take any action as a result of it. When you use Outlook, everyone whose name is on the To and Cc lists sees everybody else's name, so all recipients know who sees the message.

Sometimes you want to send a copy of a message to someone without other recipients knowing. That's when you send a *blind carbon copy* (bcc). The recipients of blind carbon copies see all the names on the To and Cc lists; the people on the To and Cc lists don't see the names on the Bcc list.

Tip #16 from

Gordon Padwick

Blind carbon copy is also useful when you want to send a message to a mailing list without revealing the names of everyone on the list to all recipients.

→ To learn how you can create a distribution list and send a message to everyone on that list, **see** "Creating a Distribution List," **p. 333**.

The header of the Outlook Message form contains a <u>C</u>c box. You can add names and e-mail addresses into it in the same way you add names and addresses to the To box. One minor difference is that if you select names from those listed in your Address Book, you choose Cc-> to copy names into the appropriate Message Recipients list.

The Message form's default header doesn't contain a Bcc box. To make this box available, choose View, Bcc Field in the form's menu bar. After you've done that, you can enter names and addresses into that field in the same way that you add them into the To field.

Note

If you use the Select Names dialog box to copy names into the Bcc list, Outlook automatically expands the Message form's header to show the Bcc box.

ENTERING A MESSAGE SUBJECT

To enter a subject for a message, move the insertion point into the Subject box, type the text of the subject, then press Tab to move the insertion point into the message box. As soon as you press Tab, the subject text replaces the original "Untitled" at the left end of the message form's title bar.

You should use succinct and meaningful subjects for your messages. Remember that what you enter in the subject box is what recipients subsequently see in their inboxes. If the subject doesn't look interesting and relevant, recipients may choose to ignore your message. Busy people often only look at messages they perceive to be important.

Note

Some people deliberately omit entering a subject for their messages, maybe because they're too lazy to do so or maybe because they think curiosity will ensure that recipients open those messages. You should avoid this practice because most people regard it as discourteous.

Although Outlook allows you to enter as many as 256 characters in the Subject box, you should use only four or five well-chosen words.

ENTERING THE MESSAGE TEXT

Say what you have to say briefly and clearly.

Because I'm assuming that you're using the HTML message format, you might expect to find detailed information about HTML here so that you can create beautifully formatted messages. However, this book is about Outlook. If you want to learn all about HTML, consult a book on that subject.

If possible, don't quickly type your message and then send it. Take some time to review what you've typed and make sure it's really what you want to say.

→ To learn about saving a draft of a message that you're not ready to send, **see** "Saving a Message Draft," **p. 110**.

FORMATTING A MESSAGE

The Formatting toolbar isn't enabled until you move the insertion point into the message box that occupies the bottom part of the Message form.

Tip #17 from

Gordon Podbielski

If the Formatting toolbar isn't displayed, choose <u>V</u>iew on the Message form's menu bar, move the pointer onto <u>T</u>oolbars, and choose Formatting.

In the Office 2000 style, the first part of the Formatting toolbar is displayed at the right of the Message form's Standard toolbar to provide as much vertical space as possible within the message box. As a result, you don't see all the buttons in the Standard and Formatting toolbars. To see all the buttons in the Formatting toolbar, click the button at the right end of the part that's displayed. You'll see the buttons in a box, as shown in Figure 3.33.

Figure 3.33
This box shows all the Formatting toolbar buttons that aren't displayed in that toolbar.

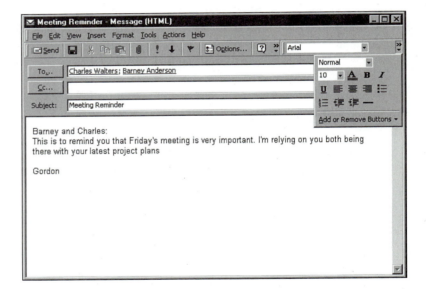

You can also drag the vertical bar at the left end of the Formatting toolbar down to display the entire toolbar below the message form's Standard toolbar, or drag it further to display the toolbar as a floating toolbar on top of the form. When you don't need to see the complete Formatting toolbar, you can drag it back to its original position.

The buttons available in the Formatting toolbar when you're using the HTML message format are listed in Table 3.2.

TABLE 3.2   FORMATTING TOOLBAR BUTTONS

Button Name	Purpose
Style	Select HTML format from a list of formats
Font	Select a font from a list of fonts installed on your computer
Font Size	Select a font size from a list
Font Color	Select a font color from a list
Bold	Make selected text bold
Italic	Make selected text italic
Underline	Underline selected text
Align Left	Left-align selected paragraphs
Center	Center selected paragraphs
Align Right	Right-align selected paragraphs
Bullets	Add bullets to selected paragraphs
Numbering	Number selected paragraphs
Decrease Indent	Decrease left indent of selected paragraphs
Increase Indent	Increase left indent of selected paragraphs
Insert Horizontal Line	Insert horizontal line

Note

No formatting is available if you're using the Plain Text message format. Most of the same formats are available if you're using the Rich Text message format. If you're using Word Mail as your editor, most of Word's formatting capabilities are available.

You might be wondering whether you can count on recipients seeing your messages exactly as you formatted them. If you use Outlook's HTML message format and the people who receive your messages use an e-mail program that's completely compatible with Outlook (such as Outlook or Outlook Express), those people will see your messages exactly as you created them. However, HTML is an evolving standard; it's quite possible that people who receive your messages use an HTML-compatible e-mail program that doesn't interpret HTML in exactly the same way as Outlook. Likewise, you might receive HTML-formatted e-mail messages from other people that Outlook doesn't interpret properly.

If you want to be sure people see your messages exactly as you create them, use Plain Text format. As mentioned previously, one significant advantage of Plain Text is that it results in significantly smaller messages which are faster to send and receive.

USING STATIONERY

When you're using HTML as your message format and the native Outlook editor as your editor, you can choose a stationery to provide a background for your messages.

Note

Stationeries were not available in Outlook 97, but were introduced in Outlook 98.

By default, Outlook creates messages on a plain background using whatever scheme you've selected for Windows Appearance (in the Windows control panel). The default Windows Standard scheme provides a white background. You can choose a stationery that provides a background appropriate for certain kinds of messages.

Tip #18 from

Using a stationery increases the size of your messages so that they take longer to send and receive. Most people prefer not to receive business messages that have a stationery. I recommend that you use stationeries only for personal messages to your friends.

To select a stationery:

1. Close any message form that you have open.
2. Choose Tools, Options and select the Mail Format tab shown previously in Figure 3.25. The Stationery and Fonts section of the Mail Format tab initially shows <None> as the default stationery.
3. Open the Use This Stationery by Default drop-down list to display a list of available stationeries.
4. Select one of the listed stationeries, then choose OK. If you haven't previously used the stationery you selected, you'll be asked to insert the Office 2000 CD-ROM disc into your drive so that Outlook can load that stationery.

The next time you start to create a message, you'll see the stationery you selected as a background for the your message. After you've chosen a stationery, Outlook uses that stationery for all your messages. To return to a plain background, go back to the Option dialog box's Mail Format tab and select <None> as your stationery.

Note

To create your own stationery or colored background, choose Stationery Picker and then choose New.

→ For detailed information about specifying mail formats, **see** "Mail Format Options," **p. 867**.

SIGNING MESSAGES

You can have Outlook automatically sign the messages you send. First, you have to create your signature.

To create a signature:

1. From any Information viewer, choose Tools, Options to display the Options dialog box, and select the Mail Format tab shown previously in Figure 3.25.

2. If you've previously created one or more signatures, open the drop-down Use This Signature by Default list, then select a signature. If want to create a new signature, go to step 3.

3. Near the bottom of the Mail Format tab, choose Signature Picker to display the Signature Picker dialog box which, if you've previously created signatures, shows a list of them. To create a new signature, choose New to display the dialog box shown in Figure 3.34.

Figure 3.34
Use this dialog box to create a new signature.

4. Enter a name for your signature in the Enter a Name for Your New Signature box. You can use names such as Personal, Business, and so on. Then choose Next > to display the dialog box shown in Figure 3.35.

5. Enter the text of your signature in the large box that occupies the upper part of this dialog box, then choose OK three times. The next time you start a message, Outlook automatically includes your signature at the end of the message.

As you can see in Figure 3.35, Outlook offers much more than just creating signatures with text. Here are some of the things you can do:

- Enter text in the box that occupies most of the upper part of the Edit Signature dialog box. By default, Outlook uses 10-point Arial as the font.
- Choose Font to open the standard Windows Font dialog box in which you can select a font name, style, size, and color.
- Choose Paragraph to select Left, Center, or Right alignment for text.

- Choose <u>C</u>lear to delete the existing signature.
- Choose A<u>d</u>vanced Edit to open Word so that you can use all of Word's formatting capabilities (including inserting pictures and objects) to create the signature.
- Attach an electronic business card (vCard) to the signature.

Figure 3.35
This is the dialog box in which you create your signature.

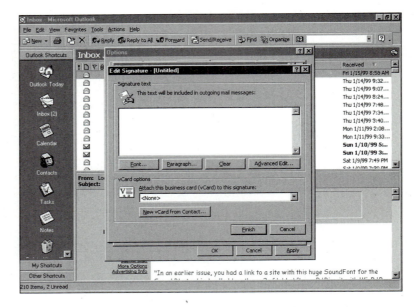

→ For detailed information about saving Contact items, **see** "Saving a Contact Item," **p. 318**.

You can create as many signatures as you like, each with a different name (Personal, Business, and so on). If you create more than one signature, select the one you want to use for a specific message by choosing <u>I</u>nsert, <u>S</u>ignature in the message form's menu bar.

MESSAGE INSERTIONS

In the early days of e-mail it was possible only to send standard alphanumeric characters. Now, e-mail messages can contain almost anything, including:

- Character sets other than US *ASCII*
- Images (still and moving)
- Sounds
- Computer files

In Outlook, you can also insert Outlook items within messages.

This capability depends on senders' and recipients' computers having the capability to encode and decode non-ASCII inclusions. IMO Outlook uses the *Multipurpose Internet Mail Extensions* (MIME) for this purpose.

INSERTING FILES

You can insert any file into a message from a disk on your computer or from a disk on another network computer that's available for sharing.

To insert a file:

1. In the Message form's menu bar, choose Insert, File to display the dialog box shown in Figure 3.36.

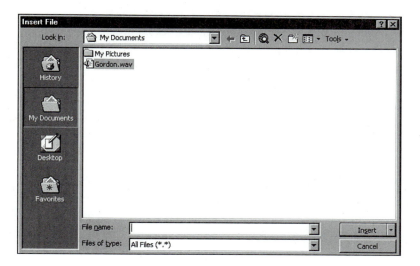

Figure 3.36
The Insert File dialog initially displays the files and folders in your default folder, My Documents for Windows 95 and Windows 98, or Personal for Windows NT.

PART
II

CH
3

2. You can choose any of the buttons in the bar at the left to select specific file locations. After choosing one of those buttons, open the drop-down Look In list to see the relevant folder structure in which you can select a folder and then select a file within that folder. You can also navigate in the Insert File dialog box in the conventional way to select a file.

3. Choose Insert. A pane opens at the bottom of the Message form and the file you selected is displayed in that form, as shown in Figure 3.37.

Figure 3.37
Inserted files are displayed as icons in a pane at the bottom of the message form. In this form, the icon on the left represents a file and the icon on the right represents an Outlook item.

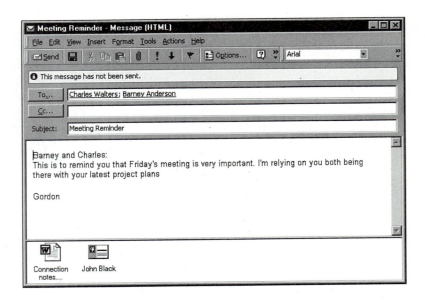

The preceding procedure described how to add attachments to a message. You can also insert a text file as text within a message. In Step 3, instead of choosing Insert, choose the button marked with a black triangle immediately at the right of the Insert button. When you do so, a menu containing Insert, Insert as Text, and Insert as Attachment appears. Choose Insert as Text to insert the text file into the message.

Tip #19 from

To delete an inserted file or item, select it and then press Delete.

INSERTING OUTLOOK ITEMS

You can insert any of your Outlook *items (page 19)* as text into a message and you can attach items to a message.

To attach an Outlook item:

1. In the Message form's menu bar, choose Insert, Item to display the dialog box shown in Figure 3.38.

2. Select the folder that contains the item you want to include in the message. You may have to use the vertical scrollbar to find the folder you want.

3. Scroll down the bottom pane to locate a specific item, then click that item to select it.

4. Make sure Attachment is selected in the Insert As section of the dialog box, then choose OK. The attachment appears as an icon in the pane at the bottom of the Message form, as shown previously in Figure 3.37.

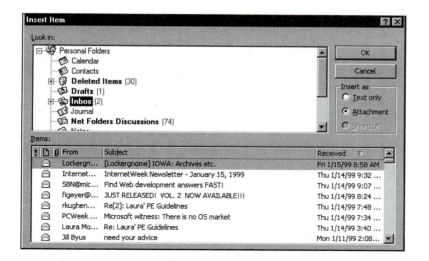

Figure 3.38
The top pane in the Insert Item dialog box shows the folders in your Personal Folders file with one folder selected. The bottom pane shows the items in the selected folder.

Instead of attaching an item, you can insert the item as text within the message. To do so, follow the steps described previously for attaching an item, with the exception that in Step 4, make sure Text Only is selected (instead of Attachment). Figure 3.39 shows an example of a Text Only insertion.

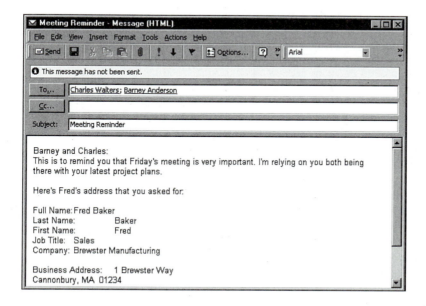

Figure 3.39
In this example, an Outlook Contact item has been inserted as Text Only into a message.

PART

II

CH

3

Note

You can also attach an Outlook item to a message by dragging that item from an Outlook folder into the message. You can't insert an item as text by dragging.

INSERTING A SIGNATURE

To insert a signature into a message, choose Insert, and then move the pointer onto Signature to see a list of signatures you've previously created. Select the signature you want to insert.

→ For information about creating a signature **see** "Signing Messages," **p. 94**.

Note	Outlook places the inserted signature at the end of a new message. If you insert a signature into your reply to a message you've received, Outlook inserts your signature at the end of your reply, not at the end of the text you're replying to. Likewise, if you insert a signature into a message you're forwarding, Outlook inserts the signature at the end of any comments you add to the original message, not at the end of the entire message.

INSERTING A HORIZONTAL LINE

If you're using the HTML message format, you can insert a horizontal line in a message.

To insert a horizontal line:

1. Place the insertion point where you want the horizontal line to appear.
2. In the Message form's menu bar, choose Insert, Horizontal Line. The horizontal line appears in your message, as shown in Figure 3.40.

Figure 3.40
The horizontal line extends over almost all the width of the form.

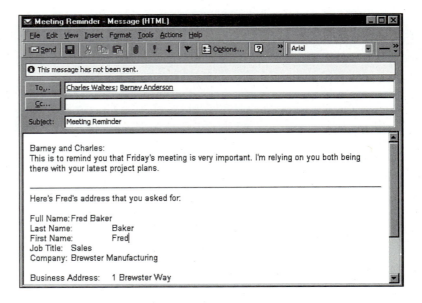

You can adjust the width and thickness of the line by selecting it so that handles appear. Drag one of the handles at the left or right ends of the line to change its width; drag one of the handles at the center of the line to change its thickness.

Note

If you're not using a stationery, you can select a horizontal line in the form, then select the Font Color button ▲ in the Formatting toolbar, and choose a color for the line. If you use certain stationeries, you can't change the color of a horizontal line.

INSERTING A PICTURE

If you're using the HTML message format, you can insert pictures into a message. An inserted picture appears in the message at the same size it was in its original file. If you want to have a reduced size version of a picture in a message, create a reduced size version before you insert the picture into your message, in order to minimize the size of the message you send.

Note

You can insert pictures saved in the .art, .bmp, .gif, .jpg, .wmf, and .xbf file formats. However, you should use only .gif and .jpg formats because are compatible with most e-mail clients, and also because they occupy less space than other formats.

To insert a picture:

1. Place the insertion point where you want the picture to appear in the message.

2. In the Message form's menu bar, choose Insert, Picture to display the dialog box shown in Figure 3.41.

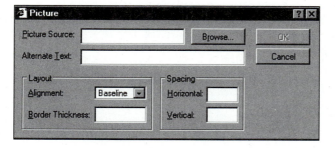

Figure 3.41
Use the Picture dialog box to identify the picture you want to insert and how you want that picture to appear.

3. In the Picture Source box, enter the complete path and file name of the picture. Alternatively, you can choose Browse and then navigate to the file.

4. In the Alternate Text box, enter text that you want to be displayed if the recipients' computers can't display pictures.

5. Open the drop-down Alignment list and choose how you want the picture to be aligned in the message.

6. If you want the picture to be displayed with a border, enter a number in the Border Thickness box. The number you enter represents the thickness of the border in pixels.

7. In the Spacing section of the dialog box, enter the space you want to have at the sides of the picture in the Horizontal box, and enter the space you want above and below the picture in the Vertical box.

8. Choose OK to place the image in the box.

Tip #20 from

After the picture appears in the message you can drag it to a different position. You can also click the picture to select it, in which case handles appear at the center of its edges and at its corners. You can drag these handles to change the size of the picture. Double-click a picture in a message to open a graphics editor in which you can edit the picture.

INSERTING A HYPERLINK

One way to insert a hyperlink into a message is simply to type the hyperlink. Outlook automatically recognizes anything you type in hyperlink format as a hyperlink. For example, if you type http://www.mcp.com (or just www.mcp.com), Outlook shows you it has recognized a hyperlink by changing the color of what you typed to blue and underlining it.

The other way to enter a hyperlink, if you're using the HTML message format, is to follow these steps:

To insert a hyperlink:

1. Place the insertion point where you want the hyperlink to be.

2. In the Message form's menu bar, choose Insert, Hyperlink to display the dialog box shown in Figure 3.42.

Figure 3.42
The Hyperlink dialog box initially assumes you want to create a hyperlink to a Web site.

3. Open the drop-down Type list and select the type of hyperlink you want to create. Outlook places the first part of the hyperlink in the URL box, according to the type you select.

4. In the URL box, complete the hyperlink, then choose OK to insert the hyperlink into the message.

FLAGGING A MESSAGE

You can flag a message to draw recipients' attention to it. Here's one way to flag a message.:

To flag a message:

1. In the Message form's menu bar, choose Actions, Flag for Follow Up, or choose the Flag for Follow Up button in the Message form's Standard toolbar, to display the dialog box shown in Figure 3.43.

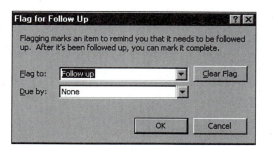

Figure 3.43
Use the Flag for Follow Up dialog box to select a type of flag.

PART

II

CH

3

2. Open the drop-down Flag To list to display a list of flag types. Select the type of flag you want to use.

Note

You are not limited to the listed names of flags. You can select any flag so that its name appears in the Flag To box, then replace that name with whatever words are appropriate.

3. If you don't want to specify a date in the flag, ignore the Reminder box. If you want to include a date with the flag, open the drop-down Reminder box to display a calendar. In that calendar, select a date. After you select a date, that date appears in the Reminder box.

→ Instead of selecting a date from the calender, you can enter descriptive words such as tomorrow, next week, and so on, and also abbreviations such as "1d" for tomorrow and "1w" for next week. **See** "Describing a Date," **p. 364**.

Note

By default, when you choose a date, Outlook automatically shows the time that corresponds to the end of your workday (set in the Options dialog box with the Preferences tab selected and Calendar Options chosen). You can replace the time Outlook displays with whatever time is appropriate.

4. Choose OK. The flag you entered appears in the InfoBar near the top of the Message form, above the To box, as shown in Figure 3.44.

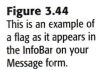

Figure 3.44
This is an example of a flag as it appears in the InfoBar on your Message form.

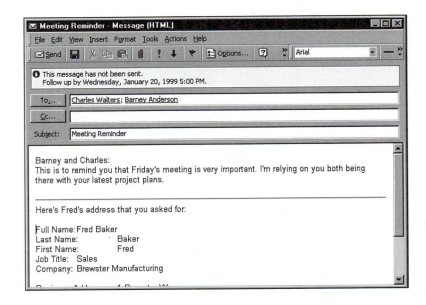

Flags you attach to messages in the manner just described are flags that are delivered with the message; they are intended for the message recipients. When a person receives a flagged message, that message is normally saved in the person's Inbox. Outlook displays reminders at the appropriate time for flagged messages in the Inbox, but only if those messages remain in the Inbox; Outlook doesn't create reminders if recipients move messages to folders other than the Inbox.

SPELL CHECKING A MESSAGE

With Outlook you can easily check the spelling in the messages you create. Doing so is well worth the few moments it takes. You surely don't want recipients to think less of you because you make spelling errors.

To check the spelling in a message, choose Tools, Spelling. After you do so, Outlook highlights words that may be misspelled and suggests corrections.

You can also choose an option that makes Outlook automatically check spelling when you send a message. I strongly recommend you use this option.

To check spelling automatically:

1. With any Outlook Information viewer displayed, choose Tools, Options and select the Spelling tab shown in Figure 3.45.
2. Check Always Check Spelling Before Sending.

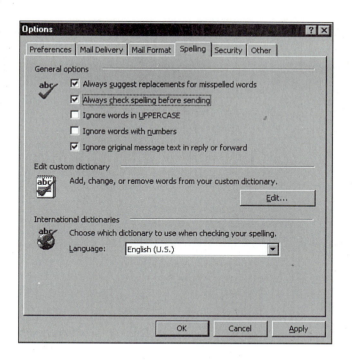

Figure 3.45
This is where you can select spelling options.

With this option selected, Outlook checks the spelling of the subject and text of each message when you choose Send in the Message form's Standard toolbar. If Outlook finds words that are not in the spelling dictionary, it displays the Spelling dialog box, such as that shown in Figure 3.46.

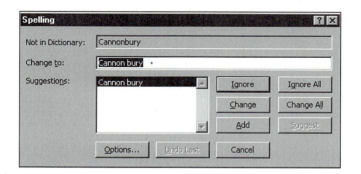

Figure 3.46
When Outlook detects a possible spelling error, it highlights the problem word and displays a dialog box that suggests correct spellings.

Use the Spelling dialog box to correct a spelling error, just as you do in Word.

SETTING MESSAGE OPTIONS

Choose Options in the Message form's Standard toolbar to display the dialog box shown in Figure 3.47.

Figure 3.47
Use this dialog box to
set various message
options.

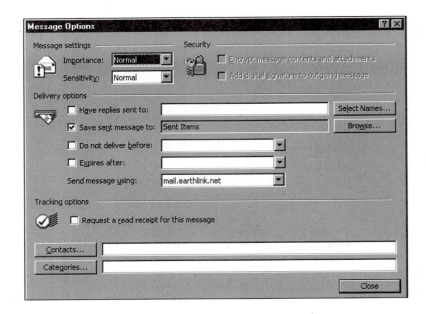

> **Note**   The Security section at the top-right is not available unless you have previously obtained a
> *security certificate.*

→ To learn how you can obtain a security certificate, **see** "Obtaining a Certificate," **p. 1004**.

MESSAGE SETTINGS

In the Message Settings section of the dialog box you can select the Importance and
Sensitivity of a message. By default, Outlook sets both of these to Normal.

Open the drop-down Importance list, and choose among Low, Normal, and High. Instead
of making this choice in the Options dialog box, you can choose the High Importance button or Low Importance button in the Message form's Standard toolbar.

Open the drop-down Sensitivity list, and choose among Normal, Personal, Private, and
Confidential.

SETTING SECURITY

If you have obtained and installed a security certificate on your computer, the two check
boxes in the Security section of the Options dialog box are enabled; otherwise they are
disabled.

Use these check boxes to encrypt a message and to authenticate a message by adding a
digital signature (page 53).

DELIVERY OPTIONS

This section of the Message Options dialog box is where you can specify several aspects of how a message is to be delivered.

When a recipient receives a message and replies to it, the reply is normally sent automatically to your e-mail address. You can, if you like, specify a different e-mail address to which replies should be sent. You might do this if you have an assistant who handles replies, or if you're going to be out of the office for a while.

To have replies automatically sent to an e-mail address other than your own, check the Have Replies Sent To box, and enter the e-mail address in the adjoining box. Instead of entering an e-mail address, you can choose Select Names to display your Address Book, and select a name there.

By default, Outlook saves a copy of messages you send in your Sent Items folder. If you don't want to save a copy of this message, uncheck the Save Sent Message To box.

PART

II

CH

3

Note

Instead of saving messages you send in your Sent Items folder, you may prefer to always include yourself in the list of message recipients. In that case, messages you send arrive in your Inbox folder.

If you want to save a copy of this message in a folder other than your Sent Items folder, leave the Save Sent Message To box checked, choose Browse, and select the Outlook folder in which you want to save a copy of the message.

In IMO Outlook, if you check Do Not Deliver Before and then select or enter a date, Outlook keeps the message in your Outbox until the date you specify. The first time you send messages after that date, the message is sent.

Also, in IMO Outlook, if you check Expires After and then select or enter a date, Outlook keeps the message in your Outbox until the specified date, or until (prior to that date) you send messages. The first time you open Outlook after the specified date, the message is automatically deleted from your Outbox.

If you have several Internet e-mail accounts, you can choose which account you want to use for each message. To do so, open the Send Message Using drop-down list, and choose the account you want to use for the current message.

REQUESTING A READ RECEIPT

You can check Request a Read Receipt in the Tracking Options section of the Options dialog box. When you do that, you're asking for a message to be automatically sent from the recipient when that person opens the message to read it.

You can't rely on getting read receipts when you request them. You, and other Outlook users, can set up Outlook so that it always or never sends Read Receipts when these are requested, or asks your permission before sending a response. To do this, choose Tools, Options and, with the Preferences tab in the Options dialog box selected, choose E-mail Options. In the E-mail Options dialog box, choose Tracking Options to display the dialog box shown in Figure 3.48.

Figure 3.48
Use this dialog box to choose whether you want to respond to requests for read receipts.

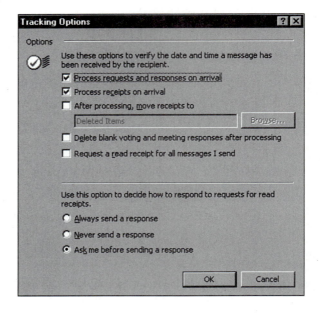

By default, Ask Me Before Sending a Response is selected. If you always want Outlook to send a response to requests for read receipts, select Always Send a Response; if you never want Outlook to respond, select Never Send a Response.

If you send a message that requests a read response, and the recipient allows read responses to be sent, you'll receive a message in your Inbox when the recipient opens the message to read it providing the recipient receives the message in Outlook and hasn't turned off responding to read receipts. However, if a recipient receives the message by way of a mail server, that server and the messaging client the recipient uses may not have the capability of processing read receipts.

The bottom line is: If you request a read receipt and receive one, you know the message recipient opened your message—that doesn't necessarily mean the recipient read it. On the other hand, if you request a read receipt and don't receive one, you really don't know whether the recipient opened the message or not.

ASSIGNING CONTACTS TO A MESSAGE

When you're creating messages (and other Outlook items) keep in mind how you might subsequently want to find those items. You can easily use Outlook to find messages based on the names of the people to whom you sent those messages. There are times, though, when you might send a message that contains information about one of your contacts, but you don't send a copy to that person.

One possible scenario is that you, as a supervisor, want to send a message to your manager regarding some action you intend to take concerning an employee. In that case, you probably won't send a copy to the employee, but you want to be able to find the message based on that employee's name.

In cases like this, you can enter a person's name in the Contacts box in the Message Options dialog box.

To enter a name in the Contacts box:

1. Choose Contacts to display the dialog box shown in Figure 3.49.

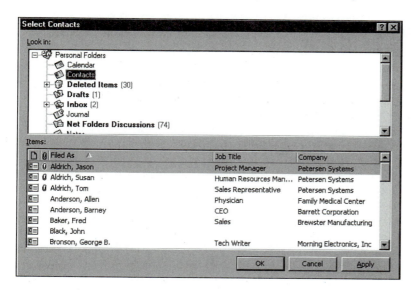

Figure 3.49
Use this dialog box to select one or more contacts.

PART
II

CH
3

2. Select the contacts whose names you want to insert into the Contacts box in the Message Options dialog box.

3. Choose OK to return to the Message Options dialog box, which now has the names you selected in the Contacts box.

ASSIGNING CATEGORIES TO A MESSAGE

As frequently mentioned in this book, assigning *categories (page 604)* to Outlook items is key to keeping yourself organized. Choose Categories at the bottom of the dialog box to open the Categories dialog box, in which you can assign categories to the message.

→ For detailed information about assigning categories to e-mail messages, **see** "Assigning and Changing Categories in E-mail You Create," **p. 610**.

After making choices in the Message Options dialog box, choose Close to return to the Message form.

SAVING A MESSAGE DRAFT

After you've created a message, you don't have to send it immediately; you can save it as a draft to be reviewed or completed later. In fact, while you're creating a message, Outlook automatically saves it periodically as a draft.

To set how often Outlook saves a draft:

1. In any Information viewer, choose Tools, Options, and select the Preferences tab.

2. Choose E-mail Options, and then choose Advanced E-mail Options to display the dialog box shown in Figure 3.50.

Figure 3.50
Use the Advanced E-mail Options tab to specify where unsent messages should be saved, and how often.

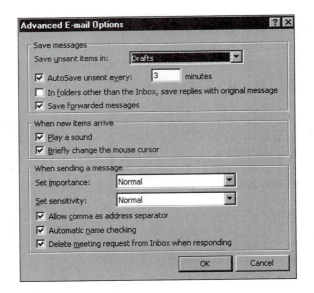

3. By default, Outlook saves unsent messages in your Drafts folder. If you want to save them in a different folder, open the drop-down Save Unsent Items In list and choose an Outlook folder.

4. Also by default, the Autosave Unsent Every box is checked so that unsent items are saved. Uncheck this box (you shouldn't) if you don't want to save unsent items.

5. In the adjacent box, enter a number that specifies the number of minutes between each time Outlook automatically saves unsent items—the default is three minutes.

Tip #21 from

Gordon Padwick

> To manually save an unsent message, in the Message form's menu bar, choose File, Save.

Subsequently, you can continue working on the message. To do so, choose the My Shortcuts group in the Outlook Bar, and choose Drafts to see a list of draft messages. Double-click the one you want to work on to display it in the Message form.

Note

> Alternatively, with any *Information viewer (page 17)* displayed, you can choose View, move the pointer onto Go To, and choose Drafts to display a list of draft messages.

SENDING A MESSAGE

Sending a message is a two-step process. First, you send a message from the Message form to your Outbox. Then Outlook sends the message from your Outbox to your mail server, keeping a copy of the message in your Sent Items folder.

PART

II

CH

3

Note

> You can set up Outlook so that it attempts to send messages to your mail server immediately after you choose Send in the Message form's Standard toolbar. To do this, with any Information viewer displayed, choose Tools, Options, and select the Options dialog box's Mail Delivery tab. Check Send Messages Immediately When Connected. After you do this, Outlook attempts to establish a dial-up connection to your mail server when you choose Send.

If you have only one Internet e-mail account, choose Send in the Message form's Standard toolbar, or press Alt+S. Outlook immediately sends the message to your Outbox folder. You can choose the My Shortcuts group in the Outlook Bar, and then choose Outbox to see the messages in your Outbox, as shown in Figure 3.51.

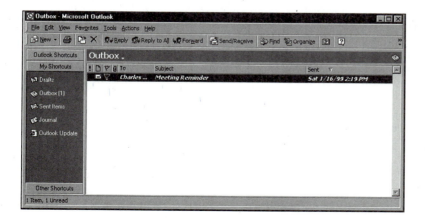

Figure 3.51
Messages waiting to be sent are listed in the Outbox Information viewer.

Note

You don't need to display the Outbox Information viewer in order to send messages. However, it's reassuring to take a look at the Outbox Information viewer while, or after, you've actually sent messages to your mail server to make sure that all messages have actually been sent.

If you have two or more Internet e-mail accounts and you designated one of these as the default, choose Send in the Message form's Standard toolbar (or press Alt+S) to send the message to your Outbox, ready to be sent from the default e-mail account. If you want the message to be sent from other than your default e-mail account, choose File in the Message form's menu bar, move the pointer onto Send Using, and choose the name of the Internet e-mail account from which the message is to be sent.

→ To find out about creating Internet e-mail accounts, **see** "Creating an Internet Account," **p. 63**.

To send messages from your Outbox to your Internet mail server (using any number of accounts on the same server), display any Information viewer, and choose Tools, Send. If necessary, Outlook establishes a connection to the server. Outlook starts sending messages. While messages are being sent, Outlook displays progress in a dialog box such as that shown in Figure 3.52.

Figure 3.52
This is an example of the dialog box in which Outlook displays the progress of messages being sent. Outlook hides this dialog box as soon as all messages have been sent.

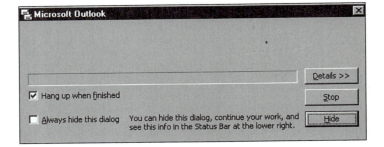

Note

Instead of choosing Tools, Send, you can choose Tools, move the pointer onto Send and Receive, and then choose All Accounts or a specific Internet mail account. This is described in the next section.

Sometimes, messages you send will be undeliverable. This may be because you have addressed them incorrectly, or because your server, the recipients' servers, or something in between, is not working. If that happens, you might receive a message in your Inbox from System Administrator. If this happened, check the e-mail address you used and try sending the message again.

Another common reason for messages being undeliverable is your POP3 or SMTP settings may have become corrupted.

→ To find information about setting up Dial-up Networking, **see** "Setting up Dial-up Networking," **p. 60**.

> **Note**
>
> In many ways, e-mail is like *snail mail*: it works almost all the time. When you send a letter by snail mail, the only way you know that the recipient received it is when you receive a response from that recipient. Similarly, when you send e-mail, the only way you know recipients have received it is when they respond.

RECEIVING INTERNET E-MAIL

You can use IMO Outlook to receive e-mail from Internet mail servers that use either the POP3 or IMAP4 protocols. When you create Internet accounts, you must properly identify which of these protocols is used by each mail server.

→ To find out how to select the POP3 or IMAP4 protocol, **see** "Creating an Internet Account," **p. 63**.

To receive e-mail that's waiting for you on your mail server, choose, Tools, move the pointer onto Send and Receive, and, if you have only one Internet mail account, choose that account name. If you have two or more Internet e-mail accounts, you can choose the account you want to use to send and receive messages. Alternatively, if you have several accounts on the same mail server, you can choose All Accounts.

> **Note**
>
> If you have many mail items to download from the server, or if there are items with large attachments, you don't have to wait until downloading is finished. Outlook can download messages in the background while you're working on other tasks.

Outlook displays the headers of messages you receive in the Inbox Information viewer, which is described in the next section.

UNDERSTANDING THE INBOX INFORMATION VIEWER

Figure 3.53 shows an example of Outlook's default Inbox Information viewer. Outlook displays message headers in your Outbox, Sent Items, and Drafts folders in similar Information viewers.

If you ever forget what the icons at the top of the Inbox viewer (or any other Table view of Outlook items) represent, move the pointer onto an icon and pause briefly. After a second or so, a ScreenTip appears that contains the icon's name.

The Message pane in the top part of the Information viewer shows message headers and, if AutoPreview is enabled, the first three lines of each message. Four columns at the left of each message contain symbols that provide information about each message.

PART

II

CH

3

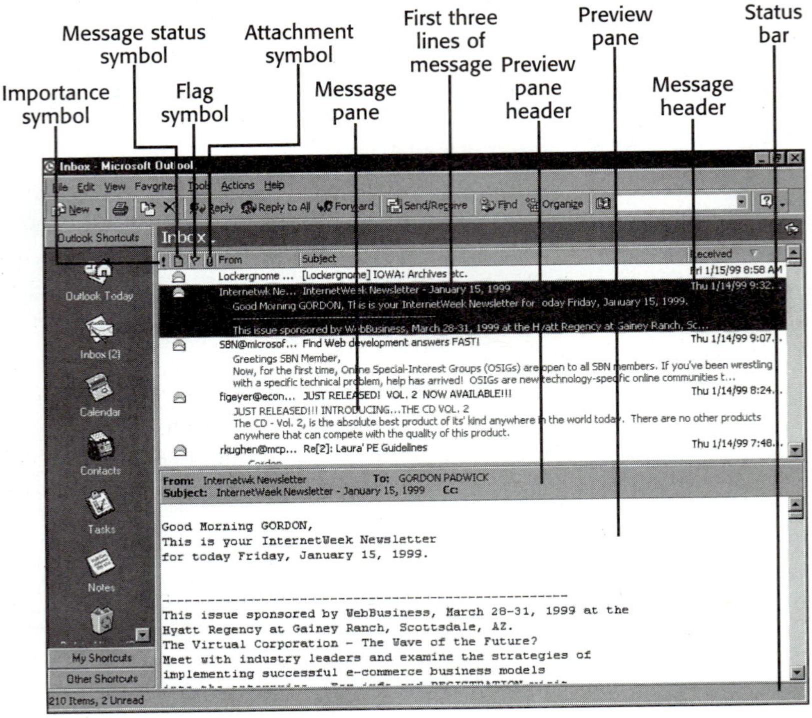

Figure 3.53
This is an example of an Inbox Information viewer.

The Message pane shows messages in a table, although the absence of grid lines might not make that obvious. The four columns at the left are identified by symbols in the row at the top of the table. The other three columns are named.

Initially, the Information viewer lists messages in the order you received them, with the most recent at the top. You can click the symbol or name at the top of each column to order messages according to what's in that column. Click the symbol or name at the top of a column again to reverse the order of the messages according to what's in that column.

For example, click From in the row at the top of the list of messages to display messages in alphabetical order by sender; click From again to display messages in reverse alphabetical order by sender.

To display messages listed by type, click the symbol at the top of the second column from the left. That lists messages with unread messages at the top. Click the same symbol again to list unread messages at the bottom.

MESSAGE HEADERS

Each message header contains the sender's name, the subject of the message, and the date the message was received by your mail server (not the date Outlook received it). You can customize Outlook to show additional information, such as the message category, in the header. This is done by modifying the message view.

→ To learn how to create custom views, **see** "Creating Custom Views," **p. 973**.

PREVIEWING MESSAGES

AutoPreview, which is turned on by default, is Outlook's ability to display the first three lines of messages below message headers. With AutoPreview, Outlook lets you see what a message is about without having to open it. You can disable AutoPreview (and subsequently enable it) by choosing View, AutoPreview.

VIEWING A MESSAGE IN THE PREVIEW PANE

The Preview pane occupies the lower part of the Information Viewer. After you click a message in the Message pane to select that message, the complete message is available in the Preview pane. You can scroll down the Preview pane to see the entire message. Like AutoPreview, the Preview pane provides a way for you to see messages without having to open them.

> **Note**
>
> You can also use the Preview pane to view messages in your Sent Items folder. You can't use the Preview pane to view messages in your Outbox folder.

You can remove the Preview pane to enlarge the Message pane so that more message headers are visible. To do so, choose View, Preview pane. After you've removed it, choose the same command to bring it back.

> **Tip #22 from**
> *Gordon Padwick*
>
> Instead of removing the Preview pane, you can drag the horizontal border between that pane and the Message pane down to increase the size of the Message pane, or up to increase the size of the Preview pane.

By default, the Preview pane has a header in which the sender's name, message subject, message recipients' names, and the names of the people to whom the message is sent as a carbon copy are shown. Also, if the message has attachments, the right end of the header contains an icon (a yellow paper clip).

To customize the Preview pane, right-click its header to display a context menu. Use the commands in this menu as follows:

- Preview Pane—Remove the Preview pane.
- Header Information—Remove the Preview pane's header. To bring the header back, right-click the top border of the Preview pane to display the same context menu.
- Preview Pane Options—Display the Preview Pane dialog box, shown in Figure 3.54.

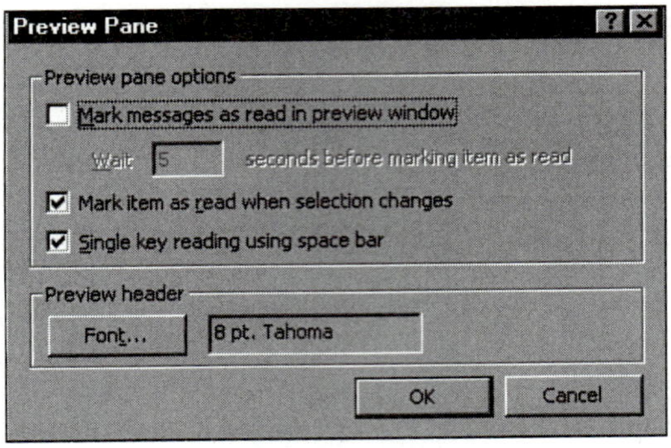

Figure 3.54
Use this dialog box to modify the Information viewer's behavior and to change the font used in the Preview pane's header.

MESSAGE SYMBOLS

The Message pane contains four columns at the left, each column being used for a specific kind of *symbol*.

→ "Outlook Symbols," **p. 1313**, contains a list of Outlook's symbols and identifies what each means.

The first column is where an Importance symbol may be shown. If a message has Normal importance, no symbol appears. Otherwise the column contains the Importance: High symbol [!] or the Importance: Low symbol [↓].

The second column always contains a symbol. In most cases, that symbol represents an envelope. Unread messages are marked with a closed envelope and messages you've read are marked with an open envelope. Various other symbols are used: for example, a message you've replied to is marked with an open envelope with a red arrow. Other symbols appear in this column in the case of mail server messages that warn of a problem with a message you've sent.

The third column contains a symbol that is supposed to look like a flag (most people think it looks like a flower). This symbol is present for messages that are flagged.

The fourth column contains a paper clip icon in the case of messages that have one or more attachments.

MESSAGE SUMMARY

The status bar at the bottom of the Information viewer displays the total number of messages in your Inbox and the number of those that are unread.

OPENING A MESSAGE

When a message arrives in your Inbox and its header is displayed in your Inbox Information viewer, there are several things you can do. The following sections describe many of these.

DELETING A MESSAGE

If, from the message header, or from the first few lines in the AutoPreview, you quickly decide you don't want to bother with a message, you can immediately delete it. To do so, click the message to select it, then choose the Delete button ⌧ in the Information viewer's Standard toolbar. In some cases, you might want to take a quick look at the message in the Preview pane before deleting it.

Tip #23 from

> When you delete a message in this way, Outlook moves it to your Deleted Items folder, from which you can retrieve it if necessary.

→ For more information about deleting messages, **see** "Deleting Messages and Other Outlook Items," **p. 124**.

READING A MESSAGE

As explained a couple of pages previously, you can read a message by selecting it in the Message pane so that's it's displayed in the Preview pane, and then scroll down the message in that pane.

Alternatively, you can double-click the message to display it in a Message form that's similar to the form you use to create new messages, as shown in Figure 3.55.

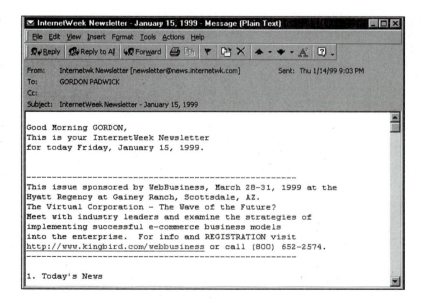

Figure 3.55
All the information in the Message form in which you can see messages you've received is read-only if it was created using the HTML or Plain Text formats. You can directly edit messages that were created in the Rich Text format.

You can use this form's menus and toolbars to work with the message in various ways.

As the message first appears, you can't edit it (unless it was created in Rich Text). However, you can choose Edit, Edit Message to make the received message editable.

You can choose the Flag for Follow Up button [▼] in the form's Standard toolbar to add a flag to the message—something you might often want to do to remind yourself to do something about the message.

DISPLAYING A MESSAGE THREAD

Outlook's ability to display related messages in a single list is a very powerful tool, particularly if you send and receive many e-mail messages.

A message thread, sometimes referred to as a conversation, is a sequence of messages about a specific topic. If you send a message to several people, each of whom reply, you create a thread. The thread is identified by text in the Conversation field in each message. This field initially contains the text in the original message's Subject field. When people reply to the original message, Outlook automatically places the same text in the Conversation field of each reply, even if respondents enter different text in the Subject fields of their replies.

> **Note**
>
> The preceding explanation applies when the sender and respondents all use Outlook as their e-mail program. If some participants in a conversation use e-mail programs that don't support the Conversation field, their messages won't be automatically identified as part of a thread.

As explained previously, you can easily sort messages in the Inbox and Sent Items Information viewers in several ways. Outlook also provides a way for you to list all items in a thread.

To display messages in a thread:

1. Display an Information viewer that contains one or more messages in a thread, usually your Inbox or Sent Items Information viewer.

2. Select any message in the thread.

3. Choose Actions, move the pointer onto Find All, and choose Related Messages. Outlook displays the Advanced Find dialog box with all the messages in the thread listed, as shown in Figure 3.56.

→ For complete information about the Advanced Find dialog box, **see** "Using Advanced Find to Find Words and Phrases," **p. 532**.

By default, Outlook searches the Inbox, Drafts, and Sent Items folders in your Personal Folders file for items that have the same text in the Conversation field as the message you originally selected.

> **Note**
>
> If you select the Advanced tab in the Advanced Find dialog box (as shown in Figure 3.56), you'll see that Outlook has automatically set the search criterion as the content of the Conversation field is exactly the text in the Conversation field of the message you originally selected.

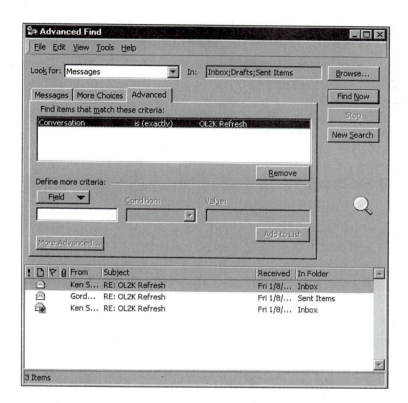

Figure 3.56
Messages in the thread are listed at the bottom of this dialog box. You can double-click any message in this list to open it in a Message form.

EXAMINING MESSAGE PROPERTIES

You can examine the properties of a message you've received and change a message's importance.

To examine a message's properties:

1. Double-click a message in the Inbox Information viewer to display that message in the Message form.

2. In the form's menu bar, choose File, Properties to display a dialog box similar to the one shown in Figure 3.57.

3. If you want to change the importance assigned by the sender, open the drop-down Importance list and select Low, Normal, or High.

4. If you want to exclude the message from AutoArchiving, check the Do Not AutoArchive This Item box.

→ To understand how Outlook archives items, **see** "AutoArchiving Outlook Items," **p. 592**.

Although this dialog box provides some information about a message, it doesn't provide a means of tracing the source of a message (something you might want to do if you receive anonymous junk mail).

Figure 3.57
This dialog box displays the message properties.

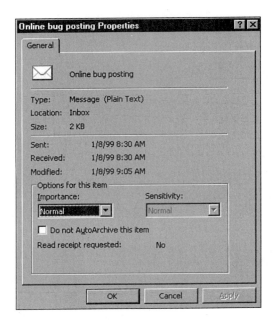

To trace a message, right-click the message header in the Inbox Information viewer to display the context menu. Choose Options in the context menu to display the dialog box shown in Figure 3.58.

Figure 3.58
Information about the message source and routing is displayed in the Internet Headers box in the lower part of the dialog box.

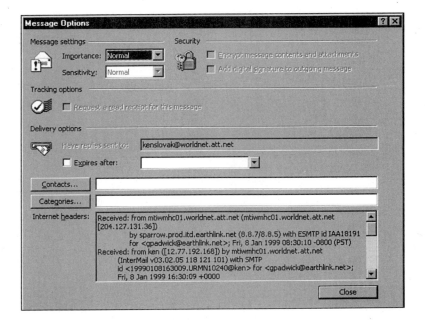

PRINTING A MESSAGE

To print a message you've received, select the message in the Inbox Information viewer's Message pane, then choose File, Print. Outlook displays the Print dialog box shown in Figure 3.59.

Tip #24 from

You're not limited to selecting only one message. You can select as many messages as you like in the Message pane.

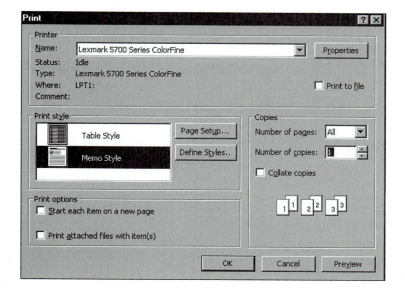

Figure 3.59
Use this dialog box to choose how you want to print the message.

PART
II

CH
3

In most cases, the default settings in the Print dialog box are what you want to use. If the message contains attachments, you can check the Print Attached Files with Item(s) box if that's what you want to do, otherwise leave this box unchecked. Choose OK to print the selected message.

REPLYING TO A MESSAGE

To reply to a message, select the message in the Inbox Information viewer, then choose Reply in the viewer's Standard toolbar. Alternatively, if you want to send a reply to everyone to whom the original message was addressed (including those people on the Cc list), choose Reply to All. You can't send replies to people the message originator placed on the Bcc list because the message you receive doesn't identify those people.

Note

You can make the same choices when you open a message in the Message form.

Outlook opens a form similar to the form you use to create new messages. In this case, though, the text of the message you're replying to appears in the form with some space above the original message for you to enter your reply. Enter your reply in the space at the top of the form. You can also make *comments* within the text of the original message (known as annotating the message). If the original message is long, you might want to delete all but it's first few lines, leaving just enough to remind the originator about the message—there's little point in cluttering up e-mail servers and other people's inboxes with copies of this material.

Note

The preceding information about replying to a message covers Outlook's default behavior. To modify the default behavior, display any Outlook Information viewer, choose Tools, Options, and select the Preferences tab in the Option dialog box. Choose E-mail Options. Choose the options you want in the On Replies and Forwards section of the dialog box.

→ To find out about changing the default settings that determine how Outlook replies to messages, **see** "On Replies and Forwards, " **p. 853**.

When you've finished, send the message in the same way that you send messages you create. If the message you're replying to contained attachments, Outlook doesn't send the attachments with the reply.

FORWARDING A MESSAGE

You can forward a message to other people. Forwarding a message is similar to replying to a message. Select the message in your Inbox Information viewer, then choose Forward in the viewer's Standard toolbar. Alternatively, open the original message in a Message form, and choose Forward.

Enter any introductory comments to the message, *annotate* the message as you wish, and send it. Unlike when you reply to a message, Outlook does send all attachments with forwarded messages. You can choose options to modify Outlook's defaults for forwarding messages.

→ To find out about changing the default settings that determine how Outlook forwards messages, **see** "On Replies and Forwards," **p. 853**.

SAVING A MESSAGE AS ANOTHER OUTLOOK ITEM

Buried within Outlook are many capabilities that are not widely known. One of these is the ability to create one type of Outlook item from a different type of Outlook item.

You may, for example, receive an e-mail message that asks you to do something. Being an organized person, you want to add that request to your to-do list. Simple! Just drag the message into your Tasks folder. Here's how.

To convert a message into a *task (page 412)*:

1. With your Inbox Information viewer displayed, scroll to find the relevant message.

2. Drag the message onto Tasks in the Outlook Bar. When you release the mouse button, Outlook displays the Tasks form with the subject of the message in that form's Subject box and the text of the message in the form's Notes box, as shown in Figure 3.60.

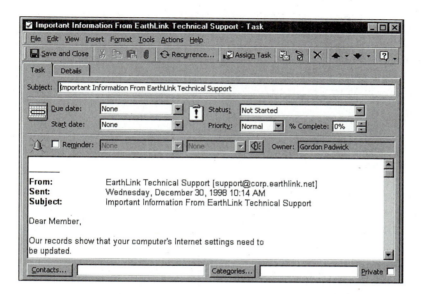

Figure 3.60
The Tasks form contains information from the message.

PART

II

CH

3

4. Make whatever entries are required in the Tasks form, such as specifying the Due Date.

→ For detailed information about using Outlook to save information about tasks, **see** "Managing Tasks," **p. 411**.

The preceding is just one example of how you can create one type of Outlook item from another, a process Microsoft calls AutoCreate. In general, you can drag any type of Outlook item into a folder of a different type to create the type of Outlook item that folder contains.

OPENING AND SAVING ATTACHMENTS

Outlook displays message attachments as icons in the Message form and also as a symbol in the Preview pane header.

To open an attachment, double-click its icon in the Message form or its symbol in the Preview pane's header.

Outlook uses the Windows list of associations to find an application installed on your computer that's capable of opening a file, based on the file name extension. If Windows contains an association for the attached type of file, that application is opened and used to open and display the file. If no association exists, you are asked to choose the application that should be used to open the file.

DELETING MESSAGES AND OTHER OUTLOOK ITEMS

This chapter deals with Outlook messages, those you send and those you receive; the information in this section, however, applies to all types of Outlook items. Unless you choose otherwise, Outlook saves copies of messages you send in your Sent Items folder; it saves messages you receive in your Inbox bolder. You can choose Sent Items in the Outlook Bar to see the headers of messages you've sent in the Sent Items Information viewer, and you can choose Inbox in the Outlook Bar to see headers of messages you've received in the Inbox Information viewer.

To delete a message from either of these Information viewers, click the message header to select it, then choose the Delete button ☒ in the Information viewer's Standard toolbar.

Deleting a message doesn't delete the message from your disk, it just moves the message from the Sent Items or Inbox folder to the Deleted Items folder. If you want to recover the deleted message, choose Deleted Items in the Outlook Bar to display the Deleted Items Information viewer. In that viewer, locate the deleted item and drag it back to Sent Items or Inbox in the Outlook Bar.

If you want to completely remove a deleted item from your disk, choose Deleted Items in the Outlook Bar. In the Deleted Items Information viewer, select the items you want to delete, and choose the Delete button ☒ in the Standard toolbar. After you've done that, you won't be able to recover the deleted items.

Even though you delete items from your Deleted Items folder, you don't necessarily recover the space those items previously occupied on your hard disk. To recover that space, you have to compact your Personal Folders file. Here's how you do that.

To compact your Personal Folders file:

1. Right-click Outlook Today in the Outlook Bar to display a context menu.
2. In the context menu, choose Properties to display the Personal Folders Properties dialog box. Choose Advanced to display the dialog box shown in Figure 3.61.
3. Choose Compact Now to compact the selected Personal Folders file.
4. Choose OK twice to close the dialog boxes.

Now, all the space previously occupied by deleted Outlook items is recovered.

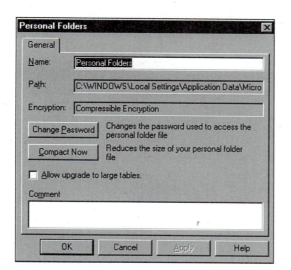

Figure 3.61
You can use this dialog box to compact the selected Personal Folders file.

Troubleshooting: Repairing Your Personal Folders File

Although Outlook does a good job of keeping your Personal Folders file (the file in which IMO Outlook saves Outlook items) in good shape, problems can occur. If you're having problems with a Personal Folders file, the Inbox Repair tool can probably fix them. Although the file's name suggests that it deals only with your Inbox folder, the file actually deals with your entire Personal Folders file.

The Inbox Repair file named Scanpst.exe is automatically installed on your computer when you install Windows 95, Windows 98, or Windows NT.

To use the Inbox Repair tool:

1. Close Outlook, choose Start on the Windows Taskbar, and move the pointer onto Find. Choose Files and Folders to display the Find: All Files dialog box.

2. In the Named box, enter Scanpst.exe and choose Find Now. Windows locates Scanpst.exe on your computer.

3. Double-click Scanpst.exe to display the Inbox Repair Tool dialog box in which you are asked to enter the name of the file you want to scan. Enter the full path name of your Personal Folders file, or choose Browse to navigate to that file, then choose Open to open that file.

Note

Your Personal Folders file is probably C:\Windows\Local Settings\Application Data\Microsoft\Outlook\outlook.pst, though it can be located elsewhere and can have a different file name.

4. Choose Options and select Replace Log, Append to Log, or No Log as you wish.

5. Choose Start to scan the file and attempt to correct errors in it.

After it has completed scanning your file, the Inbox Repair tool displays a summary of what it found and what it did. Choose OK to close the summary.

If you chose to create a log, that log is named Outlook.log. You can use WordPad (or any other text editor) to display what that file contains.

SENDING AND RECEIVING FAXES WITH INTERNET MAIL ONLY OUTLOOK

In this chapter   *by Gordon Padwick*

USING OUTLOOK TO SEND AND RECEIVE FAXES

You can use *IMO Outlook (page 53)* to send and receive faxes, providing you have a fax modem and access to a phone line. Instead of creating a fax in a word processor, printing it, and then lining up at the fax machine to send it, you can use Outlook to create and send a fax directly from your computer. If you have a phone number to which people can send you faxes, those faxes arrive in your Outlook Inbox folder in much the same way as e-mail arrives.

There are several ways that Outlook can be used to send and receive faxes:

- With IMO Outlook running under Windows 95, Windows 98, or Windows NT, you can use WinFax Starter Edition (WinFax SE). WinFax SE is licensed from Symantec by Microsoft and is supplied with Outlook 2000. WinFax SE is covered in this chapter.

- With *C/W Outlook (page 54)* running under Windows 95 or Windows 98, you can use Microsoft Fax (supplied with Windows 95 and Windows 98).

→ To learn more about faxing with C/W Outlook, **see** "Sending and Receiving Faxes with Corporate/Workgroup Outlook," **p. 233**.

- You can use various add-on fax programs available from other companies. One of these is WinFax Pro from Symantec. WinFax Pro contains many facilities that aren't in Microsoft Fax or WinFax SE.

> **Note**
>
> Some of the screens you'll see while you work with WinFax SE refer to it as Outlook Fax.

> **Note**
>
> Much of the information in this chapter is based on material originally written by Russ Valentine and Sue Mosher, and published on the Slipstick Web site. The Slipstick Web site is an excellent resource for information about Outlook— http://www.slipstick.com.

SETTING UP WINFAX SE

The default Office 2000 installation marks WinFax SE to be installed the first time you attempt to use it. This section assumes you installed Office 2000 in that way. If you chose to install WinFax SE when you installed Office, you can skip ahead to "Using the WinFax Setup Wizard."

> **Note**
>
> If you installed WinFax SE on your hard disk at the time you installed Office 2000, you won't see the message about needing to install WinFax SE now.

To set up WinFax SE, start as if you were going to send an e-mail message.

To begin, display the Inbox Information viewer, then either:

- Choose File, move the pointer onto New, and choose Fax Message
- Choose Actions, New Fax Message

The first time you do this after installing Outlook, you might see a message telling you that Outlook can't use Symantec WinFax Starter Edition because this feature is not currently installed. The message asks "Would you like to install it now?" Choose Yes to proceed with the installation.

After a couple of seconds, the installation procedure asks you to insert the Microsoft Office CD-ROM. Do so and choose OK. Reading from the CD-ROM takes only a few seconds. When it's complete, a message tells you "To complete the installation of the fax software you have to restart Outlook." Choose OK to return to the Inbox Information viewer. Choose File, Exit to close Outlook, then restart it.

Using the WinFax Setup Wizard

If you followed the procedure described in the preceding section, when Outlook starts, it displays the first Symantec WinFax Starter Edition Setup Wizard window, shown in Figure 4.1. If you installed WinFax SE at the time you installed Office 2000, the same wizard window is displayed the first time you attempt to use WinFax SE.

PART
II

CH
4

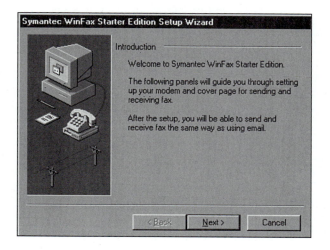

Figure 4.1
The WinFax Starter Edition Setup Wizard guides you through the process of preparing to send and receive faxes.

Note

Use the Setup Wizard to set up initial faxing parameters. You can subsequently change these parameters.

The following procedure is based on the assumption that you already have a modem installed on your computer and that you have verified it is working satisfactorily by sending and receiving e-mail.

To set up WinFax SE:

1. With the first wizard window displayed, choose <u>N</u>ext > to display the second wizard window, shown in Figure 4.2.

Figure 4.2
Use this window to provide information about yourself.

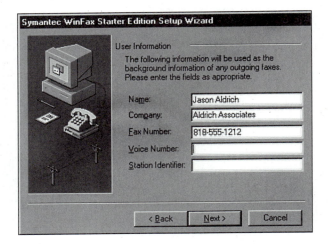

2. Enter information about yourself into any or all of the boxes in this window. WinFax SE uses the information you supply here in fax headers and cover sheets. Choose <u>N</u>ext > to display the next wizard window, shown in Figure 4.3.

3. Enter your postal address into the boxes in this window. WinFax SE uses the information you supply here in fax cover sheets. Choose <u>N</u>ext > to display the next wizard window, shown in Figure 4.4.

4. In the Auto Receive section at the top of the window, check <u>A</u>utomatic Receive Fax if you want WinFax SE to automatically receive incoming faxes.

5. Use the Ans<u>w</u>er After spin button to set the number of rings after which WinFax SE should receive an incoming fax. Alternatively, replace the default number of rings with the appropriate number.

Tip #25 from

Gordon Crock

The minimum value you should choose for Answer After is 2. Although you can set the Answer After value to 1, you might find that WinFax SE doesn't reliably detect incoming faxes if you do.

6. In the Retries section in the middle of the window, use the Number of <u>R</u>etries spin button to set the number of times WinFax SE should attempt to call a fax number.

7. Use the Retries Every spin button to set the interval between retries.

8. Choose Setup Modem to display the Modem Properties dialog box shown in Figure 4.5.

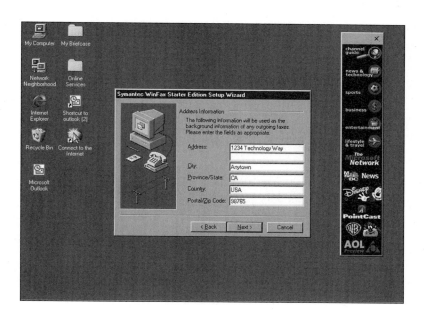

Figure 4.3
Use this window to provide your postal address.

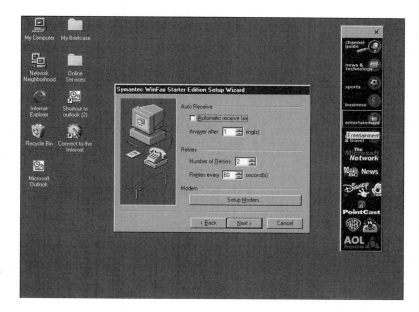

Figure 4.4
Use this window to control how Outlook receives and sends faxes.

Figure 4.5
This dialog box lists the modems installed in your computer.

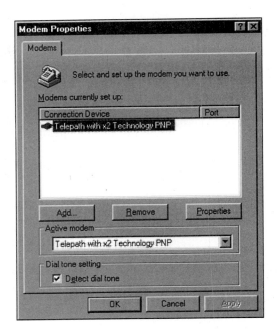

9. Select the modem you want WinFax SE to use. You can choose Properties to verify that the modem is correctly set up and, if necessary, make changes to the modem's parameters. After you've set up your modem, choose OK. A message tells you that it's necessary to restart Outlook before you can use WinFax SE. Choose OK. Another message appears telling you that the selected modem has not been configured to work with WinFax SE and inviting you to run the WinFax Modem Configuration Wizard. Choose Yes to display the first Modem Configuration Wizard window, shown in Figure 4.6.

Figure 4.6
The wizard tests and verifies the modem you intend to use.

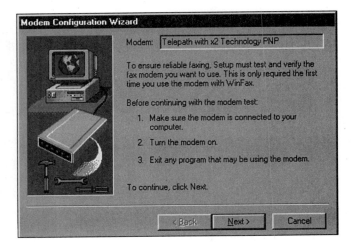

10. Follow the instructions in the first Modem Configuration Wizard window, then choose Next >. The wizard tests your modem and then, after a minute or so, displays a window such as the one shown in Figure 4.7.

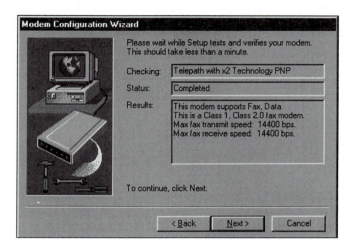

Figure 4.7
Once you've verified your modem, the wizard displays the modem's basic specifications.

PART

II

CH

4

Tip #26 from

If this window doesn't confirm that your modem is satisfactory, you'll have to find out why and remedy the problem before continuing. If you're using an external modem, one possible problem might be that the modem isn't turned on.

Windows Help contains the Modem Troubleshooter, which offers a long list of possible modem problems and leads you through the steps necessary to solve them. Choose Start in the Windows taskbar, then choose Help in the Start menu. Enter Modem as the search keyword, then select Troubleshooting.

The Microsoft Knowledge Base contains many articles about solving modem problems. To get a list of these articles, search the Knowledge Base for articles about Windows 98, and for the keyword "modem." Look for the article "Solving Problems with Modems in Windows 98." When you open that article, you'll see a list of possible problems; one or more of these probably relate to your difficulty. Select that problem to see how to solve it.

11. If the window indicates that your modem is satisfactory, choose Next > to display the final Modem Configuration Wizard window, which merely states that your modem has been successfully configured. Choose Finish to return to the WinFax Setup Wizard window previously shown in Figure 4.4. Choose Next > to display the wizard window shown in Figure 4.8.

12. Uncheck Send Cover Page if you don't want to send a cover page with your faxes. If you leave that box checked, open the drop-down Template list and select the template you want to use. The Preview section of the window provides an idea of what the selected cover page looks like. Choose Next > to display the final wizard window, shown in Figure 4.9.

Figure 4.8
Use this window to specify whether you want to send faxes with a cover page and, if so, which cover page you want to use.

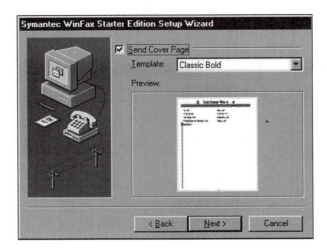

Note

Five cover pages are supplied with WinFax SE. You can't use WinFax SE to modify the design of the supplied cover pages, nor can you create your own. You can, however, create custom cover pages if you use Microsoft Fax with C/W Outlook, as described in Chapter 7, "Sending and Receiving Faxes with Corporate/Workgroup Outlook."

You can choose to send a cover page with every fax or not to send cover pages with any fax.

Tip #27 from

You'll notice that the cover pages supplied with WinFax SE contain a Symantec copyright notice, which most likely will not suit your professional needs. There is a simple workaround, however. Uncheck Send Cover Page in the wizard window shown in Figure 4.8. Create your own cover page in Word and insert that as the first page of faxes you send.

If you have access to WinFax Pro, you can use that application to modify the cover pages supplied with WinFax SE, although you can't create additional cover pages.

13. Choose Finish to display the first WinFax Registration Wizard window, shown in Figure 4.10.

14. Supply the information in the series of Registration Wizard windows and send your registration. Alternatively, you can choose Skip to skip registration at this time and return to the Inbox Information viewer.

Note

If you skip registration at this time, you can register later by choosing About Symantec in the Fax tab of the Options dialog box.

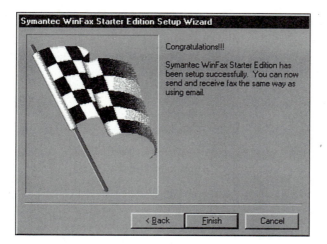

Figure 4.9
This window confirms that you have set up WinFax SE satisfactorily.

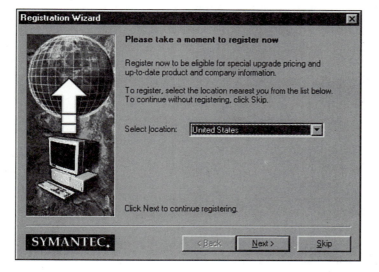

Figure 4.10
Use this window to begin the process of registering WinFax SE with Symantec.

PART

II

CH

4

After completing the steps in the WinFax SE Setup Wizard, you're ready to start using WinFax SE.

Tip #28 from

Gordon Crook

The easiest way to become familiar with WinFax SE and to verify that it's working properly is to send faxes to yourself and receive faxes from yourself. To do this, you need two phone lines, one connected to your modem and the other connected to a separate fax machine (or another computer capable of sending and receiving faxes). Failing that, you need to find a colleague with whom you can trade faxes.

EXAMINING AND MODIFYING YOUR FAX SETUP

The WinFax SE installation process adds a Fax tab to the Options dialog box. To display this tab, choose Tools, Options, and select the Fax tab, shown in Figure 4.11. Alternatively, you can run olfsetup.exe from the Windows desktop to redisplay the WinFax SE Setup Wizard.

Figure 4.11
You can use this dialog box to change the information you supplied and the choices you made in the WinFax SE Setup Wizard

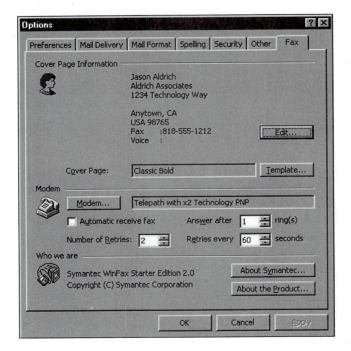

Tip #29 from

Gordon Crood

If you don't have a Fax tab for your Options dialog box, try this. Select the Other tab in the Options dialog box, choose Advanced Options, and choose Add-In Manager. In the list of Add-ins, make sure Symantec WinFax Starter Edition Extension is checked.

To examine or change WinFax SE options:

1. The top section of the Fax tab displays the cover page information you supplied while working through the WinFax SE Setup Wizard. To change any of this information, choose Edit to display a dialog box similar to the one previously shown in Figure 4.2. You can change the information in any of the boxes. Choose OK to return to the Fax tab in the Options dialog box.

2. The same tab section also displays the name of the fax cover page you selected while you were working with the WinFax SE Setup Wizard. If you want to select a different cover page, choose Template to display a dialog box similar to that previously shown in

Figure 4.8. In this dialog box you can check or uncheck $\underline{S}$end Cover Page according to whether you want to send a cover page with your faxes. You can also open the drop-down $\underline{T}$emplate list and select a template. Choose OK to return to the Fax tab in the Options dialog box.

3. The Modem section of the tab displays the name of the modem you selected while you were working with the WinFax SE Setup Wizard. Choose $\underline{M}$odem if you want to select a different modem. Outlook displays a dialog box similar to that previously shown in Figure 4.5. You can use this dialog box to select a different modem, to add or delete a modem, and to change the selected modem's properties. Choose OK to return to the Fax tab in the Options dialog box.

4. The same section of the tab also contains information about how WinFax SE receives and sends faxes. You can change any of this information.

5. Choose About Symantec if you haven't already registered WinFax SE with Symantec. Outlook displays the dialog box shown in Figure 4.12. This dialog box reminds you that "Symantec markets a fully featured product called WinFax Pro." Choose OK to return to the Fax tab of the Options dialog box.

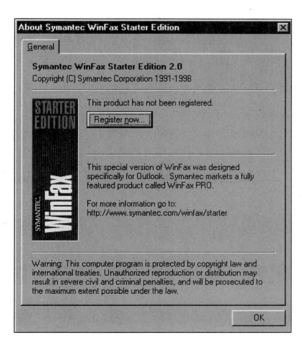

Figure 4.12
Choose Register $\underline{N}$ow to display the first Registration Wizard dialog box, then follow through the registration steps.

PART
II

CH
4

6. Choose About the $\underline{P}$roduct to open Internet Explorer and access the Web site http://www.symantec.com/winfax/starter/, which that provides information about upgrading to WinFax Pro, information about other Symantec products, and access to

technical support from Symantec. Close Internet Explorer to return to the Fax tab of the Options dialog box.

In addition to creating the Fax tab in the Options dialog box, the WinFax SE Setup Wizard also creates an entry in Outlook's Internet accounts list, but this is somewhat confusing and, if you're not careful, may cause you problems. I suggest you read what follows very carefully.

With any Outlook Information viewer displayed, choose Tools, Accounts to display a dialog box similar to the one shown in Figure 4.13.

Figure 4.13
This dialog box opens with the Mail tab selected. It contains a list of your e-mail and fax accounts.

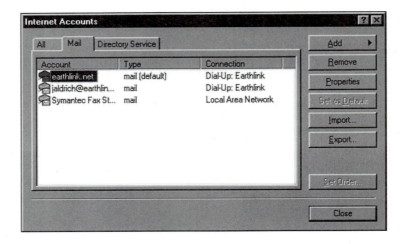

Here's the confusing part. You'll notice that the Symantec Fax Starter Edition is listed as a Mail account and that its connection is to your Local Area Network. That doesn't seem to be right. Strangely enough, though, it is correct. You can't change it, so don't try.

Caution

Don't select the Symantec Fax Starter Edition account and choose Remove unless you are sure you don't want to use WinFax SE. After you remove Winfax in this way, you'll have to reinstall it by using Add/Remove Programs in the Windows Control Panel.

Here's a brief explanation of the anomaly. WinFax SE is based on WinFax Pro, which requires *MAPI (page 39)* support. IMO Outlook doesn't provide MAPI support but, instead, uses the *TAPI* communications protocol. To overcome this problem, the WinFax Setup Wizard installs WinFax SE as if it were an e-mail account that runs over a LAN.

Despite the appearance to the contrary, WinFax SE does send and receive faxes by way of your modem.

If you select Symantec Fax Starter Edition in the Internet Accounts dialog box and then choose Properties, you'll see a four-tabbed dialog box that contains many settings that don't make sense. Don't worry about these. Even if you change them, WinFax SE restores the changes to its default settings. While all this may leave you wondering about what's happening, your only option is to ignore the properties and be happy that WinFax SE works.

USING WINFAX SE TO SEND A FAX

Sending a fax is much like sending an e-mail message. The significant difference is that you send a fax to a fax phone number instead of to an e-mail address.

SPECIFYING A FAX PHONE NUMBER

Two ways exist for you to specify a fax phone number:

- Enter the fax phone number in the To box on the Message form in the format fax@18185551212.

  For reasons explained later, it's best not to include any parentheses or hyphens.

  Outlook recognizes "fax" and sends your message as a fax by way of your modem.

- Enter the name of a contact for whom you have supplied a fax number in your Address Book.

→ If you've not already set up your Outlook Contact items, **see** "Creating a Contact Item," **p. 301**.

Tip #30 from	To avoid potential problems when you send your first fax, start by using the "fax@" phone number format. Also, if possible, send your first fax to a local phone number to avoid possible problems with area codes.
Gordon Prod	There's more information about fax numbers in the "Troubleshooting" section at the end of this chapter.

CREATING AND SENDING A FAX

To create a fax message, start with the Inbox Information viewer displayed. Then choose File, move the pointer onto New, and choose Fax Message to display the Fax form shown in Figure 4.14.

Figure 4.14
Apart from FAX in the title bar, this form is identical to a Message form. The form shown here contains a message ready to be sent.

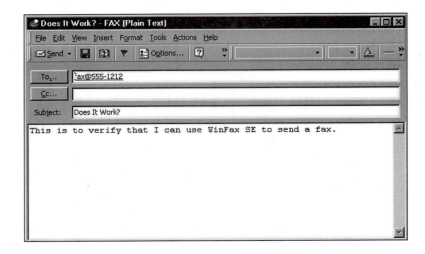

To create a fax and send it to a fax number:

1. In the To box, enter the addressee's fax number in the format shown in Figure 4.14. Make sure you enter the number without including a hyphen.

Note

Figure 4.14 shows a local phone number in the To box. If you're sending a fax to another area code, you must include the "1" before the area code. Don't place parentheses around the area code. The number you enter should be in the format fax@18185551212.

2. Enter a subject for the fax in the Subject box.

3. Enter the text of the message in the unnamed notes box.

4. Choose Send in the form's Standard toolbar. Outlook displays the dialog box shown in Figure 4.15.

Figure 4.15
This dialog box displays the fax number to which you have addressed the message.

5. If necessary, correct the fax number, then choose Send to proceed. Outlook uses your modem to call the number. While the number is ringing, WinFax generates a tone that's used by the receiving fax machine to recognize the incoming call as a fax. As soon

as communication is established, Outlook sends the fax, saving a copy in your Sent Items folder. Outlook displays the box shown in Figure 4.16 while calling the number and transmitting the fax.

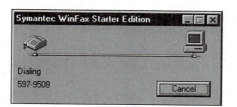

Figure 4.16
This dialog box confirms the process of calling a number and transmitting the fax.

Whether the fax is successfully transmitted or not, Outlook displays the fax header in your Sent Items information viewer.

Note

If the fax transmission fails, perhaps because the number you're calling is busy, WinFax SE saves a copy of the fax in your Sent Items folder. You'll also see a message in your Inbox Information viewer from Fax Server with the subject "Fax Undeliverable." The viewer's Preview pane contains a status report that contains information about the failed transmission.

Sending a fax by entering a fax number in the To box has a significant problem if you use a cover page; there's no opportunity for you to enter the recipient's name and organization name in the cover page. The only way to overcome this problem is to disable the use of a cover page and create your own as the first page of each message.

As mentioned previously, instead of specifying a fax number for the addressee, you can choose a recipient by name, providing your Address Book contains that person's name with a fax number. This method overcomes the problem mentioned in the preceding paragraph. By choosing a person from your address book, WinFax SE automatically inserts that person's name and organization name in the appropriate fields of the cover page, using the information in your Address Book.

To address a fax to a person by name, use the five steps just described, with only one difference. Choosing To in step 1, instead of entering a fax number, displays the dialog box shown in Figure 4.17.

In the Select Names dialog box, select the name of the contact to whom you want to send a fax, then choose To-> to display that contact's name in the Message Recipients box. You must, of course, select a contact for whom there is a fax number. If the selected contact doesn't have a fax number, that contact's name still appears in the Message Recipients box; if the selected contact has two or more fax numbers, that contact's name appears two or more times in the Message Recipients box.

PART

II

CH

4

Figure 4.17
This dialog box lists the names of your contacts.

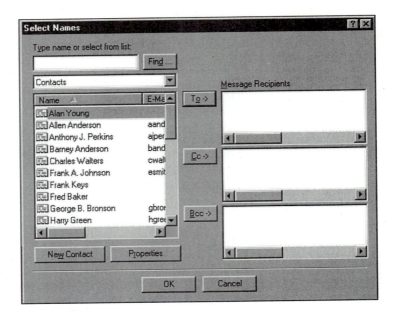

The Select Names dialog box doesn't show fax numbers. You just have to remember the contacts for whom you have supplied fax numbers.

After you've moved the recipient's name into the Message Recipients box, choose OK to return to the Fax form that now contains the recipient's name in the To box. Enter a Subject for the fax, enter its text, and then choose Send in the Standard toolbar to send the fax.

If you select the name of a contact for whom you haven't supplied a fax number, WinFax displays the dialog box shown in Figure 4.18.

Figure 4.18
You can use this dialog box to enter the fax number for a contact for whom no fax number exists in your address book.

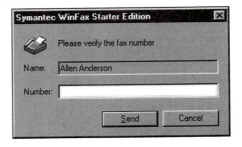

After entering the recipient's fax number, choose Send to continue.

SENDING A FAX TO MORE THAN ONE PERSON

Just as with e-mail, you can send a fax to more than one person. To do so, enter more than one fax number in the To box on the Fax form (separating one from the next with a semicolon) or, alternatively, choose To to open the Select Names dialog box and select the names of contacts for whom you have supplied fax numbers.

SENDING A FAX TO A PERSON WHO HAS MORE THAN ONE FAX NUMBER

If you use the Select Names dialog box to choose the name of a person who has more than one fax number, WinFax SE displays the dialog box shown in Figure 4.19 when you attempt to send the fax.

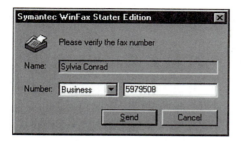

Figure 4.19
This dialog box displays one of the addressee's fax numbers.

Open the drop-down Number list and select the fax number to which you want to send the message, then choose Send to continue. If you are sending the fax to several people, this dialog box appears for each person who has more than one fax number.

ADDING ATTACHMENTS TO FAXES

You can insert Windows files and Outlook items into a fax in the same way that you insert them into an e-mail message. In the Fax form, choose Insert, File or Insert Item and then select the file or item you want to insert.

At the time you send a fax, Outlook opens each of the attachments using the applications associated with the attached files. Outlook *rasterizes* the contents of each file; that is, it converts the contents into a format suitable for transmission as a fax that can be printed by the receiving fax machine.

USING WINFAX SE TO RECEIVE AND PRINT A FAX

If you have set up WinFax SE to receive faxes and Outlook is running with Automatic Receive Fax enabled, WinFax listens for incoming calls that contain the tone identifying a message as a fax. When such a call arrives, WinFax automatically sends an acknowledgment signal to the sender. At that time, the sender responds by starting to transmit the fax. Outlook displays a dialog box similar to that previously shown in Figure 4.16 while the fax is arriving. In this case, the bottom-left corner contains the word "Receiving."

Note

To verify that Outlook is set up to receive faxes, choose Tools, Options, and select the Fax tab; make sure that Automatic Receive Fax is checked. Uncheck Automatic Receive Fax to disable receiving faxes.

If WinFax SE is not set up to automatically receive faxes, you can use it to receive faxes manually. To do this, you must have an ordinary voice telephone on the same phone line as your modem. When the phone rings, pick up the receiver and if you hear the characteristic fax sound, in Outlook choose Tools, Receive Fax.

The incoming fax arrives in your Outlook Inbox, just like any other message. Some fax machines automatically send the phone number of the sending machine, in which case the Inbox Information viewer lists that number in the From column. If the sending machine does not transmit its number, the From column is blank.

The Subject column in the Inbox Information viewer contains the words "Fax Received." The Received column shows the time WinFax SE received the fax.

The fax you receive is a graphical image, not the text you receive in e-mail messages. The Inbox preview pane shows only a report of the fax, not its details. Figure 4.20 shows a typical preview pane.

Figure 4.20
The preview pane confirms that you have received a fax.

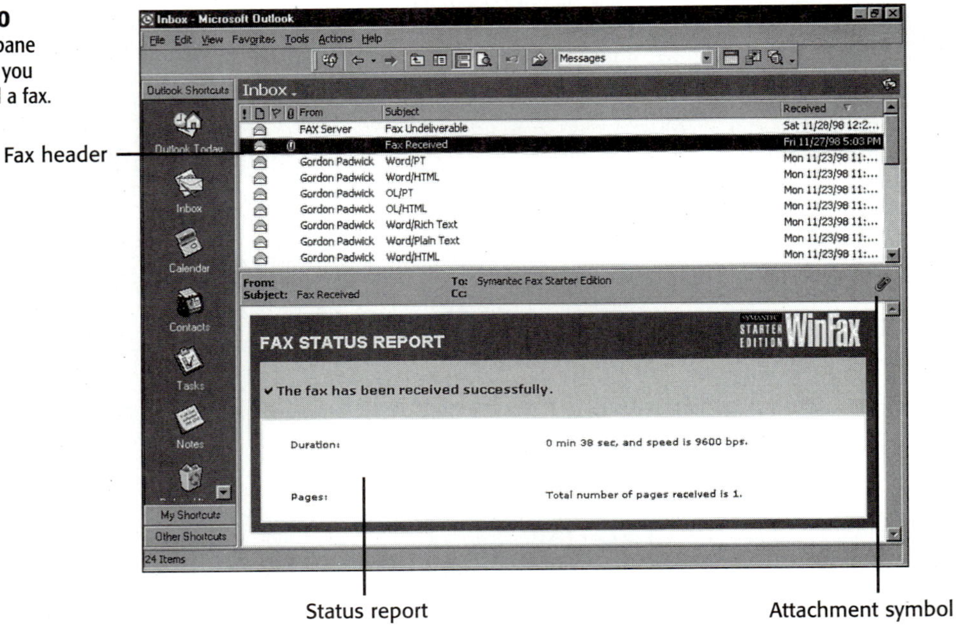

Fax header

Status report

Attachment symbol

If you have the preview header enabled, you'll see the paperclip attachment icon at the right end of the header, as shown in Figure 4.20. The attachment is the graphics file that contains the fax. You can double-click the attachment icon to see the name of the file that contains the attachment, then double-click that file name to display the dialog box shown in Figure 4.21.

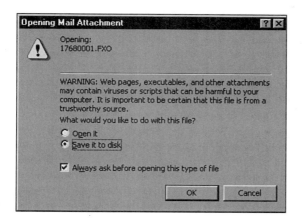

Figure 4.21
You can choose whether you want to save the attachment as a file, or open it.

If you don't have the Preview pane open, double-click the message header in the Inbox Information viewer to display a Message form, such as that shown in Figure 4.22.

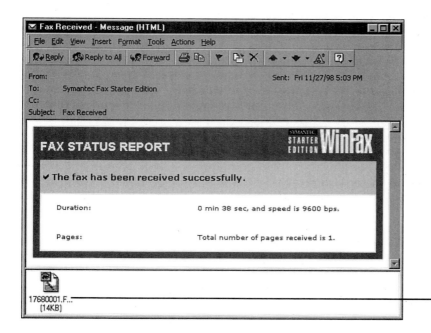

Figure 4.22
The Message form contains a fax status report with an icon representing the file that contains the fax at the bottom.

Attachment

Double-click the file icon at the bottom of the message form to display the dialog box previously shown in Figure 4.21.

You probably want to open the file so that you can see what's in the fax. In the Opening Mail Attachment dialog box, choose Open It and then choose OK. Outlook displays the fax in a Quick Fax Viewer, such as that shown in Figure 4.23.

Figure 4.23
The Quick Fax Viewer initially shows the fax at 25 percent magnification. If the sender used a conventional fax machine, the image may well be upside down, as in this example.

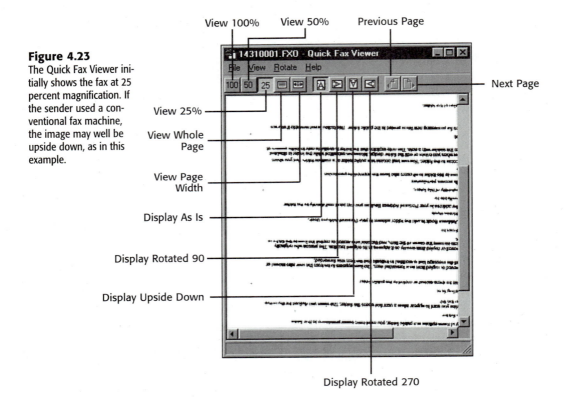

View 100%   View 50%   Previous Page

View 25%

View Whole Page

View Page Width

Display As Is

Display Rotated 90

Display Upside Down

Next Page

Display Rotated 270

Choose the buttons in the Fax Viewer's toolbar to change the image magnification and rotate it, and also to display various pages of a multi-page fax.

To print the fax, choose File, Print (or press Ctrl+P).

SENDING AN OFFICE DOCUMENT AS A FAX

After you've created an Office document, such as some text in Word or a workbook in Excel, you can directly send that document as a fax. The following paragraphs describe how to send a Word document as a fax; sending an Excel workbook is quite similar.

Tip #31 from

Gordon Padwick

The following two sections describe two ways to send an Office document, the first—using the Fax Wizard—is the method suggested in Microsoft's documentation. If you have trouble with that, try the second method (the WinFax SE Printer).

USING THE FAX WIZARD TO FAX AN OFFICE DOCUMENT

Word uses the Fax Wizard to send a document as a fax. After creating a Word document, choose File, move the pointer onto Send To, and choose Fax Recipient. The first time you do this, Word displays a dialog box saying it "can't start this wizard" because this "feature is not currently installed." To install the wizard, choose Yes. You'll be asked to insert the Office 2000 CD-ROM into your CD-ROM drive. Word installs the Fax Wizard and displays the first wizard window, as shown in Figure 4.24.

Figure 4.24
Word uses the Fax Wizard to fax a document.

PART

II

CH

4

Note

When you subsequently want to fax a Word document, the Fax Wizard is displayed without having to install it.

Follow through the steps in the Fax Wizard to fax the document. When you come to the final step, choose the Send Fax Now button. Outlook opens if it's not already running and sends the fax.

USING THE WINFAX SE PRINTER TO FAX A DOCUMENT

After you've installed WinFax SE, Symantec Fax Starter Edition is listed as an available printer in Windows applications. You can select this as a printer in order to fax a document.

To fax a document:

1. With a Windows document open in an application such as Word, choose File, Print to display the Print dialog box.

2. In the Print dialog box, open the drop-down Name list and select Symantec Fax Starter Edition.

3. Make the usual selections in the Print dialog box (page range, number of copies, and so on).

4. Choose OK. After a few seconds delay (substantially more than a few seconds if the document is long or complex), Outlook's Fax message form is displayed with an icon representing the document at the bottom.

5. Address the fax, provide a subject, and add any text in the notes section.

6. Choose Send to send the fax.

DEACTIVATING WINFAX SE

To deactivate WinFax SE, but leave it readily available to be reactivated, choose Tools, Options, and select the Other tab. Choose Advanced Options and then Add-In Manager to display a list of installed *add-ins*, one of which is Symantec WinFax Starter Edition. Uncheck that add-in.

If you want to completely remove WinFax SE from your computer, you must delete a key in the Windows registry, and delete specific files. Refer to the Microsoft Knowledge Base article Q183946 *"How to Remove and Reinstall WinFax Starter Edition"* for complete information about this.

Note
The Knowledge Base article referred to in the preceding paragraph applies specifically to Outlook 98. You can use the information in that article for Outlook 2000 by changing references in registry key names from "Office\8.0" to "Office\9.0". By the time you read this book, there will undoubtedly be many Knowledge Base articles about Outlook 2000, including an updated version of the one mentioned here.

REPLACING WINFAX SE WITH WINFAX PRO

If you only send and receive occasional faxes, you can probably make do with WinFax SE's somewhat limited capabilities. However, if you're a regular fax user, you should consider replacing WinFax SE with WinFax Pro.

Note
The remaining pages of this chapter refer specifically to WinFax Pro version 9. Some of the material doesn't apply to earlier versions of WinFax Pro.

Some of the capabilities of WinFax Pro that aren't available in WinFax SE are:

- Previewing Faxes—You can see exactly what a fax will look like before you send it.
- Custom Cover Pages—You can design your own cover pages, even including graphics such as your organization's logo.
- Optical Character Recognition (OCR)—You can convert text in a fax you receive into text you can edit in a word processor.
- Automatic Paging—WinFax Pro can automatically send a message to your pager when faxes arrive.
- Automatic Forwarding—WinFax Pro can automatically forward faxes it receives to another fax number.
- Broadcasting Faxes—Sending faxes to people whose fax numbers are in a group list.
- Fax Sharing—A workgroup consisting of up to 20 people can share one fax modem and one phone line.

There's much more, but this short list should be enough to convince regular fax users that upgrading to WinFax Pro is something they should consider.

For a detailed comparison between WinFax SE, WinFax Pro, and TalkWorks Pro, go to the Symantec Web site:

```
http://www.symantec.com/winfax/starter/compare.html
```

TROUBLESHOOTING

TROUBLESHOOTING FAX NUMBERS

Although you can sometimes get away with using the ordinary format for entering recipients' fax numbers for your contacts, this doesn't always work. To be on the safe side, you should always use the international, known as the canonical, format for fax numbers.

Outlook can create phone numbers formatted in this way automatically. After you've entered a phone number in a Contacts form, press Tab to move the insertion point to a different box. Then double-click the phone number. Outlook displays a Check Phone Numbers dialog box with the number converted to the international format. Choose OK to close the dialog box. You can use the same method to convert a phone number in an existing Contact item to the international format.

Briefly, the international format (as used for telephone numbers in North America) consists of this sequence of characters:

- The plus character (+) followed by the country code
- A single space

- The area code enclosed within parentheses
- A single space
- The local number (seven digits in North America)

An example of a telephone number in this format is:

+1 (818) 5551212

You can optionally insert the conventional hyphen between the first three and last four digits of the local number.

Tip #32 from

Consult the article *Microsoft Outlook Phone Numbers* for detailed information about how Outlook handles phone numbers. You can access this article at `http://www.slipstick.com/exchange/olphone/.htm#international`.

CHECKING WHETHER WINFAX SE IS AVAILABLE

To send and receive faxes, Outlook must have WinFax SE loaded and your modem must be initialized. If you run into problems, this might be because WinFax SE is not loaded or because your modem is not initialized.

If you're running Outlook under Windows 95 or Windows 98, press Ctrl+Alt+Del to display the Close Program dialog box.

This dialog box displays a list of running programs and should include:

- OLFax MOD (followed by the name of your modem) if your modem is initialized
- Wfxmsrvr if WinFax SE is loaded

If you're running Outlook under Windows NT, right-click the Windows taskbar to display its context menu and then choose Task Manager, which lists currently running programs. The list should include OLFax MOD and Wfxmsrvr.

If Wxsmsrvr is not listed, that means WinFax SE is not loaded. To remedy that, in Outlook choose Tools, Options then choose Modem to display the Modem Properties dialog box. Choose Properties to display the Properties For dialog box. In that box, open the Initialize At drop-down list and select the speed at which the modem should be initialized. Initialization should normally be set to 19200.

WHAT TO DO IF WINFAX SE HANGS UP

From time to time, you might find that received faxes don't appear in your Inbox Information viewer or that you can't send faxes. If this happens, try choosing Tools, Options and then close the Optional dialog box. That often gets WinFax SE working again.

CHAPTER 5

CREATING PROFILES FOR CORPORATE/WORKGROUP OUTLOOK

In this chapter

by Gordon Padwick

WHAT ARE PROFILES?

This chapter applies only to C/W Outlook. That's because everyone who uses C/W Outlook has at least one Outlook *profile*, whereas IMO Outlook users don't have an Outlook profile. You don't need to read this chapter if you're using IMO Outlook.

Before going into detail about Outlook profiles, it's important to understand that Windows uses several types of profiles. In addition to the Outlook profiles that are the subject of this chapter, Windows has hardware profiles and user profiles. Each hardware profile defines a computer hardware configuration. Each user profile defines user *settings (page 19)* such as a user's preferred desktop settings.

> **Note**
>
> Throughout this book, the word *profile* refers to an Outlook profile.

Outlook profiles are quite separate from hardware and user profiles. If you use *C/W Outlook (page 54)*, profiles are an essential part of your Outlook environment. Your profile contains information that defines how Outlook works for you.

The main reason for choosing to install C/W Outlook is that you want to be able to access services provided by specific mail servers such as Exchange Server, Microsoft Mail, or cc:Mail. If you don't need to access these mail servers or other facilities that depend on *MAPI (page 39)* services, you should probably be using IMO Outlook.

> **Note**
>
> Outlook does not support OpenMail (Hewlett-Packard), Groupwise (Novell), or Notes Mail (Lotus). Lotus does provide a MAPI transport that works with Outlook but that's supported by Lotus, not by Microsoft.

When you install C/W Outlook, you automatically have one profile. You can modify this profile to satisfy your specific needs and you can create additional profiles. This chapter explains how to do so.

A profile contains the following information:

- Information Services—A list of information services and the properties of each of them.
- Delivery—The location to which new e-mail should be delivered, and where other Outlook items are saved. Delivery also defines the order in which you want Outlook to use information services when attempting to send e-mail.
- Addressing—The default address book to use when addressing e-mail, the address book in which you want to save information about new contacts, and the order in which address books should be searched to verify recipients' e-mail addresses.

You may have more than one profile. For example, suppose you have a laptop. Most of the time you use the laptop in your office and have it connected to your *LAN*. You take your laptop with you when you travel—it's not connected to anything when you use it on a plane; it may be connected to your LAN by way of a dial-up connection when you're in your hotel room. In this situation, it's convenient to have three profiles:

- One to use when you're in your office
- Another to use while you're flying
- Yet another to use in your hotel room

Or, suppose you share a computer with other people. Each person should have his or her own profile in order to keep Outlook information separate from other users' information.

VIEWING A PROFILE FROM THE WINDOWS DESKTOP

You can examine and modify a profile either from the Windows desktop or from within Outlook. You can create additional profiles from the Windows desktop or from within Outlook, and also copy and delete profiles from the Windows desktop but not from within Outlook. This section first describes how to work with profiles from the Windows desktop.

If you've not previously used Outlook or Windows Messaging on your computer, you'll have the default Outlook profile named Microsoft Outlook Internet Settings; if you have previously used Outlook or Windows Messaging, you'll have whatever profile or profiles you've previously used. The following paragraphs assume that you've just installed C/W Outlook and haven't previously created or modified profiles.

To view a Profile from the Windows desktop:

1. Choose Start, move the pointer onto Settings, and choose Control Panel to display the Control Panel.
2. In the Control Panel, choose Mail (or Mail and Fax) to display the Properties dialog box that contains information about your current default profile, as shown in Figure 5.1.

PART

II

CH

5

Note

An alternative to steps 1 and 2 is to right-click the Outlook icon on the Windows desktop to display a context menu and then choose Properties.

Figure 5.1
The information ser-
vices listed in your
profile are probably
different from those
you see here.

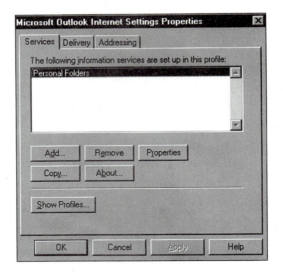

3. Choose Show Profiles to display a list of profiles available on your computer, as shown in Figure 5.2.

Figure 5.2
Only one profile is
listed if you haven't
previously used
Outlook or Windows
Messaging.

EXAMINING AND MODIFYING INFORMATION SERVICES

Open the Windows Control Panel and choose Mail (or Mail and Fax) to display the information services in your default profile. If you want to work with a different profile, choose
Show Profiles, select the profile you want to use, and choose Properties to display the

profile's Properties dialog box that lists the information services in that profile, as shown previously in Figure 5.1. Notice that the Properties dialog box opens with the Services tab selected.

Depending on whether you're looking at the Outlook default profile or a previously used profile, you may see one or more of the following information services listed in the profile. Each *information service* provides a way for Outlook to handle information:

- Internet E-mail—Provides the capability to communicate with Internet and intranet mail servers.
- Microsoft Exchange Server—Provides the capability to communicate with Exchange Server.
- Microsoft Fax—Provides the capability to send and receive faxes. You may see a fax information service other than Microsoft Fax.
- Microsoft Mail—Provides the capability to send and receive e-mail by way of a Microsoft Mail postoffice.
- Outlook Address Book—Provides access to e-mail addresses and fax numbers in your Contacts folder.
- Outlook Support for Lotus cc:Mail—Provides access to cc:Mail post office facilities.
- Personal Address Book—Provides access to e-mail addresses and fax numbers in your Personal Address Book.
- Personal Folders—Provides access to Outlook items in folders within your Personal Folders file (your e-mail, calendar, contacts list, tasks list, and personal journal).

If you've installed Outlook *add-ins* and *add-ons*, you may see other information services listed. These can include services that give Outlook the capability to connect to information providers such as AOL and CompuServe, and to send messages to pagers.

You can add any or all of these information services to your profile.

Note

Add only those information services you intend to use. The more information services you add, the more time Outlook takes to open.

→ For information about adding specific information services to your profile, **see** "Adding a Personal Address Book Information Service to a Profile," **p. 336**, "Adding the Personal Folders Information Service to a Profile" **p. 172**, "Adding the Exchange Server Information Service to a Profile," **p. 665**, and "Adding the Microsoft Mail Information Service to a Profile," **p. 765**.

ADDING AN INFORMATION SERVICE TO A PROFILE

This chapter provides general information about adding information services to a profile. Information that's specific to each information service is included in the chapter that covers that information service.

PART

II

CH

5

You can add information services to a profile by choosing A<u>d</u>d in the Properties dialog box to open the Add Service to Profile dialog box, shown in Figure 5.3.

Note

You can add multiple instances of some information services to a profile, but not other information services. Outlook warns you if you attempt to add a duplicate that isn't permitted. If you're not using Outlook as a client for Exchange, you must have the Personal Folders information service in your profile.

Figure 5.3
This dialog box con-
tains a list of informa-
tion services supplied
with Outlook,
together with any
other services you
have installed as add-
ins or add-ons.

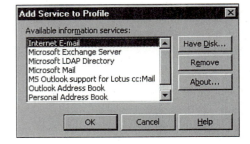

→ **See** Appendix A for information about Outlook add-ins and add-ons.

You can easily add any of the information services supplied with Outlook to a profile. For example, to add the Outlook Address Book information service, select it in the list of available services, and then choose OK. As soon as you do, you'll see the new information service listed in the Services tab of the Microsoft Outlook Properties dialog box.

Note

Some information services are immediately added to a profile and available for use, as described here. If you add some other information services to a profile from within Outlook, you have to close and re-open Outlook to be able to use the new service; Outlook usually displays a message if this is necessary.

REMOVING AN INFORMATION SERVICE FROM A PROFILE

You can remove an information service from a profile by selecting that service in the Properties dialog box and then choosing R<u>e</u>move. If you don't have access to Microsoft Exchange Server, for example, you should remove that service from the list.

Caution

Be careful not to delete an information service that you're using. After deleting some information services, considerable work is needed to re-establish them.

EXAMINING AN INFORMATION SERVICE'S PROPERTIES

To find out about, or modify, how an information service works, select that service in the Properties dialog box and then choose Properties to display a dialog box, as shown in Figure 5.4.

The Personal Folders properties dialog box contains only one tab. The dialog boxes for some other information services contain several tabs.

Each information service has different properties. Rather than attempt to cover all the information services Outlook can use in this chapter, the properties of individual information services are described in the chapters that deal with each of those services.

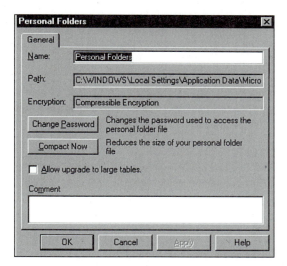

Figure 5.4
This dialog box shows the properties of the Personal Folders information service.

COPYING AN INFORMATION SERVICE

You can copy an information service from one profile to another. You might want to do this when you've created an information service that has complex settings and you subsequently need to create another profile that contains an identical, or almost identical, information service.

To copy an information service:

1. In the profile's Properties dialog box, with the Services tab selected, select the information service you want to copy to another profile.

2. Choose Copy to display the dialog box shown in Figure 5.5.

3. Select the profile into which you want to copy the information service and choose OK.

Figure 5.5
This dialog box lists the profiles available on your computer.

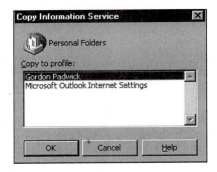

GETTING INFORMATION ABOUT AN INFORMATION SERVICE

To display information about an information service in a profile, display the profile's Properties dialog box, select the information service, and choose About. Outlook displays an information box similar to the one shown in Figure 5.6.

Figure 5.6
This is the information box for the Personal Folders information service.

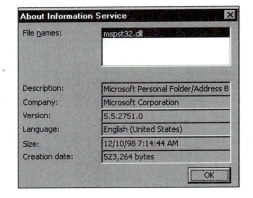

DELIVERING E-MAIL

As you've already seen, the Properties dialog box has three tabs: the Services tab is where you define the information services available in a profile. The other two tabs—Delivery and Addressing—are where you define various aspects of sending and receiving e-mail.

Note

In Outlook's terminology, *delivering* refers to both sending and receiving e-mail. Mail you send is delivered from you; mail you receive is delivered to you.

Choose the Delivery tab to display a dialog box similar to the one shown in Figure 5.7.

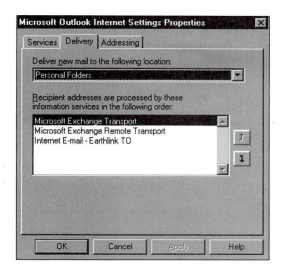

Figure 5.7
Use this dialog box to specify where e-mail messages you receive should be saved and how Outlook should save other Outlook items you create. Also use this dialog box to specify the priority Outlook should use when sending e-mail messages.

Note

Whereas IMO Outlook stores all Outlook *items (page 19)* in one or more Personal Folders files, C/W Outlook lets you store Outlook items in one or more Personal Folders files, in an Offline Store, in Mailbox folders on the Exchange Server, or in Public Folders on the Exchange Server. Refer to the Microsoft Knowledge Base article Q181406 *Purpose and Capacity of Outlook Storage Folders* for detailed information.

The Deliver New Mail to the Following Location box is where you specify where you want to save the e-mail messages you receive, as well as other Outlook items. If you have the Microsoft Exchange Server and Personal Folders information services in the your profile, you can choose to save Outlook items in your Personal Folders file on your local hard disk or in your Exchange Server store.

Tip #33 from
Gordon Padwick

If you sometimes travel with a laptop computer, you should save your incoming messages on your e-mail server so you can easily access them from a remote location. Also, if you're using a PC that doesn't have a local hard drive, you'll have no option but to save your messages on the mail server.

To choose where your incoming mail and other Outlook items are to be saved, open the Deliver New Mail to the Following Location drop-down list on the Delivery tab, and select from the listed locations. If your profile does not contain the Microsoft Exchange Server information service you'll only be able to choose Personal Folders.

It's possible to install the Personal Folders information service two or more times, each with a different name; in that case, you can select which of the Personal Folders files you want to use.

PART
II
CH
5

If you do have the Microsoft Exchange Server information service installed, choose your Exchange mailbox if you want to save your Outlook items in the Exchange Server store, or choose Personal Folders to save your Outlook items in your Personal Folders file on your local hard disk.

The lower part of the Delivery tab deals with how your computer sends e-mail messages. You can use Outlook to send messages by way of various messaging systems.

In most cases, Outlook automatically sends messages by way of the appropriate messaging system. One exception to this, however, occurs when you have the Internet E-mail and Microsoft Exchange Server information services in your profile, and you send a message to an Internet e-mail address. Outlook can handle this message either by directly accessing an Internet e-mail server from your workstation by way of a dial-up connection or by requesting Exchange Server to access an Internet e-mail server.

Outlook chooses which way to handle Internet e-mail messages according to the order in which those services are listed in the Delivery tab of the Services dialog box. If Internet E-mail is above Microsoft Exchange Server in the list of services, Outlook attempts to send your Internet e-mail messages directly to your Internet e-mail server. If Microsoft Exchange Transport comes above Internet E-mail in the list, Outlook calls on Exchange Server to handle your Internet e-mail messages.

To set the order in which Outlook attempts to send e-mail messages, adjust the order of the information services in the lower box on the Delivery tab. You can do this by selecting a service and then clicking one of the arrow buttons at the right side of the tab. You have two ways of sending Internet e-mail messages (by way of Exchange Server on your LAN or by a dial-up connection from your workstation). By placing Microsoft Exchange Transport above Internet E-mail, Outlook first attempts to send your messages by way of Exchange Server but, if that's not available, sends them by way of your dial-up connection.

Tip #34 from

Unfortunately, Outlook isn't always smart enough to try one way of handling Internet e-mail and, if that fails, try an alternative way. If you send e-mail by way of the Internet, after you've sent the mail, look in your Sent Items folder to make sure the e-mail actually was sent.

ADDRESSING E-MAIL

The Addressing tab of the Services dialog box, shown in Figure 5.8, defines various aspects of addressing and sending e-mail messages.

One way to address an e-mail message is to open one of your address lists and select a recipient. When you choose the To button on the Message form, Outlook automatically opens your default address list. If the name you want isn't in that list, you can open a list of address lists and select one of them.

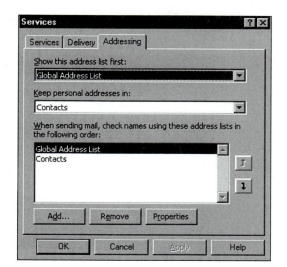

Figure 5.8
This tab is where you can specify the address list you primarily use when addressing e-mail messages.

In the Addressing tab of the Services dialog box, you can choose which of your address lists is the default. You should, of course, select the one that contains the people to whom you most often send messages.

To select a default address list, open the Show This Address List First drop-down list at the top of the tab to see a list of address lists. Then select the appropriate one.

Open the Keep Personal Addresses In drop-down list in the Addressing tab and choose where to save new personal addresses. The address book or list you choose here is where Outlook will propose to save information about people who send you e-mail.

→ For information about how you can add the name and e-mail address of a person from whom you receive a message to your list of contacts, **see** "Saving an E-mail Sender as a Contact Item," **p. 329**.

When you send an e-mail message, or when you choose Check Names on the Message form, Outlook compares recipients' names with names in your address lists. The When Sending Mail, Check Names Using These Address Lists in the Following Order list in the bottom part of the Addressing tab shows the order in which Outlook searches your address books and lists.

You can choose Add to add address books and lists to the list of those to be searched, or you can choose Remove to remove address lists from those to be searched. You can also select one of the address books and lists in the list, then choose one of the arrow buttons at the right side of the list to move the selected one up or down.

→ For more information about working with contacts, **see** "Managing Contacts," **p. 297**.

CREATING A NEW PROFILE

You can create a new profile by copying an existing profile, or you can create a new profile from scratch. If the new profile is to be similar to an existing profile, it's easier to copy an existing profile and then make changes to it. You can create a new profile from the Windows desktop or from within Outlook. The following sections first describe how to create a new profile from the Windows desktop and subsequently describe how to perform the same task from within Outlook.

CREATING A NEW PROFILE BASED ON AN EXISTING PROFILE

You can create a new profile that's similar to an existing profile, starting from the Windows desktop.

To create a new profile based on an existing one:

1. Choose Start in the Windows taskbar, move the pointer onto Settings, and choose Control Panel.

2. In the Control Panel, choose Mail (or Mail and Fax) to display your default profile's Properties dialog box.

3. Choose Show Profiles to display the Mail (or Mail and Fax) dialog box that displays the names of existing profiles.

4. Select the profile on which you want to base the new profile.

5. Choose Copy to display the dialog box shown in Figure 5.9.

Figure 5.9
The Copy Profile dialog box proposes to use the name of the profile you're copying as the name for the new profile.

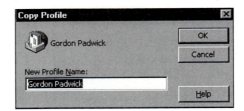

6. Replace the name in the New Profile Name box with a different name for the new profile, then choose OK. Outlook now displays the Mail (or Mail and Fax) dialog box with the name of the new profile listed.

7. With the new profile name selected, choose Properties to display that profile's Properties dialog box.

8. In the new profile's Properties dialog box, add or remove services, and modify services, as described previously in this chapter.

CREATING A NEW PROFILE FROM SCRATCH

If a new profile is to be quite different from an existing profile, you can create that profile from scratch.

To create a new profile from scratch:

1. Choose Start in the Windows taskbar, move the pointer onto Settings, and choose Control Panel.

2. In the Control Panel, choose Mail (or Mail and Fax) to display your default profile's Properties dialog box.

3. Choose Show Profiles to display the Mail dialog box that contains a list of existing profiles.

4. In the Mail dialog box, choose Add to display the Microsoft Outlook Setup Wizard's first window, shown in Figure 5.10.

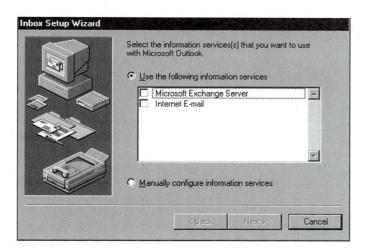

Figure 5.10
The Outlook Setup Wizard's first window invites you to create a profile that contains certain information services, or to manually configure information services.

5. If you want to create a profile that contains one of more of the listed information services, check the services you want, then choose Next.

Note

If you don't want any of these information services, see the information after this series of steps. You can set up a profile that contains any or all of the listed information services and subsequently add other information services to that profile.

6. After you've checked the information services you want in the new profile, choose Next.

7. The Wizard now leads you through a series of windows in which you set up the information services you've chosen to include in the new profile. Refer to Chapter 6, "Sending and Receiving Internet E-mail with Corporate/Workgroup Outlook," for information about setting up the Internet E-mail information service; to Chapter 25, "Adding the Exchange Server Information Service to a Profile," for information about setting up the Microsoft Exchange Server information service; and to Chapter 29,

PART

II

CH

5

"Adding the Microsoft Mail Information Service to a Profile," for information about setting up the Microsoft Mail information service.

If you want to create a new profile that contains information services other than those proposed in the window shown in Figure 5.10, choose Manually Configure Information Services, and then choose Next to display the window shown in Figure 5.11.

Figure 5.11
Use this wizard window to enter a name for your new profile.

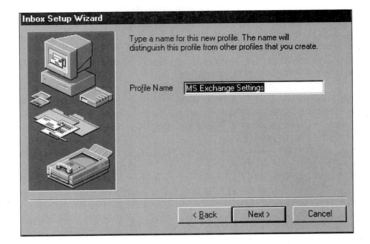

The name you enter must be different from the name of an existing profile. Now, proceed as follows:

To manually configure information services:

1. After entering a name for the new profile, choose Next to display the dialog box shown in Figure 5.12.

2. Choose Add to display the Add Service to Profile dialog box, shown previously in Figure 5.3.

3. Select an information service you want to add to the new profile and choose OK.

4. According to which information service you choose, Outlook displays an appropriate Properties dialog box that may have several tabs.

5. Enter the information required in this dialog box to define the service's properties. You can find information about doing this in the chapters of this book that cover specific services. Choose OK when you've finished defining the service properties to return to the new profile's Properties dialog box, in which you can choose another information service to add to the profile.

6. When you've finished adding services to the profile, choose OK.

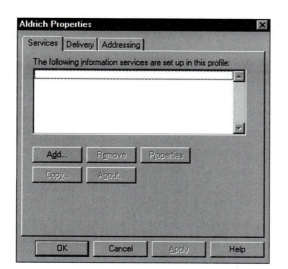

Figure 5.12
Initially, this dialog box shows no information services in the new profile.

VIEWING AND MODIFYING A PROFILE FROM WITHIN OUTLOOK

The preceding pages described how to view and modify a profile from the Windows desktop, and how to create and delete profiles. One advantage of using that method is that you can easily select any profile that's available to you.

You can also examine and modify a profile from within Outlook, but only the profile that Outlook is currently using. Before Outlook can start, it must know which profile to use. After it has started, it can't switch to another profile.

Note

If you add an information service to a profile from within Outlook, it's sometimes necessary to close and restart Outlook before the new information service is available. Outlook displays a message when this is necessary.

To examine or modify a profile from within C/W Outlook, start Outlook and choose Tools, Services. When you do so, Outlook displays the Services dialog box that contains a list of services in the profile Outlook is currently using. This dialog box is similar to the one you see when you choose a profile from the Control Panel, shown previously in Figure 5.2. The differences are that this dialog box has the title Services in the title bar, and doesn't have a Show Profiles button. In the Services dialog box, you can:

- Choose Add to add an information service to the profile
- Choose Remove to remove an information service from the profile
- Choose Properties to examine and change an information service's properties
- Choose Copy to make a copy of an information service
- Choose About to see information about an information service

PART

II

CH

5

CREATING A NEW PROFILE WHEN YOU START OUTLOOK

As explained in Chapter 1, "How Outlook Works," when you start C/W Outlook you may see the Choose Profile dialog box shown in Figure 1.5. If you don't see that dialog box when Outlook starts, refer to the same chapter for information about configuring Outlook's options so that dialog box does appear when Outlook starts.

→ **See** "Controlling How Outlook Starts," **p. 26**.

Choose New in the Choose Profile dialog box to display the first Microsoft Outlook Setup Wizard window, shown previously in Figure 5.10. Follow the steps described previously in this chapter to create a new profile.

→ **See** "Creating a New Profile from Scratch," **p. 162**.

REMOVING A PROFILE

If you no longer need a profile, you should remove it from your computer. You can do so from the Control Panel, but not from within Outlook.

To remove a profile:

1. Follow the first three steps in the "Creating a New Profile from Scratch" section to display a list of profiles.
2. Select the profile you want to remove and then choose Remove. Windows displays a message asking you to confirm that you want to remove the profile. Choose Yes. The Mail dialog box lists the remaining profiles.

TROUBLESHOOTING PROFILES

Occasionally, when you start Outlook, you may see a message that tells you that a certain information service has become corrupted. If that happens, you have to remove the information service and then add it again to the profile.

For that reason, it's a good idea to keep accurate paper records about all the information services you've added to profiles. If you have those records, you can quickly and easily re-create a corrupted information service.

The best way to keep records of each of your information services is to make screen captures of each of the dialog boxes used to set up information services, and print copies of those screen captures.

You can use a screen capture application such as Collage Complete from InnerMedia, Inc. (the application used to capture the screen images printed in this book). You can find information about Collage Complete on the Web site
`http://www.innermedia.com`.

SENDING AND RECEIVING INTERNET E-MAIL WITH CORPORATE/ WORKGROUP OUTLOOK

In this chapter

by Gordon Padwick

HOW OUTLOOK HANDLES INTERNET E-MAIL

The material covered in this chapter applies specifically to *C/W Outlook (page 54)*. If you're using IMO Outlook, refer to Chapter 3, "Sending and Receiving E-mail with Internet Mail Only Outlook," for information about sending and receiving Internet e-mail.

If you have an Internet e-mail account with an *Internet service provider* (ISP), you can use Outlook to exchange e-mail messages with anyone who also has an Internet e-mail account. You can also use Outlook to exchange e-mail messages by way of an intranet that uses Internet protocols. Outlook sends messages to your mail server, which routes those messages to recipients' mail servers. Messages addressed to you are delivered to your mail server, from which you can retrieve them.

By default, Outlook saves copies of messages you send in the Sent Items folder within your Personal Folders file or, if you're using Outlook as a client for Exchange, in your Personal Folders file within the Exchange store. Also by default, Outlook saves messages you receive in your Inbox folder within your Personal Folders file or Exchange store.

Note

This chapter refers primarily to saving messages in your Personal Folders file. Refer to Chapter 24, "Exchange Server Overview," for information about saving items in the Exchange store.

INSTALLING THE TCP/IP PROTOCOL

One of the common mistakes people make when they first try to connect to an ISP is not making sure that the *TCP/IP* protocol is installed on their computers. All Internet communication depends on the TCP/IP protocol, so you must have it installed in order to access Web sites, interact with newsgroups, or to send and receive Internet e-mail. You don't need to understand TCP/IP, just make sure it's installed.

For information about installing TCP/IP under Windows 95, Windows 98, or Windows NT, see the Windows Help topic "Connecting to the Internet." If you follow the instructions carefully, you shouldn't have any problems. However, if you do have difficulty, your ISP's technical support people will probably be glad to help.

SETTING UP DIAL-UP NETWORKING

Outlook uses your computer's modem to connect to your ISP and to send information to, and receive information from, your mail server. The dial-up networking capability within Windows is used to place the phone call.

Note

If you're using Outlook to send and receive intranet messages by way of a LAN, you don't need to set up a dial-up connection.

To verify that you have dial-up networking installed, open My Computer from your Windows desktop. One of the icons in the My Computer window should be Dial-Up Networking. If that icon isn't present, you must install dial-up networking in Windows. For information about doing that, look at the Dial-Up Networking topic in Windows Help.

Choose Dial-Up Networking in the My Computer window to open the Dial-Up Networking dialog box, which should be similar to the one shown in Figure 6.1.

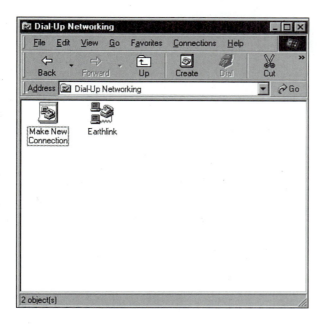

Figure 6.1
If you already have a dial-up connection, information about it is shown in this dialog box. If you haven't already defined a dial-up connection, the text boxes are empty.

Note

The illustrations and procedures in this chapter are based on Outlook running under Windows 98. In some cases, there are differences if you're running Windows 95 or Windows NT.

To define a new dial-up connection:

1. In the Dial-up Networking dialog box, double-click Make a New Connection to display the dialog box shown in Figure 6.2.

Figure 6.2
This dialog box displays the name of the software driver that controls your modem.

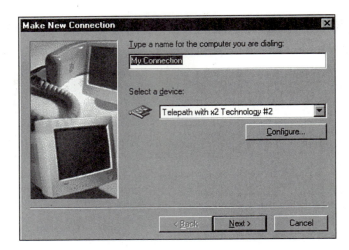

2. Replace "My Connection" in the <u>T</u>ype a Name for the Computer You Are Dialing box with the name you want to use for the computer to which you will establish a dial-up connection. If you're creating a connection to an Internet service provider, you can use the ISP's name.

3. The Select a <u>D</u>evice box contains the name of your modem driver. If you have more than one modem installed on your computer, open the drop-down list and select the appropriate modem driver.

Note

After selecting a modem driver, you can choose <u>C</u>onfigure to configure the modem. If the modem is already working, this isn't necessary.

4. Choose <u>N</u>ext > to display the next dialog box shown in Figure 6.3.

Figure 6.3
Use this dialog box to specify the phone number you want to call.

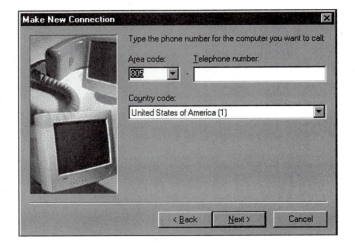

5. Enter the area code, telephone number, and country you want to call (your ISP's phone number), then choose <u>N</u>ext > to display the final dialog box shown in Figure 6.4.

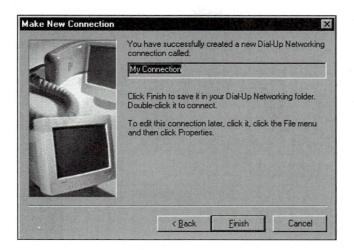

Figure 6.4
This dialog box con-firms that you have created a new dial-up connection.

6. Choose <u>F</u>inish to return to the Dial-up Networking dialog box, which now contains an icon representing the new dial-up connection.

Note

Although the preceding steps provide a phone connection to an ISP, in most cases more is required to be able to log on to the Internet and on to mail servers provided by that ISP. For example, you may have to specify Internet Protocol (IP) addresses. The settings required are different for each ISP. Your ISP will provide detailed information about the required settings and how you must set up dial-up networking.

CREATING AN INTERNET ACCOUNT

First, you have to establish an account with an Internet service provider (ISP), then you have to add the Internet E-mail information service into your Outlook profile.

Establishing an account with an ISP usually involves choosing an ISP and then making a phone call to that ISP, or using your Web browser to connect to that ISP's Web site. Either way, you'll have to give the ISP your name, suggest a name for your account, provide a password, and agree to some way that the ISP will bill you (the usual method is to provide a credit card number that will be billed on a monthly basis). After you've done that, the ISP will provide whatever information is necessary for you to log on to your account.

PART

II

CH

6

CHOOSING AN INTERNET SERVICE PROVIDER

Don't take choosing an ISP lightly. Although you can change your ISP at any time, remember that when you change your ISP, your Internet e-mail address changes.

You can choose from among many ISPs, many of whom offer different services. Consider the following:

- Some ISPs have local access telephone numbers in many parts of the country, while others have local access numbers only for one city or region. If you're likely to want to connect to your ISP while traveling, choose an ISP that has local access numbers in the places you expect to visit.

- Some ISPs allow you to have more than one e-mail address for your account so that people who share the account can keep their e-mail separate. This is particularly useful for a small business or family. Not all ISPs offer this service.

- Some ISPs accommodate various type of connections, including high-speed modem, ISDN, and others. If you expect to become a frequent Internet user, choose an ISP that offers high-speed connections, even if you don't use those connections initially.

- Some ISPs offer free or low-cost disk space you can use to create your own Web site; others don't. If you anticipate having your own Web site, investigate the cost of it being hosted by the ISP before you make your choice.

- Most ISPs provide access to Internet newsgroups. If there are some newsgroups you need to use, make sure the ISP you choose provides access to them.

After you've evaluated ISPs based on these criteria, ask around to get the opinions of people who use the services you're interested in. What you need is an ISP that provides the services you require and one to which you can usually gain fast access. Only people's experience can give you the information you need to make your choice.

CHOOSING WHERE TO SAVE MESSAGES

You can save messages you receive and copies of messages you send in a Personal Folders file on your local hard drive. Alternatively, if you're using Outlook as a client for Exchange, you can save messages in the Exchange store.

ADDING THE PERSONAL FOLDERS INFORMATION SERVICE TO YOUR PROFILE

This chapter assumes you plan to save messages in a Personal Folders file. In order to do so, you need to have a Personal Folders information service in your profile. If that service doesn't already exist, add it to your profile using the method described in the following steps.

To add the Personal Folders information service:

1. With any Outlook Information viewer displayed, choose Tools, Services to display the Services dialog box shown in Figure 6.5.

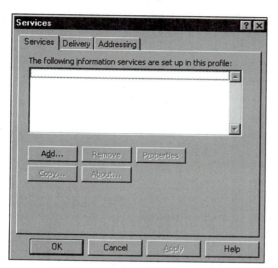

Figure 6.5
The Services dialog box opens with the Services tab showing a list of information services (if any) already in your profile.

If you already have the Personal Folders information service in your profile, you don't need to continue. Choose Cancel to close the dialog box. Although you don't usually need more than one Personal Folders information service in a profile, Outlook permits you to have several.

2. Choose Add to display the Add Service to Profile dialog box shown in Figure 6.6.

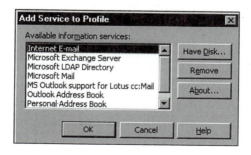

Figure 6.6
This dialog box lists the information services available to be added to your profile.

PART
II

CH

6

3. Select Personal Folders (scroll down if necessary to see Personal Folders) and then choose OK. Outlook displays the Create/Open Personal Folders File dialog box shown in Figure 6.7.

Figure 6.7
This dialog box opens displaying a list of Personal Folders files that already exist in the Windows default folder (My Documents for Windows 95 and Windows 98, Personal for Windows NT).

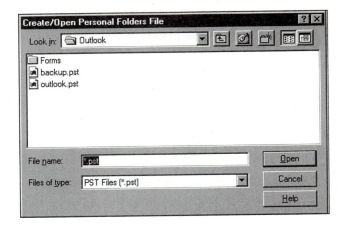

4. Enter a name for the new Personal Folders file in the File Name box. Your own last name, initials, or server account name are good choices for a file name. Outlook automatically adds the file name extension .pst to the name you enter. Choose Open to display the Create Microsoft Personal Folders dialog box shown in Figure 6.8.

Figure 6.8
This dialog box displays the complete path name of the file, using the file name you entered in the preceding step.

Note

Each Personal Folders file has two names. One of these is its file name, the name you see when you use Windows Explorer to look for files. The second is a name by which the file is listed in the Outlook folder list.

5. By default, Outlook proposes to give the new Personal Folders file the name "Personal Folders." You can accept this name if you intend to have only one Personal Folders file. If you might have two or more Personal Folders files, change the default name in

the Name box to something that identifies its purpose—to keep things simple, it's a good idea to use the same name as the file name you entered in the preceding step.

6. In the Encryption Setting section of the dialog box, select an encryption level. For most purposes, select the default Compressible Encryption.

Note

You have to select an encryption setting at the time you create a Personal Folders file. You can't subsequently change the encryption setting. The default is Compressible Encryption, a format that allows your Personal Folders file to be compressed if you have a compression program active on your computer. You can select No Encryption or Best Encryption. Best Encryption is a format that provides the best degree of protection for the information in your Outlook folders. If you select Best Encryption and you have a compression program active on your computer, your Personal Folders file is compressed, but to a lesser degree than allowed by Compression Encryption.

7. If you want to password-protect your Personal Folders file, enter a password in the Password box and again in the Verify Password box.

8. Leave the Save This Password in Your Password List box unchecked so that anyone else who uses your computer doesn't have access to your Personal Folders file.

9. Choose OK to close the dialog box and return to the Services dialog box shown previously in Figure 6.3 but with the new Personal Folders file now listed.

Note

If you password-protect a Personal Folders file, you have to provide a password to open Outlook. Once Outlook is running, you (or anyone else) can open another password protected Personal Folders file without supplying the password.

ADDING THE INTERNET E-MAIL INFORMATION SERVICE TO YOUR PROFILE

After you signed up with an Internet service provider (ISP) and added the Personal Folders information service to your profile, your next step is to connect to that account from Outlook. You do this by adding the Internet E-mail information service to your profile. The steps described here apply specifically to accessing Internet e-mail by way of an ISP. If you're accessing intranet e-mail, the procedure is similar.

PART

II

CH

6

Make sure that C/W Outlook is running before starting the following procedure.

To add the Internet E-mail information service:

1. Choose Tools, Services to open the Services dialog box previously shown in Figure 6.5.

2. Choose Add to display the Add Services dialog box previously shown in Figure 6.6.

3. Select Internet E-mail and then choose OK to add that service. Outlook displays the Mail Account Properties dialog box shown in Figure 6.9.

Figure 6.9
This dialog box opens with the General tab selected. The dialog box is shown here with typical information entered.

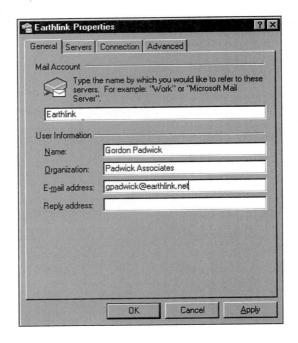

4. Enter a name for the information service in the Mail Account box. If you intend to have only one Internet E-mail information service, you can simply call this service Internet. If you expect to use more than one Internet E-mail service, enter a more specific name such as Internet Personal or the name of your ISP.

5. Enter your own name or pseudonym in the Name box. The name you enter here is the name that will appear on messages you send.

6. Enter the name of your organization, if appropriate, in the Organization box. You can leave this box empty.

7. Enter your e-mail address in the E-mail Address box. This is the address that recipients of your messages use to send replies to you, unless you enter a different e-mail address in the Reply Address box.

8. If you want to have replies sent to an e-mail address other than your own (or a separate e-mail address you use for replies), enter that e-mail address in the Reply Address box. Leave this box empty if you want replies sent to the e-mail address you entered in step 7.

9. After you've entered information into the boxes in this tab, select the Servers tab shown in Figure 6.10.

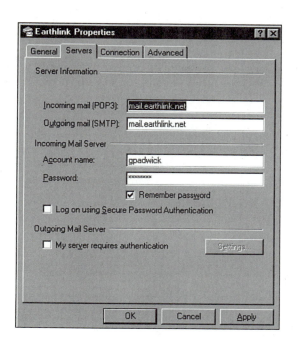

Figure 6.10
Use this tab to pro-
vide information
about your mail
servers. The dialog
box shown here has
typical information
entered.

10. Enter the name of the server you will use for messages you receive in the Incoming
    Mail (POP) box. Your ISP should have told you the name of that server at the time you
    subscribed to the account.

Note

> Unlike IMO, C/W Outlook only allows you to receive e-mail from a server that uses the
> POP protocol. POP stands for Post Office Protocol.

11. Enter the name of the server you will use for messages you send in the Outgoing Mail
    (SMTP) box. Your ISP should have told you the name of that server at the time you
    subscribed to an account with that ISP.

Note

> SMTP stands for Simple Mail Transfer Protocol, the protocol Outlook uses to send mes-
> sages to an Internet mail server. The servers used for incoming and outgoing mail may
> have the same or different names.

12. Most ISPs don't require secure password authentication. If your ISP or intranet
    server does require secure password authentication, ignore this step and go directly to
    step 16.

PART

II

CH

6

Normally, accept the default selection of Log on Using, then follow the next three steps. If you're using an ISP that doesn't require secure password authentication, but you want enhanced security, select Log on Using Secure Password Authentication (in that case you'll have to enter your username and password each time you access the server) then proceed to step 17.

13. Enter your Internet account name in the Account Name box.

14. Enter your Internet password in the Password box.

15. Leave the Remember Password box if you don't want to be prompted for your password each time you access the mail servers. Alternatively, check the box if you do want to be prompted. By checking this box, you have the security that anyone who accesses your Outlook profile can't access your e-mail without providing your password. Proceed directly to step 17.

16. Check the My Server Requires Authentication box if your outgoing server requires authentication. After you do so, you'll have to provide your username and password before you can send messages.

17. After completing this tab, select the Connection tab shown in Figure 6.11.

Figure 6.11
Use this tab to specify how you will connect to an Internet or intranet server. The tab is shown here with a phone connection to an ISP specified.

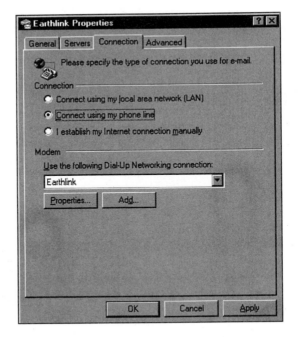

18. Select the type of connection you intend to use. If you select Connect Using My Phone Line, the Modem drop-down list becomes available. Open this list and select from among the dial-up connections you've previously created. You can examine and, if necessary, modify an existing connection by selecting that connection and choosing Properties, and you can add a new dial-up connection by choosing Add.

19. After you've specified how you intend to connect to the mail server, select the Advanced tab shown in Figure 6.12.

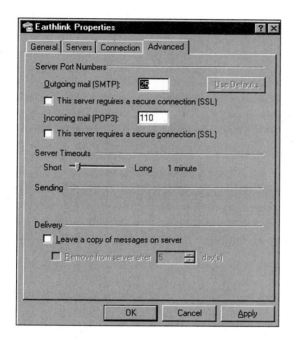

Figure 6.12
Make changes in the Advanced tab only if the default settings give you problems or if you are told to do so by your ISP.

20. In most cases, you won't need to make any changes in this dialog box, so choose OK to accept all the information you've entered and selected in all four tabs.

Although the preceding steps suggested that you accept the default choices in the Advanced tab, there may be times when you need to make some changes. The following paragraphs explain what's in this tab.

The Server Port Numbers section at the top of the Advanced tab contains information that's usually correct. Don't change the information in this section unless you have specific instructions from your ISP or server administrator to do so.

PART
II

CH
6

If you find that you are frequently disconnected from your mail server before the connection is completed, you may have to increase the time specified in the Server Timeouts section. In most cases the default value of one minute is adequate. If necessary, you can drag the pointer in this box to the right to increase the timeout, giving the server more time to process your request for service.

After you've downloaded a message waiting for you on a server, that message is normally automatically deleted from the server. You may be able to leave messages on your server after you've read them. Not all servers allow this; some that do limit the space you can use for this purpose and limit the period for which messages can be saved.

Tip #35 from

Gordon Padwick

> You can choose one of the computers you use as your main e-mail reader. When you use other computers to read e-mail, leave that e-mail on the server. Allow the server to delete messages only when you read e-mail from your main computer. In that way, you make sure all your mail is stored on your main computer.

If you want to leave messages you've read on the server, check the Leave a Copy of Messages on Server box. When you do so, the next two check boxes become enabled. If you leave these boxes unchecked, messages will remain on the server as long as the server administrator permits. You can check the Remove from Server After box and specify a certain number of days in the adjoining text box.

After you've finished setting up an Internet E-mail information service, choose OK. Outlook displays a message telling you to choose File, Exit and Log Off to close Outlook. Do that, and then restart Outlook to enable the new information service.

LOGGING INTERNET MAIL CONNECTIONS

If you run into problems connecting with an Internet mail server (or an intranet server that uses Internet protocols) you may see the message "The connection to the server has failed." The problem may be in your mail server or TCP/IP settings. Detailed information about correcting these problems is beyond the scope of this book, but Microsoft offers some suggestions in the Knowledge Base article Q154578, *Troubleshooting Problems Connecting to Mail Servers*.

If you encounter problems accessing Internet accounts, it's useful to be able to log certain aspects of the connection. Outlook provides no direct way to do that, but you can activate logging by making changes to the Windows *registry (page 605)*.

Caution

> Always make a backup copy of the registry before making changes to it. See Appendix F, "Working with the Windows Registry," for information about backing up the registry and making changes to it.

To enable logging:

1. If Outlook is open, choose File, Exit and Log Off to close it.
2. Choose Start on the Windows taskbar, and then choose Run in the Start menu. Enter regedit in the Open box to start the Registry Editor.
3. Using the method explained in Appendix F, access the key: HKEY_CURRENT_USER\Software\Microsoft\Office\9.0\Outlook\Options\Mail. The top of the Registry Editor window should show the selected registry key, as shown in Figure 6.13.

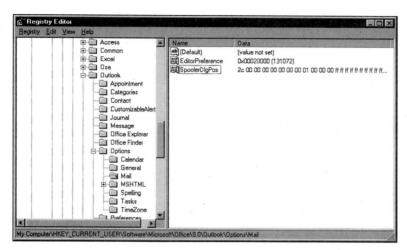

Figure 6.13
The Registry Editor window shows the original values in the selected key.

4. Choose Edit, move the pointer onto New, and choose DWORD Value. The value name New Value #1 is added to the list of value names.
5. Enter Logging to replace New Value #1 and press Enter.
6. With Logging selected, Choose Edit, Modify to open the Edit DWORD Value dialog box shown in Figure 6.14.

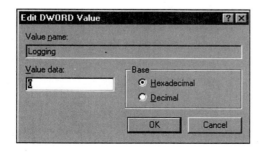

Figure 6.14
The new key initially contains the value 0 (zero).

PART

II

CH

6

7. Enter 1 (the number one) in the V̲alue Data box then choose OK. The Registry Editor now shows the new key and its value, as shown in Figure 6.15.

Figure 6.15
This is how the Registry Editor should look after you've added the new value.

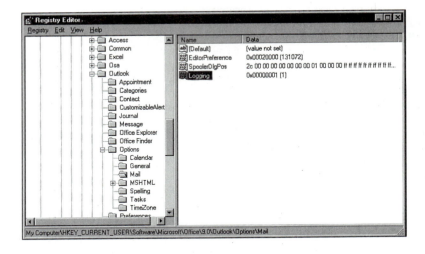

8. Choose R̲egistry, E̲xit to close the Registry Editor.

The next time you use Outlook to connect, or attempt to connect, to an Internet account, three files will be created in the Windows\Temp\Outlook Logging folder (Windows 95 or Windows 98) or in the WINNT\Temp\Outlook Logging folder (Windows NT):

- InetXP.txt—Logs the Internet session
- Pop3log.txt—Logs mail retrieval
- Smtplog.txt—Logs mail sending

 See Microsoft Knowledge Base articles Q155455, *How to Enable and Interpret the Smtp.log File*, and Q155515, *How to Enable and Interpret the Pop3.log File* for information about interpreting data in the three logging files.

After you've finished troubleshooting, you can use the Registry Editor again to turn off logging by setting Logging to 0.

SELECTING A MESSAGE FORMAT AND E-MAIL EDITOR

Outlook lets you choose from among three formats in which you can send messages. It also lets you create messages using two different editors. Outlook 2000 handles these capabilities more conveniently than previous Outlook versions did.

MESSAGE FORMAT CAPABILITIES

You can choose to send messages in HTML, Outlook Rich Text, or Plain Text formats. Table 6.1 compares these formats.

Note

> Don't assume the people to whom you send e-mail messages will be able to receive your messages with all the formatting you create, nor that they will be able to open attachments to your messages. In some cases, you may have to send sample messages to ascertain whether the e-mail programs recipients use are capable of receiving what you send.

TABLE 6.1   MESSAGE FORMATS

Format	Description
HTML	The *Hypertext Markup Language* (HTML) format offers you the ability to quickly and easily create highly formatted pages that include horizontal lines, pictures, animated graphics, and multimedia files. You can also select a *stationery* that provide background designs for your messages. Use this format only if you know message recipients use e-mail programs that can read HTML.
Outlook Rich Text	Outlook Rich Text is the standard Exchange format, so it's appropriate for C/W Outlook used as a client for Exchange. You can select fonts, font sizes, and font colors, and you can format paragraphs. You can embed objects, including pictures, within the text. Don't use this format to send messages that contain attachments to people who aren't using Outlook or Windows Messaging to receive e-mail. Instead of seeing the attachments you sent, recipients will see attachments called Winmail.dat that don't contain meaningful information.
Plain Text	This format does what you'd expect: you can use it for unformatted text; you can attach files and Outlook items to Plain Text messages. Despite its limitations, this format is your best choice for general e-mail and for messages to newsgroups. Use this format when you're sending messages to people who aren't using Outlook or Windows Messaging as their e-mail programs. You can, of course, use this format for messages to people who do use Outlook or Windows Messaging.

To be on the safe side, use Plain Text for Internet e-mail unless you really need the formatting capabilities of HTML. If you do use HTML, be prepared for the fact that some recipients may not receive your messages as you intended. An advantage of the Plain Text format is that it results in smaller files, something that's important for people who pay for Internet access by the minute, or pay long-distance phone charges.

As described subsequently in this chapter, you can use any of these mail formats to send messages that have attachments.

→ **See** a book about Internet Explorer, such as *Using Internet Explorer 4*, published by Que, for detailed information about HTML.

PART
II

CH
6

SELECTING A MESSAGE FORMAT

You can select a default message format, the format you expect to use for most of your messages, and you can select a format other than the default for specific messages (but only if you're not using WordMail as your editor).

Note

Unless you have a good reason for doing otherwise, select Plain Text as your default message format.

To select a default message format:

1. Choose Tools, Options and select the Mail Format tab shown in Figure 6.16.

Figure 6.16
Use this dialog box to select a default mail format.

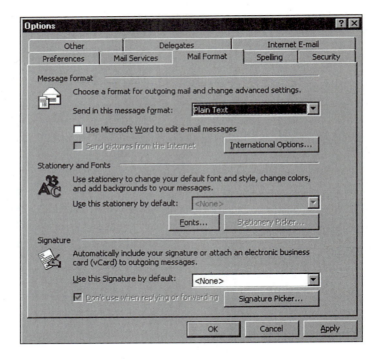

2. Open the Send in This Message Format drop-down list, and select HTML, Microsoft Outlook Rich Text, or Plain Text. Choose OK to close the dialog box.

Note

After you choose HTML, and have not checked Use Microsoft Word to Edit E-mail Messages, you can choose a default stationery.

Subsequently, when you create a message, Outlook will use the default format.

When you reply to a message you've received, Outlook automatically uses the same message format as the message you received. Similarly, if you want to annotate a message you've received and then forward the message, Outlook uses the same format as the message you received.

Note

> As described subsequently in this chapter, you can change the message format from the one Outlook automatically proposes.

→ **See** "Formatting a Message" later in this chapter for information about stationery, **p. 195**. **See** "Mail Format Options," **p. 867** for complete information about the Options dialog box's Mail Format tab.

SELECTING A MAIL EDITOR

The mail editor is a tool you use to create messages. No matter which Mail format you select, you can use Outlook's native editor or WordMail as your editor. WordMail provides access to many of the components of Word 2000 and is available only if you have Word 2000 installed on your computer.

If you have Word 2000 installed on your computer, you have the choice of using Outlook's native editor or WordMail. The disadvantages of using WordMail are the slight delay incurred in loading Word the first time in any Outlook session in which you start doing some editing, not being able to use stationery, and not being able to select message formats for individual messages. Another disadvantage of using WordMail is that recipients of your messages who aren't also using WordMail often see attachments as meaningless Winmail.dat files.

The advantages of using WordMail are that you can use Word's capabilities, such as justification and creating borders that aren't available in Outlook's native editor.

Note

> Outlook doesn't let you use any editor or word processor other than WordMail or the Outlook native editor.

To select an e-mail editor, open the Options dialog box's Mail Format tab, shown previously in Figure 6.16. Check Use Microsoft Word to Edit E-mail Messages if you want to use Word; leave the box unchecked if you want to use Outlook's native editor.

After you select WordMail as your editor and you start to create a new message with Plain Text selected as your message format, you'll have menus and toolbars similar to those available in Word at your disposal, as shown in Figure 6.17.

PART
II

CH
6

Figure 6.17
These are the menus and toolbars available when you use WordMail as your editor.

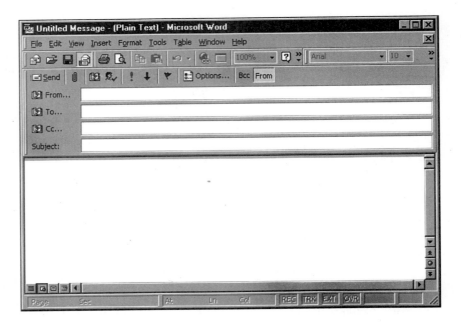

After you select Outlook's native editor and start to create a new message with Plain Text selected as your message format, you'll have the menus and toolbars shown in Figure 6.18 available.

Figure 6.18
These are the menus and the toolbars available when you use Outlook's native editor.

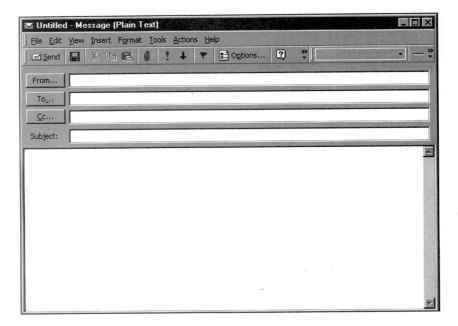

CREATING A MESSAGE

The following information assumes you're using Outlook's native editor and have selected HTML as your default message format, as described previously in this chapter.

SENDING A MESSAGE FROM WORD

In Word, or another Office application, you can create a document and send that document to an e-mail recipient. Here's how.

To create a message in Word and send it by e-mail:

1. Open Word and create the message.
2. Choose File, move the pointer onto Send To, and choose Mail Recipient. The Document form expands to show To, Cc, and Subject boxes at the top.
3. Choose To to open the Select Names dialog box, which displays a list of your contacts.
4. Select one or more people to whom you want to send the message, choose To-> to move the name or names into the Message Recipients list, then choose OK to return to the Document form in which the recipients names are displayed.
5. If appropriate, choose Cc to select the names of people to whom you want to copy the message.
6. Enter a subject of the message in the Subject box.
7. Choose Send a Copy in the form's toolbar to send the document as a message. When you do that, the document is placed in Outlook's Outbox, ready to be sent. The document is actually sent the next time you send messages from Outlook to your mail server.

Note

The preceding procedure referred specifically sending a message from Word. You can use similar steps to send messages from other Office applications.

OPENING THE MESSAGE FORM

To create a message, start by choosing Inbox in the Outlook Bar to display the Inbox Information viewer. Choose the New button at the left end of the Standard toolbar. Outlook displays a message form similar to that shown in Figure 6.18. Notice that the form's title bar reminds you which message format you have chosen as the default.

If you've chosen WordMail as your default editor or, as explained in the preceding tip, chosen WordMail for the current message, Outlook displays the message form shown previously in Figure 6.17.

CHOOSING INTERNATIONAL OPTIONS

Something new in Outlook 2000 is the importance of International Options. In the Mail Format tab of the Options dialog box, shown previously in Figure 6.16, choose International Options to display the dialog box shown in Figure 6.19.

Figure 6.19
By default, Western European (ISO) encoding is selected for outgoing and unmarked received messages.

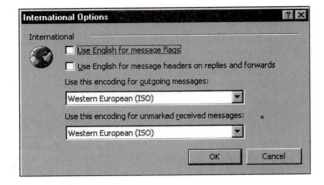

> **Note**
>
> "Encoding" refers to the relationship between the digital representations of characters in a message (or other file) and the way those characters appear onscreen or in print, and also the digital codes that are recorded by pressing keys on your keyboard. Encoding is controlled in the Windows environment by code pages, each of which contains a table of characters with a numeric index assigned to each character.

Normally, accept the defaults in this dialog box. You can open the drop-down Use This Encoding for Outgoing Messages and Use This Encoding the Unmarked Received Messages lists and select encoding other than the default.

> **Note**
>
> If you select encoding other than Western European (ISO), people who receive your messages using Outlook 97 or Outlook 98 will not be able to send replies to your messages.

If you use a non-English version of Outlook, you can check:

- Use English for Message Flags. After you do so, such flags as High Importance and Flag for Follow-up appear in English.
- Use English for Message Headers on Replies and Forwards. After you do so, the headers of message replies and forwarded messages use English for field name labels such as From, To, Sent, and Subject.

CHANGING THE MESSAGE FORMAT

If you want to use a message format other than your default, choose F<u>o</u>rmat in the Message form's menu bar to display the menu shown in Figure 6.20. You can select an alternative format either before or after you've entered the message text.

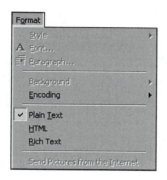

Figure 6.20
The Format menu contains your default format, Plain <u>T</u>ext in this case, which is checked, and also <u>H</u>TML and <u>R</u>ich Text.

Select <u>H</u>TML or <u>R</u>ich Text if you want to change to either of those formats. The message format name in the form's title bar changes to show the new format.

After you've switched to HTML or Rich Text, or if you had chosen HTML or Rich Text as your default format, you can change to Plain Text. To do so, choose F<u>o</u>rmat in the form's menu bar to see a menu that contains Plain <u>T</u>ext as well as <u>H</u>TML or <u>R</u>ich Text. Choose Plain <u>T</u>ext to switch to that format. When you do so, you'll see a message warning you about losing formatting. Choose <u>Y</u>es if you want to continue.

Changing from HTML to Rich Text, or vice versa, is a two step process. First change from HTML (or Rich Text) to Plain Text. With the Plain Text format selected, choose F<u>o</u>rmat in form's menu bar to display a menu in which you can select HTML or Rich Text.

> **Note**
>
> When you change the message format in this way, the change affects only the current message. Subsequent messages use the default format. The only place to change the default format is to choose <u>T</u>ools, <u>O</u>ptions and select the Mail Format tab.

The remainder of this section assumes you're using the HTML message format, even though I recommend using Plain Text for most purposes. This is so that I can describe several capabilities offered by HTML that aren't available in Plain Text. You'll find minor differences if you're using the Plain Text or Rich Text formats.

You can also use the Message form's Format menu to change encoding from the default encoding. Move the pointer onto <u>E</u>ncoding and select from a list of available encoding formats. This is something you normally shouldn't have to do and, in fact, shouldn't do unless you completely understand the implications.

ADDRESSING THE MESSAGE

The blank message form shown previously in Figure 6.18 contains the message header consisting of the To, Cc, and Subject boxes. If you see only the To box, choose View, Message Header in the form's menu bar to display the complete message header.

Figure 6.21 shows a typical message form with recipient addresses, subject, and message text entered.

Figure 6.21
This message form is ready to send.

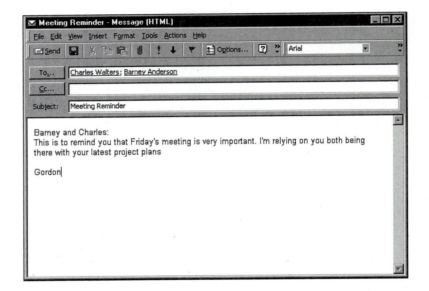

To address the message, enter one or more recipient e-mail addresses in the To box. You can do so in several ways, each of which is convenient in specific circumstances.

→ **See** "Managing Contacts," **p. 297**.

Note

The following sections make frequent reference to your Contact list. To use the information in these sections, you must already have Contact entries in your address book.

MANUALLY ENTERING AN E-MAIL ADDRESS

If you know recipients' e-mail addresses, you can enter those addresses in the To box, separating one address from the next with a semicolon. After you've completed entering addresses, press Tab to move to the next box. At that time, Outlook attempts to verify the e-mail addresses you entered by comparing them with information in your address book, a process referred to as *resolving* addresses.

Note

The term *address book* in the preceding and subsequent paragraphs refers to your Contacts folder and, possibly, to other places where you keep addresses. Refer to Chapter 9, "Managing Contacts," for detailed information about this.

When Outlook finds an address you've entered in your address book, Outlook replaces the address with the person's name and underlines that name. If Outlook doesn't find the e-mail address in your address book, but does recognize the address as being in acceptable Internet format, Outlook simply underlines the address you entered. If Outlook doesn't recognize the address as being in Internet format, Outlook leaves the name as you entered it without underlining it.

If you enter several recipients' e-mail addresses, some of them may be in your address book, but not others. If that's the case, the To box contains a mixture of e-mail addresses and people's names.

ENTERING RECIPIENTS' NAMES

If you're sending a message to recipients whose names and e-mail addresses are in your address book, you can enter names instead of e-mail addresses. After you enter one or more names, separating one from the next with a semicolon, press Tab to move to the Cc box. At that time, Outlook looks for the names in your address book. If Outlook finds a name, Outlook underlines the name to indicate that it is acceptable.

To be sure the e-mail address is correct, right-click the person's name to display a context menu. Choose Properties in the context menu to display the form shown in Figure 6.22.

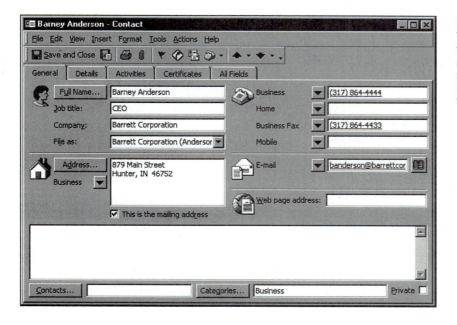

Figure 6.22
This form displays the information about a contact that's saved as a Contact item in your Contacts folder.

PART

II

CH

6

Caution

The fact that Outlook underlines a name in the To box on the Message form indicates only that the name exists in your address book, not that the address book contains an e-mail address for the contact. That's why you should always check Properties to make sure an e-mail address is available.

ENTERING PARTIAL RECIPIENT NAMES

Instead of entering the complete names of recipients, you can enter partial names. For example, you could enter Frank and press Tab. Outlook searches your address book and, if it finds only one Frank, it displays that Frank's full name and underlines it. You should check the name's properties, as previously described, to ensure that Outlook has chosen the correct e-mail address.

If there are two or more Franks in your address book and you haven't previously sent e-mail to either of them, Outlook places a squiggly red line under the name you entered to indicate that you have to make a decision. Right-click the name you entered and Outlook displays a list of all the Franks in your address book. Select the one to whom you want to send this message.

If there are two or more Franks in your address book and you have previously sent e-mail to any of them, Outlook assumes you want to send e-mail to the most recent Frank address you used and displays that person's name in the To box. To select a different Frank, right-click the name in the To box and then select the name you want to use.

SELECTING NAMES IN YOUR ADDRESS BOOK

Instead of entering recipients' names or e-mail addresses, you can select these names from those in your Contacts folder or other list of contacts. In the Message form, choose To to display the contacts in one of your address books, as shown in Figure 6.23.

Figure 6.23
The Select Names dialog box shows the names in one of your address books. These names are listed at the left side of the dialog box. The name of the address book is shown in the Show Names from The box.

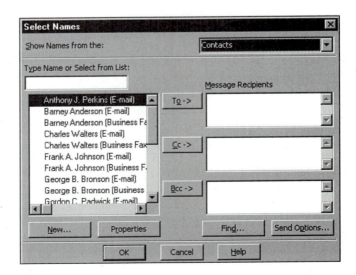

If you have more than one address book, you can open the drop-down Show Names from The box to see a list of available address books, as shown in Figure 6.24.

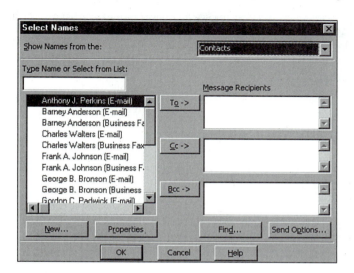

Figure 6.24
In this example, the Contacts address book is available as an Outlook Address Book.

→ For detailed information about address books, **see** "Using a Personal Address Book," **p. 336**.

Select any address book in the drop-down list. After you do so, Outlook displays the names in that address book in the Select Names dialog box.

You can use three methods to select recipients from the names in the selected address book.

One method is to scroll down the list of names, select the name of one recipient, and choose To-> to copy that name into the Message Recipients list at the right side of the dialog box. Then choose OK to return to the Message form in which the name you selected is displayed in the To box.

Tip #36 from

Gordon Padwick

To designate more than one recipient, select the first, then hold down Ctrl while you select others. To select recipient names that are listed consecutively, select the first name, then hold down Shift while you select the last name.

Alternatively, you can repeatedly choose To on the message form to add names one at a time.

PART

II

CH

6

Instead of scrolling through the list, you can enter a person's name (or partial name) in the Type Name or Select from List box. When you do that, Outlook finds the first name in the list that matches what you enter.

A third alternative is to choose Find. When you do that, Outlook displays a dialog box in which you can enter a contact's name, e-mail address, address, or phone number, and then press Find. Outlook then finds the contact.

Tip #37 from

Many names listed in the Select Names dialog box occur more than once. In fact, there's a separate entry for each e-mail address and fax number saved in each contact item. To be sure you select the correct name, use the horizontal scroll bar at the bottom of the list of names to scroll to the right. That way, you'll be able to see the e-mail addresses associated with the names. You can also select a name, then choose Properties to see all the information about a contact.

After you've selected recipients, choose OK to return to the Message dialog box that now shows recipients' names in the To box.

SENDING CARBON COPIES AND BLIND CARBON COPIES OF MESSAGES

A traditional business practice is to send messages *to* people whom you expect to take some action as a result of the message, and to send *carbon copies* (cc) to people who should know about the message but aren't expected to take any action as a result of it. When you use Outlook, everyone whose name is on the To and Cc lists sees everybody else's name on the messages they receive, so all recipients know who sees the message.

Sometimes you want to send a copy of a message to someone without other recipients knowing. That's when you send a *blind carbon copy* (bcc). The recipients of blind carbon copies see all the names on the To and Cc lists; the people on the To and Cc lists don't see the names on the Bcc list.

Tip #38 from

Blind carbon copy is also useful when you want to send a message to a mailing list without revealing the names of everyone on the list to all recipients.

→ For information about creating a distribution list, **see** "Creating a Distribution List," **p. 333**.

The header of the Outlook Message form contains a Cc box. You can add names and e-mail addresses into it in the same way you add names and addresses to the To box. One minor difference is that if you select names from those listed in your Address Book, you choose Cc-> to copy names into the appropriate Message Recipients list.

The Message form's default header doesn't contain a Bcc box. To make this box available, choose View, Bcc Field in the form's menu bar. After you've done that, you can enter names and addresses into that field in the same way that you add them into the To field.

Note

If you use the Select Names dialog box to copy names into the Bcc list, Outlook automatically expands the Message form's header to show the Bcc box.

ENTERING A MESSAGE SUBJECT

To enter a subject for a message, move the insertion point into the Subject box, type the text of the subject, then press Tab to move the insertion point into the message box. As soon as you press Tab, the subject text replaces the original "Untitled" at the left end of the message form's title bar.

You should use succinct and meaningful subjects for your messages. Remember, what you enter in the subject box is what recipients subsequently see in their inboxes. If the subject doesn't look interesting and relevant, recipients may choose to ignore your message. Busy people often only look at messages they perceive to be important.

Note

Some people deliberately omit entering a subject for their messages, maybe because they're too lazy to do so or maybe because they think curiosity will ensure that recipients open those messages. You should avoid this practice because most people regard it as discourteous.

Although Outlook allows you to enter as many as 256 characters in the Subject box, you should use only four or five well-chosen words.

ENTERING THE MESSAGE TEXT

Say what you have to say briefly and clearly.

Because I'm assuming that you're using the HTML message format, you might expect this section to provide detailed information about HTML so that you can create beautifully formatted messages. However, this book is about Outlook. If you want to learn all about HTML, consult a book on that subject.

If possible, don't quickly type your message and then send it. Take some time to review what you've typed and make sure it's really what you want to say.

→ For information about saving a message that your're not yet ready to send, **see** "Saving a Message Draft," **p. 215**.

FORMATTING A MESSAGE

The Formatting toolbar isn't enabled until you move the insertion point into the message box that occupies the bottom part of the Message form.

Tip #39 from

Gordon Padwick

If the Formatting toolbar isn't displayed, choose <u>V</u>iew on the Message form's menu bar, move the pointer onto <u>T</u>oolbars, and choose Formatting.

In the Office 2000 style, the first part of the Formatting toolbar is displayed at the right of the Message form's Standard toolbar to provide as much vertical space as possible within the message box. As a result, you don't see all the buttons in the Formatting toolbar. To see all the buttons in the Formatting toolbar, click the button at the right end of the part that is displayed to see the buttons in a box, as shown in Figure 6.25.

Figure 6.25
This box shows all the buttons in the Formatting toolbar.

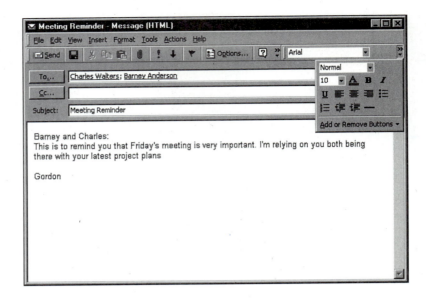

You can also drag the vertical bar at the left end of the Formatting toolbar down to display the entire toolbar below the message form's Standard toolbar, or drag it further to display it as a floating toolbar on top of the form. When you don't need to see the complete Formatting toolbar, you can drag it back to its original position.

The buttons available in the Formatting toolbar when you're using the HTML message format are listed in Table 6.2.

TABLE 6.2   FORMATTING TOOLBAR BUTTONS

Button Name	Purpose
Style	Select HTML format from a list of formats.
Font	Select a font from a list of fonts installed on your computer.
Font Size	Select a font size from a list.
Font Color	Select a font color from a list.
Bold	Make selected text bold.
Italic	Make selected text italic.
Underline	Underline selected text.
Align Left	Left-align selected paragraphs.
Center	Center selected paragraphs.
Align Right	Right-align selected paragraphs.

Button Name	Purpose
Bullets	Add bullets to selected paragraphs.
Numbering	Number selected paragraphs.
Decrease Indent	Decrease left indent of selected paragraphs.
Increase Indent	Increase left indent of selected paragraphs.
Insert Horizontal Line	Insert horizontal line.

Note

No formatting is available if you're using the Plain Text message format. Most of the same formats are available if you're using the Rich Text message format. If you're using WordMail as your editor, most of Word's formatting capabilities are available.

You might be wondering whether you can count on recipients seeing your messages exactly as you formatted them. If you use Outlook's HTML message format and the people who receive your messages use an e-mail program that's completely compatible with Outlook (such as Outlook or Outlook Express), those people will see your messages exactly as you created them. However, HTML is an evolving standard; it's quite possible that people who receive your messages use an HTML-compatible e-mail program that interprets some HTML code a little differently from Outlook. Likewise, you might receive HTML-formatted e-mail messages from other people that Outlook doesn't interpret properly.

If you want to be sure people see your messages exactly as you create them, use Plain Text format. As mentioned previously, one significant advantage of Plain Text is that it results in significantly smaller messages which are faster to send and receive.

USING STATIONERY

When you're using HTML as your message format and the native Outlook editor as your editor, you can choose a *stationery* to provide a background for your messages.

Note

Stationeries were not available in Outlook 97, but were introduced in Outlook 98.

By default, Outlook creates messages on a plain background using whatever scheme you've selected for Windows Appearance (in the Windows control panel). The default Windows Standard scheme provides a white background. You can choose a stationery that provides a background appropriate for certain kinds of messages.

PART

II

CH

6

Tip #40 from

Using a stationery increases the size of your messages so that they take longer to send and receive. Most people prefer not to receive business messages that have a stationery. I recommend that you use stationeries only for personal messages to your friends.

To select a stationery:

1. Close any message form that you have open.

2. Choose Tools, Options and select the Mail Format tab shown previously in Figure 6.16. The Stationery and Fonts section of the Mail Format tab initially shows <None> as the default stationery.

3. Open the Use This Stationery by Default drop-down list to display a list of available stationeries as shown in Figure 6.26.

Figure 6.26
You can scroll down this list to see many more stationeries.

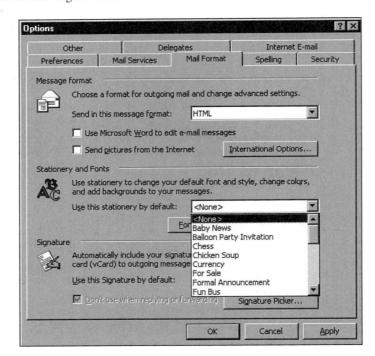

4. Select one of the listed stationeries, then choose OK. If you haven't previously used the stationery you selected, you'll be asked to insert the Office 2000 CD-ROM disc into your drive so that Outlook can load that stationery.

The next time you start to create a message, you'll see the stationery you selected as a background for your message. After you've chosen a stationery, Outlook uses that stationery for all your messages. To go back to a plain background, go back to the Option dialog box's Mail Format tab and select <None> as your stationery.

Note

To create your own stationery or colored background, choose Stationery Picker and then choose New.

→ For more information about mail formats, **see** "Mail Format Options," **p. 867**. .

SIGNING MESSAGES

You can have Outlook automatically sign the messages you send. First, you have to create your signature.

To create a signature:

1. From any Information viewer, choose Tools, Options to display the Options dialog box, and select the Mail Format tab shown previously in Figure 6.16.

2. If you've previously created one or more signatures, open the drop-down Use This Signature by Default list, then select a signature. If you want to create a new signature, go to step 3.

3. Near the bottom of the Mail Format tab, choose Signature Picker to display the Signature Picker dialog box which, if you've previously created signatures, shows a list of them. To create a new signature, choose New to display the dialog box shown in Figure 6.27.

Figure 6.27
Use this dialog box to create a new signature.

PART
II

CH
6

4. Enter a name for your signature in the Enter a Name for Your New Signature box. You can use names such as Personal, Business, and so on. Then choose Next > to display the dialog box shown in Figure 6.28.

Figure 6.28
This is the dialog box in which you create your signature.

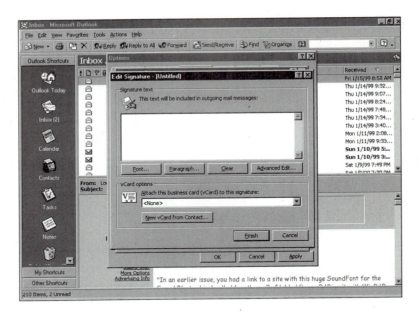

5. Enter the text of your signature in the large box that occupies the upper part of this dialog box, then choose OK three times. The next time you start a message, Outlook automatically includes your signature at the end of the message.

As you can see in Figure 6.28, Outlook offers much more than just the ability to create signatures with text. Here are some of the things you can do:

- Enter text in the box that occupies most of the upper part of the Edit Signature dialog box. By default, Outlook uses 10-point Arial as the font.
- Choose Font to open the standard Windows Font dialog box in which you can select a font name, style, size, and color.
- Choose Paragraph to select Left, Center, or Right alignment for text.
- Choose Clear to delete the existing signature.
- Choose Advanced Edit to open Word so that you can use all of Word's formatting capabilities (including inserting pictures and objects) to create the signature.
- Attach an *electronic business card (vCard) (page 330)* to the signature.

Note

Just because you can create a fancy signature doesn't mean you should! Such additions as graphics, sound, and vcards add significantly to the size of messages and may not be compatible with some recipients' e-mail client software.

→ For information about saving Contact items, **see** "Saving a Contact Item," **p. 318**.

You can create as many signatures as you like, each with a different name (Personal, Business, and so on). If you create more than one signature, select the one you want to use for a specific message by choosing Insert, Signature in the message form's menu bar.

MESSAGE INSERTIONS

In the early days of e-mail it was possible only to send standard alphanumeric characters. Now, e-mail messages can contain almost anything, including:

- Character sets other than US *ASCII*
- Images (still and moving)
- Sounds
- Computer files

You can also include Outlook items within messages.

This capability depends on senders' and recipients' computers having the capability to encode and decode non-ASCII inclusions. Outlook uses the *Multipurpose Internet Mail Extensions* (MIME) *(page 97)* for this purpose.

Note

Although MIME is the default encoding method, C/W Outlook can also use UUENCODE to encode non-ASCII inclusions in Internet e-mail messages. To select UUENCODE, choose Tools, Options and select the Options dialog box's Internet E-mail tab. You can select MIME or UUENCODE in the Internet E-mail Sending Format section of that tab.

INSERTING FILES

You can insert any file into a message from a disk on your computer or from a disk on another network computer that's available for sharing.

To insert a file:

1. In the Message form's menu bar, choose Insert, File to display the dialog box shown in Figure 6.29.
2. You can choose any of the buttons in the bar at the left to select specific file locations. After choosing one of those buttons, open the drop-down Look In list to see the relevant folder structure in which you can select a folder and then select a file within that folder. You can also navigate in the Insert File dialog box in the conventional way to select a file.
3. Choose Insert. A pane opens at the bottom of the Message form and the file you selected is displayed in that form, as shown in Figure 6.30.

Figure 6.29
The Insert File dialog box initially displays the files and folders in your default folder, My Documents for Windows 95 and Windows 98, or Personal for Windows NT.

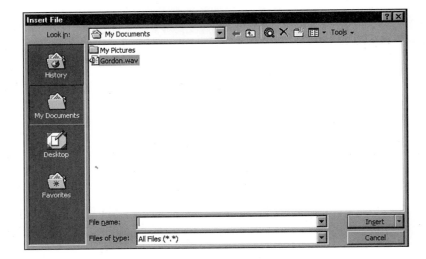

Figure 6.30
Inserted files are displayed as icons in a pane at the bottom of the message form. In this form, the icon on the left represents a file and the icon on the right represents an Outlook item.

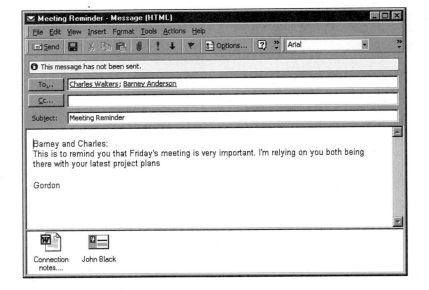

The preceding procedure described how to add attachments to a message. You can also insert a text file as text within a message. In step 3, instead of choosing Insert, choose the button marked with a black triangle immediately at the right of the Insert button. When you do so, a menu containing Insert, Insert as Text, and Insert as Attachment appears. Choose Insert as Text to insert the text file into the message.

Tip #41 from

Gordon Padwick

To delete an inserted file or item, select it and then press Delete.

INSERTING OUTLOOK ITEMS

You can insert any of your Outlook items as text into a message and you can attach items to a message.

To attach an Outlook item:

1. In the Message form's menu bar, choose Insert, Item to display the dialog box shown in Figure 6.31.

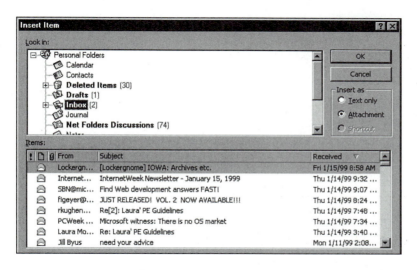

Figure 6.31
The top pane in the Insert Item dialog box shows the folders in your Personal Folders file with one folder selected. The bottom pane shows the items in the selected folder.

Note

If you're using Outlook as a client for Exchange, you can also access items in the Exchange store.

2. Select the folder that contains the item you want to include in the message. You may have to use the vertical scroll bar to find the folder you want.

3. Scroll down the bottom pane to locate a specific item, then click that item to select it.

4. Make sure Attachment is selected in the Insert As section of the dialog box, then choose OK. The attachment appears as an icon in the pane at the bottom of the Message form, as shown previously in Figure 6.30.

Instead of attaching an item, you can insert the item as text within the message. To do so, follow the steps described previously for attaching an item, with the exception that in Step 4, make sure Text Only is selected (instead of Attachment). Figure 6.32 shows an example of a Text Only insertion.

Figure 6.32
In this example, an Outlook Calendar item has been inserted as Text Only into a message.

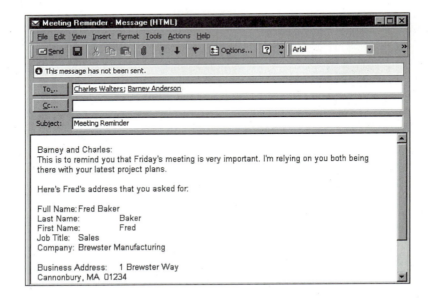

Note

You can also attach an Outlook item to a message by dragging that item from an Outlook folder into the message. You can't insert an item as text by dragging.

INSERTING A SIGNATURE

To insert a signature into a message, choose Insert, and move the pointer onto Signature to display a list of signatures you've previously created. Select the signature you want to insert.

→ For information about creating signatures, **see** "Signing Messages," **p. 199**.

Note

Outlook places the inserted signature at the end of a new message. If you insert a signature into your reply to a message you've received, Outlook inserts your signature at the end of your reply, not at the end of the text you're replying to. Likewise if you insert a signature into a message you're forwarding, Outlook inserts the signature at the end of any comments you add to the original message, not at the end of the entire message.

INSERTING A HORIZONTAL LINE

If you're using the HTML message format, you can insert a horizontal line into a message.

To insert a horizontal line:

1. Place the insertion point where you want the horizontal line to appear.

2. In the Message form's menu bar, choose Insert, Horizontal Line. The horizontal line appears in your message, as shown in Figure 6.33.

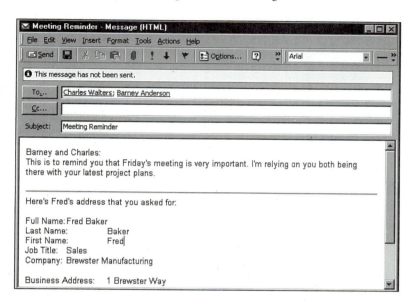

Figure 6.33
The horizontal line extends across almost the entire width of the form.

You can adjust the width and thickness of the line by selecting it so that handles appear. Drag one of the handles at the left or right ends of the line to change its width; drag one of the handles at the center of the line to change its thickness.

Note

If you're not using a stationery, you can select a horizontal line in the form, then select the Font Color button [A] in the Formatting toolbar, and choose a color for the line. If you use certain stationeries, you can't change the color of a horizontal line.

PART
II

CH
6

INSERTING A PICTURE

If you're using the HTML message format, you can insert pictures into a message. An inserted picture appears in the message at the same size it was in its original file. If you want to have a reduced size version of a picture in a message, create a reduced size version before you insert the picture into your message in order to minimize the size of the message you send.

Note

You can insert pictures saved in the .art, .bmp, .gif, .jpg, .wmf, and .xbf file formats. However, you should only use .gif and .jpg formats because these are compatible with most e-mail clients, and also because they occupy less space than other formats.

To insert a picture:

1. Place the insertion point where you want the picture to appear in the message.
2. In the Message form's menu bar, choose Insert, Picture to display the dialog box shown in Figure 6.34.

Figure 6.34
Use the Picture dialog box to identify the picture you want to insert and how you want that picture to appear.

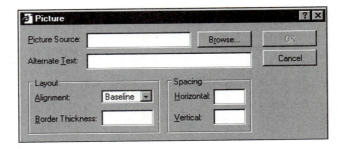

3. In the Picture Source box, enter the complete path and file name of the picture. Alternatively, you can choose Browse and then navigate to the file.
4. In the Alternate Text box, enter text that you want to be displayed instead of the picture if the recipients' computers can't display pictures.
5. Open the drop-down Alignment list and choose how you want the picture to be aligned in the message.
6. If you want the picture to be displayed with a border, enter a number in the Border Thickness box. The number you enter represents the thickness of the border in pixels.
7. In the Spacing section of the dialog box, enter the space you want to have at the sides of the picture in the Horizontal box, and enter the space you want above and below the picture in the Vertical box.
8. Choose OK to place the image in the box.

Tip #42 from

After the picture appears in the message you can drag it to a different position. You can also click the picture to select it, in which case handles appear at the center of its edges and at its corners. You can drag these handles to change the size of the picture. Double-click a picture in a message to open a graphics editor in which you can make changes to the picture.

INSERTING A HYPERLINK

One way to insert a hyperlink into a message is simply to type the hyperlink. Outlook automatically recognizes anything you type in hyperlink format as a hyperlink. For example, if you type http://www.mcp.com (or just www.mcp.com), Outlook shows you it has recognized a hyperlink by changing its color to blue and underlining it.

The other way to enter a hyperlink, if you're using the HTML message format, is to follow these steps:

To insert a hyperlink:

1. Place the insertion point where you want the hyperlink to be.

2. In the Message form's menu bar, choose Insert, Hyperlink to display the dialog box shown in Figure 6.35.

Figure 6.35
The Hyperlink dialog box initially assumes you want to create a hyperlink to a Web site.

3. Open the drop-down Type list and select the type of hyperlink you want to create. Outlook places the first part of the hyperlink in the URL box, according to the type you select.

4. In the URL box, complete the hyperlink, then choose OK to insert the hyperlink into the message.

FLAGGING A MESSAGE

You can flag a message to draw recipients' attention to it. The following is one way to flag a message:

To flag a message:

1. In the Message form's menu bar, choose Actions, Flag for Follow Up, or choose the Flag for Follow Up button in the Message form's Standard toolbar, to display the dialog box shown in Figure 6.36.

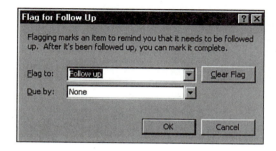

Figure 6.36
Use the Flag for Follow Up dialog box to select a type of flag.

2. Open the drop-down <u>F</u>lag To list to display a list of flag types. Select the type of flag you want to use.

> **Note**
>
> You are not limited to the listed names of flags. You can select any flag so that its name appears in the <u>F</u>lag To box, then replace that name with whatever words are appropriate.

3. If you don't want to specify a date in the flag, ignore the Reminder box. If you want to include a date with the flag, open the drop-down <u>R</u>eminder box to display a calendar. In that calendar, select a date.

→ Instead of selecting a date from the calendar, you can enter descriptive words such as "tomorrow," "next week," and so on, and also abbreviations such as "1d" for tomorrow and "1w" for next week. **See** "Describing a Date," **p. 364**.

> **Note**
>
> By default, when you choose a date, Outlook automatically shows the time that corresponds to the end of your workday (set in the Options dialog box with the Preferences tab selected and <u>C</u>alendar Options chosen). You can replace the time Outlook displays with whatever time is appropriate.

4. Choose OK. The flag you entered appears in a box on the Message form, above the To box, as shown in Figure 6.37.

Figure 6.37
This is an example of a flag as it appears in your Message form.

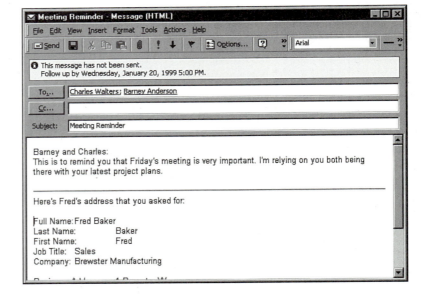

Flags you attach to messages in the manner just described are flags that are delivered with the message; they are intended for the message recipients. When a person receives a flagged message, that message is normally saved in the person's Inbox. Outlook displays reminders at the appropriate time for flagged messages, but only if those messages remain in the Inbox; Outlook doesn't create reminders if recipients move messages to folders other than the Inbox.

You can also attach a flag to the copy of a message you send (that's saved in your Sent Items folder) as a reminder to yourself. After you've sent a message, Outlook saves a copy of that message in your Sent Items folder. You can open that copy and, using the method just described, attach a flag to the copy of the message. That flag is a reminder to yourself. Flagged messages in the Sent Items folder don't create reminders. Instead, message headers displayed in the Sent Items Information viewer change to red when the flagged action becomes due.

SPELL CHECKING A MESSAGE

With Outlook you can easily check the spelling in the messages you create. Doing so is well worth the few moments it takes. You surely don't want recipients to think less of you because you make spelling errors.

To check the spelling in a message, choose Tools, Spelling. After you do so, Outlook highlights words that may be misspelled and suggests corrections.

You can also choose an option that makes Outlook automatically check spelling when you send a message. I strongly recommend you use this option.

To check spelling automatically:

1. With any Outlook Information viewer displayed, choose Tools, Options and select the Spelling tab shown in Figure 6.38.
2. Check Always Check Spelling Before Sending.

With this option selected, Outlook checks the spelling of the subject and text of each message when you choose Send in the Message form's Standard toolbar. If Outlook finds words that are not in the spelling dictionary, it displays the Spelling dialog box, such as that shown in Figure 6.39.

PART

II

CH

6

Figure 6.38
This is where you can select spelling options.

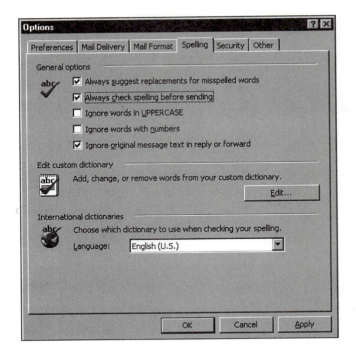

Figure 6.39
When Outlook detects a possible spelling error, it highlights the problem word and displays a dialog box that suggests correct spellings.

Use the Spelling dialog box to correct a spelling error, just as you do in Word.

SETTING MESSAGE OPTIONS

Choose Options in the Message form's Standard toolbar (or Choose View, Options) to display the dialog box shown in Figure 6.40.

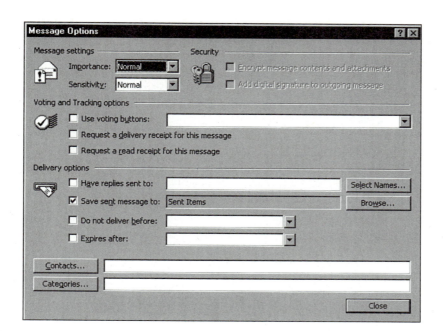

Figure 6.40
Use this dialog box to set various message options.

Note

The Security section at the top-right isn't available unless you have previously obtained a security certificate.

→ For more information about obtaining a security certificate, **see** "Obtaining a Certificate," **p. 1004**.

MESSAGE SETTINGS

In the Message Settings section of the dialog box you can select Importance and Sensitivity for a message. By default, Outlook sets both of these to Normal.

Open the drop-down Importance list, and choose from among Low, Normal, and High. Instead of making this choice in the Options dialog box, you can choose the High Importance button [!] or Low Importance button [↓] in the Message form's Standard toolbar.

Open the drop-down Sensitivity list, and choose from among Normal, Personal, Private, and Confidential.

SETTING SECURITY

If you have obtained and installed a security certificate on your computer, the two check boxes in the Security section of the Options dialog box are enabled; otherwise they are disabled.

Use these check boxes to encrypt a message and to authenticate a message by adding a digital signature.

VOTING AND TRACKING OPTIONS

Voting and Tracking options mostly require MAPI functionality, which is available in C/W Outlook but not in IMO Outlook. The capabilities described here can be used when you and your message recipients are using C/W Outlook (or another MAPI-compliant e-mail client) as a client for a MAPI-compliant e-mail system such as Exchange and Microsoft Mail.

REQUESTING DELIVERY AND READ RECEIPTS

One exception to the statements in the preceding paragraph is requesting delivery and read receipts, a capability that's only available for Internet e-mail messages. Depending on the services provided by your e-mail server, you may be able to request receipts. To do so, check the Request a Delivery Receipt for This Message and Request a Read Receipt for This Message box. If the service is available, you'll receive notification in your Inbox when each message is delivered to a recipient's mail server and when the recipient opens your message.

You can't rely on getting read receipts when you request them. You, and other Outlook users, can set up Outlook so that Outlook always or never sends read receipts when these are requested. To do this, choose Tools, Options and, with the Preferences tab in the Options dialog box selected, choose E-mail Options. In the E-mail Options dialog box, choose Tracking Options to display the dialog box shown in Figure 6.41.

Figure 6.41
Use this dialog box to choose whether you want to respond to requests for read receipts.

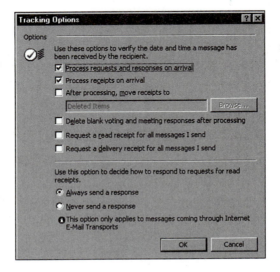

By default, Always Send a Response is selected. If you don't want Outlook to send responses, select Never Send a Response.

If you send a message that requests a read response, and the recipient allows read responses to be sent, you'll receive a message in your Inbox when the recipient opens the message to read it, providing the recipient receives the message in Outlook and hasn't turned off responding to read receipts. However, if a recipient receives the message by way of a mail server, that server and the messaging client the recipient uses may not have the capability of processing read receipts.

The bottom line is: If you request a read receipt and receive one, you know the message recipient opened your message—that doesn't necessarily mean the recipient read it. On the other hand, if you request a read receipt and don't receive one, you really don't know whether the recipient opened the message or not.

Using Voting Buttons

Because this chapter is about Internet e-mail messages (which is not a MAPI environment), voting (which depends on MAPI), is not covered here.

→ For information about using voting buttons, **see** "Using Voting Buttons," **p. 687**.

Delivery Options

This section of the Message Options dialog box is where you can specify several aspects of how a message is to be delivered.

When a recipient receives a message and replies to it, the reply is normally sent automatically to your e-mail address. You can, if you like, specify a different e-mail address to which replies should be sent. You might do this if you have an assistant who handles replies, or if you're going to be out of the office for a while.

To have replies automatically sent to an e-mail address other than your own, check the Have Replies Sent To box, and enter the e-mail address in the adjoining box. Instead of entering an e-mail address, you can choose Select Names to display the Have Replies Send To dialog box which, except for the name in the title bar, is the same as the Select Names dialog box shown previously in Figure 6.23. If necessary, open the drop-down Show Names from The list and select an address book. Then select the name of the person to whom you want replies to be sent.

By default, Outlook saves a copy of the message you send in your Sent Items folder. If you don't want to save a copy of this message, uncheck the Save Sent Message To box.

Note

Instead of saving messages you send in your Sent Items folder, you may prefer to always include yourself in the list of message recipients. In that case, messages you send arrive in your Inbox folder.

If you want to save a copy of this message in a folder other than your Sent Items folder, leave the Save Sent Message To box checked, choose Browse, and select the Outlook folder in which you want to save a copy of the message.

PART

II

CH

6

The Do Not Deliver Before and Expires After boxes allow you to enter dates. This functionality is not usually available in the Internet environment. If you want to use these, check with your mail server administrator to see if the mail server offers these capabilities. In each case, open the drop-down list to display a calendar and select a date in that calendar.

If your e-mail server offers the service, your message won't be delivered until the Do Not Deliver Before Date. Also, if your e-mail server offers the service, your message will be automatically erased if it hasn't been read by the Expires After date.

ASSIGNING CONTACTS TO A MESSAGE

When you're creating messages (and other Outlook items) keep in mind how you might subsequently want to find those items. You can easily use Outlook to find messages based on the names of the people to whom you sent those messages. There are times, though, when you might send a message that contains information about one of your contacts, but you don't send a copy to that person.

One possible scenario is that you, as a supervisor, want to send a message to your manager regarding some action you intend to take concerning an employee. In that case, you probably won't send a copy to the employee, but you want to be able to find the message based on that employee's name.

In cases like this, you can enter a person's name in the Contacts box in the Message Options dialog box.

To enter a name in the Contacts box:

1. Choose Contacts to display the dialog box shown in Figure 6.42.

Figure 6.42
Use this dialog box to select one or more contacts.

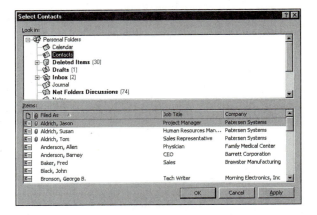

2. Select the contacts whose names you want to insert into the Contact box in the Message Options dialog box.

3. Choose OK to return to the Message Options dialog box, which now has the names you selected in the Contacts box.

ASSIGNING CATEGORIES TO A MESSAGE

As frequently mentioned in this book, assigning categories to Outlook items is key to keeping yourself organized. Choose Categories at the bottom of the dialog box to open the Categories dialog box, in which you can assign categories to the message. Refer to Chapter 21 for detailed information about categories.

→ For detailed information about assigning categories to e-mail messages, **see** "Assigning and Changing Categories in E-mail You Create," **p. 610**.

After making choices in the Message Options dialog box, choose Close to return to the Message form.

SAVING A MESSAGE DRAFT

After you've created a message, you don't have to send it immediately; you can save it as a draft to be reviewed or completed later. In fact, while you're creating a message, Outlook automatically saves it periodically as a draft.

To set how often Outlook saves a draft:

1. In any Information viewer, choose Tools, Options and select the Preferences tab.

2. Choose E-mail Options, and then choose Advanced E-mail Options to display the dialog box shown in Figure 6.43.

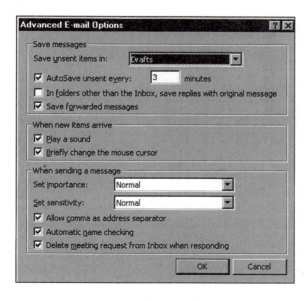

Figure 6.43
Use the Advanced E-mail Options tab to specify where unsent messages should be saved, and how often.

PART
II

CH
6

3. By default, Outlook saves unsent messages in your Drafts folder. If you want to save them in a different folder, open the drop-down Save Unsent Items In list and choose an Outlook folder.

4. Also by default, the Autosave Unsent Every box is checked so that unsent items are saved. Uncheck this box (you shouldn't) if you don't want to save unsent items.

5. In the adjacent box, enter a number that specifies the number of minutes between each time Outlook automatically saves unsent items—the default is three minutes.

To manually save an unsent message, in the Message form's menu bar, choose File, Save, or choose the Save button in the form's Standard toolbar.

Subsequently, you can continue working on the message. To do so, choose the My Shortcuts group in the Outlook Bar, and choose Drafts to see a list of draft messages. Double-click the one you want to work on to display it in the Message form.

Note

Alternatively, with any Information viewer displayed, you can choose View, move the pointer onto Go To, and choose Drafts to display a list of draft messages.

SENDING A MESSAGE

Sending a message is a two-step process. First, you send a message from the Message form to your Outbox. Then Outlook sends the message from your Outbox to your mail server, keeping a copy of the message in your Sent Items folder.

Choose Send in the Message form's Standard toolbar, or press Ctrl+Enter. Outlook immediately sends the message to your Outbox folder. You can choose the My Shortcuts group in the Outlook Bar, and then choose Outbox to see the messages in your Outbox, as shown in Figure 6.44.

Figure 6.44
Messages waiting to be sent are listed in the Outbox Information viewer. If no messages are waiting to be sent, a message tells you so.

Note

You don't need to display the Outbox Information viewer in order to send messages. However, it's reassuring to take a look at the Outbox information viewer while, or after, you've actually sent messages to your mail server to make sure that all messages have actually been sent.

→ To find out about creating Internet e-mail accounts, **see** "Creating an Internet Account," **p. 171**.

To send messages from your Outbox to your Internet mail server, display any Information viewer, and choose Tools, Send. If necessary, Outlook establishes a connection to the server. Then Outlook starts sending messages. While messages are being sent, Outlook displays the information box shown in Figure 6.45.

Figure 6.45
This is the information box C/W Outlook displays while messages are being sent. Unlike IMO Outlook, C/W Outlook doesn't give you any information about the progress of sending messages. Outlook hides this information box as soon as all messages have been sent.

Note

Instead of choosing Tools, Send, you can choose Tools, move the pointer onto Send and Receive, and then choose All Accounts or a specific Internet mail account. This is described in the next section. Also, with the Inbox Information viewer displayed, you can choose Send/Receive to send and receive messages from all accounts.

Sometimes, messages you send will be undeliverable. This may be because you have addressed them incorrectly, or because your server, the recipients' servers, or something in between is not working. If that happens, you might receive a message in your Inbox from System Administrator. If this happens, check the e-mail address you used and try sending the message again.

Another common reason for messages being undeliverable is your POP3 or SMTP settings may have become corrupted.

→ To find information about setting up Dial-up Networking, **see** "Setting up Dial-up Networking," **p. 168**.

PART

II

CH

6

Note

In many ways, e-mail is like *snail mail*: it works almost all the time. When you send a letter by snail mail, you only know that the recipient received it when you receive a response from that recipient. Similarly, when you send e-mail, the only way you know recipients have received it is when they respond to you.

RECEIVING INTERNET E-MAIL

You can use C/W Outlook to receive e-mail from Internet mail servers that use the POP3 protocol. Unlike IMO Outlook, C/W Outlook can't receive e-mail messages from servers that use the IMAP4 protocol.

Note

The preceding statement applies to using C/W Outlook to directly receive Internet e-mail. If you're using C/W Outlook as a client for Exchange and use Exchange to receive Internet e-mail, you can receive IMAP4 messages.

To receive e-mail that's waiting for you on your mail server, choose Tools, move the pointer onto Send and Receive, and, if you have only one Internet mail account, choose that account name. If you have two or more Internet e-mail accounts, you can choose the account you want to use to send and receive messages. Alternatively, if you have several accounts on the same mail server, you can choose All Accounts.

Note

With the Inbox Information viewer displayed, you can choose Send/Receive on the Standard toolbar to send messages to, and receive messages from, several accounts on the same mail server.

Note

If you have many mail items to download from the server, or if there are items with large attachments, you don't have to wait until downloading is finished. Outlook can download messages in the background while you're working on other tasks.

Outlook displays the headers of messages you receive in the Inbox Information viewer, which is described in the next section.

UNDERSTANDING THE INBOX INFORMATION VIEWER

Figure 6.46 shows an example of Outlook's default Inbox information viewer. Outlook displays message headers in your Outbox, Sent Items, and Drafts folders in similar Information viewers.

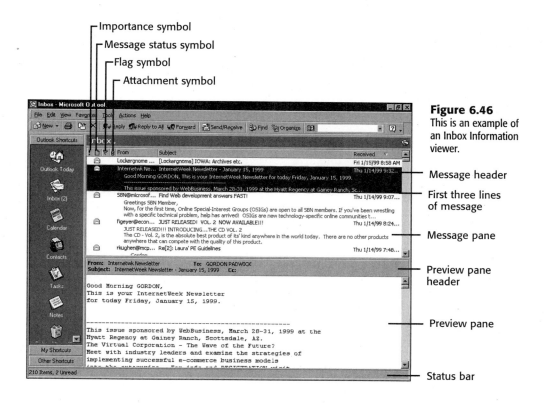

Importance symbol
Message status symbol
Flag symbol
Attachment symbol

Figure 6.46
This is an example of an Inbox Information viewer.

Message header

First three lines of message

Message pane

Preview pane header

Preview pane

Status bar

If you ever forget what the icons at the top of the Inbox viewer (or any other Table view of Outlook items) represent, move the pointer onto an icon and pause briefly. After a second or so, a ScreenTip appears that contains the icon's name.

The Message pane in the top part of the Information viewer shows message headers and, if AutoPreview is enabled, the first three lines of each message. Four columns at the left of each message contains symbols that provide information about each message.

The Message pane shows messages in a table, although the absence of grid lines might not make that obvious. The four columns at the left are identified by symbols in the row at the top of the table. The other three columns are named.

Initially, the Information viewer lists messages in the order you received them, with the most recent at the top. You can click the symbol or name at the top of each column to order messages according to what's in that column. Click the symbol or name at the top of a column again to reverse the order of the messages according to what's in that column.

For example, click From in the row at the top of the list of messages to display messages in alphabetical order by Sender; click From again to display messages in reverse alphabetical order by sender.

PART
II

CH
6

To display messages listed by type, click the symbol at the top of the second column from the left. That lists messages with unread messages at the top. Click the same symbol again to list unread messages at the bottom.

MESSAGE HEADERS

Each message header contains the sender's name, the subject of the message, and the date the message was received by your mail server (not the date Outlook received it). You can customize Outlook to show additional information, such as the message category, in the header. This is done by modifying the message view.

→ To learn how to create custom views, **see** "Creating Custom Views," **p. 973**.

PREVIEWING MESSAGES

AutoPreview, which is turned on by default, is Outlook's ability to display the first three lines of messages below message headers. By doing this, Outlook lets you see what a message is about without having to open it. You can disable, and subsequently enable, AutoPreview by choosing View, AutoPreview.

VIEWING A MESSAGE IN THE PREVIEW PANE

The Preview pane occupies the lower part of the Information Viewer. After you click a message in the Message pane to select that message, the complete message is available in the Preview pane. You can scroll down the Preview pane to see the entire message. Like AutoPreview, the Preview pane provides a way for you to see messages without having to open them.

Note

You can also use the Preview pane to view messages in your Sent Items folder. You can't use the Preview pane to view messages in your Outbox.

You can remove the Preview pane to enlarge the Message pane so that more message headers are visible. To do so, choose View, Preview Pane. After you've removed it, choose the same command to bring it back.

Tip #43 from

Instead of removing the Preview pane, you can drag the horizontal border between that pane and the Message pane down to increase the size of the Message pane, or up to increase the size of the Preview pane.

By default, the Preview pane has a header in which the sender's name, message subject, message recipients' names, and the names of the people to whom the message is sent as a carbon copy are shown. Also, if the message has attachments, the right end of the header contains an icon (a yellow paper clip).

To customize the Preview pane, right-click its header to display a context menu. Use the commands in this menu as follows:

- Preview Pane—Remove the Preview pane.

- Header Information—Remove the Preview pane's header. To bring the header back, right-click the top border of the Preview pane to display the same context menu.

- Preview Pane Options—Display the Preview Pane dialog box, shown in Figure 6.47.

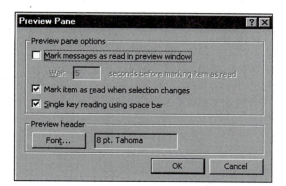

Figure 6.47
Use this dialog box to modify the Information viewer's behavior and to change the font used in the Preview pane's header.

MESSAGE SYMBOLS

The Message pane contains four columns at the left, each column being used for a specific kind of symbol. Refer to Appendix D for detailed information about Outlook's symbols.

→ "Outlook's Symbols," **p. 1313**, contains a list of Outlook's symbols and identifies what each means.

The first column is where an Importance symbol may be shown. If a message has Normal importance, no symbol appears. Otherwise the column contains the Importance: High symbol ▯ or the Importance: Low symbol ▯.

The second column always contains a symbol. In most cases, that symbol represents an envelope. Messages you've not read are marked with a closed envelope, messages you've read are marked with an open envelope. Various other symbols are used: for example, a message you've replied to is marked with an open envelope with a red arrow. Other symbols appear in this column in the case of messages from the mail server that warn you of a problem with a message you've sent.

The third column contains a symbol that is supposed to look like a flag (most people think it looks like a flower). This symbol is present for messages that are flagged.

The fourth column contains a paper clip icon in the case of messages that have one or more attachments.

PART
II
CH
6

MESSAGE SUMMARY

The status bar at the bottom of the Information viewer displays the total number of messages in your Inbox and the number of those that are unread.

OPENING A MESSAGE

When a message arrives in your Inbox and its header is displayed in your Inbox Information viewer, there are several things you can do. The following sections describe many of these.

DELETING A MESSAGE

If, from the message header, or from the first few lines in the AutoPreview, you quickly decide you don't want to bother with it, you can immediately delete it. To do so, click the message to select it, then choose the Delete button ☒ in the Information viewer's Standard toolbar. In some cases, you might want to take a quick look at the message in the Preview pane before deleting it.

Tip #44 from

When you delete a message in this way, Outlook moves it to your Deleted Items folder, from which you can retrieve it if necessary.

→ For more information about deleting messages, **see** "Deleting Messages and Other Outlook Items," **p. 229**.

READING A MESSAGE

As explained a couple of pages previously, you can read a message by selecting it in the Message pane so that it's displayed in the Preview pane, and then scroll down the message in that pane.

Alternatively, you can double-click the message to display it in a Message form that's similar to the form you use to create new messages, as shown in Figure 6.48.

You can use this form's menus and toolbars to work with the message in various ways.

As the message first appears, you can't edit it (unless it was created in Rich Text). However, you can choose Edit, Edit Message to make the received message editable.

You can choose the Flag for Follow Up button ▼ in the form's Standard toolbar to add a flag to the message—which you might want to do to if the message reminds you of something you need to take care of.

DISPLAYING A MESSAGE THREAD

Outlook's ability to display related messages in a single list is a very powerful tool, particularly if you send and receive many e-mail messages.

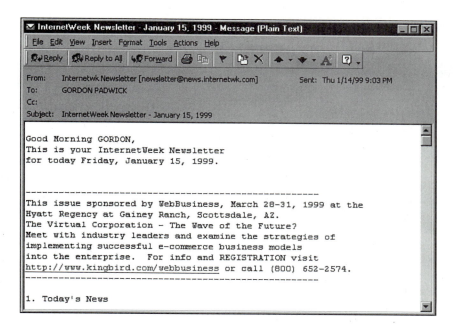

Figure 6.48
All the information you see in the Message form in which you can see messages you've received is initially read-only if it was created using the HTML or Plain Text formats. You can directly edit messages that were created in the HTML format.

A message thread, sometimes referred to as a conversation, is a sequence of messages about a specific topic. If you send a message to several people, each of whom reply, you create a thread. The thread is identified by text in the Conversation field in each message. This field initially contains the text in the original message's Subject field. When people reply to the original message, Outlook automatically places the same text in the Conversation field of each reply, even if respondents enter different text in the Subject fields of their replies.

Note

The preceding explanation applies when the sender and respondents all use Outlook as their e-mail program. If some participants in a conversation use e-mail programs that don't support the Conversation field, their messages won't be automatically identified as part of a thread.

As explained previously, you can easily sort messages in the Inbox and Sent Items Information viewers in several ways. Outlook also provides a way for you to list all items in a thread.

To display messages in a thread:

1. Display an Information viewer that contains one or more messages in a thread, usually your Inbox or Sent Items Information viewer.

2. Select any message in the thread.

3. Choose <u>A</u>ctions, move the pointer onto F<u>i</u>nd All, and choose <u>R</u>elated Messages. Outlook displays the Advanced Find dialog box with all the messages in the thread listed, as shown in Figure 6.49.

Figure 6.49
Messages in the thread are listed at the bottom of this dialog box. You can double-click any message in this list to open it in a Message form.

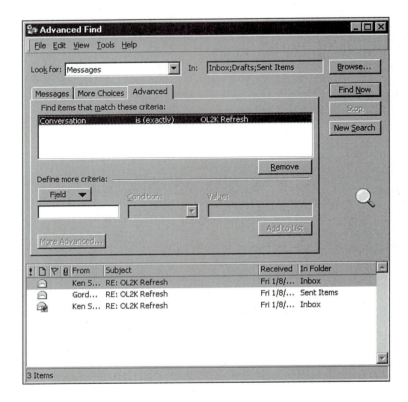

→ For more complete information about the Advanced Find dialog box, **see** "Using Advanced Find to Find Words and Phrases," **p. 532**.

By default, Outlook searches the Inbox, Drafts, and Sent Items folders in your Personal Folders file for items that have the same text in the Conversation field as the message you originally selected.

Note

If you select the Advanced tab in the Advanced Find dialog box (as shown in Figure 6.49), you'll see that Outlook has automatically set the search criterion as the content of the Conversation field is exactly the text in the Conversation field of the message you originally selected.

EXAMINING MESSAGE PROPERTIES

You can examine a message's properties and change its importance.

To examine a message's properties:

1. Double-click a message in the Inbox Information viewer to display the message in the Message form.

2. In the form's menu bar, choose File, Properties to display the Properties dialog box, similar to the one shown in Figure 6.50.

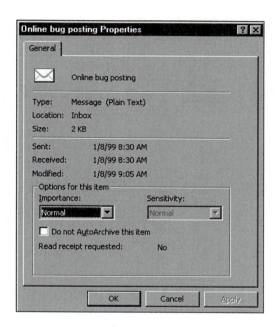

Figure 6.50
This dialog box displays the message properties.

3. If you want to change the importance assigned by the sender, open the drop-down Importance list and select Low, Normal, or High.

4. If you want to exclude the message from AutoArchiving, check the Do Not AutoArchive this item box.

→ To understand how Outlook archives items, **see** "AutoArchiving Outlook Items," **p. 592**.

Although this dialog box provides some information about a message, it doesn't provide a means of tracing the source of a message (something you might want to do if you receive anonymous junk mail).

PART

II

CH

6

To trace a message, right-click the message header in the Inbox Information viewer to display the context menu. Choose Options in the context menu to display the dialog box shown in Figure 6.51.

Figure 6.51
Information about the message source and routing is displayed in the Internet Headers box in the lower part of the dialog box.

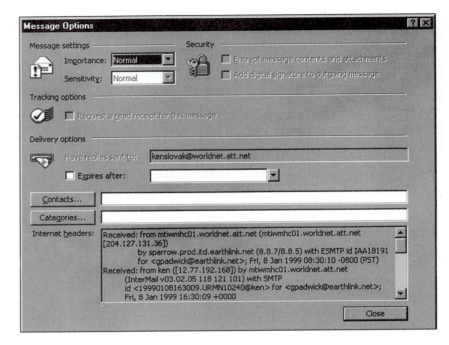

PRINTING A MESSAGE

To print a message you've received, select the message in the Inbox Information viewer's Message pane, then choose File, Print. Outlook displays the Print dialog box shown in Figure 6.52.

Tip #45 from

You're not limited to selecting only one message. You can select as many messages as you like in the Message pane.

In most cases, the default settings in the Print dialog box are what you want to use. If the message contains attachments, you can check the Print Attached Files with Item(s) box if that's what you want to do; otherwise leave this box unchecked. Choose OK to print the selected message.

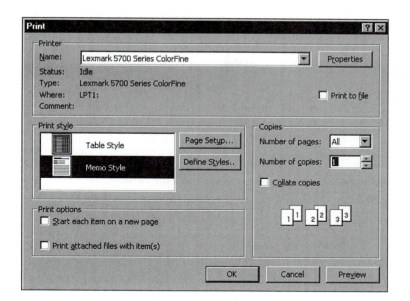

Figure 6.52
Use this dialog box
to choose how you
want to print the
message.

REPLYING TO A MESSAGE

To reply to a message, select that message in the Inbox Information viewer, then choose Reply in the viewer's Standard toolbar. Alternatively, if you want to send a reply to everyone to whom the original message was addressed (including those people on the Cc list), choose Reply to All. You can't send replies to people the message originator placed on the Bcc list because the message you receive doesn't identify those people.

Note

You can make the same choices when you open a message in the Message form.

Enter your reply in the space at the top of the form. You can also make comments within the text of the original message (known as *annotating* the message). If the original message is long, you might want to delete all but it's first few lines, leaving just enough to remind the originator about the message—there's little point in cluttering up e-mail servers and other people's inboxes with copies of this material.

Note

The preceding information about replying to a message covers Outlook's default behavior. To modify the default behavior, display any Outlook Information viewer, choose Tools, Options, and select the Preferences tab in the Option dialog box. Choose E-mail Options. Choose the options you want in the On Replies and Forwards section of the dialog box.

PART

II

CH

6

When you've finished, send the message in the same way that you sent a message you create. If the message you're replying to contained attachments, Outlook doesn't send the attachments with the reply.

FORWARDING A MESSAGE

You can forward a message to other people. Forwarding a message is quite similar to replying to a message. Select the message in your Inbox Information viewer, then choose Forward in the viewer's Standard toolbar. Alternatively, open the original message in a Message form and choose Forward.

Enter any introductory comments to the message, annotate the message as you wish, and send it. Unlike when you reply to a message, Outlook sends all attachments with forwarded messages. You can choose options to modify Outlook's defaults for forwarding messages.

SAVING A MESSAGE AS ANOTHER OUTLOOK ITEM

Buried within Outlook are many capabilities that are not widely known. One of these is the ability to create one type of Outlook item from a different type of Outlook item.

You may, for example, receive an e-mail message that asks you to do something. Being an organized person, you want to add that request to your to-do list. Simple! Just drag the message into your Tasks folder. Here's how.

To convert a message into a task:

1. With your Inbox Information viewer displayed, scroll to find the relevant message.
2. Drag the message onto Tasks in the Outlook Bar. When you release the mouse button, Outlook displays the Tasks form with the subject of the message in that form's Subject box and the text of the message in the form's Notes box, as shown in Figure 6.53.
3. Make whatever entries are required in the Tasks form, such as specifying the Due Date.

→ For detailed information about using Outlook to save information about tasks, **see** "Managing Tasks," **p. 411**.

The preceding is just one example of how you can create one type of Outlook item from another, a process Microsoft calls AutoCreate. In general, you can drag any type of Outlook item into a folder of a different type to create the type of Outlook item that the folder contains.

OPENING AND SAVING ATTACHMENTS

Outlook displays message attachments as icons in the Message form and also as a symbol in the Preview pane header.

To open an attachment, double-click its icon in the Message form or its symbol in the Preview pane's header.

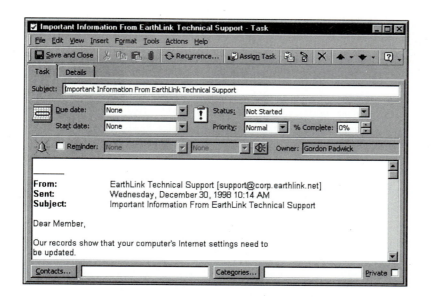

Figure 6.53
The Tasks form contains information from the message.

Outlook uses the Windows list of associations to find an application installed on your computer that's capable of opening the file, based on the file name extension. If Windows contains an association for the attached type of file, that application is opened and used to open and display the file. If no association exists, you are asked to choose the application that should be used to open the file.

DELETING MESSAGES AND OTHER OUTLOOK ITEMS

This chapter deals with Outlook messages, those you send and those you receive; the information in this section, however, applies to all types of Outlook items. Unless you choose otherwise, Outlook saves copies of messages you send in your Sent Items folder; it saves messages you receive in your Inbox bolder. You can choose Sent Items in the Outlook Bar to see the headers of messages you've sent in the Sent Items Information viewer, and you can choose Inbox in the Outlook Bar to see headers of messages you've received in the Inbox Information viewer.

To delete a message from either of these Information viewers, click the message header to select it, then choose the Delete button ☒ in the information viewer's Standard toolbar.

Deleting a message doesn't delete the message from your disk, it just moves the message from the Sent Items or Inbox folder to the Deleted Items folder. If you want to recover the deleted message, choose Deleted Items in the Outlook Bar to display the Deleted Items Information viewer. In that viewer, locate the deleted item and drag it back to Sent Items or Inbox in the Outlook Bar.

If you want to completely remove a deleted item from your disk, choose Deleted Items in the Outlook Bar. In the Deleted Items Information viewer, select the items you want to delete, and choose the Delete button ☒ in the Standard toolbar. After you've done that, you won't be able to recover the deleted items.

Even though you delete items from your Deleted Items folder, you don't necessarily recover the space those items previously occupied on your hard disk. To recover that space, you have to compact your Personal Folders file. The following procedure shows you how you do that.

To compact your Personal Folders file:

1. With any Information viewer displayed, choose <u>V</u>iew, Fold<u>e</u>r List to display a list of your Personal Folder files and the folders they contain.

Note

If you're using Outlook as a client for Exchange, you'll also see folders in the Exchange store to which you have access.

2. Right-click the Personal Folder file you want to compact to display its context menu.

3. In the context menu, choose Prope<u>r</u>ties to display the Personal Folders Properties dialog box. Choose Ad<u>v</u>anced to display the dialog box shown in Figure 6.54.

Figure 6.54
You can use this dialog box to compact the selected Personal Folders file.

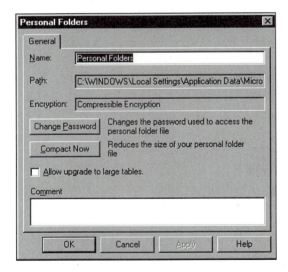

4. Choose <u>C</u>ompact Now to compact the selected Personal Folders file.

5. Choose OK twice to close the dialog boxes.

Now, all the space previously occupied by Outlook items deleted from that folder is recovered.

TROUBLESHOOTING: WHAT IF YOUR PERSONAL FOLDERS FILE BECOMES CORRUPTED?

Although Outlook does a good job of keeping your Personal Folders file (the file in which C/W Outlook can save Outlook items) in good shape, problems can occur. If you're having problems with a Personal Folders file, the so-called Inbox Repair tool can probably solve these problems. Although the file's name suggests that it deals only with your Inbox folder, the file actually deals with your entire Personal Folders file.

The Inbox Repair file named Scanpst.exe is automatically installed on your computer when you install Windows 95, Windows 98, or Windows NT.

Note

> Before attempting to recover a corrupted Personal Folders file, make a copy of that file just in case anything goes wrong.

To use the Inbox Repair tool:

1. On the Windows taskbar, choose Start and move the pointer onto Find. Choose Files and Folders to display the Find: All Files dialog box.

2. In the Named box, enter Scanpst.exe and choose Find Now. Outlook locates the Scanpst.exe on your computer.

3. Double-click Scanpst.exe to run it. Outlook asks you to enter the name of the file you want to scan. Enter the full path name of your Personal Folders file, or choose Browse to navigate to that file then choose Open to open that file.

4. Choose Start to scan the file and attempt to correct errors in it.

Note

> It's sometimes necessary to run the Inbox Repair tool more than once to recover a corrupted Personal Folders file.

If you move or rename your Personal Folders file, Outlook won't be able to find it. You can solve this problem by following these steps.

To use a moved or renamed Personal Folders file:

1. If Outlook is running, choose File, Exit and Log Off to close it.

Note

> Always choose Exit and Log Off, not Exit, to close C/W Outlook. This command closes MAPI services and removes active references to Personal Folder files.

2. From the Windows taskbar, choose Start, move the pointer onto Find, then choose Files and Folders to open the Find: All Files dialog box.

PART

II

CH

6

3. In the <u>N</u>amed box, enter `*.pst`, in the <u>L</u>ook In box, select My Computer, then choose F<u>i</u>nd Now. Windows searches your entire environment to look for any files that have .pst as their file name extensions.

4. Right-click the name of the Personal Folders file that's giving you problems to display its context menu.

5. Choose Rename in the context menu, replace the current name with a new name and press Enter. Close the Find dialog box.

6. Start Outlook. You'll see a message telling you that the old Personal Folders file can't be found. Choose OK to create the Create/Open Personal Folders File dialog box that contains the new name you entered in the previous step. Select that name, and choose <u>O</u>pen. Usually Outlook opens with your Personal Folders file available.

CHAPTER 7

SENDING AND RECEIVING FAXES WITH CORPORATE/WORKGROUP OUTLOOK

In this chapter

by Gordon Padwick

USING OUTLOOK TO SEND AND RECEIVE FAXES

You can use Outlook to send and receive faxes providing you have a fax modem and access to a phone line. Instead of creating a fax in a word processor, printing it, then lining up at the fax machine to send it, you can use Outlook to create and send a fax directly from your computer. If you have a phone number to which people can send you faxes, those faxes arrive on your computer in much the same way as e-mail arrives.

There are several ways Outlook can be used to send and receive faxes:

- With *C/W Outlook (page 54)* running under Windows 95 or Windows 98, you can use Microsoft Fax (supplied with Windows 95 and Windows 98). Microsoft Fax is covered in this chapter.

Note

Microsoft Fax is also referred to in various places as "Microsoft at Work Fax" and as "Microsoft At Work PC Fax."

- With *IMO Outlook (page 53)* running under Windows 95, Windows 98, or Windows NT, you can use WinFax Starter Edition (WinFax SE). WinFax SE is licensed from Symantec by Microsoft and is supplied with Outlook 2000.

→ If you are using IMO Outlook to send faxes, **see** "Sending and Receiving Faxes with Internet Mail Only Outlook," **p. 127**.

- You can use various add-on fax programs available from other companies. One of these is WinFax Pro from Symantec. WinFax Pro contains many facilities that aren't in Microsoft Fax or WinFax SE.

SETTING UP MICROSOFT FAX

You must add the Microsoft Fax information service to your profile and set its properties. You may also have to add files to and modify some files in your Windows environment.

MAKING MICROSOFT FAX AVAILABLE UNDER WINDOWS 98

The files necessary to support Microsoft Fax aren't installed with Windows 98 or Office 2000. However, you can separately install them from the Windows 98 CD-ROM. The files are also available from Microsoft's Office 2000 Update Web site.

Tip #46 from

Gordon Crook

Make sure you have the latest copy of the Microsoft Fax files installed on your computer. If you previously used Microsoft Fax with Outlook 97, you'll experience some incompatibility problems if you attempt to use its file with Outlook 2000. You may experience the same problem if you previously used Microsoft Fax with Outlook 98.

To make Microsoft Fax available under Windows 98:

1. Insert the Windows 98 CD-ROM into your drive. After a few seconds, you'll see the start-up screen.

2. Choose Browse This CD to display the top-level folders on the CD.

3. Navigate to the folder Tools\OldWin95\Message\US. That folder contains three files, one of which is Awfax.exe.

4. Double-click Awfax.exe. A message appears saying "This will install Microsoft Fax on your system." It also says that one of these programs must be installed: Windows Messaging, Microsoft Exchange Client, or Microsoft Outlook 97. Don't worry about the "Outlook 97" part; Outlook 2000 is okay, too. Choose Yes to continue. You'll see several files being installed and then a message saying that you must restart your computer. Choose Yes.

After your computer restarts and you start Outlook, you're almost ready to install the Microsoft Fax information service. Unfortunately what comes next is somewhat of a pain, but it's necessary. It helps to retain your good spirits by remembering that you only have to go through this once!

Ideally, you should make Microsoft Fax available under Windows before you install Outlook. If you didn't know about this before you installed Outlook, there's a possible incompatibility problem. For that reason, when you first open Outlook after performing the steps just described, Outlook displays a message saying "A recently installed program may cause Microsoft Office or other e-mail-enabled programs to function improperly…" The message also asks "Do you want Outlook to resolve this problem?" If you see this message, choose Yes.

After you do that, Outlook attempts to reload some files from the Office 2000 CD-ROM. At this stage, you probably have your Windows 98 CD-ROM in your drive (after just installing the Microsoft Fax files from that disk). The Office installation routine prompts you to insert your Office 2000 CD-ROM, which you must do. Choose OK to continue. During the process, you may be asked to close down your computer and restart Windows. If that happens, close all open dialog boxes, close Outlook, then restart Windows. Restart Outlook.

That's it! Now you really are ready to install the Microsoft Fax information service.

ADDING THE MICROSOFT FAX INFORMATION SERVICE TO YOUR PROFILE

You can add the Microsoft Fax information service to your profile either from within Outlook or in the Windows Control Panel. The following procedure adds the information service from within Outlook.

PART

II

CH

7

To add Microsoft Fax to your profile:

1. With any Outlook Information viewer displayed, choose Tools, Services to display the dialog box shown in Figure 7.1.

Figure 7.1
This dialog box lists the information services currently in your profile.

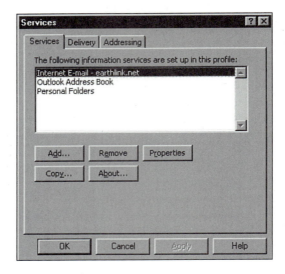

2. If your profile doesn't already contain the Microsoft Fax information service, choose Add to display the dialog box shown in Figure 7.2.

Figure 7.2
This dialog box contains a list of available information services, including Microsoft Fax.

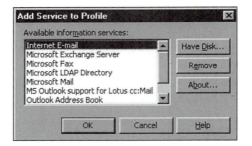

Note

If Microsoft Fax isn't included in the list of available services, that's because you haven't followed the steps in the preceding section. You must follow those steps for Microsoft Fax to appear.

3. Select Microsoft Fax, then choose OK. Outlook displays a message saying that you must specify your name, fax number, and fax modem before you can send a fax, and asks whether you want to do this now. Choose <u>Y</u>es. Outlook displays a dialog box such as the one shown in Figure 7.3.

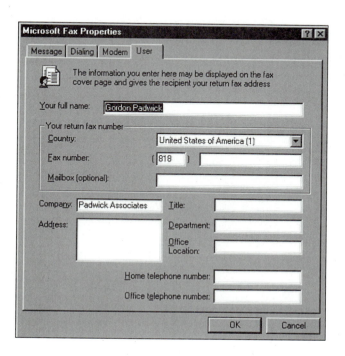

Figure 7.3
This dialog box opens with information about you that's obtained from the information you supplied when you installed Office and other applications.

4. Microsoft Fax insists that you enter your name, country, and fax number. Apart from that, you can enter as much information as you like in this dialog box. Subsequently, you can use the information you provide here to create a fax cover page.

5. After you've entered information in the User tab, select the Message tab shown in Figure 7.4. The default properties in this tab are usually satisfactory for your initial use of Microsoft Fax. A subsequent section of this chapter contains information about these properties.

➔ If you need to change the default properties, **see** "Creating and Sending a Special Fax," **p. 250**.

The default properties in this tab are usually satisfactory for your initial use of Microsoft Fax.

Select the Dialing tab, shown in Figure 7.5, to set your dialing properties.

PART

II

CH

7

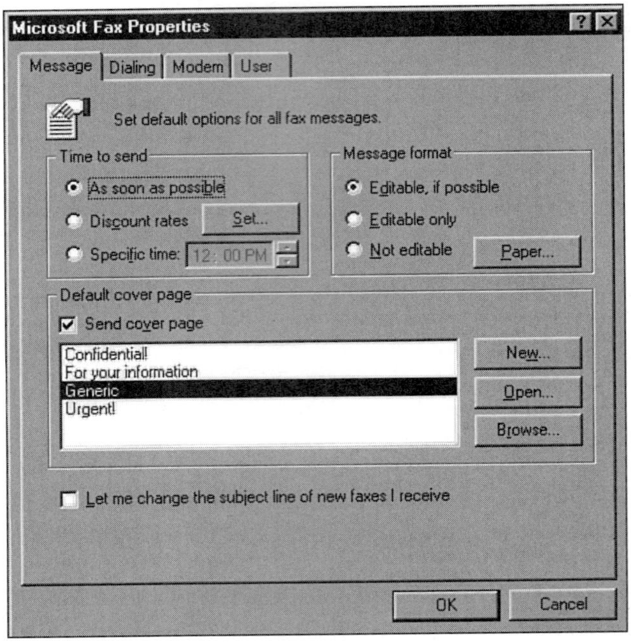

Figure 7.4
This dialog box contains properties for faxes you send.

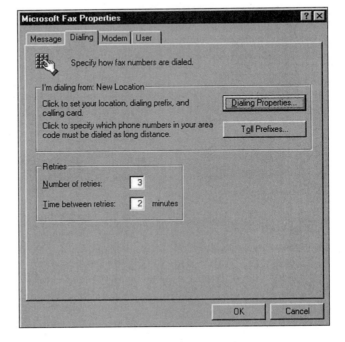

Figure 7.5
Use this tab to verify your dialing properties.

Microsoft Fax initially assumes you'll use the default properties set in Windows Dial-up Networking. To confirm these properties, choose Dialing Properties to display the dialog box shown in Figure 7.6.

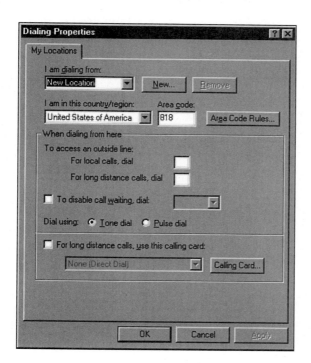

Figure 7.6
You can change your dialing properties in this dialog box.

After you've checked your dialing properties and, if necessary, made changes, choose OK to return to the Dialing tab. If there are phone numbers within your area that must be dialed as long distance, choose Toll Prefixes and select the necessary prefixes.

In the Retries section, change the default Number of Retries and Time Between Retries to whatever you want to use. Select the Modem tab shown in Figure 7.7.

If you have two or more modems installed, select the one you want to use from the list and then choose Set as Active Fax Modem. You can also use this tab to add and remove modems, to set modem properties, and to share your modem with other people who have network access to your computer.

With the Modem tab displayed, choose Properties to display the dialog box shown in Figure 7.8.

PART
II

CH
7

Figure 7.7
Use this tab to select and
configure your modem.

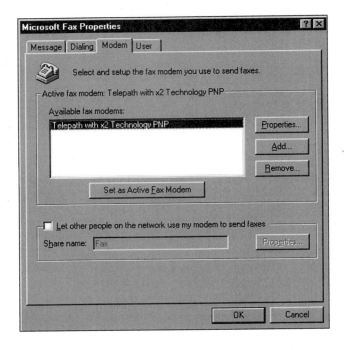

Figure 7.8
Use this dialog box to
set up your fax
modem properties.

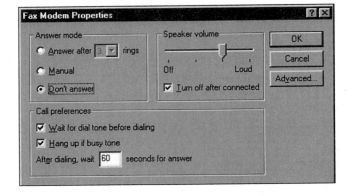

To set the fax modem properties:

1. In the Answer Mode section of the dialog box, select one of the three option buttons. If you want Microsoft Fax to receive incoming faxes automatically, select Answer After then specify the number of rings after which it should answer incoming fax calls (the minimum is two rings). If you select Manual, Microsoft Fax displays a message when an incoming call arrives asking whether you want it to receive a fax. Select Don't Answer if you don't want Microsoft Fax to answer calls.

2. In the Speaker Volume section of the dialog box, move the slider to set the speaker volume. If you enjoy hearing the strange sounds of a fax, uncheck Turn Off After Connected.

3. In the Call Preferences section of the dialog box, normally leave the two check boxes checked. You might want to change the After Dialing, Wait time.

4. Choose Advanced to display the dialog box shown in Figure 7.9. Change the settings in this dialog box only if different settings are recommended by the manufacturer of your fax modem.

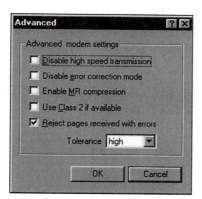

Figure 7.9
The default settings in this dialog box are suitable for most fax modems.

Note

The Disable High Speed Transmission check box, if checked, limits the speed at which your modem transmits faxes to 9600 bits per second. If you uncheck this, your modem will be able to transmit at up to 14,400 bits per second. Microsoft reports that some fax modems are unreliable at the higher speed. Uncheck this box only if you know your fax modem can reliably handle the higher speed.

After you've set Microsoft Fax properties in all four tabs, choose OK four times to return to Outlook.

Note

You can change Microsoft Fax properties at any time by choosing Tools, Services to display the Services dialog box. Select Microsoft Fax, and then choose Properties.

CHANGING MICROSOFT FAX PROPERTIES

After you've initially set properties for Microsoft Fax, you can change those properties at any time. To do so, choose Tools, move the pointer onto Microsoft Fax Tools, and choose Options to display the Microsoft Fax Properties dialog box with the Message tab selected, as previously shown in Figure 7.4. You can use the four tabs in this dialog box to change the various properties of Microsoft Fax.

PART

II

CH

7

Note

The Microsoft Fax Tools item appears on the Tools menu when you add the Microsoft Fax information service to your profile.

In addition to giving you access to Microsoft Fax properties, Microsoft Fax Tools also contains:

- Request a Fax—Lets you call a fax information service to request a fax
- Advanced Security—Provides access to security keys
- Show Outgoing Faxes—Provides a display of the progress of outgoing faxes

SHARING YOUR FAX MODEM

You can share your fax modem so that other network users can use it to send faxes. This can be useful if several people have occasional need to send faxes because only one fax modem and dedicated phone line are needed.

SETTING UP A MICROSOFT FAX SERVER

After you've added Microsoft Fax to your profile and set its properties, you can modify it so that it becomes a *fax server*. However, if you don't want to use your computer as a fax server, ignore this section.

In order to share a modem, you have to allow other people access to files on your computer, as described in the following procedure. If you already have file sharing enabled, the first four steps in this procedure are unnecessary.

Tip #47 from

Gordon Padwick

Be aware that file sharing can be a boon, but it might be a bane. If you enable file sharing, other people might be able to access files on your computer's disks that you don't want them to see. This can be a particular problem if you use a cable TV system to access the Internet. In that case, by enabling file sharing, your neighbors who use the same service can access files on your computer. You can, of course, prevent access by password-protecting your files.

To share your fax modem:

1. In the Windows taskbar, choose Start, move the pointer onto <u>S</u>ettings, and choose <u>C</u>ontrol Panel. Double-click Network to display the dialog box shown in Figure 7.10.

2. Choose <u>F</u>ile and Print Sharing to display the dialog box shown in Figure 7.11.

3. Check I Want to Be Able to Give Others Access to My <u>F</u>iles, then choose OK. After a few seconds delay, the Network dialog box reappears. Choose OK to return to the Control Panel. You are asked to insert the Windows CD-ROM so that some files can be read from it. Do so, then after the files have been read, choose <u>Y</u>es to restart your computer.

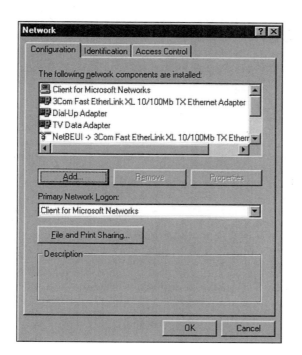

Figure 7.10
Use this dialog box to enable file sharing.

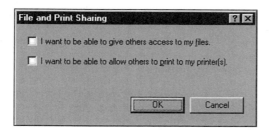

Figure 7.11
Use this dialog box to allow access to your files and printers.

4. After your computer restarts, start Outlook, and choose Tools, Services to display the Services dialog box with the Services tab selected. Select the Microsoft Fax information service and choose Properties. Select the modem tab, previously shown in Figure 7.7.

5. Check Let Other People on the Network Use My Modem to Send Faxes. When you do so, a dialog box asks you to select the drive to use for fax messages. Select a drive on your computer that has plenty of available space. Check OK. By default, the share name for the shared fax service is Fax.

6. Choose Properties at the right of the Share Name box to display the dialog box shown in Figure 7.12.

PART
II

CH
7

Figure 7.12
You can change the
share name in this
dialog box.

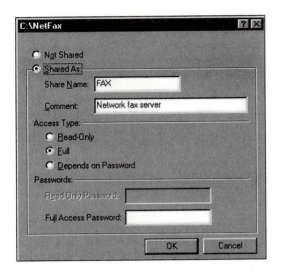

7. Replace the default Share Name with another name if you want. Make sure the Full Access Type option button is selected. Choose OK to return to the Microsoft Fax Properties dialog box. Choose OK to close that dialog box to close the Services dialog box.

Now your computer is set up as a fax server.

SETTING UP A MICROSOFT FAX CLIENT

After you've set up Microsoft Fax as a fax server on one computer, as described in the preceding section, you can add Microsoft Fax as a client to profiles on other networked computers running Outlook 97, C/W Outlook 98, or C/W Outlook 2000. The following procedure assumes you have one of these versions of Outlook installed on network computers.

To add Microsoft Fax as a fax client:

1. With any Outlook Information viewer displayed, choose Tools, Services to display the Services dialog box.

2. Choose Add to display the Add Service to Profile dialog box. Select Microsoft Fax, and choose OK to display a dialog box telling you that you must specify your name, fax number, and modem, and asking whether you want to do that now. Choose Yes to display the Microsoft Fax Properties dialog box with the User tab selected, as previously shown in Figure 7.3.

3. Enter your fax number and whatever other information you want to appear on cover pages. Select the Modem tab, shown previously in Figure 7.7.

4. Choose Add to display the Add a Fax Modem dialog box, shown in Figure 7.13.

Figure 7.13
If the computer is connected by way of a network to a fax server, Network Fax Server is available to be added.

5. Select Network Fax Server and choose OK to display the dialog box shown in Figure 7.14. The dialog box is initially displayed with the Path box empty.

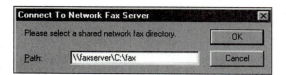

Figure 7.14
The dialog box shown here has the path to the shared network fax folder already entered.

6. In the Path box, enter the path to the shared network fax folder, using the format shown in Figure 7.14, and choose OK to return to the Microsoft Fax Properties dialog box with the Modem tab selected. The list of available fax modems contains the path to the shared network fax folder.

Note

> The computer must be connected to the computer on which the fax server is installed and Outlook must be running on that computer at the time you enter the path name in the Connect to a Network Fax Server dialog box. Otherwise, you'll see an error message when you attempt to define the fax server.

7. Select the path to the shared network fax folder and then choose Set an Active Fax Modem. Choose OK twice to close the dialog boxes and return to the Information viewer.

Now the person who uses the client can send faxes by way of the fax server and the fax server's modem and phone line, just as if the client computer had its own modem and phone line.

Note

> A fax client set up in this way can only send faxes by way of the fax server. Incoming faxes are received by the fax server and saved in the Outlook Inbox folder on that computer. You can use e-mail to distribute incoming faxes to the appropriate recipients, something that can be done manually or automated by the use of rules.

→ Outlook provides useful tools to help you slog through mundane tasks, such as distributing incoming faxes to the proper recipients; **see** "Using the Rules Wizard to Create Rules That Manage Incoming Messages," **p.624**.

CREATING AND SENDING A FAX

After you have Microsoft Fax in your C/W Outlook Profile, you can create and send a fax.

Before getting started, you should know that there are two ways to create text for a fax. If the fax is short and simple, the easiest way is to enter the text in one of the New Fax Wizard windows. See the following section "Creating and Sending a Simple Fax."

However, if the fax is long, it's usually better to create the fax as a Word document and then, after you've finished revising that document, add it to the fax. See "Creating and Sending a Special Fax" later in this chapter.

CREATING AND SENDING A SIMPLE FAX

The following steps describe how you create and send a simple fax, using the fax properties you've previously set.

To create a simple fax:

1. With the Inbox information viewer displayed, choose <u>A</u>ctions, New Fa<u>x</u> Message to display the first Compose New Fax Wizard window shown in Figure 7.15.

Figure 7.15
This window displays the name of the location from which you're dialing.

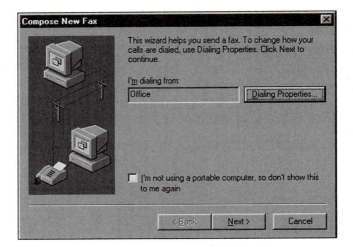

Note

You can't choose File, move the pointer onto New, and choose New Fax, as you can when using WinFax SE under IMO Outlook.

2. Choose <u>D</u>ialing Properties if you want to change the name of your location or other dialing properties. If you do so, Outlook displays the dialog box shown in Figure 7.16.

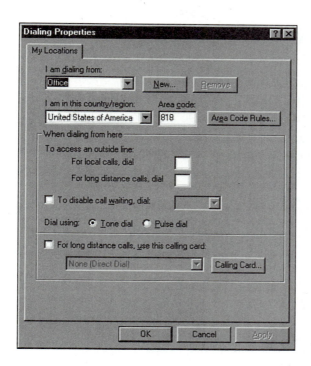

Figure 7.16
Make any changes to your dialing properties in this dialog box.

3. After making changes to your dialing properties, choose OK to return to the Compose New Fax Wizard window. If you're using a desktop computer that's always in the same place, check the box near the bottom of the window, otherwise leave the box unchecked. Choose <u>N</u>ext > to display the second wizard window, shown in Figure 7.17.

4. Enter the recipient's name in the <u>T</u>o box, enter the recipient's fax number in the <u>F</u>ax # boxes, and choose <u>A</u>dd to List to display the recipient's name in the R<u>e</u>cipient List box. Alternatively, you can choose Address Book to select one or more recipients from your address books. Choose <u>N</u>ext > to display the next wizard window, shown in Figure 7.18.

Note

You can select one of the four cover pages supplied with Windows: Confidential, For Your Information, Generic, and Urgent. You can also select any custom cover pages you have created.

→ Most likely, you'll want to create your own custom fax cover pages; **see** "Creating a Fax Cover Page," **p. 262**.

PART
II

CH
7

5. Choose No if you don't want to send a cover page, or choose Yes if you do want to send one. If you choose Yes, select the cover page you want to use. Choose Next > to display the next wizard window, shown in Figure 7.19.

Figure 7.17
Use this window to identify the recipient.

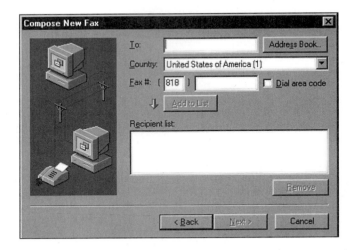

Figure 7.18
Select a cover page in this window.

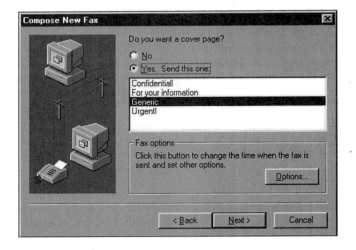

6. Enter the subject of the fax in the Subject box and the text of the fax in the Note box. Uncheck Start Note on Cover Page if you want to start the note on a separate page. Choose Next > to display the next wizard window, shown in Figure 7.20.

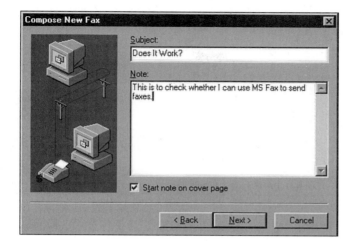

Figure 7.19
Enter the subject and text of the fax in this window.

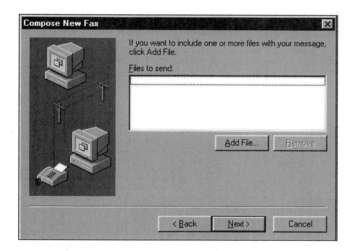

Figure 7.20
You can use this window to add files to the fax, something you probably don't want to do in the case of a simple fax.

7. Choose <u>N</u>ext > to display the final wizard window, shown in Figure 7.21.

8. Choose <u>F</u>inish to send the fax.

PART

II

CH

7

Figure 7.21
This window confirms that the fax is ready to send.

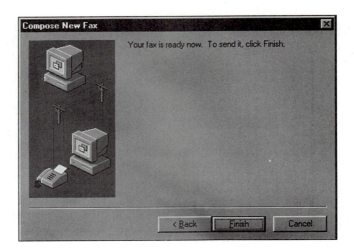

The wizard window closes when you choose Finish. Almost immediately a message box is displayed to keep you informed about the progress of sending the message. In sequence, the message box displays:

- Processing Fax—Displayed while the text of the message is being converted into a graphics image ready for sending.
- Initializing Modem—Displayed while your modem is being initialized.
- Dialing Recipient—Displayed while your modem is dialing the recipient and waiting for a response.
- Connecting—Displayed while your Microsoft Fax and the recipient's fax machine or fax software are establishing communications.
- Sending—Displayed while the fax is being sent. During this time, the message box displays the number of the page currently being sent and the percentage of that page that has been sent.

CREATING AND SENDING A SPECIAL FAX

From time to time, you'll want to create a fax that requires more attention to details than described in the preceding section. On those occasions you'll need to use some of the steps described here. Don't be put off by the large number of steps; you'll rarely need to use more than a few of them.

To create and send a special fax:

1. Create, or identify, the text and graphics files you want to send as part of the fax.
2. With the Inbox Information viewer displayed, choose Actions, New Fax Message to display the first Compose New Fax Wizard window shown in Figure 7.22.

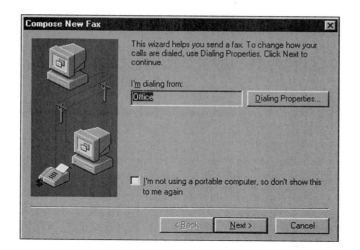

Figure 7.22
This window identifies
your dialing location.

3. If you're dialing from a location other than the one identified in the I'm Dialing From box, choose Dialing Properties to open the Dialing Properties dialog box shown in Figure 7.23.

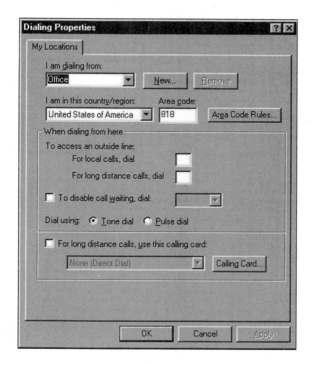

Figure 7.23
Use this dialog box to
select a different dial-
ing location, or to cre-
ate a new one.

4. After you've selected the appropriate location, choose OK to return to the Wizard window. Choose <u>N</u>ext > to display the second wizard window, shown in Figure 7.24.

Note

If you always dial from the same location, check <u>I</u>'m Not Using a Portable Computer…. After you do that, the first wizard window isn't subsequently displayed.

Figure 7.24
Use this window to identify the person to whom you want to send the fax.

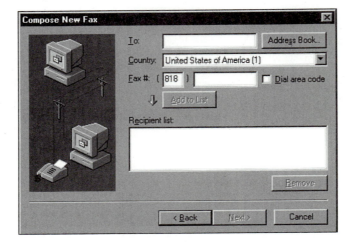

5. Choose Address Book to open the dialog box shown in Figure 7.25.

Figure 7.25
The Address Book dialog box is shown here with a recipient selected.

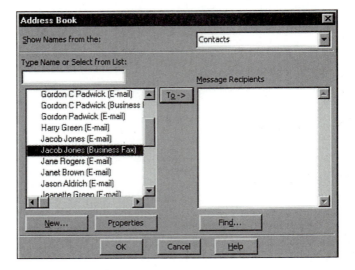

Note

Instead of choosing a name from your address book, you can enter a person's name in the To box, open the Country drop-down list and select the person's country, and enter the person's fax number in the Fax # boxes. Then choose Add to List to move the person's name into the Recipient List box.

6. Select the name of a person for whom you have a fax number, choose To-> to copy that person's name into the Message Recipients list, and then choose OK to return to the wizard window in which the selected person's name is shown in the Recipient List.

Note

You can add more than one recipient into the Recipient List by choosing names from your address book or by entering names. You can delete a name from the Recipient List by selecting that name and then choosing Remove.

7. If you're sending a fax to someone within your own telephone area code, Windows Dial-up Networking normally doesn't dial the area code. If you want the area code to be dialed, check Dial Area Code. Choose Next > to display the next wizard window, shown in Figure 7.26.

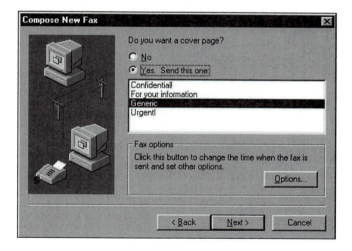

Figure 7.26
Use this window to select a cover page and to specify when the fax should be sent.

8. Select No if you don't want to send a cover page, or Yes if you want to do so. If you select Yes, Microsoft Fax uses the default cover page you selected when you set up properties, unless you select a different one in the list. You can select one of the cover pages provided with Windows or a custom cover page you've created.

9. If you want to change the default fax properties, choose Options to display the dialog box shown in Figure 7.27.

Figure 7.27
Use this dialog box to select fax properties for the current message.

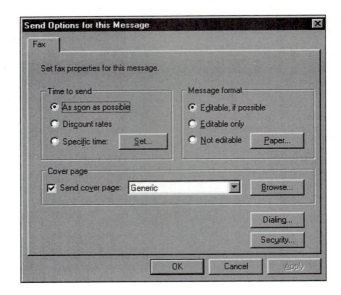

10. In the Time to Send section of the dialog box, select one of the three option buttons. If you select Specific Time, choose Set to open the dialog box shown in Figure 7.28.

Figure 7.28
Specify the time at which the fax should be sent in this dialog box.

11. In the Message Format section of the Send Options to This Message dialog box, select one of the three option buttons.

Note

Normally, select Editable, if Possible (the default). If you do so, Microsoft Fax sends the fax in *editable,* binary format if you and the recipient both have Class 1 fax capability; if either of you has Class 2 capability, Microsoft Fax sends the fax in *facsimile* format.

When you send faxes in editable, binary format recipients can read and edit them just like an e-mail message. If you include a file as an attachment to an editable fax, the file is transmitted in its native format.

If you select Editable Only, Microsoft Fax sends the fax only if the recipient's fax capability supports the editable, binary format. If not, the fax isn't sent.

If you select Not Editable, Microsoft Fax sends the fax in facsimile format.

12. Also in the Message Format section of the dialog box, you can choose Paper to display the dialog box shown in Figure 7.29. In this dialog box, open the Paper Size drop-down list and select a paper size, open the Image Quality drop-down list and select a quality, and select Portrait or Landscape orientation.

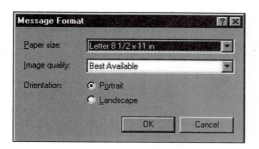

Figure 7.29
Use this dialog box to specify the message format.

13. Choose Dialing if you want to change your dialing properties. Microsoft Fax displays a dialog box in which you can change how a call is dialed.

14. Choose Security to display the dialog box, shown in Figure 7.30, in which you can choose various security options.

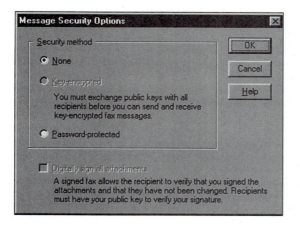

Figure 7.30
Use this dialog box to select security options for the fax.

→ To learn more about keeping your e-mail from prying eyes, **see** "Using Outlook Securely," **p. 993**.

15. After you've completed any changes to fax options, choose Next > to display the next wizard window, shown in Figure 7.31.

PART

II

CH

7

Figure 7.31
This is where you compose the fax.

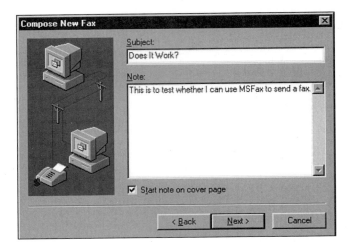

16. Enter a subject for the fax in the Subject box and the text of the fax in the Note box. If you want to start the fax on the cover page, leave Start Note on Cover Page checked, otherwise uncheck it. Choose Next > to display the next wizard window, shown in Figure 7.32.

Figure 7.32
You can use this window to add files to the fax.

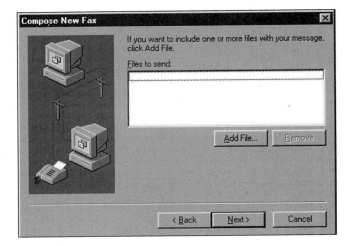

17. To add one or more files to the fax, choose Add File to display the dialog box shown in Figure 7.33.

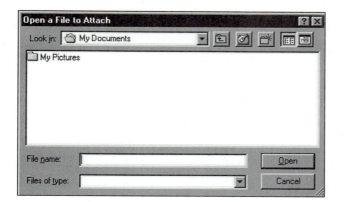

Figure 7.33
You can use this dialog box to select files you want to add to the fax.

18. Navigate to a file you want to add to the fax, select that file, and choose <u>O</u>pen to return to the wizard window previously shown in Figure 7.33 in which the path and file names of the selected file are now shown in the Files to Send box.

19. Repeat steps 17 and 18 as many times as necessary to add more files to the fax. Choose <u>N</u>ext > to display the final wizard window, shown in Figure 7.34.

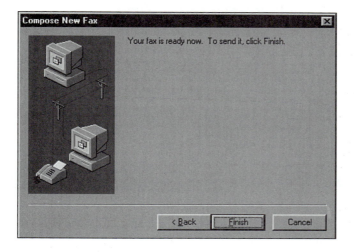

Figure 7.34
You've finished creating the fax.

20. Choose <u>F</u>inish to send the fax.

SENDING AN OFFICE DOCUMENT AS A FAX

After you've created an Office document, such as some text in Word or a workbook in Excel, you can directly send that document as a fax. The following paragraphs describe how to send a Word document as a fax; sending an Excel workbook is quite similar.

Tip #48 from

The following two sections describe two ways to send an Office document, the first being the method—the Fax Wizard—suggested in Microsoft's documentation. If you have trouble with that, try the second method (Microsoft Fax).

USING THE FAX WIZARD TO FAX AN OFFICE DOCUMENT

Word uses the Fax Wizard to send a document as a fax. After creating a Word document, choose File, move the pointer onto Send To, and choose Fax Recipient. The first time you do this, Word displays a dialog box saying it "canít start this wizard" because this "feature is not currently installed." To install the wizard, choose Yes. Youíll be asked to insert the Office 2000 CD-ROM into your ROM drive. Word installs the Fax Wizard and displays the first wizard window, as shown in Figure 7.35.

Figure 7.35
Word uses the Fax Wizard to fax a document.

Note

When you subsequently want to fax a Word document, the Fax Wizard is displayed without having to install it.

Follow through the steps in the Fax Wizard to fax the document. When you come to the final step, choose the Send Fax Now button. Outlook opens if itís not already running and sends the fax.

USING MICROSOFT FAX TO FAX A DOCUMENT

After you've installed Microsoft Fax, Microsoft Fax is listed as an available printer in Windows applications. You can select this as a printer in order to fax a document.

To fax a document:

1. With a Windows document open an application such as Word, choose File, Print to display the Print dialog box.
2. In the Print dialog box, open the drop-down Name list and select Microsoft Fax.
3. Make the usual selections in the Print dialog box (page range, number of copies, and so on).
4. Choose OK. After a few seconds delay (substantially more than a few seconds if the document is long or complex), Outlook's Compose New Fax Wizard is displayed.
5. Use the various wizard windows to prepare the fax for sending. The window in which you can add a file is not displayed, because the Office document is already added.
6. Microsoft Fax sends the Office document as a fax when you choose Finish on the last wizard window.

RECEIVING A FAX

If you're using a dedicated phone line for your fax modem and are prepared to leave your computer turned on with Outlook running (probably in the background) you can use Microsoft Fax to receive incoming faxes. Two of the benefits of doing this are

- You can subsequently use your computer printer to print faxes—much better than using the thermal printer in many fax machines.
- You can preview faxes and only print those you need to have as hard copy, thus reducing your use of expensive thermal paper.

To enable Microsoft Fax to automatically receive incoming faxes you must have selected Answer After in the Fax Modem Properties dialog box shown previously in Figure 7.8.

Note

If you selected Manual in the Fax Modem Properties dialog box, Microsoft Fax displays a dialog box when an incoming fax is received. If you want Microsoft Fax to receive the fax, choose Yes in that dialog box.

VIEWING RECEIVED FAXES

When Microsoft Fax answers an incoming message, it displays a message box with the following sequence of messages:

- Ringing—Displayed while the incoming message is ringing and before Microsoft Fax picks up the call.

PART
II
CH
7

- Initializing Modem—Displayed while Microsoft Fax is initializing your modem.
- Answering Call—Displayed while Microsoft Fax is sending an acknowledgment to the caller.
- Connecting—Displayed while Microsoft Fax is establishing communications with the calling fax machine.
- Receiving Page—Displayed while Microsoft Fax is receiving pages. The current page number and number of bytes received are displayed. This message is displayed only if Outlook is open in a window, not if Outlook is running in the background.
- Receive Successful—Displayed briefly when the sending fax machine sends an end-of-fax signal.
- Idle—Displayed briefly while Microsoft Fax turns off your modem.

The incoming fax arrives in your Outlook Inbox folder. A few seconds after the fax arrives, you can see the message header in the Inbox Information viewer just as you see incoming e-mail messages.

Note

> The delay between the time the fax arrives and the time its header appears in your Inbox Information viewer is caused by your computer processing the fax. This delay might be considerably more than a few seconds if you have a slow computer or receive a long fax.

The Icon column in the message header contains an icon that identifies the message as a fax. The From column contains the sender's fax number if that was transmitted with the fax; otherwise the column contains "Unknown Fax Machine". The Subject column contains "Fax". The Received column contains the date and time you received the fax.

If you have the Preview pane enabled, that pane contains an icon representing the fax. That's because a fax is received as a graphics image, not as text.

To display the fax, double-click the message header or the icon in the Preview pane to display the dialog box shown in Figure 7.36.

Choose Open It and choose OK to display a message image, such as the one shown in Figure 7.37.

What you're seeing here is Imaging for Windows, software Microsoft licenses from Eastman Software and included in the Office 2000 package. Imaging for Windows contains much more than you'll ever need for manipulating received faxes.

Tip #49 from

Gordon Padwick

> While you have a fax open in the Imaging for Windows window, you can annotate the fax before forwarding it to someone else. You can also use the Rubber Stamp button to mark the fax.
>
> You can investigate these and other capabilities of Imaging for Windows by choosing Help, Imaging Help and Help, Imaging Preview Help.

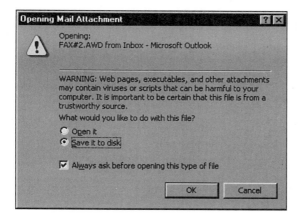

Figure 7.36
This dialog box offers the choice of opening the message or saving it on a disk.

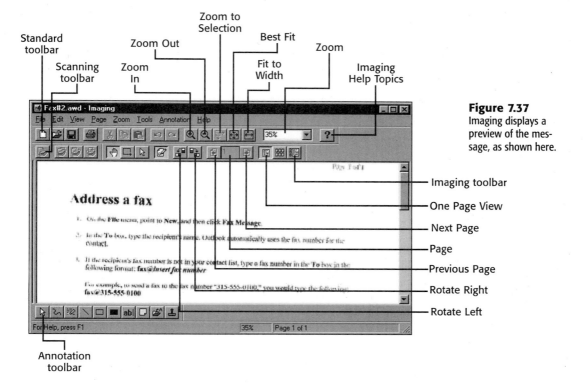

Figure 7.37
Imaging displays a preview of the message, as shown here.

Standard toolbar

Scanning toolbar

Zoom In

Zoom Out

Zoom to Selection

Fit to Width

Best Fit

Zoom

Imaging Help Topics

Imaging toolbar

One Page View

Next Page

Page

Previous Page

Rotate Right

Rotate Left

Annotation toolbar

While working with faxes you've received, you'll sometimes find it useful to use Zoom in the Standard toolbar to change the magnification of a displayed fax, and also the Rotate Left and Rotate Right buttons in the Imaging toolbar so that a fax is displayed in the correct orientation on your screen.

Note

One of the things you can't do in Imaging for Windows is convert the fax text into editable format. However, if you own a scanner, that scanner probably came with an *Optical Character Recognition (OCR)* application that converts an image of text into editable text. You can probably use that application to convert the text in a fax to text you can edit using a word processor.

PRINTING A RECEIVED FAX

You can't print a received fax from the Inbox Information viewer.

To print a fax you've received, double-click the message header in the Inbox Information viewer to display it in the Imaging window. Then choose File, Print.

CREATING A FAX COVER PAGE

After you've installed Microsoft Fax on your computer, you can use the Fax Cover Page Editor to modify the four standard cover pages and also to create your own cover pages.

Note

One of the benefits of using Microsoft Fax (only available with C/W Outlook) is that you can create custom cover pages. WinFax SE (for IMO Outlook) doesn't let you do that.

To start the Cover Page Editor, choose Start in the Windows taskbar, move the pointer onto Programs, Accessories, Fax, and choose Cover Page Editor to display the window shown in Figure 7.38.

The Style and Drawing toolbars contain many tools you can use to create a cover page. Choose Help, Help Topics to find detailed information about these tools and about creating cover pages.

The default Microsoft cover pages are in the files:

- Confidential!.cpe
- For Your Information.cpe
- Generic.cpe
- Urgent.cpe

These are normally in your C:\Windows folder.

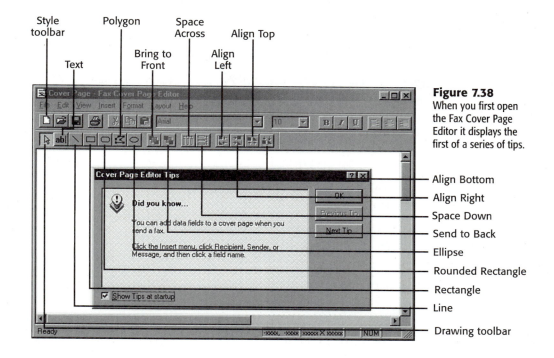

Style toolbar

Polygon

Space Across

Align Top

Text

Bring to Front

Align Left

Figure 7.38
When you first open the Fax Cover Page Editor it displays the first of a series of tips.

Align Bottom

Align Right

Space Down

Send to Back

Ellipse

Rounded Rectangle

Rectangle

Line

Drawing toolbar

MODIFYING A SUPPLIED COVER PAGE

You'll probably find that the four cover pages supplied with Microsoft Fax are usable, but aren't quite what you'd like to have. For example, you might like to have your company logo on the cover pages. You can easily do that if you have the logo available as a graphics file.

To add a logo to a cover page:

1. With the Fax Cover Page Editor displayed, choose File, Open to display the Open dialog box.

2. In the Open dialog box, navigate to the Windows folder that contains the supplied cover pages (probably C:\Windows), and select a cover page (such as Generic.cpe). Choose Open to display the cover page, as shown in Figure 7.39.

3. To insert a logo (or other graphics), choose Insert, Object to display the dialog box shown in Figure 7.40.

4. Choose Create from File, navigate to the folder that contains the graphics file you want to insert, select that file, and choose Insert to return to the Insert Object dialog box. Choose OK to insert the image into the cover page at the top-left corner.

PART

II

CH

7

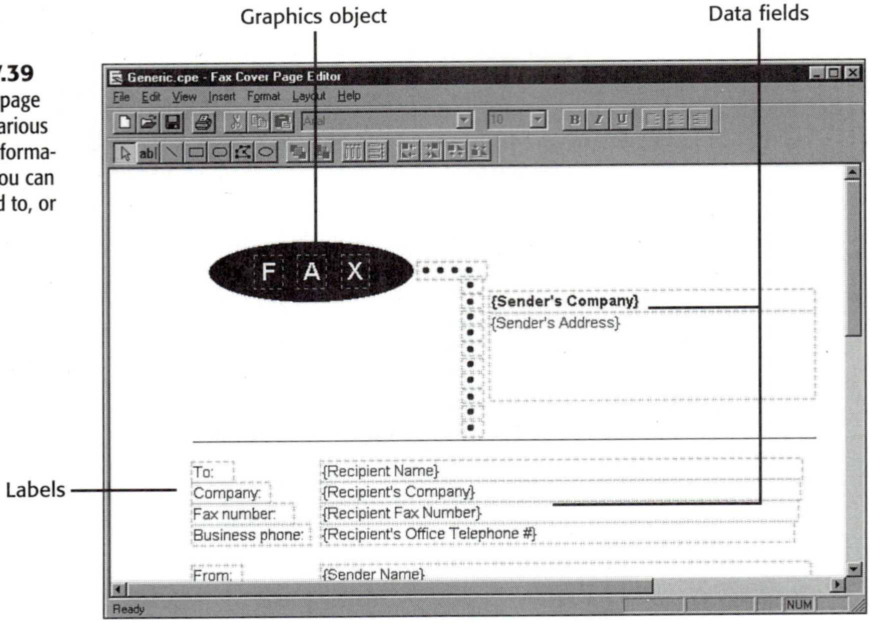

Graphics object

Data fields

Figure 7.39
The cover page contains various fields of information that you can delete, add to, or change.

Labels

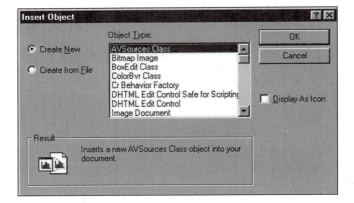

Figure 7.40
You can use this dialog box to create an object as well as to insert an existing file.

Note

Instead of seeing the graphics image on the cover page, you may only see an icon representing the graphics file. That happens if Windows doesn't associate the type of graphics file you selected with a graphics application that can open it. For information about associating files with applications, refer to "Associating File Types with Programs" in Windows Help.

5. Click the graphics image to select it. You know it's selected when handles appear at the four corners and at the middle of each edge. You can change the size of the image by dragging any of the handles; you can move the image by pointing onto the image (anywhere but on a handle) and dragging. Figure 7.41 shows a cover page with an inserted image.

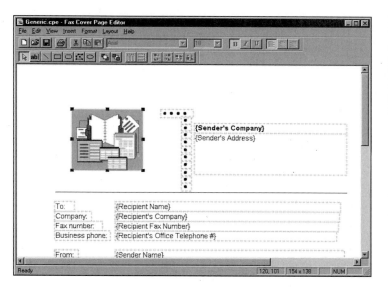

Figure 7.41
This is the generic cover page with an inserted image. The image shown here is one of the clipart images supplied with Office.

In addition to graphics, a cover page contains various text fields. Some of these are labels that always appear on the cover page; others are data fields that display information you provide when setting up Microsoft Fax properties.

You can select any label or data field by selecting it and then you can

- Delete it by pressing Delete. Alternatively, choose Edit, Delete.
- Move it by dragging.
- Change its size by dragging a handle.
- Change the font by choosing Format, Font to display the Windows Font dialog box, in which you can select a font name, style, and size. Alternatively, open the drop-down Font Name list in the Style toolbar and select a font; open the drop-down Font Size list and select a size; choose the Bold, Italic, or Underline buttons.

To change a label's text, select the label, point onto the text, and use conventional editing techniques to delete and insert characters.

To insert a label, choose the Text button in the Drawing toolbar, move the pointer to the approximate position where you want the label to be, press the mouse button, and drag to create a rectangle. Click within the rectangle to create an insertion point, type the label text, and click outside the rectangle. You can drag the label's handles to change the size of the rectangle, and you can drag the label to a different position on the cover page.

You can insert new data fields into the cover page. Choose Insert, and then

- Move the pointer onto Recipient to display a list of recipient-related fields: Name, Fax Number, Company, Street Address, City, State, Zip Code, Country, Title, Department, Office Location, Home Telephone Number, Office Telephone Number, To: List, and CC: List.
- Move the pointer onto Sender to display a list of sender-related fields: Name, Fax Number, Company, Address, Title, Department, Office Location, Home Telephone Number, and Office Telephone Number.
- Move the pointer onto Message to display a list of message-related fields: Note, Subject, Time Sent, Number of Pages, and Number of Attachments.

Select a data field in one of these lists. When you do so, a label containing the name of the selected field and that field appear on the cover page, with both selected. At this point, you can

- Drag the label and data field together to any position on the cover page.
- Drag the data field by itself. To do this, click on an unoccupied place on the cover page to deselect the label and the data field. Then click the data field to select it. Now you can drag the data field without moving the label.
- Change the text in the label, as described previously in this section.

After you've finished making changes to the cover page, choose File, Save As to display the normal Windows Save As dialog box, enter a name for the changed cover page, and choose Save. By default, the Fax Cover Page Editor saves the file in your Windows folder that also contains the supplied cover page files.

Tip #50 from

Gordon Padwick

Save the changed cover page with a name other than that of the original cover page so that you can subsequently use the original cover page if the need arises.

CREATING A NEW COVER PAGE

Unless you want to create a cover page that's completely different from one of the supplied pages, it's usually easier to modify an existing page instead of creating one from scratch. You can create a cover page from scratch if you prefer to do that.

To create a new cover page:

1. Choose Start in the Windows taskbar, then move the pointer onto Programs, move the pointer onto Accessories, move the pointer onto Fax, and choose Cover Page Editor to display an empty cover page.

2. To add a data field to the empty page, choose Insert, move the pointer onto Recipient, Sender, or Message to display a list of data fields, and select the data field you want to add. Drag the data field and its label into position on the page.

3. Repeat step 2 to add more data fields.

4. To add graphics objects to the cover page, choose Insert, Object to display the Insert Object dialog box previously shown in Figure 7.40. Choose Create from File, identify the file you want to insert, and choose OK to insert the object in the page. Drag the object into position.

5. Repeat step 4 to add more graphics objects.

6. Choose File, Save As to display the Save As dialog box. Enter a name for the new cover page and choose Save to save it.

Note

By default, Outlook saves the cover page file in your Windows folder, which is the folder that contains the supplied cover page files.

Tip #51 from

You can set up Outlook's Journal to keep a record of faxes you send to specific people. See "Recording Faxes in Your Journal," in Chapter 12 to learn more.

REPLACING MICROSOFT FAX WITH WINFAX PRO

If you only send and receive occasional faxes, you'll probably find that Microsoft Fax satisfies your needs. However, if you're a regular fax user, you should consider replacing Microsoft Fax with WinFax Pro, which is available from Symantec.

Note

The remaining pages of this chapter refer specifically to WinFax Pro version 9. Some of the information doesn't apply to earlier versions of WinFax Pro.

Some of the capabilities of WinFax Pro that aren't available in Microsoft Fax are

- Previewing Faxes—You can see exactly what a fax will look like before you send it.
- Optical Character Recognition—You can convert text in a fax you receive into text you can edit in a word processor.
- Automatic Paging—WinFax Pro can automatically send a message to your pager when faxes arrive.
- Automatic Forwarding—WinFax Pro can automatically forward faxes it receives to another fax number.
- Fax Sharing—A workgroup consisting of up to 20 people can share one fax modem and one phone line.

PART

II

CH

7

There's much more, but this short list should be enough to convince regular fax users that upgrading to WinFax Pro is something they should consider.

DISCOVERING MORE ABOUT MICROSOFT FAX

This chapter is intended to provide all the information you need to install and use Microsoft Fax. You can find additional information in Chapter 27 of the Microsoft Windows 95 Resource Kit.

The Resource Kit chapter contains information about security issues, including the use of passwords and encryption. The section "Technical Notes for Microsoft Fax" contains detailed information about the formats used to send messages and the Windows registry keys used by Microsoft Fax. Although written specifically for Windows 95, the information appears to apply equally to Windows 98.

Note

The Microsoft Windows 98 Resource Kit does not contain detailed information about Microsoft Fax.

ACCESSING THE INTERNET

In this chapter

by Gordon Padwick

ACCESSING THE INTERNET WORLD

 You'll find the information in this chapter useful if you're using IMO Outlook, or if you're using C/W Outlook and have an Internet Information service in your profile.

 Outlook 2000 is tightly integrated with Windows (including Internet Explorer), and with other Office 2000 components. Instead of duplicating functionality that's already in Windows, Outlook seamlessly links to Windows. Similarly, Outlook shares functionality with the other components of the Office suite.

Much of this component-sharing goes on behind the surface and isn't immediately obvious to Outlook users. However, when you use Outlook in the Internet environment, it's apparent that Outlook relies on other Windows and Office components. Specifically, Outlook uses components of Internet Explorer to provide access to the Internet and to intranet sites, and to provide access to Internet newsgroups.

Some vocal Microsoft critics complain about this sharing of functionality; they say, for example, that Outlook should have its own newsreader, instead of relying on Outlook Express (a component of Internet Explorer). I don't understand that perspective; I think it's great to be able to use the same keyboard and mouse for whatever application I'm using. In the same way, I'm happy to use the same Outlook Express to access Internet newsgroups, whether I'm doing so directly, from Internet Explorer, or from within Outlook.

Note
> Unfortunately, Microsoft hasn't taken integration quite far enough. There's no direct way to save information from newsgroups in the data store that Outlook uses for messages, contacts, and so on.

The fact is that Outlook uses components of Internet Explorer for many purposes including, by default, browsing the Internet and interacting with Internet Newsgroups. If you're an Outlook user, you might as well accept that and get on with using it.

The required components of Internet Explorer and Outlook Express are automatically installed when you install Outlook.

ACCESSING THE INTERNET

From any Outlook Information viewer, you can easily access Web pages and participate in Internet newsgroups.

ACCESSING WEB SITES

With any Outlook Information viewer displayed, choose <u>V</u>iew, move the pointer onto <u>G</u>o To, and choose Web Bro<u>w</u>ser. Outlook opens Internet Explorer. You can now use Internet Explorer in the normal way to access Web sites.

Tip #52 from

Gordon Padwick

If you frequently access the Internet from within Outlook, you'll find it handy to add buttons for this purpose to an Outlook toolbar.

→ To learn more about accessing other programs from your Outlook toolbar, **see** "Adding a Button to a Toolbar," **p. 824**.

Initially, when you choose Web Bro<u>w</u>ser, Outlook may tell you "This page cannot be displayed." That happens when Internet Explorer isn't configured to connect automatically to the Internet. Choose <u>F</u>ile, <u>W</u>ork Offline to continue.

At this stage, you can configure Internet Explorer so that it automatically connects to your Internet service provider (ISP). The following procedure assumes your computer is already set up to connect to the Internet and that you already have an account with an ISP.

To configure Internet Explorer to connect automatically to your ISP:

1. Start Internet Explorer, choose <u>T</u>ools, Internet <u>O</u>ptions, and select the Connections tab to display the dialog box shown in Figure 8.1.

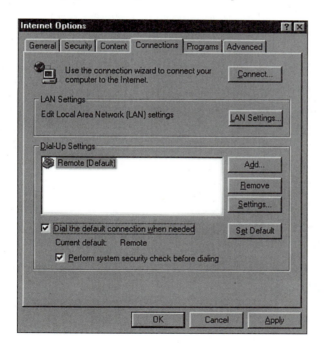

Figure 8.1
The Dial-Up Settings section of this dialog box lists your existing dial-up connections to the Internet.

Tip #53 from

Gordon Padwick

If you don't already have an ISP, choose <u>C</u>onnect. You can then use the Internet Connection Wizard to lead you through the process of finding an ISP and establishing an account.

2. Select the dial-up setting you want to use and choose Set Default.

3. Make sure Dial the Default Connection When Needed is checked.

4. Choose OK to close the dialog box.

5. Choose File, Close to close Internet Explorer.

The next time you choose View, move the pointer onto Go To, and choose Web Browser, Internet Explorer opens with your default home page displayed.

This book is primarily about Outlook; it assumes you're familiar with using Internet Explorer. However, here are a few hints about how you can use Internet Explorer and Outlook together.

With any Web page displayed by Internet Explorer, you can send that page, or a link to that page, to other people by e-mail.

To send a Web page by e-mail:

1. In Internet Explorer, display the Web page you want to send.

2. Choose File, move the pointer onto Send, and choose Page By E-mail to display a Message form similar to the one shown in Figure 8.2.

Figure 8.2
This message form automatically contains the Web page as an attachment.

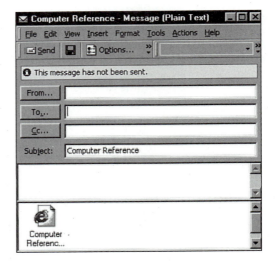

3. Address the message in the same way that you address any other Outlook message (as explained in Chapter 3).

➔ For information about how to address messages with Web page attachments, **see** "Addressing the Message," **p. 87**.

4. The Subject box automatically contains the Web page's URL. You can change the contents of this box if you want to.

5. The notes box is empty. You can enter text there to explain why you're sending the Web page.

6. Choose Send in the Message form's Standard toolbar to send the message.

But why send the complete page? Instead, just send a link to that page. By doing so, you send a much smaller message.

To send a link to a Web page, use the previous procedure with the exception that, in step 2, you must choose File, move the pointer onto Send, and choose Link By Email.

After you've finished using Internet Explorer, choose File, Close to return to Outlook.

ACCESSING FAVORITE WEB PAGES

If you have been browsing Web pages for a while, you're undoubtedly familiar with making those pages you visit frequently readily accessible by adding them to your list of favorites. In Internet Explorer, you can select a favorite to open it immediately without having to enter its URL.

You can also go directly to a favorite Web page from within Outlook. One way to do this is to open the Other Shortcuts section of the Outlook Bar and choose Favorites to see a list of shortcuts to your favorite Web pages. You can select any shortcut to start Internet Explorer and open the page associated with the shortcut. You see the Web page in the Outlook Information viewer.

Alternatively, with any Outlook Information viewer displayed, choose Favorites in the menu bar to display a list of favorites. You can select any name from the list to start Internet Explorer and open a Web page.

You can also add a shortcut to a Web page on the Outlook Bar.

→ To learn more about placing shortcuts to a Web page or a local HTML page on the Outlook Bar, **see** "Creating a Shortcut to a Web Page," **p. 811**.

PARTICIPATING IN NEWSGROUPS

You can easily participate in Internet newsgroups from within Outlook. Outlook uses Outlook Express, a component of Internet Explorer, to provide access to newsgroups.

Tip #54 from

Gordon Crooks

Outlook Express, a component of Internet Explorer, which, in turn, is a component of Windows, provides capabilities to send and receive Internet e-mail and to participate in Internet Newsgroups. If you're using Outlook, you should be using that to send and receive all your e-mail so all your messages are saved in one place. This chapter deals only with using Outlook Express to participate in newsgroups.

If you already have an Internet account with an ISP and have set up Internet Explorer to use that account, Outlook Express automatically uses the same account. From within Outlook Express, you can choose a different Internet account, though it's unlikely you would want to do that.

To participate in Internet newsgroups:

1. With any Outlook Information viewer displayed, choose <u>V</u>iew, move the pointer onto <u>G</u>o To, and choose New<u>s</u> to display Outlook Express, as shown in Figure 8.3.

Figure 8.3
You can use Outlook Express to send and receive e-mail messages as well as to participate in newsgroups.

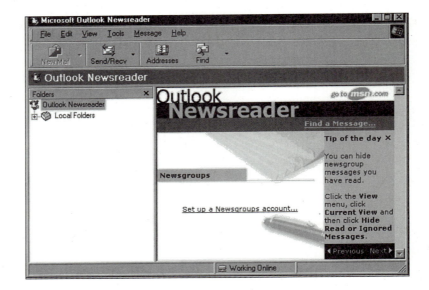

> **Note**
>
> If your computer is already connected to the Internet, you'll immediately see the window shown in Figure 8.3. If your computer is not connected to the Internet, it will attempt to connect and, after establishing a connection, display that window.

2. Choose Tools, Accounts to display the Internet Accounts dialog box and select the News tab. Outlook Express displays a list of your news accounts, such as the one shown in Figure 8.4.

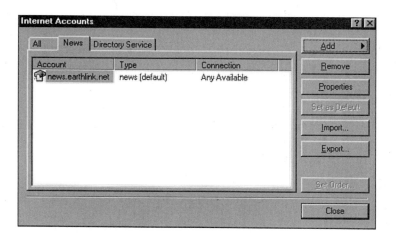

Figure 8.4
If you already have several accounts, one of them is marked as the default.

3. To add a news account, choose Add, News to open the Internet Connection Wizard, shown in Figure 8.5.

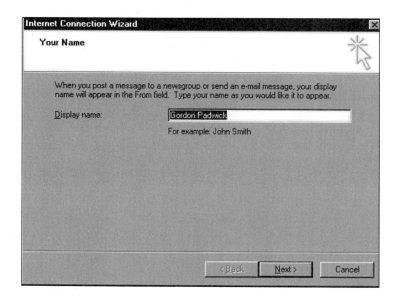

Figure 8.5
This wizard window displays the name you provided when you installed Office as your display name.

4. If you want messages you post on a newsgroup to have a different name, replace the displayed name with that name. Choose <u>N</u>ext > to display the next wizard window, shown in Figure 8.6.

Figure 8.6
This wizard window contains your e-mail address.

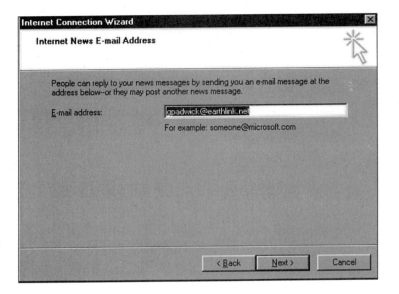

5. When people read messages you post on a newsgroup, they can reply by way of the newsgroup or by sending you an e-mail message. If you want people to use an e-mail address that's different from the one displayed in this window, enter the address you want people to use. Choose <u>N</u>ext > to display the next wizard window, such as that shown in Figure 8.7.

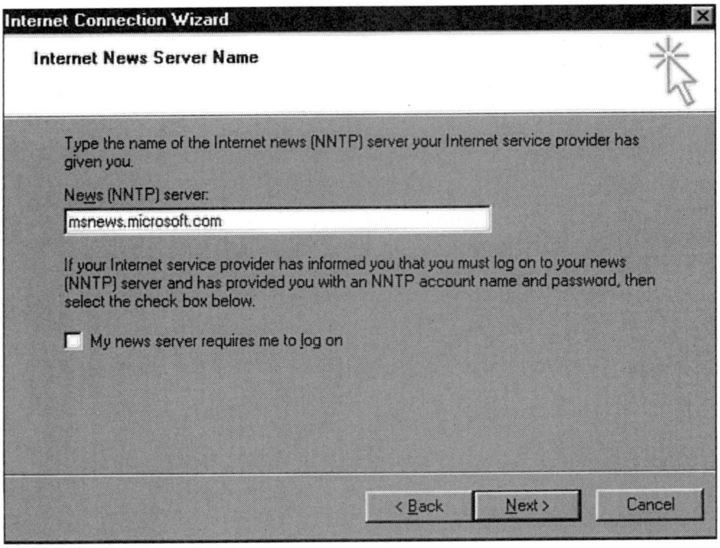

Figure 8.7
Use this window to iden-
tify the news server you
want to access. In this
example, the Microsoft
news server is identified.

6. Enter the name of the news server you want to use (such as msnews.microsoft.com) into the News (NNTP) Server box. If you're identifying a private news server that requires people to provide a name and password, check the My News Server Requires Me to Log On box. Choose Next > to display a window, the final wizard window. Choose Finish to close that window and return to the Internet Accounts dialog box that includes the new news server in the list of servers. Choose Close to close the Internet Accounts dialog box and return to the Outlook Express window previously shown in Figure 8.2.

You can use the buttons at the right side of the Internet Accounts dialog box to manage your news server accounts:

- Add—Choose this button to add a new account.
- Remove—Select an account, then choose this button to remove an account from the list.
- Properties—Select an account, then choose this button to inspect and possibly change an account's properties.
- Set as Default—Select an account, then choose this button to make that account your default account.
- Import—Import a news account from a file.
- Export—Export a news account to a file.

For more detailed information about setting up and maintaining news accounts, refer to a book about Internet Explorer, such as *Special Edition Using Microsoft Internet Explorer 4*, published by Que.

After you've set up news accounts, you can access any of the newsgroups available on those accounts. Some news servers, particularly those provided by ISPs, provide access to thousands of newsgroups. In order to easily access newsgroups you frequently use, you can subscribe to them. After you subscribe to certain newsgroups, Outlook Express makes it easy to go to those newsgroups.

Tip #55 from

Gordon Padwick

You don't have to subscribe to a newsgroup to have access to it. Subscribing merely makes it easy for you to return to newsgroups.

To subscribe to newsgroups:

1. In Outlook, choose <u>V</u>iew, move the pointer onto <u>G</u>o To, and choose New<u>s</u> to display the Outlook Express Window, shown previously in Figure 8.2.

2. In the top-left pane, select the news server that provides access to the newsgroups to which you want to subscribe. If you haven't previously accessed that news server, Outlook Express displays a message saying that you are not subscribed to any newsgroups and asking if you would like to see a list of newsgroups. Choose <u>Y</u>es. Outlook downloads a list of available newsgroups. Depending on the number of newsgroups available on the server, downloading may take several minutes. Eventually, you see the beginning of a list of newsgroups, such as that shown in Figure 8.8.

Figure 8.8
This is the beginning of a list of newsgroups available on the Microsoft news server.

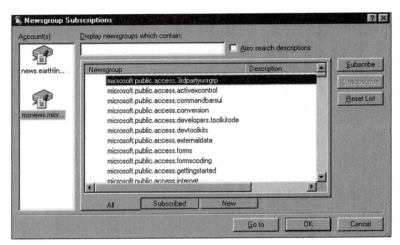

Tip #56 from

Instead of downloading the entire list of newsgroups available on a news server, you can download only those whose names contain a certain word. For example, if you want to see which newsgroups have "Outlook" in their names, enter "Outlook" in the Dis<u>p</u>lay Newsgroups Which Contain box before you start the download.

---

3. After you've downloaded a list of newsgroups, scroll down the list until you find the first one to which you want to subscribe. Select that newsgroup, then choose <u>S</u>ubscribe. An icon at the left of the newsgroup name indicates you've subscribed to it.

Tip #57 from

To cancel your subscription to a newsgroup, select that newsgroup and then choose <u>U</u>nsubscribe.

After you've subscribed to newsgroups, those newsgroups are listed in the Folders pane in the Outlook Express window, as shown in Figure 8.9.

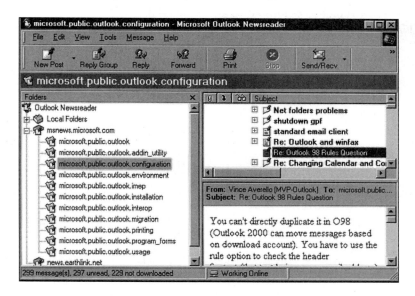

Figure 8.9
The Folders pane contains a list of the newsgroups to which you've subscribed.

Now you can use Outlook Express to participate in newsgroups. To access a newsgroup, select that newsgroup in the Folders pane. After a few seconds delay, you'll see a list of message headers in the top-right pane. You can select any message header to see the complete message in the bottom-right pane.

With a message selected, you can choose these toolbar buttons:

- New Post to create a message you want to send to the newsgroup
- Reply Group to make your reply available to all newsgroup participants
- Reply to send your reply as e-mail to the person who posted the original message
- Forward to forward the selected message as e-mail to someone
- Print to print the selected message
- Stop to stop sending and receiving messages
- Send/Receive to send messages waiting to be sent and to receive messages waiting for you

To create your own message, choose New Post in the toolbar. Outlook Express displays a Message form similar to the Outlook Message form. Enter your message and then choose Send in the toolbar to post your message on the newsgroup.

Tip #58 from

Gordon Cook

Instead of choosing Send/Receive, you can choose the small button marked with a triangle at the right of Send/Receive. That displays a menu from which you can choose Send and Receive All, Receive All, or Send All.

PARTICIPATING IN ONLINE MEETINGS

Two other Internet facilities available to you are NetMeeting and NetShow. Although you can use NetMeeting and NetShow from within Outlook, these are separate applications that come with Internet Explorer.

USING NETMEETING

NetMeeting allows any number of people to participate in a meeting without being physically present. The meeting participants are connected to each other by way of the Internet or an intranet. During the meeting, participants can exchange information in various ways:

- Talking with other people. To use this, participants' computers must have a sound card installed and a headset with earphones and a microphone.

- Sending typed messages to other people. The text each person enters is displayed on all the other participants' screens.

- Using video to see other people and to let other people see you. To use this component, each participant's computer must have a video camera installed.

- Cooperating with other people while working with word processing, spreadsheets, and other documents.

- Sharing applications and files with other people. When you share an application that's installed on your computer, meeting participants can use that application even though they don't have it installed on their computers.

- Drawing on a shared whiteboard using drawing tools that are similar to those in Microsoft Paint. Each participant can see what the others draw.

Although all this is possible, it's hardly practical unless all participants have high-speed, bi-directional Internet access such as is available by way of an ISDN, T1 line, or other high-speed connection. You can use a modem to get a feel for how NetMeeting works, but not for real-world meetings.

Tip #59 from

Gordon Cook

If you plan to use NetMeeting's audio capabilities, you should have a headset that has earphones and a microphone. Although you can use loudspeakers and a separate microphone, this setup causes feedback problems (unless the microphone is highly directional); the microphone picks up sound from the loudspeakers, resulting in a loud howling sound.

Although you can access NetMeeting from within Outlook, it's really a separate application that's not a part of the Office suite. If you ever need to remove Office from your computer, you have to remove NetMeeting separately.

SETTING UP NETMEETING

The first step in preparing to use NetMeeting is to go through the steps in the NetMeeting Wizard. These steps provide your identification (so that meeting participants can see who you are) and also adjust the audio levels.

Because NetMeeting uses audio, make sure your computer's audio setup is working correctly before you start the NetMeeting Wizard.

Note

Windows 95, Windows 98, and Windows NT have audio capabilities, but the details are different. The sound card in your computer is controlled by drivers, normally provided by the sound card's manufacturer. There's no way that this book can deal with all the possibilities. For information about setting up your sound card so that it can work with NetMeeting, refer to the information provided with your sound card or available on the manufacturer's Web site. You can also find some information in the Microsoft Knowledge Base and in the Windows 95, Windows 98, and Windows NT Resource Kits, published by Microsoft.

To set up NetMeeting:

1. With any Outlook Information viewer displayed, choose <u>V</u>iew, move the pointer onto <u>G</u>o To, and choose Internet Ca<u>l</u>l to display the first Microsoft NetMeeting Wizard window, shown in Figure 8.10.

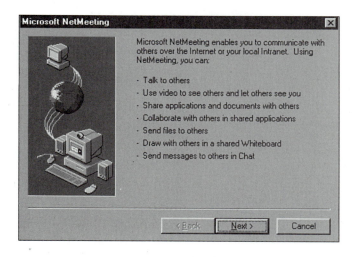

Figure 8.10
This window summarizes NetMeeting's capabilities.

Note

The NetMeeting Wizard appears the first time you choose Internet Call after installing Office. When you subsequently choose Internet Call, the NetMeeting dialog box, shown in Figure 8.18 later in this chapter, is displayed.

2. Choose <u>N</u>ext > to display the wizard window shown in Figure 8.11.

Figure 8.11
Select the directory server you want to use in this wizard window.

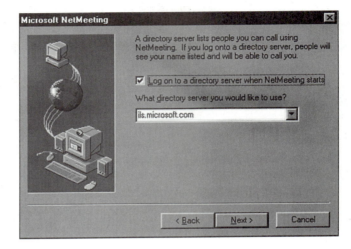

3. Open the drop-down list of directory servers and select one of them. Leave <u>L</u>og on to a Directory Server when NetMeeting Starts checked. Choose <u>N</u>ext > to display the next wizard window, shown in Figure 8.12.

Figure 8.12
Enter information about yourself in this wizard window. The information you supply in this window is available to NetMeeting participants.

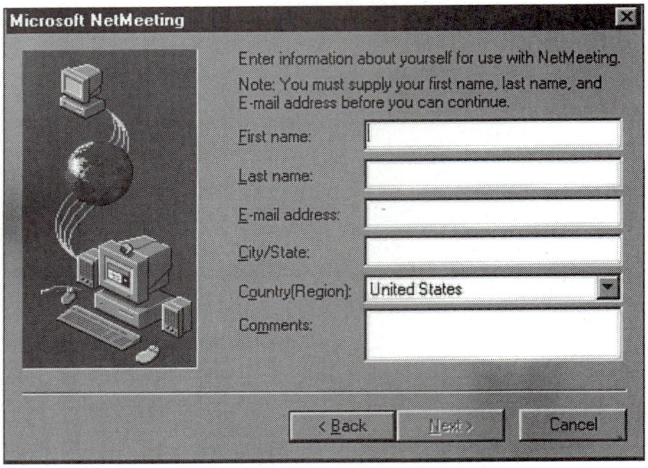

4. Enter your first name, last name, and e-mail address in the first three boxes. You can also, but don't have to, enter the name of your city or state, and also enter whatever is appropriate in the Comments box. You must select a country or region in the drop-down Country(Region) list. Choose Next > to display the next wizard window, shown in Figure 8.13.

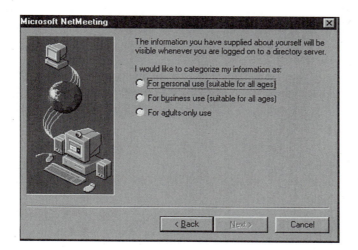

Figure 8.13
Select a category for the personal information you previously supplied.

5. Select one of the three information categories, then choose Next > to display the next wizard window, shown in Figure 8.14.

Note

The Next > button is disabled when this window first appears. The button becomes enabled when you select an information category.

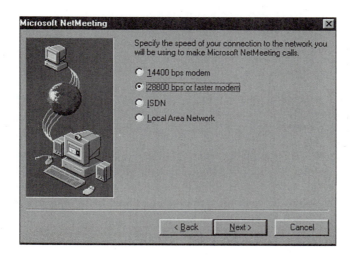

Figure 8.14
Select the type of network connection you use.

6. Select one of the four types of network connections you use, then choose <u>N</u>ext > to display the next wizard window, shown in Figure 8.15.

NetMeeting automatically adjusts itself to provide the optimum performance available according to the type of network connection you specify.

Figure 8.15
Follow the instructions in
this wizard window.

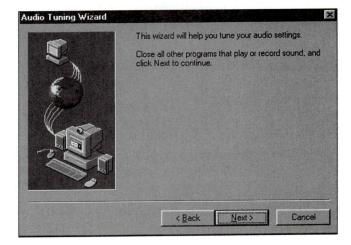

7. Choose <u>N</u>ext > to display the next wizard window, shown in Figure 8.16.

Figure 8.16
Use this wizard window
to adjust the loudness of
the sound you hear.

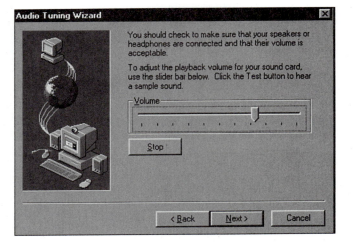

8. Choose <u>T</u>est. You should hear sound in your earphones (the label in the Test button changes to Stop). Adjust the <u>V</u>olume slider until the sound is at a comfortable level, then choose <u>S</u>top. Choose <u>N</u>ext > to display the next wizard window, shown in Figure 8.17.

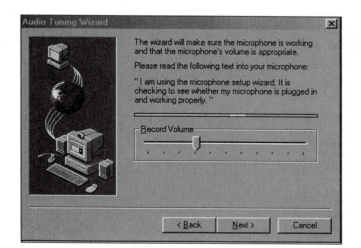

Figure 8.17
Use this wizard window to adjust your micro-phone's sensitivity.

9. With your headset's microphone in its normal position (normally within two to three inches of your mouth), speak the text shown in the window at your normal voice level. As you speak, the shallow bar above <u>R</u>ecord Volume shows green, yellow, and red seg-ments. The wizard automatically adjusts the microphone sensitivity so that the level of your speech is within an acceptable range.

Tip #60 from

Gordon Crook

If, while you speak, you don't see anything in the shallow bar above Record Volume, drag the <u>R</u>ecord Volume slider all the way to the right (for maximum sensitivity), and try again. If you still don't see anything in the shallow bar, that means your microphone isn't work-ing. Check to make sure your microphone is plugged into your computer and, if the micro-phone has an on/off switch, that it's turned on. If it still doesn't work, that means you have problems with your computer's audio system, a subject that's beyond the scope of this book.

If you drag the slider all the way to the right and then start speaking, you'll probably see the shallow bar completely filled. While you continue speaking, the slider automatically moves to the left until it reaches the optimum position.

The automatic adjustment of microphone level works only from high sensitivity downward. If you set the sensitivity too low, the slider doesn't move to the right to increase sensitivity.

Later, while you're using NetMeeting, if people complain about your microphone's level, you can return to this window and drag the slider to adjust your microphone sensitivity.

After you've adjusted your microphone sensitivity, choose <u>N</u>ext > to display the final wizard window. This window confirms that you have completed setting up NetMeeting. Choose <u>F</u>inish to close the wizard and display the NetMeeting window shown in Figure 8.18.

Tip #61 from

After you've initially set up NetMeeting, as described in the preceding pages, you can make changes. To do so, display the NetMeeting window shown in Figure 8.18, then choose Tools, Options to display the Options dialog box. You can select the six tabs in that dialog box to examine and change NetMeeting's options.

STARTING A MEETING

To start using NetMeeting from within Outlook, display any Outlook Information viewer, then choose <u>V</u>iew, move the pointer onto <u>G</u>o To, and choose Internet Ca<u>l</u>l to display the window shown in Figure 8.18.

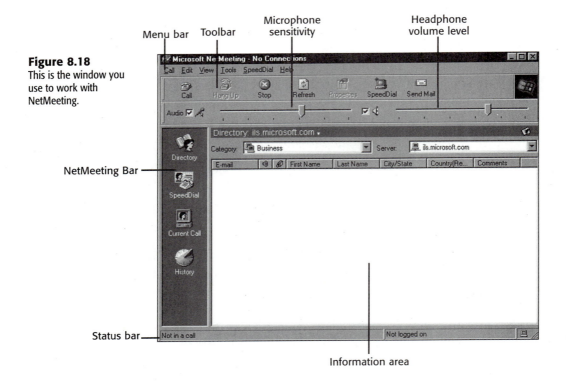

Figure 8.18
This is the window you use to work with NetMeeting.

Menu bar   Toolbar   Microphone sensitivity   Headphone volume level

NetMeeting Bar

Status bar

Information area

If you know the e-mail address of the person with whom you want to have a meeting, the easiest way to start the meeting is to call the person. To do so, choose Call on the NetMeeting toolbar to display the dialog box shown in Figure 8.19.

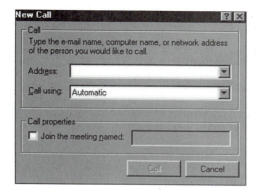

Figure 8.19
Use this dialog box to initiate a meeting.

To start a meeting with a specific person:

1. Enter the person's e-mail address into the Address box. Alternatively, if you have previously called the person, open the drop-down Address list and select the person's address.

2. Leave Call Using at the default Automatic selection.

3. If you want to give the meeting a name, check Join the Meeting Named, and enter a name in the adjacent text box.

Tip #62 from

Gordon Padwick

Providing a name for a meeting makes it easy for other people to request to be admitted to the meeting.

---

4. Choose Call. If you are not already logged on to the Internet, the Dial-up Connection dialog box is displayed and you can use it to connect. When you have a connection to the Internet, NetMeeting sends a request to the person to join the meeting.

If the person with whom you're attempting to establish a meeting can't be located or doesn't have NetMeeting available, you see a message similar to that shown in Figure 8.20.

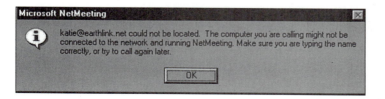

Figure 8.20
You see a message like this if the person you're calling can't be found.

The person you're calling can respond by choosing <u>A</u>ccept, in which case the meeting starts, or Ignore, in which case your computer displays a message informing you that the person has rejected your call.

Another possibility is that the person you're calling is already using NetMeeting to participate in a meeting. In that case, your computer displays a message to that effect. You may be invited into that meeting and can, if you like, accept the invitation.

While you're participating in a meeting, the NetMeeting window contains the Current Call Information viewer, such as that shown in Figure 8.21.

Figure 8.21
The Current Call Information viewer displays the names of people participating in the meeting with information about their capabilities.

Participant's name —

Audio available —

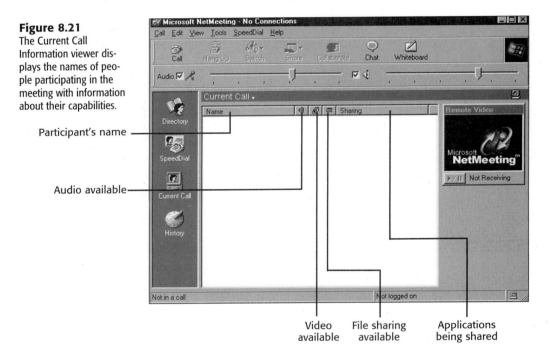

Video available   File sharing available   Applications being shared

Once you have a meeting started, you can use NetMeeting's capabilities to share information. This is fairly intuitive, so this book doesn't go into details about that. You can find detailed information in books about Internet Explorer, such as *Special Edition Using Microsoft Internet Explorer 4*, published by Que.

The preceding pages are based on the assumption that you know how to contact the person with whom you want to have a meeting. Another way to use NetMeeting to have an electronic meeting with other people is to use an *Internet Locator Server* (ILS) directory.

Internet Locator Servers are servers maintained by Microsoft and some other organizations that maintain lists of people who allow their names to be available. To see a list of publicly available ILS directories, display NetMeeting's Directories Information viewer, then open the drop-down Server list box and select one of the available directories. After a few seconds delay, you'll see the beginning of a list such as that shown in Figure 8.22.

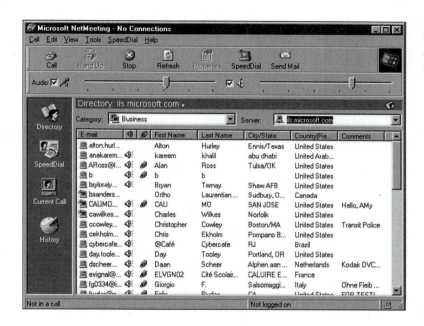

Figure 8.22
You can scroll through this list to see all the available names.

A red asterisk superimposed on the computer symbol in the left column of the list indicates that the person is currently participating in a meeting.

Each ILS directory maintains several categories of names. To see the names available in a specific category, open the drop-down Category list box and select a category. After you've selected a category, only names in that category are listed.

Tip #63 from	Each time you select a category or an ILS directory, the displayed list of names is regenerated.
Gordon Padwick	You can sort the list according to the information in any column by clicking the column title.

To establish a meeting with one of the listed people, select that person's name, then choose Call in the NetMeeting toolbar to display the New Call dialog box with the person's address displayed. Choose Call to attempt to start a meeting.

SCHEDULING A NETMEETING

If you've tried to initiate a NetMeeting either by calling a person directly or by selecting a name in an ILS directory, as described in the previous section, you probably weren't successful. The reason for that is that the people you called were probably not expecting to be invited to join a meeting and so they didn't have NetMeeting running. One way around that problem is to schedule a meeting ahead of time.

Tip #64 from

For scheduling to work correctly, it's imperative that all meeting participants have the time and time zone correctly set on their computers.

To schedule a NetMeeting:

1. With Outlook's Calendar Information viewer displayed, choose <u>A</u>ctions, New Meeting Request to display the Meeting form shown in Figure 8.23.

Figure 8.23
This is the form that's most often used to create an Outlook Appointment item.

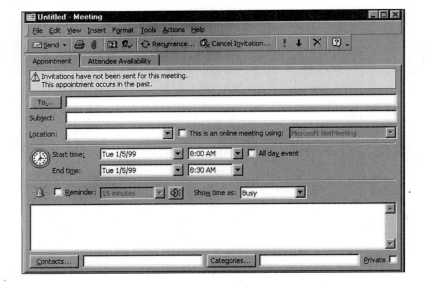

➜ For detailed information about entering information in the Meeting form, **see** "Inviting People to Meetings," **p. 400**.

2. Enter the e-mail addresses of the people with whom you want to have a NetMeeting in the To box.

➜ To learn more about entering e-mail addresses in the To box, **see** "Addressing the Message," **p. 87**.

3. Enter a name for the NetMeeting in the Subject box.

4. Check This Is an Online Meeting Using. As soon as you do so, the Meeting form changes to that shown in Figure 8.24.

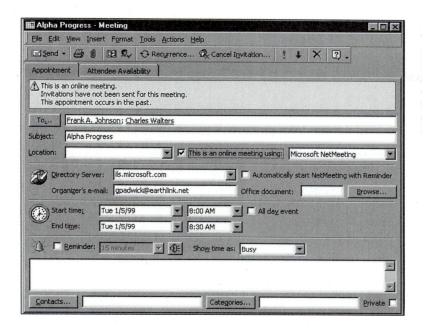

Figure 8.24
This version of the Meeting form provides boxes for NetMeeting-specific information. By default, the box at the right of This Is an Online Meeting Using contains Microsoft NetMeeting.

5. Open the drop-down Directory Server list and select the directory server that will host the meeting.

6. If you want a document to be available to participants when the NetMeeting starts, enter the full path name of that document into the Office Document box.

7. Enter a date and time for the meeting to start in the Start Time boxes.

8. Enter a date and time for the meeting to end in the End Time boxes.

9. If you want to be automatically connected to the NetMeeting a few minutes before the meeting is scheduled to start, choose Reminder to check that box, open the adjacent drop-down list and select the number of minutes prior to the meeting, and check Automatically Start NetMeeting with Reminder.

10. Choose Send in the form's Standard toolbar to send messages to people asking them to participate in the meeting.

The meeting request you create in this way is sent by e-mail to the people you want to participate in the NetMeeting. Those people receive messages in their inboxes and they can reply to those messages.

→ Asking people to attend a NetMeeting is much the same as asking people to attend a face-to-face meeting. **See** "Inviting People to Meetings," **p. 400**.

Having sent requests for people to participate in a NetMeeting, and having received responses from them, everyone is ready at the appointed time, so there should be no problem in establishing the necessary connections.

Although you will normally schedule a NetMeeting so participants can prepare for it, you can immediately start a NetMeeting.

STARTING REGULAR NETMEETINGS

If you have regular meetings with the same people, you might find it convenient to add information about setting up a NetMeeting to the other information you have about those people in your Outlook Contacts folder.

To add NetMeeting information for a contact:

1. Choose Contacts in the Outlook Bar to display the Contacts Information viewer.
2. Double-click the name of the contact with whom you want to have the NetMeeting to display information about that contact in a Contact form.

→ For information about adding contacts to your Contacts folder, **see** "Creating a Contact Item," **p.301**.

3. Select the Contact form's Details tab, shown in Figure 8.25.

Figure 8.25
Use the Online NetMeeting Settings section to define how you want a NetMeeting to be configured.

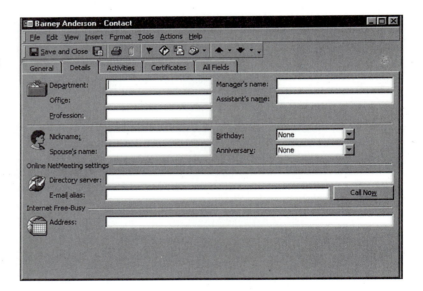

4. Enter the name of the Internet Locator Server you want to use in the Directory Server box.

Tip #65 from

Gordon Padwick

If you intend to use the Internet for your NetMeeting, you'll probably choose a public Internet Locator Server; if you plan to use an intranet, choose a private one.

5. Enter the contact's e-mail address in the E-mail Alias box.

6. Choose Save and Close in the form's toolbar to save the information.

Subsequently, to start a NetMeeting with the contact, select the contact, select the Details tab, and choose Call Now. Alternatively, with the contact's information displayed in a Contact form, choose Actions, Call Using NetMeeting.

USING NETSHOW

NetShow allows one person to give a presentation that other people can see at remote locations. The presentation, which can contain audio and video, is sent from a Web server by way of the Internet to one or more Web clients, such as Internet Explorer.

→ Scheduling a NetShow is very similar to scheduling a NetMeeting. **See** "Scheduling a NetMeeting," **p. 290**.

In the form shown previously in Figure 8.24, check This Is an Online Meeting Using, then open the adjoining drop-down list and select NetShow Services. Complete the remainder of the form in the same way you schedule a NetMeeting and then send the invitation to receive the NetShow.

When you receive an invitation to view a NetShow and respond by accepting the invitation, Outlook places an item in your calendar. A few minutes before the NetShow is scheduled, double-click the Calendar item to open it in an Appointment form. In that form, choose Actions, View NetShow to connect to the server and view the show.

As an alternative to manually joining the NetShow, you can check Reminder in the Appointment form, and select a *reminder* for a few minutes before the show is scheduled to begin. After you've done that, Outlook automatically connects you to the show at the appointed time.

Tip #66 from

It's imperative that you and the person who is giving the show have the time set correctly on your computers and also have selected the correct time zone.

GETTING HELP FOR INTERNET EXPLORER

This book is, of course, primarily about Outlook. Although the book includes information about accessing the Internet from within Outlook, by using components of Internet Explorer, there isn't space to cover this subject in detail. If you have problems accessing Web pages or participating in newsgroups, you should consult a book about Internet Explorer, such as *Special Edition Using Microsoft Internet Explorer 4*, published by Que.

You can also use a *text editor* such as Windows Notepad to open the text file IE.txt where you'll find information about installing and running Internet Explorer.

PART **III**

USING OUTLOOK AS A PERSONAL INFORMATION MANAGER

CHAPTER 9

MANAGING CONTACTS

by Gordon Padwick

In this chapter

WHAT ARE CONTACTS?

A *contact* in Outlook is a person or an organization. Outlook can save information about contacts in various places, as described in this chapter. Typically, Outlook saves such information as a contact's name, address, phone and fax number, and e-mail address. But Outlook can save much more information than this, including a contact's photograph.

Outlook uses contacts for various purposes:

- Addressing e-mail messages
- Addressing conventional mail
- Placing phone calls
- Sending faxes
- Arranging meetings
- Assigning tasks

Because so much of what you do with Outlook involves contacts, an understanding of how Outlook deals with contacts is crucial to your efficient use of Outlook.

WHERE OUTLOOK SAVES CONTACT INFORMATION

Outlook saves the information about each contact, a person or an organization, as a *Contact item*. Each Contact item contains many fields of information, only a few of which you use for most contacts.

Outlook saves Contact items in the *Outlook Address Book* that provides access to information in the Contacts folder within your Personal Folders file or, if you're using C/W Outlook as a client for Exchange, in the Contacts folder within your Exchange store; you can choose one or the other. In addition, C/W Outlook can access information about contacts stored in your *Personal Address Book* (PAB), in a *Global Address Book* (GAB), or other address book maintained by Exchange.

The first part of this chapter covers using the Outlook Address Book. Later parts of this chapter cover the additional capabilities in C/W Outlook.

PREPARING TO SAVE CONTACTS

If you're working with C/W Outlook and intend to save Contact items in a *Personal Folders file* on your computer, you must have a profile that contains the Personal Folders information service. This isn't necessary if you're using IMO Outlook.

Also in C/W Outlook, if you intend to use items in your Contacts folder as an address book, you must add the Outlook Address Book information service to your profile.

To add the Outlook Address Book information service:

1. Choose <u>T</u>ools, Ser<u>v</u>ices to display the Services dialog box.

2. Choose A<u>d</u>d to display the Add Service to Profile dialog box.

3. Select Outlook Address Book and choose OK. Outlook displays a message telling you that the new service won't be available until you exit and restart Outlook. Choose OK to return to the Services dialog box and choose OK to close that dialog box.

4. Choose <u>F</u>ile, Exit and <u>L</u>og Off to exit from Outlook. Then restart Outlook.

5. Choose <u>V</u>iew, Fold<u>e</u>r List to display your list of folders.

6. Right-click Contacts to display its context menu and choose Proper<u>t</u>ies to display the Contacts Properties dialog box. Select the Outlook Address Book tab shown in Figure 9.1.

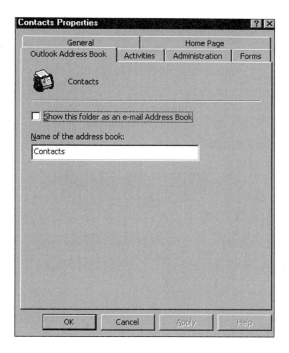

Figure 9.1
This dialog box has two additional tabs if you have the Exchange Server information service in your profile.

7. Make sure the <u>S</u>how This Folder as an E-mail Address Book box is checked.

8. Outlook proposes to call this address book Contacts. You can replace that name with another name. Choose OK to close the dialog box.

Having made sure your Contacts folder is designated as an address book, you can select your contacts as e-mail and fax recipients.

USING MULTIPLE CONTACTS FOLDERS

Most people use just one Contacts folder to hold all their Contact items. You can, if you want, create additional Contacts folders in IMO and C/W Outlook. You might, for example, want to have one Contacts folder for your business contacts and another for your personal contacts. I don't advise that though, due to the problem that arises when a person is both a business and a personal contact.

Note

You can create additional Contacts folder within an existing Personal Folders file, as described here. You can also create one or more additional Personal Folders files and place new Contacts folders in them. Refer to Chapter 37 for information creating Personal Folders files.

→ To learn more about creating Outlook folders and subfolders, **see** "Creating Folders and Subfolders, " **p. 922**.

To create an additional Contacts folder within your Personal Folders file:

1. With any Outlook Information viewer displayed, choose <u>F</u>ile, move the pointer onto Folder, and choose Fold<u>e</u>r to display the dialog box shown in Figure 9.2.

Figure 9.2
Use this dialog box to create a new Outlook folder.

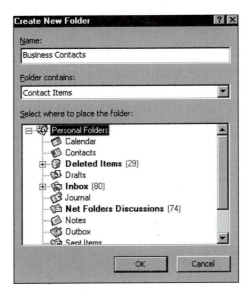

2. Enter a name for the new folder in the <u>N</u>ame box. The name you enter must not be the same as that of a folder that already exists.

3. Open the drop-down <u>F</u>older Contains list and select Contact Items.

4. In the Select Where to Place the Folder box. For example, if you want the new folder to be in your Personal Folders file, at the same level as the existing folder, select Personal Folders; if you want the new folder to be under an existing folder, such as your Contacts folder, select that folder.

5. Choose OK. Outlook asks if you want to create a shortcut to the new folder in the Outlook Bar. Choose Yes or No as you prefer.

After completing these steps, you can choose View, Folder List to see the new folder in your folder list.

PART

III

CH

9

Note

You can use any number of Contact folders as address books for addressing e-mail and faxes. You must designate one Contact folder as the default in which Outlook saves information about new contacts.

CREATING A CONTACT ITEM

You can use Outlook to save as much or little information about your contacts (people and organizations) as you like.

SELECTING CONTACT OPTIONS

Outlook offers several ways in which you can name Contact items and also how your Contact items are displayed in lists.

When you open a list of Contact items for such purposes as addressing e-mail, Outlook lists those items in alphabetical order by contacts' first name, middle name, and last name. You can change that so that contacts are listed by last name and then first name. After you've changed the listing order, that change affects only new Contact items you subsequently create; it doesn't affect the way existing items are listed.

Tip #67 from

Gordon Padwick

The effect of choosing the option that lists contacts by last name and then first name is to control what happens when you create a new Contact item. The contact's first name is placed in the lastname field, and the contact's last name is placed in the firstname field. I don't recommend selecting this option.

When you create Contact items you can choose a "File As" name by which Outlook lists items in the Contacts Information viewer when a Card view is selected. Outlook constructs the "File As" name for a person from various combinations of that person's name and company. You can choose a default combination and then, when you create a new Contact item, Outlook proposes to use that combination but, on an item by item basis, you can choose an alternative combination. "File As" names are covered in more detail later in this chapter.

→ **See** "Selecting a File As Name," **p. 305**.

To control how Outlook names and lists Contact items:

1. With any Outlook Information viewer displayed, choose <u>T</u>ools, <u>O</u>ptions and, with the Preferences tab selected, choose Contact <u>O</u>ptions to display the dialog box shown in Figure 9.3.

Figure 9.3
Use this dialog box to select how you want Contact items to be named and filed.

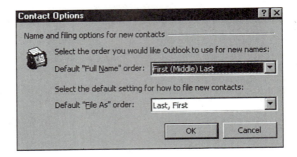

2. Open the Default "Full <u>N</u>ame" Order drop-down list and select the order you want to use.
3. Open the Default "<u>F</u>ile As" Order drop-down list and select the order you want to use.

STARTING TO CREATE A CONTACT ITEM

Start by displaying the Contact form in which you enter information about a contact.

To open the Contact form:

1. Choose Contacts in the Outlook Bar to display the Contacts Information viewer.
2. Choose <u>N</u>ew in the Standard toolbar or choose Actio<u>n</u>s, <u>N</u>ew Contact to display the Contact form shown in Figure 9.4.

Note

The Contact form is shown here as displayed by C/W Outlook. In IMO Outlook, the Contact form contains a check box labeled Send Using Plain Te<u>x</u>t immediately below the E-mail box. You can check this box if you always want to send messages to a specific contact using the *Plain Text format (page 183)*.

The General tab is where you enter most of the information about a contact.

Note

In addition to the General tab, the Details and All Fields tabs are sometimes used when creating a Contact item.

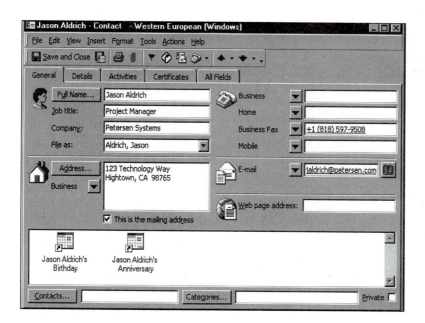

Figure 9.4
The Contact form opens with the General tab selected. The form is shown here with typical information entered.

ENTERING A CONTACT'S NAME, JOB TITLE, AND COMPANY

Note

An apology from the author: The information in this section (and throughout the book) is based on English usage. I've not had the opportunity to work with the versions of Windows and Outlook available from Microsoft for other languages. If some of the information I provide is not accurate for the language version of the product you're using, please accept my apologies.

If the contact is a person, enter that person's name in the Full Name box. If the contact is an organization, leave this box empty.

Note

Some contact-related Outlook functions, such as phone call logging, aren't available if a contact name isn't provided.

Here are some examples of how you might enter a person's name:

- Jean Morrows
- John Seivers
- Bonnie Y. Carter
- C. Jason Smith
- Dr. Brian Humphrey
- Stephanie Green, PhD

In addition to entering a person's name in first, middle, last order, you can enter the last name, a comma, and then the first and middle names. For example, instead of Bonnie Y. Carter, you could enter Carter, Bonnie Y.

If a contact has a hyphenated last name, such as "Ron Smith-Caruthers," Outlook parses the name correctly. But, what if a contact has two last names that are not hyphenated? You can deal with this situation in two ways:

- Use the Check Full Name dialog box (described subsequently) and enter the two last names in the Last box
- Enter the name as "Smith Caruthers, Ron"

After you enter a name in any of these ways, Outlook parses the name into its components. To see these components, choose Full Name to display the Check Full Name dialog box shown in Figure 9.5. This dialog box shows how Outlook saves the name you entered.

Figure 9.5
Outlook saves the name you enter in five separate fields.

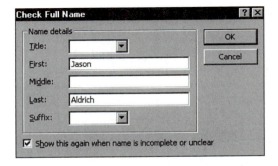

For information about setting an option that controls how Outlook separates the name you enter into the five separate fields shown in this figure, **see** "Contact Options," **p. 861**.

You don't have to check the name you enter in this way. Outlook almost always correctly parses the name into its components. However, if you've any doubt, you can do this to confirm that Outlook correctly understands the name you entered. With the Check Full Name dialog box displayed, you can edit the five individual components of a name.

Note

If Outlook doesn't understand the format of a name you enter into the Full Name box, it usually displays the Check Full Name dialog box automatically so that you can make any necessary changes. You can't rely on this happening all the time. Make sure Show This Again When Name Is Incomplete or Unclear is checked in the Check Full Name dialog box.

After you enter a name in the Full Name box, or leave that box empty if the contact is an organization, press Tab to move the insertion point into the Job Title box. If you entered a name in the Full Name box, that name replaces "Untitled" in the form's title bar. Also, the name appears a little lower on the form in the File As box with the family name first (if you enter Peter Smith in the Full Name box, the name appears as Smith, Peter in the File As box), unless you have changed "Save As" default, as described previously in this chapter.

→ To find out how you can control the way Outlook proposes to list a contact in the File As box, **see** "Selecting Contact Options," **p. 301**.

You don't have to enter anything into the Job Title box. If the contact is a person, enter that person's job title if appropriate, otherwise leave the box empty. Press Tab to move the insertion point into the Company box.

If the contact is an organization, and you left the Full Name box empty, you must provide an organization name. However, if the contact is a person, you can leave this box empty. If appropriate, enter the name of the contact company or organization in this box, then press Tab. If you've left the Full Name box empty, the name you enter in the Company box replaces "Untitled" in the form's title bar and also appears in the File As box.

SELECTING A FILE AS NAME

The File As name for a contact is the name by which contacts are normally alphabetized in the Contacts Information viewer.

As mentioned previously, Outlook suggests one File As name as soon as you enter a person's name in the Full Name box or an organization's name in the Company box. If you enter a person's name and an organization's name, Outlook creates several File As names from which you can select one.

After you entered a person's name and an organization name, Outlook proposes a File As name based on the selection you made in the Contact Options dialog box, as described previously in this chapter.

→ For information about how you can control the way Outlook proposes to list a contact in the File As box, **see** "Selecting Contact Options," **p.301**.

If you want to have a different File As name, open the drop-down File As list to see the File As names Outlook suggests, as shown in Figure 9.6.

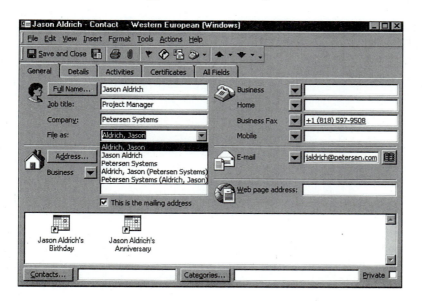

Figure 9.6
You can select any of the File As names Outlook proposes.

Instead of selecting one of the File As names Outlook proposes, you can enter any name you like (a nickname, for example) in the File As box.

Tip #68 from

Be consistent in your choice of File As names to make it easy to find contacts in the Contacts Information viewer. I suggest you choose the first format in the File As drop-down list for personal friends and the last format in the list for business contacts.

ENTERING PHONE AND FAX NUMBERS

Although the Contact form has only four boxes for phone and fax numbers (Business, Home, Business Fax, and Mobile) you can enter as many as 19 numbers for each contact. To see the available numbers, choose one of the buttons marked with a triangle between one of the phone labels and that label's text box. Outlook displays a list of phone and fax numbers, as shown in Figure 9.7.

Figure 9.7
These are the available phone and fax numbers. Those for which you have previously entered numbers are checked.

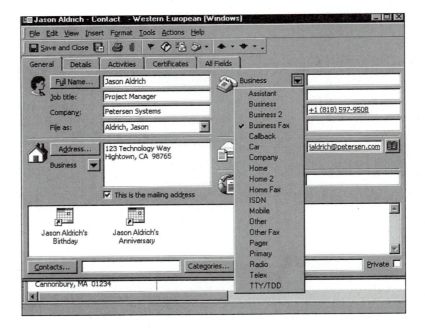

You can select any name in the list. After you do so, that name replaces the label displayed on the form. Although the form displays only four numbers at any one time, Outlook can save all 19 numbers.

Note

You can't change the labels Outlook provides for phone and fax numbers. Although you will rarely want to enter as many as 19 numbers for a contact, you might sometimes want to enter a number with a different label, for example, if a contact has three home phone numbers. In cases like that, you have to use one of the existing labels, such as "Other" for the third home phone.

To enter a phone or fax number:

1. If necessary, choose one of the buttons marked with a triangle between a label and a text box to display the list of phone and fax numbers, as previously shown in Figure 9.7. Select the type of phone number you want to enter.

2. With the insertion point in the appropriate text box, enter the phone or fax number, then press Tab. See the following notes about formatting phone and fax numbers.

Use the same steps to enter additional phone or fax numbers.

FORMATTING PHONE AND FAX NUMBERS

Here are some facts you need to know about phone and fax number formats. These facts are based on the assumption that you've set Regional Settings to English (United States) in the Windows Control Panel. There may be some differences if you're using a different Regional Setting.

- When entering a phone number, it's optional whether or not you group numbers by using spaces, hyphens, or parentheses. When you press Tab to signify you've finished entering the number, Outlook automatically formats the number according to the conventions of the Regional Settings you've selected in the Windows Control Panel.

- Always enter the complete phone number including, in North America, the area code (even if it's your local area code that you don't need to dial). If Dial-up Networking is set correctly in Windows, the local area code is ignored if it's not needed. By including the area code with the phone number, you can use your contact information when you're traveling or after your area code changes. If you omit an area code, Outlook automatically inserts your local area code.

- Don't enter a 1 before the area code. Dial-up Networking automatically inserts the 1 before area codes. However, if you do enter the 1, Outlook ignores it.

- Enter international phone numbers in the format

  +021(982)494-4321

  where 021 is the country code. The parentheses and the hyphen are optional.

- Outlook saves any text you enter after the phone number, but doesn't use that text when placing phone calls. You can, for example, append a contact's extension number after the phone number. When you place a call, the extension number is there for you to refer to. If you precede the extension number with an alphabetical character such as "x," the following numbers aren't dialed. Without the alphabetical characters, the numbers are dialed but most telephone systems ignore them.

When you enter a phone or fax number and press Tab, Outlook might, in North America, insert +1 in front of the number. As explained below, you can choose whether Outlook does this. Microsoft claims that preceding a phone number with +1 provides

- Better handling of 10-digit phone numbers
- Better parsing of international phone numbers
- Automatic validation of fax numbers

After you entered a phone or fax number and pressed Tab, you can double-click that number to display the dialog box shown in Figure 9.8. You can correct the number in that dialog box if necessary.

Figure 9.8
This dialog box shows how Outlook parses a telephone number you've entered.

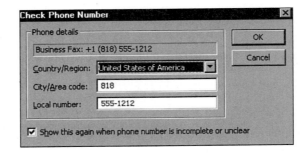

If Outlook does insert +1 before phone numbers and this seems to be giving you trouble, you can disable this functionality.

To disable the insertion of +1:

1. Display the Contacts Information viewer and select any contact.
2. Choose the Dial button 🕾 in the Standard toolbar to display the dialog box shown in Figure 9.9.

Figure 9.9
The New Call dialog box displays the name of the selected contact and one of that contact's phone numbers.

3. Choose Dialing Options (be careful not to choose Dialing Properties) to display the dialog box shown in Figure 9.10.

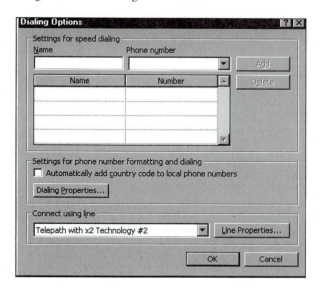

Figure 9.10
You can use this dialog box to set up speed dialing.

4. Uncheck the Automatically Add Country Code to Local Phone Numbers box. Choose OK and then Close to return to the Information viewer.

SOLVING PHONE NUMBER PROBLEMS

The preceding information covered most of what you need to know about phone numbers. In some cases, though, there's more to take care of. Microsoft has published several Knowledge Base articles that explain how to deal with some of these problems. You can probably also get help from your local telephone company.

Some regional phone companies in North America employ area code overlays that use two or more area codes for the same geographic area. If you live or work in such an area, you may have to dial an area code even if it's the same as your own. The Microsoft Knowledge Base article Q129049, *How to Perform 10-digit Dialing in Windows 95 and Windows NT*, describes three ways in which you can solve this problem.

Windows keeps a list of international telephone access codes in a file named Telephon.ini. From time to time, some countries change their access codes. When this happens, if you rely on Telephon.ini, you can add a CountryOverrides section to that file. The Microsoft Knowledge Base article Q142328, *How to Change International Dialing Access Codes* explains how to update the file and also contains an updated list of international access codes.

The best resource I've found for detailed information about how Outlook handles phone numbers is the article *Microsoft Outlook Phone Numbers* that's available on the Slipstick Web site. Go to

`http://www.slipstick.com/exchange/olphone.htm`

ENTERING POSTAL ADDRESSES

Outlook can save three postal addresses for each contact: Business, Home, and Other. These address labels are built into Outlook; you can't change them.

By default, Outlook expects you to enter a Business address. If you want to enter a different address, choose the button with the triangle icon just below Address to display the three address labels and select the one you want to use.

Entering a postal address is similar to entering a contact's name:

- You can enter the complete address in the large text box at the right of Address.
- You can choose Address to display the Check Address dialog box that contains separate boxes for each element of an address, as shown subsequently in Figure 9.11.

For straightforward home addresses you should normally enter the complete address in the large text box.

To enter an address:

1. Select Business, Home, or Other as appropriate.
2. Enter the street address on the first line and press Enter.
3. Enter the city name, a comma, the state or province abbreviation, and a space, and then the postal (ZIP) code. Press Enter.
4. If the address is for a country or region other than your own, enter the country or region name and press Enter.
5. Press Tab to signify that you've finished entering the address.

Tip #69 from

Gordon Padwick

If you need to save more than three postal addresses for a contact, you'll have to create two or more Contact items for that contact.

When you press Tab, Outlook attempts to parse the address into its components. If there's a problem, Outlook automatically displays the Check Address dialog box shown in Figure 9.11. If you want to confirm that Outlook has parsed the address correctly, choose Address to display the Check Address dialog box.

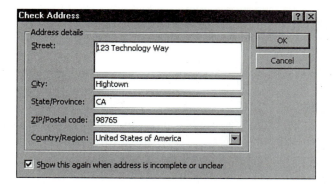

Figure 9.11
This dialog box displays the individual components of the address in separate boxes.

Notice that Outlook automatically provides the name of your own country or region, unless you entered a different one. The country or region name is derived from the Regional Setting in the Windows Control Panel.

If the text in any of the boxes is incorrect you can make corrections using normal editing techniques. Choose OK when you're satisfied with the address.

Tip #70 from

Leave the Show This Again when Address Is Incomplete or Unclear box checked. If you uncheck this box, Outlook won't display the Check Address dialog box when you enter what Outlook considers to be incomplete or unclear addresses.

To enter complex addresses, such as many business addresses, you're usually better off choosing Address and then entering the individual components of the address in the individual text boxes in the Check Address dialog box. You can enter as many lines of information as necessary in the Street box, but only one line of information in each of the other four boxes. You can open the Country/Region drop-down list and select a country or region; alternatively, you can enter a country or region name (either one that's in the drop-down list or one that isn't). After you've entered an address in this way, press OK to close the Check Address dialog box.

When you start entering the first address for a contact, Outlook automatically checks the This Is the Mailing Address box. If you don't want to mark that address as the mailing address, uncheck the box. Only one of the three postal addresses for each contact can be marked as the mailing address.

Note

The address marked as the mailing address is the one Outlook uses when you use Contact items to address letters. It's also the address that's displayed in the Contacts Information viewer with the Address Cards view selected.

ENTERING E-MAIL ADDRESSES

Outlook can save three e-mail addresses for each contact—identified as E-mail, E-mail 2, and E-mail 3. These labels are built into Outlook; you can't change them.

To enter the first e-mail address, place the insertion point in the E-mail box and then enter the address in the normal manner, such as:

■ For an Internet address: essmith@company.com

■ For an AOL address: essmith@aol.com

■ For a CompuServe address: 99999.999@compuserve.com or essmith@compuserve.com

If you already have an e-mail address in another Outlook address book, you can copy the address from there.

To copy an e-mail address:

1. Choose the button that has a book icon at the right of the E-mail box to display the Select Name dialog box.

2. Open the drop-down Show Names from The list and select the address book you want to use.

3. Select a name from the list and choose OK to close the Select Name dialog box. The E-mail box in the Contact form now contains the name you selected, underlined to indicate the name is a valid e-mail address.

After you've entered one e-mail address, you can choose the button with the triangle icon (at the left of the E-mail box) to open a drop-down list, choose E-mail 2 or E-mail 3, and enter another e-mail address.

Tip #71 from

If you need to save more than three e-mail addresses for a contact, you'll have to create two or more Contact items for that contact.

ENTERING A WEB PAGE ADDRESS

To enter a contact's Web Page address, place the insertion point in the Web Page Address box and enter the address, normally in the following format:

```
http://www.company.com
```

Tip #72 from

It's not necessary to enter "http://". If you omit those characters, Outlook provides them automatically when you press Tab to leave the box. You can also drag URLs from your favorites folder into the Web Page Address box.

INSERTING NOTES AND ATTACHMENTS

You can use the large, unnamed (notes) text box that occupies most of the lower part of the Contact form to enter miscellaneous notes about the contact. You can also choose Insert in the form's menu bar to insert a File, an Outlook Item, or an Object. Inserting attachments is quite similar to making insertions in mail messages.

Note

You can drag (or copy and paste) such things as graphics files, such as a photograph of a person, and Outlook items into the notes text box.

→ For information about attaching information to Contact items, **see** "Message Insertions," **p. 96** if you're using IMO Outlook, or **see** "Message Insertions," **p. 201** if you're using C/W Outlook.

ASSOCIATING A CONTACT WITH OTHER CONTACTS

The ability to associate a contact with other contacts is new in Outlook 2000. You will find this very useful in several circumstances:

- When you're creating Contact items for friends, you can associate each contact with others in the same family.
- When you're creating Contact items for business associates, you can associate each person with that person's supervisor and colleagues.

To associate a contact with other contacts:

1. In the Contacts form, choose Contacts to display the Select Contacts dialog box shown in Figure 9.12.

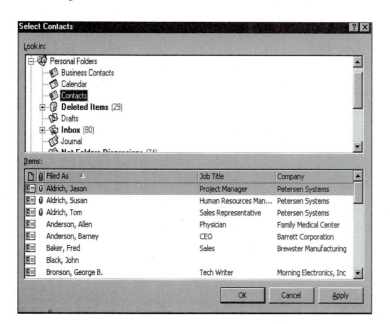

Figure 9.12
The Select Contacts dialog box lists Contact items in your default Contacts folder. If you have more than one Contacts folder, you can select one of them in the upper pane to see a list of the contacts it contains in the lower pane.

PART
III

CH
9

2. Select one or more contacts, then choose OK. The dialog box closes and the selected contacts are listed in the Contact form's Contacts box.

ASSIGNING CATEGORIES TO A CONTACT

You should get into the habit of assigning one or more categories to every Outlook item, including Contact items. By doing so, you can easily display all the items that have the same category, as well as group and filter items by category.

→ **See** "Using Categories and Entry Types," **p. 603**.

To assign categories to a contact:

1. Choose Categories to display the Categories dialog box shown in Figure 9.13.

Figure 9.13
The Categories dialog box lists your categories. If you have already assigned categories to the current Contact item, those categories are listed in the Item(s) Belong to These Categories box.

2. Select one or more categories for the Contact item, then choose OK to close the dialog box. The Contact form now shows the selected categories in the Categories box.

MARKING A CONTACT AS PRIVATE

If you intend to share the contents of your Contacts folder with other people, but you don't want other people to see information about some contacts, check the Private box at the bottom-right of the Contact form for those contacts you want to keep private.

If you're using C/W Outlook as a client for Exchange, you can allow specific people with whom you share your folders to see Private items.

→ For information about making your private items available to specific other people, **see** "Giving Permission to Access Your Folders," **p. 724**.

ENTERING MORE CONTACT DETAILS

In many cases, you can enter all the information you need to save about a contact in the Contact form's General tab. However, you can add more information in the Details tab shown in Figure 9.14.

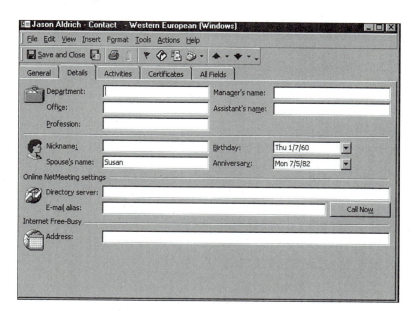

Figure 9.14
Use this dialog box to enter more information about a contact.

To enter information into any of the boxes in the top section of the tab, place the insertion point in that box and enter the information.

Tip #73 from

Instead of entering the names of the contact's manager and assistant, it's usually better to create separate Contact items for those people and associate those items with the current one (using Contacts on the General tab). By doing so, you can save other information about the manager and assistant, such as their phone numbers and e-mail addresses.

You can also enter a contact's nickname and spouse's name in the second section of the tab. If you want to save more information than just a name for the spouse, create a separate Contact item and create an association with it.

You can enter the contact's birthday and anniversary either by typing dates or by choosing the button at the right end of the Birthday or Anniversary box to display a calendar and selecting a date from the calendar. One problem with entering birthdays and anniversaries is that Outlook insists on including a year and you frequently don't know the year. My workaround for this problem is to use the year 1900 when I don't know the correct year (none of my contacts was born or married in 1900).

Note

If you enter a date without a year (such as 11/14), Outlook automatically provides the current year.

If you include a contact's birthday or anniversary, when you save the Contact item, Outlook automatically creates a recurring event in the Calendar folder. Also, the next time you open the Contact item, you'll see links to the Calendar items in the notes section of the Contact form.

→ For information about the way Outlook handles dates, **see** "Creating a One-time Appointment in the Calender Information Viewer," **p. 358** and "Creating Recurring Appointments and Events," **p. 371**.

The bottom section of the Details tab contains NetMeeting-related information. If the contact is someone with whom you have NetMeetings, and that contact is listed in a directory server, enter the name of that server in the Directory Server box. You can also enter the contact's e-mail address in the E-mail Alias box. After you've provided this information, you can initiate a *NetMeeting* by choosing Call Now.

Note

Outlook uses Internet Explorer to provide NetMeeting functionality.

→ To read about online meetings, **see** "Participating in Online Meetings," **p. 280**.

USING OTHER CONTACT FIELDS

Outlook saves each piece of information you provide about a contact in a separate storage location known as a field. Separate fields exist for each of the five components of a full name: Title, First, Middle, Last, and Suffix. Likewise, separate fields exist for each component of an address, as well for all the other elements of information you can save for each contact.

You can enter information into the fields you most often use in the Contact form's General tab. You can access a few more fields in the Details tab. To access other fields you have to use the All Fields tab. When you first open this tab you'll probably see no fields listed. That's because, by default, the tab lists User Defined Fields in This Item. Unless you have created one of more user-defined fields, no fields are available to be listed.

→ For information about creating custom fields, **see** "Creating and Using Custom Fields," **p. 1093**.

To see some of the predefined fields, open the Select From drop-down list and select Frequently-Used Fields, as shown in Figure 9.15.

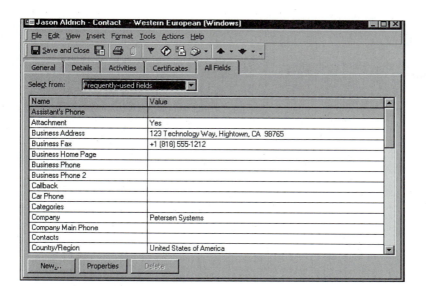

Figure 9.15
The Frequently-Used Fields list contains fields listed in alphabetical order.

You can scroll down the list to see those fields not initially visible.

Outlook has two kinds of fields: those you can edit, and those you can't. The Assistant's Phone field at the top of the list is an example of a field you can edit. Notice that this is a field that isn't accessible from the General or Details tabs. If you click anywhere on the Assistant's Phone field, the insertion point appears in the Value column. You can now enter a phone number for the Assistant.

The second field in the list is Attachment, a field whose value you can't change. This field reports the presence or absence of an attachment to the currently selected Contact item. The Value column shows Yes if the Contact item has an attachment, or No if the item doesn't have an attachment. If you click the Attachment field, the entire row becomes blue; there's no insertion point because you can't change the value of this field in this tab.

Note

> The only way to change No to Yes is to open the General tab and insert an attachment into the item. Likewise, the only way to change Yes to No is to remove all attachments.

The third field is Business Address. If you have entered a business address for the selected contact, this field contains that address. Because this is information you entered, you might expect to be able to change it. But you can't. The reason is that Business Address contains information that Outlook has constructed from other fields, specifically from the Business Address City, Business Address Country, Business Address Postal Code, Business Address State, and Business Address Street fields (you can see these fields if you open the list of Address Fields). You can edit the information in these individual fields and, after you do, the changes appear in the Business Address field.

Now that you understand that some fields are editable and others are not, you can go ahead and use this tab to enter contact information you can't enter from the General and Details tabs.

The only reason for entering information about a contact is so that you can subsequently see that information. Outlook displays information in various Information viewers, but viewers supplied with Outlook display only a few of the available fields. To display information you've entered in the All Fields tab, you have to either modify a standard view or create a custom view.

→ For information about creating custom Information viewers, **see** "Creating Custom Views," **p. 73**.

FLAGGING A CONTACT ITEM

You can flag a Contact item at the time you create it or anytime thereafter. To do so, choose the Flag for Follow Up button ⏷ on the Contact form's Standard toolbar to display the Flag for Follow Up dialog box, shown in Figure 9.16.

Figure 9.16
Use this dialog box to select a flag and, if appropriate, a due-by date.

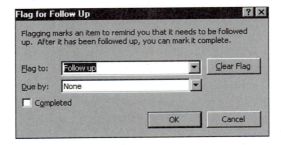

Flag a Contact item in the same way that you flag an e-mail message.

Tip #74 from
Gordon Crook

As explained in Chapters 3 and 6, you can replace the flag names available in Outlook with any appropriate words. If you select a Due By date, Outlook displays that date together with a time—the end of your workday. You can change that time to any other time.

→ To refresh your memory about flagging messages, **see** "Flagging a Message," **p. 103** if you're using IMO Outlook, or **see** "Flagging a Message," **p. 207** if you're using C/W Outlook.

SAVING A CONTACT ITEM

After you've completed entering information for a Contact item, you can save that item by choosing Save and Close in the Contact form's Standard toolbar. Alternatively, you can open the form's File menu and choose:

- Save—This saves the item and leaves the form open. Information about the current item is displayed in the form.

- Save and New—This saves the item and leaves the form open with all fields empty, ready for you to enter information about another contact.
- Save As—This saves the item in a specific format, as described in the following paragraphs.

When you choose Save As, Outlook opens the Save As dialog box, in which you can choose where you want to save the item and in what format you want to save it, as shown in Figure 9.17.

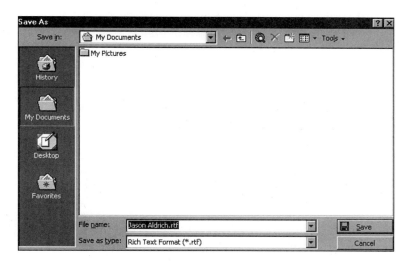

Figure 9.17
Outlook initially proposes to save the contact information in Rich Text Format.

Navigate in the Save As dialog box to locate the Windows folder where you want to save the item. Then open the drop-down Save as Type list to display a list of types. The available types are as follows:

- Text Only (.txt)—Use this if you want to use the Contact information in an application that accepts text files.
- Rich Text Format (.rtf)—Use this if you want to use the Contact information in an application that accepts files in rich text format.
- Outlook Template (.oft)—Use this if you want to save the item as an Outlook template from which you can create other Outlook items.
- Message Format (.msg)—Use this if you want to save the item so that it's compatible with clients such as Exchange client.
- vCard Files (.vcf)—Use this to save the contact in the industry-standard vCard format so that you can share it with people who use various clients other than Outlook.

Outlook proposes to save the file with the contact's full name as the filename and an extension appropriate for the file type. You can choose a different filename, but you normally won't want to. Choose Save to save the file.

CREATING DUPLICATE CONTACT ITEMS

If you create a Contact item for a person who has the same name as an existing contact, Outlook alerts you when you save the new item by displaying the dialog box shown in Figure 9.18.

Note

The ability to detect possible duplicate contacts and to merge information from one Contact item into another is known as AutoMerge Contact.

Figure 9.18
This dialog box alerts you to the fact that you're about to save a duplicate contact.

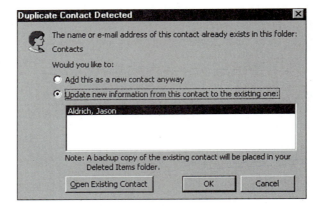

You can:

- Choose Add This as a New Contact Anyway to create the duplicate Contact item
- Choose Update New Information from This Contact to the Existing One to merge information from the new Contact item into the existing Contact item

To examine the existing contact, choose Open Existing Contact.

CREATING SIMILAR CONTACT ITEMS

Outlook keeps information about each contact as a separate Contact item. Although each Contact item has a Spouse field, you can only save the spouse's name—there are no fields for the spouse's birthday or other personal information. Similarly, each Contact item has a Children field (this field is available in the All Fields tab). You can use the Children field to list children's names but there are no fields for other information about a contact's children. For your family contacts, therefore, you'll usually want to create a separate Contact item for each family member.

In the case of Contact items for organizations, one set of fields exists for a person's name. If you have several contacts within an organization, you'll need to have separate Contact items for each member of the organization.

Another way to create several similar Contact items is to create and use an Outlook template.

→ For more information about creating similar Contact items, **see** "Creating Similar Contact Items," **p. 524**.

PART

III

CH

9

CREATING CONTACT ITEMS FOR MEMBERS OF A FAMILY

You probably have better things to do with your time than to create separate Contact items from scratch for each family member. You don't have to. Instead, create a Contact item for one member of the family, copy that item as many times as necessary, then edit the individual items so that each has the correct name, birthday, and other personal information.

To create multiple Contact items for family members:

1. Create a complete Contact item for one family member. Save that Contact item.

2. Locate the Contact item you just created in the Contacts Information viewer.

3. Create a copy of that Contact item by holding down Ctrl while you drag the item onto Contacts in the Outlook Bar.

4. Repeat step 3 as many times as necessary to create additional copies of the Contact item.

5. Double-click each of the new Contact items to open them one at a time in the Contact form. Edit each contact item as necessary, then choose Save and Close in the form's Standard toolbar to save the changes.

This procedure saves time by eliminating the need to enter such information as the postal address and phone numbers separately for each family member.

CREATING CONTACT ITEMS FOR MEMBERS OF AN ORGANIZATION

You can use the method described in the previous section to create Contact items for members of an organization. However, Outlook offers a more convenient method.

To create Contact items for organization members:

1. Create a Contact item for one member of the organization. Save that Contact item.

2. Select the Contact item you just created in the Contact Information viewer.

3. Choose Actions, New Contact from Same Company. Outlook creates a new Contact item and displays that item in the Contact form with the organization's name, postal address, business phone, and business fax numbers already entered. All other phone and fax numbers are not copied into the new Contact item.

4. Complete the new Contact item by entering the person's name and whatever other information is appropriate.

VIEWING AND PRINTING CONTACT ITEMS

After you've entered several Contact items, you can use an Information viewer to display those items. After you install Outlook you have several Contact Information viewers at your disposal. You can use any of these viewers, modify them, or create custom views.

→ For detailed information about displaying and printing Contact items, **see** "Creating Views and Print Styles," **p. 943**.

DISPLAYING CONTACT ITEMS IN THE ADDRESS CARDS VIEW

The Address Cards view of Contact items, as supplied with Outlook, shows Contact items in a manner similar to how information about contacts is often written on index cards.

Outlook can also show information about contacts in the Detailed Address Cards view. This view is similar to the Address Cards view, but contains additional information. The next section explains how to select alternative views.

To display Contact items in the Address Cards view:

1. Select Contacts in the Outlook Bar.
2. Choose View, move the pointer onto Current View, and choose Address Cards.

Now you see your contacts in the Address Cards view, as shown in Figure 9.19.

Figure 9.19
The Address Cards view shows basic information about each contact. Cards are listed in alphabetical order by File As name. Each card shows the information you've previously entered for the contact.

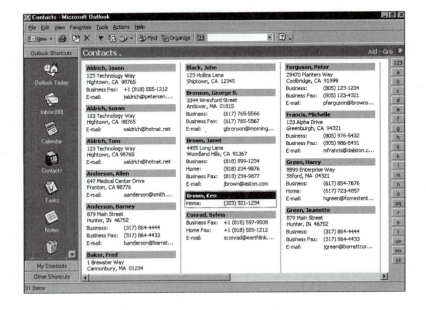

You can find information about a specific contact in several ways:

- Use the horizontal scrollbar at the bottom of the Information viewer to scroll through the cards.

- Choose one of the index buttons at the right side of the viewer to locate a card according to the first letter of its File As name.

- Press an alphanumeric key on your keyboard to find cards that have a File As name starting with a specific character.

You can double-click on any contact to display the information about that contact in a Contact form. In the Contact form, you can edit any information field and add new information.

VIEWING CONTACTS IN OTHER INFORMATION VIEWERS

You can view contacts in other ways than the default Card view. To choose a different view of Contact items, choose View and move the pointer onto Current View. Then select one of the listed views.

Address Cards and Detailed Address Cards views show contacts in index-card format. The remaining views show Contact items in table format.

CONTROLLING THE SORT ORDER FOR CONTACTS

By default, contacts are listed in alphabetical order by their File As names. You can change this sort order. The example that follows illustrates this by showing how to arrange contacts in order by organization. You can use the same technique to arrange contacts in order by other fields.

To change the sort order:

1. With any Contact Information viewer displayed, choose View, move the pointer onto Current View, and choose Customize Current View to display the dialog box shown in Figure 9.20.

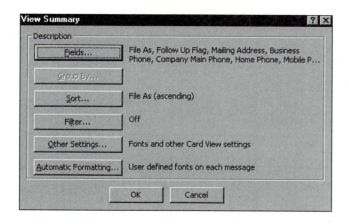

Figure 9.20
Use this dialog box to select how you want to customize the view.

PART
III

CH
9

2. Choose <u>S</u>ort to display the Sort dialog box, as shown in Figure 9.21.

Figure 9.21
Use this dialog box to
define how you want
to sort Contact items.

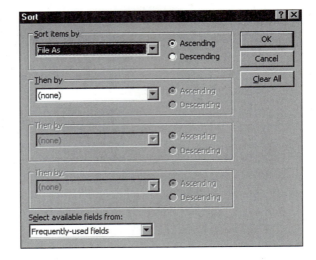

3. Open the <u>S</u>ort Items By drop-down list and select the field on which you want to sort Contact items.

Note

You are not limited to sorting on fields that are displayed in the view. Outlook initially listed Frequently-used Fields. You can select other fields by opening the drop-down <u>S</u>elect Available Fields From list at the bottom of the dialog box and selecting another group of fields.

4. Choose OK twice and then Close. Now Items are sorted by the field you specified.

Tip #75 from

With the Address Cards or Detailed Address Cards view displayed, you can right-click any white space to display a context menu and, in that menu, choose So<u>r</u>t to display the dialog box shown in Figure 9.21.

With any table view displayed, you can click any field name in a column heading to sort the table by that field. Click the field name again to sort the table in reverse order based on that field. This method allows you to sort only on displayed fields, in contrast with the method described in the preceding procedure which allows you to sort based on any field, displayed or not.

→ For more information about modifying Outlook's views and creating custom views, **see** "Creating Views and Print Styles," **p. 943**.

PRINTING CONTACT ITEMS

Outlook offers several formats for printing Contact items. With the Address Cards or Detailed Address Cards view of Contact items selected, choose <u>F</u>ile, and move the pointer onto Page Setup to choose from this list of print styles:

- Card Style
- Small Booklet Style
- Medium Booklet Style
- Memo Style
- Phone Directory Style

PART

III

CH

9

With a Table view of Contact items selected, you can choose either Table Style or Memo Style.

→ To find out about modifying the standard print styles and creating your own, **see** "Creating Views and Print Styles," **p. 943**.

When you choose a print style, Outlook displays the Page Setup dialog box, in which you can refine the page layout. After you've done that, choose <u>P</u>rint.

ORGANIZING CONTACT ITEMS

Many people start using Outlook quite casually and don't think through all the implications before they start creating Outlook items, Contact items among them. People are busy; they grab onto what they need and start charging ahead. New users often ignore Outlook's categories but later wish they hadn't. By that time, they maybe have several hundreds of Outlook items, too many to go back and individually assign categories to.

Here's a way to simplify assigning categories to existing Contact items. Once you've done that, you can easily assign colors to each category.

ASSIGNING CATEGORIES TO EXISTING CONTACT ITEMS

You can use Outlook's Organizer to assign categories to existing Outlook items. This is much easier than opening each Contact item separately in the Contact form and assigning categories to it.

To assign categories to existing Contact items:

1. Display any view of the Contacts Information viewer. In this case, a table view is likely to be more convenient than a card view.
2. Choose Organi<u>z</u>e in the Information viewer's Standard toolbar.
3. In the Organizer pane, select Using Categories.

4. Open the drop-down Add Contacts Selected Below To list, then select the category you want to assign to Contact items.

5. While holding down Ctrl, select the items you want to assign to that category.

6. After you've selected all the items to which you want to assign the category, choose Add. Outlook assigns the category to the selected items.

You can repeat these steps as often as necessary to assign other categories to items.

TO APPLY COLORS TO ITEMS ACCORDING TO THEIR CATEGORIES

After you've assigned categories to items, you can display items in colors according to their categories. The procedure described here applies only to a specific view of an item; to display certain Contact items in a specific color in a card view, you must have that view selected.

This procedure assumes you have assigned a category named Alpha to certain Contact items and that you want to display those Contact items in red in the Address Cards view.

To assign colors to Contact items:

1. Display the view of the Contacts Information viewer in which you want certain Contact items to be colored.

2. Choose Organize in the Information viewer's Standard toolbar.

3. In the Organizer pane, select Using Views.

4. Choose Customize Current View near the top-right of the Organizer pane to display the View Summary dialog box shown in Figure 9.22.

Figure 9.22
The View Summary dialog box shows a summarized description of the current view.

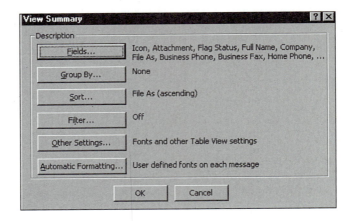

5. Choose <u>A</u>utomatic Formatting to display the dialog box shown in Figure 9.23.

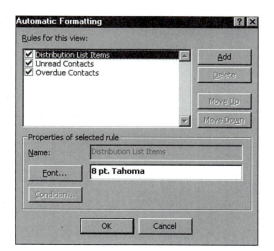

Figure 9.23
This dialog box lists the rules that already exist for the currently selected view. The checked rules are enabled.

Note

Rules (page 618) control how Outlook automatically processes items, such as placing certain items in specific folders or, in this case, automatically coloring items.

→ For detailed information about rules, **see** "Creating and Using Rules," **p. 617**.

6. Choose <u>A</u>dd to add a new rule, as shown in Figure 9.24. Outlook automatically enables the new rule by checking the box adjacent to its name. The steps that follow create a new rule that displays all Contact items to which the category Alpha is assigned in red.

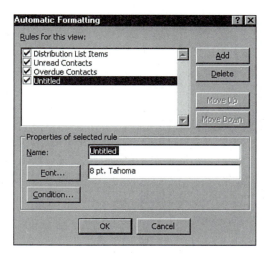

Figure 9.24
Outlook proposes to call the new rule Untitled.

7. Replace the name of the new rule using the name of the category (such as Make Alpha Red) for which you want to color Contact items.

8. Choose Font to display the standard Windows Font dialog box.

9. Open the Color drop-down list, select a color (red in this case), and then choose OK to return to the Automatic Formatting dialog box.

10. Choose Condition to display the Filter dialog box. Select the More Choices tab shown in Figure 9.25.

Figure 9.25
The More Choices tab opens with the Categories box empty.

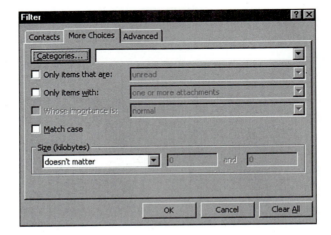

11. Choose Categories and select the category for which you want to color items (alpha in this case).

12. Choose OK four times to close the dialog boxes. Close the Organizer pane. Now the items with the specified category are colored red.

The new rule applies to all existing items and to any new Contact items you create.

If you want to disable a rule, open the Automatic Formatting dialog box, previously shown in Figure 9.24, and remove the check mark from the box adjacent to its name. To delete a rule, open the Automatic Formatting dialog box, select the rule you want to delete, and choose Delete.

USING OTHER WAYS TO CREATE CONTACT ITEMS

So far in this chapter, we've considered only one way to create Contact items—by opening the Contact form and entering information. Outlook provides several other ways in which you can create new Contact items.

SAVING AN E-MAIL SENDER AS A CONTACT ITEM

When you receive an e-mail message, that message normally contains the sender's e-mail address. If you want to keep a record of that sender's e-mail address, you can easily create a new Contact item.

After you've received an e-mail message, the header of that message is listed in your Inbox Information viewer. Follow these steps to create a Contact item for the message sender.

To create a Contact item:

1. Double-click the message header in the Inbox Information viewer to display it in the Message form.
2. Right-click the sender's name at the top of the message to display a context menu.
3. Choose <u>A</u>dd to Contacts to display a Contacts form with the sender's name and e-mail address in the appropriate boxes.
4. Enter information in any other boxes on the form (at least enter a category), and then choose <u>S</u>ave and Close in the form's Standard toolbar.

Here's a simpler way to create a Contact item for a person who has sent you a message.

To create a Contact item:

1. Drag the message header from the Inbox Information viewer onto the Contacts icon in the Outlook Bar. The sender's name and e-mail address are displayed in their appropriate boxes on a Contact form.
2. Enter information in any other boxes on the form, then choose <u>S</u>ave and Close in the form's Standard toolbar.

Using either of these methods, you might accidentally attempt to duplicate an existing Contact item. If this happens, Outlook displays the Duplicate Contact Detected dialog box, previously shown in Figure 9.18. You can use this dialog box to decide whether you want to add the duplicate contact or update information in the existing item, as described previously in this chapter.

→ **See** "Creating Duplicate Contact Items," **p. 320**.

IMPORTING CONTACTS FROM A MAIL MERGE DATA FILE

You can create Contact items from an existing Word Mail Merge data file. The data file must be in the comma-delimited format. If the Word file is in the form of a Word table, you must first convert that table into the comma-delimited format. Also the field names in Word must match the field names in Outlook.

For detailed information about importing contacts from a Word Mail Merge data file, refer to the Microsoft Knowledge Base article Q180087, *How to Import a Word Mail Merge Data Source File*.

SHARING CONTACT INFORMATION WITH VCARDS

vCards are electronic business cards that use an industry-standard format that's recognized by Outlook and by several other e-mail clients. You can find detailed information about vCards on the Internet Mail Consortium's Web page:

```
http://www.imc.org/pdi/vcardwhite.html
```

Each vCard is a file that has .vcf as its file name extension. You can:

- Save a Contact item as a vCard file
- Attach a vCard to an e-mail message
- Import information from a vCard file as an Outlook item
- Receive a vCard in an e-mail message and save its contents as a Contact item

The following procedures explain each of these in detail.

To save a Contact item as a vCard file:

1. With any Contacts Information viewer displayed, select the contact you want to save as a vCard.
2. Choose File, Save As to open the Save As dialog box. Navigate to the folder in which you want to save the file.
3. Open the Save As Type drop-down list and select vCard Files (*.vcf).
4. The File Name box contains the name of the contact you selected in step 1, followed by .vcf as the file name extension. You can change the filename if you want to.
5. Choose Save to save the vCard.

Note

As an alternative to step 1, you can display a Contact item in a Contact form and then choose File, Save As in the form's menu bar.

To send a vCard by e-mail:

1. With any Contacts Information viewer displayed, select the Contact item you want to send as a vCard.
2. Choose Actions, Forward as vCard. Outlook opens a Message form with a vCard shown as an attachment.
3. Complete and send the message in the normal way.

Note

As an alternative to step 1, you can display a Contact item in a Contact form and then choose Actions, Forward as vCard in the form's menu bar.

To import information from a vCard file as a Contact item:

1. With any Outlook Information viewer displayed, choose File, Import and Export to display the first Import and Export Wizard window.

2. Select Import a VCARD file (.vcf), then choose Next > to display the VCARD File dialog box. Navigate to the Windows folder that contains the vCard file you want to import.

3. Select the vCard file, then choose Open. Outlook imports the vCard into your Contacts folder.

Note

Outlook doesn't detect duplicates when you import in this way from a vCard.

To save a vCard you've received by e-mail as a Contact item:

1. In the Inbox Information viewer, double-click the header of the message to which a vCard is attached to display that message in a Message form. The attachment is displayed as an icon at the bottom of the form.

2. Double-click the vCard icon. Outlook displays the information from the vCard in a Contact form.

3. Choose Save and Close in the form's Standard toolbar to save the item.

IMPORTING CONTACT INFORMATION FROM OTHER APPLICATIONS

Outlook can import Contact information from various other applications. Refer to Chapter 19 for detailed information about this.

→ **See** "Exporting Items to, and Importing Items from, Other Applications," **p. 575**.

Various add-ins are available from other companies for sharing Contact (and other) Outlook items with other applications. One of these is Address Magic from Connected Software. You can find information about this product at

`http://www.empire.net/~level/AdddressMagic.html`

FINDING A CONTACT

Chapter 18 deals with finding Outlook items in general. You can use the information in that chapter to find Outlook items.

→ For detailed information about finding Outlook items, **see** "Finding Outlook Items," **p. 530**.

In addition to the general methods available, Outlook has a QuickFind Contact tool for finding Contact items.

With any Outlook Information viewer displayed, the Standard toolbar contains the Find a Contact box, as shown in Figure 9.26.

Figure 9.26
You can use the Find a Contact box to quickly find a Contact item.

Find a Contact box

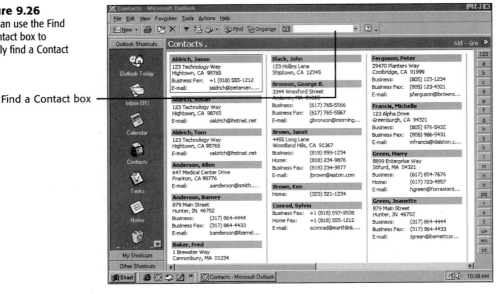

To find a contact, place the insertion point into the Find a Contact box, type all or part of the contact's name you want to find, and press Enter.

If what you type is sufficient to uniquely identify one (and only one) of the contacts in your Contacts folder, Outlook displays information about that contact in a Contact form. If two or more contacts match what you type, Outlook displays a Choose Contact dialog box such as that shown in Figure 9.27.

Figure 9.27
This box displays the names of all the contacts who match what you type.

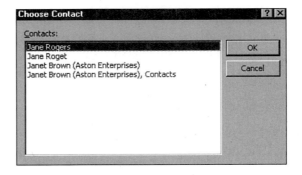

Select a contact and choose OK to display information about that contact in a Contact form.

Outlook remembers each entry you make in the Find a Contact box. After you've made entries, you can choose the small button marked with a black triangle at the right end of the Find a Contact box to display a list of your previous entries. Select a previous entry to find that contact again.

> **Note**
>
> If you have two or more Contacts folders, Outlook looks in all of them.

WORKING WITH DISTRIBUTION LISTS

After saving Contact items in a Contacts folder, you can use those items to create an e-mail distribution list. After you've created a distribution list, you can use that list as an address for e-mail messages to send a message to everyone on the list.

PART

III

CH

9

> **Note**
>
> This is a new capability in Outlook 2000 that works the same way for C/W and IMO. In Outlook 97 and in C/W Outlook 98, you had to use a Personal Address Book if you wanted to create a distribution list. IMO Outlook 98 had a different way of creating distribution lists.

Instead of using a distribution list to send messages to a group of people, you can create and use a template, as described in Chapter 17.

→ **See** "Using Templates for Distributing Messages," **p.523**.

CREATING A DISTRIBUTION LIST

To create an e-mail distribution list:

1. With a Contacts Information viewer displayed, choose Actions, New Distribution List to display the dialog box shown in Figure 9.28.

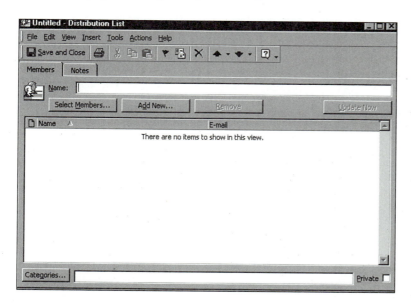

Figure 9.28
The Distribution List dialog box opens, displaying an empty list.

2. To add contacts to the distribution list, choose Select <u>M</u>embers. Outlook displays the dialog box shown in Figure 9.29.

Figure 9.29
This dialog box (shown here for C/W Outlook) shows the Contact items in your Contacts folder. The equivalent dialog box for IMO Outlook is slightly different.

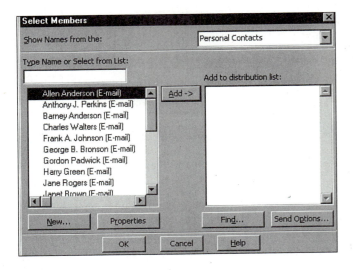

If you're using C/W Outlook, you can open the <u>S</u>how Names from The drop-down list and select other address books to which Outlook has access. IMO Outlook only gives access to your Contacts folders that are enabled as Outlook Address Books.

3. Scroll down the list of contacts and select the contacts you want to have in the distribution list, choose <u>A</u>dd-> to move those contacts into the Add to Distribution List box, then choose OK to return to the Distribution List dialog box, as shown in Figure 9.30.

If you have a long list of contacts, instead of scrolling to find those you want in your distribution list, you can choose Fin<u>d</u> to locate contacts.

4. If you want to add names and e-mail addresses that aren't in your Contacts folder (or other address books if you're using C/W Outlook), choose <u>A</u>dd New to display the dialog box shown in Figure 9.31.

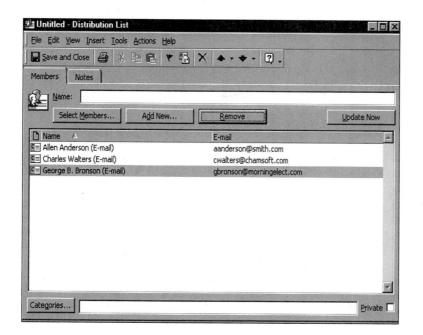

Figure 9.30
The selected contact names and their e-mail addresses are listed.

Figure 9.31
Use this dialog box to add a new contact to the distribution list and, optionally, to your Contacts folder.

5. Enter the new contact's name in the <u>D</u>isplay Name box and the contact's e-mail address in the <u>E</u>-mail Address box.

6. If the e-mail address is not an Internet address, open the drop-down Address <u>T</u>ype list and select the appropriate address type. This is available in C/W Outlook, but not in IMO Outlook.

7. If you want to add the new contact to your Contacts folder, check the <u>A</u>dd to Contacts box.

8. Choose OK to return to the Distribution List dialog box with the new contact listed.

9. Enter a name for the distribution list in the <u>N</u>ame box.

10. Choose Categories and assign one or more categories to the distribution list.

11. If you intend to share your Contacts folder but want to keep the distribution list private, check the <u>P</u>rivate box.

12. Choose <u>S</u>ave and Close in the Standard toolbar to save the distribution list in your Contacts folder.

The distribution list appears in Contacts Information viewers with the name of the distribution list as a File As name. A distribution list is identified in a card view by a pair of heads near the right end of a card's title. It's identified in a table view by a pair of heads superimposed on the Contact item symbol in the Icon column.

MODIFYING A DISTRIBUTION LIST

To examine or modify a distribution list, double-click the list's name in a Contact Information viewer. Outlook opens the distribution list in the Distribution List dialog box.

At this point, you can:

- Add more people to the distribution list. Choose Select Members to add people from your Contacts folders (or other address books if you're using C/W Outlook). Choose Add New to enter a new name and e-mail address.
- Remove people from the distribution list. Select the names you want to remove, then choose Remove.
- Update the distribution list. If you've made changes to items in your Contacts folder (or other folders you used to add names into the distribution list) since you created the list, choose Update Now to update the distribution list with those changes.

After you've made changes to the distribution list, choose Save and Close to save the changed list.

USING A PERSONAL ADDRESS BOOK

If you're using C/W Outlook, you can have a Personal Address Book in addition to a Contacts folder. In previous versions of Outlook, it was necessary to have a Personal Address Book if you wanted to create distribution lists. However, now that you can create distribution lists based on Contact items, it's no longer necessary to have a Personal Address Book for that reason.

The main benefit of having a Personal Address Book is that it gives you one place in which to keep information about contacts you frequently use. In a networked situation, you may have to look in several places for various contacts. If you have a Personal Address Book, you can copy contact information from those various places into your Personal Address book to make that information readily available.

ADDING THE PERSONAL ADDRESS BOOK INFORMATION SERVICE TO YOUR PROFILE

In order to use a Personal Address Book, you must add the Personal Address Book information service to your profile. When you do so, you create a file on your hard disk in which items in your Personal Address Book are saved.

Note

You can add the Personal Address Book information service only once into a profile.

To add the Personal Address Book information service:

1. With any Information viewer displayed, choose Tools, Services to display the Services dialog box with the Services tab selected.

2. Choose Add to display the Add Service to Profile dialog box. Select Personal Address Book and then choose OK to display the Personal Address Book dialog box shown in Figure 9.32.

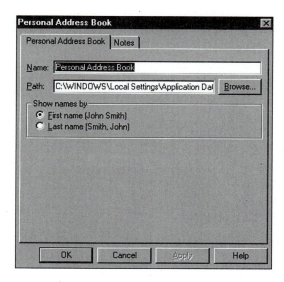

Figure 9.32
The Personal Address Book dialog box opens with a proposed name displayed in the Name box and path displayed in the Path box.

3. Outlook proposes to use the name Personal Address Book as the name used within Outlook.

4. Outlook proposes to name the Personal Address Book file Mailbox.pab. It's a good idea to replace this name with your own last name or initials.

5. Select whether you want names to be listed in first name or last name order.

6. You can select the Notes tab in which you can enter notes about your Personal Address Book.

7. Choose OK. Outlook displays a message telling you that you must exit and restart Outlook before the service can be used. Choose OK twice.

8. Choose File, Exit and Log Off to close Outlook. Then restart Outlook.

If you choose Tools, Services, you'll see that the Personal Address Book information service is now in your profile.

ENTERING INFORMATION MANUALLY INTO YOUR PERSONAL ADDRESS BOOK

This section describes how to enter information into your Personal Address Book manually. You can also copy information into your Personal Address Book, as explained in the next section.

To open your Personal Address Book, display the Inbox Information viewer and choose the Address Book icon in the Standard toolbar. Outlook displays the Address Book dialog box with your Contacts folder selected in the Show Name from The box. Open the Show Names from The drop-down list and select Personal Address Book, as shown in Figure 9.33.

Figure 9.33
The Address Book dialog box initially opens with no contacts displayed.

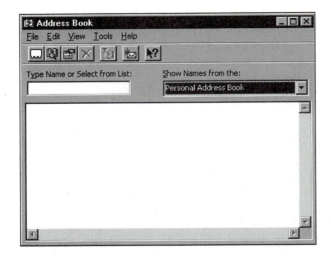

To create a new entry, choose the New Entry button in the toolbar. Outlook displays the dialog box shown in Figure 9.34.

Figure 9.34
Use this dialog box to specify whether you want to create a new contact or a new distribution list and where you want to save it.

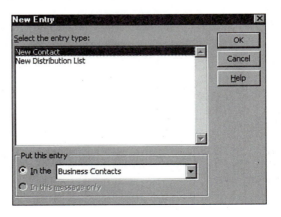

To create a new contact and save it in your Personal Address Book:

1. Select the New Contact in the Select the Entry Type list.

2. If necessary, open the drop-down In The list and select Personal Address Book. Outlook displays the New Entry dialog box shown in Figure 9.35.

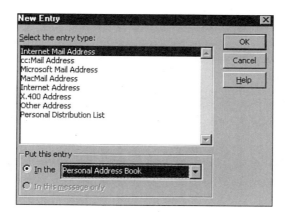

Figure 9.35
This dialog box contains a list of entry types.

3. Select the appropriate entry type for the new entry, then choose OK to display the dialog box shown in Figure 9.36.

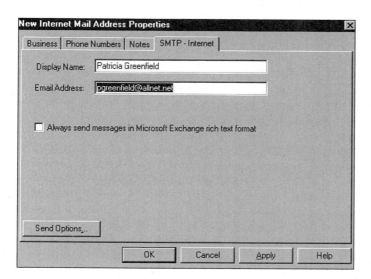

Figure 9.36
Use the four tabs in this dialog box to enter information, such as that shown here, about the new contact.

4. With the SMTP-Internet tab selected, enter the new contact's name and e-mail address in the Display Name and Email Address boxes.

Note If you chose an entry type other than Internet, this tab has a different name.

5. If appropriate, check the Always Send Messages in Microsoft Exchange Rich Text Format (do this if you always send messages by way of an Exchange server to this person).

6. If you want to use UUEncode instead of MIME for message encoding, or if you wish to change the way body text is formatted, choose Send Options to display the dialog box shown in Figure 9.37.

Figure 9.37
When this dialog box opens, the check box is unchecked and the option buttons are disabled.

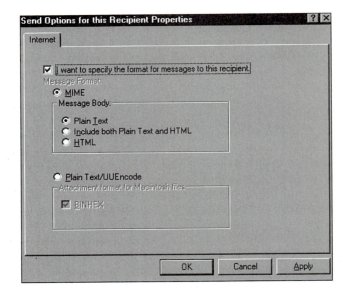

7. Select the other three tabs to enter additional information about the contact, then choose OK to save the contact information and return to the Address Book dialog box.

You can use the Address Book menus and toolbar to do such things as:

- Enter and edit contact information
- Find a contact
- Display and change a contact's properties
- Delete contacts
- Create a message to a contact
- Access help

COPYING CONTACT INFORMATION INTO THE PERSONAL ADDRESS BOOK

You can selectively copy contact information from other address books into your Personal Address Book.

To copy contact information into your Personal Address Book:

1. Choose Inbox in the Outlook Bar to display the Inbox Information viewer.
2. Choose the Address Book button 📖 in the Standard toolbar to display the Address Book dialog box previously shown in Figure 9.33.
3. Open the Show Names from The drop-down list to display a list of available address books.
4. Select the address book from which you want to copy Contact items. The Address Book dialog box displays a list of Contact items in the selected address book.
5. Select those contacts that you want to copy into your Personal Address Book.
6. Choose the Add to Personal Address Book button in the Address Book toolbar.

USING CONTACT ITEMS

You can use Contact items in many ways, some of which are described in the following sections.

ADDRESSING E-MAIL AND FAXES

You can use contacts' e-mail addresses to address e-mail messages and fax numbers to send faxes.

→ For information about addressing an e-mail message, **see** "Addressing the Message," **p. 87** if you're using IMO Outlook, or **see** "Addressing the Message," **p. 190** if you're using C/W Outlook. For ingormation about addressing a fax, **see** "Creating and Sending a Fax," **p. 139** if you're using IMO Outlook, or **see** "Creating and Sending a Fax," **p. 246** if you're using C/W Outlook.

You can also AutoCreate a message by dragging a Contact item onto the Inbox icon in the Outlook Bar. When you do so, Outlook creates a message form with the contact's e-mail address already in the To box.

USING CONTACTS FOR MASS E-MAILING

One way to use contacts for mass e-mailing is to create a distribution list and insert that distribution list into the Message form's To box.

→ For information about distribution lists, **see** "Working with Distribution Lists," **p. 333**.

Another way to use contacts for mass e-mailing is to assign a category to all the contacts to whom you want to send the mailing. Then display contact items in the By Category View. Drag the Category header onto the Inbox icon in the Outlook Bar. Outlook uses AutoCreate to open the Message form with the e-mail addresses of the contacts to which the category is assigned in the To box.

PLACING A PHONE CALL

To place a phone call, your computer must have a modem with direct access to a phone line.

To place a phone call, select a contact in one of the Contact Information viewers and choose the Autodialer button 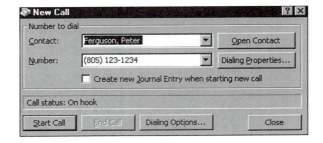 in the Standard toolbar to display the dialog box shown in Figure 9.38.

Figure 9.38
The dialog box opens with the contact's name in the Contact box and one of the contact's phone numbers in the Number box.

If the number you want to call is displayed in the Number box, choose Start Call to place the call. You can open the Number drop-down list to select one of the contact's other phone numbers.

WRITING A LETTER TO A CONTACT

Select a contact in one of the Contact Information viewers, then choose Actions, New Letter to Contact to open Word with the first Letter Wizard window displayed, as shown in Figure 9.39.

Figure 9.39
Use the Letter Wizard to complete your letter.

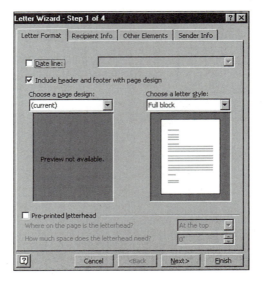

Follow through the steps of the Letter Wizard to address and write the letter. The wizard uses the postal address you designated as the mailing address on the Contact form.

CREATING A FORM LETTER

You can use Outlook contacts as a data source for Mail Merge documents you create in Word. In Word, create a form letter as you normally do. You can use an Outlook distribution list as a data sources for addressing form letters. Refer to a book about Word, such as *Special Edition Using Microsoft Word 2000*, published by Que, for information about this.

SETTING UP A MEETING WITH A CONTACT

Select a contact in one of the Contact Information viewers, then choose Actions, New Meeting Request with Contact to display the Meeting form shown in Figure 9.40.

PART
III
CH
9

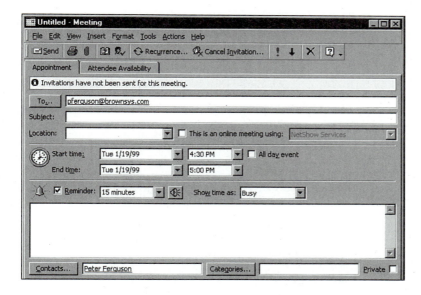

Figure 9.40
The Meeting form opens with the contact's e-mail address in the To box.

Complete the form and then send it as an e-mail message.

→ To learn about creating one-time appointments, **see** "Creating a One-Time Appointment in the Calender Information Viewer," **p. 358**.

MAKING A NOTE OF AN APPOINTMENT WITH A CONTACT

Select a contact in one of the Contact Information viewers, then choose Actions, New Appointment with Contact to display the Appointment form shown in Figure 9.41.

Figure 9.41
The Appointment form opens with the contact's name in the Contacts box at the bottom of the form.

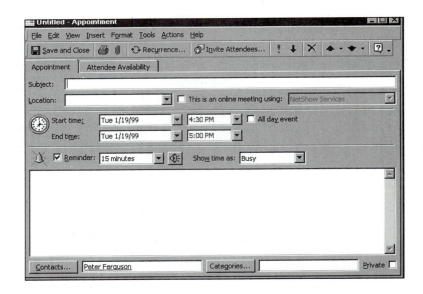

Complete the form and then save it as a Calendar item in your Calendar folder.

SENDING A TASK TO A CONTACT

Select a contact in one of the Contact Information viewers, then choose Actions, New Task for Contact to display the Task form shown in Figure 9.42.

Figure 9.42
The Task form opens with the contact's name in the Contacts box at the bottom of the form.

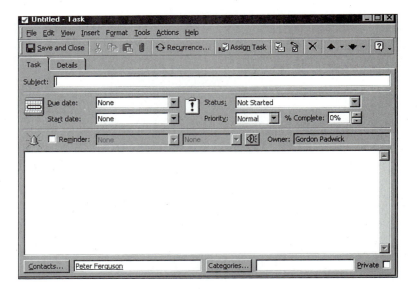

Complete the form and then choose the Assign Task button in the form's Standard toolbar to send the task assignment as an e-mail message.

→ For information about assigning tasks, **See** "Assigning a Task to Someone Else," **p. 430**.

CREATING A MAP SHOWING A CONTACT'S LOCATION

You can display and print a map showing any contact's location in the United States and some other countries. To do so, you must have an Outlook Internet account if you're using IMO Outlook, or the Internet Information service in your profile if you're using C/W Outlook. You must also have an account with an Internet service provider.

Double-click a Contact item in one of the Contact Information viewers to display the details of that contact in a Contact form. If you have entered more than one postal address for the contact, make sure the one you want to see on the map is displayed on the form.

To map the contact's location, choose the Display Map of Address button in the Contact form's Standard toolbar. Outlook establishes a connection to your Internet service provider, finds the Microsoft Expedia Maps site, and displays a map of your contact's location, as shown in Figure 9.43.

PART

III

CH

9

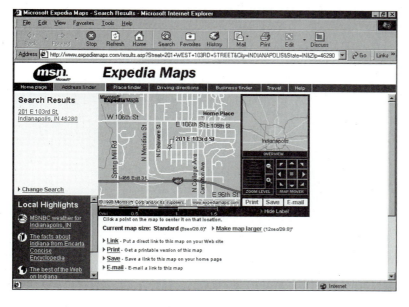

Figure 9.43
The contact's location is marked with a red push-pin on the map.

You can do several things at this stage:

■ Change the scale of the map by clicking the buttons in the ZOOM LEVEL box on the right side of the map

■ Change the area covered by the map by clicking the buttons in the MAP MOVER box on the right side of the map

- Put a direct link to the map on your Web site
- Print the map
- Save a link to the map on your home page
- Send an e-mail message containing a link to the map

Notice, also, the Local Choices box at the left. In that, you can get information about the mapped area:

- The local weather
- Facts from the Encarta Concise Encyclopedia
- The "best on the Web" about the locality
- Local news

TRACKING A CONTACT'S ACTIVITIES

You can use Outlook to track various activities of a contact, such as appointments, documents, e-mail, notes, and tasks. To display a contact's activities, double-click that contact in any Contact Information viewer to display details of that contact in the Contact form. Select the Activities tab, as shown in Figure 9.44.

Figure 9.44
The Activities tab initially lists a summary of the contact's activities.

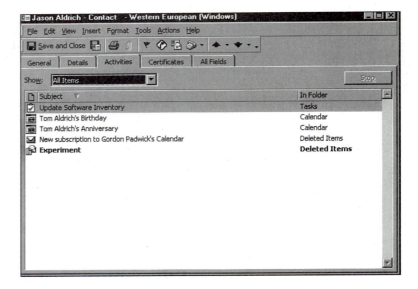

The list of activities contains one row for each activity and has three columns. From left to right, these columns are:

- Icon—An icon in each row signifies the type of activity
- Subject—This is the text in each item's Subject box
- In Folder—This is the name of the Outlook folder that contains the item

You can open the Show drop-down list to select various types of activities in more detail. You can select All Items, Contacts, E-mail, Journal, Notes, or Upcoming Tasks/Appointments.

If you choose e-mail, for example, the Activities tab contains additional columns, as shown in Figure 9.45.

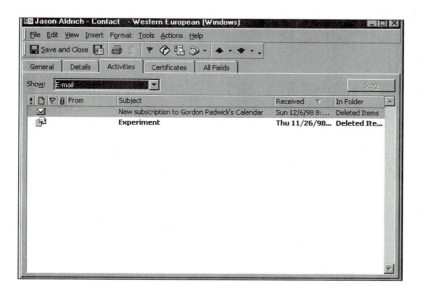

Figure 9.45
With E-mail selected, the Activities tab contains these columns.

PART
III

CH
9

<table>
<tr><td>Tip #76 from</td><td>You can click the headings at the top of the columns to sort the activities according to the contents of any column.</td></tr>
</table>

EXAMINING A CONTACT ITEM'S PROPERTIES

To examine a Contact item's properties:

1. Double-click a Contact item in the Contacts Information viewer to display that item in the Contact form.

2. In the form's menu, choose File, Properties to display the Properties dialog box, as shown in Figure 9.46.

Figure 9.46
The Properties dialog box shows information about the selected Contact item.

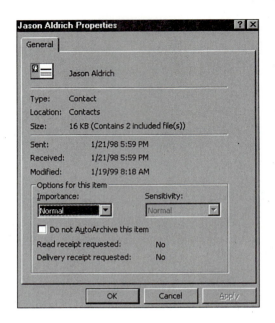

SHARING CONTACTS WITH OTHER OUTLOOK USERS

You can share individual Contact items with other Outlook users, and you can share your entire Contacts folder.

SHARING INDIVIDUAL CONTACT ITEMS

To share an individual Contact item, you can send that item in an e-mail message. In any Contact Information viewer, right-click a Contact item to display its context menu. Choose Forward and Outlook displays a Message form with the selected Contact item as an attachment.

You can drag additional Contact items from the Contact Information viewer in the message.

Send the e-mail message in the normal manner. When a recipient receives the message, that recipient drags the attached Contact item from the message onto the Contacts icon in the Outlook Bar. Outlook adds the contact into the recipient's Contacts folder.

Note

You can also save or forward contact information as a vCard, as explained previously in this chapter.

SHARING YOUR CONTACTS FOLDER

Several ways exist to share folders, including Contacts folders, between Outlook users.

One way to share a folder with someone else is to export the folder to a file from one computer, and then import it into the other computer. You can use this method for networked computers. You can also use it for computers that aren't connected to a network. Be aware, though, that Outlook folders often contain much more information than can be saved on an ordinary floppy disk. You will probably have to use high capacity disks (such as Iomega's ZIP disks) or use a utility such as WinZip to compress the file and save it on several, perhaps many, floppy disks.

→ For information about importing and exporting Outlook items, **see** "Importing and Exporting Outlook Items," **p. 565**.

You can share a file by way of the Internet (or an intranet) using Outlook's Net Folders.

→ To learn about Net Folders, **see** "What Is a Net Folder?," **p. 466**.

If you're using C/W Outlook as a client for Exchange and have your Contacts folder in the Exchange store, you can make that folder sharable and allow specific users to have access to it.

→ To understand how you can share a Contacts folder, **see** "Using Exchange Server to Share Information," **p. 703**.

USING DIRECTORY SERVICES

Outlook supports the *Lightweight Directory Access Protocol* (LDAP) that provides access to Internet directories. An Internet directory is similar to one of your own address books, but provides access to worldwide Internet addresses. You can set up Outlook to have access to various Internet directories and subsequently use those directories in much the same way as you use your own address books.

ACCESSING DIRECTORY SERVICES WITH IMO OUTLOOK

 To access LDAP directory services, you must add directory services to your accounts. You can access those directory services that are available from your ISP.

The procedure that follows applies specifically to IMO Outlook.

To add LDAP directory services to your accounts:

1. With any Outlook Information viewer displayed, choose Tools, Accounts to display the Internet Accounts dialog box.

2. Select the Directory Service tab, choose Add, and choose Directory Service to display the dialog box shown in Figure 9.47.

3. Enter the name of an available directory service, then choose Next > to display the dialog box shown in Figure 9.48.

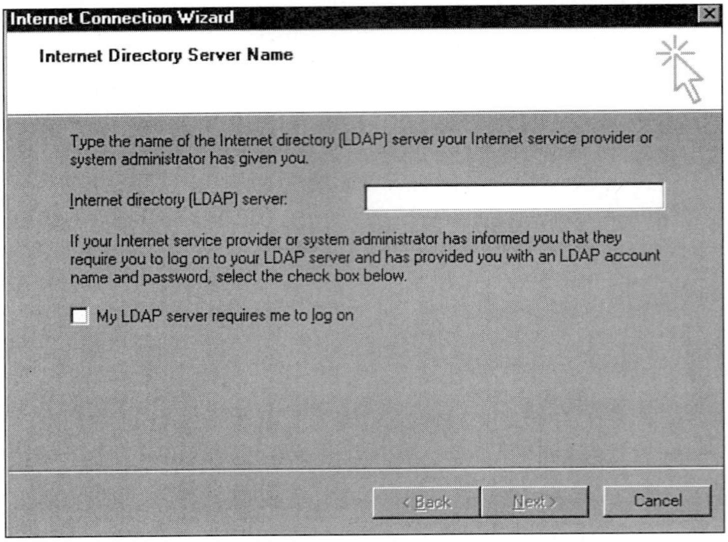

Figure 9.47
Use this dialog box to identify one of the Internet directory servers available from your ISP.

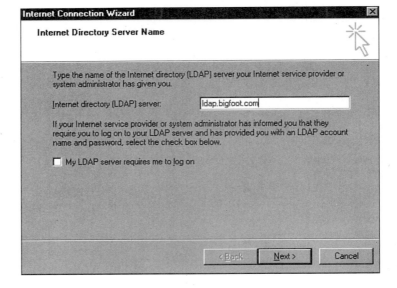

4. You most likely don't want to access the directory service each time you address a message, so choose <u>N</u>ext > to accept the default.

5. Choose <u>F</u>inish to close the dialog box and return to the Internet Accounts dialog box in which the directory service is listed.

Figure 9.48
Use this dialog box to specify whether you want to use the directory service to check e-mail addresses.

ACCESSING DIRECTORY SERVICES WITH C/W OUTLOOK

To access LDAP directory services, you must add the Microsoft LDAP Directory information service to your profile.

To add the Microsoft LDAP Directory information service to your profile:

1. With any Outlook Information viewer displayed, choose <u>T</u>ools, Ser<u>v</u>ices to display the Services dialog box.

2. Choose A<u>d</u>d to display the Add Service to Profiles dialog box.

3. Select Microsoft LDAP Directory and choose OK. After a few moments, Outlook displays the LDAP Directory Service dialog box shown in Figure 9.49.

Note

You may be asked to insert your Office 2000 CD-ROM into the drive in order to add this service.

Figure 9.49
You can use this dialog box to customize your access to the default directory service.

4. Choose OK to accept the default directory service properties. Outlook displays a message telling you to close and restart Outlook. Choose OK twice.

5. Choose <u>F</u>ile, Exit and <u>L</u>og Off to close Outlook. Then restart Outlook. Now you have directory services available.

USING DIRECTORY SERVICES

After you've set up Outlook to use Directory Services, you can access an Internet directory service in much the same way that you access one of your Outlook address books.

PART
III
CH
9

To find a person using IMO Outlook:

1. With the Inbox Information viewer displayed, choose Address Book 📖 in the Standard toolbar to display the dialog box shown in Figure 9.50.

Figure 9.50
The Address Book dialog box initially displays names in your Contacts folder.

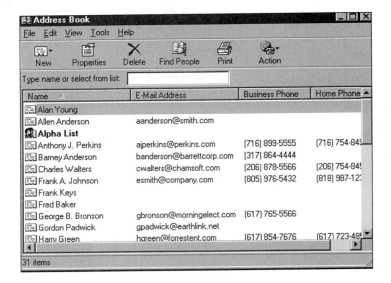

2. Choose Find People in the toolbar to display the dialog box shown in Figure 9.51.

Figure 9.51
You can use this dialog box to search in any directory to which you have access.

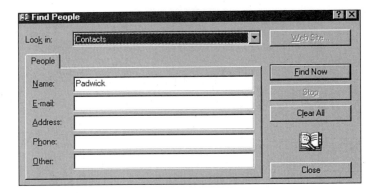

3. Open the Look In drop-down list and select the name of a directory server. The Find People dialog box changes to that shown in Figure 9.52.

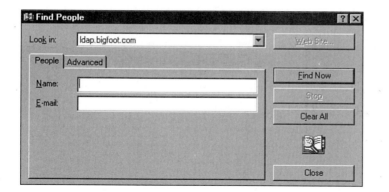

Figure 9.52
This where you specify a name or e-mail address you want to search for.

4. Enter a person's name in the Name box, or an e-mail address in the E-mail box, then choose Find Now. After a few seconds, Outlook displays the beginning of a list of people it finds, showing names, e-mail addresses and, if available home and business phone numbers, as shown in Figure 9.53.

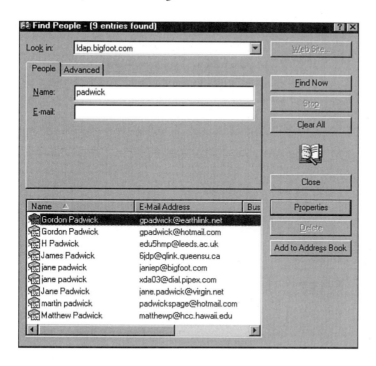

Figure 9.53
This a typical list of names and e-mail addresses found by a directory service.

You can select any name on the list, and then choose Add to Address Book, to add that name into your address book. You can also select a name and choose Properties to see what other information about a person is available.

To find a person using C/W Outlook:

1. With the Inbox Information viewer displayed, choose Address Book 📇 in the Standard toolbar to display the dialog box shown in Figure 9.54.

Figure 9.54
The Address Book dialog box initially displays names in your Contacts folder.

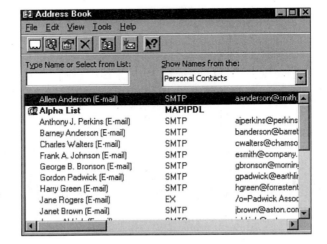

2. Open the Show Names from The drop-down list and select a directory server.
3. Choose Find Items 🔍Find in the toolbar to display the dialog box shown in Figure 9.55.

Figure 9.55
Use this dialog box to specify the name of a person you want to find.

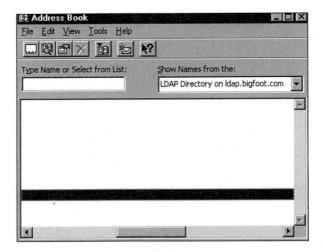

4. Enter a person's name (or partial name) in the Find All Internet Names Containing box, then choose OK. After a few seconds, Outlook displays a list of names and e-mail addresses.

TROUBLESHOOTING

On the whole, I've found that creating and using Contact items in Outlook works smoothly and reliably. The main problems with Contact items are caused by incorrect entries and by not keeping entries up to date.

Rather than being about solving problems after they occur, this section is principally about steering clear of problems. Some of the most common problems people have are caused by using too many address books and lists.

My first suggestion is that you use IMO Outlook if that satisfies your needs. IMO is simpler than C/W Outlook and, in some ways, performs better.

In IMO Outlook you initially have one Contacts folder, though you can create more. It may be tempting to have several Contacts folders, one for business contacts, one for friends, another for members of a society you belong to, and so on. But what if some people move to a different address or change their phone numbers? Do you want to go to the trouble of making changes in several folders, and will you always remember to do so? It's far better, in my opinion, to keep information about everyone in a single folder. You can use Outlook's categories to group people as you wish, assigning more than one category to a contact where that's appropriate. You can also create distribution lists based on contacts in a folder; Outlook can automatically update information in those lists if you change any information in your Contacts folder.

So, before you create more than one Contacts folder in IMO Outlook, think carefully about why you want to, and look for a way to achieve your objective while using only one Contacts folder.

Of course, in a business situation, you may have to use C/W Outlook because you need to use it as a client for Exchange or other servers. If you're using Outlook as a client for Exchange server and are deskbound, you can keep your Contacts folder, and other Outlook folders, on your local computer or on the server. Each approach has advantages and disadvantages. To get the best of both worlds, you can keep information on both and regularly synchronize the two sets of folders. That way, you have access to your folders when the server goes down or there's a LAN problem; also you can easily share information with other people.

Until the arrival of Outlook 2000, the only way to conveniently create distribution lists was to add a Personal Address Book to your C/W Outlook profile. Now, you can create distribution lists based on your Contacts folder, so that reason for having a Personal Address Book has gone away. However, if you're using C/W Outlook with access to a mail server, particularly if you have access to several mail servers, there is still a good reason for using a Personal Address Book. You can copy information about the people with whom you regularly communicate into your Personal Address Book so that you have them all in one place and don't have to hunt around on various servers to find them.

The bottom line in working with contacts is to use as few address books and lists as possible, be very careful to enter information correctly, be meticulous about keeping your Contact items up to date and, as I repeatedly say, always assign a category to every Outlook item.

CHAPTER 10

MANAGING CALENDARS

In this chapter

by Gordon Padwick

WHAT IS OUTLOOK'S CALENDAR?

You can use Outlook's Calendar to plan your future activities and also to refer back to previously planned activities.

The Calendar deals with three principal types of activities:

- Appointments—Activities that occur at specific times on specific days. Some appointments are with another person; others may be times you set aside to work by yourself.
- Meetings—Times when you meet with other people, usually a group. You can use Outlook to schedule meetings at times when other people are available. Like appointments, meetings occur on specific days at specific times.
- Events—Occasions, such as birthdays and holidays, that occur on specific days, but not at particular times on those days.

Any of these activities can be one-time or recurring. Recurring activities can be daily, weekly, monthly, or yearly.

These activities are created as Calendar items, saved in your Calendar folder, and displayed in a Calendar Information viewer.

Tasks (page 412) are strongly related to your calendar, but Outlook deals with them separately. This is because tasks usually, but not necessarily, have a start date and a due date; they aren't usually associated with specific times on specific days.

→ For information about how you can use Outlook to save information about tasks, **see** "Managing Tasks," **p. 411**.

CREATING A ONE-TIME APPOINTMENT IN THE CALENDAR INFORMATION VIEWER

We'll use the example of a one-time appointment to explain most of what you need to know about creating any kind of Calendar item.

Two ways exist to create an appointment: You can do so in the Calendar Information viewer or in the Appointment form.

Begin by choosing Calendar in the Outlook Bar to display whichever Calendar Information viewer was most recently displayed. Choose View, move the pointer over Current View, and inspect the list of views shown in Figure 10.1.

Choose Day/Week/Month to close the list and display the calendar in that view.

Choose Day in the Information viewer's Standard toolbar to display a daily calendar, as shown in Figure 10.2.

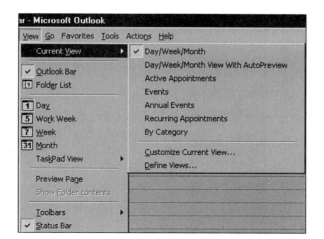

Figure 10.1
The checked view is the one that's currently displayed.

Appointment Area

Date Navigator

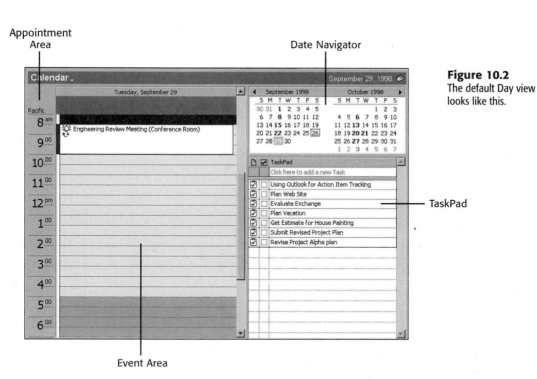

TaskPad

Event Area

Figure 10.2
The default Day view looks like this.

By default, the Appointment Area that occupies most of the left half of the viewer divides the day into half-hour segments. To change the scale, right-click anywhere in the Appointment Area to display a context menu. Choose Other Settings in that menu to display the dialog box shown in Figure 10.3.

Figure 10.3
You can use this dialog box to change the appearance of the calendar.

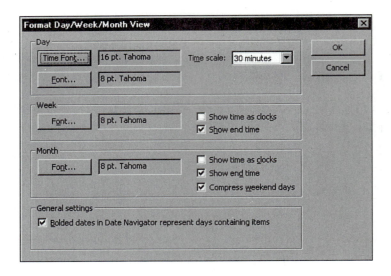

Open the drop-down Time Scale list near the top of the dialog box, and choose the time scale you want to use.

Note

The time increment you choose for the time scale is also the default duration Outlook uses for meetings.

To create an appointment:

1. If the appointment you want to create is for a month not shown in the Date Navigator at the top-right of the Information viewer, click the black triangle at the right end of the Date Navigator's banner until the correct month is displayed.

2. Click the date of the appointment in the Date Navigator. The Appointment Area now shows the hours in the selected day. That day's date is displayed at the top of the Appointment Area and has a gray background in the Date Navigator.

3. Point onto the time segment at which the appointment is to start, press the mouse button, drag down to select the period of the appointment, then release the mouse button. The period of the appointment is shown in blue.

Tip #77 from

Gordon Padwick

You can only create appointments that start and end on the time increments marked in the Appointment Area. If necessary, you can adjust start and end times in the Appointment form, as described subsequently.

4. Press Enter to signify you've finished defining the period for the appointment. The selected appointment period changes to white with a blue top, left, and bottom border. The insertion point is at the top-left of the white area.

5. Enter a few words to describe the meeting and then press Enter. The new appointment is displayed as shown in Figure 10.4.

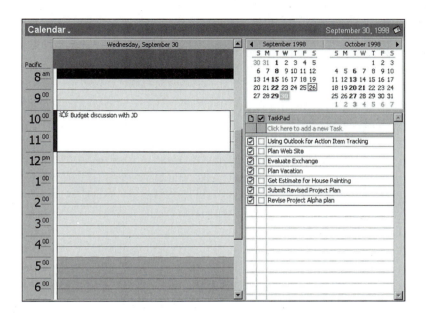

Figure 10.4
A small bell symbol appears at the left of the message's description to indicate that Outlook will give you a reminder 15 minutes before the meeting.

Note

By default, a *reminder* occurs 15 minutes before a meeting. You can change this default and you can specify how long before individual meetings you want a reminder.

→ For information about setting reminders, **see** "Setting a Reminder," **p. 366**.

Although these five steps provide a quick and easy way to enter appointments, they don't give you access to Outlook's capabilities to include additional information with Appointment items. To see more about the additional information you could include, double-click the appointment you just created to show it in the Appointment form, shown subsequently in Figure 10.5.

CREATING A ONE-TIME APPOINTMENT IN THE APPOINTMENT FORM

You can begin creating an Appointment item in the Calendar Information viewer, as described in the preceding section, and then fill in more details in the Appointment form. Alternatively, you can enter all the information for the Appointment item in the Appointment form, as described here.

To begin creating an Appointment item, display a Calendar Information viewer, then choose <u>N</u>ew in the viewer's Standard toolbar to display the Appointment form shown in Figure 10.5.

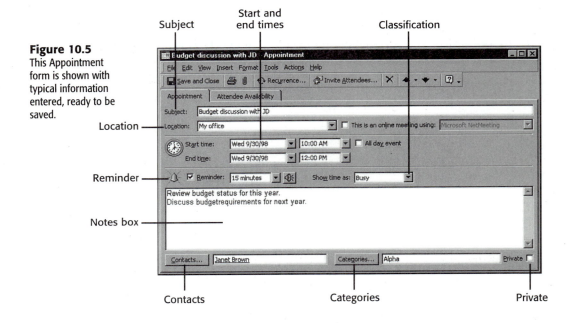

Figure 10.5
This Appointment form is shown with typical information entered, ready to be saved.

Subject

Start and end times

Classification

Location

Reminder

Notes box

Contacts

Categories

Private

By default, when you open the Appointment form, it assumes you want to create a 30-minute appointment at the beginning of the current day. The St<u>a</u>rt Time date box contains the current date and the time box contains 8:00 AM; the End Ti<u>m</u>e date box contains the same date and the time box contains 8:30 AM.

> **Note**
>
> The Appointment form defaults to the current date and a 30-minute appointment. The default appointment duration is the setting you choose for the Appointment Area's time scale, as described previously in this section. You can change the default start time by displaying an Information viewer and choosing <u>T</u>ools, <u>O</u>ptions, <u>C</u>alendar Options to display the Calendar Options dialog box. In that dialog box, you can change the <u>S</u>tart Time to a time other than 8:00 AM.

If you opened the Appointment form after the default start time, the InfoBar near the top of the form tells you "This appointment occurs in the past." That message goes away when you change the start time to a later time in the current day or to a subsequent day.

Note

Outlook is pretty smart about telling you when the appointments and other activities you create might cause problems. In addition to alerting you when you try to create an appointment in the past, the InfoBar also warns you if you attempt to create an appointment that conflicts with an existing appointment.

ENTERING THE SUBJECT AND LOCATION FOR AN APPOINTMENT

When the Appointment form opens, the insertion point is in the Subject box. Enter a few words to describe the appointment. Try to place key words at the beginning of what you enter so that the nature of the appointment is obvious in the limited space available in the Calendar Information viewers.

Tip #78 from

Gordon Padwick

Even though Outlook 2000 shows you all the text in the subject of an appointment when you point onto it in a Calendar view, you should name appointments so that the first one or two words indicate the nature of each appointment.

After you've entered a subject for the appointment, press Tab to move the insertion point into the Location box.

Outlook remembers all previous locations you've entered. If the location for the appointment you're creating is the same as the location for previous appointments (such as My Office, Conference Room, or Home), click the button at the right end of the Location box to display a drop-down list of existing locations and select the appropriate one. Alternatively, enter a brief description of the location.

Note

If the appointment is for an online meeting, click the check box at the left of This Is an Online Meeting Using; otherwise leave that check box unchecked. If you do check that box, the adjoining drop-down list is enabled—you can open that list to select the type of online meeting, according to what's installed on your computer.

After you've selected or entered a location, you can specify the start and end times for the appointment.

SPECIFYING START AND END TIMES

Start and end times are specified in a similar manner. For each, you specify a date and a time. Although most appointments are for a specific date, you can specify an appointment that starts on one day and ends on another.

Leave the All Day Event box unchecked. If you check this box, the appointment becomes an event.

→ For information about creating events, **see** "Creating a One-Time Event," **p. 368**.

ENTERING A DATE

What follows describes how you specify a start date. When you specify a start date, Outlook automatically uses the same date as the end date. You can use the information in this section to specify a different end date.

As mentioned previously, when you open the Appointment form, the Start Time date box contains the current date. You can replace the displayed date by entering a different date. When you do so, you must use a date format that's compatible with your Windows Regional Settings. For example, if you want to create an appointment for July 5, 1999, and you've set your Windows Regional Settings for English (United States), you enter 7/5/99; however, if you've set your Windows Regional Settings to English (United Kingdom), you enter 5/7/99.

SELECTING A DATE

Instead of entering a date, you can select it from a calendar. To select a date, click the button at the right end of the Start Time date box to display a calendar that shows the current month, as shown in Figure 10.6.

Figure 10.6
Outlook displays a calendar for the current month.

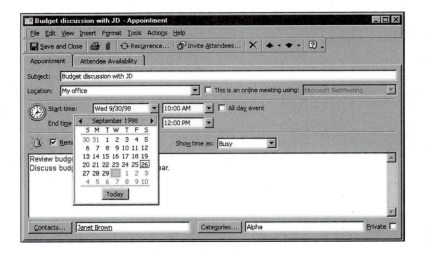

If you want to create an appointment within the current month, click the day within the month. To create an appointment for a subsequent month, click the right-pointing triangle in the month's banner to display subsequent months. With the appropriate month displayed, click the day for the appointment to return to the Appointment form with the selected day shown in the Start Time date box.

DESCRIBING A DATE

You can avoid the problem of defining dates in a way that's compatible with your Windows Regional Settings by describing dates instead of defining them.

Instead of entering a date in the Start Time or End Time date boxes, you can enter words or phrases such as:

- Tomorrow—Outlook displays the date of the day after today.
- Next Week—Outlook displays the date of the day one week after today.
- Next Month—Outlook displays the date of the month one month after today.
- Three Days from Now—Outlook displays the date three days after today.
- First Day of Next Week—Outlook displays the date of the first day of next week.
- Third Day of Next Week—Outlook displays the third day of next week.

Tip #79 from

Gordon Padwick

In addition to describing dates in words, you can use abbreviations. For example, "5m" means five minutes from now, "10d" means ten days from now, "3w" means three weeks from now, "2mo" means two months from now, and "5y" means five years from now. In each case, "now" is the date shown in the Start Time box, not the current date as indicated by your computer's internal clock. You can combine these abbreviations. For example, 1mo 3d means one month and three days from now.

PART

III

CH

10

These are just some examples of descriptive phrases I found Outlook understands. I also tried "Third day of month after next" and was rewarded with the "You must specify a valid month" message. There are some limitations to Outlook's intelligence.

ENTERING A TIME

You can enter a time in the box at the right of the Start Time date box using the 12-hour or 24-hour format. Here are some typical entries:

7:15

7:15 AM

7:15 PM

19:15

Tip #80 from

Gordon Padwick

If you enter a time without appending AM or PM, Outlook always assumes PM. To enter a time in the morning, you must append AM (or just a) to that time.

The advantage of entering a time in this manner is that you are not limited to times in a list. You can enter whatever times are appropriate. Such times as 3:17 or 18:21 are quite acceptable.

Note

Midnight is 12:00 AM. Noon is 12:00 PM.

SELECTING A TIME

To select a time, click the button at the right end of the time box to display a list of times. These times are always at half-hour intervals; you can't change that. Select a time from the list.

DESCRIBING A TIME

You can describe a time in words, just as you can describe dates in words. Some of the words you can use are

- Noon
- Midnight
- Three PM
- Ten AM

When you specify a start time, Outlook automatically changes the end time so that the duration of the appointment remains unchanged. You can separately change the end time without affecting the start time.

SETTING A REMINDER

By default, Outlook pops up a reminder on your screen 15 minutes before a meeting starts. You can change that default in the Options dialog box.

To turn off the reminder for a specific appointment, uncheck the Reminder box. To change the time ahead of the start of the appointment when the reminder appears, you can enter any number of minutes, hours, or days. Alternatively, you can click the button at the right end of the Reminder box to open a drop-down list and select from it.

Tip #81 from

Gordon Padwick

When you enter a time (instead of selecting it from a list), you can enter any number of minutes, hours, weeks, months, or years. You can use "m" as an abbreviation for minutes, "h" as an abbreviation for hours, "d" as an abbreviation for days, and "w" as an abbreviation for weeks. Outlook accepts decimal numbers such as 1.5h, 2.3d, and so on.

You can choose to have an audible reminder. To do that, click the button that has a loud-speaker icon at the right side of the Reminder box. Outlook displays the dialog box shown in Figure 10.7.

Figure 10.7
Use this dialog box to choose a sound file to play as a reminder.

You can choose any .wav sound file that's installed on your computer.

Tip #82 from

Gordon Padwick

In order to see reminders on your screen, or to hear them, Outlook must be running. That's why it's a good idea to have Outlook running (probably minimized) while you're not using it.
If Outlook isn't running when a reminder is due, you see or hear that reminder the next time you start Outlook.

PART
III

CH

10

CLASSIFYING AN APPOINTMENT

By default, Outlook classifies the time for your appointments as Busy. You can open the drop-down Show Time As box and select among Free, Tentative, Busy, and Out of Office.

When you subsequently display an appointment in the Day/Week/Month view of the Calendar Information viewer, each appointment has a colored border that identifies the appointment's classification. The colors are

- Busy—Dark blue
- Free—White
- Out of Office—Purple
- Tentative—Light blue

ADDING NOTES TO AN APPOINTMENT ITEM

You can add notes to an Appointment item in the unnamed Notes box that occupies most of the lower part of the Appointment form. It's often useful to enter notes here at the time you create the Appointment to provide information about what the meeting is about and what you intend to accomplish. During the appointment or after, you can add notes about what happened during the appointment.

To add notes, place the insertion point in the notes box, and begin typing.

While the insertion point is in the notes box, you can choose Insert in the form's menu bar and then choose File to attach a file to the Appointment item. You can also choose Item to attach an Outlook item to the Appointment item, or Object to attach a Windows object.

→ For general information about insertions, **see** "Message Insertions," **p. 96** if you're using IMO Outlook, or **see** "Message Insertions," **p. 201** if you're using C/W Outlook.

ASSOCIATING CONTACTS WITH AN APPOINTMENT ITEM

If the appointment is with one or more people who are listed in one of your address books, you can associate the Appointment item with those people.

Choose Contacts to open the Select Contacts dialog box, select the appropriate contacts, and choose OK to list those contacts in the Contacts box.

→ For more information about working with contacts in Outlook, **see** "Associating a Contact with Other Contacts," **p. 313**.

ASSIGNING CATEGORIES TO AN APPOINTMENT ITEM

As for all Outlook items, you should make a habit of assigning at least one category to every Appointment item.

Choose Categories to open the Categories dialog box, select the appropriate categories, and choose OK to return to the Appointments form in which the selected categories are listed.

→ Outlook's categories are described in Chapter 21. **See** "Using Categories and Entry Types," **p. 603**.

SAVING THE APPOINTMENT ITEM

Choose Save and Close in the Appointment form's Standard toolbar to save the Appointment item in your Calendar folder. Alternatively, you can choose File, Save or File, Save As to save the item in other formats.

→ If you need help with saving Outlook items, **see** "Saving a Contact Item," **p. 318**.

To see the Appointment item, choose the Day/Week/Month view of the Calendar Information viewer. Select Day, Work Week, Week, or Month in the Standard toolbar. Navigate to the period that contains the new appointment in the Date Navigator and you'll see the new appointment in your calendar.

→ For information about viewing appointments, **see** "Viewing Calendar Items," **p. 383**.

Note

Notice that the Day/Week/Month view with Day selected now shows the appointment location in parentheses next to the subject of the appointment.

CREATING A ONE-TIME EVENT

As mentioned earlier in this chapter, Outlook's events are very similar to appointments. The only difference is that events happen on a day or days without any times being specified, whereas appointments have start and end times. Birthdays, anniversaries, and holidays are typical events.

You can create Event items in the Day/Week/Month view of the Calendar Information viewer, or in the Event form.

CREATING A ONE-TIME EVENT IN THE INFORMATION VIEWER

Display the Day/Week/Month view of the Calendar Information viewer, then choose Day in the Standard toolbar to display the Information viewer shown previously in Figure 10.2.

Use the Date Navigator to display the day of the event. Point into the Event Area above the Appointment Area and click the mouse button. The Event Area becomes white to show it's ready for you to enter the name of an event. Type the name of the event and press Enter. Click in an unoccupied part of the Appointment Area. Now the event appears in a light gray box within the Event Area, as shown in Figure 10.8.

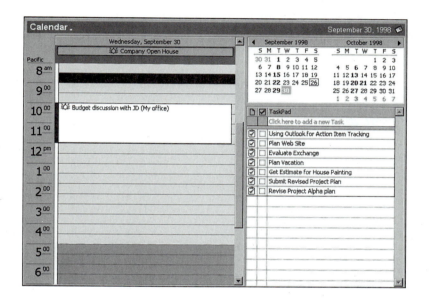

Figure 10.8
The bell symbol at the left of the event name indicates that Outlook has created a reminder for the event.

PART
III

CH
10

To create another event for the same day, point onto the dark gray area below the first event and click the mouse button. The dark gray area becomes white. Type the name of the second event. The words you type appear above the first event. Press Enter after you've finished typing the name of the second event, then click on an unoccupied part of the Appointment area. Now there are two light gray event boxes.

After you've created one or more events in this way, you can double-click an event to display that event in the Event form shown subsequently in Figure 10.9.

CREATING A ONE-TIME EVENT IN THE EVENT FORM

You can use the Event form to provide more information about an event you created in the Calendar information viewer, or you can create an Event item from scratch in the Event form, as described in the following paragraphs.

To create an Event item in the Event form, display the Calendar Information viewer and choose Actions, New All Day Event to display the Event form shown in Figure 10.9.

Figure 10.9
The Event form is almost identical to the Appointment form. The important difference is that the Start Time and End Time boxes show only dates (not times).

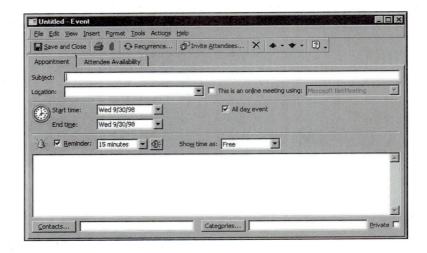

→ Enter only dates in this form in the same way that you enter dates and time in the Appointment form. **See** "Creating a One-time Appointment in the Appointment Form," **p. 361**.

CHANGING AN APPOINTMENT INTO AN EVENT AND VICE VERSA

Because appointments and events are so similar, it's easy to change one into the other.

To change an appointment into an event:

1. Display the appointment in the Day/Week/Month view of the Calendar Information viewer.

2. Double-click the appointment to display it in the Appointment form.

3. Check the All Day Event box. As soon as you do this, the times for the appointment disappear and the name of the form changes to Event.

4. Choose Save and Close in the form's Standard toolbar to return to the Calendar Information viewer. Now what was previously shown as an appointment is shown in the Event Area above the Appointment Area.

Use a similar procedure to change an event into an appointment.

To change an event into an appointment:

1. Display the event in the Day/Week/Month view of the Calendar Information viewer.

2. Double-click the event to display it in the Event form.

3. Uncheck the All Day Event box. As soon as you do this, the time boxes for the appointment appear and the name of the form changes to Appointment.

4. Enter or select appropriate start and end times for the appointment.

5. Choose Save and Close in the form's Standard toolbar to return to the Calendar Information viewer. Now what was previously shown as an event is shown in the Appointment Area.

CREATING RECURRING APPOINTMENTS AND EVENTS

Recurring Appointments and Events are those that occur regularly. A weekly appointment with your supervisor is an example of a recurring appointment. A person's birthday is an example of an annual recurring event.

The easiest way to create a recurring appointment or event is to start by creating a one-time appointment or event, and convert that into a recurring one. The following example applies specifically to an appointment. You can use almost exactly the same technique for an event.

Create a one-time appointment and display that appointment in the Day/Week/Month view of the Calendar Information viewer. Double-click the appointment to show it in the Appointment form. Choose the Recurrence button in the form's Standard toolbar to display the Appointment Recurrence dialog box shown in Figure 10.10.

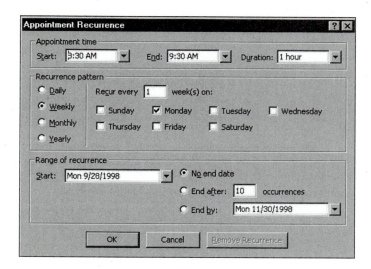

Figure 10.10
Use this dialog box to specify a weekly recurrence pattern.

MODIFYING THE APPOINTMENT TIME

The Appointment Time section at the top of the dialog box shows the start and end times of the appointment, and its duration. You can change any of these times:

- If you change the Start time, the end time changes automatically to keep the duration the same.
- If you change the End time, the duration changes to show the new duration.
- If you change the Duration, the end time changes to show the correct period between the start and end times.

If you choose OK after making changes in the Appointment Time section to go back to the Appointment form, that form shows the changed times.

SETTING THE RECURRENCE PATTERN

The Recurrence Pattern section of the dialog box is where you can select daily, weekly, monthly, and yearly recurrence. The dialog box opens with Weekly recurrence selected, as shown previously in Figure 10.10.

WEEKLY RECURRENCE

You can define the weekly interval. By default, the dialog shows 1 in the Recur Every box. You can change this to another number. For example, if the appointment occurs every other week, you would change the number to 2.

You can define the days of the week on which the recurring meeting happens. Check the appropriate days. If the meeting occurs on Mondays, check Monday and make sure no other day is checked. You can check as many days as necessary.

DAILY RECURRENCE

For a daily recurrence, choose Daily. The pattern options change to those shown in Figure 10.11.

The default daily option is Every 1 Day(s). Choose this if you have an appointment on all seven days of the week. If you have an appointment on all weekdays, choose Every Weekday.

MONTHLY RECURRENCE

For a monthly recurrence, choose Monthly. The pattern options change to those shown in Figure 10.12.

The default recurrence pattern is for one day every month. Outlook initially chooses the day number specified for the original appointment date. You can change that day number to any number in the range 1 through 31.

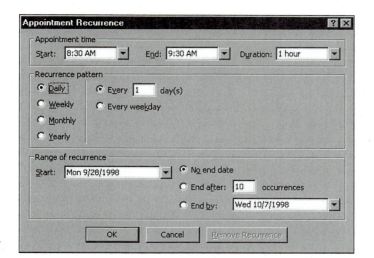

Figure 10.11
Use the Daily option to define a daily recurrence pattern.

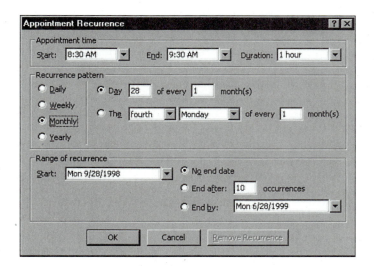

Figure 10.12
Use the Monthly option to define a monthly recurrence pattern.

Note

If you enter 29, 30, or 31 as the day number, Outlook creates the appointment for the last day of the month for those months that don't have a corresponding day.

The number 1 (for months) indicates every month. You can change this to 2 for every other month, to 3 for every third month, and so on.

Instead of specifying day numbers, you can specify a specific day. Open the drop-down list to the right of The and select among First, Second, Third, Fourth, and Last. Open the second drop-down list and select a day name. As described in the previous paragraph, you can accept the default 1 for every month, or change that to another number.

YEARLY RECURRENCE

For a yearly recurrence, choose Yearly. The pattern options change to those shown in Figure 10.13.

Figure 10.13
Use the Yearly option to define a yearly recurrence pattern.

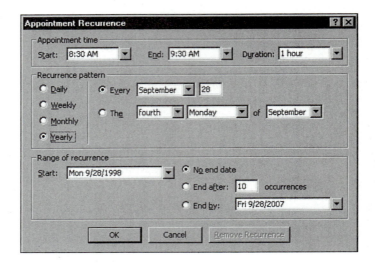

The default yearly recurrence pattern is for every year on the date specified for the original one-time appointment. You can open the drop-down list of months and select a month. You can replace the default day number with any number in the range 1 through 31.

Instead of specifying a specific date, you can define a date descriptively by checking the second option button. Open the first drop-down list at the right of The and select among First, Second, Third, Fourth, and Last. Open the second drop-down list and select a day name. Open the third drop-down list and select a month.

SETTING THE RECURRENCE RANGE

Use the Range of Recurrence section of the Appointment Recurrence dialog box to specify when the recurring appointment starts and stops.

By default, the recurrence starts on the date of the original one-time appointment. You can click the button at the right end of the Start box to display a drop-down calendar in which you can select a different start date. Alternatively, you can enter a date in the Start box.

Also by default, Outlook selects No End Date. You can choose to end the recurrence pattern after a certain number of occurrences, or at a certain date. To stop the recurrence pattern after a certain number of occurrences, choose the End After option button and replace the default 10 with the appropriate number. To stop the recurrence pattern at a certain date, choose the End <u>B</u>y option button and then click the button at the right end of the End <u>B</u>y box to open a drop-down calendar in which you can select a date. Alternatively you can enter a date in the End <u>B</u>y box.

DISPLAYING RECURRING APPOINTMENTS AND EVENTS

After you've finished defining the recurrence pattern, choose OK to display the Recurring Appointment form shown in Figure 10.14, which is similar to the Appointment form.

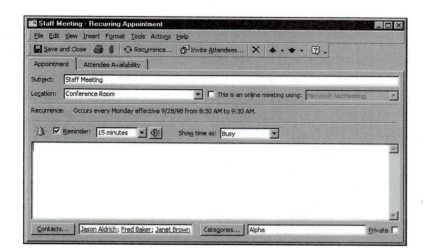

Figure 10.14
This form describes the recurring appointment instead of showing its start time and end time in boxes.

Choose <u>S</u>ave and Close in the form's Standard toolbar. Now you can use the Calendar's Day/Week/Month view to display the recurring appointment.

To display recurring appointments:

1. If necessary, choose <u>V</u>iew, move the pointer onto Current <u>V</u>iew, and choose Day/Week/Month.
2. Choose Da<u>y</u> in the Information viewer's Standard toolbar.
3. Use the Calendar Navigator to display the day calendar for the first occurrence of the recurring appointment. Figure 10.15 shows how this appointment is displayed in the calendar.

Note

The two curved arrows within the appointment indicate that you're seeing one occurrence of a recurring appointment.

4. Use the Date Navigator to select the next occurrence of the recurring appointment. This occurrence is displayed just like the first.

Figure 10.15
An occurrence of a recurring appointment is displayed in almost the same manner as a one-time appointment.

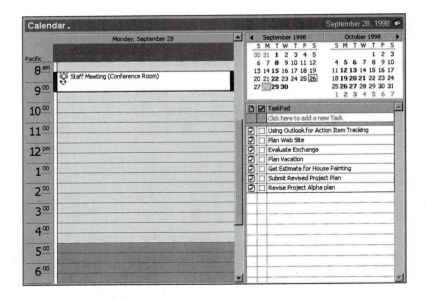

You can use the same technique to display subsequent occurrences of the recurring appointment.

CREATING RECURRING APPOINTMENTS IN ANOTHER WAY

Instead of starting from a one-time appointment, you can create a recurring appointment by using the method described in this section. Outlook doesn't offer a similar method to create recurring events.

To create a recurring appointment:

1. With any Calendar Information viewer displayed, choose Actions, New Recurring Appointment to display the Appointment Recurrence dialog box shown previously in Figure 10.10.

2. In the Appointment Time section of the dialog box, enter or select the start time in the Start box, then enter either the end time in the End box or the duration in the Duration box.

3. In the Recurrence Pattern section of the dialog box, select a recurrence pattern.

4. In the Range of Recurrence section of the dialog box, enter or select a start date in the Start box, then choose No End Date, End After, or End By.

5. Choose OK to display the Appointment Recurrence form shown previously in Figure 10.14. Enter whatever additional information is appropriate.

6. Choose Save and Close in the form's Standard toolbar to save the recurring appointment.

ENTERING HOLIDAYS AND OTHER SPECIAL DAYS

Holidays and other special days are common examples of yearly recurring events. You can create these recurring events in two ways:

- Automatically, by using Outlook's built-in lists of holidays for various countries and cultures
- Manually, by creating individual recurring events

Usually, I much prefer to do things automatically than manually—I'm all for saving time and effort—but, in this case, I recommend the manual method. I don't recommend you use Outlook's automatic method for these reasons:

- The automatic method adds holidays only over the period from January 1, 1998 to December 31, 2002. That's a problem if you want to find out the day on which a holiday occurred a few years ago, or when it will occur several years ahead.
- The automatic method creates all holidays as individual one-time events, rather than as recurring events. This means that holidays occupy much more disk space than necessary.
- If you choose two or more countries or cultures that have the same holidays, the automatic method duplicates those holidays in your calendar.
- The automatic method assigns the Holiday category to all the one-time events it creates. I prefer to reserve that category for events that really are holidays. Groundhog Day isn't a holiday for me!

One advantage of using Outlook's automatic holidays is that you have ready access to holidays for countries and cultures other than your own. Another advantage is that it provides holidays that do not have a regular recurrence pattern.

CREATING HOLIDAYS AUTOMATICALLY

Here's how you can create Calendar items for holidays automatically.

To create holidays automatically:

1. With any Information viewer displayed, choose Tools, Options to display the Options dialog box. Make sure the Preferences tab is selected.
2. Choose Calendar Options to display the Calendar Options dialog box shown in Figure 10.16.
3. Choose Add Holidays to display the Add Holidays to Calendar dialog box, shown in Figure 10.17.
4. Check those countries and cultures for which you want to add holidays, then choose OK.

PART
III
CH
10

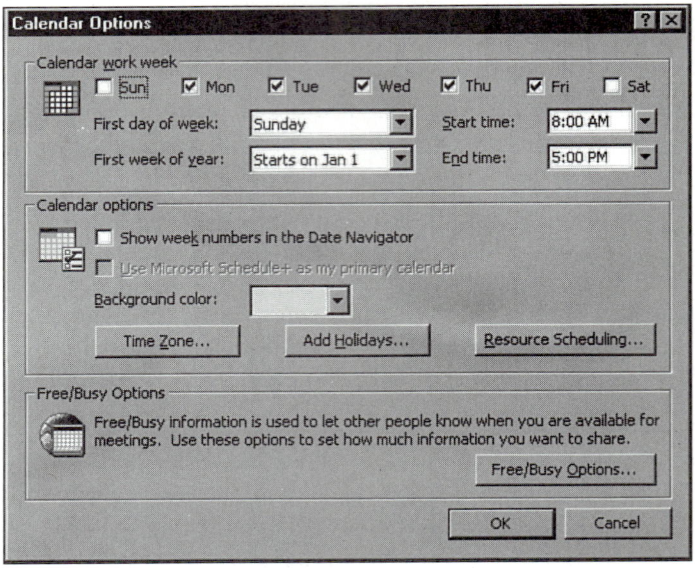

Figure 10.16
You can set several calendar options in this dialog box.

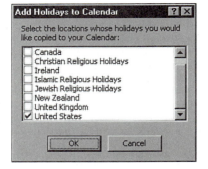

Figure 10.17
Use this dialog box to select the countries and cultures for which you want to add holidays.

After following these steps, you can examine your calendar to see the holidays that have been added.

MODIFYING OUTLOOK'S LIST OF HOLIDAYS

The holidays Outlook can add to your calendar automatically are listed in the text file Outlook.txt. You can use a text editor to make changes to this list, as explained in the Microsoft Knowledge Base article Q180985, *How to Customize Outlook Calendar Holidays*.

CREATING HOLIDAYS AND SPECIAL DAYS MANUALLY

You can use the method described previously in this chapter to enter most holidays and special days manually as recurring events. Some holidays and special days, though, have a recurrence pattern that's beyond Outlook's abilities to cope with—you have to enter these as one-time events for each year. Some examples of these are

- In the United States, income tax returns are due on April 15 unless that is a Saturday or Sunday, in which case the returns are due on the following Monday.
- In the United States, election day is the Tuesday after the first Monday in November.
- The Christian Easter Sunday is the first Sunday after the first full moon after the vernal equinox. Other Christian holy days are a certain number of days before or after Easter Sunday.

When you create Calendar events for holidays and special days, I suggest you assign Holiday as a category for items that really are holidays, such as Christmas Day and Thanksgiving Day. Assign another category, such as Special Day, for such special days as Valentine's Day that aren't really holidays.

It's not necessary for everyone in a group to individually enter holidays and other days into a calendar. One person can create a master calendar and export it to a file. Other people can import that file into their Outlook calendars.

→ For information about sharing Outlook items with other users, **see** "Importing and Exporting Outlook Items," **p. 565**.

MAKING CHANGES TO APPOINTMENTS AND EVENTS

You can make changes to

- One-time appointments and events
- All the appointments and events in a recurring series
- Individual appointments and events in a recurring series

CHANGING A ONE-TIME APPOINTMENT OR EVENT

You can change any of the information about an appointment or event by opening the item in the form in which it was created, editing information in that form, and then saving the changes.

To make changes in a form:

1. Display a Calendar Information viewer and locate the appointment or event you want to change.

2. Double-click the appointment to display it in the Appointment form, or double-click the event to display it in the Event form.

3. Change any of the information on the form.

4. Choose <u>S</u>ave and Close in the form's Standard toolbar to save the changes and close the form.

You can also make changes to an appointment or event displayed in the Day/Week/Month view of the Calendar Information viewer.

You can change the subject of an appointment or event.

To change the subject of the appointment or event:

1. Display the Day/Week/Month view of the Calendar information viewer.
2. Use the Date Navigator to locate the appointment or event whose subject you want to change.
3. Click on the appointment or event to select it. Place the insertion point where you want to make the change in the subject text, then use normal editing techniques to delete and insert characters. Press Enter when you've finished.

If you make a change to the subject of a recurring appointment or recurring event in this way, the change applies only to the single occurrence you edited. Outlook indicates this by adding a slanting line through the curved arrows that mark recurrence.

You can also change the date of an appointment or event.

To change the date of an appointment or event:

1. Display the Day/Week/Month view of the Calendar Information viewer.
2. Use the Date Navigator to locate the appointment or event you want to move.
3. Drag the appointment or event to another day in the Date Navigator.

You can change the time of an appointment.

To change the time of an appointment:

1. Display the Day/Week/Month view of the Calendar Information viewer.
2. Choose Day in the Information viewer's Standard toolbar.
3. Use the Date Navigator to locate the appointment.
4. To change the time at which the appointment starts without changing its duration, point onto the appointment and drag up or down. To change the start time without changing the end time, point onto the top border of the appointment and drag up or down. To change the end time without changing the start time, point onto the bottom border of the appointment and drag up or down.

CHANGING RECURRING APPOINTMENTS AND EVENTS

When you're dealing with recurring appointments and events, you can make changes to all the events in a series, or you can make changes to individual items within the series. You may for example want to change a regularly scheduled Monday appointment to Tuesday; in that case, you would change the series. However, if you have a regular Monday appointment, you might want to change the appointment to Tuesday if a particular Monday is a holiday. In that case, you would change only those individual appointments to Tuesday.

If you drag one occurrence of a recurring appointment or event to another date in the Date Navigator, Outlook displays a message telling you that only that one occurrence will be changed. Choose OK if that's what you want to do. Likewise, if you change the time of one occurrence of an appointment, Outlook tells you that only that one occurrence will be changed.

To have the choice of making a change to all occurrences of a recurring appointment or event or just one occurrence, follow the steps below.

To change the time of one or all appointments or events in a recurring series:

1. Display the Day/Week/Month view of the Calendar Information viewer.

2. Choose Day in the Information viewer's Standard toolbar.

3. Double-click a recurring appointment or event. Outlook displays the dialog box shown in Figure 10.18.

Figure 10.18
This dialog box is displayed if you have selected a recurring appointment or event.

4. Choose the option button according to whether you want to change only the one selected occurrence or the complete series. Then choose OK.

Proceed to make your changes.

DELETING APPOINTMENTS AND EVENTS

You can delete a one-time appointment or event, just as you delete any other Outlook item. Select that appointment or event in an Information viewer and choose the Delete button in the Standard toolbar. Outlook moves the selected item into the Deleted Items folder.

You can delete individual appointments and events from a recurring series, or you can delete the entire series.

To delete appointments and events in a recurring series:

1. Display the Day/Week/Month view of the Calendar Information viewer and use the Date Navigator to locate the item to be deleted.

2. Click an item in a recurring series of appointments or events to select that item.

3. Choose the Delete button ⊠ in the Standard toolbar. Outlook displays the Confirm Delete dialog box that asks you whether you want to delete all occurrences or just this one.

4. Choose Delete All Occurrences or Delete This One, according to what you want to do. Then choose OK.

EXAMINING A CALENDAR ITEM'S PROPERTIES

To examine a Calendar item's properties:

1. Double-click a Calendar item in the Calendar Information viewer to display that item in the Appointment, Event, or Meeting form.

2. In the form's menu bar, choose File, Properties to display the Properties dialog box, shown in Figure 10.19.

Figure 10.19
The Properties dialog box displays information about the selected Calendar item.

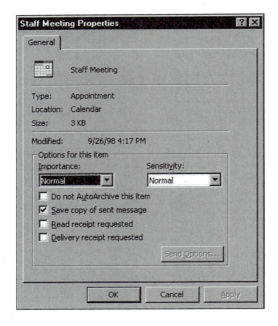

3. By default, Calendar items have Normal importance and Normal sensitivity. You can change the importance by opening the drop-down Importance list and selecting a different importance; you can change the sensitivity by opening the drop-down Sensitivity list and choosing a different sensitivity.

4. If you want to exclude the selected item from AutoArchiving, check the Do Not AutoArchive This Item box.

5. If the Calendar item is one you use to send a message (such as a Meeting Request), check or uncheck the Save Copy of Sent Message, Read Receipt Requested, and Delivery Receipt Requested boxes as appropriate.

→ To learn more about backing up your Outlook items, **see** "AutoArchiving Outlook Items," **p. 592**.

VIEWING CALENDAR ITEMS

The preceding pages of this chapter have focused on creating Calendar items. When it's been necessary to talk about viewing Calendar items you've created, I've referred mostly to the Day/Week/Month view of the Calendar Information viewer with Day selected. Now it's time to take a broader view of how you can view Calendar items.

You can view Calendar items in an Information viewer that displays those items in calendars, or you can view them in tables.

VIEWING CALENDAR ITEMS IN CALENDAR VIEWS

You can view Calendar items in four types of calendars: by the day, by the work week, by the week, or by the month.

To choose your view of a calendar, choose Calendar in the Outlook Bar to display the current default view. Then choose View in the menu bar and move the pointer onto Current View to display a menu of views. Select Day/Week/Month.

USING THE DAY VIEW

In the Standard toolbar, choose Day to display a view of the current day, with your planned activities shown in the Appointments Area as shown in Figure 10.20.

The Day view has three panes, the Appointment Area, the Date Navigator, and the TaskPad.

USING THE APPOINTMENT AREA

The Appointment Area shows your activities for the current day. The current day's date is displayed at the top of the Appointment Area. By default, the current day starts at 8:00 AM and ends at 5:00 PM. You can change the times at which your current day starts and stops in Outlook's Options.

→ For detailed information about setting Outlook's options, **see** "Setting Outlook's Options," **p. 845**.

Tip #83 from

Gordon Padwick

Use the vertical scroll bar at the right side of the Appointment Area to scroll to hours that aren't initially visible within the currently displayed day.

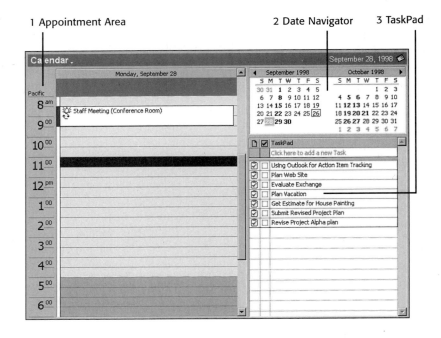

1 Appointment Area 2 Date Navigator 3 TaskPad

Figure 10.20
The Day view shows details of your appointments for a single day.

Each appointment is shown within a box in the Appointment Area that shows the duration of that appointment. If the subject of an appointment contains more text than can be displayed within the box, the subject is truncated. However, if you point onto the appointment, Outlook automatically enlarges the box to show all the text of the appointment's subject, as shown in Figure 10.21.

Figure 10.21
When you rest the pointer on an appointment that contains more text than can displayed within the space for that appointment, Outlook shows all the text in the box.

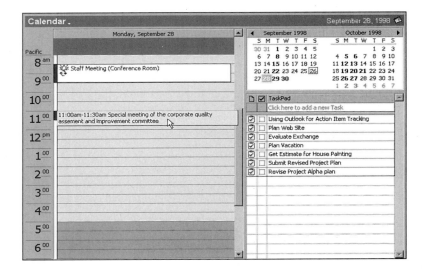

Tip #84 from

[signature]

The ability to show hidden text in this way is not limited to the Calendar Information viewer. You can use the same technique in other Information viewers.

Each event for the day is shown in a box above the Appointment Area.

As explained previously in this chapter, you can use the Appointment Area to create appointments. You can also double-click an already-existing appointment to display details about it in the Appointments form.

USING THE DATE NAVIGATOR   By default, the Date Navigator shows a calendar for the current month and the next month. You can drag the left border and the bottom border of the Date Navigator to display more months.

By default, each row in the Date Navigator shows a week from Sunday to Saturday. To choose a day other than Sunday to start each row, open the Options dialog box, select the Preferences tab, and choose Calendar Options. In the same Options dialog box, you can choose to display week numbers in the Date Navigator.

The current day, as determined by your computer's internal clock, is shown with a gray background enclosed in a red border. To display a day other than the current day, click the day you want to see in the Date Navigator.

The banner across the top of the Date Navigator has a triangle icon at the left and another triangle icon at the right. Click the triangle icon at the left to display previous months; click the triangle icon at the right to display subsequent months.

To display planned activities for a day other than the current day, click that day in the Date Navigator. After you do that, the planned activities for the selected day are shown in the Appointment Area (with that day's date above the Appointment Area), and the selected day is shown with a gray background in the Date Navigator. The current day, according to your computer's clock, is outlined in red on the Date Navigator.

You can show the activities for more than one day. To do so, click one day in the Date Navigator. Then, hold down Ctrl while you select one or more other days to select additional days in the Appointment Area, as shown in Figure 10.22.

To go back to displaying just one day in the Appointment Area, click that day in the Date Navigator.

USING THE TASKPAD   The TaskPad displays your current tasks. Refer to Chapter 11, "Managing Tasks," for information about tasks.

Figure 10.22
Here is the Appointment Area with two days displayed.

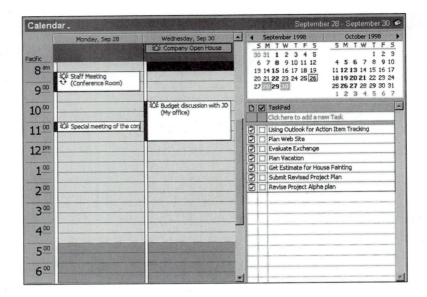

USING THE WORK WEEK VIEW

With the Day/Week/Month view of the Calendar Information viewer selected, choose Work Week in the Standard toolbar to display the Work Week view. By default, this shows a calendar with activities for Monday through Friday of the current week displayed, as shown in Figure 10.23.

Figure 10.23
The default work week is Monday through Friday. The days displayed have a gray background in the Date Navigator.

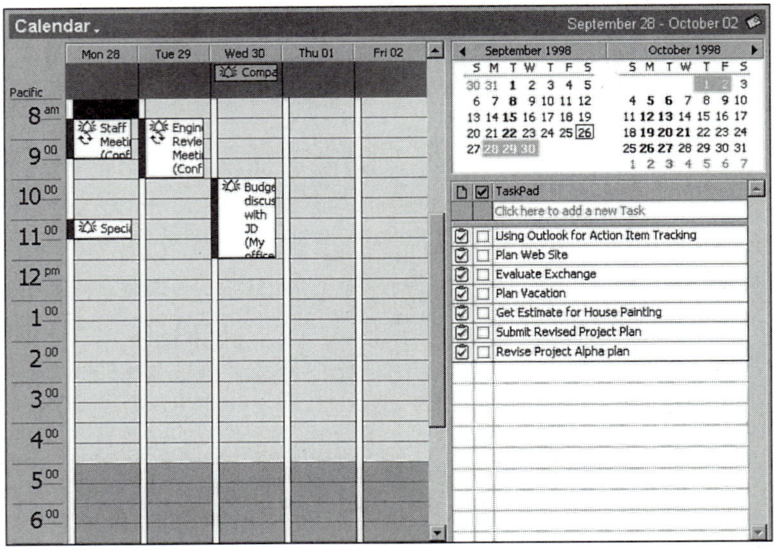

Note

> Due to the limited space in this view, only a very little of the text for each appointment and event is displayed. This is where the ability to point onto an appointment or event to see all its text is particularly useful.

The space available to display the subject of appointments and events is very limited in this view, so the text is truncated. You can display the entire text by resting the pointer on the appointment or event.

Using the Week View

With the Day/Week/Month view of the Calendar Information viewer selected, choose Week in the Standard toolbar to display the Week view. By default, this shows a calendar with activities for an entire week, as shown in Figure 10.24.

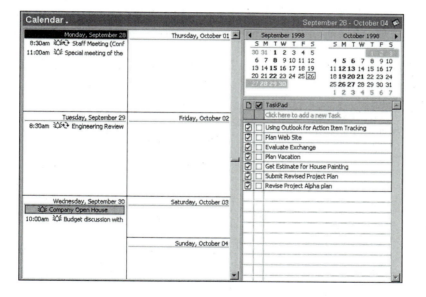

Figure 10.24
The selected week has a gray background in the Date Navigator.

Initially, Outlook displays the week that includes the current day. To display the calendar for a different week, click at the left of the week you want to see in the Date Navigator.

Tip #85 from

> Use the vertical scroll bar at the right side of the calendar to display previous and subsequent weeks.

To display more than one week, hold down Ctrl while you click at the left of the weeks you want to display in the Date Navigator.

USING THE MONTH VIEW

With the Day/Week/Month view of the Calendar Information viewer selected, choose Month in the Standard toolbar to display the Month view. By default, this shows a calendar with activities for a complete month, as shown in Figure 10.25.

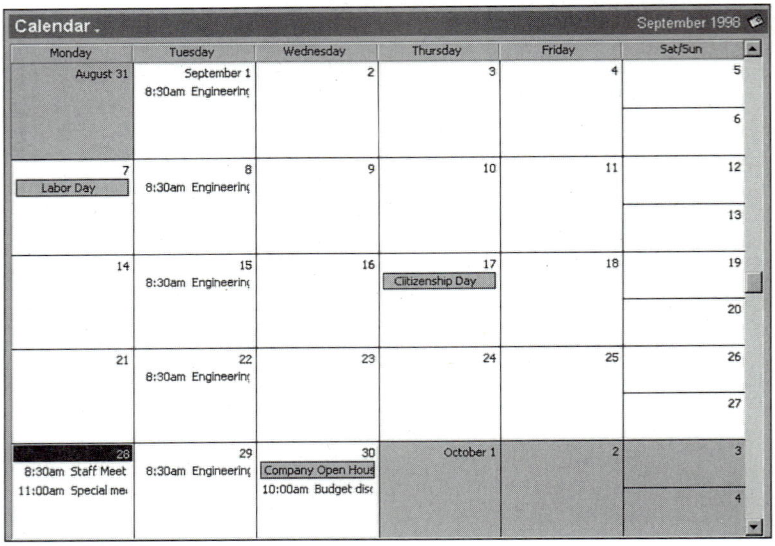

Figure 10.25
By default, the Date Navigator and TaskPad are not displayed in the Month view.

To display the Date Navigator and TaskPad, drag the right border of the Calendar to the left.

Tip #86 from

Gordon Padwick

Use the vertical scroll bar at the right edge of the calendar to move to previous and subsequent months.

By default, the Month view shows Saturday and Sunday at half the size of the other days. You can display the weekend days at the same size as the other days.

To display full-size weekend days:

1. Right-click within the Calendar to display its context menu.

2. Choose Other Settings to display the dialog box shown in Figure 10.26.

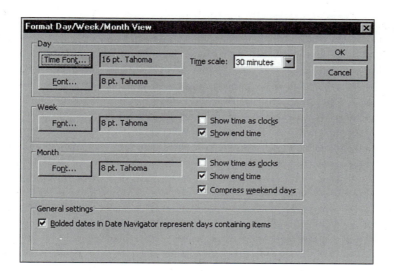

PART

III

CH

10

Figure 10.26
You can use this dialog box to change the appearance of Calendar views. The settings for the Day view also affect the Work Week view.

3. In the Month section of the dialog box, uncheck Compress Weekend Days. Choose OK to close the dialog box.

Now the Month calendar has seven columns, one for each day of the week.

MODIFYING THE DAY/WEEK/MONTH VIEW

The default Day/Week/Month view doesn't show any information you've provided for a Calendar item in the Notes box on the Appointment or Event form. You can modify this view so that information in the Notes box is displayed.

One way to do this is to use the Day/Week/Month View with AutoPreview view. To display this view, with any Calendar view displayed, choose View, move the pointer onto Current View, and choose Day/Week/Month View with AutoPreview.

After you do this, point onto an appointment or event. After a short delay, Outlook displays the details of that appointment or event with the text you entered in the Appointment or Event form's Notes box.

As an alternative, with the Day/Week/Month view displayed, choose View, Preview Pane to display the view shown in Figure 10.27.

Figure 10.27
With Preview Pane selected, the Day/Week/Month view displays a pane that summarizes an appointment or event and also the notes you've included.

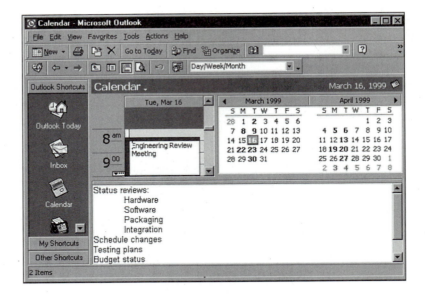

VIEWING CALENDAR ITEMS IN TABLE VIEWS

Although the Day/Week/Month views are what you will often use to see an instant picture of your plans and commitments, Outlook's table views of Calendar items provide useful insight into your Calendar items.

The standard table views of Calendar items are

- Active Appointments—Shows appointments and events for today and subsequent days listed in chronological order, grouped by recurrence
- Events—Shows only events grouped according to recurrence
- Annual Events—Shows only events that have annual recurrence
- Recurring Appointments—Shows recurring appointments and events, grouped by recurrence
- By Category—Shows all appointments and events, grouped by category

You can modify any of these standard views and you can create your own custom views.

→ For information about creating custom views of Outlook items, **see** "Creating Views and Print Styles," **p. 943**.

PRINTING CALENDAR ITEMS

You can print Calendar items in a calendar format or in a table format.

PRINTING IN CALENDAR FORMAT

To print your calendar in a calendar format, start by choosing the Day/Week/Month view of your calendar.

To print a calendar:

1. Choose File and move the pointer onto Page Setup. Outlook displays a list of available print styles, as shown in Figure 10.28.

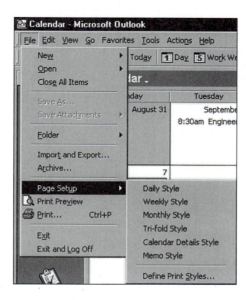

Figure 10.28
You can choose one of the predefined print styles, or you can define your own custom styles.

2. Select the print style you want to use, such as Monthly Style. Outlook displays the Page Setup dialog box, shown in Figure 10.29.

3. After defining how you want the calendar to be printed, choose Print Preview to see what your setup looks like.

Note

Notice that the text of the subject of meetings wraps within the horizontal space available for each day. This didn't happen in previous versions of Outlook.

4. If you're satisfied with the preview, choose Print to print the calendar. Otherwise, choose Page Setup to go back to the Page Setup dialog box to make changes to the setup.

Figure 10.29
Use the three tabs in
this dialog box to spec-
ify how you want the
calendar to be printed.

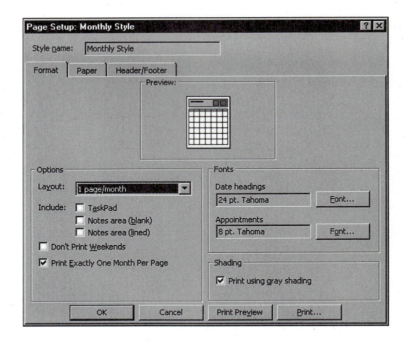

PRINTING IN TABLE OR MEMO FORMAT

If you want to print a calendar in table or memo format, select one of the table views.

To print a table view of a calendar:

1. Choose File and move the pointer onto Page Setup. Outlook offers Table Style or Memo Style.

2. Select the style you want to use to display the Page Setup dialog box.

3. Use the three tabs of this dialog box to specify how you want Outlook items to be printed.

4. Choose Print Preview to see what your setup looks like.

5. If you're satisfied with the preview, choose Print to print the Calendar items. Otherwise, choose Page Setup to return to the Page Setup dialog box.

PRINTING CALENDARS IN OTHER WAYS

You are not limited to Outlook's built-in ways of printing calendars. Instead you can

- Create your own Print Styles.
- Use Word templates.
- Use another application such as Seagate's Crystal Reports.

→ For information about printing Outlook items, **see** "Using Other Applications and Utilities to Print Outlook Items," **p. 990**.

SHARING YOUR CALENDAR

You can share your Calendar folder with other people, and you can share individual Calendar items with other people.

SHARING YOUR CALENDAR FOLDER

If you have an Internet or intranet account, you can use *Net Folders (page 453)* (sometimes referred to as Folder Publishing) to make your calendar folder available to specific other people.

If you're using C/W Outlook as a client for Exchange, you can make your calendar folder available as a *public folder (page 704)* that specific other people can access.

PART

III

CH

10

SHARING CALENDAR ITEMS

You can send selected Calendar items to other users.

To send Calendar items:

1. In any Calendar view, select one or more Calendar items you want to send.

2. Choose Acti**o**ns, Forward as v**C**alendar. Outlook opens a Message form with the appointments you selected shown as attachments, as shown in Figure 10.30.

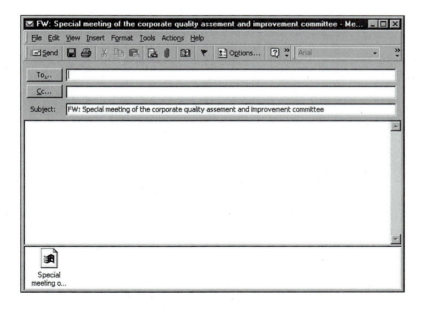

Figure 10.30
The Appointment items are shown as icons at the bottom of the Message form.

3. Address the message, give it a subject, and enter appropriate text into the notes box.

4. Choose Send to move the message into your Outbox folder.

5. Send the message in the same way that you send other messages.

When recipients receive your message, they see the icons representing your Calendar items. They can drag these icons into their Calendar folders to see them in their own calendars. Appointment items sent in this can be read by e-mail programs that are compatible with the vCalendar standard, not just Outlook.

Note   You can also right-click a Calendar item to display its context menu. In that menu, choose Forward to display a Message form with the Calendar item included as an attachment.

PUBLISHING YOUR FREE/BUSY INFORMATION

If you're using C/W Outlook and are using Exchange as your mail server, you can make your calendar accessible to specific other people.

By default, Outlook publishes your free/busy information every 15 minutes. Also, by default, Outlook publishes your free/busy information only for the next two months. You can change these defaults.

To change the free/busy time defaults:

1. Choose Tools, Options to display the Options dialog box. If necessary, select the Preferences tab.

2. Choose Calendar Options and, in the Calendar Options dialog box, choose Free/Busy Options to display the dialog box shown in Figure 10.31.

Figure 10.31
This dialog box shows your current free/busy defaults.

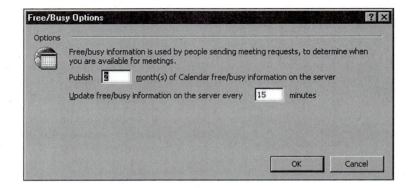

3. Enter the number of months for which you want to publish your free/busy time in the first box.

4. Enter the interval you want to have between publishing your free/busy time in the second box.

5. Choose OK three times to close the dialog boxes.

One possible problem to be aware of is that if you set the Show Time As for individual Calendar items to Free, other people will see you as free during the time of that item.

If you're using IMO Outlook, or if you're using C/W Outlook to access the Internet or an intranet, you can publish your free/busy information so that other people can know when you're available.

PUBLISHING YOUR FREE/BUSY INFORMATION

Follow these steps to publish your free/buy information on an Internet or intranet server.

To publish your free/busy times:

1. Choose Tools, Options to display the Options dialog box. Choose the Preferences tab.

2. Choose Calendar Options and choose Free/Busy Options to display the dialog box shown in Figure 10.32.

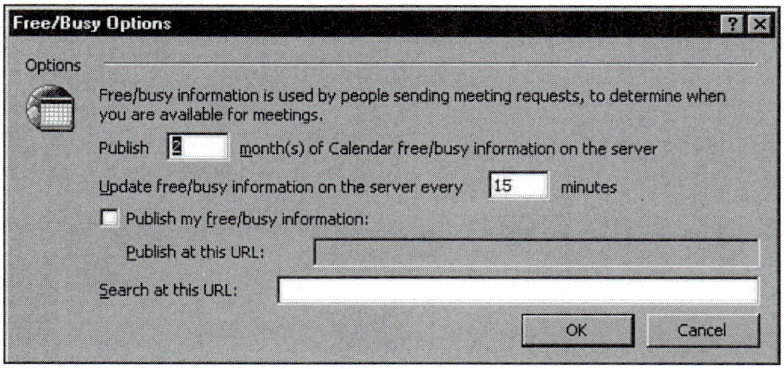

Figure 10.32
Use this dialog box to specify how you want to publish your free/busy times.

3. By default, Outlook proposes to publish your free/busy time for the next 2 Months. You can change the number of months.

4. By default, Outlook proposes to Update your free/busy time every 15 minutes. You can change this interval.

5. Make sure that the Publish My Free/Busy Information box is checked.

6. In the Publish at This URL box, enter the URL of the file in which you want to publish your free/busy information.

> **Note**
> Outlook publishes free/busy information in the industry-standard iCalendar format. In accordance with this standard, you must provide a file name that has the extension .vfb.

7. Choose OK three times to close the dialog boxes.

VIEWING A PERSON'S FREE/BUSY INFORMATION

 If you're using C/W Outlook as a client for Exchange and a person has shared his or her Calendar with you, you can view the person's free/busy information.

 If you're using IMO Outlook or using C/W Outlook and have the Internet E-mail information service in your profile, you can see a person's free/busy information if that person has published that information on the Internet or an intranet.

To see a specific person's free/busy information:

1. Display a Contacts Information viewer and double-click the contact for whom you want to see free/busy information.
2. Choose the Details tab.
3. In the Internet Free/Busy Address box, enter the URL of the file that contains the contact's free/busy information.

After you do that, the contact's free/busy information is available when you open the Appointments or Meeting form and choose the Attendee Availability tab.

USING TIME ZONES

 If there's one universal standard, it's that days consist of 24 hours. However, those 24 hours are not the same around the world. The world is divided into 24 latitudes, each of which sets its times so that midnight occurs at 0:00 and midday occurs at 12:00. That results in 5:00 in one region being 6:00, 7:00, 8:00, or whatever in other regions. The time within each latitudinal region of the world is known as a time zone.

In the days when people were only concerned with their immediate vicinity, that wasn't a problem. Now, though, many of us communicate with people throughout the world, so time zones are something we have to be concerned about.

Your computer has an internal clock that keeps track of times and dates. Using your computer's Setup utility, you can set this clock to your local time and date. In Windows, you can select Date/Time in the Windows Control Panel and, with the Date & Time tab selected, set the date and time. You can also select the Time Zone tab in which you can select your personal time zone.

Note

> Your computer's internal clock is not as accurate as a Rolex watch. You should reset your computer's clock at least once a month.
>
> Many programs are available on Internet sites that you can use to synchronize your computer's internal clock with time references available from the National Institute of Standards and Technology (NIST) or the United States Naval Observatory (USNO). One of these is Somarsoft ACTS. You can download a trial version of this program from http://www.somarsoft.com.

After you've done that, Windows applications, including Outlook, use your computer's internal clock to time-stamp your activities. There are, however, a couple of points that need clarification:

- The time and date you send an e-mail message is the time and date you sent it from your Outbox to the mail server, not the time and date the message was sent from the Message form to your Outbox.
- The time and date you received a message is the time and date the message arrived in your mail server, not the time and date the message arrived in your Inbox.

If you're using Outlook within one physical location, time zones are not a major issue. However, if you use Outlook to communicate with people in other time zones, particularly if you want to be able to plan time-critical events such as net meetings, it's very important that you and the people with whom you communicate set up time zones properly.

SETTING THE TIME ZONE

Fundamentally, Windows saves all times as *Universal Coordinated Time* (UCT), previously known as Greenwich Mean Time (GMT). Outlook uses the Windows time-zone setting to convert UCT times into local times.

To set the time zone:

1. With any Information viewer displayed, choose Tools, Options to display the Options dialog box. With the Preferences tab selected, choose Calendar Options.
2. Choose Time Zone to display the dialog box shown in Figure 10.33.

Note

> Alternatively, with the Day/Week/Month Information viewer displayed and with Day selected, you can right-click in the list of times at the left of the Appointment Area to display a context menu. Choose Change Time Zone to display the dialog box shown in Figure 10.33.

3. Open the drop-down Time Zone list and select your local time zone.
4. If the time zone you've selected adjusts times for daylight savings time, the Adjust for Daylight Saving Time box is enabled. Check that box if you want to adjust times for daylight savings time.

5. Choose OK three times to close the dialog boxes.

Figure 10.33
Use this dialog box to
set the time zone.

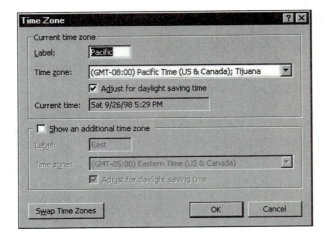

When you change from one time zone to another, Outlook automatically changes the times displayed for all Calendar items. For example, suppose your computer is set for the Eastern Time (US and Canada) time zone and you have an appointment for 9:00 AM. After you change the time zone to Pacific Time (US and Canada), Outlook shows the appointment at 6:00 AM.

Note

The time zone you select in Outlook affects Windows and applications running under Windows.

CHANGING THE TIME ZONE WITHOUT CHANGING CALENDAR TIMES

You might occasionally want to change the time zone without changing times for Calendar items. This can happen, for example, if you start using Outlook and subsequently find the time zone is incorrect.

To do this, export the items in your Calendar folder to a file, change your Windows time zone, and then import the Calendar items back into Outlook. The Microsoft Knowledge Base article Q181170, *Changing the Time Zone Without Changing Appointment*, describes this process in detail.

→ For information about importing and exporting Outlook items, **see** "Importing and Exporting Outlook Items," **p. 565**.

WORKING WITH TWO TIME ZONES

In the Day/Week/Month view of the Calendar Information viewer, with Day selected, the Appointment Area normally shows the hours of the day for the time zone you've selected.

Outlook can display hours of the day for two time zones. This is useful, for example, if you have frequent contact with people in a different time zone.

Start by displaying the Time Zone dialog box, shown previously in Figure 10.33.

To display a second time zone:

1. In the Label box, enter a short name, such as Pacific, for the current time zone.

2. Check the Show an Additional Time Zone box.

3. In the Label box (the one in the lower part of the dialog box), enter a short name, such as East, for the second time zone.

4. Open the Time Zone drop-down list (the one in the lower part of the dialog box), and select the second time zone.

5. If appropriate, check the Adjust for Daylight Saving Time box (the one in the lower part of the dialog box).

6. Choose OK three times to close the dialog boxes. The Day/Week/Month view of the Calendar Information viewer, with Day selected, now shows times in the two time zones, as shown in Figure 10.34.

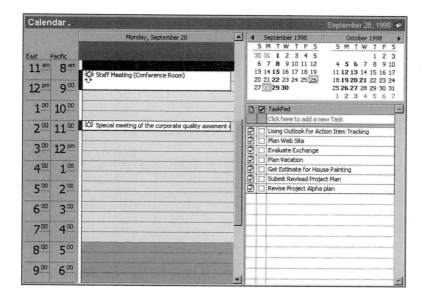

Figure 10.34
The names at the top of the two time columns are the names you entered in the Time Zone dialog box.

Times in the primary time zone are shown in the right column; times in the secondary time zone are shown in the left column. You can swap these two columns by clicking Swap Time Zones in the Time Zone dialog box.

INVITING PEOPLE TO MEETINGS

Outlook provides two ways for you to invite people to a meeting:

- You can decide when the meeting will occur and send e-mail messages inviting people to attend.
- If you have access to other people's calendars, you can choose a time for the meeting when other people are free and then send e-mail messages inviting people to attend.

UNDERSTANDING RESOURCES

Meetings involve resources as well as people. Resources are such things as:

- A room in which to hold the meeting
- Audio-visual equipment
- Remote conferencing facilities

You can set up an account for each of the meeting resources available in your organization. Then, when you arrange a meeting, you can "invite" the necessary resources.

INVITING PEOPLE TO ATTEND A MEETING

If you have decided on a time for a meeting, you can invite people to attend and reserve the resources you need.

To request people to attend a meeting:

1. With any Calendar Information viewer displayed, choose Actions, New Meeting Request. Outlook displays the Meeting form shown in Figure 10.35.

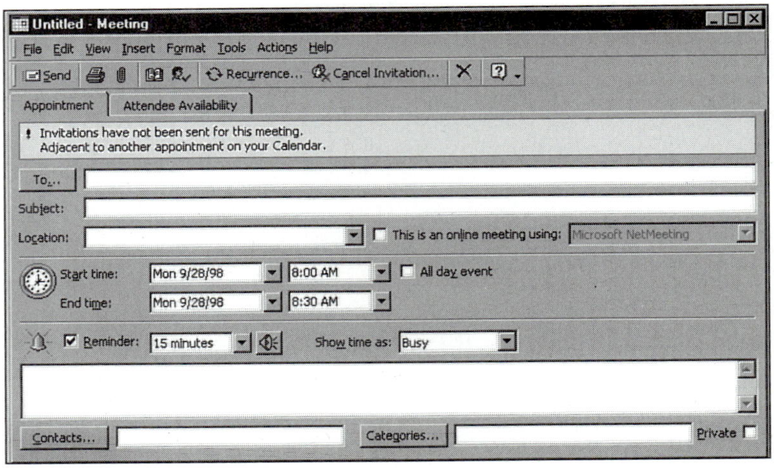

Figure 10.35
Use this form to create an e-mail message that invites people to attend a meeting.

2. Choose To to display the Select Attendees and Resources dialog box, shown in Figure 10.36, in which you can invite people to attend the meeting and ask for resources to be available.

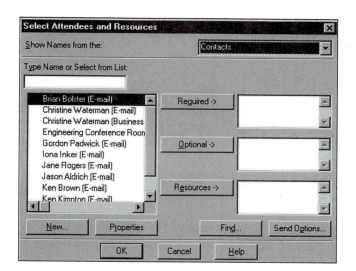

Figure 10.36
Select people and resources in much the same way that you address e-mail messages.

The dialog box shown in Figure 10.36 is what you see if you're using C/W Outlook. IMO Outlook displays a similar form.

Note

You can address attendees as Required, Optional, or Resources. Required and optional attendees are displayed in the form's To box. Resources are displayed in the Location box.

3. Enter the subject of the meeting in the Subject box and the location in the Location box.

4. Specify the Start Time and End Time in the same way that you specify start and end times for an appointment.

5. If you want a reminder before the meeting, check the Reminder box and then enter or select the time before the start of the meeting when you want to be reminded.

6. If the date and time of the meeting isn't firm, open the drop-down Show Time As list and select Tentative.

7. Use the unnamed notes box to provide information about the meeting. This might be an agenda or a statement of the purpose of the meeting.

8. You probably won't want to use the Contacts box in this form because the contacts are those people to whom you're sending the meeting invitation.

9. Choose Categories and select appropriate categories, such as the projects, that will be discussed at the meeting.

10. Choose Send in the form's Standard toolbar to send the message. The proposed meeting is added to your calendar with a meeting icon to identify it.

After you've sent the message, you can look in your Sent Items folder to see if it's been sent.

RECEIVING A REQUEST TO ATTEND A MEETING

When you receive a request to attend a meeting, that message appears in your Inbox Information viewer, as shown in Figure 10.37. If you have the Preview pane enabled, you can see the details of the message when you select the message in the Message pane.

Figure 10.37
The symbol at the left end of the message header identifies the message as a meeting request.

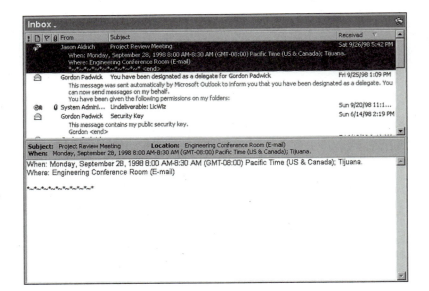

To respond to the message request, double-click the message in the Inbox Information viewer's Message pane. Outlook displays the message in the Meeting form shown in Figure 10.38.

In replying to the request, you can choose one of these buttons in the form's toolbar:

- Accept—Outlook creates an item on your calendar and marks the time as busy.
- Tentative—Outlook creates an item on your calendar and marks the time as tentative.
- Decline—Outlook creates an item in your Deleted Items folder.

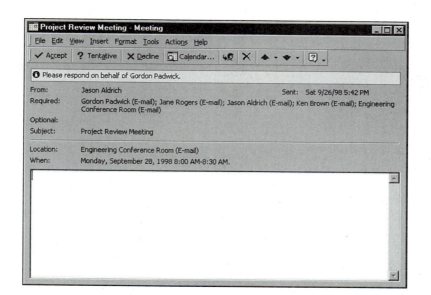

Figure 10.38
The InfoBar asks you to respond and alerts you to any conflicts with items in your calendar.

In each case, you can choose to:

- <u>E</u>dit the Text in the Notes Box Before Sending the Response
- <u>S</u>end the Response Immediately
- <u>D</u>on't Send a Response

After you accept the request, the meeting is displayed in your calendar with a dark blue border, as shown in Figure 10.39. After you tentatively accept a meeting, it appears in your calendar with a light blue border.

When you send a response to a request to attend a meeting, that response is sent as an e-mail message to the original sender. You can see that the response has been sent by looking at your Sent Items folder.

RECEIVING A RESPONSE TO A REQUEST TO ATTEND A MEETING

A response to a request to attend a meeting appears as a message in your Inbox Information viewer, as shown in Figure 10.40. Any comments the respondent has included with the response are shown in the Preview pane.

Double-click the response to see its details in the Meeting Response form, such as that shown in Figure 10.41. Notice that the InfoBar states whether the respondent has accepted, tentatively accepted, or declined your request.

Meeting icon

Figure 10.39
The meeting is identified in your calendar by a meeting icon (the two faces).

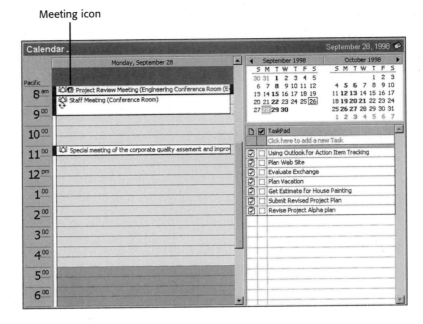

Meeting request icon

Figure 10.40
The icon (two heads) at the left of the message header in the Message pane identifies the message as a response to a meeting request.

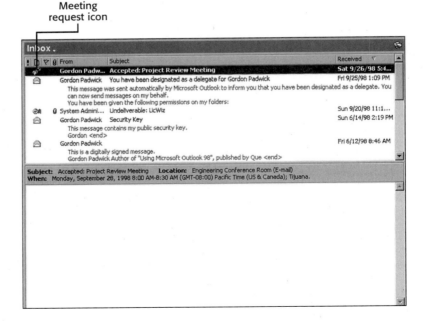

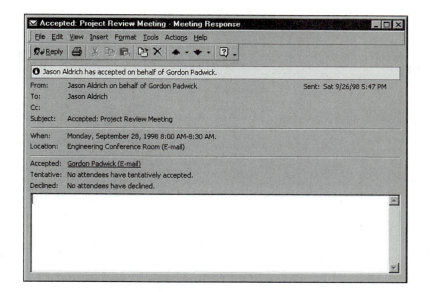

Figure 10.41
The meeting response form shows the message from the respondent and also contains a summary of who has accepted, tentatively accepted, and declined your request.

PLANNING A MEETING

In Outlook's terminology, planning a meeting is the process by which you find a time for a meeting when the people you want to attend and the resources you need are available.

FINDING A TIME FOR A MEETING

Outlook's tool for planning meetings can be used in several ways. The following paragraphs suggest one way you can use this tool.

Start by selecting the earliest time you would like to have the meeting in the Day/Week/Month Calendar Information viewer with Day selected. Then choose Actions, Plan a Meeting to display the dialog box shown in Figure 10.42.

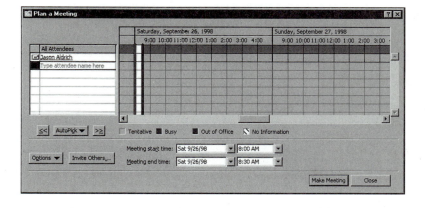

Figure 10.42
The Plan a Meeting dialog box opens with the time you marked in the Calendar Information viewer shown as a white column.

Initially the dialog box shows only your own schedule. You need to add the schedules of the people you want to attend the meeting and also for any resources you need.

To add schedules for people and resources:

1. Choose Invite Others to display the Select Attendees and Resources dialog box shown in Figure 10.43.

Figure 10.43
The list at the left contains the names of people and resources who have mailboxes on your server.

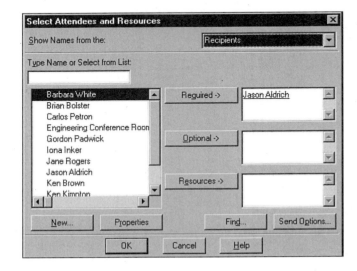

2. Select the people and resources and choose Required, Optional, or Resources to move the selected names into the boxes at the right side of the dialog box.
3. Choose OK to return to the Plan a Meeting dialog box that shows schedules for the selected people and resources, as shown in Figure 10.44.

Figure 10.44
The free/busy information for the people and resources you selected is displayed in this dialog box.

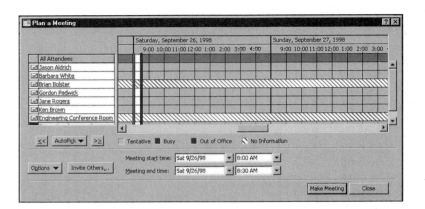

> **Note**
>
> If the schedule for a person or resource isn't available, the corresponding row is hatched.

4. If you're lucky, the date and time you originally proposed for the meeting doesn't conflict with the schedule of any of the people or resources. It's likely, though, that there are some conflicts, in which case you have to change the date or time of the meeting, as subsequently explained.

> **Tip #87 from**
>
> *Gordon Padwick*
>
> The row above the top person's schedule contains the combined schedule for all the people and resources listed. The information in this row is particularly useful if you have more schedules than can be seen at one time.

PART
III
CH
10

One way to change the time for the meeting is to let Outlook automatically find the first available period when people and resources are available. To do so, choose AutoPick. You can choose:

- All Invitees
- All People and One Resource
- Required People
- Required People and One resource

After making your choice, choose >≥ to have Outlook look for a time after the time you initially proposed, or choose <≤ to have Outlook look for a time before the time you initially proposed. When you do so, the white column moves to the right or left and suggests a time for the meeting.

Another way to change the time for the meeting is to drag the green vertical bar that marks the beginning of the meeting and the brown bar that marks the end of the meeting.

Yet another way to change the meeting time is to replace the dates and times in the Meeting Start Time and Meeting End Time boxes.

NOTIFYING ATTENDEES

Once you have established what appears to be a time when all the people and resources are available, you still need to notify those people and resources. By default, Outlook can send e-mail messages to all the people and resources. This default is signified by the envelope icons at the left of people and resource names in the dialog box. If, for any reason, you don't want to send an e-mail notification to a specific person or resource, click the icon and select Don't Send Meeting to This Attendee.

To prepare e-mail ready to send, choose Make Meeting. Outlook displays the Meeting form with the attendees' names in the To box, and with the resources' names in the Location box, as shown in Figure 10.45.

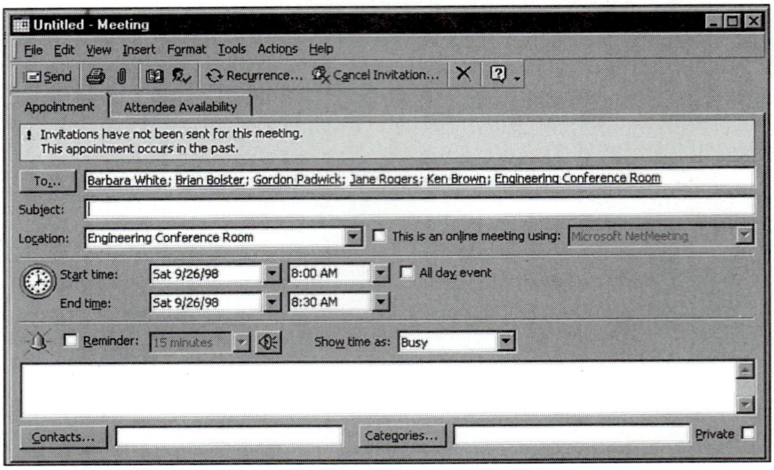

Figure 10.45
You can enter infor-
mation about the
meeting in the notes
box.

Choose $\underline{S}$end in the form's toolbar to send the messages.

Attendees receive the message and can reply to it in the manner described previously in this chapter.

→ For information about inviting people to meetings, **see** "Inviting People to Meetings," **p. 400**.

SENDING UPDATES TO ATTENDEES

After you have invited people to attend a meeting, you may want to send updated information. To do so, double-click the meeting on your calendar to open the original meeting
request in the Meeting form.

Make any changes to the information on that form and then choose Sen$\underline{d}$ Update on the
form's Standard toolbar. Outlook sends an updated message to the attendees.

YEAR 2000 COMPLIANCE

Microsoft states that Outlook is Year 2000 compliant. For a complete definition of *compliant*
in this context, see the Microsoft Year 2000 Compliance statement on the Web page

http://www.microsoft.com/ithome/topics/year2k/y2kcomply/y2kcomply.htm.

The Microsoft Knowledge Base article Q190167, *Year 2000 Compliance for Outlook 98* gives
detailed information about Year 2000 issues for Outlook 98. The information in this article
appears to apply to Outlook 2000. Presumably, Microsoft will either update this article or
publish another one soon after Outlook 2000 is released.

Although Outlook itself is Y2K-compliant, Outlook relies on other products being Y2K-compliant. In particular, you may have Y2K problems due to your computer's BIOS. Even though the software you use is Y2K compliant, you may have to update your computer's BIOS in order to use your computer after December 31, 1999.

If you use Outlook as an e-mail client, you must make sure that your e-mail server and all other parts of your e-mail environment (client transports, server connectors, gateways, and so on) are Y2K-compliant.

In places where you enter dates into Outlook, you can use a four-digit or two-digit format. If you use the two-digit format, Outlook employs a date window that extends from 30 years prior to the current date to 70 years forward of the current date.

MANAGING TASKS

In this chapter

by Gordon Padwick

Understanding Tasks

C/W

IMO

Tasks are activities planned for the future, but not things you must do on a specific day or at a specific time, though they may have a start date and a due date. This is in contrast to appointments that always have a specific date and time, and events that always occur on a specific day or days.

Here are a couple of examples to clarify the distinction between tasks and appointments. When you arrange a visit to the dentist, you create an appointment for a specific date and time. On the other hand, when your boss says, "It's time we had a Web page. I'd like to have it up and running by the end of next month," that's a task. No specific date and time are set when you must work on the project, but you must have it done by a certain date.

Tasks can be categorized in several ways, one of which is if they have a start date or due date, or both:

- Unscheduled tasks are those that don't have to be done by a certain date—the "when I get around to it" type of thing.
- Tasks that must be completed by a certain date.
- Tasks you plan to start working on by a certain date.
- Tasks you plan to start working on by a certain date and must have completed by a certain date.

Like appointments and events, tasks can be either one-time or recurring.

You can

- Create a task for yourself.
- Create a task for someone else.
- Receive a task someone created for you.

Outlook can display tasks in the TaskPad in the Day/Week/Month view of the Calendar Information viewer. It can also display tasks in various views of the Tasks Information viewer.

You can work with tasks in four places:

- In Outlook Today
- In the TaskPad
- In the Tasks Information viewer
- In a Task form

USING OUTLOOK TODAY TO WORK WITH TASKS

The Outlook Today window shows a summary of your uncompleted tasks:

- Those that don't have a start or due date (shown in black)
- Those that have a start date on or after today (shown in black)
- Those you marked today as completed (shown in gray)
- Those that are overdue (shown in red)

Tip #88 from

You can change the colors of overdue and completed tasks. To do so, choose Tools, Options, select the Preferences tab, and choose Task Options.

MARKING A TASK AS COMPLETE

Each task in the Outlook Today window has a small, empty box at the left of the subject, as shown in Figure 11.1.

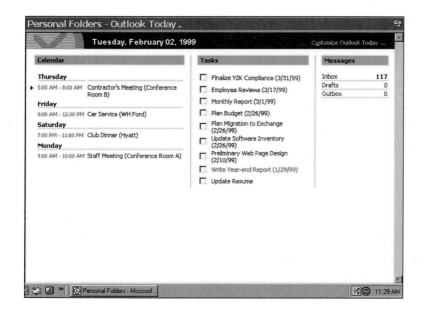

Figure 11.1
The Outlook Today window shows your current tasks with their due dates in the center column.

PART

III

CH

11

You can mark a task as complete in this window by clicking in the small box. When you do so, a check mark appears within the box and the subject is displayed in gray with strikethrough marks. Tasks marked as complete are not displayed the next time you open the Outlook Today window.

Note

> If you mark a task as complete by mistake, click the small box again to restore the task to the original status. The check mark disappears from the small box and the task subject is again displayed in black without the strikethrough.

DISPLAYING DETAILED TASK INFORMATION

To display details about a task, click the task subject. Outlook displays information about the task in a Task form.

→ For detailed information about using the Task form, **see** "Using the Task Form to Examine Tasks and to Create New Tasks," **p. 419**.

USING THE TASKPAD TO WORK WITH TASKS

As described in Chapter 10, "Managing Calendars," the TaskPad is usually displayed in the Day/Week/Month Calendar Information viewer with the Day or Week view selected.

You can use the *TaskPad*, shown in Figure 11.2, to examine your to-do list, to create tasks for yourself, and to mark tasks as completed.

Figure 11.2
The TaskPad is at the bottom-right of the Day/Week/Month Calendar Information viewer. It contains a list of your current tasks.

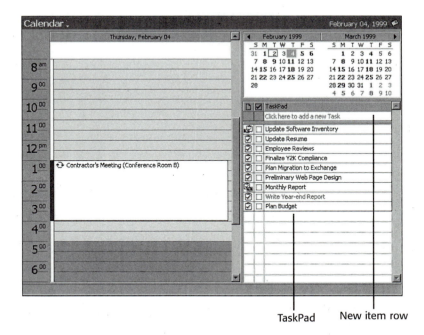

TaskPad   New item row

Tip #89 from

The TaskPad isn't normally shown in the Month view. You can drag the right border of the Month view to the left to reveal the TaskPad.

The TaskPad is like a miniature table view of an Information viewer. The default TaskPad contains three columns. From left to right, these are:

- Item Type—This column contains the Task symbol (a checked clipboard) in every row. Recurring tasks are marked with two curved arrows.

- Completion—For uncompleted tasks, this column contains an empty box. For completed tasks, this column contains a checked box.

- Subject—This column contains the subject of the task.

→ You can customize the TaskPad in much the same way that you can customize table views of Information viewers; **see** "Modifying a View," **p. 950**.

CREATING A TASK

Although limited in scope, the default TaskPad offers a quick and easy way to create new tasks.

To create a new task in the TaskPad:

1. Display the Day/Week/Month view of the Calendar Information viewer, as shown previously in Figure 11.2.

2. Click the New Item row of the TaskPad in the place that initially contains the words "Click here to add a new Task." When you click, those words disappear.

3. Enter the subject for a new task and press Enter. The subject of the new task moves into the list of current tasks.

Tip #90 from

Put the key words of the subject at the beginning. Then, if you list tasks in alphabetical order (as subsequently described) related tasks are listed in consecutive rows.

Also, try to use only a few words as the subject of each task–there's not much space in the TaskPad.

A task you create in this way has no start date and no due date. As explained subsequently in this chapter, you can add start and due dates, as well as other information, later.

→ To create a new task from scratch, **see** "Creating a New Task," **p. 420**.

EXAMINING TASKS IN THE TASKPAD

The TaskPad initially shows tasks in the order you created them, with the most recent task at the top. Completed tasks are indicated by a checked box in the Completed column and by the subject of the task being struck through. Overdue tasks are shown in red.

Tip #91 from

If you don't remember what a column in the TaskPad is for, point onto the heading of that column and pause. Outlook displays a ScreenTip that identifies the column.

You can change the order of tasks by clicking in the title row. Click once in the title of the Subject column to arrange tasks in alphabetical order; click again to arrange tasks in reverse alphabetical order. Click once in the title of the Completed column to sort tasks so that uncompleted tasks are listed above completed tasks; click again to list completed tasks at the top.

→ To examine a task in detail, double-click that task's subject in the TaskPad. Outlook displays information about the task in a Task form. **See** "Using the Task Form to Examine Tasks and to Create New Tasks," **p. 419**.

MARKING A TASK AS COMPLETE

To mark a task as complete, click the empty box in the Completed column (the second column from the left). You can also change a task that's marked completed to uncompleted by clicking the checked box in the Completed column.

DELETING A TASK

To delete a task, select that task in the TaskPad, then choose the Delete button in the Calendar Information viewer's Standard toolbar.

CUSTOMIZING THE TASKPAD

Several ways exist to customize the TaskPad. You can add columns to the TaskPad in the same way you can add columns to a Table view of an Information viewer.

→ Customizing the TaskPad is a straightforward process; **see** "Adding a Field to a View," **p. 955**.

Tip #92 from

I find it useful to add a Due Date column to the TaskPad. After doing that, I display tasks in due-date or reverse due-date order by clicking the title of the due-date column.

By default, the TaskPad contains your current tasks. These are

- All tasks that don't have a due date.

- All uncompleted tasks that do not have a start date or have a start date on or after today.

- All tasks you've marked as completed during your current Outlook session.

You can change the tasks listed in the TaskPad by choosing <u>V</u>iew, and moving the pointer onto TaskPa<u>d</u> View to display the menu shown in Figure 11.3.

Figure 11.3
You can use this menu to select various groups of tasks.

You can also change the tasks displayed in the TaskPad by setting a filter for it, just as you can set filters for table views of *Information viewers (page 17)*.

To set a filter for the TaskPad:

1. Right-click anywhere in the title row of the TaskPad to display the context menu shown in Figure 11.4.

Figure 11.4
You can use this context menu to customize the TaskPad.

PART

III

CH

11

2. Choose <u>C</u>ustomize Current View to display the View Summary dialog box shown in Figure 11.5.

Figure 11.5
You can use the View Summary dialog box to change the properties of the TaskPad.

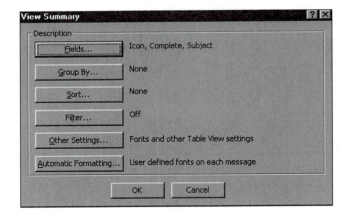

3. Choose Fi<u>l</u>ter to set a filter. Proceed from there in the same way that you set a filter for a table view of an Information viewer, as described in Chapter 38, "Creating Views and Print Styles."

You can use the context menu, previously shown in Figure 11.4, and the View Summary dialog box, previously shown in Figure 11.5, to further customize the TaskPad.

→ Customize the TaskPad using context menu; **see** "Modifying a View," **p. 950**.

CHANGING THE COLOR IN WHICH TASKS ARE DISPLAYED

By default, the TaskPad shows:

- Tasks that are not complete and not overdue in black
- Tasks that are overdue in red
- Tasks that are completed in gray

Note

The default TaskPad shows only completed tasks you have marked as completed during the current Outlook session.

You can change the colors in which the TaskPad displays overdue and completed tasks. Outlook always displays other tasks in black.

To change the color of tasks in the TaskPad:

1. With any Outlook Information viewer displayed, choose Tools, Options to display the Options dialog box. Select the Preferences tab.

2. Choose Task Options to display the dialog box shown in Figure 11.6.

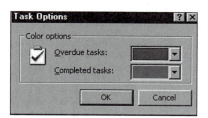

Figure 11.6
You can use this dialog box to change the colors of overdue and completed tasks. Although you can't see it on this page, the box at the right of Overdue Tasks is red and the box at the right of Completed Tasks is gray.

3. Open the drop-down Overdue Tasks list to display a list of colors. Select the color in which you want Outlook to display overdue tasks.

4. Open the drop-down Completed Tasks list to display a list of colors. Select the color in which you want Outlook to display completed tasks. Green might be a more appropriate color than the default gray.

PART
III
CH
11

USING THE TASK FORM TO EXAMINE TASKS AND TO CREATE NEW TASKS

While you can use the TaskPad to create tasks, as described previously in this chapter, that method is more appropriate for creating a personal to-do list. You should use the *Task form* to create Outlook items that contain detailed information about tasks. You can use the Task form to examine and modify existing tasks as well as to create new tasks.

EXAMINING AND MODIFYING EXISTING TASKS

You can display information about any task in the Task form and then add information to that task or modify existing information.

To display an existing task in the Form, double-click that task in:

- Outlook Today
- The TaskPad
- Any Tasks Information viewer

The Task form displays information about the selected task, as shown in Figure 11.7.

Figure 11.7
This Task form dis-
plays information
about a task created
in the TaskPad.

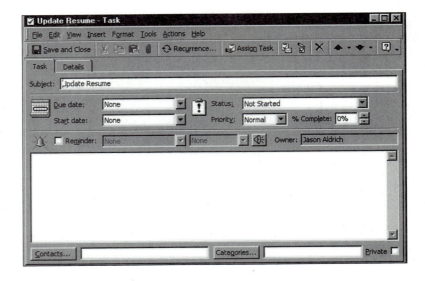

The Task form shows only the information you previously entered for the task. When you create a task in the TaskPad, the only information you supply is the subject of the task, so only the Subject box in the Task form contains information you entered in the TaskPad; all other boxes on the form are either empty or contain default values.

CREATING A NEW TASK

You can use the Task form to create a task for yourself or a task you want someone else to work on. In either case, start by defining the task.

To define a task:

1. Select Tasks in the Outlook Bar to display a Tasks Information viewer.

2. Choose New in the Standard toolbar to display the form shown in Figure 11.8.

3. Enter the subject of the task in the Subject box. Remember the suggestions earlier in this chapter to enter key words at the beginning of the subject and to use only a few words.

4. By default, the Due Date is shown as None. If you want to specify a due date, open the drop-down Due Date list to display a calendar and select the due date in that calendar. Alternatively, enter the due date using a date format that's compatible with your Windows Regional Settings. After you specify a due date, Outlook displays an InfoBar near the top of the Task form that tells you the number of days from now until the due date.

5. By default, the Start Date is shown as None. If you want to specify a start date, open the drop-down Start Date list to display a calendar and select the start date in that calendar. Alternatively, enter the start date using a date format that's compatible with your Windows Regional Settings. If you specify a start date that's later than the due date, Outlook changes the due date to the same as the start date.

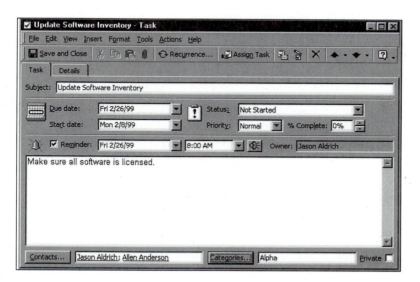

Figure 11.8
The Task form is displayed with the Task tab selected. The form is shown here with typical entries.

PART
III

CH
11

Note

If you select or enter a Start Date without having entered a Due Date, Outlook automatically makes the Due Date the same as the Start Date. Also, if you attempt to set a Start Date while the Due Date is set to None, Outlook automatically sets the Due Date to the same as the Start Date. Outlook doesn't allow you to set a Start Date without also setting a Due Date.

6. By default, Outlook displays the Status of a new task as Not Started. When you create a new task (or sometime later), you can open the Status drop-down list and select Not Started, In Progress, Completed, Waiting on Someone Else, or Deferred.

7. By default, Outlook displays the Priority of a new task as Normal. When you create a new task (or sometime later), you can open the Priority drop-down list and select Low, Normal, or High.

8. By default, Outlook displays 0% in the % Complete box. When you create a new task (or sometime later), you can enter a different percentage (or click the spin button at the right of the box to change the percentage).

Note

When you set the percentage to 0, Outlook automatically sets the status to Not Started; when you set the status to 100%, Outlook sets the status to Completed; when you set the status to any other value, Outlook sets the status to In Progress.

Also, when you select Not Started as the status, Outlook sets the percentage to 0; when you select Completed, Outlook sets the percentage to 100. When you set the Status to Waiting on Someone Else, or to Deferred, changing the percentage to anything other than 100% has no effect on the Status; changing the percentage to 100% changes the Status to Completed.

9. Initially, the Reminder box is unchecked. However, as soon as you enter a Due Date, Outlook automatically checks the Reminder box and sets the reminder date to the same as the due date, with the reminder time set to the beginning of your work day. When working with reminders, there are several points to keep in mind:

   - If you haven't entered a Due Date, you can check the Reminder box. When you do so, Outlook sets the reminder date to the current day and the reminder time to the beginning of your work day.

   - You can change the reminder date in the same way that you set the Due Date and the Start Date (see steps 4 and 5).

   - You can change the reminder time by opening the drop-down list of times and selecting a reminder time (this provides only half-hour time increments). Alternatively, you can enter a reminder time (in which case you aren't limited to half-hour increments).

Tip #93 from

The default reminder time is always the beginning of your work day. You can change the beginning of your work day in the Preferences tab of the Options dialog box.

10. If you've chosen to be reminded about a task, Outlook displays a message at the time the reminder becomes due (providing Outlook is running). To have Outlook play a sound when a reminder is due, choose the button at the right of the time box to display the dialog box shown in Figure 11.9.

Figure 11.9
Use this dialog box to select a sound file for Outlook to play when the reminder becomes due.

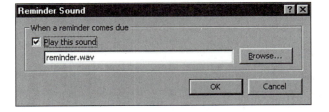

11. You can insert whatever notes are appropriate in the unnamed notes box that occupies most of the lower part of the form. You can also insert Windows files and Outlook items in this box, just as you can for Calendar items.

→ Use the notes box to help you keep track of Calendar items; **see** "Adding Notes to an Appointment Item," **p. 367**.

12. To associate one or more contacts with the task, choose Contacts to display the Select Contacts dialog box, in which you can select contacts.

13. To assign one or more categories to the task, choose Categories to display the Categories dialog box, in which can select categories.

14. If you intend to share your Tasks folder with other people but want to keep this task private, check the Private box.

15. Unless you want to enter more details about the task, choose Save and Close in the form's Standard toolbar.

Tip #94 from

You can enter more details about a task by selecting the Task form's Details tab, as described later in this chapter.

PART

III

CH

11

OWNING A TASK

Every task is owned by someone. Only the person who owns a task can change any information about that task.

Initially, a task is owned by the person who created it. In Figure 11.8, the Owner box contains the name of the person who created the task. That name has a gray background to indicate that you can't change it.

Note

Each Task item has an Owner field which is normally read-only. If you create a Table view of tasks, you can display the content of the Owner field. Outlook allows you to change the name in the Owner field in the Table view but, when you move out of that field, Outlook displays a message stating "You must be in a public folder to change the Owner field of a task. The original owner name will be restored." Sure enough, when you close the Outlook message, the original owner name reappears.

If you're working on a computer that's only used by you, your own name appears in the name box. However, if several people have Windows profiles on the computer you use, the name that appears in the Owner box is the name of the last person who used Outlook to send an e-mail message.

Tip #95 from

If a name other than yours appears in the Owner button, cancel the task you're creating, send an e-mail message to yourself, then re-create the task. This time, your own name should appear as the owner.

If you create a task, offer it to someone else, and that person accepts the task, Outlook automatically transfers ownership of the task to that person. After that, you can't make changes to the task; only the new owner can do that.

→ If you're a manager, assigning tasks is something you'll do frequently; **see** "Assigning a Task to Someone Else," **p. 430**.

ENTERING MORE INFORMATION ABOUT A TASK

While you can use the preceding procedure to enter all the information you'll normally need about a task, you can enter more information in the Task form's Details tab, shown in Figure 11.10. This tab is particularly useful in the case of tasks for which you need to keep billing records.

Figure 11.10
Use this tab to enter more information about a task.

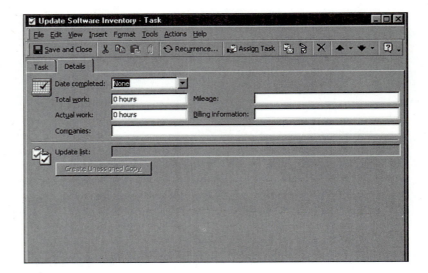

Use the boxes in this tab as follows:

- Date Completed—This box initially contains None. When the task is completed, open the drop-down calendar and select the completion date (or enter the completion date). When you do so, Outlook automatically sets the Status box in the Task tab to Completed and the % Complete box to 100. If you change Status in the Task tab to Completed, the Date Completed box in the Details tab contains the date on which you marked the task as completed. Likewise, if you open the drop-down Date Completed calendar on the Details tab and choose None, Status on the Task tab changes to In Progress and % Complete changes to 75.

- Total Work—Use this box for your estimate of the total amount of time required to complete the task.

- Actual Work—Use this box to keep track of the time you actually spend on the task.

- Mileage—Use this box to keep track of the number of miles you travel in connection with the task.

- Billing Information—Use this box for any information related to billing, such as the hourly rate to be charged.

- Companies—Enter the names of organizations associated with the task, such as the name of the client for whom the task is being performed.

The Update List box and Create Unassigned Copy button are used when you assign a task to someone else.

→ Once you've been assigned a task, you have the option of accepting or rejecting it. **See** "Accepting a Task," **p. 435**.

Tip #96 from 	If you need a more versatile and powerful way of keeping track of tasks, consider integrating Outlook with Microsoft Team Manager. **See** "Going Further with Task Management," **p. 437**.

USING THE TASKS INFORMATION VIEWER TO WORK WITH TASKS

While the TaskPad provides a useful way for you to keep up to date with your current tasks, it doesn't provide all the information you need to see or enter about tasks. The Tasks Information viewer displays more detailed information.

Choose the Tasks shortcut in the Outlook Bar to display the Tasks Information Viewer, shown in Figure 11.11.

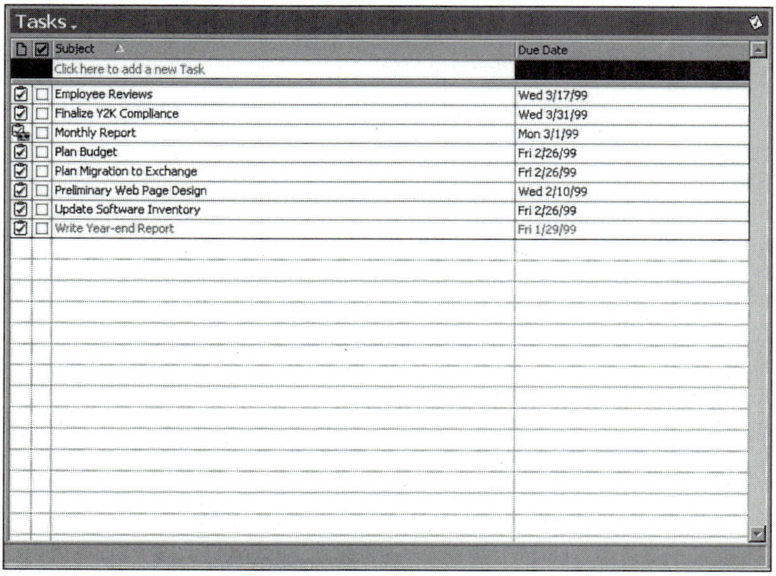

PART

III

CH

11

Tasks		Due Date
Subject	Click here to add a new Task	
Employee Reviews		Wed 3/17/99
Finalize Y2K Compliance		Wed 3/31/99
Monthly Report		Mon 3/1/99
Plan Budget		Fri 2/26/99
Plan Migration to Exchange		Fri 2/26/99
Preliminary Web Page Design		Wed 2/10/99
Update Software Inventory		Fri 2/26/99
Write Year-end Report		Fri 1/29/99

Figure 11.11
Outlook initially displays the Simple Task view of the Tasks Information viewer in which the Subject and Due Date of all tasks are listed.

If you see a different view on your computer, choose View, move the pointer onto Current View, and choose Simple List.

The Simple List view is much like the TaskPad described previously in this chapter. You can use it in the same way as the TaskPad.

With the Simple List, or another, view of tasks displayed you can choose View, Preview Pane so that you can see more information about a selected task, as shown in Figure 11.12.

Figure 11.12
The Preview pane header shows the Subject, Status, Due Date, and Owner of a task selected in the list. The pane also shows any information about the task you entered in the notes box on the Task form.

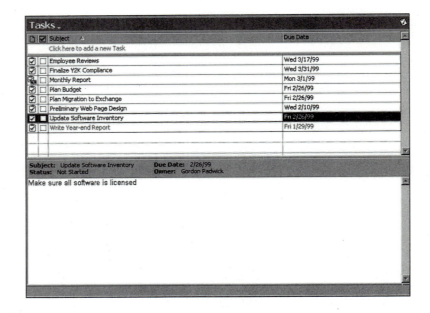

Refer to Chapters 3 and 6 for more information about the Preview pane.

Note

You can't create a Preview pane in the TaskPad.

→ For information about using the Preview pane in IMO Outlook, **see** "Viewing a Message in the Preview Pane," **p. 115**.

→ To learn more about using the Preview pane in C/W Outlook, **see** "Viewing a Message in the Preview Pane," **p. 220**.

In addition to the Simple List view shown here, you can select various other Table views and one Timeline view.

→ If none of the existing views suits your needs, **see** "Creating Views and Print Styles," **p. 943**.

USING THE TASKS INFORMATION VIEWER TO CREATE TASKS

You can use the Simple List view of the Tasks Information viewer, shown previously in Figures 11.11 and 11.12, to create a new task in much the same way that you can use the TaskPad.

→ If you need to create a new task, **see** "Creating a Task," **p. 415**.

If you don't see the New Item row on your computer screen, follow these steps.

To display the New Item row:

1. With the Simple List view of the Tasks Information viewer displayed, choose View, move the pointer onto Current View, and choose Customize Current View to Display the View Summary dialog box shown previously in Figure 11.5.

2. Choose Other Settings to display the dialog box shown in Figure 11.13.

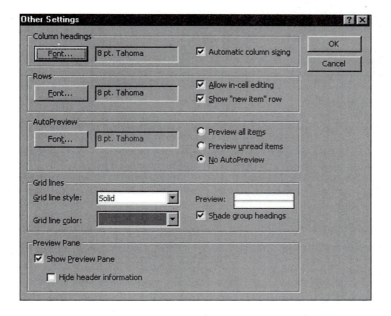

Figure 11.13
You can use this dialog box to change the appearance of a view.

3. Check the Show "New Item" Row box, then choose OK twice to close the dialog boxes. Now you should see the New Item row at the top of Simple List view of tasks.

To create a new task in the Simple List view of the Tasks Information viewer, click within the words "Click here to add a new task." The New Item row changes to show two cells, one for the subject of the new task and one for the due date. Enter the subject, optionally enter the due date, and press Enter. Outlook moves the new task into the list of tasks.

You're not limited to entering only the subject and due date for a new task in this way. You can, for example, use the Detailed List view of the Tasks Information viewer to enter more information for a new task.

To display the Detailed List view, choose <u>V</u>iew, move the pointer onto Current <u>V</u>iew, and choose Detailed List. A Detailed List view is shown in Figure 11.14.

Figure 11.14
You can use this view to enter additional information about a new task.

			Subject	Status	Due Date	% Complete	Categories
			Click here to add a new Task				
☑			Write Year-end Report	Not Started	Fri 1/29/99	0%	Alpha
☑			Preliminary Web Page Design	In Progress	Wed 2/10/99	50%	Company
☑			Update Software Inventory	Not Started	Fri 2/26/99	0%	Alpha
☑			Plan Migration to Exchange	In Progress	Fri 2/26/99	10%	Company
☑			Plan Budget	Not Started	Fri 2/26/99	0%	Alpha
			Monthly Report	Not Started	Mon 3/1/99	0%	Alpha
☑			Employee Reviews	Not Started	Wed 3/17/99	0%	Alpha
☑			Finalize Y2K Compliance	In Progress	Wed 3/31/99	50%	Company

Tip #97 from

If you enabled the Preview pane for the Simple List view and then switch to the Detailed List view, you'll probably notice that the Preview pane isn't there. That's because Outlook keeps information about each view separately. If you want to have the Preview pane displayed for the Detailed List view, you have to choose <u>V</u>iew, Preview Pa<u>n</u>e while the Detailed View is displayed.

USING THE TASKS INFORMATION VIEWER TO VIEW TASKS

You can use the Tasks Information viewer to see tasks in various Table views and in one Timeline view:

- Simple List contains all tasks and displays only the Subject and Due Date fields.

- Detailed List contains all tasks and displays the Subject, Status, Due Date, % Complete, and Categories fields.

- Active Tasks is a filtered list containing tasks that have a status of Not Started, In Progress, or Waiting On Someone Else, and displays the same fields as the Detailed List.

- Next Seven Days is a filtered list containing tasks due in the next seven days and displays the same fields as the Detailed List.

- Overdue Tasks is a filtered list containing tasks due before today and displays the same fields as the Detailed List.

- By Category contains all tasks grouped by category and contains the same fields as the Detailed List.

- Assignment contains tasks offered to you and accepted by you and displays the Subject, Owner, Due Date, and Status fields.

- By Person Responsible contains all tasks grouped by Owner and displays the Subject, Requested By, Owner, Due Date, and Status fields.

- Completed Tasks is a filtered list containing only completed tasks and displays the Subject, Due Date, Date Completed, and Categories fields.
- Task Timeline contains all tasks arranged chronologically.

→ You can modify these standard views and create custom views. **See** "Creating Views and Print Styles," **p. 943**.

In any of the Table views you can use the techniques described in the section of this chapter about using the TaskPad to:

- Change the order in which tasks are listed
- Mark tasks as completed
- Delete tasks
- Edit the contents of the displayed fields (providing you have Allow In-cell Editing enabled)
- Double-click a task to display it in a Task form

→ If you prefer to use the TaskPad, **see** "Using the TaskPad to Work with Tasks," **p. 414**.

CREATING RECURRING TASKS

PART
III
CH
11

The preceding pages of this chapter have described only one-time tasks. You can create recurring tasks just as you can create recurring appointments.

→ To learn more about recurrence, **see** "Creating Recurring Appointments and Events," **p. 371**.

Whereas you can create a recurring appointment from scratch or create one based on an existing one-time appointment, you can only create a recurring task based on an existing one-time task.

To create a recurring task:

1. With a Tasks Information viewer displayed, double-click a task to display that task in a Task form.
2. Choose Recurrence in the form's Standard toolbar to display the dialog box shown in Figure 11.15.
3. Select the Daily, Weekly, Monthly, or Yearly option button according to how often the task recurs.
4. In the Recurrence Pattern section of the dialog box, choose the check boxes and option buttons according to the recurrence pattern you want.
5. In the Range of Recurrence section of the dialog box, specify the start and end of the recurrence pattern.
6. Choose OK to return to the Task form in which the InfoBar summarizes the recurrence pattern.
7. Choose Save and Close in the form's Standard toolbar to save the recurring task.

Figure 11.15
Use this dialog box to
define the task's
recurrence pattern.
The dialog box opens
with a Weekly recur-
rence pattern selected.

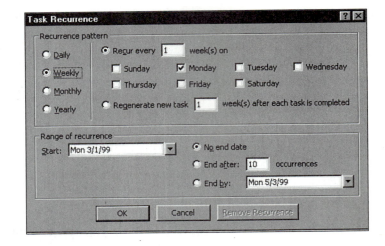

Recurring tasks are indicated in the TaskPad and in Table views of the Tasks Information
viewer by the symbol in the Icon column. Instead of the checked clipboard icon, recurring
tasks are indicated by the checked clipboard icon on which a pair of curved arrows is superimposed.

Note

The Outlook Today window doesn't indicate that a task is recurring. It shows only the next
occurrence of a recurring task.

ASSIGNING A TASK TO SOMEONE ELSE

You can assign a task to someone else. Although Outlook uses the word "assign," you can't
actually assign a task to someone else. Instead, you can offer a task to someone and that
person has the option of accepting or declining the task.

You can offer a task to someone else in two ways:

- By creating a task for yourself and then offering it to someone else
- By creating a task request

When you offer a task to someone else, you can choose whether you want to keep a copy of
the task in your task list. If you choose to do that and the person accepts the task, any
changes that person makes to the task are automatically copied to the copy of the task that
you keep. If you don't keep a copy of the task, you relinquish all knowledge of it.

Also, when you offer a task to someone else, you can request a report when the task is complete. If you do that, and the person accepts the task, an automatic report is sent to you
when that person marks the task as complete.

If the person to whom you offer a task declines to accept it, the task remains as one of your personal tasks.

ASKING SOMEONE TO ACCEPT AN EXISTING TASK

After creating a task for yourself, you can offer that task to someone else by sending an e-mail message.

To offer an existing task to someone else:

1. With any view of the Tasks Information viewer displayed, double-click a task to display it in a Task form.

2. Choose Assign Task in the form's Standard toolbar. Outlook modifies the Task form, as shown in Figure 11.16.

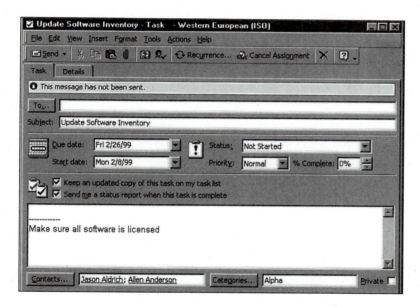

Figure 11.16
The InfoBar near the top of the form indicates that the message has not been sent.

3. Choose To to display a dialog box such as that shown in Figure 11.17.

Note

The dialog box shown in Figure 11.17 is similar to the one you see if you're using Outlook to create an e-mail message. You can open the drop-down Show Names from The list of address books to select an address book from which you want to select a person's name.

Figure 11.17
Use this dialog box to select the person to whom you want to offer the task.

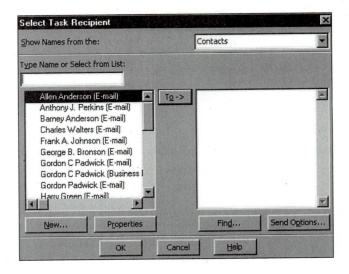

4. Select the name of the person to whom you want to offer the task from the list at the left, choose To-> to copy that name into the list on the right, and choose OK to return to the Task form. The selected person's name is now in the To box on the Task form.

5. If you want to retain the task and be updated about the progress of the task (should the person accept it), check the Keep an Updated Copy of This Task on My Task List box.

6. If you want to receive a status report when the task is marked complete (should the person accept the task), check the Send Me a Status Report when This Task Is Complete box.

7. Choose Send in the form's Standard toolbar to send the message that offers the task. If you had previously asked to be reminded when the task becomes due, Outlook displays a message saying you are no longer the owner of the task so the task reminder has been turned off.

Tip #98 from

Gordon Padwick

> By default, the Keep an Updated Copy of This Task on My Task List and Send Me a Status Report when This Task Is Complete boxes are checked. You can choose an option for either or both of these boxes so that the default is to check them. To change these defaults, choose Options, select the Other tab, choose Advanced Options, and choose Advanced Tasks. Check the appropriate boxes in this dialog box.

If you don't check the Keep an Updated Copy of This Task on My Task List box (step 5 in the preceding procedure), the task disappears from your task list when you send the message that offers the task, but reappears if that person declines to accept the task. If you do check that box, the message remains in your task list; the task symbol in the TaskPad and Tasks Information viewer has a sending hand supporting it to indicate the task has been offered.

As is the case for any other message, when you choose Send, Outlook moves the task message to your Outbox folder and the message stays there until Outlook has access to your mail server. If you're using C/W Outlook as a client for an Exchange server (and your network is operational) the message is immediately sent to the server. However, in other cases, the message stays in your Outbox until Outlook establishes a connection to the server. If you change your mind about sending the message while it's still in your Outbox, you open the Outbox Information viewer, select the message and delete it.

CREATING A TASK REQUEST FOR A GROUP

So far, the method of asking someone to accept a task that's been described assumes that you are asking only one person to accept the task. But, what if you want to ask several people to accept a task, or a similar task?

You could, of course, create individual tasks for each person, in the manner just described. A more efficient way is to create a task and save that task as an *Outlook template (page 520)*. Having created the template, you can now easily create identical tasks to send to several people, or create modified task requests to send to individual people.

Tip #99 from	If you only want to send identical tasks to several people, you can create a distribution list in your Contacts folder (new in Outlook 2000) and send a task to the distribution list.

If you send a task to more than one person, Outlook can't update you with each person's progress on the task.

→ If you need to assign tasks to more than one person, possibly the members of a workgroup, **see** "Assigning Tasks to a Team," **p. 524**.

→ You're stretching Outlook beyond what it's really intended to do when you try to use it to assign tasks to several people. If that's what you need to do, consider integrating Outlook with Microsoft Team Manager. **See** "Going Further with Task Management," **p. 437**.

SENDING A TASK REQUEST

Instead of creating a task and then offering it to someone else, you can create a task request.

To create and send a task request:

1. With any Tasks Information viewer displayed, choose Actions, New Task Request to display the Task form previously displayed in Figure 11.8.
2. Use this dialog box to create a new task, as described previously in this chapter.
3. Follow steps 3 through 7 in the procedure previously described to send the task request.

→ If you want to offer an existing task to another person, **see** "Asking Someone to Accept an Existing Task," **p. 431**.

After you've sent a task to someone else, you can send an unassigned copy of that task to another person by choosing Create Unassigned Copy in the Details tab of the Task form. You can use this to send a "for your information" copy of the task. When you choose this button, Outlook warns you "If you create an unassigned copy of this task, you will own the copy, and you will no longer receive updates for the task you assigned."

RESPONDING TO A TASK REQUEST

When you receive a task request, you'll see a message header in your Inbox Information viewer that contains the subject of the task that's being offered to you, the task's status, and the percent complete. The symbol at the left indicates the message is offering you a task, as shown in Figure 11.18.

Figure 11.18
This is how a message offering you a task appears in the Inbox Information viewer.

You can double-click the message header in the Inbox Information viewer to see details of the task in a Task form, as shown in Figure 11.19.

Figure 11.19
The InfoBar shows who is offering the task and when the message was sent.

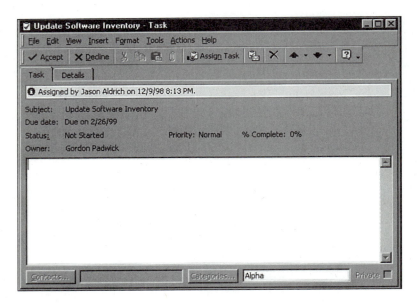

The Task form's Standard toolbar contains <u>A</u>ccept and <u>D</u>ecline buttons.

ACCEPTING A TASK

Choose the Accept button if you agree to accept the task. When you do so, Outlook displays the dialog box shown in Figure 11.20.

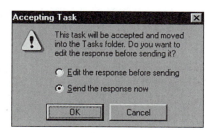

Figure 11.20
You can choose to just send your acceptance or to send your acceptance with some comments.

To send comments with your acceptance, choose Edit the Response Before Sending and choose OK. Outlook redisplays the Task form in the format shown in Figure 11.21.

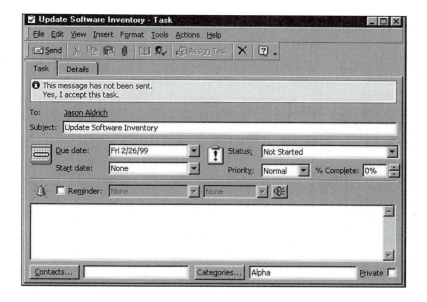

Figure 11.21
The InfoBar summarizes the status of your response.

PART

III

CH

11

Enter your comments in the unnamed notes box in the lower part of the form, then choose Send in the form's Standard toolbar to send your response.

To send your acceptance without any comments, choose the Send Immediately button. Outlook immediately sends your response to the person who offered you the task.

In addition to sending your response back to the person who offered the task to you, Outlook:

- Adds the task into your Tasks folder
- Makes you the new owner of the task, as you can see if you double-click the task in your Tasks Information viewer to see that task in a Task form

You can now double-click the task you've accepted in your Tasks Information viewer to see its details in a Task form. Because you now own the task, you have full access to the information about the task and you can use the Tasks and Details tab to keep that information updated. If the person who offered you the task chose to keep a copy of that task, Outlook automatically updates that person's copy each time you make a change to the information about the task.

Note

If the person who offered the task kept a copy of the task, that person's name appears in the Update List box in the Details tab of the Task form on your computer.

DECLINING A TASK

To decline an offered task, choose the Decline button in the Task forms Standard toolbar (previously shown in Figure 11.19). Outlook displays the Declining Task dialog box that's the same, except for the title, as the Accepting Task dialog box previously shown in Figure 11.20.

You can send a message declining the task with or without comments, just as you can for an acceptance message. In this case, Outlook doesn't add the task to your task list.

RECEIVING A RESPONSE TO A TASK REQUEST

When you receive a response from someone to whom you offered a task, you see a *message header* in your Inbox Information viewer, such as the one in Figure 11.22.

Figure 11.22
A message header indicates whether a task has been accepted or declined.

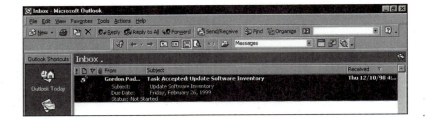

You can double-click the message header to see any comments the person might have sent with the message.

When you offer a task to someone and don't choose to keep a copy of that task in your Tasks folder, Outlook temporarily removes that task from your Tasks folder. If the person declines the task, Outlook restores that task into your Tasks folder. You can double-click the task in the Inbox Information viewer, as shown in Figure 11.23.

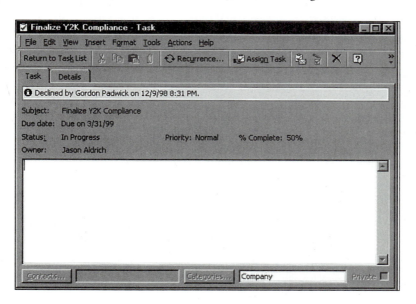

Figure 11.23
The InfoBar reminds you that the task has been declined and that you are still its owner.

PART

III

CH

11

When someone accepts the task you offered, Outlook permanently removes that task from your Tasks folder unless you chose to keep a copy of the task. In this case, the InfoBar reminds you that the task has been accepted and also indicates that the task is now owned by the person who accepted it.

GOING FURTHER WITH TASK MANAGEMENT

You can use Microsoft's Team Manager to extend Outlook's capabilities for working with tasks. Team Manager gives you the ability to delegate tasks to a team and to monitor the work of that team. To quote from Microsoft's Design Goals for Team Manager, "Microsoft Team Manager is a new workgroup tool that helps everyone on the team stay in sync by consolidating, coordinating, and tracking team activities." Team Manager can be integrated with Outlook.

You can find detailed information about Team Manager on the following Web site:

`http://www.microsoft.com/teammanager/`

Team Manager integrates with Outlook by synchronizing task lists. Synchronization occurs when you open or close Team Manager, and when you accept a team member's settings messages or a team task update message from the team manager.

Team members can create and track their own tasks using Team Manager, Outlook, or Schedule+; Team Manager keeps those tasks synchronized.

Team Manager has many capabilities, some of which are similar to those in Outlook. Other Team Manager capabilities, not available in Outlook, are

- Actual Work—Actual work tracking is available in several project-management applications. It keeps track of and displays work hours, overtime work hours, costs, work completed, and changes in the number of hours worked.
- Best Fit Scheduling—Best fit scheduling analyzes workloads to determine whether team members can complete their tasks within the available time, based on priorities and deadlines. It can also suggest schedule adjustments.
- Consolidated Status Reporting—This capability combines individual team members' reports into a consolidated report.
- Work Calendar Views—This view provides information about what members are working on by day, week, or month.
- Workload Graph—This graph provides a visual summary of team members' workloads.
- Vacation Tracking—This capability allows scheduled vacations to be taken into account when planning projects.

If you find Outlook doesn't provide all you need as far as task management is concerned, consider integrating Team Manager into Outlook.

CHAPTER **12**

KEEPING YOUR JOURNAL

In this chapter

by Gordon Padwick

WHAT IS OUTLOOK'S JOURNAL?

If you have a perfect memory, you probably don't need Outlook's Journal. However, if you sometimes forget things you've done or when you did them, the Journal can be a very useful memory supplement.

Note

Outlook 2000 retains the journaling capability that is also in Outlook 97 and Outlook 98. However, Outlook 2000 has introduced Contact Activity Tracking, which is, in many ways, more convenient than journaling. Contact Activity Tracking, though, doesn't completely replace journaling. Refer to Chapter 9 for information about Contact Activity Tracking.

→ For information about tracking your contacts' activities, **see** "Tracking a Contact's Activities," **p. 346**.

Outlook's Journal is a place where you can keep records of your daily activities. The Journal can automatically record such activities as:

- E-mail messages you send to, and receive from, specific contacts, including messages that request appointments or attendance at meetings, and those about accepting task assignments
- Telephone calls you make
- Each time you work with an Office document
- Net Folder events

In addition, you can use the Journal to manually record activities such as:

- Letters, memos, and other paper documents you receive
- Telephone calls you receive
- Conversations you have
- Items you purchase
- Anything else you do or experience

Outlook saves a record of each activity as a Journal item in the Journal folder in your Personal Folders file on your computer's hard disk or, if you're using C/W Outlook as a client for Exchange, in your Journal folder in the Exchange store. You don't need to have Outlook running for file activities to be automatically saved as Journal items.

You choose what you want Outlook to save as Journal items. You can see the items Outlook has saved in your Journal folder by opening the Journal Information viewer.

Tip #100 from

Gordon Padwick

In Outlook 97 and Outlook 98, the Outlook Shortcuts section of the Outlook Bar contained the Journal icon. In Outlook 2000, that icon is in the My Shortcuts section.

Much of this chapter is about the Timeline view of Journal items; that's because Journal items are most often displayed in a timeline. I'd like to remind you that, although Outlook doesn't offer a built-in Timeline view for other types of items, you can create display any Outlook items in a timeline. You might find it convenient, for example, to create a timeline view for items in your Inbox and Sent Items folders so that you can easily search for messages by date.

→ All the information about timelines in this chapter applies equally to timelines to display any type of Outlook item. **See** "Creating Custom Views," **p. 973**.

Using Automatic Journaling

Journaling is initially disabled after you install Outlook. The first time you choose Journal in the Outlook Bar, Outlook displays a message box that says "…the Activities tab on the contact item is the best way to track e-mail and does not require the Journal." If you're principally interested in tracking only e-mail, and don't intend to use the Journal, choose No in this box so that the Journal is not activated. If you do want to use the Journal, choose Yes to activate the Journal. The remainder of this chapter assumes you have chosen Yes.

When you choose Yes, Outlook displays the Journal Options dialog box shown in Figure 12.1.

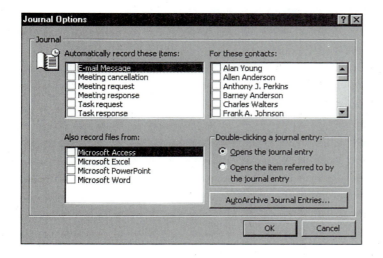

Figure 12.1
This is where you select what activities the Journal automatically records.

PART
III

Cн
12

Tip #101 from You can also open the Journal Options dialog box from any Outlook *Information viewer* *(page 17)*. Choose Tools, Options. In the Preferences tab, choose Journal Options.

The Journal Options dialog box contains four sections:

- Automatically Record These Items—Use this section to select which types of e-mail messages the Journal should record.

- For These Contacts—Use this section to select the message senders and recipients for whom the Journal should record message activity.

- Also Record Files From—Use this section to select Office Applications for which the Journal should record file activity.

- Double-clicking a Journal Entry—Use this section to select what Outlook displays when you double-click a Journal item.

The first three sections each contain several check boxes, all of which are initially unchecked. With all the check boxes unchecked, the Journal records nothing. You must check appropriate check boxes, as described in the next section, before the Journal starts recording anything.

SETTING UP AUTOMATIC JOURNALING

You set up automatic journaling in the Journal Options dialog box, shown previously in Figure 12.1. Check the check boxes in this dialog box to select what you want the Journal to record automatically.

Start by checking the types of e-mail messages you want the Journal to record. Although you check one or more types, the Journal won't record anything unless you check some contact names in the For These Contacts list.

The For These Contacts list shows the beginning of the list of names in your principal Address Book, none of which is initially checked. Scroll down this list and check those *contacts (page 298)* whose messages (messages you send to them and messages they send to you) that you want the Journal to automatically record.

Whenever you add a new name to your address book, Outlook automatically adds that name into the For These Contacts list, but leaves the new name unchecked. If you want the Journal to record mail to and from that person, you must open the Journal Options dialog box and check the new name.

Tip #102 from

You can replace Outlook's standard Contact form with a *custom form (page 1032)* that you can use to add Contact items to your Contact folder and automatically designate any of those contacts as people for whom you want the Journal to record mail.

→ For general information about creating custom forms, **see** "Creating and Using Custom Forms," **p. 1031**.

The Also Record File From list includes the Office and Office-compatible applications installed on your computer for which the Journal can automatically record file activity. Check those applications you want the Journal to record.

Tip #103 from

Gordon Padwick

You should be aware that having the Journal record file activity for an application increases the time it takes for an application to open and close files.

After you've checked an application, the Journal subsequently records each time you work with one of that application's files.

Tip #104 from

Gordon Padwick

You may find that some Office-compatible applications installed on your computer aren't listed in the Journal Options dialog box. This can occur if you install Outlook after installing the other application. In many cases, you can solve this problem by opening Outlook and, while Outlook is open, start the other application. With the application open, open and then close one of its files. See the "Troubleshooting" section at the end of this chapter for more information about this.

Outlook starts journaling the selected activities automatically as soon as you choose OK twice to close the Options dialog box.

JOURNALING PHONE CALLS

Outlook can automatically create Journal items for phone calls you make, providing you use Outlook to place those calls.

→ For information about using Outlook to make phone calls, **see** "Placing a Phone Call," **p. 342**.

You can set an Outlook option to automatically record phone calls you make to specific people. Unfortunately, before you can set that option, you have to make a change in the Windows registry. Before you begin, take at look at the current Journal options.

To examine the Journal options:

1. Choose Tools, Options to display the Options dialog box. Make sure the Preferences tab is selected.

2. Choose Journal Options to display the Journal Options dialog box.

3. Examine the list of items in the top-left box.

If the list of items already contains an item named Phone Call, you don't need to modify the registry. Most likely, though, the list doesn't contain Phone Call. In that case follow the steps in the next procedure.

→ For detailed information about the Journal Options dialog box, **see** "Journal Options," **p. 863**.

PART

III

CH

12

Caution

As always, be aware that information in the registry controls how Windows and the applications under Windows run. Any incorrect change you make to the registry could affect Windows or an application, or even make your computer unusable. Always make a backup copy of the registry before making any changes to it. See Appendix F for detailed information about this.

To modify the Windows registry so that you can record information phone calls in the Journal:

1. Choose Start, Run on the Windows taskbar to display the Run dialog box.

2. In the Open box, enter Regedit and choose OK to start the Registry Editor.

3. Navigate to the registry key
   HKEY_CURRENT_USER\Software\Microsoft\Shared Tools\Outlook\Journaling\
   Phone Call

4. Select the Phone Call key to display the values it contains in the Registry Editor's right pane.

5. Select the AutoJournaled value, then choose Edit, Modify to display the Edit DWORD Value dialog box.

6. Replace 0 (zero) in the Value Data box with 1 (one) then choose OK.

7. Choose Registry, Exit to close the Registry Editor.

After making this change to the registry, choose Tools, Options to display the Options dialog box again and make sure the Preferences tab is selected. Now you should see Phone Call listed as one of the items in the top-left box. This means that the Journal has the capability to record information about phone calls. However, it remains for you to activate it.

To activate journaling information about phone calls:

1. Make sure Phone Call in the top-left box of the Journal Options dialog box is checked.

2. In the top-right box that lists your contacts, check the names of all the contacts for whom you want to record phone calls you initiate.

From now on, whenever you use Outlook to place a phone call to one of the people whose names you checked, Outlook will record information about the call in your Journal.

UNDERSTANDING ENTRY TYPES

Each Journal item has a specific entry type. There's a separate entry type for each type of e-mail message and for each application listed in the Journal Options dialog box. When Outlook creates automatic Journal items, each item has the appropriate entry type assigned to it.

→ You'll learn more about entry types later in this chapter. **See** "Creating Journal Items Manually," **p. 448**.

DISPLAYING JOURNAL ITEMS

By default, Outlook displays Journal items in a timeline view, as shown in Figure 12.2.

To display a timeline view of Journal items:

1. Click Journal in the My Shortcuts section of the Outlook Bar to display the Journal items in the Journal Information viewer.

2. If a timeline view isn't displayed, choose <u>V</u>iew, move the pointer onto Current <u>V</u>iew, and choose By Type to display a view similar to that in Figure 12.2.

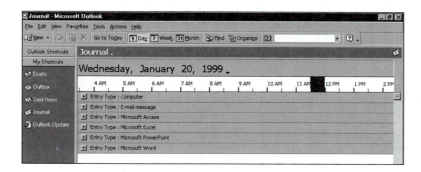

Figure 12.2
The Timeline view initially shows only headers for the entry types for which Outlook has saved Journal items. The timeline shown here displays Journal items for a day.

To expand an entry type, click the button marked with a plus sign at the left end of the appropriate entry-type header. After you do so, the space under that header expands to show details about the Journal items of that entry type, as shown in Figure 12.3.

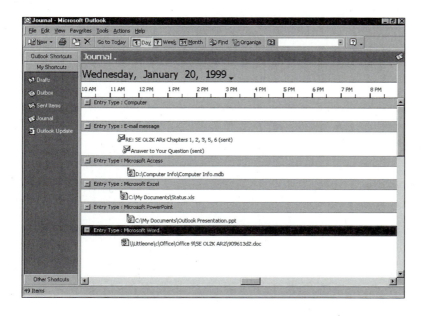

Figure 12.3
The E-mail entry type is expanded to show each Journal item.

PART
III

CH

12

You can choose the Day, Week, or Month button in the Standard toolbar to vary the scale of the timeline. You can use various ways to scroll backward and forward in time, one of which is to use the horizontal scrollbar near the bottom of the viewer (other ways are described later in this chapter). The status bar at the bottom of the viewer shows the total number of items in your Journal folder.

When you have Day selected, as in Figure 12.3, text adjacent to each icon provides detailed information about what that icon represents; the same is true when you have Week selected. However, with Month selected, only icons are displayed; in that case, you can move the pointer onto an icon and pause briefly to see a ScreenTip that describes that icon.

To see the details of any Journal item, double-click that item to display it in a Journal Entry form, as shown in Figure 12.4.

Figure 12.4
This Journal item is for an e-mail message. You can double-click the message icon in the Notes box to open the message.

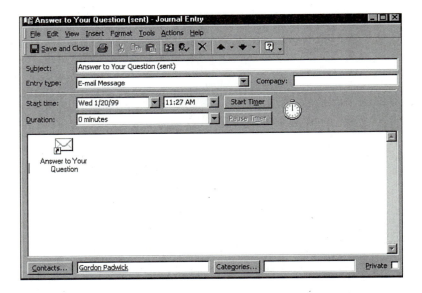

Tip #105 from

The Journal's behavior when you double-click an item in the timeline is the default. You can, in the Journal Options dialog box shown previously in Figure 12.1, select Opens the Item Referred to by the Journal Entry (in the Double-clicking a Journal Entry section). Subsequently, when you double-click a item in the Timeline view, Outlook displays the item itself instead of an icon representing the item.

→ You can, of course, choose other views of Journal items, as described later in this chapter. **See** "Viewing and Printing Journal Items," **p. 454**.

MOVING AROUND IN A TIMELINE

As mentioned previously, you can move backward and forward in time by using the horizontal scroll bar. That's adequate when you only want to move a short distance. Other ways of moving around are often more convenient. The following two sections separately describe how to move by date and time, and how to move from one item to another. These sections refer to using several keyboard keys.

→ Refer to Appendix G for detailed information about keyboard shortcuts, many of which are not described in this chapter. **See** Table G.17 and Table G.18, **p. 1346**.

MOVING BY DATE AND TIME

You may have noticed that there are two time scales at the top of the timeline:

- The top time scale shows the currently displayed date in Day view, or the currently displayed month in Week and Month views
- The lower time scale shows hours in Day view, or days in Week and Month views

When you first open a timeline, the lower time scale is active with a blue marker showing the current time in Day view, or the current day in Week and Month views. With the lower time scale enabled, you can press the right-arrow and left-arrow keys to move by the hour or day increment in that scale.

To activate the upper time scale, press Shift+Tab. Now pressing the right arrow key or left arrow keys moves the displayed time one day at a time with Day view selected, one week at a time with Week view selected, or one month at a time with Month view selected.

To return to having the lower time scale active, press Tab.

Whether the upper or lower time scale is active, you can choose the triangle at the right of the date or month in the upper time scale to display a calendar, as shown in Figure 12.5.

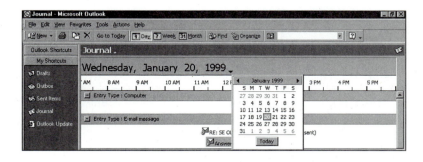

Figure 12.5
The calendar shows the days of the month corresponding to the date or month adjacent to the triangle you chose.

PART

III

CH

12

With a calendar displayed, you can:

- Choose any day in the calendar to view the part of the timeline that covers that day
- Choose one of the arrows in the calendar's banner to move from month to month
- Choose Today to view the part of the calendar that covers the current day

In the Journal Information viewer's menu bar, you can choose <u>V</u>iew, move the pointer onto <u>G</u>o To, and choose Go to To<u>d</u>ay (to display the current day's part of the timeline) or Go to Dat<u>e</u> (to display a dialog box in which you can enter a date or open a calendar).

Wherever you are in the timeline, you can choose Go to Today in the Information viewer's Standard toolbar to return to the current day.

MOVING BY ITEM

When you click an item on a timeline, that item is selected. With an item selected, you can press the left-arrow key to select the previous item within a group, or press the right-arrow key to select the next item within a group. For example, if you have a message item selected, pressing an arrow key selects the previous or next message item.

You can also press Home to select the first item within a group, or End to select the last item within a group.

CREATING JOURNAL ITEMS MANUALLY

In addition to letting Outlook create Journal items automatically, you can use Outlook to create items manually.

SAVING JOURNAL ITEMS FOR THINGS YOU DO

You might like to use Outlook to chronicle the significant events in your life. I find it particularly useful, for example, to record when I install new hardware and software on my computer and make changes to its configuration. I also use Outlook to record when I have work done on my car. If you're a gardener, you might like to record various jobs you do in your garden, such as planting and fertilizing.

To manually create a Journal item:

1. Choose Journal in the My Shortcuts section of the Outlook Bar to display any Journal Information viewer.
2. Choose New in the Standard toolbar to display the Journal Entry form shown in Figure 12.6.
3. Enter a subject for the Journal item in the Subject box. After you've entered a subject and moved the pointer out of the Subject box, the text of the subject replaces Untitled in the form's title bar.
4. Open the drop-down Entry Type list and select one of the available entry types.

Note

You must select one of the entry types in the list. Outlook doesn't let you enter other entry types in the Entry Type box.

→ There's more information about creating your own entry types later in this chapter. **See** "Creating Custom Entry Types," **p. 450**.

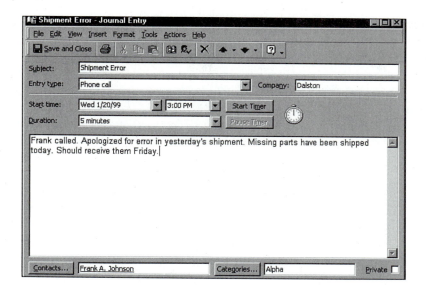

Figure 12.6
The Journal Entry form initially displays the current date and time in the Start Time boxes. This figure shows a typical completed form.

5. If the Journal item has something to do with one or more of your contacts, choose Contacts to open the Select Contacts dialog box, in which you can select contacts from your Address Book. When you choose OK in that dialog box, the selected contacts' names appear in the Contacts box. If the Journal item has something to do with people whose names aren't in your Address Book, enter their names in the Contacts box. You can leave this box empty.

6. If the Journal item has something to do with an organization, enter that organization's name in the Company box. You can leave this box empty.

7. By default, the Start Time boxes contain the date and time you opened the Journal Entry form. You can open a drop-down calendar from the date box and select a different date. You can also open a drop-down list of times from the Time box and select a different time. You can enter a date and time instead of selecting them (be careful to use standard Windows formats for dates and times you enter). You can't leave the Date and Time boxes empty.

8. If a duration is associated with the Journal item, you can enter that duration in the Duration box. You can't leave this box empty. Use the default 0 minutes to mean that the duration is not relevant.

PART

III

CH

12

Tip #106 from

Gordon Crush

> If you're recording an event such as an incoming phone call while it's happening, you can use Outlook's built-in timer to keep track of the duration of the event.

→ There's information about keeping track of a phone call's duration later in this chapter. **See** "Journaling Phone Calls," **p. 443**.

9. Enter whatever text is appropriate in the unnamed Notes box that occupies most of the lower part of the form. With the insertion point in the Notes box, you can (using the form's menu bar) choose Insert, Item to insert an icon representing an Outlook item into the Notes box, or choose Insert, Object to insert a Windows object (such as a picture) into the Notes box. You can leave the Notes box empty.

10. Choose Categories to open the Categories dialog box and select one or more categories to assign to the Journal item. You can, but shouldn't, leave the Categories box empty.

11. Choose Save and Close in the Standard toolbar to save the item.

CREATING CUSTOM ENTRY TYPES

The drop-down Entry Type list on the Journal Entry form contains entry types that relate to Outlook items and Office applications. You can add your own entry types to the list but, to do this, you have to edit the Windows *registry (page 605)*.

→ For detailed information about adding entry types, **see** "Creating New Entry Types," **p. 614**.

JOURNALING OUTGOING PHONE CALLS

You can use Outlook to create Journal items for outgoing and incoming phone calls. These Journal items record the fact that you made the phone calls and, optionally, the duration of the calls; they don't record your phone conversation. Outlook's ability to record the duration of phone calls (and other activities) is particularly useful to people who bill clients based on time.

The easiest way to create a Journal item for an outgoing call is to use your computer's modem to dial the call. To use this method, your computer's modem must be connected to the same phone line as your telephone.

Note

If you don't have a *modem (page 60)* that's connected to the same phone line as your telephone, you must record phone calls manually, as described in the next section, "Journaling Incoming Phone Calls."

To journal an outgoing phone call:

1. Choose Contacts in the Outlook Bar to display items in your Contacts folder in any Information viewer.

2. Select the contact you want to call.

3. Choose the Dial button [icon] in the Standard toolbar to display the dialog box shown in Figure 12.7.

4. If the contact has several phone numbers and the number you want to use isn't displayed in the Number box, open the drop-down Number list and select the appropriate number. If the number you want to call isn't in the list, you can manually enter the number in the Number box.

Figure 12.7
The New Call dialog box opens with the selected contact's name and one of that contact's phone numbers displayed.

5. Make sure that the Create New Journal Entry when Starting New Call box is checked, as shown in Figure 12.7.

6. Choose Start Call. Outlook immediately dials the number and displays a message telling you to "Lift the receiver and click Talk."

7. Pick up the phone and choose Talk. The Journal Entry form appears and the timer automatically starts. During the conversation, the timer registers the duration in one-minute increments.

8. When you've finished the conversation, choose Hang Up and hang up the phone. The Journal Entry form contains information about the call, including its duration.

9. Enter any notes about the conversation in the Notes box on the form.

10. Choose Save and Close on the Standard toolbar to save the item and close the form.

JOURNALING INCOMING PHONE CALLS

You have to create Journal items manually for incoming phone calls because Outlook can't tell when one begins and ends.

Note

> You can use the method described in this section to create a Journal item for a face-to-face conversation.

To create a Journal item for an incoming phone call:

1. Choose Journal in the My Shortcuts section of the Outlook Bar to display any Journal Information viewer.

2. Choose New in the Standard toolbar to display the Journal Entry form shown previously in Figure 12.6.

3. When the call starts, choose Start Timer. As soon as you do that, the hand in the clock icon starts moving around the clock to indicate that Outlook is timing the call.

4. Either while the call is in progress or after it has finished, enter information into the various boxes on the form. Don't forget to select the Phone Call entry type.

5. At the completion of the call, choose Pause Timer to stop the clock.

6. Choose Save and Close in the Standard toolbar to save the item and close the form.

If you're using this method to create an Outlook item for a face-to-face conversation, there may be interruptions, such as when a phone call arrives. In that case, choose the Pause Timer button to stop the clock. When the conversation resumes, choose Start Timer to continue timing.

ADDING APPOINTMENTS AND TASKS TO YOUR JOURNAL

Appointment items show when an *appointment (page 358)* is supposed to happen, but don't indicate whether or not they actually did. Likewise, Task items show when *tasks (page 412)* are due, not when you actually worked on them. You might find it useful to create Journal items for Appointments that happened and for Task items on which you spent some time.

Here's one way you can create a Journal item from a Calendar item. You can use the same method to create a Journal item from a Task item. Outlook's capability to create one type of item from another is known as AutoCreate.

To create a Journal item from an Appointment:

1. Choose Calendar in the Outlook Bar to display the Calendar Information viewer. Choose a view in which you can conveniently see the Calendar item you want to use.

2. While holding down Ctrl, drag the Calendar item onto the Journal icon in the My Shortcuts section of the Outlook Bar. When you release the mouse button, the Journal Entry form is displayed with information from the Calendar item.

Notice these points:

- The subject of the Journal item is the same as the subject of the appointment.
- The Journal item's entry type is Meeting, which is often appropriate. If it isn't appropriate, you can choose a different entry type. You might have to create one or more custom entry types, as described earlier in this chapter.
- The Start Time for the Journal item is the same as the Start Time of the Appointment item. The Duration for the Journal item is correctly calculated as the difference between the Calendar item's End Time and Start Time.
- The Journal form's notes box contains an icon that represents the original Calendar item. You can double-click it to display the Calendar item.

Step 2 in the preceding procedure describes what happens when you drag in the usual manner with the left mouse button pressed. If, instead, you drag with the right mouse button pressed, Outlook offers a choice when you release the mouse button:

- Copy Here as Journal Entry with Shortcut—Outlook creates a new Journal item with a shortcut to the Calendar item in the Notes box.
- Copy Here as Journal Entry with Attachment—Outlook creates a new Journal item with a copy of the Calendar item attached (represented by an icon in the Notes box).

- Move Here as Journal Entry with Attachment—Outlook creates a new Journal item with the Calendar item moved into that item's Notes box. The Calendar item no longer exists in the Calendar folder.

- Cancel—Cancel creating the new Journal item.

JOURNALING NET FOLDER EVENTS

As you'll learn in Chapter 14, "Sharing Information with Other People," *Net Folders* are folders you can share with other Outlook users by way of the Internet or an intranet.

After you've made a folder sharable as a Net Folder, you can use Outlook's Journal to keep a record of events that affect the folder, such as when someone else adds items to it.

→ For more information about Net Folders, **see** "What Is a Net Folder?," **P. 466**.

To journal Net Folder events:

1. With any Information viewer displayed, choose View, Folder List to display Outlook's folder list.

2. Right-click the name of the shared folder to display its context menu. Choose Properties in the context menu to display the folder's Properties dialog box. Unlike folders that aren't shared, this dialog box contains a Sharing tab. Choose the Sharing tab shown in Figure 12.8.

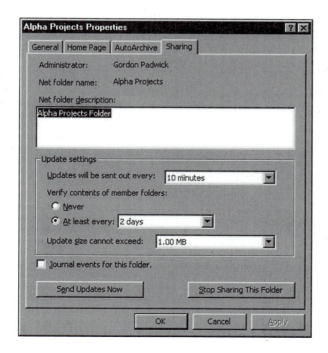

Figure 12.8
The Properties dialog box's Sharing tab is where you can enable journaling of Net Folder events.

PART

III

CH

12

3. Check the Journal Events for This Folder box.

From now on, Outlook will journal events for the Net Folder.

VIEWING AND PRINTING JOURNAL ITEMS

By default, Outlook displays the Journal Information viewer using the By Type Timeline view, in which items are grouped by entry type, as shown previously in Figure 12.2. Outlook can also display timeline views with Journal items grouped by Contact or by Category.

If you choose View, Preview Pane, Outlook displays a preview pane below the timeline, as shown in Figure 12.9. The Journal displays an icon representing the selected item in the Preview pane. You can double-click the icon to see the items details.

Tip #107 from

Gordon Padwick

The Preview pane always displays an icon. The selection you make in the Double-clicking a Journal Entry section of the Journal Options dialog box doesn't affect this.

Figure 12.9
With Preview Pane enabled, you can select any item in the timeline to see the details of that item in the Preview Pane.

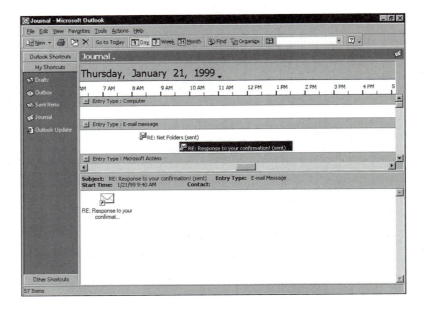

In addition to timeline views, Outlook can display Journal items in these table views:

- Entry List—A tabular view of all Journal items
- Last Seven Days—A tabular view of Journal items created or modified during the last seven days
- Phone Calls—A tabular view that includes only Phone Call entry type items

To select a view:

1. Start with any Journal Information viewer displayed.
2. Choose <u>V</u>iew and move the pointer onto Current <u>V</u>iew to see a list of available views.
3. Select the view you want to use.

→ You can modify the views supplied with Outlook and you can create your own. **See** "Creating Views and Print Styles," **p. 943**.

You can print Journal items based on a Table view, but not based on a Timeline view. You can, however, print individual items selected in a Timeline view.

To print Journal items based on a Table view:

1. Select a Table view of Journal items, as described in the previous section.
2. Choose <u>F</u>ile, <u>P</u>rint to display the Print dialog box.
3. With Table Style selected, choose OK to print the table.

To print Journal items selected in a Timeline view:

1. Select a Timeline view of Journal items.
2. Select one or more items in the view.
3. Choose <u>F</u>ile, <u>P</u>rint to display the Print dialog box. Memo Style is the only print style available.
4. Choose OK to printed the selected Journal items.

→ For more detailed information about printing Outlook items, **see** "Viewing and Printing Contact Items," **p. 322**.

VIEWING JOURNAL ITEMS FOR A CONTACT

You can easily display the Journal items related to a specific contact.

To see a contact's Journal items:

1. Choose Contacts in the Outlook Bar to display any Contacts Information viewer.
2. Double-click a contact to display information about that contact in a Contact form.
3. Select the Activities tab.
4. Open the drop-down Sho<u>w</u> list and select Journal to see all Journal items related to the selected contact.

TROUBLESHOOTING

As explained earlier in this chapter, you can set up the Journal so that it records file activities associated with some Office and Office-compatible applications. You do this by checking application names in the Journal Options dialog box's Also Record Files From section.

PART
III

CH
12

Normally, when you install Office 2000, all the principal Office applications are available to be checked. If you install Office-compatible applications, such as Microsoft's Project and Team Manager, after you've installed Outlook, the names of these applications should automatically be added to the list in the Outlook Options dialog box. If that doesn't happen, try the method suggested earlier in this chapter for adding applications to the list.

→ For information about adding applications to be journaled, **see** "Setting Up Automatic Journaling," **p. 442**.

If that method doesn't work, an alternative is to add applications to the list by editing the Windows registry.

Using the method described in Appendix F, access the registry key:
My Computer\HKEY_CURRENT_USER\Software\Microsoft\Shared Tools\Outlook\Journaling

Within that key, add a registry key corresponding to a missing application, using the same format as the existing keys.

→ For information about working with registry keys, **see** "Working with the Windows Registry," **p. 1323**.

In addition to some Windows applications available from Microsoft, you can make some applications from other companies accessible to the Journal. This capability depends on the required functionality being present within each application.

CHAPTER 13

USING OUTLOOK TO KEEP NOTES

In this chapter

by Gordon Padwick

WHAT ARE NOTES?

 Think of Notes in Outlook as the computer equivalent of the sticky yellow paper notes decorating your computer monitor and desk in your office, and your refrigerator door at home.

 You can use Outlook's Notes to jot down reminders, ideas, phone numbers, and suggestions—all those pieces of information you mustn't forget, but can't immediately take the time to file in their proper places. Later, you can review your notes, act on them, or move the information they contain into appropriate Outlook folders or other folders on your computer.

Many people who use Outlook either ignore Notes or use Notes when they should be using a different Outlook facility. After reading this chapter, you'll understand the value of Notes and, I hope, start giving Notes the opportunity to help you work more efficiently.

SETTING UP NOTES

After installing Outlook on your computer, Notes is set up and ready to use.

You can make some minor changes to how Outlook displays Notes by making choices in the Options dialog box. By default, notes have a yellow background, are of medium size, and use the 10-point Comic Sans MS font. You can change any of these defaults.

CREATING A NOTE

In this book, I've previously recommended that you always keep Outlook running, probably minimized, while you're working with other applications. If you do so, Outlook is always ready for you to make a note.

Note

Another advantage of keeping Outlook running is that reminders always pop up on your screen at the appropriate time.

To create a note:

1. If Outlook is minimized, click the Outlook button in the Windows taskbar to display an Information viewer.
2. Choose Notes in the Outlook Bar to display the Notes Information viewer, such as that shown in Figure 13.1.

Figure 13.1
The Notes Information viewer appears with existing notes displayed.

3. Choose <u>N</u>ew on the Standard toolbar to display the Notes form shown in Figure 13.2.

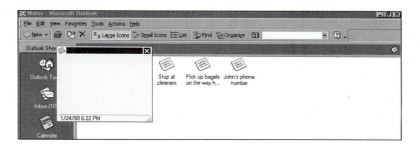

Figure 13.2
The Notes form pops up on top of the Information viewer with the current date and time at the bottom.

Note

If you have any Outlook Information viewer displayed, you can click the black triangle at the right of New to display a menu. Select <u>N</u>ote in the menu to display the Notes form. Another way to display the Notes form is to press Ctrl+Shift+N from just about anywhere within Outlook.

4. Type your note, then click the X at the top-right of the Notes form to save and close the note; after you do so, the Notes Information viewer contains an icon representing that note. Alternatively, you can click outside the note to save it, hide it behind whatever else is displayed, display a button representing the note in the Windows taskbar, and display an icon representing that note in the Notes Information viewer.

As you type a note, the text automatically wraps within the width of the Notes form. If you enter more text than will fit within the height of the form, the text automatically scrolls vertically.

You can change the size of the Notes form by dragging its borders or by dragging the shaded bottom-right corner.

After you save or hide a note Outlook displays that note as an icon with the first few words of the text in the Notes Information viewer. You can see the entire note by double-clicking the icon.

PART

III

CH

13

If you choose View, Preview Pane, Outlook displays a preview pane in the bottom part of the Notes Information viewer. Then, when you select any note, the text of that note appears in the Preview pane.

WORKING WITH A NOTE

To work with a note, right-click the note's icon in the Notes Information viewer to display its context menu as shown in Figure 13.3. You can use this menu to open or print the note, to forward the note to someone, to change the color of the note, to assign categories to it, to delete it, or to move it to a folder.

Figure 13.3
A note's context menu contains several commands you can use in addition to the Print command.

OPENING AND PRINTING A NOTE

To open a note displayed as an icon in the Notes Information viewer, either double-click the note or right-click it and choose Open on the context menu.

To print all the notes in your Notes folder, choose File, Print to display the Print dialog box. Choose OK to start printing.

To print an individual note, right-click that note in Notes Information viewer to display its context menu, shown previously in Figure 13.3, then choose Print. The selected note is immediately printed.

Note

You can select as many notes as you like. If you select two or more notes, the Print dialog box gives you the option of starting each note on a new page or printing notes one after the other on pages.

FORWARDING A NOTE

Open the note's context menu and choose Forward. Outlook displays a Message form with the note inserted as an attachment. Complete the message form in the normal way and send the note.

CHANGING A NOTE'S BACKGROUND COLOR

Open the note's context menu and move the pointer onto Color to display a list of five colors. Select the background color you want.

ASSIGNING CATEGORIES TO A NOTE

Because notes are usually temporary items, it's usually not necessary to assign categories to them. However, you can assign categories to notes if you want to do so.

Tip #108 from	If you're in the habit of creating a lot of notes, you might find it convenient to assign categories to each of them. Subsequently, you can view your notes grouped in categories.

Open the note's context menu and choose Categories to display the Categories dialog box. Select the categories you want to assign to the note and choose OK.

DELETING A NOTE

Click the note in the Notes Information viewer to select it, then choose the Delete button ☒ in the Standard toolbar. Alternatively, open the note's context menu and choose Delete. Outlook moves the note from the Notes folder to the Deleted Items folder.

MOVING AND COPYING A NOTE TO ANOTHER FOLDER

To move or copy a note to another folder, drag the note icon in the Notes Information viewer onto the other folder's icon in the Outlook Bar. Hold down Shift while you drag to move the note; hold down Ctrl to copy the note.

Tip #109 from	You can also choose View, Folder List to display your folder list, and then move or copy the note into any folder in the list.

When you move or copy a note to another Outlook folder, the note appears in that folder's form with the text of the notes in the form's Notes box.

VIEWING NOTES

Outlook provides five built-in views of notes, the default being the Icons view, shown previously in Figure 13.1. You can choose buttons in the Standard toolbar to modify the appearance of this view:

- Large Icons—Each note is represented by a large icon with the first few words of its text beneath it. Icons are displayed side-by-side in rows in the Information viewer.

- Small Icons—Each note is represented by a small icon with the first few words of the note's text at the icon's right. Notes that contain only a few words of text are shown side-by-side.

PART

III

CH

13

- List—Each note is represented by a small icon with the first few words of the note and text at the icon's right. Each note starts a new row in the Information viewer.

To select other views, choose View and move the pointer onto Current View to see a list of views. Select the view you want to use from:

- Icons—Notes represented by icons arranged in the date order
- Notes List—Table view of all notes sorted by the date they were created or last modified
- Last Seven Days—Table view of notes created or modified during the last seven days
- By Category—Table view of notes grouped by categories and sorted within each category by order of creation or modification dates
- By Color—Table view of notes grouped by color and sorted within each color by order of creation or modification dates

→ You can modify these standard views and create your own views. **See** "Creating Views and Print Styles," **p. 943**.

COPYING A NOTE INTO AN OFFICE DOCUMENT

You can easily copy a note into an Office document.

To copy a note into a Word document:

1. Display the Outlook Notes Information viewer and the Word document side-by-side on your monitor.
2. Locate the place in the Word document where you want to insert the note.
3. Hold down the Ctrl key while you drag the note into the Word document.

Alternatively, you can copy the note into the Windows clipboard, then paste it into the document.

COPYING A NOTE ONTO THE DESKTOP

You can copy a note to the Windows desktop by dragging in the normal way. If you drag with the right mouse button pressed, you can choose whether you want to copy or move the note to the desktop.

When you close or minimize Outlook, notes you've dragged onto the desktop remain there. You can right-click a note icon on the desktop to see the context menu shown in Figure 13.4, even if Outlook isn't running.

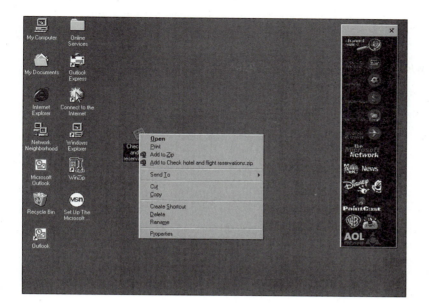

Figure 13.4
Among other things, you can use this context menu to send a note as a mail message or save it on a floppy disk.

If you open notes by double-clicking them within Outlook and then close Outlook, the open notes remain displayed on the desktop. You can close notes displayed on the desktop by clicking the Close button at the right end of the note's title bar.

HINTS ABOUT USING NOTES

Here are some hints that might help you to use Outlook's Notes productively.

- Use notes only as a temporary place to keep information. Remove each note as soon as you've done what the note is intended to remind you of, or when you've copied the information it contains to an appropriate folder. At the end of each day, move any outstanding notes into the appropriate Outlook folder, such as your Calendar, Contacts, or Tasks folders.

- Don't bother to assign categories to notes that are there to remind you to do something before the end of the current day. Do be meticulous about assigning categories to notes that you will convert into permanent Outlook items. The categories you assign to notes stay with those notes when you convert them into another type of Outlook item.

- Use colors to identify different types of notes. You have five colors to choose from.

- If an idea for an e-mail message flashes into your mind, but you haven't time to deal with it immediately, write the gist of it as a note. Subsequently, choose Forward in the note's context menu to create an e-mail message based on the note.

- Use only a few key words in the first line of a note so that you can easily identify a note in the Notes Information viewer.

PART
III

CH
13

- With the Preview pane enabled, you can select the text in a note, copy that text to the Windows Clipboard, and paste that text into another Outlook item or Windows application.

- If you save a URL in a note and have the Preview pane enabled, you can select that URL to activate it.

- By default, Outlook provides only one Notes folder. You can create as many other Notes folders as necessary so that you can save various kinds of notes in appropriate folders.

- Don't use notes as a substitute for inserting comments in individual items' Notes boxes. For example, if you want to make a note about a contact, open the information about that contact in a Contact form, and insert the note in that form's Notes box.

SHARING INFORMATION WITH OTHER PEOPLE

OUTLOOK AS A SHARING TOOL

You can use Outlook as a means of keeping your personal information organized and, if you have IMO or C/W Outlook installed, as a means of sharing information with other people. Using e-mail to send and receive messages is, of course, the most obvious way you can share information. In addition, you can use Outlook to share information contained in your Outlook folders.

If you use Outlook to connect to the Internet, you can make your Outlook folders available to be shared by specific people as Net Folders. The people with whom you share those folders see those folders the same as they see their own. This chapter describes how to use Net Folders. The primary purpose of Net Folders is to share Outlook folders by way of the Internet, which you can do with IMO Outlook and also with C/W Outlook if you have an Internet Information Service in your profile. In addition, you can share Net Folders by way of Microsoft Mail.

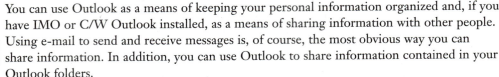

Tip #110 from

[signature]

You can use Net Folders only if you or the people you're sharing folders with access a POP3 mail server, not an IMAP server.

→ Another way to use Outlook to share information, if you're using C/W Outlook as a client for an Exchange server, is to use public folders. **See** "Using Public Folders," **p. 704**.

WHAT IS A NET FOLDER?

A *Net Folder* is an Outlook folder that's shared by way of the Internet or an intranet among two or more people. You can create a folder, make it sharable, and give permission to specific people to access the folder. You can give each person permission to:

- Only read what's in the folder
- Read what's in the folder and add new items to it
- Read what's in the folder, add new items to it, and also to edit and delete items that person has added
- Read what's in the folder, add new items to it, and also to edit and delete all items

A person to whom you offer access to a Net Folder can choose whether or not to subscribe to it. If the person agrees to subscribe, the Net Folder appears on the subscriber's Outlook folder list.

Outlook sends the contents of your shared folder to subscribers by way of the Internet or an intranet at intervals you specify. When it's time to send the folder, Outlook automatically places a copy of it in your Outbox and subsequently sends it as soon as your computer is connected to the mail server. Outlook doesn't save a copy of the shared folder in your Sent Items folder.

In addition to sending updates of a shared folder at regular intervals, you can manually send updates at any time.

Subscribers receive the updated folder from their mail servers. The updated folder appears in their folder lists, not in their Inboxes.

INSTALLING THE NET FOLDERS ADD-IN

In order to share a folder as a Net Folder with other people, or to access a Net Folder that someone shares with you, you must have the Rules Wizard and Net Folders add-ins installed on your computer. The Rules Wizard is normally installed automatically when you install Outlook. The Net Folders add-in, though, is not installed automatically.

To check whether you have the Net Folders add-in installed, open any Information viewer then open the File menu. If the File menu contains Share, you have the Net Folders add-in installed. If the File menu does not contain Share, you don't have the Net Folders add-in installed.

To install the Net Folders add-in:

1. With any Outlook Information viewer displayed, choose Tools, Options to display the Options dialog box. Select the Other tab.

2. Choose Advanced Options and then, in the Advanced Options dialog box, choose Add-In Manager to display the dialog box shown in Figure 14.1.

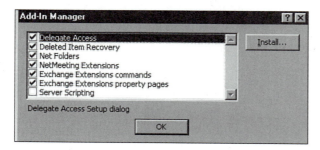

Figure 14.1
This dialog box lists the add-ins you have installed. The installed add-ins that are enabled are checked. This dialog box shows Net Folders installed and enabled.

3. If Net Folders is listed but not checked, check it; ignore the following steps in this procedure. If Net Folders is not listed, proceed to step 4.

4. Choose Install to display the dialog box shown in Figure 14.2.

Figure 14.2
This dialog box contains the names of add-in files.

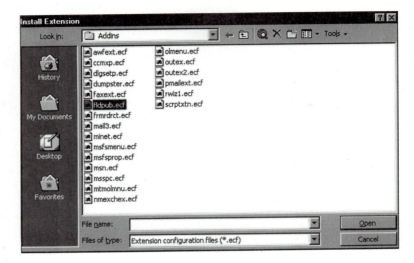

5. Select fldpub.ecf, then choose Open to return to the Add-In Manager dialog box that now lists Net Folders. Make sure Net Folders is checked.

6. Choose OK three times to close the dialog boxes.

Now your File menu should contain Share.

PUBLISHING A NET FOLDER

You can publish most of your Outlook folders as Net Folders, but not your Inbox or Outbox folders. Also, if you're using C/W Outlook as a client for an Exchange server, you can't publish Exchange folders or Exchange Offline folders.

To publish a Net Folder:

1. If you want to share a folder other than your Calendar, Contacts, or Tasks folder in the currently active Personal Folders file, open the Information viewer that displays the contents of the folder you want to share.

2. Choose File, then move the pointer onto Share to display the menu shown in Figure 14.3.

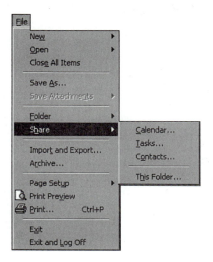

Figure 14.3
Use this menu to select the folder you want to share.

3. Choose Calendar, Contacts, Tasks, or This Folder to display the first Net Folder Wizard window, similar to that shown in Figure 14.4.

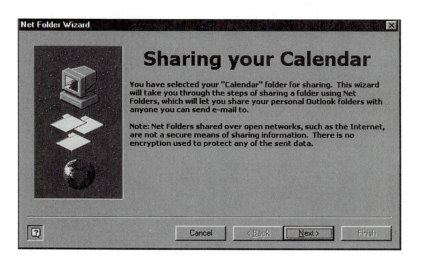

Figure 14.4
The wizard window contains the name of the folder you're sharing if it's your Calendar, Contacts, or Tasks folder.

Note If you attempt to share a folder that can't be shared, Outlook displays an error message.

4. Choose <u>N</u>ext > to display the wizard window shown in Figure 14.5.

Figure 14.5
This window will subsequently display a list of the people with whom you are sharing the folder.

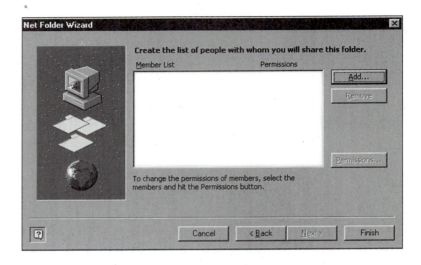

5. Choose <u>A</u>dd to add the names of the people with whom you want to share the folder. Outlook displays the dialog box shown in Figure 14.6.

Figure 14.6
Select the names of people with whom you want to share the folder in the same way that you select recipients for an e-mail message.

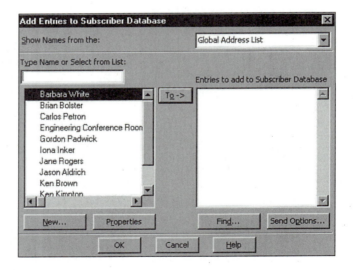

➔ For information about selecting message recipients, **see** "Addressing the Message," **p. 87**.

6. After you've selected people's names and chosen OK, Outlook displays those names in the wizard window, as shown in Figure 14.7.

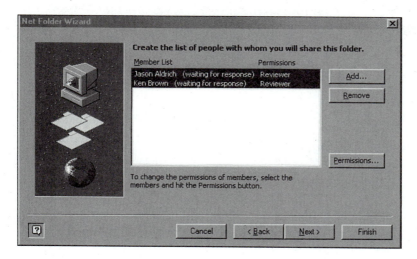

Figure 14.7
Outlook gives each person Reviewer (read-only) permission to access the shared folder. You can subsequently change this permission.

> **Note**
>
> The words "waiting for response" adjacent to each name indicate that people haven't responded to your offer to share the folder. Of course, that's because you haven't yet sent the offer to them.

7. To change a person's permissions, select that person's name and choose <u>P</u>ermissions to display the dialog box shown in Figure 14.8.

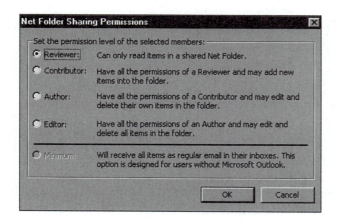

Figure 14.8
You can choose among these permissions for each subscriber.

PART

III

CH

14

8. Select a permission, then choose OK to return to the wizard window that now indicates the new permission.

Tip #112 from

[signature]

You can remove a subscriber by selecting a name and then choosing <u>R</u>emove.

9. When you've finished adding subscribers and setting permissions, choose <u>N</u>ext > to display the window shown in Figure 14.9.

Figure 14.9
Enter a description of the folder for subscribers to see.

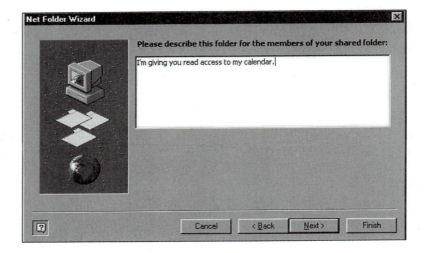

10. Choose <u>N</u>ext > to display the window shown in Figure 14.10.

Figure 14.10
This window tells you that you've finished making the folder available for sharing.

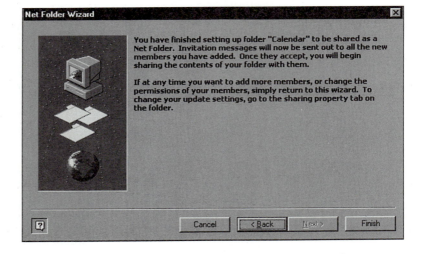

11. Choose Finish to close the wizard. Outlook displays a message telling you that invitations to share the folder have been successfully sent. Choose OK.

Although Outlook tells you that invitations have been sent, that probably isn't true. In fact, invitations have been placed in your Outbox ready to be sent the next time you access your mail server.

When you do connect to your mail server, Outlook sends a message to the people to whom you've offered subscriptions, keeping a copy of that message in your Sent Items folder. You can double-click the message header in your Sent Items Information viewer to see the message.

RECEIVING A SUBSCRIPTION INVITATION

Invitations you receive to subscribe to a folder arrive from your mail server and are saved in your Inbox. The Inbox Information viewer displays the message header in the same way that it displays headers for other incoming messages. However, the information isn't displayed in the Preveiw pane.

RESPONDING TO AN INVITATION

Double-click the message header in the Inbox Information viewer to view the message in a Message form, as shown in Figure 14.11.

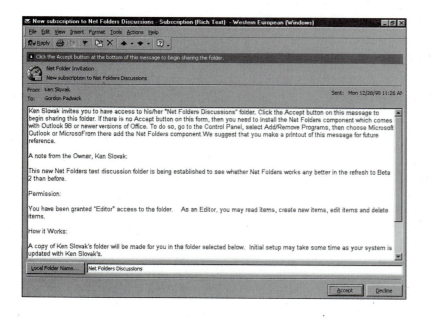

Figure 14.11
This is the message Outlook sends to let you know you've been invited to subscribe to a net folder.

The message briefly describes how Net Folders work. The wide box near the bottom of the form contains the name of the form you're being invited to subscribe to. If you intend to accept the invitation, you can change the folder's name to something more meaningful to you. By default, when you accept the invitation, Outlook places the Net Folder in your active Personal Folders file. You can choose a different location.

Tip #113 from

Ignore the following procedure if you intend to accept the invitation with the default name and to place the invitation in your Personal Folders file. Also, ignore the procedure if you don't intend to accept the invitation.

To change the name of a folder you subscribe to:

1. Choose <u>L</u>ocal Folder Name to display the dialog box shown in Figure 14.12.

Figure 14.12
This dialog box lists the top-level folders in your folder list.

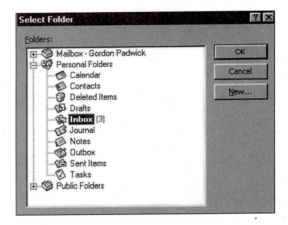

2. Choose <u>N</u>ew to display the dialog box shown in Figure 14.13.

3. Enter a name for the folder in the <u>N</u>ame box.

4. Open the drop-down <u>F</u>older Contains list and select the type of items the folder will contain. For example, for a Calendar folder, select Appointment Items.

5. In the <u>S</u>elect Where to Place the Folder box, select the folder under which the new folder should be listed.

6. Choose OK to close the Create New Folder dialog box. Outlook asks whether you want to have a shortcut for this folder in your Outlook Bar. Choose <u>Y</u>es or <u>N</u>o according to your preference. Outlook displays the Select Folder dialog box with the new folder shown in its proper place in your folder list. Choose OK to return to the Message form, which now contains the new name.

Figure 14.13
Use this dialog box to name the folder, select the type of items it will contain, and to position it in your folder list.

To accept the invitation, choose Accept. Outlook displays a message confirming that you have accepted the Net Folder and telling you that the contents of the folder will be sent to you shortly. Choose OK.

A short while later, you can access your mail server to receive the contents of the shared folder. After you've done so, you can look at that folder by opening your folder list and selecting the Net Folder in that list.

If you want to decline the invitation, choose Decline. Outlook asks you to confirm you want to decline the invitation; choose OK. Outlook creates a message in your Outbox, ready to send to the person who originally sent the invitation to you. This message is sent the next time you connect to your mail server.

SETTING THE PROPERTIES OF A NET FOLDER

After you've sent invitations to people to subscribe to a shared folder, you can examine and set certain sharing properties.

To examine and set sharing properties:

1. Choose View, Folder List, and right-click a shared folder to display its context menu.

PART

III

CH

14

2. In the context menu, choose Properties. Select the Sharing tab shown in Figure 14.14. This tab exists only for shared folders.

Figure 14.14
This is the Sharing tab for a Calendar folder.

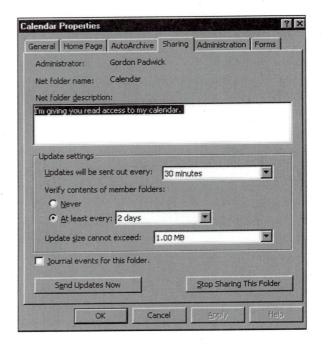

3. The Net Folder Description contains the text you entered when you originally shared the folder. You can edit this text.

4. Change the period in the Updates Will Be Sent Out Every box. The default 30 minutes is probably much too frequent if you're using a dial-up connection to the Internet. You can open the drop-down list and select a longer interval.

5. By default, Outlook compares the content of your folder with the contents of the Net Folders on all subscribers' computers every two days and makes corrections if necessary. If you're confident that the updating process is reliable, select Never; otherwise, open the drop-down list and select an appropriate number of days.

6. By default, Outlook limits the size of updates to one megabyte. You can open the drop-down list and select a different size limit.

Tip #114 from

Gordon Padwick

The size limit you specify here affects only what Outlook is able to send. Your Internet or intranet server may impose a smaller limit than you specify. If you're having problems with updating Net Folders, ask the server administrator if there is a limit and, if necessary, request an increase.

7. Check Journal Events for This Folder if you want Outlook to record changes to the shared folder in the Journal.

8. You can choose S̲end Updates Now to immediately send updates to the folder.

9. You can choose S̲top Sharing This Folder if you want to stop sending updates to subscribers. When you do so, Outlook automatically sends a message to all subscribers telling them that the folder is no longer shared. Subscribers retain the folder with its most recent updates, but receive no subsequent updates.

ADDING AND REMOVING SUBSCRIBERS

When you first use the Net Folder Wizard you offer to share a folder with specific people. You can subsequently remove people from the list of subscribers and add other people to it.

To change the subscriber list:

1. Choose V̲iew, Fold̲er List, and select the shared folder for which you want to add or remove subscribers.

2. Choose F̲ile, move the pointer onto S̲hare, and choose T̲his Folder to open the first Net Folder Wizard window, previously shown in Figure 14.4.

3. Choose N̲ext > to display the second wizard window that contains a list of current subscribers.

4. To remove a subscriber, select that subscriber and choose R̲emove.

5. To add a new subscriber, choose A̲dd to display the Add Entries to Subscriber Database dialog box, previously shown in Figure 14.6. Select a subscriber to add, choose T̲o >, and choose OK.

CHANGING SUBSCRIBERS' PERMISSIONS

When you add a Net Folder subscriber, Outlook automatically gives Reviewer permissions to that person. Reviewer permissions only allow the subscriber to read the contents of the shared folder. You may want to give certain subscribers additional permissions.

To change a subscriber's permissions:

1. Follow the first three steps in the preceding procedure.

2. Select the subscriber for whom you want to change permissions, then choose P̲ermissions to display the Net Folder Sharing Permissions dialog box, previously shown in Figure 14.8.

3. Select the permission level you want to assign to the person.

PART

III

CH

14

CANCELING A NET FOLDER SUBSCRIPTION

Any subscriber to a Net Folder can cancel that subscription.

To cancel a subscription to a Net Folder:

1. Choose View, Folder List to display your folder list.
2. Right-click the Net Folder for which you want to cancel your subscription to display its context menu.
3. Choose Properties to display the Properties dialog box. Select the Sharing tab.
4. Choose Cancel Membership.

After you do this, you no longer receive updates to the folder but the folder remains in your folder list and that folder contains all its existing items.

UNSHARING A FOLDER

You can stop sharing a folder you've previously been sharing. Here's one way to do that.

To stop sharing a folder:

1. Choose View, Folder List to display your folder list.
2. Select the folder you no longer want to share.
3. Choose File, move the pointer onto Share, and choose This Folder to display the first Net Folder Wizard window.
4. Choose Stop Sharing This Folder.

After you do this, the folder is no longer shared. All subscriptions to the folder are erased. Previous subscribers still have the subscribed folder with its most recent updates, but don't receive any changes you make to the folder.

TROUBLESHOOTING

After you accept an invitation to subscribe to a Net Folder, you'll probably find that things go quite smoothly at first. However, if you reformat your hard disk, you'll no longer have access to the shared folder. This happens even if you back up your Personal Folders file that contains your copy of the shared folder, reformat your disk, reinstall Windows and Outlook, and import the saved Personal Folders file.

The solution to this problem is for the person who owns the shared Net Folder to cancel your subscription, and then issue a new invitation to you to subscribe.

If you've been successfully using a subscription to Net Folders and then run into problems, these problems are usually solved in the same way.

One problem you might experience with Net Folders is duplication of posted messages. This can happen if a subscriber who has permission to add or modify items in the shared folder has two or more profiles that allow connection to the same store. If a subscriber uses one profile and accesses the Net Folder on the owner's computer, the local copy of the folder is updated. If the subscriber subsequently uses another profile to access the Net Folder on the owner's computer, the local copy is again updated, with the result that the local copy now has duplicates of any new postings.

When Outlook synchronizes the Net Folder on the local computer with the Net Folder on the owner's computer, the duplicate postings are copied to the owner's computer. Subsequently, the duplicate postings are copied to the Net Folder copies on all other subscriber's computers.

Outlook doesn't currently have any fix for this problem, so it's important for people to use only one profile to access Net Folders.

CHAPTER 15

MANAGING OUTLOOK FOLDERS

In this chapter

by Gordon Padwick

HOW OUTLOOK SAVES INFORMATION

Outlook saves items of information you create and receive in what are called *folders* (page 18). These aren't the type of folders you see on your disks when you use Windows Explorer. Rather, they are information containers that are either within a Personal Folders file on your computer's hard disk or, if you're using C/W Outlook as a client for Exchange, maybe in your Exchange store.

In addition to items of information, Outlook saves setup and reference information in several other files, some of which contain the Windows registry database. For example, the categories you can assign to items are saved within the registry. In various places in this book, there are references to information in the registry, along with a description of how you can access that information if you need to change it.

If several people have individual Windows profiles on a computer, the information that Outlook saves in the registry is saved separately for each person. As a result, each person can have a separate set of categories and other Outlook settings.

ACCESSING FOLDER LISTS

When you choose an icon in the Outlook Bar, Outlook opens the folder associated with that icon and displays the items contained in the folder in an Information viewer.

You can also select a folder and see its contents by choosing View, Folder List, and then choosing the name of a folder. Another way to display the folder list if you have the Advanced toolbar displayed is to choose the Folder List button in that toolbar.

Yet another way to display the Folder List is to click the name of the currently displayed Information viewer in that viewer's banner. When you do this, the folder list pops up on top of the Information viewer. If you subsequently click anywhere outside the folder list, the list disappears. To convert this pop-up folder list into the normal one that's displayed by the other methods, click the yellow pushpin at the top of the list.

To hide the normal folder list, click the X at the top-right, choose View, Folder List, or choose the Folder List button in the Advanced toolbar.

If you're using IMO Outlook you'll probably see a folder list similar to that shown in Figure 15.1.

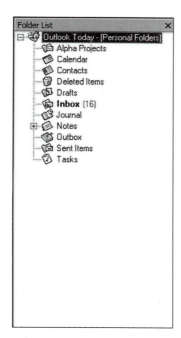

Figure 15.1
This typical folder list contains Outlook's standard folders under the heading Outlook Today-[Personal Folders].

Tip #115 from

If you see only the heading, click the small box that contains a plus sign at the left of the heading to expand the list so that the names of all the folders are shown.

The folder list shown in Figure 15.1 contains Outlook's default folders and some custom folders. The default folders are

- Calendar
- Contacts
- Deleted Items
- Drafts
- Inbox
- Journal
- Notes
- Outbox
- Sent Items
- Tasks

At the right of some folder names are numbers in parentheses. These numbers indicate how many items are waiting for your attention:

- The number adjacent to the Drafts folder indicates how many message drafts are in that folder.
- The number adjacent to the Inbox folder indicates how many incoming messages are waiting to be read.
- The number adjacent to the Outbox folder indicates how many messages are waiting to be sent to your mail server.

You're not limited to having only one Personal Folders file and one set of folders. As you'll see in this chapter, you can create additional Personal Folders files. After you do so, you'll see them all in the folder list. You must designate one Personal Folders file as the default file, the one in which Outlook normally saves items.

 If you're using C/W Outlook, but don't use it as a client for Exchange, the folder list is just the same as the one you see if you're using IMO Outlook, as previously described.

 If you're using C/W Outlook as a client for Exchange, and use the Exchange store to save Outlook items, the folder list shows the folders within your Exchange store. However, you can have a Personal Folders file on your local hard disk and save your Outlook items there. If you do have a Personal Folders file on your hard disk, you must choose whether you want to save Outlook items there or in your Exchange store.

WORKING WITH FOLDERS

 With the folder list displayed, you can access the contents of any folder by clicking the name of the folder. You can also right-click the name of a folder to display a context menu. The following sections describe some of what you can do from the context menu.

Note

Some of the menu items in the context menu are available only for folders you create, not for Outlook's standard folders. You can't move, delete, or rename a standard folder.

OPENING A FOLDER

In the context menu, choose Open Folder to display the contents of the folder. This command is somewhat redundant because you can do the same just by clicking the name of the folder.

OPENING A FOLDER IN A NEW WINDOW

In the context menu, choose Open in New Window to open the selected folder in its own Outlook Window. By doing this, you can have two or more Outlook folders visible at the same time. This can be very useful when you want to refer to information in one Outlook folder while you're working with information in another. It's also very convenient when you want to move or copy items from one folder into another.

Tip #116 from

Gordon Padwick

You'll ordinarily work with Outlook maximized. When you display two or more Outlook windows simultaneously, you should choose the Restore button near the right end of the windows' title bars and arrange the individual windows on your monitor so that you can see what you need. Alternatively, you can tile two or more windows by clicking an empty place in the Windows taskbar and choosing Tile Windows Horizontally or Tile Windows Vertically.

FINDING ITEMS IN A FOLDER

To find items in a folder, open that folder's context menu and choose Advanced Find.

→ For information about Advanced Find, **see** "Using Advanced Find to Find Words and Phrases," **p. 532**.

COPYING AND MOVING FOLDERS

You can copy any folder, including its contents, to another location within your folder list. You can move only those folders you've created, not the standard Outlook folders, to a new location. With only that difference, copying and moving are quite similar.

Open the folder's context menu and choose either Copy or Move (in each case the menu item includes the name of the folder) to open the Copy Folder or Move Folder dialog box. Figure 15.2 shows the Copy Folder dialog box.

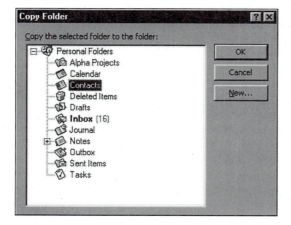

Figure 15.2
The Copy Folder dialog box shows your folder list. The Move Folder dialog box does the same.

Whether you're moving or copying the folder, select the name of the folder under which you want the folder to be, and choose OK.

Note

You can move a folder you've created (but not a standard Outlook folder) by dragging it to a new location within the folder list.

Yet another way to copy or move a folder is to point onto a folder name in the folder list, press the right mouse button, and drag to the new location. When you release the mouse button, a menu containing Move, Copy, and Cancel appears. Choose Move to move the folder, Copy to copy the folder, or Cancel to do neither.

DELETING A FOLDER

You can delete a folder you've created, but not one of Outlook's standard folders.

To delete a folder, open its context menu and choose Delete (Delete is followed by the folder name). Outlook displays a message asking you to confirm that you want to delete the folder by moving the folder and its contents into the Deleted Items folder. Choose Yes if you want to delete the folder and its contents.

RENAMING A FOLDER

You can rename a folder you've created, but not one of Outlook's standard folders.

To rename a folder, open its context menu and choose Rename (Rename is followed by the folder name). Outlook makes the folder name available for editing. Replace the original folder name with a new name, then press Enter.

CREATING A NEW FOLDER

You can create a new folder within your Personal Folders file or, if you're using C/W Outlook as a client for Exchange, within your Exchange store. The new folder can be a top-level folder at the same level as the standard Outlook folders, can be a subfolder under a top-level folder (either one of the standard Outlook folders or a top-level folder you've created), or can be a subfolder under a subfolder.

To create a new folder, right-click your Personal Folders file in the folder list or right-click your Exchange store, if you want the new folder to be a top-level folder. Alternatively, right-click the existing folder under which you want to create a new subfolder. Whichever you do, Outlook displays a context menu. In that context menu, choose New Folder to display the dialog box shown in Figure 15.3. Another way to display this dialog box is to choose File, move the pointer onto Folder, and choose New Folder.

Figure 15.3
Use the Create New
Folder dialog box to
define the new
folder.

To define a new folder:

1. Enter a name for the new folder in the Name box. The name should be different from the name of any folder that already exists at the same level as the new folder.

2. Open the drop-down Folder Contains list and select the type of items you will place in the new folder. Each folder can contain items of only one type.

3. In the Select Where to Place the Folder box, select the folder below which you want to place the new folder.

4. Choose OK to create the folder.

After you've completed these steps, the new folder appears in the folder list.

ADDING A FOLDER ICON TO THE OUTLOOK BAR

The Outlook Shortcuts and My Shortcuts group in the Outlook Bar initially contain icons representing the standard Outlook folders. If you create folders you're going to access frequently, it's convenient to add icons representing those folders to the Outlook Bar. You can add icons to the standard groups of the Outlook Bar, or you can create one or more custom groups in the Outlook Bar for these icons.

→ To find out how to add groups to the Outlook Bar, **see** "Renaming, Adding, and Removing Outlook Bar Groups," **p. 805**.

To create an Outlook Bar icon for a folder:

1. Select the Outlook Bar group in which you want to place the folder icon.

2. In the folder list, right-click the folder for which you want to create an Outlook Bar icon to display its context menu.

3. In the context menu, choose Add to Outlook Bar.

The icon appears in the Outlook Bar section.

> **Note** You can also drag a folder name into an Outlook Bar group.

If you subsequently want to remove the icon from the Outlook Bar, right-click the icon in the Outlook Bar and choose Remove from Outlook Bar. Outlook asks you to confirm you want to remove the icon. Choose Yes.

COPYING AND MOVING OUTLOOK ITEMS

You can copy and move Outlook items from one folder to another. Each folder can hold only one type of Outlook item. If you copy or move an item from one folder to another folder of the same type, the item is unchanged. When you copy or move an item to a folder of a different type, Outlook changes the item to the type of the new folder. For example, if you copy or move an item from a Calendar folder to a Task folder, the item becomes a Task item.

When you copy an item, Outlook creates a new item in another folder, leaving the original item in its folder. When you move an item, Outlook places the item in another folder, deleting it from the original folder.

The methods of copying and moving described in this section are primarily used when you want to handle individual items. To move groups of items, it's often more convenient to use Outlook's Organize capability.

→ For information about organizing items, **see** "Organizing Outlook Items," **p. 560**.

COPYING AND MOVING ITEMS BETWEEN SIMILAR FOLDERS

Although a specific example is used here to illustrate copying and moving items, the methods described can be used with all types of items.

Suppose you are involved with several projects. In that case, you may find it convenient to create several Tasks folders, one for each project, and keep the tasks for each project in the appropriate folder. If you presently have all your tasks in the standard Tasks folder, you can easily move individual tasks into separate folders. The first step is to create the new folders, as explained previously in this chapter.

→ For information about creating Outlook folders, **see** "Creating a New Folder," **p. 486**.

Figure 15.4 shows an example of a folder list with two subfolders for tasks.

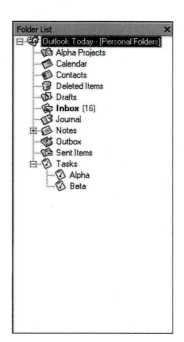

Figure 15.4
This folder list shows subfolders named Alpha and Beta under the standard Tasks folder.

Tip #117 from

To avoid the possible confusion that's likely to happen if you have two versions of each item, you should move items from the standard Tasks folder to the new subfolders, not copy them.

With the folder list displayed, as shown previously in Figure 15.4, drag items from the Tasks Information viewer onto the appropriate subfolder name in the folder list. Outlook assumes you want to move items, so there's no need to hold down the Shift key while you drag. When you release the mouse button, the item you dragged disappears from the list of tasks in the Tasks Information viewer. To confirm that the task is in the subfolder, you can click the subfolder name in the folder list to show its contents in that task's Information viewer.

Tip #118 from

Gordon Padwick

If, for some reason, you want to copy an item instead of move it, hold down Ctrl while you drag.

You can select several items and drag them all in one operation. To do so, select the first item, then hold down Ctrl while you select additional items. After you've selected all the items you want to move, drag one of them onto the subfolder name. All the selected items move.

Note

To select consecutive items, select the first item, then hold down Shift while you select the last item.

If you have an icon on the Outlook Bar corresponding to the target folder, you can drag items onto that icon instead of onto the folder name in the folder list.

COPYING ITEMS INTO A DIFFERENT TYPE OF FOLDER

One of Outlook's most useful capabilities is being able to change one type of Outlook item into another type, a process known as AutoCreate. Suppose you receive e-mail asking you to get something done by a certain date. To make sure you don't forget, you can add that request to your to-do list. One way to do so is to create a new Task item from scratch. An easier way is to copy the e-mail message into your Tasks folder to automatically create a Task item; you may have to make a few adjustments to it, but that's less work than creating a Task item from scratch.

CREATING A NEW ITEM IN A FOLDER OF A DIFFERENT TYPE

To use AutoCreate to create a new item, display the Information viewer that includes the item you want to start with. For example, if you want to start with an e-mail message you've received, display the Inbox Information viewer.

You probably want to leave the original item in its folder, so you'll copy the item, not move it. Drag the item either onto an icon in the Outlook Bar or onto a folder name in the folder list. For example, if you want to create a new task in the standard Outlook Tasks folder, drag the item onto the Tasks icon in the Outlook Bar. When you release the mouse button, Outlook displays the Task form with the subject of the original message in the Subject box and the text of the message in the form's Notes box, as shown in Figure 15.5. All you have to do is enter the appropriate due date (if there is one) in the Due Date box, then choose Save and Close in the form's Standard toolbar.

The preceding paragraph describes what happens when you drag in the normal way (holding down the left mouse button). If you drag holding down the right mouse button, Outlook gives you a choice when you release the mouse button. The options are:

- Copy Here as Task with <u>T</u>ext—This has the same effect as dragging with the left mouse button pressed. The original message remains in your Inbox folder.

- Copy Here as Task with <u>S</u>hortcut—Instead of copying the text of the message into the Task's Notes box, a shortcut to the message is copied into the Task's Notes box. The original message remains in your Inbox folder. You can double-click the shortcut in the Task's Notes box to see the original message.

- <u>C</u>opy Here as Task with Attachment—Instead of copying the text of the message into the Task's Notes box, the message is attached to the task and an icon representing the attachment is displayed in the Task's Notes box. The original message remains in your Inbox folder. You can double-click the attachment in the Task's Notes box to see the original message.

- <u>M</u>ove Here as Task with Attachment—The only difference between this and the previous option is that the original message is deleted from your Inbox folder.

- <u>C</u>ancel—The operation is canceled. Nothing is added to your Tasks folder and the original message remains in your Inbox folder.

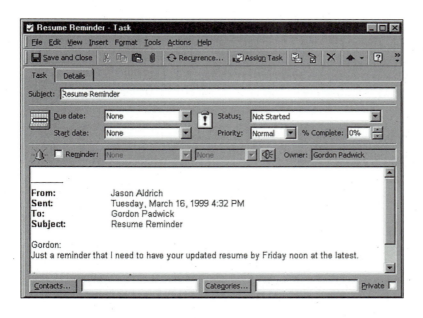

Figure 15.5
This is a Task form with a new task created from an e-mail message by AutoCreate.

In most case, dragging with the left mouse button pressed is a good choice. However, if you're creating an item from an item in another folder, and you have permanent access to the other folder, you might consider copying the item as a shortcut to minimize the disk space occupied.

If you're copying an item other than incoming e-mail, copying as a shortcut is sometimes useful. If you do that, you see any change to the original item when you open the shortcut. This is not useful if you've copied incoming e-mail because you can't change a message you've received. However, it could be useful if you copy a Calendar item to a Task item, or something similar.

Copying as an attachment can be useful if you need to copy many items. You might, for example, have many e-mail messages you want to use to create a new task. You can select all those items in your Inbox Information viewer and then, with the right mouse button pressed, drag to your Tasks folder. Choose Copy Here as Task with Attachment. Then you see icons representing each of the e-mail messages in the Task item's Notes box. You can then readily see what attachments you have and double-click any of them to display their details.

You'll probably rarely use the Move Here as Task with Attachment option. It's available if you want to move an Outlook item out of one folder into another.

Note

If you want to add a shortcut to another Outlook item, or add an attachment, to an existing item, open the existing item, then use Insert, Item.

USING MORE THAN ONE PERSONAL FOLDERS FILE

Outlook doesn't limit you to having only one Personal Folders file although, in most cases, you don't need more than one. If you do have more than one, you must designate which one you want Outlook to use as the default for items you create and receive.

One possible purpose of having a second Personal Folders file is to have a place where you can experiment with Outlook and learn how to use it. Use the primary Personal Folders file for your normal work; have a second Personal Folders file in which you can work without the risk of damage to your work items.

CREATING A PERSONAL FOLDERS FILE

 When you install IMO Outlook on a computer that hasn't previously had Outlook or Windows Messaging installed, it automatically creates a Personal Folders file in your C:\Windows\Local Settings\Application Data\Microsoft\Outlook folder. Depending on the choices you make when you install C/W Outlook, a Personal Folders file may or may not be created.

Note

> If you install Outlook on a computer on which a previous version of Outlook or Windows Messaging has been installed, Outlook usually detects and uses your previous Personal Folders file, in whichever Windows folder it exists.

Here's how you create a new Personal Folders file.

Note

> The method of creating a new Personal Folders file described here works equally well with IMO or C/W Outlook. In C/W Outlook, you can also create a new Personal Folders file by adding a Personal Folders information service to your profile.

To create a new Personal Folders file:

1. Choose File, move the pointer onto New, and choose Personal Folders File (.pst) to display the dialog box such as that shown in Figure 15.6.

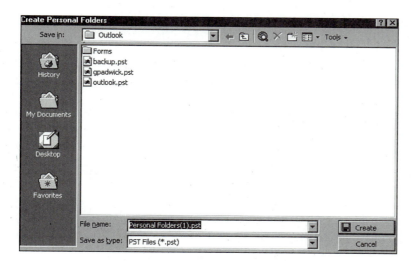

Figure 15.6
The Create Personal Folders dialog box opens, displaying a list of files in your C:\Windows\Local Settings\Application Data\Microsoft\Outlook folder.

2. You can create a new Personal Folders file in any folder, but it makes sense to create the new file in the same folder as any existing Personal Folders files. If you want to create the new Personal Folders file in a different folder, navigate to that folder.

3. Enter a name (such as your initials or last name) for the new Personal Folders file in the File Name box. You don't need to enter a file name extension because Outlook automatically uses .pst.

4. Choose Create to display the dialog box shown in Figure 15.7.

Figure 15.7
The Create Microsoft Personal Folders dialog box displays the full path name of the new file and proposes to show it with the name Personal Folders in the folder list.

> **Note**
>
> Each Personal Folders file has two names. One name is the file name you see in Windows Explorer. The other is the name you see in the Outlook folder list. The name in the Name box of this dialog box is the name that appears in the folder list.

5. Change the proposed name Personal Folders in the Name box to a name that identifies the purpose of the new Personal Folders file. This can be the same as the file name you entered in the previous dialog box.

6. In the Encryption Setting section of the dialog box, select the level of encryption you want to use.

> **Note**
>
> The only time you can set the encryption setting for a Personal Folders file is when you create the file. After you've created the file, you can't subsequently change its encryption.

7. If you want to password-protect the new file, enter a password in the Password box and again in the Verify Password box.

> **Note**
>
> You can subsequently password-protect a Personal Folders file that you didn't password-protect at the time you created it. You can subsequently change the password for a Personal Folders file.

8. Leave the Save This Password in Your Password List box unchecked.

9. Choose OK to complete creating the file.

You'll see the new Personal Folders file listed in the folder list, as shown in Figure 15.8. Initially, this file contains only the Deleted Items folder.

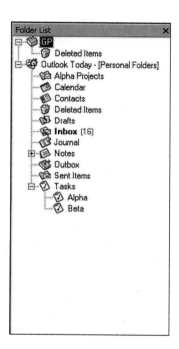

Figure 15.8
Notice that the original Personal Folders file has what looks like a house superimposed on its logo, whereas the new Personal Folders file doesn't.

Outlook shows the default file that is currently being used to save items by the small house superimposed on the file's icon in the folder list.

ACTIVATING A NEW PERSONAL FOLDERS FILE

You can activate a new Personal Folders file, that is, make it the default file in which Outlook saves items.

ACTIVATING A NEW PERSONAL FOLDERS FILE IN IMO OUTLOOK

Start by choosing View, Folder list to display the folder list.

To activate a Personal Folders file:

1. In the folder list, right-click the name of the Personal Folders file that you want to activate to display its context menu.

2. In the Context menu, choose Properties to display the file's Properties dialog box, as shown in Figure 15.9.

Figure 15.9
The Properties dialog box is displayed with the General tab selected.

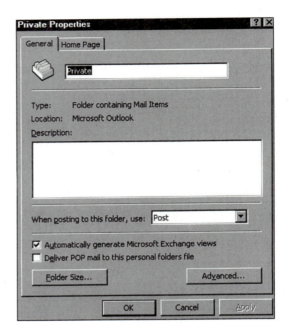

3. If you like, you can enter some comments about the purpose of the Personal Folders file in the Description box.

4. To make this Personal Folders file the active one, check the Deliver POP Mail to This Personal Folders File box.

Note

Although the name of the check box referred to in the preceding step refers only to POP Mail, in fact all Outlook items are delivered to (saved in) the new Personal Folders file.

5. Choose OK to close the dialog box. A message appears telling you that the location where mail will be delivered will not change until you exit and restart Outlook.

6. Exit and restart Outlook. When Outlook restarts, you see a long message about the location change. Choose Yes.

7. Open the folder list. Now you see the new Personal Folders file's icon has the house superimposed on it, indicating that file is where Outlook now saves items. Also, if you expand the file, you see that the new file contains all the standard Outlook folders, not just Deleted Items as previously.

ACTIVATING A NEW PERSONAL FOLDERS FILE IN C/W OUTLOOK

In C/W Outlook, you use the Services dialog box to choose which information service Outlook uses to save items.

To activate a Personal Folders file:

1. Choose Tools, Services and select the Delivery tab to display the dialog box shown in Figure 15.10.

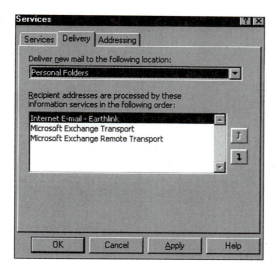

Figure 15.10
Use this dialog box to specify where Outlook should save items.

2. Open the drop-down Deliver New Mail to the Following Location list.

3. Select the name of the Personal Folders file that you want Outlook to use.

4. Choose OK. Although Outlook doesn't tell you, you must choose File, Exit and Log Off to close Outlook, and then restart Outlook before the new Personal Folders file will be used.

5. Restart Outlook. If necessary, choose View, Folder List to display the folder list. Now, the "house" icon appears over the name of the new Personal Folders file, indicating that is where Outlook will save items.

Removing a Personal Folders File

If you no longer need a certain Personal Folders file, you can detach it from Outlook so that it no longer appears in the folder list. You can't detach a currently activated Personal Folders file. If you want to detach the currently activated Personal Folders file, you must first activate a different Personal Folders file.

After you've detached a Personal Folders file, that file still exists on your hard drive, it just isn't available to Outlook. If you've really finished with the file, you can delete it from your hard drive under Windows in the same way that you delete any other file.

Caution	Don't delete a Personal Folders file from your hard drive without first detaching it from Outlook. If you do, Outlook will complain that it can't find the file.

The method you use to detach a Personal Folders file is different for IMO and C/W Outlook.

Detaching a Personal Folders File from IMO Outlook

Before you detach a Personal Folders file, make sure Outlook isn't using that file for saving items. To do so, open the folder list. If the file you want to detach is marked with a house on its icon, it is currently being used to save items. If that's the case, follow these steps to deactivate the file and then detach it. If the file is not currently being used, ignore steps 1 through 7.

To detach a Personal Folders file from IMO Outlook:

1. Open the Outlook folder list and right-click the name of a Personal Folders file other than the one you want to detach.

2. In the context menu, choose Properties.

3. Check Deliver POP Mail to This Personal Folders file.

4. Choose OK. Outlook displays a message telling you to close and restart Outlook. Choose OK.

5. Choose File, Exit to close Outlook.

6. Restart Outlook. Outlook displays a message about a change of location. Choose Yes. Outlook reopens.

7. If necessary, choose View, Folder List to display the folder list. Now the "house" is superimposed on a Personal Folders file name other than the one you want to detach from Outlook.

8. Right-click the name of the Personal Folders file you want to detach to display its context menu.

9. Choose Close. The name of that Personal Folders file disappears from the folder list.

Now, you can safely use Windows Explorer to delete the unwanted Personal Folders file from your Windows file environment.

To reattach a Personal Folders file (a file that you've detached but haven't deleted from your hard drive) to Outlook, use the procedure described previously for creating a Personal Folders file. The differences are, in step 1, choose File, Open (instead of File, New), and in Step 2, select the name of the existing file instead of entering a new name.

→ For information about creating a Personal Folders file, **see** "Creating a Personal Folders File," **p. 492**.

DETACHING A PERSONAL FOLDERS FILE FROM C/W OUTLOOK

Before you detach a Personal Folders file, make sure Outlook isn't using that file for saving items. To do so, open the folder list. If the file you want to detach is marked with a house on its icon, it is currently being used to save items. If that's the case, follow these steps to deactivate the file and then detach it. If the file is not currently being used, ignore steps 1 through 4.

To detach a Personal Folders file from C/W Outlook:

1. Choose Tools, Services to open the Services dialog box, then choose the Delivery tab.
2. Open the drop-down Deliver New Mail to the Following Location list and choose an information service other than the Personal Folders file you want to detach.
3. Choose File, Exit and Log Off to close Outlook.
4. Restart Outlook and, if necessary, open the folder list.
5. Right-click the Personal Folders file you want to detach to display its context menu.
6. Choose Delete (followed by the name of the file). That file disappears from the folder list.

Now, you can safely use Windows Explorer to delete the unwanted Personal Folders file from your Windows file environment.

To reattach a Personal Folders file (a file that you've detached but haven't deleted from your hard drive) to Outlook, use the procedure described previously for creating a Personal Folders file. The differences are, in step 1, choose File, Open (instead of File, New), and in step 2, select the name of the existing file instead of entering a new name.

→ For information about creating a Personal Folders file, **see** "Creating a Personal Folders File," **p. 492**.

USING PROPERTIES

Your Personal Folders file and the folders it contains all have properties that you can inspect and, in most cases, change.

UNDERSTANDING PROPERTIES OF A PERSONAL FOLDERS FILE

Right-click the name of a Personal Folders file in the folder list to display the file's context menu. In that menu, choose Properties to display a dialog box such as that shown in Figure 15.11.

Figure 15.11
The Properties dialog box contains two or more tabs.

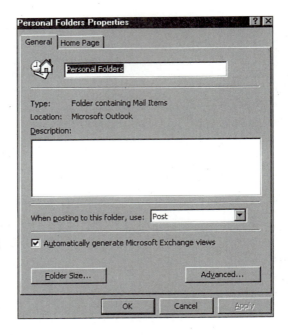

The icon at the top-left of the General tab has a house superimposed if the Personal Folders file you're currently accessing is the one Outlook uses to save items; the icon represents a file drawer if you're accessing any other Personal Folders file. The name of the folder appears at the right of the icon. Although it looks as though you can change the name, in fact you can't do so in this dialog box. To change the name, choose the Advanced button, as described subsequently in this section.

You can use the Description box to enter information about the Personal Folders file.

The When Posting to This Folder, Use box contains the name of the default form used to enter information. You can open the drop-down list to choose other available forms.

Leave the Automatically Generate Microsoft Exchange Views checked if you intend to share this folder with other people who use Exchange Client (Windows Messaging) as their e-mail client. Otherwise uncheck this box.

The Deliver POP Mail to This Personal Folder File (available only if you're using IMO Outlook) should be checked if you want Outlook to use the current Personal Folders File to save items; otherwise it should be unchecked.

Note
This check box can't be unchecked if you have only one Personal Folders file. You must have one Personal Folders file activated for IMO Outlook to use for saving items.

→ For information about activating a Personal Folders file, **see** "Activating a New Personal Folders File," **p. 495**.

IMO   C/W

Choose the Folder Size button to open a dialog box similar to the one shown in Figure 15.12.

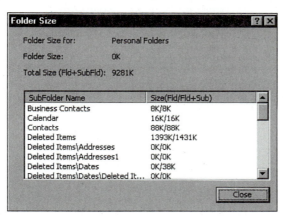

Figure 15.12
The Folder Size dialog box shows the size of the folder and also the size of all the subfolders it contains.

Note
The folder size shown here is considerably less than the space occupied by the file on your hard drive. Apparently what is shown here is the size in terms of the number of bytes within your Personal Folders file. It does not take account of any overhead, nor does it take account of information such as settings, views, and links that are saved in a Personal Folders file.

Choose Advanced to open the dialog box shown in Figure 15.13.

Figure 15.13
You can use this Personal Folders dialog box to change the name by which the Personal Folders file is listed in the folder list.

Note

The only time you can select an encryption level is when you create a Personal Folders file. You can't subsequently change the encryption level.

Choose the Change Password button to change the file's current password, or to start protecting the file with a password.

Choose Compact Now to recover the space previously occupied by items you've deleted from the Deleted Items folder.

Check Allow Upgrade to Large Tables to increase the Outlook's capacity if you need to. If this box is unchecked, Outlook is limited to approximately 16,000 folders per file and 16,000 items per folder. With this box checked, Outlook can accommodate approximately 64,000 folders per file and 64,000 items per folder. That should be more than enough for even the wildest e-mail junkie!

Note

By checking Allow Upgrade to Large Tables, you change the format in which Outlook saves items. After you check this, folders you export cannot be imported into Outlook on another computer in which Large Tables is not enabled. Outlook 97 doesn't support large tables, so compatibility with Outlook 97 is lost if you use Large Tables in Outlook 98 or Outlook 2000.

After you've finished with this dialog box, choose OK to close it and return to the General tab.

The Web Views tab provides access to a Web view you want to make available in the form.

→ For information about displaying Web views, **see** "Using Web Views," **p. 503**.

UNDERSTANDING FOLDER PROPERTIES

Right-click the name of a folder in the folder list to display its context menu. Choose Properties in the context menu to display the dialog box shown in Figure 15.14.

If you have the Net Folders add-in installed, the Properties dialog box for some individual folders includes a Sharing tab.

With the exception of the Contacts folder, the Properties dialog boxes for folders have the same tabs as the Personal Folders file Properties dialog box, but also have an AutoArchive tab. Notice that some boxes in the General tab that are in the Personal Folders file Properties dialog box are missing from the folders' Properties dialog boxes.

The AutoArchive tab is used to define how Outlook archives items within a folder.

→ For information about AutoArchiving, **see** "AutoArchiving Outlook Items," **p. 529**.

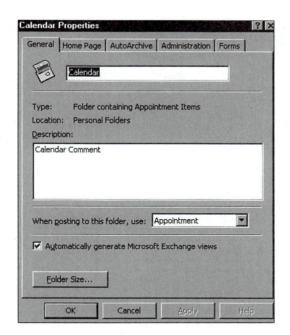

Figure 15.14
The Properties dialog box for most folders is similar to the Properties dialog box for a Personal Folders file.

The Properties dialog box for the Contacts folder doesn't have an AutoArchive tab because Outlook doesn't automatically archive Contact items. This dialog box does have two other tabs: Outlook Address Book and Activities.

The Outlook Address Book tab is where you can choose to have Outlook use the contents of a Contacts folder as an e-mail and fax address book.

The Activities tab is where you can define the activities Outlook associates with contacts.

→ For information about how you can track a Contact's Activities, **see** "Tracking a Contact's Activites" **p. 346**.

USING WEB VIEWS

In previous versions of Outlook, the Information viewers could be used to display the contents of Outlook folders and, if the Integrated File Management component of Outlook is installed, the contents of folders and files within the Windows environment. In addition to these capabilities, Outlook 2000 Information viewers can be used to display Web pages.

Briefly, it works like this. You can associate a Web page with any Outlook folder. The Web page can be designated as the default view Outlook displays when you select the folder, or it can be available as an optional view.

ASSOCIATING A WEB PAGE TO AN OUTLOOK FOLDER

Here's a practical example of how you might like to use Web Views. You can easily adapt the example for other purposes.

While I'm working with Outlook, I often want to refer to Microsoft's Outlook Web page to get information. Using the method described here, you can do the same. You can assign the Web page to one of Outlook's standard folders, but it's usually better to create a folder and assign the Web page to that.

To associate a Web page with an Outlook folder:

1. With any Outlook Information viewer displayed, choose File, move the pointer onto New, and choose Folder to create a new folder within your Personal Folders file. Give that folder a name, such as Outlook Information, and select Mail Items in the Folder Contains drop-down list.

2. Choose View, Folder List, right-click the new folder to display its context menu, and choose Properties. Select the Home Page tab in the Properties dialog box, as shown in Figure 15.15.

Figure 15.15
The Home Page tab is shown here with a Web page address entered.

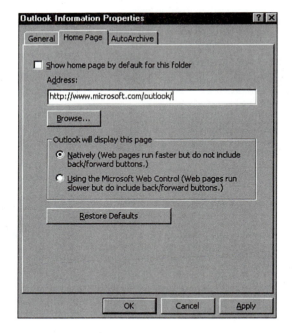

3. Enter the address (URL) of the Web page you want to associate with the folder in the Address box near the top of the dialog box. To provide access to Microsoft's Outlook Web page, enter `http://www.microsoft.com/office/Outlook/`.

4. Select the option you prefer in the Outlook Will Display This Page section of the dialog box. Choose OK to close the dialog box.

Tip #120 from

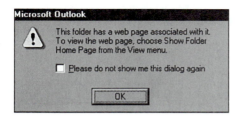

In step 3, you can choose <u>B</u>rowse to open the Find Web Files dialog box, select Favorites, and then choose a Web page from your favorites.

If you subsequently want to remove the association, open the Web Views tab and choose Restore Defaults.

VIEWING A FOLDER THAT HAS AN ASSOCIATED WEB PAGE

To view a Web page, open the Outlook folder to which you've associated a Web page. Outlook displays the message shown in Figure 15.16, telling you that the folder has a Web page associated with it. Choose OK to close the message box. At this point, the folder's Information viewer contains a list of Outlook items in the folder.

Figure 15.16
This message appears only when you select a folder with which a Web page is associated.

To display the Web page associated with the folder, open the <u>V</u>iew menu. The menu contains an item that wasn't there before you associated a Web page with the folder—Show Folder <u>H</u>ome Page. Choose Show Folder <u>H</u>ome Page to display the Web page in the Information viewer, as shown in Figure 15.17.

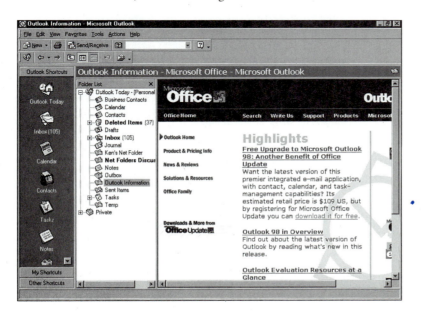

Figure 15.17
The Information viewer displays the Web page after whatever time it takes for your computer to connect to the Internet and access the page.

To switch back to the normal view of the folder's contents, choose View, Show Folder Home Page.

You can associate a Web page (only one) with any Outlook folder, default folders as well as folders you create. Here's an example of how you might associate a Web page with Outlook's Calendar folder. Suppose someone in your organization maintains a corporate calendar and posts that calendar on a Web page. You could associate that Web page with the Calendar folder on your computer. Then you can easily switch between viewing your personal calendar and the corporate calendar.

TROUBLESHOOTING

Sometimes Outlook's folders get corrupted and can't be opened. When that happens, you can often restore your Personal Folders file by using the Inbox Repair Tool, a utility that's on the Office 2000 CD-ROM. Despite the tool's name, it examines your Personal Folders file's structure and item headers, and attempts to recover all folders and items.

To run the Inbox Repair Tool, close Outlook, then choose Start in the Windows taskbar, move the pointer onto Programs, move the pointer onto accessories, move the pointer onto System Tools, and choose Inbox Repair Tool.

Alternatively, if you don't find the Inbox Repair Tool listed, you can choose Start in the Windows taskbar, move the pointer onto Find and choose Files and Folders to display the Find dialog box; in that dialog box, enter Scanpst.exe in the Named box and press Find Now. Double-click Scanpst.exe to run the file.

When you run the Inbox Repair Tool, the dialog box shown in Figure 15.18 appears.

Figure 15.18
You can choose Help in this dialog box to see information about the Inbox Repair Tool.

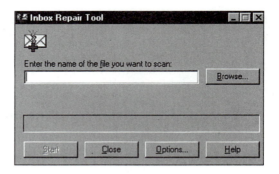

Enter the file name of the Personal Folders file you want to repair; alternatively, choose Browse to scan your disk for files that have .pst as their file name extensions and select the file.

Note

Personal Folders files are normally in the folder C:\Windows\Local Settings\ Application Data\Microsoft\Outlook.

After naming the file, choose <u>S</u>tart. A progress bar keeps you informed as the tool runs through eight phases. The process takes only a few seconds if no problems are found. However, if the tool does find problems, the process may take quite a while, particularly if you have a large Personal Folders file.

At the end of the process, the tool displays an information box that contains a list of recovered folders and items.

MANAGING YOUR COMPUTER ENVIRONMENT

Accessing Files

Integrated File Management is an optional Outlook component that gives you access to files on your computer's local hard drives as well as network hard drives from within Outlook.

This chapter describes some of the facilities available when you have Integrated File Management installed.

Using Other Shortcuts in the Outlook Bar

You can use the shortcut icons in the Other Shortcut section of the Outlook Bar as an alternative to Windows Explorer.

Using My Computer

Choose My Computer in the Other Shortcuts section of the Outlook Bar to display the Desktop Information viewer such as the one shown in Figure 16.1.

Figure 16.1
The viewer opens, displaying information about your Windows desktop.

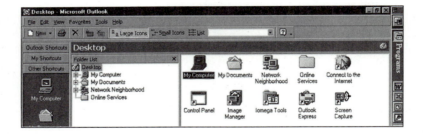

Like Windows Explorer, the Desktop Information viewer has two panes. The left pane lists major regions of your environment. After you select a region in the left pane, the contents of that region are shown in the right pane and the name of the selected region appears in the viewer's banner.

Unlike Windows Explorer, the Desktop Information viewer has the Standard toolbar shown in Figure 16.1. The buttons in this toolbar make the viewer more convenient to use than Windows Explorer.

Notice also that the Desktop Information viewer has a Print button in the toolbar. You can use this button to print what's displayed in the right pane, something you can't easily do in Windows Explorer.

You can expand any of the desktop components, just as you can in Windows Explorer. Figure 16.2 shows an example of expanded folders.

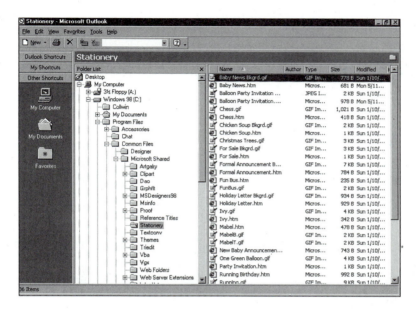

Figure 16.2
The folder structure is expanded here to show the contents of a low-level folder.

As in Windows Explorer, you can click any of the column titles in the right pane to display a folder's contents listed alphabetically by Name or Type, numerically by Size, or by date. If you select a folder than contains documents, you can click the Author column to display documents sorted by author.

Tip #121 from

Dates are listed with the abbreviation of day names preceding the date. Consequently, if you click Modified, the folder's contents are listed in alphabetical order by day name, instead of by date.

You can click a column title a second time to reverse the sort order.

The Information viewer can show various views of a folder's contents in addition to the Icon view shown in Figure 16.1. To select a different view, choose View and move the pointer onto Current View to display the available views:

- Icons—Shows folder contents as icons as shown in figure 16.1. You can choose Large Icons, Small Icons, or List buttons in the toolbar to display icons in various ways.
- Details—Shows folder contents as shown in Figure 16.2.
- By Type—Groups folder contents by file type.

You can also choose Customize Current View to customize the standard views, Define Views to define a new view, or Format Columns to display the Format Columns dialog box in which you can define how you want the columns in the viewer to appear.

→ For information about customizing views, **see** "Creating Views and Print Styles," **p. 943.**

You can choose Format Columns to display the dialog box shown in Figure 16.3.

Figure 16.3
You can use this dialog box to format the individual columns of the My Computer Information viewer.

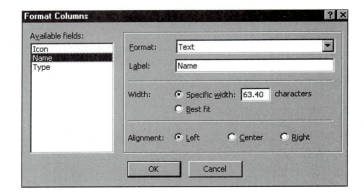

To format a column:

1. In the Available Fields list, select the column you want to format.
2. Open the drop-down Format list. If alternative formats are available for the column you've selected, select the format you want to use.
3. If you want to change the name for the column, edit the default name displayed in the Label box.
4. Use the Width section of the dialog box to select (or specify) the width of the column.
5. Select Left, Center, or Right alignment.
6. Repeat steps 1 through 5 to format other columns.

If you choose <u>V</u>iew, Fold<u>e</u>r List, the left pane disappears and the right pane is enlarged. Choose the same command again to restore the left pane.

You can choose <u>V</u>iew and move the pointer onto <u>T</u>oolbars to see a list of available toolbars. In addition to the Standard toolbar, which is displayed by default, you can display the Advanced toolbar, the Web toolbar, and the private toolbar. You can also choose <u>C</u>ustomize to customize menus and toolbars.

→ For information about customing toolbars, **see** "Customizing Command Bars," **p. 815**.

USING THE MY DOCUMENTS OR PERSONAL BUTTON

If you're running Outlook under Windows 95 or Windows 98, the Other Shortcuts section of the Outlook Bar contains a My Documents button. Choose My Documents to display an Information viewer that's similar to the one displayed when you choose My Computer. In this case, the viewer opens displaying the contents of your My Documents folder.

If you're running Outlook under Windows NT, the Other Shortcuts section of the Outlook Bar contains a Personal button. Choose Personal to display an Information viewer that's similar to the one displayed when you choose My Computer. In this case, the viewer opens displaying the contents of your Personal folder.

USING THE FAVORITES BUTTON

Choose the Favorites button in the Other Shortcuts section of the Outlook Bar to display an Information viewer that's similar to the one displayed when you choose My Computer. In this case, the viewer opens displaying the contents of your Favorites folder.

You can add folders, files, and URLs to your Favorites folder in several ways. Two of these are

- In Internet Explorer, open a Web page and choose F<u>a</u>vorites, <u>A</u>dd to Favorites. After choosing how you want to save the page, choose OK.
- Choose My Computer in the Outlook Bar and navigate through the folder tree to display the folder or file you want to add to your favorites in the right pane. Drag the file or folder onto the Favorites icon in the Outlook Bar.

Any changes you make to your Favorites in either of these ways affects what you see in Internet Explorer and Outlook.

If you want to organize your favorites, you'll probably find that it's more convenient to do so in Outlook, rather than in Internet Explorer.

CREATING AN OUTLOOK BAR SHORTCUT FOR A FOLDER

You can add shortcut buttons into any group in the Outlook Bar to provide shortcuts to folders. The following steps describe how to add such a shortcut to a group in the Outlook Bar.

To add a shortcut to the Outlook Bar:

1. Select a group in the Outlook Bar, such as the Other Shortcuts group.
2. Right-click the background of the Outlook Bar to display its context menu.
3. Choose Outlook Bar Shortcut to display the dialog box shown in Figure 16.4.

Figure 16.4
You can use this dialog box to find Outlook folders and folders in the Windows file system.

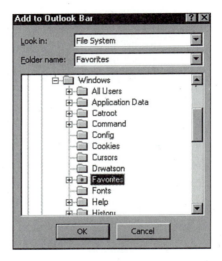

4. If necessary, open the Look In drop-down list and select File System.
5. Navigate to the Windows folder for which you want to create a shortcut.
6. Select the folder and choose OK. A shortcut to the folder appears in the Outlook Bar.

Note Refer to Chapter 33 for more detailed information about customizing the Outlook Bar.

→ **See** "Adding Shortcut Icons to an Outlook Bar Group," **p. 807**.

To delete a shortcut from the Outlook Bar, right-click the shortcut icon in the Outlook Bar to display its context menu. Choose Remove from Outlook Bar.

SEARCHING THE FILE SYSTEM FOR A FILE

You can search the Windows file system from within Outlook to find a file.

To find a file:

1. With any Outlook Information viewer displayed, choose Tools, Advanced Find to display the Advanced Find dialog box shown in Figure 16.5.

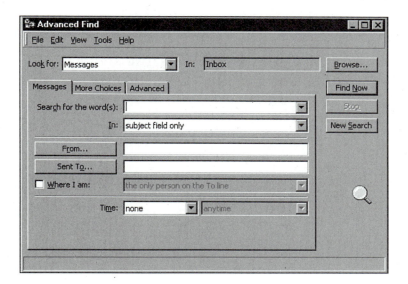

PART

III

CH

16

Figure 16.5
The Advanced Find dialog box opens, expecting you to want to find Outlook items in whatever Outlook folder you previously had selected.

2. Open the Look For drop-down list and select Files.

Note

Make sure you select Files, not Files (Outlook/Exchange).

3. Enter the name of the file you want to find in the Named box. If the file doesn't have a standard Office extension to its file name, you must include the extension with the file name.

4. Choose Find Now to initiate the search.

→ For detailed information about using Advanced Find, **see** "Finding Files," **p. 554**.

MANAGING OUTLOOK

CHAPTER 17

USING OUTLOOK TEMPLATES

In this chapter

by Gordon Padwick

WHAT ARE TEMPLATES?

Instead of creating every Outlook item from scratch, you can create templates from items, and then create other Outlook items based on those templates.

For example, you may have to create a monthly report of your activities in a standard format. That report may well have boilerplate text that changes very little from month to month, it may contain standard sections, and perhaps tables that contain budget and expense information that changes each month. Instead of creating all this from scratch every month, you can create and save a template. Subsequently, all you have to do each month is fill in the blanks. This can be a great time saver. With the help of templates you might even get your monthly reports in on time!

Outlook saves templates as files in the Windows file system. Each template is a separate file with .oft as it's file name extension.

CREATING AN E-MAIL TEMPLATE

You create a template for an e-mail message in the same way that you create any other e-mail message. In this case, though, instead of creating the complete message, just create a skeleton containing any boilerplate text, section headings, and tables.

→ If you usually assign the same *categories (page 604)* to certain kinds of messages, you can save yourself some time by creating templates that have those categories assigned to them. **See** "Creating a Message with Predefined Categories," **p. 611**.

After you've created the template, instead of choosing Send in the toolbar to send it, choose File in the form's menu bar, and then choose Save As to open the dialog box shown in Figure 17.1.

The dialog box opens with the subject of the message as the proposed file name and with the same file type in which you created the template, Text Only in this case.

Open the drop-down Save as Type list to see the list of available file formats, as shown in Figure 17.2.

Select Outlook Template. Outlook proposes to save the message as a template in your Templates folder with a file name that has .oft as its extension. The file name Outlook proposes is still the same as the subject of the message. You can change this to another name, but leave the file name extension as .oft.

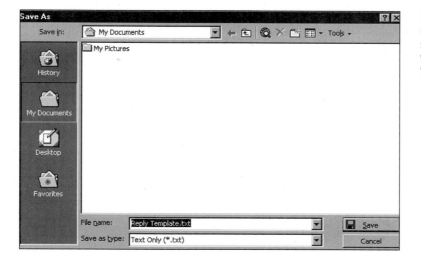

Figure 17.1
Use this dialog box to specify the type of file you want to save and where you want to save it.

PART

IV

CH

17

Figure 17.2
These are the available file types.

Caution

> Don't be tempted to choose a folder other than the default Templates folder for saving templates. If you do, Outlook won't be able to find your templates.

Choose <u>S</u>ave to save the template. Close the Message form. When Outlook asks if you want to save changes to the form, you could choose <u>N</u>o because you've already saved the form as a template. However, it's a good idea to choose <u>Y</u>es to save the form as an Outlook item. The reason for this is to provide a way to recover your work if, for some reason, the template isn't saved properly. There is more about this in the "Troubleshooting" section at the end of this chapter. Once you're satisfied that the template has been saved properly and is available for your use, you can safely delete the Outlook item.

See "Troubleshooting," **p. 526**.

USING AN E-MAIL TEMPLATE

When it comes time to write a monthly report, or whatever other message you created the template for, follow these steps to open the template.

To open a template:

1. In the Outlook Bar, click the type of icon you would normally choose if you were creating an Outlook item from scratch. For an e-mail message, click Inbox in the Outlook Bar.

2. Choose <u>T</u>ools, move the pointer onto <u>F</u>orms, and choose Ch<u>o</u>ose Form to display the dialog box shown in Figure 17.3.

Figure 17.3
The Choose Form dialog box opens, expecting you to choose a form in the Standard Forms Library.

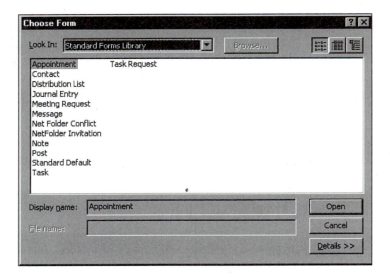

3. Open the drop-down Look In list and select User Templates in File System to display the dialog box shown in Figure 17.4.

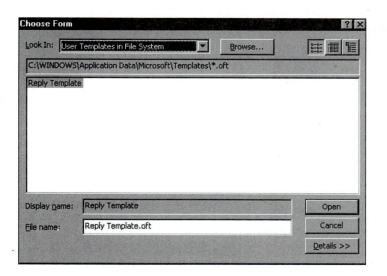

Figure 17.4
This dialog box shows the templates available in your templates folder.

4. Select the template you want to use and choose Open to display the form (a Message form in this case) with the information in the template displayed.

5. Use this template to finish creating your message.

6. When you've finished, choose Send in the form's toolbar to send the message.

USING TEMPLATES FOR DISTRIBUTING MESSAGES

If you frequently send messages to a group of people, you can create a distribution list and send each message to the distribution list. Creating and using distribution lists is covered in Chapter 9, "Managing Contacts."

→ For information about distribution lists, **see** "Working with Distribution Lists," **p.333**.

Create a prototype message, as described earlier in this chapter.

→ To learn how to create a prototype message, **see** "Creating an E-mail Template," **p. 520**.

Enter the e-mail addresses of all the people to whom you want to send the message in the To box. If there's any boilerplate text that's usually in each message, enter that in the notes box. Save the prototype message as a template.

When you want to send a message to the group, open the template, enter the text, and send the message in the normal way.

USING TEMPLATES FOR OTHER TYPES OF OUTLOOK ITEMS

You can use a similar method to create templates for other types of Outlook items. Here are some examples.

SENDING REGULAR MEETING REQUESTS

If you regularly send meeting requests to people, you can create a template of a meeting request. Then, instead of creating the meeting request from scratch, you can open the template, fill in the specific details, and send it.

→ To find out about Outlook to invite people to meetings, **see** "Inviting People to Meetings," **P. 400**.

CREATING SIMILAR CONTACT ITEMS

Perhaps you want to create many contact items for people in the same organization. Although you can use Outlook's Create Contact from Same Company option, you may find this doesn't do exactly what you want. In that case, you can create and save a prototype Contact item as a template. Then use that template to create individual Contact items.

→ For information about creating similar Contact items, **see** "Creating Similar Contact Items," **p. 320**.

ASSIGNING TASKS TO A TEAM

As a manager of a team, you might need to assign a similar task to several team members. The Task items you need to create for each member probably contain some text that's the same for everyone, and some text that's specific to each person. In that case, create a Task item that contains all the information that goes to everybody and save that as a template. Using the template, you can customize the Task item for each team member without having to retype everything.

→ To learn about using Outlook to assign tasks, **see** "Assigning a Task to Someone Else," **p. 430**.

MODIFYING A TEMPLATE

After you've created a template, you'll probably want to modify it from time to time. That's easy to do.

To modify an existing template:

1. In the Outlook Bar, click the type of icon you would normally choose if you were creating an Outlook item from scratch. For an e-mail message, click Inbox in the Outlook Bar.
2. Choose Tools, move the pointer onto Forms, and choose Choose Form to display the dialog box shown previously in Figure 17.3.

3. Open the drop-down <u>L</u>ook In list and select User Templates in File System to display the dialog box previously shown in Figure 17.4.

4. Double-click the name of the template you want to modify to open the template in a Template form, which is similar to a message form.

5. Make any changes to the template, such as changing e-mail addresses in the To box, text in the Subject box, and boilerplate text in the notes box.

6. Choose <u>F</u>ile, <u>S</u>ave to save the modified template, then close the template.

Note

If you want to save the original template and the modified template, in Step 6, choose <u>F</u>ile, Save <u>A</u>s to display the Save As dialog box in which you must give the modified template a name that's different from that of the original template. Make sure you select Outlook Template in the Save as <u>T</u>ype drop-down list; if you don't you won't be able to use the modified template.

SHARING TEMPLATES

Each template is a separate file in your Windows file system so it's easy to copy a file to another computer either by way of a network or by way of a floppy disk. In Windows Explorer, locate the folder that contains templates, usually C:\Windows\Application Data\Microsoft\Templates and copy the file either directly to the other computer by way of a network or onto a floppy disk.

Make sure you copy the template into the folder on the other computer that Windows uses for templates. That may not be the same folder as on your computer.

Tip #122 from

Gordon Padwick

To locate the folder in which Windows stores templates, choose Start in the Windows taskbar, move the pointer onto <u>F</u>ind, and choose <u>F</u>iles or Folders. In the Find dialog box, enter *.oft in the Named box and choose F<u>i</u>nd Now. After a few seconds, a list of template files is displayed; the list shows the folder that's used for template files.

But what if there are no templates already saved? In that case, you'll have to create a simple template on that computer and save it. Then you can use the method explained in the preceding paragraph to locate where templates are saved.

Another possible problem is that you'll see templates saved in several folders. That can happen if a previous version of Office has been used on that computer. The folder you need is most likely the folder in which the most recently created template is saved. If you've any doubt, create a simple template and look to see where it's saved.

Outlook and other Office applications automatically recognize template files and make them available as long as they are in the correct folder and have .oft as their file name extensions.

TROUBLESHOOTING

You're unlikely to have much trouble with templates. The only problem I recall people having is when Outlook can't find a template. The most likely reasons for this are if you forget to save a template you've created as an Outlook template, or if you save it in the wrong folder. When you have finished creating an Outlook item that you want to use as a template, choose File, Save As to display the Save As dialog box. There, you *must* open the drop-down Save as Type list and select Outlook Template. If you don't, the file will be saved as a text file. Outlook won't subsequently display the file in the list of templates, so you won't be able to use it.

As far as I know, there's no way to convert the file you saved as a text file to a template file. That's why, previously in this chapter, I recommended that you save a new template as an Outlook item until you're certain the template has been properly saved and is available to be used.

If you save a template in the wrong folder, use Windows Explorer to move it to the correct folder. The tip in the previous section explains how to find the folder in which template files should be saved.

CHAPTER 18

FINDING AND ORGANIZING OUTLOOK ITEMS

In this chapter   *by Gordon Padwick*

SEARCHING FOR INFORMATION

After you've used Outlook for several months, you're likely to have a lot of information stashed away in your folders; some of it is easy to find, but finding other *items (page 19)* isn't always so easy.

It's easy to find the e-mail you sent to a certain person. Just open your Sent Items folder and click To at the top of the table view of items you've sent to see all the items listed alphabetically by the name of the person to whom you sent mail. Similarly, you can click Sent to see items listed in date order, or Subject to see items listed alphabetically by subject.

Tip #123 from

In either case, click the column heading a second time to the reverse the sort order.

Finding an item by subject, though, presents problems because, quite often, the first word of an item's subject doesn't define what a message is really about. Outlook's Find capability offers a solution to this problem. This chapter describes how to solve this problem by using Outlook's Find and Advanced Find capabilities.

USING THE QUICKFIND CONTACT TOOL

Before we get deeply into finding items, let's take a quick look at the QuickFind Contact tool that's new in Outlook 2000.

Apparently, Microsoft found that the most frequent information Outlook users wanted to find was information about contacts. Microsoft's answer to that need is the QuickFind Contact tool that's available near the right end of each Information viewer's Standard toolbar, as shown in Figure 18.1.

QuickFind Contact tool

Figure 18.1
The empty box near the right end of an Information viewer's Standard toolbar provides access to the QuickFind Contact tool.

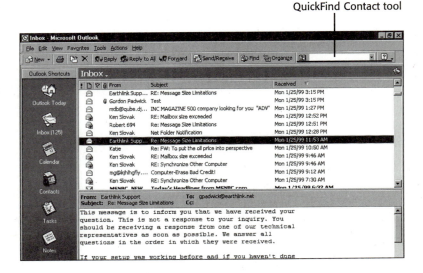

No matter what Information viewer is displayed, you can use the QuickFind Contact tool to get information about one of your contacts.

To display information about a contact:

1. Place an insertion point in the QuickFind Contact tool.
2. Enter a name or partial name. If there's only one name that matches, Outlook displays a Contact form containing information about that contact, such as that shown in Figure 18.3. If two or more names match, Outlook displays a dialog box, such as that shown in Figure 18.2, which lists matching contacts.

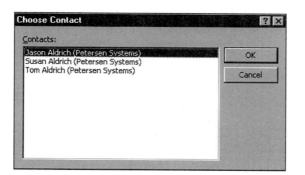

Figure 18.2
This dialog box lists all contacts that match your entry.

3. Select the contact for whom you want to see information, then choose OK to see information about that contact in a form such as that shown in Figure 18.3.

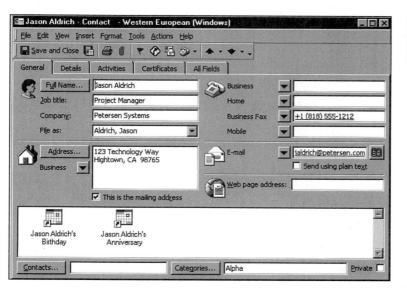

Figure 18.3
Outlook displays information about the contact in a Contact form.

FINDING OUTLOOK ITEMS

As an introduction to using Outlook's Find capability, we'll look specifically at how you can find messages you've received. You can use the same technique to find other types of Outlook items. This section describes only Outlook's basic Find capability. If you don't see what you need here, look later in this chapter for information about Advanced Find.

→ To learn more about using the Outlook Advanced Find capabilities, **see** "Using Advanced Find to Find Words and Phrases," **p. 532**.

Note

> The basic method of finding items described in this section looks only in one Outlook folder at a time, the folder you're currently accessing. You can use Advanced Find, described later in this chapter, to look in more than one folder.

To find all e-mail messages that contain certain text, display the Inbox Information viewer. Choose Find in the Standard toolbar (alternatively, choose Tools, Find). When you do so, the Find Items in Inbox pane appears at the top of the Information viewer, as shown in Figure 18.4.

Figure 18.4
The Find Items pane provides an easy way to look for text in a message.

Find Items pane

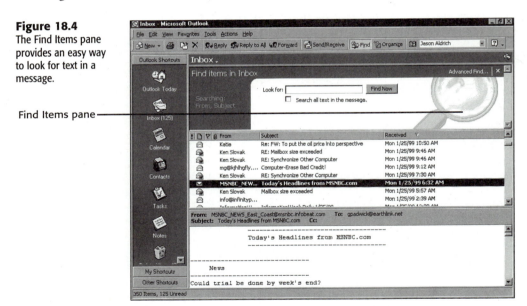

Note

> If you don't see Find in the toolbar, choose the More Buttons button ⬛ to display a box that contains Find.

To find messages in your Inbox folder:

1. In the Look For box, enter the word or phrase you want to find.

2. Leave the Search All Text in the Message check box unchecked if you want to search only the headers of messages. Check this box if you want to search the entire contents of messages.

3. Choose Find Now to initiate the search. Outlook displays the results of the search in a table, as shown in Figure 18.5.

Note

The Preview pane works the same for search results as it does in the Inbox Information viewer. If the Preview pane is not enabled, you see just a list of message headers. If the Preview pane is enabled, you see two panes; the upper pane shows a list of message headers and the lower pane shows the contents of any message you select in the upper pane. You can double-click any message header in the upper pane to display that message in a Message form.

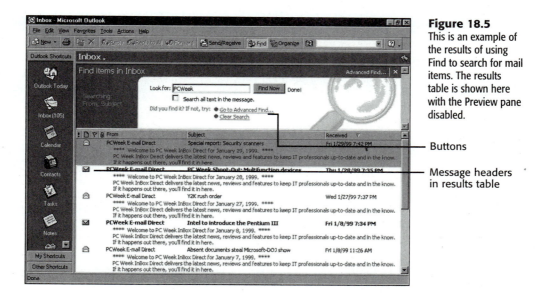

Figure 18.5
This is an example of the results of using Find to search for mail items. The results table is shown here with the Preview pane disabled.

Buttons

Message headers in results table

Note

In this example, the search characters are "PC Week" and the search is limited to message headers. Outlook finds all messages from any sender that has "PC Week" in its name or those characters in its subject.

If you search only for message headers, the search is quite fast. Almost immediately a list of messages with headers that match your search word or phrase appears as shown in Figure 18.5. If you check Search All Text in the Message, to search through the entire content of messages, the search takes much longer. In either case, if no matches are found, Outlook displays "No items found" at the top of the message headers pane. Additionally, at the completion of the search, two small buttons labeled Go to Advanced Find and Clear Search appear in the Find pane.

Outlook searches only those messages displayed in the current view. If the current view is filtered to show only messages that satisfy certain conditions, only messages that satisfy those conditions will be found. For example, if you are using the Last Seven Days view of your Inbox, the search results displayed contain only messages you received in the last seven days. If Outlook doesn't find what you're looking for, you may have to choose a different view and then try Find again.

After making one search, you can choose Clear Search to clear the list of found items and also to clear the search text. Then you can enter another search word or phrase and begin another search. When you've finished searching, close the Find pane by clicking the X at the top-right of the pane or by again choosing Find in the Information viewer's Standard toolbar.

Note   The Find pane closes when you display a different Information viewer.

You can use the same technique to search for Outlook items in any folder. For example, to find specific contacts, open the Contacts Information viewer, and choose Find to display the Find pane. To find a contact based on the text you entered in the various boxes on the General tab on the Contact form (but not the Notes box or the Categories box), leave the Search All Text in Contact check box unchecked. Check this box if you want to include text in the Notes box of each Contact item in your search.

Outlook displays most search results in a Table view (an exception is when you search a Card view of Contact items, the search results are displayed in a Card view). You can double-click any item in the search results to display that item in the form in which it was created. You can also click the header of any column of a search results table to sort the search results in order based on the contents of that column.

USING ADVANCED FIND TO FIND WORDS AND PHRASES

Although the Find pane described in the previous section provides an easy way to find certain types of information, it won't always provide what you need. You can't use the Find pane to find Outlook items that contain specific text in certain fields. For example, you can't find contacts who have a specific telephone area code in this way. Advanced Find can make these sorts of searches and much more.

ACCESSING ADVANCED FIND

Outlook's Advanced Find provides many ways to find Outlook items as well as Windows files. You can access Advanced Find in several ways:

- With any Information viewer displayed, choose Tools, Advanced Find to display the dialog box as shown in Figure 18.6.

- With the Inbox or Sent Items Information viewer displayed, choose Actions, move the pointer onto Find All, and choose Messages from Sender to display a dialog box similar to that shown in Figure 18.6.

- With any Information viewer displayed, choose Find in the Standard toolbar to display the Find Items pane, then choose Advanced Find near the right end of the pane's banner to display a dialog box similar to that shown in Figure 18.6.

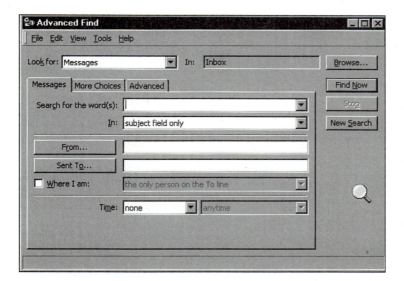

Figure 18.6
The Advanced Find dialog box opens with the first tab selected.

Tip #124 from

After you've completed a search initiated from the Find pane, Outlook asks you "Did you find it?" At this point, you can choose Go to Advanced Find.

The Advanced Find dialog box contains a three-tabbed subform. The name of the first tab corresponds to the name of the Information viewer that was displayed when you opened the Find pane. Figure 18.6 shows this tab as Messages because the Inbox Information viewer was displayed when Advanced Find was chosen in this example. The other two tabs are always named More Choices and Advanced.

SPECIFYING THE TYPE OF ITEM TO FIND

Outlook assumes you want to find items of the type contained in the currently open folder and displayed in the current Information viewer. If Outlook is displaying *Contact items (page 298)* in your Personal Folders file when you start Advanced Find, the first tab within the dialog box is named Contacts, the Look For box contains Contacts, and the In text box contains the name of the folder or folders Outlook proposes to search in; what's in the In text box depends on how you opened Advanced Find.

If you want to look for a different type of item, open the Look For drop-down list in which you can select:

- Any type of Outlook item
- Appointments and Meetings
- Contacts
- Files
- Files (Outlook/Exchange)
- Journal entries
- Messages
- Notes
- Tasks

Tip #125 from

Gordon Padwick

Choosing Any Type of Outlook Item is particularly useful if you want to find all the Outlook items that relate to a particular subject, such as a person or project.

Select a type of item in the Look For drop-down list. After you do so, the name of the item type you select appears as the name for the first tab in the Advanced Find dialog box's sub-form.

DECIDING WHERE TO LOOK FOR THE ITEM

Outlook items may be in various places. If you haven't changed the default folders, items are usually in one of two places:

- In the folders within your Personal Folders file (if you're not using Outlook as a client for Exchange Server)
- In the folders within your Exchange store (if you are using C/W Outlook as a client for an Exchange server)

When you first open the Advanced Find dialog box, the In text box (near the top-right) is gray and contains the name of an Outlook or Exchange folder (sometimes more than one), Personal Folders, or Mailbox. This means that Outlook is ready to search for items in those places. After you open the Look For drop-down list and select a type of item, Outlook replaces the initial folder name with the name of the folder in which the type of item you've selected is normally kept. For example, if you select Tasks, Outlook expects to find Task items in the Tasks folder.

If the name in the In text box isn't where you want to search, choose Browse to open the dialog box shown in Figure 18.7.

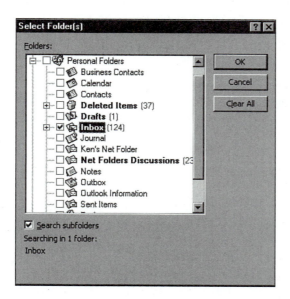

Figure 18.7
The Select Folder(s) dialog box lists the available folders. The folder or folders in which Outlook proposes to search are checked.

PART
IV
CH
18

In the Select Folder(s) dialog box, expand the appropriate top-level folder if necessary, deselect any folders you don't want to search, select the folder or folders in which you want Outlook to search, then choose OK. The names of the folders you select appear in the In text box.

| Note | You can select any number of folders in this way. If you select two or more folders, one folder name is separated from the next in the In text box by a semicolon. |

→ To learn more about working with Outlook folders, **see** "Creating Folders and Subfolders" **p. 922**.

STARTING YOUR SEARCH

Suppose you want to search for a contact. You've selected Contacts to look for and you accept Outlook's proposal to search in the Contacts folder. Now select the Contacts tab if it isn't already selected.

Tip #126 from

Gordon Crock

Advanced Find searches for items that satisfy criteria specified in all three tabs of the Advanced Find dialog box. Before you start specifying a new search, choose New Search to remove all existing search criteria. This ensures that any criteria in tabs you're not using won't interfere with the search. This isn't strictly necessary when you first open Advanced Find because all search criteria are initially cleared. However, it is necessary if you use Advanced Find two or more times while it is open.

To set up your search:

1. Enter the word or phrase you want to search for in the Search for the Word(s) box.

Tip #127 from

Gordon Crock

If you've previously searched for the same word or phrase, you can open the Search for the Word(s) drop-down list and select that word or phrase.

2. If you don't want to search in the field proposed in the In text box (the one in the Contacts tab, not the In text box at the top of the dialog box), open the In drop-down list and select the fields in which you want to search. The selection available varies according to the type of item you're looking for.

3. In many cases, the information you've entered and selected so far is all that's necessary. Choose Find Now to initiate the search. Outlook displays the results of the search in a table at the bottom of the Advanced Find box, as shown in Figure 18.8.

Figure 18.8
Outlook displays the result of the search in a table.

You can double-click any item in the search results table to open that item in the Outlook form in which that item was originally created.

UNDERSTANDING HOW OUTLOOK SEARCHES

In the preceding pages of this section, you've been told to enter the word or phrase you want Advanced Find to search for. There's more to know than you might expect about how Outlook interprets a word or phrase.

LOOKING FOR SEVERAL WORDS

When you enter several words, Outlook searches for those words as a phrase. The entire phrase must exist for Outlook to find it.

Outlook can also search for items that contain one word or another—this is sometimes referred to as a *Boolean* search. For example, if you want to search for an item that contains the word "apple" or the word "orange," you enter these words in the Search for the Word(s) box with a comma or semicolon separating one word from the next. If you enter

```
apple orange
```

Outlook searches for items that contain the phrase "apple orange." If you enter

```
apple,orange
```

or

```
apple;orange
```

Outlook searches for items that contain either "apple" or "orange" or both words.

Instead of single words, you can use phrases. For example, if you enter

```
sweet apples,bitter oranges
```

Outlook searches for items that contain either the phrase "sweet apples" or the phrase "bitter oranges," or both phrases.

PUNCTUATION MARKS

If you want to search for a phrase that contains punctuation marks, you must enclose the entire phrase within double quotation marks. For example, if you want to search for items that contain the phrase "apple, orange, or banana" enter

```
"apple, orange, or banana"
```

If you omit the quotation marks, Outlook will search for items that contains either "apple," "orange," or "or banana."

PLURALS AND VERB FORMS

If you ask Outlook to search for "apple" it finds items that contain "apple" and also items that contain "apples." However, if you ask Outlook to search for "apples" it only finds items that contains "apples"—not items that contain "apple."

PART

IV

CH

18

Outlook's capability to find plurals when you specify a singular noun extends to nouns that have slightly irregular plural forms. For example, if you specify "box," Outlook finds items that contain "box" or "boxes." Outlook isn't smart enough, however, to find "mice" when you specify "mouse." If you want to find "mouse" or "mice" you have to enter

```
mouse,mice
```

Tip #128 from

To be on the safe side, if you want Outlook to find singular and plural forms of nouns that have irregular plurals, specify both forms (separated by a comma or semicolon) in the search text.

The same principle applies to verb forms. For example, if you search for "play," Outlook will also find "plays" and "played." Don't expect Outlook to find various forms of irregular verbs.

FINDING SPECIFIC OUTLOOK ITEMS

You can use Advanced Find to find words and phrases in any type of item. You can also look for items based on something other than words or phrases. What you can search for depends on the type of item for which you're searching.

FINDING CALENDAR ITEMS

After you select Appointments and Meetings in the Look For drop-down list, Outlook assumes you want to search for items in your Calendar folder; the Appointments and Meetings tab contains three sections, as shown in Figure 18.9.

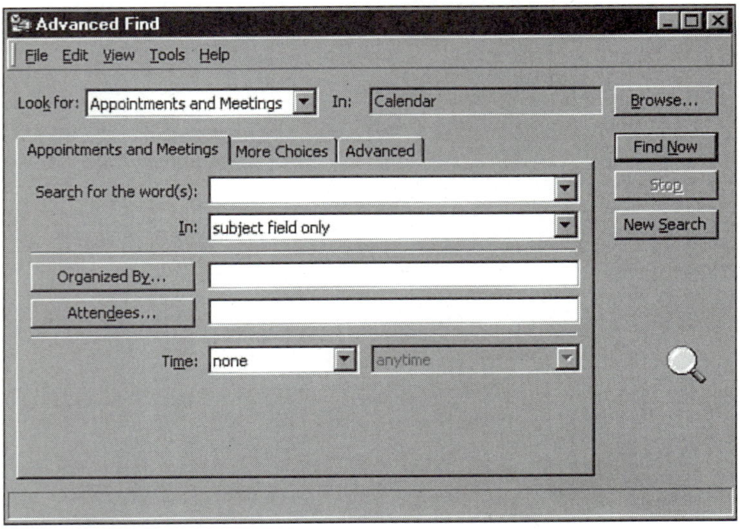

Figure 18.9
You can search for words, meeting organizers, meeting attendees, and times in calendar items.

![Advanced Find dialog box showing the Appointments and Meetings tab with Look for: Appointments and Meetings, In: Calendar, Search for the word(s), In: subject field only, Organized By, Attendees, Time: none, anytime fields]

You can enter search criteria in any one or more of the sections in the Advanced Find dialog box's Appointments and Meetings tab. It's important to understand that all the criteria you enter must be satisfied in order for Outlook to find an item. Suppose, for example, you enter the word Alpha in the Search for the Word(s) box, and you enter the name of an attendee (such as Jane Rogers) in the Attendees box. Outlook then finds those appointments and meetings for which the subject contains the word Alpha and the people with whom you had the appointment or attended the meeting includes Jane Rogers.

The top section of the Appointments and Meetings tab is where you can enter a word or phrase to search for, as already described.

The second section applies to calendar items that represent meetings. In this section, you can specify one or more people who organized meetings and one or more people who were invited to attend meetings. Choose Organized By to display the Select Names dialog box in which you can select organizers' names from your address books. Choose Attendees to select attendees names from your address books. Alternatively, you can enter the names of people.

The third section applies to all types of calendar items. By default, none appears in the Time box—time is not used as a basis for finding items. Open the Time drop-down list and select from the following: None, Starts, Ends, Created, and Modified. After you select any of these except None, the adjacent drop-down list is enabled with Anytime selected. Open this drop-down list and select from the twelve timeframes. For example, you can direct Outlook to search for items received or created today, tomorrow, in the last seven days, and so on. This feature narrows your search, thus helping you find items quickly.

Enter the appropriate search criteria in all three sections of this tab.

→ For more information about making the most of Outlook searches, **see** "Creating Precise Searches," **p. 546**.

FINDING CONTACT ITEMS

After you select Contacts in the Look For drop-down list, Outlook assumes you want to search in your Contacts folder; the Contacts tab contains three sections, as shown in Figure 18.10.

Use the top section of this tab to enter words and phrases to search for, as previously described.

In the second section, you can enter a complete or partial e-mail address. You can use this to find all your contacts who have e-mail addresses on a certain server by entering the name of the server. For example, enter the name of that server (such as hotnet.net) in the E-mail box. Outlook will subsequently find all your contacts who have an e-mail account on that server.

PART

IV

CH

18

Figure 18.10
You can search for words, e-mail addresses, and times in contact items.

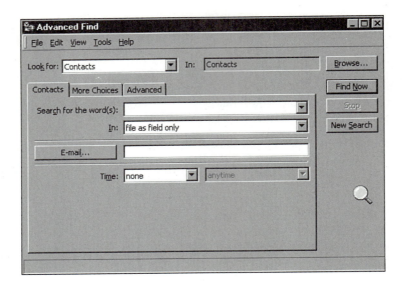

The third section is similar to the third section of the Appointments and Meetings tab (described previously in this chapter), but with fewer selections. You can choose among:

- None
- Created (the time the item was originally created)
- Modified (the most recent time the item was modified)

FINDING JOURNAL ITEMS

After you select Journal Entries in the Look For drop-down list, Outlook assumes you want to search in your Journal folder; the Journal Entries tab contains three sections, as shown in Figure 18.11.

By now you should be getting the picture. You can search each type of Outlook item for words and also define times. In addition, special search criteria are available for each type of item.

For Journal items, you can open the Journal Entry Type drop-down list and select all entry types or a specific type of Journal entry. You can also choose Contact to open the Select Names dialog box in which you can select a contact's name (or several contacts' names).

→ To learn more about Outlook's advanced searching capabilities, **see** "Using Advanced Find to Find Words and Phrases," **p. 532**.

FINDING MESSAGE ITEMS

After you select Messages in the Look For drop-down list, the Messages tab contains three sections, as shown in Figure 18.12.

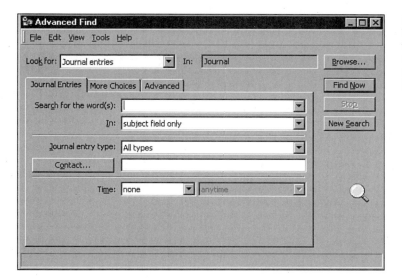

Figure 18.11
You can search for text, specific Journal entry types, contacts, and times in Journal items.

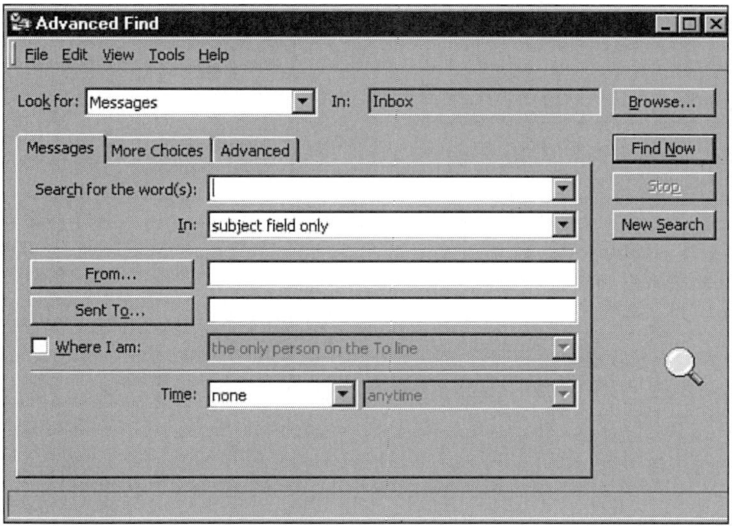

Figure 18.12
You can search for words in a message, names of message senders and recipients, for your involvement with the message, and for times in Message items.

As always, you can enter a word or words to search for in the Search for the Word(s) box, or open the drop-down list and select previous words you've searched for. You can open the drop-down In list and select Subject Field Only, Subject Field and Message Body, or Frequently-used Text Fields.

Choose From or Sent To (or both) to open the Select Names dialog box to select the name or names of people to whom you've sent messages or from whom you've received messages. Alternatively, instead of selecting names, you can enter names in either or both text boxes.

If you want to have your involvement in the message as one of the search criteria, check the Where I Am box to activate the drop-down list at its right. Open the drop-down list and select from:

- The only person on the To line
- On the To line with other people
- In the CC line with other people

You can open the drop-down Time list and select among:

- None
- Received
- Sent
- Due
- Expires
- Created
- Modified

After you select anything other than None, the box on the right becomes enabled with "anytime" initially displayed. If you select "received" in the Time drop-down list, you are asking Outlook to find messages you've received on any date or time.

Instead of accepting the default "anytime" you can open the drop-down list and select among:

- Anytime
- Yesterday
- Today
- In the Last 7 Days
- Last Week
- This Week
- Last Month
- This Month

To specify dates and times more precisely than is possible by making selections here, you can use the Advanced tab, as explained subsequently in this chapter.

→ To learn more about effectively narrowing your Outlook searches, **see** "Defining Advanced Find Criteria," **p. 549**.

FINDING NOTES ITEMS

After you select Notes in the Look For drop-down list, the Notes tab contains two sections, as shown in Figure 18.13. Outlook gives you the options to search Notes for words in the subject field or in the contents of notes. You can also search based on time constraints:

- None
- Created
- Modified

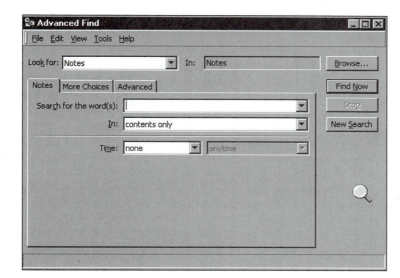

Figure 18.13
You can use text and times as search criterion in Notes items.

PART
IV

CH
18

> **Note**
>
> The Subject field of a note contains the first paragraph of that note. The Contents field of a note contains the entire text, including the first paragraph.

The drop-down Time lists contain the selections available when you're specifying criteria for finding messages, as described in the preceding section.

FINDING TASK ITEMS

After you select Tasks in the Look For drop-down list, the Tasks tab contains three sections, as shown in Figure 18.14.

Open the Status drop-down list and select from:

- Doesn't Matter
- Not Started
- In Progress

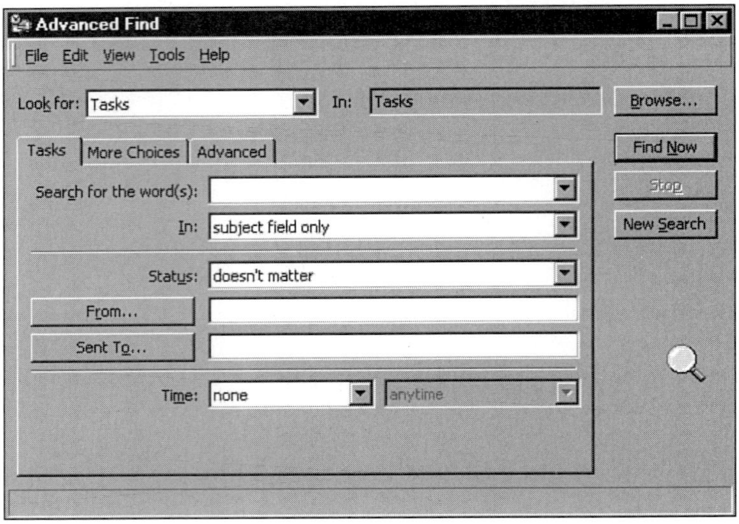

Figure 18.14
You can search for words, task status, whom you received tasks from, to whom you sent tasks, and times.

- Completed
- Waiting on Someone Else
- Deferred

Choose From or Sent To (or both) to open the Select Names dialog box to select the name or names of people to whom you've sent tasks or from whom you've received tasks. Alternatively, you can enter names in these boxes.

Open the drop-down Time list and select among:

- None
- Due
- Starts
- Completed
- Created
- Modified

If you select any of these other than None, the adjacent box becomes enabled with "anytime" inside it. You can open the drop-down list and select among:

- Anytime
- Yesterday
- Today
- Tomorrow
- In the Last 7 Days

- In the Next 7 Days
- Last Week
- This Week
- Next Week
- Last Month
- This Month
- Next Month

Viewing Find Results

Outlook displays the results of a search, whether you start from the Find pane or the Advanced Find dialog box, as a table in a default view. The default view Outlook uses depends on the type of item you're finding. If you're using Advanced Find, you can easily choose a different view of the results of the search.

After you've used Advanced Find to search for items, the items that match your search criteria are displayed in a table at the bottom of the Advanced Find dialog box. To see the items in a different view, choose View in the Advanced Find menu bar, move the pointer onto Current View, and select the view in which you want to see the search results. In the case of messages, you can also choose AutoPreview in the Advanced Find's View menu to display the first three lines of message texts.

Part
IV
Ch
18

Note

The AutoPreview menu item isn't available until the results of a search are displayed.

Saving and Reusing Search Criteria

After you've constructed a set of search criteria (and confirmed that it satisfies your needs) you can save it so it's immediately available to be used again.

To save your search criteria:

1. Choose File in the Advanced Find menu bar and choose Save Search to display the Save Search dialog box.
2. Navigate through your folder structure to find the folder in which you want to save the search or, alternatively, create a new folder.
3. Enter a name for the search file. Outlook provides .oss as the file name extension; this is the same file name extension used for saved searches in other Office applications.
4. Choose OK to save the search.

To reuse saved search criteria:

1. Open the Advanced Find dialog box.
2. Choose File in the Advanced Find menu bar and choose Open Search. If you already have search criteria defined in the Advanced Find dialog box, Outlook warns you that your current search will be cleared if you proceed. Choose OK.
3. Navigate to the folder in which you saved searches and select the one you want to use.
4. Choose OK to import the saved search criteria into the Advanced Find dialog box.
5. Choose Find Now to run the saved search.

MODIFYING A SAVED SEARCH

You can make changes to an existing saved search and then resave it. Save it with its existing file name if you want to replace the original saved search; save it with a different name if you want to save it in addition to the existing saved search.

Use the two procedures in the preceding section. Start by using the first four steps of the second procedure to open the existing saved search, make your changes, and then use the first procedure to save those changes.

CREATING PRECISE SEARCHES

What you've learned about searching for items with Advanced Find so far in this chapter might be all you'll ever need. Chances are, however, that there will be times when you need more. That's when you'll use the More Choices and Advanced tabs within the Advanced Find dialog box.

Before going any further, you need to understand one thing clearly. You can specify search criteria in any or all three tabs of the Advanced Find dialog box. When you choose Find Now, Outlook looks for items that satisfy all the criteria specified in all three tabs. Although you can only see one tab at a time, Outlook sees all three. If you're not getting the search results you expect, a likely cause is that there are search criteria in one of the tabs you haven't looked at.

I strongly recommend that, before you start creating a set of criteria, you choose New Search. When you do that, all search criteria in all three tabs are cleared. That way you know you're starting from scratch. Now, any criteria set in the tabs you're not looking at can't affect your search.

REFINING YOUR SEARCH

Choose the More Choices tab in the Advanced Find dialog box, shown in Figure 18.15, to see the additional criteria you can use to narrow your search.

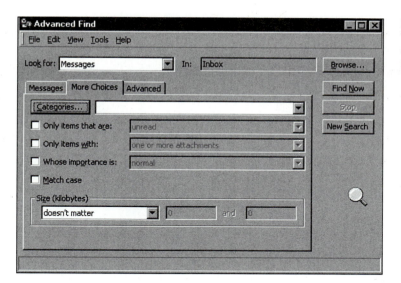

Figure 18.15
The More Choices tab offers additional search criteria.

The most useful part of this tab is the Categories button. I can't stress too strongly the benefits of assigning categories to all your Outlook items. If you want to take advantage of Outlook's capability to give you control over your personal and business activities, you must assign one or more categories to every Outlook item (with the exception of Note items that you'll deal with before the end of the day).

→ To learn more about assigning categories to your Outlook items, **see** "Using Categories and Entry Types," **p. 603**.

Suppose you are involved in a project called Alpha and you create a category named Alpha. Each time you create an appointment or meeting item related to the project, you should assign the category Alpha to that calendar item; the same goes for every Alpha-related message you send and receive, contacts involved with the project, and tasks. Every Outlook item having to do with project Alpha should have the Alpha category assigned to it.

Now you can easily find every Outlook item that relates to project Alpha by using the steps in the following procedure.

To find Outlook Items to which specific categories are assigned:

1. Open Advanced Find and choose New Search to make sure no search criteria exist.

2. In the Look For list, select Any Type of Outlook Item.

3. If the In text box doesn't correctly identify where you want to look for items, choose Browse to select the appropriate locations.

4. Open the More Choices tab and choose Categories to display the Categories dialog box that lists the categories in your personal Master Category List.

5. In the Available Categories list, check Alpha (or whatever other category you want to search for). You can select more than one category. After selecting one or more categories, choose OK. Outlook displays the Advanced Find dialog box with the selected category in the Categories box.

6. Choose Find Now to display a list of all Outlook items to which the category Alpha (or whichever category you specified) is assigned. The list shows the Outlook folder that contains each item found by the search.

Note

Instead of selecting *categories (page 604)*, you can enter categories. If you enter more than one category, separate one category from the next with a comma or semicolon. Outlook finds all the items to which at least one of the categories is assigned.

Being able to search by category is a powerful capability, but only if you're meticulous about assigning categories to all Outlook items.

The five other choices you can make in the More Choices tab are:

- Only Items that Are—Check this and then select either Unread or Read.
- Only Items With—Check this and then select One or More Attachments or No Attachments.
- Whose Importance Is—Check this and then select Normal, High, or Low.
- Match Case—Check this if you want the search for text specified in the first tab to be matched for case (uppercase or lowercase).
- Size (Kilobytes)—By default, Doesn't Matter is selected. You can open the drop-down list and then select from among Doesn't Matter, Equals (Approximately), Between, Less Than, or Greater Than. After you select any of these options other than Doesn't Matter, one or both of the boxes on the right become enabled so you can enter the size in kilobytes.

Tip #129 from

Gordon Padwick

Each type of Outlook item contains a Size field that contains the item's size in kilobytes. The value isn't displayed in any standard view. However, you can add the Size field to a table view. Refer to "Modifying Standard Information Views" in Chapter 38, "Creating Views and Print Styles," for information about how to do so.

You can also display the size of individual items, as explained in Chapter 20.

→ For more information about displaying Outlook item sizes, **see** "Displaying the Size of Outlook Items," **p. 584**.

DEFINING ADVANCED FIND CRITERIA

Choose the Advanced tab in the Advanced Find dialog box if you want to get serious about your searches. In this tab, you can define conditions and values for one or more fields in an item. You can create search criteria above and beyond what's available in the other two tabs. You can, for example, use a date field as a criterion to search for items that contain a specific date, or range of dates, in a date field.

The top part of this tab contains the Find Items That Match These Criteria box. Initially this box is empty except for text that says Add Criteria from Below to This List, as shown in Figure 18.16.

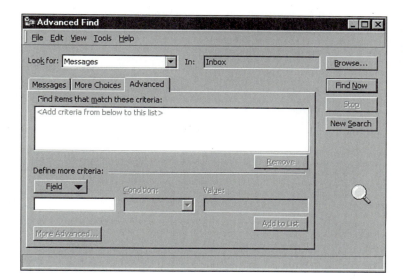

Figure 18.16
You can use this tab to be creative in defining searches.

The following example illustrates how you create Advanced find criteria.

Suppose you want to search for contacts whose home phone number is within a certain area code. If you already have search criteria in any of the three tabs, choose New Search to remove all those criteria.

To search for Contacts who have a specific telephone area code:

1. Open the Look For drop-down list at the top of the dialog box and choose Contacts.
2. In the Advanced Find dialog box's Advanced tab, choose Field to display a list of field types, and move the pointer onto Phone Number Fields. Outlook displays the list of phone number fields shown in Figure 18.17.

Figure 18.17
Outlook displays a list
of all phone number
fields.

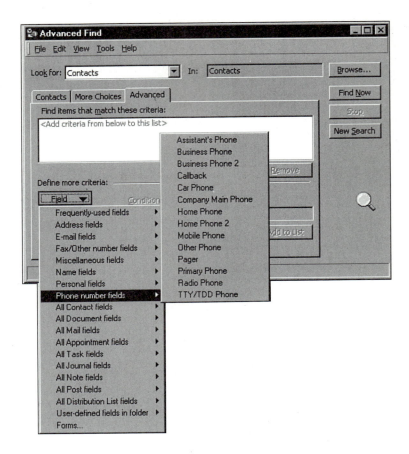

3. Select a type of phone number, such as Home Phone. The field you select appears in the Field box. Now the Condition box is enabled as shown in Figure 18.18.

4. You can open the Condition drop-down list to select one of these conditions: Contains, Is (Exactly), Doesn't Contain, Is Empty, and Is Not Empty. In this case, Contains is what you want.

5. In the Value box, enter the area code you want to find, such as (818). Make sure you enclose the number within parentheses.

Note

Outlook automatically formats phone numbers you enter for contacts according to regional conventions. If you're running Outlook under Windows in which Regional Settings is set to English (United States), Outlook automatically encloses telephone area codes within parentheses.

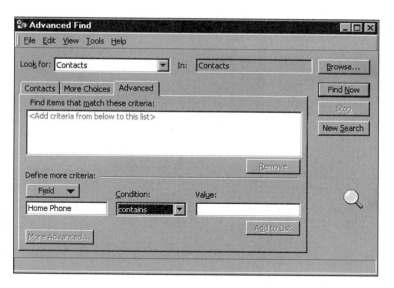

Figure 18.18
The Condition box initially contains the word "contains."

6. Choose A<u>d</u>d to List to add the criterion into the Find Items That <u>M</u>atch These Criteria box, as shown in Figure 18.19.

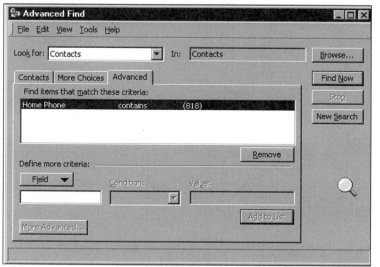

Figure 18.19
The Find Items That Match These Criteria list contains a summary of the criteria you've defined.

7. Choose Find <u>N</u>ow to start the search.

Outlook searches your Contacts folder and displays all items in which the Home Phone field contains the area code you specified.

The preceding example showed only one criterion specified. You can make your search more specific by adding more criteria. For example, you could add a criterion that specifies a certain last name. The following steps show how to add a second criterion to the one you just created.

To search for items by multiple criteria:

1. With the Advanced tab of the Advanced Find dialog box already containing one search criteria, such as that described in the preceding steps, choose Field, select a group of fields such as Name Fields, and then select a specific name field such as Last Name.

2. As previously, "contains" in the Condition box is what you want. Enter a value, such as a person's last name, in the Value box.

3. Choose Add to List to add the second criterion into the Find Items That Match These Criteria box. The Advanced tab now contains two search criteria, as shown in Figure 18.20.

Figure 18.20
This is an example of a search based on two criteria.

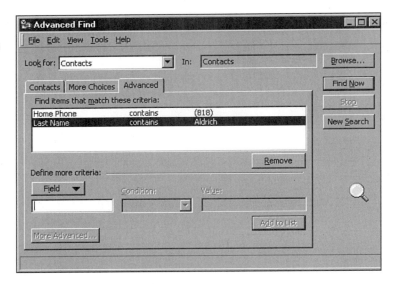

4. Choose Find Now to initiate the search.

This search finds only those contacts who have the specified area code and the specified last name.

Microsoft doesn't specify any limit to the number of criteria you can specify in this way. If after creating a criterion, you want to remove it from the list, select that criterion and choose Remove.

FINDING ITEMS BASED ON DATES AND TIMES

When you're using Advanced Find to look for messages, items in your calendar, or task-related items, you'll probably want to search by date and, perhaps, by time. Recall that the first tab provides some capability to search by time, but only in certain broad categories, such as last week, or next month. You can use Advanced criteria to specify exact dates and also exact times (with a one-minute resolution).

Suppose you want to look for messages that arrived this morning before 11:00 AM. For the sake of this example, we'll assume today's date is 1/26/99.

To search for messages received within a certain range of time:

1. With Messages selected in the Advanced Find dialog box's Look For box, select the Advanced tab.

2. Choose Field to display the list of field groups and move the pointer onto Date/Time Fields. Outlook displays the available date/time fields, as shown in Figure 18.21.

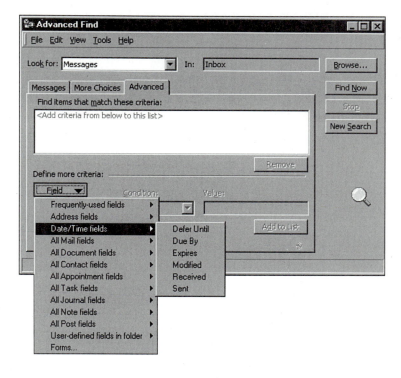

Figure 18.21
These are the available date/time fields.

3. Because you're looking for messages you've received, select Received in the list of available fields. The Condition box becomes enabled with "anytime" inside it.

4. Open the drop-down Condition list. You can select from quite a long list of conditions including "between," which is the one to select.

5. In the value box, enter

   `1/26/99 0:00 AM and 1/26/99 11:00 AM.`

6. Choose A<u>d</u>d to List to display the criterion in the Find Items That <u>M</u>atch These Criteria box, as shown in Figure 18.22.

Figure 18.22
Make sure the search criterion as it appears here is correct.

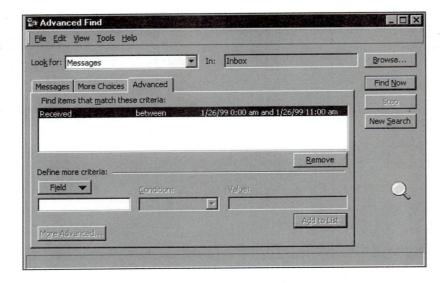

7. Choose Find <u>N</u>ow to start the search.

Tip #130 from

The examples given here are meant to get you started. It's worth taking time to explore what's available in the Advanced tab and practice creating searches.

FINDING FILES

So far in this chapter we've looked only at finding Outlook items. You can also use Advanced Find to find files on any disk accessible to your computer. In order to use Outlook to find files, you must install Outlook's Integrated File Management component.

→ To learn more about installing Outlook's Integrated File Management component, **see** "Installing Outlook 2000," **p. 1277**.

SPECIFYING FOLDERS TO FIND

To find files:

1. Start with any Outlook Information viewer displayed. Choose Tools, Advanced Find to open the Advanced Find dialog box.

2. Open the Look For drop-down list and choose Files to display the dialog box shown in Figure 18.23. Notice that the first tab is named Files.

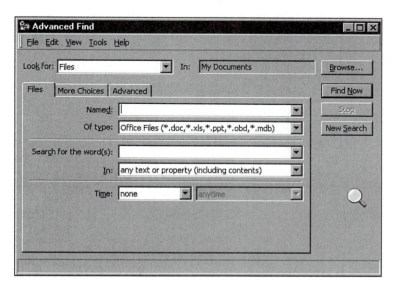

Figure 18.23
Outlook proposes to search for files in your Personal folder if you're working under Windows NT, or in your My Documents folder if you're working under Windows 95 or Windows 98.

3. If you want to search in a folder other than Personal (or My Documents), choose Browse to open the Select Folders dialog box and navigate in it to the folder in which you want to search. Choose OK to close the dialog box.

Specifying File Names and Types

You can specify the file you want to search for by file name and extension.

Outlook initially assumes you want to search for an Office file, so the Of Type box contains the standard file name extensions for Office files. You can open the drop-down list of types and select from:

- All Files (*.*)
- Office Files (*.doc, *.xls, *.ppt, *.obd, *.mdb)
- Documents (*.doc)
- Workbooks (*.xls)
- Presentations (*.ppt)
- Binders (*.odb)
- Databases (*.mdb)
- Templates (*.dot, *.xlt, *.oft, *.pot, *.obt)

Note

You can't enter any other file name extension; you can only choose from the list. Don't worry about this if you want to search for a different type of file. A little later in this chapter, you'll learn an easy way to accomplish this.

After selecting the appropriate file name extension, enter the name of the file or files you want to search for in the Named box. If you want to search for just one file and you know its exact name, enter that name without the extension. If you want to search for several files, enter the file names, separating one from the next by a semicolon.

If you don't know exact file names, or you want to search for several files with similar names, you can use these *wildcard* characters:

- Use * to represent any number of characters.
- Use ? to represent a single character.

Note

As the following examples show, the * wildcard character behaves a little differently than it does within the DOS environment.

For example, if you enter catfish*, Outlook will find files with such names as catfish, catfish01, catfish02, catfish23, catfishfood, and so on. If you enter *fish, Outlook will find files with such names as fish, catfish, dogfish, and so on. If you enter catfish0?, Outlook will find files with such names as catfish01, catfish02, but not catfish23 or catfishfood. One more example: If you enter *fish*, Outlook will find such names as fish, catfish, fish01, and so on.

What if you want to find a file with a name that doesn't have one of the standard Office extensions, such as Readme.txt? In that case, enter the complete file name and extension in the Named box. When you enter a file name with an extension, Outlook ignores whatever extensions are in the Of Type box.

After you've specified one or more file names, choose Find Now. Outlook searches in the folder you specified in the In box and in all its subfolders and displays a list of all the files that match the file name and extension you specified. You can double-click any name in the list to open the file.

NARROWING THE SEARCH FOR FILES

You can narrow the search for files by entering a word or phrase in the Search for the Word(s) box. The method described here significantly increases the time it takes Outlook to find files because it has to search within files.

To specify where Outlook should search for the words or phrases you've specified, open the In list to select:

- Any text or property (including contents)
- Contents only

By default, the Time box contains None, meaning that Outlook doesn't consider times and dates when it searches for files. You can open the Time drop-down list and select Modified, in which case the adjacent drop-down list is available. Open that list, and select from:

- Anytime
- Yesterday
- Today
- In the Last 7 Days
- Last Week
- This Week
- Last Month
- This Month

MAKING MORE CHOICES

The More Choices tab contains two check boxes and a drop-down list when you're searching for files, as shown in Figure 18.24.

Figure 18.24
You can refine your search by making selections in the More Choices tab.

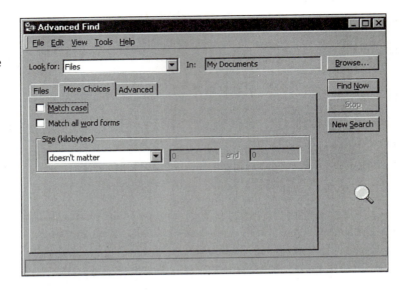

Outlook normally searches for the file contents you specify in Search for the Word(s) (in the Files tab) without regard for case. Check Match Case if you want the search to be case sensitive.

Outlook normally searches for files that contain exactly the word you specify in Search for the Word(s). If you check Match All Word Forms, Outlook locates files that contain variations of the words you specify. For example, if you specify write, Outlook finds files that contain variations of write, such as writes, wrote, and written.

You can also specify the size of files you want Outlook to find by opening the Size drop-down list and selecting from the following:

- Doesn't Matter
- Equals (approximately)
- Between
- Less Than
- Greater Than

After you select anything other than Doesn't Matter, enter the file size in the two adjacent boxes.

USING THE ADVANCED TAB

The Advanced tab contains the same elements as the Advanced tab described earlier in this chapter for use when finding Outlook items. One difference, however, is that the Fields drop-down list contains fields associated with files instead of those in Outlook items. You can choose either Frequently-Used Fields (which contains Created, Modified, and Size), or

All File Fields (which contains a long list of fields, only some of which are associated with any particular type of file). You can select specific fields in documents, and create criteria based on the values in those fields.

USING FIND FROM THE WINDOWS DESKTOP

You can use Outlook's Find feature from the Windows desktop without starting Outlook.

To use Outlook's Find feature from the Windows desktop:

1. Choose Start on the Windows taskbar to open the Start menu.
2. Move the pointer onto Find on the Start menu to display the menu shown in Figure 18.25.

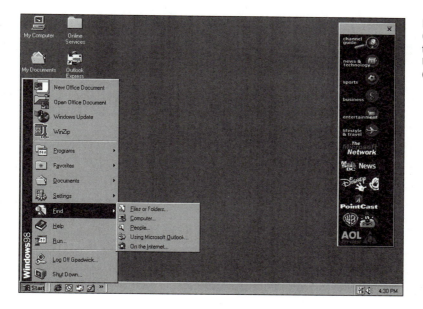

Figure 18.25
One of the items in the Find menu is Using Microsoft Outlook.

PART
IV
CH
18

3. Choose Using Microsoft Outlook. The Advanced Find dialog box is displayed with Files in the Look For box.
4. Use Find to locate files, as described earlier in this chapter.

→ For more information about using Outlook's Find capabilities, **see** "Finding Files," **p. 554**.

To look for Outlook items, open the Look For drop-down list and choose a type of Outlook item. Outlook opens so that you can proceed.

ORGANIZING OUTLOOK ITEMS

Finding items, as described in the preceding pages of this chapter, temporarily organizes items into a table based on criteria you enter. You can also organize Outlook items permanently by moving selected items into specific folders.

Outlook offers two ways for you to organize items: one is by using the Organize capability described here. The other is to create rules that automatically place e-mail messages you receive and copies of e-mail messages you send in specific folders.

→ To learn more about automating how Outlook works with your e-mail, **see** "Creating and Using Rules," **p. 617**.

The following pages refer specifically to organizing e-mail messages you've received, but also apply to all types of Outlook items.

ORGANIZING E-MAIL MESSAGES

Instead of keeping all the e-mail messages you receive in your Inbox folder, you can create folders for specific types of messages and move appropriate messages into those folders. For example, you can create a folder for all messages relating to a specific project so that you can keep those messages in one place.

CREATING A FOLDER FOR SPECIFIC MESSAGES

The first step in organizing your e-mail messages into folders is to create these folders. The subject of creating folders is covered in detail in Chapter 37. The information given here covers this subject only briefly.

→ For more detailed information on creating Outlook folders, **see** "Creating Folders and Subfolders," **p. 922**.

To create a folder for e-mail messages:

1. Display the Inbox Information viewer.

2. Choose <u>F</u>ile, move the pointer onto <u>F</u>older, and choose <u>N</u>ew Folder to display the dialog box shown in Figure 18.26.

3. Enter a name for the new folder, such as a project name, in the <u>N</u>ame box. Outlook won't let you use the name of an existing folder.

4. Outlook proposes that the new folder is to be used for Mail Items and that it is to be placed under the Inbox folder. Choose OK.

5. Outlook asks you if you want to create a shortcut to the new folder on the Outlook Bar. Choose <u>Y</u>es or <u>N</u>o as you prefer.

6. Repeat steps 2 through 5 to create more new folders.

7. If the folder list isn't displayed, choose <u>V</u>iew, Fold<u>e</u>r List. You should now see your new folders in the folder list, as shown in Figure 18.27.

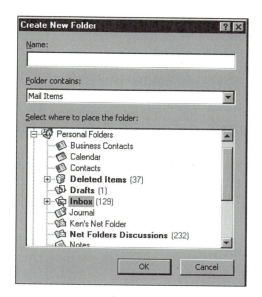

Figure 18.26
This dialog box opens with Inbox selected because you started from the Inbox Information viewer.

New folders

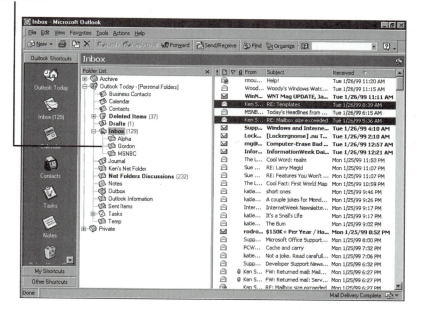

Figure 18.27
The new folders, named Alpha, Gordon, and MSNBC in this case, are shown in the folder list.

MOVING SELECTED MESSAGES INTO A NEW FOLDER

Having created new folders, you can organize your mail by moving specific messages into them. Use the steps that follow if you wanted to move only one or two messages into a new folder.

To organize e-mail messages you've received:

1. With the Inbox Information viewer displayed, select one message you want to move into a new folder. Then hold down the Ctrl key while you select additional messages.

2. Choose Organize in the Standard toolbar to display the Ways to Organize Inbox pane shown in Figure 18.28.

Figure 18.28
The pane initially proposes to move the selected messages to the folder you most recently created.

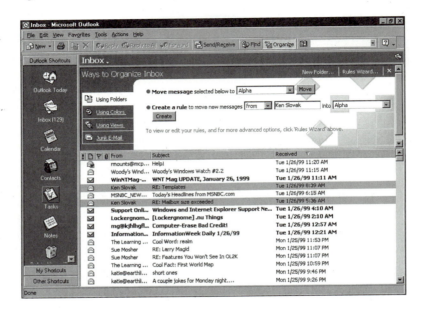

> **Note**
>
> The Organize pane has four buttons at the left. Make sure the Using Folders button is selected if you want to move selected messages into a specific folder.

3. If the folder Outlook proposes to move the selected messages to isn't correct, open the drop-down list, choose Other Folder, and then select the folder you want to use.

4. Choose Move to move the selected messages into the new folder.

You probably noticed that the Organize pane invites you to create a rule that will automatically move messages you receive in the future into the new folder. We'll postpone dealing with that subject until Chapter 22.

➔ To learn more about having Outlook help to organize your email automatically, **see** "Creating and Using Rules," **p. 617**.

USING FIND TO LOCATE MESSAGES TO MOVE

The method described in the preceding steps is fine if you only have a few messages to move. But, if you want to move many messages, finding all those messages in the Inbox Information viewer can be time-consuming and tedious. You can simplify the process by using Outlook's Find capability to find specific messages.

If you're moving messages relating to a specific project into a new folder, you should have assigned the project name as a category to all those messages. If you haven't been meticulous about assigning categories, it's likely that many of the messages contain the project name in the Subject box. You can use Find, as described previously in this chapter, to find all the messages that have a specific category assigned or have the project name in the subject box. After you've found messages in this way, select those messages in the Results table, and then use Organize to copy the messages into the new folder. You should look carefully through the messages in the Results table to make sure that all the messages there really do relate to the project. If some don't, make sure those messages are not selected before you use Organize.

To select all the messages in the Results table, choose Edit, Select All (or press Ctrl+A). To select or deselect specific messages, hold down the Ctrl key while you click those messages.

You might have to use Find several times to make sure you find all the projected related messages. For example, you could look for messages from specific people who are involved in the project.

ORGANIZING MESSAGES BY COLOR

You can also use the Organize pane to display selected messages in a specific color.

Select the messages you want to color either manually or by using Find to identify messages to which specific categories are assigned or which contain some other identifying characteristic. Then, choose Using Colors at the left of the Organize pane. The Organize pane changes to that shown in Figure 18.29.

At this stage, you can:

- Open the drop-down list at the right of Color Messages, and select "sent to" instead of "from"
- Replace the name in the text box
- Open the drop-down list of colors and select a color other than red

Choose Apply Color to color the selected messages. Outlook colors all the messages from the selected person in the new color so that you can easily identify them.

PART
IV

CH
18

Figure 18.29
The Organize pane proposes to color the messages you selected in red.

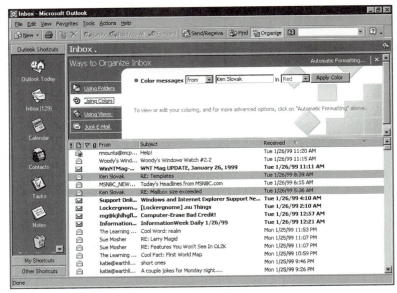

TROUBLESHOOTING

You're not likely to find problems with the QuickFind tool. It works as advertised. Just enter one or more letters in a contact's name and you'll see a list of contacts whose File As names contain those characters.

When you use Find, pay attention to whether Search All Text in the Message is checked. If it is checked, Outlook checks all the text in all the messages in whatever folder you've selected for the characters you type, a process that can take quite a while. If you only want Outlook to check message headers, make sure the Search All Text in the Message check box is not checked.

When you use Advanced Find, remember that Outlook searches based on all three panes of the Advanced Find dialog box. If you don't find what you're looking for, choose New Search to clear out all search criteria, then go back into each of the panes and carefully set up criteria in each of them.

CHAPTER 19

IMPORTING AND EXPORTING OUTLOOK ITEMS

In this chapter

by Gordon Padwick

WORKING WITH DATA FROM OTHER APPLICATIONS

Although Outlook is a very powerful application, it doesn't exist in a world of its own. Most Outlook users work with several other applications and receive files created in other applications from other people.

If you've previously used another application such as Access, Excel, Word, or a Personal Information Manager to keep your personal records, you'll probably want to bring these records into Outlook's integrated environment. And when you receive information from other sources, you'll want to combine that information with information you already have in Outlook folders.

This chapter contains information about several techniques you can use to bring information into Outlook's folders, and also how you can export information from Outlook into other applications.

IMPORTING WHEN YOU FIRST RUN OUTLOOK

The first time you run Outlook, it examines your computer environment to see if you have other applications installed that you might have used to save such things as appointments and information about contacts. If it finds such applications, it displays a list of them and asks you if you want to import information from them. You can select any or all of the listed applications or, if you don't want to import from any of them, select None. If you select any existing applications, Outlook imports information from them into the appropriate Outlook folders.

Note
> Outlook can import calendar and contact information from various *PIMs (page 14)* from other companies. It's possible, though, that you have been using a PIM that Outlook doesn't recognize.

If you choose not to import your existing calendar and contact information the first time you run Outlook, you can import that information later, as described in the next section.

IMPORTING FROM OUTLOOK EXPRESS

If you've previously used Outlook Express or another messaging application to send and receive e-mail, you can import messages and your address book from that application into Outlook. The following steps refer specifically to Outlook Express. You can use the same technique to import messages and your address book from some other applications.

To import Outlook Express messages:

1. With any Outlook Information viewer displayed, choose File, Import and Export to display the first Import and Export Wizard window shown in Figure 19.1.

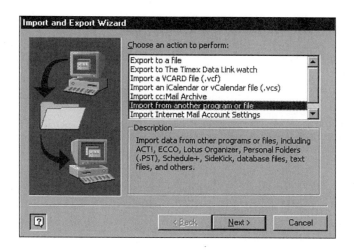

Figure 19.1
The first wizard window asks you want you want to do.

2. In the first wizard window, choose Import Internet Mail and Addresses, then press Next > to display the second wizard window, shown in Figure 19.2.

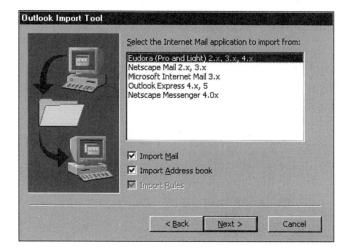

Figure 19.2
The second wizard window asks you which e-mail application you want to import messages from.

PART
IV

CH
19

3. Select Outlook Express or whichever other e-mail application you want to import from.

4. If you select Outlook Express, the wizard proposes to import your Outlook Express mail, address book, and rules. If you select any of the other sources, the option to import rules is not available. Uncheck Import Mail if you don't want to import messages; uncheck Import Address Book if you don't want to import the address book; uncheck Import Rules if you don't want to import rules. Choose Next > to display the third wizard window, shown in Figure 19.3.

Figure 19.3
Use this wizard window to specify where you want addresses to be imported into and what to do about duplicates.

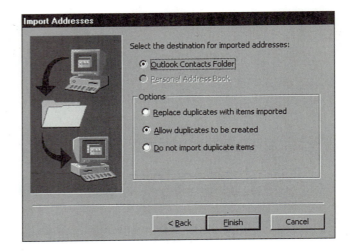

5. In most cases, accept the defaults in this dialog box, then choose Finish to import the data.

Note

The option to import into your Personal Address Book is available only if you're using C/W Outlook. That's because IMO Outlook doesn't support the use of a Personal Address Book.

As an alternative to importing into Outlook from Outlook Express, you can export from Outlook Express into Outlook.

SAVING OUTLOOK ITEMS AS FILES

You can save any Outlook item as a file in several formats. The following example refers specifically to a message item, but you can use the same technique for other types of Outlook items.

To save a message as a file:

1. Choose Inbox in the Outlook Bar to display the Inbox Information viewer if you want to save a message in your Inbox folder. Choose Sent Items in the Outlook Bar if you want to save a message in your Sent Items folder.

2. Select the message you want to save.

3. Choose File, Save As to display the Save As dialog box shown in Figure 19.4.

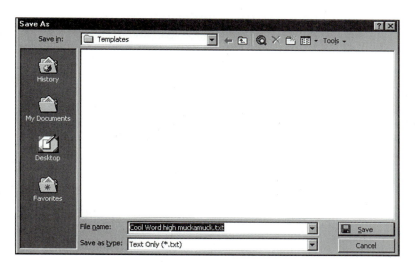

Figure 19.4
By default, Outlook proposes to save the message in the mail format (HTML, RTF, or TXT) in which you received or created it.

4. Open the drop-down Save as Type list to display a list of available file types. You can select Outlook Template, Message Format, or the format in which the message was originally created. Select the format you want to use. Outlook provides a file name extension in the File Name box to match the file type you selected.

> **Note**
>
> If the message was originally created in HTML or RTF format, you can save it in TXT format.

5. By default, Outlook proposes to use the subject of the message as the name of the file. You can replace this name, but don't change the extension.

6. If you want to save the file in a folder other than the one Outlook proposes, navigate to that folder.

7. Choose Save to save the message.

> **Note**
>
> The preceding procedure refers to saving one mail item at a time. You can also select several items and save them all in a single file. In that case, Outlook doesn't propose a file name for the saved items; you have to provide a name for the file in which the items are saved.

PART
IV

CH

19

Table 19.1 lists the file formats available for various Outlook items.

TABLE 19.1	AVAILABLE FILE FORMATS					
Item	Text Only	Rich Text	Outlook Template	Message	vCalendar	vCard
Message	Yes	Yes	Yes	Yes	No	No
Calendar	Yes	Yes	Yes	Yes	Yes	No
Contact	Yes	Yes	Yes	Yes	No	Yes
Journal	Yes	Yes	Yes	Yes	No	No
Task	Yes	Yes	Yes	Yes	No	No

Tip #134 from

Gordon Crosh

An alternative way to save an item as a file is to drag that item into a folder using Windows Explorer. The created file is in Message format with .msg as its file name extension.

You can also drag an item onto the Windows desktop to create an icon on the desktop that represents a file in Message format.

Text Only and *Rich Text Format (page 183)* are general-purpose formats you can use when you want to access Outlook items in various applications.

Use the Outlook Template format when you want to create a template based on one item that you can use as the basis for similar items, as explained in Chapter 17. Use the vCalendar format to exchange calendar information, and use the vCard format to exchange contact information, in industry-standard formats with other people, including those who use applications other than Outlook that support these formats.

Use the Message format to move individual Outlook items from one computer to another when you don't have e-mail connectivity.

→ To learn more about generating Outlook items, **see** "Using Outlook Templates," **p. 519**.

→ For additional information about sharing your contact information with other Outlook users, **see** "Sharing Contact Information with vCards," **p. 330**.

SHARING ITEMS WITH OTHER OUTLOOK USERS

One way to share Outlook items with other Outlook users is to export items to a Personal Folders file so that other people can import items from that folder into their own Personal Folders file or Exchange store. This is particularly convenient when you want to share items by way of a LAN.

It's less convenient if you can't share the file by way of a LAN because the Personal Folders file is likely to be too large to copy to a standard floppy disk and probably larger than you want to send by e-mail. In that case, you have to resort to using a utility such as WinZip to copy the file onto several floppy disks, or to using high-capacity disks such as Iomega's Zip disks.

EXPORTING ITEMS TO A PERSONAL FOLDERS FILE

You can use Outlook's Import and Export Wizard to copy Outlook items to a Personal Folders file, as well to other file formats.

To export Outlook items to a Personal Folders file:

1. With any Outlook Information viewer displayed, choose File, Import and Export to display the first Import and Export Wizard window, shown previously in Figure 19.1.

2. Select Export to a File and then choose Next > to display the second wizard window, shown in Figure 19.5.

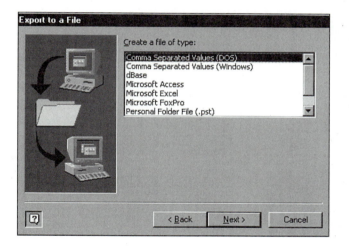

Figure 19.5
The second wizard window asks you what sort of file you want to create.

3. Select Personal Folder File (.pst) and then choose Next > to display the third wizard window, shown in Figure 19.6.

4. By default, Outlook selects the folder that was displayed in an Information viewer when you started using the wizard. If you want to export from a different folder, select that folder. If you want to export items from all your folders, select Personal Folders.

5. If your folder structure contains subfolders and you want to export items from the selected folder and all its subfolders, make sure Include Subfolders is checked. If you don't want to export from subfolders, make sure that box is unchecked.

PART
IV

CH
19

Figure 19.6
The third wizard window asks which Outlook folder you want to export from.

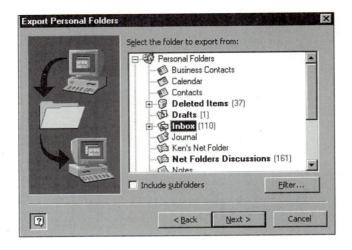

6. If you want to export all items from the selected folder, go to step 8. If you want to export only certain items, choose Filter to display the Filter dialog box shown in Figure 19.7.

Figure 19.7
The Filter dialog box has three tabs in which you can define how you want to filter items.

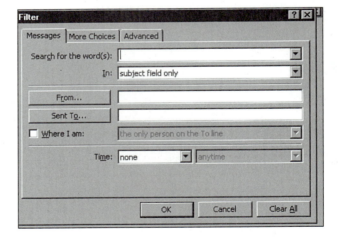

7. Set up filter conditions in the same way that you set up an Advanced Find, as explained in Chapter 18, "Finding and Organizing Outlook Items." After you've set up the filter conditions, choose OK to return to the third wizard window. Choose Next > to display the fourth wizard window.

→ To learn more about Outlook's Advanced Find abilities, **see** "Using Advanced Find to Find Words and Phrases," **p. 532**.

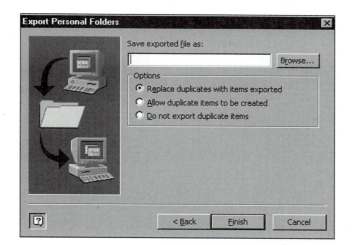

8. Either enter a full path name for the new file in the Save Exported File As box, or choose Browse, navigate to the folder in which you want to create the file, and enter a file name.

9. It doesn't usually matter which option button you choose in the Options section of the dialog box because you probably want to create a new file that doesn't already contain any Outlook items. Choose Finish. Outlook creates the new file.

Note

If you want to copy Outlook items to a file that already contains items, follow the steps in the preceding procedure. In that case, though, it's important to make the appropriate selection in the Options section of the dialog box shown in Figure 19.8.

IMPORTING ITEMS FROM A PERSONAL FOLDERS FILE

The process of importing items from a Personal Folders file is very similar to the process of exporting items, which is described in the preceding section.

To import Outlook items from a Personal Folders file:

1. With any Outlook Information viewer displayed, choose File, Import and Export to display the first Import and Export Wizard window, shown previously in Figure 19.1.

2. Select Import from Another Program or File and then choose Next > to display the second wizard window, shown in Figure 19.9.

3. Scroll down the list and select Personal Folder File (.pst). Then choose Next > to display the third wizard window, shown in Figure 19.10.

Figure 19.9
The second wizard window asks you what type of file you want to import from.

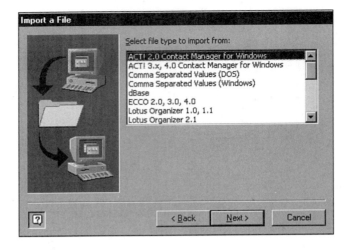

Figure 19.10
The third wizard window asks which file you want to import.

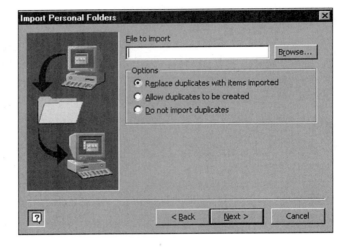

4. Enter the full path name of the file you want to import into the File to Import box, or choose Browse, navigate to the file, select the file and choose Open.

5. In the Options section of the dialog box, choose an option button according to how you want Outlook to deal with duplicate items. Either the first or third option is usually appropriate. Choose Next > to display the fourth wizard window, shown in Figure 19.11.

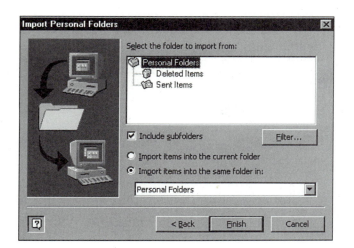

6. If you want to import all the items in all the folders in the Personal Folders file, select Personal Folders and check the Include Subfolders box. If you want to import the items in only one folder, select that folder (Outlook lets you select only one folder). If you want to import all items, choose Next > and go to step 8. To select certain items to import, choose Filter to display the Filter dialog box shown previously in Figure 19.7.

7. Set up filter conditions in the same way that you set up an Advanced Find, as explained in Chapter 18. After you've set up the filter conditions, choose OK to return to the fourth wizard window.

→ To learn more about setting up filter conditions, **see** "Using Advanced Find to Find Words and Phrases," **p. 532**.

8. Choose whichever of the two options buttons is appropriate. If you choose Import Items into the Current Folder, Outlook imports items into whichever folder you had open when you started using the Import and Export Wizard. If you choose Import Items into the Same Folder In, Outlook imports items into a folder of the same type as the one from which items are being imported; the name of the folder into which items will be imported is shown in the box below the second check box. If you have more than one Personal Folders file or Exchange store, you can open the drop-down list and choose the one into which items will be imported.

9. Choose Finish. Outlook copies items into the specified folders.

EXPORTING ITEMS TO, AND IMPORTING ITEMS FROM, OTHER APPLICATIONS

Outlook can export items directly to, and import items directly from, various other applications.

PART

IV

CH

19

IMPORTING INFORMATION FROM PIMs

If you've previously been using a *Personal Information Management (PIM) (page 14)* program to maintain your calendar, contact information, and so on, you can probably use Outlook's Import and Export Wizard to import information directly into Outlook. To do so, open the wizard (as explained in the previous two sections) and, in the first wizard window, choose Import from Another Program or File. Choose Next > to open the second wizard window. In that window, you can select these PIMs:

- ACT! 2.0 Contact Manager for Windows
- ACT! 3.X, 4.0 Contact Manager for Windows
- ECCO 2.0, 3.0, 4.0
- ECCO Pro 4.0
- Lotus Organizer 1.0, 1.1
- Lotus Organizer 2.1
- Lotus Organizer 97
- Schedule+ 1.0
- Schedule+ 7.0
- Sidekick 95
- Sidekick for Windows 2.0

Although Outlook can import from these applications, it can't export to them.

IMPORTING FROM, AND EXPORTING TO, WINDOWS APPLICATIONS

Outlook can directly import information from, and export information to, dBASE, Microsoft Access, Excel, and FoxPro.

Use the Outlook Import and Export Wizard to import from files created by these applications, and to export to files that can be read by these applications. The methods for doing this are quite similar to those described previously for importing from, and exporting to, a Personal Folders file. Some specific points relating to this are covered subsequently in this chapter.

→ For more information about using database information with Outlook, **see** "Importing Data from a Database," **p. 578**.

→ To learn more about using Excel data with Outlook, **see** "Importing from an Excel Worksheet," **p. 581**.

IMPORTING FROM, AND EXPORTING TO, MORE APPLICATIONS

Outlook can directly import information from dBASE and export information to dBASE and other applications that create files in the .dbf format.

If there are other applications that you want to import from and export to, but you don't see these applications listed in the Import and Export Wizards dialog boxes, there are two ways to solve the problem.

One way is to use an intermediate file format. Suppose, for example, you have been keeping your contact information in a Paradox database and want to import that information into an Outlook Contacts folder. Unfortunately, Outlook can't directly import from Paradox. What you can do is to use Access to convert the Paradox files into Access format. After you've done that, you can import the information in Access format into Outlook.

Note

> The preceding paragraph contains just one example of how you can use an intermediate application. Various Microsoft applications can import information from other applications; also some other applications can export information in a format that's compatible with Microsoft applications.

Another way to import information from, and export information to, other applications is to use industry-standard formats. Outlook and many other applications support:

- Comma Separated Values (otherwise known as comma-delimited values) for DOS
- Comma Separated Values (otherwise knows as comma-delimited values) for Windows
- Tab Separated Values (otherwise known as tab-delimited values) for DOS
- Tab Separated Values (otherwise known as tab-delimited values) for Windows

You can use these formats to transport information between Outlook and other applications.

These four formats are all text file formats. In the case of comma separated values, one field of information is separated from the next by a comma. In the case of tab separated values, one field of information is separated from the next by a tab character.

PART

IV

CH

19

Tip #135 from

Gordon Woodcock

> If the application you're importing from encloses the information in text fields within quotation marks, Outlook doesn't regard commas or tabs within fields as field-separation characters. However, if you're importing text that's not enclosed within quotation marks and that text includes commas or tab characters, you can expect problems.

In these formats, one record is separated from the next by a sequence of two characters: carriage return and line feed.

Note

> For more information about using these formats, refer to the Microsoft Knowledge Base article Q179556, *How to Import and Export Text Data with Outlook*.

IMPORTING DATA FROM A DATABASE

Importing information from a database involves copying data from specific database fields into specific Outlook fields. Outlook fields have specific names, as listed in Appendix C. The database you're importing from has fields with different names, usually names assigned by the person who created the database. There's no automatic way by which Outlook can know the name of the fields in the database that should be imported into Outlook's fields. For that reason, it's necessary to use a process known as Field Mapping to define the relationships between Outlook fields and database fields. The process of field mapping is described in the following procedure that uses importing contact information from an Access database as an example.

To import contact information from an Access database:

1. Choose File, Import and Export to display the first Import and Export Wizard window, previously shown in Figure 19.1.

2. Select Import from Another Program or File and choose Next > to display the wizard window previously shown in Figure 19.9.

3. Select Microsoft Access and choose Next >. If you haven't previously imported from Access, Outlook displays a message box telling you that it can't start the Import/Export engine because the feature is not currently installed and asking whether you would like to install it now. Choose Yes. Outlook attempts to install the Import/Engine from the Office 2000 CD-ROM (if the CD-ROM isn't in your drive, a message tells you to insert it). After you do so, the wizard window shown in Figure 19.12 is displayed.

Figure 19.12
This is where you specify the Access file to import.

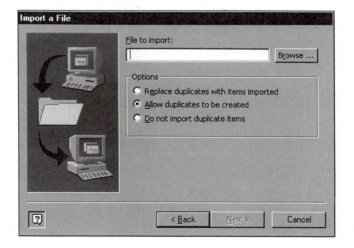

4. Either enter the path name of the file you want to import, or choose B<u>r</u>owse to locate the file.

5. In the Options section, select how you want Outlook to handle duplicates. It's unlikely that Outlook will recognize any items in your Access database as duplicates, so accept the default "Allow Duplicates to Be Created." Choose <u>N</u>ext > to display the wizard window shown in Figure 19.13.

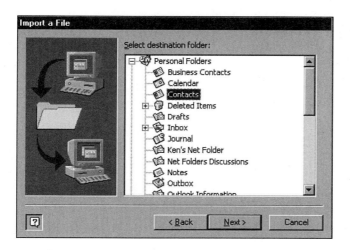

Figure 19.13
This window displays the structure of your Outlook folders.

6. Select the Outlook folder into which you want to import information from the database, then choose <u>N</u>ext > to display the dialog box shown in Figure 19.14.

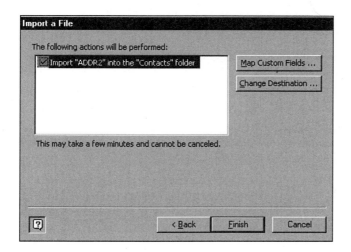

Figure 19.14
This dialog box displays the file name of the database you've chosen to import and the name of the Outlook folder into which you want to import data.

PART

IV

CH

19

7. Choose <u>M</u>ap Custom Fields to display the dialog box shown in Figure 19.15.

Figure 19.15
Use this dialog box to establish relationships between fields in the source database and Outlook fields.

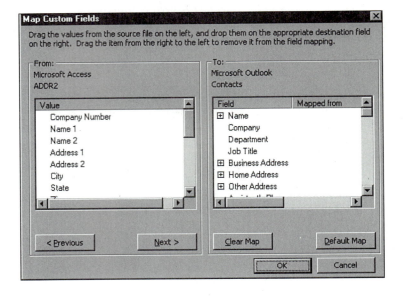

Note

The Map Custom Fields dialog box contains two lists. The list on the left displays the names of fields in the database from which you want to import. The list on the right contains the names of Outlook fields and groups of fields; group names are indicated by a box at the left of the name containing +; to see individual field names within a group, click the +.

The list of Outlook fields has two columns, the left field containing field names; the right column (initially empty) is for the names of database fields to be copied into each Outlook field.

8. Point onto a field in the list of database fields. Press the mouse button, and drag to the corresponding field in the list of Outlook fields. The name of the database field appears in the right column of the Outlook list of fields, indicating that you want the information from that database field to be copied to the Outlook field.

9. Repeat step 8 for each field of the database you want to import into Outlook. When you've finished, choose OK to return to the Import a File dialog box, previously shown in Figure 19.14.

10. Choose <u>F</u>inish to begin importing data from the database into Outlook.

Note

> You can use the Previous and Next buttons in the Map Custom Fields dialog box to display data in specific database fields. Choose the Clear Map button to remove all relationships between database and Outlook fields. Choose the Default Map button to automatically create relationships between database and Outlook fields that have the same name.

IMPORTING FROM AN EXCEL WORKSHEET

To import information from an Excel worksheet into Outlook, the information must be in a named range. Also, the top row of the named range must contain field names that correspond to Outlook field names.

To create a named range in an Excel worksheet, select the block of cells you want to have in the range, then choose Insert, move the pointer onto Name, and choose Define to open the Define Name dialog box. Enter a name for the range into the Names in Workbook box, and choose OK. Choose File, Save to save the workbook with the named range.

Note

> The name you give the range must not be the same as any of the field names in the top row of the named range. Also, range names cannot contain spaces.

PART

IV

CH

19

CHAPTER 20

COMPACTING FOLDERS AND ARCHIVING OUTLOOK ITEMS

In this chapter

by Gordon Padwick

UNDERSTANDING ARCHIVING AND BACKING UP

Two reasons exist for backing up or archiving Outlook:

- To avoid keeping unnecessarily large files on your hard disk. Archiving is intended for this purpose.
- To be able to restore Outlook after a disk crash, or move your Outlook configuration to another disk. Backing up is used for this purpose.

Outlook saves two kinds of information. The most obvious kind of information is your Outlook items—e-mail messages, information about contacts, your calendar, and so on. The other kind of information is what can collectively be called Outlook's settings.

If you're using C/W Outlook as a client for Exchange, you can choose to keep your Outlook items in an Exchange store on the server, or you can save those items in a Personal Folders file on your hard drive. If you're using C/W Outlook but not as a client for Exchange, or if you're using IMO Outlook, you have no choice but to save your Outlook items in a Personal Folders file on your hard drive. Whichever Outlook options you are using, Outlook's settings are saved in various files on your hard drive.

This brings us back to the two reasons for archiving and backing up Outlook. You can use three techniques to minimize the space occupied by Outlook items:

- Deleting Outlook items you don't need to keep
- Compacting folders so that they occupy as little space on your hard drive as possible
- Archiving items by moving them from your hard drive to another storage medium

Backing up Outlook involves copying all the Outlook items you need to keep (and also the files that contain Outlook's settings) onto another storage medium.

This chapter is principally about deleting Outlook items, compacting folders, and archiving items.

DISPLAYING THE SIZE OF OUTLOOK ITEMS

If you use Outlook regularly, your Personal Folders file (or Exchange store) can grow very rapidly. You can easily find out the size of individual items.

To determine the size of an Outlook item:

1. Choose one of the shortcut icons on the Outlook Bar to display an Information viewer.

Note

You can also choose View, Folder List to display a list of Outlook folders in which you can select a folder. This method provides a way to open folders for which there is no corresponding icon in the Outlook Bar.

2. Double-click an item to display that item in a form.

3. In the form's menu bar, choose File, Properties, to display a Properties dialog box such as that shown in Figure 20.1.

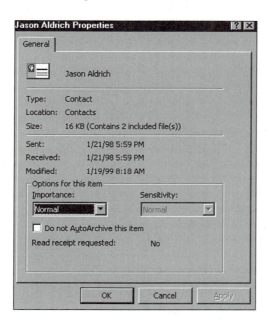

Figure 20.1
This dialog box shows the properties of a Contact item.

The fourth row in the dialog box shows the size (in bytes) of the selected item. If the item contains attachments, the indicated size includes those attachments. Message items, particularly those that have attachments, can occupy much more space than *Contact items (page 298)*.

Another way to keep track of the size of Outlook items is to add the Size field to one of the standard Outlook views or create a custom view that contains the Size field. You can use a view that contains the Size field to display the size of all Outlook items of a specific type.

→ For information about modifying and creating views, **see** "Adding a Field to a View," **p. 955**.

It's a little-known fact that message format has a significant effect on message size; this applies to messages you create and save in your Sent Items folder as well to messages you receive and save in your Inbox folder. Messages in *Plain Text format (page 183)* are much smaller than messages in HTML or Rich Text format. For example, one particular 50-line message in Plain Text format (with no attachments) occupies 1kB. The same message in *HTML (page 183)* or *Rich Text format (page 183)* occupies 8kB.

The much smaller size of Plain Text messages is a good reason for preferring this format unless you really need the formatting capabilities of HTML or Rich Text.

PART

IV

CH

20

→ For information about selecting a message format, **see** "Selecting a Message Format," **p. 81**, and "Selecting a Message Format and E-mail Editor," **p. 182**.

Tip #136 from	Another way to minimize the space occupied by mail is to take advantage of Outlook's ability to automatically reject junk e-mail. Note, though, that this places junk mail in your Deleted Items folder; you have to delete items from that folder to recover the disk space they occupy.

→ For information about automatically deleting junk mail, **see** "Dealing with Junk E-mail," **p. 623**.

DELETING OUTLOOK ITEMS

After understanding how much space individual items occupy, you won't be surprised to learn that a frequent user's Outlook items can easily occupy several tens of megabytes of disk space.

Note	The remaining part of this section describes how you can manually delete items. Archiving, which you can set up to automatically delete items, is described later in this chapter.

→ To learn about AutoArchiving, **see** "Managing AutoArchiving," **p. 595**.

You can delete an item from an Outlook folder in several ways. When you delete an item from any Outlook folder other than the Deleted Items folder, Outlook moves the item into the Deleted Items folder. After selecting an item to be deleted, either:

- On the Standard toolbar, choose the Delete button
- Choose Edit, Delete
- Press Ctrl+D
- Press Delete
- Drag the item onto the Deleted Items icon on the Outlook Bar
- Drag the item onto the Deleted Items folder in the Outlook folder list
- Drag the item onto the Windows Recycle Bin (even though you drag to the Recycle Bin, the item moves into the Outlook Deleted Items folder)

You can use the same methods to delete an Outlook folder you've created, but not one of Outlook's standard folders. When you delete a folder, Outlook moves that folder (and all the items it contains) into the Deleted Items folder, creating a new subfolder within the Deleted Items folder.

MOVING ITEMS INTO THE DELETED ITEMS FOLDER

Your first line of defense in keeping the amount of disk space Outlook uses under control is to make a regular habit of deleting all items you don't need to keep. Each time you download e-mail, for example, immediately delete items you don't want to keep.

To delete Outlook items:

1. Open the Information viewer that displays items you want to delete. For example, to delete unwanted mail items you've received, open the Inbox Information viewer.

2. Select one item you want to delete. To select additional items, hold down Ctrl while you select those items.

3. Choose the Delete button ✖ in the Standard toolbar. Outlook immediately removes the selected items from the Information viewer.

These steps don't actually delete items from your hard drive. All they do is move items from their original folder (the Inbox folder in the case of mail items you've received) into the Deleted Items folder. As you'll see in a moment, you can easily move any items you deleted accidentally back into their original folders.

Note

Because you can easily restore deleted items to their original folders, Outlook doesn't ask you to confirm that you really want to delete items.

RESTORING ITEMS TO THEIR ORIGINAL FOLDERS

You can easily restore items in the Deleted Items folder back into their original folders.

To restore deleted items:

1. Choose Deleted Items in the Outlook Bar to display the Deleted Items Information viewer.

2. Select one or more items in the Deleted Items Information viewer. All the items you select must be intended to be restored to the same folder.

3. Drag the selected items onto the Outlook Bar shortcut icon that represents the folder into which you want to restore the items. If you've selected several items in the Deleted Items Information viewer, all items are restored when you drag one of them.

   If you want an alternative to dragging, after you've selected items in the Deleted Items Information viewer, choose Edit, Move to Folder. The Move to Folder dialog box then appears. Select the folder to which you want to move the items and choose OK.

PART

IV

CH

20

Tip #137 from

Gordon Crook

If you want to restore a deleted item into a folder for which a corresponding icon doesn't exist on the Outlook Bar, open the folder list and drag the item onto the folder name there.

DELETING ITEMS FROM THE DELETED ITEMS FOLDER

To completely delete items from your hard drive, you must delete items from your Deleted Items folder. You can delete all items or delete only specific items. You can delete items from the Deleted Items folder manually or set an Option so that Outlook automatically deletes everything in that folder when you close Outlook, as described subsequently in this section.

To delete all items from the Deleted Items folder, right-click the Deleted Items icon in the Outlook Bar to display its context menu. Then choose Empty "Deleted Items" Folder. Outlook asks you to confirm that you want to permanently delete all the items and folders in the Deleted Items folder. Choose Yes.

Instead of deleting everything in the Deleted Items folder, you can delete specific items or folders.

To delete specific items or folders from the Deleted Items folder:

1. Choose Deleted Items in the Outlook Bar to display the Deleted Items Information viewer.
2. Select the items you want to delete.
3. Choose the Delete button ✗ in the Standard toolbar. Outlook displays a message asking you to confirm that you really want to delete the items. Choose Yes if you do want to delete the items, No if you don't. If you choose Yes, Outlook permanently deletes the items.

You can set an option to automatically empty the Deleted Items folder when Outlook closes.

To automatically empty the Deleted Items folder:

1. With any Information viewer displayed, choose Tools, Options to display the Options dialog box.
2. Select the Other tab shown in Figure 20.2.
3. Check Empty the Deleted Items Folder upon Exiting.

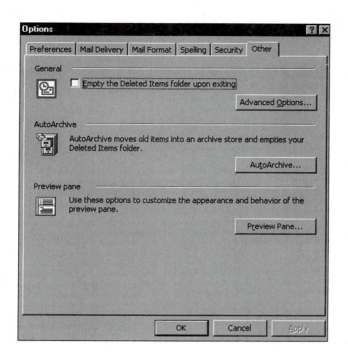

Figure 20.2
Use this dialog box to set miscellaneous options.

COMPACTING YOUR PERSONAL FOLDERS FILE

After you've deleted items from the Deleted Items folder in your Personal Folders file, Outlook doesn't always release the space those items previously occupied. To get the space back, you must compact your Personal Folders file.

To see how much space is recovered by compacting your Personal Folders file, you can find out its size before and after compacting.

To see the size of your Personal Folders file:

1. With any Outlook Information viewer displayed, choose View, Folder List to display your list of folders, as shown in Figure 20.3.

2. Right-click the name of your Personal Folders file, not one of the individual folders within that file, to display its context menu.

3. Choose Properties to display the Personal Folders Properties dialog box, which opens with the General tab selected.

4. Choose Folder Size to display the dialog box shown in Figure 20.4.

PART

IV

CH

20

Figure 20.3
The folder list opens with your currently active Personal Folders file expanded to show the folders it contains.

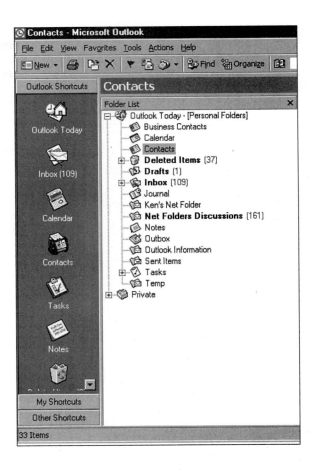

Figure 20.4
This dialog box shows the size of the file and the sizes of the individual folders within it.

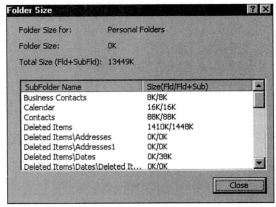

The sizes shown apparently represent the space occupied by Outlook items. A Personal Folders file is considerably bigger than the size indicated in this dialog box due to the overhead in the file. In one case in which the dialog box shows a size of 775kB, Windows Explorer shows the size of the file to be 1,008kB.

The top section of this dialog box contains three rows:

- The name of the Personal Folders file (Personal Folders in this case)
- The size of any data within the file but not within individual folders (normally 0K)
- The total size of data within folders and subfolders

The bottom section contains a table that lists the size of individual folders and subfolders. Two numbers, separated by a slash, are shown for each folder. The first number represents the data in the folder itself, excluding data in any subfolders; the second number represents the data in the folder itself and the data in any subfolders.

To compact your Personal Folders file:

1. With any Outlook Information viewer displayed, choose View, Folder List to display your list of folders as shown previously in Figure 20.3.

2. Right-click the name of your Personal Folders file, not one of the individual folders within that file, to display its context menu.

3. Choose Properties to display the Personal Folders Properties dialog box, which opens with the General tab selected.

4. Choose Advanced to display the dialog box shown in Figure 20.5.

5. Choose Compact Now to recover unused space within your Personal Folders file.

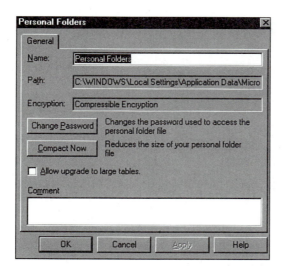

Figure 20.5
You can use this dialog box to change your password and to compact your Personal Folders file.

PART

IV

CH

20

> **Note**
>
> Compacting a file just once doesn't necessarily make the file as small as possible. You may have to compact it two or three times.
>
> Some people recommend compacting from the Windows Control Panel instead of from within Outlook. In the Control Panel, double-click Mail to display a Properties dialog box, select the Personal Folders file, and choose Properties. Choose Compact Now to compact the file.

AUTOARCHIVING OUTLOOK ITEMS

AutoArchiving is the process by which Outlook either copies or deletes items from your Outlook folders periodically. Outlook can AutoArchive items in all folders except your Contacts folder.

→ As explained subsequently in this chapter, you can archive items manually. **See** "Archiving Items Manually," **p. 597**.

The items that Outlook AutoArchives are those that are expired. You can specify the expiry period for items in each folder and you can specify the interval at which Outlook performs AutoArchiving.

DEFINING EXPIRATION PERIODS

Each folder has a default expiration period for the items it contains, as listed in Table 20.1.

TABLE 20.1	DEFAULT EXPIRATION PERIODS		
Folder	**Period**	**Default**	**Basis**
Calendar	6 months	Yes	Item start date or date of last item modification
Contacts	None	NA	Not archived
Deleted Items	2 Months	Yes	Date item moved into folder
Drafts	3 months	No	Date item created or last modified
Inbox	3 months	No	Date message received or last modified
Journal	6 months	Yes	Entry date or date of last modification
Notes	3 months	No	Entry date or date of last modification
Outbox	3 months	No	Creation date or date of last modification
Sent Items	2 Months	Yes	Date item was sent
Tasks	6 months	Yes	Completion date or date of last modification. Uncompleted tasks are not archived

Note

> The Period and Default for custom folders depends on the type of item each folder contains. If you create a custom folder to hold Task items, for example, that folder has the same Period and Default as the standard Outlook Tasks folder.

➜ For information about custom folders and subfolders, **see** "Creating Folders and Subfolders," **p. 922**.

Although each folder has a default AutoArchive period, AutoArchiving is only initially activated for those folders marked Yes in the Default column in Table 20.1.

ENABLING AND DISABLING AUTOARCHIVING

As Table 20.1 shows, some folders have AutoArchiving turned on by default, and others do not. You can change these defaults.

To turn AutoArchiving on or off for a folder:

1. Right-click the shortcut icon in the Outlook Bar (or the folder name in the folder list) corresponding to the folder for which you want to turn AutoArchiving on or off to display the folder's context menu.

2. Choose Properties in the context menu to display the folder's Properties dialog box.

3. Select the AutoArchive tab (available for all folders except the Contacts folder), as shown in Figure 20.6.

4. Check the Clean Out Items Older Than box to turn AutoArchiving on; uncheck that box to turn AutoArchiving off.

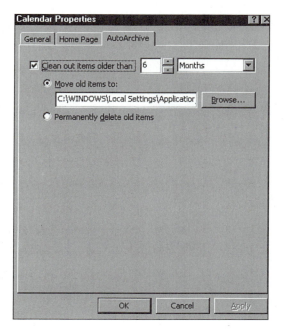

Figure 20.6
This dialog box shows whether AutoArchiving is turned on and the period between AutoArchiving.

PART

IV

CH

20

CHANGING AUTOARCHIVING PERIODS

You can change the intervals between which Outlook performs AutoArchiving.

To change the AutoArchive period:

1. Follow steps 1 through 3 in the preceding procedure.
2. In the box at the right of Clean Out Items Older Than, change the number. Open the adjacent drop-down list and select Months, Weeks, or Days.

CONTROLLING WHAT AUTOARCHIVING DOES

By default, AutoArchiving moves Outlook items from your Personal Folders file into an archive file. You can determine, separately for each folder, the location of the archive file. You can also choose whether AutoArchiving should permanently delete items or move them to an archive folder. If you choose to move items into an archive folder, those items are added to items already in that folder.

→ Although what follows applies to all items in a folder, you can separately mark individual items to be excluded from AutoArchiving, as explained in the following section. **See** "Excluding Individual Items from AutoArchiving.

To control what AutoArchiving does:

1. Follow Steps 1 through 3 in the procedure in the "Enabling and Disabling AutoArchiving" section previously in this chapter.
→ For detailed descriptions of these steps, **see** "Enabling and Disabling AutoArchiving," **P. 593**.
2. If you want to move eligible items to another folder, enter the full pathname of the folder into the Move Old Items To box; alternatively, choose Browse and navigate to the file in which you want to save the archived items.

   If you want to delete, instead of move, eligible items, choose the Permanently Delete Old Items option button.

Caution

If you choose Permanently Delete Old Items, items are not moved to your Outlook Deleted Items folder; they are permanently deleted.

EXCLUDING INDIVIDUAL ITEMS FROM AUTOARCHIVING

By default, the AutoArchiving properties you define for a folder apply to all items in that folder. You can, however, mark specific items to be excluded from AutoArchiving. Suppose, for example, there is a specific Calendar item that you want to retain in your Calendar folder, even though that item is eligible for being AutoArchived.

To exclude a Calendar item from AutoArchiving:

1. Open the Calendar Information viewer and double-click the item you want to exclude from AutoArchiving to display the item in the form in which it was created.

2. In the form's menu bar, choose File, Properties to display the item's Properties dialog box, such as that shown in Figure 20.7.

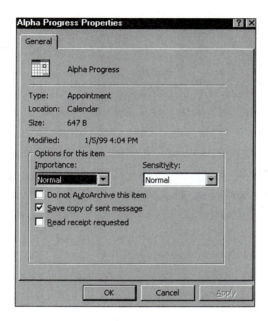

Figure 20.7
This dialog box shows the properties of the selected item.

3. Check the Do Not AutoArchive This Item box to exclude the item from AutoArchiving.

Note

You can use this procedure to exclude any type of item from AutoArchiving.

PART
IV

CH
20

MANAGING AUTOARCHIVING

Now that you understand how Outlook AutoArchives items, you need to see what control you have over the entire AutoArchiving process.

To set up AutoArchiving:

1. With any Outlook Information viewer displayed, choose Tools, Options to display the Options dialog box. Select the Other tab, and choose AutoArchive to display the dialog box shown in Figure 20.8.

Figure 20.8
Use this dialog box to define how you want AutoArchive to work.

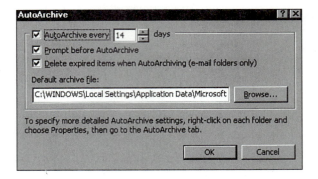

2. By default the AutoArchive Every box is checked, meaning that AutoArchive is turned on. Leave it checked and choose OK if you want AutoArchive to be enabled. If you don't want to use AutoArchive, uncheck the box.

Tip #138 from

Gordon Brook

When you open Outlook, it checks to see if it should AutoArchive items. If you leave your computer on with Outlook running all the time, Outlook never checks to see if AutoArchive is due. If you do leave your computer on all the time, close down Outlook each evening and open it again each morning in order for Outlook to check whether AutoArchive is due.

Windows 98 has a Scheduled Task Wizard you can use to automatically start and stop Outlook (or any other application) on a regular basis. From the Windows taskbar, choose Start, move the pointer onto Programs, move the pointer onto Accessories, move the pointer onto System Tools, and choose Scheduled Tasks to display the Scheduled Tasks dialog box. Choose Add Scheduled Task to display the first Scheduled Task Wizard, then follow the instructions in the wizard.

3. If you checked the AutoArchive Every box, enter the AutoArchive period (number of days) in the adjoining box.

4. Leave the Prompt Before AutoArchive checked if you want Outlook to let you know it's about to start AutoArchiving. Uncheck this box if you want Outlook to proceed with AutoArchiving without giving you prior notification.

5. By default, Outlook deletes (rather than archives) expired e-mail items. Uncheck the Delete Expired Items when AutoArchiving (E-mail Folders Only) box if you prefer to archive these items.

6. The Default Archive File box proposes where Outlook will save the archived items. You can enter a different file (using its full path and file name), or you can choose Browse to navigate to the folder in which you want to save the archived items.

Caution

Step 5 in the preceding procedure refers to the fact that by default Outlook deletes, rather than archives, e-mail items. Organizations may want to make it corporate policy that everyone uses this default.

The reason is that e-mail tends to be a free-wheeling environment in which people say things that could be used to their disadvantage. Recent legal proceedings have involved subpoenas for e-mail records that have had a significant adverse effect on a corporation's standing.

For this reason, it's usually advisable to keep only those e-mail records that you specifically decide are needed.

Note, though, that any contract you may have with a government agency may require you to keep records of all communications.

Whether you choose to have AutoArchiving move items to another folder or delete items, items are deleted from your Personal Folders file. As previously stated in this chapter, Outlook doesn't necessarily recover the space previously occupied by items that have been deleted.

→ You should regularly compact your Personal Folders file. **See** "Compacting Your Personal Folders File," **p. 589**.

ARCHIVING ITEMS MANUALLY

If you have not turned on AutoArchiving, or if you have turned on AutoArchiving and you want to archive items before AutoArchiving is due, you can use manual archiving. Although AutoArchiving never archives Contact items, you can manually archive these items.

To manually archive items:

1. With any Outlook Information viewer displayed, choose File, Archive to display the dialog box shown in Figure 20.9.

Figure 20.9
The Archive dialog box opens with the folder corresponding to the Information viewer you started from selected.

2. Leave the Archive This Folder and All Its Subfolders option button selected if that's what you want to do. Alternatively, select the Archive All Folders According to Their AutoArchive Settings option button.

3. If you selected Archive This Folder..., select the folder you want to archive.

4. Also, if you selected Archive This Folder..., open the Archive Items Older Than drop-down calendar and select the age of the items you want to archive. You can, alternatively, enter a date in the box.

5. Also, if you selected Archive This Folder..., check Include Items with "Do Not AutoArchive" checked if that's what you want to do. Otherwise, leave this box unchecked.

6. Also, if you selected Archive This Folder..., enter the full path and file name of the file into which you want to archive items in the Archive File box. Alternatively, choose Browse and navigate to the file.

7. Choose OK to proceed with archiving.

If you choose Archive All Folders According to Their AutoArchive Settings, Outlook does exactly the same as it does when AutoArchiving occurs. It AutoArchives now, rather than waiting for the appointed AutoArchive time. This option moves items into the file that AutoArchiving uses, adding items to those already in the file or, if you've so specified, deletes items.

→ For a full description of AutoArchiving, **see** "Managing AutoArchiving", **p. 595**.

By choosing Archive This Folder and All Subfolders, you can control which folders are archived, the age of the items in those folders that are archived, and the file into which the archived items are moved. If you choose a file that doesn't already exist, Outlook creates that file. Each time you manually archive, Outlook adds items to the items already in the archive file.

MANAGING ARCHIVE FILES

The purpose of archiving is to avoid filling your hard drive with Outlook items. It makes no sense, therefore, to use a folder on your hard drive for your archive; you need to choose another medium.

When considering which medium to use for your archive, you should also consider how you will retrieve archived items when you need them. After all, you archive items because you might want to access them at some future time. You need to be sure you can conveniently retrieve archived items.

CHOOSING AN ARCHIVE MEDIUM

Here are some suggestions for archive media.

- If your computer is connected to a network, create an archive file on the server and let the network administrator worry about space on the server disks. Remember, though, that the network administrator may copy old files to tape. When you want old Outlook items, you may need to ask the administrator to mount old tapes to access your items.

- If you want to maintain your own archive files, use such media as Iomega Zip or Jaz disks (or other high-capacity disks, writable CD-ROMs, or the like).

Don't let your archive file get too large. If you want to access archived items, you may have to copy the archive file back onto your hard drive. Rather than have one enormous archive file, it's usually better to create new archive files periodically. Depending on your Outlook usage, you should create a new archive file every month, quarter, or year. To be on the safe side, donít let your archive files grow to a size that's larger than you can copy back to your hard drive.

RETRIEVING ARCHIVED ITEMS

You can use three ways to retrieve archived items:

- Import archived items into the file in which they were created.

- Choose File, move the pointer onto Open, and choose Personal Folders File (.pst) to display the Open Personal Folders dialog box. In that dialog box, navigate to the archive file, select it, and choose OK.

Tip #139 from

If you intend to use this method, don't save your archive on a CD-ROM of the write-once kind. That's because Outlook requires read/write access to a Personal Folders file.

- Create a new Personal Folders file and import the archived items into that.

IMPORTING ARCHIVED ITEMS INTO THE ORIGINAL FOLDER

You can choose to retrieve all items from an archive file or folder within that file, or only items from a folder within that file.

To import all items:

1. With any Information viewer displayed, choose File, Import and Export to display the first Import and Export Wizard window.

2. Select Import from Another Program or File and choose Next.

3. Select Personal Folder File and choose Next.

4. In the File to Import box, enter the full path and file name of the archive file, or choose Browse and then navigate to the file.

PART

IV

CH

20

5. Select one of the options in the Options section of the dialog box. To avoid the possibility of overwriting existing items, the best choice is usually <u>A</u>llow Duplicates to Be Created. Choose <u>N</u>ext.

6. In this wizard window, select either the entire file or a folder within the file. Outlook lets you select either the entire file or just one folder within it. By default, Outlook proposes to import subfolders. You can uncheck the Include <u>S</u>ubfolders box.

7. If you want to import only items that satisfy certain criteria, you can choose <u>F</u>ilter and then define criteria for the files to be imported. Choose Finish to import the files from your archive.

IMPORTING ARCHIVED ITEMS INTO A NEW FOLDER

Instead of importing archived items into their original folders, you may want to import them into a separate folder. To do so you have to create a new Personal Folders file.

To create a new Personal Folders file:

1. With any Information viewer displayed, choose <u>F</u>ile, move the pointer onto Ne<u>w</u>, and choose Personal Folders <u>F</u>ile to display the dialog box shown in Figure 20.10.

Figure 20.10
This dialog box lists the names of Personal Folders files that already exist.

2. Enter a name for the new file into the File <u>N</u>ame box.

3. Choose Create to begin creating the new file. Outlook displays the dialog box shown in Figure 20.11.

4. Change the suggested Outlook name "Personal Folders" to something appropriate.

Figure 20.11
Specify the new folder in
this dialog box.

5. Choose an encryption setting.

6. Enter a password, if you want to have one, and verify that password by entering it a second time.

7. Choose OK to finish creating the file.

Now you have a new Personal Folders file into which you can import items from your archive. Don't forget to make use of the Filter capability in order to selectively import only the items you need.

➔ For information about importing items, **see** "Importing Items from a Personal Folders File," **p. 573**.

BACKING UP OUTLOOK

Backing up your Outlook configuration so that you can install it on another disk or another computer involves saving all your Outlook items and saving Outlook's settings.

The preceding sections of this chapter explain how you can save the Outlook items you've created or received. To completely back up Outlook, you also have to save all the files that contain all of Outlook's *settings (page 19)*.

Many of Outlook's settings are saved within the Windows *registry (page 605)*, so one thing you must do is to save the registry.

➔ For detailed information about backing up the regstry, **see** "Backing Up and Restoring the Registry," **p. 1324**.

PART

IV

CH

20

Microsoft hasn't published a complete list of all the files that contain information that Outlook uses. However, some of these files are:

- Personal Folders—These are files that have .pst as their file name extension and contain Outlook items you've saved in a Personal Folders file.

- Offline Folders—These are files that have .ost as their file name extension and contain Outlook items you've saved for offline use. You'll only have these files if you're using Outlook as a client for Exchange.

- Personal Address Book—These are files that have .pab as their file name extension and contain contact information you have in your Personal Address Book.

- Outlook Configuration Files—Some of the other files that Outlook uses have .dat (Outlook forms, menus, toolbars, and views), .fav (Outlook Bar shortcuts) .inf (default settings), .nick (Outlook nicknames), .rwz (rules), and .rtf, txt, and htm (AutoSignatures) as their file name extensions.

→ For more information about Outlook files, **see** "Outlook Files," **p. 1296**.

TROUBLESHOOTING

The most likely problem you might run into when importing into, or exporting from, Outlook is that you run out of disk space due to the size of the information. If that happens, the operation aborts without losing any data. Your only loss is the time wasted.

To avoid this problem, it's good practice to find out the size of the information you're going to import or export before you begin, and compare that with the space available. You can, of course, use My Computer or Windows Explorer to find out the size of complete files and how much space is available on a disk.

→ You can use the methods previously described in this chapter to find out the size of Outlook folders and individual Outlook items. **See** "Displaying the Size of Outlook Items," **p. 584** (this chapter) and "Compacting Your Personal Folders File." **p. 589**.

CHAPTER 21

USING CATEGORIES AND ENTRY TYPES

In this chapter

by Gordon Padwick

WHAT ARE CATEGORIES?

A *category (page 604)* is a word or phrase you can assign to any Outlook item so that you can easily group like items together. For example, you can create a category for each project you work on. After you've created a category for a project, you can assign that category to all messages, contacts, appointments, tasks, and notes that have anything to do with the project. Subsequently, you can easily find all Outlook items related to the project.

Categories are key to keeping your information organized and easy to find. If you discipline yourself to assign categories to all your Outlook items, you'll be amazed at how organized you are. On the other hand, if you ignore categories you'll have the electronic equivalent of piles of paper on your desk.

Some of your items might relate to several projects. No problem! You can assign as many categories as you like to any Outlook item.

Outlook considers every piece of information to be an *item*. Each mail message, calendar activity, task, and so on, is an item. You can assign one or more categories to each item either by

- Entering the category in a form's Categories box.
- Selecting from a master list of categories, as explained in the next section.

Tip #140 from *Gordon Padwick*	You should normally select from a Master Category List to ensure that you use consistent category names. If the Master Category List doesn't contain the categories you need, you can add more categories.

→ For information about adding categories to, and deleting categories from, your Master Category List, **see** "Customizing Your Personal Master Category List," **p. 606**.

USING A MASTER CATEGORY LIST

Outlook has a default Master Category List. You can see this list in two ways:

- Open an Information viewer that displays items in one of Outlook's folders (such as the Inbox Information viewer) and choose Edit, Categories to display the Categories dialog box (the Categories menu item is dimmed and not available if there aren't any items in the selected Information viewer). Choose Master Category List to display the dialog box shown in Figure 21.1.
- Open one of the forms in which you create a new item (such as the Appointment form), choose Categories to display the Categories dialog box, and then choose Master Category List to display the dialog box shown in Figure 21.1.

The Message form doesn't have a Categories button. In this form, choose Options in the Standard toolbar to display the Message Options dialog box that contains a Categories button.

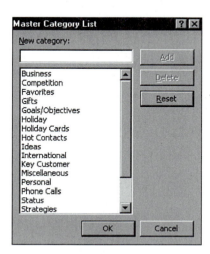

Figure 21.1
The default Master Category List contains a variety of pre-defined categories listed in alphabetical order.

HOW OUTLOOK SAVES CATEGORY LISTS

Before going any further, you need to understand that Outlook maintains at least two Master Category Lists.

The process of installing Outlook writes the default Master Category List into the Windows *registry*—a database that contains information about the settings for Windows itself, applications that run under Windows, and computer users.

The information in each user's Windows profile is also maintained in the registry; each user's profile contains a copy of the Master Category List—the user's personal Master Category List. Users can easily make changes to their personal Master Category Lists, but not to the default Master Category List.

→ To make changes to Outlook's default Master Category List, you have to edit the Windows registry. **See** "Customizing Outlook's Default Master Category List," **p. 606**.

Each Outlook user can restore the categories in that user's own profile by choosing Master Category List in the Categories dialog box and then choosing Reset in the Master Category List dialog box. This deletes all the categories in that user's personal Master Category List and then copies the default categories into it.

PART

IV

CH

21

CUSTOMIZING YOUR PERSONAL MASTER CATEGORY LIST

When you begin to use Outlook, the default Master Category list is copied into your personal Master Category List. More than likely, the categories in the default Master Category List supplied with Outlook won't suit your personal needs. It's easy to delete those categories in your personal Master Category List that you don't expect to use and add categories that you will use.

PLANNING YOUR MASTER CATEGORY LIST

It's worth taking the time to give some serious thought to planning categories, just as you would before setting up a file system for paper documents. You'll probably want to have categories for business and personal items. Categories you might need for business items include

- Separate categories for each project you're involved with
- Separate categories for each type of business contact
- Separate categories for each of your organization's departments

Categories you might need for personal items include

- Separate categories for each type of personal contact (family, friend, medical, finance, legal, and so on)
- Separate categories for each of your interests and hobbies
- Separate categories for each type of family activity

These are just suggestions to start you thinking. While planning your categories, remember that you can assign several categories to each item. When you assign several categories to one item, Outlook saves the item only once, but when you display items sorted by category you'll see the item listed several times, once under each category assigned to the item.

Tip #142 from

Gordon Padwick

> Try to make your list of categories fairly complete. Although you may add categories at any time, doing so may make it necessary to change the categories you've already assigned to items—a time-consuming process.

DELETING AND ADDING CATEGORIES

After you have a reasonably complete list of the categories you want in your personal list, display the Categories dialog box. Then choose Master Category List to display the dialog box previously shown in Figure 21.1. This dialog box displays categories in alphabetical order.

To delete categories from your personal Master Category List:

1. In the Master Category List dialog box, select the category or categories you want to delete. As soon as you select a category, the <u>D</u>elete button becomes enabled.

Note

You can select several categories and delete them all at the same time. To select several categories, select one category, then hold down the Ctrl key while you select others. To select consecutive categories, select the first category, then hold down the Shift key while you select the last category.

2. Choose <u>D</u>elete. The selected category or categories are immediately deleted from your personal Master Category List.

To add categories to your personal Master Category List:

1. In the Master Category List dialog box, shown previously in Figure 21.1, place the insertion point in the <u>N</u>ew Category box.

2. Type a word or short phrase to name the new category. As soon as you type the first character, the <u>A</u>dd button becomes enabled.

3. Choose <u>A</u>dd. The new category immediately appears in your Master Category List in its correct alphabetical position.

Note

If the word or phrase you type already exists in the category list, Outlook doesn't add a duplicate when you choose <u>A</u>dd.

4. Repeat the preceding three steps to add as many new categories as you need.

5. When you've finished deleting and adding categories, choose OK to close the Master Category List dialog box. Now you can use your new Master Category List to assign categories to items.

ADDING CATEGORIES ON-THE-FLY

Sometimes you won't be able to find the category you want to assign to an item in your personal Master Category List. You can, of course, use the method described in the previous section to add a new category to your Master Category List, but there's an even faster way to add a new category.

To add a category on-the-fly:

1. Double-click an item to which you want to assign a category. Outlook displays that item in a form, which, except for message items, contains a Categories button.

PART

IV

CH

21

2. Choose Categories to display the Categories dialog box shown in Figure 21.2.

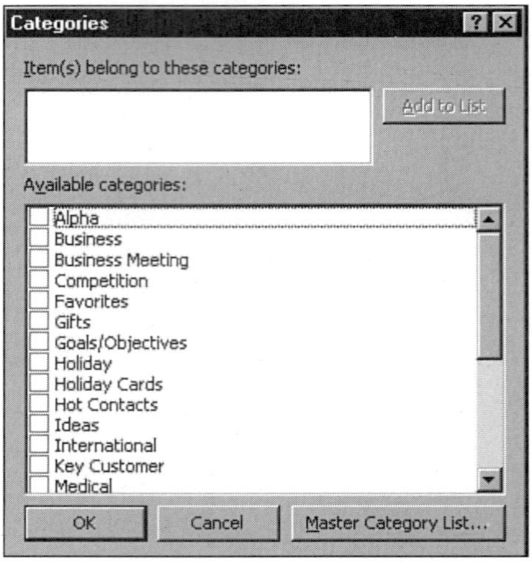

Figure 21.2
This is the dialog box
you use to assign cat-
egories to items.

3. Enter the name of the new category in the Item(s) Belong to These Categories box, as
   shown in Figure 21.3. As soon as you enter the first character, the Add to List button
   becomes enabled.

Figure 21.3
Enter a new category
directly into the
Categories dialog
box.

4. Choose Add to List to add the new category to your personal Master Category List.
   The new category immediately appears in the list of Available Categories. It's automatically checked to indicate it will be assigned to the Outlook item you're creating.
5. Choose OK to assign the category to the Outlook item.

The next time you open your personal Master Category List (as described earlier in this chapter) you'll find the new category is listed.

HOW CATEGORIES ARE ASSIGNED TO ITEMS

Each Outlook item consists of many predefined fields, including a Category field. When you assign a category to an item, the name of the category is copied into the item's Category field. Like many Outlook fields, the Category field can contain as many as 256 characters, so you can assign many categories to an item. When two or more categories are assigned to an item, a comma separates one category from the next. You normally won't assign more than two or three categories to an item.

After you've assigned categories to an item, it doesn't matter whether those categories still exist in your personal Master Category List. When you delete a category from your Master Category List, Outlook doesn't delete that category from the items to which you previously assigned it. However, when you open an item to which a category that's not in your personal Category List is assigned and open the Categories dialog box, you'll see that the category is marked as "not in Master Category List."

I recommend that you assign categories to items by choosing categories from your Category List, not by typing category names into a form's Categories box. If you insist on doing so, however, nothing prevents you from just entering category names into the Categories box on a form.

The problem that arises when you enter, rather than select, categories is that you probably won't always enter category names consistently. If you use the singular form of a category name one time and the plural form another time, Outlook sees two category names. Even the slightest difference between one category name and another results in separate categories. Avoid this potential problem by always choosing categories from your personal Master Category List.

Items in Outlook folders have categories assigned to them in yet another way when you receive Outlook items from other people. If someone creates an e-mail message, assigns categories to it, and sends it to you, the item in your Inbox folder has those categories assigned to it, whether or not those categories are in your Master Category List.

→ Within a single organization, people should be encouraged to use the same Master Category List. **See** "Sharing Your Personal Category List," **p. 612**.

Of course, you have no control over the categories assigned to Outlook items by people outside your own organization. When you receive those messages, however, you can change the assigned categories to those in your own Master Category List. By doing so, Outlook items you receive are organized in a way that is consistent with the organization of items you create.

PART

IV

CH

21

DETERMINING AND CHANGING CATEGORIES

Tip #143 from

Within your own group, it's preferable that everyone has the same personal Master Category List. Refer to the next section for information about sharing Category Lists.

You can find out what categories are assigned to any item and, if necessary, change those categories. In this section, you'll find out how you can look at categories assigned to a message you've received. Remember, of course, that categories can be assigned to any Outlook item, including e-mail messages, calendar items, and so on.

CHANGING A MAIL ITEM'S CATEGORIES

Note

You can use the method described here to determine and change categories in mail items in your Sent Items folder as well as items in your Inbox folder.

To display, and possibly change, the categories assigned to an e-mail item you've received:

1. Open the Inbox Information viewer and select the message.

2. Choose Edit, Categories to display the Categories dialog box shown previously in Figure 21.2. The Item(s) Belong to These Categories box contains the names of the categories already assigned to the item. Also, the individual categories assigned to the message are checked in the Available categories box. Any categories assigned to the message that don't exist in your personal Master Category List are marked in the list as "not in Master Category List."

Note

If the message is open in a message form, choose View, Options to display the Message Options dialog box and then choose Categories to display the Categories dialog box.

3. If you want to change the categories assigned to the message to be consistent with the way you assign categories, remove the check marks from categories you don't want to use and check those categories you do want to use. Choose OK to close the Categories dialog box.

ASSIGNING AND CHANGING CATEGORIES IN E-MAIL YOU CREATE

To assign or change categories in a message you're creating, choose Options in the Message form's Standard toolbar to display the Message Options form shown in Figure 21.4.

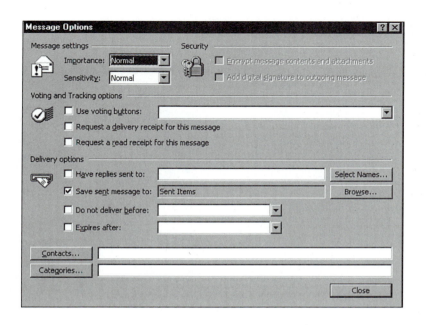

Figure 21.4
The Message Options form contains a Categories box at the bottom.

To assign or change the categories assigned to the message:

1. Choose the Categories button to display the Categories dialog box.

2. Check the categories you want to assign to the message. If necessary, uncheck already-assigned categories you don't want to assign to the message.

3. Choose OK to return to the Message Options form in which the assigned categories are displayed in the Categories box.

4. Choose Close to return to the Message form.

CREATING A MESSAGE WITH PREDEFINED CATEGORIES

Instead of individually assigning categories to every message you create, you can create any number of message *templates (page 520)*, each with specific categories assigned, as explained in Chapter 17.

→ For information about creating a message template, **see** "Creating an E-mail Template," **p. 520**.

After creating these templates, you can use any of them as the basis for messages. This method several advantages:

- It saves you the time and trouble of separately assigning categories to each message
- It avoids the possibility of forgetting to assign categories to messages
- It helps you to assign the same categories to every message of each type

PART
IV
CH
21

ASSIGNING AND CHANGING CATEGORIES FOR OTHER ITEMS

The forms you use to create Outlook items other than messages all contain a Categories box similar to that in the Appointments form shown in Figure 21.5. Choose Categories and then follow the four steps described in the preceding section to assign or change categories.

Figure 21.5
The Appointment form contains a Categories box at the bottom-right.

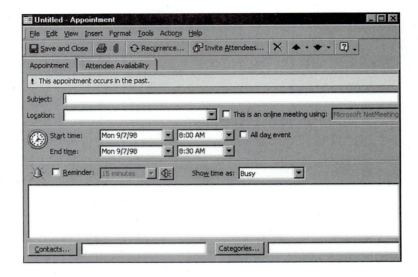

> **Note**
>
> You can create templates for all types of Outlook items with each template containing predefined categories. Refer to the previous section in which this concept is explained in the context of e-mail messages.

SHARING YOUR PERSONAL CATEGORY LIST

The "Understanding How Outlook Saves Category Lists" section earlier in this chapter explained that Outlook keeps the default Master Category List and your personal Master Category List in the Windows registry.

If you want to share your Master Category List with someone else, you must export part of the registry from one computer into a file and then import that file into the registry of the other computer (as described later in this section). This also works well if you want to copy the personal Master Category List you use at home onto the computer you use in your office.

After customizing your personal Master Category List, close or minimize Outlook, then proceed as follows.

→ For information about backing up the Windows registry, **see** "Working with the Windows Registry," **p. 1323**.

Appendix F contains a detailed description of the method you can use to export any registry key to a file, and then import that file into another computer's registry. The registry key that contains your personal Master Category List is

```
HKEY_CURRENT_USER\Software\Microsoft\Office\9.0\Outlook\Categories
```

If you administer a workgroup or LAN, consider using this procedure to copy a standard Master Category List to everyone's computer.

Customizing Outlook's Default Master Category List

In all probability, the sample categories supplied with Outlook are not what you want to use. If you manage a group of Outlook users, you might want to change Outlook's default Master Category List so that it contains more appropriate categories.

You can use the technique described in Appendix F to modify Outlook's default Master Category List. The registry key you need to use for this purpose is

```
HKEY_LOCAL_MACHINE\Softwarw\Microsoft\Office\9.0\Outlook\Categories.
```

After you've changed the default Master Category List on one computer, you can save the Categories key to a file, then copy that file into the registry on other computers. Outlook users in a group can then use the customized Master Category List as a basis for the Outlook categories they assign to Outlook items.

Understanding Entry Types

When you manually create entries in Outlook's *Journal (page 440)*, you can assign categories to each Journal item. In addition, you must assign an entry type to each item.

→ For information about creating Journal Items, **see** "Creating Journal Items Manually," **p. 448**.

Outlook contains a built-in list of entry types. These are:

Conversation	Meeting request	Note
Document	Meeting response	Phone call
E-mail message	Microsoft Access	Remote session
Fax	Microsoft Excel	Task
Letter	Microsoft	Task request
Meeting	PowerPoint	Task response
Meeting cancellation	Microsoft Word	

As you see, all the entry types in this built-in list relate to Outlook items and office applications. What if you want to record in your journal items such as adding hardware or software to your computer, buying something, having your car serviced, and so on? None of the entry types is suitable for these activities.

CREATING NEW ENTRY TYPES

Whereas you can easily tailor Outlook's categories, as explained in the first part of this chapter, there's no simple way to modify Outlook's list of entry types. Like categories, Outlook's list of entry types is in the Windows registry. To modify that list, you have to resort to editing the registry.

Caution

As always, be aware that information in the registry controls how Windows and the applications under Windows run. Any incorrect change you make to the registry could affect Windows or an application, or even make your computer unusable. Always make a backup copy of the registry before making any changes to it. See Appendix F for detailed information about this subject.

Suppose you want to add a new entry type, such as Computer, to the list.

To add an entry type:

1. Choose Start, Run on the Windows taskbar to display the Run dialog box.
2. In the Open box, enter Regedit and choose OK to start the Registry Editor.
3. Navigate to the registry key
   `HKEY_CURRENT_USER\Software\Microsoft\Shared Tools\Outlook\Journaling`

   and right-click this key to display its context menu.
4. Point onto New in the context menu, and choose Key. New Key #1 appears in the Registry Editor's Key pane.
5. Replace New Key #1 with the name of the new entry type, such as Computer, and press Enter.

6. Right-click the new key to display its context menu, move the pointer onto New, and choose String Value. New Value #1 appears in the registry's Value pane.

7. Replace New Value #1 with the word Description and press Enter to display the Edit String dialog box in which the Value Name box contains Description.

8. In the Value Data box, enter the name of the new entry type, such as Computer, and choose OK. The registry's Value pane now contains a value named Description with its data shown as "Computer."

9. Choose Registry, Exit to close the Registry Editor.

You can add as many new item types as you like in this manner.

→ Form more information about working with the registry, **see** "Working with the Windows Registry," **p. 1323**.

SELECTING AN ENTRY TYPE

The next time create a new Journal item, you can assign one of the entry types you've created to that item.

To create a journal item having a custom entry type:

1. Start Outlook and choose Journal in the Outlook Bar.

2. Choose New in the Standard toolbar to display the Journal Entry form.

3. Open the drop-down Entry Type list that contains the standard Outlook entry types together with the custom entry types you created.

4. Select an entry type from the drop-down list.

→ **See** "Creating Journal Items Manually," **p. 448**.

TROUBLESHOOTING

Outlook's default Master Category List and your personal Master Category List are saved in keys in the Windows registry, as explained previously in this chapter. You can run into trouble with categories, therefore, if your registry becomes corrupted, you accidentally remove keys, or you enter data in the wrong format.

In anticipation that this might happen, you should regularly make a backup copy of your registry using the methods described in Appendix F. Then you can restore your registry if problems occur.

→ For information about backing up the registry, **see** "Backing up and Restoring the Registry," **p. 1234**.

Note

The advice about making regular backups of the registry doesn't apply only to solving possible problems with Outlook's categories. It's good advice that applies to using Windows and all applications that run under Windows.

PART
IV

CH
21

CHAPTER 22

CREATING AND USING RULES

In this chapter

by Gordon Padwick

WHAT IS A RULE?

A *rule* is a set of conditions, actions, and exceptions that controls how Outlook processes and organizes messages. The conditions determine which types of messages a rule applies to; the actions are what the rule does; the exceptions determine when a rule does not apply to certain messages. Some rules work on messages you receive; other rules work on messages you send.

These two examples will help you understand the sorts of things rules can do:

- You can create a rule that forwards all messages you receive from a specific person to another person.
- You can create a rule that moves copies of messages you send to a specific person into a certain folder.

To create basic rules, choose Organize in the Inbox Information viewer's toolbar. To create more sophisticated rules, use Outlook's Rules Wizard.

You can create and edit rules to do things such as:

- Perform an action when a message arrives
- Perform an action before a message is sent
- Move incoming messages that satisfy certain conditions into a specific folder
- Notify you when certain messages arrive
- Automatically delete messages that satisfy certain conditions
- Assign a flag to certain messages
- Automatically reply to certain messages
- Notify you when recipients read certain messages

You can combine these and other actions in many ways to create various rules, as described in the rest of this chapter.

Tip #144 from

> Outlook 2000 contains rule conditions and actions that weren't available in previous versions of Outlook. The Outlook Help topic "Rule Conditions and Actions that Work Only in Outlook 2000" contains information about what's new in Outlook 2000.

This chapter focuses on rules that run under Outlook on your computer. If you're using *C/W Outlook (page 54)* as a client for Exchange, you can create rules that run on the server under Exchange.

Note

> In previous versions of Outlook, rules could be used only on Internet messages received from a POP3 server. Outlook 2000 rules can also be used on messages received from an IMAP server.

→ For information about using rules for C/W Outlook used as a client for an Exchange server, **see** "Using Server-Based Rules," **p. 697**.

USING ORGANIZE TO CREATE RULES

Chapter 18 introduced Outlook's Organize capability. That chapter describes how you can use Organize to move existing messages you've received from the Inbox folder to another folder. You can also use Organize to create rules that move new messages to a different folder when those messages arrive.

→ For information about using organize to create rules, **see** "Organizing E-mail Messages," **p. 560**.

CREATING A NEW FOLDER

Before creating a rule to move incoming messages to a folder, that folder must exist. If the folder you want to move messages to doesn't exist, follow these steps to create it.

To create a new folder:

1. With your Inbox Information viewer displayed, choose File, move the pointer onto Folder, and choose New Folder to display the dialog box shown in Figure 22.1.

Figure 22.1
Because you started from the Inbox Information viewer, Outlook proposes to create a new folder for Mail Items.

2. Enter a name for the new folder in the Name box. If you intend to use the folder for mail from a certain person, use that person's name as the name for the folder.

3. Use the Select Where to Place the Folder box to identify where the new folder should be placed in your folder structure. Because you started from the Inbox Information viewer, Outlook proposes to place the new folder as a subfolder for the existing Inbox folder.

4. Choose OK. Outlook asks if you want a shortcut to this folder added to the Outlook Bar. You probably don't, so choose <u>N</u>o.

→ For more detailed information about creating folders, **see** "Creating Folders and Subfolders," **p. 922**.

Tip #145 from

[signature]

You can, if you like, choose <u>V</u>iew, Fold<u>e</u>r List to confirm that the new folder is correctly placed in your folder structure.

CREATING THE RULE

Rules you create in IMO Outlook and in C/W Outlook that's not a client for Exchange always run within Outlook on your computer. In contrast, some rules you create in C/W Outlook that is a client for Exchange run either within Outlook on your computer or within the server. In the case of Outlook used as an Exchange client, Outlook evaluates each rule you create. If the rule can be run in either place, Outlook gives you a choice of running the rule within the client or server.

Here's how you use Organize to create a rule that moves incoming mail to a new folder.

To create a rule that moves incoming messages to a specific folder:

1. With the Inbox Information viewer displayed, choose Organi<u>z</u>e in the viewer's toolbar to display the Organize pane shown in Figure 22.2.

Figure 22.2
The second line in the Organizer pane assumes you want to create a rule based on the names of the sender and recipient of the currently selected e-mail item.

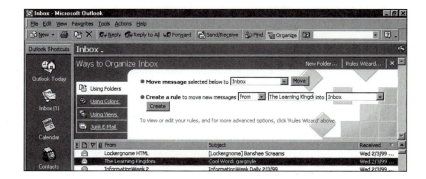

2. The first box in the second line initially contains the word "from." You're creating a rule that applies to messages from someone, so this appropriate.

Note

You can open the drop-down list and select "sent to" if you want to create a rule that affects messages sent to someone.

3. The second box in the second line contains the name of the sender of the currently selected message. Replace that name with the name of the sender whose messages you want the rule to apply to. You can enter the name or, if you already have a message from that person, select that message in the message headers listed below the Organize pane.

Tip #146 from

Depending on various factors, a sender's name might not always appear in the same way. For example, you might sometimes see a sender's name in the From box, and at other times see a sender's e-mail address. You must create a separate rule for each way a sender's name appears.

4. Open the drop-down list at the beginning of the third line in the Organize pane to see a list of some of your Outlook folders, as shown in Figure 22.3.

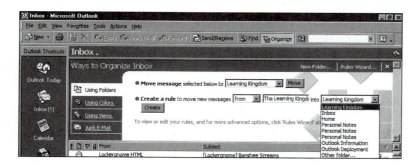

Figure 22.3
The list contains the names of one or more custom folders that you've previously created.

5. If the name of the folder into which you want to move incoming mail is in the list, select that name. If the name of the folder isn't in the list, choose Other Folder to display the Select Folder dialog box that lists all your Outlook folders; select the folder you want to use and choose OK. The name of the selected folder appears in the box at the left end of the third line in the Organize pane.

6. Choose Create in the Organize pane. A message appears stating that the "new rule will be applied to new messages as they are received." The message also asks if you want "to run this rule on the current contents of the folder."

7. Choose Yes if you want the rule to apply to the existing folder contents, or choose No if you want the rule to apply only to new messages. At this point, if you're using C/W Outlook as a client for Exchange and if the new rule could be run either on the client or on the server, Outlook displays the dialog box shown in Figure 22.4. If you're using IMO Outlook or C/W Outlook not as a client for Exchange, you don't see this dialog box, so proceed to step 8.

8. If the dialog box shown in Figure 22.4 does appear, you should normally choose Server so that messages are processed by the rule when you're not running Outlook and when your computer is turned off.

Figure 22.4
This dialog box appears only if you're running Outlook as a client for Exchange and only if the new rule could be run either on the client or on the server.

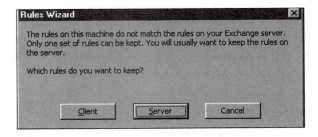

9. After a short delay, the word Done appears to signify that the rule has been created and will be applied to all incoming messages.

10. Choose X at the top-right corner of the Organize pane, or choose Organize in the Standard toolbar, to close the Organize pane.

After you create a rule in this way, Outlook tests each incoming message to see if it is from the sender you specified in step 3 of the preceding procedure. If the message is from that sender, Outlook immediately moves the message into the folder you specified in step 5. If the message is not from that sender, Outlook saves the incoming message in the usual folder, normally your Inbox folder.

CREATING A RULE TO COLOR MESSAGES

You can use Organize to create rules that make message headers in the Inbox Information viewer appear in various colors according to the sender's or recipient's name. You might, for example, want all messages from your supervisor to show up in red and all messages from important customers to be blue.

Note

You can color message headers in the Sent Items folder or a custom folder that contains messages in the same way.

At the left edge of the Organize pane, choose Using Colors to display the pane shown in Figure 22.5.

Figure 22.5
Use this pane to color messages from specific people.

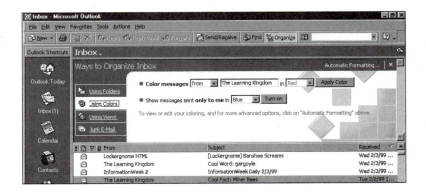

Note
The window shown in Figure 22.5 is for C/W Outlook. The corresponding window for IMO Outlook doesn't contain the second line in the Organize pane.

To color message headers:

1. The Organize pane opens with From in the first box in the top line. If you want to color message headers in your Sent Items Information viewer, open the drop-down list and choose Sent To.

2. Enter the name of the person whose messages you want to color in the second box.

3. Open the drop-down list of colors and select the color you want to use.

4. To apply a color to messages already in your Inbox or Sent Items Information viewer, choose Apply Color.

5. In C/W Outlook, if you want to apply a color to messages sent only to you, open the drop-down color list in the second line and choose a color.

6. In C/W Outlook, choose Turn On to apply the rule to future messages you receive or send. A few moments after you do so, the label on the Turn On button changes to Turn Off. Choose that button if you want to turn the rule off.

CHANGING A VIEW

The Using Views button at the left side of the Organize pane has nothing to do with creating rules. It just provides a quick way to change the view in which Outlook displays messages.

→ For detailed information about views, **see** "Using Default Views," **p. 944**.

DEALING WITH JUNK E-MAIL

You can use the Junk E-mail button at the left side of the Organize pane to set up how Outlook automatically processes junk e-mail.

→ For information about automatically dealing with junk e-mail, **see** "Dealing with Junk E-mail," **p. 623**.

CHANGING A RULE

While you can create additional rules in the manner just described, you can't deactivate, delete, or (with one exception) change a rule from the Organize pane. You must use the Rules Wizard to do any of these things. The remainder of this chapter describes how you can use the Rules Wizard.

The exception mentioned in the previous paragraph is this: If you use the Organize pane to create a rule that moves incoming messages from one person to a certain folder, Outlook creates a rule to do that. If you subsequently create a rule to move incoming messages from another person to the same folder, Outlook doesn't create a second rule. Instead, Outlook modifies the existing rule so that incoming messages from one person or the other are moved to the folder. However if you choose a different folder for messages from the second person, Outlook creates a second rule.

USING THE RULES WIZARD TO CREATE RULES THAT MANAGE INCOMING MESSAGES

Normally, Outlook places all the messages you receive in your Inbox folder. If you receive only a few messages each day, that's no problem. However, if you're one of those people who receive many messages each day, you might prefer to organize those messages by having Outlook automatically assign certain types of messages to separate folders.

Tip #147 from	Instead of organizing messages by saving them in different folders, you might prefer to organize messages by assigning categories to them. Subsequently, you can display messages sorted by category.

The next section describes in detail how you create a specific rule. There's more general information about creating rules later in this chapter.

DELIVERING MESSAGES TO FOLDERS AUTOMATICALLY

You can use the Outlook Rules Wizard to create a rule that Outlook uses to place messages that satisfy certain conditions into a custom folder.

Suppose you want Outlook to save all the messages you receive in the future from Jane Rogers in a separate folder. The first step is to create a custom folder for these messages, as described previously in the chapter. Although you don't have to, it helps to keep your folder structure organized if you create custom folders for mail messages as subfolders to your Inbox folder.

→ For information about creating folders, **see** "Creating a New Folder," **p. 619**.

CREATING THE RULE

Here's how you create the rule that automatically moves messages from Jane Rogers into the Jane Rogers folder.

To create the rule:

1. With the Inbox Information viewer displayed, choose Tools, Rules Wizard to display the first Rule Wizard window, as shown in Figure 22.6.

2. Choose New to start creating a new rule. Outlook displays the second wizard window, shown in Figure 22.7.

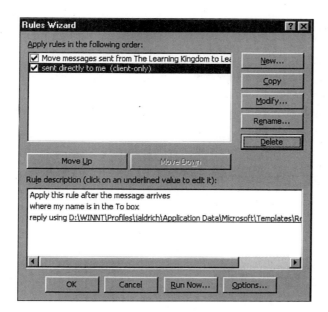

Figure 22.6
The first time you open the Rules Wizard, the two large boxes are empty. Subsequently, these boxes show information about existing rules.

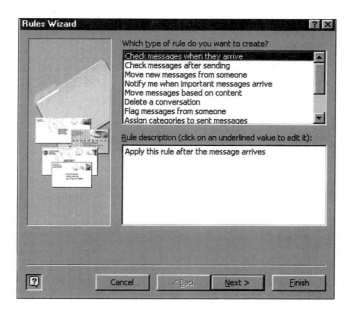

Figure 22.7
The types of rules you can create are listed in the upper box.

3. In the upper box, select Move New Messages from Someone. A description of this rule appears in the lower box, as shown in Figure 22.8.

Figure 22.8
The underlined words in the description (they are usually blue on your monitor) require definitions.

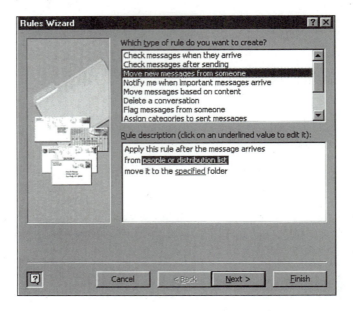

4. Choose Next > to display the next wizard window, which displays a list of conditions that must be satisfied for the rule to be applied. Each condition has a check box adjacent to it, as shown in Figure 22.9.

5. Check those conditions that apply. You can check as many as you like. All the checked conditions must be satisfied for the rule to be applied. In this case, the From People or Distribution List is already checked, which is what you want.

6. Click the first underlined words—people or distribution list—in the Rule Description box. Outlook displays the dialog box shown in Figure 22.10.

7. Select one or more people to whom you want the rule to apply (or you can select one or more distribution lists). Then choose From-> to move the selected names into the Specify the Address of the Sender box and choose OK. The name or names you select replace the underlined words in the wizard window.

Tip #148 from
Gordon Padwick

The colors in which various elements within windows and dialog boxes appear depend on what you select in the Appearance tab of the Display Properties dialog box, accessible from the Windows Control Panel.

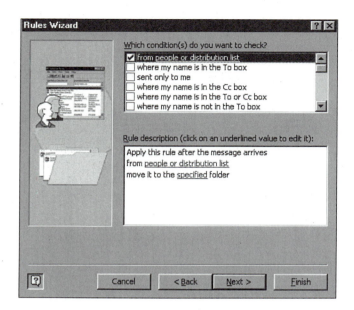

Figure 22.9
You can scroll through the list to see all the available conditions.

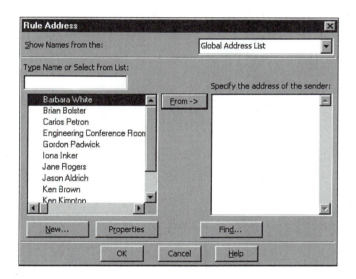

Figure 22.10
This dialog box displays a list of people in one of your address books.

Note

If you're using IMO Outlook, you usually have only one address book, although you can have more than one. If you're using C/W Outlook, you may have several address books, in which case you can choose the address book from which you want to select a name or distribution list.

8. Select the second underlined word or phrase in the lower wizard window—specified in this example. Outlook displays your folder list, as shown in Figure 22.11.

Figure 22.11
You may have to expand the folder list to see the name of a custom folder.

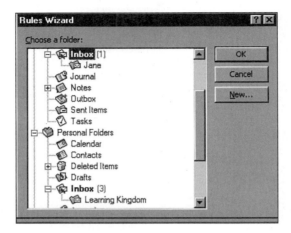

9. Select the folder into which you want Outlook to place items, then choose OK to return to the wizard window, which now looks like that in Figure 22.12.

Figure 22.12
Both the original underlined words or phrases in the lower box are replaced with your selections and are now displayed in black.

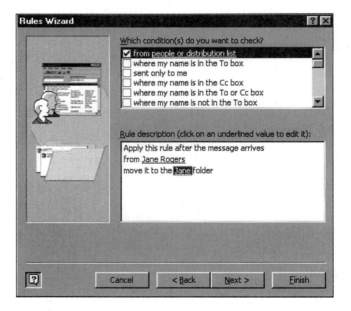

10. Choose <u>N</u>ext > to display the next wizard window, in which you can choose what you want to do with messages that satisfy the conditions you've previously specified.

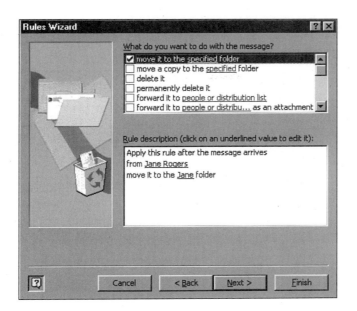

Figure 22.13
This window asks you what you want to do with the message.

11. You probably want to move messages that satisfy the conditions you've specified in previous wizard windows to the folder you've specified. This action is already checked. You can, of course, check other actions.

12. Choose <u>N</u>ext > to display the next wizard window, shown in Figure 22.14, in which you can specify exceptions to the rule.

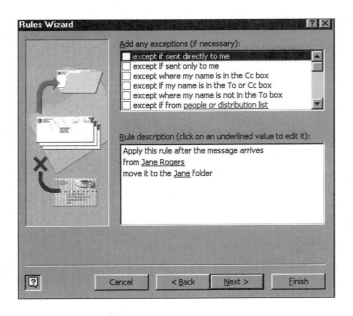

Figure 22.14
Use this window to select exceptions to the rule.

13. You don't have to select any exceptions, but you can check any appropriate exceptions. When you select an exception, a description of that exception is added to the rule description in the lower box. As an example, if you want to make messages marked as high importance exceptions, scroll down the list of exceptions and check Except if It Is Marked as Importance, as shown in Figure 22.15.

Figure 22.15
Now there's another underlined word (usually colored) in the description of the rule.

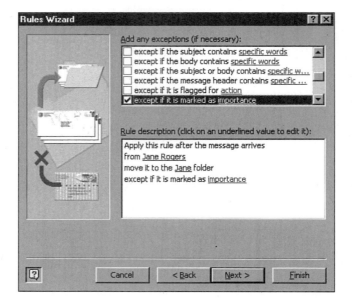

14. Click Importance in the lower box. Outlook displays the importance dialog box in which you can select Low, Normal, or High. Choose High, and then choose OK to return to the wizard window. The description now includes the importance you selected, as shown in Figure 22.16.

15. Choose Next > to display the final wizard window in which you supply a name for the rule, as shown in Figure 22.17.

16. Replace the suggested name with something more meaningful.

17. If you want to move messages you've previously received from Jane Rogers into the new folder, check Run This Rule Now on Messages Already in "Inbox."

18. If you want this new rule to begin testing incoming messages immediately, make sure Turn on This Rule is checked.

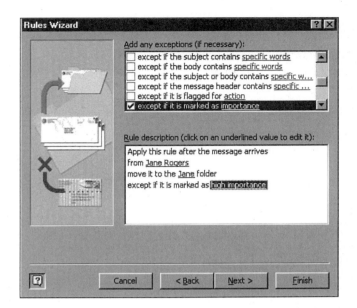

Figure 22.16
The rule description now shows that messages of high importance are excluded.

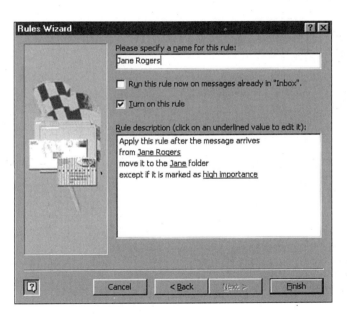

Figure 22.17
Outlook suggests the first replacement you made in the description box as the name for the new rule.

19. Choose Finish. Choose OK to return to the first wizard window that displays the name of the rule and its final description, as shown in Figure 22.18.

Figure 22.18
This is how the wizard window displays the completed rule.

Notice that the name of the rule appears in the upper box and the name is checked. Being checked, Outlook applies the rule to every message you receive and, if a message satisfies the conditions and doesn't contain anything that satisfies the exclusions, the actions of the rule occur. If you uncheck the rule name, Outlook doesn't apply the rule to incoming messages.

TESTING THE RULE

One way to test a rule is to receive a message that satisfies the rule's conditions and doesn't satisfy the rule's exclusions, and then verify that the actions of the rule occur. In the detailed example described in the preceding section, ask the person whose messages are specified in the rule to send you a message and see what happens. If the rule does what you intend, everything is probably alright. On the other hand, if the rule doesn't do what you intend, you'll have to modify it.

Outlook 2000 offers another way to test a rule—by running it now.

RUNNING A RULE NOW

Normally a rule that applies to incoming messages runs when messages are received. This was the only way to run a rule in Outlook 97 and Outlook 98. Outlook 2000 adds the capability to run a rule now.

Running a rule now means running a rule for messages that already exist in your folders. In the case of a rule that affects incoming messages, this means applying the rule to messages already in your Inbox folder. You can use this to test a rule you've just created and also to apply a new rule to messages that already exist in one of your folders.

Tip #149 from

Gordon Pool

Of course, if you chose in the final wizard window to apply the rule to existing messages in a folder, you'll be able to see if the rule works without running it now.

The rule described previously in this chapter affected incoming messages from a specific sender. If you already have messages from that sender in your Inbox, you can apply the rule to those messages.

To run a rule now:

1. Choose View, Folder List, and select the folder containing messages you want to use to test the rule.

2. Choose Tools, Rules Wizard to display the Rules Wizard.

3. Choose Run Now to display the dialog box shown in Figure 22.19.

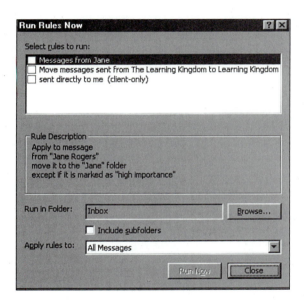

Figure 22.19
This dialog box shows all the available rules.

4. Check the rule you want to test. The Run in Folder box displays the name of the folder that contains the messages you want to use for the test. You can choose Browse to select a different folder.

5. Check Include Subfolders if you want to include messages in the selected folder's sub-folders in the test. Usually leave this box unchecked.

6. Open the Apply Rules To drop-down list and select All Messages, Unread Messages, or Read Messages.

7. Choose Run Now to run the rule.

8. Choose Close and then OK to close the dialog boxes.

9. If the folder list isn't already open choose <u>V</u>iew, Fold<u>e</u>r List and select the folder into which the rule should have moved messages. You should see the messages that satisfied the rule's conditions in the folder. If that's the case, your rule is working as it should. If that's not the case, you need to make changes to the rule.

MODIFYING A RULE

You can use the Rules Wizard to make changes to an existing rule.

To modify a rule:

1. With any Outlook Information viewer displayed, choose <u>T</u>ools, Ru<u>l</u>es Wizard to display the first wizard window that shows a list of existing rules.

2. Select the rule you want to modify, then choose <u>M</u>odify to display the wizard window shown previously in Figure 22.6, with the type of rule highlighted.

3. Make whatever changes are necessary by choosing another type of rule in the upper box or by clicking underlined text in the lower box to make different selections. You can choose <u>N</u>ext > to progress to subsequent wizard windows to make changes in them.

4. In any wizard window, choose Finish to signify you've finished making changes to the rule.

CREATING OTHER TYPES OF RULES FOR MESSAGES

The preceding example used one example of a rule to explain how rules for incoming messages are created and how they work.

You can use the Rules Wizard to create many types of rules for incoming and outgoing messages. These rules are

- Check Messages When They Arrive
- Check Messages After Sending
- Move New Messages from Someone
- Notify Me When Important Messages Arrive
- Move Messages Based on Content
- Delete a Conversation
- Flag Messages from Someone
- Assign Categories to Sent Messages
- Assign Categories Based on Content
- Move Messages I Sent to Someone
- Stop Processing All Following Rules

When you choose any of these types of rules, a description of that rule appears in the lower wizard window. The descriptions include underlined words or phrases (displayed in blue) that require more information. You can click on the underlined words or phrases to open a dialog box in which you can enter or select the required information.

Far too many combinations of rule types and added information required exist than can be covered individually in this chapter. The preceding example of a rule that applies to incoming messages (and the example later in this chapter of a rule that applies to outgoing messages) should give you the general idea about creating rules, and serve as examples for creating your own rules.

AUTOMATICALLY REPLYING TO MESSAGES

 If you're using C/W Outlook as a client for Exchange, you can create rules that automatically send replies to messages. For example, if you're going to be out of town for a few days, you can create a rule that detects messages from certain people, or about certain subjects, and sends a reply explaining you're away and will reply when you get back. This rule can be created to run on the server, so it works even though your computer is turned off or you've taken it with you.

Note

> You can create the same rule to run on IMO Outlook or on C/W Outlook that isn't a client for Exchange. In this case, though, you would have to leave your computer on with Outlook running for the rule to operate.

Outlook uses a *template (page 520)* for the message to be sent as a reply. Your first task, therefore, is to create the message you want sent as a reply and save it as an Outlook template.

→ For information about creating e-mail templates, **see** "Creating an E-mail Template," **p. 520**.

After creating the template, follow these steps to create the rule. Because the steps are similar to those previously described, most of them are described only in outline form.

To create a rule that sends an automatic response to a message:

1. In the first Rules Wizard window, check Check Messages When They Arrive.

2. In the second wizard window, check Where My Name Is in the To Box.

3. In the third wizard window, check Reply Using a Specific Template.

4. In the Description box, select the underlined words A Specific Template. Outlook displays the dialog box shown in Figure 22.20.

5. Open the Look In drop-down list and choose User Templates in System to see a list of the templates you created.

6. Select the message template you want to use for the reply then choose Open to return to the wizard window that now contains the complete file name of the template.

7. Choose Finish to save the rule.

Figure 22.20
This dialog box initially displays your standard templates.

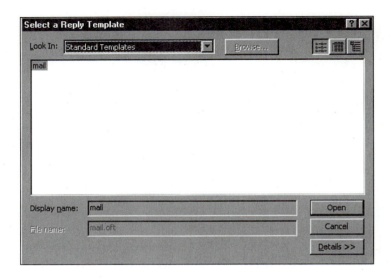

If, while you're away, somebody sends you a message that requests your reply be sent to someone else, the Outlook rule sends the reply to the message sender instead of to the person designated to receive the reply. For detailed information on this point, refer to the Microsoft Knowledge Base article Q186691, *Inbox Assistant Replies to Sender not Alternate Recipient*.

CREATING A RULE BASED ON A MESSAGE

Instead of creating a rule from scratch, as described previously in this chapter, you can create a rule based on some of the information in a message you've received. For example, you may want to create a rule that applies to future messages you receive from a specific sender.

To create a rule based on a message you've received:

1. In the Inbox Information viewer, double-click a message from the person for whom you want to create a new rule to display that message in a Message form.

2. In the form's menu bar, choose Actions, Create Rule. Outlook displays the first Rules Wizard window, as shown in Figure 22.21.

The first four conditions offered by the wizard are based on

- Who sent the message
- Who the message was addressed to
- The subject of the message

You can use these conditions, or the others available, to create a rule.

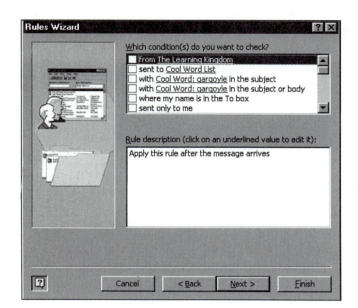

Figure 22.21
This wizard window contains some conditions based on the message.

CREATING RULES FOR OUTGOING MESSAGES

The process of creating rules to be applied to messages you send is the same as creating rules to be applied to incoming messages. The most frequently used rule of this type is one that saves copies of certain messages you send in a folder other than the usual Sent Items folder.

The following steps describe the creation of a rule that saves messages in which a specific word or phrase appears in the subject of the message into a folder other than the Inbox folder. Because the details of creating such a rule are the same as those described previously in this chapter, the following steps merely outline the procedure.

To create a rule that saves copies of messages you send in a specific folder:

1. In the first Rules Wizard window, choose Move Messages I Send to Someone.
2. In the second wizard window, choose a condition such as With Specific Words in the Subject.
3. Choose the underlined words in the Description box and replace those words with explicit words or phrases.
4. Choose Next and then define any exceptions to the rule.
5. Choose Next and then enter a name for the rule.
6. Choose Finish.

MANAGING RULES

The Rules Wizard automatically saves the rules you create in a file with the file name extension .rwz. If you're using IMO Outlook, this file is Microsoft Outlook Internet Settings.rwz; if you're using C/W Outlook, this file has the name of your profile as its file name.

Outlook imposes a maximum size of 32 kB for the rules you save. The size of each rule varies according to its complexity. You can typically save between 40 and 50 rules. If you attempt to save a rule when no more space for rules is available, Outlook displays a message telling you "Changes to the rule could not be saved. There is not enough memory or the rules are too complex. Try deleting some rules."

RENAMING A RULE

You can easily rename a rule. To do so, display the first Rules Wizard window, shown previously in Figure 22.6. Select the rule you want to rename, then choose Rename to display the dialog box shown in Figure 22.22.

Figure 22.22
The current name of the selected rule is displayed in the New Name of Rule box.

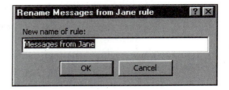

Edit the current name.

COPYING A RULE

A convenient way to create a new rule that's similar to an existing one is to copy the existing rule. To do so, display the first Rules Wizard window, shown previously in Figure 22.6. Select the rule you want to copy, then choose Copy. Outlook adds the copied rule to the list of rules. The copy has a name starting with "Copy of" followed by the name of the rule that was copied. Choose Rename to change the name to something more appropriate.

You can make changes to the rule's actions, conditions, and exceptions in much the same way you create a new rule. You can select any of the underlined words and phrases in the Rule Description box to make changes.

DELETING A RULE

To delete a rule, select it in the first Rules Wizard window, then choose Delete. Outlook displays a dialog box in which you are asked to confirm the deletion. Choose Yes.

REORDERING RULES

Outlook applies rules to messages in the order those rules are listed in the Rules Wizard. In the case of incoming messages, Outlook applies rules to messages as they arrive in your Inbox folder. If a rule moves a message from the Inbox folder to another folder, rules are no longer applied to that message. In the case of an Outgoing message, Outlook applies rules to messages as they arrive in the Sent Items folder.

To change the order in which rules are applied to messages, display the list of rules in the first Rules Wizard window. Select a rule you want to move up or down in the list and then choose Move Up or Move Down.

EXPORTING AND IMPORTING RULES

You can export a set of rules to a file, and you can import a set of rules from a file.

Tip #150 from

To copy a set of rules from one computer to another, export the rules from the first computer then import those rules into the second computer. You can import rules from a computer running Outlook 98, but you can't import rules from Outlook 97.

To export a set of rules:

1. Choose Options in the first Rules Wizard window to display the dialog box shown in Figure 22.23.

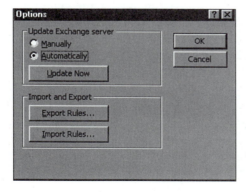

Figure 22.23
Use this dialog box to export or import a set of rules.

Note

The dialog box shown here is what you see if you're using C/W Outlook as a client for Exchange. If you're using C/W Outlook and don't have the Microsoft Exchange Server information service in your profile, or if you're using IMO Outlook, a smaller dialog box containing only the Export Rules and Import Rules button is displayed.

2. Choose Export Rules to display the dialog box shown in Figure 22.24.

Figure 22.24
Outlook proposes to save the exported rules in a file named Untitled.rwz. The dialog box is shown here after the name Outlook proposes has been changed.

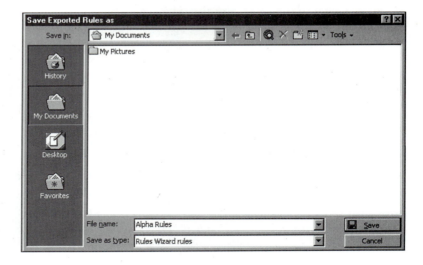

3. Navigate to the Windows folder in which you want to save the rules.

4. Change the name of the file that will be created to something meaningful (Outlook automatically supplies .rwz as the file name extension) and choose OK to save the file.

Use similar steps to import rules from a file. In this case, choose Import Rules in the Options dialog box to display the Import Rules From dialog box. Navigate to the Windows folder that contains the file to be imported, select the file, and choose Open.

CREATING CONDITIONAL RULES

If you create several rules, Outlook normally executes the rules in the order they're listed in the Apply Rules in the Following Order box, such as in the example previously shown in Figure 22.18. You can also create a set of rules in such a way that one rule executes under certain conditions and a different rule executes under other conditions. For example, you might want to create rules that:

- Copy all messages addressed directly to you into a specific folder
- Copy all messages that have specific Subject text to a different folder

You can do this by using Stop Processing More Rules, as described in the following procedure.

To create conditional rules that move messages addressed to you into a folder named Personal Messages and other messages that contain "Alpha" in the subject box to a folder named Alpha Messages:

1. If the folders into which you want to move incoming mail messages don't already exist, create them. The remaining steps assume you named the two folders Personal Messages and Alpha Messages.

→ For information about creating new folders, **see** "Creating Folders and Subfolders," **P. 922**.

2. Choose Tools, Rules Wizard to display the first Rules Wizard dialog box shown previously in Figure 22.18.

3. Choose New to display the second wizard window.

4. In the Which Type of Rule Do You Want to Create list, select Check Messages When They Arrive, then choose Next > to display the next wizard window.

5. Check Where My Name Is in the To Box, then choose Next > to display the next wizard window.

6. Check Move a Copy to the Specified Folder then select the underlined word "Specified" in the Rule Description box to display the dialog box in which you can select a folder.

7. Select the folder into which you want messages addressed to you moved (Personal Messages in this case), then choose OK to return to the wizard window in which the Rule Description box now contains the name of the folder you selected.

8. Scroll down to the bottom of the What Do You Want to Do with the Message box and check Stop Processing More Rules.

Note

At this point, the Rule Description box contains this description of your rule:

Apply this rule after the message arrives
where my name is in the To box
move a copy to the Personal Messages folder
and stop processing more rules

9. Choose Next > to display the next wizard window. You probably don't want any exceptions, so choose Next > to display the final wizard window.

10. Enter an appropriate name for the rule (such as Messages to Me), then choose Finish. That completes creating the first rule. You can see its name listed in the first Rules Wizard window.

11 Choose New to begin creating the second rule that will move messages with "Alpha" in the subject into the Alpha Messages folder.

12. Select Check Messages When They Arrive, then choose Next >.

13. Select the condition With Specific Words in the Subject.

14. Select the underlined words "Specific Words" in the Rule Description box to display

the Search Text dialog box. Enter "Alpha" in the Add New box, then choose Add. The word you entered is now listed in the Search List box. Choose OK to return to the wizard window in which the Rule Description box contains the word you just specified. Choose Next > to display the next wizard window.

15. Select Move a Copy to the Specified Folder, then select the underlined word "Specified" in the Rule Description box. Select the folder into which you want to move Alpha messages (as previously described in step 7) then choose OK to return to the wizard window. Choose Next > to open the next wizard window.

16. Select any exceptions to the rule in this window, then choose Next > to open the final wizard window.

17. Enter a name for the rule (such as Alpha Messages), then choose Finish. The two rules are now listed in the first Rules Wizard window.

You haven't quite finished yet. The Rules Wizard automatically lists rules in alphabetical order by the name you give them. If you've followed the previous procedure, you'll have two rules: Alpha Messages followed by Messages to Me. If you leave the messages listed in this way, Outlook will process the Alpha Messages rule first and then the Messages to Me rule.

At this point, you have to consider what you want to happen to a message that's addressed to you and has Alpha in its subject. As things stand now, the first rule copies such a message to the Alpha Messages folder, leaving the original message in your Inbox bolder. Then, the second rule runs, copying the message into your Personal Messages folder. You now have copies of the message in the Alpha Messages folder and in the Personal Messages folder.

If you change the order of the two rules so that the Messages to Me rule runs first, the result is different. The Messages to Me rule makes a copy of the message in your Personal Messages folder but the Alpha Messages rule doesn't run (due to Stop Processing More Rules in the Messages to Me rule). So, you only have a copy of the message in your Personal Messages folder.

Before leaving this subject, let's consider one more possibility. If you had included Stop Process More Rules in the Alpha Messages rule and that rule is processed first, a message addressed to you with Alpha in its Subject would be copied only to the Alpha Messages folder.

→ For information about changing the order of rules, see "Reordering Rules," p. 639.

Note

Although it might take some head scratching, you can set up quite complex rule processing, much like the If and Case constructs you'll be familiar with if you've done any programming. When you enable two or more conditions within a rule, all those conditions must be satisfied for the rule to run. If you want the rule to run if any one of several conditions is satisfied, you must place each condition in a separate rule. Use Stop Processing More Rules in specific rules, as described in this section, to prevent subsequent rules running.

Plan ahead before you start creating a set of conditional rules. One way to do that is to create a diagram of what you want to achieve. Then you can base the design of individual rules on that diagram.

DEALING WITH JUNK MAIL

If you use Outlook to receive Internet e-mail, you probably receive a lot of junk mail that you'd rather not have to bother with. Outlook contains a built-in filter you can turn on so that messages containing certain words and phrases in the subject or body are ignored. If you don't turn the filter on, messages containing these words and phrases are handled normally.

To see the list of words and phrases that Outlook looks for, open the file named Filters.txt. This file is usually in the same Windows folder as Outlook. The easiest way to find it is to use the Windows Find command or, from within Outlook, choose Tools, Advanced Find. Double-click the file name to open it in Windows Notepad or another text editor.

Note

The purpose of opening Filters.txt is to see what words and phrases Outlook uses to identify junk mail. Don't attempt to edit this file.

TURNING ON JUNK MAIL FILTERS

With the Inbox Information viewer displayed, choose Organizer in the Standard toolbar. At the left side of the Organizer pane, choose Junk E-mail to display the pane shown in Figure 22.25.

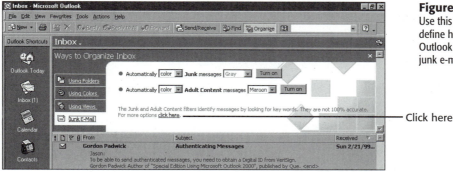

Figure 22.25
Use this pane to define how you want Outlook to handle junk e-mail.

Click here

If you looked at the contents of the Filters.txt file previously mentioned, you saw that the file lists two types of unwanted mail: Junk and Adult Content. You can determine how you want Outlook to handle these two types of mail. For each type, you can tell Outlook to

- Color or move the mail
- If you choose to move it, which folder to move it to

Make these selections by opening the drop-down lists in the pane and selecting from them.

After you've made your selections, choose Turn On to turn the filters on. After you choose Turn On, the button labels change to Turn Off. Choose the Turn Off buttons to turn the filters off.

Tip #151 from

I suggest you initially choose to color Junk and Adult Content messages. Use Outlook that way for a few days to see which type of messages Outlook detects. After that, if you're satisfied, you might prefer to have Outlook automatically send Junk and Adult Content messages to a Junk E-mail folder that Outlook automatically creates.

ADDING A SENDER TO THE JUNK OR ADULT CONTENT LIST

To add the name of a sender to the Junk or Adult Content lists, right-click a message from that sender in the Inbox Information viewer to display a context menu. Move the pointer onto Junk E-mail and choose either Add to Junk Senders List or Add to Adult Content Senders List. Outlook displays a message confirming that the selected name has been added to the list you chose.

You can also add names to the Junk and Adult Content lists, and remove names you previously added by displaying another view of the Organize pane. To display this view, choose Click Here in the pane shown previously in Figure 22.22. The new view is shown in Figure 22.26.

Figure 22.26
Use this pane if you want to edit your lists of junk and adult content mail senders.

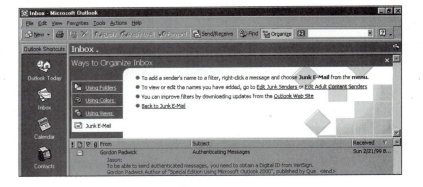

Choose Edit Junk Senders to display the dialog box shown in Figure 22.27. Choose Edit Adult Content Senders to display a similar dialog box.

The pane shown previously in Figure 22.26 invites you to visit Microsoft's Outlook Web site to download improved filters. At the time this book was written, the only improved filters offered was Omron's MailJail. One of these is MailJail Lite for Outlook 98. Perhaps a version for Outlook 2000 will become available.

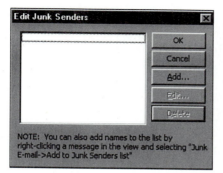

Figure 22.27
You can use this dialog box to add or delete senders, or to edit existing senders. The dialog box is shown here with no junk senders identified.

IMPROVING HOW OUTLOOK HANDLES JUNK E-MAIL

So far, you've learned how to use the Organize pane to set up Outlook so that it detects junk e-mail. You can gain more control over this by using the Rules Wizard to create a customized rule.

→ For information about using the Rules Wizard to create rules, **see** "Using the Rules Wizard to Create Rules That Manage Incoming Messages," **p. 624**.

To create a customized rule that handles junk e-mail:

1. Choose Tools, Rules Wizard to open the Rules Wizard.

2. In the first wizard window, choose New.

3. In the second wizard window, select Check Messages When They Arrive.

4. In the third wizard window, select Suspected to Be Junk E-mail or from Junk Senders.

5. Choose 'Junk Senders'. Outlook displays the Edit Junk Senders dialog box.

6. Use the Edit Junk Senders dialog box to add senders to your list, or to edit or delete existing senders.

7. In the fourth wizard window, select what you want Outlook to do when it detects suspected junk e-mail. You'll probably want to select Move It to a Specified Folder.

8. Choose Specified. Outlook displays a dialog box that lists your folders. Select the folder into which you want Outlook to move suspected junk e-mail.

9. In the fifth wizard window, select any exceptions to the new rule.

10. In the sixth wizard window, name the new rule and make sure it's turned on.

11. Choose Finish to return to the first wizard window that lists the new rule.

You can follow an almost identical procedure to create a customized rule for detecting messages that contain suspected adult content.

CREATING RULES WITH OR CONDITIONS

Most of the rules you create by using the Rules Wizard test for only one condition such as:

- Where My Name Is in the To Box
- Sent Only to Me

However, if you examine the list of conditions offered by the Rules Wizard, you'll find some that contain the word "or." You can use these conditions to test for one thing or the other. Some examples of these are

- From People or Distribution List
- Suspected to Be Junk E-mail or from Junk Senders

TROUBLESHOOTING RULES

If you're careful while you go through the steps of the Rules Wizard, you'll probably find that your individual rules work. But, if a rule doesn't work as you intend, it's probably because you made an incorrect selection or supplied invalid information. The only solution to this is to carefully examine each Rules Wizard window and make the necessary corrections.

After you've created several rules, those rules are listed in the first Rules Wizard window. Outlook runs those rules that are checked in the order they are listed. If you run into trouble with processing rules, the first step is to make sure that each rule works individually. You can do that by having only one rule checked at a time.

When you're satisfied that each rule runs as intended by itself, consider the order of the rules. One common problem is that a rule may move an incoming message to a folder other than the folder on which the rules operate. If this happens, subsequent rules won't operate on the message that's been moved.

You may be able to correct a problem with multiple rules by changing their order. To do this, display the list of rules in the Rules Wizard, select a rule you want to move, and then choose the Move Up or Move Down button.

The most difficult rule problems to solve are those that can (and do) occur if you're using Stop Processing More Rules to create conditional rule processing.

→ For information about Stop Processing More Rules, **see** "Creating Conditional Rules," **p. 640**.

You may well find that a set of conditional rules work fine most of the time but, under some circumstances, don't do what you intend. Welcome to the world of computer programming! Only systematic analysis can solve these types of problems. One technique is to create a diagram (programmers call it a flow chart) that illustrates how you want your rules to work. Having done that, examine the details of each rule to check that each one is constructed properly.

CHAPTER **23**

MANAGING OUTLOOK FOR A WORKGROUP

In this chapter   *by Gordon Padwick*

WHAT IS A WORKGROUP?

Like many other words we often use, *workgroup* means different things to different people. A workgroup may be just a few people who work together in a small office; at the other extreme, a workgroup may be a large number of people who work in many different locations.

This chapter focuses on a small number of people, all of whom work in the same location. It's way beyond the scope of this book to deal with managing large, scattered, groups of people; for information on that subject, I refer you to books about managing networks such as *Using Networks*, published by Que.

Microsoft provides extensive information about deploying and supporting the Office suite in a workgroup and enterprise environment in the Office Resource Kit.

→ For information about what's in the Office 2000 Resource Kit, **see** "Using the Office 2000 Resource Kit," **p. 1291**.

BEING CONSISTENT

Consistency is the key to productivity in a workgroup. By consistency, I mean:

- Everyone uses the same suite of Office applications. Because this book is about a member of Microsoft's Office suite, I assume all members of the workgroup use Word for word processing, Excel for spreadsheets, Outlook for communications and personal information management, and so on.

- Everyone uses the same version of all applications. Because this book is about a member of the Office 2000 suite, I assume all members of the workgroup are using that.

- Everyone upgrades from a previous version of the chosen suite at the same time, or within as short a period as possible. Unfortunately, files created in one version of an application can be incompatible with another application.

Tip #152 from

Gordon Padwick

The Office 2000 Resource Kit contains information about dealing with file incompatibilies between versions of Office.

- Everyone sets up applications in the same way.
- Data that several people use is exactly the same for everyone. By shared data, I mean spelling dictionaries, address lists, templates, styles, graphics images, Outlook's categories and entry types, and so on.

I realize that this ideal is not always possible; however, it should be the objective.

One possible problem is that some workgroup members may need to share files with customers, clients, and suppliers. This may mean that those people need to have applications in addition to the standard workgroup applications.

Another possible problem may be that some workgroup members do work at home where they already have applications other than the workgroup standard in use. It's unfortunate that continually converting files from one format to another causes time-consuming problems. It takes a wise and tactful manager to provide those people with legal copies of the applications used in the office, and to persuade the home workers to use those applications for office work.

Getting everyone's cooperation to use a common set of applications is rarely easy. Human nature being what it is, the more skilled and experienced a person is, the more difficult it often is to persuade that person to accept a standard that's different from their preference.

PART

IV

CH

23

In my experience, the effective approach is to get everyone together and first focus on getting agreement to the concept that it is best for everyone if they all use the same applications and the same setups for those applications. After getting agreement on that, it should be possible to get everyone to buy into the idea of debating the benefits of various possibilities and accepting the majority opinion. In a large organization, such an approach isn't possible. In that case, a decision has to be made from on high. Then employees have to understand that if they want to work in the organization, they use the applications provided.

The remainder of this chapter and, in fact, this entire book assumes that the workgroup is using, preferably by consensus, Office 2000 as the standard suite of Office applications.

USING IMO OR C/W OUTLOOK

All the members of a small workgroup should use the same Outlook installation option: either IMO or C/W.

Although the subject is dealt with elsewhere in this book, I'll take a few moments here to remind you about them. Both options allow you to use Outlook as a *personal information manager (PIM) (page 14)* to maintain your personal calendar, keep an address book, have a to-do list, and keep track of what you've done, but the two installation options differ in the way you send and receive e-mail messages and faxes, and how you collaborate with other people. Here are the essential differences:

- Internet Mail Only (IMO)—You can use the IMO installation of Outlook to send and receive e-mail by way of the Internet or an intranet that uses the standard Internet protocols. You can share information with other people by way of Net Folders. You can use IMO Outlook to send and receive messages from an Exchange Server providing that server is set up to support the IMAP4 protocol. You can send and receive faxes using WinFAX SE.

- Corporate/Workgroup (C/W)—With this installation option, you can add services to your profile that allow you to send and receive e-mail by way of the Internet and an intranet, and also by way of messaging systems based on Microsoft's Exchange Server, Microsoft Mail, Lotus cc:Mail, or other MAPI-compatible e-mail systems. If you're using Exchange Server, you can share information in public folders, but you can't do that with Microsoft Mail or Lotus cc:Mail. An add-on available from Lotus gives C/W Outlook the ability to use Lotus Notes for e-mail and sharing information. You can send and receive faxes using Microsoft Fax.

Tip #153 from

[signature]

If you only occasionally send and receive faxes, WinFAX SE (used with IMO Outlook) will probably satisfy your needs. Microsoft Fax (used with C/W Outlook) provides more capabilities, including the ability to share one fax line between several computers for sending, but not receiving, faxes. You can replace WinFax SE or Microsoft Fax with a third-party fax application, such as Symantec's WinFax Pro, to obtain enhanced faxing capabilities in IMO or C/W Outlook.

Because the simple approach that works is usually the best, you should first consider whether IMO Outlook can satisfy your needs. IMO Outlook has several advantages over C/W Outlook:

- It's less demanding of system resources (disk space and RAM)
- It starts up and closes down faster
- It provides a faster, and more informative, way to send and receive Internet e-mail

On the downside, each person using IMO Outlook usually needs a connection (modem and phone line) to an Internet service provider (ISP) and an account with that ISP.

If workgroup members don't use the phone much for voice or fax communications, and don't send and receive many e-mail messages, IMO Outlook is probably a good choice. On the other hand, if workgroup members regularly use the phone for voice communication as well as for sending and receiving e-mail messages, each person will need a separate modem and phone line to connect with their ISP. For a home office, IMO Outlook usually works well; it's less satisfactory for a business office.

Small offices in which people need to send frequent e-mail messages to each other should probably install C/W Outlook, interconnect their computers by way of a peer-to-peer LAN using Ethernet, and use Microsoft Mail to send messages to each other. A peer-to-peer LAN using Microsoft Mail doesn't need a server; any computer on the network can host a postoffice that routes messages between workgroup members. If workgroup members need to send and receive external e-mail messages, they need to have separate modems and phone lines to connect to the ISP.

Members of a busy workgroup that handles many internal and external e-mail messages need a server-based LAN. Microsoft offers the Small Business Server package, which includes Windows NT Server and Microsoft Exchange with licenses for up to 25 users. With this package installed on a server, workgroup members can send messages and exchange information among themselves, and can use one or more shared modems to send and receive Internet e-mail messages and faxes.

Tip #154 from

> If you choose to go with Microsoft Exchange, you need to have one person to administer it, a task that is definitely more than trivial. If your business depends on being able to communicate, and you use Exchange as the basis of your communications, your business depends on Exchange being up and running. Your Exchange Administrator should take the time to not only understand how to create accounts, but also to learn how to get things up and running when Exchange goes down.

After reviewing this, if you're alone in a home office or a member of a small workgroup, you should probably choose IMO Outlook. If you're a member of anything more than a very small workgroup, you should probably choose C/W Outlook. Of course, if you have access to a mail server other than an Internet server, you must choose C/W Outlook.

Tip #155 from

> If you choose a server-based network, the computer used as the server should not have any software other than that required by the server installed on it. Don't install Office or any other user application on the server. If you do, you can expect to experience network crashes.
>
> The reason is this: If you install Office applications (or other applications) on the server, you will use them from time to time. Many applications aren't as good as they ought to be about managing memory. The result is that using applications (even after closing them) can result in memory being locked up. Managing a network requires adequate access to memory. If you've locked memory due to using an errant application, the server crashes.
>
> Microsoft's Windows NT Server has been undeservedly given the reputation of being unreliable. This, I think, is due to the fact that network managers can easily install and use applications under Windows Server. Don't do that. Other servers are perceived as being more reliable because they can't easily be used to run applications and don't, therefore, invite the problem.
>
> Install Windows Server on a computer that's used as a server. Don't try to use applications on the server.

HAVING CONSISTENT OUTLOOK CONFIGURATIONS

Having made the decision that all workgroup members use the same Outlook service option, either IMO or C/W, the next thing to consider is how to share information such as address books and categories.

Outlook keeps information in two places:

- Files saved on users' hard disks or on the server
- The Windows registry

SHARING FOLDERS

Consider contact lists as an example. Each user should have one contact list for keeping personal information; that list doesn't need to be shared. In addition, there should be a shared list for business contacts. Using a shared list for business contacts eliminates the trouble of manually adding new contact information and updating old information separately on each computer.

If the workgroup computers aren't interconnected by way of a LAN, you can keep a master contact list on one computer. At regular intervals, use Outlook's Import and Export capability, described in Chapter 19, to export the master contact list to a removable disk. Subsequently, import the master list to other computers.

→ For information about sharing Outlook items and settings among users, **see** "Sharing Items with Other Outlook Users," **p. 570**.

If the workgroup uses IMO Outlook, you can use *Net Folders (page 453)* to share information. One person creates a Net Folder that contains a Contacts folder, and makes the Net Folder available to others for sharing. The person who creates the Net Folder can allow specific people access to the folder and specify whether each person can read, write, or edit items in the folder, as explained in Chapter 14. The contents of the Net Folder on each computer are synchronized at specified intervals by way of the Internet.

→ For information about Net Folders, **see** "What Is a Net Folder?," **p. 466**.

If the workgroup uses C/W Outlook with an Exchange server, you can use public folders, saved in the Exchange store, to share information. Public folders on an Exchange server work much like Net Folders. The significant difference is that each workgroup member normally has instant access to information in *public folders (page 704)*.

→ For information about public folders, **see** "Using Public Folders," **p. 704**.

The three ways of sharing a contact list described here are examples of what can be done. Other ways are available depending on the type of server the workgroup uses. Also, note that sharing information isn't limited to a contact list. You can, for example, share a workgroup calendar, project information, product information, or whatever other type of information the workgroup uses.

SHARING INFORMATION IN THE REGISTRY

Outlook, like Windows and other Windows applications, keeps a lot of information about itself in the Windows registry. In addition to information about itself, Outlook also keeps certain information provided by users in the registry. Two important examples are

- A user's Outlook categories (used to organize all types of Outlook items)
- A user's list of entry types (used when creating journal items)

As I've mentioned several times in this book, one of the keys to using Outlook efficiently is to be meticulous about consistently assigning categories to all Outlook items. All workgroup members should use the same master category list in order to share items so that each member can easily organize them.

→ For information about coordinating category lists within a workgroup, **see** "Sharing Your Personal Category List," **p. 612.**

Tip #156 from	Sharing a master category lists requires working with the Windows registry. Appendix F, "Working with the Windows Registry," contains an introduction to this subject. For more detailed information, refer to *Using the Microsoft Windows 98 Registry*, published by Que.

Although not as important as categories, it's certainly desirable for all workgroup members to share the same set of Outlook Entry Types so that members can share Journal items in an organized manner. Entry types are saved in the Windows registry, though in a format that's different from Categories.

Tip #157 from	One of the CD-ROMs for the Premium Edition of Office 2000 contains a file named RegKey.xls. That file contains a complete list of registry keys used by all Office 2000 applications.

Using Outlook as a Client for Exchange Server, Microsoft Mail, and cc:Mail

CHAPTER 24

EXCHANGE SERVER OVERVIEW

In this chapter

by Gordon Padwick

OUTLOOK AS A CLIENT FOR EXCHANGE

Outlook is Microsoft's premier client for Exchange server. Although Outlook can be used as a client for other e-mail servers, it is as an Exchange client that Outlook offers its full capabilities.

Note You don't have to use Outlook to access e-mail and other information in Exchange. You can use various applications available from Microsoft and other companies.

The next four chapters provide detailed information about using Outlook as a client for Exchange. This chapter briefly explains what Exchange is and what it can do. This chapter doesn't provide detailed information about administering Exchange. Refer to a book such as *Using Microsoft Exchange Server 5.5, Special Edition*, published by Que, for that information.

If you're already familiar with Exchange Server, you should probably skip this chapter.

WHAT IS EXCHANGE?

Before going any further, I should point out that Microsoft has used the name Exchange for two completely different products. Windows 95 contained an application known as Exchange that was a mail client intended for use with Microsoft Mail, Internet e-mail, and a few other e-mail systems. It was, in fact, the precursor of Outlook, which became available in Office 97. This Exchange is now known as Windows Messaging.

The other Exchange, the one that's the subject of this chapter, is a mail server. It became available in 1996.

Exchange is the heart of corporate messaging and collaboration systems. It includes facilities for:

- Transmitting e-mail messages between computer users
- Connecting to other e-mail systems including the Internet, Lotus Notes, Lotus cc:Mail, Microsoft Mail, and IBM PROFS
- Automatically responding to messages according to user-defined rules
- Recalling and replacing messages you've previously sent but haven't been read by recipients
- Providing a way for people to vote on issues and for the results of those votes to be tallied
- Allowing individual users to assign delegates
- Allowing users to work offline and from time-to-time to synchronize their information with that maintained on an Exchange server
- Acting as an information store that can be used to publish information
- Acting as an electronic bulletin board

- Organizing Web pages for a group to share
- Scheduling group activities such as meetings
- Hosting online meetings
- Creating and distributing electronic forms

The preceding list is intended to give you an idea of the scope of Exchange's capabilities, and is by no means comprehensive.

Exchange can be used as a messaging and collaboration system by groups of almost any size. It's available as part of Microsoft's Small Business Server package with licenses for only five people. At the other end of the spectrum, Exchange can be used by international enterprises with hundreds of thousands of employees.

Note

> At the time this chapter was written, Microsoft was shipping Exchange version 5.0 with the Small Business Server package. This chapter, as well as other information about Exchange throughout this book, primarily deals with version 5.5, the latest version of Exchange.

Exchange runs under Windows NT Server and is, in many ways, integrated with NT Server. For example, Exchange can be installed in such a way that each user can have a single password to log on to the server network and on to Exchange. Exchange can be set up to share user account information with Windows NT, thus simplifying an administrator's tasks.

PART
V

CH
24

STORING INFORMATION

Exchange saves information in what's known as information *stores*. There are three information stores: *Public*, *Private*, and *Directory*. Prior to version 5.5, each of these stores had a maximum capacity of 16 GB. While this is more than sufficient for small organizations, it is not adequate for large enterprises. In version 5.5, the maximum capacity of each store has been increased to 16,000 GB.

Each user keeps e-mail and other personal information in the Private store. An Exchange administrator can limit the amount of space available to each user. Shared information is kept in the Public store.

Note

> If you use Outlook as a client for Exchange, you can choose whether you want to save e-mail messages and other information in the Exchange store or in a Personal Folders file on your computer's hard drive.

When a person sends a message to a number of people, Exchange saves that message only once, a technique known as *single-instance message storage*. The message remains in the store until the last recipient deletes it.

SENDING AND RECEIVING E-MAIL

You can send and receive e-mail within the Exchange environment. You can also use Exchange to connect to other e-mail environments.

WORKING IN THE EXCHANGE ENVIRONMENT

With Outlook as your mail client, you can create messages and choose Send. As long as your computer is connected to Exchange Server, your messages are immediately sent to the Exchange information store and, from there, to the recipients' inboxes. Similarly, messages sent to you arrive from the Exchange information store in your inbox.

SENDING AND RECEIVING INTERNET MESSAGES

You can use Exchange to send and receive e-mail messages and other information by way of the Internet or an intranet. Exchange supports many Internet *protocols (page 39)*, including the following:

- Simple Mail Transfer Protocol (SMTP)—Used to send e-mail messages to an Internet or intranet e-mail server
- Post Office Protocol 3 (POP3)—The most common protocol used to retrieve messages from an Internet or intranet e-mail server
- Internet Mail Access Protocol 4 (IMAP4)—Another protocol used to retrieve messages from an Internet or intranet e-mail server
- Network News Transfer Protocol (NNTP):—Used to send and receive newsgroup messages
- Lightweight Directory Access Protocol (LDAP)—Used to read and write information to Internet or intranet directories
- Hypertext Transport Protocol (HTTP)—Used for sending hypertext documents on the Internet or an intranet
- Hypertext Markup Language (HTML)—A language used to create hypertext documents
- Simple Security Layer (SSL)—Used to protect data traveling on the Internet
- Secure MultiPurpose Internet Mail Extensions (S/MIME)—Used to secure attachments to e-mail messages

The preceding list contains only the major Internet protocols Exchange supports.

Because Exchange supports all the major Internet protocols, you can use Outlook and any other Internet e-mail client to send and receive messages from your Exchange information store.

COMMUNICATING WITH OTHER MESSAGING SYSTEMS

You can interchange e-mail messages with users who use other messaging systems.

Quite often, organizations that have been using earlier messaging systems such as cc:Mail want to upgrade to Exchange but can only do so in phases. That's not a problem because Exchange includes a cc:Mail connector that makes it possible to send messages to, and receive messages from, cc:Mail users.

IBM's Lotus Notes and Microsoft Exchange are today's major contenders for enterprise e-mail and collaboration systems. It doesn't have to be one or the other. With the recent acquisition of Linkage Software, Microsoft has been able to enhance and integrate Linkage technology into Exchange version 5.5 to provide reliable connectivity with Lotus Notes.

Many large organizations have invested substantial resources into creating messaging systems based on IBM's PROFS OfficeVision and SNADS messaging systems running on mainframe computers and minicomputers. Exchange version 5.5 includes Linkage technology that can link Exchange to these systems.

AUTOMATING MESSAGING

You can create rules to automate how Exchange deals with e-mail. For example, you can use a rule, known as the Out-of-Office Assistant, to deal with e-mail that arrives while you're not logged on to Exchange. You can use this rule to send an automatic response to the sender saying that you're out of the office until a certain date and will respond to the message when you return. Or, you can use the rule to automatically route the message to someone else.

You can use Exchange rules in many other ways. For example, you could create a rule that redirects a message in which a certain word or phrase is mentioned to another person.

DELEGATING YOUR WORK

You can give one or more people delegate access to any of your Outlook folders. These people must, of course, have Exchange accounts. For each delegate, you can provide access to one or more of your Outlook folders. You can assign three levels of access for each person to each folder:

- Reviewer access—This only allows the delegate to read items in a folder
- Author access—This allows the delegate to read items and create new items in a folder
- Editor access—In addition to being able to read items and create new items, this allows the delegate to modify existing items

Although you grant a delegate access to read items in your folders, by default, Outlook doesn't allow delegates to read items you've marked as private. However, you have the option of granting specific delegates permission to see your private items.

→ To learn more about granting access to your private Outlook items, **see** "Delegating Access to Your Folders," **p. 691**.

If you have delegate access to someone else's Exchange account, you can send e-mail messages on behalf of that person. Recipients see messages sent in this way with the actual sender's name and the name of the person on behalf of whom the message was sent.

SHARING YOUR FOLDERS

You can share the Outlook folders that you keep in the Exchange store with specific other people, giving each person one or more of these following permissions:

- Read items
- Create items
- Delete items
- Create subfolders

A person with whom you have shared your folders can open those folders to see your Outlook items and, subject to the permissions you gave, create and delete items.

USING PUBLIC FOLDERS

Sharing folders, as described in the preceding section, is appropriate when you want to share information with one other person, or perhaps a small group. When you want to share information with many people, it's better to use Exchange's public folders.

Any Outlook user can create a public folder that resides within the Exchange store. The person who creates the folder owns it and can allow specific people or groups to access it. As with shared folders, the owner decides which permissions each person has.

Public folders are typically used to make information available to many people. For example, an organization might place its employee policy manual in a public folder, something that has advantages over printing and distributing paper copies: it's a lot less expensive and much easier to update. This is an example of a public folder to which everyone has read access, but only one person has permission to edit.

You can use public folders as an electronic bulletin board that people can use to exchange ideas. Used in this way, a public folder is much like an Internet newsgroup. The bulletin board can be *unmoderated*, in which case anyone can post whatever they like on it. Alternatively, it can be *moderated*, in which case people submit their contributions to a moderator, who decides whether to publish each contribution in the public folder.

WORKING REMOTELY

Using Exchange as an e-mail system is particularly useful for people who travel. You can create an offline Outlook folder on your laptop's hard disk. After doing so, you can copy information from your folders in the Exchange store into the *offline folder (page 731)* so that you can work with Outlook while you're not connected to Exchange.

While you're away from the office, you can connect to Exchange using a dial-up connection to receive information from, and send information to, Exchange. While connected, you can *synchronize* the information on your remote computer with that in your Exchange store so that your folders in both locations have the latest information. Similarly, when you return to your office, you can again synchronize so that you can continue to work with the latest information while your computer is connected to Exchange.

→ For more information on synchronizing folders, **see** "Understanding Offline Folders," **p. 731**.

PLANNING MEETINGS

As explained in Chapter 10, "Managing Calendars," with Exchange as your server, you can plan meetings at times when other people and the resources you need are available.

→ To learn more about scheduling meetings and resources using Outlook, **see** "Planning a Meeting," **p. 405**.

SYNCHRONIZING EXCHANGE FOLDERS

The subject of synchronizing folders was mentioned in the "Working Remotely" section of this chapter. That was in the context of updating your offline folders and your folders in the Exchange store so that both sets of folders contained the latest (and the same) information. Exchange also uses synchronization when an organization has two or more separate Exchange installations.

Many large enterprises have business units in various locations. In these circumstances, it's common for each business unit to have its own Exchange server. The various Exchange installations are interconnected and, at times chosen by the administrators, synchronize the information in their stores.

GETTING MORE INFORMATION ABOUT EXCHANGE SERVER

This chapter gives you a brief overview of what you can do with Exchange. You can find more detailed information in two books: *Introducing Exchange* and *Exchange in Business*, both published by Microsoft Press.

Refer to *Special Edition Using Microsoft Exchange Server 5.5*, published by Que, for detailed information about administering Exchange Server.

CHAPTER 25

ADDING THE EXCHANGE SERVER INFORMATION SERVICE TO A PROFILE

In this chapter   *by Gordon Padwick*

ACCESSING EXCHANGE SERVER

This chapter applies only to C/W Outlook. You won't ordinarily use *IMO Outlook (page 53)* to access an Exchange server.

Tip #158 from	You can use IMO Outlook to send and receive e-mail by way of an Exchange server. If the Exchange server is set up to support the IMAP4 protocol, you can set up an IMAP account in IMO Outlook to access mail on an Exchange server. However, this method of connecting to an Exchange server doesn't provide access to the server's capabilities other than e-mail.

In order to use Outlook as a client for Exchange you should have the Microsoft Exchange Server information service in your profile. This chapter explains how to add that service to your profile and how to set the service's properties.

This chapter explains how to add the information service into your profile from within Outlook. You can also add it to your profile from the Windows Control Panel.

ADDING THE EXCHANGE SERVER INFORMATION SERVICE

You add the Exchange Server information service to a profile in the same way that you add other information services. If this information service already exists in your profile, you can't add it a second time. After you've added the service, you must close and restart Outlook before you can use it.

To add the service:

1. With any Outlook Information viewer displayed, choose Tools, Services to display the Services dialog box shown in Figure 25.1.

Figure 25.1
The Services dialog box lists the information services already in your profile.

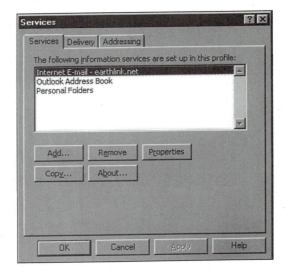

2. Choose Add to display the Add Service to Profile dialog box, which lists available information services.

3. Select Microsoft Exchange Server and choose OK. Outlook displays the Microsoft Exchange Server dialog box, shown subsequently in Figure 25.2.

Note

If the Exchange Server information service is already in your profile, Outlook displays a message saying that you can't add Exchange Server a second time.

RE-ADDING THE SERVICE

You may run into a problem if you have the Exchange Server information service in your profile and, after experiencing problems with connectivity to Exchange, decide to remove the service and then add it back into your profile.

To remove the service, choose Tools, Services, to display the Services dialog box. Select Microsoft Exchange Server in the list of services, and choose Remove. Outlook removes the service from the list.

At that point, you might be tempted to immediately add the service back into your profile. That won't work! Although the service isn't listed, it remains active until you close and restart Outlook. If you do go ahead, you'll find that you can't set the properties of the service you just added. If you attempt to set its properties, Outlook displays a message saying "Changes cannot be made while mail is running."

The solution to this problem is to close (use File, Exit and Log Off) and restart Outlook after you've removed the service. With Outlook restarted, you can go ahead and add the service back into your profile and set its properties.

SETTING THE PROPERTIES

The Microsoft Exchange Server dialog box shown in Figure 25.2 is displayed when you choose OK in the Add Service to Profile dialog box to add the service to your profile. After you've completed setting the Information service's properties, you can redisplay this dialog box by selecting the service in the Properties dialog box and then choosing Properties.

SETTING THE GENERAL PROPERTIES

You can set the principal properties of the Exchange Server information service in the General tab. The first step is to identify the Exchange server on which your mail account is installed and to identify your mailbox. If you don't know the names of the Exchange Server and your mailbox, you'll have to ask the Exchange administrator for this information.

PART
V

CH
25

Figure 25.2
The Microsoft Exchange Server properties dialog box opens with the General tab selected.

If you're setting up Outlook as a client for Exchange on a local network, you'll probably only be concerned with the settings in the General tab.

While you're adding the Exchange Server information service to your profile, you have to provide the names of the Exchange server and your mailbox on that server. Subsequently, if you open the Microsoft Exchange Server dialog box, the Microsoft Exchange Server and Mailbox boxes are gray; you can't change the server or mailbox names. To change the server or mailbox names, you must remove the information service from your profile, close and restart Outlook, and add the information service into your profile again.

To identify your Exchange mailbox:

1. Enter the name of the of the Exchange server into the Microsoft Exchange Server box.

2. Enter the name of your Exchange mailbox in the Mailbox box. The Check Name button becomes enabled after you've entered the server and mailbox names.

3. Choose Check Name to verify the server and mailbox names. After a short delay, Outlook underlines these names to signify they are valid, and disables the Check Name button. If one or both of the server and mailbox names are not valid, Outlook displays a message saying "The name could not be resolved." If that happens, check with your Exchange administrator for the correct names to use.

You may see a message that says "Network problems are preventing connection to the Microsoft Exchange Server computer." This is a problem to be solved by the LAN or Exchange administrator.

Use the lower part of the General tab to specify what happens when Outlook starts.

If you're setting up Outlook on a desktop computer that's permanently connected to the server, you should select the default Automatically Detect Connection State.

If you're setting up Outlook on a laptop computer that's only sometimes connected to the server, you'll probably have two or more profiles.

- In the profile you use when the computer is connected to the server, select Automatically Detect Connection State.

- In the profile you use when you are out of the office, select Manually Control Connection State. In most cases, leave Choose the Connection Type When Starting unchecked and select Work Offline and Use Dial-up Networking. If you select Choose the Connection Type When Starting, a dialog box is displayed when you start Outlook, asking whether you want to work offline or connect to your network.

The Seconds Until Server Connection Timeout box at the bottom of the dialog box is where you specify how long Outlook tries to connect to the server before telling you that a connection cannot be established. The default 30 seconds is usually more than enough for a local connection. However, if you're connecting from a remote location, particularly if you're using dial-up networking, you may have to increase the default time significantly. Refer to *Special Edition Using TCP/IP*, published by Que, for specific TCP/IP dial-up networking information.

SETTING THE ADVANCED PROPERTIES

Choose the Advanced tab to set advanced properties of the information service. The Advanced tab is shown in Figure 25.3.

The top section of the dialog box is where you can identify Exchange mailboxes (other than your own) that you want to access. The owners of those mailboxes must, of course, give you permission to access those mailboxes. In some circumstances you might own more than one mailbox. In that case, you identify the principal one in the General tab and others in this tab.

→ For information about granting and using delegate access, **see** "Delegating Access to Your Folders," **p. 691**.

To identify an Exchange mailbox to which you have delegate access, enter the name of the mailbox in the Open These Additional Mailboxes box. After you've entered the mailbox name, choose Add. You can list as many mailboxes as you need in this way.

Note

The Add button is not enabled if you selected Work Offline and Use Dial-up Networking. Nor is it available if you didn't enter your mailbox name and chose Check Name in the General tab.

Figure 25.3
You can use the
Advanced tab to set more
properties.

If you want to remove a mailbox from the list, select that mailbox and choose Remove.

By default, Outlook doesn't encrypt messages that you send to Exchange. If you want to encrypt messages, check one or both of the boxes in the Encrypt Information section of the dialog box.

As explained in Chapter 24, "Exchange Server Overview," Exchange can be set up to share passwords with Windows NT Server. You can choose how you want the Exchange Server information service to handle passwords. Select one of these:

- NT Password Authentication—Choose this if you want to log on to Exchange Server with the same password you use to log on to NT Server.

- Distributed Password Authentication—Choose this if the server you're accessing makes use of Microsoft's Membership Directory Services.

- None—After you choose this, you'll be asked for a password when you open Outlook.

Check the Enable Offline Use box if you want to work offline and enable automatic offline synchronization.

Choose Offline Folder File Settings to display the dialog box shown in Figure 25.4.

→ To learn more about working with Outlook while you're offline, **see** "Using Outlook Offline," **p. 738**.

SETTING THE DIAL-UP NETWORKING PROPERTIES

You need to use this tab, shown in Figure 25.5, only if you're setting up Outlook to connect to Exchange by Dial-up networking.

Make sure Dial Using the Following Connection is selected, then open the drop-down list of available connections and, if the one you want to use is available, select it.

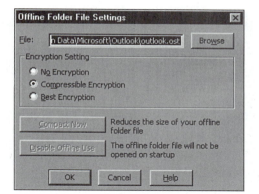

Figure 25.4
Use this dialog box to specify how you will work offline.

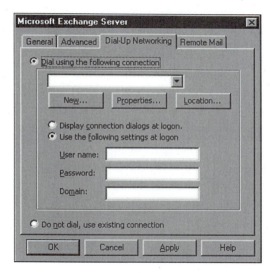

Figure 25.5
Use this tab to define how Outlook connects to Exchange by dial-up networking.

> **Note**
>
> If you haven't previously set up the dial-up connection, you can use the New, Properties, and Locations buttons to set up a dial-up connection.

➔ For information on adding dial-up connections, **see** "Setting up Dial-up Networking," **p. 60**.

Enter your mailbox name in the User Name box, your password in the Password box, and your server domain name in the Domain box.

SETTING REMOTE MAIL PROPERTIES

You need to use this tab, shown in Figure 25.6, only if you're setting up Outlook to use remote mail.

Figure 25.6
Use this tab to define
how Outlook sends and
receives remote mail.

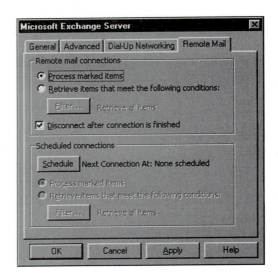

→ For information about setting up remote mail, **see** "Working Remotely," **p.729**.

MAKING THE INFORMATION SERVICE AVAILABLE

After setting up properties in the General tab and any of the other three tabs that are appropriate, choose OK. Outlook displays a message telling you to close Outlook and restart it. Choose OK to close the message box, choose OK to close the Services dialog box, and then choose File, Exit and Log Off to close Outlook. The Microsoft Exchange Server information service is available the next time you start Outlook.

TROUBLESHOOTING

Troubleshooting connections to an Exchange server is a matter for the Exchange administrator, not the Outlook user, to solve. If you've correctly identified the name of your Exchange server and the name of your account on that server, you should have a connection. If that fails, there's not much you can do from your end—that's what administrators are for.

If you set up Outlook with the Microsoft Exchange Server information service, and can't get access to the Exchange server, the only advice I can give is to contact your LAN or Exchange administrator and ask for help in solving the problem.

CHAPTER **26**

USING EXCHANGE SERVER FOR E-MAIL

In this chapter

by Gordon Padwick

USING OUTLOOK AS A CLIENT FOR EXCHANGE

This chapter is about sending and receiving e-mail messages between people who use Outlook as clients for an Exchange server. The subjects covered here are only relevant to people who have *C/W Outlook (page 54)* installed and have an e-mail account on an Exchange server.

SETTING UP OUTLOOK AS AN EXCHANGE CLIENT

To use Outlook as an Exchange client, you must have C/W Outlook installed on your computer, have the Microsoft Exchange Server information service in your profile, have a LAN connection to a server on which Exchange Server is installed, and have an e-mail account on that Exchange Server.

To check whether you have C/W Outlook installed on your computer, with Outlook running, choose <u>H</u>elp, <u>A</u>bout Microsoft Outlook to display a dialog box similar to the one shown in Figure 26.1.

Figure 26.1
The second line in this dialog box contains the phrase "Corporate or Workgroup" if you have C/W Outlook installed.

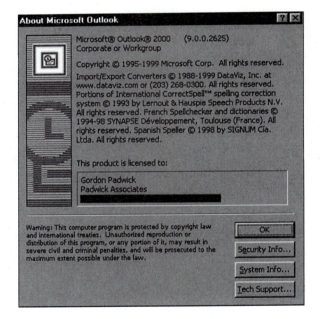

If you have IMO Outlook installed, you can't usually access Exchange Server. You'll have to change your Outlook service option.

Note

If your Exchange server has the IMAP service installed, you can use an IMO Outlook IMAP account to access Exchange server's e-mail services. See "Changing from One Service Option to Another," in Appendix A.

To check whether you have the Microsoft Exchange Server information service in your profile, choose <u>T</u>ools, Ser<u>v</u>ices to display the dialog box shown in Figure 26.2.

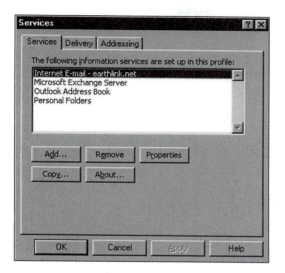

Figure 26.2
The list of information services should include Microsoft Exchange Server.

→ If Microsoft Exchange Server isn't listed, you'll have to add that information service to your profile. **See** "Adding the Exchange Server Information Service to a Profile," **p. 655**.

The subjects of connecting to a LAN and setting up e-mail accounts on Exchange Server are beyond the scope of this book.

Tip #159 from

If you need to set up e-mail accounts for your Exchange Server, I suggest picking up a copy of Special Edition Using Microsoft Exchange Server 5.5, published by Que.

PART
V

CH
26

SELECTING A STORAGE LOCATION

If you use IMO Outlook, or C/W Outlook without connectivity to Exchange Server, Outlook stores your e-mail and all other Outlook items in a Personal Folders file on your hard drive. However, if you use C/W Outlook with connectivity to Exchange Server, you can choose from three places to store your e-mail and other Outlook items:

- A Personal Folders file on your local hard drive
- The Exchange Server information store
- An Offline Folders file on your local hard drive

This chapter assumes that you're using a computer that's permanently connected to Exchange Server, so the chapter considers only the first two places where you can save Outlook items.

→ If you need to work with offline folders, **see** "Understanding Offline Folders," **p. 731**.

You should keep your Outlook items in the Exchange Server information store in order to take advantage of Exchange Server's capabilities. If you and other Outlook users do that, you can easily share such information as Calendar and Contact items, and be able to replicate your offline folders with the information store. The downside of doing that is each time you work with Outlook items you create traffic on the LAN. If you have a reliable, high-performance LAN, you should keep your Outlook items in the Exchange Server information store. Only if you experience LAN problems should you consider saving Outlook items locally.

Note

The decision about where you save Outlook items is usually made by the Exchange administrator.

FINDING OUT WHERE OUTLOOK ITEMS ARE SAVED

You can easily see where Outlook items are stored. With any Outlook Information viewer displayed, choose <u>V</u>iew, Fold<u>e</u>r List to display the list of folders. If the only place you have available for saving Outlook items is the Exchange store, you'll see a list of folders such as that shown in Figure 26.3.

Figure 26.3
The top-level folder in this case is named Outlook Today – {mailbox – Jason Aldrich}. The word "mailbox" in this name indicates that your Outlook items are saved in an Exchange mailbox.

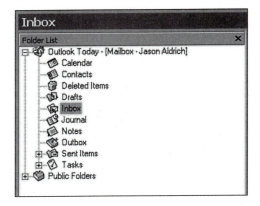

The name Jason Aldrich is the name of the fictitious person who owns the mailbox. In your case, your own name or pseudonym is there instead of Jason Aldrich.

Note

This list shows two top-level folders. The one with the name that starts with the words "Outlook Today" contains your Outlook items. Public Folders is an area of the Exchange store you can use to share information with other people. See Chapter 27, "Using Exchange Server to Share Information."

If you have a mailbox on an Exchange server and a Personal Folders file in your local disk, the folder list looks something like that shown in Figure 26.4.

Current storage ———

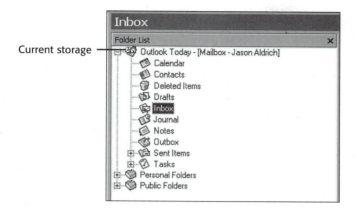

Figure 26.4
This folder list has an additional top-level folder named Personal Folders.

In this case, you can select either your mailbox on the Exchange server or your Personal Folders file on your local disk as the place to save your Outlook items. Outlook can save items in one or the other.

Note

You can access more than one Personal Folders file and more than one mailbox on the Exchange Server from a single profile.

The place where Outlook currently saves your Outlook items is indicated in two ways:

- By the image of a house superimposed over a top-level folder icon
- By the words "Outlook Today" at the beginning of a top-level folder's name

PART
V
CH
26

CHANGING WHERE OUTLOOK ITEMS ARE STORED

Use these steps to change where Outlook saves items.

To select where Outlook saves items:

1. With any Outlook Information viewer displayed, choose Tools, Services to display the Services dialog box. Select the Delivery tab, shown in Figure 26.5.
2. Open the drop-down Deliver New Mail to the Following Location list to display a list of available locations.

Note

Although the name of the box refers specifically to mail, Outlook uses the same location for all items.

Figure 26.5
The Delivery tab shows where Outlook items are currently saved, the Exchange store in this case.

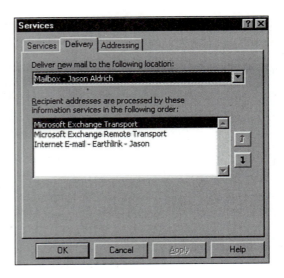

3. Select the location in which you want to save Outlook items. Select a location that has a name starting with "Mailbox" to save Outlook items in the Exchange store; select the name of a Personal Folders file to save Outlook items on your local hard drive.

4. Choose OK to close the dialog box. The new delivery location doesn't take effect until you choose File, Exit and Log Off to close Outlook and then restart it.

Tip #160 from	Outlook doesn't tell you that you must close and restart Outlook before the new delivery location takes effect. However, that step is necessary.

After you restart Outlook, the folder list looks like the one in Figure 26.6.

Figure 26.6
Now, the house image and the words "Outlook Today" indicate that the location in which Outlook saves items is the Personal Folders file.

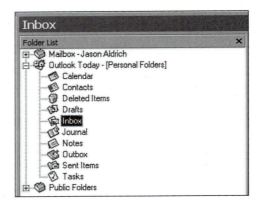

If you want to use the Exchange server's store to save Outlook items, you must have that selected. The remainder of this chapter assumes that you're using the Exchange store.

COPYING ITEMS TO THE MAILBOX FOLDER

If you have previously been using a Personal Folders file to save your Outlook items, you may want to copy those items to a Mailbox folder on Exchange Server.

→ You must display the items to be copied in a Table-type view. **See** "Creating Views and Print Styles," **p. 943**.

To copy Outlook items from a Personal Folders file to a server Mailbox:

1. With any Table-type Outlook Information viewer displayed, choose <u>V</u>iew, Fold<u>e</u>r List.

2. If necessary, expand your Personal Folders file to display the names of the folders it contains. Also, if necessary, expand your Mailbox to display the folders it contains.

3. In the folder list, select the folder in your Personal Folders file from which you want to copy items.

4. Select one or more items. If you want to select all items in the folder, choose <u>E</u>dit, Select A<u>l</u>l.

5. Hold down Ctrl while you drag the selected item or items onto the folder in your Mailbox into which you want to copy items. If you want to move items from one folder to the other instead of copying them, hold down Shift while you drag.

SENDING AND RECEIVING E-MAIL

Sending and receiving e-mail messages using Exchange Server as the mail server is almost the same as sending and receiving Internet e-mail messages. One difference is that, because your computer is permanently connected to the server, you don't have to do anything to send messages from your Outbox to the server, nor do you have to do anything to collect messages waiting for you on the server. Outlook automatically sends messages you create to the server and saves copies of them in your Sent Items folder, and automatically collects messages waiting for you on the server and places them in your Inbox folder.

In addition to sending messages on you own behalf, you can send messages on behalf of another person.

When you create messages to be sent to other people who have accounts on an Exchange server, you should normally use the Microsoft Outlook Rich Text mail format because that's the native format used by Exchange. By using this format, you can be sure recipients will see your messages exactly as you create them. However, for messages that go to people outside your Exchange environment who may not be using message clients that accept Rich Text Format, it's better to use Plain Text.

Tip #161 from

[signature: Gordon Woods]

You might, under some circumstances, run into formatting problems if you send messages using the HTML format. Refer to the Microsoft Knowledge Base article Q183668, *HTML Formatting Not Retained on Exchange 5.5* for detailed information about this.

The remainder of this chapter describes messaging capabilities provided by Exchange Server that are in addition to the basic processes of sending and receiving messages.

CHANGING DELIVERY OPTIONS FOR MESSAGES

You can set several delivery options for messages you send by way of Exchange Server.

REDIRECTING REPLIES

Normally, when you send a message and recipients reply to it, the replies are automatically sent to you. You can, however, request that replies to specific messages are automatically sent to someone else.

To redirect replies:

1. At any time while you're creating a message in the Message form, choose Options in the form's toolbar to display the Message Options dialog box, shown in Figure 26.7.

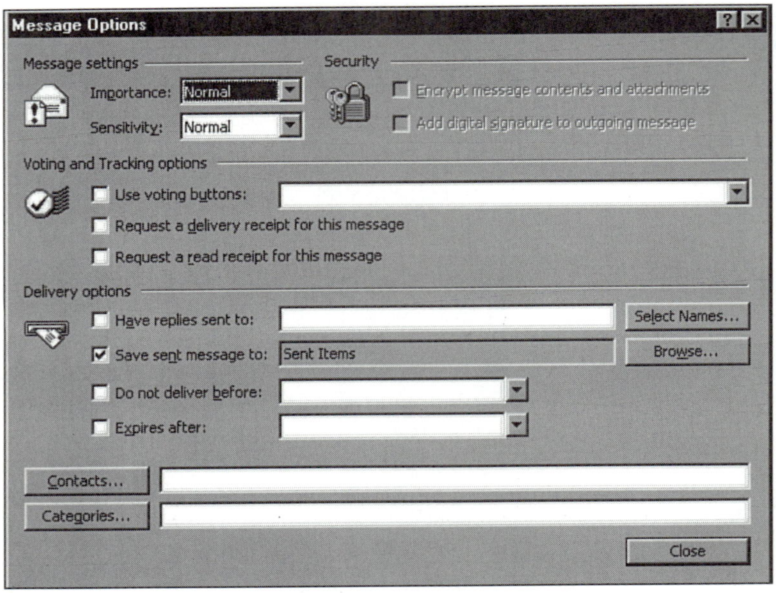

Figure 26.7
Use this dialog box to change the delivery options for a message.

2. In the Delivery Options section of the dialog box, check H_ave Replies Sent To. When you do so, your own name appears in the adjacent text box. The name is underlined to indicate the name is an alias for an e-mail address.

3. If you know the e-mail address of the person to whom you want replies to be sent, you can replace your own name with the e-mail address of the person to whom you want replies to be sent. Otherwise, choose Se_lect Names to display the Have Replies Sent To dialog box shown in Figure 26.8.

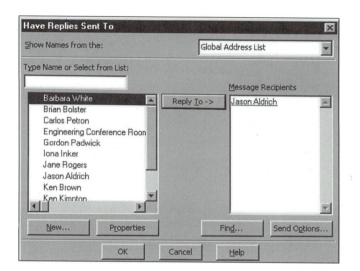

Figure 26.8
This dialog box initially shows your name in the M_essage Recipients box.

Note

This dialog box may be a little confusing. The box labeled Message Recipients is actually where the name of the person who should receive replies to your message appears, not a list of the people who receive your messages.

4. Delete your own name from the M_essage Recipients list.

5. In the list of names on the left, select the name of the person to whom you want replies to be directed. Then choose Reply T_o-> to copy that name into the Message Recipients list.

6. Choose OK to return to the Message Options dialog box that now shows the name of the person you selected in the Have Replies Sent To box.

The name you select in this manner applies only to the message you're currently creating.

Note

If the person who receives messages has created a rule that generates automatic replies to messages, that automatic reply is sent to you, not to the person you designate to receive replies.

→ Outlook helps you automate repetitive tasks. **See** "Creating and Using Rules," **p. 617**.

When recipients receive a message in which replies have been redirected, they won't see anything unusual about the message. The message header contains the name of the sender as usual. However, when a user replies to the message, the reply will be addressed to the person designated in the Have Replies Sent To box in the original message.

SCHEDULING A MESSAGE FOR LATER DELIVERY

In the Exchange messaging environment, you can create a message and mark it not to be delivered until a certain time and date. After you create the message and send it, Outlook sends it to Exchange in the normal way. Exchange holds the message until the date and time you specify and then sends it to the recipients.

To schedule a message for later delivery:

1. At any time while you're creating a message in the Message form, choose Options in the form's toolbar to display the Message Options dialog box, shown previously in Figure 26.7.
2. In the Delivery Options section of the dialog box, check Do Not Deliver Before. Outlook proposes tomorrow's date and 5:00 PM.
3. You can edit the proposed date and time. Alternatively, click the button at the right end of the box to display a calendar on which you can select a date.

Outlook saves copies of messages that are set for delayed delivery in your Sent Items folder in the same way that it saves ordinary messages. You can see these messages listed in the Sent Items Information viewer. You can double-click a message in the Information viewer to display it in a Message form. The InfoBar near the top of the Message form contains the delayed delivery information.

SETTING AN EXPIRATION DATE AND TIME

You can set an expiration date and time for a message. After you do so, Exchange automatically deletes the message if the recipient hasn't opened it by the date and time you specify. The procedure for setting an expiration time and date is the same as that described in the preceding section. Instead of checking the Do Not Deliver Before box, check the Expires After box.

You can see the headers of messages you've sent that have an expiration date in your Sent Items Information viewer. You can double-click a message header to display it in a Message form. The InfoBar near the top of the form contains the expiration information.

REQUESTING RECEIPTS

You can ask Outlook to send you two types of delivery receipts, either for all messages you send or for individual messages. You can request delivery receipts for a specific message by checking boxes in the Message Options dialog box, shown previously in Figure 26.7.

To request a receipt when a message arrives in a recipient's Inbox, check Request a <u>D</u>elivery Receipt for This Message. To request a receipt when a recipient opens a message, check Request a <u>R</u>ead Receipt for This Message.

The following steps describe how you request delivery receipts for all messages you send. These steps apply to delivery receipts, to responses you get from meeting requests you send, and from messages you send that include voting buttons.

→ Outlook allows you to poll message recipients. **See** "Using Voting Buttons," **p. 687**.

→ While in the planning stage for your meeting, you'll need to arrange a time when everyone in your workgroup can meet. **See** "Planning a Meeting," **p. 405**.

To request delivery receipts for all messages:

1. With any Outlook Information viewer displayed, choose <u>T</u>ools, <u>O</u>ptions, and select the Preferences tab in the Options dialog box.

2. Choose E-<u>m</u>ail Options and then, in the E-mail Options dialog box, choose <u>T</u>racking Options to display the Tracking Options dialog box, shown in Figure 26.9.

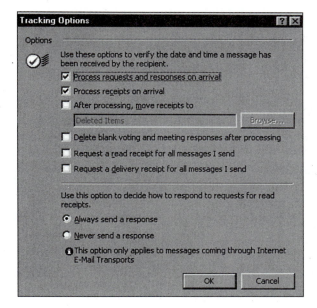

Figure 26.9
Use this dialog box to set tracking options that apply to all the messages you create.

PART
V

CH
26

Tip #162 from

Within your Exchange Server environment, tracking options work as explained here. If you're using Outlook as an Exchange client and are communicating with people who have other messaging environments, some of the choices you make here may not operate as you expect.

3. If you want to keep delivery receipts and other responses in a folder other than your Inbox folder, check After Processing, Move Receipts To. When you do that, Outlook proposes to move receipts and responses to your Deleted Items folder. You can choose Browse to open the Select Folder dialog box, in which you can select any other Outlook folder (or create a new folder and select that).

4. If you want to delete voting and meeting responses that contain no text, check the Delete Blank Voting and Meeting Request Responses After Processing. By doing so, these responses are deleted from your Inbox (or other folder that you specified). Even though the response messages are deleted, those responses are still tallied.

5. To request a read receipt for all messages you send, check the Request a Read Receipt for All Messages I Send box.

6. To request a delivery receipt for all messages you send, check the Request a Delivery Receipt for All Messages I Send box.

7. Choose the Always Send a Response option button if you are willing to respond to requests for read receipts. Alternatively, check the Never Send a Response if you don't want to respond to requests for read receipts. This choice applies only to responses requested by way of an Internet mail server.

After you've set receipt options that apply to all messages, you can use the Message form's Message Options dialog box to make other choices for individual messages.

After you send messages for which you request one or both receipts, Exchange automatically sends receipt messages to your Inbox.

Tip #163 from

Gordon Padwick

When you receive a read receipt, all you know is that a recipient opened the message, or marked it as read. You have no guarantee the recipient actually read it. If you really want to know that a recipient has read the message, you should request the recipient to send an acknowledgment to you.

TRACKING MESSAGE RECEIPTS

If you send a message in which you have requested a delivery receipt, a read receipt, or both to several people, you can easily see a tally that shows which people have read your message.

To see a tally of people who have read your message:

1. With any Outlook Information viewer displayed, select the My Shortcuts section of the Outlook Bar and select Sent Items to display the Sent Items Information viewer.

2. In the Sent Items Information viewer, double-click the message for which you want to see the tally. Outlook displays a message form that now has two tabs. The Message tab is selected—it contains your original message.

3. Select the Tracking tab shown in Figure 26.10.

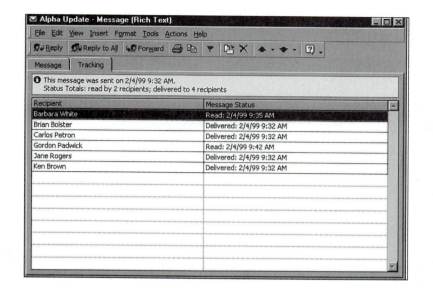

Figure 26.10
The Tracking tab contains a table that lists the message recipients to whom you sent the original message and shows which of those recipients have read it. Notice the status totals at the top of the table.

4. If you want to print a copy of the response tally, open the form's File menu and choose Print.

Tip #164 from

You can arrange the list of recipients in alphabetical order by clicking the title at the top of the Recipient column. To send a copy of some or all rows in the list to someone else, select the rows you want to send, press Ctrl+C to copy the list into the Clipboard, create a new message, and press Ctrl+V to paste the selected rows into that message.

RECALLING MESSAGES

Subject to certain conditions, you can recall a message that you've previously sent. For a message recall to be successful:

- The recipient must have Outlook running
- The recipient must be logged on to Exchange
- The recipient must not have opened the message
- The message must be in the recipient's Inbox folder

As mentioned in various places in this book, it should be normal practice for all users to keep Outlook running (probably minimized) while their computers are turned on. If that happens, the first of these conditions is satisfied.

Normally, when a user logs on to Windows NT Server, that user is automatically logged on to Exchange Server. That satisfies the second condition.

The third condition is common sense. A recipient who has opened a message has probably read it, or at the least knows it's waiting to be read. You wouldn't want to open a message and subsequently find that somebody else has deleted it from your Inbox.

The last condition is the one that's likely to give you the most trouble. That's because many users employ Rules in Outlook or Exchange to place messages in specific folders other than their Inbox folders. Because of that, many of the messages you send are likely to be in folders other than Inbox folders on users' computers or in their Exchange stores.

Here's another point to be aware of. In order for Outlook on your computer to know whether a recipient has opened a message, you must have sent the message with a read receipt requested. If you sent the message you're trying to recall without requesting a read receipt, Outlook won't receive a read receipt even though the recipient has opened the message. As a result, Outlook will report "No recipients have reported reading the message" even though some may have done so. This will make you think that you can successfully recall the message when in fact you can't. For this reason, you should consider requesting a read receipt for all messages you send by way of Exchange.

Note

The disadvantages of requesting receipts are that it increases network traffic and also increases each Outlook user's storage requirements.

Caution

Because there's a strong possibility that you won't be able to recall messages, be careful what you send.

Knowing that message recall works only some of the time, here's how you attempt to recall a message.

To recall a message:

1. With any Outlook Information viewer displayed, select the My Shortcuts section of the Outlook Bar and choose Sent Items to display the Sent Items Information viewer.

2. Double-click the message you want to recall to display that message in the Message form.

3. Choose Actions, Recall This Message to display the dialog box shown in Figure 26.11.

Figure 26.11
This dialog box warns you that you may not be able to recall the message from some recipients.

4. Choose the <u>D</u>elete Unread Copies of This Message option button and go to step 6. Alternatively, choose the Delete Unread Copies and <u>R</u>eplace with a New message option button and go to step 5.

5. Edit the original message that Outlook automatically displays in a Message form. Then choose <u>S</u>end in the form's toolbar to send the revised message. If the recall is successful, the revised message replaces the original message in the recipients' Inboxes.

6. Normally, leave the <u>T</u>ell Me if a Recall Succeeds or Fails for Each Recipient box checked.

Within a short time, you should have messages in your Inbox telling you whether your recalls have succeeded or failed.

USING VOTING BUTTONS

You can send a message that asks a question to which you want people to reply with one of a set of possible answers. The message can include Outlook's built-in voting buttons, or voting buttons you define.

Outlook includes three sets of predefined voting buttons:

- Approve; Reject
- Yes; No
- Yes; No; Maybe

You can define your own voting buttons with as many choices as you like. However, each message can contain only one set of voting buttons.

CREATING A MESSAGE THAT CONTAINS VOTING BUTTONS

Start by creating a message in the normal way. At any time while you're creating the message, choose Op<u>t</u>ions in the Message form's toolbar to display the Message Options dialog box, shown previously in Figure 26.5. Then proceed as follows.

To create a message containing voting buttons:

1. Check the Use Voting B<u>u</u>ttons box. Outlook displays the first built-in choice of voting buttons: Approve; Reject, as shown in Figure 26.12.

2. If you want to use a different set of built-in voting buttons, click the button at the right end of the Use Voting B<u>u</u>ttons box to display a list and select from that list. If you want to define your own voting buttons, enter the names of these buttons in the Use Voting Buttons box, separating one button name from the next with a semicolon, as shown in Figure 26.13.

PART

V

CH

26

Figure 26.12
Outlook initially suggests Approve; Reject as the names of the voting buttons.

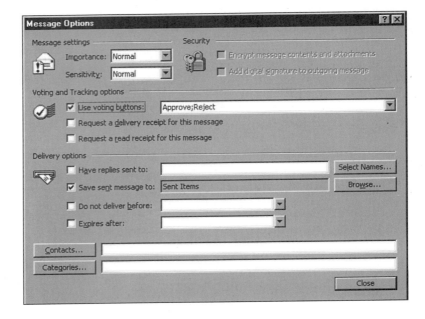

Figure 26.13
These voting buttons ask recipients to choose a color.

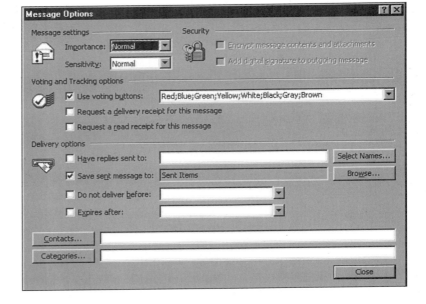

3. Choose Close to close the Message options dialog box and return to the Message form.

4. Complete the message and send it in the normal manner.

REPLYING TO A MESSAGE THAT CONTAINS VOTING BUTTONS

When you receive a message that contains voting buttons you don't see the voting buttons in your Inbox Information viewer, nor is there any indication of them in the Preview pane. To see the voting buttons, you must double-click the message header in the Inbox Information viewer to display the message in a Message form, as shown in Figure 26.14.

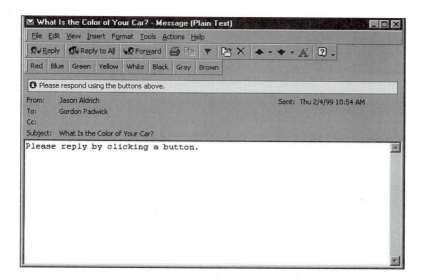

Figure 26.14
The Message form shows the voting buttons immediately below the toolbar.

Notice that the InfoBar draws your attention to the voting buttons with the words "Please respond using the buttons above." As usual, the InfoBar has a bright yellow background, so it's immediately obvious.

To reply to the message, click one of the buttons. Outlook displays the dialog box shown in Figure 26.15.

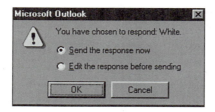

Figure 26.15
This dialog box confirms which voting button you chose.

If you accept the default option button <u>S</u>end the Response Now and then choose OK, Outlook immediately sends your response back to the sender. The InfoBar in the Message form changes to show which voting button you chose as well as the date and time you sent the response.

If you choose <u>E</u>dit the Response Before Sending and then choose OK, Outlook displays a Message form that's addressed to the sender of the original message with the name of the voting button you selected in the Subject box. You can enter a message to the original sender, and then choose <u>S</u>end in the form's toolbar to send your and message back to the original sender.

RECEIVING VOTING RESPONSES

When you receive responses to a message containing voting buttons that you sent, those responses appear as usual in your Inbox Information viewer. The message header there contains the name of the respondent in the From column and the name of the voting button that respondent selected in the Subject column. You can double-click the message header to see the message in a Message form, as shown in Figure 26.16.

If the respondent sent a message with the response, that message is displayed in the notes box.

Figure 26.16
The InfoBar near the top of the Message form tells you which voting button the respondent selected.

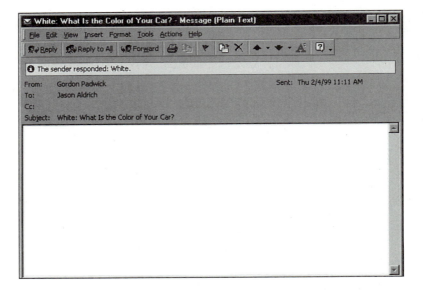

DISPLAYING A TALLY OF VOTING RESPONSES

Follow these steps to display a tally of responses to the message you sent.

To see a tally of responses:

1. With any Outlook Information viewer displayed, select the My Shortcuts section of the Outlook Bar and choose Sent Items to display the Sent Items Information viewer.

2. Double-click the original message containing voting buttons that you sent to display that message in a Message form that now has two tabs. The Message tab showing the original message is initially selected.

3. Select the Tracking tab, shown in Figure 26.17.

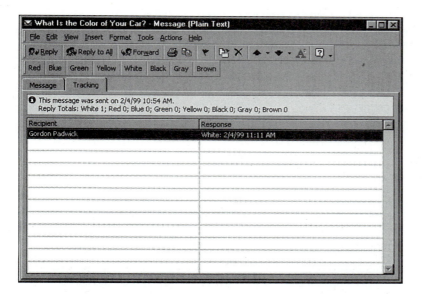

Figure 26.17
The InfoBar near the top of the Tracking tab contains a summary of the responses you've received. The table shows the voting button chosen by each respondent, only one in this case.

As described previously in this chapter, you can sort the table that contains details of responses, print it, and copy it into another message.

→ If you send a message in which you have requested a delivery receipt, you can easily see who has read the message. To learn more, **see** "Tracking Message Receipts," **p. 684**.

Part V
Ch
26

DELEGATING ACCESS TO YOUR FOLDERS

When using Exchange as your messaging system, you can let other people act as delegates on your behalf.

If you have a trusted administrative assistant, you can give that assistant full delegate access to any or all of your Outlook folders. That's quite different from allowing your assistant to log on as you because you can control which of your Outlook folders your assistant can access.

If you're going to be out of the office for a while, you can give one of your colleagues delegate access to your mail folders so that person can respond to mail on your behalf while you're away.

DELEGATING ACCESS TO YOUR E-MAIL

Here's how you give another person delegate access to your e-mail. Although Outlook allows you to select more than one delegate, it's usually best to select only one.

Note

The procedure described here is based on the assumption that you save your Outlook items in the Exchange store. If you save your Outlook items in a Personal Folders file or an Offline Folders file, a delegate can only send mail on your behalf, not access your folders.

To give delegate access to your mail:

1. With any Outlook Information viewer displayed, choose Tools, Options to display the Options dialog box.

2. Select the Delegates tab shown in Figure 26.18 (this tab is available only if you have the Microsoft Exchange Server information service in your profile).

Figure 26.18
The tab is shown here with a delegate already added.

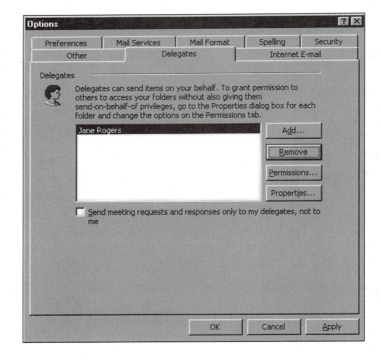

3. If you want to add a delegate, choose Add to display the Add Users dialog box shown in Figure 26.19.

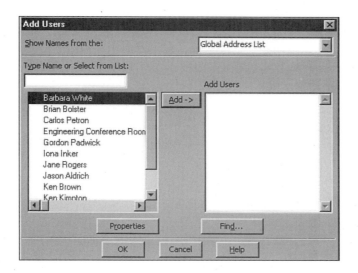

Figure 26.19
The left box shows the
names of users in
your primary address
book.

4. If necessary, open the drop-down <u>S</u>how Names from The list to access other address
   books. Choose another address book if necessary to display the names in that address
   book. The address book you choose should be one that contains the names of people
   who have accounts on your Exchange server.

5. Select the name of the person you want to appoint as your delegate. Then choose
   <u>A</u>dd-> to add that person's name to the Add Users list.

6. Choose OK to return to the Delegates tab, then choose OK to display the Delegate
   Permissions dialog box shown in Figure 26.20.

PART
V

CH
26

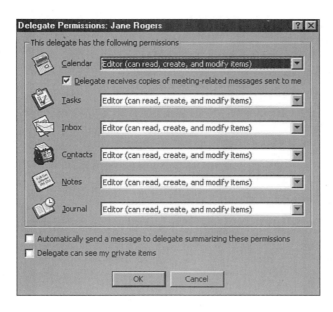

Figure 26.20
Use this dialog box to
select the Outlook
folders to which you
want the delegate to
have access.

7. For each of the types of Outlook items you can choose to allow the delegate to have these permissions:

   ■ None

   ■ Reviewer

   ■ Author

   ■ Editor

   Open the drop-down list box for each type of Outlook item and select the permission you want to give (each type of permission is defined in the drop-down list). If you only want the delegate to have access to your e-mail, all item types except Inbox should have the None permission. If you want the delegate to fully act on your behalf as far as e-mail messages are concerned, the e-mail permission should be Editor.

8. To have Outlook Send a message to the delegate to inform that person about the permissions you've given, check Automatically Send a Message to Delegate Summarizing These Permissions. After you do so, Outlook sends a message that appears in that delegate's Inbox Information viewer.

9. If you have assigned the delegate permission to access one or more of your folders that contains items you've marked as Private, check Delegate Can See My Private Items if the delegate is indeed a trusted assistant. Make sure this box is unchecked if you don't want the delegate to see your private items.

10. After you've assigned permissions, choose OK to return to the Delegates tab, then choose OK to close the Options dialog box.

Note

You can reopen the Delegates tab in the Options dialog box at any time to change a delegate's permissions. To do so, select the delegate, then choose Permissions. To remove a delegate, select that delegate's name in the Delegates tab of the Options dialog box, and choose Remove.

ACCESSING FOLDERS FOR WHICH YOU HAVE DELEGATE ACCESS

After you've been granted delegate access to someone else's folders, you can open that person's folders as well as your own.

When you click a shortcut icon in the Outlook Bar, Outlook opens your own Outlook folders in the normal manner.

To open someone's folders for which you have delegate permission:

1. With any Outlook Information viewer displayed, choose File, move the pointer onto Open, and choose Other User's Folder. Outlook displays the dialog box shown in Figure 26.21.

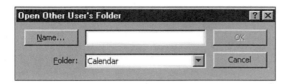

Figure 26.21
Use this dialog box to specify the folder you want to open.

2. In the <u>N</u>ame box, enter the name of a person who has given you delegate access. Alternatively, choose <u>N</u>ame to display the Select Name dialog box in which you can select a person's name.

3. Open the <u>F</u>older drop-down list and select the folder you want to open. Choose OK. If the person you named has not given you delegate permission at all, or if the folder you select is not a folder for which you've been given delegate permission, Outlook displays a message stating "Unable to display folder." If the person you named has given you delegate permission for the selected folder, Outlook displays that folder in an Information viewer superimposed over your Information viewer, as shown in Figure 26.22.

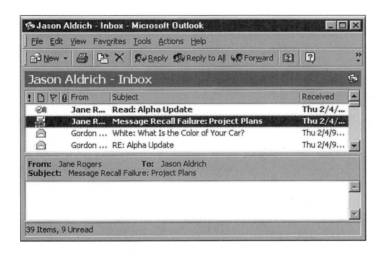

Figure 26.22
This is an example of an Inbox Information viewer displayed using delegate access. Notice that the name of the person who owns the folder is displayed in the banner.

PART

V

CH

26

With the other person's folder displayed in an Information viewer, you can work with the information in that viewer in the same way that you work with information in your own folders. You are, of course, subject to the permissions the folder's owner granted to you. For example, if you only have permission to read information, you won't be able to create new items or edit existing ones.

After you've finished working with the other person's folder, you can close that Information viewer by clicking the X at the right end of the viewer's banner.

The next time you choose <u>F</u>ile and move the pointer onto <u>O</u>pen, you'll see a list of folders you recently opened. You can choose any folder from the list to open that folder again.

SENDING MESSAGES ON SOMEONE ELSE'S BEHALF

You need delegate permission in order to send messages on another person's behalf.

To send a message on behalf of someone else:

1. Starting from Outlook running under your own profile, display the Inbox Information viewer.
2. Choose New in the Standard toolbar to display the Message form.
3. In the Message form's menu bar, choose View, From Field to add the From box near the top of the form, as shown in Figure 26.23.

Figure 26.23
The Message form now has a From box.

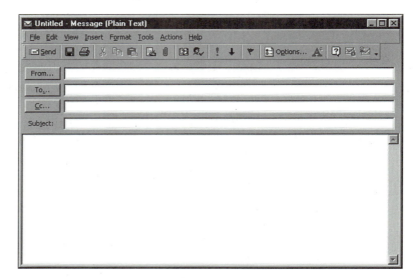

4. Enter the name of the person on behalf of whom you're sending into the From box. Alternatively, choose From to display the Choose Sender dialog box and select the person's name in that dialog box.
5. Complete the remaining parts of the form as you normally do. Then choose Send in the form's Standard toolbar to send the message.

As usual, Outlook saves a copy of the message you sent in your Sent Items folder. If you open that copy, you'll see something like the message shown in Figure 26.24.

Note

If you attempt to send a message on behalf of someone who hasn't given you delegate permissions, it might initially appear that you have been able to do so. However, soon after you send the message, Exchange will send you a message that will appear in your Inbox Information viewer: "The originator does not have permission to submit the message." The person to whom you sent the message will not receive it.

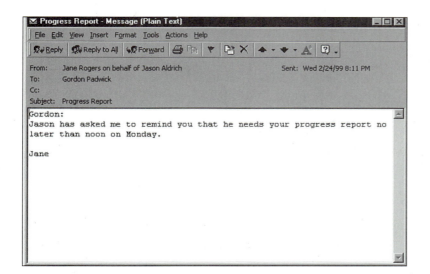

RECEIVING A MESSAGE SENT ON BEHALF OF ANOTHER PERSON

When you receive a message that was sent on behalf of someone other than the actual sender, the message header appears in your Inbox Information viewer. The message appears to be from the person on behalf of whom it was sent, not from the actual sender. Similarly, the message displayed in the Preview pane gives no indication that it was actually sent by someone else. You only find out that the message was sent on behalf of the person it appears to be from when you double-click the message header to display the message in a Message form, just like the one previously shown in Figure 26.4.

USING SERVER-BASED RULES

Chapter 22, "Creating and Using Rules," introduced you to rules that can process incoming and outgoing messages automatically. That chapter focused on rules that run on your computer and are only active when your computer is turned on and Outlook is running.

If you use Outlook as a client for Exchange, you can also set up rules that run on the server—rules that operate whether or not your computer is turned on providing, of course, the server is up and running.

One of the examples in Chapter 22 was a rule that automatically sends a reply to messages you receive. As stated in that chapter, you have to leave your computer turned on with Outlook running for the rule to work. If you're using Outlook as a client for Exchange, a better solution exists—it's called the Out of Office Assistant.

PART
V

CH
26

USING THE OUT OF OFFICE ASSISTANT

Using Outlook as a client for Exchange, you can use the Out of Office Assistant running on Exchange to process your e-mail automatically, even when your computer is turned off. After you turn on the Out of Office Assistant, it automatically sends whatever reply you choose to senders. You can also set up the Out of Office Assistant to process rules you create. Of course, the Out of Office Assistant deals only with e-mail you receive by way of Exchange. It doesn't, for example, know anything about Internet e-mail that arrives directly to your computer.

To turn on the Out of Office Assistant:

1. With any Outlook Information viewer displayed, choose Tools, Out of Office Assistant to display the dialog box shown in Figure 26.25.

Figure 26.25
This dialog box opens with I Am Currently In the Office selected.

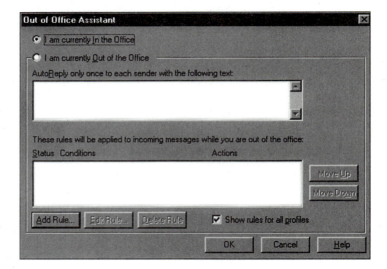

2. Choose I Am Currently Out of the Office.
3. In the box labeled AutoReply Only Once to Each Sender with the Following Text box, enter the message you want to be sent. Choose OK.

From now on, the message you entered in step 3 will be automatically sent whenever the first message from each sender arrives in your Exchange store.

When you return to the office and are ready to respond to messages, open the Out of Office Assistant dialog box again and choose I Am Currently In the Office.

You can use the Out of Office Assistant to do much more than just send an automatic reply. With the Out of Office Assistant dialog box open, choose Add Rule to display the dialog box shown in Figure 26.26. You can use this dialog box to create several rules.

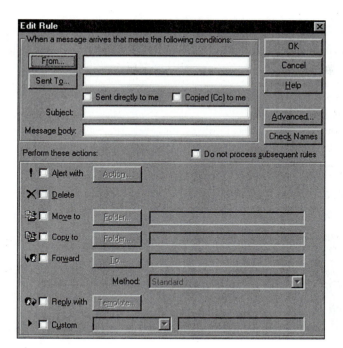

Figure 26.26
Use this dialog box to define a rule than runs on the server when a message arrives in your mailbox in the Exchange store.

The top section of the dialog box contains boxes in which you can define certain aspects of incoming messages. The rule is applied only if it satisfies all the criteria you define in these boxes.

The bottom section of the dialog box is where you can define what the rule does. The choices you make here should be obvious, particularly if you've read Chapter 22, so they're not covered in detail here.

You can make more precise definitions of the message to be acted on by choosing Advanced to display the dialog box shown in Figure 26.27.

RUNNING OUTLOOK RULES ON EXCHANGE

When you've finished designing a rule using the Rules Wizard, you choose Finish to save that rule. At that time, Outlook examines the rule to see if it can run on Exchange without access to your computer. If for some reason that's not possible—for example, if the rule involves saving a message in a folder on your computer's hard drive—Outlook displays a message stating "This rule is a client-only rule, and will process only if Outlook is running." When you see that message you have no alternative but to choose OK. Outlook saves the rule and the wizard window lists the rule with the words "client only" after the rule's name.

PART
V

CH

26

Figure 26.27
Use this dialog box to specify additional criteria about messages to be responded to.

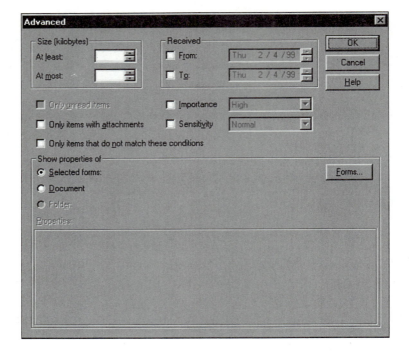

If you create a rule that can be run on the server and doesn't need access to your computer, by default Outlook automatically saves that rule on the server instead of on your computer's hard disk. In that case, the rule's name is displayed in the wizard window without the words "client only" being added.

You know, therefore, that rule names displayed in the wizard window with the words "client only" appended refer to rules that operate only when Outlook is running on your computer; rule names without those words appended run on the server whether or not Outlook is running on your computer.

You can control whether or not Outlook saves rules on the server. To do so, choose Tools, Rules Wizard to open the Rules Wizard dialog box, and then choose Options to display the dialog box shown in Figure 26.28.

By default, Automatically is selected in the Update Exchange Server section of this dialog box. If you want to manually control whether Outlook saves rules on the server, select Manually.

Tip #165 from

Outlook saves the Automatically or Manually selection from one Outlook session to the next. If you select Manually and subsequently exit from Outlook, that setting will be in effect the next time you start Outlook.

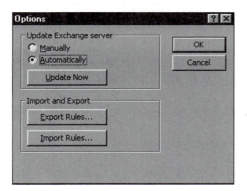

Figure 26.28
Use this dialog box to choose whether Outlook automatically saves new rules on the server.

After you select <u>M</u>anually, Outlook saves rules on your computer. To move those rules that can run on the server from your computer to the server, choose <u>U</u>pdate Now in the Rules Wizard Options dialog box.

USING WEB SERVICES

If your Exchange Server administrator has set up and enabled Outlook Web Access on Exchange, you can create and access forms in HTML format from within Outlook. In this situation, the new command Web Form appears on Outlook's Actions menu. When you choose this command, you can choose a form that your default Web browser automatically opens.

For detailed information about Outlook Web Access, refer to the Microsoft publication *Outlook Web Access Deployment and Troubleshooting Guide* which is available on the Web site `http://support.microsoft.com/support.exchange/content/whitepapers/whitepapers.asp`. You can also find information in books about Exchange Server, such as *Special Edition Using Microsoft Exchange Server 5.5*, published by Que.

TROUBLESHOOTING

Everyone has troubles, from time to time, with e-mail. It's not easy to find out the cause of those troubles; it's less easy to correct them. That's because e-mail is a very complex process that involves hardware and software on your computer, the physical connection between your computer and your e-mail servers, the paths between your servers and your recipients' servers, and the hardware and software your recipients use. You can only be responsible for your own hardware and software.

If you have trouble sending and receiving e-mail, you can try to isolate the problem by sending a message to yourself. By doing that, you're limiting the problem to what happens on your local computer and your account on the local Exchange server. If that works okay, you know that what you've set up is satisfactory. If that doesn't work, you need to ask for help from your local network or Exchange administrator.

PART
V
CH
26

Once you've been able to send a message to yourself, you know that your end of Outlook is fine. Now try sending messages to a colleague who has an account on the same Exchange server. Gradually expand your horizon until you find out where the difficulty arises. Once you've identified the problem, the only thing you can do is talk (yes, plain old telephone) to the person responsible for the system where the problem occurs to get help in resolving it.

CHAPTER 27

Using Exchange Server to Share Information

by Gordon Padwick

In this chapter

SHARING INFORMATION

When you're using C/W Outlook as a client for an Exchange server, you can choose among three ways to share information with other people who have Exchange accounts:

- Delegate Access—To give someone permission to access your Outlook folders and act on your behalf. For example, designating delegate access is useful if you are a manager and need an assistant to act on your behalf while you are away.

- Public Folders—To make information available throughout a group or organization.

- Shared Folders—To share information in your folders with several or many people in a work group.

→ If you want to designate another person to have delegate access to your folders, **see** "Delegating Access to Your Folders," **p. 691**.

This chapter focuses on public and shared folders.

USING PUBLIC FOLDERS

Public folders on the server are used to make information available to members of a group of any size. Common uses of public folders are to publish company-wide information such as Employee Policy Manuals and corporate calendars.

> **Note**
>
> The process of putting information into a public folder is known as *posting*.

You can use public folders for such purposes as:

- Posting information for many people to see—Normally, one person has permission to post, edit, and delete information in a public folder of this type, while everyone has permission to read that information.

- Maintaining an unmoderated electronic bulletin board—Used in this way, a public folder is very similar to an Internet newsgroup. Everyone has permission to post and read information. Normally, one person has permission to delete information.

- Maintaining a moderated bulletin board—People offer items to a moderator who decides which items to post on the bulletin board. Only the moderator has post and delete permissions; everyone has read permission.

- Sharing Outlook items with other people—The people who own the items copy those items to a public folder and give specific people permission to read them.

- Sharing files created in other applications, such as documents created in Word, worksheets created in Excel, and databases created in Access—The people who own the files copy them to a public folder and give specific other people whatever permissions are appropriate.

CREATING A PUBLIC FOLDER

Public folders are created within an existing public folder in the *Exchange store*. Exchange Server provides up to 16 gigabytes of space for public folders; the Exchange administrator can limit the size of individual public folders. You must have permission to create a folder in order to create a folder within an existing public folder.

Note

> The Exchange Server administrator uses Exchange Server Administrator to control permissions for creating folders on the server. This subject is beyond the scope of this book. For information about this, I recommend picking up a copy of *Special Edition Using Microsoft Exchange Server 5.5*, also published by Que.

This chapter assumes you have the permission required to create public folders. If that's not the case, ask your Exchange Server administrator to grant you the necessary permission.

To create a public folder:

1. With any Outlook Information viewer displayed, choose View, Folder List to display your folder list, such as the one shown in Figure 27.1.

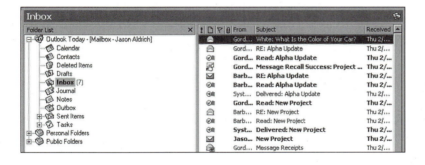

Figure 27.1
If you have the Microsoft Exchange Server information service in your profile, your folder list should contain a folder named Public Folders.

2. Expand the Public Folders folder and then expand the All Public Folders folder, as shown in Figure 27.2.

Note

> The All Public Folders folder in Figure 27.2 contains four folders. Your Public Folders folder may be empty or may contain a long list of folders. The icon at the left of each folder name indicates the type of item that folder contains.

3. Right-click All Public Folders to display its context menu (be careful to right-click All Public Folders, not Public Folders). Choose New Folder in the context menu to display the dialog box shown in Figure 27.3.

4. Enter a name for the new public folder in the Name box.

Figure 27.2
The Public Folders folder contains a Favorites folder and an All Public Folders folder.

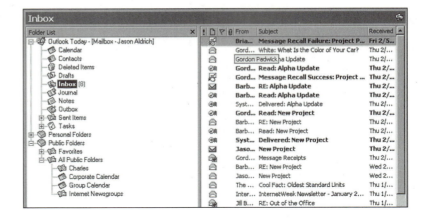

Figure 27.3
Use this dialog box to create a public folder.

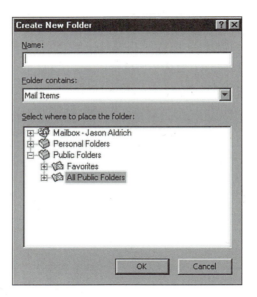

5. Unless you specifically intend to use the new folder for a particular type of Outlook item, leave Mail Items in the <u>F</u>older Contains box. You can open the drop-down list and select another type of Outlook item.

> **Note**
> Use Mail Items in the <u>F</u>older Contains box if you're setting up a public folder to use for general information or as a bulletin board.

6. Because you started creating the new folder with All Public Folders selected in the folder list, Outlook proposes to save the new folder as a subfolder of All Public Folders. Don't change that, unless you want the new folder to be a sub-folder under an existing folder.

7. Choose OK to finish creating the new folder.

8. Outlook asks if you want to add a shortcut to the new folder on the Outlook Bar. Choose <u>Y</u>es if you expect to access the public folder frequently; otherwise, choose <u>N</u>o. The dialog box closes and the new folder is shown in the folder list as a subfolder of All Public Folders.

The name of the new public folder appears in your folder list in its correct alphabetical position.

GIVING PEOPLE ACCESS TO A PUBLIC FOLDER

After you create a public folder, you own it and control who has access to it. The only other person who can control access is the Exchange administrator. You can give access to individual people or to groups. Outlook gives you two ways to do this. You can give specific permissions to people or groups, or you can assign roles to people or groups. The available permissions are listed in Table 27.1; predefined roles are listed in Table 27.2.

TABLE 27.1   AVAILABLE PERMISSIONS

Permission Types	Individual Permissions
Access	Create items, Read items, Edit own items, Edit all items, Create subfolders, Folder visible
Ownership	Folder owner, Folder contact
Delete	Delete own items, Delete all items

TABLE 27.2   OUTLOOK'S PREDEFINED ROLES

Role	Permissions
Author	Create, read, modify, and delete own items and files
Contributor	Read items; Submit items and files
Custom	Any combination of permissions
Editor	Create, read, modify, and delete all items and files
Non-Editing Author	Create and read items; Delete own items
Owner	Create, read, modify, and delete all items and files; Create subfolders; Set permissions for other people to access the folder
Publishing Author	Create and read items; Modify and delete own items; Create subfolders
Publishing Editor	Create, read, modify, and delete all items and files; Create subfolders
Reviewer	Read items

PART

V

CH

27

EXAMINING THE DEFAULT PERMISSIONS

With a public folder (one that you own) for which you want to assign permissions visible in the folder list, right-click the name of that folder to display its context menu. In the context menu, choose Properties to display the folder's properties dialog box. Choose the Permissions tab to display the dialog box shown in Figure 27.4. The Properties dialog box has a Permissions tab only for the public folders you own.

Figure 27.4
The dialog box opens with some names listed, each with a specific role.

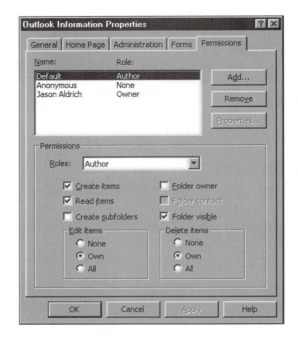

Note

> After you right-click the name of a public folder that someone else created and, therefore, owns, the dialog box has a Summary tab instead of a Permissions tab. Choose the Summary tab to see, but not change, the permissions you have for that folder.

Outlook defines default permissions to three names: Default, Anonymous, and your own name.

- Default defines the permissions everyone who has an Exchange Server account gets unless you specifically give a person different permissions. Outlook assigns Author permissions to default users.

- Anonymous defines the permissions given to people who don't have an Exchange Server account but, if the server administrator allows, log on to Exchange Server as Anonymous. The same permissions apply to people who log on as Anonymous by way of Outlook Web Access or an Active Server Page. Outlook assigns no permissions to anonymous users.

Note

For information about Outlook Web Access, see *Special Edition Using Microsoft Exchange Server 5.5*, published by Que. For more information about Active Server Pages (ASP) see *Special Edition Using Microsoft FrontPage 2000*, also published by Que.

- Your own name defines the permissions you have as the owner of the public folder. Outlook assigns Owner permissions to the folder owner.

When the dialog box first appears, the first name in the list—Default—is selected. The permissions section in the bottom part of the dialog box shows the permissions given to default users. You can select the other two names to see the permissions given to them.

For each name in the list of users, the Permissions section of the dialog box shows permissions in two ways. The <u>R</u>oles box shows permissions in terms of a predefined role. Below that are check boxes and option buttons that show the individual permissions associated with the role.

CHANGING PEOPLE'S PERMISSIONS

You don't have to accept the default permissions Outlook assigns. For example, you may want to change the permissions for Default to None, so that only those people you specifically assign permissions to can access the public folder. If the public folder is intended to contain information available for everyone on the LAN to read, you should change the permissions for Anonymous to Read Items.

To change a person's or group's role:

1. Select the person or group in the list in the upper part of the dialog box.
2. Open the drop-down <u>R</u>oles list and select the role you want to assign. The role in the second column of the list of users changes to the role you selected. Also, the check boxes and option buttons below Roles change to show the individual permissions associated with the new role.

To assign specific permissions to a person or group:

1. Select the person or group in the list in the upper part of the dialog box.
2. Check the check boxes and select the option buttons in the lower part of the dialog box to assign specific permissions. If you select a combination of check boxes and option buttons that correspond to a predefined role, the name of that role appears in the Roles box. Otherwise, the Roles box contains the word Custom.

PART
V

CH
27

Tip #166 from

If you don't want a group, such as Anonymous, to see the public folder, remove the check mark from the Folder Visible box.

ADDING PERMISSIONS

You can add people and groups to the permissions list.

To add permissions for a person or group:

1. In the Permissions tab of the public folder's Properties dialog box, choose Add to display the dialog box shown in Figure 27.5.

Figure 27.5
This dialog box opens showing a list of people who have accounts on the Exchange server.

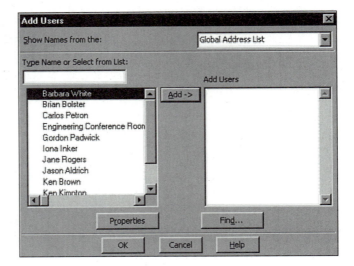

2. Choose the name of a person (or of several people) for whom you want to assign permissions.

3. Choose Add-> to move the selected names into the Add Users list, then choose OK to return to the dialog box that shows the names you selected with the permissions you previously assigned to Default users.

4. Select the new users (you can select them individually or select any combination of them).

5. Either assign a role to the new user (or users) or select the individual permissions you want them to have.

WITHDRAWING A USER'S PERMISSIONS

To withdraw the permissions you've previously given for a user to access the public folder, select that user's name in the Permissions tab, then choose Remove. Outlook immediately removes the user's name from the list of users.

GETTING INFORMATION ABOUT A USER

To see information about a user, select that user's name in the list of users in the Permissions tab. Then choose Properties. Outlook displays the selected user's Properties dialog box, such as the one shown in Figure 27.6.

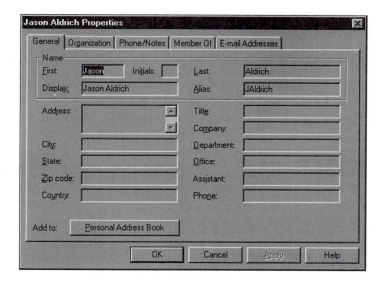

Figure 27.6
Individually select the five tabs in this dialog box to see information about the selected user.

POSTING INFORMATION ON A PUBLIC FOLDER

You can post Outlook items or files on a public folder for which you have Create Items permission. After you post an item in a public folder, other people who have permission to create items can respond to it. The chain of responses is known as a *conversation*. A conversation has a name that's the same as the subject of the message that started the conversation.

POSTING A MESSAGE

Posting information in a public folder is much like sending an e-mail message.

To post information in a public folder:

1. Select the public folder into which you want to post information. If you have a shortcut icon for the public folder in your Outlook Bar, choose it. Otherwise, open your folder

PART
V

CH

27

list and choose the public folder. Either way, Outlook displays an Information viewer that shows items already in the public folder.

2. Choose the <u>N</u>ew at the left end of the viewer's Standard toolbar to display the Discussion form shown in Figure 27.7.

Figure 27.7
The Discussion form opens with the name of the public folder near the top. The form shown here is ready to post.

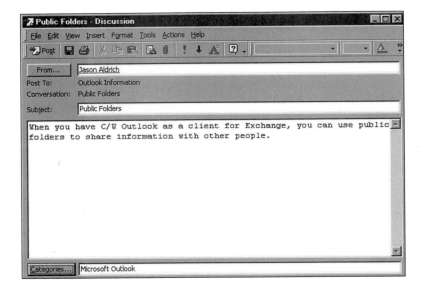

3. Enter a subject for the item in the Subject box and press Enter or Tab to move the insertion point into the large text box. The subject text appears as the name of the conversation in the header.

4. Enter text into the large box that occupies most of the form.

5. If you want your post to include insertions, choose <u>I</u>nsert in the form's Standard toolbar and choose <u>F</u>ile (to insert a file), It<u>e</u>m (to insert an Outlook item), or <u>O</u>bject (to insert a Windows object).

6. Choose <u>C</u>ategories to display the Categories dialog box, in which you can select one or more categories for the item.

7. Choose Po<u>s</u>t in the form's Standard toolbar to post your item into the public folder.

An item posted in this way appears in the public folder's Information viewer in much the same way as received e-mail appears in the Inbox Information viewer. You, or anyone else who has access to the public folder, can double-click the posted items header in the viewer to see the item in the Discussion form.

Note

A public folder's Information viewer can be displayed with or without a Preview pane. Choose View, Preview Pane to display or hide the Preview pane.

RESPONDING TO A POST

When you read something that another person has posted in a public folder, you may want to ask a question or add information, something you can do if you have permission to create items. Instead of creating a new post, you should reply to the existing one. In that way, you create a conversation in which your reply is linked to the original message, as subsequently described in this chapter.

→ You can use Public Folders as a conversation forum. **See** "Using a Public Folder as an Unmoderated Bulletin Board," **p. 714**.

POSTING A FILE

You can post a file created in an Office, or Office-compatible, application into a public folder.

To post an Office file into a public folder:

1. Open the file you want to post using the Office application in which the file was created.

2. Choose File, move the pointer onto Send To, and choose Exchange Folder. After a few moments delay, a dialog box such as that shown in Figure 27.8 is displayed. Initially, only top-level folders are listed. You have to expand these folders to see individual folders.

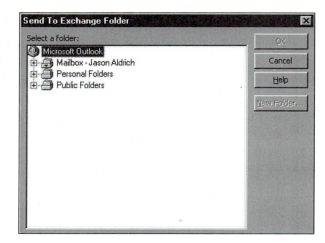

Figure 27.8
This dialog box initially lists the available, top-level folders.

Note

The folders listed in this dialog box are those available on your computer as well as the folders on your Exchange Server.

3. Expand Public Folders, expand All Public Folders, and select the public folder into which you want to post the file.

4. Choose OK to post the file in the selected public folder.

After following these steps, you'll find the file available in the public folder's Information viewer, as shown in Figure 27.9.

Figure 27.9
The symbols at the left of item names identify whether an item is a message or a file. If the item is a file, the item's name becomes the subject of the file.

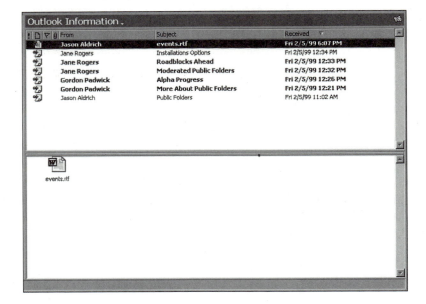

USING A PUBLIC FOLDER AS AN UNMODERATED BULLETIN BOARD

You can use a public folder as a bulletin board, a community resource people can use to discuss whatever is on their minds. Anyone who has Create Item permission for the public folder can post items on the bulletin board and respond to items already posted there.

To use a public folder you've created in this way, you should probably set the Default role as Author. Having done that, anyone who has an Exchange account can post items in the folder, read whatever anyone else has posted, and respond to posted items. You might consider, though, whether you want to allow users to edit and delete items they've previously posted, both of which are permissions included in the Author role.

In the Permissions tab of the public folder's dialog box, you can change the Default permissions to include only Create and Read items. After you've done that, users can't change or delete items once they've posted them—more in the spirit of a bulletin board.

When a public folder is used as a bulletin board, users can post items onto that board. Other users see those items when they open the bulletin board public folder, and they can double-click the item header to see the item in full in the Discussion form shown in Figure 27.10.

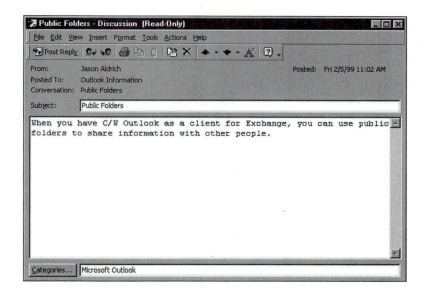

Figure 27.10
The text in this form is read-only because the public folder's owner assigned Author permissions to other people.

> **Note**
>
> *Author permissions* allow a user to read items, to create new items, and to edit only items that user has created.

To respond to an item, after double-clicking the item header in the public folder's Information viewer to display the item in a Discussion form, choose Post Reply in the form's Standard toolbar. Now you see the original post with space above it for your response, as shown in Figure 27.11.

Responding to a post is much like replying to an e-mail message. After completing your response, choose Post in the Discussion form's Standard toolbar to post the reply. After you've posted your response, you're left with the original post displayed in the Discussion form. Close that form when you've finished reading what it contains.

Figure 27.11
The form you use for a response already has the original post's subject as the name of the conversation, but the Subject box is empty. You should provide a subject for your response.

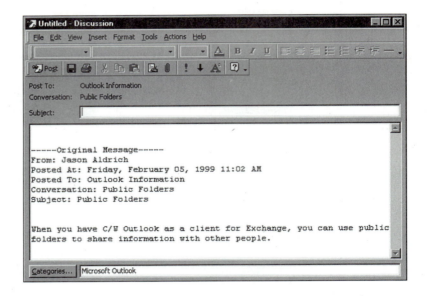

VIEWING A CONVERSATION

A public folder used as a bulletin board may contain many conversations, each started by someone who posts a message. Any number of people can respond to the original message; other people can respond to those responses. Before long, the bulletin board contains many conversations, each with several (perhaps many) responses.

You can group messages by conversation so that you can easily follow through a thread of messages. To do so, display the public folder's Information viewer, choose View, move the pointer onto Current View, and choose By Conversation Topic. Outlook displays conversation topics, initially with all of them collapsed so that you can't see the items within each conversation. Choose the + at the left of a conversation topic to expand that topic, as shown in Figure 27.12.

Figure 27.12
The By Conversation Topic view indents items to show their relationships.

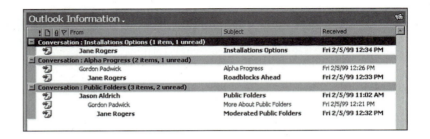

In this view, double-click any message to display it in the Discussion form.

Sending an E-mail Response to a Conversation Item

People should normally respond to bulletin board messages on the bulletin board so that everyone can benefit from those responses. There are times, though, when you might want to send a private response to a person who posted a message. You can do so by sending e-mail directly to that person.

Also, you might want to send a copy of a bulletin board message to someone who doesn't have access to the bulletin board. You can do so by using e-mail.

To e-mail a conversation item or send e-mail to someone who posted an item:

1. Display the public folder's Information viewer.
2. Select the conversation item you want to send by e-mail.
3. Choose Reply in the viewer's toolbar if you want to send a reply to the person who posted the conversation item; alternatively, choose Forward if you want to send the item to someone. In either case, Outlook displays a Message form that contains the conversation item.
4. Proceed in the normal way to send the message.

Using a Public Folder as a Moderated Bulletin Board

A moderated bulletin board is one for which people can submit items for posting on the bulletin board to a moderator. The moderator decides whether to post those items.

To designate a public folder as a moderated bulletin board, you must be the owner of that public folder. Proceed as follows.

To create a moderated bulletin board.

1. In the folder list, right-click the name of a public folder for which you have Owner permission to display the folder's context menu.
2. Choose Properties to display the folder's Properties dialog box. Select the Administration tab to display the dialog box shown in Figure 27.13.
3. Choose Moderated Folder to display the dialog box shown in Figure 27.14.
4. Check Set Folder up as a Moderated folder. When you do so, the boxes and buttons in the lower part of the dialog box become available.
5. Choose To to display a dialog box in which you can select the name of a moderator to whom items submitted to the moderated folder will be forwarded for consideration.

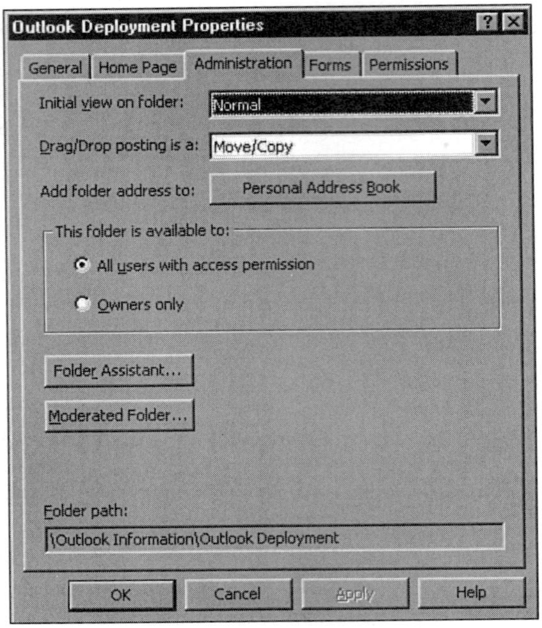

Figure 27.13
Choose Help at the bottom of this dialog box if you want to see information about what it contains.

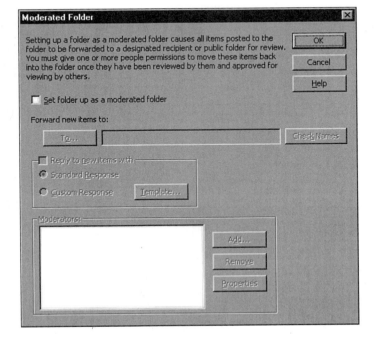

Figure 27.14
Read the text at the top of this dialog box to get a brief description of how moderated folders work.

> The person you select here is who Outlook automatically sends submissions to, not necessarily the person who accepts or rejects submissions. The people who actually accept or reject submissions are selected in step 7. Instead of naming a person, you can name another public folder where submitted messages are to be saved for review by the moderators.

6. If you want Outlook to automatically reply to all submissions, check Reply to <u>N</u>ew Items With. To use Outlook's automatic response, accept the default Standard <u>R</u>esponse; otherwise select <u>C</u>ustom Response (in which case you must have a response previously saved as an Outlook template; choose <u>T</u>emplate to select that template).

→ To save a response as a template, **see** "Using Outlook Templates," **p. 519**.

7. Choose A<u>d</u>d to select the Select Additional Moderators dialog box. Select one or more moderators and then choose OK. The names of the moderators you selected are displayed in the <u>M</u>oderators box at the bottom of the Moderated Folder dialog box.

After you've selected one or more moderators, all items submitted to the public folder are automatically forwarded to those moderators. Those moderators need to have Create Item permission to the public folder so that, if they approve items, they can post them in the folder.

USING CUSTOM FORMS WITHIN PUBLIC FOLDERS

By default, public folders offer the Post form, shown in the preceding sections of this chapter, for people to use when posting items. However, you can use public folders for many specialized purposes that require a public folder to offer a *custom form (page 1032)*.

→ To learn more about creating Outlook forms, **see** "Creating and Using Custom Forms," **p. 1031**.

After you've created a custom form, you can associate that form with a public folder. You must have Owner permission to do so.

To associate a custom form with a public folder:

1. Display your folder list and right-click the name of the public folder to which you want to associate a form.

2. Choose Propert<u>i</u>es in the public folder's context menu and select the General tab, shown in Figure 27.15.

3. Open the drop-down box labeled When <u>P</u>osting to This Folder, Use. Most likely, you'll see only Post and Forms listed. Choose Forms to display the dialog box shown in Figure 27.16.

4. Open the drop-down <u>L</u>ook In list and select the forms library in which you have saved the custom form (probably Personal Forms Library).

5. Select the form you want to associate with the public folder and choose Open to return to the Properties dialog box in which the name of the form you chose is shown.

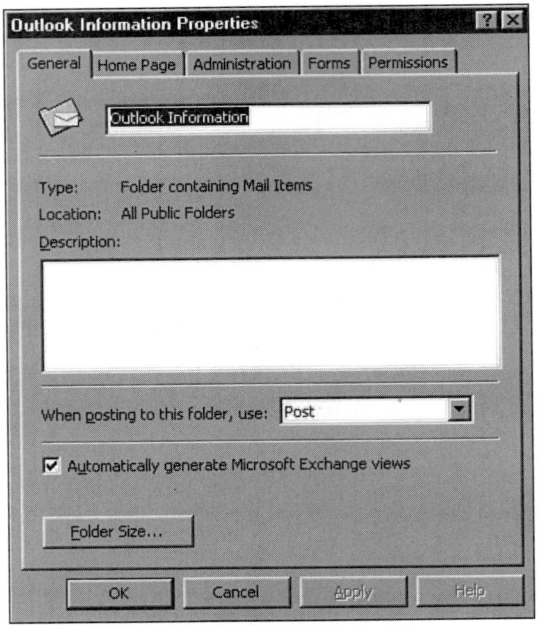

Figure 27.15
By default, public folders offer the Post form.

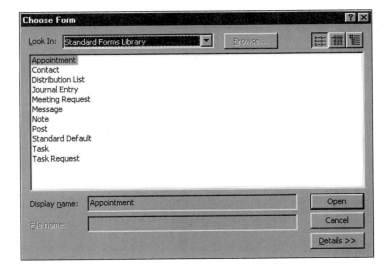

Figure 27.16
This dialog box opens showing a list of forms in the Outlook Standard Forms Library.

Subsequently, when a person chooses <u>N</u>ew in the public folder's Information viewer toolbar, Outlook displays the form you specified.

MAKING A PUBLIC FOLDER AVAILABLE OFFLINE

Normally, public folders are available when your computer is connected to Exchange Server. However, there are times when people need access to a public folder when they're working offline. The following procedure shows you how to do just that.

To make a public folder available offline:

1. Display your folder list.

2. Point onto the name of the folder you want to be able to use offline. Press the mouse button and drag the public folder onto the Favorites subfolder (under Public Folders). Now you have a copy of the public folder in your Favorites folder.

3. Expand Favorites and right-click the folder you just dragged into Favorites to display its context menu.

4. Choose Properties in the context menu to open the Properties dialog box. Select the Synchronization tab, as shown in Figure 27.17.

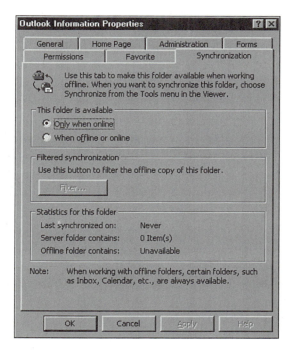

Figure 27.17
Use this dialog box to enable offline use of the public folder.

PART

V

CH

27

5. In the This Folder Is Available section of the dialog box, select When Offline or Online.

When you work offline, any changes you make to the contents of your copy of the public folder don't affect the actual public folder on the server. Likewise, any changes other people make to the public folder on the server don't affect your offline copy. Later, when you're again online, you can synchronize your offline copy of the public folder with the actual public folder on the server. The *synchronization (page 732)* process updates both folders so that each of them contains the most recent information.

→ To learn more about synchronizing your remote folders, **see** "Synchronizing Your Offline Folders ," **p. 740**.

CREATING RULES FOR A PUBLIC FOLDER

You can create rules for a public folder in a similar manner to creating rules in the Out of Office Assistant.

→ **See** "Using the Out of Office Assistant," **p. 698**.

Note   You must have Owner permission for a public folder in order to create rules for it.

To create rules for a public folder:

1. Display your folder list and right-click the name of a public folder to display its context menu.

2. Choose Properties in the context menu to display the Properties dialog box. Select the Administration tab, shown previously in Figure 27.13.

3. Choose Folder Assistant to display the dialog box shown in Figure 27.18.

Figure 27.18
Initially, this dialog box contains no rules.

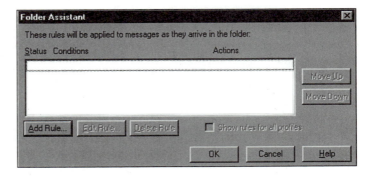

4. Choose Add Rule to display the Edit Rule dialog box, shown in Figure 27.19, in which you can enter and select information to define a rule.

5. After you've defined the rule, choose OK to return to the Folder Assistant dialog box that lists the rule you created.

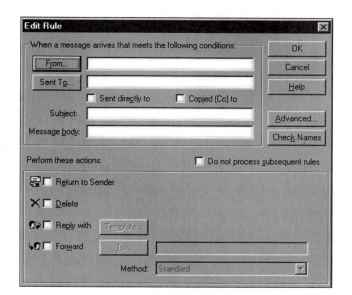

Figure 27.19
This dialog box provides facilities for you to specify the details of a rule for a public folder.

Note

Chapter 22, "Creating and Using Rules," contains detailed information about creating rules for e-mail messages. Much of the information there applies to creating rules for public folders.

USING THE FAVORITES FOLDER

The word "favorites" in the Outlook environment has two completely different meanings:

- The Favorites shortcut in the Other Shortcuts section of the Outlook Bar provides access to files, folders, and shortcuts (including URL shortcuts) in the Windows Favorites folder.

- Favorites in the folder list is an Outlook public folder that contains a subset of the public folders available in the Exchange store.

This section deals with the second meaning of the word.

The Exchange store in a large organization might contain hundreds, if not thousands, of public folders, only a few of which each person accesses regularly. To simplify access to frequently used public folders, each person can copy those public folders from the All Public Folders section of the folder list into the Favorites section.

To copy a public folder from the All Public Folders section to the Favorites section, simply drag the name of the public folder from one section to the other. After you've done that, you can access a public folder by selecting from the few folders listed in the Favorites section instead of from the many folders listed in the All Public Folders section.

PART
V

CH
27

As explained previously in this chapter, you can make public folders listed in the Favorites section of Public Folders available for offline use, something you can't do for public folders only listed in the All Public Folders section.

SHARING YOUR FOLDERS

If you're using C/W Outlook as a client for Exchange and you save your Outlook items in the Exchange store, you can give other people access to your folders. You can't share folders in your Personal Folders file.

Note
You can, of course, share your entire Personal Folders file within the Windows environment. When you do that, you have no control over sharing individual folders within the file.

GIVING PERMISSION TO ACCESS YOUR FOLDERS

Sharing your own folders has much in common with sharing public folders. Most organizations use public folders to create a long-term resource available throughout a large group or even the entire enterprise. Individual people who want to share information with a few colleagues often prefer to share information in their own existing folders instead of taking the time to create a public folder. Whereas you need to have the appropriate permission from the Exchange Server administrator to create a public folder, you don't require any such permission to share your own folders.

To share a single Outlook folder:

1. Display your folder list and right-click the name of a folder you want to share to display its context menu.

2. Choose Properties to display the Properties dialog box. Select the Permissions tab, as shown in Figure 27.20.

3. To give someone access to your folders, choose Add to display the Add Users dialog box, shown previously in Figure 27.5, in which you can select the names of people who have accounts on Exchange to whom you want to grant access permission.

4. Select the names of one or more people whom you want to have access to your folder. Choose Add-> and then choose OK to return to the folder's Properties dialog box, which now shows the people's names you just selected. Each has the same role (None) as the Default.

5. Select one or more of the names you selected in the previous step.

6. To assign a role to the selected names, open the Roles drop-down list and select a role. Alternatively, check individual permissions and select option buttons. This is similar to granting permissions for a public folder, described previously in this chapter.

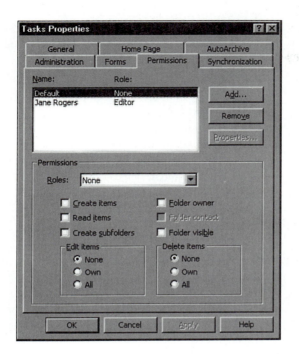

Figure 27.20
The Permissions tab initially shows that Default users have None as their permissions, meaning that nobody has access to your folders.

→ If others in your workgroup need to access your public folders, **see** "Giving People Access to a Public Folder." **p. 707**.

Now, the people you selected have the permissions you assigned to access your folders. At any time you can return to this dialog box to change these permissions:

- You can select a person's name and then choose Remove to remove all the permissions you gave that person.

- You can select a person's name and then change the role or individual permissions you gave that person.

ACCESSING ANOTHER PERSON'S FOLDERS

After other people have granted you access to their folders in the Exchange store, you can open those folders.

To open another person's Outlook folders:

1. With any Outlook Information viewer displayed, choose File, move the pointer onto Open, and choose Other User's Folder to display the dialog box shown in Figure 27.21.

2. Choose Name to display the Select Name dialog box. Use that dialog box to select the name of the person who has granted you folder access.

3. Open the drop-down Folder list and select the folder to which you have been granted access.

4. Choose OK to display the folder.

Figure 27.21
The dialog box is shown here with a user's name and one of that user's folders selected.

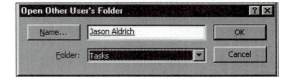

Subject to the permissions the folder's owner granted, you can now work with the other person's folder.

TROUBLESHOOTING

Public Folders are quite simple at the Outlook level; the types of problems you'll run into there are mainly to do with permissions. However, public folders are maintained on your Exchange server, so you might well run into all sorts of connectivity problems, just as you might do when using your network for other purposes. Fortunately for you, connectivity problems are the province of the network administrator, they're not for you to solve (unless you have the misfortune to be that person).

One of the key concepts of public folders is ownership. Depending on the permissions the Exchange administrator gives to you, you can create public folders. You own those folders and can grant permissions to other people to access your folders. The only other person who can change permissions is the Exchange administrator. You can delete your own public folders; the Exchange administrator can too, but only after granting himself ownership permissions to your public folders.

If the owner of a public folder hasn't granted you specific permissions to access that folder, you get only default permissions which usually means you have no access to the folder. If you can't access a public folder, or can't do what you think you ought to be able to do within the folder, your only recourse is to contact the folder's owner and ask that person to change your permissions.

But what if the owner has left the organization? In that case, you can contact the Exchange administrator. That person can grant ownership permissions to himself or herself (or to someone else), so that changes can be made to your permissions.

You may find that access to public folders is slow. Apart from the obvious problem of a slow network, the speed problem might be caused by the way Exchange handles views. Whenever you or another person creates a new view or sort order for a public folder, Exchange creates a new index and stores that index in a temporary cache. The process of creating the new index can take a considerable amount of time if the folder is large. By default, Exchange keeps indexes for eight days and then deletes them (the Exchange administrator can change this default).

As a result of this mechanism, your access to a public folder may be slow the first time you create a new view. Also, if you haven't accessed a public folder for eight days, or whatever other aging period the Exchange administrator has set, you'll have to wait while Exchange creates a new index. To minimize this problem, create new views only when you really need them; also, make a habit of opening public folders to which you want fast access once a week.

CHAPTER 28

WORKING REMOTELY

In this chapter   *by Gordon Padwick*

WHEN YOU'RE OUT OF THE OFFICE

Quite a lot of people use Outlook in more than one place. If you're like many people who work in an office, you probably do most of your Outlook work there; sometimes, perhaps often, you use Outlook at home.

If you travel on business, you probably take a laptop computer with you. You may use the same laptop with a connection to your server while you're in the office, or you may use a desktop computer that stays on your desk. You don't have a permanent connection to the server while you're traveling with your laptop.

In these and other circumstances you need a way to use Outlook while you're not connected to the server, and you need a way to keep your Outlook data on two or more computers synchronized, to ensure that the same and most recent data is on all the computers.

Outlook offers several ways for you to solve these problems.

Note

Let me be honest with you. Setting up a computer to work remotely in the Exchange environment isn't simple. That's because Outlook has to deal with various configuration matters, not because Outlook is inherently difficult to use. If you work for a large enterprise, you will probably be issued with a laptop for your remote work, all set up and ready to go. Lucky you! If you have to set up a laptop by yourself for remote use, and you've never done it before, be prepared for some headaches.

UNDERSTANDING OUTLOOK'S SOLUTIONS

The following paragraphs deal with IMO Outlook and C/W Outlook separately. The techniques described here assume you use one computer in your office and another computer in other places.

WORKING REMOTELY WITH IMO OUTLOOK

You can use IMO Outlook to send and receive only Internet e-mail, as well as to manage your calendar, contacts list, to-do list, and journal. Outlook saves all the items you create and receive in folders within your Personal Folders file. If you use one computer in your office and another computer somewhere else, you have a separate Personal Folders file on each computer.

Prior to Outlook 2000, it was difficult (some would say next to impossible) to keep separate Personal Folders files on two computers synchronized. One of the major improvements in Outlook 2000 is the ability to synchronize Personal Folders files.

The only e-mail you can send and receive with IMO Outlook is Internet e-mail. Providing you have an e-mail account with an ISP that has local access phone numbers for your office and other location, receiving and sending e-mail presents no problems.

Tip #168 from

[signature]

> Configure Internet e-mail so that the location you use less frequently keeps messages on the mail server after you've read them. When you're in the other location, download messages including those you've previously read at the other location. This ensures that you have all the messages you've received in one Personal Folders file. Of course, copies of messages you send are in the Sent Items folder on the computer from which you send those messages.
>
> I find that much more convenient than exporting a Personal Folders file from one computer to a large-capacity removable disk and then importing the file from the disk to another computer.

WORKING REMOTELY WITH C/W OUTLOOK

The situation is potentially more complex if you use C/W Outlook because C/W Outlook has more capabilities than IMO Outlook and you can set up Outlook in various ways. The remainder of this chapter covers some of the possibilities in detail, including:

- Using C/W Outlook but not as an Exchange client, in which case Outlook items are saved in a Personal Folders file.
- Using C/W Outlook as an Exchange client, in which case Outlook items on your desktop computer are usually saved in an Exchange store.
- Using Exchange as your messaging system.
- Using a system other than Exchange for messaging.

WORKING REMOTELY IN AN EXCHANGE ENVIRONMENT

The scenario considered here is that of a corporate environment in which desktop computers use a LAN on which Exchange Server is used as an e-mail system. People use C/W Outlook on their computers as clients for Exchange. In order to take advantage of the collaboration facilities available in Exchange, people save their Outlook items in the Exchange store.

People who work away from the office use laptop computers on which C/W Outlook is installed and use an Offline Folders file to save Outlook items while the computers aren't connected to the server.

UNDERSTANDING OFFLINE FOLDERS

An Offline Folders file is similar to a Personal Folders file. The file contains folders that are used to save Outlook items.

PART

V

CH

28

Although a Personal Folders file and an Offline Folders file are similar in that they both contain folders used to store Outlook items, there is a significant difference between the two. A Personal Folders file contains a set of Outlook folders that are independent of any other Outlook folders.

In contrast, an Offline Folders file contains Outlook folders that are closely related to Outlook folders in the Exchange store. When you create an Offline Folders file, that file contains a copy of the Outlook folders you have in your Exchange store. While you work with Outlook, you can synchronize the Outlook folders in your Offline Folders file with your Outlook folders in the Exchange store so that both contain the most recent data.

Personal Folders files have .pst as their file name extensions; Offline Folders files have .ost as their file name extensions.

When your laptop computer is connected to a LAN you can synchronize the information in your Offline Folders file with information from your Exchange store. Then you can disconnect the computer from the LAN and work with Outlook while you're traveling or in a different location. Sometime later, when your computer is again connected to the LAN, you can again synchronize your Offline Folders file with your Exchange store.

Note

Synchronization is the process by which two sets of folders are compared and updated so that the most recent items are saved in both sets of folders.

CREATING A PROFILE FOR OFFLINE USE

If you're going to use your computer offline (not connected to Exchange) you must create a profile for that purpose. You should do that after you've created a profile for working with Outlook when your computer is connected to Exchange.

Note

If you already have a profile for working online with Exchange, the offline profile you create automatically contains the folder structure in your online profile and the individual folders contain the Outlook items in your Exchange store.

To create a profile for offline use:

1. If Outlook is already running, choose File, Exit and Log Off to close Outlook.

2. Choose Start on the Windows taskbar, move the pointer onto Settings, and choose Control Panel.

3. In the Control Panel, double-click Mail (or Mail and Fax) to display the Properties dialog box.

4. Choose <u>S</u>how Profiles to display the Mail dialog box that contains a list of existing profiles.

5. Choose A<u>d</u>d to display the Microsoft Outlook Setup Wizard, as shown in Figure 28.1.

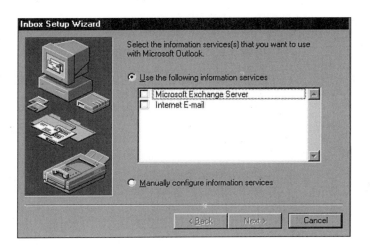

Figure 28.1
The wizard offers two information services you can include in a new profile.

6. Check Microsoft Exchange Server, then choose Next > to display the second wizard window, as shown in Figure 28.2.

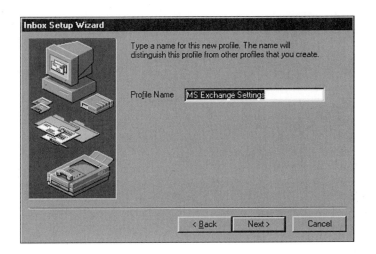

Figure 28.2
The wizard proposes a name for the new profile.

7. Replace the suggested name with something more appropriate, such as Offline. Choose Next > to display the third wizard window, as shown in Figure 28.3.

Figure 28.3
Use this window to specify your Exchange server and the name of your mailbox on that server.

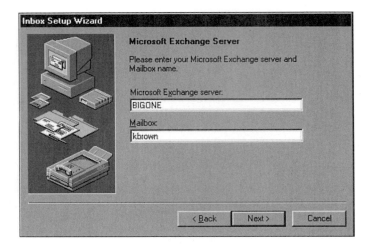

8. Enter the name of your server and the name of your mailbox. Choose Next > to display the fourth wizard window, shown in Figure 28.4.

Figure 28.4
This is the window in which you let the profile know that you will be working offline.

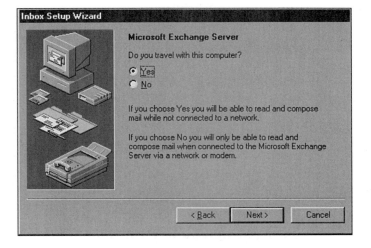

9. The window asks "Do you travel with this computer?" Choose <u>Y</u>es to indicate that you will be working offline. Choose Next > to display the final wizard window, shown in Figure 28.5.

Figure 28.5
This wizard window says you've completed creating the new profile.

10. Choose Finish to display the dialog box shown in Figure 28.6. Don't close this dialog box yet.

Figure 28.6
This dialog box lists the profiles available on your computer, including the one you just created.

PART

V

CH

28

Now you have to set the properties of the new profile, as explained in the next section.

Note

If you intend to use the Internet for e-mail while you're traveling, you should also add the Internet E-mail information service to your profile. You'll also need to make sure you have the TCP/IP protocol installed in Windows and that your computer is set up for Dial-up Networking.

→ If you need to install the TCP/IP protocol, **see** "Installing the TCP/IP Protocol," **p. 60**.

→ To set up your computer for dial up connections, **see** "Setting up Dial-up Networking," **p. 60**.

CREATING AN OFFLINE FOLDERS FILE

To create and use an Offline Folders file, you must have C/W Outlook installed on your computer and you must have created a profile for using Outlook offline, as explained in the preceding section.

The following steps continue from those in the preceding section.

To create an Offline Folders file:

1. After creating a profile for offline use, as described in the preceding section, select that profile in the Mail dialog box previously shown in Figure 28.6 and choose Properties to display the dialog box for that profile, as shown in Figure 28.7.

Figure 28.7
This dialog box opens with the Services tab selected, showing the information services in your profile.

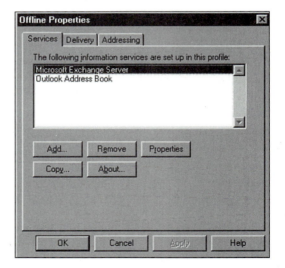

2. Select the Microsoft Exchange Server information service and choose Properties to display the Properties dialog box. Select the Advanced tab, shown in Figure 28.8.

Figure 28.8
Use this dialog box to begin creating an Offline Folders file.

3. Choose Offline Folder File Settings to display the dialog box shown in Figure 28.9.

Figure 28.9
Windows proposes to create an Offline Folders file named outlook.ost.

4. Enter the full path name for the Offline Folders file you want to use in the File box. Alternatively, choose Browse to navigate to a folder and enter a file name.

Tip #169 from

[signature]

It's a good idea to replace the default file name with your own name or e-mail account name. For example, if your e-mail account name is kbrown, use kbrown.ost as the file name.

5. Choose the encryption setting you want to use.

Note

You have to select an encryption setting at the time you create an Offline Folders file. You can't subsequently change the encryption setting.

6. Choose OK three times and then close the Control Panel.

After completing these steps, you have on your computer an Offline Folders file that contains a duplicate of the folders and Outlook items in your Exchange store.

The next time you open Outlook, you may see the Choose Profile dialog box. In that case select the offline profile you just created.

If Outlook starts without displaying the Show Profile dialog box, you need to change Outlook's options so that this dialog box does appear. To do so, with any Information viewer displayed, choose Tools, Options to display the Options dialog box. Select the Mail Services tab and, in the Startup Settings section, select Prompt for a Profile to Be Used, then choose OK to save that option. After doing that, when you start Outlook, you'll see the Choose Profile dialog box and be able to select the profile you want to use—either the one you use when your computer is connected to the server or the one you use offline.

USING OUTLOOK OFFLINE

After completing the steps described in the preceding two sections, you can unplug your computer from the network and use Outlook offline.

Start Outlook in the normal way. If, as suggested in the previous section, you set the Outlook option to Prompt for a Profile to be Used, Outlook displays the Choose Profile dialog box. Open the drop-down list of profiles, select your offline profile, and choose OK. Outlook opens in the normal way.

To see that you have Outlook open with access to your Offline folder, you can choose View, Folder List to see a list of folders, as shown in Figure 28.10.

From here, you can continue to work with Outlook in the normal way.

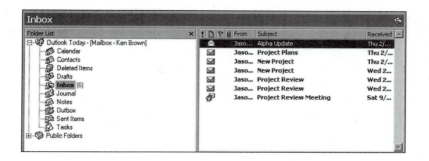

Figure 28.10
Each of the folder icons has a superimposed box containing a plus sign to indicate you're accessing offline folders.

COPYING AN ADDRESS BOOK INTO YOUR REMOTE COMPUTER

If you intend to send e-mail while you're working remotely you need to have a list of e-mail addresses available. One way you can do this is to copy the Global Address Book from your Exchange server into your remote computer.

With your remote computer connected to the LAN and with Outlook running under your offline profile, proceed as follows:

To copy the Global Address Book:

1. With any Outlook Information viewer displayed, choose Tools, move the pointer onto Synchronize, and choose Download Address Book. Outlook displays the dialog box shown in Figure 28.11.

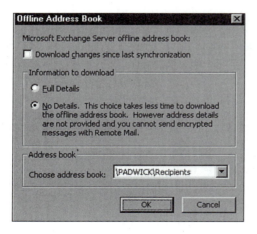

Figure 28.11
Use this dialog box to specify what you want to download.

2. The first time you copy the Global Address Book, uncheck Download Changes Since Last Synchronization. When you subsequently copy the Global Address Book, check this box.

PART
V

CH
28

3. In the Information to be Downloaded section of the dialog box, you'll normally want to leave the default Full Details selected.

4. Open the drop-down Choose Address Book list and select the address book you want to download.

5. Choose OK to start downloading.

SYNCHRONIZING YOUR OFFLINE FOLDERS

The process of synchronizing your offline folders compares the contents of your folders in the Exchange store with the contents of your offline folders. If a later version of an item is in the Exchange store, that item is copied into the corresponding offline folder. If a later version of an item is in an offline folder, that item is copied into the corresponding folder in the Exchange store.

> **Note**
>
> During synchronization, an item that's been deleted from an offline folder is deleted from the corresponding server folder. Likewise, any item that's been deleted from the server folder is deleted from the corresponding offline folder.

As mentioned previously in this chapter, when you create an Offline Folders file on your remote computer, the items currently in your Exchange store are automatically copied into your offline folders. However, in the interval between setting up your remote computer and going on a trip, some of the items in your Exchange store will have changed, so you must synchronize to bring your offline folders up to date.

MANUALLY SYNCHRONIZING FOLDERS

To synchronize your folders, start with any Outlook Information viewer displayed, then open the Tools menu and move the pointer onto Synchronize and choose All Folders, if you want to synchronize all folders. Alternatively, if you want to synchronize only the folder that the current Information viewer displays, choose This Folder.

AUTOMATICALLY SYNCHRONIZING FOLDERS

You can set up Outlook so that offline folders are automatically synchronized with corresponding folders in the Exchange store at certain times.

To configure automatic synchronization:

1. With any Outlook Information viewer displayed, choose Tools, Options to display the Options dialog box. Select the Mail Services tab, shown in Figure 28.12.

2. Check Enable Offline Access. When you do that, the check boxes within the Enable Offline Access section of the dialog box become available.

3. To automatically synchronize all offline folders whenever you exit from Outlook, check the first check box.

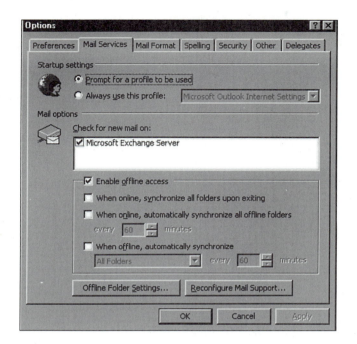

Figure 28.12
The Mail Options section of this dialog box provides facilities for setting automatic synchronization.

4. To automatically synchronize all offline folders while you're online, check the second check box and specify the number of minutes between each synchronization.

5. To automatically synchronize all offline folders while you're offline, check the third check box and specify the number of minutes between each synchronization.

Note

After you check When Offline, Automatically Synchronize, Outlook attempts to make an online connection at the defined intervals. For this to happen successfully, you must have a physical connection to the server either by way of a network or dial-up networking.

CHOOSING OFFLINE FOLDER SETTINGS

The Offline Folders file always contains the standard Outlook folders: Calendar, Contacts, Deleted Items, Drafts, Inbox, Journal, Notes, Outbox, Sent Items, and Tasks. If you have created custom folders in your Outlook store, you can choose whether you want to have these custom folders available when you're working remotely.

To make this choice, open the Tools menu from any Outlook Information viewer, move the pointer onto Synchronize, and choose Offline Folder Settings to display the dialog box shown in Figure 28.13.

PART

V

CH

28

Figure 28.13
Choose which folders
you want to use offline.

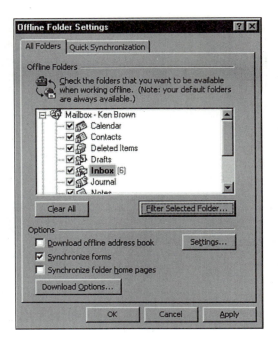

You can also open this dialog box by choosing Offline Folder Settings in the Mail Services tab of the Options dialog box.

By default, all the standard Outlook folders are checked. If you uncheck one of these, Outlook displays a message saying this folder can't be unselected. If you want to work with custom folders, check those folders, then choose OK.

To uncheck all checked custom folders, choose Clear All.

By default, synchronization involves all items in folders. If you want to filter items so that only those that satisfy specific criteria are synchronized, select a folder and choose Filter Selected Folder. When you do this, Outlook displays the dialog box shown in Figure 28.14.

Apart from the name in its title bar, the Filter dialog box works the same as the Advanced Find dialog box that's described in detail in Chapter 19, "Importing and Exporting Outlook Items." Use this dialog box to define criteria for the items you want to synchronize.

➔ To search for content in your Personal Folders, **see** "Using Advanced Find to Find Words and Phrases," **p. 532**.

Notice that the Filter dialog box has three tabs. You can define criteria in all three tabs. Initially, each tab contains no criteria. Items must satisfy criteria defined in all three tabs to be included in the synchronization process.

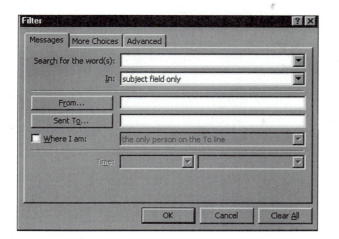

Figure 28.14
Use this dialog box to specify criteria for the items you want to synchronize.

USING PUBLIC FOLDERS REMOTELY

When you're working offline, you can't access Exchange public folders directly. You can, however, access copies of public folders that have been created in Exchange's public folders Favorites folder.

As explained in Chapter 27, "Using Exchange Server to Share Information," the person who owns a public folder can create a copy of that folder in the public folders Favorites folder.

While you're working offline you can access the Favorites folder that contains the information that existed the last time you synchronized. Any offline changes you make are copied to your Favorites folder in the Exchange store the next time you synchronize.

→ If you need to see the information in your Personal Folders as it existed the last time you synchronized, **see** "Using the Favorites Folder," **p. 723**.

CONNECTING TO YOUR EXCHANGE MAILBOX

You can set up the Microsoft Exchange Server information service on your remote computer so it can send and receive e-mail messages by way of your Exchange mailbox.

Your Exchange Server administrator has probably set up Exchange Server so that remote users can connect by way of a dial-up connection. The details of this depend on how the dial-up connection at the server end is configured to maintain the necessary level of security. To connect to the server, you may have to provide one or more passwords. In some cases, after you have provided those passwords, you may be instructed to disconnect and wait for the server to call you back. All this is necessary to avoid the possibility of unauthorized people gaining access to your account on the server.

Your first step, then, is to ask the Exchange administrator for information about the connection procedure.

PART

V

CH

28

Then, you have to set up the Microsoft Exchange Server information service on your computer. Use the Dial-up Networking and Remote Mail tabs to do so.

SETTING UP DIAL-UP NETWORKING

With any Outlook Information viewer displayed, choose Tools, Services to display the Services dialog box. In that dialog box, select the Microsoft Exchange Server information service, and then choose Properties. Select the Dial-up Networking tab, as shown in Figure 28.15.

Figure 28.15
Use this dialog box to define the dial-up connection to your Exchange Server.

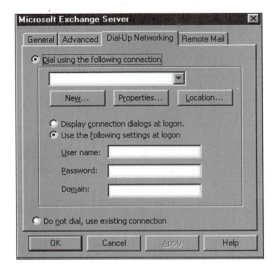

If you have a permanent dial-up connection to the server, select Do Not Dial, Use Existing Connection (at the bottom of the dialog box).

Otherwise, accept the default Dial Using the Following Connection and proceed as follows.

To select a dial-up connection:

1. Open the drop-down list of existing dial-up connections and select the one you want to use.

Note

If you haven't previously created a dial-up connection to the Exchange Server phone number, choose New to create a new connection.

If you want to check, or change, the properties of an existing connection, choose Properties.

If you want to check, or change, the location from which you're calling, choose Location.

2. Enter your username for your Exchange account in the User Name box.

3. Enter your password for your Exchange account in the Password box.

4. Enter the name of the NT domain in which your Exchange account is available in the Domain box.

SETTING UP REMOTE MAIL

With any Outlook Information viewer displayed, choose Tools, Services to display the Services dialog box. In that dialog box, select the Microsoft Exchange Server information service, and then choose Properties. Select the Remote Mail tab, as shown in Figure 28.16.

Figure 28.16
This is where you can specify how you want your remote computer to interact with your Exchange mailbox.

In the Remote Mail Connections section of the dialog box you can choose:

- Process Marked Items—After you do so and connect to your Exchange mailbox, you'll see a list of items waiting for your attention. You can select the items you see to have them transmitted to you.

- Retrieve Items that Meet the Following Conditions—After you do this, the Filter button becomes available. Choose this button to display the dialog box shown in Figure 28.17.

In the Remote Mail Connections section in the Microsoft Exchange Server dialog box, you can leave Disconnect After Connection Is Finished checked if you want to disconnect automatically or uncheck it if you want to remain connected. With the Filter dialog box (shown in Figure 28.17) displayed, you can be even more selective by choosing Advanced to display the dialog box shown in Figure 28.18.

PART
V

CH
28

Figure 28.17
Use this dialog box to specify the mail items you want to receive.

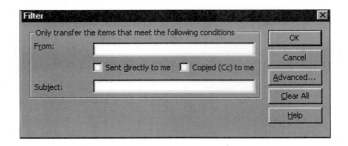

Figure 28.18
Here are more choices you can make to define which mail messages you want to receive.

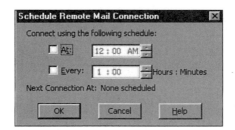

You can use the Scheduled Connections section of the Remote Mail dialog box to select automatic connection to the Exchange server at specified times. To do so, choose Schedule to display the dialog box shown in Figure 28.19.

Figure 28.19
Use this dialog box to schedule the next connection to Exchange and the subsequent interval between connections.

You can use the two options buttons and the Filter button to further control which messages are transmitted from and to Exchange server.

When your remote computer connects to your Exchange server, it receives messages waiting for you according to the criteria you've defined.

Any outgoing messages you create on your remote computer are saved in your Outbox until a connection to your Exchange server is established. When that happens, the messages in your Outbox are transmitted to your Outbox in the Exchange store and then processed as they would be if you'd created those messages locally.

USING REMOTE MAIL

Note

In order to use Outlook's Remote Mail capabilities, you must be using C/W Outlook, but not necessarily as a client for an Exchange server.

Remote Mail is an alternative way to send and receive e-mail. You can use Remote Mail for such purposes as receiving e-mail from, and sending e-mail to, an e-mail server:

- From your desktop computer
- From a computer you use at another location, such as a laptop computer you have with you while you're traveling

With Remote Mail, you can access e-mail in:

- A Personal Folders file on another computer
- An e-mail server such as your Internet server

You're probably wondering why you would want to use Remote Mail to send and receive e-mail when Outlook already provides other ways to do so. The answer to that question is that, although Remote Mail is somewhat less convenient, it has the advantage that you can use it to download only message headers and subsequently download only the complete messages you want to see.

The primary purpose of Remote Mail is to provide a way for you to receive important e-mail messages from a remote location without incurring the expense of high long-distance phone charges for messages you don't need. However, Remote Mail also provides a way for you to save time when you're working at your desk by not downloading unnecessary messages.

PREPARING TO USE REMOTE MAIL

You must have the Personal Folders information service in your profile. To check whether you have that service, display any Outlook Information viewer and choose Tools, Services. Examine the list of services to see if Personal Folders is listed. If it isn't listed, you must add that service into your profile and set its properties as described in Chapter 6.

→ Before using remote mail, you'll need to check your profile for the Personal Folders Information Service. **See** "Adding the Personal Folders Information Service to Your Profile." **p. 172**.

Tip #171 from

Gordon Padwick

You may find it convenient to create a separate profile that contains the Personal Folders information service to use when you're working with Remote Mail.

Although having an address book available if you're working with a remote computer isn't essential, it is very convenient. You can copy the server's Global Address Book to your remote computer using the method described previously in this chapter.

➔ If your address book isn't copied onto your remote computer, **see** "Copying an Address Book into Your Remote Computer," **p. 739**.

RECEIVING AND SENDING MESSAGES

This section describes how to use Remote Mail, with accessing your Internet mail as an example.

The first step in setting up the computer you will use for remote mail is to create a dial-up networking connection, as described in Chapter 3. After you've created a dial-up connection to the number you'll be calling, you're ready to use Remote Mail.

➔ If you haven't already set up your dial-up networking, **see** "Setting up Dial-up Networking," **p. 60**.

To use Remote Mail:

1. With the Inbox Information viewer displayed, choose <u>T</u>ools, move the pointer onto <u>R</u>emote Mail, and choose Connec<u>t</u> to display the first Remote Connection Wizard window, shown in Figure 28.20.

Figure 28.20
The wizard shows the available connections to information services.

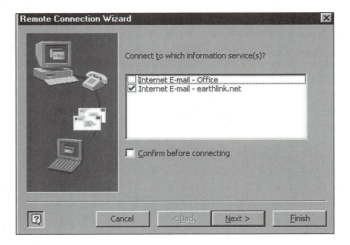

2. Check the information service you want to use. If you want Outlook to ask you for confirmation before beginning to establish a connection, check <u>C</u>onfirm Before Connecting. Choose <u>N</u>ext > to display the second wizard window, shown in Figure 28.21.

Note

The large box always contains "Retrieve new message headers…" In addition, the box contains a list of any messages in your Outbox waiting to be sent.

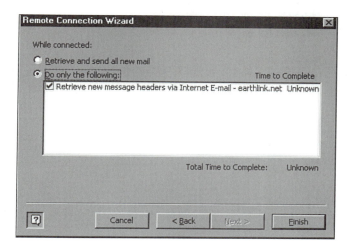

Figure 28.21
You can select
whether you want
to retrieve and send
all messages or just
perform specific
tasks.

3. In this wizard window, select the top option button if you want the server to retrieve
   and send all waiting messages. If you want to specify certain tasks, select the second
   option button then check the tasks to be done and uncheck those not to be done.
   Choose Next > to display the third wizard window shown in Figure 28.22.

Tip #172 from

If all you want to do is to download the headers of messages waiting for you, make sure
only that task is checked.

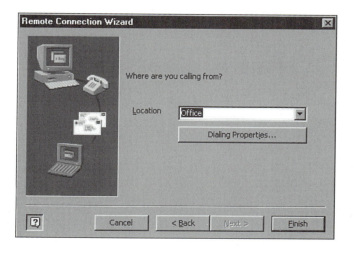

Figure 28.22
Use this wizard
window to select
your dialing location.

4. Open the drop-down Location list and select your dialog location. After doing that, you can choose Dialing Properties if you want to verify or change those properties.

5. Choose Finish. Outlook starts the process of connecting to the server, and then either retrieving and sending all messages, or just downloading the headers of waiting messages. If you chose to retrieve and send messages, Outlook saves retrieved messages in your Inbox folder and copies of sent messages in your Sent Items folder. If you chose to download only the headers of waiting messages, only the headers of waiting messages are saved in your Inbox folder. Figure 28.23 shows how these headers appear.

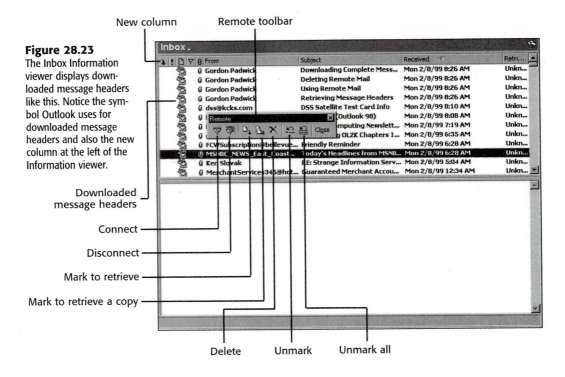

Figure 28.23
The Inbox Information viewer displays downloaded message headers like this. Notice the symbol Outlook uses for downloaded message headers and also the new column at the left of the Information viewer.

New column

Remote toolbar

Downloaded message headers

Connect

Disconnect

Mark to retrieve

Mark to retrieve a copy

Delete   Unmark   Unmark all

The Remote toolbar, which is automatically displayed when you use Remote Mail to access messages and is shown in Figure 28.23, is a floating toolbar. You can drag it to any convenient place on your screen. The buttons on this toolbar correspond to the items in the Remote Mail submenu.

You can also display the Remote toolbar by choosing View, moving the pointer onto Toolbars, and choosing Remote.

After you've used Remote Mail to retrieve message headers, you can select one or more of those headers in the Inbox Information viewer and then choose one of these buttons in the Remote toolbar:

- Mark to Retrieve—Choose this button to mark selected messages to be downloaded from the mail server and, after doing that, delete those messages from the mail server. When you do this, another symbol column appears in the Inbox Information viewer. The symbol in this column indicates that the message has been marked to be retrieved and then deleted from the server.

- Mark to Retrieve a Copy—Choose this button to mark selected messages to be downloaded from the mail server and, after doing that, leave those messages on the mail server. When you do this, another symbol column appears in the Inbox Information viewer. The symbol in this column indicates that the message has been marked to be retrieved but not deleted from the server.

- Delete—Choose this button to delete selected messages from the mail server without downloading them. After you do this, the message header is deleted from your Inbox folder and from the list in the Inbox Information viewer.

You can also select one or more message headers and then choose the Unmark button in the Remote toolbar to unmark the selected message headers. Choose Unmark All to unmark all message headers.

After you've identified how you want to deal with each message in this way, the new column in the Inbox Information viewer contains symbols indicating how each mail item is to be dealt with, as shown in Figure 28.24.

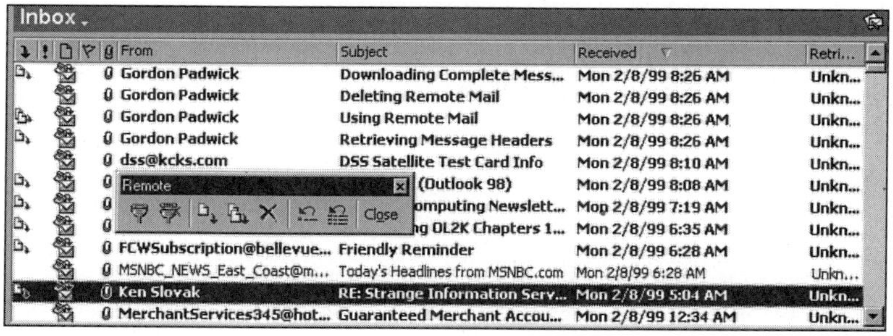

Figure 28.24
Now you're ready to use Remote Mail again to download complete messages.

Choose Tools, and move the pointer onto Remote Mail again, and choose Connect (alternatively, choose Connect on the Remote toolbar) to return to the Remote Connection Wizard. You probably won't have to make any changes to the first and third wizard windows. However, the large box in the second wizard window lists all mail messages you previously marked for delivery. You can uncheck any that you don't want to download now.

PART
V

CH
28

When you choose Finish in the third wizard window, the complete messages you marked are downloaded.

To close down Remote Mail, choose Tools, move the pointer onto Remote Mail, and choose Disconnect.

REFINING REMOTE MAIL

The preceding section described the default way Remote Mail works. You can gain more control over Remote Mail by setting some properties of the Microsoft Exchange Server information service. Start by choosing Tools, Services to display the Services dialog box. Select Microsoft Exchange Server and choose Properties and then select the Remote Mail tab shown in Figure 28.25.

Figure 28.25
By default, Process Marked Items is selected in the Remote Mail Connections section of the dialog box.

Note

By default, Disconnect After Connection Is Finished is checked. If you're using Remote Mail for long distance calls, it's worth making sure this box is checked so that you don't get charged for connection time you're not using.

With Process Marked Items selected, Remote Mail works as described in the preceding section. To gain more control, select Retrieve Items that Meet the Following Conditions. When you do so, the Filter button becomes available. Choose Filter to display the dialog box shown in Figure 28.26.

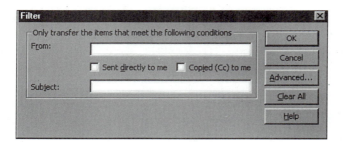

Figure 28.26
You can use this dialog box to specify criteria that messages must satisfy in order to be downloaded.

To specify criteria:

■ In the From box, enter the names of one or more senders. Separate one name from the next with a semicolon.

■ Check one or both of the check boxes to create criteria based on how messages are addressed to you.

■ Enter one or more words that must be in messages' subjects. Separate one word from the next with a semicolon.

Tip #173 from

A message must satisfy all the criteria you specify here in order to be downloaded. If you specify criteria in the Advanced dialog box (described next), messages must additionally satisfy those criteria.

To specify more criteria, choose Advanced to display the dialog box shown in Figure 28.27.

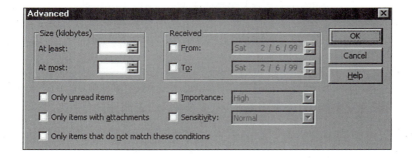

Figure 28.27
You can hone in on specific messages by making choices in this dialog box.

Notice that you can:

■ Restrict the size of messages

■ Specify a range of dates on which the message was received in the server or folder

■ Check various characteristics of messages

PART

V

CH

28

The usefulness of these items depends on the circumstances in which you're using Remote Mail. For example, if you're using a distant phone connection, you might well want to limit the messages you retrieve by choosing only those that are unread and have high importance.

Tip #174 from

The check box marked Only Items that Do Not Match These Conditions deserves your particular attention. If you only want to retrieve messages that do not have attachments, check this box and also the one marked Only Items with Attachments.

SCHEDULING REMOTE MAIL

Choose Schedule in the Remote Mail tab (shown previously in Figure 28.25) to display the dialog box shown in Figure 28.28.

Figure 28.28
You can specify a time for your next connection and also the interval between connections.

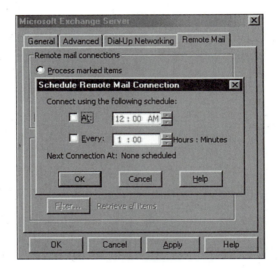

To specify the time for the next connection, check At and then enter a time in the adjacent box. After you do so, the scheduled time for the next connection is displayed near the bottom of the dialog box.

To specify an interval between connections, check Every and then enter the interval in the adjacent box.

TROUBLESHOOTING

Outlook's abilities to work remotely mostly work quite smoothly. However, that's not always the case. Problems can cause painful headaches.

If you're at a remote location and find that you can't send or receive e-mail messages, the most likely reason is that your server is down, or there's some interconnection problem.

To be prepared for this type of problem, set up and test Remote Mail while you're at home base. That way, you can get assistance from your local administrator before you travel. After getting Remote Mail working locally, try it from your home computer before you travel. Again, if you have problems, you have a local resource to help you solve your problems.

You may find that folders you've previously had access to are no longer available to you. That could be because the people who own those folders have changed the access permissions. If you can't access a folder you think should be shared, contact the owner of that folder to verify that you have access.

Perhaps you can access a folder but can't see all the items in it. That may be because the view you're using applies a filter. Examine your view and, if necessary, remove the filter.

Do you find that it takes a long time to open a public folder? That could be because you're using a view that is no longer available on the server and the server has to rebuild it. Make a habit of opening your important public folders regularly so that Exchange doesn't delete your views. You'll have to ask your Exchange administrator how frequently Exchange discards unused views (the default is eight days, but the administrator might have changed that).

CHAPTER 29

SETTING UP MICROSOFT MAIL

by Gordon Padwick

In this chapter

USING MICROSOFT MAIL FOR E-MAIL

You must have C/W Outlook installed on your computer in order to use Microsoft Mail.

If you share information with other computer users by way of a peer-to-peer network or small LAN, you probably use Microsoft Mail to exchange e-mail messages. To use Microsoft Mail, you must have the Microsoft Mail information service in your profile. Also, of course, you must have a network adapter installed in your computer with cabling to the other computers on the network.

To be able to use Microsoft Mail, one of the computers to which you have access (possibly your own) must act as a postoffice that consists of a set of files. These files store e-mail messages that are waiting to be delivered and manage the flow of messages.

CREATING A MICROSOFT MAIL POSTOFFICE

If your network doesn't already have a Microsoft Mail postoffice, you or one of your colleagues must create one and subsequently manage it.

CREATING A POSTOFFICE FOLDER

The postoffice files must be in a folder that's shared with everyone who wants to send and receive e-mail. This folder can be anywhere within the folder structure on any computer. The important thing is that whoever creates that folder makes it sharable.

You can give the postoffice folder any name you like, but it makes sense to call it Postoffice.

INSTALLING MICROSOFT MAIL POSTOFFICE

The file you need to run in order to install a Microsoft Mail Postoffice is Wms.exe. This file is somewhat hidden on the Windows 98 CD-ROM. The U.S. version of the file is Tools\Oldwin95\Message\Us\Wms.exe; the international version of the file is Tools\Oldwin95\Message\Intl\Wms.exe.

> **Note**
>
> Although the U.S. and international files have the same name, they are different as is apparent by the fact that their sizes are not the same.

> **Note**
>
> If your Windows Control Panel has a Microsoft Mail Postoffice icon, you can ignore this section.

To install a postoffice:

1. Close Outlook.

2. Insert your Windows 98 CD-ROM in the drive. Close the Windows 98 window.

3. Choose Start on the Windows taskbar and then choose R̲un in the startup menu to display the Run dialog box.

The next step is based on the assumption that D: is your CD-ROM drive. Substitute the appropriate drive letter at the beginning of the command if necessary. The step also assumes you want to install the U.S. version of the postoffice. Replace "US" with "Int" if you want to install the international version.

4. In the O̲pen box, enter

   `D:\Tools\Oldwin95\Message\US\Wms.exe`

   and choose OK.

5. When a message appears asking you to confirm that you want to install Windows Messaging, choose Y̲es.

6. Read the license agreement and, if you accept it, choose Y̲es. Windows copies the necessary files from the CD-ROM onto your hard drive.

7. When a message appears stating that setup is complete, choose OK.

8. On the Windows taskbar, choose Start, move the pointer onto S̲ettings, and choose C̲ontrol Panel. Now you should see an icon labeled Microsoft Mail Postoffice.

CONFIGURING A POSTOFFICE

After you've created a sharable folder for the postoffice, continue as follows, working on any computer that has access to the shared postoffice folder.

To install the postoffice:

1. If Outlook is running, choose F̲ile, Exit and L̲og Off to close Outlook and return to the Windows desktop.

2. Choose Start in the Windows taskbar, move the pointer onto S̲ettings, and choose C̲ontrol Panel to display the Control Panel.

3. In the Control Panel, double-click Microsoft Mail Postoffice to display the Microsoft Workgroup Postoffice Admin Wizard's first window, shown in Figure 29.1.

4. S̲elect Create a New Workgroup Postoffice then choose Next > to display the second wizard window shown in Figure 29.2.

5. Either enter the full path name of the postoffice folder, or choose Br̲owse, navigate to the folder, select the folder, and choose OK. After you've entered or selected the folder name, choose Next > to display the third wizard window, as shown in Figure 29.3.

If the postoffice folder is on a computer other than the one you're working on, you must enter the folder name using the *Universal Naming Convention* (UNC) format that includes the name of the computer, as shown in Figure 29.3.

Figure 29.1
You can select whether you want to administer an existing postoffice or create a new one.

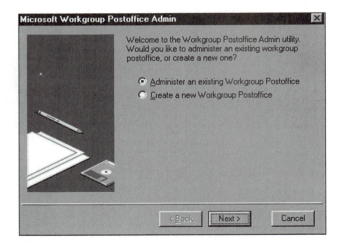

Figure 29.2
Use this window to specify the location and name of the postoffice folder. The window here is shown after the location and name of the postoffice folder has been entered.

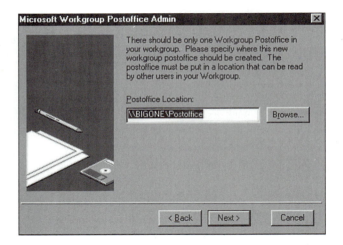

6. If you're satisfied with the postoffice folder, choose Next > to display the dialog box shown in Figure 29.4.

7. Enter a name for the postoffice administrator (such as Admin) in the Name box.

8. Enter a name for a mailbox people can use to send messages to the postoffice administrator (such as Admin) in the Mailbox box.

Note

The name you use for the postoffice administrator's mailbox should be different from the name of your personal mailbox for two reasons. You probably don't want e-mail about the postoffice to get mixed up with your personal e-mail. Also, if you pass the task of administering the postoffice on to someone else, you won't have to change the name of the administrator's mailbox.

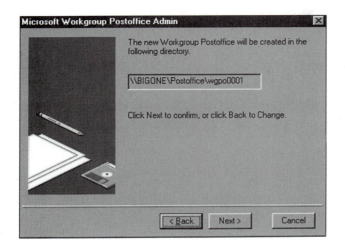

Figure 29.3
Windows creates a subfolder with the name such as wpgo0001 within the postoffice folder you previously created.

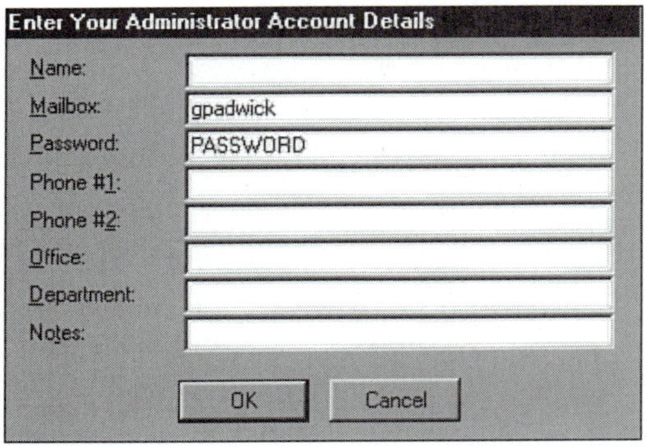

Figure 29.4
Use this dialog box to name the postoffice, and to provide information about yourself as the administrator.

9. Replace the default PASSWORD with the password you want to use to read e-mail sent to the postoffice administrator and to administer the postoffice.

Caution

It's very important that you remember your postoffice administrator password and keep it private. Without that password, neither you nor anyone else can administer the postoffice. If you forget the password, you'll have to remove the postoffice and create an entirely new one. That process deletes all messages waiting to be delivered in the postoffice. Not the recommended way to win a popularity contest!

10. You can leave the remaining five boxes empty or enter information in them as you want. After you've finished with this dialog box, choose OK. Windows displays a message reminding you that you must share the folder. Choose OK to return to the Windows Control Panel. Close the Control Panel.

11. If you haven't already made the postoffice folder available for sharing, open Windows Explorer, right-click the Postoffice folder to display its context menu, choose Properties, and select the Sharing tab, shown in Figure 29.5.

Figure 29.5
Use this dialog box to share the postoffice folder.

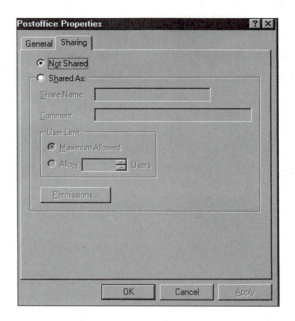

12. Choose Shared As to share the folder. Windows automatically displays the name of the folder as the Share Name, that is, the name by which other users access the folder. By default, Windows allows as many people as permitted by the LAN server (if you're using Microsoft Mail on a LAN) to simultaneously access the postoffice. There's no limit if you're using a peer-to-peer network. You can, if you like, limit the number of people who have simultaneous access.

13. Choose Permissions, and make sure that Full Access permissions are granted so that everyone can send and receive e-mail.

14. Choose OK to close the Properties dialog box. Windows displays a warning if the share name, such as Postoffice, contains more than eight characters—in that case the folder won't be accessible from some MS-DOS workstations. You can ignore that message because Microsoft Mail runs under Windows. Choose Yes to continue. Close Windows Explorer.

Tip #175 from

If some people are still using Windows for Workgroups, you must not use a share name that has more than eight characters.

CREATING MAILBOXES

In order to send and receive e-mail, each workgroup member must have a mailbox in the postoffice. Only the postoffice administrator can create, delete, or change mailboxes.

As the administrator, you already have an administrator's mailbox in the postoffice, but you need to create a mailbox for your ordinary mail. Use the following steps to create your personal mailbox and the same steps to create a mailbox for each workgroup member. You create a mailbox from within Windows so, if Outlook is running, choose File, Exit and Log Off to close Outlook.

To create a mailbox:

1. Choose Start in the Windows taskbar, move the pointer onto Settings, and choose Control Panel to open the Control Panel.

2. Double-click Microsoft Mail Postoffice to display the first Microsoft Workgroup Postoffice Admin Wizard window, shown previously in Figure 29.1.

3. Accept the default Administer an Existing Workgroup Postoffice, and choose Next to display the second wizard window, shown previously in Figure 29.2. This window should automatically display the Postoffice Location. If it doesn't, enter the full *UNC* name of the postoffice; alternatively, choose Browse, navigate to the postoffice folder, select the folder, and choose OK. Choose Next > to display the third wizard window shown in Figure 29.6.

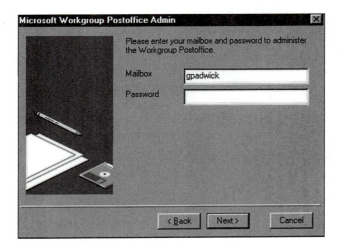

Figure 29.6
You must enter the name of the administrator's mailbox and the administrator's password to proceed.

4. Enter the administrator's name and password, then choose Next. If you enter the correct name and password, Windows displays the dialog box shown in Figure 29.7. If you enter the incorrect name or password, you see a message telling you that the postoffice can be managed only by the user who created it.

Figure 29.7
This dialog box lists the names of existing mailboxes. Immediately after you have created a postoffice, only the administrator's mailbox exists.

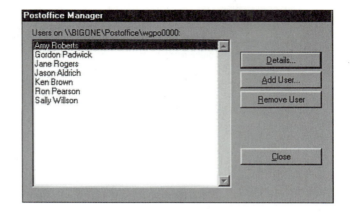

5. Choose Add User to display the dialog box shown in Figure 29.8, in which you can create a new mailbox.

Figure 29.8
Use this dialog box to provide information about a new mailbox.

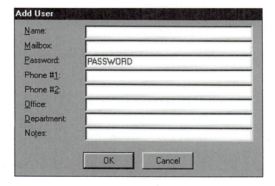

6. To create a mailbox for yourself, enter your name (such as Brian Bolster) in the Name box.

7. Enter a name for the mailbox (such as bbolster) in the Mailbox box.

> **Note**
>
> Most workgroups have a convention for naming mailboxes. A common convention is to use a person's first initial and last name.

8. You can leave the default PASSWORD as the password, because each person should change the password to something only that person knows.

9. You can enter information into the remaining five boxes or not, as you want.

10. Choose OK to return to the Postoffice Manager window that now lists the mailbox you just created.

You can repeat the steps just described to add any number of mailboxes to the postoffice.

MANAGING MAILBOXES

You can use the Postoffice Manager window, shown previously in Figure 29.1, to manage mailboxes. To manage a mailbox, select that mailbox. After you've selected it you can:

- Choose Details to display a dialog box that contains information about the owner of a mailbox. You can make changes to any of the information you provided at the time you created the mailbox.

- Choose Remove User to remove the selected mailbox. Windows asks you to confirm that you want to delete the mailbox. You'll want to do this when a person leaves your organization.

Note

People often forget their passwords. When this happens, select the user's name in the Postoffice Manager dialog box—the old password is shown as a group of asterisks. Delete those asterisks and either leave the Password field empty or enter a generic password such as "password." Instruct the user to open the mailbox and immediately enter a new password.

ADDING THE MICROSOFT MAIL INFORMATION SERVICE TO A PROFILE

All the people who want to use Outlook to send and receive e-mail messages must have the Microsoft Mail information service in their profiles.

To add the Microsoft Mail information service to a profile and set the service's properties:

1. With any Outlook Information viewer displayed, choose Tools, Services to display the Services dialog box with the Services tab selected. The information services already in the profile are listed.

Note

If Microsoft Mail is listed, it is already in your profile. You can't add it more than once, so choose Cancel to close the dialog box.

2. Choose Add to display the Add Service to Profile dialog box.

3. Select Microsoft Mail and choose OK. Outlook displays the Microsoft Mail dialog box with the Connection tab selected, as shown in Figure 29.9.

Figure 29.9
Use this tab to identify your Microsoft Mail postoffice and how you want to connect to it.

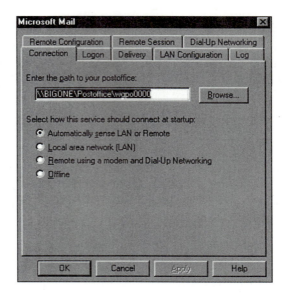

SETTING THE CONNECTION PROPERTIES

As explained in the first part of this chapter, Microsoft Mail uses a postoffice located in a shared folder on the network to maintain information about users and to distribute e-mail. The postoffice must be created before you can set up Microsoft Mail.

In the Microsoft Mail dialog box's Connection tab, shown previously in Figure 29.9, proceed as follows.

To set up connections:

1. If the Enter the Path to Your Postoffice box doesn't already show the correct path to the postoffice folder, either enter the path name using the *Universal Naming Convention* (UNC) format or choose Browse, navigate to the folder, select it, and choose OK. The postoffice is normally, but not necessarily, in a folder named \Postoffice\wgpo0000\.

2. Choose one of the four option buttons to define how you want Outlook to connect to the postoffice when Outlook starts. Usually the default Automatically Sense LAN or Remote is satisfactory.

If you've chosen Automatically Sense LAN or Remote as the connection option, Outlook automatically determines whether the computer is connected to the postoffice by way of a LAN or a dial-up connection; if no connection is available, a dialog box offers you the choice of working offline. If you want to disable access to Microsoft Mail without removing the Microsoft Mail information service from your profile, choose the last option, Offline, in step 2.

SETTING THE LOGON PROPERTIES

Select the Microsoft Mail dialog box's Logon tab, shown in Figure 29.10, to set the Logon properties.

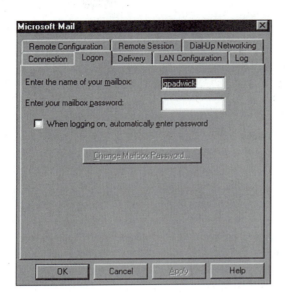

Figure 29.10
Enter your mailbox name and password in this dialog box.

To identify yourself:

1. Enter your mailbox name in the Enter the Name of Your <u>M</u>ailbox box.

2. Enter your mailbox password in the Enter Your Mailbox <u>P</u>assword box.

You should normally leave the When Logging on, Automatically <u>E</u>nter Password box unchecked. If you check this box, anyone who gains access to Outlook on your computer has access to your Microsoft Mail mailbox.

At the time you initially set your Logon properties, the <u>C</u>hange Mailbox Password button isn't available. After you've finished setting the Microsoft Mail information services properties, you can return to this dialog box and choose the Change Mailbox Password button. This displays a dialog box you can use to change the password initially assigned by the postoffice administrator to a password that's known only to you.

SETTING DELIVERY PROPERTIES

After you've set the Logon properties, select the Delivery tab to display the dialog box shown in Figure 29.11.

Figure 29.11
Use this tab to select how you want mail to be delivered.

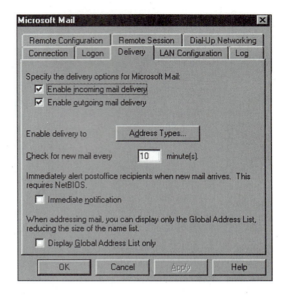

To set delivery properties:

1. Leave the Enable Incoming Mail Delivery and Enable Outgoing Mail Delivery boxes checked unless, for some reason, you don't want to receive or send mail.

2. By default, Outlook sends all types of e-mail to the Microsoft Mail postoffice. If there are some types of messages (such as faxes) that you don't want to send to the Microsoft Mail postoffice, choose Address Types to display a list of message types and uncheck the types of mail you don't want to send to the Microsoft Mail postoffice.

3. By default, Outlook attempts to send mail to and receive mail from your Microsoft Mail postoffice every ten minutes. You can change that to any number of minutes you prefer.

4. Check the Immediate Notification box if you want to immediately be notified when mail arrives from the Microsoft Mail postoffice. You must have NETBIOS installed on the network to use this capability.

5. Ignore the Display Global Address List Only check box. It has no effect when you're using Outlook as a client for Microsoft Mail.

SETTING THE LAN CONFIGURATION PROPERTIES

After you've finished setting the Delivery properties, select the LAN configuration tab shown in Figure 29.12.

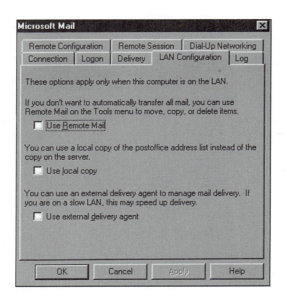

Figure 29.12
The properties in this dialog box apply only when your computer is connected to the Microsoft Mail postoffice by way of a LAN.

If you prefer to receive only message headers rather than complete messages, check Use Remote Mail. Subsequently, you can choose Tools, Remote Mail to select the messages you want to receive in full.

The Use Local Copy and Use External Delivery Agent check boxes have no effect when you're using Outlook as a client for the Microsoft Mail postoffice.

SETTING LOG PROPERTIES

After you've set the LAN Configuration properties, select the Log tab to display the dialog box shown in Figure 29.13.

By default, Outlook maintains a log of Microsoft Mail events. This log is a text file with either the default name or a name you specify. You can open this log in Windows Notepad or another text editor to see the history of your connections to the Microsoft Mail postoffice. The events this log records include:

- Each time you connect to the postoffice
- The connection speed (number of bytes per second)
- The number of mail items you send and receive during each session
- Any errors that occurred when you attempted to connect to the postoffice or when you attempted to send or receive mail

If you experience problems with Microsoft Mail, this log provides information that might help you understand the cause of those problems.

Figure 29.13
Use this dialog box to
turn message logging
on or off.

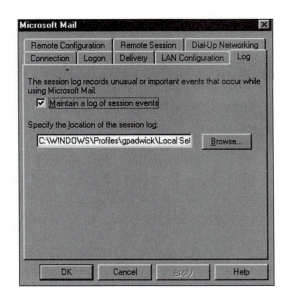

You can uncheck the <u>M</u>aintain a Log of Session Events box if you don't want to maintain a log. You can change the location of the log by specifying another file in the Specify the <u>L</u>ocation of the Session Log box.

Tip #176 from

If your connections to the Microsoft Mail postoffice work well, delete the information in the session log from time to time. Otherwise, it will continue to grow, occupying your disk with unneeded information.

SETTING THE REMOTE CONFIGURATION PROPERTIES

After you've set the Log properties, select the Remote Configuration tab if you intend to access the Microsoft Mail postoffice from a remote location.

The settings in this tab apply only when your computer has a dial-up connection to the Microsoft Mail postoffice. The settings are identical to those in the LAN Configuration tab, previously described and previously shown in Figure 29.12.

SETTING THE REMOTE SESSION PROPERTIES

After you've set the Remote Configuration properties, select the Remote Session tab to display the dialog box shown in Figure 29.14.

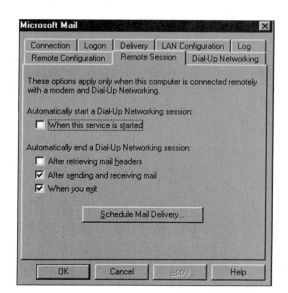

Figure 29.14
Use this dialog box to specify how Outlook communicates from a remote location with the Microsoft Mail postoffice.

If you want Outlook to attempt to connect to the Microsoft Mail postoffice whenever you start Outlook, check the When This Service Is Started box.

You can check or uncheck any combination of the lower three check boxes to control how the connection to the Microsoft Mail postoffice is terminated. By choosing the appropriate check boxes, you can avoid unnecessarily high telephone charges.

To schedule regular automatic dial-up connection, choose Schedule Mail delivery to display the dialog box shown in Figure 29.15.

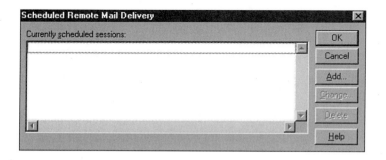

Figure 29.15
This dialog box opens with no scheduled dial-ups listed.

To schedule a regular dial-up, choose Add to display the Add Schedules Session dialog box, in which you can choose a dial-up connection and the frequency with which you want automatic dial-up connection to occur.

SETTING THE DIAL-UP NETWORKING PROPERTIES

After you've set the Remote Session properties, select the Dial-up Networking tab to display the dialog box shown in Figure 29.16.

Figure 29.16
Use this dialog box to set dial-up properties.

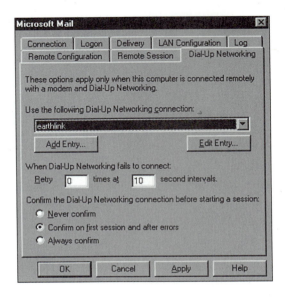

The settings in this tab apply only when your computer has a dial-up connection to the Microsoft Mail postoffice.

Open the Use the Following Dial-up Networking Connection drop-down list to display a list of dial-up connections available on your computer and select the one that provides a connection to the Microsoft Mail postoffice. You can choose Add Entry to create a new dial-up connection and Edit Entry to modify an existing connection.

In the center of the dialog box, you can specify the number of times Outlook should try to connect to the postoffice, and the interval between those tries.

In the bottom part of the dialog box, choose an option button according to how you want to be notified about the success or failure of an attempt to connect to the postoffice.

COMPLETING THE MICROSOFT MAIL POSTOFFICE SETUP

After you've worked your way through all these tabs, choose OK to close the Microsoft Mail dialog box. You must choose File, Exit and Log Off to close Outlook and then restart Outlook before you can access the Microsoft Mail postoffice.

TROUBLESHOOTING

With the exception of setting up a Microsoft Mail postoffice on a computer running Windows 98, the information in this chapter is quite straightforward and is unlikely to cause significant problems.

After you've successfully set up a Microsoft Mail postoffice, you shouldn't experience many problems. One thing to watch out for, though, is that there's enough space on the disk used by the postoffice. The postoffice saves mail until the last person to whom the mail was addressed downloads it. If users send mail with large attachments and the people to whom that mail is addressed don't download that mail, the disk space occupied by the postoffice can grow rapidly. If the disk used by the postoffice runs out of space, Microsoft Mail won't work for anybody.

Although this book is about Outlook, it's appropriate to mention that you don't have to use Outlook to access your Microsoft Mail postoffice. You can also do so from Windows Messaging, which is available as a feature of Windows 95 and Windows 98.

CHAPTER 30

USING MICROSOFT MAIL FOR E-MAIL

In this chapter   *by Gordon Padwick*

MICROSOFT MAIL CAPABILITIES

Microsoft Mail provides e-mail and some collaboration facilities suitable for use by members of a workgroup whose computers are interconnected by a peer-to-peer network or small LAN. To use Microsoft Mail, one computer on the network must contain a postoffice folder that's accessible by all workgroup members. All workgroup members must have a Microsoft Mail client, such as C/W Outlook, installed on their computers.

Refer to Chapter 29, "Setting Up Microsoft Mail," for information about setting up a postoffice and adding the Microsoft Mail information service to people's profiles.

> **Note**
>
> You must have *C/W Outlook (page 54)*, not IMO Outlook, installed on your computer in order to send and receive Microsoft Mail messages.

STARTING OUTLOOK

If you have the Microsoft Mail information service in your profile and have not, as suggested in Chapter 29, saved your Microsoft Mail password, you'll see the dialog box shown in Figure 30.1 when you start Outlook.

Figure 30.1
This dialog box asks for your Microsoft Mail password.

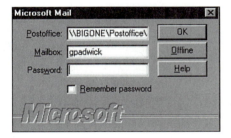

If your computer is connected to the Microsoft Mail postoffice, enter your Microsoft Mail mailbox name and password and choose OK to continue the process of starting Outlook. If your computer isn't connected to the postoffice, choose Offline and then choose OK.

SENDING AND RECEIVING E-MAIL MESSAGES

Sending and receiving Microsoft Mail e-mail messages is much like sending and receiving Internet and Exchange e-mail messages, so these subjects are described only briefly in this chapter.

→ For information about sending and receiving Internet e-mail messages with C/W Outlook, **see** "Sending and Receiving Internet E-mail with Corporate/Workgroup Outlook," **p. 167**.

The information in this chapter assumes you have access to a Microsoft Mail postoffice on your network and you have added the Microsoft Mail information service to your profile.

→ If you need to set up access to a Microsoft Mail postoffice, **see** "Creating a Microsoft Mail Postoffice," **p. 758**.

→ If you need to modify your profile, **see** "Adding the Microsoft Mail Information Service to a Profile," **p. 765**.

CREATING AN E-MAIL MESSAGE

You can choose from three message formats when you send a message: HTML, Plain Text, and Rich Text, as explained in Chapter 6. Within a workgroup, it's a good idea for everyone to use the same format. Generally, your first choice should be Plain Text because this results in smaller messages and, therefore, less traffic on the network than the other two formats.

- If all members of the workgroup use an e-mail client such as Outlook 98 or Outlook 2000 that has HTML capabilities, you can use the HTML format.
- If some members of the workgroup use an e-mail client that isn't HTML-compatible, but has graphics capabilities, you can use the Rich Text format.
- If some members of the workgroup use an e-mail client that can only display unformatted text, your only choice is to use the Plain Text format.

Tip #177 from

Gordon Padwick

If you experience problems sending or receiving e-mail, try the Plain Text format. Although this may lack glamour, it usually get's the job done.

You can use either Outlook's built-in editor or Word to create your messages. Use whichever you prefer.

→ If you have yet to select a default message format and e-mail editor, **see** "Selecting a Message Format and E-mail Editor," **p. 182**.

The remainder of this chapter is based on the assumption that you're using the Plain Text format (except where otherwise noted) and Outlook's built-in editor. You'll notice some differences if you use a different message format or if you use Word as your e-mail editor.

To create an e-mail message:

1. With the Inbox Information viewer displayed, choose <u>N</u>ew in the Standard toolbar to display the Message form shown in Figure 30.2.
2. Choose To to open the Select Names dialog box. Open the drop-down <u>S</u>how Names from The list and select Postoffice Address List as shown in Figure 30.3.

Figure 30.2
The Message form is shown here with a message ready to send.

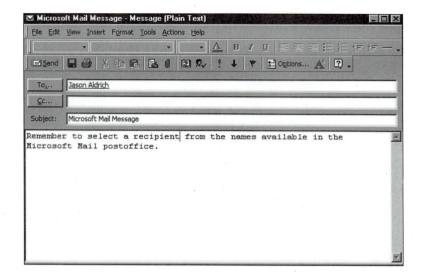

Figure 30.3
This dialog box lists the names of people who have accounts on the Microsoft Mail postoffice.

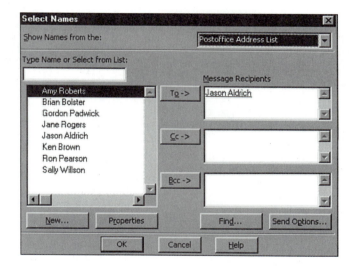

3. Select the name of the person, or names of the people, to whom you want to address the message, choose To-> to move the selected name or names into the Message Recipients list, then choose OK to return to the Message form in which the selected name or names appear in the To box.

Note

You can use the same method to select people who should receive carbon copies (Cc) and blind carbon copies (Bcc) of the message.

4. Enter a subject for the message in the Subject box, then press Enter or Tab to move the insertion point into the large text box that occupies the lower part of the form. When you do so, the subject of the message replaces "Untitled" in the form's title bar.

5. Enter the message in the large text box. You can choose Insert in the form's menu bar to insert files, Outlook items, and a signature.

→ If you're using the HTML message format, you can also insert horizontal lines, pictures, and hyperlinks into the message. **See** "Message Insertions," **p. 201**.

6. Choose Options in the form's Standard toolbar to display the dialog box shown in Figure 30.4.

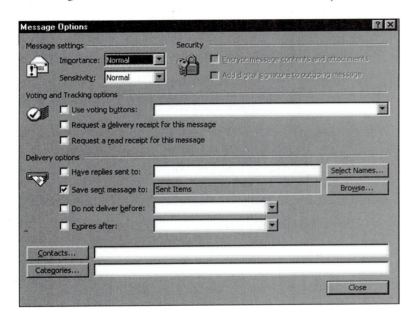

Figure 30.4
You can use the boxes in this dialog box to set options for the message.

7. In many cases, the only options you'll want to use are Contacts and Categories. If the message refers to other people who are listed in your Contacts folder, but are not recipients of this message, choose Contacts to display the dialog box shown in Figure 30.5.

8. Choose Categories to open the dialog box shown in Figure 30.6.

9. Choose Close to return to the Message form. Now the message is ready to send.

Note

Although the Message Options dialog box contains the same options available when you're sending a message using Exchange, not all of these options are available in Microsoft Mail. Those you can use are described subsequently in this chapter.

Figure 30.5
Select the names of
people to whom the
message relates, then
choose OK to return
to the Message
Options dialog box.

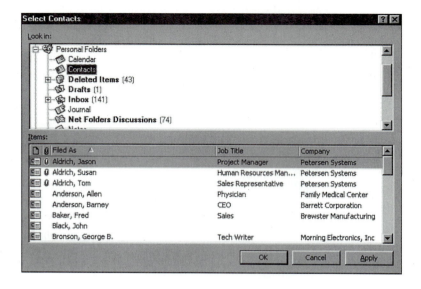

Figure 30.6
Check one or more
categories that apply
to the message, then
choose OK to return
to the Message
Options dialog box.

SENDING AN E-MAIL MESSAGE

After you've created an e-mail message, choose <u>S</u>end in the Message form's Standard tool-bar to send the message. Outlook moves the message to your Outbox folder. At scheduled intervals (the default is every 10 minutes) Outlook sends messages in your Outbox to the Microsoft Mail postoffice and keeps a copy of the message in your Sent Items folder.

→ If you haven't already, you'll want to set Outlook's delivery properties; **see** "Setting Delivery Properties," **p. 767**.

If you want to send messages in your Outbox immediately, choose <u>T</u>ools, Se<u>n</u>d.

RECEIVING AN E-MAIL MESSAGE

When a message for you arrives in the postoffice, it stays there until the version of Outlook running on your computer accesses the postoffice, at which time the message moves into your Inbox folder. You can see the message header by opening the Inbox Information viewer.

→ To learn more about the Inbox Information viewer, **see** "Understanding the Inbox Information Viewer," **p. 218**.

REPLYING TO A MESSAGE

Outlook provides two ways to reply to a message you've received. One way is to select the message in the Inbox Information viewer and then choose Reply in the viewer's Standard toolbar. The other way is to double-click the message in the Inbox Information viewer to display the message in the Message form; then choose Reply in the form's Standard toolbar.

In either case, Outlook displays the message you're replying to in a Message form with space at the top for you to enter your reply. You can make annotations to the original message, or you can delete all or some of the original message. When you've completed your reply, choose Send in the Message form's Standard toolbar to send the reply in the same way you send any other message.

→ For more information about replying to messages, **see** "Replying to a Message," **p. 227**.

FORWARDING A MESSAGE

Forwarding a message is similar to replying to a message. To do so, choose Forward in the Inbox Information viewer's Standard toolbar or choose Forward in the Message form's Standard toolbar.

→ For more information about forwarding a message, **see** "Forwarding a Message," **p. 228**.

USING MESSAGE OPTIONS

The Message Options dialog box, shown previously in Figure 30.4, contains several options, only some of which Microsoft Mail supports.

MESSAGE SETTINGS

You can open the Importance drop-down list and select an importance other than normal. You can also open the Sensitivity drop-down list and select a sensitivity other than normal.

When a recipient receives a message that has importance other than normal, an importance symbol appears in the left column of the Inbox Information viewer, but there's no indication that the sensitivity is other than normal. If the recipient double-clicks the message header in the Inbox Information viewer to see it in the Message form, the InfoBar near the top of the form contains information about other-than-normal importance and sensitivity, as shown in Figure 30.7.

Figure 30.7
The InfoBar in this form shows that the message is private and of high importance.

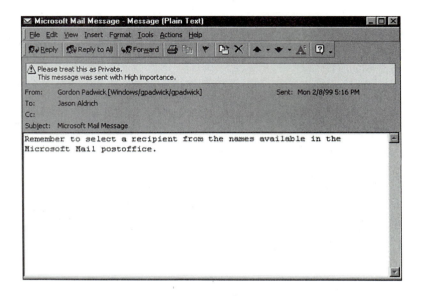

Microsoft Mail does not support security options.

VOTING AND TRACKING OPTIONS

You can use Microsoft Mail to send messages with voting buttons. Refer to Chapter 26, "Using Exchange Server for E-mail," for detailed information about sending and replying to messages with voting buttons.

If you check Tell Me When This Message Has Been Delivered, the Microsoft Mail postoffice sends a confirming message to your Inbox folder when the message arrives in the postoffice; not, as you might expect, when the message arrives in the recipient's Inbox folder.

If you check Tell Me When This Message Has Been Read, you receive a confirming message in your Inbox folder when the recipient double-clicks the message to display it in the Message form.

DELIVERY OPTIONS

You can use the Have Replies Sent To option. You can check that box and enter a name other than your own in the adjoining text box (or select a name in the Postoffice Address List). The recipient receives the message as normal. When the recipient chooses Reply, the name you entered in the Have Replies Sent To box is shown in the To box, and the reply is sent to that person.

You can choose not to have Outlook save copies of messages you send by removing the check mark from the Save Se_n_t Message To box. You can also choose Browse to display a list of your Outlook folders and choose a folder other than the default Sent Items folder.

The Do Not Deliver _B_efore and E_x_pires After capabilities are not supported by Microsoft Mail.

Tip #178 from 	You can, and should, assign *categories (page 604)* to e-mail messages you send by Microsoft Mail. If you assign categories to messages, you can subsequently find those messages easily.

USING MICROSOFT MAIL REMOTELY

The previous pages of this chapter are based on the assumption that you and other workgroup members connect to the Microsoft Mail postoffice by way of a LAN. You can also set up a Microsoft Mail postoffice so that people can send and receive e-mail messages from a remote location using a dial-up connection. To do so, the computer that contains the postoffice folder must have a modem that's set up to answer incoming phone calls.

→ The Microsoft Mail postoffice must be set up to work with remote mail; **see** "Setting the LAN Configuration Properties," **p. 768**.

With the Microsoft Mail postoffice set up to handle remote mail, you can use remote mail in much the same way you can when you have Exchange as your e-mail system.

→ To learn more about working remotely with the Microsoft Mail postoffice, **see** "Working Remotely," **p. 729**.

TROUBLESHOOTING

If you're not able to send and receive messages by way of Microsoft Mail, the problem might be

- On your computer
- On the computer used by the person with whom you're trying to communicate
- On the network connections between your computer and the computer
- On the network connections between the computer used by the person with whom you're trying to communicate
- On the computer that supports the Microsoft Mail postoffice

Suppose you're trying to send an e-mail message to or receive an e-mail message from Mary, and it doesn't work. One thing to do is to ask a colleague who also has a Microsoft Mail postoffice account to try sending a message to and receiving a message from Mary. If that works, you know the problem must be with your computer or its network connections.

If that doesn't work, it's a postoffice problem. Perhaps the disk on the postoffice server is full, or perhaps the postoffice computer is no longer connected to the network. The person responsible for the postoffice computer has to solve those problems.

If it comes down to the fact that the problem must be with your computer, check out your network connections first. Using Windows Explorer, can you use Network Neighborhood to see other computers? If you can, you have network access; if you can't, maybe the problem is as simple as the LAN connector is no longer plugged into your computer, or there's some other disconnection.

If you can access the network and other people can use the Microsoft Mail postoffice, the problem has to be inside your own computer. Most likely, for whatever reason, the Microsoft Mail information service has become corrupted. Check that carefully and make whatever corrections are necessary.

Keep in mind that problems you experience with Outlook might not be directly caused by the Outlook software itself—it could be an operating system error, or a hardware conflict or failure. For help in resolving these types of problems, consult books such as *Using Microsoft Windows 98*, *Windows 98 Installation & Configuration Handbook*, or *Upgrading and Repairing PCs, 10th Anniversary Edition*, all published by Que, *Peter Norton's Guide to Upgrading and Repairing PCs, published by Sams*, or a host of other books available.

CHAPTER 31

SETTING UP LOTUS CC:MAIL

In this chapter

by Gordon Padwick

WHAT IS CC:MAIL?

cc:Mail is a messaging system from Lotus that is widely used by many organizations. In basic concept, cc:Mail messaging is similar to Microsoft Mail and Exchange. Each of these systems uses a central postoffice to direct e-mail messages from a sender to one or more recipients. Senders and recipients all use a client application to access the postoffice.

If you're in an organization that uses cc:Mail for e-mail, you probably have the cc:Mail client application installed on your computer. While the cc:Mail client provides access to the cc:Mail postoffice, it doesn't, by itself, provide access to other e-mail systems.

Note

Some e-mail servers, such as Microsoft Exchange Server and Lotus Notes Server, can be configured with connectors to cc:Mail servers. Such a configuration gives the cc:Mail client the ability to interchange messages with people who use other messaging environments.

C/W Outlook, on the other hand, is a versatile e-mail client. It gains its versatility by having the ability to use information services added to a user's profile to access various messaging systems. As you've seen in previous chapters, you can add information services to provide access to Internet, Exchange, and Microsoft Mail e-mail systems. You can also add an *information service* that provides access to cc:Mail. That's the subject of this chapter.

By using Outlook as your cc:Mail client, one big advantage is that the cc:Mail messages you receive arrive in your Outlook Inbox, which also contains messages you receive from the Internet and other mail systems. Likewise, Outlook saves copies of cc:Mail messages you send in your Sent Items folder. Another advantage is that you can send and receive cc:Mail and other messages from one mail client, instead of having to use a separate client for cc:Mail.

In addition to providing access to cc:Mail messages, the MS Outlook Support for the Lotus cc:Mail information service described in this chapter provides access from Outlook to cc:Mail folders and bulletin boards.

INSTALLING VENDOR INDEPENDENT MESSAGING FILES

Vendor Information Messaging (VIM) is an interface provided by Lotus that allows communication between cc:Mail and other applications. This interface consists of several files that must be installed on a computer on which applications are to communicate with cc:Mail. You must install these files on the computer on which you run Outlook if you want Outlook to send and receive cc:Mail messages.

At the time this book was written, the VIM files you need to access cc:Mail from Outlook could be downloaded from Lotus. These files were, and probably still are, available in a 705-kilobyte compressed file named Vdlw32.zip. You can download this file from various Web sites, one of which is `http://ftp.support.lotus.com/ftp/pub/comm/ccmail/dev_tools`.

Tip #179 from

[signature]

The following procedure refers to "unzipping" files. Chances are you're quite familiar with this process. For those of you who aren't familiar with zipping and unzipping, I'll offer a brief explanation.

Operating systems such as DOS and Windows can only work with files that have a specific format. In many cases, this format occupies more space, often a lot more space, than is required by data. "Zipping" refers to the process of compressing a file in a way that all its data, but not its format, is retained. "Unzipping" refers to restoring a zipped file to its original format.

Many files available for downloading by way of the Internet are zipped to minimize transmission time. These files have .zip as their file name extensions.

Although several compression methods are available, by far the most common is the Zip format, first introduced by PKWare as a DOS application. In the Windows world, WinZip (from Niko Mak Computing) is generally used to zip and unzip files. You can download a trial version of WinZip from `http://www.winzip.com`.

Some compressed files available for downloading are self-extracting; these files have .exe as their file name extensions. You can double-click a file of this type that you have downloaded to run its built-in unzipping capability to re-create the original, uncompressed files.

To install the VIM files:

1. Use your Web browser to access this Web site and select Vdlw32.zip to display the File Download dialog box. Select Save This File to a Disk to download it.

2. Unzip the file to a new folder on your hard drive—the unzipped files occupy a total of 1.5 megabytes.

3. Copy all the files except Readme.txt to your Windows System folder, normally C:\Windows\System.

ADDING THE CC:MAIL INFORMATION SERVICE TO A PROFILE

After you've installed the VIM files, you're ready to add the MS Outlook Support for Lotus cc:Mail information service to your profile.

To add support for cc:Mail to your profile:

1. Make sure your computer has a network connection to the cc:Mail postoffice. If you're already using the cc:Mail client on your computer, the easiest way to check your cc:Mail connection is to use the cc:Mail client to access the postoffice.

2. With any Outlook Information viewer displayed, choose Tools, Services to display the Services dialog box.

3. Choose Add to display the Add Service to Profile dialog box.

4. Select MS Outlook Support for Lotus cc:Mail and choose OK. After a short delay, a message tells you to insert your Office 2000 CD. Do so, and choose OK. Outlook reads the required files from the CD and then displays the dialog box shown in Figure 31.1 with the Logon tab selected.

Figure 31.1
Use this dialog box to identify your cc:Mail postoffice and to provide your account information.

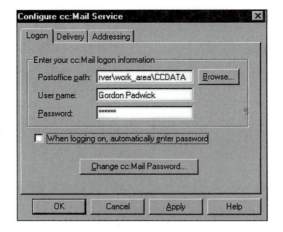

5. Enter the full path name to your cc:Mail postoffice in the Postoffice Path box. Alternatively, choose Browse, navigate to the postoffice, and select it. The cc:Mail postoffice is usually named CCDATA, but it can have a different name.

6. Enter your cc:Mail username in the User Name box and enter your cc:Mail password in the Password box.

7. If you want Outlook to remember your password so that you don't have to enter it each time you want to access cc:Mail, check the When Logging on, Automatically Enter Password box.

Note
If you check When Logging on, Automatically Enter Password, anyone who opens Outlook on your computer and has access to your profile also has access to your cc:Mail. That means other people can read your e-mail and send e-mail under your name. It's usually best not to check this box.

8. If you want to change your cc:Mail password, choose Change cc:Mail Password. Outlook displays the dialog box shown in Figure 31.2, in which you're asked to enter your existing password, and then enter the new password twice.

Figure 31.2
Use this dialog box to change your cc:Mail password.

9. Select the Delivery tab, shown in Figure 31.3.

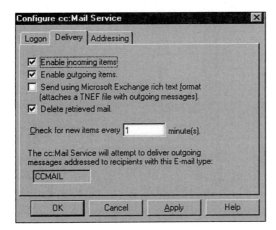

Figure 31.3
Use this dialog box to define how you want Outlook to handle cc:Mail messages.

PART

V

Cʜ

31

10. Enable Incoming Items and Enable Outgoing Items are both initially checked. You can uncheck either or both of these, but it's unlikely you would want to do that.

11. Send Using Microsoft Exchange Rich Text Format is initially unchecked. You can check this box, but read the information that follows this procedure before you do.

12. By default, messages are deleted from the cc:Mail postoffice when they arrive in your Inbox. Uncheck Delete Retrieved Mail if you want messages to remain in the cc:Mail postoffice.

13. By default, Outlook checks for cc:Mail messages every minute. You can change the number of minutes in the Check for New Mail Every box.

14. Select the Addressing tab, shown in Figure 31.4.

15. By default, you have access to the cc:Mail address book in the postoffice. If you prefer to access a copy of the cc:Mail address book on your local disk, check Use Local Copy. To do this, you must copy the address book from the postoffice to your local disk, as explained in step 17.

16. If you have already copied the cc:Mail address book from the postoffice, the file name of the local copy is displayed in the File Name box. You can change this name if you want to have a new local copy.

Figure 31.4
Use this tab to select
how you want to use
address books.

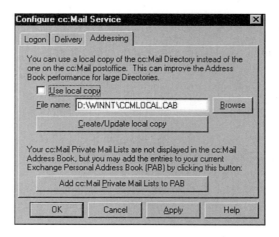

17. Choose Create/Update Local Copy to create a local copy of the cc:Mail address book or to update an existing copy.

18 If you have private mail lists in the cc:Mail postoffice, you can choose Add cc:Mail Private Mail Lists to PAB to copy entries in those lists to your Outlook Personal Address Book. Choose OK to close the Configure cc:Mail Service dialog box. Outlook tells you to close and restart Outlook to use the cc:Mail information service.

The Send Using Microsoft Exchange Rich Text Format check box in the Delivery tab provides a way for you to send enhanced messages by way of cc:Mail. These enhancements can be seen only by recipients who use Outlook or Windows Messaging as their e-mail, not by recipients who use the cc:Mail client. If you check this box, you can create messages that use the rich text formatting capabilities, embedded objects, embedded messages, and the location of inserted files. The enhancements are included in a *Transport Neutral Encapsulation* (TNEF) file that Outlook attaches to the message you create.

After you're set up the cc:Mail information service, then closed and restarted Outlook, the Tools menu contains an additional item, cc:Mail Service tools. Move the pointer onto that item to have access to

- Update cc:Mail Bulletin Boards
- Import cc:Mail Bulletin Boards
- Import cc:Mail Folders
- Update Local Copy of cc:Mail Address Book
- Import cc:Mail Private Lists to Personal Address Book

UPGRADING TO CONNECTORWARE 2.0

Microsoft licenses MS Outlook Support for Lotus cc:Mail from Transend Corporation. That company also offers an enhanced version called ConnectorWare 2.0.

You can obtain detailed information about ConnectorWare 2.0 from the Web site `http://www.transend.com/datasheet.html`.

You can also download a trial version from that site.

One of the significant enhancements in ConnectorWare 2.0 is its ability to access cc:Mail version 6.x postoffices.

TROUBLESHOOTING

You might well have some troubles when trying to use Outlook 2000 as a client for cc:Mail. Some of these are due to the fact that you're trying to get software from two major companies to collaborate. Both of these companies, Microsoft and Lotus, want to rule the messaging and collaboration environments. Although the two companies claim to be collaborating to solve communication issues, it's probable that this collaboration has some limits.

If you run into problems, your first priority should be to make sure you're using the latest Vendor Independent Messaging (VIM) file available from Lotus. You can download these files from `http://ftp.support.lotus.com/ftp/pub/comm/ccmail/dev_tools/`.

After that, make sure your path to the cc:Mail program files is correct. To do that, look in the registry key:

HKEY_LOCAL_MACHINE\Software\Transend\Ccmsvc

 If this fails, you may have to completely remove and reinstall the cc:Mail information service. Refer to the Microsoft Knowledge Base article Q190083 for detailed information about how to do so.

CHAPTER 32

USING CC:MAIL FOR E-MAIL

In this chapter   *by Gordon Padwick*

Using cc:Mail

After you've added the MS Outlook Support for cc:Mail information service to your profile, you can use Outlook to send messages to and receive messages from people who have accounts on a cc:Mail postoffice.

Sending and Receiving E-mail

You send e-mail to a recipient with a cc:Mail account in much the same way as you send any other e-mail. With the Inbox Information viewer displayed choose New in the Standard toolbar to display the Message form.

You can choose To to select recipient addresses from the cc:Mail address book, or you can enter a recipient's address in the To box, using the cc:Mail format. For example, to send a cc:Mail message to a person who has an account on the cc:Mail postoffice named CCPOST and whose cc:Mail address is Brown_T, enter the address as:

[CCMail:Brown_T at CCPOST]

Note

> Note these important points. The entire address must be enclosed with brackets. Also, the word "at" with a space both before and after it is required in cc:Mail addresses rather than the "@" seen in traditional addresses.

After you've completed the message, choose Send to send the message to your Outbox.

The next time Outlook accesses the cc:Mail postoffice, your message is automatically sent.

Note

> By default, Outlook accesses the cc:Mail postoffice at one-minute intervals. You can change this interval in the Delivery tab of the Configure cc:Mail Service dialog box.

→ To learn more about configuring Outlook to retrieve e-mail from cc:Mail, **see** "Setting Up Lotus cc:Mail," **p. 785**.

When Outlook accesses the cc:Mail postoffice, it downloads any messages waiting for you and places them in your Inbox. You can see these messages in your Inbox Information viewer in the same way that you see messages from other sources.

When you reply to a message you've received from a cc:Mail account, Outlook automatically sends the reply to that account in the cc:Mail postoffice.

With the MS Outlook Support for cc:Mail information service in your profile, you can send messages to people with an Internet e-mail address, without having the Internet E-mail information service in your profile.

Note

An Internet mail connector must be installed in the cc:Mail server in order to do this.

To send a message to a person who has an Internet e-mail account, enter the address as:

[CCMail:Brown_T@company.com at fastnet]

where the recipient's Internet e-mail address is Brown_T@company.com on an Internet mail server named fastnet.

Tip #180 from

The entire address must be enclosed within brackets. The spaces before and after "at" are required.

TROUBLESHOOTING

If you've been using cc:Mail 7.x or 8.x and then install Outlook, you'll probably see an error message the next time you try to use cc:Mail. The reason for this is that the Outlook installation replaces some *Messaging Application Programming Interface (MAPI) files (page 39)* and the new files are not compatible with the cc:Mail client. The solution to this problem is to have both sets of MAPI files on your computer, one for use with Outlook and most other Windows applications, and the other to use with the cc:Mail client. After you've installed the MS Outlook Support for cc:Mail information service, use the following procedure to do this.

To be able to use Outlook and the cc:Mail client on the same computer:

1. Locate the file named Wmail32.exe. Make a note of the name of the folder that contains this file.
2. Use Windows Explorer to copy the file named Mapisp32.exe from your Windows\System folder into the same folder as Wmail32.exe.
3. Use Windows Explorer to copy the file named Mapi32.dll from your Office 97 CD-ROM into the same folder as Wmail32.exe.
4. Restart your computer.

After following these steps, you have the Outlook version of Mapi32.dll and Mapi32.exe in your Windows\System folder; you have the same version of Mapi32.exe, but an older version of Mapi.dll, in the folder that contains other cc:Mail-related files.

PART

V

CH

32

CUSTOMIZING OUTLOOK

CHAPTER 33

CUSTOMIZING THE OUTLOOK BAR

In this chapter   *by Gordon Padwick*

THE IMPROVED OUTLOOK BAR

The Outlook Bar, displayed at the left edge of Outlook's Information viewers, contains shortcut icons you can choose to gain immediate access to the standard Outlook folders and, if you have the Integrated File Management component of Outlook installed, to your Windows folder structure.

The default Outlook Bar has three groups of shortcut icons:

- Outlook Shortcuts group—This group contains shortcut icons that provide access to most of the standard Outlook folders.

- My Shortcuts group—This group contains shortcut icons that provide access to folders containing e-mail messages you're preparing to send or have sent to your Outlook Journal folder, and to the Outlook Update Web page.

- Other Shortcuts group—This group contains shortcut icons that access your Windows folder structure.

Note

> The Outlook Update Web page contains information about updates to Outlook and other Office 2000 applications that are available from Microsoft. The Web page URL is http://officeupdate.microsoft.com/welcome/outlook.htm.

The default Outlook Bar gives only basic access to your Outlook and Windows folders. You can add more shortcut icons to any group and you can add more groups to the Outlook Bar to provide fast access to your entire information environment.

In this chapter, you'll learn how to add shortcuts to existing Outlook Bar groups and add more groups to the Outlook Bar. You'll also learn how to add shortcuts your Windows folders and files, and to Web pages—something that's new in Outlook 2000.

SELECTING AN OUTLOOK BAR GROUP

By default, Outlook displays the Outlook Shortcuts group of shortcut icons, as shown in Figure 33.1.

Tip #181 from

> To see hidden shortcut icons, click the triangle button near the bottom of the Outlook Shortcuts group. After you've done that, you can click the triangle button near the top to see hidden icons above those you can see.

With the Outlook Shortcuts group displayed, you can choose the My Shortcuts or Other Shortcuts button to display those Outlook Bar groups. With either of those groups displayed, you can choose the Outlook Shortcuts button to display that group again.

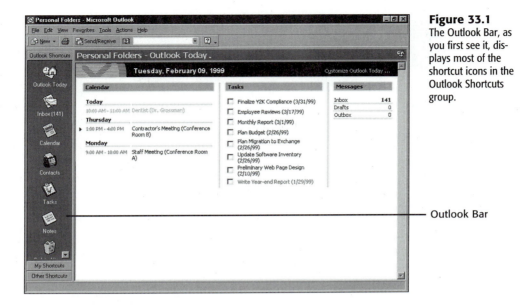

Figure 33.1
The Outlook Bar, as you first see it, displays most of the shortcut icons in the Outlook Shortcuts group.

Outlook Bar

DISPLAYING AND HIDING THE OUTLOOK BAR

By default, Outlook displays the Outlook Bar at the left edge of all *Information viewers (page 17)*, but it doesn't have to be displayed. Chapter 1, "How Outlook Works," contains information about modifying the Outlook startup so that an Information viewer is displayed without the Outlook Bar. This has the advantage that Information viewers are enlarged so that you can see more of what's in them.

→ To get tips on altering your Information viewers' startup appearance, **see** "Controlling How Outlook Starts," **p. 26**.

With any Outlook Information viewer displayed, you can choose <u>V</u>iew, <u>O</u>utlook Bar to hide or unhide the Outlook Bar.

Tip #182 from

If you frequently hide and then redisplay the Outlook Bar, you can create a button on one of the toolbars for this purpose. Choosing that button is somewhat more convenient than choosing <u>V</u>iew, <u>O</u>utlook Bar—one click instead of two.

→ For more information on creating a toolbar button, **see** "Adding a Button to a Toolbar," **p. 824**.

CHANGING THE APPEARANCE OF THE OUTLOOK BAR

You can make the Outlook Bar narrower or wider by moving the pointer onto the border between the Outlook Bar and an Information viewer. When the pointer icon changes to a pair of vertical lines with left- and right-pointing arrows, press the mouse button and drag to the left or to the right.

CHOOSING SMALL ICONS

When you have the Outlook Shortcuts group displayed, you can't see all its shortcuts (unless you have a big monitor that displays a large number of pixels). After you use the techniques described in this chapter to add more shortcut icons to a group on the Outlook Bar, you'll probably wish that more could be seen at one time.

You can choose to have small icons, instead of the default large icons, displayed in the Outlook Bar. This choice is available separately for each Outlook Bar group.

To have small icons in an Outlook Bar group, select that group, then right-click within the Outlook Bar group (not on an icon) to display the Outlook Bar's context menu, shown in Figure 33.2.

Choose Small Icons. Instead of the large icons previously displayed in the Outlook Bar, you now have small icons, as shown in Figure 33.3.

You'll probably prefer to use Outlook with small icons in the Outlook Bar, unless you're displaying Outlook on a small screen. You can, of course, go back to large icons by again displaying the Outlook Bar context menu and choosing Large Icons.

Figure 33.2
This is the menu you use to customize the Outlook Bar.

CHANGING THE ORDER OF ICONS

You can change the order of icons in a group so that those you use most often are close together. You can also move icons from one group to another.

To move a shortcut icon within a group:

1. Point onto the shortcut icon you want to move and press the mouse button.
2. Drag up or down. As you drag, a black bar appears between icons. Stop dragging when a bar appears at the position where you want the icon you're dragging to be.
3. Release the mouse button. The icon moves to the new position.

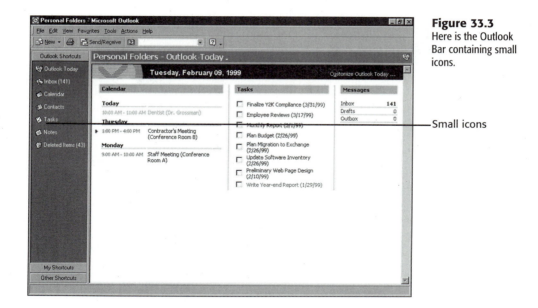

Figure 33.3
Here is the Outlook Bar containing small icons.

You can use a similar method to move a shortcut icon from one group to another. Here's an example.

To move the Deleted Items shortcut icon from the Outlook Shortcuts group to the My Shortcuts group:

1. With the Outlook Shortcuts group displayed, point onto the Deleted Items icon and press the mouse button.

2. Drag down onto the My Shortcuts group button. The My Shortcuts group appears with a black bar representing the icon you're dragging below the last icon in that group.

3. Drag up to place the Deleted Items icon where you want it to be within the My Shortcuts group, then release the mouse button.

PART
VI
CH
33

Tip #183 from

Whether you're dragging a shortcut icon within a group, or from one group to another, if you drag onto a group name and then release the mouse button, Outlook displays a message stating that you can't do that. If that happens, choose OK to close the message. Try the process again, this time making sure you don't release the mouse button while you're pointing onto a group name.

USING A SHORTCUT ICON'S CONTEXT MENU

Right-click a shortcut icon to see its context menu, as shown in Figure 33.4.

Figure 33.4
This is a shortcut icon's
context menu.

Choose an item on the context menu, according to what you want to do:

- Open Folder—Open the Outlook folder represented by the shortcut icon to display its contents in an Information viewer. This is the same thing that happens when you click a shortcut icon.

- Open in New Window—Open the Outlook folder represented by the shortcut icon in a separate window on your screen. This allows you to have two or more windows visible, each showing the contents of a separate folder.

- Advanced Find—Open the Advanced Find dialog box. The Advanced Find dialog box opens ready to search in the folder corresponding to the Outlook Bar shortcut you're working with.

→ For information about working with Advanced Find, **see** "Using Advanced Find to Find Words and Phrases," **p. 532**.

- Remove from Outlook Bar—Remove the icon from the Outlook Bar.

- Rename Shortcut—Rename the shortcut icon.

- Properties—Display the shortcut icon's properties. Properties are explained in the next section.

UNDERSTANDING A SHORTCUT ICON'S PROPERTIES

When you choose Properties in a shortcut icon's context menu, you have access to the properties of the folder to which the icon is a shortcut. For example, if you right-click the Contacts shortcut icon and then choose Properties, you see the dialog box shown in Figure 33.5.

You can use this dialog box to examine and, if necessary, change the properties of the Contacts folder, as explained in Chapter 9, "Managing Contacts."

→ To learn more about adjusting the settings for Contacts, **see** "Examining a Contact Item's Properties," **p. 347**.

For information about the properties of other folders, refer to the chapters in which specific types of Outlook items are described.

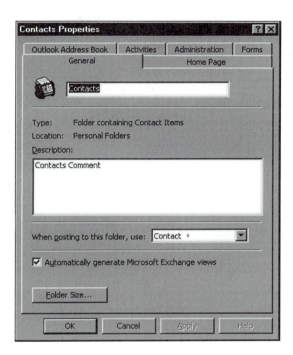

Figure 33.5
This is the Contacts
Properties dialog box.

Note The Properties dialog box tabs vary according to the Outlook Bar shortcut you're looking at, according to whether you're using IMO or C/W Outlook, and, if you're using C/W Outlook, which Information Services are in your profile.

RENAMING, ADDING, AND REMOVING OUTLOOK BAR GROUPS

If you're like me, you don't particularly like the names Microsoft has given to two of the default Outlook Bar groups. Outlook Shortcuts may be okay, but My Shortcuts and Other Shortcuts? You can change the names of the Outlook Bar shortcuts to whatever seems more appropriate. You can also add groups to, and delete groups from, the Outlook Bar.

Note Outlook saves your Outlook Bar configuration in a file named Microsoft Outlook Internet Settings.Fav. After you've customized the Outlook Bar, you can restore it to its default. Close Outlook and delete the Microsoft Outlook Internet Settings.Fav file. When you restart Outlook, a new file based on the default settings is automatically created.

RENAMING AN OUTLOOK BAR GROUP

Suppose you want to change the name of the My Shortcuts group to E-mail Shortcuts.

To change the name of an Outlook Bar group:

1. In the Outlook Bar, right-click the group name you want to change to display the group's context menu, shown previously in Figure 33.2.

2. Choose <u>R</u>ename Group in the context menu. The group name button changes to white with the name selected, as shown in Figure 33.6.

Figure 33.6
This is how the group name appears when it's ready for editing.

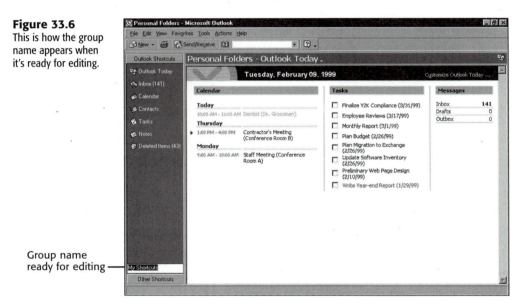

Group name ready for editing

3. Edit the group name in the normal way, then press Enter. Now the group has the new name.

ADDING A GROUP

The default Outlook Bar has three groups of shortcut icons. The maximum number of groups allowed is 12, so you can add up to nine more.

To add a group to the Outlook Bar:

1. Right-click any group name to display that group's context menu, shown previously in Figure 33.2.

2. Choose <u>A</u>dd New Group. A button appears at the bottom of the Outlook Bar with the temporary name "New Group" selected.

3. Change the temporary name to the name you want the new group to have, then press Enter.

Tip #184 from

Each new group you create always appears below the existing group buttons in the Outlook Bar. There appears to be no straightforward way to change the order of group buttons in the Outlook Bar.

 If you must change the group order, one possible workaround is suggested at the end of this chapter. **See** "Troubleshooting," **p. 813**.

REMOVING A GROUP

You can remove any group from the Outlook Bar, including the default groups.

To remove an Outlook Bar group:

1. Right-click the name of the group you want to remove to display its context menu.

2. Choose Remove Group in the context menu. Outlook asks you to confirm that you want to remove the group.

Caution

When Outlook asks you to confirm that you want to remove the group, it doesn't name the group you've selected. Be sure, in step 1, the group you select is really the one you intend to remove. After you've removed a group, you can't undo the remove. You can, however, re-create the group, but that's a considerable amount of work.

3. Choose Yes to remove the group.

ADDING SHORTCUT ICONS TO AN OUTLOOK BAR GROUP

Whenever you create a new Outlook folder, Outlook asks you if you want to create a shortcut to that folder in the Outlook Bar. If you choose not to create a shortcut at that time, you can do so later.

In addition to creating Outlook Bar shortcuts to Outlook items, you can also create shortcuts to Windows folders and files, to Web pages, and to items on the Windows desktop.

CREATING A SHORTCUT ICON WHEN YOU CREATE AN OUTLOOK FOLDER

Chapter 15, "Managing Outlook Folders," explains how to create a new Outlook folder and how you can add a shortcut icon to the Outlook Bar to access that folder.

→ To gain fast access to a new folder by creating a shortcut to it on the Outlook Bar, see "Adding a Folder Icon to the Outlook Bar," **p. 487**.

CREATING A SHORTCUT TO AN EXISTING OUTLOOK FOLDER

You can add a shortcut to any Outlook Bar group to provide easy access to that folder.

PART
VI

CH
33

To add an Outlook folder shortcut icon to an Outlook Bar group:

1. Select the Outlook Bar group into which you want to add a shortcut icon.

2. Choose View, Folder List to display the Outlook folder list.

3. If necessary, expand the folder list so that the name of the folder for which you want to create a shortcut icon is visible.

4. Drag the folder name into the Outlook Bar group.

Tip #185 from

> If you subsequently change your mind about which Outlook Bar group you want the new shortcut to be in, you can drag it to another group.

→ You can make your Outlook Bar more convenient to use by placing those icons you use most often at the top of a group. To learn more, **see** "Changing the Order of Icons," **p. 802**.

If you're using C/W Outlook as a client for Exchange, you can create Outlook Bar shortcut icons for public folders in the Exchange store. Expand your folder list to display the names of public folders, then drag a folder name into the Outlook Bar.

CREATING A SHORTCUT TO A WINDOWS FOLDER OR FILE

C/W

IMO

You can create a shortcut to any folder or file in your Windows folder structure, including folders and files on other network computers to which you've been granted access. You can use the first method described in this section to create a shortcut only to a folder; you can use the second method to create a shortcut to a folder or file.

To add a Windows folder shortcut icon to an Outlook Bar group:

1. Select the Outlook Bar group into which you want to add a shortcut icon.

2. Right-click that Outlook Bar group to display its context menu.

3. Choose Outlook Bar Shortcut to display the dialog box shown in Figure 33.7.

4. Open the drop-down Look In list and select File System. The list now shows you the Windows desktop structure, as shown in Figure 33.8.

Tip #186 from

> Notice that the folder structure includes Network Neighborhood. You can expand that to see folders on other computers to which you have access and create shortcut icons on the Outlook Bar to those folders.

5. Expand the list to display the folder for which you want to create a shortcut.

6. Select that folder and choose OK. The shortcut icon appears in the Outlook Bar.

Here's a way to add shortcuts representing Windows folders or files into an Outlook Bar group.

Figure 33.7
Use this dialog box to add shortcuts to Outlook folders as well as to Windows folders.

Figure 33.8
You can expand this list to show any part of your Windows folder structure.

PART

VI

CH

33

To add a shortcut to a Windows folder or file into the Outlook Bar:

1. Display Outlook and Windows Explorer together on your screen, as shown in Figure 33.9.

2. Drag whichever folder or file you want from the left or right panes of the Windows Explorer window into the Outlook Bar.

Figure 33.9
Adjust the size of the
windows so that the
Outlook Bar is visible
and you can see as
much as you need in
the Windows Explorer
window, as shown
here.

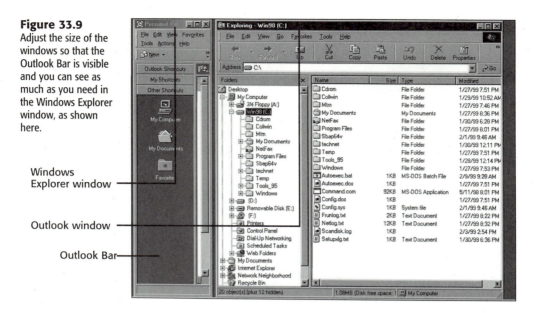

Windows
Explorer window ——

Outlook window ——

Outlook Bar ——

After adding a shortcut representing a Windows folder or file to the Outlook Bar, you can choose the icon in the Outlook Bar to access that folder or file.

What happens when you choose an icon in the Outlook bar depends on what that icon represents:

- If the icon represents a Windows folder, the Information viewer displays a list of files and folders in that folder
- If the icon represents a document, Windows opens the application associated with that type of document and displays that document
- If the icon represents an executable file, Windows runs the file

CREATING A SHORTCUT TO THE WINDOWS DESKTOP

You already know that you can create icons on your Windows desktop to provide fast access to applications. For example, while writing this book, I often need to use the Collage Complete Screen Capture and Image Manager applications. By having shortcuts to those applications on my desktop, I can quickly open them.

However, if I have Outlook maximized, I can't see shortcuts on my desktop. Here's where Outlook simplifies my life. I can drag shortcuts from my Windows desktop into the Outlook Bar. Now I have shortcuts in the Outlook Bar that are copies of the shortcuts on my desktop.

Tip #187 from

If you often want to open other applications while you're working with Outlook, consider using the method described here to place shortcuts to those applications in your Outlook Bar.

Here's another example of the versatility and usefulness of creating shortcuts in the Outlook Bar. Do you often want to take a look at something in the Windows Control Panel? If so, you can create a shortcut to it in the Outlook Bar. First create a shortcut to the Control Panel on the Windows desktop. Then drag that shortcut into the Outlook Bar. Here are the details.

To create a shortcut to the Control Panel in the Outlook Bar:

1. Open Windows Explorer and select your Windows folder.

2. Scroll down the list of files in the Windows folder to find Control.exe.

3. Drag Control.exe onto the Windows desktop. Now you have a shortcut to the Control Panel on your Windows desktop.

4. Open Outlook, restore it so that it occupies only a part of your screen, and select the Outlook Bar group in which you want to have the Control Panel shortcut.

5. Drag the Control Panel shortcut from your Windows desktop to the Outlook Bar.

Now, from within Outlook, you can instantly bring up your Control Panel.

Tip #188 from

This technique has many possibilities. You might, for example, find it useful to create an Outlook Bar shortcut that instantly displays your Printers dialog box.

CREATING A SHORTCUT TO A WEB PAGE

You can create shortcuts in your Outlook Bar to get direct access to specific Web pages.

Note

The Outlook Update shortcut in the default My Shortcuts Outlook Bar group is a shortcut to a Web page.

To create a shortcut in the Outlook Bar to a Web page:

1. Use Internet Explorer to access an Internet Web page.

2. Display the Web page for which you want to create a shortcut on an Outlook Bar.

3. Open Outlook and arrange the Internet Explorer and the Outlook windows on your screen, as shown in Figure 33.10.

PART

VI

CH

33

Figure 33.10
You see a part of the
Windows Explorer screen
on the left and a part of
the Outlook screen on the
right.

Internet Explorer
window

Web page icon

Outlook window

Outlook Bar

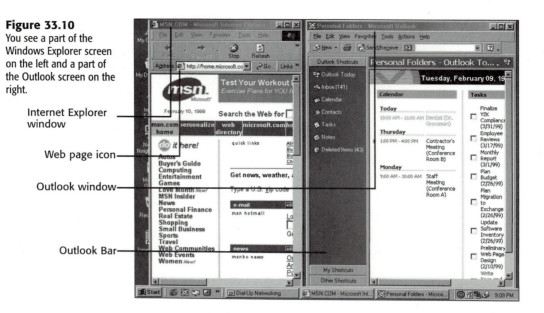

4. Drag the Web page icon shown in Figure 33.10 into the Outlook Bar in the Outlook window.

After you've done that, you can choose the new shortcut in the Outlook Bar to access whatever Web site you specified.

Tip #189 from

> You can also drag existing shortcuts in the Favorites Information viewer into the Outlook Bar.

After you've created a shortcut to a Web page, you simply choose the shortcut in the Outlook Bar to display that Web page.

→ For more detailed information about opening a Web page from within Outlook, **see** "Accessing Web Sites," **p. 270**.

REMOVING SHORTCUT ICONS FROM THE OUTLOOK BAR

You can remove any shortcut icon from the Outlook Bar.

To remove a shortcut icon:

1. Right-click the shortcut icon you want to remove to display its context menu.

2. Choose Remove from Outlook Bar. Outlook asks you to confirm that you want to remove the selected shortcut icon.

3. Choose Yes.

TROUBLESHOOTING

As mentioned previously in this chapter, while you can easily change the order of shortcut items within a group, you can't change the order of groups within the Outlook Bar. Suppose, for example, you create a new group and you want to have that group at the top of the Outlook Bar so that it's the one displayed when you open Outlook. Here's a workaround you can use.

To create a new Outlook Bar group at the top of the Outlook Bar:

1. Add a new group to the Outlook Bar.

→ For details on how to add new groups to the Outlook Bar, **see** "Adding a Group," **p. 806**.

2. Drag the existing shortcuts from the Outlook Shortcuts group into the new group.

→ To learn more about reordering icons on your Outlook Bar, **see** "Changing the Order of Icons," **p. 802**.

3. Insert new shortcuts into the group you just emptied.

→ For additional information about shortcuts and the Outlook Bar, see "Adding Shortcut Icons to an Outlook Bar Group," **p. 807**.

4. Rename the two Outlook Bar groups.

→ To learn the steps for changing group names, **see** "Renaming an Outlook Bar Group," **p. 806**.

PART

VI

CH

33

CHAPTER 34

CUSTOMIZING COMMAND BARS

In this chapter   *by Gordon Padwick*

WHAT ARE COMMAND BARS?

If you're upgrading from Outlook 97 to Outlook 2000, you're probably used to thinking of the menu bar and toolbars as separate components of the user interface. While they're visually separate in Outlook 2000, they have a lot in common, so much so that Microsoft now uses the term *Command Bars* for both.

> **Note**
>
> The similarity between the menus and toolbars extends to what's in them. Toolbars can contain menus and menus can contain tools.

One of the limitations of Outlook 97 was that you couldn't customize the menu bar or toolbar. That limitation disappeared in Outlook 98. In Outlook 2000 you can customize command bars—the menu bar and the toolbars.

In common with the other Office 2000 applications, Outlook 2000 offers adaptive menus and toolbars that use Microsoft IntelliSense technology to adapt automatically to how you work with Outlook. By default Outlook's menus and toolbars group together the menu items and tools you use frequently and temporarily hide others.

> **Tip #190 from**
>
>
>
> The illustrations in this book were saved with adaptive menus and toolbars turned off to make the book easier to follow. To turn adaptive menus and toolbars on or off, choose Tools, Customize to display the Customize dialog box. Select the Options tab. Check Menus Show Recently Used Commands First to turn on adaptive menus and toolbars; uncheck it to turn off adaptive menus and toolbars. The setting you choose applies to all Office 2000 applications.

COMMAND BARS IN THE DEFAULT USER INTERFACE

The default Outlook user interface has a menu bar at the top and a single toolbar under the menu bar, as shown in Figure 34.1.

Unlike Outlook 97, the menu bar in Outlook 2000 contains the same menus for all the Information viewers that display Outlook items—with only one slight difference when an Information viewer that displays Windows folders is open. Many of the items in the menus are also the same. Many of the tools in the toolbars, however, are different for each Information viewer because the tools provide quick access to various types of Outlook items.

The Outlook 2000 toolbar contains fewer tools than the Outlook 97 toolbar. The toolbar is easier to use because the icons for the most frequently used tools are supplemented by words. In addition, if you move the pointer onto a tool and pause for a moment, a ScreenTip containing the name of the tool appears.

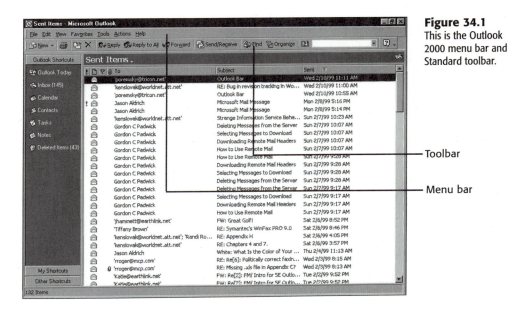

Figure 34.1
This is the Outlook 2000 menu bar and Standard toolbar.

DISPLAYING AND HIDING TOOLBARS

The toolbar initially displayed by Outlook 2000 is more properly called the Standard toolbar. You can also display a toolbar, known as the Advanced toolbar, that's similar to the Outlook 97 toolbar by choosing <u>V</u>iew, moving the pointer onto <u>T</u>oolbars, and choosing Advanced. The Advanced toolbar appears at the right side of the Standard toolbar, as shown in Figure 34.2.

> **Note**
>
> You can also right-click any button in a displayed toolbar to display a list of available toolbars, and then select from that list.

 When the two toolbars are displayed side by side, there isn't room for all the tools. To see any tools that aren't displayed, choose the More Buttons icon at the right end of the toolbar. Any tools not visible in the toolbar are now available in a box, as shown in Figure 34.3.

> **Tip #191 from**
>
> *Gordon Padwick*
>
> To change the number of visible tools in each toolbar, move the pointer onto the Advanced toolbar's *handle* (the vertical bar near the left edge of the toolbar). You're pointing onto the correct place when the pointer changes to a four-headed arrow. Drag the handle to the left or right to change the number of tools visible in each toolbar.

PART
VI
CH
34

Figure 34.2
The Advanced toolbar initially appears at the right of the Standard toolbar to leave as much vertical space as possible for the Information viewer.

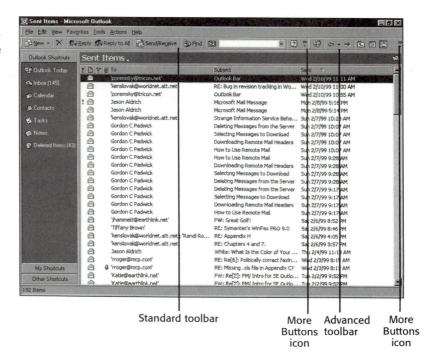

Standard toolbar   More   Advanced   More
                          Buttons   toolbar   Buttons
                          icon   icon

Figure 34.3
You can choose tools in this box just as you can choose tools displayed in the toolbar.

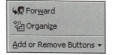

The Web toolbar initially appears as a floating toolbar that you can drag to anywhere on your screen. See Figure 34.4.

Figure 34.4
This toolbar is useful when you use Outlook to display Web pages.

→ For information about using the Web toolbar, **see** "Accessing Web Sites," **p. 270**.

When you're using the Inbox Information viewer in C/W Outlook, you can also display the Remote toolbar, shown in Figure 34.5.

Figure 34.5
The Remote toolbar contains tools that duplicate those in the Remote Mail menu.

The Remote toolbar initially appears as a floating toolbar that you can drag to wherever you like on your screen. This toolbar is useful only if you're working with remote mail.

→ For detailed information about working with remote mail, **see** "Using Remote Mail," **p. 747**.

To remove a toolbar, choose <u>V</u>iew, move the pointer onto <u>T</u>oolbars, and choose the name of the toolbar you want to remove. You can also remove a floating toolbar by clicking the X at the right end of its title bar.

MOVING A TOOLBAR

The Standard and Advanced toolbars are initially displayed in the docked position at the top of an Outlook window.

You can drag a docked toolbar to another docked position. For example, if you have the Standard and Advanced toolbars displayed side by side, as previously shown in Figure 34.2, you can drag the Advanced toolbar down and to the left so that it's immediately below the Standard toolbar. To do so, point onto the Advanced toolbar's handle (the vertical bar near its left edge). When you're pointing onto the correct position, the pointer changes to a four-headed arrow. Now, drag down and to the left until the Advanced toolbar is in the position shown in Figure 34.6.

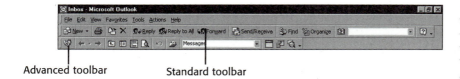

Advanced toolbar   Standard toolbar

Figure 34.6
With the Advanced toolbar in this position, all the tools in the Standard and Advanced toolbars are visible.

Tip #192 from

Gordon Padwick

To return the Advanced toolbar to its original position at the right of the Standard toolbar, point onto the Advanced toolbar's handle and drag it into the Standard toolbar.

You can also drag a toolbar that's docked at the top of the window to a docked position at the left, right, or bottom of the Outlook window. Point onto a docked toolbar's handle and drag to a different edge of the window.

You can convert a docked toolbar to a floating toolbar. To do so, point onto the toolbar's handle and drag the toolbar away from the window border, as shown in Figure 34.7.

Toolbar name   Title bar   Close

Figure 34.7
Here is the Standard toolbar in a floating position.

As Figure 34.7 shows, a floating toolbar has a title bar that contains the name of the toolbar. To move a floating toolbar, point into the title bar and drag. You can also choose the X at the right end of the title bar to close the toolbar.

Whereas a docked toolbar always consists of a single row or column of tools, that isn't so for a floating toolbar. To change a floating toolbar to an array with several rows and columns of tools, point onto one of the toolbar's borders. If you point onto the left or right border, you can drag to the right or left; if you point onto the top or bottom border, you can drag up or down. Figure 34.8 shows the result of doing this.

Figure 34.8
Here is the Standard toolbar as an array.

To return a floating toolbar to the docked position, point onto the toolbar's title bar and drag to one of the borders of the window.

SAVING AND RESTORING TOOLBARS

Outlook automatically saves the status of toolbars in a file named Outcmd.dat. Status indicates:

- Which toolbars are displayed
- Whether each toolbar is docked or floating
- The position of each toolbar
- In the case of a floating toolbar, the size of the array
- Any changes you've made to the contents of the default toolbars
- Complete information about any custom toolbars you've created

Note

Any changes you make to the menu bar and the individual menus are also saved in Outcmd.dat.

Outlook saves this file separately in each user's Windows profile. As a result, if several people have a Windows account on one computer, each person can have separate customized toolbars and menus.

Outlook refers to Outcmd.dat on startup so that toolbars and menus appear as they were when you previously closed Outlook.

After you've made changes to Outlook's toolbars, menu bar, or individual menus, you can restore the defaults. This process removes any custom toolbars you've created.

Tip #193 from

Gordon Woodcock

If you inherit a computer from someone who has customized Outlook's toolbars, you might want to restore the default toolbars. You can use the steps in the following procedure to do that.

To restore Outlook's default toolbars, menu bar, and individual menus:

1. Exit Outlook.
2. Use the Windows Find command to locate Outcmd.dat.
3. Rename Outcmd to something like Outcmd.old.
4. Restart Outlook. On startup, Outlook looks in your Windows profile for Outcmd.dat and, if it's not available, creates a new one based on the built-in defaults.

CUSTOMIZING A TOOLBAR

Having described what you can do with Outlook's default toolbars, it's time now to think about how you can modify the existing toolbars and create new ones. A word of warning is appropriate before getting started with this. This warning applies to modifying menus as well as to modifying toolbars.

By changing toolbars and menus, you're changing Outlook's user interface. If you work by yourself with Outlook and never ask anyone for help, change the toolbars and menus as much as you like. You've made the changes, you know what they are, and you have to solve any problems that arise.

However, if you work in a group and rely on other people for support, you're heading for problems if you make more than minor changes to toolbars and menus. This is particularly the case if you rely on support by telephone from a help desk. A support person can't guide you through a process if your Outlook installation doesn't have the standard toolbar buttons and menu items (or, perhaps, customized toolbars and menus that match a group standard).

Groups of users should either not make changes to toolbars and menus or, if changes are necessary, every member of the group should have the same customized toolbars and menus. Think about that before making changes.

The remainder of this chapter describes how you can customize toolbars and the menu bar.

You can change the size of toolbar buttons, delete buttons from a toolbar, and add buttons to a toolbar. You can also create custom toolbars.

Tip #194 from

Before you start making changes to toolbars, the menu bar, and individual menus, you should save a copy of the original Outcmd.dat file. Then, if things go wrong, you can restore the saved file to return to your configuration before you started to make changes.

CHANGING THE SIZE OF TOOLBAR BUTTONS

By default, all toolbar buttons are small. You can, however, choose to have large buttons displayed.

To display large toolbar buttons:

1. With any Outlook Information viewer displayed, choose Tools, Customize to display the Customize dialog box. Select the Options tab, shown in Figure 34.9.

Figure 34.9
Use this dialog box to select options that apply to all Office 2000 applications.

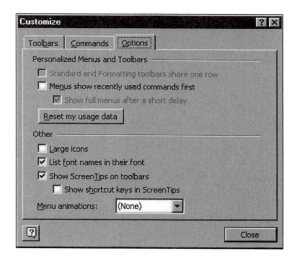

2. Check Large Icons and then choose Close. The Outlook window now has large icons, as shown in Figure 34.10.

Figure 34.10
After you've chosen Large Icons, Outlook 2000 and all other Office 2000 applications display large toolbar icons.

Tip #195 from

Gordon Crabtree

In most cases, you won't want to use large icons. However, if you're using a laptop with a small screen or work in difficult lighting conditions, large icons might be preferable to the standard small icons. Also, people who have poor vision might prefer to use large icons.

Unless you want to keep large icons, return to the Customize dialog box, previously shown in Figure 34.9, and uncheck Large Icons.

While you have the Options tab open, notice the other choices it offers:

- Standard and Formatting Toolbars Share One Row—This option applies to forms such as Outlook's Message form, in which Standard and Formatting toolbars are available. With this option checked, the Standard and Formatting toolbars are in the same row at the top of the form; with the item unchecked, the two toolbars are in separate rows.

- Menus Show Recently Used Commands First—Check this to enable Office 2000's adaptive menus and toolbars capability, described at the beginning of this chapter. Uncheck this box to turn the capability off. What you select here affects all Office 2000 applications.

- Reset My Usage Data—Choose this button to restore the default menus and toolbars in Outlook (and other Office 2000 applications) when you have checked Menus Show Recently Used Commands First.

- Large Icons—Check this to display large icons. Uncheck it to display small icons.

- List Font Names in Their Font—Check this if you want Office 2000 applications to show lists of fonts with each font's name displayed in that font.

- Show ScreenTips on Toolbars—Check this if you want a ScreenTip to display a tool's name when you move the pointer onto a tool.

- Show Shortcut Keys in ScreenTips—Check this if you want ScreenTips to display shortcut keys for those tools that have shortcut keys.

- Menu Animations—Open the drop-down list and select among None, Random, Unfold, and Slide.

Note

Instead of attempting to describe menu animations, I'll leave it to you to try them out and decide if there's an animation you'd like to use.

DELETING A TOOLBAR BUTTON

If you want to add your own buttons to a toolbar, you might like to remove some standard buttons that you rarely use to make room for the new buttons.

To delete a toolbar button:

1. Display the toolbar from which you want to delete a button.
2. Point onto the button you want to delete.

PART
VI

CH
34

3. Hold down the Alt key while you drag the button off the toolbar. When you release the Alt key, the button disappears from the toolbar.

ADDING A BUTTON TO A TOOLBAR

You can add a new button to a toolbar, or replace a button you previously removed from a toolbar.

To add a button to a toolbar:

1. Display the toolbar to which you want to add a button.

2. Choose Tools, Customize to display the Customize dialog box.

Tip #196 from

Gordon Padwick

Alternatively, right-click any tool in a toolbar to display the context menu, and choose Customize in that menu.

---

3. Select the Commands tab to display the dialog box shown in Figure 34.11.

Figure 34.11
This dialog box displays the commands available to be added as buttons to a toolbar.

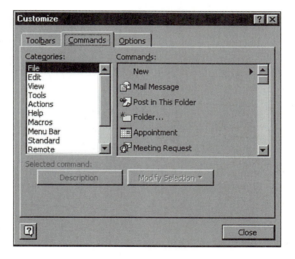

4. In the Categories list at the left side of the dialog box, select the category of the command you want to add. For example, if you want to add an Outlook Today button to a toolbar, select the View category. The right side of the dialog box now lists the commands in that category, as shown in Figure 34.12.

5. Move the pointer onto the command you want to add, press the mouse button, and drag the command to the position where you want it on the toolbar. When you release the mouse button, the new command appears within a black-bordered box on the toolbar.

6. Choose Close in the Customize dialog box. The black-bordered box in the toolbar disappears, leaving the new button as a normal button.

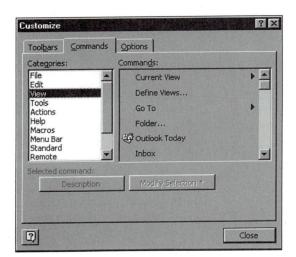

Figure 34.12
With the View category selected, the Commands list contains the commands available in that category.

Tip #197 from

In the Customize dialog box, with the Commands tab selected, you can select a command in the list on the right and then choose Description to see a description of the selected command.

ADDING A CUSTOM MENU TO A TOOLBAR BUTTON

Toolbars can contain buttons that display menus as well as conventional buttons. For example, choose the black triangle near the right edge of the New button in the Inbox Information viewer's Standard toolbar to see a menu. You can add buttons that display menus to Outlook's toolbars.

Note

Outlook identifies each menu button in toolbars with a black triangle near its right edge.

PART
VI

CH
34

To add a button that displays a menu into a toolbar:

1. Display the toolbar into which you want to insert the button.

2. Choose Tools, Customize and select the Commands tab shown previously in Figure 34.11.

3. Scroll down in the Categories list and select New Menu. When you do so, New Menu appears in the Commands list, as shown in Figure 34.13.

Figure 34.13
With New Menu selected in the Categories list, the Commands list contains only New Menu.

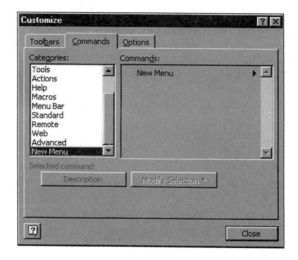

4. Drag New Menu from the Commands list into the toolbar in which you want to have the new button. While the mouse button is pressed, you see only a black vertical bar in the toolbar. Drag the black bar horizontally to the position where you want to have the button, then release the mouse button. The new button appears in the menu, as shown in Figure 34.14.

Figure 34.14
In this case, the new button has been added near the right end of the Advanced toolbar.

Inserted button

5. Right-click the new button to display it's context menu, as shown in Figure 34.15.

6. Change the temporary name to an appropriate name for the button, then press Enter. You can either close the Customize dialog box at this stage, or continue on to the procedure to add items into the menu.

Figure 34.15
The third item in the context menu contains the temporary name New Menu.

When entering a name for the button, place an ampersand immediately before the character to be underlined in the menu name. That character becomes a hot key. Subsequently, hold down Alt and type that character to open the menu. Be careful not to choose a hotkey character that is already used in the menu bar or any other displayed toolbar.

At this stage, you have a button that provides access to a menu, but that menu is empty. Now you can add items to the menu.

To add items to a menu:

1. If the Customize dialog box isn't displayed, choose Tools, Customize to display it. Make sure the Commands tab is selected.
2. Choose the menu button that you previously placed in the toolbar. An empty box appears immediately below the button.
3. Scroll, if necessary, in the Categories list and select a command category to display commands in that category in the Commands list.
4. Scroll, if necessary, down the commands in the Commands list to find a command you want in the menu.
5. Drag that command into the empty box below the toolbar button. When you release the mouse button, the box expands horizontally to provide space for the command. The command's name and, if available, its icon appear in the box, as shown in Figure 34.16.

PART
VI

CH
34

Figure 34.16
Here's how the menu appears after you've added one item to the menu.

6. Repeat steps 3 through 5 to add more commands into the menu.

7. Close the Customize dialog box.

You can choose the new button in the toolbar to display the menu you've just created, and then choose any item in that menu.

CHANGING THE POSITION OF A TOOLBAR BUTTON

To change the position of a toolbar button, point onto the button, hold down the Alt key, and drag the button to a new position. You can use this method to move a button within a toolbar and also to move a button from one toolbar to another.

INSERTING AND DELETING SEPARATORS BETWEEN TOOLBAR BUTTONS

If you look closely at one of Outlook's toolbars, you'll notice vertical gray lines that divide buttons into groups; these lines are known as *separators*. You can insert separators into toolbars and remove separators from toolbars.

To insert a separator at the left of a button, hold down the Alt key while you drag the button a short distance to the right. The separator appears when you release the Alt key.

To delete a separator at the right of a button, hold down the Alt key while you drag the button a short distance to the left. The separator disappears when you release the Alt key.

MODIFYING A TOOLBAR BUTTON

You can make changes to an existing toolbar button, but only if the Customize dialog box is displayed. With the Customize dialog box displayed, right-click a button to display the context menu shown in Figure 34.17.

Figure 34.17
These are the items available in a toolbar button's context menu.

Use a toolbar button's context menu as follows:

- Reset—Reset all aspects of a button to what it was before you made changes to it by using any other command in this menu. Choosing this doesn't restore the button to its original default condition.
- Delete—Delete the selected button.
- Name—Change the name of a button. The current name of the button, if any, is displayed in the menu with an ampersand (&) preceding the underlined character as it appears on the button. You can change the displayed name and change the position of the ampersand so that a different character becomes underlined and acts as the hot key. When you change a button's name, make sure the ampersand precedes a character that's not underlined in any other button on the toolbar. The changed name also appears as a ScreenTip when you point onto a button and pause briefly.
- Copy Button Image—Copy the button image (not the button text) to the Clipboard.
- Paste Button Image—Replace the image (not the text) on the selected button with an image previously copied to the Clipboard.
- Reset Button Image—Reset the button image (not its text) to what it was before you made changes to it.
- Edit Button Image—Open the Button Editor dialog box to display the image's individual pixels, as shown in Figure 34.18.

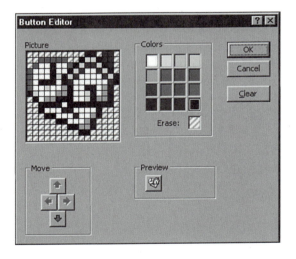

Figure 34.18
You can use this dialog box to make changes to a button's image, or to create an image for a button that previously didn't have one.

Tip #198 from

Although functional, this image editor is somewhat limited. If you make more than occasional small changes to images, consider using a graphics editor such as Windows Paint or a specialized image editor, saving the image to the Clipboard, and pasting it from there.

- Change Button Image—Select a button image from an available set of images.
- Default Style—Display only the default image in the selected button (no text). If there's no default image, the button is just an empty box.
- Text Only (Always)—Display only text in the button.
- Text Only (In Menus)—With a toolbar button selected, this command has the same effect as Default Style. With a menu item selected, display only text.
- Image and Text—Display an image and text in the selected button.
- Begin a Group—Insert a separator at the left of the selected button.
- Assign Hyperlink—Create a button that accesses a file on your computer, a file on another computer to which you have network access, or to a Web page. You can also use this to prepare pre-addressed Message forms.

By using these commands you can customize a toolbar to satisfy your personal taste and requirements. For example, you can add text to a button that, by default, contains only an icon; you might consider doing this for people who have difficulty remembering what some buttons are for. You can also remove text from buttons to make them smaller; this can be useful if you want to make room for several custom buttons.

→ For detained information about adding buttons to a toolbar, **see** "Adding a Button to a Toolbar," **p. 824**.

The ability to create toolbar buttons that enable hyperlinks is very powerful, though you need some practice to become fully comfortable with it. The next four sections provide an introduction to this subject. All four sections assume you have chosen the Assign Hyperlink command in a toolbar button's context menu, as described in this section.

LINKING TO A FILE OR WEB PAGE

After you choose Assign Hyperlink, the Assign Hyperlink dialog box is displayed, such as the one shown in Figure 34.19.

You can use the buttons at the left of the list to select:

- Recent Files—The most recent files you've had open.
- Browsed Pages—Web pages you've most recently used.
- Inserted Links—Links you've most recently created or entered into your browser's Address box.

Note

The first time you choose Assign Hyperlink, the dialog box that appears has Assign Hyperlink in its title bar. After you've assigned a hyperlink to a button, and choose Assign Hyperlink, the dialog box has Edit Hyperlink in its title bar.

Either enter the name of the file or Web page name to which you want to create a link in the Type the File or Web Page Name box, or select any file in this list to create a link between the toolbar button and that file. You can also choose File or Web Page to find files and Web pages that are not listed.

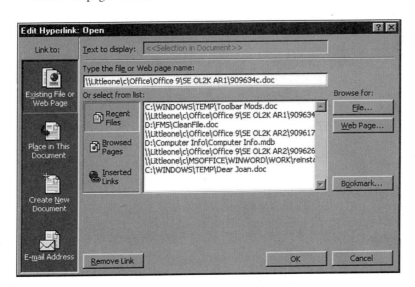

Figure 34.19
This list contains the names of recent Office files you have had open.

Select any file in this list to create a link between the toolbar button and that HTML page. The selected HTML address appears in the Type the File Web Page Name box near the top of the dialog box.

After having established a link from the toolbar button and an item in one of the three lists, you can choose the toolbar button to activate the link.

With one of the three lists displayed, you can choose:

- The File button to open the Link to File dialog box, in which you can navigate through the Windows file system to find a file to which you want to link
- The Web Page button to start your Web browser to find a Web page to which you want to create a link

With the Recent Files or Browsed Pages lists displayed, select an item in one of the lists. Alternatively, you can choose File to look for files in your Windows file system or Web Page to look for a URL. If you choose Bookmark, you'll find it doesn't do anything; that's because Bookmark isn't applicable to Outlook and should be grayed. If you work with Word, you'll find that Bookmark provides access to Word's bookmarks.

LINKING TO A PLACE IN A DOCUMENT

After you choose Assign Hyperlink, the Assign Hyperlink dialog box is displayed. If you choose Place in This Document you'll see a message that states, "Internal hyperlinks are disabled in this mode." Apparently Microsoft plans some functionality here that isn't yet available.

CREATING A NEW DOCUMENT

After you choose Assign Hyperlink, the Assign Hyperlink dialog box is displayed. Choose Create New Document to display the dialog box shown in Figure 34.20.

Figure 34.20
Use this dialog box if you want the toolbar button to create a new document.

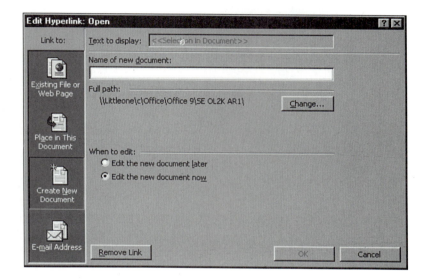

Enter the name of the new document you want the toolbar button to create in the Name of New Document box.

The Full Path section of the dialog box contains the path name you most recently accessed. Choose Change if you want to select a different path. After you do so, Outlook displays a dialog box in which you can navigate to a new path.

In the When to Edit section of the dialog box, you can select an option button that controls what happens when you subsequently choose the toolbar button. Select from the following:

- Edit the New Document Later if you want the new document to be created but not displayed ready for editing

- Edit the New Document Now if you want the new document to be created and displayed in its associated application ready for editing

CREATING A PRE-ADDRESSED MESSAGE FORM

If you frequently send e-mail messages to the same people, you can make your life a little easier by creating a separate toolbar button for each of them. After doing so, just click one of those buttons to display a Message form that's already addressed. The following procedure describes how to create a custom toolbar button for this purpose.

To add a toolbar button that creates an e-mail message:

1. Display the toolbar in which you want to create the new button.

2. Add a new button to the toolbar, as explained previously in this chapter. It doesn't much matter which command you choose for that button because you're subsequently going to assign a hyperlink to the button. After you do that, the button represents that hyperlink, not the command it originally represented.

→ For detailed information about adding a button to a toolbar, **see** "Adding a Button to a Toolbar," **p. 824**.

3. If the Customize dialog box isn't displayed, choose <u>T</u>ools, <u>C</u>ustomize to display it. By having the Customize dialog box open, you have access to Outlook's customization capabilities, even though you don't use the dialog box itself during this procedure.

4. Right-click the new button you just created to display its context menu, shown previously in Figure 34.17.

5. Move the pointer onto Assign <u>H</u>yperlink in the context menu, and choose <u>O</u>pen to display the Assign Hyperlink: Open dialog box. Select the E-mail Address button at the left to display the dialog box shown in Figure 34.21.

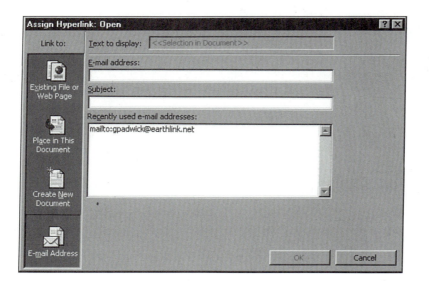

Figure 34.21
This is where you enter an e-mail address and subject for a message.

6. Enter a contact's e-mail address into the <u>E</u>-mail Address box and, optionally, a subject for the message in the <u>S</u>ubject box. Outlook automatically inserts "mailto:" in front of the e-mail address you enter.

Note

> You have to enter the recipient's e-mail address; you can't select it from an address book.

7. Choose OK to return to and close the Assign Hyperlink dialog box. Although you've replaced the new button's original purpose, it retains the image and, perhaps, the text of the original purpose.

8. Right-click the button to open its context menu again. You can use this menu to change the button's image and text to whatever is appropriate for its new purpose, as explained previously in this chapter.

Tip #199 from

> If you have sufficient space in your toolbar, select Text Only (always) and change the button's name to the recipient's name. If you have limited space in the toolbar, choose Default Style so that only an icon appears in the button. When you point onto the button and pause, the ScreenTip shows the recipient's name, and, if you have entered a subject, also the subject.

→ For detailed information about modifying a toolbar button, **see** "Modifying a Toolbar Button," **p. 828**.

9. Close the Customize dialog box.

Subsequently, when you choose the new button, Outlook displays a Message form with the e-mail address and subject you entered in step 6 already there.

CHANGING THE WIDTH OF A DROP-DOWN LIST

Some toolbars contain drop-down lists. For example, the Inbox Information viewer's Standard toolbar contains a drop-down Find a Contact list. The box from which this list drops down is quite wide to provide enough space for contacts' names. To conserve space in the toolbar, you might want to make the box somewhat narrower.

To change the width of a drop-down list:

1. Display the toolbar that contains the drop-down list.

2. Choose Tools, Customize to display the Customize dialog box shown previously in Figure 34.11. It doesn't matter which tab is selected.

Note

> The only purpose of displaying the Customize dialog box is to enable toolbar customization. You don't actually use the dialog box in this procedure.

3. In the toolbar, click the box from which the list drops down. The border of the box changes from gray to black.

4. Point onto the left or right border of the box, press the mouse button, and drag to change the width of the box.

5. Close the Customize dialog box.

RESETTING INDIVIDUAL BUILT-IN TOOLBARS

After you've made changes to one of Outlook's built-in toolbars, you can reset that toolbar to its original condition—so that it has the original buttons in their original positions.

→ For information about resetting all toolbars, the menu bar, and individual menu items to their default states, **see** "Saving and Restoring Toolbars," **p. 820**.

To reset a toolbar:

1. Choose Tools, Customize to display the Customize dialog box. Select the Toolbars tab shown previously in Figure 34.16.

Tip #200 from

You can also display the Customize dialog box by right-clicking a toolbar button and then choosing Customize.

---

2. Select the toolbar you want to reset.

3. Choose Reset to reset the selected toolbar to its original condition.

Note

You can't rename or delete Outlook's built-in toolbars.

The Toolbars box in the Toolbars tab lists the Menu Bar and the available toolbars with a check box adjacent to each. You can check an item in the list to display it or uncheck an item to hide it.

You can also reset individual toolbars in another way. The method is slightly different depending on whether the toolbar is docked or floating:

- For a docked toolbar, choose the black triangle at its right end.
- For a floating toolbar, choose the arrow at the left of the toolbar name in the title bar.

In either case, this opens a menu that contains only one item—Add or Remove Buttons. Choose that menu item to display a menu. Choose Reset Toolbar near the bottom of that menu.

Notice that the Add or Remove Buttons menu contains a list of the default buttons in the selected toolbar. Each name in the list has a check box that's checked if the current toolbar contains that button. You can uncheck these boxes to remove individual buttons from the toolbar and subsequently check these boxes to restore individual buttons.

Each Add or Remove Buttons menu also contains Customize—yet another way to open the Customize dialog box.

PART

VI

CH

34

WORKING WITH CUSTOM TOOLBARS

There are at least two reasons why you might want to create custom toolbars:

- You may want to have more toolbar buttons than there's space for on an existing toolbar.
- You may want to create a set of buttons useful for a specific task.

CREATING A CUSTOM TOOLBAR

Each Outlook *Information viewer (page 17)* and *form (page 24)* has its own set of toolbars and its own menu bar. You have to customize existing toolbars and the menu bar separately for each viewer and form. Similarly, you have to create custom toolbars separately for each viewer and form.

To create a custom toolbar:

1. Open the Information viewer or form for which you want to create a custom toolbar.
2. Choose Tools, Customize to display the Customize dialog box. Select the Toolbars tab, shown subsequently in Figure 34.23.
3. Choose New to display the dialog box shown in Figure 34.22.

Figure 34.22
Outlook proposes to create a new toolbar named Custom 1.

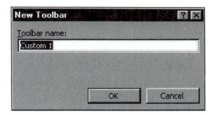

4. Replace the proposed name with something more descriptive, then choose OK to return to the Customize dialog box, which now lists the name of the new toolbar. In addition, a prototype of the new toolbar is displayed, as shown in Figure 34.23.
5. Select the Customize dialog box's Commands tab, select a Category for the first button you want to have in the new toolbar, select a command in that category, and drag the command into the new toolbar.
6. Repeat step 5 as many times as necessary to place more buttons in the new toolbar. The width of the new toolbar automatically increases each time you drag a button into it.
7. Choose Close to close the Customize dialog box.
8. Drag the new toolbar to a docked position or wherever you want it to be displayed.

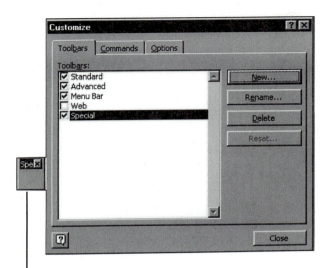

Figure 34.23
The prototype of the new toolbar has room for only one button.

Prototype of new toolbar

ADDING MORE BUTTONS TO A CUSTOM TOOLBAR

After you've created a custom toolbar you can add more buttons to it and remove buttons from it in the same way that you can with the built-in Outlook toolbars (described previously in this chapter).

→ For detailed information about adding a button to a toolbar, **see** "Adding a Button to a Toolbar," **p. 824**.

Another way to add buttons to a toolbar (custom or built-in) is to drag buttons from one toolbar to another. To do this, you must first enable toolbar editing by opening the Customize dialog box; choose Tools, Customize to do so.

Select the toolbar button you want to move by pointing onto it and pressing the mouse button. When you do so, the button's border becomes black. Drag the selected button into another toolbar and release the mouse button. Close the Customize dialog box.

RENAMING AND DELETING A CUSTOM TOOLBAR

You can rename or delete custom toolbars. You can't rename or delete Outlook's built-in toolbars.

To rename or delete a custom toolbar:

1. Display the Information viewer that contains the custom toolbar.

2. Choose Tools, Customize to display the Customize dialog box. Select the Toolbars tab.

3. Select the custom toolbar you want to rename or delete, as shown in Figure 34.24.

PART
VI

CH
34

Figure 34.24
The Rename and Delete buttons are enabled when you select a custom toolbar.

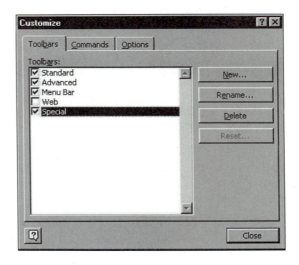

4. Choose Rename if you want to rename the toolbar; Outlook displays a dialog box in which you can edit the toolbar's name. Choose Delete if you want to delete the toolbar; Outlook asks you to confirm that you want to delete it.

> **Note**
> You can't reset a custom toolbar because there's no default to go back to.

CUSTOMIZING THE MENU BAR

Outlook handles the menu bar in much the same way as a toolbar. You can add menus to the menu bar and delete menus from the menu bar; you can add menu items to, and delete menu items from, each menu; you can also change the order of menu items in a menu.

One thing you can't do is create a custom menu bar. Outlook can have only one menu bar.

REMOVING A MENU ITEM FROM A MENU

To remove a menu item from a menu, start by displaying the Customize dialog box, even though you don't actually use that dialog box. It's necessary to have this dialog box open to make menus available for editing. You can't edit menus without having the Customize dialog box displayed.

To remove a menu item from a menu:

1. With the Outlook Information viewer or form from which you want to remove a menu item displayed, choose Tools, Customize. It doesn't matter which tab is selected.

2. In the viewer's or form's menu bar (not in the Customize dialog box), select the menu item you want to remove, as shown in Figure 34.25.

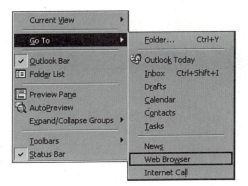

Figure 34.25
The selected menu item name is enclosed in a black box. The black box signifies that the menu is available for editing.

3. Drag the selected menu item out of the menu.

4. Close the Customize dialog box.

ADDING A MENU ITEM TO A MENU

Outlook's menus contain menu items the application's designers expected to be useful. You can easily add menu items to Outlook's menus.

To add a command to a menu:

1. Display the Information viewer to which you want to add a menu command.

2. Choose Tools, Customize to display the Customize dialog box.

3. Select the Commands tab to display the dialog box previously shown in Figure 34.11.

4. In the Categories list at the left side of the dialog box, select the category of the command you want to add. The right side of the dialog box now lists the commands in that category, as previously shown in Figure 34.12.

5. Move the pointer onto the command you want to add, press the mouse button, and drag the command onto the name of the menu into which you want to add the command. The menu opens. Keeping the mouse button pressed, drag down to the position where you want the command to be in the menu. Release the mouse button. The new command is enclosed within a black border.

6. Close the Customize dialog box. The black-border disappears, leaving the new command as a normal-looking command.

Note

You can use the procedure just described to add commands to submenus.

CHANGING THE POSITION OF A MENU ITEM IN A MENU

You can change the position of a menu item in a menu.

PART
VI

CH
34

To change the position of a menu item in a menu:

1. With the Information viewer or form in which you want to change the position of a menu item displayed, choose Tools, Customize to display the Customize dialog box.

2. In the viewer's or form's menu bar (not in the Customize dialog box), select the menu that contains the menu item you want to move.

3. Point onto the menu item and drag it up or down.

4. Release the mouse button when the item is in the position where you want it.

5. Close the Customize dialog box.

Tip #201 from	You can use this procedure to create submenus.

ADDING AND DELETING SEPARATORS IN A MENU

Outlook's menus contain horizontal, gray separator bars that divide menu items into related groups. You can add more *separators (page 828)* and delete separators.

To insert or delete separators:

1. With the Information viewer or form in which you want to change the position of a menu item displayed, choose Tools, Customize to display the Customize dialog box.

2. In the viewer's or form's menu (not in the Customize dialog box), point onto the menu item above which you want to add or remove a separator.

3. Press the mouse button and drag down slightly to insert a separator, or press the mouse button and drag up slightly to remove a separator.

4. Close the Customize dialog box.

DELETING A MENU

You can delete Outlook's default menus as well as custom menus.

To delete a menu and all the menu items it contains, move the pointer onto the menu item, then press and hold down Alt while you drag the menu out of the menu bar.

Caution	As you see, removing a menu from the menu bar is very easy, probably too easy, to do. One simple drag, and the menu's gone. There's no Undo for this action. While you can easily reset the menu bar to its default state, you can't easily reset the menu bar to what it was before you dragged the menu out of it. Refer to "Troubleshooting" at the end of this chapter for more information about this.

ADDING A NEW MENU TO THE MENU BAR

Instead of adding menu items to existing menus, you can create new menus. The procedure that follows is not necessarily intuitively obvious, so pay close attention.

To add a new menu to the menu bar:

1. With the Information viewer or form to which you want to add a new menu displayed, choose Tools, Customize to display the Customize dialog box, and then select the Commands tab.

2. Scroll to the bottom of the Categories list and select New Menu. The Commands list at the right shows New Menu.

3. Drag New Menu from the Commands list into the position you want to have the new menu in the menu bar. This step is the one people sometimes miss; make sure you do it. The new menu appears in the menu bar with the name "New Menu" in a box with a black border.

4. In the Customize dialog box, choose Modify Selection to display a context menu in which the proposed name "New Menu" is selected. Replace the suggested menu name "New Menu" with an appropriate name and press Enter.

Note

Alternatively, with the Customize dialog box displayed, you can right-click the new menu name in the menu bar to display the context menu.

5. Close the Customize dialog box.

Tip #202 from

Just as you can add menus to toolbars, you can add buttons to menus. You can also add hyperlinks to menus, just as you can add hyperlinks to toolbars, as described previously in this chapter.

At this stage you have a new menu, but it contains no menu items and no separators. Use the methods previously described in this chapter to add menu items and separators into the new menu.

→ For detailed information about adding menu items and separators to a menu, **see** "Adding a Menu Item to a Menu," **p. 839** and "Adding and Deleting Separators in a Menu," **p. 840**.

CREATING SEPARATORS IN THE MENU BAR

The default menu bar contains no separators. You can insert vertical lines that separate the menus in the menu bar into groups.

PART
VI

CH
34

To insert a separator at the left of a menu name:

1. Choose Tools, Customize to display the Customize dialog box. Select the Commands tab.

2. In the Outlook menu bar, choose the menu to which you want to add a vertical separator. Outlook displays the menu name with a black border.

3. Choose Modify Selection in the Customize dialog box to display the context menu shown in Figure 34.26.

Figure 34.26
The Modify menu appears like this.

4. Choose Begin a Group, then choose Close. Now there's a vertical separator at the left of the menu you chose.

RESETTING THE MENU BAR

After you've made changes to the menu bar or to the contents of individual menus, you can reset the entire Outlook menu structure to its default condition.

To reset the menu structure and contents:

1. Choose Tools, Customize to display the Customize dialog box.

2. Select the Toolbars tab.

3. In the Toolbars list, select Menu Bar.

4. Choose Reset. Outlook asks you to confirm that you want to reset the menu bar. Choose OK.

5. Close the Customize dialog box.

TROUBLESHOOTING

As is so often the case, the best way to solve problems is to anticipate them before they happen and have a strategy prepared. It's too late to buy health insurance when you're in the hospital facing huge medical bills!

Outlook's insurance policy for toolbar and menu bar problems is the Outcmd.dat file, which was described earlier in this chapter. This file contains complete information about all changes you have made to the default toolbars, the menu bar, and individual menus. If several people use the same computer, there's a separate Outcmd.dat file in each person's Windows profile.

→ For detailed information about saving and restoring toolbars, **see** "Saving and Restoring Toolbars," **p. 820**.

I strongly recommend that you make a copy of your Outcmd.dat file before you make any significant changes to your toolbars or menu bar. Then, if something goes wrong, you can restore the file you saved to get Outlook back to the condition it was in before you started to make changes.

If you don't save your Outcmd.dat file, you can still reset Outlook's toolbars and menu bar to their default conditions, but in doing so, you lose any previous toolbar and menu bar customizations you've made. To do so, in Windows find and then delete the Outcmd.dat file. The next time you start Outlook, it automatically creates the default menu bar and toolbars and also creates a new Outcmd.dat file.

PART

VI

CH

34

CHAPTER 35

SETTING OUTLOOK'S OPTIONS

In this chapter   *by Gordon Padwick*

OUTLOOK'S OPTIONAL SETTINGS

Outlook has many optional settings. If you install Outlook from the Office 2000 CD-ROM, you'll start off with certain default settings. However, if you install Outlook from your organization's LAN, you might have completely different settings chosen by your LAN administrator

Note

The optional settings described in this chapter are those you can change after Outlook is installed. Refer to Appendix A, "Installing Outlook," for information about installation options.

The options available depend on which Outlook service option you have installed: Corporate/Workgroup, Internet Only, or No E-Mail. Also, any Outlook Add-Ins you have installed can affect the options available.

This chapter covers the Outlook options you most likely have available. You may not have some of those mentioned, and you may have others that are not covered.

ACCESSING OUTLOOK'S OPTIONAL SETTINGS

With any Information viewer displayed, choose Tools, Options to display the Options dialog box that has several tabs, the most common of which are covered in the following pages. Some of the tabs are different according to which Outlook service option you have

Note

You'll most likely be concerned with only a few of Outlook's options. If you're using Outlook on a standalone computer, most of the options set when you install Outlook are probably what you need. If you're using Outlook as a network client, your network administrator has probably set the options appropriate for the network.

Some of the dialog boxes you use to select options are different depending on whether you have IMO Outlook or C/W Outlook installed. In cases where the dialog boxes are significantly different, this chapter contains illustrations of both. Where the differences are minor, they're covered in the text. Also, there are some differences according to whether certain Outlook Add-ins are installed and, in the case of C/W Outlook, which information services are in your profile.

When you choose Tools, Options, Outlook displays the Options dialog box with the Preferences tab selected. This dialog box, an example of which is shown in Figure 35.1, has five or more tabs. Some points to note are

■ The second tab from the left is named Mail Delivery in IMO Outlook; it's named Mail Services in C/W Outlook.

- C/W Outlook has a tab named Internet E-mail if you have the Internet E-mail information service in your profile.

- The dialog box you see may have several additional tabs.

→ For information about adding the Internet E-mail information service to C/W Outlook, **see** "Adding the Internet E-mail Information Service to Your Profile," **p. 175**.

PREFERENCES OPTIONS

Select the Preferences tab shown in Figure 35.1 to set your preferences for each type of Outlook item.

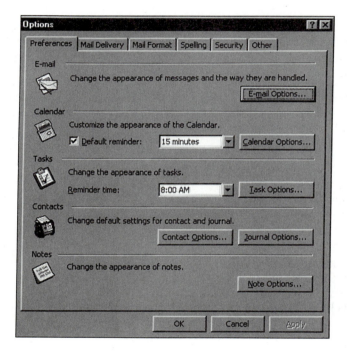

Figure 35.1
This tab contains five sections in which you can set options for the major types of Outlook items.

E-MAIL OPTIONS

In the E-mail section of the Preferences tab, choose E-mail Options to display the E-mail Options dialog box shown in Figure 35.2.

Note

The dialog box shown here is from IMO Outlook. The corresponding C/W dialog box is almost the same: it doesn't have the Automatically Put People I Reply to In check box near the bottom.

PART

VI

CH

35

Figure 35.2
Use this dialog box to
define how you want
Outlook to handle mes-
sages.

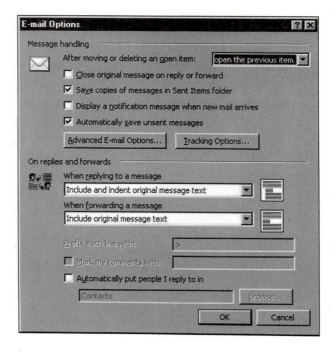

MESSAGE HANDLING   Open the After Moving or Deleting an Open Item drop-down list to
select what happens while you're using the Inbox, Outbox, and Sent Items Information
viewers. Choose from:

- Open the Previous Item
- Open the Next Item
- Return to the Inbox

Check or uncheck the four list boxes according to your preferences:

- Close Original Message on Reply or Forward
- Save Copies of Messages in Sent Items Folder
- Display a Notification Message When New Mail Arrives
- Automatically Save Unsent Messages

Choose Advanced E-mail Options to display the dialog box shown in Figure 35.3, in which
you can specify more detailed actions relating to messages.

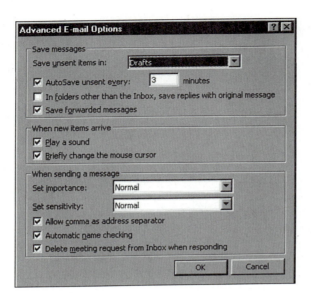

Figure 35.3
Use this dialog box to further customize how Outlook handles messages.

By default, Outlook saves message drafts in the Drafts folder every three minutes. The purpose of this is, of course, to minimize the amount of work you lose in the event of a power failure. You can open the drop-down Save Unsent Items In list to select a different folder and you can change the default interval to a different number of minutes. If you don't want Outlook to automatically save drafts while you're working, uncheck the AutoSave Unsent Every box.

Tip #203 from

Gordon Padwick

If you have AutoSave enabled, you'll notice while you're typing that Outlook hesitates momentarily from time to time. That happens while AutoSave occurs. If you reduce the AutoSave interval too much, this can become irritating. On the other hand, if you make the AutoSave period too long, you might lose a lot of your work in the event of a power failure or other disaster.

By default, Outlook saves replies you create to incoming messages in the Sent Items folder. If you're replying to a message you've saved in a folder other than the Inbox, you can check the In Folders Other Than the Inbox, Save Replies with Original Message box. After you do that, Outlook saves your replies in the same folder as the original message.

By default, Outlook saves copies of messages you forward in your Sent Items folder. If you don't want to save copies of messages you forward, uncheck the Save Forwarded Messages box.

PART

VI

CH

35

Outlook normally plays a sound and briefly changes the mouse pointer each time a message arrives in your Inbox. You can uncheck either or both of the Play a Sound and Briefly Change the Mouse Cursor boxes if you don't want that to happen.

You can use the bottom section of the Advanced E-mail Options dialog box to change the default Normal importance and Normal sensitivity settings for messages you send. Open the drop-down Set Importance list and drop-down Set Sensitivity list and select the defaults you want Outlook to use.

When you enter multiple addresses in the To, Cc, or Bcc boxes in the Message form, one address is separated from the next by a semicolon. With the Allow Comma as Address Separator box checked, Outlook also recognizes a comma as an address separator.

If you enter recipients' names into the Message form (instead of selecting names from an address book) Outlook normally checks your address books to make sure those names have valid addresses. If you don't want that checking to occur, uncheck the Automatic Name Checking box.

Note

The process of associating a person's name with that person's e-mail address is known as "resolving."

With the Delete Meeting Request from Inbox When Responding box checked, Outlook automatically deletes a meeting request from your Inbox when you reply to that meeting request. If you select Accept or Tentative, Outlook creates an appointment in your calendar. To keep the meeting request in your Inbox, uncheck this box.

After making whatever choices are appropriate in this dialog box, choose OK to have Outlook accept those choices. Outlook returns you to the E-mail Options dialog box.

In the E-mail Options dialog box, choose Tracking Options to display a dialog box in which you can specify whether and how Outlook should let you know when the messages you send are received. There are some differences between the dialog boxes displayed by IMO and C/W Outlook. The two dialog boxes are shown in Figures 35.4 and 35.5.

Note

The tracking options depend on functionality of recipients' e-mail software and their e-mail servers. Just because these options are available in Outlook doesn't necessarily mean they'll work in all e-mail environments. Refer to the chapters of this book about specific e-mail environments for some additional information.

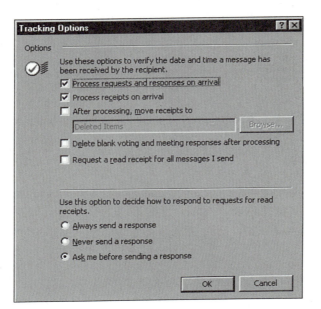

Figure 35.4
This is the Tracking Options dialog box displayed by IMO Outlook.

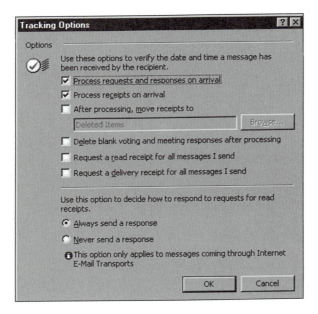

Figure 35.5
This is the Tracking Options dialog box displayed by C/W Outlook.

→ Detailed information about the options you can select in this dialog box is in various chapters of this book. For information about setting and using delivery options, **see** "Delivery Options," **p. 107**. To learn more about Outlook's voting and tracking options, **see** "Voting and Tracking Options," **p. 212** and **p. 782**. And for information about receipts for messages you send with Outlook, **see** "Tracking Message Receipts," **p. 684**.

The Request a Delivery Receipt for All Messages I Send check box, shown in Figure 35.4, is not present in the IMO Outlook dialog box. That's because current Internet standards don't support delivery receipts. The Internet does, however, support read receipts.

By default, the first two check boxes in these dialog boxes are checked so that Outlook processes requests, responses, and receipts on arrival.

If you check After Processing, Move Receipts To, Outlook automatically moves receipts to your Deleted Items folder (or to another folder if you choose Browse and select a different folder).

The voting and meeting responses you receive are considered blank if they contain no comments. Outlook normally retains voting and meeting responses you receive in your Inbox folder. However, if you check Delete Blank Voting and Meeting Responses After Processing, Outlook deletes blank voting and meeting responses; it doesn't delete those that contain comments.

Check Request a Read Receipt for All Messages I Send if it's your normal practice to request read receipts. With this box checked or not, you can still request, or not request, read receipts on a message by message basis. The operative word here is "request." Even though you request a read receipt, your recipients can choose whether they want to send one to you.

In C/W Outlook, but not in IMO Outlook, your can request a delivery receipt for all messages you send by checking Request a Delivery Receipt for All Messages I Send.

The option buttons near the bottom of the dialog box affect how Outlook responds on your computer to incoming messages you receive that request a read receipt. The first two options are available in IMO and C/W Outlook. In C/W Outlook, though, they apply only to Internet e-mail messages you receive. You can choose here whether you want Outlook to always or never send acknowledgments when incoming messages request a read receipt. In IMO Outlook you have the additional possibility of being notified on a message-by-message basis when an incoming message requests a read receipt, and deciding at that time whether you want to send one—this is the default in IMO Outlook. In C/W Outlook, the default is to automatically send read receipts when you open a message or select it and read it in the Preview pane.

Tip #204 from

Gordon Padwick

You can tell whether Outlook consider a message to have been read by the icon in the second column of the Inbox Information viewer. If the icon looks like an open envelope, the message has been read; if the icon looks like a closed envelope, the message hasn't been read.

After you've made your choices in this dialog box, choose OK to return to the E-mail Options dialog box.

ON REPLIES AND FORWARDS   This section of the E-mail options dialog box deals with how you want to reply to and forward messages.

Open the When Replying to a Message drop-down list and choose from:

- Do Not Include Original Message
- Attach Original Message
- Include Original Message Text
- Include and Indent Original Message Text
- Prefix Each Line of the Original Message

Open the When Forwarding a Message drop-down list and choose from:

- Attach Original Message
- Include Original Message Text
- Include and Indent Original Message Text
- Prefix Each Line of the Original Message

If you choose to prefix each line of the original message, either for messages you reply to or for messages you forward, you can specify the character used as a prefix in the Prefix Each Line With box (but not if you're using Microsoft Word as your message format). Outlook offers > as the default character.

Note

> The Prefix Each Line With box is enabled only if you have selected Prefix Each Line of the Original Message in one or both of the preceding list boxes.
>
> If a message is in *Plain Text format (page 183)* the original message that you reply to or forward is never indented.
>
> If a prefix character is used, the spell checker doesn't ignore the original message if you spell check replies before sending them.

You can add comments to a message you reply to or forward, and you can identify those comments with your name or other text. To change the identification, check Mark My Comments With and enter the identification you want to use in the adjoining box. This capability is available only if you've selected Rich Text as your default mail format; otherwise, it's unavailable as shown in Figure 35.2.

PART

VI

CH

35

If you're using IMO Outlook, you can check A<u>u</u>tomatically Put People I Reply to In to automatically create Contact items for people to whom you send replies to messages. If you check this box, Outlook creates *Contact items (page 298)* for these people in your Contacts folder. You can choose <u>B</u>rowse to select a different folder in which to create Contact items for these people.

If you have this box checked and reply to a lot of messages, your Contacts folder will become large very quickly. It's usually better to leave this box unchecked and manually choose which senders you want to add to your Contacts folder.

Tip #205 from

Gordon Padwick

Although C/W Outlook offers no automatic way to save senders' addresses, you can create rules to do so. You can also use a commercially available Outlook add-on such as ExLife for this purpose. You can download a trial version of ExLife from `http://www.mokry.cz`.

When you're finished setting E-mail options, choose OK to return to the Preferences tab of the Options dialog box.

CALENDAR OPTIONS

In the Calendar section of the Preferences tab (shown previously in Figure 35.1) you can choose whether or not you want Outlook to create *reminders* automatically. Check <u>D</u>efault Reminder if you want automatic reminders. After you check this, you can open the adjacent drop-down list and choose the time prior to calendar events when you want to be reminded.

Be aware that Outlook displays (or sounds) reminders only for items in the default Calendar folder.

→ For more information about Calendar reminders in Outlook, **see** "Setting a Reminder," **p. 366**.

Tip #206 from

Gordon Padwick

The drop-down list provides only specific times such as 5 minutes, 10 minutes, 15 minutes, 1 hour, 1 day, and so on. Instead of selecting one of these times, you can enter a time as a certain number of minutes, hours, or days. When entering a time, you can use the abbreviations "m" for minutes, "h" for hours, and "d" for days.

Choose <u>C</u>alendar Options to display the dialog box shown in Figure 35.6.

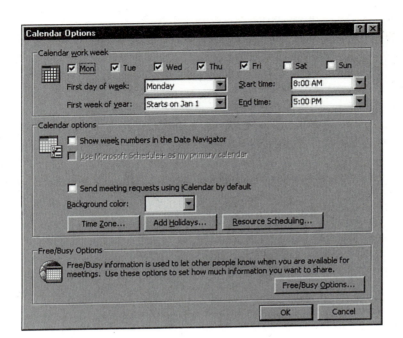

Figure 35.6
The Calendar Options
dialog box contains
three sections.

Note

The dialog box shown here is from C/W Outlook. The corresponding IMO Outlook dialog box is almost the same. The only difference is that it doesn't contain the Always Use Local Calendar check box.

CALENDAR WORK WEEK The top section of this dialog box is where you define your work week.

By default, Outlook considers Monday through Friday to be the work week, as shown by the checked boxes at the top of the Calendar Options dialog box in Figure 35.6. If, with this default setting, you display the Calendar Information viewer with the Day/Week/Month view selected and choose Work Week, Outlook displays your calendar for Monday through Friday.

Unfortunately, Outlook doesn't give you complete flexibility about choosing your work week. One limitation is that the Work Week view always displays consecutive days, even if the days checked in the Calendar Options dialog box aren't consecutive. Another limitation is that the number of days displayed in the Work Week view corresponds to the number of days checked in the Calendar Options dialog box, but not necessarily the checked days.

For example, if you check Sunday, Wednesday, Thursday, Friday, Saturday in the Calendar Options dialog box, Outlook's calendar displays Wednesday through Sunday as the work week, as you might expect. If you uncheck Thursday in the Calendar Options dialog box, you might expect the Calendar to show Wednesday, Friday, Saturday, Sunday as the work week, but that's not what happens. In fact, the Calendar shows Wednesday, Thursday, Friday, Saturday as the work week.

Note

What seems to be happening is that Outlook assumes the first checked day after two or more unchecked days is the beginning of the work week. Then, Outlook counts the number of checked days and assumes the work week consists of that number of consecutive days. Perhaps a subsequent version of Outlook will correct this problem.

Anyway, with this limitation in mind, check and uncheck days at the top of the dialog box to define your workweek.

The First Day of Week box controls how the Calendar view's Date Navigator displays monthly calendars. With the default Sunday in this box, the day check boxes at the top of the Calendar Options dialog box has Sunday at the left; also the Calendar Information viewer's Date Navigator shows weeks starting on Sunday.

You can open the First Day of Week drop-down list and select a different day. After you do that, the day check boxes at the top of the Calendar Options dialog box has the selected day at the left; also the Calendar Information viewer's Date Navigator shows weeks beginning on the day you selected.

Open the Start Time drop-down list and choose the time your working day starts. Open the End Time drop-down list and choose the time your working day ends. The times you set in these boxes affect the Calendar Information viewer when you use the Day view. Times before the start time and times after the end time are shaded.

Note

Instead of choosing from the drop-down lists, you can enter times. You have to do this if the times you want are not in the drop-down lists. You can use the abbreviations "a" for AM and "p" for PM.

Although you can enter any time you like, the Calendar Information viewer, with Day view selected, approximates start and end time to the nearest time increment selected for that view.

Open the First Week of Year drop-down list and choose how you want the calendar to select the first week of the year. The selection you make here affects how Outlook displays and prints calendars. You can choose from:

- Starts on Jan 1
- First 4-day Week
- First Full Week

CALENDAR OPTIONS SECTION OF THE CALENDAR OPTIONS DIALOG BOX You can select miscellaneous calendar options in the middle section of the dialog box.

Check Show Week Numbers in the Date Navigator if you want weeks to be numbered. After you do so, week numbers appear at the left of each week in the Calendar Information viewer's Date Navigator.

If, when you installed Outlook on your computer, you enabled Schedule+, you can check Use Microsoft Schedule+ as My Primary Calendar, if that's what you want to do.

 If you're using C/W Outlook as a client for an Exchange server, you can choose whether to use the calendar on your local computer or the calendar on the server. By default, Always Use Local Calendar is checked. Uncheck this box if you want to use the calendar on the server.

 By default, Outlook doesn't send meeting requests in iCalendar format. Check the Send Meeting Requests Using iCalendar by Default box if you want to use the iCalendar format.

 By default, the background color in the Day and Work Week view of the calendar is yellow so that appointments, shown in white, stand out clearly on a yellow background. You can open the drop-down Background Color list and select a different color.

Note

Outlook doesn't provide any way for you to color-code Calendar items. They always appear in white. This capability has been requested by many users and could possibly appear in a future version of Outlook.

Choose Time Zone to display the dialog box, shown in Figure 35.7, in which you can select your primary time zone and, optionally, a secondary time zone. In both cases, you can check a box to enable Outlook to adjust for daylight savings time (not available for some time zones). If you choose a secondary time zone, Outlook shows times for both zones in the Day view of the calendar.

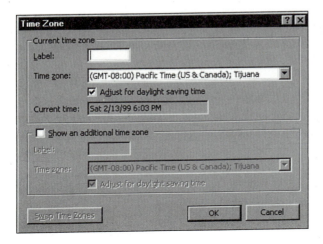

Figure 35.7
Use the Time Zone dialog box to specify your current time zone and, optionally, a secondary time zone.

You can choose S<u>w</u>ap Time Zones to make your secondary time zone the primary one, and the primary time zone the secondary one.

→ For detailed information about how Outlook works with time zones, **see** "Using Time Zones," **p. 396**.

Tip #207 from

As mentioned in Chapter 10, if you use Outlook to communicate with people in time zones other than your own, it's very important to make sure your computer's internal clock is set correctly and that you have the correct time zone selected. If you don't do this, you'll be confused by the incorrect dates and times Outlook associates with messages.

After you've chosen options in the Time Zone dialog box, choose OK to return to the Calendar Options dialog box.

Choose Add <u>H</u>olidays if you want Outlook to automatically add holidays to your calendar; Outlook displays the dialog box shown in Figure 35.8.

Figure 35.8
Use this dialog box to select locations or cultures for which you want Outlook to create holiday items in your calendar.

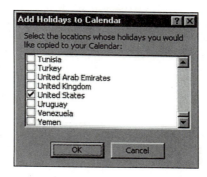

You can choose one or more geographic locations or cultures and Outlook will add holidays appropriate for them. Beware, though, of these limitations:

- Outlook adds most holidays as one-time events, not as recurring events.
- Outlook adds holidays for only a few years.
- If you choose two or more locations or cultures, and the same holidays are listed for more than one of them, you'll have those holidays marked several times in your calendar.
- Outlooks assigns the category "Holiday" to all items, whether or not they really are holidays.

→ Outlook's list of holidays is in the text file Outlook.txt. For more information, **see** "Modifying Outlook's List of Holidays," **p. 378**.

Instead of using Add Holidays, consider manually adding holidays as recurring events, and assigning appropriate categories to each of them.

Tip #208 from

Gordon Pooch

You should use the category "Holiday" only for those days that really are holidays, and use the category "Special Day" for other recognized days that are not holidays.

If you don't want to use Outlook's automatic holidays, choose Cancel to return to the Calendar Options dialog box.

RESOURCE SCHEDULING Choose Resource Scheduling if you're responsible for coordinating *resources*; Outlook displays the dialog box shown in Figure 35.9.

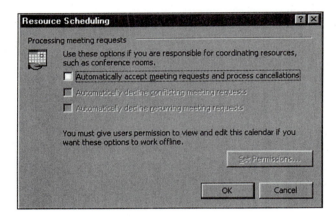

Figure 35.9
You can make choices about how Outlook automatically responds to requests for resources.

By default, only the Automatically Accept Meeting Requests and Process Cancellations check box is available and it's not checked. Check this box if you want your resources to automatically respond to requests and cancellations. When you check this box, the next two check boxes become available and are initially unchecked. Check these boxes if appropriate.

The Set Permissions button is available in C/W Outlook but not in IMO Outlook. If you want users to be able to create resource requests while working offline, you must give those people access to your Calendar folder. Choose Set Permissions to display the Calendar Properties dialog box. Select the Permissions tab, shown in Figure 35.10, to give people access to your calendar.

→ To learn about how you can share your calendar with other people, **see** "Sharing Your Calendar," **p. 393**.

PART

VI

CH

35

Figure 35.10
You can give specific people or groups access to
your Calendar folder in
this dialog box.

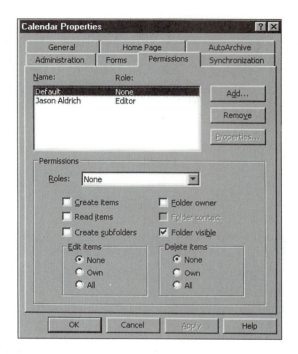

After giving permissions in the Calendar Properties dialog box, choose OK to return to the Resource Scheduling dialog box. Choose OK to return to the Calendar Options dialog box.

FREE/BUSY OPTIONS   Choose Free/Busy Options to open the dialog box shown in Figure 35.11.

→ For more details about using Free/Busy information to schedule meetings, **see** "Publishing Your Free/Busy Information," **p. 395**.

By default, Outlook proposes to publish your calendar information for the next two months, and does so every 15 minutes. You can change the number of months for which you want to publish information and you can change how often the information is published.

Even though the period ahead and frequency are specified, Outlook doesn't publish your Free/Busy information unless you check Publish My Free/Busy Information. When you do so, the Publish at This URL box becomes available. Enter the Web page address in that box (if you publish your Free/Busy information on a Web page) or the full path name in *UNC* format (if you publish your Free/Busy information on an Exchange server). Instead of specifying a URL, you can enter the address of a server in which to search for Free/Busy information in the Search at This URL box.

After you've set the Free/Busy options, choose OK to close the dialog box and return to the Calendar Options dialog box. Choose OK to return to the Options dialog box.

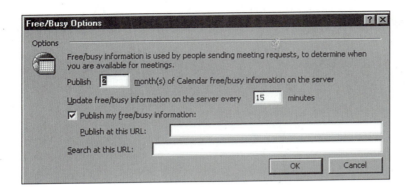

Figure 35.11
Use this dialog box to specify how many months ahead you want to publish your calendar information on a server and to identify the server.

TASK OPTIONS

In the Tasks section of the Preferences tab (shown previously in Figure 35.1) you can specify the reminder time-of-day you want to appear in task items. Open the Reminder Time drop-down list and select a time. Instead of selecting a time, you can enter a time—you're not limited to the times in the drop-down list.

→ To learn more about setting task reminders, **see** "Using the Task Information Viewer to Work with Tasks," **p. 425**.

Choose Task Options to display the dialog box shown in Figure 35.12.

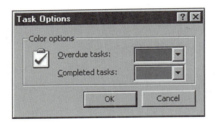

Figure 35.12
Use this dialog box to select colors in which tasks are displayed.

Open the Overdue Tasks drop-down list and select the color in which you want overdue tasks to be displayed in the Tasks Information viewer and in the TaskPad. Open the Completed Tasks drop-down box and select the color in which you want completed tasks to be displayed.

Choose OK to return to the Options dialog box.

CONTACT OPTIONS

In the Contact section of the Preferences tab (shown previously in Figure 35.1), choose Contact Options to display the dialog box shown in Figure 35.13.

PART

VI

CH

35

Figure 35.13
Use this dialog box to select how Outlook formats and files people's names.

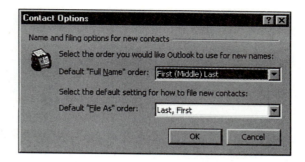

The choices you make in the Contact Options dialog box control how Outlook parses people's names you enter in the Contact form and how Contact items are filed.

Open the drop-down Default "Full Name" Order list and select the name order you want Outlook to use. The choices are

- First (Middle) Last—If you enter three names, Outlook considers the first to be the first name, the second to be the middle name, and the third to be the last name. If you enter two names, Outlook considers the first to be the first name and the second to be the last name.

- Last First—If you enter three names, Outlook considers the last two to be the first name and the first to be the last name. If you enter two names, Outlook considers the first to be the last name and the last to be the first name.

- First Last1 Last2—If you enter two or more names, Outlook considers the first to be the first name and all the others to be the last name.

Note

The last default choice is intended to allow easy creation of Contact items for people who have multiple last names.

Open the drop-down Default "File As" Order list. In this list select the default way you want Outlook to construct a File As name for a new contact. Select from:

- Last, First
- First, Last
- Company
- Last, First (Company)
- Company (Last, First)

Note

The terms in parentheses are included in the File As name only if text for those fields is available.

After making your selections in this dialog box, choose OK to return to the Options dialog box.

JOURNAL OPTIONS

In the Contacts section of the Preferences dialog box, shown previously in Figure 35.1, choose Journal Options to display the dialog box shown in Figure 35.14.

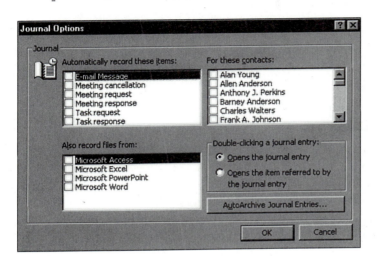

Figure 35.14
Use this dialog box to select the activities Outlook automatically records in the Journal.

> **Note**
>
> Outlook's Journal is not activated when you install Outlook. The first time you attempt to display the Journal Information viewer, you are asked whether you want to activate the Journal. If you choose to do so, then the dialog box shown in Figure 35.14 is displayed.

The top-left section of the Journal Options dialog box contains a list of six types of Outlook message items. Check the message type you want Outlook to record in the Journal.

> **Note**
>
> In addition to the six types of messages listed in the Journal Options dialog box, Outlook can also automatically record the time and duration of outgoing telephone calls (those initiated from within Outlook). This capability can't be set up from within the Options dialog box—it requires editing the Windows registry.

→ For details on using Outlook to record information about your phone calls, **see** "Journaling Phone Calls," **p. 443**.

In addition to selecting one or more types of messages, you must also choose the people from whom these messages are received or to whom you send them. The For These Contacts box at the top-right of the Journal Options dialog box contains a list of the names of all the people in your default Contacts folder. Outlook creates automatic Journal items only for the types of Message items you select in the Automatically Record These Items box, and only messages from or to those people you check in the For These Contacts box.

In addition to creating automatic Journal items based on messages you receive and send, Outlook can also create a Journal item each time you work with an Office or Office-compatible application file. You must check those applications for which you want Outlook to create Journal items. Use the Also Record Files From list at the bottom-left of the Journal Options dialog box to do so.

You can also choose what you want Outlook to do when you double-click a Journal item in the Journal Information viewer. In the Double-clicking a Journal Entry section of the dialog box, you can select between two options. The selection affects only what happens when you double-click a Journal item for an Office file in the Journal Information viewer. With either option selected, if you double-click a Journal item for a Message item, Outlook displays the message in the Journal Entry form.

In the case of Journal items created when you work with Office files, you can choose from:

- Opens the Journal Entry—Outlook displays the Journal Entry form with an icon representing that file in the Notes box.

- Opens the Item Referred to by the Journal Entry—Outlook displays a dialog box in which you can choose whether you want to open the file or save it on a disk. If you choose to open the file, Windows displays the file in the associated application. For example, if the Journal item represents a Word file, Windows starts Word and displays the file in a Word window.

Choose AutoArchive Journal Entries to display the Journal Properties dialog box with the AutoArchive tab selected, as shown in Figure 35.15.

By default, Outlook AutoArchives Journal items every six months and saves them in a file named Archive.pst within the Outlook folder on your hard disk. Because the purpose of archiving is to save space on your hard disk, you should choose somewhere else, such as a high-capacity, removable disk as your archive medium.

→ Detailed information about AutoArchiving can be found in "AutoArchiving Outlook Items," p. 592.

After you've finished working with Journal's AutoArchive properties, choose OK to return to the Journal Options dialog box, then choose OK to return to the Options dialog box.

NOTE OPTIONS

In the Notes section of the Preferences tab (shown previously in Figure 35.1), choose Note Options to display the dialog box shown in Figure 35.16.

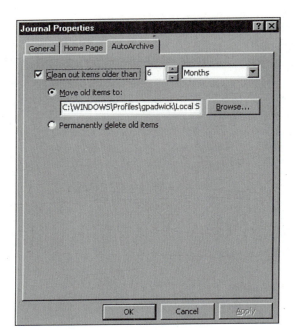

Figure 35.15
You can use this dialog box to examine and change Journal's AutoArchive properties.

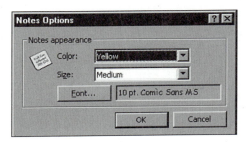

Figure 35.16
Use this dialog box to specify the appearance of notes.

Open the Color drop-down list and select a default color for notes.

Next, open the Size drop-down list and select a default size for notes.

Choose Font to open a dialog box in which you can select the font to be used in notes.

When you've finished setting Notes options, choose OK to return to the Options dialog box.

MAIL SERVICES OPTIONS

The Mail Services tab is available only if you're using C/W Outlook.

Select the Mail Services tab of the Options dialog box, shown in Figure 35.17, to set your preferences for Outlook startup settings and mail options.

PART

VI

CH

35

Figure 35.17
The Mail Services tab contains Startup Settings and Mail Options sections.

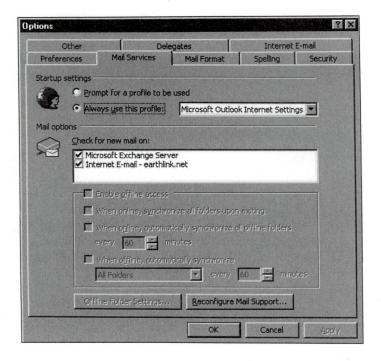

STARTUP SETTINGS

This section contains two option buttons:

- Prompt for a Profile to Be Used—Choose this if you want Outlook to offer a choice of profiles when it starts.

- Always Use This Profile—Choose this if you want Outlook to always start using a specific profile. Open the drop-down list and select the profile you want Outlook to use.

MAIL OPTIONS

The Check for New Mail On list contains the names of all the information services in your profile that are capable of sending and receiving mail. Check those you want Outlook to check for mail (checking, in this context, means receiving and sending).

The Enable Offline Access options are intended for use by people who use Outlook on a computer that's sometimes connected, and sometimes not connected, to Exchange. This check box and those below it are available only if you have the Microsoft Exchange Server information service in your profile and have enabled Offline Folders.

If your computer is permanently connected by way of a LAN to Exchange, this box should be unchecked. If your computer is only sometimes connected to the server, check this box and then choose the conditions under which you want your offline folders to be synchronized with your folders in the Exchange store.

→ Synchronizing is the process of copying items between your local folders and the Exchange store so that the most recent information is saved on both. For additional information, **see** "Synchronizing Your Offline Folders," **p. 740**.

If you check When Online Automatically Synchronize All Offline Folders or When Offline Automatically Synchronize All Offline Folders, you can change the interval between synchronizations.

RECONFIGURING MAIL SUPPORT

If you want to change from using C/W Outlook, choose Reconfigure Mail Support. When you do so, Outlook displays a dialog box in which you can select Internet Only. After you select that, Outlook displays a message summarizing what happens if you make the change. Choose OK if you want to continue. Outlook immediately closes down.

The next time you start Outlook, it will look for some installation files and, if it can't find them, will ask you to insert Office 2000 CD-ROM. After you do so, the necessary files are installed and, eventually, IMO Outlook opens.

MAIL FORMAT OPTIONS

Select the Mail Format tab of the Options dialog box, shown in Figure 35.18, to set your preferences for message format and related subjects.

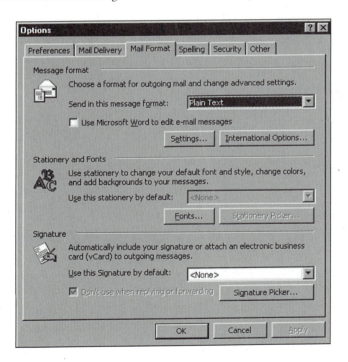

Figure 35.18
This is the Mail Format tab for C/W Outlook. The corresponding tab for IMO Outlook is quite similar.

The Mail Format tab for IMO Outlook does not have the Send Pictures from the Internet check box. It does have a Settings button that's not on the tab for C/W Outlook. Both these differences are covered in this section.

MESSAGE FORMAT

In this section you can select one of three default formats for messages you create:

Message Format	Purpose
HTML	Use this format if you send messages to recipients who use an e-mail application that can accept HTML. This format provides easy-to-use message formatting that will appear on recipients' screens as you intended.
Microsoft Outlook Rich Text	Use this format if you send messages to recipients who use an e-mail application that can accept Microsoft Rich Text.
Plain Text	Use this format if you send messages to recipients who may be using a text-based e-mail application. Also, use this format if you want to minimize the size of messages.

The message format you select here is the default Outlook proposes to use when you create a new message. You can select other than the default message format for individual messages.

 If you're using C/W Outlook, but not IMO Outlook, and you select the HTML message format, you can check the Send Pictures from the Internet box. With this box checked, all pictures, including background images, are sent with your messages. If this box is unchecked, only references (pointers) to pictures are sent.

  With the Use Microsoft Word to Edit E-mail Messages box unchecked, you use Outlook's built-in editor to create and edit messages. With this box checked, you use Word. Your choice of the built-in editor or Word affects only the editing capabilities you use; it has no effect on the format of messages you send.

 The Settings button (available in IMO Outlook but not in C/W Outlook) provides access to certain Plain Text and HTML settings. The Settings button isn't available if you select the Rich Text message format.

Note

 In C/W Outlook, if you have the Internet E-mail information service in your profile, the Options dialog box has an Internet E-mail tab. This tab provides access to equivalent settings.

→ For detailed information about the Internet E-mail tab that's available in C/W Outlook, **see** "Internet E-mail Options," **p. 892**.

 With the Plain Text message format selected, choose Settings to display the dialog box shown in Figure 35.19.

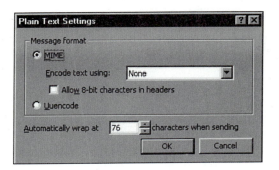

Figure 35.19
Use this dialog box to refine how IMO Outlook uses MIME when you have the Plain Text message format selected.

Note

MIME, which is supported by Outlook, provides a way to send messages that contain other than binary files and text that uses other than ASCII characters.

Use the default Plain Text settings unless you're instructed by an e-mail administrator to choose other settings.

Select Uuencode instead of MIME if your message recipients use that standard.

Tip #209 from

MIME and Uuencode are both standards that allow binary data (such as graphics) to be sent by way of a messaging system that's intended to support only text. For this to work, the sender and recipient must both use the same standard. By default, Outlook uses MIME. If you send messages from Outlook to recipients who don't have a MIME-compatible mail client application, you may be able to send messages that include binary information by switching to the Uuencode standard.

→ You can find much more information about MIME and Uuencode later in this chapter. **See** "Internet E-mail Sending Format," **p. 892**.

A box near the bottom of the Plain Text Settings dialog box defines the line length for messages you send.

Tip #210 from

In some cases, the default value of 76 for the line length is too high and results in extra line breaks in messages your recipients see. If that happens, try changing this value to 72.

PART

VI

CH

35

If you select HTML as your default message format and then choose Settings, Outlook displays the dialog box shown in Figure 35.20.

Figure 35.20
This is the Settings dialog box when you've selected HTML as your default message format.

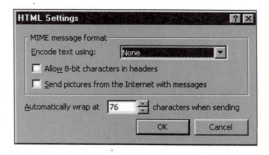

This dialog box is similar to the corresponding dialog box for Plain Text settings. Notice that this dialog box has a check box for Send Pictures from the Internet with Messages. The purpose of this check box is explained previously in this section.

If you're using a non-English version of Outlook, you can send English versions of *message headers*, even though the text of the message is in a different language. To do so, choose International Options to display the dialog box shown in Figure 35.21.

Figure 35.21
Use this dialog box to specify English headers in messages that use a different language.

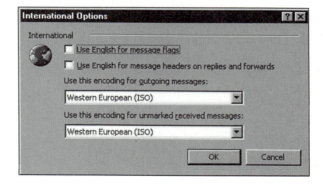

Check Use US English for Message Headers on Replies and Forwards if you want to have headers in English. Leave the box unchecked if you want to retain the original language.

You can open the two drop-down lists to select specific encoding for outgoing and incoming messages.

Choose OK to return to the Options dialog box.

STATIONERY AND FONTS

The Stationery and Fonts choices are available only if you have selected Outlook's built-in editor, not if you've selected Word as your editor. Also, Stationery is only available if you've selected HTML as your default message format.

Stationery refers to an overall design of a message, including a background pattern.

Open the Use This Stationery by Default drop-down list and select the stationery you want (I strongly recommended <none>).

Choose Fonts to display the dialog box shown in Figure 35.22.

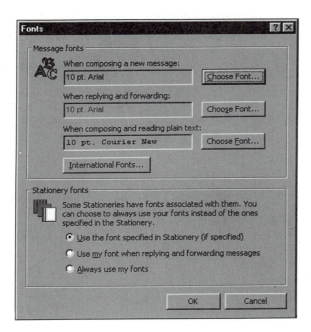

Figure 35.22
Use this dialog box to select the default fonts you want to use in your messages.

You can use this dialog box to specify a font to use for three purposes. In each case, choose the Choose Font button to open the standard Windows Font dialog box, in which you can select a font, font style, font size, font effects, and font color.

Don't be led astray into thinking that, because Stationery and Fonts are grouped together in this dialog box, the fonts you specify here apply only to stationery. That's not the case. This is where you set default fonts for your messages.

Tip #211 from

Because you have no control over the fonts installed on recipients' computers, it's usually best to use only the standard Windows fonts.

In addition to choosing fonts, you can choose International Fonts to display the dialog box shown in Figure 35.23.

Figure 35.23
Use this dialog box to select font settings other than the default Western European.

In the Fonts dialog box, you can also choose to override the fonts specified in some stationeries.

Choose OK to return to the Options dialog box.

Choose Stationery Picker (only available when you have the HTML message format selected) to open the dialog box shown in Figure 35.24.

Figure 35.24
Use this dialog box to select existing stationeries, edit stationeries, and create new ones.

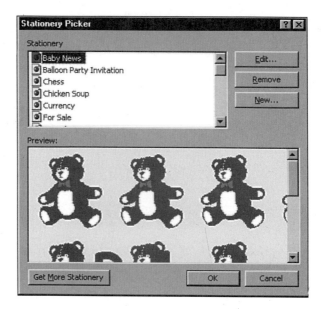

To select an existing stationery, scroll down the Stationery list and select one. The large box in the lower part of the dialog box shows what the stationery you've selected looks like.

If you can't find a suitable stationery, choose Get More Stationery. If your computer can connect to the Internet, your Web browser automatically opens a Microsoft Web page where more stationeries are available, as shown in Figure 35.25.

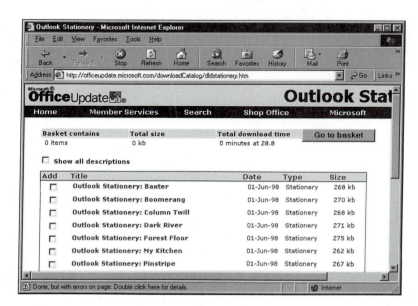

Figure 35.25
Scroll down the list of items available for downloading to find stationeries.

Check one or more stationeries that you want to download, then choose Go to Basket to download that item.

You can choose these buttons:

- Edit—Makes changes to an existing stationery
- Remove—Removes a stationery from the list
- New—Creates a new stationery

Tip #212 from

You can easily create a new stationery that contains only text. If you want your stationery to include graphics, you must already have a graphics file in jpg, jpeg, gif, or bmp format.

Stationeries are, in fact, HTML files. You can find these files in the Windows folder C:\Program Files\Common Files\Microsoft Shared\Stationery folder if you accepted the default file locations when you installed Outlook.

PART
VI
CH
35

Tip #213 from

Gordon Padwick

> You can locate your stationeries files by using Windows' Find to look for one of them, such as Baby News.htm.

To make changes to a stationery file, double-click the file name in Windows Explorer to open the file in Internet Explorer. Choose View, Source to see the HTML code. You can make whatever changes you want in the HTML code and then save those changes.

Choose OK to return to the Options dialog box.

SIGNATURE

Signatures are available only if you've selected Outlook's built-in editor as your message editor instead of Word.

Tip #214 from

Gordon Padwick

> You can use an Outlook add-on such as ExSign if you want more powerful signature capabilities than exist within Outlook. A trial version of ExSign is available for downloading from http://www.mokry.cz.

If you've already created one or more signatures, open the Use This Signature by Default drop-down list and select the default signature you want to attach to outgoing messages.

After you've selected a signature, you can check Don't Use when Replying or Forwarding, if you don't want Outlook to automatically sign replies you send or messages you forward. Uncheck the box if you do want replies and forwarded messages to be signed.

To change an existing signature or create a new one, choose Signature Picker to display the dialog box shown in Figure 35.26.

To select an existing signature, select it in the list of signatures, then choose OK.

To edit an existing signature, select it in the Signature box, then choose Edit to display the dialog box shown in Figure 35.27.

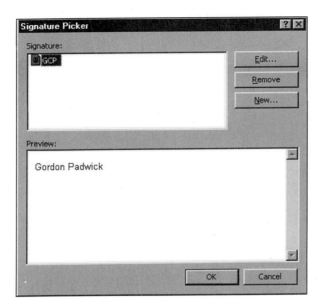

Figure 35.26
Use this dialog box to select or edit an existing signature, or to create a new one.

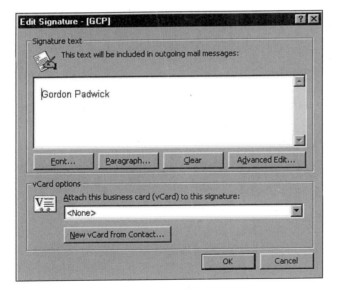

Figure 35.27
Use this dialog box to edit an existing signature.

In this dialog box, you can:

- Edit the existing text.

- Select text and choose Font to display the standard Windows Font dialog box—in which you can select a font, font style, font size, underlining, and font color.

- With the insertion point in a paragraph of the signature, choose Paragraph to display a dialog box in which you can select the alignment of the selected paragraph. You can also choose to add bullets to the selected paragraph.

- Choose Clear to delete the entire selected signature.

- Choose Advanced Edit to open Word so that you can use Word's capabilities while creating the signature.

If you have vCards (electronic business cards) available on your computer, you can open the drop-down Attach This Business Card (vCard) to This Signature and select a vCard to be part of the signature. You can also choose New vCard from Contact to open a dialog box in which you can select one of your existing contacts (including yourself) and automatically create a vCard.

After you've finished making choices in the Mail Format dialog box, choose OK to return to the Options dialog box.

SPELLING OPTIONS

Use the Spelling tab of the Options dialog box, shown in Figure 35.28, to set your preferences for spell checking.

GENERAL OPTIONS

Check boxes in the General Options section specify how you want spell checking to function. These boxes are self-explanatory.

EDIT CUSTOM DICTIONARY

Choose Edit to open a Notepad window that contains words in your custom dictionary. You can add words to this dictionary, delete words from it, and edit existing words.

Note

Outlook shares standard dictionaries and a custom dictionary with other Office 2000 applications such as Word and Excel, but not with Outlook Express. Your custom dictionary is in the file Custom.dic.

INTERNATIONAL DICTIONARIES

Open the Language drop-down list to select the dictionary you want to use to check your spelling. The list includes those dictionaries you selected when you installed Outlook.

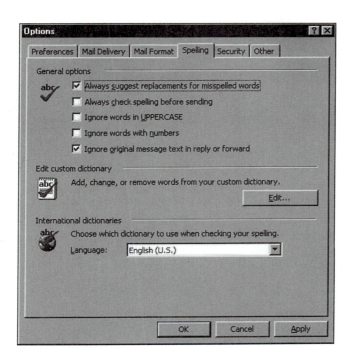

Figure 35.28
The Spelling tab has General Options, Edit Custom Dictionary, and International Dictionaries sections.

SECURITY OPTIONS

Use the Security tab shown in Figure 35.29 to set your preferences for message security.

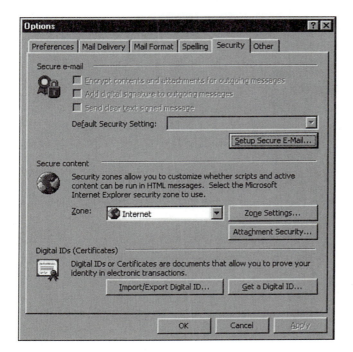

Figure 35.29
The Security tab has Secure E-mail, Secure Content, and Digital IDs (Certificates) sections.

PART
VI

CH
35

SECURE E-MAIL

You can use the Secure e-mail section of this tab only if you have a Digital ID installed on your computer. Use this section to specify the security options you want to use for all outgoing Internet messages.

Note

The following paragraphs are based on the assumption that you have a Digital ID installed.

→ If you're not already familiar with Digital IDs, before attempting to set options in the Security Options tab, **see** "Using Outlook Securely," **p. 993**.

If you already have one or more Digital IDs (certificates) installed on your computer, the Default Security Setting box displays the name of the ID you're currently using. You can open the drop-down Default Security Setting list to select a different ID (if more than one exists on your computer).

CHANGING SECURITY SETTINGS   Choose Setup Secure E-Mail to open the Change Security Settings dialog box shown in Figure 35.30.

Figure 35.30
Use this dialog box to change security settings.

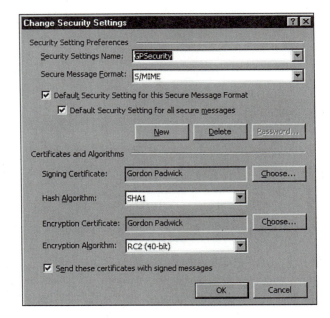

The Security Settings Name box shows the security setting you chose in the previous dialog box. You can open the drop-down list to choose a different one.

Choose <u>N</u>ew to create a new security setting, as explained in Chapter 39. You can create several security settings based on the same digital ID, each one having different security options.

→ For detailed information about creating security settings, **see** "Creating New Security Settings," **p. 1013**.

To delete an existing security setting, select that setting, then choose <u>D</u>elete Setting.

SECURE CONTENT

The Secure Content section of the Security tab (shown previously in Figure 35.29) contains choices you can make about Internet Explorer's security zones. The choices you make in this section apply only to messages you receive from an Internet or intranet mail server.

Security zones affect the way scripts and other active contents of messages are handled by Outlook.

Note

> Outlook relies on some of the functionality of Internet Explorer, which is why the Outlook installation process automatically installs Internet Explorer. For detailed information about Internet Explorer's security zones, refer to a book such as *Using Microsoft Internet Explorer 4*, published by Que.

To examine, and possibly modify, Internet zones, open the drop-down <u>Z</u>one list and select Internet. Then choose Zo<u>n</u>e Settings. Outlook displays a message box with some information about security settings. Choose OK to display the dialog box shown in Figure 35.31.

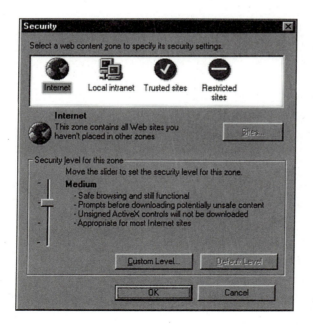

Figure 35.31
Use this dialog box to examine the default security zones, make change to those zones, and to create your own security zones.

Select the zones one at a time. When you select a zone, the lower part of the dialog box shows you whether that zone has High, Medium, Medium-low, or Low security. The text at the right of the slider summarizes what the selected security level means. You can change a zone's security level by dragging the slider up or down.

To create a custom security zone, choose Custom Level to display the dialog box shown in Figure 35.32.

Figure 35.32
In this dialog box, you can choose how you want your custom security zone to handle various types of active message content.

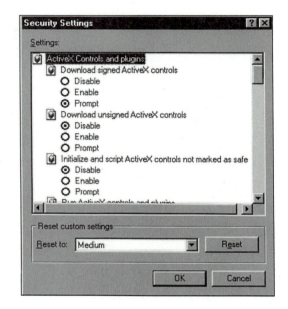

→ For detailed information about Security Zones, **see** "Using Security Zones," **p. 1023**.

DIGITAL IDS (CERTIFICATES)

Use this section of the Security tab (shown previously in Figure 35.29) to request a digital ID, to export the ID to a file, and to import the ID from a file.

→ The process of obtaining a Digital ID from VeriSign is described in Chapter 39. **See** "Obtaining a Certificate," **p. 1004**.

OTHER OPTIONS

Use the Other tab of the Options dialog box, shown in Figure 35.33, to set your preferences for how you want Outlook to deal with items in the Deleted Items folder, to access some advanced options, how you want AutoArchive to work, and to customize the Preview pane.

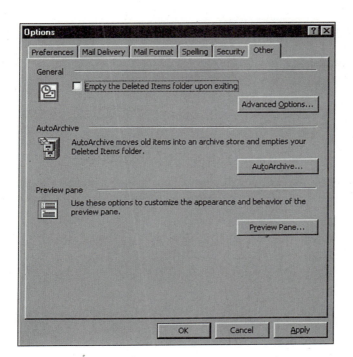

Figure 35.33
The Other tab has General, AutoArchive, and Preview Pane sections.

GENERAL OPTIONS

By default, Outlook saves the contents of your Deleted Items folder when you close Outlook. The next time you work in Outlook, any items you delete are appended to the items already in the Deleted Items folder. Over time, therefore, the Deleted Items folder can become quite large.

You can check Empty the Deleted Items Folder upon Exiting. After you do that, Outlook automatically deletes all items in the Deleted items folder when you exit Outlook.

In most cases, checking that box is a good thing to do. However, you should probably make a habit of checking what's in your Deleted Items folder each time you prepare to exit from Outlook. By doing that, you'll eliminate the possibility of losing items you might want to keep.

Choose Advanced Options to display more general options in the dialog box shown in Figure 35.34.

PART

VI

CH

35

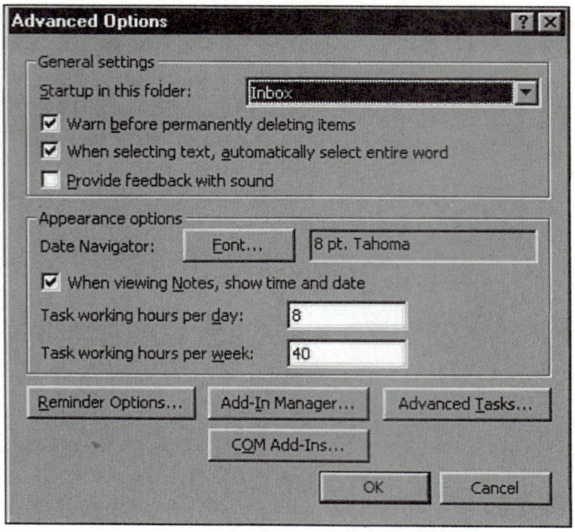

Figure 35.34
This tab has General Settings and Appearance Options sections and some buttons that provide access to even more options.

GENERAL SETTINGS   Open the Startup in this Folder drop-down list and select the folder you want Outlook to display when it starts. You can choose from:

- Calendar
- Contacts
- Inbox
- Journal
- Notes
- Outlook Today
- Tasks

In most cases, the best choice is Outlook Today because that window gives you an overview of your current activities.

Check or uncheck the following boxes:

- Warn Before Permanently Deleting Items—Outlook displays a warning message before you permanently delete items.
- When Selecting Text, Automatically Select Entire Word—Outlook selects an entire word and the space after it when you select one or more characters within a word.
- Provide Feedback with Sound—Outlook plays a sound when you perform certain actions.

APPEARANCE OPTIONS   You can select the font used by the Calendar Information viewer's Date Navigator. Choose Font to display a dialog box similar to the standard Windows Font dialog box, in which you can choose the font used by the Date Navigator. You can't choose a font color.

If you don't want Notes to display the time and date they were created, uncheck When Viewing Notes, Show Time and Date.

Enter the appropriate number of hours in the Task Working Hours Per Day Box.

Enter the appropriate number of hours in the Task Working Hours Per Week Box.

REMINDER OPTIONS Choose Reminder Options to display the Reminder Options dialog box, shown in Figure 35.35.

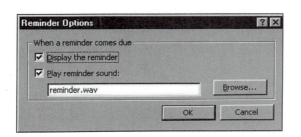

Figure 35.35
Use this dialog box to choose whether Outlook should display a reminder and play a sound when a reminder becomes due.

If you want Outlook to display reminders, check the Display the Reminder box.

If you want Outlook to play a sound, check the Play Reminder Sound box. After you do so, you see the name of the sound file that Outlook will play by default. To select a different sound file, choose Browse to display the Reminder Sound File dialog box; navigate to find the sound file you want to use.

Note

Outlook displays and sounds reminders only for Calendar items in the default Calendar folder.

ADD-IN MANAGER Choose Add-In Manager to display the Add-In Manager dialog box shown in Figure 35.36.

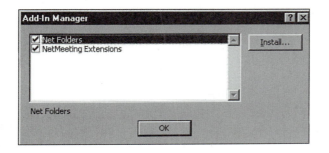

Figure 35.36
This dialog box contains a list of the Outlook Add-ins currently installed.

PART

VI

CH

35

The Add-ins listed depend on choices you made when you installed Outlook and which Add-ins you may have subsequently installed.

A check box adjacent to each Add-in name indicates whether that Add-in is active. Make sure the Add-ins you want to use are checked.

You can press the down-arrow key on your keyboard to select each Add-in in turn. The dialog box displays text that shows the purpose of the selected Add-in.

You can install Add-ins in three ways:

■ Install standard Outlook Add-ins by opening the Windows Control Panel and choosing Add/Remove Programs. Select Outlook 2000 from the list of installed software, and choose Add/Remove. Choose Add New Components and then follow the on-screen instructions.

■ Install Add-ins available on disk by choosing Install in the Add-In Manager dialog box.

■ Installing certain third-party Add-ins in the same way that you install other Windows applications.

Note

Some Add-ins are automatically installed in Outlook when you install other applications on your computer. Symantec's WinFax Pro is one application that does this.

ADVANCED TASKS   Choose Advanced Tasks to display the dialog box shown in Figure 35.37.

Figure 35.37
You can check or
uncheck three options
in this dialog box.

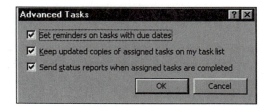

These options are fairly self-explanatory. You can find more information about them in Chapter 11.

■ Set Reminders on Tasks with Due Dates

■ Keep Updated Copies of Assigned Tasks on My Task List

■ Send Status Reports when Assigned Tasks Are Completed

➔ For detailed information about the task-related activities affected by these options, **see** "Creating a New Task," **p. 420**.

CUSTOM FORMS   The Custom Forms button is available only in C/W Outlook.

Choose <u>C</u>ustom Forms to display the dialog box shown in Figure 35.38.

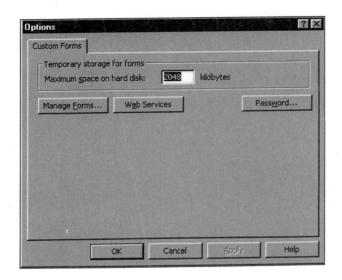

Figure 35.38
Use this dialog box to work with custom forms.

Use the Maximum <u>S</u>pace on Hard Disk box to assign a certain amount of temporary storage for forms.

Choose Manage <u>F</u>orms to display the dialog box shown in Figure 35.39.

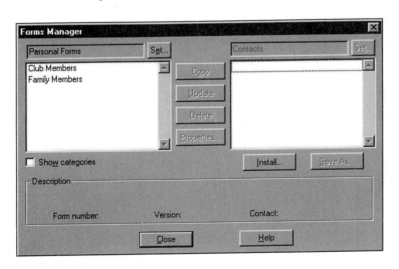

Figure 35.39
Use this dialog box to work with existing forms.

You can use this dialog box to

- Copy a form
- Update a form

- Delete a form
- View and modify the properties of a form
- Set up a form
- Save a form as a file

→ For comprehensive information about creating your own forms, **see** "Creating and Using Custom Forms," **p. 1031**.

Choose W<u>e</u>b Services to open the dialog box shown in Figure 35.40.

Figure 35.40
Use this dialog box to set Outlook so that it opens a form it doesn't recognize in HTML format and then uses your browser to display the form.

You can also use this dialog box to add a command to the Actions menu that provides a link to a Web page library of HTML forms.

Choose Pass<u>w</u>ord to display the dialog box shown in Figure 35.41.

Figure 35.41
Use this dialog box to change your server password.

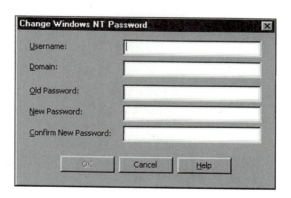

The reference to Windows NT refers to your network's Windows NT Server.

COM ADD-INS   COM Add-ins are executable files or dynamic link libraries that add extra functionality to Outlook. You can find examples of COM files in the Microsoft Office Update Web site, which you can reach by choosing <u>H</u>elp, Office on the <u>W</u>eb.

Choose C<u>O</u>M Add-ins to display the dialog box shown in Figure 35.42.

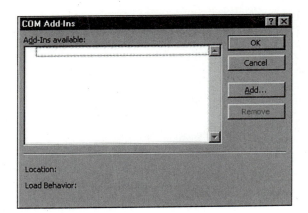

Choose <u>A</u>dd to display the Add Add-in dialog box, in which you can select more COM add-ins.

To remove a COM add-in, select that add-in and then choose Remove.

After you've finished working with Advanced Options, choose OK to return to the Other tab of the Options dialog box.

AUTOARCHIVE

Outlook's AutoArchive facility moves old items into an archive file and deletes items in your wastebasket. By default, Outlook AutoArchives items at the following ages:

Item Type	Age
Calendar	6 months
Deleted items	2 months
Journal	6 months
Sent items	2 months
Task	6 months

Contact, Draft, Inbox, and Note items are, by default, not AutoArchived.

Note

To change the default AutoArchive properties for a type of item, right-click the name of the folder for that type of item in the folder list, choose Properties in the context menu, and choose the AutoArchive tab of the Properties dialog box.

Choose AutoArchive to display the AutoArchive dialog box shown in Figure 35.43.

Figure 35.43
Use this dialog box to
set default
AutoArchiving
conditions.

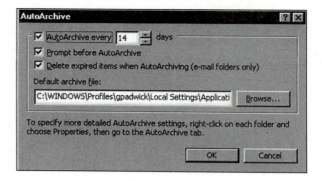

Check AutoArchive Every to enable AutoArchiving; uncheck it to disable AutoArchiving. If you have AutoArchiving enabled, you can choose the interval at which AutoArchiving occurs. AutoArchiving occurs the first time you start Outlook after the prescribed number of days.

If you've enabled AutoArchiving, you can check Prompt Before AutoArchive if you want cto be alerted before AutoArchiving starts. Otherwise AutoArchiving starts without any warning.

Check Delete Expired Items when AutoArchiving (E-mail Folders Only) if you want e-mail items to be deleted instead of being saved in the archive file.

The Default Archive File box displays the full path name of the file Outlook proposes to use for archiving. If you want to choose a different path, choose Browse and navigate to the folder that contains the file you want to use.

Tip #215 from

Gordon Padwick

> The default AutoArchive file is on your hard disk. This defeats the purpose of AutoArchiving, which is to minimize the space on your hard disk occupied by Outlook items. You should replace the default AutoArchive file with a file on a high-capacity, removable disk or, perhaps, a file on your server.

PREVIEW PANE

Choose Preview Pane to display the dialog box shown in Figure 35.44.

Check Mark Messages as Read in Preview Window if you want Outlook to automatically mark messages as read when they have been displayed in the preview pane for a certain period. By default, that period is 5 seconds. To change that period, enter your preferred period in the Wait box.

Check Mark Item as Read when Selection Changes if you want Outlook to automatically mark a selected message as read when you select a different message.

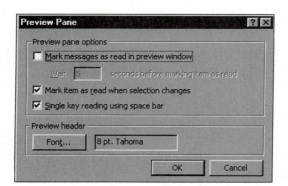

Figure 35.44
Use this dialog box to customize the appearance and behavior of the preview pane.

Note

If you don't check one or both of the preceding items, Outlook doesn't automatically mark items as read. In that case, you can open the Edit menu and choose Mark as Read to mark an item as read.

Check Single Key Reading Using Spacebar if you want to be able to press the spacebar to select one message after another.

Choose Font to open a dialog box (similar to that used in other Office applications) in which you can select the font to be used in the preview header that contains the From, To, Cc, and Subject fields.

DELEGATES OPTIONS

The Delegates tab, shown in Figure 35.45, is only available if you're using C/W Outlook and have the Microsoft Exchange Server information service in your profile.

The Delegates box lists the names of people who can send items on your behalf. You can choose these buttons to modify this list:

- Add—Display the Add Users dialog box shown in Figure 35.46 in which you can choose a name listed in the Global Address List.

- Remove—Removes the selected name from the list of delegates.

- Permissions—Displays the Delegate Permissions dialog box shown in Figure 35.47, in which you can specify the folders you want to give the selected delegate access to, and the permission level for that delegate. This button isn't available if you're using Offline Folders or a Personal Folders file to store Outlook items.

- Properties—Displays the Properties dialog box shown in Figure 35.48, in which you can view and modify a selected delegate's properties, providing you have appropriate permissions.

PART
VI
CH
35

Figure 35.45
Use the Delegates tab to allow other people to send messages on your behalf.

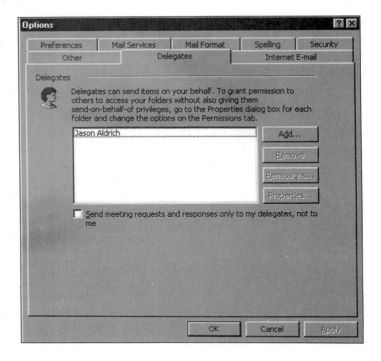

Figure 35.46
Use the Add Users dialog box to name delegates.

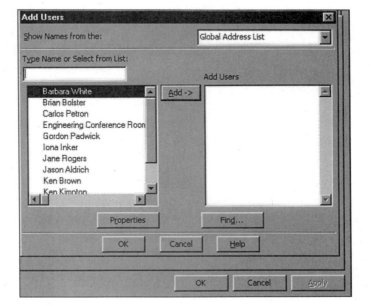

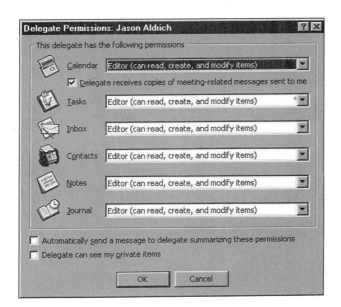

Figure 35.47
Use the Permissions
dialog box to modify
a delegate's permissions.

Figure 35.48
Use the Properties
dialog box to examine and modify a delegate's properties.

You can check the Send Meeting Requests and Responses only to My Delegates, Not to Me box. After you do so, meeting requests and responses sent to you aren't added to your Inbox folder and aren't displayed in your Inbox Information viewer. This option is available when you give editor permission for your Calendar folder to a delegate, and then select Delegate Receives Copies of Meeting-related Messages Sent to Me in the Delegate Permissions dialog box.

INTERNET E-MAIL OPTIONS

This tab, shown in Figure 35.49, is available only in C/W Outlook and only if you have the Internet information service in your profile.

Note

The equivalent tab in IMO Outlook is the Mail Delivery tab.

Figure 35.49
This tab has an Internet E-mail Sending Format section and several check boxes.

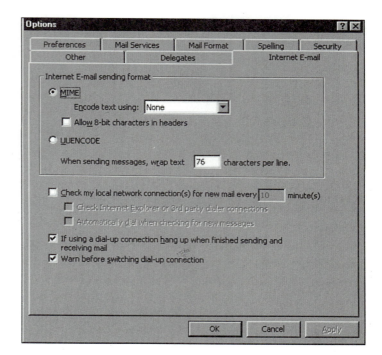

INTERNET E-MAIL SENDING FORMAT

Originally, the Internet was able to send only text messages. UUENCODE was created as a means of converting other-than-text information at the sender's end into information that, to the Internet, appeared to be text. In tandem, UUDECODE was created to be used by recipients to change UUENCODE information back to its original format.

More recently, the Multipurpose Internet Mail Extensions (MIME) format has been created to enable any sort of information to be included in Internet messages.

By default, Outlook uses MIME to send files, graphics, Outlook items, and other non-text attachments to messages. This format is recognized by most e-mail applications and is what you should normally use. If your recipients are using e-mail applications that aren't MIME-compatible, you can choose to use UUENCODE.

If you choose MIME, Outlook uses the Quoted Printable format to encode text. You can open the Encode Text Using drop-down list and choose None, Quoted Printable, or Base 64. None (the default) means that text is not encoded; Quoted Printable and Base 64 are two ways of representing 8-bit data with just 7-bit text.

Outlook treats characters in headers in the same way as other message characters. You can check Allow 8-bit Characters in Headers so that Outlook allows headers to contain foreign character sets, high ASCII, or double-byte character sets in the message header.

Outlook automatically starts a new line in a message after a certain number of characters, 76 by default. You can change this number of characters in the When Sending Messages, Wrap Text At box.

CHECK BOXES

Check the Check My Local Network Connection(s) for New Mail Every box if you want Outlook to regularly check your Internet e-mail server for new messages and send messages from your Outbox. When this box is checked, you can

- Specify how often Outlook checks for Internet e-mail
- Check Check Internet Explorer or 3rd Party Dialer Connections if you want to use a dialer application and settings other than dial-up networking to connect to your Internet service provider
- Check Automatically Dial when Checking for New Messages if that's what you want to do

You can also

- Check If Using a Dial-up Connection Hang up when Finished Sending and Receiving Mail
- Check Warn Before Switching Dial-up Connection if you have two or more dial-up connections and you want to be able to cancel a connection that isn't working

MAIL DELIVERY OPTIONS

This tab, shown in Figure 35.50, is available only in IMO Outlook.

Note

The equivalent tab in C/W Outlook is the Mail Services tab.

Figure 35.50
This tab has an Accounts Manager, Mail Account Options, and Dial-up Options sections.

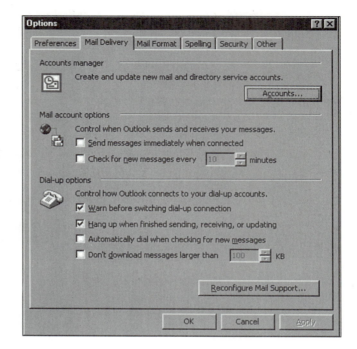

ACCOUNTS MANAGER

Choose Accounts to display the dialog box shown in Figure 35.51 with the Mail tab selected.

The most frequent use for this dialog box is to select a default account. If you have only one account, that is, of course, your default. If you have two or more accounts, select the one you want to be the default, and then choose Set as Default.

Note

The Set as Default button is dimmed if you select your current default account.

You can create a new Internet E-mail account from this dialog box. To do so, choose Add and, in the menu that appears, choose Mail. This leads you into the process described in Chapter 3.

→ For detailed information about creating an Outlook Internet account, **see** "Creating an Outlook Internet Account," **p. 64**.

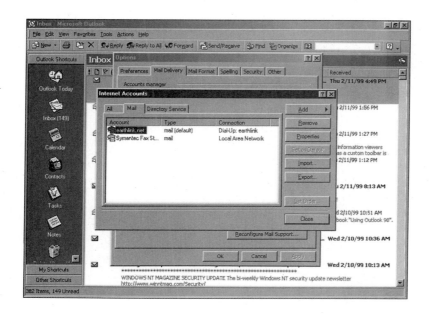

Figure 35.51
This dialog box lists your current e-mail and fax accounts.

To remove an account, select that account and then choose Remove. Outlook asks you to confirm that you want to remove the account. Choose Yes to proceed.

To examine or change an account's properties, select the account and then choose Properties to display the dialog box shown in Figure 35.52.

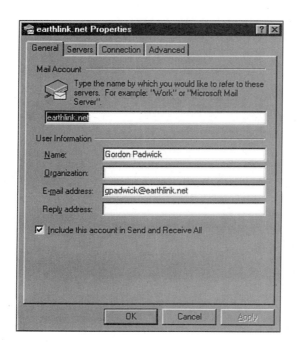

Figure 35.52
You can select the four tabs in this dialog box to examine and change the account's properties.

MAIL ACCOUNT OPTIONS

The two check boxes in this section of the dialog box allow you to control how Outlook sends and receives e-mail.

The Send Messages Immediately box is, by default, unchecked. If you check this box, Outlook attempts to send messages as soon as you choose Send in the Message form to place a message in your Outbox folder.

The Check for New Messages Every box is, by default, checked and the adjoining box contains 10; Outlook automatically sends messages in your Outbox, if there are any, every 10 minutes and gets any messages waiting for you on the server. Uncheck this box if you don't want Outlook to automatically send and receive messages. If the box is checked, you can change the interval between Outlook's attempts to send and receive messages.

DIAL-UP OPTIONS

The four check boxes in this section of the dialog box have to do with how Outlook connects to, and disconnects from, a dial-up connection to an Internet mail server.

With the Warn Before Switching Dial-up Connection box checked, as it is by default, Outlook warns you and asks for your permission before switching from one dial-up connection to another.

Hang up When Finished Sending, Receiving, or Updating, which is checked by default, causes Outlook to disconnect automatically when it has finished sending and receiving messages. Having this checked can save you a lot of money if you're using a long-distance connection.

Automatically Dial When Checking for New Messages is unchecked by default. This means that you have to establish a dial-up connection manually. If you check this option, Outlook dials automatically.

Don't Download Messages Larger Than is unchecked by default. If you want to put a limit on the size of messages Outlook will download, check this option. You can change the size limit to whatever you want.

RECONFIGURING MAIL SUPPORT

If you want to change from using IMO Outlook to using C/W Outlook, choose Reconfigure Mail Support. When you do so, Outlook displays a dialog box in which you can select Corporate or Workgroup. After you select that, Outlook displays a message summarizing what happens if you make the change. Choose OK if you want to continue. Outlook immediately closes down.

The next time you start Outlook, it will look for some installation files and, if it can't find them, will ask you to insert the Office 2000 CD-ROM. After you do so, the necessary files are installed and, eventually, C/W Outlook opens.

OTHER TABS

You may see tabs in addition to those described in this chapter. For example, if you're using IMO Outlook and have installed WinFax SE, a Fax tab is available.

Various Add-ins have their own options and provide tabs in the Options dialog box to provide access to those options.

CHAPTER 36

CUSTOMIZING OUTLOOK TODAY

In this chapter

by Gordon Padwick

OUTLOOK TODAY OVERVIEW

  Outlook Today appeared first in Outlook 98. The view provides a concise "at-a-glance" view of your current activities in the attractive style of a Web page, as shown in Figure 36.1.

Figure 36.1
Outlook Today shows you what's on your plate.

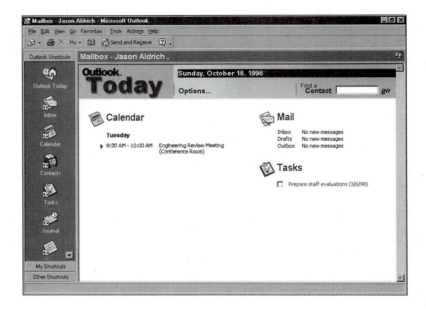

Tip #216 from

If Outlook Today isn't displayed, click Outlook Today in the Outlook Bar.

You can choose an Outlook option so that Outlook Today always appears when you start Outlook.

→ For information about configuring Outlook Today to launch upon startup, **see** "Startup Options," **p. 901**.

By default, Outlook Today shows:

- The activities on your calendar for today and the next few days
- Tasks that you should currently be working on
- The number of unread messages in your Inbox folder
- The number of unfinished message drafts in your Drafts folder
- The number of messages waiting to be sent in your Outbox folder

All the information displayed by Outlook Today is hyperlinked to the underlying Outlook items. You can click any information displayed by Outlook Today to see details about it. You can also check off completed tasks in Outlook Today.

But that's just Outlook Today in Outlook as it comes out of the box. You can customize Outlook Today to make it even more useful.

CHOOSING OUTLOOK TODAY'S OPTIONS

You can customize Outlook Today to suit your personal preferences.

To access Outlook Today's options, choose Customize Outlook Today to display the Customize Outlook Today window shown in Figure 36.2.

Note

Customize Outlook Today is usually at the top-right of the Outlook Today window. In the case of the Winter style, however, it's at the bottom-right.

Figure 36.2
This window offers several choices about what Outlook Today displays.

STARTUP OPTIONS

If the Startup check box is unchecked Outlook starts up with the Information viewer specified in the Options dialog box.

Note

Choose Tools, Options, select the Other tab, and choose Advanced Options. In the Advanced Options dialog box, the Startup in This Folder contains the name of the Information viewer Outlook displays on startup.

If you want Outlook to display Outlook Today on startup, irrespective of the setting in the options dialog box, check the Startup box in the Customize Outlook Today window. After you save the changes in the Customize Outlook Today window, you can subsequently select the Other tab in the Options dialog box. There, you can choose Advanced Options where you'll see Outlook Today specified as the startup folder. Likewise, after you choose Outlook Today as the startup folder in the Advanced Options dialog box, you can return to the Customize Outlook Today window where you'll find that the Startup check box is checked.

Note

If you've had Outlook set up so that Outlook Today is the startup folder, and then uncheck the Startup check box in Customize Outlook today, Outlook will subsequently start with the Inbox Information viewer displayed.

DISPLAYING YOUR CALENDAR ACTIVITIES

By default, Outlook Today displays activities on your calendar for five days, today and the next four days. You can open the Calendar drop-down Show list and select any number of days in the range one through seven.

DISPLAYING YOUR TASKS

You can make several choices about how Outlook Today displays your *tasks (page 412)*.

You can select:

- All Tasks—Outlook Today shows all the tasks in your Tasks folder.
- Today's Tasks—Outlook Today shows only those incomplete tasks that are due today or are overdue.

Check the Include Tasks with No Due Date (only available if you've selected Today's Tasks) if you want to include those tasks in the list displayed by Outlook Today.

The two drop-down lists allow you to choose how you want tasks to be sorted. Open the sort My Task List By drop-down list and select the primary sorting criterion from:

- None
- Importance
- Due Date
- Creation Time
- Start Date

If you select any of these except None, you can open the Then By drop-down list and select a secondary sorting criterion from the same list.

You can select Ascending or Descending separately for the primary and secondary sorting criteria, as long as you haven't selected None.

SELECTING AN OUTLOOK TODAY STYLE

By default, Outlook displays Outlook Today in the Standard (three-column) format shown previously in Figure 36.1. You can open the Style drop-down list and choose from these alternative styles:

- Standard
- Standard (two column)
- Standard (one column)
- Summer
- Winter

The Summer style has a yellow background; the Winter style has a white background. Both of these styles use a two-column format.

DISPLAYING MESSAGES

By default, Outlook Today displays a count of the outstanding mail items in your Inbox, Drafts, and Outbox folders.

If you've created other folders for Mail items, you can have Outlook display the outstanding mail in these folders, too. To do so, choose the Choose Folders button in the Customize Outlook Today window to display the dialog box shown in Figure 36.3.

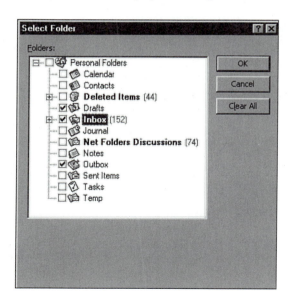

Figure 36.3
This dialog box shows your Outlook folder structure with the Drafts, Inbox, and Outbox folders checked.

You can uncheck folders for which you don't want to see a count of outstanding mail. You can also check additional folders to have a count of outstanding Mail items in those folders displayed in Outlook Today.

Note

> Although you can, in the Check Folders dialog box, check folders that contain items other than mail items, Outlook Today doesn't display information about these folders.

SAVING THE OPTIONS YOU'VE SPECIFIED

After you've customized Outlook Today, as described in the preceding sections, choose Save Changes to display Outlook Today with your changes incorporated.

EXTENDING OUTLOOK TODAY

You can extend Outlook Today far beyond choosing the options described in the previous section of this chapter. That's because Outlook Today is defined by *HTML (page 183)* code, to which you have access, and which you can modify.

You can customize and extend Outlook today by

- Adding text, links, and images
- Adding script
- Adding ActiveX components
- Changing styles for the background and fonts

This chapter covers only basic customization of Outlook Today. For more comprehensive information, refer to the Microsoft Publication *Microsoft Outlook 2000 Deployment Kit*.

BASIC CUSTOMIZATION

When you use basic customization, you save your Outlook Today page as an .htm file on your local hard disk, a shared network disk, or Web server.

Note

> To customize the Outlook Today page, you need to be familiar with the Windows registry and with HTML. Appendix F, "Working with the Windows Registry," provides an introduction to the Windows Registry. For detailed information about the Windows registry, see *Using the Microsoft Windows 98 Registry*, published by Que. For information about HTML, refer to a book such as *Special Edition Using HTML 4, Fifth Edition*, published by Que.

The next few sections describe how you can change Outlook so that the Outlook Today window depends on a file you can edit without any special tools, instead of the default Outlwvw.dll file that isn't ordinarily editable.

OBTAINING THE OUTLOOK TODAY SOURCE CODE

Customizing involves making changes to the Outlook Today source code that's in the file Outlwvw.dll, a file that's automatically installed on your computer when you install Outlook. You need to know where that file is.

To locate Outlwvw.dll:

1. Close Outlook if it's running.

2. Choose Start on the Windows taskbar, move the pointer onto Find, and choose Files or Folders to display the dialog box shown in Figure 36.4.

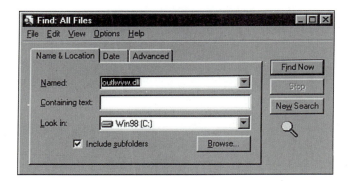

Figure 36.4
You can use this dialog box to find any file or folder in your Windows file system.

3. In the Named box enter Outlwvw.dll.

4. Leave the Containing Text box empty.

5. Open the drop-down Look In list and select the disk on which you have installed Outlook.

6. Choose Find Now to start the search. Windows displays a results box, as shown in Figure 36.5.

Note

If you installed Outlook in the default location, Outlwvw.dll is in the C:\Program Files\ Microsoft Office\Office\1033 folder.

When you know where Outlwvw.dll is, you can use Internet Explorer to get the Outlook Today source code.

To get the Outlook Today source code:

1. Click the Internet Explorer icon on the Windows desktop to open Internet Explorer.

2. If Internet Explorer automatically connects you to a Web page, choose File, Work Offline.

3. Enter the following address into the Internet Explorer Address box
   res://C:\Program Files\Microsoft Office\Office\1033\outlwvw.dll/outlook.htm.

Figure 36.5
When Windows finds the file, it displays the file's name and location in the results box. Make a note of the file's location.

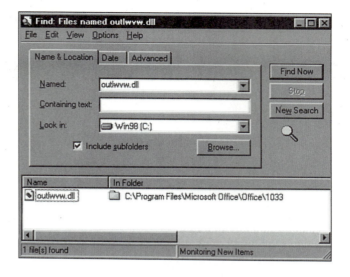

> **Note**
>
> The entry shown in step 3 is based on the assumption that you installed Outlook in the default folder. If that's not the case, change the path to the correct path for your computer.
>
> Note very carefully the use of forward and backward slashes. There are two forward slashes after res: and one forward slash before Outlook.htm. All others are backward slashes.

4. After you've entered the address, check it to make sure it's correct, then press Enter.

5. The Internet Explorer Script Error box appears because the code is not being hosted by Outlook. Choose OK to hide the Script Error box. Internet Explorer now displays Outlook Today as it appears without being linked to any data, as shown in Figure 36.6.

Figure 36.6
This is the Outlook Today background.

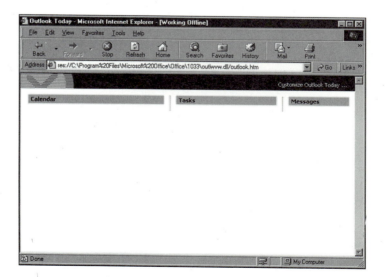

6. Choose <u>V</u>iew, Sour<u>c</u>e to display the HTML code that creates Outlook Today, part of which is shown in Figure 36.7.

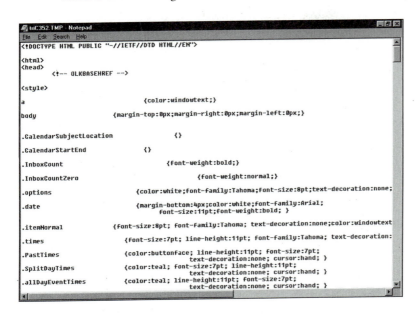

Figure 36.7
The source code is displayed in a Windows Notepad window.

7. At this point, you can choose <u>F</u>ile, <u>P</u>rint to print the HTML code for your reference.

Note

If you intend to develop a custom Outlook Today window, this code provides a good starting point.

8. Choose <u>F</u>ile, Save <u>A</u>s to open the Save As dialog box and save the file with the name Outlook.htm. Make a note of the location of the file.

After you've saved the file, you have to make three small changes. This is because the original file was designed to be saved as a .dll file and loaded with the res:// protocol. Instead, you will be using it as a .htm file and loading it with either the http:// or file:// protocol.

The text `display:none` occurs in three places in the file. Use Windows notepad to search for these three and replace `display:none` with `display:`. After you've made these changes, save and close the file.

MODIFYING THE WINDOWS REGISTRY

You have to make a change in the Windows registry so that Outlook Today will use the file you just created instead of Outlwvw.dll.

Caution

Always make a backup copy of the registry files before making any change to their contents. Refer to Appendix F of this book for information about backing up the registry.

→ For general information about working with the registry, **see** "Working with the Windows Registry," **p. 1323**.

To modify the registry:

1. Choose Start in the Windows taskbar, then choose Run to open the dialog box shown in Figure 36.8.

Figure 36.8
Use this dialog box to name the program you want to run.

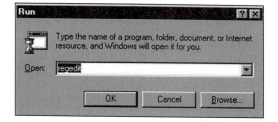

2. In the <u>O</u>pen box, enter regedit and then choose OK to open the *Registry Editor*, as shown in Figure 36.9.

Figure 36.9
The Registry Editor initially displays the My Computer tree with six subtrees listed in the left pane.

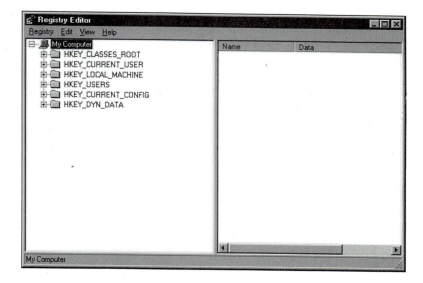

3. Expand the HKEY_CURRENT_USER subkey.

4. Continue expanding subkeys until you reach
   HKEY_CURRENT_USER\Software\Microsoft\Office\9.0\Outlook\Today.

5. Select Today to see the values in that key listed in the right pane, as shown in Figure
   36.10.

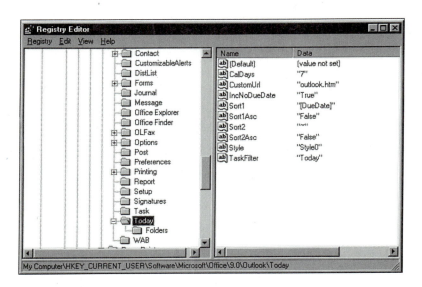

Figure 36.10
Look to see if one of the values listed has the name CustomUrl.

> **Note**
>
> The values in this registry key correspond to the selections you made in the Customize Outlook Today window, as described previously in this chapter.

→ For information about interactive changes you can make to the Outlook Today window, **see** "Choosing Outlook Today's Options," **p. 901**.

6. Select the value named CustomUrl.

7. Choose Edit, Modify to display the dialog box shown in Figure 36.11.

Figure 36.11
The Value data box contains the current data in the CustomUrl value.

Tip #217 from

[signature]

Make a note of the current data in the Url value because you might subsequently want to restore Outlook to use the default Outlook today window.

8. Replace the current data with the complete path name of the Outlook.htm file you cre- ated in the previous section, specifying the file protocol.

Note

If you saved Outlook.htm in the C:\My Documents folder, enter the new value as `File://C:\My Documents\Outlook.htm`.

9. Choose OK. The new value for CustomUrl is now shown in the right pane.

10. Choose Registry, Exit to close the Registry Editor.

TESTING OUTLOOK TODAY

After you've created an Outlook.htm file and made a change in the registry that makes Outlook Today depend on that file, you can test what happens.

Start Outlook and display Outlook Today. You should see the same Outlook Today window as you normally do. One difference, though, is that Outlook Today opens more slowly. That's because it now uses the separate .htm file instead of using the normal .dll file.

The big difference is that you can make changes to the .htm file that result in changes to what Outlook Today displays. That's something you can't do if Outlook Today runs from Outlwvw.dll (as it normally does).

Note

A customized Outlook Today doesn't have to be slower than the original one. After you've made changes to Outlook.htm, you can use a resource editor such as Microsoft Developer Studio to save the customized file in .dll format.

MAKING CHANGES TO OUTLOOK TODAY

The Outlook.htm file contains HTML code and uses cascading style sheets to describe the Outlook Today page. You can modify this file in the same way that you can modify any other HTML page. Details of the techniques for doing this are beyond the scope of this book. You can find general guidance in the *Microsoft Outlook 2000 Deployment Kit*. For detailed information, you'll have to consult a book about HTML that contains information about Cascading Style Sheets. One such book is *Special Edition Using HTML 4, Fifth Edition*, published by Que.

Tip #218 from

[signature]

I particularly recommend the fifth edition of *Using HTML 4* if you're interested in working with Cascading Style Sheets.

After you've made changes to your Outlook.htm file, you can see the effects of those changes the next time you open Outlook Today.

DEVELOPING OUTLOOK TODAY FURTHER

This chapter provides only a broad introduction to the subject of customizing Outlook Today. Regard the Outlook Today that comes with Outlook as only an example of what Outlook Today can be.

If you're using Outlook on a home computer, you'll probably find the default Outlook Today provides a useful summary of your current calendar, tasks, and messages. However, if you're responsible for deploying Outlook throughout your organization, give some thought to the potential of Outlook Today.

As stated previously in this chapter, Outlook Today is an HTML page that Outlook displays. Whatever you can display on an HTML page can be displayed in Outlook Today—it's not limited to information about Outlook items, nor is it limited to information available in files on a local computer. You can use Outlook Today to present a wide variety of information to Outlook users. This information can include, but is by no means limited to:

- Organization and industry news
- The current group or organization calendar
- A daily motivational message
- An up-to-date progress summary—sales statistics for marketing and sales people, bugs fixed for software people, network performance for people who support the network, orders received and orders shipped for the shipping department, and so on

In short, if information is available somewhere on your network, it can be displayed on the Outlook Today window people see when they start Outlook.

At the time this chapter was written, Microsoft hadn't published specific information about customizing Outlook Today in Outlook 2000. However, the Outlook 98 information in the Microsoft Knowledge Base article Q194978, "Finding Information on How to Customize "Outlook Today," appears to apply equally to Outlook 2000.

CHAPTER 37

CUSTOMIZING THE FOLDER LIST

In this chapter

by Gordon Padwick

UNDERSTANDING OUTLOOK'S FOLDERS

If you're using IMO Outlook or C/W Outlook, but not as a client for Exchange, Outlook saves items of information in a Personal Folders file. While your Personal Folders file is usually on your local hard drive, it can be on any other network disk to which you have access. If you're using C/W Outlook as a client for Exchange, Outlook can save items of information in a Personal Folders file on a local or network disk, and can also save items in the Exchange store.

Whether you've set up Outlook to save items on a local hard drive, a network drive, or the Exchange store, items are saved in a set of ten folders, one folder for each type of Outlook item. These folders are

- Calendar—For Outlook items that describe dated activities
- Contacts—For Outlook items that contain information about people or organizations
- Deleted Items—For Outlook items that you've deleted from other Outlook folders
- Drafts—For messages you're working on but aren't ready to send
- Inbox—For messages you've received
- Journal—For Outlook items that record information about messages you've sent to, and received from, specific people, Office files you've worked with, and various other activities
- Notes—For Outlook items you create to save temporary information
- Outbox—A temporary place where Outlook saves messages you've created until a connection to a mail server is available
- Sent Items—For copies of messages you've sent
- Tasks—For tasks you've created for yourself, asked other people to accept, or accepted from other people

You can create additional folders, and you can create subfolders below the original ten folders and below any other folders you create. This chapter explains how to create additional folders.

Note

A *folder* is space on a disk that is a container for information. Within the context of Windows, a folder contains files or other folders, all of which can be seen by Windows Explorer. Within the Outlook context, a folder is space within a Personal Folders file or Exchange store that contains Outlook items and other Outlook folders, and also can be used to store Windows files.

Each Outlook folder can contain one type of Outlook *item (page 19)*, other Outlook folders, and files. If you attempt to save an Outlook item of one type in an Outlook folder that's intended for Outlook items of a different type, Outlook automatically converts the item being saved into an Outlook item of the type the folder holds. For example, if you drag a Message item into a folder that holds Calendar items, Outlook saves the Message item as a Calendar item.

> **Note**
>
> The process of creating one type of Outlook item from a different type of Outlook item is known as *AutoCreate*.

Although an Outlook folder can contain Outlook items of only one type, it can contain Outlook subfolders that contain Outlook items of a different type.

EXAMINING THE OUTLOOK FOLDER LIST

With any Outlook Information viewer displayed, choose <u>V</u>iew, Fol<u>d</u>er List to see a list of Outlook folders. If you've just installed Outlook, you'll see a list of folders similar to that shown in Figure 37.1.

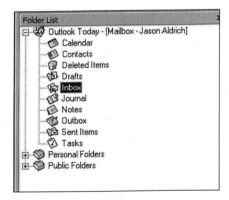

Figure 37.1
This is a list of folders such as you might see if you're using C/W Outlook as a client for an Exchange server.

> **Note**
>
> The Folder List shown in Figure 37.1 is typical of what you'll have after installing C/W Outlook as a client for an Exchange server. After installing C/W Outlook not as a client for an Exchange server, or having installed IMO Outlook, you'll have only one root folder.

After you, or other people, have been working with Outlook for a while, you may see many more folders than shown in Figure 37.1.

The folders are arranged in a tree structure with the root name at the top. This root name represents a Personal Folders file or an Exchange store. The folders in which Outlook saves items are listed under the root name.

Tip #219 from

Gordon Padwick

If you only see a root name, that name has a small box containing a + sign at the left. Click that box to expand the root so that the Outlook folders are displayed. After you've expanded the root, the small box contains a – sign. You can click that box to collapse the list of Outlook folders. After you've done so, the small box contains a + sign.

In Figure 37.1, the name of the root is Outlook Today - [Mailbox - Jason Aldrich]. This indicates that your Outlook folders are in an Exchange store. You'll see roots with names like this only if you're using C/W Outlook as a client for an Exchange server.

Note

The name "Jason Aldrich" used in this book is a fictitious mailbox name. You'll see the name of your own mailbox.

If you had installed IMO Outlook, or C/W Outlook but not as a client for an Exchange server, the name of the root is usually "Outlook Today - [Personal Folders]." The root always has a name like this if you're using IMO Outlook or C/W Outlook but not as a client for an Exchange server.

Note

The default name Outlook uses for your Personal Folders file is "Personal Folders." You can change that name to something different, such as "Master Folders." In that case, the name for the root folder in the Folder List would be "Outlook Today - [Master Folders]."

Note

If you're using Personal Folders files or an Exchange store you created while using a previous version of Outlook, the names for root folders might be different from what's described here. For example, the name of your Personal Folders file might just be "Personal Folders."

You can choose any folder name in the list to see the Outlook items in that folder listed in an Information viewer in the right pane. You can also right-click a folder name to display that folder's context menu, as described subsequently in this chapter.

→ A folder's context menu provides a convenient way to do many things with a folder. **See** "Using a Folder's Context Menu," **p. 921**.

To hide the list of folders, choose the X at the right end of the Folder List's title bar, or choose <u>V</u>iew, Fold<u>e</u>r List.

DISPLAYING A TEMPORARY FOLDER LIST

The Folder List that's displayed when you choose View, Folder List, as described in the preceding section, remains displayed until you hide it either by clicking the X in the list's title bar or by choosing View, Folder List again.

You can also display your Folder List by displaying any Outlook Information viewer, and then clicking that Information viewer's name. The Folder List you get by doing this, shown in Figure 37.2, is almost identical to the one shown in Figure 37.1.

Push pin

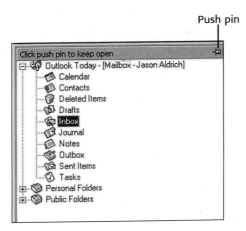

Figure 37.2
The Folder List shown here has a push pin icon at the right end of its title bar.

This Folder List is temporary—it disappears when you click anywhere in the right pane or when you choose a folder in the list.

You can use this Folder List only for selecting a folder. You can't right-click a folder name to display its context menu.

You can easily convert a temporary Folder List to the more permanent one described in the preceding section. To do so, click the push pin in its title bar.

ACTIVATING AN OUTLOOK LOCATION

The Folder List shown in Figures 37.1 and 37.2 contains several root names. Notice that the icon at the left of the root name has a small image of a house superimposed on it. The superimposed house indicates that the root is the default location where Outlook currently saves items. That's of little significance if you have only one root—in that case, only one location exists where Outlook can save items, so you don't need to be shown which location that is.

CREATING ADDITIONAL PERSONAL FOLDERS FILES

Whether you have IMO or C/W Outlook, you can have several Personal Folders files, each containing many folders. In C/W Outlook used as a client for an Exchange server, you always have your Exchange mailbox as a root; in addition, you may have one or more Personal Folders files.

To create a Personal Folders file:

1. With any Outlook Information viewer displayed, choose File, move the pointer onto New, and choose Personal Folders File to display the dialog box shown in Figure 37.3.

Figure 37.3
This dialog box displays a list of Personal Folders files in your Outlook folder.

2. Replace the name in the File Name box with the Windows file name you want to use for the new Personal Folders file. You can also change the Windows folder in which the new Personal Folders file will be saved.

3. Choose Create to display the dialog box shown in Figure 37.4.

Figure 37.4
Use this dialog box to specify the new Personal Folders file.

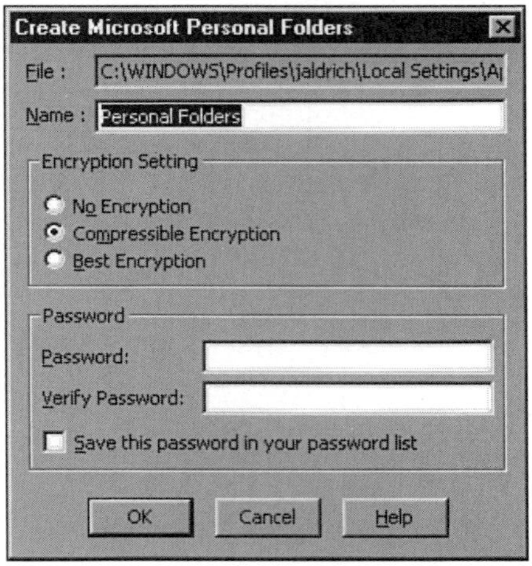

4. Replace the proposed name "Personal Folders" with a more meaningful name.

Tip #220 from

Gordon Paddle | If you don't change this name, you'll have two or more root folders in your Outlook Folder List all named "Personal Folders" and you won't know which is which.

5. Choose an encryption setting.

6. If you want to protect the new Personal Folders file with a password, enter a password in the Password box and enter the same password in the Verify Password box.

7. Normally, leave Save This Password in Your Password List unchecked.

8. Choose OK to create the new folder.

The next time you open your Folder List, you'll see the name of the new folder listed. If you click the + at the left of its name to see the individual folders it contains, you'll find that it only contains a Deleted Items folder. If you subsequently designate this folder as your default Outlook store, Outlook automatically creates the ten standard folders in it (nine in addition to the Deleted Items folder).

DESIGNATING A DEFAULT OUTLOOK STORE

Figure 37.1 shows a Folder List for C/W Outlook (used as a client for an Exchange server) that contains one Personal Folders file and two Exchange stores (one for your personal Outlook items and one for public folders). One of these four roots has the house superimposed over its icon. That's the default store in which Outlook is currently set to save items.

If you have two or more sets of Outlook folders, you need to be able to select which set Outlook uses as the location to save items. The set of folders in which Outlook saves items is known as your default store. The method by which you designate the default store is different for IMO and C/W Outlook.

 To specify where IMO Outlook saves items:

IMO

1. Choose View, Folder List to display your Folder List.

2. Right-click the root name of the Personal Folders file you want to use as your default store to display its context menu.

3. Choose Properties to display the properties dialog box for that Personal Folders file, shown in Figure 37.5.

4. If Deliver POP Mail to This Personal Folders File is checked and not available, that Personal Folders file is already designated as your default store, so choose OK to close the dialog box. Don't follow the remaining steps in this procedure.

   If Deliver POP mail to This Personal Folders File is not checked, check it, then choose OK to close the dialog box. Outlook displays a message stating that the location will not change until you exit and restart Outlook.

5. Choose OK to close the message.

6. Choose File, Exit to close Outlook, then restart Outlook. When you restart Outlook, you'll see a message about changed locations. Choose Yes to continue.

Figure 37.5
This dialog box opens with the General tab selected.

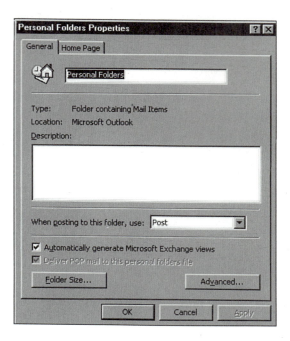

When Outlook restarts, display the Folder List—you'll see that the Personal Folders file you chose in step 3 is now the default store, as indicated by the house superimposed on its icon. If you expand the newly selected root folder, you'll see that it now contains the standard ten folders.

Subsequently, when you create new Outlook items and save them, they are saved in the folder that you just designated as your default store.

To specify where C/W Outlook saves items:

1. Choose Tools, Services to display the Services dialog box. Select the Delivery tab shown in Figure 37.6.

Note

The name of this box is misleading because it refers specifically to mail. In fact, the location named in this box is the default store where Outlook saves all items.

When you create a new Outlook item, Outlook normally saves that item in the default store. However, if you open the Folder List and select a store other than the default and then create an Outlook item, Outlook saves that item in the selected store instead of in the default store.

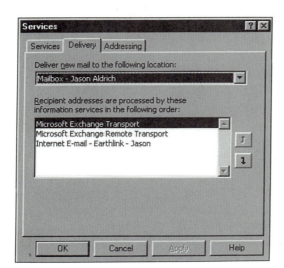

Figure 37.6
The Deliver New Mail to the Following Location box shows the current location in which Outlook saves items—your current default store.

2. Open the drop-down Deliver <u>N</u>ew Mail to the Following Location list to display a list of the available locations. The locations listed include your Personal Folders files and (if you're using C/W Outlook as a client for an Exchange server) the Exchange mailboxes to which you have access.

3. Select the location in which you want Outlook to save items.

4. Choose OK to close the Services dialog box.

5. Choose <u>F</u>ile, Exit and <u>L</u>og Off.

6. Restart Outlook. Although you don't have to, you can choose <u>V</u>iew, Fold<u>e</u>r List to confirm that Outlook is now set to save items in the location you chose in step 3—that location now has the house superimposed on its icon.

Note

After you've changed the location in which Outlook saves items, you must exit from Outlook and restart it before Outlook uses the new location as your default store.

USING A FOLDER'S CONTEXT MENU

Many of the remaining sections of this chapter refer to a folder's *context menu*. You can display a folder's context menu by right-clicking that folder's name in the Folder List. Figure 37.7 shows a typical context menu.

Several of the items in a context menu are not available for Outlook's built-in folders. This is because you can only move, delete, or rename folders you create, not Outlook's built-in folders. With the exception of <u>S</u>end Link to This Folder, all the context menu items are available for folders and subfolders you create. Send Link to This Folder is available only for public folders. Figure 37.9, shown subsequently, is an example of a context menu for a folder you've created.

Figure 37.7
Many of the items in the context menu contain the name of the folder you selected.

CREATING FOLDERS AND SUBFOLDERS

Within an Outlook storage location, such as a Personal Folders file or an Exchange store, you can create as many Outlook folders as you need, and you can create subfolders within existing folders.

The reasons you create additional Outlook folders are the same as those for creating Windows folders. You save information so that you can access it when you need to do so. Accessing information is simplified if you have the information organized into separate folders.

→ You can use two ways, and combinations of those two ways, to organize Outlook items. One way is to save items in specific folders. The other way is to assign categories to items. To learn more about how to do this, **see** "How Categories Are Assigned to Items," **p. 609**.

CREATING A NEW FOLDER OR SUBFOLDER

You can create as many new Outlook folders and subfolders as you like within a Personal Folders file or, if you're using C/W Outlook as a client for an Exchange server, in the Exchange store. The procedure that's described here creates folders and subfolders within the currently active location. The first step, if you have more than one Outlook storage location available, is to make sure the location in which you want to create a folder or subfolder is the active one.

→ For information about making a specific store the default in which Outlook saves items, **see** "Activating an Outlook Location," **p. 917**.

Tip #221 from	You can drag folders and subfolders you create, but not Outlook's default folders, to different places within the folder structure.

To create a folder or subfolder:

1. With any Outlook Information viewer displayed, choose File, move the pointer onto Folder and choose New Folder to display the dialog box shown in Figure 37.8. Alternatively, right-click a folder name in the Folder List to display the folder's context menu, then choose New Folder.

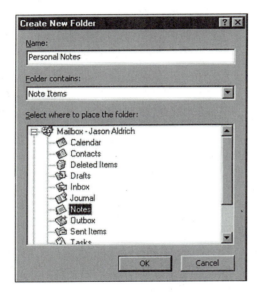

Figure 37.8
Use this dialog box to create a new folder or subfolder.

2. In the Name box, enter a name for the new folder. The name should, of course, be different from any existing name within the folder branch in which you intend to place it.

3. Open the drop-down Folder Contains list and select the type of Outlook item you intend to save in the new folder or subfolder.

4. In the Select Where to Place the Folder box, select the root name if you're creating a folder that's to be at the same level in the folder structure as the built-in Outlook folders. Alternatively, if you're creating a subfolder, select the existing folder below which you want the new subfolder to be placed.

5. Choose OK. Outlook asks whether you want to place a shortcut to the new folder on the Outlook Bar. Choose Yes or No according to your preference.

6. If you like, you can choose View, Folder List to confirm that the new folder exists in the position you intended in the Folder List.

CREATING A FOLDER SHORTCUT IN THE OUTLOOK BAR

When you create a new folder or subfolder, Outlook offers to create a shortcut in the Outlook Bar, as mentioned in step 5 of the preceding procedure. If you decline to create a shortcut at that time, you can subsequently create a shortcut.

To create a folder shortcut:

1. Select the Outlook Bar group in which you want to create the shortcut.

2. In the Folder List, right-click the folder or subfolder for which you want to create the shortcut to display its context menu.

3. Choose Add to Outlook Bar in the context menu. The shortcut immediately appears in the Outlook Bar.

Here's an alternative way to create an Outlook Bar shortcut for a folder you've created.

To drag a shortcut onto the Outlook Bar:

1. Display the Folder List.

2. Select the Outlook Bar group into in which you want to place the new shortcut.

3. Drag the folder name from the Folder List into the Outlook Bar. The new shortcut appears in the Outlook Bar when you release the mouse button.

→ For more detailed information about creating shortcuts in the Outlook Bar, **see** "Adding Shortcut Icons to an Outlook Bar Group," **p. 807**.

To remove a shortcut from the Outlook Bar, right-click the shortcut icon in the Outlook Bar to display its context menu, then choose Remove from Outlook Bar. Outlook asks you to confirm that you want to remove the shortcut. Choose Yes.

DELETING A FOLDER OR SUBFOLDER

You can delete a folder or subfolder you've created, but not one of Outlook's built-in folders. There are several ways to delete a folder. When you delete a folder, Outlook moves that folder and its contents into the Deleted Items folder. In each case, start by displaying the Folder List.

To delete a folder or subfolder by using that folder's context menu:

1. Right-click the folder you want to delete to display its context menu, shown in Figure 37.9.

2. Choose Delete in the context menu. Outlook asks you to confirm that you want to delete the folder and its contents.

3. Choose Yes. The folder immediately disappears from the Folder List.

COPYING A FOLDER DESIGN

 In C/W Outlook you can copy the various Permissions, Rules, Description, Forms, and Views properties of one folder, as described subsequently in this chapter, to another folder.

Tip #223 from

This capability is available only if you have the Microsoft Exchange Server information service in your profile.

You copy folder designs within your Exchange store, within your Personal Folders files, and from one store to another, such as from a folder within your Exchange store to a folder within a Personal Folders file.

PART
VI

CH
37

To copy the design of a folder:

1. Display the Folder List and select the folder to which you want to copy the properties of another folder.

2. Choose File, move the pointer onto Folder, and choose Copy Folder Design to display a dialog box such as that shown in Figure 37.11.

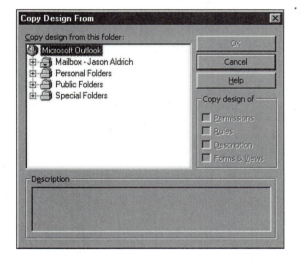

Figure 37.11
The Copy Design From dialog box shows the folder structure with all roots collapsed.

3. Expand the root folder that contains the folder that has the properties you want to copy, then select that folder to display the dialog box shown in Figure 37.12.

4. Check any combination of Permissions, Rules, Description, and Forms & Views, that you want to copy.

5. Choose OK. Outlook displays a message saying that the target folder's existing properties will be replaced by the new properties. Choose Yes. Outlook copies the folder design.

Figure 37.12
Use this dialog box to
check the properties
you want to copy to
the another folder.

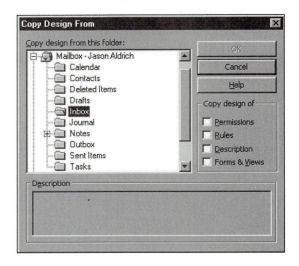

SETTING FOLDER PROPERTIES

Each Outlook folder has a set of properties that you can customize. To display a folder's properties, right-click a shortcut icon in the Outlook Bar or right-click a folder name in the Folder List to display the folder's context menu. In the context menu, choose Properties to display the folder's Properties dialog box.

If you're using IMO Outlook, most folders display a dialog box with three tabs, as shown in Figure 37.13.

SETTING THE GENERAL PROPERTIES

The box at the top of the dialog box contains the name of the folder. You can't change the name of Outlook's built-in folders, but you can change the name of a folder or subfolder you've created.

The Description box is initially empty. You can enter text in that box to describe the purpose of the folder. There's no need to do so for Outlook's built-in folders, but you may want to do so for folders and subfolders you create.

The When Posting to This Folder, Use box contains the name of the form associated with the folder. For example, if you're looking at the properties of the Calendar folder, the form name displayed is Appointment because that's the form you use when you create a Calendar item. You won't normally change to a different form in the case of Outlook's built-in folders.

If you have created folders, you may also have created custom forms to use for entering data into those folders. If that's the case, you can open the When Posting to This Folder, Use drop-down list and choose Forms. That takes you to the dialog box shown in Figure 37.14.

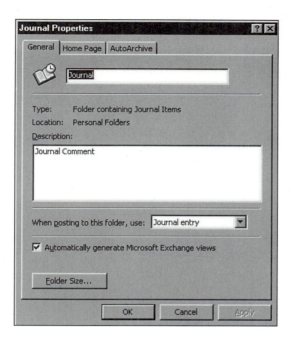

Figure 37.13
The Properties dialog box opens with the General tab selected.

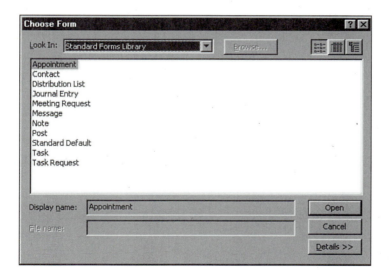

Figure 37.14
You can select a form from the Standard Forms Library shown here, or open the Look In drop-down list to select a form in another forms library.

→ To learn more about Outlook's forms, **see** "Creating and Using Custom Forms," **p. 1031**.

Although the A̲utomatically Generate Microsoft Exchange View check box in the General tab of the Properties dialog box is available for all folders, it is generally applicable only to public folders in the Exchange store. Check this box for public folders that you want to make accessible to people who use Exchange Client as a client for Exchange Server. The Folder Size button has nothing to do with setting a folder's properties. You can choose this button to open the dialog box shown in Figure 37.15.

Figure 37.15
This dialog box displays the size of the folder and also the sizes of any subfolders it contains.

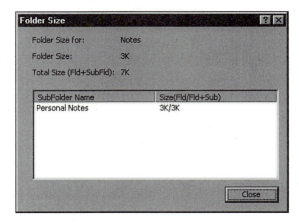

SETTING THE HOME PAGE PROPERTIES

Home Page properties are new in Outlook 2000. You can use these properties to associate a folder with a Web page or other page defined by HTML code. When you do this, Outlook uses the rendering and security services of Internet Explorer to display the HTML-defined page in a folder's Information viewer.

You can see this happening when you display Outlook Today. What you see in Outlook Today is actually a page defined by HTML code. To get an insight into this, right-click Outlook Today in the Outlook Bar to see its context menu. Choose Properties, and select the Home Page tab. The Show Home Page by Default for This Folder box is checked ; if you've installed Office 2000 in the default folders, the Address of the home page is:

```
res:\C:Program Files\Microsoft Office\Office\1033\Outlwvw.dll/outlook.htm
```

which is the location of an HTML file on your hard disk. Refer to Chapter 36 for more information on this topic.

→ For more information about working with HTML files, **see** "Obtaining the Outlook Today Source Code," **p. 905**.

For any folder, you can enter the name of an HTML page and check Show Home Page by Default for This Folder. After you do so, when you select that folder either in the Outlook Bar or the Folder List, Outlook displays the HTML page instead of the normal Information viewer. This isn't something you should do with Outlook's built-in folders, because that would mean you can't see the items in those folders in the Information viewer.

In a corporate or workgroup situation, you might find it useful to create a shared folder that displays a Web page. You can demonstrate this capability if you're working at a computer that can connect to the Internet. Do the following:

To display a Web page in an Outlook Information viewer:

1. Create an Outlook folder. Name it Home (or any other name you prefer), accept the default Mail Items for what it contains, and save the folder anywhere in your Folder List.

→ There's more detailed information about creating folders previously in this chapter. **See** "Creating a New Folder or Subfolder," **p. 922**.

2. Right-click the new folder in the Folder List, choose Properties in the context menu, and select the Home Page tab.

3. Initially, the Show Home Page by Default for This Folder check box is unavailable and the insertion point is in the text box. In the text box, enter http://www.mcp.com (the address of the Macmillan Computer Publishing home page) or another Web page address. As soon as you start typing the check box becomes available.

4. Check the check box.

5. Select one of the two option buttons, according to your preference.

6. Choose OK to close the dialog box.

This procedure created an Outlook folder that has a Web page associated with it.

Choose the new folder in the Outlook Bar (if you created a shortcut icon for the new page) or in the Folder List. Your computer is automatically connected to the Internet and the Web page you specified for the folder is displayed in the folder's Information viewer, as shown in Figure 37.16.

The preceding procedure is intended merely to give you a quick way to understand the significance of the Home Page tab in the Properties dialog box. How you use this capability in practice depends on your needs. You need to understand:

- You can create any number of folders or subfolders and associate an HTML page with each of them.

- Each HTML page can contain any type of information and can be linked to other HTML pages.

- The associated HTML pages can be anywhere—on the Web (as in the example), on your local hard disk, on a network disk to which you have access.

The Restore Defaults button in the Home Page tab of the Properties dialog box removes the check mark from the Show Home Page by Default for This Folder check box and removes the Web page address from the text box. Thereafter, the folder provides access to Outlook items.

SETTING AUTOARCHIVE PROPERTIES

All folders except folders designated to hold Contact items have an AutoArchive tab, such as the one shown in Figure 37.17.

PART
VI
CH
37

Figure 37.16
Whenever you open a folder to which a Home page is associated, you see that page like this.

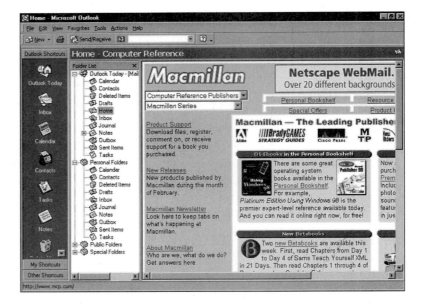

Figure 37.17
Use this tab to specify how Outlook AutoArchives items in a folder.

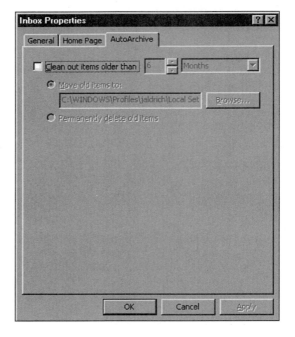

By default, AutoArchiving is turned on. Outlook defines a specific aging period for each type of item. When AutoArchiving occurs, items older than the aging period are archived. Also, by default, Outlook saves archived items in a folder named Archive.pst.

In this dialog box, you can

- Turn AutoArchiving off
- Change the aging period for the items in the folder
- Specify the Windows folder in which archived items are saved
- Choose to delete, instead of save, archived items

→ To learn how to control AutoArchiving, **see** "AutoArchiving Outlook Items," **p. 592**.

SETTING OUTLOOK ADDRESS BOOK PROPERTIES

The Properties dialog box for the Contacts folder has two tabs not available for other folders: Outlook Address Book and Activities.

The Outlook Address Book tab is shown in Figure 37.18.

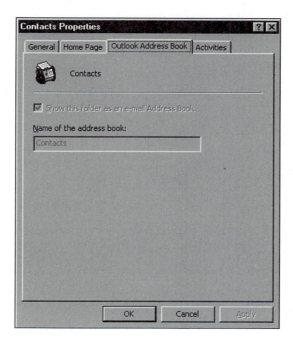

Figure 37.18
Use this tab to designate a Contacts folder as an e-mail Address book.

With <u>S</u>how This Folder as an E-mail Address Book checked, you can use the Outlook items in the Contacts folder to address e-mail and faxes.

By default, Outlook proposes to give the address book that contains information about your contacts the name Contacts. That's okay if you have only one Outlook folder for contacts. If you have two or more folders for Contact items, you should change the name to something more meaningful. For example, you might have one folder in which you keep information about personal friends, another folder in which you keep information about business contacts, and another folder in which you keep information about members of a club. If you do that, you should give each of these address books an appropriate name.

Tip #224 from

Gordon Podlach

> Although Outlook allows you to keep any number of Contacts folders, and some people recommend that you do so, in my experience it's best to use only one Contacts folder. Rather than keeping different types of contacts in different folders, it's better to assign categories to contacts. By doing that, if a contact belongs in two or more groups, you can assign two or more categories instead of duplicating the contact information in two or more folders.

The other Properties tab that's unique to Contacts is Activities, shown in Figure 37.19.

Figure 37.19
You can use this tab to define how you want to save contact activities.

→ Activities is something new in Outlook 2000. To learn more about it, **see** "Tracking a Contact's Activities," **p. 346**.

The Activities tab initially lists folders that Outlook can search for information about your contacts' activities. You can choose the buttons at the bottom of the dialog box for these purposes:

- Copy—To make a copy of a selected folder group
- Modify—To change the name of a selected folder group and to add folders to, and remove folders from that group

- Reset—To reset the contents a selected folder group to its original state
- New—To create a new folder group

Open the Default Activities View drop-down list and select the default view that's displayed in the Contact form's Activities tab.

SETTING ADMINISTRATION PROPERTIES

Properties dialog boxes in C/W Outlook have an Administration tab. Most of the boxes in this tab are unavailable if you're looking at properties for a folder in your Personal Folders file, one of your folders in the Exchange store, or a public folder in the Exchange store for which you don't have administrative permissions. Figure 37.20 shows such a tab.

PART

VI

CH

37

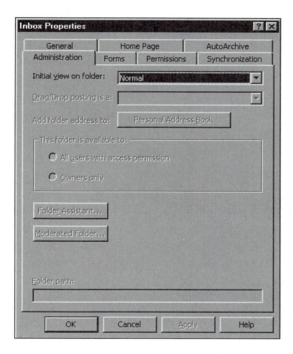

Figure 37.20
This is the Administration tab for a folder in your Personal Folders file.

In this case, only the Initial View on Folder drop-down list is available. Although it may appear otherwise, this setting applies only to the initial view for a shared public folder. You can open the drop-down list and select a view that appears when someone opens the folder. If that person chooses a different view, that view is what the person sees.

If you look at the properties of an Exchange public folder for which you do have administrative permissions and select the Administration tab, the tab is displayed as shown in Figure 37.21.

Figure 37.21
This is the Administration tab for an Exchange public folder for which you have administrative permissions.

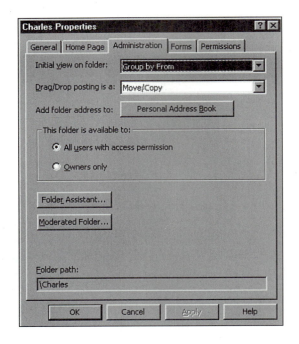

Open the drop-down Drag/Drop Posting Is A list. You can open the Drag/Drop Posting Is A drop-down list and select from the following:

- Move/Copy—This formats a moved or copied item as it was in the original location. The person who posted the item remains as the owner of the item. The item contains no reference to the person who moved or copied the item.

- Forward—This formats a moved or copied item as a forwarded item. The item appears to be from the person who moved or copied it and that person is shown as the owner of the item.

You can choose Personal Address Book to add the folder address book to your Personal Address Book.

In the This Folder Is Available To section, select an option button according to whether you want the folder to be accessible to all users who have access permission, or only to people who have Owner permission.

Choose Folder Assistant to create rules for processing items posted in the folder.

→ For information about creating server-based rules **see** "Using Server-Based Rules," **p. 697**.

Choose Moderated Folder if the public folder is to be a moderated folder. Refer to Chapter 27 for information about setting up a moderated bulletin board.

→ To find out how to use a public folder as a moderated bulletin board, **see** "Using a Public Folder as a Moderated Bulletin Board," **p. 717**.

Folder Path displays the location of the folder.

SETTING FORMS PROPERTIES

All Outlook items have an associated default form, which you can use to create an item and also to view information that's in an item. In addition to the default form, you can create any number of default forms for special purposes. For example, you may find it useful to have a special form for creating Contact items for club members or family members.

→ For detailed information about creating custom forms, **see** "Creating and Using Custom Forms," **p. 1031**.

After you've created custom forms, you have to make those forms available for use with specific folders. The Forms tab of the Properties dialog box displays the names of custom forms available to a folder as shown in Figure 37.22.

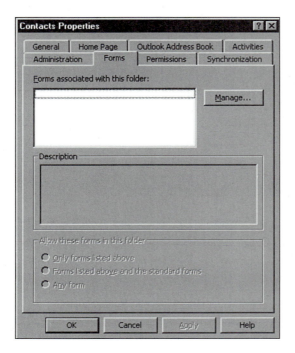

Figure 37.22
The Forms Associated with This Folder Box is initially empty because no custom forms are associated with the folder.

To associate custom forms with a folder:

1. Choose Manage in the Forms tab to display the dialog box shown in Figure 37.23.

Figure 37.23
You can use this dialog box to select forms in a forms library and associate those forms with a folder.

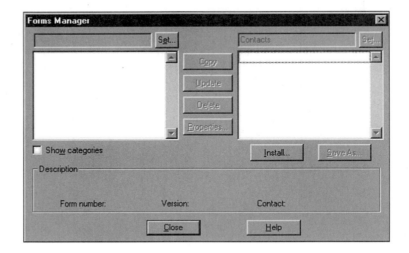

2. Choose Set to display the dialog box shown in Figure 37.24.

Figure 37.24
Select a forms library in this dialog box.

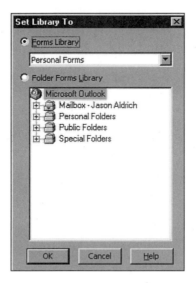

3. Select Forms Library, then open the drop-down list of forms libraries. Unless you have created forms libraries, the only one listed is Personal Forms. Select the forms library in which you've saved custom forms.

4. After you've selected a forms library, choose OK to return to the Forms Manager dialog box which now shows the forms library you selected, as shown in Figure 37.25.

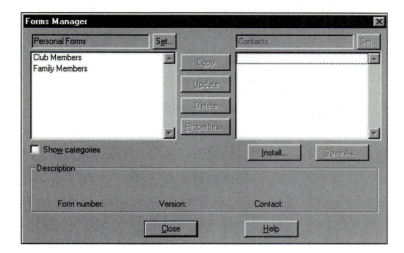

Figure 37.25
The left box in this dialog box lists the custom forms in the selected forms library.

5. Select the form you want to make available to the current folder, then choose Copy. The selected form is now listed in the right box.

6. Repeat step 5 to make additional forms available to the folder.

7. Choose Close to return to the Forms tab, as shown in Figure 37.26.

Figure 37.26
The Forms tab now lists the forms available to the folder.

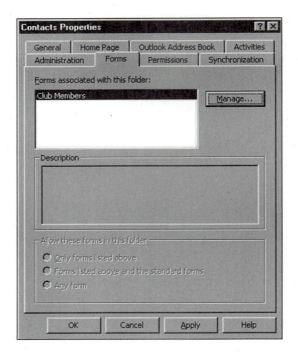

When you select a custom form in the Forms tab, the Description box contains a description of that form if you saved a description when you published the form. You can't change a form's description in this tab.

The Allow These Forms in This Folder section at the bottom of the Forms tab contains three option buttons that aren't available for your personal folders. They are available if you're working with public folders. Select an option button according to which forms are to be used with the selected folder.

SETTING PERMISSIONS PROPERTIES

The Permissions tab, shown in Figure 37.27, is available for a public folder you own. You can use this tab to grant permissions to other people to have access to the folder.

→ For details on granting and denying permissions, **see** "Giving People Access to a Public Folder," **p. 707**.
→ For more information about folder properties, **see** "Using Properties," **p. 499**.

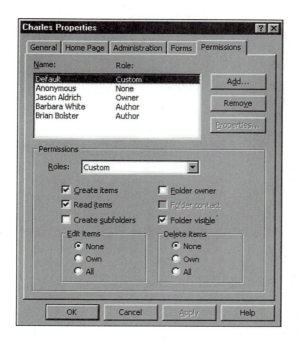

Figure 37.27
Use this dialog box to grant permissions to a public folder you own.

TROUBLESHOOTING

If you create several Personal Folders files, and neglect to give them specific Outlook names (even though the files have different names within the Windows file structure), Outlook's Folder List will show these files all with the same name—Personal Folders. This presents a problem because you don't know which is which.

To solve this problem, display the Folder List and, within one of the Personal Folders files, select one of the folders it contains. When you do that, you'll see the items within that folder. The items you see should be enough to tell you which Personal Folders file you've selected. Now, right-click the root of that folder to display its context menu and, in that menu, choose Properties to display the Properties dialog box with the General tab selected. Choose Advanced and, in that dialog box, change the name of the Personal Folders file to something that describes its contents (such as Toastmasters). When you close the dialog boxes to return to the Folder List, you'll see that the Personal Folders file now has the new name instead of the generic name.

You can repeat this process to give each of your Personal Folders files specific names.

As you've seen in this chapter, each Personal Folders file has two names: its name within the Windows file structure and the name by which itís known within Outlook. You may run into the situation in which Outlook can't find a Personal Folders file because the file's name within the Windows file structure has changed, its location has changed, or the file has become corrupted. In that case, when you attempt to access the folder from within

Outlook, you'll see a message that states "Unable to display the folder." That sentence is followed by the complete path name of the file Outlook is unable to find. Make a careful note of that path name.

If you've been meticulous about backing up your Windows files, you should be able to find the file among your backup files. In that case, copy the backup file into its original location. Now, Outlook should be able to find and use the file as it was at the time you created the most recent backup.

Another possibility is that you've moved files within your Windows file structure. In that case, use Windows Find to locate the file and restore it to its original path.

CHAPTER **38**

CREATING VIEWS AND PRINT STYLES

In this chapter

by Gordon Padwick

SEEING OUTLOOK ITEMS

  Many of the preceding chapters in this book contain examples of how you can use Outlook's Information viewers to display Outlook items. Some chapters contain information about printing Outlook items. Now, we turn to detailed information about how Outlook displays and prints items.

USING DEFAULT VIEWS

Outlook out-of-the-box has various ways to display and print items you've saved. The ways you can display items are known as *Views*; the ways you can print items are known as *Print Styles*. Each Print Style is based on a View.

Each type of Outlook item can be displayed in various Views. Each view of a particular type of item can be printed based on several Print Styles. While most of the examples in this chapter refer specifically to *Contact items*, the methods described apply to items in general (except where noted otherwise).

Outlook can display items you've saved in five types of views:

- Table View—A view in which items are displayed in a table with one row for each item. The information about each item is displayed in columns of the table. All Outlook items can be displayed and printed in a Table view. Figure 38.1 shows a typical Table view.

- Timeline View—A view in which items are displayed chronologically according to the date when they were created or received. This view can be scaled to show a day, week, or month at a time. All Outlook items can be displayed in a Timeline View. Timeline views cannot be printed. Figure 38.2 shows a typical Timeline view.

- Card View—A view in which items are displayed as they might appear on traditional index cards. Though primarily intended for Contact items, this view can be used to display and print other types of Outlook items. Figure 38.3 shows a typical Card view.

- Day/Week/Month View—A view in which items are displayed in a day, week, or month calendar. Though primarily intended for Calendar items, this view can be used to display and print other types of Outlook items. Figure 38.4 shows a typical Day/Week/Month view.

- Icon View—A view in which items are displayed as icons. This view is primarily intended for use with Notes items; it doesn't seem to be useful for other types of Outlook items. Figure 38.5 shows a typical Icon view.

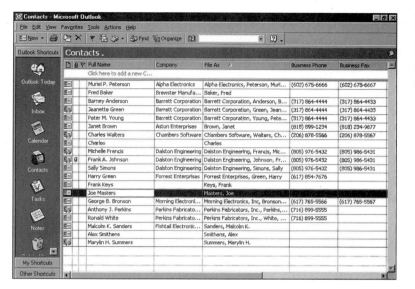

Figure 38.1
This is a typical Table view of Contact items. The top row of the table contains field names.

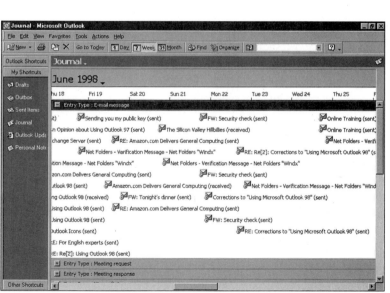

Figure 38.2
This is a typical Timeline view of Journal items.

Figure 38.3
This is a typical Card view of Contact items.

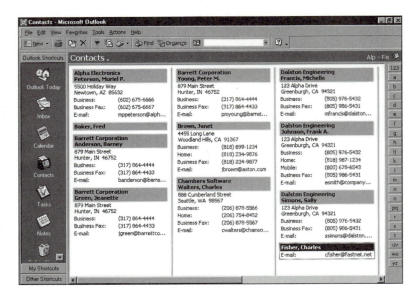

Figure 38.4
This is a typical Day/Week/Month view of Calendar items.

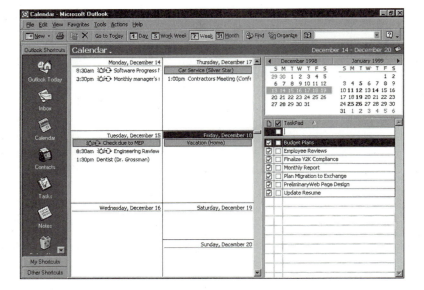

VIEWING OUTLOOK ITEMS

Outlook out-of-the-box contains various ways of viewing each type of item. To view items, choose the type of item you want to view in the Outlook Bar or Folder List. Then choose View, move the pointer onto Current View to display a list of views, and select the view you want Outlook to display. The default views are listed in Table 38.1, together with the default print styles available for each view.

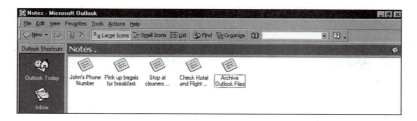

Figure 38.5
This is a typical Icon view of Notes items.

→ For detailed information about print styles, **see** "Using Print Styles," **p. 975**.

TABLE 38.1   DEFAULT OUTLOOK VIEWS

PART

VI

CH

38

Outlook Item	View	Print Styles
Calendar	Day/Week/Month	Daily, Weekly, Monthly, Tri-fold, Calendar Details, Memo
	Day/Week/Month with AutoPreview	Daily, Weekly, Monthly, Tri-fold, Calendar Details, Memo
	Active Appointments	Table, Memo
	Events	Table, Memo
	Annual Events	Table, Memo
	Recurring Appointments	Table, Memo
	By Category	Table, Memo
Contacts	Address Cards	Card, Small Booklet, Medium Booklet, Memo, Phone Directory
	Detailed Address Cards	Card, Small Booklet, Medium Booklet, Memo, Phone Directory
	Phone List	Table, Memo
	By Category	Table, Memo
	By Company	Table, Memo
	By Location	Table, Memo
	By Follow Up Flag	Table, Memo
Inbox	Messages	Table, Memo
	Messages with AutoPreview	Table, Memo
	By Follow Up Flag	Table, Memo
	Last Seven Days	Table, Memo
	Flagged for Next Seven Days	Table, Memo
	By Conversation Topic	Table, Memo

continues

TABLE 38.1 CONTINUED

Outlook Item	View	Print Styles
	By Sender	Table, Memo
	Unread Messages	Table, Memo
	Sent To	Table, Memo
	Message Timeline	see tip
Journal	By Type	see tip
	By Contact	see tip
	By Category	see tip
	Entry List	Table, Memo
	Last Seven Days	Table, Memo
	Phone Calls	Table, Memo
Tasks	Simple List	Table, Memo
	Detailed List	Table, Memo
	Active Tasks	Table, Memo
	Next Seven Days	Table, Memo
	Overdue Tasks	Table, Memo
	By Category	Table, Memo
	Assignment	Table, Memo
	By Person Responsible	Table, Memo
	Completed Tasks	Table, Memo
	Task Timeline	see tip

Deleted Items, Drafts, Outbox, and Sent Items have the same views as the Inbox.

Tip #226 from

Timeline views cannot be printed as such. However, you can select one or more items in a Timeline view and print those items in Memo style.

UNDERSTANDING WHAT'S IN A VIEW

Each view contains information about one type of Outlook item but only some of the fields of information about each item. Some views contain information about only those items that satisfy certain conditions.

Views that contain only those items that satisfy certain conditions are known as *filtered*. For example, the Last Seven Days Inbox view is a filtered view because it contains only the e-mail you've received during the last seven days. All filtered views contain the phrase "Filter Applied" at the right end of the view's banner.

To understand how you find out what a particular view displays, we'll use the Address Cards view of Contact items as an example. Outlook displays Contact items in the Address Cards view, as previously shown in Figure 38.3. The information displayed in Card view contains all your Contact items but only some of the information for each contact.

To see which fields of information are displayed in the Card view:

1. Choose Contacts in the Outlook Bar to display the Contacts Information viewer.

2. Choose <u>V</u>iew, move the pointer onto Current <u>V</u>iew, and choose Address Cards. Now you have the Address Cards view of Contacts displayed.

3. Choose <u>V</u>iew, move the pointer onto Current <u>V</u>iew, and choose <u>C</u>ustomize Current View to display the dialog box shown in Figure 39.6.

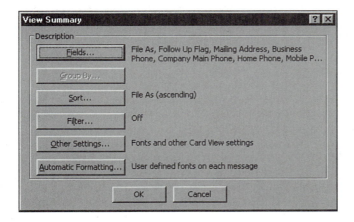

Figure 38.6
You can choose the buttons near the left edge of this dialog box to get information about the current view.

4. Choose <u>F</u>ields to display the dialog box shown in Figure 38.7.

5. Choose Cancel to return to the View Summary dialog box shown previously in Figure 38.6.

In this dialog box, Group By is not available. For some views, you can choose Group By to see how items are grouped in the view. You can choose <u>S</u>ort to see how items are sorted (ascending order by File As name in this case), and Fi<u>l</u>ter to see how items are filtered (Off indicates items aren't filtered). The <u>O</u>ther Settings and <u>A</u>utomatic Formatting buttons provide other ways you can control the appearance of a view.

Figure 38.7
The list on the right shows the names of fields that are displayed (but only if they contain data) in the Card View.

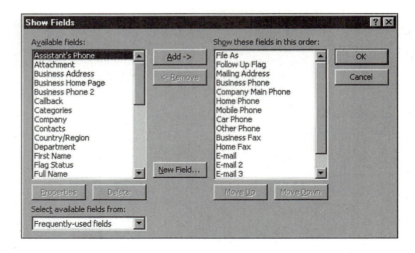

6. Choose Cancel to close the dialog box.

→ For information about the six buttons in the View Summary dialog box, **see** "Modifying a View," **p. 950**.

MODIFYING A VIEW

You can modify any of Outlook's default views and you can create additional views. This section covers modifying a default view, primarily using the Phone List view of Contact items as an example.

Tip #229 from

You can use all of the techniques described here to modify Table views. Some of these techniques are not available in other types of views.

To display the Phone List view, start with any Contacts Information viewer displayed, then choose <u>V</u>iew, move the pointer onto Current <u>V</u>iew, and choose Phone List. Outlook displays the view shown in Figure 38.8.

CHANGING THE WIDTH OF COLUMNS

By default, Outlook displays this Table view (and other Table views) with the width of each column compressed so that all fields are partially visible. You can change the width of individual columns by pointing onto the vertical line that separates one column name from the next and dragging to the right or left. If you increase the width of one column, Outlook automatically decreases the width of other columns so that at least a part of each column is visible.

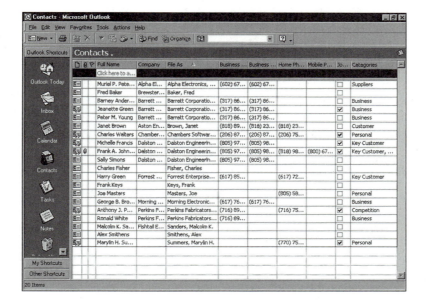

Figure 38.8
The Phone List view is a table that lists some of your contacts' phone numbers.

You can add a horizontal scroll bar at the bottom of a Table view. After you do so, you can set the width of any column to whatever you like without affecting the width of other columns. If you increase the width of columns, some columns are no longer visible, but you can use the scroll bar to see them.

Tip #230 from

You have to add a horizontal scroll bar separately for each Table view.

To add a horizontal scroll bar to a Table view:

1. With a Table view displayed, choose <u>V</u>iew, move the pointer onto Current <u>V</u>iew, and choose <u>C</u>ustomize Current View to display the View Summary dialog box previously shown in Figure 38.6.

2. Choose <u>O</u>ther Settings to display the dialog box shown in Figure 38.9.

3. Uncheck Automatic Column Si<u>z</u>ing and choose OK twice to close the dialog boxes. The Table view now has a scroll bar at the bottom.

Figure 38.9
This dialog box is used to change the appearance of a Table view.

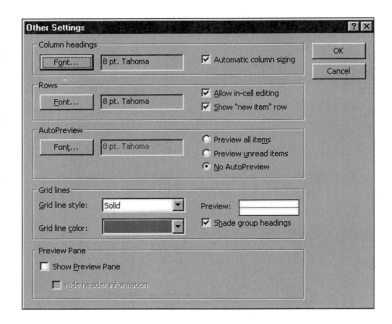

You can now increase the width of one or more columns without affecting the width of other columns, as shown in Figure 38.10.

Figure 38.10
You can use the horizontal scroll bar at the bottom of the Table view to see hidden columns.

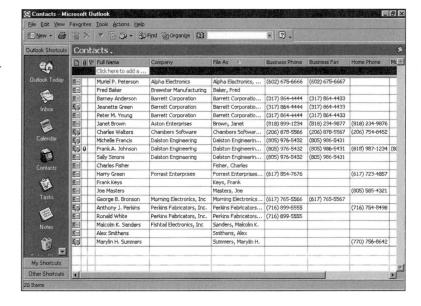

Tip #231 from

Open the Other Settings dialog box (shown in Figure 38.9) and check Automatic Column Sizing to return to the default Table view in which all columns are partially visible.

All the columns in a Card view have the same width. You can change the width of the columns in this view by dragging one of the vertical lines that separate one column from the next. By dragging one of these vertical lines, you change the width of all the columns.

CHANGING THE ORDER IN WHICH ITEMS ARE LISTED

Table views initially list information about Outlook items in a table in the order you created (or received) those items.

Tip #232 from

You can use the method described here to change the order of any type of Outlook item displayed in a Table view.

You can change the order in which *contacts (page 298)* are listed in the Phone List view by clicking in the title of a column. For example, click the title of the File As column to list the contacts alphabetically by File As name. After you do so, the items are immediately listed in File As order and a gray triangle at the top of the File As column indicates the File As field is being used to control the sort order.

→ For information about a contact's File As name, **see** "Entering a Contact's Name, Job Title, and Company," **p. 303**.

Initially the gray triangle points upward to indicate that items are listed in ascending order. You can click the File As column heading again to reverse the sort order. After you do that, the triangle points down and the Contact items are listed in reverse (descending) alphabetical order. Click the column heading again to go back to ascending order.

You can click any column heading to make it the column that controls sort order. Click once for ascending sort order, click again for descending sort order, click once more to go back to ascending sort order.

→ Another way to change the order in which items are listed is to sort items. You can use this with Table and other types of views. **See** "Sorting Items," **p. 964**.

CHANGING THE FIELDS DISPLAYED IN A VIEW

Each view displays only some of the fields of information available for Outlook items. To see which fields are displayed in the current view, choose <u>V</u>iew, move the pointer onto Current <u>V</u>iew, and choose <u>C</u>ustomize Current View to display the View Summary dialog box previously shown in Figure 38.6.

You can use this dialog box to control which fields the view displays and the order in which those fields are displayed.

CHANGING THE ORDER OF FIELDS IN A VIEW

You can use several methods to change the order in which fields are displayed in a view. You can use the first two methods described here to change the order of fields displayed in any Table or Card view.

To change the order in which fields are displayed in a Table or Card view:

1. In the View Summary dialog box shown previously in Figure 38.6, choose Fields to display the Show Fields dialog box, previously shown in Figure 38.7.
2. Select the field you want to move in the Show These Fields in This Order list at the right. When you do so, the Move Up and Move Down buttons become available.

Note

> Only the Move Down button is available if you select the top item in the list. Only the Move Up button is available if you select the bottom item in the list.

3. Choose Move Up or Move Down to change the position of the selected field in the list.

Here's another way to change the order of fields in a Table or Card view.

To change the order in which fields are displayed in a Table or Card view:

1. In the View Summary dialog box shown previously in Figure 38.6, choose Fields to display the Show Fields dialog box, previously shown in Figure 38.7.
2. In the Show These Fields in This Order list at the right, point onto the field you want to move.
3. Drag up or down to move the field to a different position in the list.

In a Table view (but not in any other view) you can change the order of columns by dragging column titles.

To change the order of columns in a Table view:

1. Display a Table view of Outlook items, such as the Phone List view of Contact items, previously shown in Figure 38.1.
2. Point onto the title of a column you want to move.
3. Press the mouse button and drag to the left or to the right until two red arrows appear above and below the left edge of the new position for the column you want to move.
4. Release the mouse button. The column moves to the new position.

REMOVING FIELDS FROM A VIEW

You can use the Show Fields dialog box, previously shown in Figure 38.7, to remove fields from those that are displayed in the view.

To remove one or more fields from a view:

1. Select the field or fields you want to remove from the view in the Show These Fields in This Order List.

2. Choose <-Remove. Outlook immediately deletes the selected field from the list at the right and inserts that field in the Available Fields list at the left (in its correct alphabetical position).

3. Choose OK twice to close the dialog boxes and display the Table view that no longer contains the field you removed.

Another way to remove a column from a Table view is to drag the column heading up. As you drag, a large X appears over the field name. When you release the mouse button, the entire column disappears from the table.

Yet another way to remove a column from a Table view is to right-click a field name at the top of a column to display the context menu shown in Figure 38.11. Choose Remove This Column in the context menu.

Figure 38.11
This is the context menu that's displayed when you right-click a column heading.

ADDING A FIELD TO A VIEW

You can use the Show Fields dialog box, previously shown in Figure 38.7, to add fields to a view.

To add one or more fields to a view:

1. Select the field in the Show These Fields in This Order list after which you want the inserted field (or fields) to be inserted.

2. Select the fields you want to add in the Available Fields list.

3. Choose Add->. Outlook deletes the selected fields from the Available Fields list and inserts those fields into the Show These Fields in This Order list.

4. Choose OK twice to close the dialog boxes and display the Table view that now includes the fields you added.

When you open the Show Fields dialog box, the Available Fields list on the left contains only frequently-used fields—the Select Available Fields From box at the bottom-left of the dialog box confirms that. You can open the Select Available Fields From drop-down list and select one of these groups of fields:

- Frequently-used fields
- Address fields
- E-mail fields
- Fax/Other number fields
- Miscellaneous fields
- Name fields
- Personal fields
- Phone number fields
- All Contact fields
- User-defined fields in folder
- All Document fields
- All Mail fields
- All Appointment fields
- All Task fields
- All Journal fields
- All Note fields
- All Post fields
- All Distribution List fields
- Forms

You can select any item in the list. When you select any except the last (Forms), a list of fields appears in the Available Fields box. You can select any field and choose Add-> to add that field to the bottom of the Show These Fields in This Order list.

When you select Forms in the drop-down Select Available Fields From list, Outlook displays the dialog box shown in Figure 38.12.

Tip #233 from

Gordon Gaard

Outlook contains many standard forms, such as the Message form, in which you create messages. You can import forms from Microsoft and other sources and also create your own forms, as described in Chapter 40.

Most forms contain fields that you can add into a Table view of Outlook items.

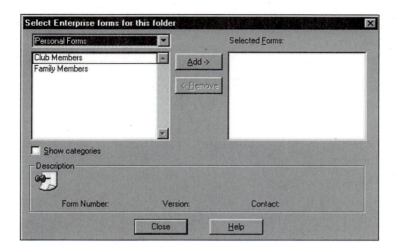

Figure 38.12
Use this dialog box to
select fields from a
form.

To select a field from a form:

1. In the Select Enterprise Forms for This Folder dialog box, open the unnamed drop-down list at the top-left and select Personal Forms if you want to select fields from a form you've imported or created, or select Applications Forms if you want to select fields from one of Outlook's standard forms. After you do that, the box below the drop-down list contains a list of available forms.

2. Select a form from which you want to select fields, and choose Add-> to add that form to the Selected Forms list on the right.

3. Repeat step 2 as often as necessary to add more forms into the Selected Forms list.

Tip #234 from

[signature]

You can remove one or more forms from the Selected Forms list by selecting forms and choosing Remove.

---

4. Select one or more forms in the Selected Forms list, then choose Close to return to the Show Fields dialog box. The fields from the selected forms are listed in the Available Fields list.

5. Select one or more fields you want to add into the Table view and choose Add->.

Another way to insert a field into a Table view is to use the Field Chooser. To display the Field Chooser, right-click anywhere in the table heading to display the context menu previously shown in Figure 38.11. Choose Field Chooser in the context menu to display the Field Chooser shown in Figure 38.13.

Figure 38.13
The Field Chooser
lists available fields.

You can open the drop-down list of field types at the top of the Field Chooser to display various lists of fields. Drag any field from the Field Chooser into the table heading and place it wherever you want. A new column appears when you release the mouse button.

CREATING A NEW FIELD

You are not limited to the information fields supplied with Outlook or available in forms. You can create your own fields.

To create a new field:

1. In the View Summary dialog box shown previously in Figure 38.6, choose Fields to display the dialog box shown previously in Figure 38.7.
2. Choose New Field to display the dialog box shown in Figure 38.14.

Figure 38.14
Use this dialog box to
create a new field.

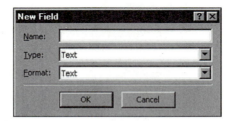

3. In the Name box, enter a name for the new field.
4. Open the drop-down Type list and select a type for the new field.
5. Open the drop-down Format list and choose a format for the new field.
6. Choose OK. The new field appears in the Show These Fields in This Order box.

→ For detailed information about creating fields, **see** "Creating and Using Custom Fields," **P. 41**.

GROUPING ITEMS

The Phone List view of Contact items shows a single list of items. Other views, such as the By Category view, arrange items in groups. For example, the By Category view of Contact items groups contacts by categories, as shown in Figure 38.15.

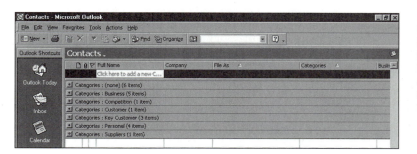

Figure 38.15
Each category has a header that contains the category name. Individual categories can be expanded to show all the items in that category.

PART
VI

CH
38

→ For detailed information about Outlook's categories, **see** "Using Categories and Entry Types," **p. 603**.

Note

If you assign more than one *category (page XXX)* to an Outlook item, that item appears in each of the categories assigned to it. A single item to which several categories are assigned is listed in each of those category groups.

Initially, this view shows only category headers. Each category header has a small box at the left containing + to indicate there are items within that category. Each category header contains the name of the category and the number of items in that category. Click the + to display all the items within the category.

The header of each expanded category (that shows all the items in that category) has a small square containing – at the left. Click that small square to collapse the category so that only the header is visible.

Another way to expand and collapse groups is to choose View and move the pointer onto Expand/Collapse Groups. You can choose:

- Collapse This Group—Collapses a selected group
- Expand This Group—Expands a selected group
- Collapse All—Collapses all groups
- Expand All—Expands all groups

You can modify grouping in existing views by:

- Adding grouping to views that are originally not grouped
- Changing grouping in views that are originally grouped

This can be done in two ways: in a dialog box or visually. The next two sections show how you can add grouping to an originally ungrouped view, using the Phone List view of Contact items as an example.

You can create as many as four levels of groupings.

USING A DIALOG BOX TO SET UP ONE LEVEL OF GROUPING

With the Contacts Information viewer displayed in the Phone List view, choose View, move the pointer onto Current View, and choose Customize Current View. Choose Group By to display the dialog box shown in Figure 38.16.

Figure 38.16
The Group Items By box contains (none) to indicate that no grouping is in effect.

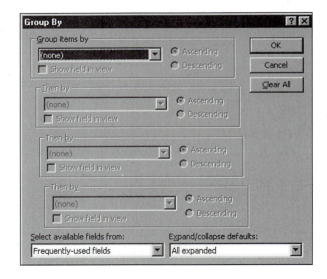

To set up one level of grouping:

1. Open the drop-down Group Items By list to display a list of fields in Contact items. This list contains all the fields in Contact items, not just those displayed in the view that you're currently working with.

2. Scroll down the list of fields and select the field by which you want to group items. For example, if you want to group Contacts by company name, select the Company field. The Group By dialog box now appears as shown in Figure 38.17.

Tip #235 from

You can group by fields that are not displayed in the view. If necessary, you can open the Select Available Fields From drop-down list at the bottom of the dialog box to select a field that is not in the Frequently-used Fields list.

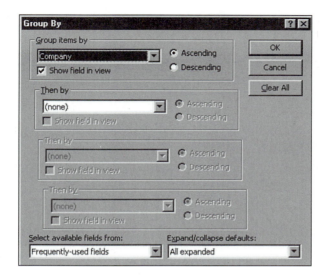

Figure 38.17
The grouping field you selected now appears in the Group Items By box.

3. By default, Outlook proposes to show the field the items will be grouped by as a column in the table. This isn't necessary because the group name appears in each group header. Normally uncheck the Show Field in View box.

4. Leave the Ascending option button selected if you want groups to be listed in ascending order. Select the Descending option button to list groups in descending order.

5. Outlook proposes to display the view with all groups expanded. You can open the drop-down Expand/Collapse Defaults list and select All Expanded, All Collapsed, or As Last Viewed.

6. Choose OK to return to the View Summary dialog box that now displays how items are grouped, as shown in Figure 38.18.

To see how items are grouped in the table, choose OK to close the View Summary dialog box. The table is now similar to that previously shown in Figure 38.15.

USING A DIALOG BOX TO SET UP MULTIPLE LEVELS OF GROUPING

The preceding procedure showed how to group items at one level, such as by category or company name. You can choose to group items with groups to as many as four levels. For example, if you have Contacts that work for companies in various countries, you might find it convenient to group contacts by category and, for each category, by company, and for each company, by country.

Figure 38.17 shows the Group By dialog box after you've defined the first level of grouping. Notice that in the dialog box the Then By section is enabled. You can open the Then By drop-down list and select a field by which you want items to be grouped within the first level of grouping. If you wanted to group items by company and then by category, you would select Category for the second level of grouping.

Figure 38.18
The text at the right of the Group By button in the View Summary dialog box shows how items are grouped.

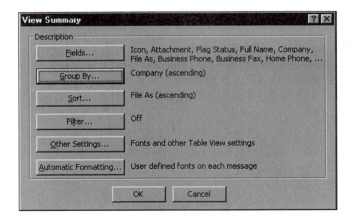

After you've selected a field for second-level grouping, the third section of the dialog box becomes available and you can select a field for third-level grouping. That makes the fourth section of the dialog box available, in which you can select a field for fourth-level grouping.

Tip #236 from

Gordon Padwick

To clear all grouping, choose Clear All in the Group By dialog box.

VISUALLY SETTING UP GROUPING

This example also uses the Phone List view of Contact items. If you've followed the previous section to set up grouping for the Phone List view, choose Clear All in the Group By dialog box so that you can follow what comes next.

To set up grouping visually:

1. With the Contacts Information viewer displayed and the Phone List view selected, choose View, move the pointer onto Toolbars, and select Advanced to display the Advanced toolbar.

2. In the Advanced toolbar, choose the Group By Box button (the third button from the right) 🔲. When you do that, a row appears at the top of the Contacts table, as shown in Figure 38.19.

3. To group by a field, drag that field from the column heading in the table into the grouping row. For example, to group the table by the Company field, drag the Company column heading into the grouping row. After you've done that, the table appears as shown in Figure 38.20.

Group By Box

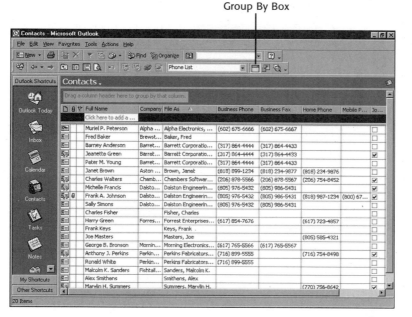

Figure 38.19
The extra row at the top of the table is where grouping fields are shown.

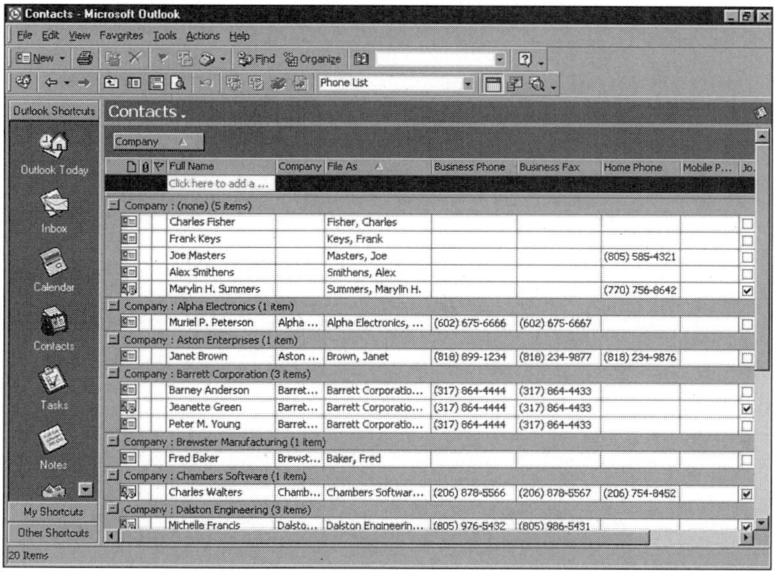

Figure 38.20
The table is now grouped, with the name of the grouping field above the column titles.

4. To create a second level of grouping, drag another field into the grouping row, as shown in Figure 38.21.

Figure 38.21
The table now has
two levels of
grouping.

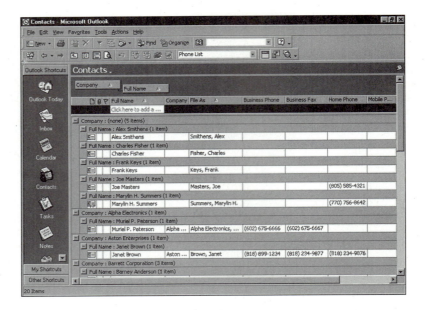

5. If necessary, repeat step 4 to create two additional levels of grouping.

When you're working visually, you can undo each level of grouping by dragging a group name from the grouping row back into its original position as a column title.

Tip #237 from

After creating groups in the Group By dialog box (shown in Figure 38.16), you can choose the Group By Box button in the Advanced toolbar to display grouping. Also, after creating groups with the Group By Box button, you can modify or clear those groups in the Group By dialog box.

To remove the Group By box at the top of a Table view, choose the Group By Box button in the Advanced toolbar. This has no effect on the grouping in the view.

The visual method of grouping just described allows you to group only on fields displayed in the table. You can group on other fields by displaying the Field Chooser, previously shown in Figure 38.13, and dragging a field from there into the Group By box.

SORTING ITEMS

Unless a specific sort order is specified, a view displays items in the order they were created or received. For example, the Phone List view of Contact items doesn't, initially, have a sort order specified, so it lists items in the order they were created. The Address Cards view of Contact items, on the other hand, is defined to display items in alphabetical order by File As name.

→ You can sort a Table view based on a single field by clicking a column header. **See** "Changing the Order in Which Items Are Listed," **p. 153**.

You can create a sort order for items displayed in a table with up to four levels of sorting. To see how this works, we'll use the Phone List view of Contact items as an example.

To sort Contact items in the Phone List view:

1. Display the Contacts Information viewer with the Phone List view selected.

2. Choose View, move the pointer onto Current View, and choose Customize Current View to display the View Summary dialog box previously shown in Figure 38.6.

3. Choose Sort to display the dialog box shown in Figure 38.22.

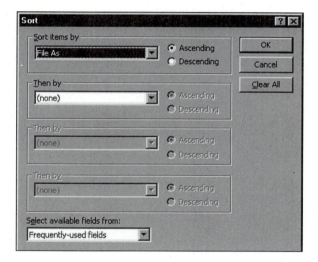

Figure 38.22
The Sort Items By box initially shows (none) to indicate that items are not sorted.

PART
VI

CH

38

4. Open the drop-down Sort Items By list and select the field by which you want items to be sorted. For example, if you want items to be sorted by Company, select the Company field.

Tip #238 from

You are not limited to sorting by fields that are displayed in the view. If necessary, you can open the Select Available Fields From drop-down list. From here you select the group of fields from which you want to select the field by which items are to be sorted.

5. Select the Ascending option button if you want items to be listed in ascending order, or select the Descending option button if you want items to be listed in descending order.

This procedure explains how to specify only one level of sorting.

→ You can choose up to four levels of sorting just as you can select up to four levels of grouping. **See** "Using a Dialog Box to Set up Multiple Levels of Grouping," **p. 961**.

FILTERING ITEMS

You can choose to filter items in a view so that a view shows only those items that satisfy certain conditions. If you have the Calendar Information viewer displayed with the Phone List view selected, the View Summary dialog box, previously shown in Figure 38.6, has Off at the right of the Filter button. This means that the view doesn't filter items, so it displays all the items in the Calendar folder.

The following example illustrates how you can create a filter, in this case so that the Phone List shows only phone numbers for a certain company.

To filter a view:

1. In the View Summary dialog box, choose Filter to display the dialog box shown in Figure 38.23.

Figure 38.23
The Filter dialog box is similar to the Advanced Find dialog box.

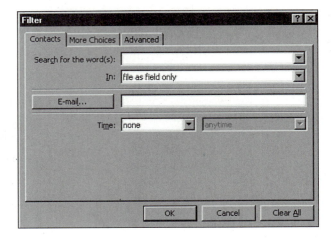

→ For detailed information about using the Advanced Find dialog box, **see** "Using Advanced Find to Find Words and Phrases," **p. 532**.

Note

The left tab in this dialog box has the name of the type of item you're working with, Contacts in this case.

2. In the Search for the Word(s) box, enter a word or phrase that appears in a particular field of items you want to have included. For example, if you want to list only items that include a specific company name, enter that company name.

3. Open the drop-down In list and select the field in which the name or phrase you entered in step 2 appears. For example, if the name or phrase appears in the Company field, select Company Field Only.

4. Choose OK to return to the View Summary field, as shown in Figure 38.24.

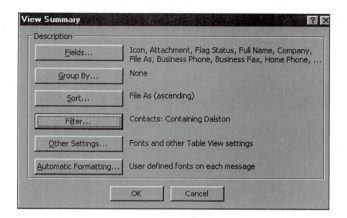

Figure 38.24
A summary of the filter you specified appears at the right of the Filter button in the View Summary dialog box.

5. Choose OK to close the dialog box and display the filtered view, as shown in Figure 38.25.

Figure 38.25
The Information viewer now contains only those items that satisfy the filter condition.

Tip #239 from

Gordon Padwick

When an Information Viewer is displaying a filtered view, the words "Filter Applied" appear at the right end of the viewer's banner, as shown in Figure 38.25. This is to remind you that the viewer probably isn't displaying all the items in the corresponding folder.

The preceding sequence of steps is only a very simple example of how you can set up filters.

→ You can create more complex filters using the same methods you employ when using Advanced Find. **See** "Using Advanced Find to Find Words and Phrases," **p. 532**.

To remove a filter from a view, open the Filter dialog box and delete the filter criteria. Choose OK twice to return to the Information viewer that now displays all items in the corresponding folder, and without "Filter Applied" in the banner.

CREATING OTHER SETTINGS

The Other Settings button in the View Summary dialog box gives you access to a dialog box in which you can select fonts and various other aspects of a table's appearance.

To change a table's appearance:

1. In the View Summary dialog box, choose Other Settings to display the dialog box shown in Figure 38.26.

Figure 38.26
Use this dialog box to control a view's appearance.

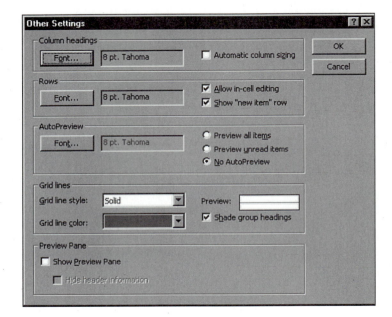

2. To change the font used for column headings, choose Font in the Column Headings section of the dialog box to display a Font dialog box that's similar to the standard Windows Font dialog box. You can use this to select a font name, style, and size, but not color.

3. To change the font used for rows in a table, choose Font in the Rows section of the dialog box.

4. If the view you're working with includes *AutoPreview*, you can change the font used for the AutoPreview by choosing Font in the AutoPreview section of the dialog box.

5. By default, Outlook creates tables with the width of columns set so that all columns are displayed—in most cases this results in columns showing truncated text. You can uncheck the Automatic Column Sizing box in the Column Headings section of the

dialog box so you can adjust column widths and show as many or as few columns as you want. After you do that, a horizontal scroll bar appears at the bottom of the table; you can use that scroll bar to see hidden columns.

6. By default, Outlook allows in-cell editing. That means you can edit the contents of fields in the displayed table. Uncheck Allow In-cell Editing in the Rows section of the dialog box to make the table read-only.

7. By default, you can't add a new item from within a table. To allow adding a new item from within a table, check Show "New Item" Row in the Rows section of the dialog box. After you do that, an empty row is displayed at the top of the table; you can use that row to create a new item.

8. Message and Calendar items can be used with AutoPreview. If you're working with a view of these types of items, you can select one of the option buttons in the AutoPreview section of the dialog box.

9. Use the Grid Lines section of the dialog box to control whether Outlook displays grid lines in the table and, if it does, the color of those grid lines. Open the Grid Line Style drop-down list and select a style. Open the Grid Line Color drop-down list and select a color. The Preview box on the right shows an example of the style and color you've selected.

10. When you choose grouping, by default Outlook displays the group headings with a gray background. To display group headings with a white background, uncheck the Shade Group Headings box.

11. Message and Calendar items can be displayed with a Preview pane. If you're working with a view of these types of items, you can select whether the Preview pane is displayed. Check the Show Preview Pane box if you want to display a Preview pane. After you check that box, check Hide Header Information if you don't want to display the Preview pane header.

AUTOMATIC FORMATTING

The Automatic Formatting button in the View Summary dialog box provides access to rules that determine how certain kinds of items are displayed. The available rules depend on the types of items you're working with. All rules may not necessarily apply to your particular Outlook configuration.

→ To learn more about rules, **see** "Creating and Using Rules," **p. 617**.

To understand how these formatting rules work, we'll use the Inbox Information viewer as an example.

With the Inbox Information viewer displayed and with the Messages view selected, choose View, move the pointer onto Current View, and choose Customize Current View to display the View Summary dialog box. Choose Automatic Formatting to display the dialog box shown in Figure 38.27.

Figure 38.27
This is the Automatic Formatting dialog box, showing the default rules for messages.

The rules in this dialog box control how Outlook displays messages in the Inbox Information viewer.

You can select a rule in the list to see how it controls the display of messages. For example, if you select the Unread Messages rule, as shown in Figure 38.27, you see that unread messages are displayed in black using the 8-point Tacoma font. You can change that by choosing Font to display the standard Windows Font dialog box, in which you can select a font name, style, size, and color.

You can create your own formatting rules to control how Outlook displays messages that satisfy certain criteria.

To create a formatting rule:

1. In the Automatic Formatting dialog box, choose Add to modify the appearance of the dialog box, as shown in Figure 38.28.

2. Change the name in the Name box to an appropriate name.

3. Choose Font and select a font in which you want Outlook to display messages that satisfy the new criteria.

4. Choose Condition to display the Filter dialog box, shown previously in Figure 38.23.

5. Use the Filter dialog box to define the conditions that must be satisfied. For example, you might want the rule to apply to messages from a certain person, or messages in which a certain word appears in the Subject box. See Chapter 18 for detailed information about this dialog box.

→ For detailed information about using Advanced Find, **see** "Using Advanced Find to Find Words and Phrases," **p. 532**.

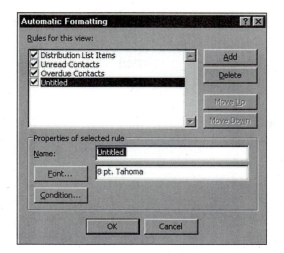

Figure 38.28
A new rule appears in
the list, tentatively
named Untitled.

PART

VI

CH

38

6. Choose OK to return to the Automatic Formatting dialog box. Now the new formatting rule is listed.

To delete a rule you've created, select that rule and choose <u>D</u>elete. You can't delete the default Outlook rules (though you can modify them).

RESETTING A VIEW TO ITS ORIGINAL STATE

If you've modified one of the views supplied with Outlook, the modified view is what Outlook subsequently uses. To go back to the original, unmodified view, you can reset the modified view to its original state.

To reset a view to its original state:

1. Display an Information viewer that displays the type of items for which you want to reset a view.

2. Choose <u>V</u>iew, move the pointer onto Current <u>V</u>iew, and choose <u>D</u>efine Views to display the dialog box shown in Figure 38.29.

3. Select the view you want to reset. If you select a view supplied with Outlook, the bottom button at the right is labeled Reset. That button is not available if you haven't modified the view; it is available if you have modified the view, as shown in Figure 38.30. If the view you select is one you've created, the bottom button is labeled Delete.

4. Choose <u>R</u>eset. Outlook asks you to confirm you want to reset the view to its original settings. Choose OK.

Figure 38.29
This dialog box lists all the views available for the type of item you selected.

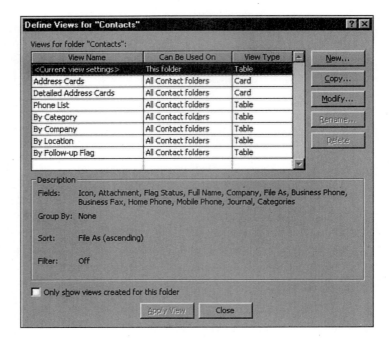

Figure 38.30
You can choose the Reset button to restore a view supplied with Outlook to its original state.

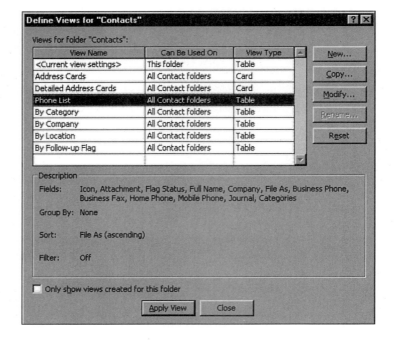

CREATING CUSTOM VIEWS

The preceding information describes how you can modify the default Outlook views of items. You can also create your own custom views.

Tip #240 from	If you're setting up Outlook for other people to use, you can prohibit access to the default Outlook views and make only the custom views you've created available.

CREATING A CUSTOM VIEW BASED ON AN EXISTING VIEW

You can define a custom view based on an existing view, or you can define a custom view from scratch. If the custom view you want to create is similar to an existing view, it's easier to start from that view and then save that view with a different name.

To create a custom view based on an existing view:

1. Start by displaying an Information viewer that displays the items you want to display in the custom view. For example, if you want to create a custom view for Contact items, display a Contact Information viewer.

2. Choose <u>V</u>iew, move the pointer onto Current <u>V</u>iew, and choose <u>D</u>efine Views to display the dialog box previously shown in Figure 38.29.

3. Select the existing view on which you want to base the custom view.

4. Choose Copy to display the dialog box shown in Figure 38.31.

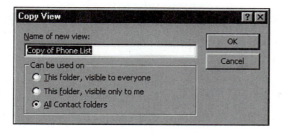

Figure 38.31
Use this dialog box to provide a name for the new view and also to select how you want the view to be used.

5. Replace the view name in the <u>N</u>ame of New View box with an appropriate name for the new view.

6. Select the option button in the Can Be Used On section of the dialog box, according to how you want the new view to be used:

   ■ <u>T</u>his Folder, Visible to Everyone—The view is available only for the folder in which you created it and can be used by everyone who has permission to access that folder.

   ■ This <u>F</u>older, Visible Only to Me—The view is available only for the folder in which you created it and can be used only by the person who created the view.

- ■ All Contact Folders—The view is available in all Contact folders. If you're creating a view for Outlook items other than Contact items, the word Contact is replaced by the appropriate item name.

7. Choose OK to display the View Settings dialog box, in which you can choose the settings for the new view. In this dialog box, you can refine what's shown in the new view, using the methods described previously in the "Modifying a View" section of this chapter.

After you've completed making the changes to the view, you have a new view with the name you chose in step 5.

CREATING A NEW VIEW FROM SCRATCH

You can create a new view without basing it on an existing view.

To create a new view from scratch:

1. Start by displaying an Information viewer that displays the items you want to display in the custom view. For example, if you want to create a custom view for Contact items, display a Contact Information viewer.

2. Choose View, move the pointer onto Current View, and choose Define Views to display the dialog box previously shown in Figure 38.29.

3. Choose New to display the dialog box shown in Figure 38.32.

Figure 38.32
Enter a name for the new view and select its type in this dialog box.

4. Replace New View in the Name of New View box with an appropriate name.

5. In the Type of View list, select the type of view you want to create.

6. In the Can Be Used On section of the dialog box, select an option button according to how you want the view to be used.

7. Choose OK to display the View Summary dialog box, shown previously in Figure 38.6, in which you can specify the settings for the new view.

MAKING ONLY CUSTOM VIEWS AVAILABLE

You can set up Outlook so that it makes available only custom views you've created, not the default views that come with Outlook. This is done separately for each type of Outlook item.

To make only custom views available for one type of Outlook item:

1. Display an Information viewer that displays one type of Outlook item.

2. Choose View, move the pointer onto Current View, and choose Define Views to display the dialog box previously shown in Figure 38.29.

3. Check the Only Show Views Created for This Folder box.

Subsequently, when a user chooses View, and moves the pointer onto Current View, the only views available are the custom views.

DELETING A VIEW

You can delete a view you've created, but you can't delete any of the default Outlook views.

To delete a view:

1. Display any Information viewer that shows the Outlook item type for which you want to delete a view.

2. Choose View, move the pointer onto Current View, and choose Define Views to display the dialog box previously shown in Figure 38.29.

3. Select the view you want to delete. If you select a view you've created, the bottom button on the right is labeled Delete.

4. Choose Delete to delete the selected view. Outlook asks you to confirm that you want to delete the view. Choose Yes.

USING PRINT STYLES

Outlook provides many ways in which you can print Outlook items. Depending on the type of item you've selected, you can choose among several print styles to control how printed pages are formatted. Each print style is based on a view.

Outlook has built-in print styles for each of its views, as listed previously in Table 38.1. As that table shows, all views except Timeline views have the Memo print style available, and all table views have a Table print style. In addition, Day/Week/Month Calendar views have several ways in which you can print calendars in the traditional calendar format; Card views of Contact items have index-card and booklet print styles.

You can modify the supplied print styles and you can supplement them by creating custom print styles. As described later in this chapter, if Outlook doesn't allow you to print in the format you need, you can export Outlook items to other applications and use the printing capabilities in them.

→ For more information about printing Outlook items, **see** "Using Other Applications and Utilities to Print Outlook Items," **p. 990**.

PRINTING TABLE VIEWS OF OUTLOOK ITEMS

With the Contacts Information viewer selected, you can choose among several Table views, such as the Phone List view used as an example previously in this chapter. You can choose the built-in Table or Memo print style to print this view. After you've selected a print style, you can make modifications to it.

The Table print style prints a table as it appears in a table Information viewer. In contrast, the Memo print style prints items in the format shown in Figure 38.33. Using the Table or Memo print style, you can print all the items displayed in the Information viewer or you can select certain items to be printed. If you want to print only certain items, select those items before step 1 in the following procedure.

To select and modify the Table print style for a Table view:

1. With a Table view, such as the Phone List view of Contact items, selected, choose File and move the pointer onto Page Setup to display the menu shown in Figure 38.34.

> **Note**
> The third item in the menu, Define Print Styles, is used when you create a custom print style. Creating custom print styles is dealt with subsequently in this chapter.

2. Choose Table Style to display the dialog box shown in Figure 38.35. The Format tab is initially selected.

3. The Fonts section of this dialog box shows the default fonts in which column headings and rows of the table are printed. You can choose Font to change the default font name, style, and size for column headings in a dialog box similar to the standard Windows Font dialog box. You can choose Font to change the font for rows of the table.

> **Note**
> The Print Using Gray Shading box has no effect on tables that are based on a view that isn't grouped. If the view is grouped, such as the By Category view, and the Print Using Gray Shading box is checked, the group headers are printed with a gray background; if it isn't checked, the group headers are printed with a white background.

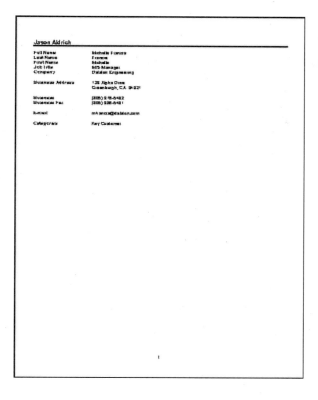

Figure 38.33
This is an example of how Outlook prints a Contact item in the Memo print style.

Figure 38.34
You can choose either Table Style or Memo Style.

Figure 38.35
The Preview section at the top of this dialog box shows a picture of the print style.

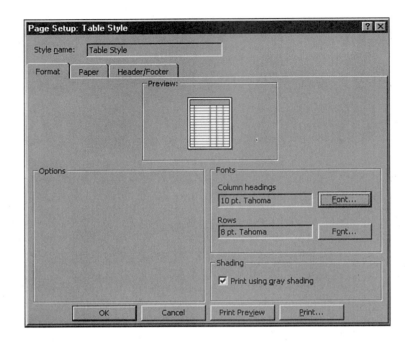

4. Select the Paper tab, shown in Figure 38.36.

Figure 38.36
You can use this tab to select the size of the paper on which the table will be printed and the layout on that paper.

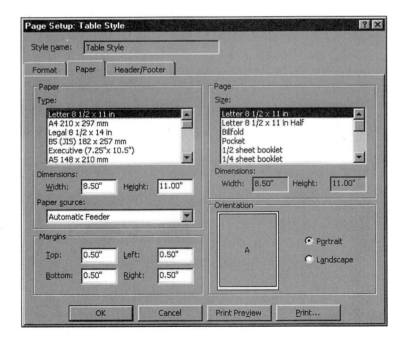

5. In the Paper section of this dialog box, select the type of paper in the Type list. The Width and Height boxes show the dimensions of the selected paper. If you're using non-standard paper, you can enter the appropriate width and height in those boxes. The image in the Orientation section shows a scaled view of the paper. If your printer has more than one paper source, open the drop-down Paper Source list and select a source.

6. In the Page section of the dialog box, select how you want the printed image to be laid out on the paper. The image in the Orientation section shows a scaled view of the layout; the width and height boxes show the size of the printed image.

7. In the Margins section of the dialog box, enter the sizes of the margins.

8. In the Orientation section of the dialog box, select Portrait or Landscape.

9. Select the Header/Footer tab shown in Figure 38.37.

10. You can enter text or any combination of five fields of information into any of the three positions in the header and into any of the three positions in the footer. Enter fields by choosing the buttons near the bottom of the dialog box. Choose Font or Font to select a font name, style, and size for the header and footer. To reverse the order of the header and footer sections on even pages, check the Reverse on Even Pages box.

11. If you'd like to see an enlarged preview of a printed page, choose Print Preview. Outlook displays a typical page, such as that shown in Figure 38.38.

PART
VI

CH

38

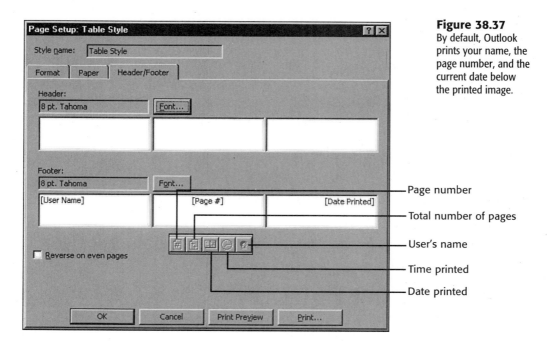

Figure 38.37
By default, Outlook prints your name, the page number, and the current date below the printed image.

Figure 38.38
You can enlarge the displayed page by choosing the Actual Size button 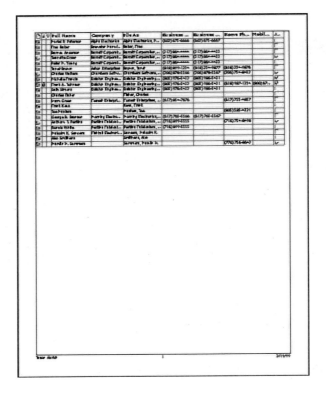 in the toolbar.

12. Choose Page Setup if you want to return to the Page Setup dialog box, or choose Print to print the table. If you choose Print, Outlook displays a dialog box such as that shown in Figure 38.39.

13. Most of the selections in this dialog box are similar to those available when you're printing other Windows documents. Notice that you can select All Rows or Only Selected Rows. Choose OK to print the table.

Selecting the Memo style and using it to print a table is similar to using a Table print style. The only significant difference is in the Print dialog box. Instead of selecting All Rows or Only Selected Rows, you can check two check boxes:

- Start Each Item on a New Page
- Print Attached Files with Item(s)

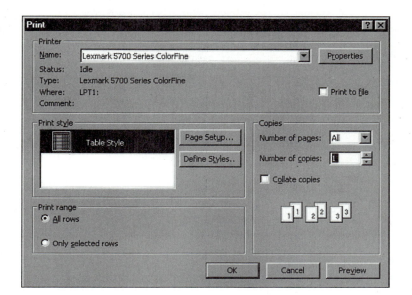

Figure 38.39
Your dialog box may be somewhat different from the one shown here, depending on the type of printer you're using.

Printing Calendar Views of Outlook Items

With the Day/Week/Month view of your calendar displayed in the Calendar Information viewer, you can print your daily, weekly, or monthly calendar (you can also print Calendar items using the Memo print style).

Note

Outlook 2000 has significantly improved calendar printing over previous Outlook versions. Whereas previous versions of Outlook truncated text that didn't fit into the available space in a calendar, Outlook 2000 automatically wraps text.

The Daily, Weekly, and Monthly print styles print calendars in almost the same way they appear in the Calendar Information viewer. Figures 38.40, 38.41, and 38.42 show previews of printed calendar pages.

Setting up the Daily, Weekly, or Monthly print style is much the same as setting up the Table print style, previously described in this chapter. One difference is in the Format tab of the Page Setup dialog box. Figure 38.43 shows the Format tab for the Daily print style.

Another difference is in the Print dialog box shown in Figure 38.44.

The Weekly and Monthly print styles have similar choices in the Page Setup and Print dialog boxes.

Figure 38.40
This is a preview of a typical calendar page printed using the Daily print style.

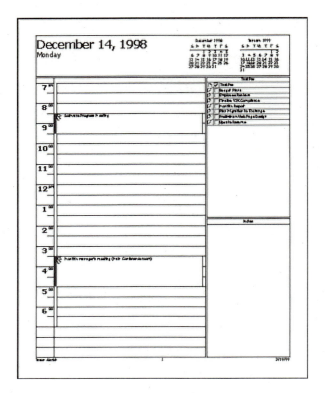

When you're using the Monthly print style, Outlook 2000 offers the ability to print exactly one month per page, something that wasn't available in previous versions of Outlook. Also, you have the choice of printing or not printing weekend days.

Tri-fold Style is another built-in print style for use with Calendar items. This style divides the printed page into three sections—you can choose what is displayed in each.

Figure 38.45 shows the Format tab of the Page Setup dialog box after you choose the Tri-fold style.

You can use this print style to print a calendar that provides a detailed view of your day in one panel, a summarized view of the month in another panel, and your to-do list in the third panel. Various other combinations are available.

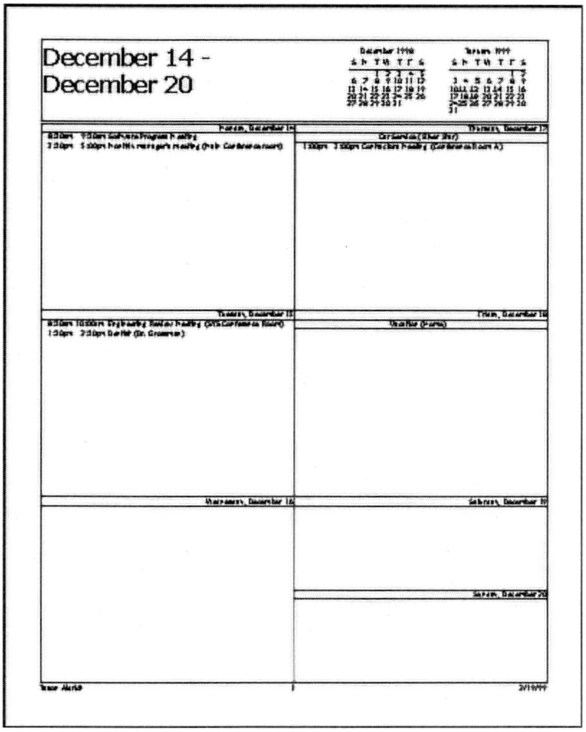

Figure 38.41
This is a preview of a typical calendar page printed using the Weekly print style.

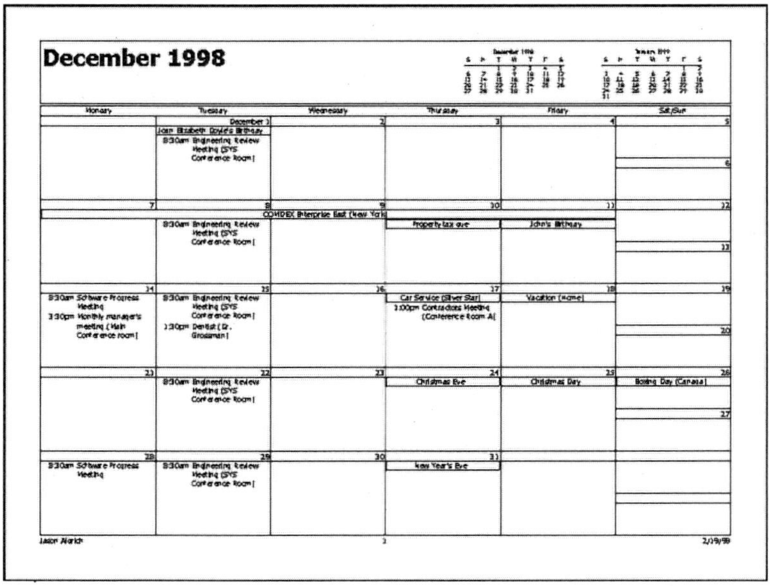

Figure 38.42
This is a preview of a typical calendar page printed using the Monthly print style.

Figure 38.43.
You can choose what you want to include in a printed daily calendar.

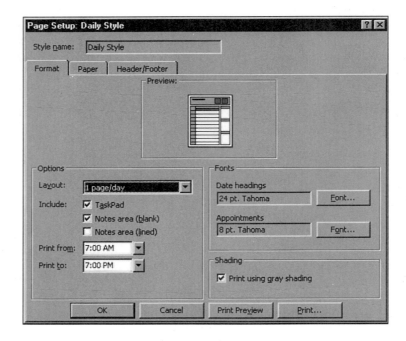

Figure 38.44
You can choose how many days of the calendar to print and whether to print items marked as private.

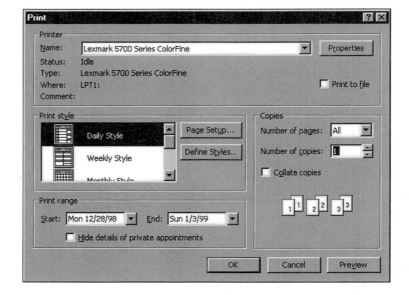

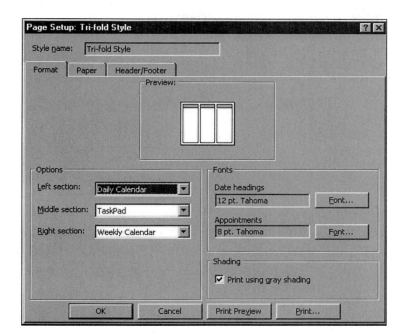

Figure 38.45
The Preview section at the top of this dialog box illustrates how the printed page is arranged in three sections.

PART

VI

CH

38

The Options section at the bottom-left of this dialog box is where you can select what goes into each section of the printed page. For example, if you open the Left Section drop-down list, you can choose among:

- Daily Calendar
- Weekly Calendar
- Monthly Calendar
- TaskPad
- Notes (blank)
- Notes (lined)

You can choose among the same items for the other two sections.

The Calendar Details Style is yet another built-in print style for calendars. This style prints details about one or more selected Calendar items. This print style is useful, for example, if you have an Appointment item for which you have entered a lot of notes. Using this print style, you can print all your notes on one or more pages, as shown in Figure 38.46.

Figure 38.46
This is the preview of
a page based on the
Calendar Details Style.

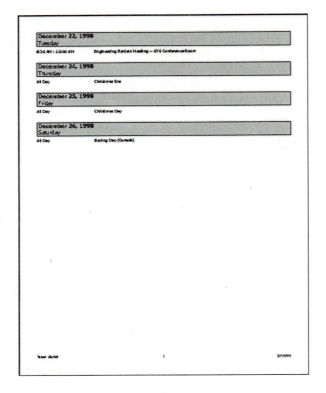

PRINTING CONTACT VIEWS OF OUTLOOK ITEMS

Just as Outlook has built-in views appropriate for Calendar items, so it has built-in views appropriate for Contact items. These are the Card, Small Booklet, Medium Booklet, and Phone Directory print styles (you can also print Contact items using the Memo print style).

You can use the Card print style to print Contact items as they might appear on traditional index cards. When you choose this style, the Page Setup dialog box's Format tab initially assumes you want to print contact information on ordinary paper, as shown in Figure 38.47.

You can make these determinations:

- Whether items follow one another in columns or each item starts a new page
- The number of columns on a page
- How many blank pages to print at the end (for you to temporarily pencil in new contacts)
- Whether you want letter tabs to be printed at the edge of pages
- Whether each alphabetical section should have a heading

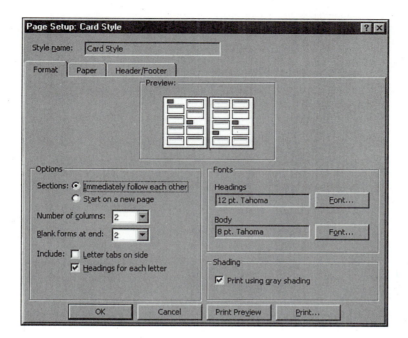

Figure 38.47
Use the Options section of this dialog box to specify how you want Contact items to be laid out on pages.

You can use the Paper tab of this dialog box to choose paper that is particularly appropriate for printing cards. In addition to standard paper sizes, you can select among several paper and card sizes suitable for printing cards, including standard index cards and various papers from Avery that can be used to print index cards on laser and inkjet printers.

The Small Booklet and Large Booklet print styles provide the capability to print contact items on pages with eight or four sections, so that the pages can be folded into booklet form.

The Phone Directory print style prints Contact items in a similar format to a typical phone book. You can choose how many columns are to be on a page.

CREATING CUSTOM PRINT STYLES

So far, you have seen how you can select a built-in print style, modify it somewhat, and use it to print Outlook items. But what if you want to use a modified version of a built-in print style regularly? You must be wondering if you have to repeat the modification each time you want to print items. No, you don't. You can solve this problem in two ways:

■ You can save the modified print style. In this case, you no longer have the original built-in print style.

■ You can save the modified print style as a custom print style. In that case you have both the original built-in print style and the modified print style.

To keep things simple, we'll use the Table print style as an example. However, what follows applies to all print styles.

To create a custom print style:

1. Display the Information viewer that contains the Outlook items for which you want to create a print style. Select the view you want to use as the basis for the new print style. For example, display the Contacts Information viewer and select the Phone List view.

2. Choose File, move the pointer onto Page Setup, and choose Define Print Styles to display the dialog box shown in Figure 38.48.

Figure 38.48
This dialog box lists the available print styles for the type of item and the view of that item you selected in step 1.

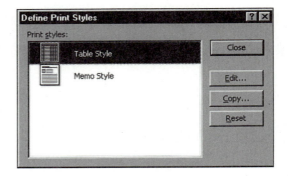

3. Select the print style, such as Table Style on which you want to base the custom view.

4. If you want to change the built-in view, choose Edit. If you want to create a new view based on the built-in view, choose Copy. After you choose Copy, Outlook displays the dialog box shown in Figure 38.49.

Note

If you had chosen Edit instead of Copy, the Style Name box would have contained the name of the built-in style (and would not be available for editing), instead of showing the print style as a copy of the built-in print style.

5. Edit the name in the Style Name box to create an appropriate name for your custom style.

6. Make whatever changes are necessary in the Format, Paper, and Header/Footer tabs of the Page Setup dialog box to create the new print style.

7. Choose OK to save the custom print style and return to the Define Print Styles dialog box, as shown in Figure 38.50.

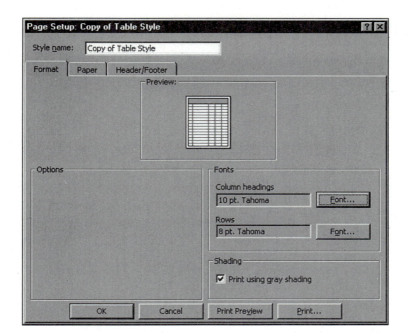

Figure 38.49
This dialog box is the same one you see when you're temporarily modifying a built-in print style.

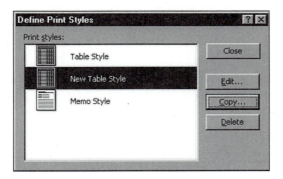

Figure 38.50
The new print style you created is now listed.

RESETTING AND DELETING PRINT STYLES

The Define Print Styles dialog box, previously shown in Figure 38.48, lists the built-in print styles and any custom print styles you've created. If you select a built-in print style, the bottom button is named Reset. After you've modified a built-in print style, you can choose that button to reset a built-in print style to its original state.

If you select a custom print style you've created, the bottom button is named Delete. You can choose that button to delete a custom print style.

USING OTHER APPLICATIONS AND UTILITIES TO PRINT OUTLOOK ITEMS

Although the variety of print styles provided by Outlook is extensive, you may have printing requirements that Outlook doesn't satisfy.

One way to obtain more printing flexibility is to export Outlook items into another application and use that application's printing capabilities. For example, you can export Outlook items into an Access table and then design an Access report that prints the Outlook items. Consult a book about Access, such as *Using Microsoft Access 2000*, for information about creating Access reports.

Tip #242 from

Gordon Pod....

> You can also use Seagate Crystal Reports Version 6.0 to print Outlook items. This report writer utility gives access to all the data fields in Outlook items, and provides much more flexibility in designing reports than is available in Outlook itself. You can find information about Crystal Reports at `http://www.seagatesoftware.com`.

TROUBLESHOOTING

While working with custom views, you must remember that each view you create is for items of a specific type. If you've created a custom view for your Inbox folder, that view can only be used for Mail items. In addition to using the new view for your Inbox folder, you can also use it for your Outbox and Sent Items folders, but not, for example, for your Calendar and Contacts folders. If you want to have a similar view for various types of Outlook items, you have to create separate views for the appropriate Outlook folders.

It's also important to remember that a custom view can be made available in three ways. If you, or someone else, can't find a view, that may be because, although the view exists, it's not available in the current circumstances. You can select:

- This Folder, Visible to Everyone—The view is available only in the folder in which it is created and is available to everyone who has permission to access the folder.

- This Folder, Visible Only to Me—The view is available only in the folder in which it is created, and only to the person who created the view.

- All Folders of a Specific Type—The view is available in all folders of a specific type. For example, if you create a view for Mail folders, you can select All Mail Folders so that the view is available in any folder that contains Mail items, and is available to everyone.

After you've created a view, you can't change its availability.

SECURITY CONSIDERATIONS

CHAPTER 39

USING OUTLOOK SECURELY

In this chapter *by Gordon Padwick*

STORING AND SHARING INFORMATION

Outlook provides facilities for saving and sharing information.

If you use Outlook on a standalone computer to which only you have access and which doesn't have a modem, your concerns about security are that Outlook accurately saves the information you enter and returns that information when you need it—and that no one steals your computer.

You probably don't use Outlook like that. If you use Outlook on a standalone computer, you probably have a modem and use Outlook to send and receive e-mail by way of the Internet or another e-mail service. If you use Outlook on a networked computer, you can share information in many ways.

When you use Outlook on a computer that's connected either by way of a phone line or a LAN to other computers, several issues arise. These include

- Can you be sure that information you want to keep private can't be accessed by other people?

- Can you be sure that information you want to share with other people is accessible only by those people with whom you want to share that information?

- When you send an e-mail message, can you be sure that message is received by, and only received by, the people to whom you addressed it?

- When people receive a message from you, can you be sure the message hasn't been tampered with?

- When you receive an e-mail message, can you be sure that message was actually sent by the person from whom it appears to be sent?

- When you receive an e-mail message, can you be sure the message hasn't been tampered with?

These and other questions are addressed in this chapter.

SECURING YOUR COMPUTER

There is no such thing as absolute security. However, there's a lot you can do to make your security close to impenetrable. The degree to which you are willing to adopt these measures depends on the value of the information stored on your computer and to which your computer has access.

Later in this chapter you'll read about *certificates*. It's particularly important to secure your computer if you have a certificate. If your computer is not secure, it's possible that other people can obtain copies of your certificate and then pass themselves off as you.

→ You can use certificates to authenticate and encrypt messages. **See** "Sending Secure Messages on the Internet," **p. 1002**.

PHYSICALLY SECURING YOUR COMPUTER

Physically securing your computer, in this case, means preventing unauthorized people from gaining access to it. If you're using a desktop computer, that might mean keeping it in a vault that's as difficult to get into as a bank's strongroom. In less demanding situations it's usually adequate to keep your computer in a room that's always locked when you're not there.

An alternative is to replace the hard drive in your computer with a removable hard drive. When you're finished working, you can remove the hard drive and either keep it with you or put it into a safe.

Note

You can't protect your data by deleting files from your hard disk because deleting removes only an index entry that points to where the data is stored. You, or someone else, can easily recover deleted files.

Laptop computers are a particular problem as far as security is concerned. Short of chaining the computer to your body, there's really no way to eliminate the possibility of the computer being stolen with all your valuable data on its hard disk. If you use a laptop and have data that must not be accessible to other people, make sure you keep that data only on a removable disk. Keep that disk in your personal possession, not plugged into the computer.

PART

VII

CH

39

PREVENTING ACCESS TO YOUR COMPUTER

The preceding section addressed the issues of preventing people from gaining access to your computer. Those methods are probably too extreme in most environments. What do you do if you live in a cubicle to which many people have access while you're at lunch or in a meeting?

One possibility is to use a so-called screen saver. While modern monitors don't seem to need any help to prevent ghost images being permanently registered on their screens, you can use a screen saver to blank out your screen while you're away from you computer. You, or someone else, can see the screen again only by entering a password.

While a screen saver can prevent a casual intruder from using your computer, it won't deter a skilled hacker.

Windows NT and Windows 98, unlike Windows 95, has a more effective way of preventing access to your computer. Running under Windows NT or Windows 98, you can set up accounts that can only be accessed by entering a username and password. This is in contrast to Windows 95, which uses a username and password only to determine a user's Windows settings.

Tip #243 from

Gordon Prod

The password security offered by Windows NT and Windows 98 is a very good reason to use those operating systems instead of Windows 95.

CREATING PRIVATE OUTLOOK ITEMS

When you create an Outlook item, you can mark that item as private. After doing so, the item is displayed just like any other Outlook item when you display Outlook items in an Information viewer. However, if someone else with whom you have shared your Outlook folder opens that folder, that person will see that the item exists but won't be able to see any information about it.

For example, if you allow your administrative assistant to have access to your Calendar, you can create an appointment and mark it private. Subsequently, your administrative assistant can see that you have blocked out time on your calendar, but cannot see the details of that item.

Tip #244 from	In C/W Outlook used as a client for an Exchange server, you can allow a delegate to see items you've marked as private. To do so, choose Tools, Options, and select the Delegates tab. Select a delegate, then choose Permissions. Check Delegate Can See My Private Items.

CONTROLLING ACCESS TO FOLDERS

Access to Outlook folders differs according to whether you're working with IMO Outlook or C/W Outlook.

WORKING WITH IMO OUTLOOK

If you're using IMO Outlook, you have access only to the Outlook folders within the Personal Folders files on the computer you're using. You can access this folder in the same way you can access other Windows files.

There's nothing to prevent anyone who has access to your computer from copying a Personal Folders file. As mentioned previously in this chapter, if you use Windows NT or Windows 98, you can protect all your files by requiring a password to start the operating system.

When you install IMO Outlook, a Personal Folders file with the name Outlook.pst is automatically created and has the standard Outlook folders. To examine the properties of the Personal Properties file, right-click Outlook Today in the Outlook Bar, and choose Properties in the context menu to display the Personal Folders Properties dialog box. Choose Advanced to display the dialog box shown in Figure 39.1.

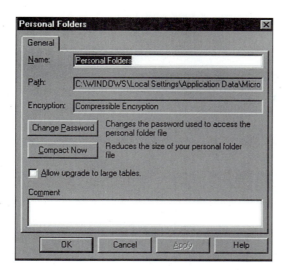

Figure 39.1
This dialog box displays information about your Personal Folders file.

This dialog box shows:

- The Name—Personal Folders—by which the file is known within Outlook. You can change that name from Personal Folders to something else.
- The Path of the file. You can't change that.
- The fact that Compressible Encryption is used to save Outlook items within the file. You can't change that.

Tip #245 from

[signature]

Although you can't change the encryption for the existing Personal Folders file, you can create another Personal Folders file and set it to Best Encryption. You can designate the new file as your default personal store.

→ For information about creating personal folders files and choosing one of them to be the default, **see** "Creating Additional Personal Folders Files," **p. 917** and "Designating a Default Outlook Store," **p. 919**.

Initially, Outlook creates your Personal Folders file without a password. To provide protection for your Outlook items saved in your Personal Folders file, you can protect the file with a password.

To protect your Personal Folders file with a password:

1. In the Personal Folders dialog box, choose Change Password to display the dialog box shown in Figure 39.2.

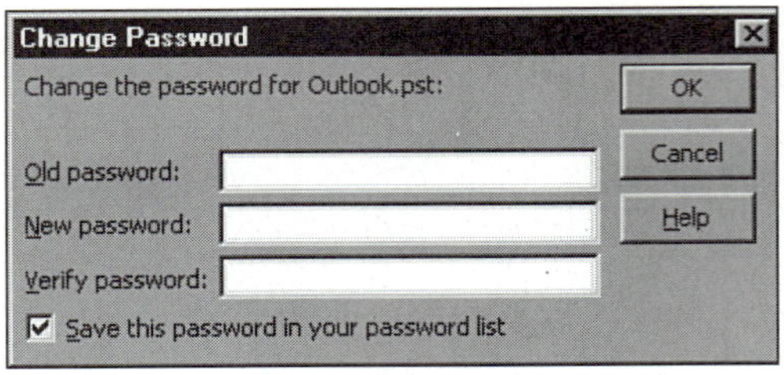

Figure 39.2
Use this dialog box to
designate a password.

2. If you haven't previously designated a password for your Personal Folders file, leave the Old Password box empty. If you have previously password-protected your Personal Folders file, enter that password in the Old Password box.

3. Enter the new password in the New Password box. Outlook remembers the characters you enter but displays asterisks in the box.

4. Enter the new password again in the Verify Password box.

Note

Passwords are case sensitive. You must enter the same combination of uppercase and lowercase characters in both boxes. Later, when you use the password to gain access to your Outlook items, you must use the correct combination of uppercase and lowercase characters.

5. Leave the Save This Password in Your Password List box unchecked. Choose OK. If you enter exactly the same characters in the New Password and Verify Password boxes, Outlook accepts the new password and closes the dialog box. If you don't enter the same characters in both boxes, Outlook tells you that both boxes must have the same content; you must correct that problem by reentering the password in both boxes.

6. Choose OK three times to close the dialog boxes.

7. Choose File, Exit to close Outlook.

The next time you start Outlook, you'll see the dialog box shown in Figure 39.3.

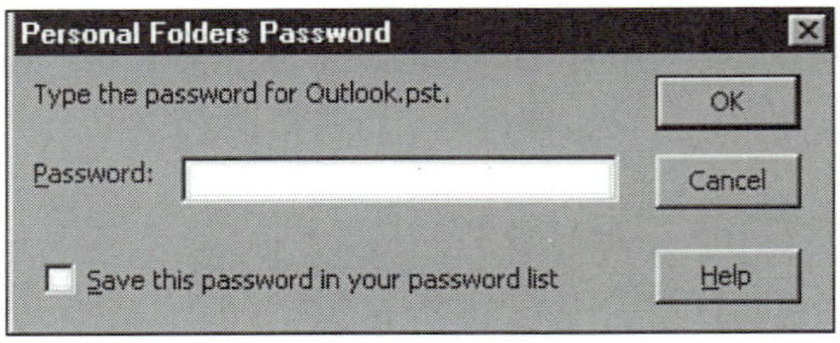

Figure 39.3
You must enter your
password before
Outlook will start.

Tip #246 from

If you enter the wrong password, Outlook displays a message about that. Choose OK to close the message box, then enter the correct password.

If you click outside the Personal Folders Password dialog box, that dialog box disappears and Outlook appears to freeze. Click the Personal Folders Password button in the Windows taskbar to redisplay the Personal Folders Password dialog box.

WORKING WITH C/W OUTLOOK

If you're using C/W Outlook, but not as a client for an Exchange server, the situation is much the same as for IMO Outlook, described in the preceding section.

If you're using C/W Outlook as a client for an Exchange server, you have access to any number of Personal Folders files and *Offline Folders files (page 731)* on your local hard drive, and also to any number of sets of Outlook folders within Exchange server stores. You can control access to any folder that you own in the Exchange store—your own Outlook folders and public folders for which you have Owner permissions.

→ For information about granting permission to access your Outlook folders and the public folders you own in the Exchange store, **see** "Delegating Access to Your Folders," **p. 691** and "Giving People Access to a Public Folder," **p. 707**.

PART
VII

CH
39

LOGGING ON

Outlook provides password protection for access to mail servers. If you're concerned about other people reading e-mail addressed to you, you should set up your e-mail accounts so a password is required before Outlook will connect to a mail server. In many cases, you don't have any choice about this because mail servers are usually set up to require a password.

LOGGING ON TO AN INTERNET MAIL SERVER

If you're running IMO Outlook and you have an Internet e-mail account, you can set up Outlook so it automatically supplies your password when you attempt to connect to the server, or so you have to provide the password each time you attempt to connect. Having Outlook automatically supply the password is convenient, but presents a security risk. If your computer is accessible to other people, it's generally better not to have Outlook automatically supply the password.

Note

Internet e-mail servers normally use the same account name and password for receiving and sending mail. If you're accessing a server that requires (or allows) separate names and passwords for receiving and sending, refer to the information about outgoing mail servers later in this section.

To have Outlook automatically supply a password for access to an Internet mail server:

1. Choose Tools, Accounts to display the Internet Accounts dialog box. With the Mail tab selected, select the Internet account for which you want to supply a password, then choose Properties and select the Servers tab, shown in Figure 39.4.

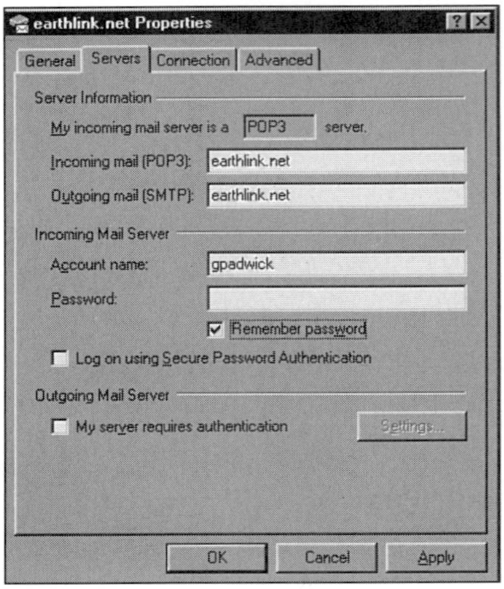

Figure 39.4
The Incoming Mail Server section of this dialog box is where you specify a password.

2. Enter your e-mail account password in the Password box.

3. Check Remember Password.

4. Choose OK to close the dialog box, then choose Close to close the Internet Accounts dialog box.

The next time you attempt to log on to your Internet e-mail server, you won't be asked for your name or password.

If you want the security protection provided by being asked for your password when you attempt to log on to your e-mail server, make sure Remember Password in the Properties dialog box shown in Figure 39.4 is not checked. After you do so, you'll see the dialog box shown in Figure 39.5 when you attempt to log on to your Internet account.

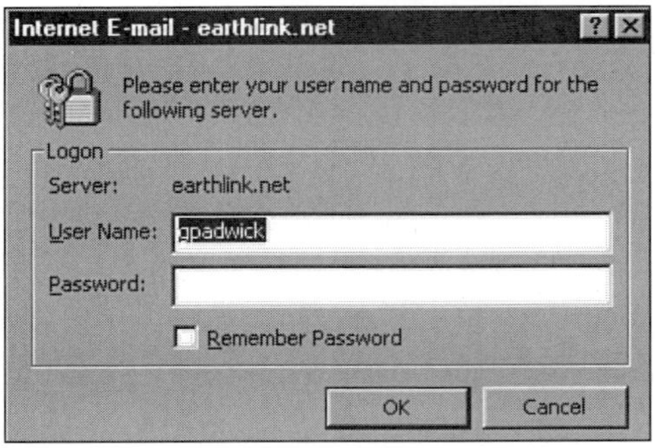

Figure 39.5
Enter your password in this dialog box to gain access to your Internet account.

Note If you access an Internet server that requires secure password authentication, select Log on Using Secure Password Authentication in the Properties dialog box, shown in Figure 39.4.

You can also set up the Internet E-mail information service to require a password before mail can be sent from the account. If you don't do that, anyone who has access to your computer can send a message that appears to recipients to be from you.

To require a password before Outlook will send Internet e-mail, check My Server Requires Authentication and then choose Settings to display the dialog box shown in Figure 39.6.

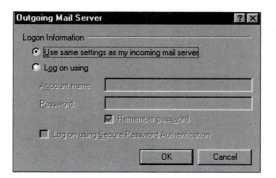

Figure 39.6
Make choices for outgoing e-mail in this dialog box in much the same way that you previously did for incoming e-mail.

PART
VII
CH
39

If you're running C/W Outlook, you set up an Internet e-mail account by adding an Internet E-mail information service to your profile. Do this in almost exactly the same way as described previously for IMO Outlook.

The only difference is the way you start. Replace the first step in the preceding section with this:

1. Choose Tools, Services to display the Services dialog box. In the Services tab, select the Internet e-mail information service, then choose Properties and select the Servers tab shown previously in Figure 39.4.

LOGGING ON TO AN EXCHANGE SERVER

If you're using C/W Outlook as a client for an Exchange server, by default when you start Outlook it automatically connects to Outlook folders in the Exchange store.

To require a password to access an Exchange server:

1. Choose Tools, Services to display the Services dialog box. Select the Microsoft Exchange Server information service and then choose Properties. Select the Advanced tab shown in Figure 39.7.

Figure 39.7
Use this dialog box to control access to the Exchange server.

By default, NT Password Authentication is displayed in the Logon Network Security box. This means that the same password you use to log on to your Windows NT server is used to log you on to your Exchange Server—convenient, but a possible security risk.

2. Open the drop-down Logon Network Security list and choose None.

3. Choose OK twice to close the dialog boxes. Choose File, Exit and Log Off to close Outlook.

The next time you start Outlook, you'll see the dialog box shown in Figure 39.8.

Figure 39.8
You must supply your Exchange password before Outlook will connect to the Exchange server.

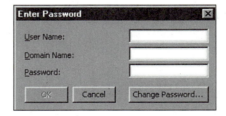

SENDING SECURE MESSAGES ON THE INTERNET

While the Internet is convenient to use, you might wonder how secure it is and what you can do to enhance the security of your Internet communications. For normal communications, the Internet seems to be at least as secure as postal mail. While it's not unusual to hear about mail being stolen from postal mailboxes, it's rare to hear about e-mail messages being stolen.

Note

This chapter covers only basic information about security on the Internet. For much more detailed information, consult books such as *Special Edition Using the Internet* (Chapter 41), published by Que, *Using Microsoft Internet Explorer 4.0* (Chapter 16), published by Que, and, for comprehensive information on the subject, to *Internet Security Professional Reference*, published by New Riders.

If the messages you send and receive contain confidential information, you should consider enhancing e-mail security by using a certificate. Outlook fully supports the use of certificates. Microsoft recommends VeriSign as a source of certificates, so this chapter focuses on certificates issued by that company. VeriSign calls certificates *Digital IDs*.

Note

Certificates rely on the *Secure Multipurpose Internet Mail Extensions* (S/MIME) protocol that Outlook supports. You can send secure e-mail messages to, and receive secure e-mail messages from, people who use Outlook or other e-mail programs that support S/MIME. E-mail programs that support S/MIME include Outlook, Outlook Express, Netscape Messenger, Deming, Frontier, Pre-mail, Opensoft, Connectsoft, and Eudora.

For detailed information about using VeriSign Digital IDs with Outlook, refer to the article "Personal IDs for Outlook Users," available at

`http://www.verisign.com/securemail/outlook98/outlook.html`.

Understanding Certificates

A certificate serves two purposes: authentication and encryption.

- Authentication means that you can send messages to other people and those people can have a high level of confidence that the messages they receive really are from you, and that those messages haven't been tampered with in any way. Authentication also means other people can send messages to you and you can have the same confidence that the messages you receive are really from the apparent senders and are the messages those people actually sent.

- Encryption is the process of converting plain text into an encoded form. If you have a certificate, you can encrypt your messages so that only a recipient who knows how to decrypt those messages can read them. Likewise, other people can send encrypted messages to you.

When you receive a certificate, you get two keys: your private key and your public key. The private key is just that—*private*. It's an entry in the Windows registry on your computer that's protected by a password. Your private key is created on your computer and resides only there. It is not known to the organization or person who issued the certificate. Your private key is used to create digital signatures and to decrypt messages encrypted with the corresponding public key.

The public key, on the other hand, is a file you can make freely available to other people. You must provide your public key to people before they can send you encrypted messages. Your public key is used to encrypt messages that can be decrypted by your private key.

Note The private key and matching public key are sometimes referred to as a *key pair*.

After you've installed a certificate on your computer, you're ready to send secure mail. If you want to send encrypted mail to someone, you must have that person's public key.

- When you send a message secured by your certificate, a recipient who uses an e-mail program that supports S/MIME can verify the message is really from you and hasn't been tampered with by anyone else.
- When people send you messages secured by their certificates, you can verify the message is really from the apparent sender and hasn't been tampered with.
- To send an encrypted message a recipient can decrypt, you must have the recipient's public key in the Contact item for that recipient in your Contacts folder.
- In order for other people to send you encrypted messages you can decrypt, those people must have your public key.

OBTAINING A CERTIFICATE

You can use Outlook to obtain a certificate from VeriSign, either a 60-day trial version at no cost, or on a subscription basis which, at the time this book was written, was available for around $10 per year.

To get a certificate from VeriSign, you have to connect to VeriSign's Web site. You must, of course, have Outlook set up to connect to the Internet.

Note VeriSign uses the term *Digital ID* as a brand name for certificates.

To obtain a VeriSign Digital ID:

1. With any Outlook Information viewer displayed, choose Tools, Options and select the Security tab shown in Figure 39.9.
2. Choose Get a Digital ID. Outlook accesses your ISP and connects you to a VeriSign Web page.
3. Follow the instructions there to apply for either an evaluation or annual subscription to a Digital ID and for installing that Digital ID on your computer.

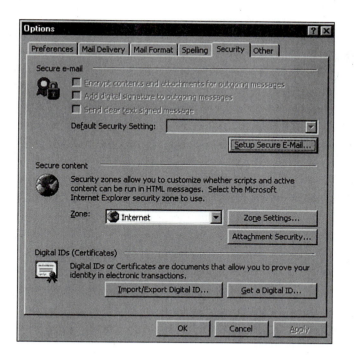

Figure 39.9
The Security tab pro-
vides access to
Outlook's security
options.

Note

A short while after you apply for a Digital ID, you'll receive an e-mail message confirming that your application has been accepted and instructing you how to proceed. You must install the Digital ID on the same computer you used to apply for the Digital ID. As explained subsequently in this chapter, you can move your Digital ID from one computer to another.

SETTING THE SECURITY LEVEL FOR YOUR PRIVATE KEY

During the process of installing your private key, you'll be asked to select a security level. Three security levels are available:

- High—Choose this if you want to password-protect your private key. You'll be asked for the password each time you use your private key.

- Medium—Choose this if you don't want to password-protect your private key. Outlook displays a message each time you use your private key.

- Low—Choose this if you want to be able to use your private key without being asked for a password and without Outlook displaying a message.

MAKING A BACKUP COPY OF YOUR DIGITAL ID

There are two reasons why you would want to make a backup copy of your Digital ID:

- So that you can restore your Digital ID if it becomes corrupted on your hard disk
- So that you can move your Digital ID to another computer or hard disk

You should normally save a copy of your Digital ID on a floppy disk and keep that disk in a secure place.

To make a copy of your Digital ID:

1. With any Outlook Information viewer displayed, choose Tools, Options to display the Options dialog box and select the Security tab, shown previously in Figure 39.9.

2. Choose Import/Export Digital ID to display the dialog box shown in Figure 39.10.

Figure 39.10
You can use this dialog box to import a previously saved Digital ID as well as to export the Digital ID on your computer.

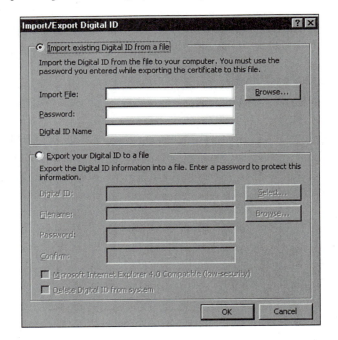

3. Select Export Your Digital ID to a File.

4. Choose Select to display a dialog box similar to that shown in Figure 39.11.

5. Select the Digital ID you want to save.

6. If you want to see information about the Digital ID, you can choose View Certificate. This step isn't required.

7. Choose OK to return to the Import/Export Security Information and Digital ID dialog box that now has the name of the Digital ID you selected in step 5 displayed in the Digital ID box.

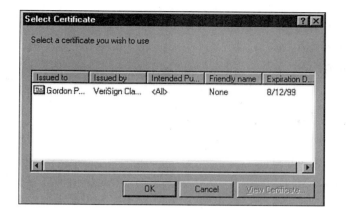

Figure 39.11
This dialog box lists information about your installed certificates.

8. Enter a full path name for the exported file in the Export File box. Alternatively, you can choose Browse, navigate to a disk, and enter a name for the exported file.

9. Enter a Password for the exported file into the Password box. Enter the password again into the Confirm box.

10. Unless you want your Digital ID to be compatible with the low-security protocol of Internet Explorer 4.0, leave the Microsoft Internet Explorer 4.0 Compatible box unchecked.

11. Choose OK to display the dialog box shown in Figure 39.12.

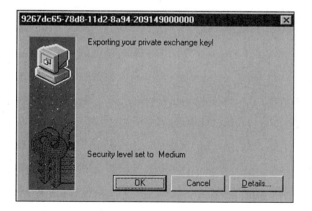

Figure 39.12
This dialog box states the security level of the private key you're about to export.

12. Choose OK to create the exported file. After a short delay, the Outlook Options dialog box reappears. Outlook saves the file with .pfx as its file name extension.

Tip #247 from

Gordon Pool

If someone else gains access to the backup copy of your Digital ID, that person could import your Digital ID onto another computer. For that reason, it's important to protect the backup file with a password and to keep the backup disk in a secure place.

REMOVING YOUR DIGITAL ID FROM A COMPUTER

When the time comes to replace your hard disk with another one, you must remember to remove your Digital ID from the old disk. Otherwise, if someone else inherits your old hard disk, that person also inherits your Digital ID. Likewise, if you replace your computer with a new one, remember to remove your Digital ID before you pass your old computer on to someone else.

To remove your Digital ID, follow the first seven steps in the preceding procedure. Then select Delete Digital ID from System, and choose OK.

Tip #248 from

Gordon Pool

"Removing" doesn't really remove information from your hard disk—it just makes that information inaccessible by normal means. Techniques are available to recover information you may have removed.

In high-security environments, any disk that contains, or has contained, confidential information that's removed from a computer should be physically destroyed to avoid any possibility that information can be recovered.

IMPORTING YOUR DIGITAL ID FROM A BACKUP DISK

The process of importing your Digital ID from a backup disk in similar to the process of exporting your Digital ID.

To import your Digital ID:

1. With any Outlook Information viewer displayed, choose Tools, Options to display the Options dialog box and select the Security tab, shown previously in Figure 39.9.

2. Choose Import/Export Digital ID to display the dialog box previously shown in Figure 39.10.

3. Select Import Existing Digital ID from a File.

4. In the Import File box, enter the full path name of the file you want to import. Alternatively, choose Browse, navigate to the disk that contains the file, select the file, and choose Open to return to the Import/Export Security Information and Digital ID dialog box, as shown in Figure 39.13.

5. In the Password box, enter the password of the saved file.

6. In the Digital ID Name box, enter the name by which you want Outlook to refer to your Digital ID. You can use any name, but your own name or mailbox name are appropriate.

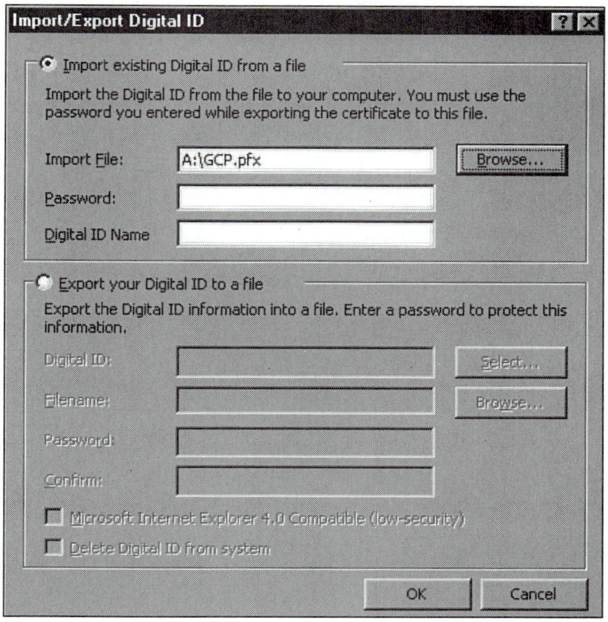

Figure 39.13
The dialog box now contains the path name of the file to be imported.

ADDING DIGITAL ID BUTTONS TO THE MESSAGE FORM'S TOOLBAR

You can add two Digital ID buttons to the Message form's Standard toolbar. After doing so, you can readily see whether your digital signature and encryption are turned on or off, and also enable and disable those options.

To add Digital ID buttons to the Message form's Standard toolbar:

1. With the Inbox Information viewer displayed, choose New in the Standard toolbar to display the Message form.

2. Choose View, move the pointer onto Toolbars, and choose Customize. Select the Commands tab, scroll down the Categories box and select Standard, as shown in Figure 39.14.

3. Scroll down to the bottom of the list of commands.

4. Drag the Encrypt Message Contents and Attachments command into the Message form's Standard toolbar, just to the right of the Office Assistant button.

5. Drag the Digitally Sign Message command into the Message form's Standard toolbar, just to the right of the Encrypt Message Contents and Attachments button.

6. Choose Close to close the Customize dialog box. The Message form's Standard toolbar now contains the two added buttons, as shown in Figure 39.15.

Figure 39.14
The right box contains a list of commands in the Standard category.

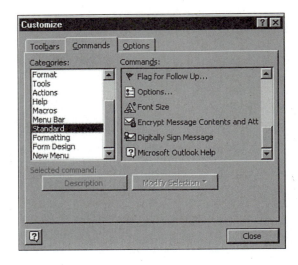

Figure 39.15
This is the Message form's Standard tool-bar with the two Digital ID buttons added.

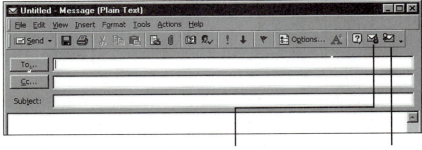

Encrypt message contents and attachments   Digitally sign message

When encryption and digital signing is turned off, the two buttons have a normal gray background. The buttons have a bright background when those options are enabled. Click a button to change from disabled to enabled and vice versa.

SENDING AND RECEIVING DIGITALLY SIGNED MESSAGES

You can set up Outlook so that the default is to send all your messages with a digital signature, or the default is to send all your messages without a digital signature. Whichever you choose as the default, you can turn the digital signature off or on for each message.

CHOOSING DIGITAL SIGNATURES AS THE DEFAULT

If you expect to digitally sign most of the messages you send, you should set this as a default.

To set digital signing as the default:

1. With any Outlook Information viewer displayed, choose <u>T</u>ools, <u>O</u>ptions to display the Options dialog box. Select the Security tab shown in Figure 39.16.

Figure 39.16
When you have a Digital ID installed, the Secure E-mail section of this dialog box is enabled.

2. Check A<u>d</u>d Digital Signature to Outgoing Messages.

3. If you want people who use e-mail applications that don't support *S/MIME (page 1003)* signatures to be able to read your messages, check Send Clear <u>T</u>ext Signed Messages.

Note

If you leave the Send Clear Text Signed Messages unchecked, only recipients who use an e-mail application that supports S/MIME signatures will be able to read your messages. Those people will also be able to verify that the message actually came from you and has not been tampered with.

If you check the Send Clear Text Signed Messages box, all recipients (whether they use an application that supports S/MIME or not) will be able to read your messages. Recipients who don't use an application that supports S/MIME won't be able to verify that the message actually came from you, nor can they be certain the message hasn't been tampered with.

EXAMINING AND CHANGING SECURITY SETTINGS

Your Digital ID has certain security settings. You can examine and change these settings by choosing Change Settings (in the Security tab of the Options dialog box) to display the dialog box shown in Figure 39.17.

Figure 39.17
You can use this dialog box to change your security settings and to create new settings.

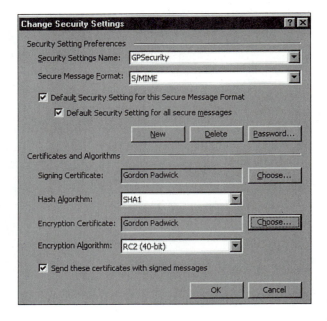

To change the Digital ID settings:

1. If you want to change the default name of your security settings, edit the name in the Security Settings Name box.

2. The default Secure Message Format is S/MIME, which is what you want if you're going to send and receive secure mail by way of the Internet or an intranet.

Note

If you're using C/W Outlook as a client for an Exchange server and will be using that messaging system, open the drop-down Secure Message Format list and select Exchange Server Security.

3. Leave Default Security Setting for This Secure Message Format checked to make the current security settings the default for the format shown in the Secure Message Format box.

4. Leave Default Security Setting for All Secure Messages checked to make the current security settings the default if you use Exchange and S/MIME.

5. If you want to create another security setting, choose New. Outlook removes the name in the Security Settings Name box. Enter a name for the new setting in that box and choose a Secure Message Format.

6. If you want to delete a security setting, select that setting and choose <u>D</u>elete.

7. By default, the Signing Certificate box contains the name of your Digital ID. If you have more than one Digital ID, choose <u>C</u>hoose to open the Select a Certificate dialog box, in which you can select the certificate you want to use for signing messages in the current set of security settings.

8. Leave the Hash Algorithm as the default SHA-1.

9. By default, the Encryption Certificate box contains the name of your Digital ID. If you have more than one Digital ID, choose C<u>h</u>oose to open the Select a Certificate dialog box, in which you can select the certificate you want to use for encrypting messages in the current security settings.

10. Leave the Encryption Algorithm as the default.

11. If you want to send your *public key (page 1004)* with messages, check the S<u>e</u>nd These Certificates with Signed Messages box. You should check this box if you want people to whom you send messages to be able to send you encrypted messages. This box is not available if you select Exchange Server Security as the Secure Message Format.

CREATING NEW SECURITY SETTINGS

PART
VII
CH
39

The preceding section assumed you needed just one set of security settings. You can have more than one set.

Starting from the Security tab in the Options dialog box, choose Change Settings to display the Change Security Settings dialog box shown previously in Figure 39.16. In that dialog box, choose Create <u>N</u>ew to clear all the boxes. You can now follow the steps in the preceding procedure to name and select security settings for another set.

When you have two or more named sets of security settings, you can open the drop-down Security Settings Name list to select the set you want to use.

DELETING A SET OF SECURITY SETTINGS

To delete a set of security settings, select that set as explained in the preceding section, then choose <u>D</u>elete Setting.

SENDING A DIGITALLY SIGNED MESSAGE

When you send a digitally signed message, that message contains your digital signature. The message recipient who uses an e-mail program that supports *S/MIME (page 1003)* can examine that signature to verify the message actually came from you. This works because only a computer on which your Digital ID is installed can send a message that contains your digital signature.

A digitally signed message contains the original message and an encrypted version of that message. When the message is received by a computer on which the e-mail program supports S/MIME, the original message and encrypted message are compared to make sure they are identical. Any difference between the two indicates that the message has been tampered with.

After you've set the default to send messages with a digital signature, create a message to be sent in the normal way. The Message form's Standard toolbar contains a button you can use to turn a digital signature on or off, as shown previously in Figure 39.15.

If you've set the default to send all messages with a digital signature, the Digitally Sign Message button has a bright background. To send the current message without a digital signature, click the button—the bright background disappears, signifying that the digital signature is turned off.

→ You can also enable and disable your digital signature by checking or unchecking the Add Digital Signature to Outgoing Message box in the Message Options dialog box. **See** "Choosing Digital Signatures as the Default," **p. 1010**.

If you've set the default to send all messages without a digital signature, the Digitally Sign Message button doesn't have a bright background. To send the current message with a digital signature, click the button—the bright background appears, signifying that the digital signature is turned on.

> **Note**
>
> If you use the Microsoft Outlook *Rich Text (page 183)* format to create a message and send that message as a secure message using your S/MIME digital signature, Outlook automatically changes the message format to *HTML (page 183)* to ensure the correct processing of your digital signature. As a result, some of the message formatting may be lost. The format change occurs when you choose Send in the Message form.
>
> Messages you create in *Plain Text (page 183)* format are sent in Plain Text format. Messages you create in HTML format are sent in HTML format.

 After you've sent a digitally signed message, you can see that message in your Sent Items folder. It is identified as a message that was sent with a digital signature by the red ribbon on the message symbol. Also, if you open the sent message in a Message form, the header contains the red ribbon.

RECEIVING DIGITALLY SIGNED MESSAGES

Some of the people to whom you send digitally signed messages may be using an e-mail program that supports S/MIME, others may not. Three possibilities exist:

- A recipient uses an e-mail application that supports S/MIME
- A recipient uses an e-mail application that doesn't support S/MIME and you haven't checked Send Clear Text Signed Message in the Security tab of the Options dialog box
- A recipient uses an e-mail application that doesn't support S/MIME and you have checked Send Clear Text Signed Message in the Security tab of the Options dialog box

The preceding section described the Send Clear Test Signed Message option.

RECEIVING A DIGITALLY SIGNED MESSAGE ON A COMPUTER THAT SUPPORTS S/MIME

The Inbox Information viewer initially displays the header for a secure message with a red ribbon superimposed on the message symbol. When you select the message header, the Preview pane's header contains a red ribbon near its right edge.

Note

The Inbox Information viewer always indicates that received secure messages have an attachment. As explained previously, a secure message contains the original message and an encrypted version of that message. The attachment is actually the encrypted version of the message.

You can double-click the message to display it in the Message form, as shown in Figure 39.18.

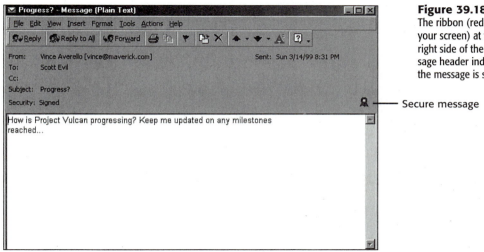

Figure 39.18
The ribbon (red on your screen) at the right side of the message header indicates the message is secure.

Secure message

PART

VII

CH

39

If you want to verify the identity of the sender, follow these steps:

To verify a sender's identity:

1. With the received message displayed in a Message form, choose File, Properties to display the Security Properties dialog box. Select the Security tab shown in Figure 39.19.

Note

All five items in this dialog box should be checked if the message is fully authenticated.

Figure 39.19
This dialog box con-
firms, or does not con-
firm, the authenticity
of the message.

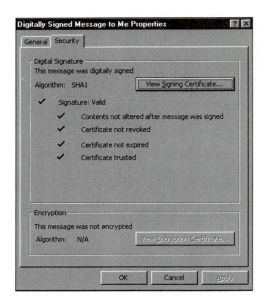

2. To obtain more information about the sender, choose View Signing Certificate to display the View Certificate dialog box, in which you can examine information about the
sender's Digital ID.

Tip #249 from

As an alternative to those two steps, you can choose the red ribbon in the message form's
header to display a dialog box that's similar to the one shown in Figure 39.19.

RECEIVING A DIGITALLY SIGNED MESSAGE ON A COMPUTER THAT DOES NOT SUPPORT S/MIME

Two possibilities exist, depending on how the sender set up Outlook, to send digitally
signed messages.

- If the sender chose to send the message with Send Clear Text Signed Messages not
enabled, recipients who use an e-mail program that does not support S/MIME to
receive messages are not able to read digitally signed messages.

- If the sender chose to send the message with Send Clear Text Signed Messages
enabled, recipients who use an e-mail program that does not support S/MIME are able
to read digitally signed messages, but are not able to verify the authenticity of those
messages.

→ For information about setting up Outlook with Send Clear Text Signed Messages enabled, **see**
"Choosing Digital Signatures as the Default," **p. 1010**.

SENDING AND RECEIVING ENCRYPTED MESSAGES

Sending an encrypted message is much like sending a secure message. However, you must have a person's public key in your Contacts folder to send an encrypted message to that person. This is because the encryption is based on information in the recipient's Digital ID.

GETTING PUBLIC KEYS

You must have a person's public key in order to send a secure message. For example, if you want to send an encrypted message to John Aldrich, you must have John Aldrich's public key and add that key to the John Aldrich item in your Contacts folder. The following paragraphs explain how you obtain the public key and add that key to a Contact item.

GETTING A PUBLIC KEY FROM ANOTHER PERSON

The easiest way to get another person's public key is to ask that person to send you a message that includes that person's public key. When you receive that message, proceed as follows.

To add a public key to an existing Contact item or create a new Contact item that contains a public key:

1. Double-click the message that contains the sender's public key to display that message in a Message form.
2. Right-click the sender's name in the Message form to display a context menu.
3. Choose <u>A</u>dd to Contacts to display a Contact form that shows the sender's name and e-mail address. Select the Certificates tab shown in Figure 39.20.

PART

VII

CH

39

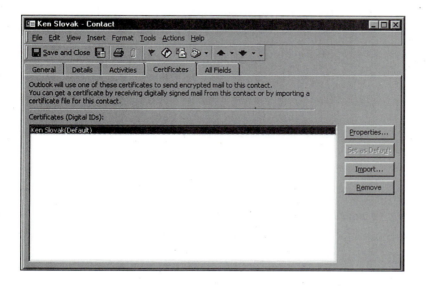

Figure 39.20
The Certificates tab contains the name of the sender's Digital ID.

4. Choose Save and Close to save the Contact item that contains the sender's public key. If a Contact item for the sender already exists, Outlook displays the Duplicate Contact Detected dialog box in which you can select whether you want to create a new Contact item or update the existing item by adding the certificate to it.

After following these steps, you have the sender's public key that you can use to send encrypted messages to that person.

DOWNLOADING A PUBLIC KEY

You can obtain public keys from the VeriSign Web page (`https://digitalid.verisign.com/services/client/index.htm`) shown in Figure 39.21.

Figure 39.21
Use this page to spec-ify the e-mail address of the person whose public key you need.

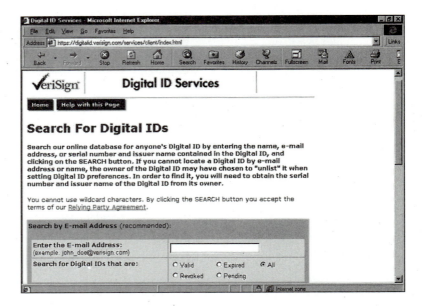

To download someone's public key:

1. Enter the person's e-mail address in the first box.

2. Choose Valid—only valid public keys are of any use to you.

3. Choose Search (not shown in the figure). After several seconds, the name of the person you're searching for is displayed.

4. Click the person's name to display a page that contains detailed information. Scroll to the bottom of that page and choose Download. The page shown in Figure 39.22 is dis-played.

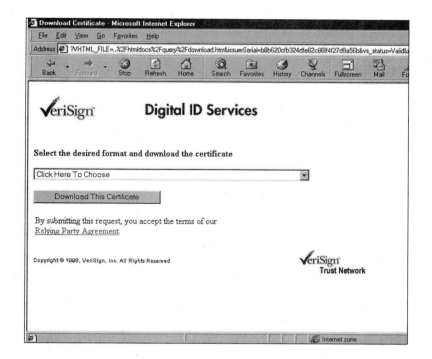

Figure 39.22
Be sure to select the
format you need
before downloading
the public key.

5. Open the Click Here To Choose drop-down list and select Someone Else's Digital ID for Microsoft IE (4.0 or Later)/Outlook Express/Outlook.

6. Choose Download This Certificate. The File Download dialog box proposes to Save This File to Disk, which is what you want to do. Choose OK to open the Save As dialog box.

7. Navigate to the folder in which you want to save the public key, change the File Name to the contact's name, and choose OK. A moment later, a Download Complete message appears. Choose OK.

You have to repeat these steps to obtain the public key for every person to whom you want to send encrypted messages.

The next step is to add the public key to a *Contact item (page 298)*.

To add a public key to a Contact item:

1. Open Outlook and choose Contacts in the Outlook Bar.

2. Locate the Contact item to which you want to add a public key.

3. Double-click the Contact item to open the item in a Contact form. Select the Certificates tab shown in Figure 39.23.

Figure 39.23
The Certificates (Digital IDs) box is initially empty.

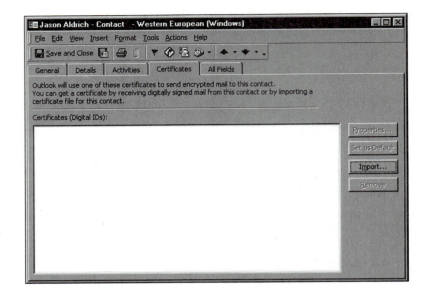

4. Choose Import to display the Locate Security Profile dialog box.

5. Navigate to the folder in which you saved the public key you previously downloaded.

6. Select the public key for the contact and choose Open. The public key is now listed in the Certificates (Digital IDs) box and the Properties button becomes available.

7. You can choose Properties to display information about the public key. This step is not required.

8. Choose Save and Close to save the Contact item.

IMPORTING PUBLIC KEYS FROM OUTLOOK EXPRESS

If, prior to using Outlook, you've been using Outlook Express to send secure messages, you have one or more public keys in your Outlook Express address book. When you import that address book into Outlook, public keys are not imported with the rest of the contact information. You have to import each public key separately.

To export a public key from Outlook Express:

1. In Outlook Express, choose Tools, Address Book to display a dialog box such as the one shown in Figure 39.24.

2. Double-click the contact whose public key you want to export to display that contact's properties. Select the Digital IDs tab.

Tip #250 from

Gordon Padwick

If you have more than one entry in your Outlook Express Address Book for a contact, make sure you select the one that contains the contact's public key.

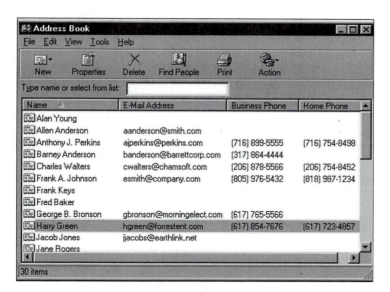

Figure 39.24
The Outlook Express address book lists your contacts. Those whose public keys you already have are marked with red ribbons.

3. Select the public key you want to export, then choose Export.

4. Enter the full path name for the file in which you want to save the exported public key, then choose Save. Outlook Express saves the file.

Note

Outlook Express automatically provides the file name extension .cer.

→ After you've exported a public key from Outlook Express, use the procedure described previously in this chapter to add that public key to the appropriate Outlook Contact item. **See** "Downloading a Public Key," **p. 1018**.

CHANGING THE TRUST STATUS OF A PUBLIC KEY

When you import someone's public key into that person's contact item, that public key has a trust status associated with it. Ideally, you should be able to absolutely trust Digital IDs, but that isn't necessarily the case.

To trust a Digital ID, you must have complete confidence that:

- The Digital ID was properly issued. This means that the issuing authority verified the identity of the person to whom the Digital ID was issued, never issues the same Digital ID to more than one person, and keeps Digital IDs completely confidential.

- The person to whom the Digital ID was issued makes sure no one else can obtain a copy of that Digital ID.

When a Digital ID is issued by a trusted certifying authority such as VeriSign, you can be sure that the Digital ID was properly issued. Only if the person to whom the Digital ID was issued installed it on a secure computer and, if a backup is made, that backup is kept in a secure place, can you be sure that the Digital ID can be trusted.

Note

Individual people usually get their Digital IDs from a reliable certifying authority such as VeriSign. However, you may come across Digital IDs issued by individuals or organizations you don't necessarily trust.

Three trust status levels are available:

- Inherit Trust from Issuer—This, the default, provides the same trust status as the one associated with the organization or person who issued the person's Digital ID.
- Explicitly Trust This Certificate—This trust status says that you trust the source, irrespective of who issued the person's Digital ID.
- Explicitly Don't Trust This Certificate—This trust status says that you distrust the source, irrespective of who issued the person's Digital ID.

To examine or change the trust status of a public key after you've added it to a Contact item:

1. With the Contacts Information viewer displayed, double-click the contact to display it in a Contact form. Choose the Certificates tab and select the public key, as previously shown in Figure 39.23, though this time with one or more certificates listed.

2. Choose Properties to display the Certificate Properties dialog box. Select the Trust tab shown in Figure 39.25.

Figure 39.25
This dialog box shows the trust status of the Digital ID.

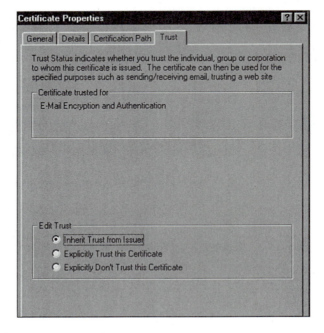

3. To change the trust status, choose the appropriate option button in the Edit Trust section near the bottom of the dialog box.

SENDING AN ENCRYPTED MESSAGE

To send an encrypted message, create the message in the usual way. In the Message form, choose the Encrypt Message Contents and Attachments button on the Standard toolbar, shown previously in Figure 39.10, then send the message in the normal way.

Note

You can also enable or disable encryption by checking or unchecking the Encrypt Message Contents and Attachments button in the Message Options dialog box.

After you send an encrypted message, you can see that message in the Sent Items Information viewer. The message symbol is marked with the blue padlock to indicate it was sent as an encrypted message.

If you double-click the message to display it in a Message form, the form's header contains the blue padlock to indicate that the message was sent encrypted.

RECEIVING AN ENCRYPTED MESSAGE

When you receive an encrypted message, the message header appears in your Inbox Information viewer with a blue padlock symbol superimposed on the message icon. When you select the message header, the Preview pane doesn't display the message; instead it states "Encrypted or encoded messages cannot be shown in the Preview Pane. Open the message to read it." After you double-click the message header to display it in the Message form, a blue padlock symbol at the right side of the form's header indicates that the message was encrypted.

Note

Encrypted messages can be decrypted only if you're using e-mail software, such as Outlook, that supports S/MIME.

USING SECURITY ZONES

Incoming e-mail messages and Web pages you access can contain scripts that run on your computer. While most of these scripts are useful, some may either accidentally or deliberately damage files on your hard disk. By taking advantage of security zones, you can control what happens when you receive messages or access Web pages that contain scripts. By choosing an appropriate zone for each Web page you access, you can prevent potentially damaging content from being downloaded, or receive a warning before potentially damaging content is downloaded.

You can choose among four zones:

- Local Intranet Zone—For sites on a local intranet that you trust.
- Trusted Sites Zone—For sites outside your local intranet that you trust.
- Internet Zone—For most Web sites.
- Restricted Sites Zone—For sites you don't trust.

By default, each zone has a security level assigned to it, as listed in Table 39.1.

TABLE 39.1 DEFAULT SECURITY LEVELS FOR ZONES

Zone	Security Level
Local Intranet Zone	Medium
Trusted Sites Zone	Low
Internet Zone	Medium
Restricted Sites Zone	High

You can change the security level for any zone.

The effect of each security level is defined in Table 39.2.

TABLE 39.2 EFFECTS OF SECURITY LEVELS

Level	Effect
High	All potentially damaging content is not downloaded to your computer.
Medium	Outlook warns you before running any potentially damaging content.
Low	Outlook accepts potentially damaging content without giving you any warning.
Custom	It's up to you to specify how Outlook handles potentially damaging content.

You're probably wondering exactly what type of potentially damaging content security levels are concerned with and exactly what zones do about potentially damaging content.

The message content and other activities that security levels detect are listed in these categories:

- ActiveX controls and plug-ins
- Cookies
- Downloads
- Java

- Miscellaneous
- Scripting
- User authentication

CHANGING THE SECURITY LEVEL FOR A ZONE

You can change the security level for each zone to other than the default. For example, you may have such complete confidence in your local intranet that you want to change its security level to Low.

To change the security level of a zone:

1. In the Options dialog box, select the Security tab, shown previously in Figure 39.10.

2. Choose Zone Settings. Outlook displays a warning message about changing security settings. Choose OK to display the dialog box shown in Figure 39.26.

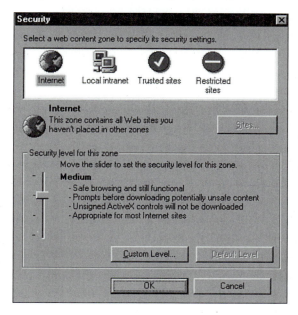

Figure 39.26
This is the dialog box you use to work with zones.

3. Select one of the four zones in the box at the top of the dialog box.

4. Move the slider at the left side of the box to set the security level for that zone.

5. To customize the security level, choose Custom Level to display the dialog box shown in Figure 39.27.

6. Select Disable, Enable, or Prompt for each security setting. Alternatively, you can open the Reset To drop-down list and select a preset combination.

Figure 39.27
This is the beginning of a list of available security settings.

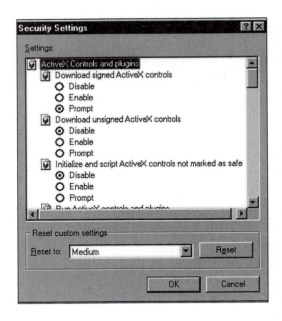

RESTORING A ZONE'S DEFAULT SECURITY LEVEL

To restore a zone's security level to the default, choose Default Level.

ASSIGNING WEB SITES TO ZONES

When you first start using Outlook, no Web sites are assigned to any zones. By default, Outlook assumes the use of the Internet Zone, so you are warned before Outlook runs any potentially damaging content.

ASSIGNING SITES TO THE LOCAL INTRANET ZONE

You define what kind of sites you want to assign to the Local Intranet Zone. You can also assign sites that are outside your local intranet to this zone.

To assign types of intranet sites and sites outside your intranet to this zone:

1. In the Security dialog box, select Local Intranet.
2. Choose Sites to display the dialog box shown in Figure 39.28.
3. By default, all three check boxes are checked. Uncheck any that are inappropriate.
4. Choose Advanced to display the dialog box shown in Figure 39.29.
5. Enter the complete URL of a site into the Add This Web Site to the Zone box, then choose Add. The URL you entered is added to the list of sites in the Web Sites box.

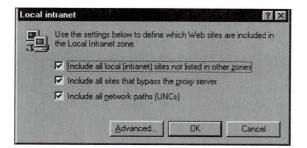

Figure 39.28
You can choose any combination of the check boxes in this dialog box.

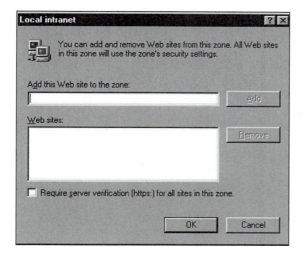

Figure 39.29
Use this dialog box to assign specific Web sites to the zone.

6. Repeat step 5 to add more URLs.

7. For added security, check the Require Server Verification (https) for All Sites in This Zone. By doing that, Outlook will use the Local Intranet Zone for sites in the Web Sites box that are accessed by a secure server.

Note

To remove a site, select that site in the Web Sites box, then choose Remove.

ASSIGNING SITES TO THE TRUSTED SITES ZONE

You can assign any Web sites to the Trusted Sites Zone.

To assign sites to this zone:

1. In the Security dialog box, select Trusted Sites.

2. Choose <u>S</u>ites to display the Trusted Sites Zone dialog box similar to the one previously shown in Figure 39.29.

3. Enter a URL in the A<u>d</u>d This Web Site to the Zone box, then choose <u>A</u>dd. The site is added to the list in the Web Sites box.

4. For added security, you can check Require <u>S</u>erver Verification (https) for All Sites in This Zone. After you do so, Outlook will use the Trusted Sites Zone only for sites that are accessed by a secure server.

ASSIGNING SITES TO THE INTERNET ZONE

You can't add specific sites to the Internet Zone. Outlook automatically assigns sites that aren't assigned to another zone to the Internet Zone.

ASSIGNING SITES TO THE RESTRICTED SITES ZONE

Assign sites to the Restricted Sites Zone in the same way that you add sites to the Trusted Sites Zone, as previously described.

SECURITY IN EXCHANGE SERVER

The sections of this chapter that cover authenticated and encrypted messages focused on Internet messages. Most of that material applies also to messaging in the Exchange environment. Security is managed by key pairs (each user having a public and private key) in the same way it's managed for Internet messages.

In this case, though, instead of using an external source, such as VeriSign, for keys, keys are generated within the Exchange server. The Exchange administrator uses Key Management Server, a component of Exchange Server, to create and manage keys.

From a user's perspective, there's little difference between using authentication and encryption for Exchange and Internet messages. One key point to note, though, is that when using the Change Security Settings dialog box, previously shown in Figure 39.17, to specify security settings, you should open the drop-down Secure Message <u>F</u>ormat list and select Exchange Server Security.

For detailed information about administering and using security in an Exchange messaging environment, see *Special Edition Using Microsoft Exchange Server 5.5*, published by Que.

PART **VIII**

DEVELOPING OUTLOOK-BASED APPLICATIONS

CHAPTER **40**

CREATING AND USING CUSTOM FORMS

In this chapter

by Helen Feddema

PART
VIII
CH
40

WHY DO YOU NEED CUSTOM FORMS?

Outlook's standard forms comprise a complete *Personal Information Manager (PIM) (page 14)* that includes all the functionality needed for many users. But Outlook is also a development environment that gives you the tools you need to create your own custom forms, based on the standard forms. This flexibility means that you are not tied down to the form design or data fields that Microsoft built into the Outlook standard forms. You can customize a copy of a standard form by adding a few custom fields (as described in Chapter 41, "Creating and Using Custom Fields"), or you can create an entirely new form.

→ To learn more about working with custom fields, **see** Chapter 41, "Creating and Using Custom Fields."

You can even create a complete application consisting of several interlinked Outlook forms, and maybe a few Office UserForms (new to Outlook 2000). If you need to interact with other applications (such as Access or Word), you can use *OLE Automation (page 1124)* to link Outlook forms to data stored in other Office applications (or vice versa), as described in Chapter 42, "Enhancing Outlook Forms with Visual Basic Script Code," Chapter 43, "Creating Application-wide Outlook Visual Basic for Applications Code," and Chapter 44, "Understanding Automation."

→ To learn more about writing code for Outlook forms, **see** Chapter 42, "Enhancing Outlook Forms with Visual Basic Script Code."

→ To learn more about writing application-wide VBA code, **see** Chapter 43, "Creating Application-wide Outlook Visual Basic for Applications Code."

→ To learn more about writing Automation code for exchanging data among Office applications, **see** Chapter 44, "Understanding Automation."

REVIEWING OUTLOOK'S BUILT-IN FORMS

Unlike Word and Excel, which let developers create a new document or worksheet from scratch, the Outlook form designer restricts developers to creating customized forms based on one of the standard Outlook forms. In the Outlook interface, the available forms are displayed in the New Object drop-down list, shown in Figure 40.1.

Tip #251 from *Helen Bell Feddema*	The order of forms in the drop-down list changes with the current Outlook folder. The default form for that folder is at the top of the list, and you can click on the icon heading the list (just to the left of the word "New") to create a new instance of the default form without dropping down the list.

The standard forms available for selection in the interface are listed in Table 40.1, which lists the forms available for developers to customize, and their IPM message class (used to reference forms in VBS or VBA code). There are some discrepancies between these lists. While Appointments, Contacts, Tasks, and Task Requests have the same name throughout, the form called Mail Message in the interface is called just Message in the Forms Library, while its IPM class is Note. The form called Note in the interface and the Forms Library has an IPM class of StickyNote, and the Post form in the Forms Library is not a selection on the drop-down New Object list in some folders. The new NetFolder Conflict and

NetFolder Invitation forms are not available from the drop-down menu, but they are available from the Choose Form dialog (though not in the Design Form dialog). Finally, Office Documents are not in the Forms Library, but they do have IPM message classes.

Figure 40.1
The available forms on the New Object drop-down toolbar list.

Tip #252 from
Helen Bell Feddema

The MessageClass property of an Outlook item is a string starting with "IPM" (an acronym for Interpersonal Message). Each of the Outlook standard items in the interface has an equivalent MessageClass value, which you can use to determine what kind of object it is, when iterating through items in a folder from VBS or VBA code.

When you create and publish a custom form, your form name is added on after the standard form name, indicating which standard form your form was based on. For example, if you create a custom form called "Sales Call" based on the Contact form, its MessageClass value will be "IPM.Contact.Sales Call." Piggybacking a custom form on the standard form allows the item to use the standard form in case a custom form is not available.

PART
VIII

CH
40

TABLE 40.1   STANDARD OUTLOOK FORM TYPES

Drop-Down List	Forms Library	IPM Class	Editable Pages
Contact	Contact	IPM.Contact	
Task	Task	IPM.Task	[None]
Task Request	Task Request	IPM.TaskRequest	[None]
Mail Message	Message	IPM.Note	Message
Appointment	Appointment	IPM.Appointment	[None]
Meeting Request	Meeting Request	IPM.Schedule.Meeting.Request	[None]

continues

TABLE 40.1   CONTINUED

Drop-Down List	Forms Library	IPM Class	Editable Pages
Distribution List	Distribution List	IPM.DistList	[None]
Journal Entry	Journal Entry	IPM.Activity	[None]
Note	Note	IPM.StickyNote	[None]
	Post	IPM.Post	Message
	Standard Default	IPM	Message
	NetFolder Conflict	IPM.Note.FolderPub.Conflict	[None]
	NetFolder Invitation	IPM.Note.FolderPub NewSubscriber	[None]
Office Document		IPM.Document.Excel.Sheet.8	
		IPM.Document.Word.Document.8	
		IPM.Document.PowerPoint.Show.8	

→ To learn how the Contact form is used in the interface, **see** Chapter 9, "Managing Contacts".

→ To learn how to work with the Appointment form in the interface, **see** Chapter 10, "Managing Calendars."

→ To learn how to work with the Task form in the interface, **see** Chapter 11, "Managing Tasks."

→ To learn how to work with the Journal in the interface, **see** Chapter 12, "Keeping Your Journal."

The Task, Mail Message, Contact, and Appointment forms are the most useful to Outlook developers, since they are the main forms users will need to work with. The Note form isn't customizable—you can't switch to design view and add custom controls to it—but it is still of some use, as you can create a Note from code and fill in the text.

In the following sections you learn the techniques you need to create a custom form and place controls on it, and in Chapter 41, "Creating and Using Custom Fields," you learn more about creating and placing custom fields on a form.

GETTING HELP FOR FORMS

There is a special Help book with information on designing Outlook forms, which has lots of useful information for form designers. To open this book, open Outlook Help, click the Contents tab, click the Advanced Customization book (it's near the bottom of the list), then select one of the books under the Advanced Customization book. Figure 40.2 shows the Working with Forms book open, with the "Change the Default Form for a Folder" Help topic selected.

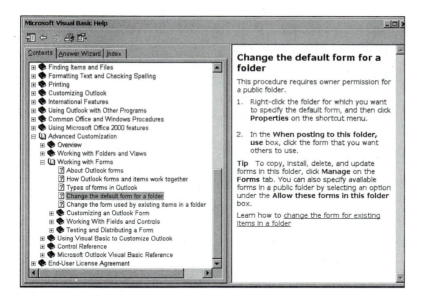

Figure 40.2
Outlook Help topics related to form design.

CREATING A NEW OR MODIFIED FORM BASED ON A BUILT-IN OUTLOOK FORM

When you create an Outlook form, you can't start with a blank form, as in Access. Every custom form must be based on one of the standard forms, so the first step in creating a custom form is to select one of the standard form types, either from the drop-down list shown in Figure 40.1 or from the list of forms on the New submenu, or by selecting the form from the Standard Forms Library. Normally, one of the first two options is preferable because these choices are more convenient. However, if you need to create a new Post form, you may need to use the longer route to select that form from the Standard Forms Library, as it is not always available from the other lists.

To select a form from the New submenu or the Standard Forms Library, implement the following steps:

1. Access the File menu on the main Outlook toolbar.

2. Select the New command from the File menu.

3. You can choose any of the standard forms directly from the list on this submenu, shown in Figure 40.3.

4. Select the Choose Form command from the New submenu to select a form from the Standard Forms Library, as shown in Figure 40.4.

5. Select the desired form from the list of standard forms, and click the Open button.

Figure 40.3
The New submenu opened from the File menu.

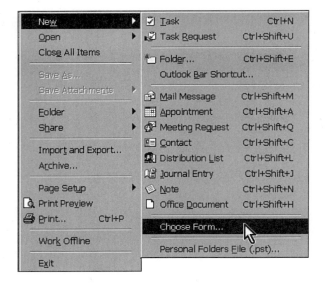

Figure 40.4
The Choose Form dialog box open to the Standard Forms Library.

Note

The Choose Form dialog box offers several choices of forms libraries. In addition to the Standard Forms Library, you can choose the Personal Forms Library (where your customized forms are stored), possibly an Organizational Forms Library (if you are attached to a network), and a number of other selections, as shown in Figure 40.5.

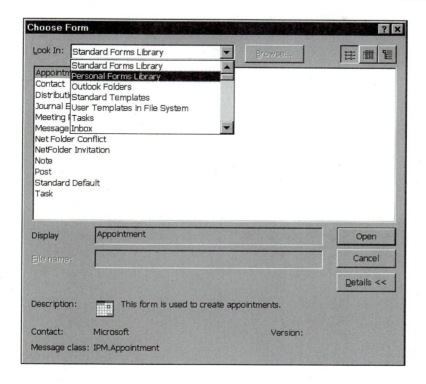

Figure 40.5
The libraries available from the Choose Form dialog box.

PART

VIII

CH

40

UNDERSTANDING A FORM'S ANATOMY

Unlike Visual Basic or Access forms, where data storage is completely separate from form design, in Outlook form data and design are stored together in each item. In Outlook 97, form data and design were very hard to separate—when you switched to design view in a form, you would see whatever data you had entered onto that item, and then when you saved the form, after making design changes, the data was saved along with the design, so if you made a new item from that saved form, it would have the item's data on it. You had to carefully strip out all the data before saving a form to avoid this problem.

Fortunately, this clumsy workaround is no longer necessary. You can now run a form from design view by dropping down the Form menu and selecting Run This Form, as shown in Figure 40.6, to open a fresh instance of the form, which you can test by entering data as needed. When you close the form instance, none of the data is saved to the form design.

Caution

If you want to save a new custom form from a filled-in item, you still need to delete the data before publishing the form; otherwise every new item you create from the form will have that data.

Figure 40.6
Running a form from the menu.

Tip #253 from
Helen Bell Feddema

To streamline your form design work, you can add the Run This Form command to the Outlook toolbar, as described in the following steps.

To create a Run This Form button:

1. Open a form and switch to Design view.

2. Right-click the gray background area on the toolbar.

3. Select the Customize command from the shortcut menu, as shown in Figure 40.7.

Figure 40.7
The first step in adding a command to a menu.

4. In the Customize dialog box click the Commands tab.

5. Select the Form category and then drag the Run This Form command to the toolbar, as shown in Figure 40.8.

6. Click the Modify Selection button, and select the Default Style selection, as shown in Figure 40.9.

Figure 40.8
Dragging a command to the toolbar.

Figure 40.9
Selecting the default style for the new toolbar button.

PART

VIII

CH

40

7. Next, right-click the new blank toolbar button, select Change Button Image from the shortcut menu, and select the runner image for the button, as shown in Figure 40.10.

8. Close the Customize dialog box by clicking the Close button.

9. Figure 40.11 shows the new button on the toolbar.

Figure 40.10
Selecting an image for
the new button.

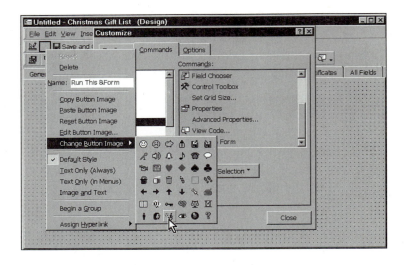

Run this form

Figure 40.11
The Run button on
the Outlook design
view toolbar.

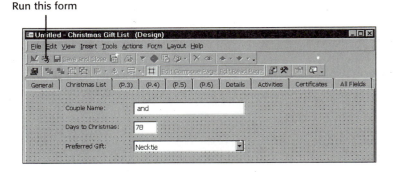

Caution

Once you have run a form, you can't switch directly back to Design view from Form view (as in Access). Instead, just close the new form instance; the form in Design view is still there, in its own window.

From the design point of view, an Outlook form is a container for controls. Most forms have a collection of pages, one or more of which are normally displayed in form view, while the others can be made visible to add more controls to the form. You cannot add a completely new page to a form, only make one of the existing extra pages visible. The Note form is an exception: it is a single-page form, which does not allow any changes to its interface. Table 40.1 (earlier in this chapter) lists the Outlook forms.

Controls are interface elements that can display data from the item's properties (called fields in the interface), or just add decorative or informative elements to the form. A control that displays data from a field is called a *bound* control, while controls that do not display field data are *unbound* controls. Some types of controls can be bound or unbound, while others cannot be bound to data, so they are always unbound controls.

Figure 40.12 shows the Toolbox floating toolbar, which is used to place controls on an Outlook form. The process of placing controls on a form is described in more detail in "Adding Controls to a Form" later in this chapter, and in Chapter 41.

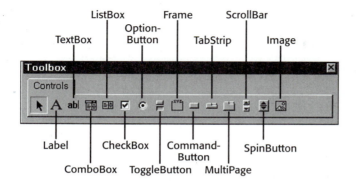

Figure 40.12
The Toolbox floating toolbar.

The most commonly used built-in Outlook controls are described in the following sections.

LABEL CONTROL

The Label control is used to display text on a form. Label controls cannot be bound to a data field. Labels are typically used either to describe an adjacent bound field (usually a text box), or to provide general information about a form, such as a caption for a group of controls.

TEXTBOX CONTROL

The TextBox control is probably the most frequently used of all the controls. A TextBox control can be (and usually is) bound to a data field, and is used to enter or modify data in the field. TextBoxes may be unbound, however; in that case they are generally used to hold the results of a formula or calculation (see the sections on Combination and Formula Fields in Chapter 41).

COMBOBOX CONTROL

The ComboBox control allows the user to select a value from a drop-down list, or enter text into a text box field at the top of the list. This control may be bound to a field, in which case the selected entry is stored in the field. The entries available in a ComboBox control's drop-down list may be hard-coded into its properties sheet, or written to the control from VBS code.

LISTBOX CONTROL

The ListBox control, like the ComboBox, displays a list of items for user choice. However, the ListBox's list is always displayed, and the user cannot enter a value that is not in the list. Because the ListBox control does not collapse into a single row when not in use, it takes up more room on a form than a ComboBox, and thus is not practical except for a very small list.

ListBox controls can be bound or unbound, like ComboBox controls. When a ListBox is bound to a field, the entries to display in its drop-down list are entered in the same way as for the ComboBox control.

CHECKBOX CONTROL

A CheckBox control is used to display a Yes/No value. Although a CheckBox control need not be bound, it usually is, since an unbound CheckBox is not of much use. When checked, the CheckBox represents a Yes value; when unchecked, it represents a No value.

OPTIONBUTTON CONTROL

The OptionButton control is similar in function to the CheckBox control; instead of a check mark, the Yes value is displayed by a black center, and the No value by a white center.

TOGGLEBUTTON CONTROL

The ToggleButton control also functions as an interface for a Yes/No field; when the button appears to be pressed, it represents a Yes value, and when it appears to be raised, it represents a No value. ToggleButtons may be bound or unbound, but like CheckBoxes and OptionButtons, they are not much use unless they are bound. The ToggleButton control is rarely used, as it takes up more room than the CheckBox or OptionButton and its meaning is not as intuitive.

FRAME CONTROL

The Frame control cannot be bound to a field (unlike the Access Frame control); it is used to contain a group of other controls, usually CheckBoxes or OptionButtons, to indicate that they are alternate choices for an option. A group of CheckBoxes or OptionButtons within a Frame is often referred to as an Option Group. Unlike option groups in Access, you can save a text value to a control in an option group. Additionally, a Frame Control can be set to a very short height, in which case it is a Line control (see the "Creating a Line Control" sidebar later in this chapter).

COMMANDBUTTON CONTROL

The CommandButton control cannot be bound to a field, and it needs a VB Script to be functional. Chapter 42, "Enhancing Outlook Forms with Visual Basic Script Code," has several examples of VB Scripts that empower CommandButton controls. When a CommandButton is clicked, the attached VB Script runs to perform a specified action.

IMAGE CONTROL

The Image control is used to display an image on a form. If it is bound, a separate image can be stored in the control for each record; an unbound Image control displays the same image on each record.

The remaining controls in the Toolbox (the TabStrip, MultiPage, ScrollBar, and SpinButton controls) are less commonly used, as they require programming to make them useful. The MultiPage control is discussed in a later section in this chapter.

In addition to the standard Outlook controls, you can also add ActiveX controls to an Outlook form. However, there is no guarantee that an ActiveX control will have full functionality on an Outlook form. Additionally, if you are going to distribute your custom form to other users, they may not be able to use the form unless they have the same version of that ActiveX control installed. For this reason, it is best to avoid ActiveX controls except in an environment where the computer setup is standardized for all users, so you can be sure that all users have the necessary support files.

Distributing ActiveX Controls

If you have Office 2000 Developer, you have a set of ActiveX controls that work with Outlook (and the other Office programs), and you can use the Package and Deployment Wizard to prepare distribution disks which include all the necessary supporting and license files to make the ActiveX controls work on users' forms.

Apart from this scenario, however, it is difficult (or impossible) to be sure your system will work on somebody else's.

CREATING A NEW OR MODIFIED FORM BASED ON A BUILT-IN OUTLOOK FORM

The first step in creating a custom form is to decide which of the built-in Outlook forms you will use as the *template (page 520)* for the form. (The available forms are listed in Table 40.1.) If the form you are designing doesn't really look like any of the standard forms, check the available built-in fields for each form to see which form type has the most useful collection of fields for your purposes.

Note

Even if you create a form based on the Standard Default form, it is still based on one of the standard forms—the Mail Message form, message class IPM.Note.

To check the available fields for a particular type of form, you don't need to open a form of that type—you can check the fields available for any type of form by implementing the following steps:

1. Create a new Contact item, and switch to design view.
2. Right-click a control, and select Properties from the shortcut menu, as shown in Figure 40.13.

3. Select the Properties sheet's Value tab, then click the Choose Field button to open the list of available field groupings, as shown in Figure 40.14.

4. Select the group you want to examine from the list. Figure 40.15 shows the list of All Task Fields, opened out to display the fields.

Figure 40.13
Opening a control's Properties sheet.

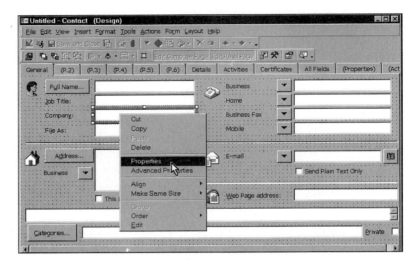

Figure 40.14
The list of available field groupings on the Value tab of a control's properties sheet.

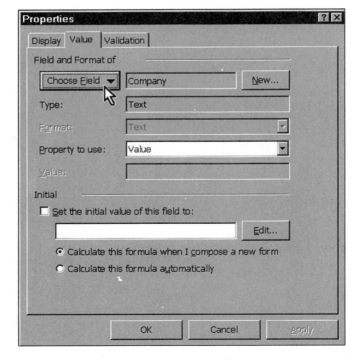

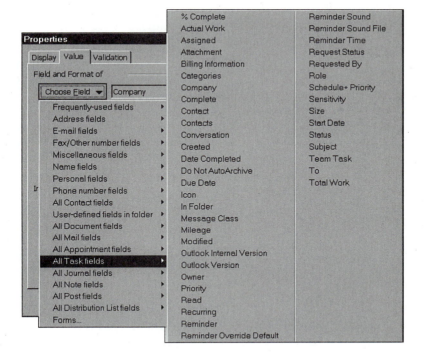

Figure 40.15
The All Task Fields list, opened out.

Tip #254 from
Helen Bell Feddema

You can see an alphabetical list of all Outlook fields and their matching properties by opening the Help topic "Outlook Fields and Equivalent Properties" as follows:

1. Open Outlook Help.
2. Click the Contents tab.
3. Expand the Advanced Customization book.
4. Expand the Working with Forms book.
5. Expand the Working with Fields and Controls book.
6. Select the Outlook Fields and Equivalent Properties Help topic, as shown in Figure 40.16.

Caution

Even though you can open a list of fields belonging to another form type from a Contact form, if you select a field that's only available on another type of form, you will get the error message shown in Figure 40.17 when you try to bind a control to that field. (The same message will appear if you try to drag an inappropriate field to a form from the Field Chooser palette.)

PART

VIII

CH

40

Figure 40.16
Opening the Outlook Fields and Equivalent Properties Help topic.

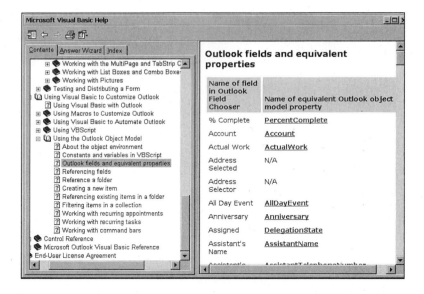

Figure 40.17
Error message resulting from trying to bind a control on a Contact form to a Task field.

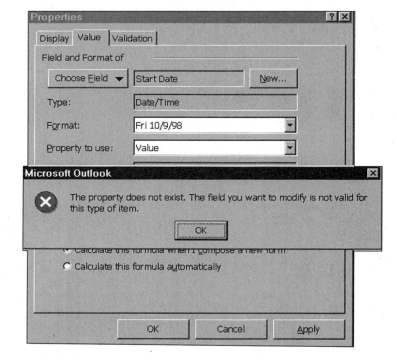

After deciding which set of fields has the best fit with your needs, you can start your customized form by creating a new form of the desired type by selecting it from the New Object drop-down list, as shown in Figure 40.18.

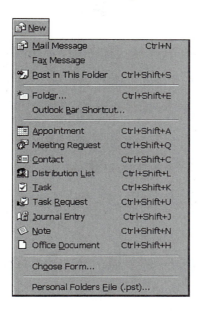

Figure 40.18
Selecting a form type for creating a new form.

Since the Contact form is the heart of an Outlook application—especially with the new Contact Linking features in Outlook 2000—the next section describes the creation of a custom Contact form in detail.

CUSTOMIZING THE CONTACT FORM

As an example, I will step you through the creation of a custom Contact form that will be used to store a Christmas card and gift list, using some of the fields created in Chapter 41. Start by creating a new Contact form, then switch to design view. The General page on the Contact form is editable, so start by deleting the e-mail and Web site controls and graphics, which aren't needed for this type of list. To delete a control, just click it and press the Delete button.

ADDING CONTROLS TO A FORM

Tip #255 from
Helen Bell Feddema

If you don't need any of the built-in controls on a form page that is normally displayed, you can hide that page by pulling down the Form menu and clicking the Display This Page command (the check mark will disappear). To make one of the extra pages (P.2 to P.6) visible, pull down the Form menu and click the Display This Page command to check it, so the page will be visible.

Next, add some family-related fields to the new blank area. There is a Spouse Name control on the Details page, but that page has lots of unnecessary information and can't be edited, so the first step is to make that page invisible. To make a page invisible, click on its tab, then drop down the Form menu and uncheck the Display This Page item, as shown in Figure 40.19.

Figure 40.19
Making a form page invisible.

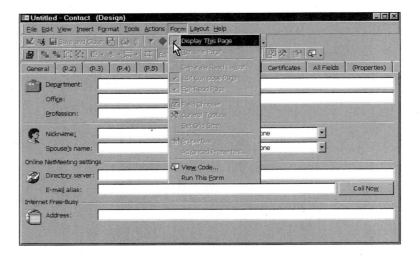

Next, switch back to the General page and insert the built-in Spouse and Children fields, and a Family label. The fields are in the Name Fields group, so they can be dragged to the page from the Field Chooser, after selecting that group, as shown in Figure 40.20. (Note that the pointer changes to a little gray box with a plus sign attached to it while the field is being dragged.)

Figure 40.20
Dragging the Spouse field to a Contact form.

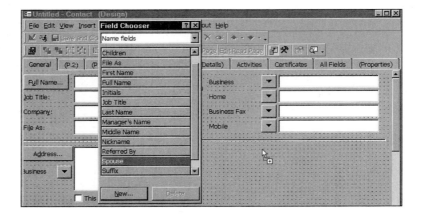

When you drag a text field to a form from the Field Chooser, it appears as a TextBox control with an attached Label control. After dragging the Children field to the form in a similar manner, the next step is to move the new fields down a bit, then insert a Label control for the group title. Since Label controls aren't bound to fields, they can't be dragged from the Field Chooser. To insert a Label control, first click the Toolbox button on the toolbar to open the Control Toolbox, as shown in Figure 40.21.

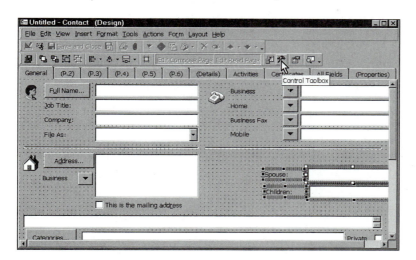

Figure 40.21
Opening the Control Toolbox.

After clicking the Label tool in the Toolbox (it's the one with the large "A"), you can either click the form to insert a default-sized Label control, or click and drag a rectangle on the form to create a Label control of the desired size. Use one of these methods to place a Label control on the form. You can change its caption directly in the control by double-clicking the original Label*n* text and replacing it with the text you want. However, you will probably want to make more changes than just the text, so right-click the new Label control and open its Advanced Properties sheet to select a different font size and color.

PART
VIII

CH
40

Tip #256 from

Helen Bell Feddema

You can modify the color properties from either the Properties sheet or the Advanced Properties sheet, but the Advanced Properties sheet lets you see the foreground and background colors, while the Properties sheet just gives you a cryptic list of various Windows attributes to select from (such as Info Text and Inactive Caption).

Note

Outlook controls have two properties sheets: The Properties sheet and the Advanced Properties sheet. While many control properties appear in both sheets, some do not–for example, you can only bind a control to a field in the Properties sheet, while the WordWrap property is only found in the Advanced Properties sheet. To make things more confusing, some properties listed in the Advanced Properties sheet (such as ControlSource) are non-functional in Outlook.

To give the Label control a caption of "Family Information," in Arial 16 pt Bold text in green, centered, on a light blue background, you need to set several properties. Start by right-clicking the new Label control and opening its Advanced Properties sheet from the shortcut menu, as shown in Figure 40.22.

Figure 40.22
Opening a control's Advanced Properties sheet.

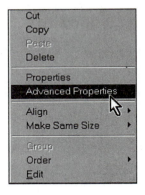

Select the Caption property row. To enter the caption "Family Information," type that text into the box at the top of the Advanced Properties sheet and click the Apply button, as shown in Figure 40.23.

Figure 40.23
Entering a caption for the new Label control.

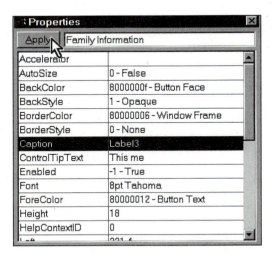

Tip #257 from
Helen Bell Feddema

You can move quickly to another property in the Advanced Properties sheet by typing its first letter.

To center the control, select the TextAlign property and either double-click the property in the sheet, or select 2 - Center from the drop-down list at the top of the Advanced Properties sheet, as shown in Figure 40.24.

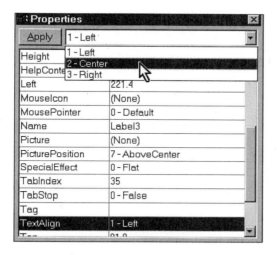

Figure 40.24
Changing the control's alignment.

Next, select the Font property. To select a different font, click the Build button next to the current font name at the top of the Advanced Properties sheet (it's the small button with the three dots), and select the desired font, size, and emphasis from the Font dialog box, as shown in Figure 40.25.

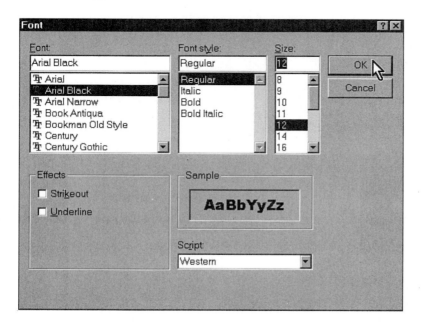

Figure 40.25
Changing the control's font name, size, and emphasis.

The BackColor and ForeColor properties are set from either a drop-down list with the same cryptic Windows components that are in the Properties sheet (see Figure 40.26), or a considerably more intuitive Color dialog box shown in Figure 40.27.

Figure 40.26
Selecting a BackColor value from the drop-down list.

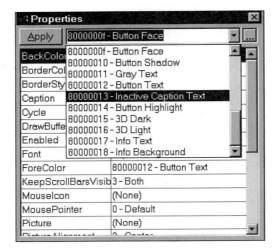

Figure 40.27
Selecting a color from the Color dialog box.

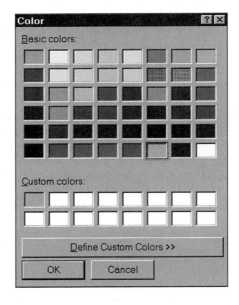

ADDING GRAPHICS TO A FORM

Finally, you can add an Image control with a Christmas theme for the family information group. Click the Image tool in the Toolbox (it's the last button on the right) to place an Image control on the form. Open the control's Advanced Properties sheet and select an image for its Picture property by clicking the Build button at the top of the sheet to open the Load Picture dialog box. Select an appropriate image, such as the reindeer image from the FrontPage collection, as shown in Figure 40.28.

Tip #258 from *Helen Bell Feddema*	Office 2000 comes with an extensive collection of clip art, which you can use for images on Outlook forms. The default location for these files is C:\Program Files\Common Files\Microsoft Shared\Clipart. Additionally, if you have the Premium Edition of Office 2000 (the one that includes FrontPage), you will have many more images to select, including the Reindeer image I picked for the Christmas List form.

Tip #259 from *Helen Bell Feddema*	You may find it more convenient to do any necessary editing or resizing of images in another program, such as Paintbrush, as Outlook offers only limited tools for manipulating images in Image controls. After resizing or editing an image, you can save it as a separate file, then just select the edited file for your Image control.

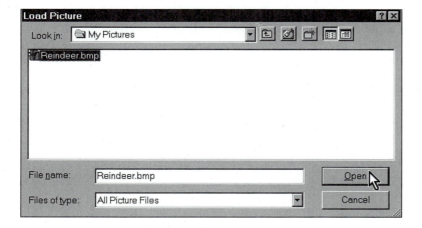

Figure 40.28
Selecting an image for an Image control.

The controls are shown in Figure 40.29. The group isn't quite done yet—the next section will show you how to align them more attractively.

Figure 40.29
The Family
Information controls.

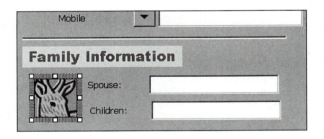

UNDERSTANDING THE CONTROL PROPERTIES SHEET

When you work with controls on a form, you will need to set many of the control properties through the Properties sheet, accessible via a control's shortcut menu. Different types of controls have somewhat different selections on their Properties sheets. Most control Properties sheets have three pages—Display, Value, and Validation. However, depending on the control type, some of the properties on one or more pages of the Properties sheet may be disabled.

For example, all the properties on a Label control's Value and Validation pages are disabled, since a Label control is not bound to a field. Most of the properties on a CommandButton control's Value and Validation pages are disabled, since CommandButtons are not bound either, except for a few special cases. The Properties sheet for a Frame or Line control is more limited: it has just a single page, Display, with all properties enabled. However, you can adjust more of a Frame or Line control's properties by opening its Advanced Properties sheet, as described in the following tip.

Tip #260 from
Helen Bell Feddema

There is no Line control in the Control Toolbox, but you can see controls named Line*n* on the General page of the default Contact form. A Line control is just a very short Frame control, so to insert a Line control on a form, start by inserting a Frame control from the Control Toolbox.

Next, open the Advanced Properties sheet for the new Frame control and set its Height property to just a few points—2 to 4 points makes a chiseled line, while 1 point makes a thin solid line. You can adjust the appearance of the line further by changing the Special Effect and BorderStyle properties in the Advanced Properties sheet.

The following discussion deals with the Properties sheet for a TextBox, ComboBox, or ListBox control, which have the fullest selection of adjustable properties.

To open a control's Properties sheet, right-click the control and select Properties from its shortcut menu, as shown in Figure 40.13 earlier in this chapter. Initially, the Properties sheet opens to the Display page, shown in Figure 40.30.

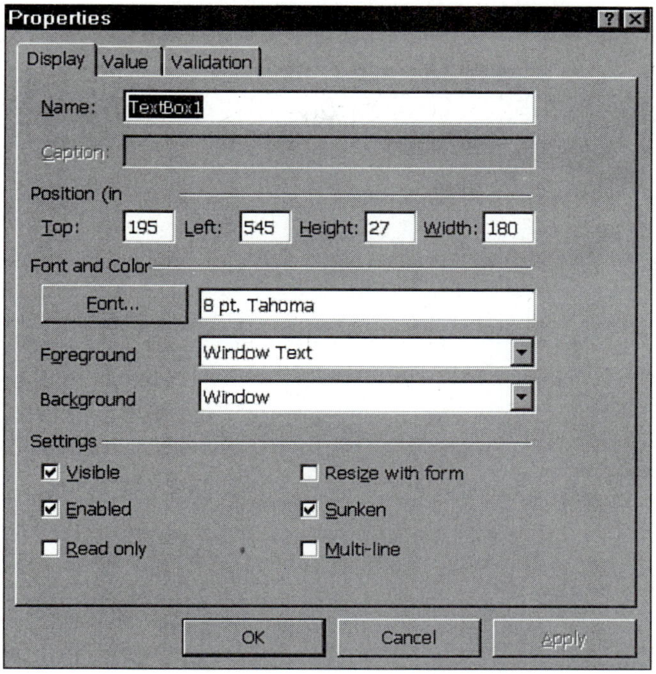

Figure 40.30
The Display page of a TextBox control's Properties sheet.

The first property shown on the Display page is the control's name—the default name is TextBox*n* for a TextBox control, and similarly for other control types. You can leave the name as is, but if you are going to write any code that references the control, it is a good idea to give it a more descriptive name, possibly using an identifying prefix from Table 40.2, based on the Leszynski Naming Convention for various dialects of Visual Basic. (The value of the LNC prefixes will become more apparent in Chapters 42–44, which deal with writing VBS and VBA code.)

PART
VIII
CH
40

TABLE 40.2 SUGGESTED CONTROL NAME PREFIXES

Control Type	Suggested Prefix
Label	lbl
TextBox	txt
ComboBox	cbo
ListBox	lst
CheckBox	chk
OptionButton	opt
ToggleButton	tgl
Frame	fra

Control Type	Suggested Prefix
Line	lin
CommandButton	cmd
TabStrip	tab
Image	img

The Caption property is grayed out for TextBox controls, but it can be filled in as desired for controls that have a visible caption, such as Label, CheckBox, and OptionButton controls.

The Position group has four controls used to set the control's position on the form. These properties set the control's Top, Left, Height, and Width in points (a point is 1/72 of an inch).

The Font button opens a standard Font dialog box where you can select a new font, size, and emphasis for the text displayed in the control, as shown in Figure 40.25 earlier in this chapter.

Finally, the Settings group lets you adjust a miscellaneous selection of properties that affect either the control's appearance or functionality:

- Visible—The control is visible if this property is checked, and invisible if it is unchecked.

- Enabled—The control is enabled if this property is checked, and disabled if it is unchecked. Disabled controls appear grayed out, and can't be used.

- Read Only—The control is read-only if this property is checked, and read/write if it is unchecked. Read-only controls look normal, but they can't be edited.

- Resize with Form—When checked, this property enables the control to be automatically resized when the form is resized; if unchecked, the control remains the same size when the form is resized. Many of the default controls on Outlook's built-in forms are resizable.

- Sunken—If this property is checked, the control has the Sunken special effect (this is the default setting for TextBox controls on the standard Outlook forms). If the property is unchecked, the control has the Flat special effect. (You can set more special effect properties from the control's Advanced Properties sheet.)

- Multi-line—If this property is checked, the control takes multiple lines of text, using the Enter key to start a new line. This is especially useful for entering address data. If the property is unchecked, the control only accepts one line of data.

The Value page of a TextBox control's Properties sheet is shown in Figure 40.31. On this page you can select a field for binding a control, as described in the next section. You can also select another property to use, though the default Value property is almost always appropriate.

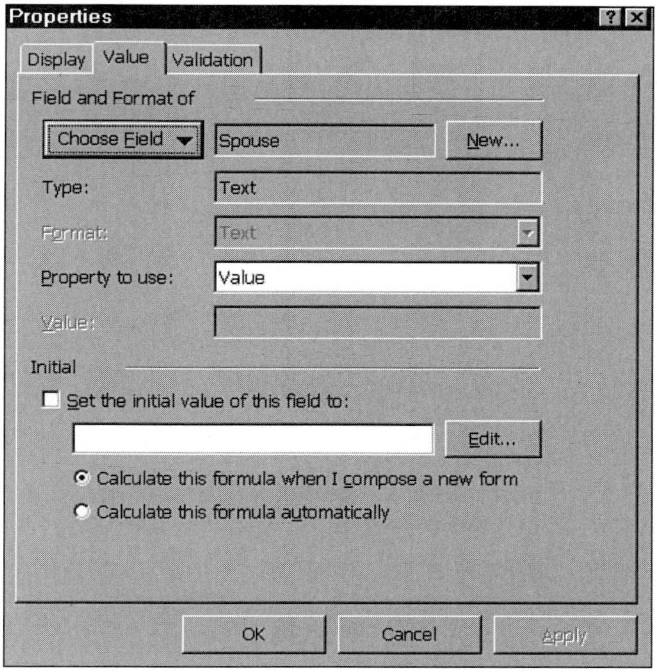

Figure 40.31
The Value page of a
TextBox control's
Properties sheet.

The read-only Type property indicates the data type of the field to which the control is bound. The Format and Value properties are disabled.

The Initial section of this page lets you enter an initial (default) value for the control; you can also use the Edit button to open a screen where you can create a Combination or Formula field, as described in Chapter 41. If you have entered a formula, you can use the two option buttons at the bottom of the page to determine whether the formula should be calculated automatically, or when a new form is created.

The Value page of a ComboBox or ListBox control (shown in Figure 40.32) is somewhat different; it has a List Type property where you can select two options for the drop-down list: Dropdown (the default) or Droplist. The combo box looks the same whichever list type you choose: the only difference is that a Droplist list type limits the user's choice to the items in the list, while a Dropdown list lets the user enter an item not in the list. (This choice is roughly equivalent to the Access Limit to List property.)

The Validation page is the final page of the Properties sheet; it is used to enter a rule for validating data entered into the control.

For example, you may want to ensure that an out-of-stock product is not shipped. To ensure that a form can't be saved with "Sprockets" entered into the Product field, enter the validation formula

PART

VIII

Cн

40

```
<> "Sprockets"
```

and the validation text

```
"Sprockets are currently out of stock"
```

in the properties on the Validation page of a control, as shown in Figure 40.33.

Figure 40.32
The Value page of a
ComboBox control's
properties sheet.

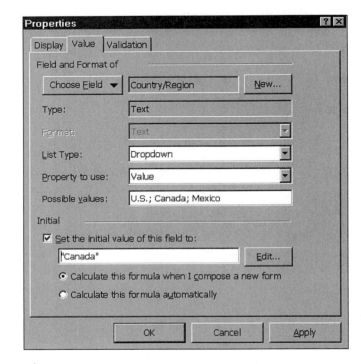

Now, if you try to save and close a form with "Sprockets" entered into the Product field, you will get the error message shown in Figure 40.34, and you won't be able to save and close the form until you delete or change the text in the Product text box.

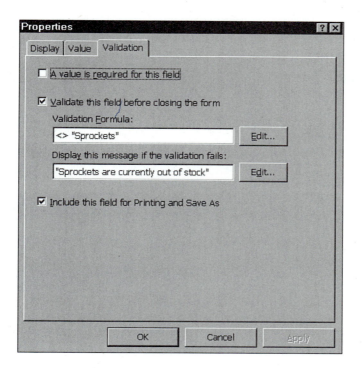

Figure 40.33
The Validation page of a TextBox control's Properties sheet.

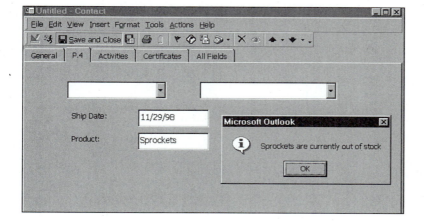

Figure 40.34
An error message for a control with a validation rule.

PART

VIII

Cʜ

40

ASSOCIATING CONTROLS WITH FIELDS

Tip #261 from
Helen Bell Feddema

If you need to validate a field before saving the entire form, you can place a validation formula on the PropertyChange or CustomPropertyChange event of the form (see Chapter 42).

→ To learn more about working with these events, **see** Chapter 42, "Enhancing Outlook Forms with Visual Basic Script Code."

In addition to dragging fields to a form from the Field Chooser, as described earlier in this chapter, you can also place a control of a specific type on a form, using the Control Toolbox, and then bind the control to a field. This technique is particularly useful when you want to associate a ComboBox or ListBox control with a field. You can bind a control to either a built-in Outlook field, or a custom field you have created.

To associate a control with a built-in field, click the Choose Field button on the Value page of a control's Properties sheet, then select one of the field groups from the drop-down list, as shown in Figure 40.35.

Figure 40.35
The list of field groups for binding a control to a field.

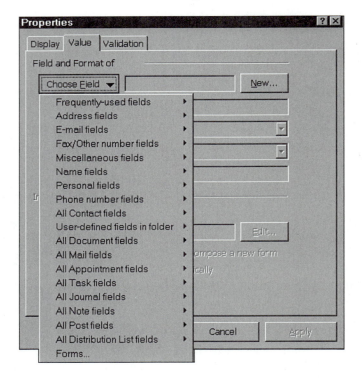

Select one of the field groups, then select a field from the group. Figure 40.36 shows the control's Properties sheet with the Personal Home Page field selected from the Frequently Used Fields group.

To bind a control to an already existing custom field in the item or folder, select the User-defined Fields in Folder list, as shown in Figure 40.37.

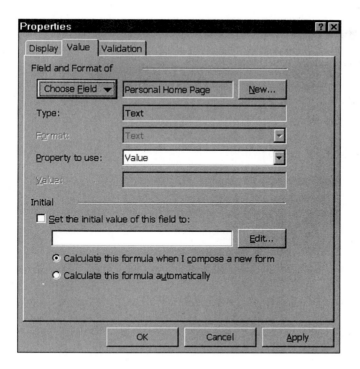

Figure 40.36
A newly inserted TextBox control bound to the Personal Home Page field.

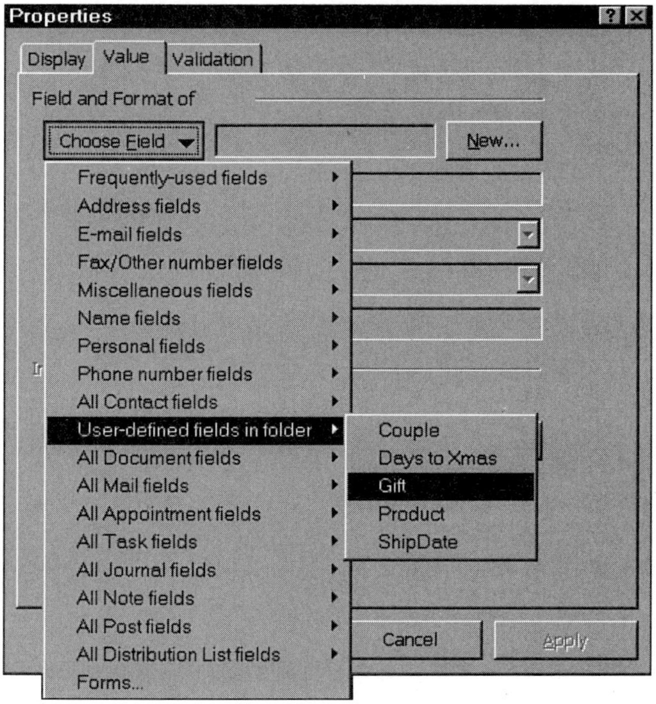

Figure 40.37
Selecting a user-defined field for a control value.

You can also create a new field for a control on-the-fly, by clicking the New button on the Value page of the Properties sheet, and filling in the properties on the New Field dialog box, as shown in Figure 40.38.

Figure 40.38
Creating a new field from a control's Properties sheet.

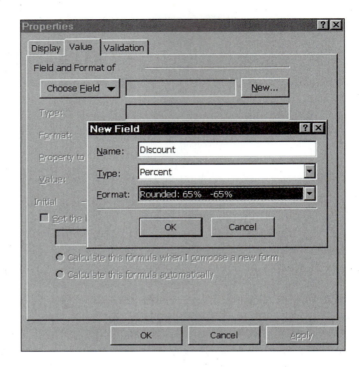

ARRANGING CONTROLS

After you have placed some controls on a form, you will generally need to rearrange them. To move a control, click on it to give it the focus (you will see little white squares—known as *sizing handles*—on each corner and the midpoint of each side), then hold the mouse down and drag the control to another location. To resize the control, click one of the sizing handles (the pointer should change into an arrow, as shown in Figure 40.39), then stretch out the control in the direction of the arrow. You can resize a control horizontally, vertically, or diagonally.

Figure 40.39
The Resize pointer.

Additionally, the Outlook form designer has a number of useful tools for this purpose. Figure 40.40 shows a customized form design toolbar, with the alignment tools on the left.

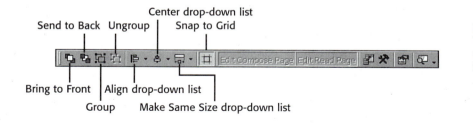

Send to Back   Ungroup   Center drop-down list   Snap to Grid

Bring to Front | Align drop-down list
            Group   Make Same Size drop-down list

Figure 40.40
The alignment tools on the form design toolbar.

BRING TO FRONT/SEND TO BACK TOOLS

If you want to position a control underneath or on top of other controls—say an Image control as a background under an option group—you can use the Bring to Front or Send to Back tools. Select the control to be brought to the front (or sent to the back) and click the appropriate tool to move the control to the front (or back). The Bring to Front and Send to Back tools are the first two tools on the Design toolbar.

GROUP/UNGROUP TOOLS

When you have a group of controls you want to treat as a unit, you can use the Group tool to create a semi-permanent group. To group controls, either draw an imaginary rectangle enclosing a part of each, or click the first control, then Shift-click the others. While all the controls are highlighted, click the Group tool to create the group, as shown in Figure 40.41.

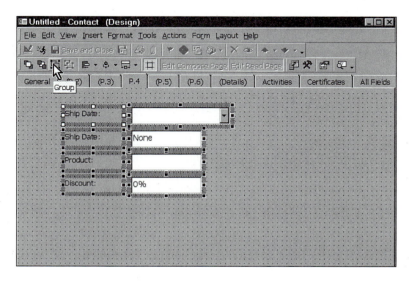

Figure 40.41
Grouping a set of controls.

To clear the group, select it and click the Ungroup button.

ALIGNMENT TOOLS

To the right of the Ungroup tool on the Design toolbar there are three drop-down lists offering choices of alignment tools. The Align drop-down list offers a choice of aligning the selected controls to the Left, Center, Right, Top, Middle, Bottom, or To Grid.

Tip #262 from

Helen Bell Feddema

The Middle selection on the Align list is especially useful for aligning a TextBox control with its Label control, as shown in Figure 40.42.

Figure 40.42
Aligning a TextBox control with its Label control.

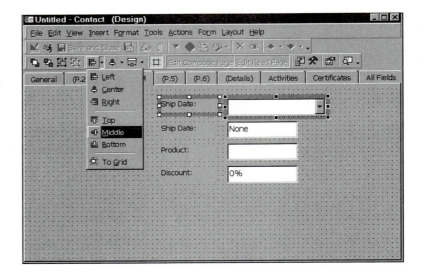

The next drop-down list, the Center list, offers a choice of centering options—Horizontally and Vertically. Finally, the Make Same Size drop-down list lets you make a group of controls the same width, height, or both, as shown in Figure 40.43.

When you align controls using these tools, they are aligned relative to the dominant control.

The Dominant Control for the Sizing and Grouping Commands

Some alignment and sizing operations for groups of controls make use of a *dominant control*—the control to which the other controls are aligned or sized. You can select a group of controls to resize or align by several methods. Each method results in a different control being the dominant control.

When you Shift-click to select controls, the first control selected is the dominant control. When you Ctrl-click to select controls, the last control selected is the dominant control, and when you draw a rectangle around a group of controls with the mouse pointer, the control nearest the pointer when you start drawing is the dominant control.

You can change the dominant control by Ctrl-clicking twice on a control; that control then becomes the dominant control. You can tell which control in a group is the dominant control by the color of its sizing handles (the little squares at its corners and the midpoints of each side—see Figure 40.42 for an example). The dominant control's sizing handles are white, while the other controls have black handles.

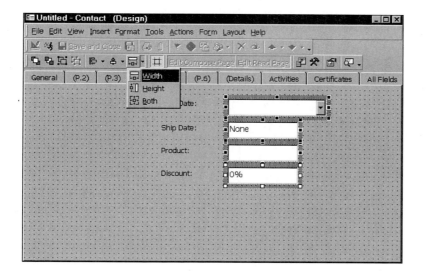

Figure 40.43
Making a group of controls the same width.

When you select a group of controls, and place the pointer over the border of one of the controls in the group, the mouse pointer turns into a double-pointed arrow, as shown in Figure 40.44, indicating that you can move the group.

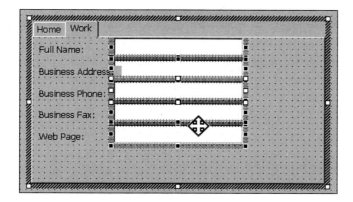

Figure 40.44
The Move Group pointer.

Figure 40.45 shows the Family Information control group, after resizing and aligning the controls.

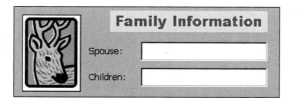

Figure 40.45
The Family Information controls after resizing and aligning.

USING THE TABSTRIP OR MULTIPAGE CONTROL TO CREATE A MULTI-PAGE FORM

Although each of the standard Outlook forms is itself a multi-page tabbed form (though some only display a single page by default), if you need a more sophisticated interface for displaying complex data, you can add a TabStrip or MultiPage control to one of the form pages. These two controls look very similar, but they have somewhat different functionality.

The MultiPage control is intended for managing large amounts of data that can be sorted into several categories (but all belonging to one record). The TabStrip control, on the other hand, is intended to present different sets of data, possibly from different data sources, in a visual group. For other Office applications, such as Access, this is a real distinction; however, Outlook offers considerably less functionality for binding controls to diverse data sources, so there is little practical difference between these controls, except that the MultiPage control is easier to work with.

You can easily place different controls on each page of a MultiPage control, which makes this control an excellent interface for displaying several sets of related information in a compact form. The user simply clicks the tab to open the appropriate page of data. To add a MultiPage control to an Outlook form page, click the MultiPage tool in the Control Toolbox and place the control on a form. Initially, a MultiPage control has two pages, called Page1 and Page2. To change the caption of a page, right-click the tab to open its shortcut menu, and select the Rename command, as shown in Figure 41.46.

Figure 40.46
Renaming a page of a MultiPage control.

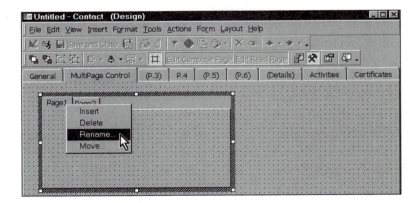

Enter the Caption, Accelerator Key, and ControlTip Text information (only the Caption is required) in the Rename dialog box, as shown in Figure 40.47.

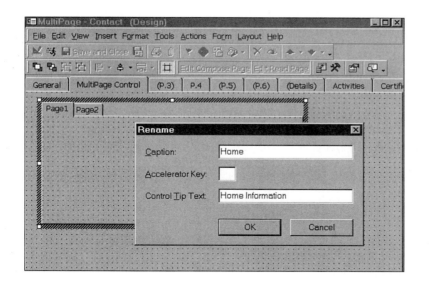

Figure 40.47
Setting a page's properties in the Rename dialog box.

You can add, delete, or move pages as needed by selecting the Insert, Delete, or Move command from the MultiPage control's shortcut menu (right-click any page tab, or the gray area to the right of the tabs, to open this menu). If you have entered an Accelerator key for a page, that letter will be displayed with an underline. Setting accelerator keys lets the user activate a page by pressing Alt+N, where N represents the letter entered as the accelerator key for that page.

Figure 40.48 and Figure 40.49 show the Work and Home pages of MultiPage control, with the appropriate home or business fields displayed.

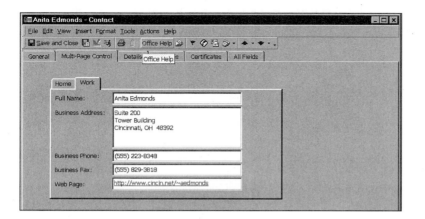

Figure 40.48
The Work page of a MultiPage control.

Figure 40.49
The Home page of a
MultiPage control.

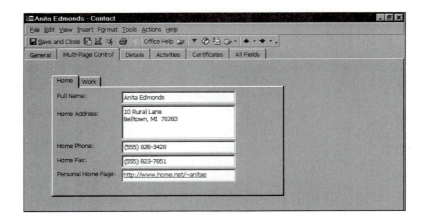

CREATING A FORM BASED ON AN OFFICE DOCUMENT

In addition to creating a form based on one of the standard Outlook forms, you can also choose to create a form in an Outlook folder based on one of four Office Document selections (Word document, Excel worksheet, Excel chart, and PowerPoint presentation). To create a form based on an Office Document, select Office Document from the New Object menu, as shown in Figure 40.50.

Figure 40.50
Creating an Office
Document in Outlook.

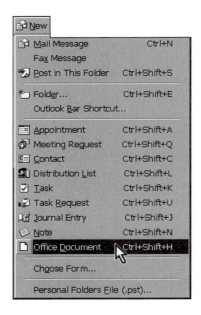

The New Office Document dialog box opens, as shown in Figure 40.51, with a choice of Excel Worksheet, Excel Chart, PowerPoint Presentation, or Word Document. Selecting one of these options opens a document of the indicated type, which is generally similar to a normal document created directly from the application, with a few extra features for interfacing with Outlook, and perhaps lacking a few standard features.

The Office document types available depend on what Office components you chose to install. If you did not install the PowerPoint component, for example, you won't have a PowerPoint selection in the Office Documents dialog box.

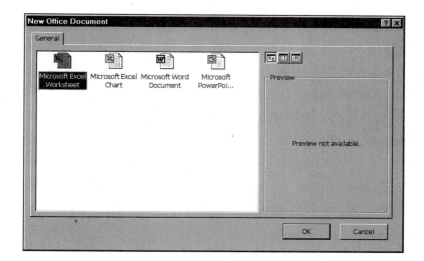

Figure 40.51
The four types of Office Documents in Outlook.

There are a number of differences between a regular Excel worksheet or chart, PowerPoint Presentation, or Word document and its Outlook Office Document counterpart. These differences will be discussed in detail for Excel worksheets; the menu differences are similar across the board, but there are some other application-specific differences which will be mentioned in the following sections.

THE EXCEL WORKSHEET OFFICE DOCUMENT

When you select an Excel worksheet, you initially get a small dialog box (shown in Figure 40.52) where you can choose to post the document in the current Outlook folder, or send it to someone by e-mail.

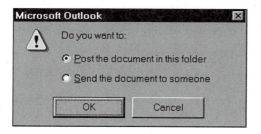

Figure 40.52
Options for creating a new Office Document.

After choosing one of the options (the Post selection is the default), a new Excel worksheet opens, looking much like a regular worksheet. However, if you examine an Office Document worksheet in comparison to a regular worksheet (see Figure 40.53), you should see some differences.

Figure 40.53
An Excel Office Document next to a regular Excel worksheet.

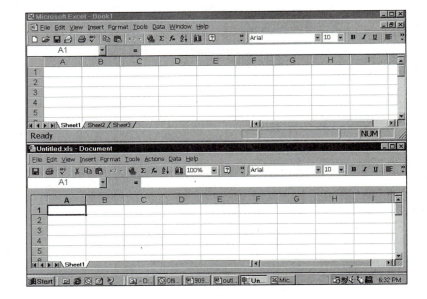

Table 40.3 lists the main interface differences between the two types of worksheets.

TABLE 40.3   REGULAR EXCEL WORKSHEET VS. EXCEL OFFICE DOCUMENT WORKSHEET

Regular Worksheet	Office Document Worksheet
MDI interface	SDI interface
Regular icon in taskbar	Special icon in taskbar
Has a Window menu	Has no Window menu
Has no Actions menu	Has an Actions menu
Has New, Open, and E-mail tools on toolbar	Lacks New, Open, and E-mail tools on toolbar

Note

MDI (Multiple Document Interface) lets you open multiple documents in one program window. Word 97 had MDI, and Excel 2000 has MDI.

SDI (Single Document Interface) requires you to open a new instance of a program for each document. Word 2000 and Access 2000 have SDI.

Additionally, there are significant differences in the selections available on several of the menus of an Excel Office Document worksheet, as opposed to the corresponding menus in a regular worksheet. Figure 40.54 compares the file menu of a regular Excel worksheet with the File menu of an Excel Office Document worksheet.

Figure 40.54
The File menu on a regular Excel worksheet.

Figure 40.55
The File menu on an Excel worksheet Office Document.

Similarly, Figure 40.56 and Figure 40.57 compare the Edit menus of the two worksheets; Figure 40.58 and Figure 40.59 compare the View menus; Figure 40.60 and Figure 40.61 compare the Tools menu; Figure 40.62 shows the Actions menu (only available in the Office Document worksheet). The Insert, Format, Data, and Help menus are the same in both worksheets, and the Window menu is only available in the regular worksheet.

Figure 40.56
The Edit menu on a regular Excel worksheet.

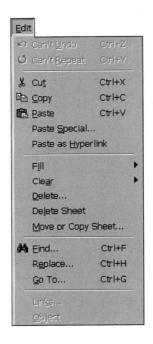

After entering the data you want in the Office Document worksheet, select the Post command from the File menu to save it to the Outlook folder, where its name (default: Untitled.xls) appears as the document's Subject.

THE EXCEL CHART OFFICE DOCUMENT

The differences between Excel Chart Office Documents and regular Excel charts are very similar to the differences between Excel worksheet Office Documents and regular Excel worksheets, so they will not be discussed in detail.

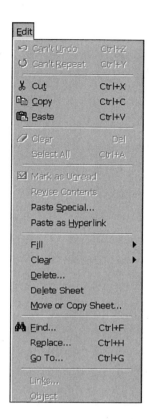

Figure 40.57
The Edit menu on an
Excel worksheet
Office Document.

Figure 40.58
The View menu on a
regular Excel
worksheet.

Figure 40.59
The View menu on an
Excel worksheet
Office Document.

Figure 40.60
The Tools menu on a
regular Excel
worksheet.

THE POWERPOINT PRESENTATION OFFICE DOCUMENT

PowerPoint has a Single Document Interface, so PowerPoint Office Document presentations are similar to regular PowerPoint presentations in that respect. There are menu differences similar to the ones in Excel, however.

Figure 40.61
The Tools menu on an Excel worksheet Office Document.

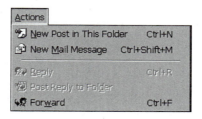

Figure 40.62
The Actions menu on an Excel worksheet Office Document.

PART
VIII

CH
40

THE WORD OFFICE DOCUMENT

Word 2000 now has an SDI interface, so there is no difference between a regular Word document and an Office Document Word document in that respect. However, if you have customized your Outlook form toolbar, you may see the new buttons in a Word Office document. The Design This Form and Run This Form buttons can be seen on a Word Office document's toolbar in Figure 40.63.

Design This Form   Post

Run This Form

Figure 40.63
The toolbar of a Word Office Document.

Clicking the Design This Form button opens a form vaguely similar to an Outlook form, with a blank Document page, a Properties page, and an Actions page. You can type text into the large white area on the Document page (and format it), and use the Properties and Actions pages as in an Outlook form. Clicking the Run This Form button returns you to the normal Word document view, and clicking the Post button posts the Word Office document to the Outlook folder.

Note

The toolbar of a Word Office Document may pick up custom tools from both the Outlook and Word toolbars; Figure 40.63 shows two custom Outlook tools (Design This Form and Run This Form) and one custom Word tool (Print This Page).

Unlike Excel documents, the default document title (Untitled.doc) is not displayed when a Word Office document is listed in an Outlook folder; instead, the Subject field of the document is displayed. By default, this field is blank, so you need to fill it in manually, from the Word document's properties sheet, in order to identify the document in the Outlook interface.

The menu differences for Word are generally similar to those in Excel.

FORM MANAGEMENT

Once you have customized a form, in order to use it again, you need to publish the form to a forms library. Outlook offers a number of options for publishing and saving custom forms, described in the following sections.

PUBLISHING A FORM TO A FORMS LIBRARY

In order to conveniently reuse the custom form on your own computer, you need to publish the form to an appropriate forms library (Personal or Organizational). To publish a custom form to the Personal Forms Library (the usual choice):

1. Open the custom form and switch to Design view.
2. Delete any sample data entered into fields on the item that you don't want on the generic form.
3. Access the Tools menu, open the Forms submenu, and select Publish Form from the pop-out Forms submenu, as shown in Figure 40.64 (or click the Publish Form button on the toolbar).
4. The Publish Form As dialog box opens, where you can select the library for storing the form, as shown in Figure 40.65.

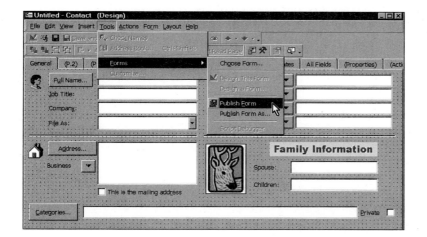

Figure 40.64
Publishing a custom form.

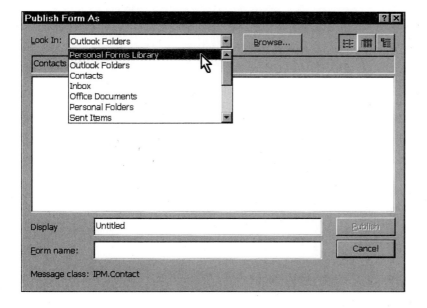

Figure 40.65
Selecting the Personal Forms Library for saving a custom form.

5. On the same dialog box you can select the library for storing the form, enter the display name and form name for the custom form, and view (but not change) the message class.

6. Finally, click the Publish button to save the custom form to the selected Forms library, as shown in Figure 40.66.

Figure 40.66
The filled in Publish
Form As dialog box.

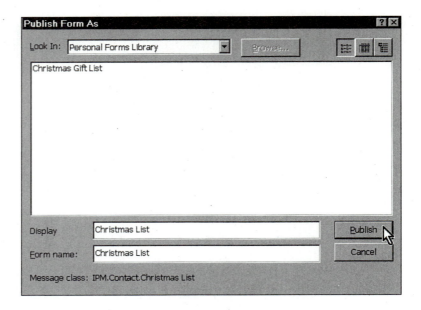

USING CUSTOM FORMS

Once you have published a form, you can select it from the Personal Forms Library to make a new custom item based on the form. To view the list of available forms in the Personal Forms Library:

1. Access the File menu on the main Outlook toolbar.

Tip #263 from
Helen Bell Feddema

Alternately, you can save a click by dropping down the New Object list and selecting Choose Form from it.

2. Select the New command from the File menu.

3. Select the Choose Form command from the New submenu, as shown in Figure 40.67.

4. The Choose Forms dialog box opens with the Standard Forms Library as the default library selection, as shown in Figure 40.68.

5. Drop down the Look In list and select the Personal Forms Library, as shown in Figure 40.69.

6. Select the desired form from the Personal Forms Library list, and click the Open button, as shown in Figure 40.70.

7. A new form opens, based on the custom form, ready to enter data.

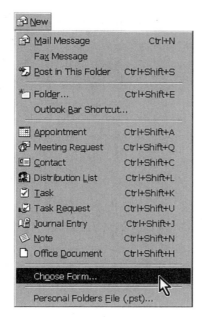

Figure 40.67
Selecting the Choose Form command from the New submenu.

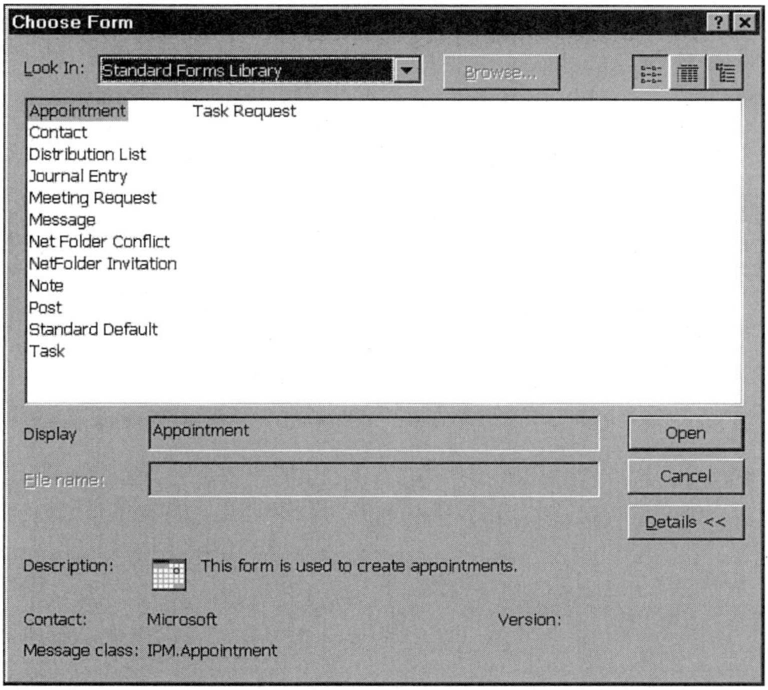

Figure 40.68
The Choose Forms dialog box with the default form library selection.

Figure 40.69
Selecting the Personal
Forms Library.

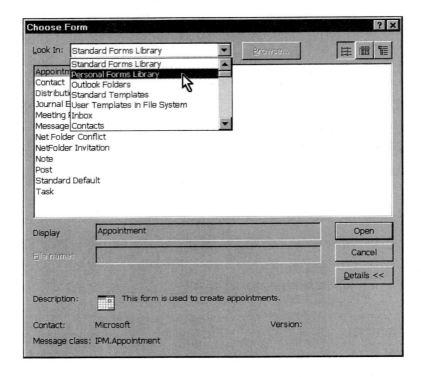

Figure 40.70
Selecting a form from
the Personal Forms
Library.

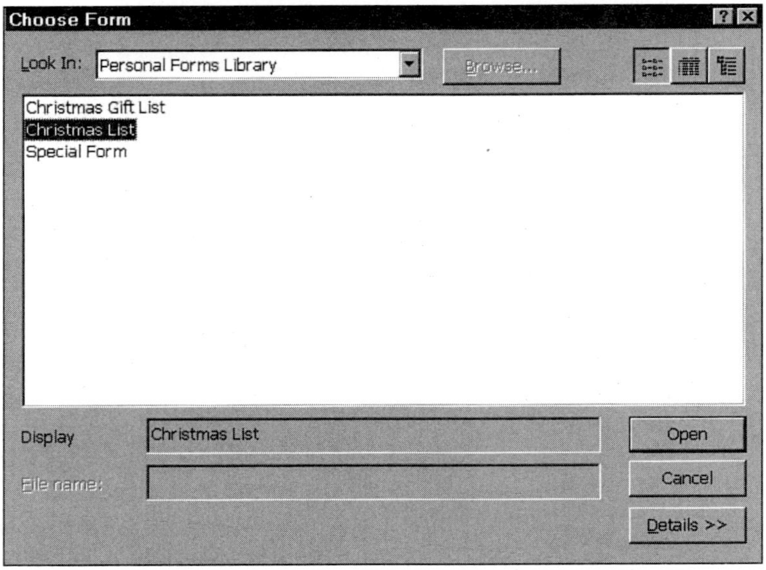

In addition to saving a form to the Personal (or Organizational) Forms Library, which makes it available on your local computer or the network to which your computer is attached, you have several other options for saving a form, described in the following sections.

SAVING A FORM IN A FOLDER

Saving a form saves an individual instance of the form with a particular set of data in its fields. *Publishing* a form saves the form design to a forms library, where it can be used to create form instances based on its design.

When you create a new instance of a form, either from a standard Outlook form or a custom form, once you click the Save and Close button (shown in Figure 40.71), the form is saved as an item in the current folder, along with any data you have entered into it. For example, your Contacts folder contains the *Contact items (page 298)* made from the standard Contact form by clicking the New Contact button, and possibly items made from a custom Contact form you have assigned to that folder, and similarly for the other folders.

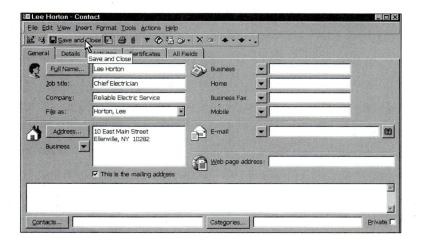

Figure 40.71
Saving a form.

SAVING A FORM AS A TEMPLATE

You can also save a form as a form template. An Outlook template is a separate file with an .oft extension (similar in functionality to the Word .dot template). Outlook templates are convenient for e-mailing to other users, or saving to a disk for transfer to another computer, or just as a convenient way of backing up your forms individually. To save a form as a template, you can start with a new blank form created from a form in a forms library, or you can use a form item (but be sure you clear it of unnecessary data before saving it in that case).

In either case, to save a form template:

1. In either form or design view, select Save As from the File menu, as shown in Figure 40.72.

2. The Save As dialog box opens with a choice of several save types, as shown in Figure 40.73.

3. Select the Outlook Template (*.oft) save format, and click the Save button.

Figure 40.72
Starting the Save
process for an item.

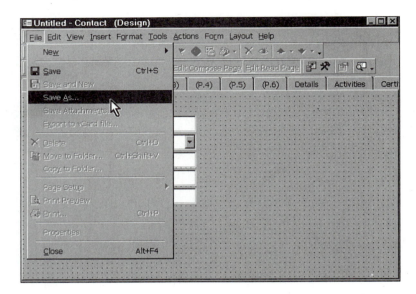

SAVING A FORM AS A FILE

There are several other options for saving an item as a file, which you can see in Figure 40.73. The *Text Only (.txt) format* saves the data in the item as unformatted text, as you would expect. The *Rich Text Format (.rtf) option (page 183)* may be disappointing if you are expecting to see the saved form as it looks in Outlook. All you get is a text output of the data in the item, with minimal formatting, as shown in Figure 40.74.

The *Message (.msg) format* produces a file that can be opened directly by double-clicking; it opens as a standard Outlook item. This is a good choice for saving an individual item to send to another person or transfer to another computer on a disk. After opening a message format file, it can be saved to a folder in the user's Outlook folders tree.

The *v-card (.vcf) option* saves a contact in a special format that can be e-mailed and then easily added to the recipient's Contacts list. A v-card file cannot be opened directly, unlike a message file.

Figure 40.73
The Save As dialog box with choice of save types.

Figure 40.74
A Contact item saved in Rich Text Format.

DISTRIBUTING A FORM

The Message and Template save options are useful for sending files to other users, as they can be attached to mail messages and then opened on the recipient's computer. Additionally, you can send a vcard directly (without the need to save a contact in vcard format first) by selecting Forward as vCard from the Actions menu of a Contact item, as shown in Figure 40.75.

Figure 40.75
Forwarding a contact as a vcard.

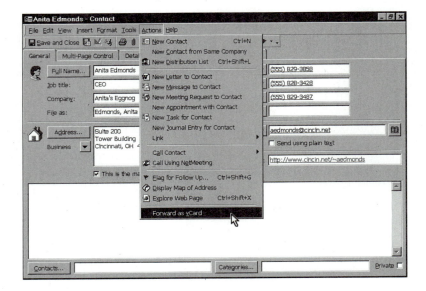

FORM LIBRARIES AND MANAGING FORMS

You can delete forms from a forms library, as well as copying and moving forms to other folders, in the Forms Management dialog box, opened from a folder's properties sheet. To open the Forms Management dialog box:

1. Go to the Tools menu, and select Options to open the Options dialog box.
2. Click the Other tab, and then click the Advanced Options button, as shown in Figure 40.76.
3. In the Advanced Options dialog box, click the Custom Forms button, as shown in Figure 40.77.
4. On the Custom Forms dialog box, click the Manage Forms button, as shown in Figure 40.78. (Yes, this is getting rather tedious!)
5. The Forms Manager dialog box opens, with two panes, one of them generally displaying your Organizational or Personal Forms Library, as shown in Figure 40.79.

6. If you see the form you want to delete, just select it and click the Delete key.

7. Otherwise, you can locate the form by clicking the Set button over one of the panes to open the Set Library To dialog box, which is shown in Figure 40.80.

8. You can either select a forms library in the Forms Library drop-down list, with the Forms Library option selected (the default) or select an Outlook folder by clicking the Folder Forms Library option button, and expanding the Personal (or Organizational) Folders tree, as shown in Figure 40.81.

9. Once you have located the folder that contains the form you want to delete, click the OK button in the Set Library To dialog box to return to the Manage Forms dialog box.

10. You can now select the form to delete from the folder you opened, and click the Delete button to delete the form.

11. In the same Manage Forms dialog box, you can also copy a form from one folder to another, or from a folder to a library. Figure 40.82 shows the Special Events Staff form being copied from the Personal Forms Library to the Company Information folder.

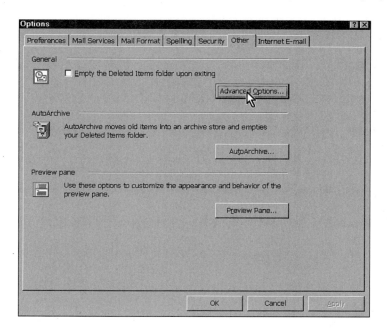

Figure 40.76
Opening the Advanced Options dialog box.

PART

VIII

CH

40

Figure 40.77
Opening the Custom
Forms dialog box.

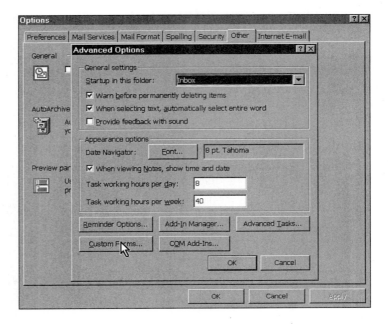

Figure 40.78
Opening the Forms
Manager dialog box.

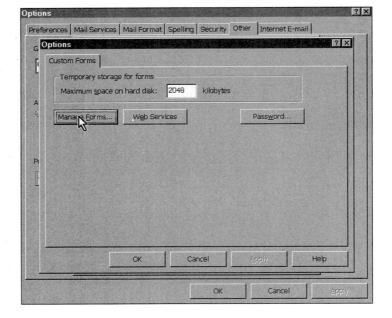

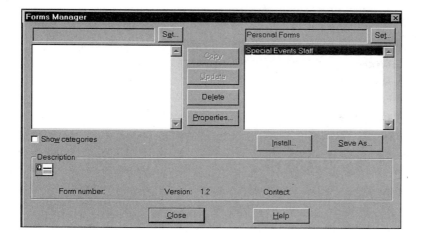

Figure 40.79
The Forms Manager dialog box, with the Personal Forms Library selected in the right pane.

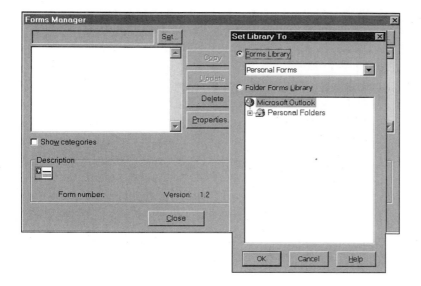

Figure 40.80
The Set Library To dialog box, with the Forms Library option selected.

Figure 40.81
The Set Library To dialog box, with the Folder Forms Library option selected and the Outlook folder tree expanded.

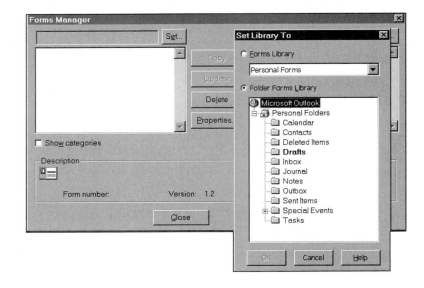

Figure 40.82
Copying a form from the Personal Forms library to an Outlook folder.

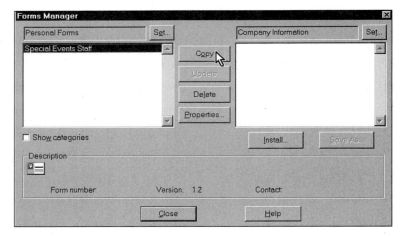

The Forms Manager dialog box is only available if you installed Outlook for Corporate/Workgroup E-mail support; it is not available if you installed Outlook for Internet Mail only.

CHANGING THE DEFAULT FORM USED BY CONTACT ITEMS

If you have created a custom Contact form and want to use it in place of the default Contact form for any contact items created in your Contacts folder, first save the custom form to your Personal Forms Library, and then select it as the form to use for the Contacts folder by implementing the following steps:

1. Right-click the Contacts icon in the Outlook bar (or the Contacts folder in the Folders List) and select Properties from the shortcut menu, as shown in Figure 40.83.

2. The default Contact form is the selection in the "When Posting to This Folder, Use:" drop-down list in the middle of the Properties sheet.

3. Drop down the list and select the Forms... entry, as shown in Figure 40.84.

4. Select the Personal Forms Library in the Look In list, then select the custom contact form you want to use, and click the Open button, as shown in Figure 40.85.

5. Now the chosen custom Contact form will be used when you create a new Contact item in the Contacts folder.

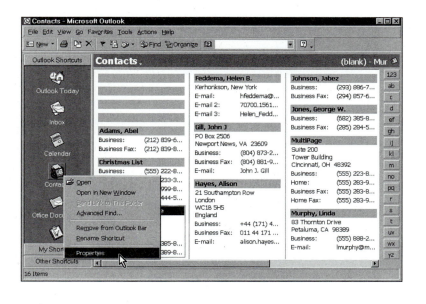

Figure 40.83
Opening the Contacts folder's Properties sheet.

PART

VIII

CH

40

Figure 40.84
Selecting the Forms…
selection in the
Contacts folder's
Properties sheet.

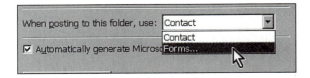

Figure 40.85
Assigning a custom
form to the Contacts
folder.

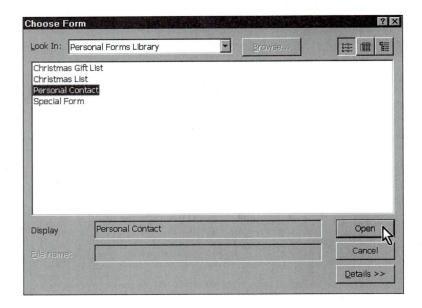

Caution

Assigning a new form to a folder ensures that any new forms created in a folder will be based on the new form, but it does not change the form type of items already present in the folder. To do that, you need to write VBS code to change the message class of all items that were in the folder before you changed its default form.

Tip #264 from
Helen Bell Feddema

If you just have a few items to change to another form, you can create a new contact with the EXACT same name and then save it. A dialog box pops up telling you that there is another contact with the same name, and asking if you want to use that data. Click OK to replace the old form with the new one. If you have numerous items to upgrade, though, you will need to write code to change them to another form.

SHARING CUSTOM FORMS

If your computer is attached to a network running Exchange Server, you can share a custom form by saving it to the Organizational Forms Library instead of the Personal Forms Library. The Organizational Forms Library is available to all users on the network, so they can all use your form to make new items.

TROUBLESHOOTING

Q: Where's my form?

A: If you can't find a form after publishing it, you may have inadvertently saved it to another folder or library than you intended. If you are using Outlook in the Corporate/Workgroup mode, open the Forms Manager dialog box to locate your form (see Figures 40.76 through 40.82).

Q: When I create a new item using a custom form I designed, it already has data on it. Why isn't it blank?

A: You probably saved the form with some test data on it. Open the form in design view, and clear out all the data (look at all the fields on the All Fields tab to make sure you have cleared all the fields), then publish it again. Now new items created from the form should be blank.

Q: Why do I get the standard form instead of my custom form when I create a new item in a folder?

A: By default, Outlook uses the standard form for a folder, such as the Contact form for the Contacts folder. If you want to use a custom Contact form for the Contact folder, assign your custom form as the form to use for that folder, as described in the "Changing the Default Form Used by Contact Items" section in this chapter.

Q: Why do items imported from Access not use my custom form?

A: When you import items from another program, Outlook always uses the standard form for that folder, even if you have assigned the folder a custom form. To use a custom form when importing, you have to write VBA or VBS code to do the import, creating new items based on your custom form. You can download a form with a VBS procedure to upgrade the message class of items in a folder from the author's Web site, `http://www.ulster.net/~hfeddema/CodeSamples.htm`.

Q: I want to delete a form from my Personal Forms Library, but I installed the Internet Mail Only version of Outlook. How can I delete the form?

A: You can temporarily switch to Corporate/Workgroup mode, open the Forms Manager to delete the form (and do any other form housekeeping you need to do), then switch back to IMO mode. To switch Outlook modes, follow these steps:

PART

VIII

CH

40

1. Drop down the Tools menu.
2. Select the Options command.
3. Click the Mail Delivery tab.
4. Click the Reconfigure Mail Support button.
5. Select the Corporate or Workgroup option and click the Next button.
6. Click the Yes button; Outlook closes automatically.
7. When you next open Outlook, it will be in the Corporate/Workgroup mode.

CREATING AND USING CUSTOM FIELDS

In this chapter   *by Helen Feddema*

OUTLOOK AS A DEVELOPMENT ENVIRONMENT

Although you normally interact with Outlook through its built-in *forms (page 24)* and actions, Outlook offers developers the opportunity to create custom forms based on Outlook's built-in forms, and also to write code to add functionality to these forms. When you need to design a very specialized form from scratch, you need the techniques covered in Chapter 40, "Creating and Using Custom Forms," which covers the creation of custom forms.

But sometimes you just need to add a few custom fields to a standard form, or use a few of the built-in fields that aren't normally displayed on the form. In this chapter you will learn how to add custom fields to a form.

A Note on Terminology

A *Field* is a piece of data associated with an Outlook item of a particular type, such as a Contact or Appointment item. You can see the item's fields and their values (if any) on the All Fields page of the item (in design view). In the Outlook interface, when you add a field to a form from the Field Chooser, it appears on the form as a bound control.

A *Built-in Field* is a field that belongs to a standard (unmodified) Outlook item, such as a Contact or Task.

A *Custom Field* is a field that you create for a customized Outlook item.

A *Control* is an interface element on the form; controls can be bound to fields (so they display data), or unbound.

A *Bound* control displays data from a particular field on a form; you can usually edit the data in bound controls.

An *Unbound* control displays text entered by the form designer for informational purposes, or serves as a decorative element (such as lines and images).

When you work with fields from VBS or VBA code, you are working with *Properties*; each property corresponds to a field belonging to the item. Fields and properties often have similar, even identical names, but there are some exceptions. See the Outlook Fields and Equivalent Properties Help topic for a listing of the Outlook fields and properties.

→ For instructions on opening this Help topic, **see** the "Getting Help on Outlook Fields and Properties" tip in Chapter 40, "Creating and Using Custom Forms."

WHY DO YOU NEED CUSTOM FIELDS?

You may find that you can enter all the information you need into the available built-in fields displayed on a standard Outlook form. In that case, you don't need to create a custom form; you can just use one of the default forms. Even if you don't see all the fields you need on a standard form, suitable fields may still be available—not all the built-in fields are displayed in controls on the standard forms.

Tip #265 from

Helen Bell Feddema

If you can use built-in fields for your needs, it's a good idea to do so—using built-in fields enables you to export data using the Import and Export command on the File menu, and simplifies referencing the fields in code, if you do need to write VBS or VBA code.

If you want to use a built-in field that isn't displayed on a standard form (say the Customer ID field, which is not displayed on the standard Contact form), you need to create a custom form, but you don't need to create a custom field. All you have to do is display the built-in field you want to use in a control on a page of your custom form.

Before creating a custom field, switch to Design view and take a look at the All Fields tab, where you can see all the available fields (you will see many fields that don't appear on the standard form). Table 41.1 lists the available fields for the standard Contact item, and notes which of them are bound to visible controls on the standard forms. The available fields for Mail Messages, Appointments, and Tasks are listed in Table 41.2 through Table 41.4.

Switching to Design View

To switch to design view for an item, first open the item, then pull down the Tools menu, and select the Forms submenu (if you don't see the Forms selection on the menu, click the downward double-arrow to expand the menu to show this item). Then select Design This Form from the Forms pop-out menu, as shown in Figure 41.1.

Tip #266 from
Helen Bell Feddema

By default, Outlook is installed with menus set to display only the most commonly used commands, with a downward-pointing double arrow you can click to expand a menu to show all the commands. To display all the menu commands all the time, right-click the menu or toolbar background, select Customize, and uncheck the "Menus show recently used commands first" check box on the Options page of the dialog box.

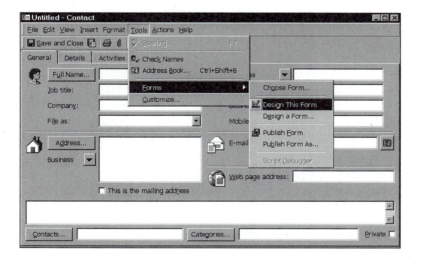

Figure 41.1
Switching to Design view.

If you plan to design custom forms on a regular basis, a Design This Form button on the on the toolbar will save you lots of time pulling down a menu and submenu every time you want to switch to Design view.

Tip #267 from Helen Bell Feddema	Implement the following steps to put the Design This Form button on the standard Outlook toolbar, to make it easier to switch to Design view.

1. Open a form (don't switch to Design view).
2. Right-click the grey background on the form menu to open the shortcut menu.
3. Select Customize from the shortcut menu, as shown in Figure 41.2.
4. In the Customize dialog box, select Tools from the Categories list, and drag the Design This Form item from the Commands list to a location on the toolbar, as shown in Figure 41.3. (Note that the pointer turns into a little button with an attached plus sign as you drag it.)
5. Click the Close button. Now you can see the new button on the Outlook toolbar, as shown in Figure 41.4.

Figure 41.2
Opening the Toolbar Customize dialog box.

Figure 41.3
Dragging a command to the toolbar.

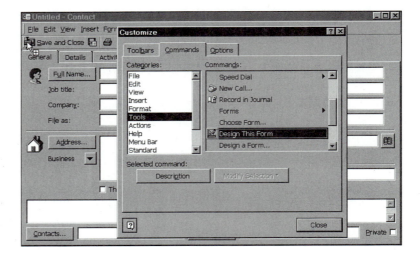

Figure 41.4
The new Design This Form button on the toolbar.

When you work with controls in Form Design view, you can use the Field Chooser dialog box, which offers a selection of lists of fields to place on the form. You can see the fields belonging to a form on the form's All Fields page, in Design view. The following tables list the standard fields for the Outlook items, and indicate whether or not they are displayed on the standard form for that item. See the list of Outlook fields and properties in Appendix H, "Outlook Fields and Equivalent Properties." for a list of all the Outlook fields, and their corresponding property names, as used in VBS and VBA code.

Caution

There are some discrepancies between the lists of built-in fields in the Field Chooser and the list on the All Fields tab. For example, the Notes field appears on the Field Chooser for a Contact item, but not on the list of fields on the All Fields tab.

TABLE 41.1 AVAILABLE FIELDS FOR THE STANDARD OUTLOOK CONTACT ITEM

Field Name	On Standard Form
Account	No
Address Selected	Yes
Address Selector	Yes
Anniversary	Yes
Assistant's Name	Yes
Assistant's Phone	No
Attachment	No
Billing Information	No
Birthday	Yes
Business Address	Yes
Business Address City	Yes
Business Address Country	Yes
Business Address PO Box	Yes
Business Address Postal Code	Yes
Business Address State	Yes
Business Address Street	Yes

continues

PART
VIII

CH
41

TABLE 41.1 CONTINUED	
Field Name	**On Standard Form**
Business Fax	Yes
Business Home Page	Yes
Business Phone	Yes
Business Phone 2	Yes
Callback	Yes
Car Phone	Yes
Categories	Yes
Children	No
City	Yes
Company	Yes
Company Main Phone	Yes
Computer Network Name	No
Contacts	Yes
Country/Region	Yes
Created	No
Customer ID	No
Department	Yes
E-mail	Yes
E-mail 2	Yes
E-mail 3	Yes
E-mail Selected	Yes
E-mail Selector	Yes
File As	Yes
First Name	Yes
Flag Status	No
Follow Up Flag	No
FTP Site	No
Full Name	Yes
Gender	No
Government ID Number	No
Hobbies	No

Field Name	On Standard Form
Home Address	Yes
Home Address City	Yes
Home Address Country	Yes
Home Address PO Box	Yes
Home Address Postal Code	Yes
Home Address State	Yes
Home Address Street	Yes
Home Fax	Yes
Home Phone	Yes
Home Phone 2	Yes
Icon	No
In Folder	No
Initials	No
Internet Free/Busy Address	Yes
ISDN	Yes
Job Title	Yes
Journal	No
Language	No
Last Name	Yes
Location	No
Mailing Address	Yes
Mailing Address Indicator	Yes
Manager's Name	Yes
Message Class	No
Middle Name	Yes
Mileage	No
Mobile Phone	Yes
Modified	No
Nickname	Yes
Notes (not in All Fields list; corresponds to Body property)	Yes
Office Location	Yes
Organizational ID Number	No

continues

TABLE 41.1   CONTINUED

Field Name	On Standard Form
Other Address	Yes
Other Address City	Yes
Other Address Country	Yes
Other Address PO Box	Yes
Other Address Postal Code	Yes
Other Address State	Yes
Other Address Street	Yes
Other Fax	Yes
Other Phone	Yes
Outlook Internal Version	No
Outlook Version	No
Pager	Yes
Personal Home Page	No
Phone 1 Selected	Yes
Phone 1 Selector	Yes
Phone 2 Selected	Yes
Phone 2 Selector	Yes
Phone 3 Selected	Yes
Phone 3 Selector	Yes
Phone 4 Selected	Yes
Phone 4 Selector	Yes
Phone 5 Selected	Yes
Phone 5 Selector	Yes
Phone 6 Selected	Yes
Phone 6 Selector	Yes
Phone 7 Selected	Yes
Phone 7 Selector	Yes
Phone 8 Selected	Yes
Phone 8 Selector	Yes
PO Box	Yes
Primary Phone	Yes
Private	Yes

Field Name	On Standard Form
Profession	Yes
Radio Phone	Yes
Read	No
Referred By	No
Reminder	No
Reminder Time	No
Reminder Topic	No
Send Plain Text Only	Yes
Sensitivity	No
Size	No
Spouse	Yes
State	Yes
Street Address	Yes
Subject	Yes
Suffix	Yes
Telex	Yes
Title	Yes
TTY/TDD Phone	Yes
User Field 1	No
User Field 2	No
User Field 3	No
User Field 4	No
Web Page	Yes
ZIP/Postal Code	Yes

TABLE 41.2   AVAILABLE FIELDS FOR THE STANDARD MAIL MESSAGE ITEM

Field Name	On Standard Form
Attachment	No
Bcc	Yes
Billing Information	No
Categories	No
Cc	Yes

continues

TABLE 41.2   CONTINUED

Field Name	On Standard Form
Changed By	No
Contacts	No
Conversation	No
Created	No
Defer Until	No
Do Not AutoArchive	No
Download State	No
Due By	No
Expires	No
Flag Status	No
Follow Up Flag	No
From	No
Have Replies Sent To	No
Icon	No
Importance	No
In Folder	No
Internet Account	No
Junk E-mail Type	No
Message (not in All Fields list)	Yes
Message Class	No
Mileage	No
Modified	No
Outlook Internal Version	No
Outlook Version	No
Read	No
Receipt Requested	No
Received	No
Relevance	No
Remote Status	No
Retrieval Time	No
Sensitivity	No
Sent	No

Field Name	On Standard Form
Size	No
Subject	Yes
To	Yes
Tracking Status	No

TABLE 41.3   AVAILABLE FIELDS FOR THE STANDARD APPOINTMENT ITEM

Field Name	On Standard Form
All Day Event	Yes
Attachment	No
Billing Information	No
Categories	Yes
Contacts	Yes
Conversation	No
Created	No
Directory Server	Yes
Do Not AutoArchive	No
Duration	No
End	Yes
Event Address	No
Icon	No
Importance	Yes
In Folder	No
Location	Yes
Meeting Status	No
Message Class	No
Mileage	No
Modified	No
NetMeetingAutoStart	Yes
NetMeeting Office Document Path	Yes
NetMeeting Organizer E-mail	Yes
Online Meeting	Yes

continues

TABLE 41.3 CONTINUED

Field Name	On Standard Form
Online Meeting Type	Yes
Optional Attendees	Yes
Organizer	No
Outlook Internal Version	No
Outlook Version	No
Read	No
Recurrence	Yes
Recurrence Pattern	Yes
Recurrence Range End	Yes
Recurrence Range Start	Yes
Recurring	Yes
Remind Beforehand	Yes
Reminder	Yes
Reminder Override Default	No
Reminder Sound	Yes
Reminder Sound File	Yes
Required Attendees	Yes
Resources	No
Response Requested	No
Sensitivity	No
Show Time As	Yes
Size	No
Start	Yes
Subject	Yes

TABLE 41.4 AVAILABLE FIELDS FOR THE STANDARD TASK ITEM

Field Name	On Standard Form
% Complete	Yes
Actual Work	Yes
Assigned	No
Attachment	No

Field Name	On Standard Form
Billing Information	Yes
Categories	Yes
Company	Yes
Complete	Yes
Contact	No
Contacts	Yes
Conversation	No
Created	No
Date Completed	Yes
Do Not AutoArchive	No
Due Date	Yes
Icon	No
In Folder	No
Message Class	No
Mileage	Yes
Modified	No
Outlook Internal Version	No
Outlook Version	No
Owner	Yes
Priority	Yes
Read	No
Recurring	No
Reminder	Yes
Reminder Override Default	No
Reminder Sound	Yes
Reminder Sound File	Yes
Reminder Time	Yes
Request Status	No
Requested By	No
Role	No
Schedule+ Priority	No
Sensitivity (bound to Private check box)	Yes

continues

TABLE 41.4 CONTINUED

Field Name	On Standard Form
Size	No
Start Date	Yes
Status	Yes
Subject	Yes
Team Task	No
To	No
Total Work	Yes

If one of the built-in fields is suitable for your needs, you don't need to create a custom field; you can just drag the field to an appropriate page of the form (where it will appear as a bound TextBox control).

Figure 41.5 shows the Billing Information field being dragged to the General page of a Contact item, in the place where the Web Address field usually appears (that control was deleted).

Tip #268 from

Helen Bell Feddema

> To delete a single control, place your cursor on it (white sizing squares should appear around its border) and click the Delete key. To delete a group of controls, select them all using Ctrl+Click, then press the Delete key.

Figure 41.5
Dragging the Billing Information field to a Contact item's General page.

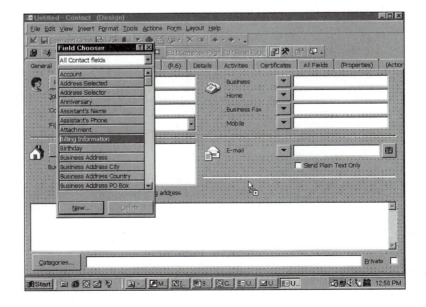

Figure 41.6 shows the same form in Form view, with the new field visible.

The grid of dots you see in Design view is helpful in lining up controls, but if you prefer to work without a grid, you can turn it off by pulling down the Layout menu on a form, and clicking the Show Grid toggle command.

To move controls on a form, drag them with the mouse. See Chapter 40, "Creating and Using Custom Forms," for more details on working with controls on forms.

Figure 41.6
The Billing Information field on the Contact item.

Or you can create another type of control and bind it to the field, as shown in Figure 41.7.

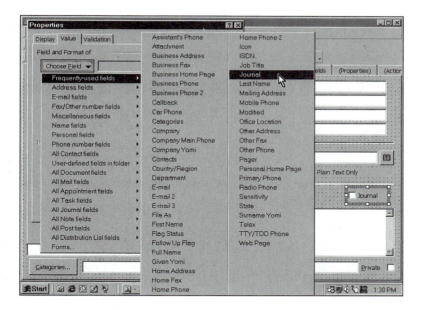

Figure 41.7
Binding a newly inserted CheckBox control to the Journal Yes/No field.

Caution

Although you can edit the General page on a Contact item or the Message page of a Mail Message item (a step up from Outlook 97), the main pages of Task and Appointment items are still read-only, so you can't add controls to these pages.

CREATING A SIMPLE CUSTOM FIELD

If you can't find an appropriate field in the list of available fields for an item, you can create a custom field in one of two ways: directly in the All Fields tab of the item, and from a control's properties sheet (discussed later in this chapter). To create a custom field directly:

1. In Design view, click the All Fields tab of an item. The User-defined Fields in This Item selection (the default) should initially show no fields.
2. Click the New…button to open the New Field dialog box.
3. Enter "Preferred" as the name for the field in the Name box.
4. Select the Yes/No field type in the Type box.
5. Select the Yes/No format in the Format box (the selection of formats depends on the chosen field type).
6. Click the OK button.
7. The new field appears in the list of User-defined Fields in This Item.

Figure 41.8 shows the new field's properties being set up, and Figure 41.9 shows the Preferred field in the list of user-defined fields. This field could be used to indicate that the contact is a Preferred customer, who will get special mailings or discounts.

Note

You can select the User-defined fields in folder selection when creating a custom field, to make the field available to all items in the folder.

Figure 41.8
Creating a new Yes/No field from the All Fields page.

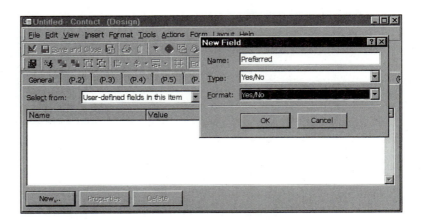

Tip #269 from
Helen Bell Feddema

In naming fields, it is best to avoid using punctuation marks such as $, #, or %, as they may cause problems later on, especially if you plan to export data from Outlook to other Office applications, using Automation. Field names without spaces or punctuation marks should be trouble-free however you use them.

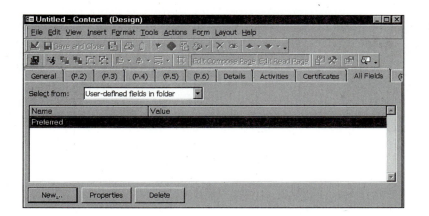

Figure 41.9
The new Preferred field in the list of user-defined fields.

ADDING A CUSTOM FIELD TO AN OUTLOOK FORM

You can also create a custom field on-the-fly, from a control's properties sheet (say after looking for a suitable built-in field and not finding one). The following steps describe this method of creating a custom field.

1. In Design view, select the tab where you want to place the control.

2. Click a tool on the Toolbox, then click on the form to insert a control of your choice on the form.

3. Right-click the control and select the Properties command to open the control's properties sheet to the Value page.

4. Click the New button to open the New Field dialog box.

5. From that point on, follow steps 3 through 6 in the preceding list to create the custom field.

Tip #270 from
Helen Bell Feddema

If you don't see the Toolbox in Form Design view, you can turn it on by clicking the Control Toolbox button on the form toolbar.

Tip #271 from
Helen Bell Feddema

If you create a custom field, then delete it from the All Fields page of a form (perhaps because you realize it is the wrong data type), it may still be in the list of user-defined fields on the Field Chooser, and you won't be able to re-create the field with the same name. Usually closing Outlook and reopening will clear out deleted custom field names.

Caution

If you drag a field from the Field Chooser to a form, it is usually a text box. If you then select a new field for binding the control, even if that field has a data type more suitable to another control type (such as a Yes/No field, which is better displayed in a check box or option button control), you can't change the control type. To prevent this problem, you need to think ahead, and either create the field in the All Fields tab first, then drag it from the Field Chooser, or place a control of the appropriate type on the form, then create a new field for the control with the right data type.

Figure 41.10 shows how you start to create a custom field from a control's properties sheet.

Figure 41.10
Creating a custom field from a control's properties sheet.

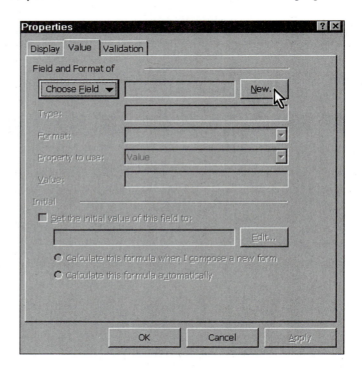

Table 41.5 lists the field types you can use when creating custom fields:

TABLE 41.5   FIELD TYPES FOR OUTLOOK CUSTOM FIELDS

Type	Usage
Combination	Combines the values of several fields and/or text into a single expression
Currency	Numeric data used for financial calculations
Date/Time	Date and time data
Duration	Numeric data as minutes, hours, or days

Type	Usage
Formula	Calculations based on standard and custom fields
Integer	Non-decimal (whole number) numeric data
Keywords	Used to group and find items, similar to Categories
Number	Non-financial numeric data
Percent	Numeric data expressed as a percentage
Text	Text, or combinations of text and numbers up to 255 characters long
Yes/No	Data that is either True or False (or Yes and No)

Most of the field types are standard; you may be familiar with Integer, Text, and Yes/No fields from Word, Access, or Excel. However, there are a few special Outlook field types, not used in other Office applications; they will be discussed in the following sections.

CREATING A COMBINATION CUSTOM FIELD

As the name suggests, a combination field concatenates data from several fields or text strings. Outlook has a number of built-in combination fields, such as the Full Name field, which combines the components of a contact's name, and the File As field, which offers several combinations of company and personal name fields. You can also create your own combination field, for example, a Couple field that combines the contact name and spouse name (for use in addressing invitations or Christmas cards), by implementing the following steps:

1. Switch to Design view in a contact item.
2. Place a TextBox control on a page of the form, by clicking on the TextBox tool in the Toolbox.
3. Right-click the control and select the Properties command from its context menu to open the properties sheet.
4. Click the New button to open the New Field dialog box.
5. Give the field a name and select Combination as the field type.
6. Click the Edit button to open the Combination Formula Field dialog box.
7. Click the Field button to select the Full Name field from the Frequently-used Fields list.
8. Type "and" after [Full Name] (without the quotes) as the connecting text between the two fields. (There is no need to use the ampersand to connect the text to the fields, or to put the text in quotes, as you would with VBS code.)
9. Click the Field button again to select the Spouse field from the Name Fields list.
10. Click the OK button to save the new combination field, then click OK on the New Field dialog box.
11. Figure 41.11 shows the entire field expression in the Combination Formula Field dialog box.

Tip #272 from
Helen Bell Feddema

If all the couples on your list have the same last names, and you just store the spouse's first name in the Spouse field, you could use the expression

[FirstName] and [Spouse] [LastName]

instead.

Figure 41.11
Creating a combination field.

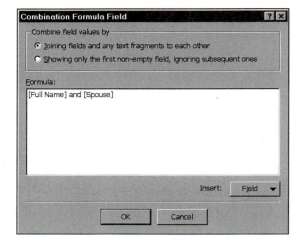

The combination field expression now appears in the text box on the control's properties sheet, as shown in Figure 41.12.

Figure 41.12
The combination field expression in the properties sheet.

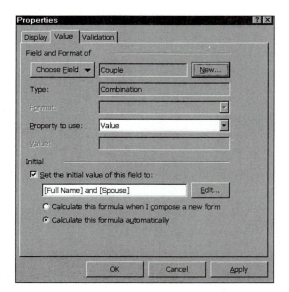

The resulting expression is shown in Form view in Figure 41.13.

To rename one of the extra pages on a form (P.2 through P.6), pull down the Form menu on a form in Design view, and click the Display This Page selection, then pull down the same menu again and click the Rename Page selection, and rename the page in the Rename dialog box.

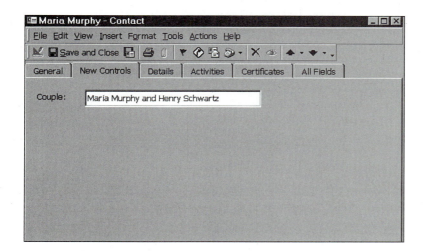

Figure 41.13
The combination field on the form.

CREATING A FORMULA CUSTOM FIELD

The other special Outlook field type is the formula field, which has some resemblance to an Excel formula, or an Access calculated field. Formula fields are started in a similar way to combination fields. Once you have the New Field dialog box open, implement the following steps to create a field that displays the number of days to Christmas:

1. Place a TextBox control on the form, as in earlier examples.
2. Select Formula as the field type.
3. Click the Edit button to open the Formula Field dialog box.
4. Use the Function button to select the functions to use in the field, and the Field button to select any fields needed to replace the function argument placeholders. (Or, if you prefer, you can type the entire expression directly.) Figure 41.14 shows the DateSerial function being selected (one of the date functions needed to create this formula).
5. Figure 41.15 shows the completed formula in the Formula Field dialog box.
6. The resulting formula field with the days to Christmas calculation is shown in form view in Figure 41.16. The entire formula is DateDiff("d", Date( ), DateSerial(Year(Date( )),12,25)).

PART

VIII

CH

41

Note

When composing formulas for formula fields, it helps to have some experience with creating formulas in Excel, or calculated fields in Access. The Outlook Help topic "Examples of Formula and Combination Fields" has some useful examples that you can adapt to your own needs.

Caution

The Help topic mentioned in the preceding note shows quotes surrounding literal text. This is incorrect; in Outlook you should omit the quotes.

Tip #274 from

Helen Bell Feddema

If you prefer, you can type in field names instead of selecting them, but selecting them guarantees that they are typed correctly.

Figure 41.14
Selecting the DateSerial function for a formula field.

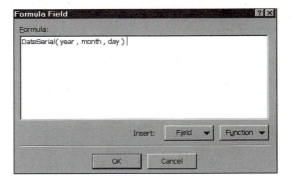

Figure 41.15
The complete formula in the Formula Field dialog box.

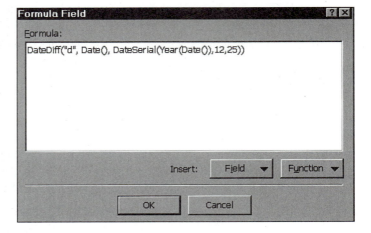

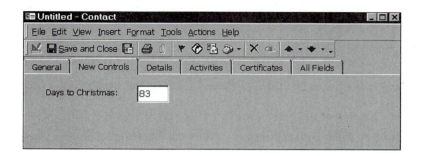

Figure 41.16
The days to Christmas formula field.

ADDING A CUSTOM FIELD TO A VIEW

I made a Christmas Gift List custom Contact form using the two preceding custom fields and one other field (Gift), bound to a combo box. The Christmas List page of this form displays the Couple Name combination field, the Days to Christmas formula field, and the Preferred Gift text field, as shown in Figure 41.17.

A *combo box control (page 1041)* allows the user to select one of several items from a drop-down list, or type in a value. In Outlook, you can either type the list choices into the control's properties sheet, or fill the list from code, using an array (a fairly advanced programming technique). You don't have the option of filling a combo box from a table of data, as in Access. To create a combo box for selecting gifts, follow the steps below:

1. Open a form, and switch to design view.
2. Place a ComboBox control on a page of the form, by clicking on the ComboBox tool in the Toolbox.
3. Right-click the ComboBox control and select Properties from its context menu.
4. On the Display tab, enter the name cboGift ("cbo" is a commonly used prefix indicating that the control is a combo box).
5. On the Value tab, create a custom field called Gift (field type Text).
6. Enter "Gold Pen; Golf Balls; Calendar" in the Possible Values box.
7. Run the form by selecting Run This Form from the Form menu.
8. Drop down the combo box's list; you should see the three selections you entered in the properties sheet.

After publishing the form to my Personal Forms library, I created a Christmas Gift List folder to store these contacts, and assigned it the custom Christmas Gift List form as the default form to use for the folder. To assign a published custom form to a folder:

1. Right-click the folder in the Shortcuts list or Folder list.
2. Select Properties from the shortcut menu, as shown in Figure 41.18.
3. Drop down the selection list in the When Posting to This Folder, Use list box, and select Forms…, as shown in Figure 41.19.

PART

VIII

CH

41

4. In the Choose Form dialog box, first select the appropriate forms library from the Look In list box, then select the form, as shown in Figure 41.20.

5. Click the Open button on the Choose Form dialog box, then the OK button on the folder properties sheet.

6. Now when you create a new contact in this folder, your custom Christmas Gift List form will be used.

Figure 41.17
Custom fields on a page of a custom Contact form.

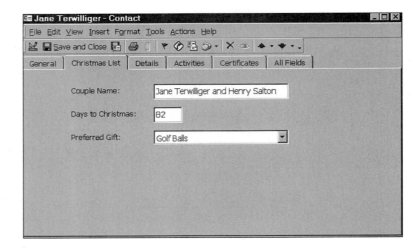

Figure 41.18
Opening a folder's properties sheet.

Figure 41.19
Selecting the Forms library for assigning a form to a folder.

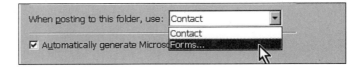

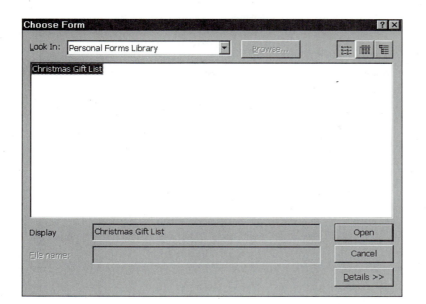

Figure 41.20
Selecting a custom
form from the Choose
Form dialog box.

Tip #275 from
Helen Bell Feddema

> To use custom fields as columns in a view, they must be created as fields in a folder, not
> just as fields in an item. To create fields in a folder, switch to Design view on a form and
> click the All Fields tab, then select the User-defined Fields in Folder selection before creat-
> ing the fields. The following discussion assumes that you have created your custom fields
> as fields in a folder.

After creating one or more custom fields to use on a custom form, and making the custom
form the default form for a folder, you may want to display a custom field as a column in a
view.

To add two of the custom fields just created to a view for a folder:

1. With the Christmas Gift List folder open, select View from the Outlook menu, then
   select Current View from the View menu, and Customize Current View from the
   Current View submenu, as shown in Figure 41.21.

2. Click the Fields button on the View Summary dialog box, as shown in Figure 41.22.

3. Select the User-defined Fields in Folder selection from the Select Available Fields
   From list box at the bottom of the Show Fields dialog box.

4. Select the Couple and Gift fields and click the Add button to add the fields to the view,
   as shown in Figure 41.23.

5. Remove any fields you don't want in the view by selecting them and clicking the
   Remove button.

6. Use the Move Up and Move Down buttons to arrange the fields in the order you want.

7. The final selection is Couple, Home Address, and Gift, as shown in Figure 41.24.

8. Click the OK button on the Show Fields dialog box, and then the OK button on the View Summary dialog box.

9. Figure 41.25 shows the finished view.

Figure 41.21
Customizing a view.

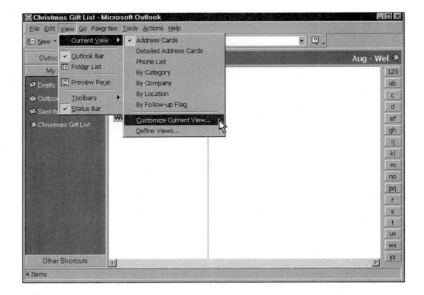

Figure 41.22
The View Summary dialog box.

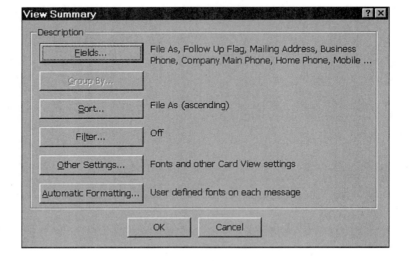

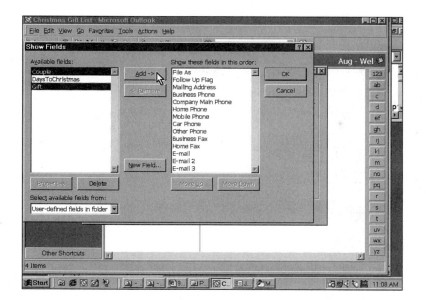

Figure 41.23
Adding custom fields to a view.

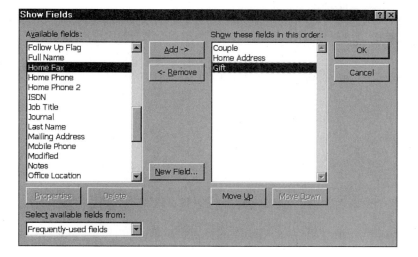

Figure 41.24
The final selection of fields for a custom view.

Figure 41.25
The finished view, showing custom fields.

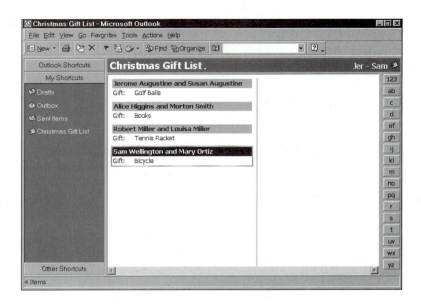

TROUBLESHOOTING

Q: **I made a custom field with the Text data type, and now I realize it should be a Date/Time field. How can I change it?**

A: Unfortunately, you can't change the data type of an Outlook custom field. You will need to delete the field from the All Fields tab, and then re-create it using the Date/Time data type.

Q: **I can change a text box to a combo box (or vice versa) in Access. How can I change a control's type in Outlook?**

A: Unfortunately, Outlook does not let you change a control's type. You must delete the control and replace it with another control of the desired type.

Q: **I have a formula that works in an Access calculated field, but it doesn't work in an Outlook formula field.**

A: There are some syntactical differences between Access calculated fields and Outlook formula fields. Some likely traps:

Access calculated fields start with an equals sign; you don't need it in Outlook.

Literal text in Access calculated fields needs to be enclosed in quotes and concatenated with ampersands; they aren't needed in Outlook formulas. Check the "Examples of Formula and Combination Fields" Help topic in Outlook for some examples of formula field expressions that work in Outlook, but be aware that quotes are used in these examples (they should be removed).

Q: **I changed a formula, and when I ran the form, the results of the formula were correct, but the old formula still displays in Design view. How can I fix it?**

A: Saving and reopening the form will usually fix this problem.

CHAPTER 42

ENHANCING OUTLOOK FORMS WITH VISUAL BASIC SCRIPT CODE

In this chapter

by Helen Feddema

WHAT IS VISUAL BASIC SCRIPTING EDITION?

For the first time, Outlook 2000 now supports Visual Basic for Applications (VBA), the Visual Basic dialect used in other Office applications. However, Outlook VBA is only supported for application-wide use, as described in Chapter 43, "Creating Application-wide Outlook Visual Basic for Applications Code." For working with forms, Outlook still uses the Visual Basic Scripting Edition (VBS) dialect of VB, which was originally developed for Internet Explorer, and is currently used in Internet Explorer, Outlook, and the Windows Scripting Host applet provided with Windows 98.

VBS is a less powerful language than VBA, and it lacks the full Visual Basic Environment (VBE) interface that developers can use while working with VBA. However, VBS has gone through a number of upgrades since the original version (VBS 1.0) that accompanied Outlook 97 (see Table 42.1), and each version has removed a few of its limitations.

Unlike earlier versions, the current version of VBS lets you use the convenient For Each...Next and With...End With constructs, but unfortunately some hoped-for enhancements didn't make it into Outlook 2000 VBS—you still can't use error handling constructs, named arguments, or named constants (other than True and False).

Additionally, VBS still lacks explicit data types (all variables are Variants), and it doesn't have a real programmer's editor.

The Script Editor remains a slightly enhanced version of Notepad, and the Outlook Object Browser falls far short of its equivalent in other Office applications; it only displays objects in Outlook's own object model, not those in other Office applications.

However, the new Microsoft Development Environment (MDE) window (successor to the Script Debugger available in earlier versions of Outlook) helps to overcome some of the limitations of the Script Editor. See the "Debugging and Editing Visual Basic Code" section later in this chapter for more details on using the MDE for stepping through and debugging Outlook VBS code.

TABLE 42.1 VBS AND OUTLOOK VERSIONS

Outlook Version	VBS Version
Outlook 97	VBS 1.0
Outlook 97	VBS 2.0*
Outlook 98	VBS 3.0
Outlook 2000	VBS 5.0**

*An add-in previously downloadable from the Microsoft.com Web site.
**The latest version of VBS 5.x can be downloaded from the Microsoft Scripting Technologies Web site at http://msdn.microsoft.com/scripting/default.htm.

GETTING HELP FOR VBS

There are several books in Outlook Help with information on Outlook VBS. They are located under the main Advanced Customization book (near the bottom of the Contents tab of the Outlook Help window). Figure 42.1 shows these topics, expanded, with the Using Visual Basic with Outlook topic selected.

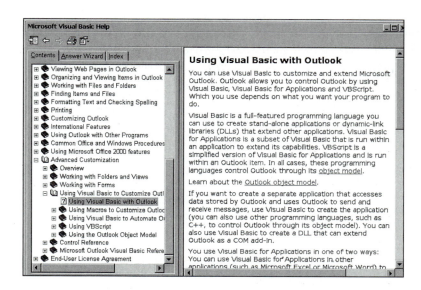

Figure 42.1
Outlook VBS Help topics.

VBS COMPARED TO VBA

Table 42.2 lists a number of VBA features that are lacking, or not fully implemented, in VBS. This table is based on a comparison of the VBS 5.0 Beta with VBA, from the Scripting Technologies page on the Microsoft Web site (the latest available reference at the time of writing). This Web site also has downloadable VBS documentation. The URL for the Scripting Technologies Web site is `http://msdn.microsoft.com/scripting/default.htm`.

TABLE 42.2   VBA FEATURES NOT IN VB SCRIPT

Category	Omitted Feature/Keyword
Array Handling	Option Base Declaring arrays with lower bound <> 0
Collection	Add, Count, Item, Remove Access to collections using ! character (e.g., MyCollection!Foo)
Conditional Compilation	#Const #If…Then…#Else
Control Flow	DoEvents GoSub…Return, GoTo On Error GoTo On…GoSub, On…GoTo Line numbers, Line labels
Conversion	CVar, CVDate Str, Val
Data Types	All intrinsic data types except Variant Type…End Type
Date/Time	Date statement, Time statement
DDE	LinkExecute, LinkPoke, LinkRequest, LinkSend

continues

TABLE 42.2 CONTINUED	
Category	**Omitted Feature/Keyword**
Debugging	Debug.Print End, Stop
Declaration	Declare (for declaring DLLs) Optional ParamArray Static
Error Handling	Erl Error Resume, Resume Next
File Input/Output	All traditional Basic file I/O
Financial	All financial functions
Object Manipulation	TypeOf
Objects	Clipboard Collection
Operators	Like
Options	Deftype Option Base Option Compare Option Private Module
Select Case	Expressions containing **Is** keyword or any comparison operators Expressions containing a range of values using the **To** keyword
Strings	Fixed-length strings LSet, RSet Mid Statement StrConv
Using Objects	Collection access using!

Caution

Outlook VBS Documentation

Most (if not all) of the available documentation on VBS is oriented toward using VBS in Internet Explorer, Access ASP, Windows Scripting Host, and other programs; it may not be completely accurate when used as a reference for Outlook VBS.

Additional help on the VBS language is available from the MDE window's Help menu, including a very useful VB Script Language Reference (see Figure 42.39 in the "Debugging and Editing Visual Basic Code" section later in this chapter).

THE OUTLOOK OBJECT MODEL

Automation (formerly OLE—*Object Linking and Embedding*—Automation) is now a feature of the Component Object Model (COM) technology, which allows developers to manipulate other applications from code. All the Microsoft Office applications support Automation, and so do many other products, both Microsoft and non-Microsoft. With Office 2000, major players such as Micrografx and Visio have entered the arena (or substantially upgraded their add-in products), with applications that support Automation with extensive object models, and even include the same dialect of VBA (v. 6.0) used in Office, making it easy to create seamless applications with enhanced functionality.

If you are writing code in a dialect of VB for a product that supports Automation, you can use the CreateObject and GetObject functions to control objects belonging to other Automation-supporting applications. For example, you can write Access Automation code to export data to Word and print letters, or Word Automation code to import appointments from Outlook and print a formatted calendar, or Outlook Automation code to export contacts to an Excel worksheet.

As with any application that supports Automation, Outlook has an object model consisting of a number of objects representing various Outlook components; these objects are available for use to other applications that support Automation.

You need a basic understanding of the Outlook object model in order to write code that works with Outlook objects such as contacts, tasks, appointments, mail messages, and folders. While there are syntactical differences between the VBS and VBA dialects of Visual Basic, as listed in Table 42.2, both dialects work with the same Outlook object model, so the following information is relevant for writing both VBS and VBA code.

The "Responding to Events" section later in this chapter shows how to write VBS code attached to Outlook forms to perform various actions on Outlook objects, while Chapter 43 covers writing VBA code to manipulate Outlook objects. More details on writing Automation code to control other applications from Outlook, or to control Outlook from other applications, are given in Chapter 44, "Understanding Automation."

Caution

An application's object model may not have objects corresponding to all of the product's functionality. For example, the Outlook 2000 object model lacks any objects representing Views, and the Access 2000 object model lacks objects corresponding to I/O specs.

The Outlook object model is shown in Figure 42.2.

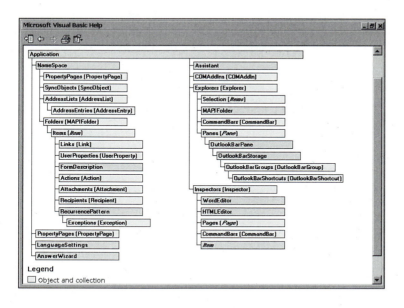

Figure 42.2
The Outlook 2000 object model.

UNDERSTANDING OUTLOOK'S EVENTS, METHODS, OBJECTS, AND PROPERTIES

When you work with Outlook VBS, you write code in the Script Editor window for a form, which contains that form's code module. To open the Script Editor window, implement the following steps:

1. Open an Outlook item.

2. Pull down the Tools menu on the item's toolbar.

3. Select the Forms submenu (if you don't see it, click the double-arrow to expand the menu).

4. Select Design This Form from the pop-up Forms menu.

5. On the Form Design toolbar, click the View Code button to open the Script Editor window.

Once you have the Script Editor window open, you can open the Outlook Object Browser by pressing F2.

Tip #276 from *Helen Bell Feddema*	For quick access to Design view, you can drag the Design This Form command to the Form toolbar, as described in the "Why Do You Need Custom Fields" section in Chapter 41, "Creating and Using Custom Fields."

Tip #277 from *Helen Bell Feddema*	The Object Browser opened from the Script editor window is limited compared to the full-featured Object Browser available from the VBE window; to open the full Object Browser, press Alt+F11 while in the main Outlook window. If the Object Browser isn't already open, press F2 to open it.

Most of the Office object models feature objects that you already know from the interface, such as Word documents and bookmarks, or Excel worksheets and charts. At first glance, the Outlook object model seems to lack the objects you would expect to find, such as Tasks, Mail Messages, and Contacts, instead featuring strangely-named object such as Explorers, Inspectors, and the Namespace object. However, once you get beyond the peculiar terminology, you will find the familiar Outlook components as items of various types under Folder objects.

Outlook objects (as seen in the Outlook object model shown in Figure 42.2) represent various Outlook components. Some of the objects are familiar from the interface, such as Folders, Items, Pages, and AddressLists; others represent more abstract functionality, such as SyncObjects and COMAddIns. If you open the Outlook Object Browser (by pressing F2 from the Script Editor window, as described previously), you can see the objects listed in the Classes list on the left side, while the Members list on the right lists the events, methods, and properties for each object, as shown in Figure 42.14.

The VBS Object Browser does not distinguish among the members of an object by using a distinctive icon for each; because of this limitation, you may find it more helpful to open the VBA Object Browser from the Outlook VBE window, as described in the preceding tip, or even the VBE window in another Office application, in order to examine Outlook objects in a richer environment. (This is particularly handy if you are planning on manipulating Outlook objects from another application.) To open the Object Browser from Access:

1. Open an Access database.

2. Open any module, or press Alt-F11.

3. The Microsoft Visual Basic window opens.

4. Open the Tools menu and select References, as shown in Figure 42.3.

5. The References dialog box opens, with the checked type libraries at the top.

6. If the Microsoft Outlook 9.0 Object Library selection is checked, you don't need to do anything; just close the dialog box.

7. If the Outlook 9.0 selection is not checked, locate it in the list of type libraries and check it, as shown in Figure 42.4.

8. Click OK to close the References dialog box.

9. Press F2 to open the Object Browser.

10. Select Outlook from the list of libraries in the drop-down list, as shown in Figure 42.5.

11. The Outlook objects are listed in the Classes list, and their events, properties, and methods in the Members list, each with a distinctive icon, as shown in Figure 42.6.

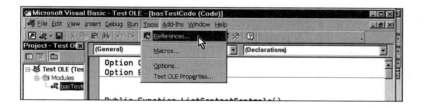

Figure 42.3
Opening the References window from the Access Visual Basic window.

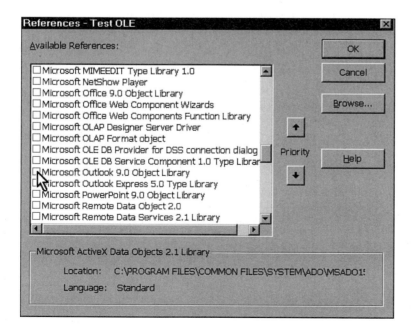

Figure 42.4
Checking the Outlook 9.0 Object Library selection in the References dialog box.

Figure 42.5
Selecting the Outlook library in the Object Browser.

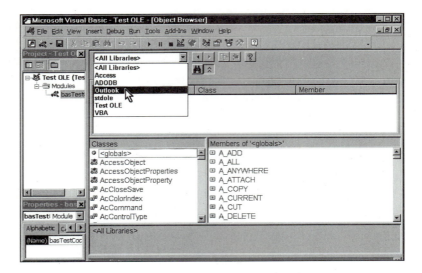

Figure 42.6
The icons used to indicate the member type in the Object Browser.

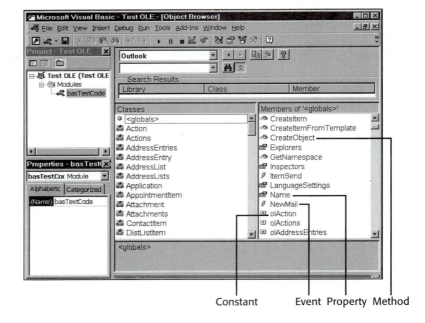

Constant   Event Property Method

Definitions of Terms

An *object* is an element of an application, such as an Outlook folder or task.

A *collection* is an object that contains one or more other objects, such as the Outlook Folders and Controls collections.

An *event* is an action recognized by an object, such as the Close event that occurs when closing an Outlook form.

A *method* is an action that an object can perform, such as the Save method for an Outlook item.

A *property* is an attribute defining one of an object's characteristics. In Outlook, each item has numerous properties, which are also called *fields* in the interface. The name and address controls on a Contact item are bound to various Outlook properties.

A *constant* is a fixed value used as an argument for a function or method, or for setting a value.

You can open the Help topic for a property, event, or method by right-clicking it and selecting Help from the context menu, as shown in Figure 42.7.

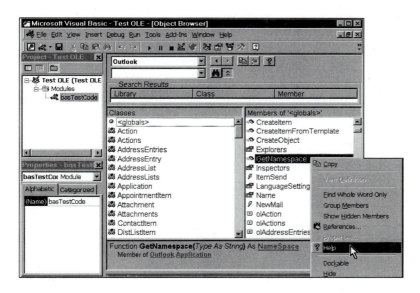

Figure 42.7
Opening the Help topic for an Outlook method.

The appropriate Help topic opens, as shown in Figure 43.8.

Caution

Not all object model components have associated Help topics.

Figure 42.8
The Close Event Help topic.

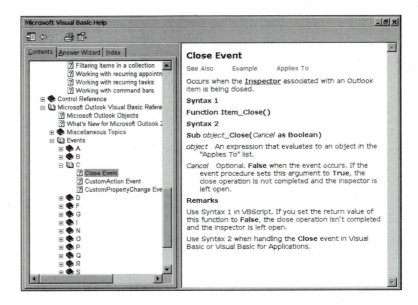

PLANNING YOUR CODE

To plan your VBS code for a form, first decide what should happen when users work with your forms—for example, you might want to automatically open another form, send a message, or post a journal entry. In some cases, these tasks can be accomplished by creating custom actions, as described in Chapter 9, "Managing Contacts," but if you want a procedure to run automatically when an event occurs (that is, without any special effort by the user) you need to write an event procedure attached to the appropriate form event.

For example, if you want to be sure that a new contact's FileAs field is always filled by the selection with the Company name first, and the contact name in parentheses, it is best to just write this selection directly to the FileAs field from the Write event, rather than expecting users to make the appropriate selection manually.

In order to write effective VBS code, you need to be familiar with the Outlook events that can be used to trigger code. Compared to other Office applications (such as Access), Outlook has few events. There is only one control event (Click), which only applies to *CommandButton controls (page 1200)*, and a limited selection of item and property events.

Outlook has 16 events in all, which are listed in Table 42.3, with the Outlook objects to which they apply. An event occurs when the user does something in the interface, such as double-clicking a Task item in a list view to open the task for editing (the Open event), clicking the Close and Save button to close a Contact item (the Save and Close events), or entering new text into a standard or custom control (the PropertyChange or CustomPropertyChange events). Detailed instructions for writing event procedures for these events are given in the next section.

TABLE 42.3   THE OUTLOOK EVENTS

Event Name	Applies To
Open	Items
Read	Items
Write	Items
Close	Items
Send	Items
Reply	Items
ReplyAll	Items
Forward	Items
*BeforeCheckNames	Items
*AttachmentAdd	Items
*AttachmentRead	Items
*BeforeAttachmentSave	Items
PropertyChange	Standard Properties
CustomPropertyChange	Custom Properties
CustomAction	Items
**Click	Various Controls—see the list in the "Click" section later in this chapter for details

New to Outlook 2000
**Not in Event Handlers drop-down list*

The Outlook events are described in more detail in the following section.

USING THE SCRIPT EDITOR

To write VBS code for an Outlook form, switch to Design view (as described in the section "The Outlook Object Model," earlier in this chapter), and click the Script Editor button on the toolbar, as shown in Figure 42.9.

Figure 42.9
Opening the Script Editor window.

The Script Editor, as you can see in Figure 42.10, looks a great deal like Notepad. It lacks the handy IntelliSense features of VBA's development environment, and it has no Debug toolbar, and therefore no way of setting a breakpoint, stepping over called procedures, and other handy debugging tools (although there is an add-on Script Debugger tool, in the form of the Microsoft Development Environment, that you can use with VBS, as described later in this chapter, in the "Debugging and Editing Visual Basic Code" section). However, despite its deficiencies, VBS is the dialect of VB you have to use when programming for Outlook forms.

Note

If your code can be run from the Application level, rather than running from a form, you would be better off writing VBA code, where you can use a more powerful dialect of VB in a much richer development environment. In many cases, you can write a function in VBA, then call the function from VBS code attached to an Outlook form.

Figure 42.10
The Script Editor window.

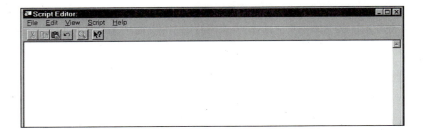

There are two selections on the Script menu, as shown in Figure 42.11.

Figure 42.11
The Script Editor's Script menu.

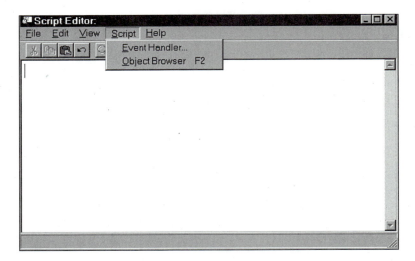

The Event Handler selection opens the Insert Event Handler dialog box, where you can insert a code stub for one of the Outlook events, as shown in Figure 42.12.

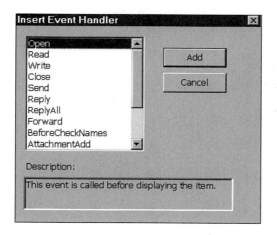

Figure 42.12
Selecting an event handler.

Figure 42.13 shows the code stub for the Close event. The events will be discussed in a later section in this chapter.

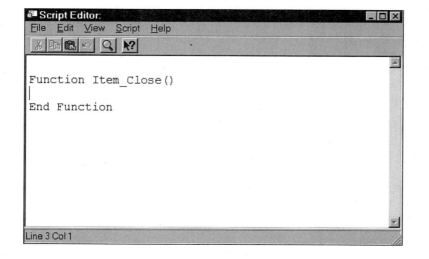

Figure 42.13
The Close event code stub.

To test the sequence of events for a form, use the Event Handler selections to insert code stubs for the Open, Read, Write, Close, and Send events. Place a message box in each procedure reporting that the event has occurred. The test code is given in Listing 42.1.

LISTING 42.1

```
Function Item_Open()

    MsgBox "Open event occurred"

End Function

Function Item_Read()

    MsgBox "Read event occurred"

End Function

Function Item_Write()

    MsgBox "Write event occurred"

End Function

Function Item_Close()

    MsgBox "Close event occurred"

End Function

Function Item_Send()

    MsgBox "Send event occurred"

End Function
```

Run the form and experiment with filling in data, closing, saving, and sending the item in various views, to familiarize yourself with the sequence of events.

The other selection on the Script menu opens the Object Browser (it can also be opened by the F2 hot key). The VBS Object Browser (shown in Figure 42.14) is a limited version of the VBA Object Browser. It lists only Outlook objects and their properties, methods, and events, and thus is of no use when writing code that manipulates other object models. However, you would most likely write such code in VBA at the Application level of Outlook, so this limitation is less of a problem than in previous versions of Outlook.

To get Help on an object, click the Object Help button; the appropriate Help topic opens, as shown in Figure 42.15.

Clicking the Insert button inserts the chosen property or method into the Script Editor window, as shown in Figure 42.16. However, it does not include any of the arguments, so it is not as helpful as the equivalent functionality in the VBA Object Browser.

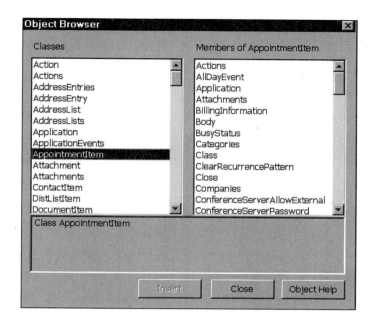

Figure 42.14
The Outlook Object Browser.

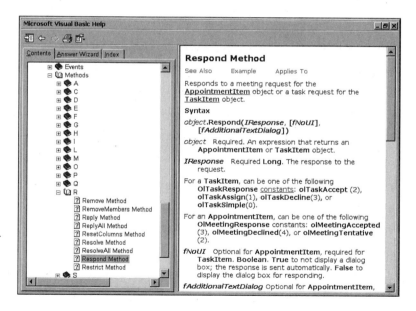

Figure 42.15
The Respond method Help topic.

Figure 42.16
A method inserted
into VBS code.

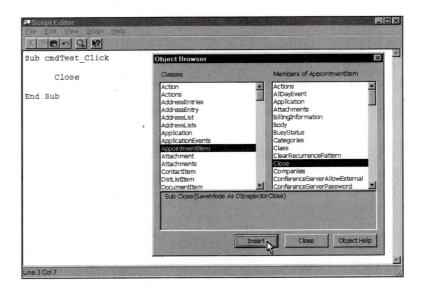

RESPONDING TO EVENTS

The events in Table 42.3 are available to all of the standard Outlook forms except the Note form—Mail Message, Appointment, Contact, Task, and Journal Entry. However, the Send, Reply, ReplyAll, and Forward events (as well as the new BeforeCheckNames, AttachmentAdd, AttachmentRead, and BeforeAttachmentSave events) are primarily useful for Mail Messages. When you are working in the VB Script window (see the Script Editor section for details), you can paste a code stub for any of these events except the Click event from the Events selection on the Script menu of the Script Editor window. The Click event, however, must be entered into your code manually, using the syntax shown in Listing 42.2, where cmdNote is the name of the CommandButton control.

LISTING 42.2

```
Sub cmdNote_Click

    'Event code here

End Sub
```

WRITING THE CODE

The Contact form is the heart of a Personal Information Management system, so let's start with a custom Contact form, and write VB Script to add functionality to its form and property events. To test the basic functioning of the Open, Read, Write, and Close events, open a blank instance of the standard Contact form. Start by dropping down the New Object menu from the main Outlook window, then select the New Contact selection. If you are in the Contacts folder, you don't have to drop down the menu, because New Contact will be the default selection, as shown in Figure 42.17.

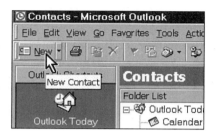

Figure 42.17
Creating a new Contact item.

For each of the events described in the following sections, open the Script Editor, as described earlier, pull down the Script menu, select the Event Handler command, and select the event from the list in the Insert Event Handler dialog box, as shown in Figure 42.18.

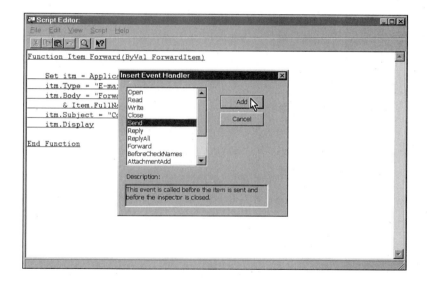

Figure 42.18
Inserting a code stub from the Insert Event Handler dialog box.

After clicking the Add button, a code stub is pasted into the Script Editor, after any existing code, as shown in Figure 42.19.

Figure 42.19
A code stub inserting into a VB Script module.

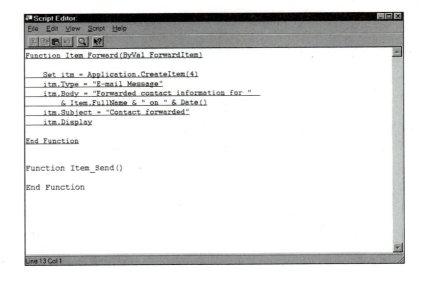

OPEN

The Open event is triggered when an item is opened, or a new item is created from a standard or custom form. The Open event does not occur when an item is selected for in-cell editing, for example, in a list view. The Open event occurs before the form is displayed. This event is useful for reminding a user that certain information must be filled in, or that the form is of a particular type. Figure 42.20 shows a message box triggered by the Open event in Listing 42.3 when a new Contact item is created from a custom form. After you click the OK button in the message box, the form opens.

LISTING 42.3

```
Function Item_Open()

    MsgBox "This is a custom form — there is no Details page"

End Function
```

Figure 42.20
A message box triggered by the Open event for a custom form.

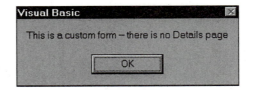

You can also use the Open event to open a custom form to a special page, other than the default page (the General page is the default page for a Contact form, and the Message form is the default page for a Mail Message).

Tip #279 from

Helen Bell Feddema

If you want to permanently turn off the General or Message page, uncheck the Display This Page option for that page on the Form menu in Design view.

The code in Listing 42.4 opens a custom Contact form to its Special Events page.

LISTING 42.4

```
Function Item_Open()

    Item.GetInspector.SetCurrentFormPage "Special Events"

End Function
```

READ

The Read event occurs when the user selects an item for editing, before the Open event. The Read event (unlike the Open event) occurs when the user selects an item for in-cell editing (in a list view, for example); such editing does not trigger the Open event. The Read event does not occur when a new item is created based on a form. Figure 42.21 shows a Read event message box that pops up when a Contact item created from a form is opened from the Address Card view, from the code shown in Listing 42.5.

LISTING 42.5

```
Function Item_Read()

    If Item.BusinessTelephoneNumber = "" Then
        MsgBox "Please enter a business phone number"
    End If

End Function
```

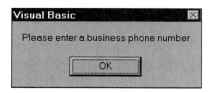

Figure 42.21
A message box triggered by the Read event for a custom form.

PART

VIII

CH

42

WRITE

When the user finishes editing an item and clicks the Save and Close or Next Item button on the toolbar (in full form view), or tabs off the item (in list view), the Write event occurs. In case the user just closes the form from the Close button (the little × in the upper-right corner of the form), the regular "Do you want to save changes?" dialog box pops up. After the user has clicked on one of its buttons, the Write event procedure fires. The Write event also occurs when a newly created item is first saved.

If the user has not edited the item, the Write event does not occur. This event is valuable for performing error-checking, or determining whether key fields on a form have been filled in.

Note	You can also check the values of fields from the PropertyChange and CustomPropertyChange events.

If you include a Cancel statement in a Write event procedure, depending on the user's actions, the Write event is canceled, as in Listing 42.6. Figure 42.22 shows a message box triggered by trying to save and close a Contact item when the Assistant Name has been entered, but not the Assistant Phone Number.

LISTING 42.6

```
Function Item_Write()

    If Item.AssistantName <> "" And Item.AssistantTelephoneNumber = "" Then
        MsgBox "Please enter " & Item.AssistantName & _
            "'s phone number"
        Cancel=False
    End If

End Function
```

CLOSE

The Close event occurs when the user saves and closes an item in Form view, or tabs away from it in List view. The Close event occurs after the Write event. If the item is just closed by clicking the form's Close button, first the "Do you want to save changes?" dialog box pops up, then after the user has clicked on one of its buttons, the Write event and then the Close event occur.

The Close event is very useful for triggering actions such as creating another item incorporating information from the item that has just been closed, for example, posting a Journal entry or sending a Mail Message.

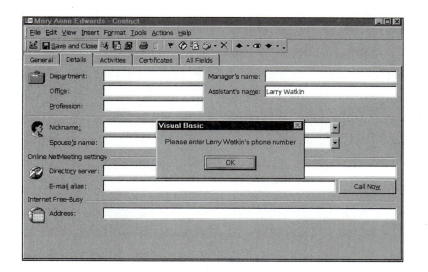

Figure 42.22
A message triggered
from the Write event
if a custom field is
not filled in.

Since the Close event occurs after the Write event, and thus after the form has passed any error-trapping code you may have placed on the Write event, it is a good place to attach code that triggers automatic generation of Outlook items. While users have commands on the Outlook Contact menu to manually create various Outlook items, sometimes it is desirable to create items automatically, without user intervention, and you can do this with a VBS script on the Close event. The code shown in Listing 42.7 automatically generates a Journal item noting that the Contact information has been updated.

Tip #280 from

Helen Bell Feddema

Code run from the Close event catches changes made to the item even if the user just closes the form, rather than clicking the Save and Close button.

Note

The Saved property of an Outlook item is True if the item has not been modified since it was last saved, and False if it has been edited but not saved.

LISTING 42.7

```
Function Item_Close()

    If Item.Saved = False Then
        Item.Save
        Set itm = Application.CreateItem(4)
        itm.Type = "Note"
        itm.Body = "Updated contact information for " & Item.FullName & " on " &
➡Date()
```

PART
VIII
CH
42

continues

LISTING 42.7   CONTINUED

```
        itm.Subject = "Address update"
        itm.Display
    End If

End Function
```

This code runs when the user tries to close the form without saving it, after making changes to the form. To ensure that the Journal entry will always be written, the same code (minus the Item.Save line) should also be placed on the Write event. Figure 42.23 shows the Journal entry created by the code in Listing 42.7.

Figure 42.23
A Journal entry automatically created by code running from the Close event of a Contact item.

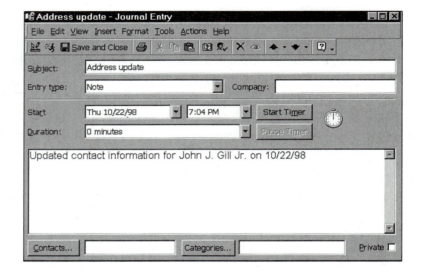

The code for creating an Outlook item in VB Script requires use of a numeric code, since VB Script does not support named arguments or constants (except for True and False). However, when you create Outlook items in VBA code, the named constants can be used. The named constants and their numeric equivalents are given in Table 42.4.

If you look at the Outlook object library in the Object Browser, you can see selections starting with the prefix "Ol." These are collections of named constants (called Enums, short for Enumerations). Each constant in an Enum has a numeric equivalent, and in VBS you have to use the numbers, not the names; the named constants only work in VBA code. For example, the following code referencing the default Calendar folder works in VBA, but not in VBS:

```
Set fld = nms.GetDefaultFolder(olFolderCalendar)
```

The VBS equivalent uses the value 9, the numeric equivalent of the olFolderCalendar constant:

```
Set fld = nms.GetDefaultFolder(9)
```

Defining Your Own Constants in VBS Code

Although you can't use the predefined Enum named constants in VBS code, you can declare your own constants using the Const keyword. This technique can be useful if you need to frequently reference the same value for an argument. The following code sample shows how to declare a constant representing the value of Pi, which you can then use in your code:

```
Const conPi = 3.14159265358979
```

Additionally, you can create your own named constants to make your code more readable, such as

```
Const ContactItem = 2
```

which would let you run the following line of code:

```
Application.CreateItem(ContactItem)
```

instead of the more cryptic

```
Application.CreateItem(2)
```

TABLE 42.4   CODES AND CONSTANTS FOR CREATING OUTLOOK ITEMS

Item Name	Named Constant	Numeric Constant
Mail Message	olMailItem	0
Appointment	olAppointmentItem	1
Contact	olContactItem	2
Task	olTaskItem	3
Journal Entry	olJournalItem	4
Note	olNoteItem	5
Post	olPostItem	6
Distribution List	olDistributionListItem	7

SEND

The Send event occurs when an item is sent, either by clicking its Send button or selecting Send from the File menu. Usually you send Mail Messages, but you can also send some other items—for example, you can send (assign) a Task item by clicking the Assign Task button on the Task item toolbar, as shown in Figure 42.24.

An Appointment item can also be sent in a similar manner, using the Invite Attendees button on the toolbar to create a Meeting Request item, as shown in Figure 42.25. See Chapter 11, "Managing Tasks," for more details on sending and assigning items in the interface.

If you create a Mail Message based on a custom form with a Send event, clicking its Send button triggers the Send event. The Send event occurs before the Write event and the Close event. The Send event can be used to automatically generate a Journal entry or a desktop Note, for example. The code in Listing 42.8 creates a desktop Note after a mail message has been sent.

PART
VIII

CH
42

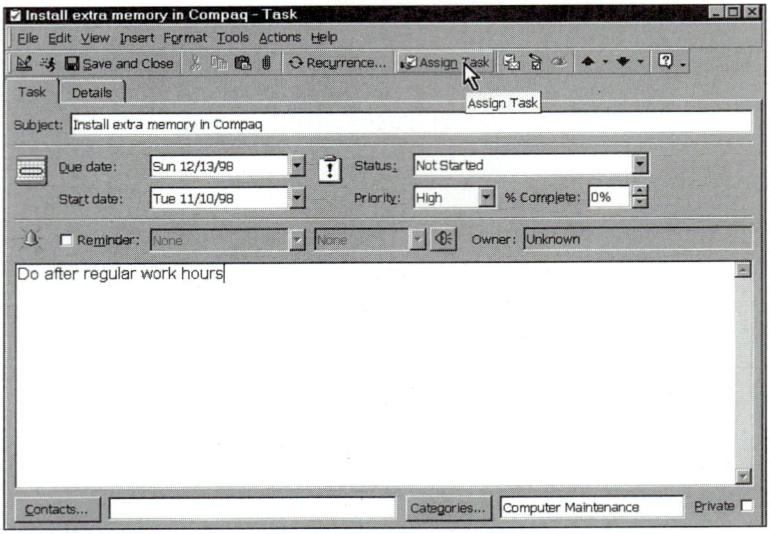

Figure 42.24
Assigning a task.

Figure 42.25
Inviting attendees to a meeting.

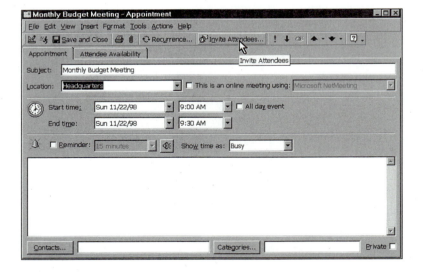

LISTING 42.8

```
Function Item_Send()

    Set itm = Application.CreateItem(5)
    strRecipient = Item.To
    itm.Body = "Call to follow up mail message to " & strRecipient
    itm.Display

End Function
```

Figure 42.26 shows the desktop Note created by the code in Listing 42.8.

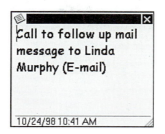

Figure 42.26
A desktop Note cre-
ated by code running
from the Send event
of a Mail Message.

REPLY, REPLYALL

The Reply event occurs when you reply to a mail message that you have received. The ReplyAll event is similar, except that it occurs when you click the ReplyAll button in a Mail Message you have received.

For the Reply event, you might want to post a Journal entry noting that you replied to the message, as shown in Listing 42.9.

LISTING 42.9

```
Function Item_Reply(ByVal Response)

    Set itm = Application.CreateItem(4)
    strSender = Item.SenderName
    itm.Body = "Replied to " & strSender & " on " & Date()
    itm.Subject = "Follow-up Response"
    itm.Type = "E-mail Message"
    itm.Display

End Function
```

Figure 42.27 shows the Journal entry created by the code in Listing 42.9.

FORWARD

You can forward an incoming Mail Message by clicking the Forward button in its toolbar, as shown in Figure 42.28, or forward a Contact item by dropping down the Actions menu and selecting either the Forward as vCard or Forward command (Corporate/Workgroup), or just the Forward as vCard command (Internet Mail Only), as shown in Figure 42.29.

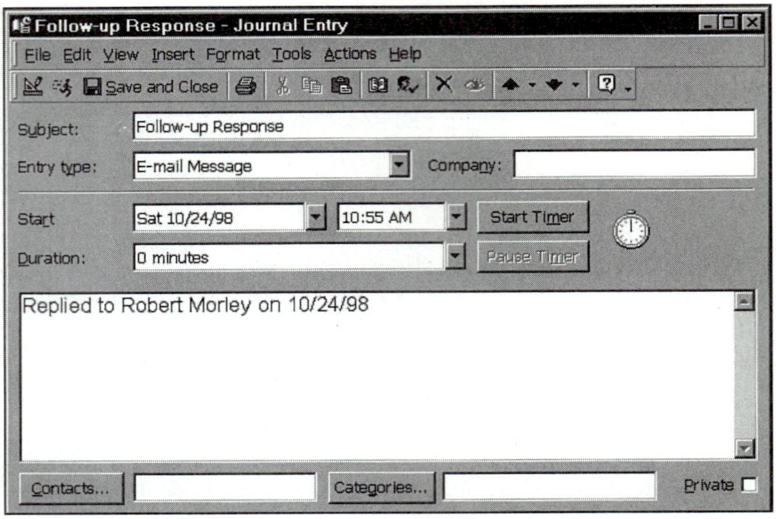

Figure 42.27
A Journal entry created by code running from a Mail Message's Reply event.

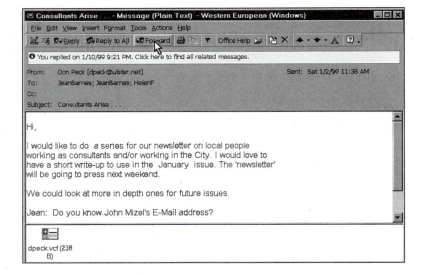

Figure 42.28
Forwarding a Mail Message.

→ For more information about forwarding items in the interface, **see** Chapter 11, "Managing Tasks."

BEFORECHECKNAMES

The BeforeCheckNames event occurs when you check e-mail names, as you might expect. You can check names manually at any point by pressing Alt-K or by selecting Check Names from the Tools menu; in any case, name checking takes place automatically when you send the mail message (unless you have turned off automatic name checking).

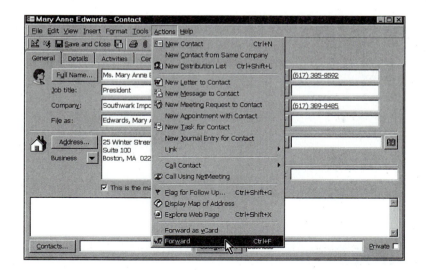

Figure 42.29
Forwarding a
Contact.

You can use this event to remind a user to check something related to e-mail, such as a reminder to check the server status, as in Listing 42.10.

LISTING 42.10

```
Function Item_BeforeCheckNames()

    MsgBox "Check e-mail server status before sending mail"

End Function
```

Figure 42.30 shows the message popped up from the code in Listing 42.10.

ATTACHMENTADD, ATTACHMENTREAD, BEFOREATTACHMENTSAVE

The three new attachment events offer Outlook programmers more control over message attachments. The AttachmentAdd event occurs when you insert an item as an attachment into a Mail Message, Task, or other item that supports attachments. The AttachmentRead event occurs when you open an attachment, usually by double-clicking it. The BeforeAttachmentSave event occurs when a newly inserted attachment is saved (right after the AttachmentAdd event).

Listing 42.11 is a VB Script with three procedures, one for each of the new attachment events. The first procedure gives a warning if the attachment exceeds 100,000 bytes. The second reminds the user to save changes to the original if the attachment is changed. The third cancels the AttachmentSave event unless the user is "Henry Johnson."

Figure 42.30
An informative message popped up from a Mail Message's BeforeCheckNames event.

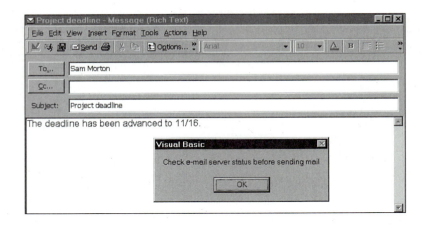

LISTING 42.11

```
Sub Item_AttachmentAdd(ByVal att)

    If att.Type = 1 Then
        Item.Save
        If Item.Size > 100000 Then
            MsgBox "This is a very large attachment; some mail servers may not be
➥able to handle it"
        End If
    End If

End Sub

Sub Item_AttachmentRead(ByVal att)
    If att.Type = 1 Then
        MsgBox "Save changes to the original if you change this file"
    End If

End Sub

Function Item_BeforeAttachmentSave(ByVal att)

    Dim nms
    Set nms = Application.GetNameSpace("MAPI")

    If nms.CurrentUser <> "Henry Johnson" Then
        MsgBox "You don't have permission to save attachments; canceling save"
        ItemBeforeAttachmentSave = False
    End If

End Function
```

The new Attachment-related events are not very reliable yet. The AttachmentSave event in particular is quite buggy, and can't be relied on to not save an attachment if it fails error-trapping.

PROPERTYCHANGE

The PropertyChange event occurs only when the user changes a standard property—most commonly, by entering or editing text in a control bound to that property. This event is triggered any time text in *any* control bound to a built-in field is changed, as opposed to the AfterUpdate event for a control in Access, for example, which occurs when text in a specific control is changed.

To make use of the PropertyChange event, you need to write a logical construct (typically a Case statement) that specifies the action to take for the control(s) with the changes you want to monitor, as shown in the code in Listing 42.12, where a change to the PersonalHomePage property triggers a reminder message.

LISTING 42.12

```
Sub Item_PropertyChange(ByVal strName)

    MsgBox "In PropertyChange event"

    Select Case strName
        Case "PersonalHomePage"
            MsgBox "Add new Web page to Favorites"
    End Select

End Sub
```

The PropertyChange event fires a lot more times than you might think. For example, if you change a contact's name, a number of name component properties are changed, as well as several variants of the FileAs *combination fields (page 1111)*, in a domino effect. The code sample in Listing 42.12 has a message box placed before the Case statement that pops up every time a property (any property) is changed; try placing this code in the Script Editor window for a contact form, then edit the contact's last name. The message box pops up 21 times, one for each combination field that is changed when the LastName field is changed.

Note

If you only need to run code when a single field is changed, an If…Then structure is most efficient; use a Case statement when you need to run code when multiple fields are changed.

CUSTOMPROPERTYCHANGE

The CustomPropertyChange event is similar to the PropertyChange event, except that it applies to custom properties (also known as fields)—in other words, the ones you create—as opposed to the built-in standard properties. The code shown in Listing 42.13 pops up an informative message when the Gift custom field is changed.

LISTING 42.13

```
Sub Item_CustomPropertyChange(ByVal strName)

    MsgBox "In CustomPropertyChange event"

    Select Case strName
        Case "Gift"
            MsgBox "New gift selected -- modify gift mailing list"
        Case "BusinessTelephoneNumber"
            MsgBox "Phone number changes -- reprint phone list"
    End Select

End Sub
```

CUSTOMACTION

The CustomAction event occurs when a custom action attached to an Outlook form is run.

CLICK

The Click event is not on the drop-down list of event handlers in the Script Editor window, and it is not listed in the Outlook Visual Basic Help file list of events; however, it is listed as an event under the Control Reference Help topic. The Click event is very useful for adding functionality to forms, such as creating new Outlook items, Word documents or Excel worksheets when the user clicks a button.

In previous versions of Outlook, the Click event only applied to the CommandButton control. In Outlook 2000, more controls have a Click event, though only if they are unbound.

Tip #281 from
Helen Bell Feddema

To respond to a change in a bound control, use the PropertyChange event (for a control bound to a built-in field) or the CustomPropertyChange event (for a control bound to a custom field).

The following controls fire the Click event when clicked:

CheckBox

CommandButton

Frame

Image

Label

OptionButton

ToggleButton

The following controls fire the Click event when the user selects an item in their list:

ComboBox

ListBox

The Click event does fire when an item is selected from the list of an unbound Listbox or ComboBox control. However, you can't enter a list of possible values in the properties sheet of an unbound Listbox or ComboBox control, so this feature is only useful when you write code to fill the list with an array, as in the simple example in Listing 42.14.

LISTING 42.14

```
Function Item_Open()

    Dim varList
    Dim itm
    Dim pgs
    Dim pg
    Dim ctls
    Dim ctl

    'Fill Listbox and ComboBox lists with data

    varList = Array("IBM", "Xerox", "Microsoft", "Apple")
    Set itm = Item.GetInspector
    Set pgs = itm.ModifiedFormPages
    Set pg = pgs("Click Test")
    Set ctls = pg.Controls
    Set ctl = ctls("lstTestClick")
    ctl.list = varList

    Set ctl = ctls("cboTestClick")
    ctl.List = varList

End Function
```

The following controls do not fire the Click event:

MultiPage

ScrollBar

SpinButton

TabStrip

TextBox

Finally, Help says that a page on the MultiPage control (though not the MultiPage control itself) fires the Click event when the user clicks on the page, but not when the user clicks on the page's tab. I found this not to be the case, but possibly Microsoft will have this feature working by release.

Since Outlook has no other control event procedures, the Outlook form designer must use command buttons or various unbound controls to run code that could be more conveniently (and automatically) run from various control events for bound controls in Access. For practical purposes, this makes the Outlook Click event primarily useful for command buttons.

If you have designed forms in Access or Visual Basic (or even Word UserForms), you will probably expect to be able to open a command button's Click event procedure by right-clicking or double-clicking on the command button in Form Design view.

However, Outlook lacks this convenient method for creating or editing a Click event procedure. Instead, you must note the name of the command button control (here is a good place to give it a meaningful name, such as cmdReminder, so your code will be more comprehensible), then open the Script Editor window from the View Code button and type in the event procedure with the control name (if you mistype the name, the code won't run, so be careful!). Listing 42.15 shows an event procedure for a command button called cmdReminder, which posts a reminder note to the desktop when the cmdReminder command button is clicked, thus triggering its Click event. Figure 42.31 shows the note.

Figure 42.31
A Note popped up from a CommandButton control on a Contact item.

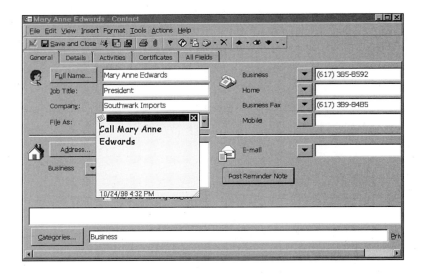

LISTING 42.15

```
Sub cmdReminder_Click

    Set itm = Application.CreateItem(5)
    strRecipient = Item.FullName
    itm.Body = "Call " & strRecipient
    itm.Display

End Sub
```

Listing 42.16 lists the code running from a command button that creates a new Word document from a custom template (the template's path and name are picked up from a TextBox control on the custom Contact form), and fills it with name and address data from the current Contact item. Figure 42.33 shows the Word document.

LISTING 42.16

```
Sub cmdMerge_Click

    Dim objWord
    Dim strWordTemplate

    strWordTemplate = Item.UserProperties("WordTemplate")

    'Open Word invisibly
    Set objWord = Item.Application.CreateObject("Word.Application")
    MsgBox "Opening document based on template: " & strWordTemplate

    'Open a new letter based on the selected template
    Set objDocs = objWord.Documents
    objDocs.Add strWordTemplate

    'Write info from contact item to Word custom doc properties
    Set prps = objWord.ActiveDocument.CustomDocumentProperties
    prps.Item("Name").Value = Item.FullName
    prps.Item("Company").Value = Item.CompanyName
    If Len(Item.JobTitle) > 0 Then
        prps.Item("Job Title").Value = Item.JobTitle
    End If
    If Len(Item.BusinessAddress) > 0 Then
        prps.Item("Address").Value = Item.BusinessAddress
    End If
    prps.Item("Salutation").Value = Item.FirstName
    prps.Item("Custom Field") = Item.UserProperties("CustomField")

    'Update fields in Word document and activate it
    objWord.Selection.WholeStory
    objWord.Selection.Fields.Update
    objWord.Selection.HomeKey 6
    objWord.Visible = True
    objWord.Activate

End Sub
```

The code in Listing 42.16 assumes some familiarity with the Word object model, which you can examine in the full-featured Object Browser in Word itself (press Alt+F11, then F2 from a Word window). Figure 42.32 shows the Word VBE window, with the Object Browser open to the Range object.

Figure 42.32
The Range object in the Word VBE Object Browser.

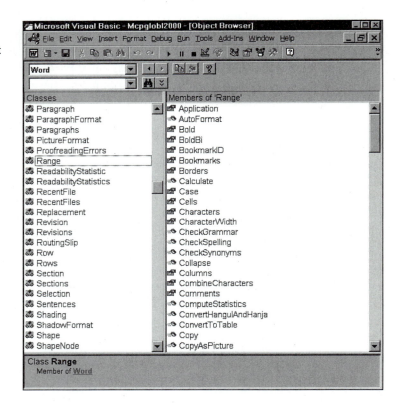

→ **See** Chapter 44, "Understanding Automation," for a more detailed discussion of exporting Outlook data to other Office applications.

USING METHODS

Each Outlook object may have one or more methods, which are used in code to perform actions on the objects, such as saving, sending, or closing them. You can see the methods for an Outlook object most clearly in the VBE Object Browser, where they are indicated by a green rectangle icon.

Figure 42.34 shows the ContactItem's members, with the Save method highlighted.

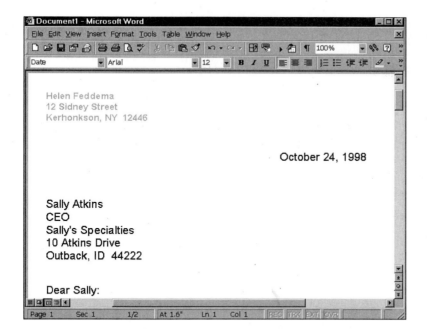

Figure 42.33
A Word document filled with data from the current Outlook Contact.

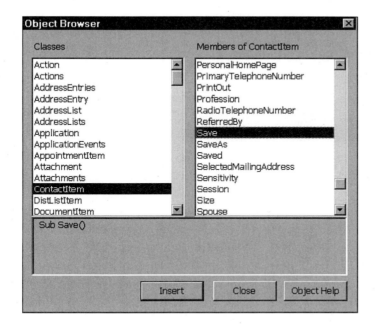

Figure 42.34
The Save method of the ContactItem object in the Object Browser.

You can use an item's methods in VBS code to simulate the actions you can perform on that type of item in the Outlook interface, or to do things you cannot easily do in the interface, such as creating a Mail Message with certain fields automatically filled in, and then sending it, as shown in Listing 42.17.

Note

When you use the Send method to send a Mail Message—as with clicking the Send button in the interface—the message is not sent immediately; it is just put into the Outbox; it will be sent the next time you click the Send/Receive Mail button.

LISTING 42.17

```
Sub cmdSend_Click

    Set nms = Application.GetNameSpace("MAPI")
    strUserName = nms.CurrentUser
    Set msg = Application.CreateItem(0)
    strRecipient = Item.Email1Address
    msg.Subject = "Call me"
    msg.Body = "Call " & strUserName
    msg.To = strRecipient
    msg.Display
    msg.Send

End Sub
```

The mail message created and sent from the code in Listing 42.17 is shown in Figure 42.35.

Figure 42.35
A Mail Message sent and filled in from code on a CommandButton control.

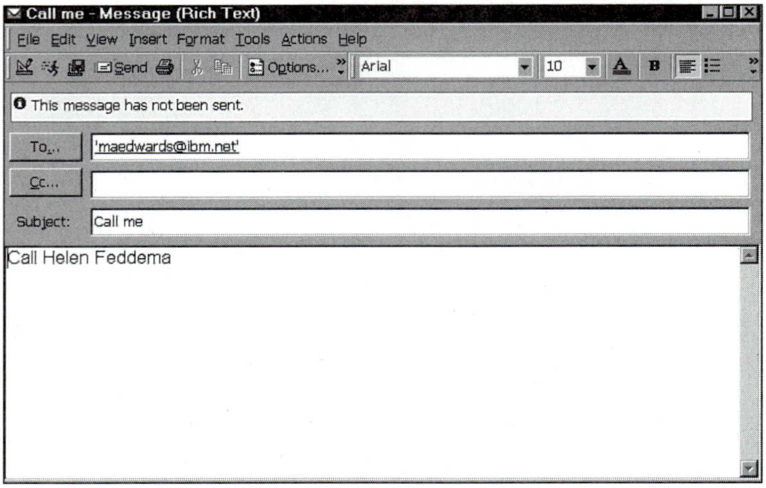

USING OUTLOOK CONSTANTS WITH YOUR CODE

Outlook constants, like those of other Office applications, are divided into groups called *enums* (short for enumerations). Each enum contains a group of related constants that can be used for specific arguments of methods or functions, as indicated in the Object Browser. Outlook enum names start with the prefix "Ol" with a capital O, while the constants themselves start with the prefix "ol" with a lowercase o.

If you look at the lower pane in the Object Browser, you can see the name of the enum(s) with constants that can be used for the arguments of a method or event. Figure 42.36 shows that the Close method of the Contact item uses the OlInspectorClose enum, which means you can supply any of the constants in this enum as values for this argument.

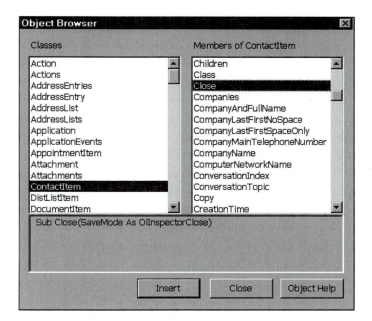

Figure 42.36
The enum used for an Outlook method's argument.

Tip #282 from
Helen Bell Feddema

You are not limited to using Outlook constants in VBS code—you can use VBA constants (they use the "vb" prefix) or DAO constants (they use the "db" prefix) as well, where they are appropriate.

The constants in an enum have two forms: named and numeric. In standard VBA, you can use the more user-friendly named constants, while in VBS you must use the numeric constants. Table 42.5 lists the Outlook enums and their constants.

TABLE 42.5   OUTLOOK CONSTANTS

Named Constant (Use in VBA Code)	Numeric Constant (Use in VBS Code)
OlActionCopyLike	
olReply	0
olReplyAll	1
olForward	2
olReplyFolder	3
olRespond	4
OlActionReplyStyle	
olEmbedOriginalItem	1
olIncludeOriginalText	2
olIndentOriginalText	3
olLinkOriginalItem	4
olOmitOriginalText	0
olReplyTickOriginalText	1000
olUserPreference	5
OlActionResponseStyle	
olOpen	0
olPrompt	2
olSend	1
OlActionShowOn	
olDontShow	0
olMenu	1
olMenuAndToolbar	2
OlAttachmentType	
olByReference	4
olByValue	1
olEmbeddedItem	5
olOLE	6

Named Constant (Use in VBA Code)	Numeric Constant (Use in VBS Code)
OlBusyStatus	
olBusy	2
olFree	0
olOutOfOffice	3
olTentative	1
OlDaysOfWeek	
olFriday	32
olMonday	2
olSaturday	64
olSunday	1
olThursday	16
olTuesday	4
olWednesday	8
OlDefaultFolders	
olFolderCalendar	9
olFolderContacts	10
olFolderDeletedItems	3
OlDefaultFolders	
olFolderDrafts	16
olFolderInbox	6
olFolderJournal	11
olFolderNotes	12
olFolderOutbox	4
olFolderSentMail	5
olFolderTasks	13
OlDisplayType	
olAgent	3
olDistList	1

continues

PART

VIII

CH

42

TABLE 42.5   CONTINUED

Named Constant (Use in VBA Code)	Numeric Constant (Use in VBS Code)
OlDisplayType	
olForum	2
olOrganization	4
olPrivateDistList	5
olRemoteUser	6
olUser	0
OlEditorType	
olEditorHTML	2
olEditorRTF	3
olEditorText	1
olEditorWord	4
OlFlagStatus	
olFlagComplete	1
olFlagMarked	2
olNoFlag	0
OlFolderDisplayMode	
olFolderDisplayFolderOnly	1
olFolderDisplayNoNavigation	2
olFolderDisplayNormal	0
OlFormRegistry	
olDefaultRegistry	0
olFolderRegistry	3
olOrganizationRegistry	4
olPersonalRegistry	2
OlGender	
olFemale	1
olMale	2
olUnspecified	0

Named Constant (Use in VBA Code)	Numeric Constant (Use in VBS Code)
OlImportance	
olImportanceHigh	2
olImportanceLow	0
olImportanceNormal	1
OlInspectorClose	
olDiscard	1
olPromptForSave	2
olSave	0
OlItemType	
olAppointmentItem	1
olContactItem	2
olDistributionListItem	7
olJournalItem	4
olMailItem	0
olNoteItem	5
olPostItem	6
olTaskItem	3
OlJournalRecipientType	
olAssociatedContact	1
OlMailingAddress	
olBusiness	2
olHome	1
olNone	0
OlMailingAddress	
olOther	3
OlMailRecipientType	
olBCC	3
olCC	2
olOriginator	0
olTo	1

PART

VIII

CH

42

continues

TABLE 42.5 CONTINUED

Named Constant (Use in VBA Code)	Numeric Constant (Use in VBS Code)
OlMeetingRecipientType	
olOptional	2
olOrganizer	0
olRequired	1
olResource	3
OlMeetingResponse	
olMeetingAccepted	3
olMeetingDeclined	4
olMeetingTentative	2
OlMeetingStatus	
olMeeting	1
olMeetingCanceled	5
olMeetingReceived	3
olNonMeeting	0
OlNetMeetingType	
olChat	2
olNetMeeting	0
olNetShow	1
OlNoteColor	
olBlue	0
olGreen	1
olPink	2
olWhite	4
olYellow	3
OlObjectClass	
olAction	32
olActions	33
olAddressEntries	21
olAddressEntry	8
olAddressList	7

Named Constant (Use in VBA Code)	Numeric Constant (Use in VBS Code)
OlObjectClass	
olAddressLists	20
olApplication	0
olAppointment	26
olAttachment	5
olAttachments	18
olContact	40
olDocument	41
olDistributionList	69
olException	30
olExceptions	29
olExplorer	34
olExplorers	60
olFolder	2
olFolders	15
olFormDescription	37
olInspector	35
olInspectors	61
olItems	16
olJournal	42
olLink	75
olLinks	76
olMail	43
olMeetingCancellation	54
olMeetingRequest	53
olMeetingResponseNegative	55
olMeetingResponsePositive	56
olMeetingResponseTentative	57
olNamespace	1
olNote	44

PART

VIII

CH

42

continues

TABLE 42.5 CONTINUED

Named Constant (Use in VBA Code)	Numeric Constant (Use in VBS Code)
OlObjectClass	
olOutlookBarGroup	66
olOutlookBarGroups	65
olOutlookBarPane	63
olOutlookBarShortcut	68
olOutlookBarShortcuts	67
olOutlookBarStorage	64
olOutlookPropertyPageSite	70
olPages	36
olPanes	62
olPost	45
olPropertyPages	71
olRecipient	4
olRecipients	17
olRecurrencePattern	28
olRemote	47
olReport	46
olSelection	74
olSyncObject	72
olSyncObjects	73
olTask	48
olTaskRequest	49
olTaskRequestAccept	51
olTaskRequestDecline	52
olTaskRequestUpdate	50
olUserProperties	38
olUserProperty	39
OlOutlookBarViewType	
olLargeIcon	0
olSmallIcon	1

Named Constant (Use in VBA Code)	Numeric Constant (Use in VBS Code)
OlPane	
olOutlookBar	1
olFolderList	2
olPreview	3
OlRecurrenceState	
olApptException	3
olApptMaster	1
olApptNotRecurring	0
olApptOccurrence	2
OlRecurrenceType	
olRecursDaily	0
olRecursMonthly	2
olRecursMonthNth	3
olRecursWeekly	1
olRecursYearly	5
olRecursYearNth	6
OlRemoteStatus	
olMarkedForCopy	3
olMarkedForDelete	4
olMarkedForDownload	2
olRemoteStatusNone	0
olUnMarked	1
OlResponseStatus	
olResponseAccepted	3
olResponseDeclined	4
olResponseNone	0
olResponseNotResponded	5
olResponseOrganized	1
olResponseTentative	2

PART

VIII

CH

42

continues

TABLE 42.5   CONTINUED

Named Constant (Use in VBA Code)	Numeric Constant (Use in VBS Code)
OlSaveAsType	
olDoc	4
olHTML	5
olMSG	3
olRTF	1
olTemplate	2
olTXT	0
olVCal	7
olVCard	6
OlSensitivity	
olConfidential	3
olNormal	0
olPersonal	1
olPrivate	2
OlSortOrder	
olAscending	1
olDescending	2
olSortNone	0
OlSyncState	
olSyncStarted	1
olSyncStopped	0
OlTaskDelegationState	
olTaskDelegationAccepted	2
olTaskDelegationDeclined	3
olTaskDelegationUnknown	1
olTaskNotDelegated	0

Named Constant (Use in VBA Code)	Numeric Constant (Use in VBS Code)
OlTaskOwnership	
olDelegatedTask	1
olNewTask	0
olOwnTask	2
OlTaskRecipientType	
olFinalStatus	3
olUpdate	2
OlTaskResponse	
olTaskAccept	2
olTaskAssign	1
olTaskDecline	3
olTaskSimple	0
OlTaskStatus	
olTaskComplete	2
olTaskDeferred	4
olTaskInProgress	1
olTaskNotStarted	0
olTaskWaiting	3
OlTrackingStatus	
olTrackingDelivered	1
olTrackingNone	0
olTrackingNotDelivered	2
olTrackingNotRead	3
olTrackingRead	6
olTrackingRecallFailure	4
olTrackingRecallSuccess	5
olTrackingReplied	7

continues

TABLE 42.5 CONTINUED

Named Constant (Use in VBA Code)	Numeric Constant (Use in VBS Code)
OlUserPropertyType	
olCombination	19
olCurrency	14
olDateTime	5
olDuration	7
olFormula	18
olKeywords	11
olNumber	3
olPercent	12
olText	1
olYesNo	6
OlWindowState	
olMaximized	0
olMinimized	1
olNormal	2

REFERENCING THE CURRENT USER

Sometimes you need to retrieve the name of the current Outlook user, say to send a Mail Message with the current user as the sender. The CurrentUser property of the namespace object returns the current user's name, as shown in Listing 42.16.

Figure 42.35 shows a Mail Message produced by the code in Listing 42.17.

REFERENCING AN OUTLOOK FOLDER

Referencing a specific folder in Outlook VBS can be complex. If you want to reference a standard folder under the Personal folders top-level folder, you can use one of the OlDefaultFolders constants (see Table 42.5 for a listing). For VBS code, you must use the numeric equivalents, not the named constants. For example, to refer to the default Calendar folder, use the syntax in Listing 42.18.

LISTING 42.18

```
Dim nms
Dim fld

Set nms = Application.GetNameSpace("MAPI")
Set fld = nms.GetDefaultFolder(9)
fld Display
```

Global and Local Variables

Since VBS does not support data typing of variables (as do Access, VB, and VBA), you can't dimension (Dim) a VBS variable as a particular data type. Instead, just use the Dim keyword, as in the following code:

```
Dim dteStart
```

You can dimension (or *declare*) a number of variables at the beginning of a VBS script, before the first procedure. These are called *global* or *module-wide* variables. Variables dimensioned within a procedure are called *local* or *procedure-wide* variables. Global variables can be used in any procedure in a module; local variables can only be used within their procedure.

Outlook VBS does not require variables to be declared, but declaring them at the top of the module (or procedure) lets you organize your code, so you know what objects you are working with, and what the variables are called. Additionally, declaring a variable with Dim allocates storage space for it in advance, although practically, with the amounts of memory likely to be available on current computers, it is quite unlikely that there would be a shortage of memory for undeclared variables.

Tip #283 from
Helen Bell Feddema

> Even though data typing isn't supported in VBS, you can still use prefixes to indicate what type of data you will be storing in the variable, as with the preceding code sample, where the "dte" prefix indicates a date.

If you need to reference a custom folder under the Personal Folders top-level folder, use the syntax in Listing 42.19; to reference a custom folder under the Public Folders top-level folder, use the syntax in Listing 42.20.

LISTING 42.19

```
Dim nms
Dim fld

Set nms = Application.GetNameSpace("MAPI")
Set fld = nms.Folders("Personal Folders").Folders("Custom Folder")
```

LISTING 42.20

```
Dim nms
Dim fld

Set nms = Application.GetNameSpace("MAPI")
Set fld = nms.Folders("Public Folders").Folders("All Public
Folders").Folders("Custom Folder")
```

Finally, to reference a folder in an Exchange mailbox, use the syntax in Listing 42.21, which references the default Calendar folder in the Exchange mailbox belonging to a user whose name is assigned to the strUserName variable. (The value of strUserName could be assigned from code, or picked up from a form; note that you will have to add a line to the code to set this variable appropriately for your needs, to get the code to run on your system.) This code defaults to the current user's local Calendar in case the Exchange Mailbox for the specified user is not found.

LISTING 42.21

```
'Set reference to Outlook Calendar folder in an Exchange mailbox
Set nms = Application.GetNamespace("MAPI")
Set rcp = nms.CreateRecipient(strUserName)
'strUserName must be the name of a valid recipient mailbox on
'the Exchange server
rcp.Resolve
If rcp.Resolved Then
    Set fld = nms.GetSharedDefaultFolder _
        (rcp, olFolderCalendar)
Else
    MsgBox "Can't find a valid mailbox for " & strUserName _
        & "; using default local calendar"
    Set fld = nms.GetDefaultFolder(olFolderCalendar)
    prps("UserName") = nms.CurrentUser
End If
```

SETTING OR RETRIEVING THE VALUE IN A FIELD

To change a value in a field, you simply set the field equal to the desired value, as in Listing 42.22, where Item references the current item. You don't need to go through a control to set a field's value (whether it is a built-in field or a custom field you created); you only need to use the more complex control reference syntax when you must change the value displayed in an unbound control (one that is not linked to a field).

Tip #284 from

Helen Bell Feddema

In some cases a newly entered or changed value in a bound control won't be picked up from the field. You can use the Save method before getting values from fields to prevent this problem.

LISTING 42.22

```
Item.FileAs = "Archer Industries (Ken Walker)"
```

SETTING OR RETRIEVING A VALUE IN AN UNBOUND CONTROL

Normally, when you work with Outlook items and their fields (properties) in VBS code, you are working directly with the item's properties. In the interface, the user edits these properties by working with controls bound to the properties, but you can change an item's properties directly from code, as described in the preceding section. However, sometimes you need to set or retrieve the value in an unbound control. In that case you need to use the more complex syntax shown in Listing 42.23, which references a control on a specific page of a Contact item.

The syntax for referencing controls on Outlook forms is quite cryptic. There is no Forms collection, as in some other Office applications; rather, you need to walk through the Outlook object model hierarchy (described in more detail in the "Outlook Object Model" section earlier in this chapter). To reference a control on a page of a custom form, you start with the Item, then the ModifiedFormPages collection, then the specific page, then the Controls collection of that page, then (finally!) the specific control.

LISTING 42.23

```
Sub cmdTest_Click

Set itm = Item.GetInspector
Set pgs = itm.ModifiedFormPages
Set pg = pgs("Special Events")
Set ctls = pg.Controls
Set ctl = ctls("chkAttendee")
    If ctl = True then
        MsgBox "Contact was an attendee"
    Else
        MsgBox "Contact was not an attendee"
    End If
End Sub
```

Figure 42.37 shows the message box popped up by clicking the test button that runs the code in Listing 42.24.

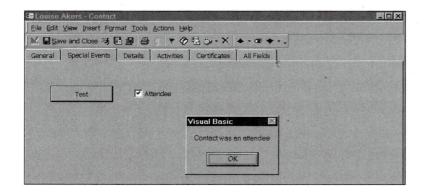

Figure 42.37
A message popped up based on the value in a CheckBox control.

PART
VIII

CH
42

It is not necessary to break down the control reference into separate components as shown in Listing 42.23; you can instead write a single long line of code like the one in Listing 42.24 to reference a control.

LISTING 42.24

```
Set ctl = Item.GetInspector.ModifiedFormPages("Special _
Events").Controls("chkAttendee")
```

However, there are some advantages to breaking the reference into its separate components—you can easily reassign the *pg* or *ctl* variable to another control with just a short line of code; and the short lines of code are more readable.

VBS now has a continuation character, so you can break a long line of code. It is the same as in VBA, a space followed by an underscore. The code segment in Listing 42.25 illustrates the use of the continuation character in VBS code.

Caution

You can only use the VBS continuation character where there is a space or a period naturally occurring in the code, and you can't break up a text string in quotes with the continuation character. If you break a line of code at an inappropriate location, you will get an error when you run the code.

LISTING 42.25

```
If strCategory = "[All Categories]" or _
    strCategory = "[Travel Expenses]" Then
```

DEBUGGING AND EDITING VISUAL BASIC CODE

Unlike other applications, where you do your debugging in design mode, in Outlook the Script Debugger is only available in runtime. To open the Script Debugger, implement the steps below:

1. Open an Outlook item that has VBS script.
2. Pull down the Tools menu on the item's toolbar.
3. Select the Forms submenu (if you don't see it, click the double-arrow to expand the menu).
4. Select Script Debugger from the pop-up Forms menu, as shown in Figure 42.38.
5. The Script Debugger window opens, as shown in Figure 42.39.

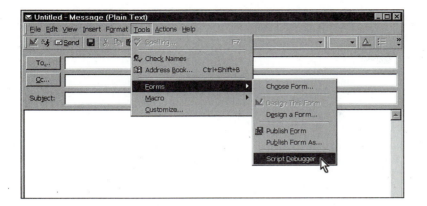

Figure 42.38
Opening the Script Debugger.

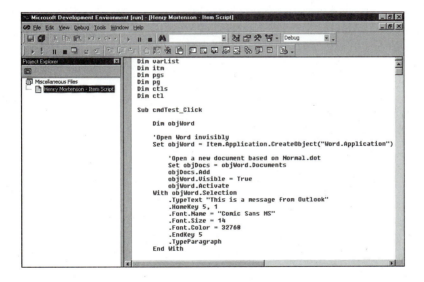

Figure 42.39
The Microsoft Development Environment window.

Note

Until fairly late in the beta of Office 2000, selecting the Script Debugger command opened a Script Debugger window. The Script Debugger has been replaced by the Microsoft Development Environment (MDE), but the menu command and button retain the old name.

Note

If you don't see a Script Debugger button on your toolbar or command on your menu, you may need to install the Script Debugger component. To do this, insert the Office 2000 CD, select the Add or Remove Features button, and select the Visual Basic Scripting Support item under the Outlook branch of the install tree.

If you have the Script Debugger installed, when you try to open a form, or click a control, and there is a runtime error, you will get the error message shown in Figure 42.40.

Figure 42.40
Error message from trying to open a form with an error in its VB Script.

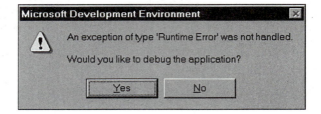

If you click the No button, you will get a message like the one in Figure 42.41, and after accepting it, you will be returned to your Outlook form in Design view, where you can open the Script Editor and try to fix the problem indicated by the error message.

Figure 42.41
An error message giving details about the VB Script error.

On the other hand, if you click the Yes button, the MDE window opens, with the same error message as if you clicked No. After closing the error message dialog box, you will see the offending line of code highlighted, so you can examine it in context. You can't edit it, though—the MDE window is read-only for Outlook VBS code.

You can also use the MDE window proactively, by opening the Script Debugger from the menu, and using the Insert Breakpoint button (or pressing F9) to set a breakpoint in your VBS code; when the code reaches the breakpoint, it will switch to the MDE window, where you can step through your code line by line, using one of the Step tools on the MDE toolbar (generally, the Step Into tool is the most useful). Figure 42.43 shows a procedure with a breakpoint set, as indicated by the dark red circle to the left of the line with the breakpoint.

The tools on the Debug toolbar in the MDE window are shown in Figure 42.44.

Note   Not all of the tools on the MDE Debug toolbar are useful for debugging VBS code.

Figure 42.45 shows a VB Script stopped at a breakpoint, to start stepping through the lines of code using the Step Into button on the Debug toolbar.

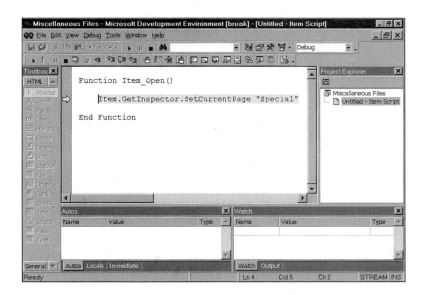

Figure 42.42
The MDE window with a line of VBS code highlighted to indicate where the error occurred.

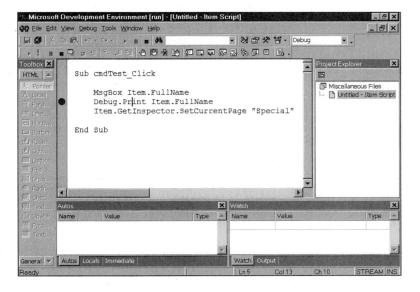

Figure 42.43
VBS code with a breakpoint set, in the MDE window.

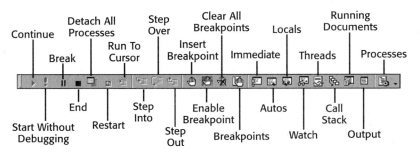

Figure 42.44
The MDE Debug toolbar.

PART

VIII

Cн

42

Figure 42.45
Ready to step through VBS code in the MDE window.

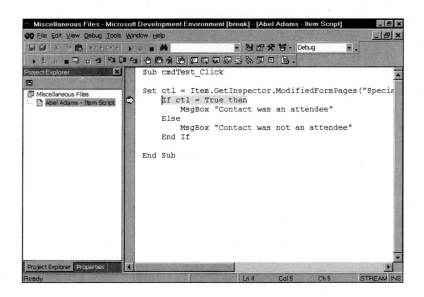

For details on the use of these tools, see the MDE Help, which contains several topics explaining the MDE interface, as shown in Figure 42.46.

Figure 42.46
The Environment User Interface Help topics in the MDE Help window.

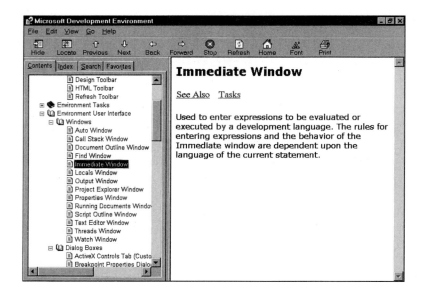

One of the most useful topics in MDE Help is the VB Script Language reference, as shown in Figure 42.47.

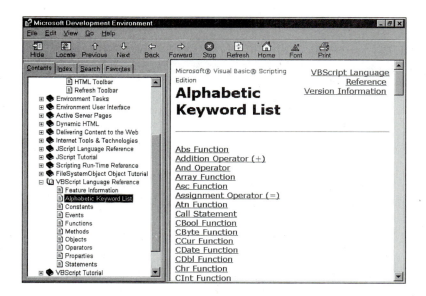

Figure 42.47
The VB Script Language Reference Help topics in MDE Help.

PREVENTING VBSCRIPT FROM RUNNING WHEN YOU OPEN AN ITEM

When you open an Outlook custom form that has VBA code attached to it, you may get the cryptic message shown in Figure 42.48.

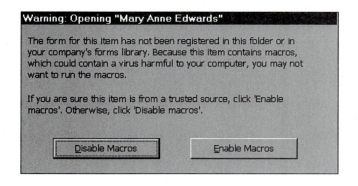

Figure 42.48
The macro virus warning message on opening a custom form with attached VBS code.

Normally, you should just click the Enable Macros button to open the form with the code enabled. If you don't want to run the form's VBS code, click the Disable Macros button. Alternatively, you can hold the Shift key while opening an item (say, by double-clicking it) in order to open it with macros enabled.

To permanently turn off the macro virus warning message for a custom form, publish the form to your Personal Forms Library, as described in Chapter 40. Then, the first time you create a new form based on the form template in the library, you will get a brief informative message telling you that the form is being installed on your machine, and the form will open without the macro virus warning message. Now that the form is installed on your system, you can make more instances of the form as needed, without any warning messages.

To suppress the macro virus warning error message globally, you can change the macro security level to a lower setting. Start by selecting Security from the Macros menu, as shown in Figure 42.49. When the Security window opens (shown in Figure 42.50), select the Low option to turn the warning off completely (Medium is the default setting for Outlook).

Figure 42.49
Opening the Macro Security dialog box.

Figure 42.50
The Macro Security window.

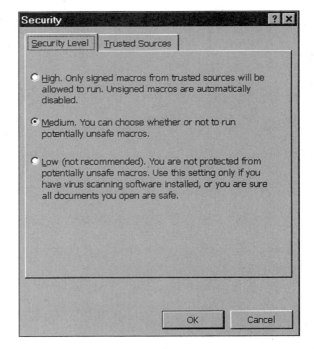

If you choose the High option in the Security window, you can only open forms with macros if they have certificates indicating that they come from a trusted source.

TROUBLESHOOTING

Q: **Why isn't the Click event on my ComboBox control running?**

A: Probably because you mistyped the control name in the event procedure, or you changed the control name after writing the procedure. Change the procedure name (or the control name) so that they match, and the procedure should run.

Q: **Why doesn't the Click event fire when I select an item from a ListBox control?**

A: Probably because the control is bound; the Click event only fires for unbound controls.

Q: **Why does my code stop with an error message on the following line?**

```
Dim dteStart As Date
```

A: VBS doesn't support data typing of variables; all variables are of the all-purpose Variant type. Change the code to

```
Dim dteStart
```

and it should run.

Q: **Why does my VBS code work on my system, but not on my colleague's?**

A: There are several possibilities:

- Your colleague may have a different version of Outlook, which doesn't support some of the features you are using in Outlook 2000.

- Your colleague may have a different version of VBS, which doesn't support some of the features you are using in VBS 5.0, such as the For Each…Next or With…End With constructs.

- Your colleague may have Outlook set up in a different e-mail configuration—for example, you might have Corporate/Workgroup while she has Internet Mail Only. Some actions work in one configuration, but not the other.

CHAPTER 43

CREATING APPLICATION-WIDE OUTLOOK VISUAL BASIC FOR APPLICATIONS CODE

In this chapter   *by Helen Feddema*

VBA VERSUS VBS

Outlook 2000, like earlier versions of Outlook, supports VBS for creating code behind forms, as described in Chapter 42, "Enhancing Outlook Forms with Visual Basic Script Code." However, in addition to VBS, Outlook now hosts real Visual Basic for Applications (VBA) for creating application-wide code—a significant advance in functionality for Outlook developers. You can write macros (procedures) in VBA, using application-wide events such as the NewMail event, which lets you control Outlook without having to attach code to a specific form. Additionally (a long-awaited feature!), you can write code for custom toolbar buttons. Office standard UserForms (new to Outlook 2000, though you may know them from Word 97) are handy for creating enhanced dialog boxes for running VBA code.

The VBA dialect of Visual Basic is considerably more powerful than the VBS dialect, which is used to create code behind forms in Outlook. The main differences between the dialects are listed in Table 43.1.

TABLE 43.1   DIFFERENCES BETWEEN THE CURRENT VERSIONS OF VBA AND VBS

VBA v. 6.0	VBS v. 5.0
Runs within the Outlook application	Runs from an Outlook form
Hosted by all Office applications (and some non-Office applications)	Hosted by Outlook (and some non-Office applications)
Has the powerful VBE developer's environment	Has the limited Script Editor development environment
Has a full-featured Object Browser, listing objects for other applications as well as Outlook objects	Has a limited Object Browser, listing only Outlook objects
Supports data typing for variables	Does not support data typing; all variables are of the Variant type
Supports named constants for function arguments and value setting	Does not support named constants for function arguments and value settings; numeric values must be used instead
Cannot be sent to another user with a form	Can be sent to another user with a form
Works with application-wide events, such as selecting a folder	Works only with form events, such as changing the value of a field on a form
Uses different syntax for some settings	Uses different syntax for some settings

Additionally, VBA comes with a sophisticated development interface, the *Visual Basic Editor* (VBE), which gives developers a set of powerful tools for creating and debugging their code.

> **Note**
>
> VBA (Visual Basic for Applications) is the dialect of Visual Basic used in Office applications. VBA code is edited in the VBE window.
>
> *VBE* (the Visual Basic Editor) is the window in which you edit VBA code; it is generally opened by pressing Alt+F11 from an Office document window.
>
> *VBS* (Visual Basic Scripting Edition) is the dialect of Visual Basic used in Outlook code behind forms. Outlook VBS code is edited in the Script Editor, and debugged in the MDE window.
>
> *MDE* (the Microsoft Development Environment) lets you view and step through Outlook VBS code in a read-only window.

USING VBA TO CREATE APPLICATION-WIDE OUTLOOK CODE

In Outlook 2000, VBA code is used to respond to *events (page 358)* at the application level and in response to events attached to many Outlook objects (Folders, Explorers, Inspectors, OutlookBarGroups, and others), as opposed to the limited number of form events and the single control event available for use in Outlook VBS code. Using the VBE development environment discussed in the following sections, you can write VBA code to respond to an application-wide event, such as the arrival of new mail, or to an event such as a user opening a new Explorer window.

Unlike VBS code (which is attached to forms), VBA code can be run regardless of whether an item is open, making it much more flexible than VBS, which only runs when the form to which it is attached is open.

As in other Office applications, VBA code resides in code modules located in VBA projects, which also may contain UserForms (see the "UserForm Window" section later in this chapter). Outlook VBA projects belong to a particular Outlook user, so each user can have a customized Outlook environment. Samples of VBA code using application-wide events will be given in later sections of this chapter.

A full discussion of using the VBA programming language is beyond the scope of this book; the following sections assume that the reader is generally familiar with Visual Basic programming from using VB or some dialect of VBA, such as Word or Excel VBA, or the older WordBasic or AccessBasic dialects. Rather than attempt to teach you VBA, this chapter introduces some of the special features of VBA used in Outlook, with an emphasis on using VBA to add useful functionality to the Outlook interface.

THE VBA DEVELOPER'S ENVIRONMENT

The Visual Basic Editor (described in detail in the next section) is used to create and edit both code modules and UserForms in Outlook VBA projects. If you have worked with Word or Excel macros and procedures in previous versions of Office, or Access code in

Office 2000, the VBE environment will be familiar to you. Office 2000 finally offers a standardized development environment for all its components, replacing the non-standard (though equally powerful) Access developer's environment with the standard VBE window, and giving Outlook the VBE environment for application-wide code, though still retaining the limited Script Editor for working with VBS code.

In Chapter 41 you learned about the Outlook form events, which are available for use in VBS code behind Outlook forms. On the application level, there are numerous other events, all new to Outlook 2000, which can be used in VBA procedures. The Outlook events are listed in Table 43.2.

TABLE 43.2 THE OUTLOOK EVENTS

Event Name	Applies to Object(s)
*Activate	Explorer, Inspector
*AttachmentAdd	Items
*AttachmentRead	Items
*BeforeAttachmentSave	Items
*BeforeCheckNames	Items
*BeforeFolderSwitch	Explorer
*BeforeGroupAdd	OutlookBarGroups
*BeforeGroupRemove	OutlookBarGroups
*BeforeGroupSwitch	OutlookBarPane
*BeforeNavigate	OutlookBarPane
*BeforeShortcutAdd	OutlookBarShortcuts
*BeforeShortcutRemove	OutlookBarShortcuts
*BeforeViewSwitch	Explorer
Close	Items
CustomAction	Items
CustomPropertyChange	Items
*Deactivate	Explorer, Inspector
*FolderAdd	Folders
*FolderChange	Folders
*FolderRemove	Folders
*FolderSwitch	Explorer
Forward	Items
*GroupAdd	OutlookBarGroups

Event Name	Applies to Object(s)
*ItemAdd	Items
*ItemChange	Items
*ItemRemove	Items
*ItemSend	Application
*NewExplorer	Explorers
*NewInspector	Inspectors
*NewMail	Application
*OnError	SyncObject
Open	Items
*OptionsPagesAdd	Application, NameSpace
*Progress	SyncObject
PropertyChange	Items
*Quit	Application
Read	Items
*Reminder	Application
Reply	Items
ReplyAll	Items
*SelectionChange	Explorer
Send	Items
*ShortcutAdd	OutlookBarShortcuts
*Startup	Application
*SyncEnd	SyncObject
*SyncStart	SyncObject
*ViewSwitch	Explorer
Write	Items

*New to Outlook 2000

UNDERSTANDING THE VBE WINDOW

To create or edit Outlook VBA code, start by opening the VBE window by dropping down the Tools menu, clicking the Macro command to open the Macros submenu, and selecting the Visual Basic Editor command, as shown in Figure 43.1.

Tip #285 from

Helen Bell Feddema

You can press Alt+F11 from the main Outlook window to open the VBE window quickly.

Figure 43.1
Opening the Visual
Basic Editor window.

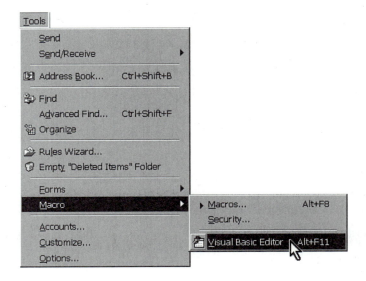

The Visual Basic Editor window opens, as shown in Figure 43.2. The VBE window is used to create (or delete) modules, to edit code in modules, and to create (or delete) UserForms. It contains a powerful Object Browser and debugging tools to aid you in figuring out problems with your code. You can also export your code to text files so you can share it with other users.

Note

The title bar of the VBE window says "Microsoft Visual Basic," but it is generally referred to as the VBE window.

The VBE window normally opens with three of its component windows (panes) visible: the Project Explorer, Properties Sheet, and Code Window. There are a number of other windows you can open as needed: the Object Browser, Immediate window, Locals window, Toolbox, UserForm window, and Watch window. All of the VBE component windows can either be paned, or used as free-floating windows or toolbars, as you prefer. The VBE component windows are discussed in the following sections.

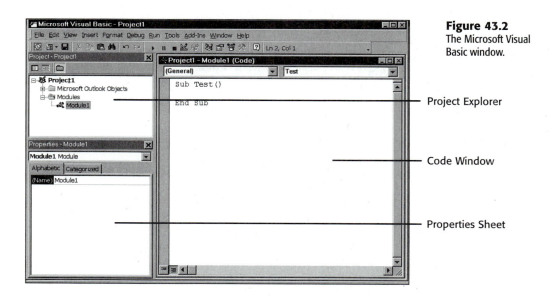

Figure 43.2
The Microsoft Visual
Basic window.

Project Explorer

Code Window

Properties Sheet

Tip #286 from

Helen Bell Feddema

> To convert a VBE component window from docked to free-floating, click its title bar and drag it to a new location. To dock a free-floating window, click and drag its title bar to the VBE window edge where you want to dock it.

Additionally, the VBE window has five toolbars; they are discussed later in this chapter.

PROJECT EXPLORER

The Project Explorer window has a tree-type display, similar to the Windows Explorer. If you see only a Project*n* node with a plus sign to its left, indicating that this node is collapsed, you can expand it (to open up the branches) by clicking on the plus sign, as shown in Figure 43.3.

Figure 43.3
The Project Explorer
window, in collapsed
mode.

View Code

View Object

Toggle Folders

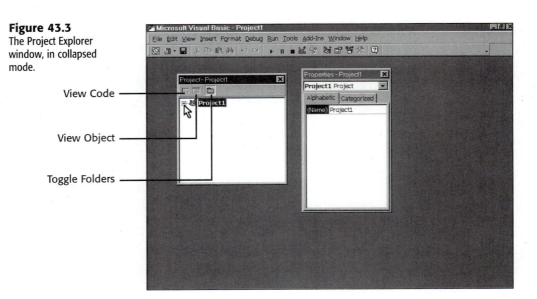

The Project Explorer window has its own toolbar, with three buttons:

View Code	Displays the Code window for the selected item
View Object	Displays the Object window for the selected UserForm
Toggle Folders	Hides or shows object folders

If you have not created any code modules, the Project Explorer will initially only have one folder, Microsoft Outlook Objects, with just one object, ThisOutlookSession, under it, representing the current Outlook session, as shown in Figure 43.4. You can create a new module in the Project Explorer by dropping down the Insert Object menu on the Standard toolbar and selecting the Module selection, as shown in Figure 43.5.

Note

You can also create a new module to contain your macros by selecting Macro from the Tools menu (see the "Macros" section later in this chapter for more details on this method). Whether you create a macro (procedure) from the Macro menu or from the VBE window, it will end up in a module you can view in the VBE window.

A new Code window opens to a blank module, as shown in Figure 43.6. Now the Project Explorer has a Modules folder, with the new module under it.

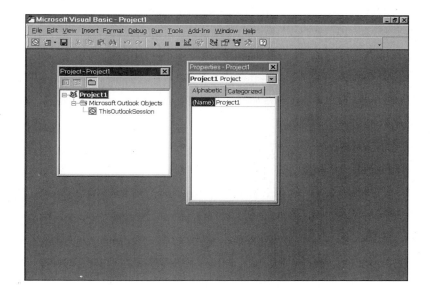

Figure 43.4
The Project Explorer window, in expanded mode.

Figure 43.5
Creating a new module in the Project Explorer.

Figure 43.6
A newly created
Code window.

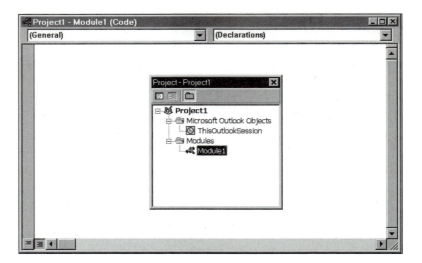

You can create new UserForms in a similar manner by selecting the UserForm selection from the New Object drop-down list on the Standard menu. As you create new objects, they are added to the Project Explorer tree. You can easily select the one you want to work on by selecting the item and pressing Enter, or by double-clicking it.

PROPERTIES WINDOW

The Properties window (similar to the Advanced Properties sheet in the Outlook form design window) lists the design-time properties of the selected object. If you have selected multiple controls, the Properties window displays just the properties common to all the selected controls.

Tip #287 from

If the Properties window is not visible, you can turn it on by clicking the Properties Window button on the Standard toolbar, as shown in Figure 43.7.

You won't see many properties in the Properties Window when a module is highlighted (see Figure 43.8); this window is primarily useful for UserForms and their controls.

The Properties window has two tabs: if you select the Alphabetic tab, the properties are listed alphabetically, in one long list. If you select the Categorized tab, the properties are categorized by property type.

Figure 43.7
The Properties
Window button on
the Standard toolbar.

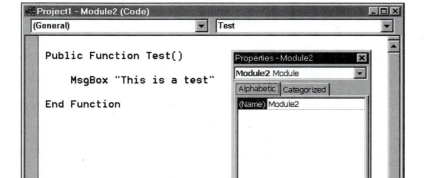

Figure 43.8
The Properties
Window for a code
module.

CODE WINDOW

The Code window displays your code, with a variety of tools for editing, running, and debugging it. Each module opens in its own Code window (see Figure 43.9), and you can have multiple Code windows open at once. On the top of a Code window, there are two drop-down lists. The one on the left is the Object Box, where you can select objects associated with the form or other object the code belongs to.

The Procedures/Events Box (on the right) displays procedures and events in the module, so you can go directly to the one you want to work with. At the top of the list there is a (Declarations) selection, which takes you to the top of the module, where you can enter options, declare global variables, and create general procedures.

On top of the vertical scrollbar is a little Split Bar, which you can drag up and down to split the Code window into two portions, each displaying a separate portion of code.

In the bottom right corner there are two icons:

Procedure View	Displays one procedure at a time in the Code window
Full Module View	Displays all the code in the module in a continuous stream

Figure 43.9
The Code window, with the Procedures/Events dialog box dropped down.

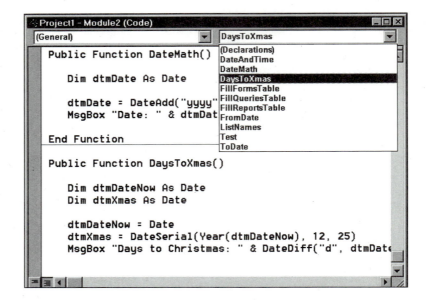

OBJECT BROWSER

The VBA Object Browser (like the VBS Object Browser) lets you examine Outlook objects and their properties, methods, and events. However, it also lets you inspect objects, properties, methods, and events belonging to other applications to which you have set a reference—a significant enhancement.

The two main components of the Object Browser window are the Classes list on the left side, where you can select a class to examine from the selected type library, and the Members list on the right, which shows the methods, properties, events and constants for the selected class.

The Project/Library dialog box lets you select the type library with the objects you want to examine, and the Search Text Box underneath it lets you enter a search string (click the Search button to run the search).

The Object Browser's toolbar buttons are described below:

Go Back	Returns to previous selection in Classes and Members list
Go Forward	Repeats original selection in Classes and Members list
Copy to Clipboard	Copies current selection to the Windows Clipboard
View Definition	Moves the cursor to the place in the Code window where the selection in the Classes or Members list is defined

Help	Opens context-specific help for the selected item
Search	Starts searching for the text string in the Search box
Show/Hide Search Results	Opens or hides the Search Results pane, with the results of the current search

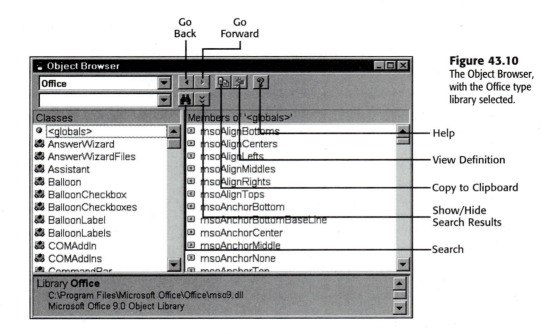

Figure 43.10
The Object Browser, with the Office type library selected.

If you want to examine the components of another Office application's object model, you need to set a reference to it. To set a reference to the Access type library, implement the following steps:

1. Open the VBE window, if it is not already open.
2. Drop down the Tools menu, and select References, as shown in Figure 43.11.
3. The References dialog box opens, with the checked type libraries at the top.
4. If the Microsoft Access 9.0 Object Library selection is checked, you don't need to do anything; just close the dialog box.

5. If the Access selection is not checked, locate it in the list of type libraries and check it, as shown in Figure 43.12.

6. Click OK to close the References dialog box.

7. Press F2 to open the Object Browser, if it is not already open.

8. Select Access from the list of type libraries in the drop-down list, as shown in Figure 43.13.

9. The Access objects are listed in the Classes list, and their events, properties, and methods in the Members list, each with a distinctive icon, as listed in Figure 43.14.

Note

For a key to the Object Browser icons, see Figure 42.6 in Chapter 42, "Enhancing Outlook Forms with Visual Basic Script Code."

Figure 43.11
Opening the References window from the Access Visual Basic window.

Figure 43.12
Checking the Access object library selection in the References dialog box.

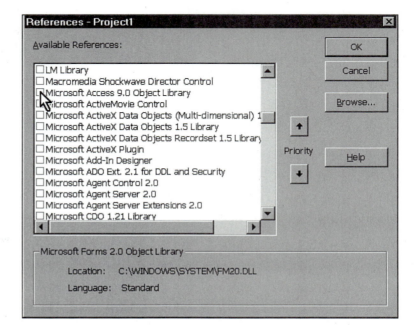

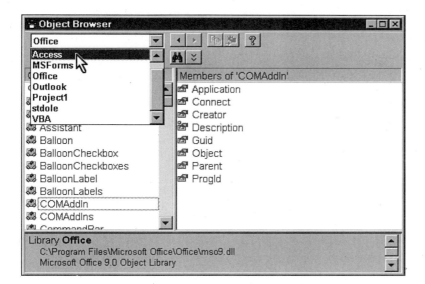

Figure 43.13
Selecting the Access
library in the Object
Browser.

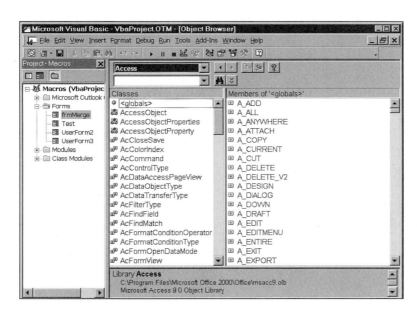

Figure 43.14
The Access object
library.

Definitions of Terms

An *object* is an element of an application, such an Outlook folder or task.

A *collection* is an object that contains one or more other objects, such as the Outlook Folders and Controls collections.

An *event* is an action recognized by an object, such as the Close event that occurs when closing an Outlook form.

A *method* is an action that an object can perform, such as the Save method for an Outlook item.

A *property* is an attribute defining one of an object's characteristics. In Outlook, each item has numerous properties, which are also called *fields*. The name and address controls on a Contact item are bound to various Outlook properties.

A *constant* is a fixed value used as an argument for a function or method, or for setting a value.

You can open the Help topic for a property, event or method by right-clicking it and selecting Help from the context menu, as shown in Figure 43.15; or you can click the Help button on the Object Browser's toolbar.

Figure 43.15
Opening the Help topic for an Access method.

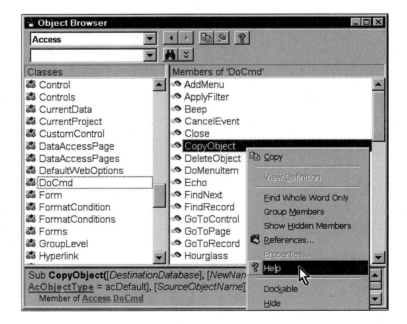

The CopyObject Help topic opens, as shown in Figure 43.16.

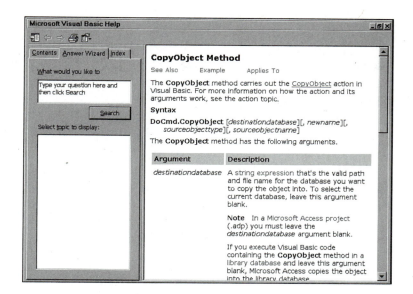

Figure 43.16
The Help topic for the Access CopyObject method.

IMMEDIATE WINDOW

The Immediate window (which you can open by pressing Ctrl+G, or by selecting the Immediate Window selection from the View menu), allows you to execute code directly, by typing it into the window and pressing Enter. While this can be handy, the major usefulness of the Immediate window is for displaying the values of variables you use in code, by using the Debug.Print method.

Using Debug.Print to display the values of variables (as opposed to using message boxes) allows you to run your code all the way through, without interruption, and if anything goes wrong, you can examine the variables in the Immediate window to see if any of them contain inappropriate information. (This technique is used in several of the code listings later in this chapter.) Figure 43.17 shows the Immediate window displaying a variable (with explanatory text) from a function that calculates the days left until Christmas.

LOCALS WINDOW, WATCH WINDOW

The Locals window and Watch window are used for advanced debugging, beyond the scope of this book.

USERFORM WINDOW

A UserForm window opens when you select UserForm from the Insert Object drop-down list on the Standard Outlook toolbar. UserForms (just as in Word) are standard Office forms on which you can place a variety of controls, using the Toolbox (see the next section).

UserForms are used to enter information, make selections, and run code—each UserForm has its own attached VBA code module, which you can edit in a Code window. However, UserForms can't be bound to data.

Figure 43.17
The Immediate window displaying the contents of a variable in a Code module.

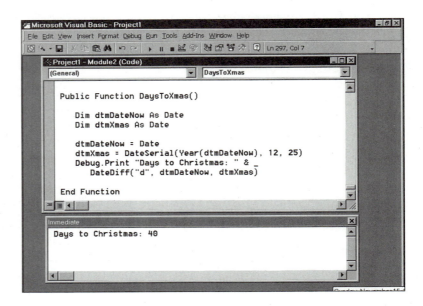

Caution

Office UserForms and Outlook forms are different types of objects; their interfaces and functionality differ significantly, so that it isn't safe to assume that if you can do something in a UserForm, you can do it in an Outlook form, or vice versa.

Tip #288 from
Helen Bell Feddema

To open a UserForm's code module, double-click its background.

Unlike regular Outlook forms, which are based on one of the standard Outlook item templates, UserForms have no built-in fields or controls; you have to populate them with controls of your choice. UserForms are very convenient for use as enhanced dialog boxes to let users make choices or enter information needed in your code.

UserForms have their own set of special toolbars, which are discussed in the following sections.

TOOLBOX   The Toolbox appears when you open a UserForm, as shown in Figure 43.18. It contains a set of standard Visual Basic controls, and possibly one or more ActiveX controls you have added to it.

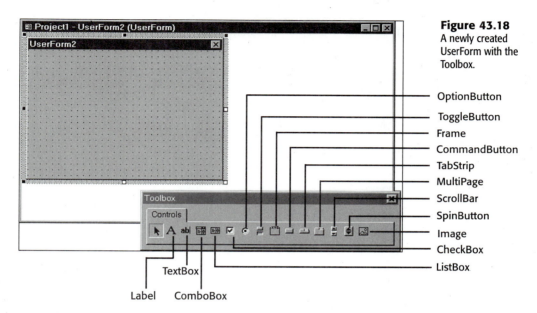

Figure 43.18
A newly created UserForm with the Toolbox.

OptionButton
ToggleButton
Frame
CommandButton
TabStrip
MultiPage
ScrollBar
SpinButton
Image
CheckBox
ListBox

TextBox

Label   ComboBox

The Visual Basic controls most commonly used on UserForms are described in the following sections.

Label Control   The Label control is used to display text on a UserForm. Labels are typically used either to describe an adjacent TextBox or ComboBox control, or to provide general information about a UserForm, such as a caption for a group of controls. Label controls can't be modified by the user.

TextBox Control   The TextBox control is used to enter or display data, which can be retrieved from code. TextBoxes on UserForms can't be bound to data.

ComboBox Control   The ComboBox control allows the user to select a value from a drop-down list, or to enter text into the box at the top of the list. Although ComboBox controls have a RowSource property, if you enter values into it (as you can do in Access), you will just get an "Invalid property setting" error message on exiting the property; apparently this property does not accept a list of values in UserForms. However, you can write values to the control's drop-down list from VBS code, using an array.

ListBox Control   The ListBox control, like the ComboBox, displays a list of items for user choice. However, the ListBox's list is always displayed, and the user can't enter a value that is not in the list. Because the ListBox control doesn't collapse into a single row when not in use, it takes up more room on a UserForm than a ComboBox, and thus is not practical except for a very small list.

CheckBox Control   A CheckBox control is used to display a Yes/No value. When checked, the CheckBox represents a Yes value; when unchecked, it represents a No value.

OptionButton Control   The OptionButton control is similar in function to the CheckBox control; instead of a check mark, the Yes value is displayed by a black center, and the No value by a white center.

ToggleButton Control   The ToggleButton control also functions as an interface for a Yes/No field; when the button appears to be pressed, it represents a Yes value, and when it appears to be raised, it represents a No value. ToggleButtons are rarely used, as they take up more room than CheckBox or OptionButton controls, and their meaning is not as intuitive.

Frame Control   The Frame control is used to contain a group of other controls, usually CheckBoxes or OptionButtons, to indicate that they are alternate choices for an option. A group of CheckBoxes or OptionButtons within a Frame is often referred to as an Option Group.

CommandButton Control   The CommandButton control is used to run a Sub procedure, which runs when it is clicked.

Image Control   The Image control is used to display an image on a UserForm.

The remaining controls in the Toolbox (the TabStrip, MultiPage, ScrollBar, and SpinButton controls) are less commonly used, as they require programming to make them useful.

In addition to the standard Visual Basic controls, you can also add ActiveX controls to a UserForm. As with adding ActiveX controls to an Outlook form, there is no guarantee that an ActiveX control will have full functionality on a UserForm.

USERFORM TOOLBAR   The UserForm toolbar (shown in Figure 43.19) has a number of useful tools for working with controls on UserForms.

Tip #289 from
Helen Bell Feddema

You can create new pages on the Toolbox, as a way of grouping your controls. To make a separate page for ActiveX controls, right-click the Toolbox background and select the New Page command from the context menu (the same menu can be used to rename, move, or delete Toolbox pages).

Figure 43.19
The UserForm
toolbar.

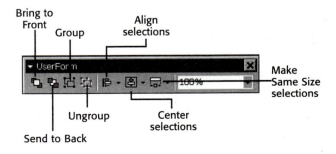

The tools on the UserForm toolbar work exactly like their counterparts on the Outlook Form Design toolbar; for details on their functionality, see the "Arranging Controls" section in Chapter 40, "Creating and Using Custom Forms."

STANDARD TOOLBAR

The VBE Standard toolbar (shown in Figure 43.20) has a number of tools to help you work with code in modules.

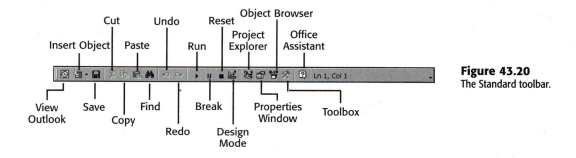

Figure 43.20
The Standard toolbar.

The buttons work as follows:

View Outlook	Switches back to the Outlook window
Insert Object	Drops down a list where you can choose a new object to insert:
	UserForm
	Module
	Class Module
	Procedure
Save	Saves the current project, including its component forms and modules
Cut	Cuts the selected object to the Clipboard
Copy	Copies the selected object to the Clipboard
Paste	Pastes the selected object from the Clipboard
Find	Opens the Find dialog box and searches for the text in the Find What box
Undo	Reverses the last edit action
Redo	Undoes the last Undo action
Run	Runs the current procedure or UserForm, or a macro if neither the Code window nor a UserForm is active
Break	Stops execution of code and switches to Break mode

Reset	Clears variables and resets the project
Design Mode	Toggles Design mode on and off
Project Explorer	Opens the Project Explorer
Properties Window	Opens the Properties Window
Object Browser	Opens the Object Browser
Toolbox	Opens the Toolbox
Office Assistant	Opens the Office Assistant (or Help, if you have turned the Office Assistant off)

EDIT TOOLBAR

The Edit toolbar (shown in Figure 43.21) contains some specialized buttons to aid you in working with code.

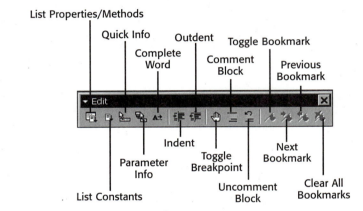

Figure 43.21
The Edit toolbar.

The buttons work as follows:

List Properties/Methods	Opens a box that lists an object's properties and methods
List Constants	Opens a box that lists the constants for a property
Quick Info	Gives the syntax for a variable, function, method, or procedure
Parameter Info	Opens a pop-up dialog box listing the parameters for a function
Complete Word	Completes the word you are typing
Indent	Shifts the selected text to the next tab stop

Outdent	Shifts the selected text to the previous tab stop
Toggle Breakpoint	Toggles a breakpoint on or off on the current line of code
Comment Block	Adds the comment character to each line of highlighted code
Uncomment Block	Removes the comment character from each line of highlighted code
Toggle Bookmark	Toggles a bookmark on or off for the current line of code
Next Bookmark	Goes to the next bookmark
Previous Bookmark	Goes to the previous bookmark
Clear All Bookmarks	Clears all bookmarks

Note

The Edit toolbar is only enabled when you have a Code window open.

DEBUG TOOLBAR

The Debug toolbar is used when you are trying to figure out why your code isn't working as you intended. The Debug toolbar buttons are shown in Figure 43.22.

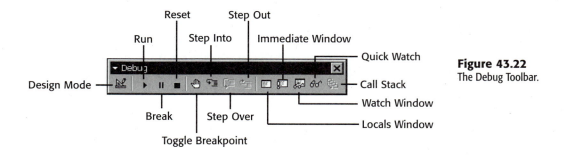

Figure 43.22
The Debug Toolbar.

Some of the buttons on the Debug Toolbar (Design Mode, Run, Break, Reset, Toggle, Breakpoint) are also on the Standard or Edit toolbars (see their descriptions in preceding sections); the others are used for advanced debugging purposes, beyond the scope of this book.

MACROS

Outlook macros don't work like macros in Word or Excel. You can't record an Outlook macro; they are actually procedures in a VBA module, similar to the modules you create directly in the VBE window. All macros are procedures, but not all procedures are macros:

In Outlook (and all other Office applications except Access) a macro is a Sub procedure that doesn't accept arguments. All your Outlook macros are stored in a single module.

Tip #290 from
Helen Bell Feddema

Although it isn't required—Outlook will just name the module containing macros Module*n*—I recommend naming it "Modules" (or "basModules" if you use a naming convention) so you will know which one it is when you look at the Project Explorer.

You can create a macro by accessing the Tools menu in the regular Outlook window, selecting the Macro selection to open the Macro submenu, and selecting the Macros command, as shown in Figure 43.23.

Figure 43.23
Creating an Outlook macro.

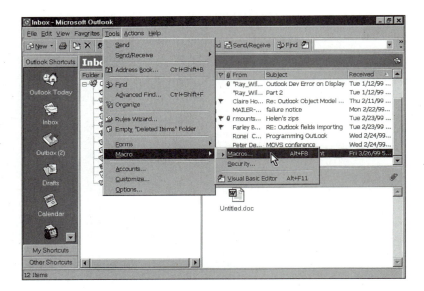

The Macros window opens (see Figure 43.24), enabling you to enter a name for the new macro, and click the Create button. The VBE window opens to a new module (or the module containing your existing macros, if this is not your first macro), containing a new Sub procedure with the name you assigned to the macro, as shown in Figure 43.25.

At this point, you are in the VBE window, and can continue working on the macro just as if you had started it from the VBE window, using the New Procedure button on the Standard toolbar.

Note

Once you have created a macro in an Outlook session, when you create additional macros, they will all be created in the same module. Procedures created in this module appear in the Macros dialog box; they are the only procedures available through the Macros dialog box.

If you have created one or more macros, when you open the VBE window, you will get the message shown in Figure 43.26. Answering Yes to this question enables the macros; answering No disables the macros. The virus warning message only appears the first time you open the VBE window in an Outlook session; if you close the VBE window and then reopen it (without closing down Outlook), it will not appear again.

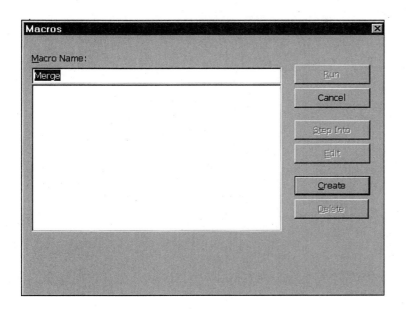

Figure 43.24
The Macros window.

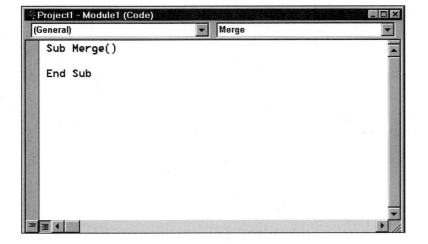

Figure 43.25
The new macro as a Sub procedure.

To turn off the session macro virus warning permanently, implement the following steps:

1. Pull down the Tools menu in the main Outlook window.

2. Click the Macro selection to open its submenu.

3. Click the Security selection, as shown in Figure 43.27.

4. The Security dialog box opens, as shown in Figure 43.28.

5. You have three choices—High, Medium, and Low security. Selecting Low turns off the warning permanently, but (as the text says), it is somewhat risky.

Figure 43.26
The Macro Virus Warning dialog box for an Outlook session.

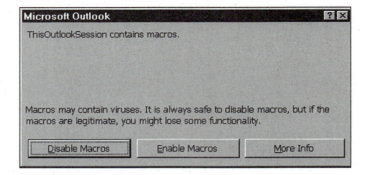

Caution

The macro virus warning described here is for the entire Outlook session; the form macro virus warning described in Chapter 40, "Creating and Using Custom Forms," can be turned off by publishing the form, as described in that chapter.

Figure 43.27
Opening the macro security dialog box.

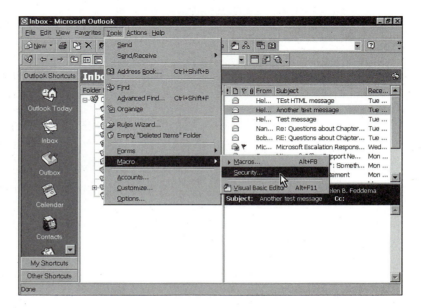

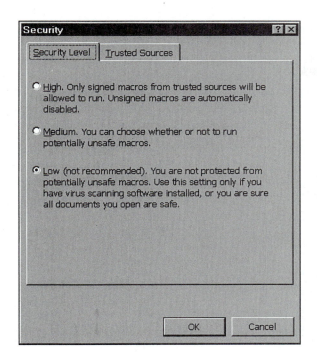

Figure 43.28
The Security dialog box.

PROGRAMMING COMMON OUTLOOK TASKS WITH VBA

With the introduction of VBA to Outlook 2000, many exciting possibilities have opened up, allowing developers much greater control of the Outlook environment and Outlook events, both from within Outlook and from other applications that support Automation. The following sections will give you an idea of how you can use Outlook VBA code to make it easier to perform common tasks, or customize the Outlook interface.

CREATING A CUSTOM TOOLBAR BUTTON TO PRINT NEW MAIL MESSAGES

Since the earliest version of Outlook, users have wanted to be able to print new mail messages automatically. With Outlook 2000, it is easy to write a macro that prints all the unread mail messages in the Inbox, and (if desired) you can place a button to run the macro on your Outlook toolbar. To create such a macro, implement the following steps:

1. From the Outlook window, press Alt+F8 to open the Macros dialog box.

2. Enter PrintMail as the macro name, as shown in Figure 43.29, and click the Create button.

3. The VBE window opens to the module containing your macros, with a code stub for the new macro, as shown in Figure 43.30.

4. Start by declaring variables to reference the Outlook objects you need—the Outlook application itself, the NameSpace object, a Folder object for the Inbox, Items for the mail messages in the Inbox, and MailItem for each message. You can select the appropriate object types for each of these objects, using the Methods/Properties list that appears after you type "Outlook." (See Listing 43.1 for the complete procedure.)

5. Next, set references to the objects just dimensioned, using the Set keyword because these are object variables.

6. Use the For Each...Next construct to loop through the mail messages in the Inbox, checking each for the value of its Unread property, and printing the message if Unread = True.

7. To check that the macro works, run it from the Code window by clicking the Run button on the toolbar.

8. After verifying that the macro works (all unread mail messages should print), you can make a toolbar button for the macro.

9. Close the VBE window (you can't customize an Outlook toolbar while the VBE window—or any modal dialog—is open).

10. Switch back to the Outlook window, if necessary.

11. Right-click the gray background of the Standard toolbar to display its context menu, then click the Customize selection, as shown in Figure 43.31.

12. Select the Commands tab on the Customize dialog box, if it is not already selected.

13. Select the Macros category from the Categories list.

14. Drag the PrintMail macro from the Commands list to the toolbar, as shown in Figure 43.32.

15. By default, the button will have a text label along with a macro icon. To change it to an icon-only button, click the Modify Selection button on the Customize dialog box and select Default Style from the menu, as shown in Figure 43.33.

16. Close the Customize dialog box by clicking its Close button.

17. Now the new PrintMail button appears on the Standard toolbar, as shown in Figure 43.34.

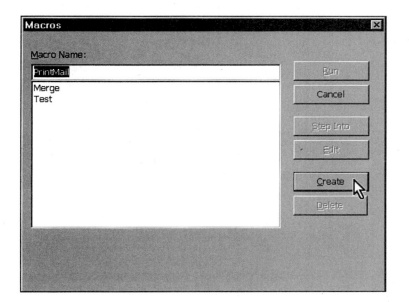

Figure 43.29
Creating a macro.

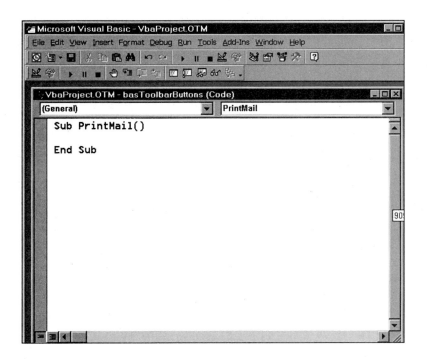

Figure 43.30
The new macro's
code stub.

Figure 43.31
Customizing a tool-
bar.

Figure 43.32
Dragging the new
macro to the toolbar.

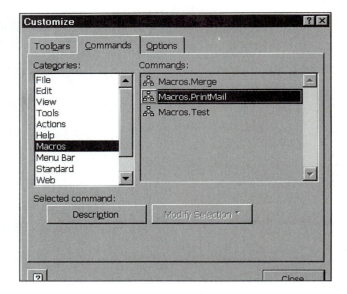

LISTING 43.1

```
Sub PrintMail()

    Dim objOutlook As Outlook.Application
    Dim fld As Outlook.MAPIFolder
    Dim nms As Outlook.NameSpace
    Dim itms As Outlook.Items
    Dim itm As MailItem

    Set objOutlook = CreateObject("Outlook.application")
    Set nms = objOutlook.GetNamespace("MAPI")
    Set fld = nms.GetDefaultFolder(olFolderInbox)
    Set itms = fld.Items

    For Each itm In itms
        If itm.UnRead = True Then
            itm.PrintOut
        End If
    Next itm

End Sub
```

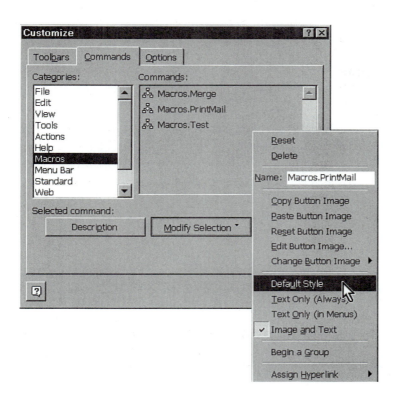

Figure 43.33
Selecting the default style for the new toolbar button.

Figure 43.34
The new PrintMail toolbar button.

Tip #291 from
Helen Bell Feddema

You don't have to leave the toolbar button called Macros.PrintMail (or even worse, Modulen.PrintMail). To rename a toolbar button, open the Customize dialog as described in the preceding steps, then right-click the button and rename it in the Name property of its menu, as shown in Figure 43.35.

Figure 43.35
Renaming a toolbar
button.

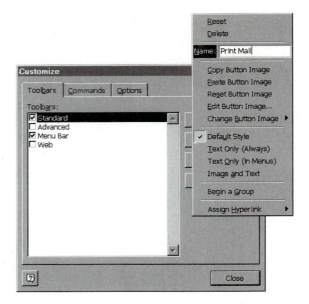

USING THE NEWMAIL EVENT TO PRINT NEW MAIL MESSAGES WHEN RECEIVED

The previous section showed you how to create a toolbar button to print unread mail messages. But what if you want to fully automate this procedure, so that every time you receive mail, the new mail messages print out automatically? You can do this by using the NewMail event, one of the new application-wide events introduced in Outlook 2000. To write an event procedure for printing new mail messages when mail is received, implement the following steps:

1. Open the VBE window by pressing Alt+F11 from the Outlook window.

2. If the Project Explorer is not visible, click the Project Explorer button on the toolbar to open it.

3. Open the Microsoft Outlook Objects folder and double-click the ThisOutlookSession selection under it to open its code module.

4. Select Application in the Object Box, and NewMail in the Procedures/Events Box in the Code window, to create a code stub for the NewMail event procedure, as shown in Figure 43.36.

5. Enter the code into the event procedure—the same code used for the preceding macro procedure will do, just omitting the line that sets the objOutlook variable, which is not needed. (See Listing 43.2 for the full procedure.)

6. Now every time you get new mail, the new mail messages will be printed automatically.

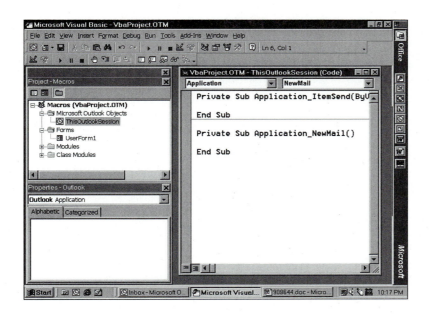

Figure 43.36
Creating an
application-wide
event procedure.

LISTING 43.2

```
Private Sub Application_NewMail()

    Dim fld As Outlook.MAPIFolder
    Dim nms As Outlook.NameSpace
    Dim itms As Outlook.Items
    Dim itm As Outlook.MailItem

    Set objOutlook = CreateObject("Outlook.application")
    Set nms = objOutlook.GetNamespace("MAPI")
    Set fld = nms.GetDefaultFolder(olFolderInbox)
    Set itms = fld.Items

    For Each itm In itms
        If itm.UnRead = True Then
            itm.PrintOut
        End If
    Next itm

End Sub
```

SELECTING CONTACTS FOR MAIL MERGE

In previous versions of Outlook, it was possible to merge an individual Outlook contact to a Word letter by using the limited built-in merge functionality, or by creating a custom contact form with a command button to run VBS code to do the merge. You could also write

Word VBA or Outlook VBS code to merge all the contacts in a folder to a Word merge letter, or to merge just the contacts with a certain value in the Categories field.

With Outlook 2000, you can go a step further: With a UserForm dialog box as a front end, you can let users select as many contacts as they want from a multi-select ListBox control, and then merge the selected contacts only. This method lets you easily select the contacts you want to send a letter to, even though they don't have the same category. To create a UserForm with code to do a mail merge, implement the following steps:

1. Open the VBE window by pressing Alt+F11 from the Outlook window.

2. Create a new UserForm by selecting UserForm from the Insert Object menu on the toolbar.

3. Open the Project Explorer and Properties Window (if they are not already open) by clicking their buttons on the toolbar.

4. Select the new UserForm in the Project Explorer, and double-click it to open the UserForm.

5. Highlight the default UserForm name in the Properties window and change it to frmMerge.

6. Similarly, give the form's Caption property the name "Merge." The renamed Name and Caption properties are shown in Figure 43.37.

Figure 43.37
A UserForm's properties sheet.

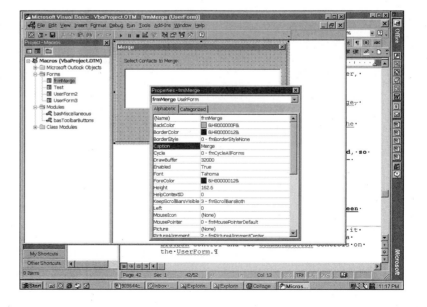

7. Using the Toolbox (open it from its button if it is not already open), place a Label control, a ListBox control, and two CommandButton controls on the UserForm.

8. Select the ListBox control and make the following selections for some of its properties, to make it a multi-select ListBox with check boxes for selecting contacts:

Name	lstMergeContacts
ColumnWidths	72 pt;256 pt
ListStyle	1 - fmListStyleOption
MultiSelect	1 - fmMultiSelectMulti

9. Using the Properties window, change the Label control's caption to "Select Contacts to Merge:", and the CommandButtons' captions to "Merge" and "Cancel," and their names to "cmdMerge" and "cmdCancel," as shown in Figure 43.38.

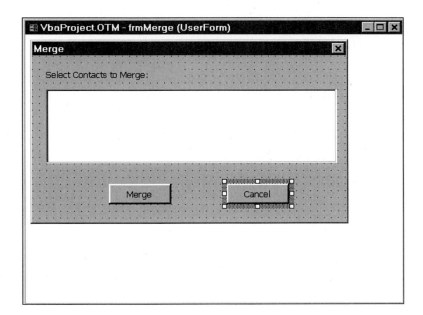

Figure 43.38
Adding controls to a UserForm.

10. Now open the UserForm's code module by double-clicking the form's background.

11. To fill the ListBox control with contact names, select the Initialize event from the Procedures/Events Box to create a code stub for the event.

12. Enter the code shown in Listing 43.3 to fill the ListBox control (lstMergeContacts) with contact names, using a two-dimensional array filled from the contacts in your default Contacts folder.

13. The two CommandButtons on the UserForm run the Sub procedures listed in Listing 43.3—the Cancel button simply closes the form without doing anything, while the Merge button merges the selected contacts to a Word mail merge letter, then closes the form.

14. Displaying the UserForm (so the user can select contacts to merge) takes a procedure in another module—for example a macro in the Macros module.

15. Open the Macros module and create a new Sub procedure, using the code in Listing 43.4.

16. If desired, put the code that opens the UserForm on a toolbar button, as in the preceding NewMail example.

17. Now when you run the macro or click the button, the UserForm opens (see Figure 43.39), and you can check off the contacts to merge, then click the Merge button to do the merge to Word.

Figure 43.39
Selecting contacts to merge from a UserForm.

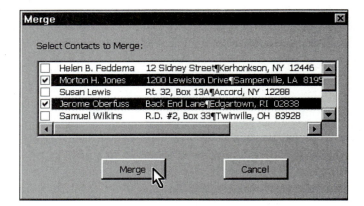

18. A new Word document is created from the template for each checked contact.

19. The Word template (located in the default User Templates folder) has two custom document properties: FullName and BusinessAddress, which are displayed in DocProperty fields in the letter. Figure 43.40 shows the custom document properties being created in the template's properties sheet, and Figure 43.41 shows the DocProperty fields in a document based on the template, which display the values in the properties.

Note

The paragraph marks (¶) in the dialog indicate a line break between the name and address.

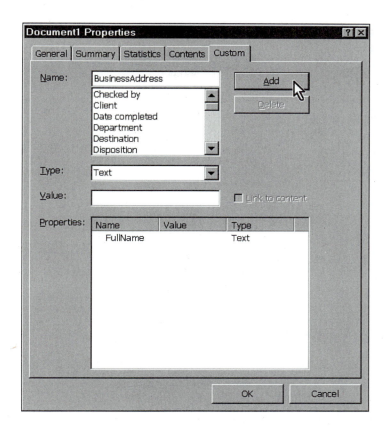

Figure 43.40
Creating custom document properties for a Word document.

Word Custom Document Properties

Word custom document properties are located on the Custom page of a document's properties sheet, as shown in Figure 43.40. When creating custom document properties, it is advisable to avoid using the same names as built-in properties, to avoid confusion when referencing the properties.

Note

You can't create an empty custom document property in Word; when you create a new text custom document property, save it with a space, or a zero for a numeric property.

Figure 43.41
A Word document created from VBA code and filled with Outlook contact information.

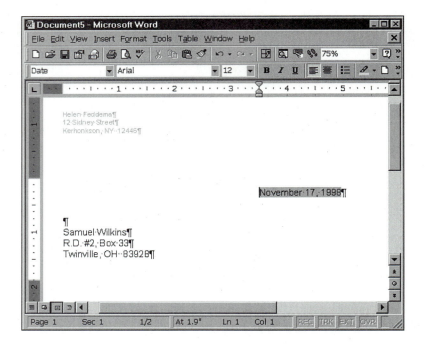

LISTING 43.3

```
Option Explicit

Dim objOutlook As Outlook.Application
Dim fld As Outlook.MAPIFolder
Dim nms As Outlook.NameSpace
Dim itms As Outlook.Items
Dim itm As Outlook.ContactItem
Dim i As Single
Dim j As Single
Dim lngContacts As Long

Private Sub UserForm_Initialize()

    Dim aryMerge()

    Set objOutlook = CreateObject("Outlook.application")
    Set nms = objOutlook.GetNamespace("MAPI")
    Set fld = nms.GetDefaultFolder(olFolderContacts)
    Set itms = fld.Items
    lngContacts = itms.Count
    Debug.Print "Number of contacts: " & lngContacts
    ReDim aryMerge(lngContacts - 1, 1)
    i = 0
    j = 0
    lstMergeContacts.ColumnCount = 2

For Each itm In itms
     If Len(itm.BusinessAddress) > 0 Then
```

```
          Debug.Print "Setting row " & i & ", column " & j
          aryMerge(i, j) = itm.FullName
          Debug.Print "Setting row " & i & ", column " & j + 1
          aryMerge(i, j + 1) = itm.BusinessAddress
          i = i + 1
          End If
      Next itm
    lstMergeContacts.List() = aryMerge

End Sub

Private Sub cmdCancel_Click()

    Unload FrmMerge

End Sub

Private Sub cmdMerge_Click()

    Dim lst As ListBox
    Dim objWord As Word.Application
    Dim strWordTemplate As String
    Dim prps As Object

    Set objOutlook = CreateObject("Outlook.application")
    Set objWord = CreateObject("Word.application")
    Set nms = objOutlook.GetNamespace("MAPI")
    Set fld = nms.GetDefaultFolder(olFolderContacts)
    Set itms = fld.Items
Set lst = lstMergeContacts
strWordTemplate = "C:\Windows\Application Data\Microsoft\Templates\Letter from
Outlook.dot"

    lngContacts = itms.Count

    For i = 0 To lngContacts - 1
       If lst.Selected(i) = True Then
          Debug.Print "Selected name: " & lst.List(i)
          'Open a new letter based on the selected template
          objWord.Documents.Add strWordTemplate

          'Write info from contact item to Word custom doc properties
          Set prps = objWord.ActiveDocument.CustomDocumentProperties
          prps.Item("FullName").Value = Nz(lst.List(i, 0))
          prps.Item("BusinessAddress").Value = Nz(lst.List(i, 1))

          'Update fields in Word document and activate it
          objWord.Selection.WholeStory
          objWord.Selection.Fields.Update
          objWord.Selection.HomeKey 6
          objWord.Visible = True
          objWord.Activate
       End If
    Next i

    Unload frmMerge

End Sub
```

LISTING 43.4

```
Sub Merge()

    Load frmMerge
    frmMerge.Show

End Sub
```

Tip #292 from

Helen Bell Feddema

You can borrow Word's Mail Merge Helper image for your Outlook Merge button by implementing the following steps:

1. Right-click the Outlook toolbar and select Customize from the menu.
2. Drag the new Merge button from the Macros list to the toolbar.
3. Leave the Customize dialog box open, and open a Word mail merge document.
4. Right-click the Word toolbar and select Customize from the menu.
5. Right-click the Mail Merge Helper toolbar button and select Copy Button Image, as shown in Figure 43.42.

Figure 43.42
Copying the Word
Mail Merge Helper
button image.

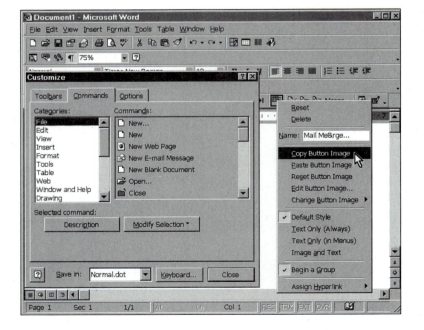

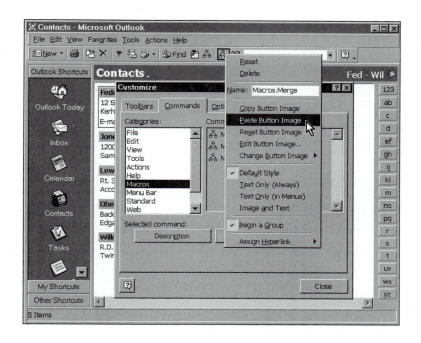

Figure 43.43
Pasting the Word button image to an Outlook toolbar button.

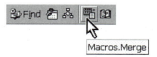

Figure 43.44
The Outlook Merge button, with the image from the Word Mail Merge Helper button.

6. Switch back to Outlook, right-click the Merge button, and select Paste Button Image, as shown in Figure 43.43.

7. Close the Outlook and Word Customize dialog boxes.

8. The Outlook Merge button now has the Mail Merge Helper image, as shown in Figure 43.44.

BUTTONS TO PASTE BOILERPLATE TEXT INTO MAIL MESSAGES

If you need more than a few signatures for your mail messages—in particular, if you want to be able to paste in paragraphs of boilerplate text—you can create one or more toolbar buttons to paste chunks of text into a mail message. If you only have a few selections, make a button for each; if you have a great number of boilerplate selections, it may be more practical to select the one you want to use from a ListBox or ComboBox control on a UserForm, using a technique similar to the one used in the last section to select a contact for a mail merge letter.

I have a Notepad document containing a collection of URLs I frequently need to paste into mail messages. To automate this process, I created a macro to run from a toolbar button. You can create such a macro by implementing the following steps:

1. Open the VBE window by pressing Alt+F11 from the Outlook window.
2. Open the Macros module and create a new procedure—say WebSites.
3. Enter the code shown in Listing 43.5 in the procedure.
4. Save the module and make a toolbar button for the WebSites macro, as in the earlier examples.
5. Start writing a mail message. At the point where you want to insert the boilerplate text, click the WebSite toolbar button.
6. Alternatively, you can run a macro that has not been assigned to a toolbar button by dropping down the Tools menu, selecting the Macro selection to open the Macro sub-menu, and selecting the Macros command to open the Macros dialog box.
7. Select the WebSites macro in the list of available macros, and click the Run button, as shown in Figure 43.45.

Figure 43.45
Running a macro from the Macros dialog box.

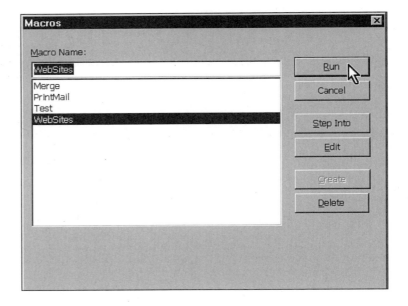

8. The text is pasted into the mail message, as shown in Figure 43.46.

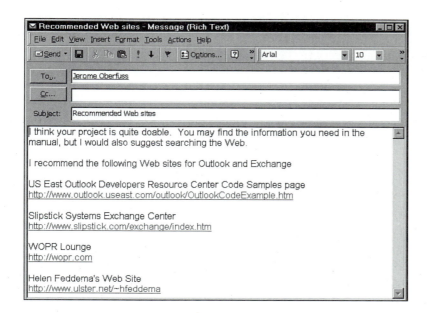

Figure 43.46
A mail message with
boilerplate text
pasted from a macro.

Tip #293 from

Helen Bell Feddema

The best place for a button (or several buttons) like this in a New Message window's toolbar; this will ensure that the focus will remain in the Message window.

Note

If the boilerplate text is pasted into a message with an automatic signature, the insertion is
placed after the signature. Also, the cursor is left positioned at the beginning of the
inserted text.

Caution

Because of a "by design" feature of Outlook 2000 (some might call it a bug), pasting text
from code into a mail message automatically converts it into a Rich Text message. If you
want the message to be Plain Text or HTML, you can select another format from the message's Format menu.

LISTING 43.5

```
Public Sub WebSites()

    Dim objOutlook As Outlook.Application
    Dim ins As Outlook.Inspector
    Dim itm As Outlook.MailItem
    Dim strText As String
```

continues

LISTING 43.5   CONTINUED

```
Set objOutlook = CreateObject("Outlook.application")
Set ins = objOutlook.ActiveInspector
Set itm = ins.CurrentItem

'Add the text to the text already in the main Body field,
'by concatenating it in chunks
strText = itm.Body
strText = strText & _
    "I recommend the following Web sites for Outlook and Exchange" & _
    vbCrLf & vbCrLf
strText = strText & _
    "US East Outlook Developers Resource Center Code Samples page" & _
    vbCrLf
strText = strText & _
    "http://www.outlook.useast.com/outlook/OutlookCodeExample.htm" & _
    vbCrLf & vbCrLf
strText = strText & _
    "Slipstick Systems Exchange Center" & vbCrLf
strText = strText & _
    "http://www.slipstick.com/exchange/index.htm" & vbCrLf & vbCrLf
strText = strText & "WOPR Lounge" & vbCrLf
strText = strText & "http://wopr.com" & vbCrLf & vbCrLf
strText = strText & "Helen Feddema's Web Site" & vbCrLf
strText = strText & "http://www.ulster.net/~hfeddema"

'Write the text back to the Body field
itm.Body = strText

End Sub
```

USING COMMANDBARS

In addition to placing new buttons on the built-in Outlook toolbars, you can also create your own CommandBars, with just the functions you need for a custom Outlook application. CommandBars come in several varieties:

Toolbar

Menu bar

Menu

Shortcut menu

Submenu

While there is a CommandBars collection in the Outlook object model, and you can add new CommandBars using the collection's Add method, you can't do much with Outlook CommandBars in VBA code. The Office object model (installed with Office 2000) has a richer set of methods, properties, and constants for its CommandBars, so if you want to create CommandBars from code, and populate them with controls, you should use the Office object model.

TROUBLESHOOTING

Q: **My code stops on a line of code with an error message, with a function highlighted, but I know the line of code is OK. What is the problem?**

A: Your code may use early binding of variables, using specific object types in declarations such as

```
Dim ctl As Control
```

If the line of code uses a method or property that is not appropriate for the declared object type, you will get an error. To fix this problem, inspect the available methods, properties, or arguments, and select one that belongs to the object you are using.

Or you may have used a function from another application's dialect of VBA, such as the Nz function from Access VBA. If you use early binding, you must have a reference set to the appropriate object library; otherwise, the object (Control in this case) won't be recognized. Similarly, if you use a function from another application's dialect of VBA, you must have a reference set to that object library. To check whether this may be a problem, implement the following steps:

1. If your code has stopped with an error message, click the OK button in the dialog box, as shown in Figure 43.47.

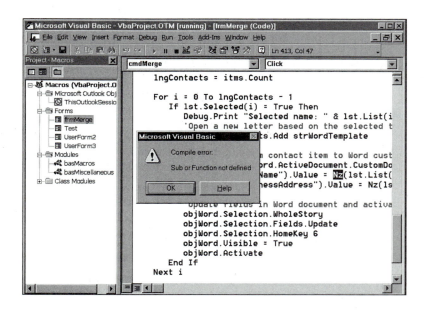

Figure 43.47
An error message highlighting the Nz function.

2. Click the Reset button on the toolbar to reset the code, as shown in Figure 43.48.

Figure 43.48
Resetting code after
an error.

3. Pull down the Tools menu and select the Reference command.

4. Locate the appropriate object library in the list and click it. In this case, the Nz function requires the Access 9.0 object library, so Figure 43.49 shows this object library being checked.

Figure 43.49
Setting a reference to
the Access 9.0 object
library.

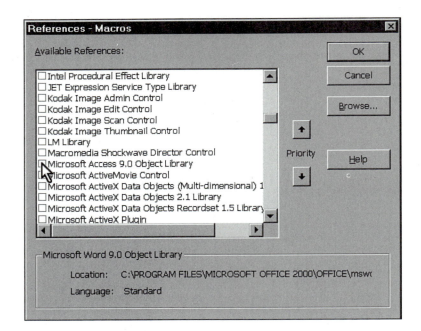

5. Close the References dialog box.

6. Try running the code again; it should run now.

Caution

Sometimes the missing object library is indicated by the word "MISSING" in the list of object libraries (next to the library's name), but you can't count on this.

Q: How can I get projects from Outlook, Access, and Word to display in the same VBE window?

A: Unfortunately, this is not possible. Each Office application opens its own VBE window.

Q: Will my Outlook VBA code work with Outlook 97 or 98?

A: No; Outlook VBA only works with Outlook 2000.

Q: My code runs without error messages, but I am not getting the results I intended. How can I find out what is wrong with the code?

A: Try using Debug.Print statements in your code to display the values of any variables you are using. (Press Ctl+G in the VBE window to open the Immediate Window, where you see the results of these statements.)

Q: My code runs correctly up to a certain point, but I can't figure out exactly where the problem is. Can I make the code execute more slowly, so I can see what is happening?

A: You can step through your code a line at a time by setting a breakpoint in the code (say, just before the problem area). To set a breakpoint, click the Break button on the toolbar, or press F9. Then press F8 repeatedly, to run the code a line at a time.

UNDERSTANDING AUTOMATION

THE HISTORY OF OFFICE DATA EXCHANGE

With every version of Office, the techniques available for interchanging data among Office applications have become more sophisticated. Starting with Windows 3.0, the Windows clipboard has allowed users to exchange text data (and, to some extent, graphic data) among Windows applications, using the Copy and Paste commands on the File menu (or their hot-key equivalents, Ctrl+C and Ctrl+V). But copying and pasting aren't very practical for transferring large amounts of Access or Excel data to another application, and these techniques require the user to perform the appropriate selection (copying, application switching, selection, and pasting operations) just right—otherwise the right data won't get into the right location in the target application.

Dynamic Data Exchange (DDE) provided a way to exchange data in various early VB dialects (WordBasic, AccessBasic, and so on). It wasn't very reliable, and the programming syntax was obscure, but it did the job for certain types of information exchange. You may still see DDE code used to transfer data among Office applications—it survives to this day in Access-to-Word Mail Merge—but it has generally been replaced by the more powerful and easier-to-use Automation technology, which lets you work directly with objects belonging to other applications' object models. You will see Automation in practice in the listings later in this chapter.

THE OUTLOOK OBJECT MODEL

An application's object model is a representation of the application's functionality (or a subset of it) as a hierarchy of objects with properties, methods, and events that can be manipulated from code. An object is simply something you work with in an application—in Outlook, that would be folders, items in folders, and the curiously named Explorer and Inspector objects, which are just Outlook's arcane ways of referring to the pane in which you see the contents of a folder (that's the Explorer), or the actual item itself, once you have opened it (that's the Inspector).

When Outlook is open, there is always an Explorer object open, but not necessarily an Inspector object. You can use the technique illustrated in Listing 44.17 to determine what type of active interface object is currently active (Explorer or Inspector), and what type of item it displays.

→ For general information about the Outlook object model, **see** Chapter 42, "Enhancing Outlook Forms with Visual Basic Script Code."

An understanding of the Outlook object model (see Figure 44.1), or at least its main components, is essential for writing code to work with Outlook, whether from Outlook VBS, Outlook VBA, or VBA from other Office (or non-Office) applications. You can get information about the objects in the Outlook object model by opening the Outlook Objects Help topic in Outlook Help, as shown in Figure 44.2.

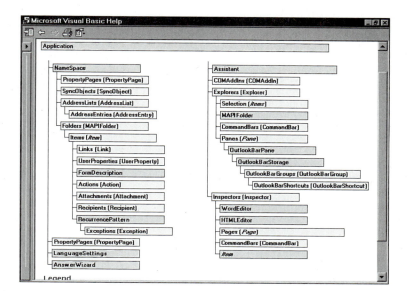

Figure 44.1
The Outlook object model Help topic gives you a schematic look at the Outlook objects you can manipulate in code.

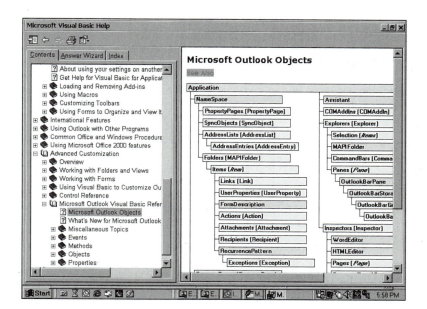

Figure 44.2
Opening the Outlook Objects Help topic.

Note   The terms *object model* and *object hierarchy* are used more or less interchangeably.

In the Outlook Objects Help topic, the blue objects are single objects, while the yellow objects are collections. You can click an object (or collection) to open its Help topic, where you can open lists of the object's properties, events, and methods by clicking the appropriate link in the topic header. Figure 44.3 shows the NameSpace Object Help topic, with its Properties list open to select the CurrentUser property.

Figure 44.3
The NameSpace Help topic, with its Properties list.

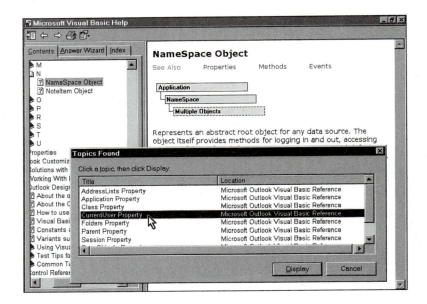

The major components of the Outlook object model—the ones you need to use in writing VBA code—are discussed in the following section.

APPLICATION

The Application object is at the top of the object hierarchy. It represents the entire Outlook application, and in order to work with any of the objects underneath it, you must set a reference to the Outlook object. In VBS code, use the Application keyword to refer to the Outlook Application object, using the syntax in Listing 44.1. In VBA code (whether in Outlook or some other application), use the syntax shown in Listing 44.2, which first dimensions the Outlook object and then sets a reference to it. Alternatively, you can dimension an Outlook object variable using the New keyword, as in Listing 44.16, in which case you don't need to set the variable.

Listing 44.1, run from a command button called cmdReminder on an Outlook form, posts a reminder note on the user's desktop.

LISTING 44.1

```
Sub cmdReminder_Click

    Set itm = Application.CreateItem(5)
    strRecipient = Item.To
    itm.Body = "Call to follow up mail message to " & strRecipient
    itm.Display

End Sub
```

Listing 44.2, which could be run from an Access module, prints all unread mail messages. If this code is run from another application than Outlook, set a reference to the Outlook 9.0 object library (see "Setting a Reference to the Outlook Object Library" later in this chapter for details on setting references).

→ For a full discussion of the following code sample, **see** Chapter 43, "Creating Application-wide Visual Basic for Applications Code."

LISTING 44.2

```
Function PrintMail()

    Dim objOutlook As Outlook.Application
    Dim fld As Outlook.MAPIFolder
    Dim nms As Outlook.NameSpace
    Dim itms As Outlook.Items
    Dim itm As MailItem

    Set objOutlook = CreateObject("Outlook.application")
    Set nms = objOutlook.GetNamespace("MAPI")
    Set fld = nms.GetDefaultFolder(olFolderInbox)
    Set itms = fld.Items

    For Each itm In itms
        If itm.UnRead = True Then
            itm.PrintOut
        End If
    Next itm

End Function
```

NameSpace

Note | MAPI is an acronym for Mail Application Programming Interface.

The oddly-named NameSpace object represents the MAPI message store where Outlook data is stored (roughly equivalent to Access tables). You need to reference the NameSpace object in order to get at items stored in folders, as in Listing 44.2. You can reference this object and objects under it whether or not any objects are open. The NameSpace object itself has a few useful properties, especially the CurrentUser property, which prints the name of the current Outlook user to the Immediate window when run from a module, as shown in Listing 44.3. If run from an application other than Outlook, set a reference to the Outlook object library before running the function.

Tip #294 from

Helen Bell Feddema

The CurrentUser property is useful when you need to extract the Outlook user's name, say to include in the header of a printed calendar.

LISTING 44.3

```
Public Function OutlookUser() As String

    Dim objOutlook As Outlook.Application
    Dim nms As Outlook.NameSpace
    Dim strUser As String

    Set objOutlook = CreateObject("Outlook.application")
    Set nms = objOutlook.GetNamespace("MAPI")
    strUser = nms.CurrentUser
    Debug.Print "Outlook User name: " & strUser
    objOutlook.Quit

End Function
```

CLOSING OUTLOOK

Some of the code samples working with Outlook in this chapter end with the line

```
objOutlook.Quit
```

to close Outlook. It is generally desirable to quit Outlook if you have created an instance of Outlook from another application, except in the special case where you need to work with the current Outlook object, as in Listing 44.10 later in this chapter. If you run the code from within Outlook, you can comment out this line of code by prefacing it with an apostrophe ('). You should also comment out the lines of code that declare and set an Outlook object, since they are not necessary. Unless otherwise stated, it is assumed that code samples in this chapter are to be run from an Access module.

FOLDERS

The Folders collection contains folders—the same folders you can see in the Folder List in the Outlook interface (see Figure 44.4).

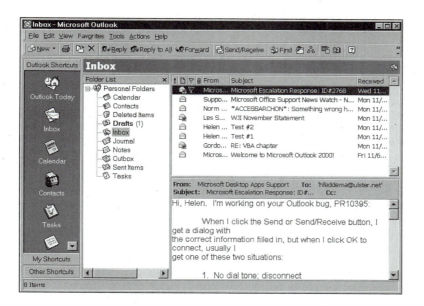

Figure 44.4
The Outlook Folder
List.

Tip #295 from
Helen Bell Feddema

If you don't see the Folder List, drop down the View menu and select Folder List, as shown
in Figure 44.5 (if you don't see this selection, click the double-arrow to expand the menu).

Tip #296 from
Helen Bell Feddema

By default, Outlook is installed with menus set to display only the most commonly used
commands, with a downward-pointing double arrow you can click to expand a menu to
show all the commands. To ensure that each menu displays all the menu commands, right-
click the menu background, select Customize, and uncheck the Menus Show Recently Used
Commands First check box on the Options page of the dialog box.

Figure 44.5
Making the Folder
List visible.

In order to work with items in a folder in VBA code, you need to reference the folder you want to work with, using one of the following methods:

- Use one of the Outlook folder reference constants in the OlDefaultFolders enum (see Table 44.1).
- Use the collection index number (rarely used, except when iterating through an entire collection of folders).
- Use the folder name (for non-default folders).

TABLE 44.1   THE OLDEFAULTFOLDERS ENUM

Named Constant	Numeric Value
olFolderCalendar	9
olFolderContacts	10
olFolderDeletedItems	3
olFolderDrafts	16
olFolderInbox	6
olFolderJournal	11
olFolderNotes	12
olFolderOutbox	4
olFolderSentMail	5
olFolderTasks	13

Folder references use a different syntax depending on whether the folder is located under your Personal Folders or Public Folders top-level folder, or is located under an Exchange mailbox. In case the folder is one of the standard Outlook folders located under your Personal Folders folder (the default location), you can use one of the named constants in Table 44.1 in VBA code (as in Listing 44.4). These constants list the subjects of all appointment items in the default calendar to the Immediate window (except for recurring appointments). If this code is run from an application other than Outlook, set a reference to the Outlook 9.0 object library (see the sidebar later in this chapter for details).

LISTING 44.4

```
Public Function ListAppts()

    Dim objOutlook As Outlook.Application
    Dim nms As Outlook.NameSpace
    Dim fld As Outlook.MAPIFolder
    Dim itms As Outlook.Items
    Dim itm As Outlook.AppointmentItem

    Set objOutlook = CreateObject("Outlook.application")
```

```
    Set nms = objOutlook.GetNamespace("MAPI")
    Set fld = nms.GetDefaultFolder(olFolderCalendar)
    Set itms = fld.Items

    For Each itm In itms
        If itm.RecurrenceState = olApptNotRecurring Then
        Debug.Print itm.Subject
        End If
    Next itm

    objOutlook.Quit

End Function
```

For folders located under the Public Folders top-level folder, use the alternate syntax shown in Listing 44.5, which lists tasks in a public folder called Special Tasks.

The code has the following requirements:

1. If the function is run from an application other than Outlook, set a reference to the Outlook 9.0 object library.

2. Create an Outlook folder called "Special Tasks" under the Public Folders top-level folder.

LISTING 44.5

```
Public Function ListPublicAppts()

    Dim objOutlook As Outlook.Application
    Dim nms As Outlook.NameSpace
    Dim fld As Outlook.MAPIFolder
    Dim itms As Outlook.Items
    Dim itm As Outlook.TaskItem

    Set objOutlook = CreateObject("Outlook.application")
    Set nms = objOutlook.GetNamespace("MAPI")
    Set fld = nms.Folders("Public Folders").Folders("All Public
➥Folders").Folders("Special Tasks")
    Set itms = fld.Items

    For Each itm In itms
        Debug.Print itm.Subject
    Next itm

    objOutlook.Quit

End Function
```

Additionally, a folder may contain subfolders. To reference a custom folder located under another folder in the Personal Folders tree, use the syntax shown in Listing 44.6. Note that you need to add a line to the following code, to set the strUserName variable appropriately for your system.

LISTING 44.6

```
Set fld = nms.Folders("Personal Folders").Folders("Special
➥Events").Folders("Schedule")
```

Finally, for folders located under an Exchange mailbox, use the syntax shown in Listing 44.7, where strUser is a valid Exchange mailbox name. This code lists the appointments in a calendar located in the user's Exchange mailbox, and defaults to the local calendar if an Exchange mailbox for the specified user can't be found.

Code requirements in this usage are:

1. A valid Exchange mailbox for the user represented by the strUser variable.
2. A Calendar folder under that mailbox.
3. Permission to access that Calendar folder.

LISTING 44.7

```
Public Function ExchangeFolder()

    Dim objOutlook As Outlook.Application
    Dim nms As Outlook.NameSpace
    Dim fld As Outlook.MAPIFolder
    Dim itms As Outlook.Items
    Dim itm As Outlook.AppointmentItem
    Dim rcp As Outlook.Recipient
    Dim strUserName As String

    Set objOutlook = CreateObject("Outlook.application")
    Set nms = objOutlook.GetNamespace("MAPI")

    'strUserName must be the name of a valid recipient mailbox on
    'Exchange server
    strUserName = InputBox("Enter Exchange Mailbox name", "User Name")
    Set rcp = nms.CreateRecipient(strUserName)
    rcp.Resolve
    If rcp.Resolved Then
        Set fld = nms.GetSharedDefaultFolder _
            (rcp, olFolderCalendar)
    Else
        MsgBox "Can't find a valid mailbox for " & strUserName _
            & "; using default local calendar"
        Set fld = nms.GetDefaultFolder(olFolderCalendar)
    End If

    Set itms = fld.Items

    For Each itm In itms
        Debug.Print itm.Subject
    Next itm

    objOutlook.Quit

End Function
```

ITEMS

Each folder may contain one or more items, which may not all be the same type. For example, you might have a few Post items and a Word Office Document in your Inbox, along with the regular Mail Message items. When writing VBA code, generally, you will want to process only items of a specific type in a folder, such as only the Mail Messages in the Inbox.

You can select the named constant for the appropriate item type from the pop-up list in the VBE window. The list pops up automatically when you type a period after an object name, as shown in Figure 44.6.

PART
VIII
CH
44

Tip #297 from	When you declare a variable for a single Outlook item, you must select a specific item type, such as MailItem or ContactItem. However, when you declare a variable for a collection of items in a folder, that variable is just declared as Items, and can represent any type of item. If you need to declare a variable for an item, but you don't know what type of item it is, just declare it as Object (see Listing 44.8 later in this chapter for an example).
Helen Bell Feddema	

Figure 44.6
Selecting an item type from the IntelliSense drop-down list in a code module.

FINDING AN OUTLOOK ITEM

How do you reference an individual item—for example, a particular person's Contact item? In Access, a table generally is indexed on a key field with a unique value, say a Customer ID or Social Security Number, so you can easily find the record you want to work with. If the table doesn't have a naturally unique field, you can create one using the AutoNumber field data type. Unfortunately, Outlook has no equivalent functionality.

While there are some built-in Outlook fields suitable for use in locating records (the Customer ID, Government ID Number, and Organizational ID fields), these fields must be filled in manually for every record (so if you forget to enter values for all items, you won't be able to use them for locating a record). Also, they don't apply to some types of data, such as contacts who are personal friends rather than business contacts. And finally, to make one of these fields a required field (so a record can't be saved unless it is filled in), you have to create a custom Outlook contact form and transfer all your existing contacts to that form— a considerable inconvenience.

Outlook does have a built-in field (UniqueID) which seems to offer the promise of a unique identifier—but unfortunately the value of this field changes when an item is moved to another folder, so it isn't really much use for locating a specific item, since your friend Jim Jensen is the same person, even when you put his contact item in another folder. Because of this flaw, if you want to have a unique identifier for items of a particular type, you must create a custom field (or use one of the three ID fields mentioned previously), set its Required property to True, and fill it yourself.

So, for now you have two choices when trying to locate a specific Outlook item: You can search for data in a field such as FullName (which may not be unique), or you can select (or create) an ID field, and carefully fill it with appropriate, unique data for each item you create, and then use that field for locating items.

EXPLORERS

Explorers and Inspectors are Outlook's active interface objects—they let you write code to manipulate the objects users have opened, even if you don't know their specific names or contents. *Explorers* are Outlook windows that display the contents of folders, and the Explorers collection includes all the currently open Explorers. You can work with Explorer windows without knowing their names, as in the code in Listing 44.8, which lists the subjects of all items in the currently open folder, whatever it may be.

Tip #298 from

Helen Bell Feddema

The code samples in this chapter and the supporting files—Word templates, Access databases, and Excel worksheets—can be downloaded from `http://www.ulster.net/~hfeddema`. In case you want to try the samples without downloading the files, you should enter the code into a code module in another Office application (I recommend Access). Next, set a reference to the Outlook 9.0 object library (see "Setting a Reference to the Outlook Object Library"), compile the code to check for typos or missing references, and then run the function by clicking the Run button on the toolbar, as shown in Figure 44.7.

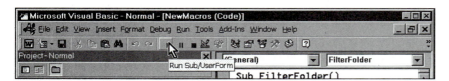

Figure 44.7
Running a function from Access.

SETTING A REFERENCE TO THE OUTLOOK OBJECT LIBRARY

1. Open the VBE window in an Office application (Access is recommended).
2. Pull down the Tools menu.
3. Select the References command.
4. Locate the Outlook 9.0 Object Library selection in the list of object libraries, and check it, as shown in Figure 44.8.
5. Click OK to close the References dialog box.

Caution

The Nz function used in many of the code samples in this chapter is specific to Access VBA. If you run code containing this function from an application other than Access, make sure you have set a reference to Access, using the References dialog box, as described in the following steps for Outlook.

Requirements for code in this instance are

1. A reference to the Outlook 9.0 object library.
2. (If not run from Access) A reference to the Access 9.0 object library.

LISTING 44.8

```
Public Function ListAESubjects()

    Dim objOutlook As Outlook.Application
    Dim exp As Explorer
    Dim fld As Outlook.MAPIFolder
    Dim itms As Outlook.Items
    Dim itm As Object

'Retrieve current Outlook object if Outlook is running,
'and otherwise create a new Outlook object
    On Error Resume Next
    Set objOutlook = GetObject(, "Outlook.Application")
    If Err.Number <> 0 Then
        'Outlook is not running; creating an Outlook object
        Set objOutlook = CreateObject("Outlook.Application")
        Err.Clear
    End If

    Set exp = objOutlook.ActiveExplorer
    Set fld = exp.CurrentFolder
    Set itms = fld.Items
    Debug.Print "Listing subjects of items in " _
        & fld.Name & ":" & vbCrLf

    For Each itm In itms
        Debug.Print Nz(itm.Subject)
    Next itm

End Function
```

EARLY BINDING VS. LATE BINDING

If you have set a reference to the Microsoft Outlook 9.0 object library (to check this, open the References dialog box from the Tools menu in a module, as shown in Figure 44.7), you can declare your variables using specific object types, as in Listing 44.7. This is called *early binding*, and it can give you better performance, but the downside is that you can only use the variable to reference the object class you specify.

If you haven't set a reference to an object library, you can't declare your variables as specific object classes in that library, and you will need to use the generic Object object instead; this is called *late binding*. Late binding may involve a slight performance hit, but such a variable can be reused for an object of a different class, which can be useful.

Late binding is also useful in case you don't know the object type a line of code will need, as in the Dim itm As Object line in Listing 44.8. In this case, since the *fld* variable refers to whatever folder the user has opened, the specific object type for items in that folder might be MailItem, AppointmentItem, or whatever—you don't know which. The generic Object type will work regardless of the actual object type.

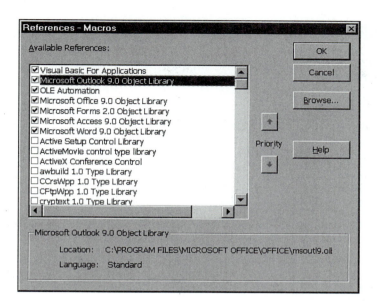

Figure 44.8
Checking the
References dialog box
for the Outlook 9.0
object library, so you
can use early binding
for Outlook objects.

INSPECTORS

Inspectors are Outlook windows displaying the contents of a specific item, such as a Contact or Task. The code in Listing 44.9 lists certain properties of the item in the currently open Inspector, using On Error Resume Next in case that property isn't relevant for that object type. The error handler in this function traps Error 91, "Object variable or With block variable not set," which occurs if you run the code when no Inspector is open.

Note

See Listing 44.11 for an alternative method of checking the object type of the active Outlook window, and taking the appropriate action.

The following code requires a reference to the Outlook 9.0 object library.

LISTING 44.9

```
Public Function ListAIProps()

On Error GoTo ListAIPropsError

    Dim objOutlook As Outlook.Application
    Dim ins As Inspector
    Dim itm As Object

    'Retrieve current Outlook object if Outlook is running,
    'and otherwise create a new Outlook object
    On Error Resume Next
    Set objOutlook = GetObject(, "Outlook.Application")
```

continues

LISTING 44.9   CONTINUED

```
    If Err.Number <> 0 Then
        'Outlook is not running; creating an Outlook object
        Set objOutlook = CreateObject("Outlook.Application")
        Err.Clear
    End If

    Set ins = objOutlook.ActiveInspector
    Set itm = ins.CurrentItem
    Debug.Print "Listing properties of " & ins.Caption
    Debug.Print "Item subject: " & itm.Subject
    Debug.Print "Item body: " & itm.Body
    On Error Resume Next
    Debug.Print "Item last name: " & itm.LastName
    On Error Resume Next
    Debug.Print "Item date received: " & itm.Received
    On Error Resume Next
    Debug.Print "Item due date: " & itm.DueDate

ListAIPropsExit:
    Exit Function

ListAIPropsError:
    If Err.Number = 91 Then
        MsgBox "There is no Inspector object open; exiting"
    Else
        MsgBox "Error No: " & Err.Number & "; Description: " & Err.Description
    End If

    Resume ListAIPropsExit

End Function
```

CONTROLLING OTHER OFFICE APPLICATIONS FROM OUTLOOK

With the introduction of VBA to Outlook 2000, it has become much easier to write Automation code to control other Office applications from Outlook. The following sections show you how to control Access, Word, and Excel from Outlook, using Automation code in Outlook macros.

IMPORTING DATA FROM AN ACCESS DATABASE INTO OUTLOOK

If you have created an Access database with a table of contacts, or other name and address-type information, you may want to import the data into Outlook, creating new Contact items from the Access data. While Outlook 2000 does include a built-in Import and Export Wizard (available from the File menu), this Wizard only imports to standard Outlook items, so if you want to import Access data into items based on a custom form, with your own selection of custom fields, you need to write VBA code to do the import.

The code in Listing 44.10 imports records from the Employees table in the sample Access Northwind database into items created from a custom Outlook form called Special Events Staff, in a custom folder. The code uses early binding of variables, so check the References dialog box (see Figure 44.7) to make sure that both the Microsoft Access 9.0 and Microsoft DAO 3.6 object libraries are checked before running the macro.

Code requirements are:

1. A custom Outlook form based on the Contact form, called "Special Events Staff" (see the following note).

2. An Outlook folder called "Special Events" under the top-level Personal Folders folder.

3. Another Outlook folder called "Company Information" under the Special Events folder (see Figure 44.9 for a view of these folders in the Outlook folder tree).

> **Note**
>
> If you are unable to download the Zip file of supporting files from http://www.ulster.net/~hfeddema, you can create the necessary Outlook custom form from scratch. The Special Events form used in Listing 44.10 is based on the Contact form, with several custom fields, arranged as shown in Figure 44.12 (or as you prefer):
>
> EmployeeID (Integer)
>
> HireDate (Date/Time)
>
> ReportsTo (Text)

➔ For general information on creating custom forms, **see** Chapter 40, "Creating and Using Custom Forms."

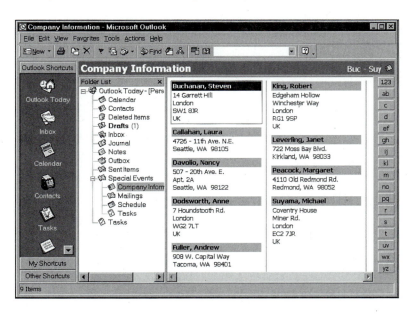

Figure 44.9
The Outlook folders tree showing the Special Events and Company Information folders.

LISTING 44.10

```
Sub ImportEmployees()

On Error GoTo ImportEmployeesError

    Dim objOutlook As New Outlook.Application
    Dim objAccess As New Access.Application
    Dim rst As Recordset
    Dim DAO As Object
    Dim wks As Workspace
    Dim dbs As Database
    Dim nms As NameSpace
    Dim fld As MAPIFolder
    Dim itms As Items
    Dim itm As ContactItem
    Dim strAccessDir As String
    Dim strFolder As String
    Dim strDBName As String
    Dim fFound As Boolean
    Dim lngRecCount As Long

    Set nms = objOutlook.GetNamespace("MAPI")

    'Pick up path to Access database directory from Access SysCmd function
    strAccessDir = objAccess.SysCmd(9)
    Debug.Print "Access Directory: " & strAccessDir
    strDBName = strAccessDir & "Samples\Northwind.mdb"
    Debug.Print "DBName: " & strDBName
    objAccess.Quit

    'Set up reference to Access database
    Set DAO = CreateObject("DAO.DBEngine.36")
    Set wks = DAO.Workspaces(0)
    Set dbs = wks.OpenDatabase(strDBName)

    'Open Access table containing data to import into Outlook
    Set rst = dbs.OpenRecordset("Employees")
    lngRecCount = rst.RecordCount
    If lngRecCount = 0 Then
        MsgBox "No employees to import"
        Exit Sub
    Else
        MsgBox lngRecCount & " employees to import"
    End If

    'Set up the Outlook folder and items and iterate
    'through the Access table, adding one contact item using
    'the custom form for each Access record

    Set fld = nms.Folders("Personal Folders").Folders("Special
➥Events").Folders("Company Information")
    Set itms = fld.Items

    Do Until rst.EOF
        Debug.Print "Importing " & Nz(rst!LastName) & "'s record"
        Set itm = itms.Add("IPM.Contact.Special Events Staff")
```

```
        'Built-in Outlook properties
        itm.LastName = Nz(rst!LastName)
        itm.FirstName = Nz(rst!FirstName)
        itm.JobTitle = Nz(rst!Title)
        itm.BusinessAddressStreet = Nz(rst!Address)
        itm.Title = Nz(rst!TitleOfCourtesy)
        itm.BusinessAddressCity = Nz(rst!City)
        itm.BusinessAddressState = Nz(rst!Region)
        itm.BusinessAddressPostalCode = Nz(rst!PostalCode)
        itm.BusinessAddressCountry = Nz(rst!Country)
        itm.Birthday = Nz(rst!BirthDate)
        itm.Body = Nz(rst!Notes)

        'Custom Outlook properties
        itm.UserProperties("EmployeeID") = Nz(rst!EmployeeID)
        itm.UserProperties("HireDate") = Nz(rst!HireDate)
        If Nz(rst!ReportsTo) = 2 Then
            itm.UserProperties("ReportsTo") = "Fuller, Andrew"
        ElseIf Nz(rst!ReportsTo) = 5 Then
            itm.UserProperties("ReportsTo") = "Buchanan, Steven"
        End If
        itm.Close (0)

        rst.MoveNext

    Loop
    rst.Close
    MsgBox "All employees imported into Company Information folder!"

ImportEmployeesExit:
    Exit Sub

ImportEmployeesError:
    MsgBox "Error No:  " & Err.Number & "; error message:  " & Err.Description
    Resume ImportEmployeesExit

End Sub
```

Since this procedure is a macro, once you have created it—either directly as a sub procedure in your Macros module, or by selecting Create from the Macros dialog box—you can run it from the Macros menu selection on the Tools menu, as shown in Figure 44.10.

The Company Information folder full of the newly imported Contact items is shown in Figure 44.11, and one of the custom Contact items is shown in Figure 44.12.

CREATING WORD LETTERS USING OUTLOOK DATA

Outlook 2000 does offer enhanced functionality for merging contacts to Word, compared to previous versions. But you still have to go through a complex procedure of copying to another folder, or applying filters, in order to gather a few contacts you might want to merge to a particular Word letter. Also, the merge functionality doesn't give you an easy way to select the fields you want to merge to the Word letter, or any way of selecting custom fields.

If you want to be able to easily merge Outlook data from the current contact to a Word letter, you can write your own Outlook macro, which will extract exactly the fields you want to use from the currently selected Contact item, and write them to Word custom document properties fields in a document created from a Word template. This method has several advantages over mail merge for a single document—the Outlook contact information is stored in the document itself, and no extra merge file is required.

Figure 44.10
Running the newly created ImportEmployees macro from the Macros dialog box.

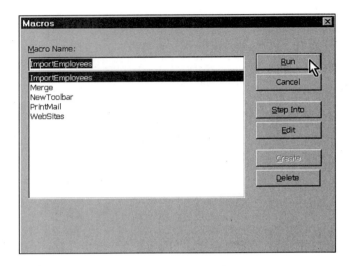

Figure 44.11
A folder full of contacts newly imported from Access, using the ImportEmployees macro.

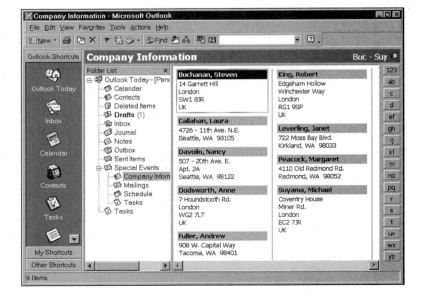

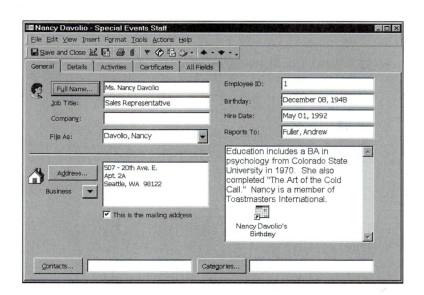

Figure 44.12
A contact imported from Access to a custom Contact form.

PART
VIII

CH
44

The macro code in Listing 44.11 creates a Word letter based on a template with the appropriate custom document properties, fills the document properties with data from Outlook, and opens the letter for the user to type in the body of the letter.

Requirements for this code are:

1. Set a reference to the Outlook 9.0 object library.
2. Set a reference to the Word 9.0 object library.
3. Set a reference to the Access 9.0 object library.
4. Copy the file "Staff Letter.dot" to the local templates folder (by default "C:\Windows\Application Data\Microsoft\Templates"). (Or you can create this template yourself, with custom document properties as described in the following Tip.)
5. Enter the code in Listing 44.11 into an Outlook macro.
6. Open an Outlook item based on the Special Events Staff custom form.
7. Run the macro.

LISTING 44.11

```
Public Sub SingleLetter()

On Error GoTo SingleLetterError

    Dim strLetter As String
    Dim strDate As String
    Dim strSalutation As String
```

continues

LISTING 44.11   CONTINUED

```
Dim strTemplateDir As String
Dim objOutlook As Outlook.Application
Dim objWord As Word.Application
Dim objDocs As Word.Documents
Dim prps As Object
Dim ins As Inspector
Dim itm As ContactItem

strDate = CStr(Date)
Debug.Print "Date: " & strDate
Set objOutlook = CreateObject("Outlook.Application")
Set ins = objOutlook.ActiveInspector
Set itm = ins.CurrentItem
Debug.Print "Selected item: " & ins.Caption
Debug.Print "Item class: " & itm.Class

If itm.Class <> olContact Then
    MsgBox "The active Inspector is not a contact item; exiting"
    Exit Sub
End If

'Open Word invisibly
Set objWord = CreateObject("Word.Application")

strTemplateDir = "C:\WINDOWS\Application Data\Microsoft\Templates\"
strLetter = strTemplateDir & "Staff Letter.dot"
'MsgBox "Opening document based on template: " & strLetter

If Nz(itm.Title) <> "" Then
    strSalutation = itm.Title & " " & itm.LastName
Else
    strSalutation = "Mr. " & itm.LastName
End If

'Open a new letter based on the selected template
Set objDocs = objWord.Documents
objDocs.Add strLetter
objWord.Visible = True

'Write info from contact item to Word custom doc properties
Set prps = objWord.ActiveDocument.CustomDocumentProperties
prps.Item("TodayDate").Value = strDate
prps.Item("Name").Value = itm.FullName
prps.Item("Address").Value = Nz(itm.BusinessAddress)
prps.Item("Salutation").Value = strSalutation
prps.Item("EmployeeID").Value = Nz(itm.UserProperties("EmployeeID"))
objWord.ActiveDocument.Fields.Update
objWord.Activate
```

```
SingleLetterExit:
   Exit Sub

SingleLetterError:
   If Err.Number = 91 Then
      MsgBox "There is no Inspector object open; exiting"
   Else
      MsgBox "Error No: " & Err.Number & "; Description: " & Err.Description
   End If

   Resume SingleLetterExit

End Sub
```

Tip #299 from

Helen Bell Feddema

Word custom document properties are used to store information in a Word document that can be displayed in the document, using DocProperty fields. You can write to custom document properties from VBA or VBS code, which makes them very handy for merging data from Outlook to Word. Compared to mail merge, custom document properties have two advantages: (1) There is no need to have the source application open, once the data has been written to the custom document properties; (2) Each document has its own data stored separately, which makes it easier to reprint or edit the individual documents.

To examine or create custom document properties, open a Word document's Properties sheet from its File menu, and click the Custom tab. The Custom tab of a Word document's Properties sheet is shown in Figure 44.13.

To insert the contents of a custom document property into a Word document, implement the following steps:

1. Drop down the Word document's Insert menu.

2. Select the Field command.

3. In the Field dialog box, select Document Information from the Categories list and DocProperty from the Field names list, then click the Options button, as shown in Figure 44.14.

4. Select the document property you want to insert from the Property list in the Field Options dialog box, as shown in Figure 44.15.

5. Click the OK button on the Field Options dialog box, then on the Field dialog box.

6. You should see the contents of the field in the Word document.

7. To see the field codes, press Alt+F9; now you should see the field codes, as shown in Figure 44.16.

This code uses the ActiveInspector object's CurrentItem property to identify which contact to use for the merge; all you have to do is open the contact to merge and click the macro's toolbar button on the form toolbar. Or, you can select the macro to run from the Macros dialog box, opened from the form's Tools menu.

Note

> Be sure to run this macro from the Tools|Macros dialog box on the Contact item menu, not the one on the main menu—if you use the main Outlook Tools|Macros selection, the active inspector won't be the Contact item any more.

Figure 44.17 shows a Word letter created by using the preceding procedure.

Figure 44.13
Viewing the values of custom document properties on the Custom page of a Word document's Properties sheet.

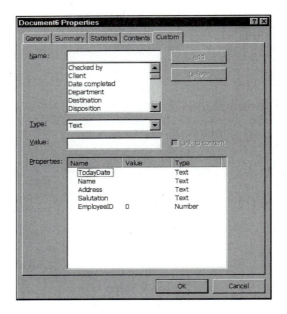

Figure 44.14
Placing a DocProperty field in a Word document.

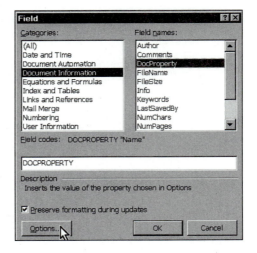

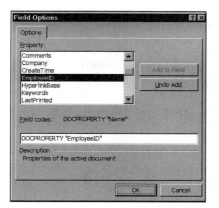

Figure 44.15
Selecting a document property for a DocProperty field.

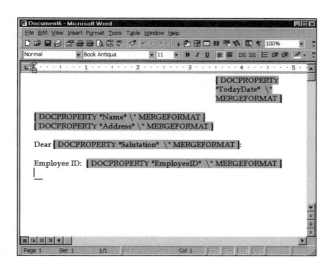

Figure 44.16
Viewing field codes in a Word document.

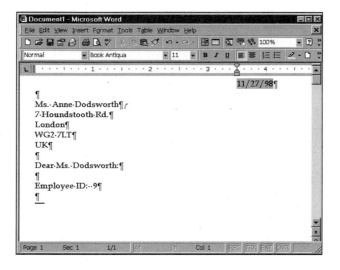

Figure 44.17
A single Word letter created from an Outlook contact.

CREATING WORD LABELS USING OUTLOOK DATA

Sometimes you want to merge a large group of contacts into a single Word document, to create a set of letters to different contacts, or perhaps sheets of labels. If you want to use just the standard contact fields, the built-in mail merge functionality may be all you need; however, if you need to use custom fields, you're out of luck, because the built-in Outlook mail merge utility only merges data in standard Outlook fields.

The code in Listing 44.12 merges data from all the contacts in the currently selected folder to a Word labels document. Instead of a mail merge document (which would require a separate data source document), the code simply iterates through the contacts in the currently selected folder (accessed via the ActiveExplorer object), and writes the data from the desired fields to cells in a Word table, formatted for Avery #5160 labels.

Code Requirements in this case include

1. Set a reference to the Outlook 9.0 object library.

2. Set a reference to the Word 9.0 object library.

3. Set a reference to the Access 9.0 object library.

4. Copy the file "Labels.dot" to the local templates folder (by default "C:\Windows\Application Data\Microsoft\Templates).

5. Alternatively, you can create this template yourself—start by dropping down the Tools menu in Word.

6. Choose the Envelopes and Labels selection, and follow the on-screen instructions to create a Labels document for Avery #5160 labels, and save it as "Labels.dot" in the local templates folder.

7. Run the macro.

LISTING 44.12

```
Public Sub PrintLabels()

On Error GoTo PrintLabelsError

    Dim objOutlook As Outlook.Application
    Dim nms As NameSpace
    Dim fld As MAPIFolder
    Dim itms As Items
    Dim itm As ContactItem
    Dim exp As Explorer
    Dim strTemplateDir As String
    Dim strLetter As String
    Dim objWord As Word.Application
    Dim objDocs As Word.Documents
```

```
    'Set a reference to the currently selected folder
    Set objOutlook = CreateObject("Outlook.Application")
    Set nms = objOutlook.GetNamespace("MAPI")
    Set exp = objOutlook.ActiveExplorer
    Set fld = exp.CurrentFolder
    Debug.Print "Folder default item type: " & fld.DefaultItemType
    If fld.DefaultItemType <> olContactItem Then
        MsgBox "Folder does not contain contact items; exiting"
        Exit Sub
    End If

    'Open Word invisibly
    Set objWord = CreateObject("Word.Application")

    'Pick up Word user templates folder from Registry
    strTemplateDir = "C:\WINDOWS\Application Data\Microsoft\Templates\"
    strLetter = strTemplateDir & "Labels.dot"

    'Open a new letter based on the selected template
    Set objDocs = objWord.Documents
    objDocs.Add strLetter

    Set itms = fld.Items

        For Each itm In itms
            objWord.Selection.TypeText Text:=itm.FullName
            objWord.Selection.TypeParagraph
            If Nz(itm.CompanyName) <> "" Then
                objWord.Selection.TypeText Text:=itm.CompanyName
                objWord.Selection.TypeParagraph
            End If
            objWord.Selection.TypeText Text:=itm.BusinessAddress
            objWord.Selection.TypeParagraph
            objWord.Selection.MoveRight Unit:=wdCell
            objWord.Selection.MoveRight Unit:=wdCell
        Next
    objWord.Visible = True
    objWord.ActiveDocument.PrintOut

PrintLabelsExit:
    Exit Sub

PrintLabelsError:
    MsgBox "Error No:   " & Err.Number & "; error message:   " & Err.Description
    Resume PrintLabelsExit

End Sub
```

The code checks whether the selected folder contains Contact items, and exits if that is not the case. It also has an If…Then loop to check whether a company name has been entered for the contact, to prevent printing a blank line when the company name is missing. Figure 44.18 shows a sheet of labels produced by running the macro.

Figure 44.18
A sheet of Word labels produced from contacts in an Outlook folder.

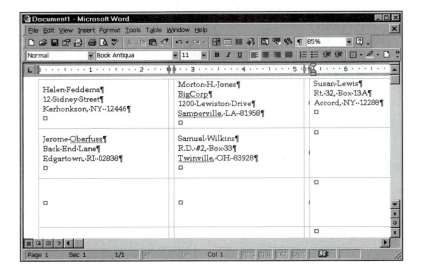

CREATING AN EXCEL WORKSHEET FILLED WITH OUTLOOK DATA

The Outlook mail merge utility lets you merge data to Word (though only in a limited fashion)—but what if you want to merge data to another application? If you want to fill an Excel worksheet with data from Outlook, for example, you need to write code, such as the code in Listing 44.13, which fills a worksheet with contact data.

Code Requirements for this type of worksheet are

1. Set a reference to the Excel 9.0 object library.
2. (If not run from Access) Set a reference to the Access 9.0 object library.
3. (If not run from Outlook) Set a reference to the Outlook 9.0 object library.
4. Copy the Excel worksheet "Contacts.xls" to the default Documents folder (usually C:\My Documents).
5. Or you can create this worksheet yourself, setting up the columns as shown in Figure 44.19.
6. Run the procedure.

LISTING 44.13

```
Public Sub ContactsToExcel()

On Error GoTo ContactsToExcelError

    Dim objExcelApp As New Excel.Application
    Dim objExcelBook As Excel.Workbook
    Dim objExcelSheets As Excel.Worksheets
    Dim objExcelSheet As Excel.Worksheet
    Dim rng As Excel.Range
    Dim strRange As String
    Dim lngASCII As Long
    Dim strASCII As String
    Dim i As Integer
    Dim lngCount As Long
    Dim objOutlook As Outlook.Application
    Dim nms As NameSpace
    Dim fld As MAPIFolder
    Dim itms As Items
    Dim itm As ContactItem
    Dim exp As Explorer
    Dim strSheet As String


    'Set a reference to the currently selected folder
    Set objOutlook = CreateObject("Outlook.Application")
    Set nms = objOutlook.GetNamespace("MAPI")
    Set exp = objOutlook.ActiveExplorer
    Set fld = exp.CurrentFolder
    Debug.Print "Folder default item type: " & fld.DefaultItemType
    If fld.DefaultItemType <> olContactItem Then
        MsgBox "Folder does not contain contact items; exiting"
        Exit Sub
    End If

    Set itms = fld.Items
    lngCount = itms.Count

    If lngCount = 0 Then
        MsgBox "No Contacts to export"
        Exit Sub
    Else
        MsgBox lngCount & " Contacts to export"
    End If

    strSheet = "C:\My Documents\Contacts.xls"
    Debug.Print "Opening Excel workbook: " & strSheet

    'Adjust the following number to be 1 less than the row number of the
    'first body row
    i = 3
```

continues

LISTING 44.13 CONTINUED

```
'Initialize column letters with 64, so the first letter used will be A
lngASCII = 64
objExcelApp.Workbooks.Open (strSheet)
Set objExcelBook = objExcelApp.ActiveWorkbook
Set objExcelSheet = objExcelBook.Sheets(1)
objExcelSheet.Activate
objExcelApp.Application.Visible = True

'Iterate through contact items in Contacts folder, and export a few fields
'from each item to a row in the Contacts worksheet
For Each itm In itms
    i = i + 1
    lngASCII = lngASCII + 1
    strASCII = Chr(lngASCII)
    strRange = strASCII & CStr(i)
    Set rng = objExcelSheet.Range(strRange)
    rng.Value = Nz(itm.Title)

    lngASCII = lngASCII + 1
    strASCII = Chr(lngASCII)
    strRange = strASCII & CStr(i)
    Set rng = objExcelSheet.Range(strRange)
    rng.Value = Nz(itm.FirstName)

    lngASCII = lngASCII + 1
    strASCII = Chr(lngASCII)
    strRange = strASCII & CStr(i)
    Set rng = objExcelSheet.Range(strRange)
    rng.Value = Nz(itm.MiddleName)

    lngASCII = lngASCII + 1
    strASCII = Chr(lngASCII)
    strRange = strASCII & CStr(i)
    Set rng = objExcelSheet.Range(strRange)
    rng.Value = Nz(itm.LastName)

    lngASCII = lngASCII + 1
    strASCII = Chr(lngASCII)
    strRange = strASCII & CStr(i)
    Set rng = objExcelSheet.Range(strRange)
    rng.Value = Nz(itm.JobTitle)

    lngASCII = lngASCII + 1
    strASCII = Chr(lngASCII)
    strRange = strASCII & CStr(i)
    Set rng = objExcelSheet.Range(strRange)
    rng.Value = Nz(itm.CompanyName)

    lngASCII = lngASCII + 1
    strASCII = Chr(lngASCII)
    strRange = strASCII & CStr(i)
    Set rng = objExcelSheet.Range(strRange)
    rng.Value = Nz(itm.BusinessTelephoneNumber)
```

```
        lngASCII = lngASCII + 1
        strASCII = Chr(lngASCII)
        strRange = strASCII & CStr(i)
        Set rng = objExcelSheet.Range(strRange)
        rng.Value = Nz(itm.BusinessFaxNumber)

        lngASCII = lngASCII + 1
        strASCII = Chr(lngASCII)
        strRange = strASCII & CStr(i)
        Set rng = objExcelSheet.Range(strRange)
        On Error Resume Next
        rng.Value = itm.UserProperties("EmployeeID")

        lngASCII = 64

        Next itm

ContactsToExcelExit:
    Exit Sub

ContactsToExcelError:
    MsgBox "Error No:  " & Err.Number & "; error message:  " & Err.Description
    Resume ContactsToExcelExit

End Sub
```

Figure 44.19 shows the filled worksheet.

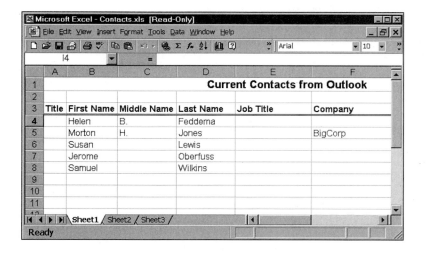

Figure 44.19
An Excel worksheet filled with Outlook contract information.

FILLING AN ACCESS TABLE WITH OUTLOOK DATA

You can fill an Access table with information from Outlook using the DAO object model (which is used to work with data in Access tables). The code in Listing 44.14 fills an Access table with contact data, then prints a report based on the table. The DAO object model is used to work with the data, and the Access object model is used to get the default database folder and print the report.

Requirements for this code include

1. Copy the Access database "Personal.mdb" into the default Office folder (usually C:\Program Files\Microsoft Office\Office).
2. This database contains a table called "tblContacts" and a report called "rptContacts."
3. Set a reference to the Access 9.0 object library.
4. Set a reference to the DAO 3.6 object library.
5. Open the Contacts folder in Outlook.
6. Create an Outlook macro with the code in Listing 44.14.
7. Run the macro.

LISTING 44.14

```
Public Sub ContactsToAccess()

On Error GoTo ContactsToAccessError

    Dim objOutlook As New Outlook.Application
    Dim objAccess As New Access.Application
    Dim rst As Recordset
    Dim dao As Object
    Dim wks As Workspace
    Dim dbs As Database
    Dim nms As NameSpace
    Dim exp As Explorer
    Dim fld As MAPIFolder
    Dim itms As Items
    Dim itm As ContactItem
    Dim strAccessDir As String
    Dim strFolder As String
    Dim strDBName As String
    Dim fFound As Boolean
    Dim lngRecCount As Long

    'Set a reference to the currently selected folder
    Set objOutlook = CreateObject("Outlook.Application")
    Set nms = objOutlook.GetNamespace("MAPI")
    Set exp = objOutlook.ActiveExplorer
    Set fld = exp.CurrentFolder
```

```
Debug.Print "Folder default item type: " & fld.DefaultItemType
If fld.DefaultItemType <> olContactItem Then
   MsgBox "Folder does not contain contact items; exiting"
   Exit Sub
End If

'Pick up path to Access database directory from Access SysCmd function
strAccessDir = objAccess.SysCmd(9)
Debug.Print "Access Directory: " & strAccessDir
strDBName = strAccessDir & "Personal.mdb"
Debug.Print "DBName: " & strDBName
objAccess.Quit

'Set up reference to Access database
Set dao = CreateObject("DAO.DBEngine.36")
Set wks = dao.Workspaces(0)
Set dbs = wks.OpenDatabase(strDBName)
Set rst = dbs.OpenRecordset("tblContacts")

Set itms = fld.Items
For Each itm In itms
   rst.AddNew
   If Nz(itm.Title) <> "" Then rst!Title = Nz(itm.Title)
   If Nz(itm.FirstName) <> "" Then _
      rst!FirstName = Nz(itm.FirstName)
   If Nz(itm.MiddleName) <> "" Then _
      rst!MiddleName = Nz(itm.MiddleName)
   If Nz(itm.LastName) <> "" Then _
      rst!LastName = Nz(itm.LastName)
   If Nz(itm.Suffix) <> "" Then _
      rst!Suffix = Nz(itm.Suffix)
   If Nz(itm.CompanyName) <> "" Then _
      rst!Company = Nz(itm.CompanyName)
   If Nz(itm.JobTitle) <> "" Then _
      rst!JobTitle = Nz(itm.JobTitle)
   If Nz(itm.BusinessAddressStreet) <> "" Then _
      rst!BusinessStreet = Nz(itm.BusinessAddressStreet)
   If Nz(itm.BusinessAddressCity) <> "" Then _
      rst!BusinessCity = Nz(itm.BusinessAddressCity)
   If Nz(itm.BusinessAddressState) <> "" Then _
      rst!BusinessState = Nz(itm.BusinessAddressState)
   If Nz(itm.BusinessAddressPostalCode) <> "" _
      Then rst!BusinessPostalCode = Nz(itm.BusinessAddressPostalCode)
   If Nz(itm.BusinessAddressCountry) <> "" Then _
      rst!BusinessCountry = Nz(itm.BusinessAddressCountry)
   If Nz(itm.HomeAddressStreet) <> "" Then _
      rst!HomeStreet = Nz(itm.HomeAddressStreet)
   If Nz(itm.HomeAddressCity) <> "" Then _
      rst!HomeCity = Nz(itm.HomeAddressCity)
   If Nz(itm.HomeAddressState) <> "" Then _
      rst!HomeState = Nz(itm.HomeAddressState)
   If Nz(itm.HomeAddressPostalCode) <> "" Then _
      rst!HomePostalCode = Nz(itm.HomeAddressPostalCode)
   If Nz(itm.HomeAddressCountry) <> "" Then _
```

continues

LISTING 44.14   CONTINUED

```
    rst!HomeCountry = Nz(itm.HomeAddressCountry)
If Nz(itm.OtherAddressStreet) <> "" Then _
    rst!OtherStreet = Nz(itm.OtherAddressStreet)
If Nz(itm.OtherAddressCity) <> "" Then _
    rst!OtherCity = Nz(itm.OtherAddressCity)
If Nz(itm.OtherAddressState) <> "" Then _
    rst!OtherState = Nz(itm.OtherAddressState)
If Nz(itm.OtherAddressPostalCode) <> "" Then _
    rst!OtherPostalCode = Nz(itm.OtherAddressPostalCode)
If Nz(itm.OtherAddressCountry) <> "" Then _
    rst!OtherCountry = Nz(itm.OtherAddressCountry)
If Nz(itm.BusinessFaxNumber) <> "" Then _
    rst!BusinessFax = Nz(itm.BusinessFaxNumber)
If Nz(itm.BusinessTelephoneNumber) <> "" Then _
    rst!BusinessPhone = Nz(itm.BusinessTelephoneNumber)
If Nz(itm.Business2TelephoneNumber) <> "" Then _
    rst!BusinessPhone2 = Nz(itm.Business2TelephoneNumber)
If Nz(itm.CallbackTelephoneNumber) <> "" Then _
    rst!Callback = Nz(itm.CallbackTelephoneNumber)
If Nz(itm.CarTelephoneNumber) <> "" Then _
    rst!CarPhone = Nz(itm.CarTelephoneNumber)
If Nz(itm.CompanyMainTelephoneNumber) <> "" Then _
    rst!CompanyMainPhone = Nz(itm.CompanyMainTelephoneNumber)
If Nz(itm.HomeFaxNumber) <> "" Then _
    rst!HomeFax = Nz(itm.HomeFaxNumber)
If Nz(itm.HomeTelephoneNumber) <> "" Then _
    rst!HomePhone = Nz(itm.HomeTelephoneNumber)
If Nz(itm.Home2TelephoneNumber) <> "" Then _
    rst!HomePhone2 = Nz(itm.Home2TelephoneNumber)
If Nz(itm.ISDNNumber) <> "" Then _
    rst!ISDN = Nz(itm.ISDNNumber)
If Nz(itm.MobileTelephoneNumber) <> "" Then _
    rst!MobilePhone = Nz(itm.MobileTelephoneNumber)
If Nz(itm.OtherFaxNumber) <> "" Then _
    rst!OtherFax = Nz(itm.OtherFaxNumber)
If Nz(itm.OtherTelephoneNumber) <> "" Then _
    rst!OtherPhone = Nz(itm.OtherTelephoneNumber)
If Nz(itm.PagerNumber) <> "" Then _
    rst!Pager = Nz(itm.PagerNumber)
If Nz(itm.PrimaryTelephoneNumber) <> "" Then _
    rst!PrimaryPhone = Nz(itm.PrimaryTelephoneNumber)
If Nz(itm.RadioTelephoneNumber) <> "" Then _
    rst!RadioPhone = Nz(itm.RadioTelephoneNumber)
If Nz(itm.TTYTDDTelephoneNumber) <> "" Then _
    rst!TTYTDDPhone = Nz(itm.TTYTDDTelephoneNumber)
If Nz(itm.TelexNumber) <> "" Then rst!Telex = Nz(itm.TelexNumber)
If Nz(itm.BillingInformation) <> "" Then _
    rst!BillingInformation = Nz(itm.BillingInformation)
If Nz(itm.Email1Address) <> "" Then _
    rst!EmailAddress = Nz(itm.Email1Address)
If Nz(itm.Email1DisplayName) <> "" Then _
    rst!EmailDisplayName = Nz(itm.Email1DisplayName)
If Nz(itm.Email2Address) <> "" Then _
```

```
                rst!Email2Address = Nz(itm.Email2Address)
        If Nz(itm.Email2DisplayName) <> "" Then _
            rst!Email2DisplayName = Nz(itm.Email2DisplayName)
        If Nz(itm.Email3Address) <> "" Then _
            rst!Email3Address = Nz(itm.Email3Address)
        If Nz(itm.Email3DisplayName) <> "" Then _
            rst!Email3DisplayName = Nz(itm.Email3DisplayName)
        If Nz(itm.Subject) <> "" Then rst!Notes = Nz(itm.Subject)
        If Nz(itm.WebPage) <> "" Then rst!WebPage = Nz(itm.WebPage)
        If Nz(itm.Categories) <> "" Then _
            rst!Categories = Nz(itm.Categories)
        Debug.Print Nz(itm.FullName) & "'s data exported to tblContacts"
        On Error Resume Next
        rst.Update
    Next itm

    rst.Close

    'Prints an Access report based on tblContacts
    Set objAccess = CreateObject("Access.Application")
    objAccess.OpenCurrentDatabase (strDBName)
    objAccess.DoCmd.OpenReport "rptContacts", acViewNormal
    objAccess.Quit

ContactsToAccessExit:
    Exit Sub

ContactsToAccessError:
    MsgBox "Error No:   " & Err.Number & "; error message:   " & Err.Description
    Resume ContactsToAccessExit

End Sub
```

Figure 44.20 shows the Access report in print preview.

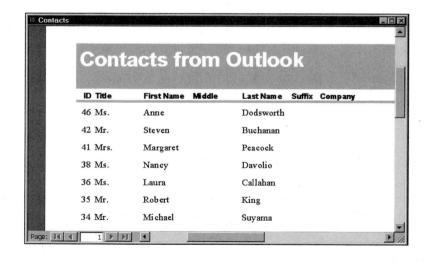

Figure 44.20
An Access report based on a table filled with data from Outlook.

PART

VIII

CH

44

CONTROLLING OUTLOOK FROM OTHER OFFICE APPLICATIONS

Just as in previous versions of Outlook, you can control Outlook from VBA in other Office applications; but now you are working with a much richer object model for Outlook. The listings in the following sections illustrate importing Outlook data into Access, Excel, and Word, working with VBA code from these applications.

IMPORTING DATA FROM OUTLOOK INTO AN ACCESS TABLE

The following Access VBA code imports data from the default Contacts folder into an Access table. You will notice many similarities to the code in Listing 44.10, which exported contact data from Outlook to Access; now that Outlook hosts standard Office VBA, it is easy to transfer large chunks of code from one Office VBA dialect to another.

Code requirements for transferring data to another dialect are

1. Copy the Access database "Personal.mdb" into the default Office folder (usually C:\Program Files\Microsoft Office\Office).
2. This database contains a table called "tblContacts."
3. Set a reference to the Access 9.0 object library.
4. Set a reference to the DAO 3.6 object library.
5. Set a reference to the Outlook 9.0 object library.
6. Run the function to import the contacts from Outlook.

LISTING 44.15

```
Public Function ImportContacts()

On Error GoTo ImportContactsError

    Dim objOutlook As New Outlook.Application
    Dim rst As Recordset
    Dim dbs As Database
    Dim nms As NameSpace
    Dim fld As MAPIFolder
    Dim itms As Items
    Dim itm As ContactItem
    Dim lngRecCount As Long

    'Set a reference to the default Contacts folder
    Set nms = objOutlook.GetNamespace("MAPI")
    Set fld = nms.GetDefaultFolder(olFolderContacts)

    'Set up reference to Access table
    Set dbs = CurrentDb
    Set rst = dbs.OpenRecordset("tblContacts")

    Set itms = fld.Items
```

```
For Each itm In itms
    rst.AddNew
    If Nz(itm.Title) <> "" Then rst!Title = Nz(itm.Title)
    If Nz(itm.FirstName) <> "" Then _
        rst!FirstName = Nz(itm.FirstName)
    If Nz(itm.MiddleName) <> "" Then _
        rst!MiddleName = Nz(itm.MiddleName)
    If Nz(itm.LastName) <> "" Then _
        rst!LastName = Nz(itm.LastName)
    If Nz(itm.Suffix) <> "" Then _
        rst!Suffix = Nz(itm.Suffix)
    If Nz(itm.CompanyName) <> "" Then _
        rst!Company = Nz(itm.CompanyName)
    If Nz(itm.JobTitle) <> "" Then _
        rst!JobTitle = Nz(itm.JobTitle)
    If Nz(itm.BusinessAddressStreet) <> "" Then _
        rst!BusinessStreet = Nz(itm.BusinessAddressStreet)
    If Nz(itm.BusinessAddressCity) <> "" Then _
        rst!BusinessCity = Nz(itm.BusinessAddressCity)
    If Nz(itm.BusinessAddressState) <> "" Then _
        rst!BusinessState = Nz(itm.BusinessAddressState)
    If Nz(itm.BusinessAddressPostalCode) <> "" _
        Then rst!BusinessPostalCode = Nz(itm.BusinessAddressPostalCode)
    If Nz(itm.BusinessAddressCountry) <> "" Then _
        rst!BusinessCountry = Nz(itm.BusinessAddressCountry)
    If Nz(itm.HomeAddressStreet) <> "" Then _
        rst!HomeStreet = Nz(itm.HomeAddressStreet)
    If Nz(itm.HomeAddressCity) <> "" Then _
        rst!HomeCity = Nz(itm.HomeAddressCity)
    If Nz(itm.HomeAddressState) <> "" Then _
        rst!HomeState = Nz(itm.HomeAddressState)
    If Nz(itm.HomeAddressPostalCode) <> "" Then _
        rst!HomePostalCode = Nz(itm.HomeAddressPostalCode)
    If Nz(itm.HomeAddressCountry) <> "" Then _
        rst!HomeCountry = Nz(itm.HomeAddressCountry)
    If Nz(itm.OtherAddressStreet) <> "" Then _
        rst!OtherStreet = Nz(itm.OtherAddressStreet)
    If Nz(itm.OtherAddressCity) <> "" Then _
        rst!OtherCity = Nz(itm.OtherAddressCity)
    If Nz(itm.OtherAddressState) <> "" Then _
        rst!OtherState = Nz(itm.OtherAddressState)
    If Nz(itm.OtherAddressPostalCode) <> "" Then _
        rst!OtherPostalCode = Nz(itm.OtherAddressPostalCode)
    If Nz(itm.OtherAddressCountry) <> "" Then _
        rst!OtherCountry = Nz(itm.OtherAddressCountry)
    If Nz(itm.BusinessFaxNumber) <> "" Then _
        rst!BusinessFax = Nz(itm.BusinessFaxNumber)
    If Nz(itm.BusinessTelephoneNumber) <> "" Then _
        rst!BusinessPhone = Nz(itm.BusinessTelephoneNumber)
    If Nz(itm.Business2TelephoneNumber) <> "" Then _
        rst!BusinessPhone2 = Nz(itm.Business2TelephoneNumber)
    If Nz(itm.CallbackTelephoneNumber) <> "" Then _
        rst!Callback = Nz(itm.CallbackTelephoneNumber)
    If Nz(itm.CarTelephoneNumber) <> "" Then _
        rst!CarPhone = Nz(itm.CarTelephoneNumber)
```

PART

VIII

CH

44

continues

LISTING 44.15 CONTINUED

```
        If Nz(itm.CompanyMainTelephoneNumber) <> "" Then _
            rst!CompanyMainPhone = Nz(itm.CompanyMainTelephoneNumber)
        If Nz(itm.HomeFaxNumber) <> "" Then _
            rst!HomeFax = Nz(itm.HomeFaxNumber)
        If Nz(itm.HomeTelephoneNumber) <> "" Then _
            rst!HomePhone = Nz(itm.HomeTelephoneNumber)
        If Nz(itm.Home2TelephoneNumber) <> "" Then _
            rst!HomePhone2 = Nz(itm.Home2TelephoneNumber)
        If Nz(itm.ISDNNumber) <> "" Then _
            rst!ISDN = Nz(itm.ISDNNumber)
        If Nz(itm.MobileTelephoneNumber) <> "" Then _
            rst!MobilePhone = Nz(itm.MobileTelephoneNumber)
        If Nz(itm.OtherFaxNumber) <> "" Then _
            rst!OtherFax = Nz(itm.OtherFaxNumber)
        If Nz(itm.OtherTelephoneNumber) <> "" Then _
            rst!OtherPhone = Nz(itm.OtherTelephoneNumber)
        If Nz(itm.PagerNumber) <> "" Then _
            rst!Pager = Nz(itm.PagerNumber)
        If Nz(itm.PrimaryTelephoneNumber) <> "" Then _
            rst!PrimaryPhone = Nz(itm.PrimaryTelephoneNumber)
        If Nz(itm.RadioTelephoneNumber) <> "" Then _
            rst!RadioPhone = Nz(itm.RadioTelephoneNumber)
        If Nz(itm.TTYTDDTelephoneNumber) <> "" Then _
            rst!TTYTDDPhone = Nz(itm.TTYTDDTelephoneNumber)
        If Nz(itm.TelexNumber) <> "" Then rst!Telex = Nz(itm.TelexNumber)
        If Nz(itm.BillingInformation) <> "" Then _
            rst!BillingInformation = Nz(itm.BillingInformation)
        If Nz(itm.Email1Address) <> "" Then _
            rst!EmailAddress = Nz(itm.Email1Address)
        If Nz(itm.Email1DisplayName) <> "" Then _
            rst!EmailDisplayName = Nz(itm.Email1DisplayName)
        If Nz(itm.Email2Address) <> "" Then _
            rst!Email2Address = Nz(itm.Email2Address)
        If Nz(itm.Email2DisplayName) <> "" Then _
            rst!Email2DisplayName = Nz(itm.Email2DisplayName)
        If Nz(itm.Email3Address) <> "" Then _
            rst!Email3Address = Nz(itm.Email3Address)
        If Nz(itm.Email3DisplayName) <> "" Then _
            rst!Email3DisplayName = Nz(itm.Email3DisplayName)
        If Nz(itm.Subject) <> "" Then rst!Notes = Nz(itm.Subject)
        If Nz(itm.WebPage) <> "" Then rst!WebPage = Nz(itm.WebPage)
        If Nz(itm.Categories) <> "" Then _
            rst!Categories = Nz(itm.Categories)
        Debug.Print Nz(itm.FullName) & "'s data exported to tblContacts"
        On Error Resume Next
        rst.Update
    Next itm

    rst.Close
    objOutlook.Quit

ImportContactsExit:
    Exit Function
```

```
ImportContactsError:
   MsgBox "Error No:  " & Err.Number & "; error message:  " & Err.Description
   Resume ImportContactsExit

End Function
```

The Access table with the imported contact data is shown in datasheet view in Figure 44.21.

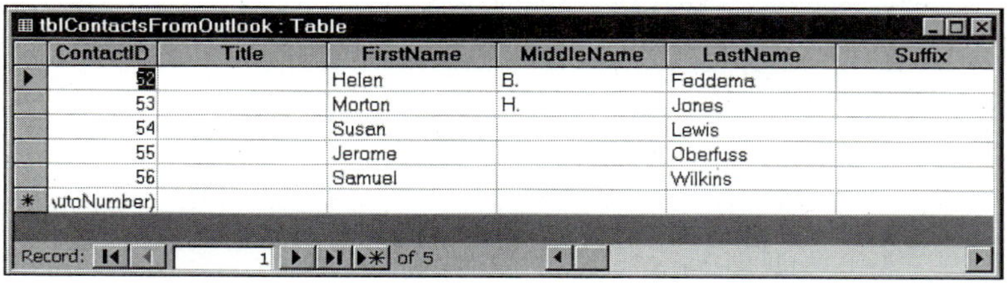

ContactID	Title	FirstName	MiddleName	LastName	Suffix
52		Helen	B.	Feddema	
53		Morton	H.	Jones	
54		Susan		Lewis	
55		Jerome		Oberfuss	
56		Samuel		Wilkins	
utoNumber)					

Figure 44.21
An Access table with data imported from Outlook contacts.

IMPORTING DATA FROM OUTLOOK INTO AN EXCEL WORKSHEET

If you want to export your Outlook Calendar to an Excel worksheet, perhaps to share it with another person who doesn't have Outlook, the code in Listing 44.16 will do the job.

This code requires:

1. Copy the Excel worksheet "Calendar.xls" into the default Documents folder (usually C:\My Documents).
2. Alternatively, create a worksheet with columns as shown in Figure 44.22, and place the code in Listing 44.16 in its code module.
3. Set a reference to the Outlook 9.0 object library.
4. Set a reference to the Access 9.0 object library.
5. Set a reference to the Excel 9.0 object library.
6. Run the procedure in the worksheet's module to import the Outlook appointments into the worksheet.

LISTING 44.16

```
Public Function ImportCalendar()

On Error GoTo ImportCalendarError

   Dim objOutlook As New Outlook.Application
   Dim nms As NameSpace
   Dim fld As MAPIFolder
   Dim itms As Items
   Dim itm As Outlook.AppointmentItem
```

continues

LISTING 44.16   CONTINUED

```
Dim lngRecCount As Long
Dim objBook As Workbook
Dim objSheets As Worksheets
Dim objSheet As Worksheet
Dim rng As Excel.Range
Dim strRange As String
Dim lngASCII As Long
Dim strASCII As String
Dim i As Integer
Dim lngCount As Long

'Set a reference to the default Calendar folder
Set nms = objOutlook.GetNamespace("MAPI")
Set fld = nms.GetDefaultFolder(olFolderCalendar)
Set itms = fld.Items
lngCount = itms.Count

If lngCount = 0 Then
    MsgBox "No Calendar items to import"
    Exit Function
Else
    MsgBox lngCount & " Calendar items to import"
End If

'Set the i variable to be 1 less than the row number of the
'first body row
i = 3

'Initialize column letter variable with 64, so the first letter used will be A
lngASCII = 64

Set objSheet = ActiveWorkbook.Sheets(1)
objSheet.Activate

'Iterate through items in Calendar folder, and export a few fields
'from each item to a row in the Calendar worksheet
For Each itm In itms
    i = i + 1

    lngASCII = lngASCII + 1
    strASCII = Chr(lngASCII)
    strRange = strASCII & CStr(i)
    Set rng = objSheet.Range(strRange)
    rng.Value = Nz(itm.Start)

    lngASCII = lngASCII + 1
    strASCII = Chr(lngASCII)
    strRange = strASCII & CStr(i)
    Set rng = objSheet.Range(strRange)
    rng.Value = Nz(itm.End)

    lngASCII = lngASCII + 1
    strASCII = Chr(lngASCII)
    strRange = strASCII & CStr(i)
```

```
            Set rng = objSheet.Range(strRange)
            rng.Value = Nz(itm.CreationTime)

            lngASCII = lngASCII + 1
            strASCII = Chr(lngASCII)
            strRange = strASCII & CStr(i)
            Set rng = objSheet.Range(strRange)
            rng.Value = Nz(itm.Subject)

            lngASCII = lngASCII + 1
            strASCII = Chr(lngASCII)
            strRange = strASCII & CStr(i)
            Set rng = objSheet.Range(strRange)
            rng.Value = Nz(itm.Location)

            lngASCII = lngASCII + 1
            strASCII = Chr(lngASCII)
            strRange = strASCII & CStr(i)
            Set rng = objSheet.Range(strRange)
            rng.Value = Nz(itm.Categories)

            lngASCII = lngASCII + 1
            strASCII = Chr(lngASCII)
            strRange = strASCII & CStr(i)
            Set rng = objSheet.Range(strRange)
            rng.Value = Nz(itm.IsRecurring)

            lngASCII = 64

    Next itm

    objOutlook.Quit

ImportCalendarExit:
    Exit Function

ImportCalendarError:
    MsgBox "Error No:  " & Err.Number & "; error message:  " & Err.Description
    Resume ImportCalendarExit

End Function
```

Figure 44.22 shows the Excel worksheet filled with Outlook Calendar data.

IMPORTING CONTACT DATA FROM OUTLOOK INTO A WORD LETTER

The code in Listing 44.17 is probably the easiest to use of all the code samples in this chapter: it runs automatically from the New event of a Word template. Because of this, whenever the user creates a new letter from this template, the code runs and automatically fills the document with data from the currently open Outlook contact.

Figure 44.22
An Excel worksheet filled with Outlook Calendar data.

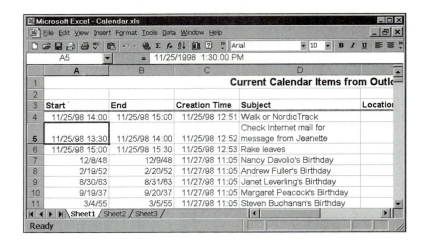

Note

Although this code runs from the New event of a Word document (see Figure 44.23), it would work equally well as an AutoNew macro; some developers prefer to use an AutoNew macro in order to keep the code in the same module as other procedures.

Figure 44.23
Code running from the New event of a Word template.

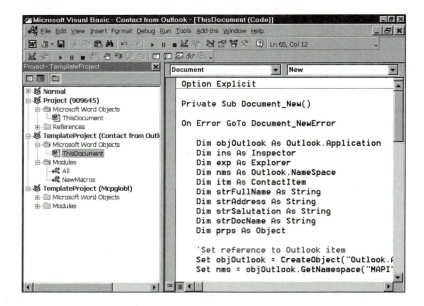

Code requirements for this task are

1. Copy the file "Contact from Outlook.dot" to the local templates folder (by default "C:\Windows\Application Data\Microsoft\Templates).

2. Alternatively, create a new Word template and paste the code in Listing 44.17 into the New event of its Document object.

3. Create the following custom document properties (data type: Text) for the template:

   Address

   Full Name

   Salutation

   Job Title

   Voice Phone

   Fax Phone

   E-mail

   Web page

4. The Custom tab of the template's Properties sheet (with the custom document properties) is shown in Figure 44.24.

5. Save the template (if necessary).

6. Open a contact item in Outlook (it may be based on the standard Contact form, or a custom form).

7. Create a new document based on the template; the code runs, importing contact data from the current Outlook contact item.

PART

VIII

CH

44

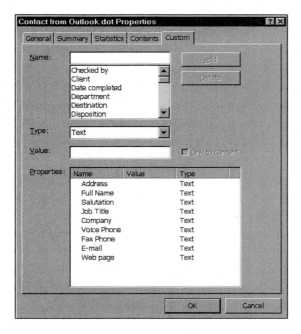

Figure 44.24
The Custom tab of a Word template's properties sheet.

LISTING 44.17

```
Private Sub Document_New()

On Error GoTo Document_NewError

    Dim objOutlook As Outlook.Application
    Dim ins As Inspector
    Dim itm As ContactItem
    Dim strFullName As String
    Dim strAddress As String
    Dim strSalutation As String
    Dim strDocName As String
    Dim prps As Object

    'Retrieve current Outlook object if Outlook is running,
    'and otherwise create a new Outlook object
    On Error Resume Next
    Set objOutlook = GetObject(, "Outlook.Application")
    If Err.Number <> 0 Then
        'Outlook is not running; creating an Outlook object
        Set objOutlook = CreateObject("Outlook.Application")
        Err.Clear
    End If

    If TypeName(objOutlook.ActiveWindow) <> "Inspector" Then
        MsgBox "No Outlook contact item open; exiting"
        ActiveDocument.Close
        Exit Sub
    End If

    Set ins = objOutlook.ActiveInspector
    Set itm = ins.CurrentItem
    Debug.Print "Selected item: " & ins.Caption
    Debug.Print "Item class: " & itm.Class

    If itm.Class <> olContact Then
        MsgBox "No Outlook contact item open; exiting"
        ActiveDocument.Close
        Exit Sub
    End If

    'Pick up variables from Outlook contact
    If Nz(itm.JobTitle) <> "" Then
        strAddress = itm.JobTitle & vbCrLf
    End If

    If Nz(itm.CompanyName) <> "" Then
        strAddress = strAddress & Nz(itm.CompanyName) & vbCrLf
    End If

    If Nz(itm.MailingAddress) <> "" Then
        strAddress = strAddress & Nz(itm.MailingAddress)
    Else
        MsgBox "No address for contact; exiting"
        Exit Sub
        ActiveDocument.Close
```

```
      End If

      If Nz(itm.Title) <> "" Then
          strSalutation = itm.Title & " " & Nz(itm.LastName)
      Else
          strSalutation = "Mr. " & Nz(itm.LastName)
      End If

      'Assign Outlook data to custom document properties
      Set prps = ActiveDocument.CustomDocumentProperties
      prps.Item("Full Name").Value = Nz(itm.FullName)
      prps.Item("Address").Value = strAddress
      prps.Item("Job Title").Value = Nz(itm.JobTitle)
      prps.Item("Salutation").Value = strSalutation
      prps.Item("Voice Phone").Value = _
          Nz(itm.BusinessTelephoneNumber)
      prps.Item("Fax Phone").Value = Nz(itm.BusinessFaxNumber)
      prps.Item("E-mail").Value = Nz(itm.Email1Address)
      prps.Item("Web page").Value = Nz(itm.WebPage)

      'Update fields in document
      Selection.WholeStory
      Selection.Fields.Update
      Selection.HomeKey Unit:=wdStory

Document_NewExit:
    Exit Sub

Document_NewError:
    MsgBox "Error No:  " & Err.Number & "; error message:  " & Err.Description
    Resume Document_NewExit

End Sub
```

TROUBLESHOOTING

Q: **Can I write Access, Word, or Excel Automation code that works with any version of Outlook?**

A: Yes, with some limitations:

- Only reference Outlook objects and methods that exist in the oldest version of Outlook you need to support.

- If there is a reference set to the Outlook object library, remove it.

- Use late binding of variables—declare all Outlook variables as Object—so the correct object library can be referenced when the code is run.

Q: **Why does my code stop on a line using the Nz function?**

A: The Nz function is specific to Access VBA; set a reference to the Access 9.0 object library, and the function will work.

Q: I tried to create Word custom document properties from Outlook VBA code, to avoid having to create them manually, but I just got an error message when I tried to run the code. How can I create custom document properties programmatically?

A: Unfortunately, you can't create custom document properties from code; the Word CustomDocumentProperties collection is a read-only collection. You must first create custom document properties in the Word interface before you can reference them in code.

PART **IX**

APPENDIXES

INSTALLING OUTLOOK 2000

In this appendix   *by Gordon Padwick*

SYSTEM REQUIREMENTS

To experience acceptable performance from Office 2000, you require:

- A PC with a Pentium (or better) processor clocked at 166 MHz or higher
- At least 32 megabytes of RAM (if you don't plan to use Word as your e-mail editor); I'd recommend at least 48 megabytes if you want to use more than one Office application simultaneously
- A CD-ROM drive (Office 2000 is not available on floppy disks) for local installation, or a network connection to a server for LAN-based installation
- A video board and VGA color monitor capable of displaying at least 256 colors (Super VGA or better is recommended) at 800×600 pixel resolution
- A Microsoft Mouse (or compatible pointing device)
- A modem capable of communicating at 9600 bits per second or more (at least 28.8 kilobits per second is recommended) if you intend to use Outlook to send and recieve messages by way of a phone line

You'll gain considerably better performance from Office 2000 if you have a computer that exceeds the recommended specifications. If you have a fast computer (a Pentium II that runs at 300 MHz or faster, and has 64 MB or more of RAM, you'll be very satisfied with the performance of Office 2000).

A typical installation of Office 2000 occupies approximately 200 megabytes of disk space. If you have the Premium or Developer editions of Office 2000 and intend to install components in addition to the standard Office applications, you'll require considerably more disk space.

Note

> If you intend to use the installation rollback features of Office 2000, set aside at least another 100 megabytes of disk space.

INSTALLING OFFICE 2000

Outlook is installed with the rest of the Office 2000 components.

Note

> Outlook is installed with one of three service options enabled: No E-mail, Internet Only E-mail, or Corporate/Workgroup. If you previously had Outlook 98 installed on your computer, Outlook 2000 is installed with the same service option as Outlook 98. If you didn't previously have Outlook 98 installed, Outlook 2000 is installed with Internet Only E-mail enabled.
>
> The procedure in the following steps describes what occurs if you haven't previously had Office installed on your computer.

→ To learn more about the various options available to you when you set up Outlook, **see** "Understanding Outlook's Service Options," **p. 51**.

The following procedure describes how to install Office 2000, including Outlook, from a CD-ROM. Consult your network administrator if you want to install from a server.

Note

Prior to installing Office 2000 (or most other applications) make sure that no other programs are running. Especially make sure that any anti-virus programs are disabled during the installation process.

To install Office 2000:

1. Insert the Office 2000 CD-ROM into your CD-ROM drive. After a few seconds a window similar to the one shown in Figure A.1 appears.

   If the window doesn't appear, choose Start in the Windows taskbar, move the pointer onto <u>S</u>ettings, and choose <u>C</u>ontrol Panel. In the Control Panel, choose Add/Remove Programs and then, with the Install/Uninstall tab selected, choose <u>I</u>nstall to display the Install Program from Floppy Disk or CD-ROM window. Choose <u>N</u>ext> and then, in the Run Installation window, choose Finish. After a few seconds the window shown in Figure A.1 is displayed.

Note

You may see a message saying that your Windows installer has been updated and you must reboot your system. Choose OK and then reboot your system.

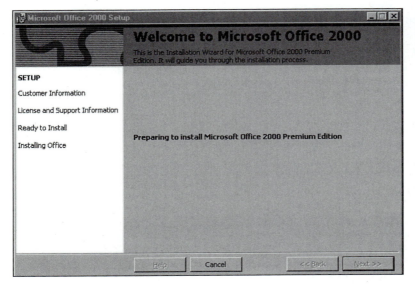

Figure A.1
This window tells you that Windows is preparing to install Office 2000.

2. Wait a few seconds until the Next button becomes enabled, then choose <u>N</u>ext >> to display the window shown in Figure A.2.

Figure A.2
This window requires you to identify yourself and enter the CD Key.

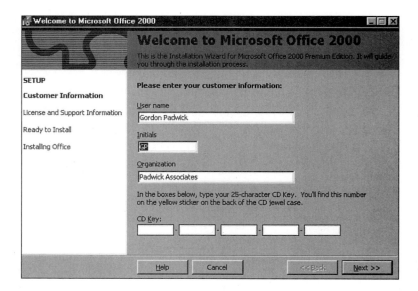

3. Windows displays a default username in the <u>U</u>ser Name box and a default organization name in the <u>O</u>rganization box. If necessary, change these defaults to the appropriate names. Enter your initials in the <u>I</u>nitials box. Enter the CD key in the CD <u>K</u>ey boxes. Choose <u>N</u>ext >> to display the window shown in Figure A.3.

Figure A.3
This window displays the Microsoft license agreement.

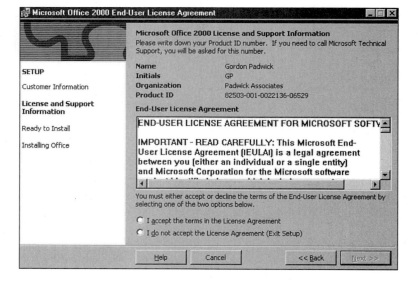

4. Read the end-user license agreement. If you agree to it, select I Accept the Terms in the License Agreement. Choose Next >> to display the window shown in Figure A.4.

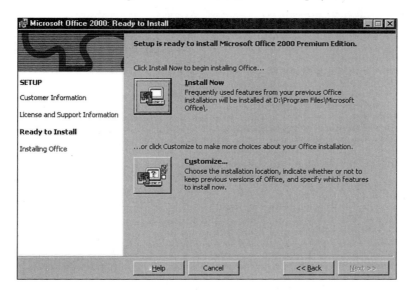

Figure A.4
Choose how you want to install Office 2000.

PART

IX

APP

A

5. At this stage, you have a choice: Install Now or Customize. The first time you install Office 2000, it's usually best to choose Install Now. This option installs Office 2000 in a similar way to any previous version of Office on your computer. Later, you can customize your Office 2000 installation. Choose Install Now to initiate the installation process. The process takes approximately 15–20 minutes. During that time, a progress bar like the one in Figure A.5 lets you know that something is happening.

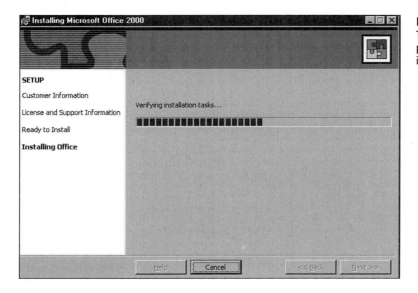

Figure A.5
This progress bar is displayed during most of the installation process.

Note
If nothing seems to be happening for a minute or two, be patient. You'll probably see the screen flicker from time to time. Eventually the installation process will get to the next step.

6. When the initial part of the installation process is complete, a message tells you that your system must be restarted. Choose <u>Y</u>es. The installer closes down Windows and restarts it. After restarting, Windows updates your system settings. If you're using Windows NT, you see it setting up the following items:

- Browsing services
- Internet tools
- Security
- System services
- Microsoft virtual machine

These details aren't displayed if you're installing Office 2000 under Windows 98. All you see is the statement "Updating System Settings," a process that takes several minutes.

Eventually, a dialog box displays the message "Finishing Microsoft Office 2000 Setup." After several more minutes, the installation process is finished and the Windows desktop is displayed containing the Microsoft Outlook icon.

RUNNING OUTLOOK FOR THE FIRST TIME

Double-click the Microsoft Outlook icon to start Outlook.

Note
The procedure described here is what happens the first time you run Outlook 2000 after you've installed it, if you have a previous version of Outlook installed on your computer. The procedure is slightly different if you've not had a previous version of Outlook installed.

The first time you start Outlook, the first Outlook 2000 Startup Wizard window, shown in Figure A.6, appears.

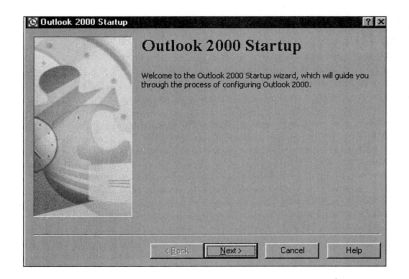

Figure A.6
This is the first of a series of wizard windows that guide you through the process of configuring Outlook.

PART

IX

APP

A

To configure Outlook:

1. With the first wizard window displayed, choose Next > to display the second wizard window, shown in Figure A.7.

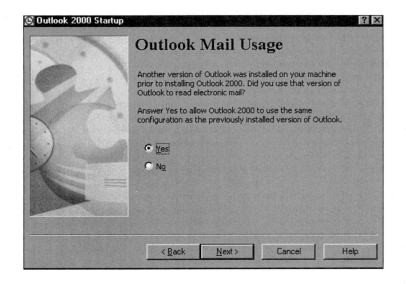

Figure A.7
This screen appears only if you had a previous version of Outlook installed on your computer.

2. Choose Yes if you want to use the same Outlook configuration as before, or No if you want to select a configuration. If you want to see what configurations are available, choose No, then choose Next > to display the window shown in Figure A.8.

Figure A.8
This dialog box lists e-mail programs already available on your computer.

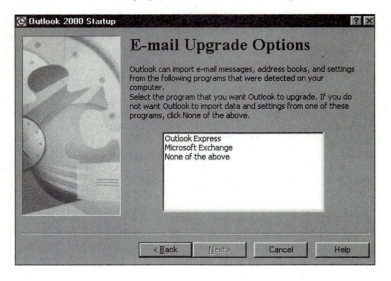

> **Note** The e-mail programs you see listed may be different from those shown here.

3. If you want Outlook to import messages, address books, and settings from an e-mail program you've been using previously, select that program from the list. Otherwise, select None of the Above. Choose Next > to display the wizard window shown in Figure A.9.

Figure A.9
Use this dialog box to select which of the Outlook e-mail service options you want to install.

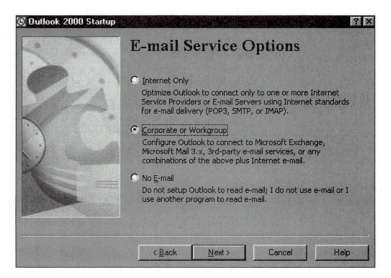

4. Select Internet Only, Corporate or Workgroup, or No E-mail. From here, the procedure depends on which service option you choose. The following step assumes you select Internet Only. Choose Next > to display the message shown in Figure A.10.

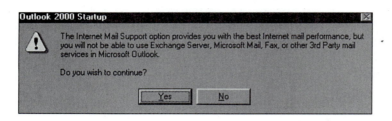

Figure A.10
The message displayed here gives information about the service option you've selected.

5. Choose Yes to continue. If you don't have the Office CD-ROM inserted, a message asks you to insert it. The files required for the e-mail service option you selected are read from the CD-ROM, and then Outlook opens.

Instead of Outlook opening, you may be asked to open an e-mail account. This happens if you're running Outlook for the first time on a computer that hasn't previously had a version of Outlook installed and you've chosen to install the Internet Only E-mail option. A wizard leads you through the process of creating an e-mail account.

You may be asked to create some *information services*. This happens if you're running Outlook for the first time on a computer that hasn't previously had a version of Outlook installed and you chose to install the Corporate or Workgroup e-mail option. A wizard leads you through the process of creating information services.

Note

You'll also be asked to create an e-mail account or some information services if the previous version of Outlook on your computer was installed with the No E-mail option, and you are now installing Outlook 2000 with either the Internet E-mail or Corporate or Workgroup options.

SWITCHING TO A DIFFERENT SERVICE OPTION

As explained previously, you can use Outlook 2000 (and Outlook 98) with one of three service options enabled: No E-mail, Internet Only Mail (IMO), or Corporate/Workgroup (C/W). In Outlook 98, it wasn't easy to switch from one service option to another. Outlook 2000 corrects this problem by providing a way to switch easily between service options.

Note

To find out which service option you currently have, display any Outlook *Information viewer (page 17)*, choose Help, About Microsoft Outlook. The second line of the About Microsoft Outlook dialog box contains the name of the current service option.

If several people share Outlook on the same computer, all of them have to use the same service option. If one person changes the service option, all the other people have to use Outlook with the new service option.

SWITCHING FROM NO E-MAIL TO INTERNET MAIL ONLY

If you initially install the No E-mail option, you can change to Internet Mail Only, but not directly to Corporate or Workgroup.

To switch from No E-mail to Internet Mail Only:

1. With any Outlook Information viewer displayed, choose Tools, Accounts to display the Internet Accounts dialog box.
2. Use this dialog box to add an Internet account, as described in Chapter 3, "Sending and Receiving E-mail with Internet Mail Only Outlook."

→ To learn more about configuring Outlook to manage your Internet e-mail, **see** "Creating an Internet Account," **p. 63**.

Outlook automatically changes to the Internet Mail Only option when you create an Internet account.

To switch back to No E-mail, remove all the Internet accounts.

SWITCHING FROM INTERNET MAIL ONLY TO CORPORATE OR WORKGROUP

If you have Outlook running with the Internet Only option, you can switch to Corporate or Workgroup.

To switch from Internet Mail Only to Corporate or Workgroup:

1. With any Outlook Information viewer displayed, choose Tools, Options, and select the Mail Delivery tab to display the dialog box shown in Figure A.11.
2. Choose Reconfigure Mail Support to display the window shown in Figure A.12.
3. Select Corporate or Workgroup, then choose Next > to display the message shown in Figure A.13.
4. Choose Yes. Outlook closes and returns you to the Windows desktop.
5. Restart Outlook. You'll be told to insert the Office 2000 CD-ROM. A series of messages is displayed while the necessary files are loaded. After a few seconds, Outlook opens, this time with the Corporate or Workgroup option.

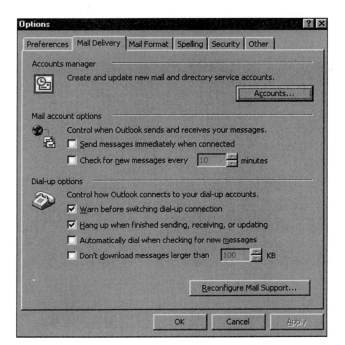

Figure A.11
IMO Outlook displays
this dialog box after you
select the Mail Delivery
tab.

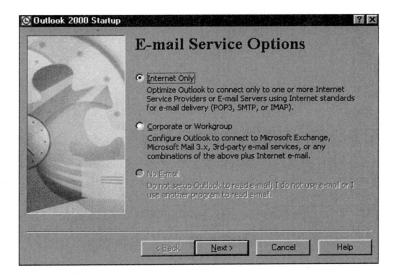

Figure A.12
This window summarizes
the capabilities of the
Internet Mail Only and
Corporate or Workgroup
service options.

Figure A.13
This message contains important information about the consequences of changing from Internet Mail Only to Corporate or Workgroup.

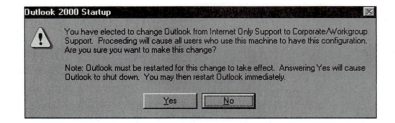

SWITCHING FROM CORPORATE OR WORKGROUP TO INTERNET MAIL ONLY

You can switch from Corporate or Workgroup to Internet Only by implementing almost the exact steps described in the preceding section. The principal differences are:

- In step 1, select the Mail Services tab
- In step 3, choose Internet Only

INSTALLING ADD-INS

When you install Outlook, you have access to many communication and information capabilities. Outlook comes with additional capabilities (known as add-ins) that you can install. In addition to the add-ins supplied with Outlook, more add-ins (some are called add-ons) are available from Microsoft and other suppliers.

Most add-ins are installed by the method described in the following steps. However, some add-ins are installed from the Control Panel in the same way as Windows applications.

To install an add-in:

1. With any Outlook Information viewer displayed, choose Tools, Options. Select the Other tab.
2. Choose Advanced Options, then choose Add-In Manager to display the dialog box shown in Figure A.14

Figure A.14
This dialog box lists the add-ins already installed.

The add-ins listed in this box are all installed. However, only those checked are enabled for use. You can disable an installed add-in by unchecking it.

3. Choose Install to display the dialog box shown in Figure A.15.

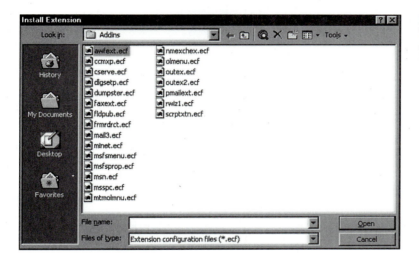

Figure A.15
This dialog box lists add-ins available for installation.

The dialog box shown in Figure A.15 lists the add-ins supplied with Outlook. If you want to install an add-in from another source, navigate to the folder that contains the add-in file.

4. Select the add-in you want to install, and choose Open to return to the Add-In Manager dialog box in which the new add-in is listed and checked.

The dialog box shown in Figure A.15 lists available add-ins by file name. Table A.1 relates file names to the functions of add-ins.

TABLE A.1   ADD-IN FILE NAMES

Add-in	File Name
Delegate Access	Dlgsetp.ecf
Exchange Extensions Commands	Outex.ecf
Exchange Extensions Property Pages	Outex2.ecf
NetMeeting Extensions	Nmexchex.ecf
TeamStatus Form	Olmenu.ecf
Rules Wizard	Rwiz1.ecf

continues

PART

IX

APP

A

TABLE A.1 ADD-IN FILE NAMES	
Add-in	**File Name**
Mail 3.0 Extensions	Mail3.ecf
Deleted Item Recovery	Dumpster.ecf
Server Scripting	scrptxtn.ecf
Internet Mail	Minet.ecf
(Corporate or Workgroup mode only)	
Net Folders	Fldpub.ecf
Fax Extension	Faxext.ecf
cc:Mail Menu Extension	Ccmxp.ecf
Digital Security	Etexch.ecf
Microsoft Fax	Awfext.ecf
Microsoft Mail 3.x Menu Extensions	Msfsmenu.ecf
Microsoft Mail 3.x Property Sheet Extensions	Msfsprop.ecf
Schedule+	Msspc.ecf
The Microsoft Network	Msn.ecf
CompuServe E-mail	Cserve.ecf
Windows CE Support	Pmailext.ecf
Outlook Forms Redirector	Frmrdrct.ecf

You can open add-in (ecf) files with a standard text editor (such as Windows NotePad) to gather more information about them. Under no circumstances, though, should you modify them. Doing so may cause an add-in to function incorrectly (if at all). Also, be aware that simply installing an add-in with the Add-in Manager does not necessarily add the functions of the add-in to Outlook. Many are dependent on other components (such as transports) without which they will not operate. An excellent example of this is Exchange add-ins, which need to have the Exchange Server service installed and functioning. Refer to Appendix E, " Outlook Resources," for information about sources of Outlook add-ins.

USING THE OFFICE 2000 RESOURCE KIT

In this appendix   *by Gordon Padwick*

WHAT IS THE OFFICE 2000 RESOURCE KIT?

The Microsoft Office 2000 Resource Kit consists of information and tools for use by people who deploy and support Office 2000. Most of the information and tools are primarily of interest to people who administer and support Office 2000 in medium- and large-sized organizations, but some are relevant to small organizations. Although power users and developers might find some of the information interesting, they won't find it useful. The Resource Kit is available on one of the CD-ROMs in the Microsoft Office 2000 Premium Edition package and also on one of the Microsoft Web sites. The *HTML (page 183)* version of the Resource Kit is also included on the Office 2000 Resource Kit CD.

While much of what's in the Resource Kit applies to the Office suite as a whole, some of the contents are specific to individual applications, including Outlook.

This appendix is intended to draw your attention to the existence of the Resource Kit, and to give you an idea about what it contains. For detailed information, refer to the Resource Kit itself.

THE RESOURCE KIT OVERVIEW

This appendix was written before the final version of the Resource Kit became available. In the beta version, Microsoft states that the final version of the Resource Kit will contain detailed explanations of why certain administrative tasks should be done as well as how to do them.

The Resource Kit text covers many important areas of information:

- The Office Environment—This section contains detailed information about how Office components fit into various Office environments. It covers such topics as client and server platforms, server tools and technologies, security, sharing data among Office components, programming techniques used for customizing Office, and deploying Office in various environments.

- Installing Office—The focus here is on installing Office within workgroups and enterprises. The information included covers the needs of desktop, laptop, and mobile users. Particular attention is given to international installations and other situations in which more than one language is used.

- Managing the Office Desktop—In a large organization it's often desirable to have some control over how users can modify and customize Office applications. The Resource Kit explains how administrators can do this by taking advantage of system policies and by locking down Office on individual computers. This section also contains advice about installing Office upgrades.

- Supporting Office Users—While each of the Office applications contains comprehensive online help that can be supplemented by help from Web sites, this information doesn't cover specific environments. The Resource Kit provides information about customizing online help and the Answer Wizard.

- Office 2000 Upgrading Reference—There's a lot of advice here about upgrading to Office 2000 from previous versions of Office, as well as from other application suites. The section also provides information about file converters you can use to manage the transition to Office 2000.

- Office and the Web—One of the key enhancements in Office 2000 is its focus on the Web. This part of the Resource Kit provides information about Office Server Extensions, FrontPage Server Extensions, and other Web subjects of interest to administrators.

- Understanding and Managing Security—Here, you'll find information about macro viruses, encryption, and digital signatures (certificates), as well as coverage of the various built-in Office security features.

- Using Office in a Multinational Organization—This section describes various multinational deployment scenarios, including how Office applications provide support for multiple languages.

Resource Kit Tools

The Resource Kit contains various tools that can help you deploy, administer, and support Office. These include

- Custom Installation Wizard—Administrators can use this tool to plan and execute deployment of Office in a manner that's tailored to the organization's needs.

- Office Profile Wizard—Administrators can use this wizard to create default user profiles that include standard locations for files and templates, as well as preset options for Office applications.

- Microsoft Internet Explorer Administration Kit—This kit lets administrators customize how Internet Explorer 5 is installed with Office.

- Office Removal Wizard—This is a standalone wizard with the same capabilities as the version removal capability built in to Office and the Custom Installation Wizard.

- System Management Server Package Definition Files—This is a sample set of package definition files that can be used as they are or modified. These files can be used to install Office and individual Office applications remotely.

- Office Converter Pack—This consists of a wide variety of converters and filters useful in environments that use various versions of Office, Office for the Macintosh, and other application suites.

- Answer Wizard Builder—Administrators can use this wizard to create automatic answers to questions unique to their organizations.

- HTML Help Workshop—This can be used to develop Help topics that provide information specific to an organization.

- Customizable Alerts—Information and tools in the Resource Kit provide what you need to customize Office error messages so that they give information specific to an organization.

PART

IX

APP

B

- Motionless Office Assistant—If Office is installed in a Windows Terminal Server environment, performance can be improved by installing the motionless Office Assistant on the server.

- Excel Date and File Utilities—These utilities can be used to detect and correct various problems relating to dates in Excel worksheets.

- PowerPoint 97/2000 Viewer—This viewer enables people who do not have PowerPoint installed on their computers to view presentations created in PowerPoint 97 and PowerPoint 2000. The viewer does not have the capability to edit PowerPoint presentations.

- FrontPage Server Extensions Resource Kit—This is a guide to installing and administering the FrontPage Server Extensions on a Web server.

- Outlook Nickname Utility—Outlook uses a nickname list to automatically check contacts' names. This utility can be used to clean out the nickname list if it becomes corrupted.

- Unbind Office Binders Utility—This utility can be used to extract individual files from Office 2000 binder files.

- Help on the Web—The Resource Kit contains information and tools that can be used to customize Help on the Web.

- Localized Setup Utility—This utility can be used to change the language used by Office applications on an individual computer after Office has been installed.

- System Policy Editor and Templates—Administrators can use the System Policy Editor to remotely control the Office options for all the computers in a workgroup. The Resource Kit contains system policy templates for all the Office applications.

OTHER INFORMATION AND RESOURCES

Some of the other information of interest to Outlook users in the Office Resourse Kit includes:

- An Excel workbook (FileList.xls) containing worksheets that list files for all Office 2000 applications

- A Word document (Formats.doc) that lists the data formats supported by Office 2000

- An Excel workbook (RegKey.xls) containing worksheets that list all the registry keys that affect Office 2000 applications

- An Excel workbook (Ie5Feats.xls) that lists Office 2000 features which rely on functionality provided by Internet Explorer 5.0

- An Excel workbook (SetupRef.xls) containing worksheets that list office 2000 setup command-line options, settings file formats, and customizable properties

- An Excel workbook (Webent.xls) containing a workbook that lists built-in connections to the Web from within Office 2000

APPENDIX

OUTLOOK'S FILES, FOLDERS, FIELDS, AND REGISTRY KEYS

In this chapter

by Gordon Padwick

WHERE OUTLOOK SAVES INFORMATION

Outlook saves configuration information and Outlook items in many different places and files. The data that you see in Outlook such as e-mail, appointments, tasks, reminders, and so on are saved in a file with a .PST extension. This file can have any name, but most often has the same name as the Outlook profile that you use. In C/W Outlook you may use a Personal Address Book that has a .PAB extension. Some configuration and customization information is kept in separate files with specific file extensions and some is kept in the Windows registry. This appendix provides details about where this information is stored.

Information is also available in the Office Resource Kit about all the files and registry keys that Outlook uses. This information is in the form of Excel workbook files.

OUTLOOK FILES

Outlook saves various kinds of information in files with standard file name extensions. Also, Outlook can import files from, and export files to, various applications, each of which have specific file name extensions. The files where Outlook saves its configuration and customization data are listed in Table C1. Many of the other file name extensions you may encounter while working with Outlook are listed in Table C.2

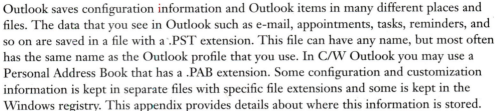

TABLE C.1 OUTLOOK CONFIGURATION AND CUSTOMIZATION FILES	
File	**Outlook Information**
Adult Content Senders.txt	Additions to the Adult Content Senders rule
Exception List.txt	Exceptions to the Junk Senders rule
Extend.dat	List of Outlook extensions and add-ins
Frmcache.dat	Forms cache
Junk Senders.txt	Additions to the Junk Senders rule
<profile name>.fav	Outlook Bar Shortcuts
<profile name>.nick	Names for the Automatic Name Check feature
<profile name>.rwz	User-created rules
Outcmd.dat	Customizations to menus and toolbars
OutlPrnt	Print settings
VbaProject.OTM	Macro and VBA code
Views.dat	Some of the information on custom views
Outlbar.inf	Setup file for Outlook Bar structure

Note

In Table C.1, <profile name> stands for the name of your Outlook Profile. For IMO Outlook, where there are no profiles, the file name is Microsoft Outlook Internet Settings.

TABLE C.2   OUTLOOK FILE NAME EXTENSIONS

Extension	Information Contained
.cal	Schedule+ 1.0 files
.cfg	Form setup files
.csv	Comma separated values files (Windows)
.dbf	ACT!, FoxPro, and dBASE files
.dll	Application extensions
.doc	Word files
.ecf	Extension configuration files
.eco	ECCO files
.exe	Executable files
.fdm	Form message files
.htm	HTML files
.inf	Profile settings
.mdb	Access files
.msg	Messages dragged onto the Windows desktop
.ocx	ActiveX controls
.oft	Outlook templates
.org,.or2	Lotus Organizer files
.oss	Saved searches
.ost	Offline storage files
.pab	Personal address book
.pst	Personal folder and AutoArchive files
.rtf	Document saved in rich text format
.sc2	Schedule+ interchange files
.scd	Schedule+ 7x files
.stf	Setup Table files
.txt	Tab separated values files, Comma separated values files (DOS), text files
.vcf	vCard files

PART

IX

APP

C

continues

Extension	**Information Contained**
.vcs	vCalendar files
.wab	Windows Address Book
.xls	Excel files

TABLE C.2   CONTINUED

OUTLOOK FOLDERS

Outlook saves items in various folders within a Personal Folders file or Exchange store. Some customization information, such as the information for customized views, is also saved in the Personal Folders file or Exchange store. The standard folders are listed in Table C.3.

TABLE C.3   STANDARD OUTLOOK FOLDERS

Folder Name	**Items Contained**
Calendar	Appointments, events, and meetings
Contacts	Information about people and organizations
Deleted Items	Items deleted from other folders
Inbox	Messages received from a mail or fax server
Journal	Activities saved in the Journal
Notes	Notes
Outbox	Messages waiting to be sent
Sent Items	Items sent to a mail or fax server
Tasks	Tasks created, assigned to others, and received as assignments
Junk E-mail	This folder is created if the Junk E-mail or Adult Content Rules are enabled

OUTLOOK FIELDS

Outlook maintains a database that contains various tables of information. Each table contains many fields that have the data you see in the various Outlook forms. Some fields are used only in one table while others are used in more than one table. Table C.4 lists all the data fields available in Outlook.

Tip #300 from

You can create an unlimited number of custom fields in addition to the standard fields listed here.

Field Name	Data Type	Write	Notes	Calendar	Contact	Journal	Note	Post	Task	Document
% Complete	Percent	Y	Percentage of task completed.						X	
Account	Text	Y	Description of account.		X					
Actual Work	Duration	Y	Time spent on task. Saved in minutes.						X	
Address Selected	Reserved	N								
Address Selector	Reserved	N								
All Day Event	Yes/No	Y	If set to Yes, the Duration field is set to 1440 minutes.	X						
Anniversary	Date/Time	Y	When this field has a value, a Calendar item is attached to a Contact, and the Attachment field is set to Yes.		X					
Assigned	Number	N	0 - not assigned						X	
			1 - assigned by me							
			2 - assigned to me							
Assistant's Name	Text	Y	Name of assistant.		X					
Assistant's Phone	Text	Y	Phone number of assistant.	X						
Attachment	Yes/No	N	For Contact: Yes when Birthday or Anniversary date is provided. Otherwise No.	X	X	X	X		X	X
Author	Text	N	Original document author							X
BCC	Text	Y	Names of blind copy recipients.					X		
Billing Information	Text	Y	Information about person or organization to be billed	X		X	X		X	X
Birthday	Date/Time	Y	For Contact, when a birthday date is provided, a Calendar item is attached to the Contact and the Attachment field is set to Yes.		X					

continues

PART

IX

APP

C

Field Name	Data Type	Write	Notes	Calendar	Contact	Journal	Note	Post	Task	Document
Business Address	Combination	N	Complete business address. Combination of individual business address fields.		X					
Business Address City	Text	Y	Business address city		X					
Business Address Country	Text	Y	Business address country		X					
Business Address PO Box	Text	Y	Business address post office box		X					
Business Address Postal Code	Text	Y	Business address postal code		X					
Business Address State	Text	Y	Business address state		X					
Business Address Street	Text	Y	Business address street address		X					
Business Fax	Text	Y	Business fax number		X					
Business Home Page	Text	Y	Business URL		X					
Business Phone	Text	Y	Business first phone number		X					
Business Phone 2	Text	Y	Business second phone number		X					
Bytes	Number	N	Document size							X
Callback	Text	Y	Callback phone number		X					
Car Phone	Text	Y	Contact's car phone number		X					
Categories	Text	Y	Used to group and find related Outlook items. Multiple categories are separated by commas.	X	X	X	X	X	X	X
Category	Text	N	Document category							X
CC	Text	Y	Names of copy recipients					X		
Characters	Number	N	Characters in document							X
Children	Text	Y	Names of children		X					
City	Text	Y	Home city name		X					

Field Name	Data Type	Write	Notes	Calendar	Contact	Journal	Note	Post	Task	Document
Color	Number	Y	0 - blue					X		
			1 – Green							
			2 - Pink							
			3 - Yellow							
			4 - White							
Comments	Text	N	Document comments							X
Company	Text	Y	Company or organization name	X	X				X	X
Company Main Phone	Text	Y	Company or organization main phone number		X					
Complete	Yes/No	Y	Whether task is complete							X
Computer Network Name	Text	Y	Name of computer network		X					
Contacts	Combination	N	Contacts' names			X				X
Content	Text	Y	Text in a note					X		
Conversation	Derived	N	Value of the Subject field in the first message	X			X		X	X
Country/Region	Text	Y	Home country		X					
Created	Date/Time	N	Date and time item was created	X	X	X	X	X	X	X
Customer ID	Text	Y	Customer identification		X					
Creation Time	Date/Time	N	Date and time document created							X
Date Completed	Date/Time	Y	Date and time task completed							X
Defer Until	Date/Time	Y	Date and time message to be delivered					X	X	
Department	Text	Y	Department name		X					
Distribution List Name	Text	N	Name of distribution list		X					
Do Not AutoArchive	Yes/No	N	Whether to AutoArchive item	X		X	X	X	X	X

continues

Field Name	Data Type	Write	Notes	Calendar	Contact	Journal	Note	Post	Task	Document
Document Subject	Test	N	Subject of document							X
Due By	Date/Time	Y	Date and time action associated with a message flag is to be completed. When this field has a value, the Flag Status field is set to 2.				X			
Due Date	Date/Time	Y	Date and time task is due.							X
Duration	Reserved	N	Minutes. 1440 for All Day Events. Otherwise the difference between the End Time and the Start Time.	X	X					
E-mail	Text	Y	First e-mail address		X					
E-mail 2	Text	Y	Second e-mail address		X					
E-mail 3	Text	Y	Third e-mail address		X					
Edit Time	Number	N	Minutes spent editing document							X
End	Date/Time	Y	End date and time	X	X					
Entry Type	Text	N	Type of entry for Journal item (selected from list)			X				
Expires	Date/Time	Y	Date and time message expires				X	X		
File As	Combination	N	Name under which Contact item is filed		X					
First Name	Text	Y	Contact's first name		X					
Flag Status	Number	N	0 – Normal				X			
			1 - Completed							
			2 - Flagged							
Follow Up Flag	Yes/No	N	Flag exists				X			
FTP Site	Text	Y	FTP site name		X					
From	Text	N	Message sender				X	X		
Full Name	Combination	Y	Title, first name, second name, last name, and suffix.		X					

Field Name	Data Type	Write	Notes	Calendar	Contact	Journal	Note	Post	Task	Document
Gender	Number	Y	0 - Unspecified		X					
			1 - Female							
			2 - Male							
Governent ID Number	Text	Y	Government identification		X					
Have Replies Sent To	Text	N	Contact to whom replies are to be sent.					X		
Hidden Slides	Text	N	Hidden PowerPoint slides							X
Hobbies	Text	Y	Hobbies and interests		X					
Home Address	Combination	N	Complete home address. Combination of individual home address fields.		X					
Home Address City	Text	Y	Home address city		X					
Home Address Country	Text	Y	Home address country		X					
Home Address PO Box	Text	Y	Home address post office box		X					
Home Address Postal Code	Text	Y	Home address postal code		X					
Home Address State	Text	Y	Home address state		X					
Home Address Street	Text	Y	Home address street address		X					
Home Fax	Text	Y	Home fax number		X					
Home Phone	Text	Y	Home phone number		X					
Home Phone 2	Text	Y	Second home phone number	X						
Icon	Icon	N	Icon exists	X	X	X	X	X	X	X
Importance	Number	Y	0 - Low Importance	X			X		X	
			1 - Normal Importance							
			2 - High Importance							
In Folder	Text	N	Name of folder that contains item	X	X	X	X	X	X	X
Initials	Text	Y	Contact's initials		X					
ISDN	Text	Y	ISDN phone number		X					

continues

Field Name	Data Type	Write	Notes	Calendar	Contact	Journal	Note	Post	Task	Document
Job Title	Text	Y	Job title		X					
Journal	Yes/No	Y	Whether contact activities are to be journaled		X					
Keywords	Text	N	Document keywords							X
Language	Text	Y	Contact's language		X					
Last Author	Text	N	Most recent editor							X
Last Name	Text	Y	Contact's last name		X					
Last Saved Time	Date/Time	N	Date and time document most recently saved							X
Lines	Number	N	Lines in document							X
Location	Text	Y	Contact's location		X					
Mailing Address	Reserved	N	Identifies mailing address		X					
Manager	Text	N	Document manager's name							X
Manager's Name	Text	Y	Manager's name		X					
Meeting Status	Number	N	0 - None	X						
			1 - Meeting organizer							
			2 - Tentatively accepted							
			3 - Accepted							
			4 - Declined							
			5 - Not yet accepted							
Message	Text	Y	Text of message				X	X		
Message Class		N	See list of message classes	X		X	X	X	X	X
Message Flag	Text	Y	Action associated with message flag. When an action exists, the Flag Status field is set to 2.				X			
Middle Name	Text	Y	Middle name		X					
Mileage	Text	Y	Mileage information	X	X	X	X		X	X
Mobile Phone	Text	Y	Mobile phone number		X					

Field Name	Data Type	Write	Notes	Calendar	Contact	Journal	Note	Post	Task	Document
Modified	Date/Time	N	Last time item modified	X	X	X	X	X	X	X
Multimedia Clips	Text	N	File names of multimedia clips							X
Nickname	Text	Y	Contact's nickname		X					
Notes	Text	Y	Text in notes box	X	X	X			X	X
Office Location	Text	Y	Contact's office location		X					
Optional Attendees	Text	Y	Names of optional attendees at meeting or appointment (each name separated from next by a semicolon).	X						
Organizational ID Number	Text	Y	Contact's organization ID number		X					
Organizer	Text	Y	Organizer of meeting or appointment.	X						
Other Address	Combination	N	Complete Other address. Combination of individual Other address fields.		X					
Other Address City	Text	Y	Other address city		X					
Other Address Country	Text	Y	Other address country		X					
Other Address PO Box	Text	Y	Other address post office box		X					
Other Address Postal Code	Text	Y	Other address postal code		X					
Other Address State	Text	Y	Other address state		X					
Other Address Street	Text	Y	Other address street address		X					
Other Fax	Text	Y	Other fax number		X					
Other Phone	Text	Y	Other first phone number		X					
Outlook Internal Version		N	For administrative use only	X	X	X	X	X	X	X
Outlook Version	Text	N	Outlook version in which item created	X	X	X	X	X	X	X
Owner	Text	N	Task owner's name							X

continues

Field Name	Data Type	Write	Notes	Calendar	Contact	Journal	Note	Post	Task	Document
Pager	Text	Y	Pager phone number		X					
Pages	Number	N	Number of document pages							X
Paragraphs	Number	N	Number of document paragraphs							X
Personal Home Page	Text	Y	Contact's personal URL		X					
PO Box	Text	Y	PO Box number		X					
Presentation Format	Text	N	PowerPoint presentation format							X
Primary Phone	Text	Y	Primary phone number		X					
Printed	Date/Time	N	Date and time last printed							X
Priority	Number	N	0 - Low							X
			1 - Normal							
			2 - High							
Private	Number	N	0 - Not private	X	X		X	X	X	X
			1 - Private							
Profession	Text	Y	Contact's profession		X					
Radio Phone	Text	Y	Radio phone number		X					
Read	Yes/No	N	Whether an item has been read	X	X	X	X	X	X	X
Received	Date/Time	N	Date and time message received by recipient's mail box					X	X	
Recurrence	Number	N	0 - None	X						X
			1 - Daily							
			2 - Weekly							
			3 - Monthly							
			4 - Yearly							
Recurrence Pattern	Combination	N	Combination of values in Recurrence, Start, and End fields	X						X

Field Name	Data Type	Write	Notes	Calendar	Contact	Journal	Note	Post	Task	Document
Recurrence Range End	Date/Time	N	Last date and time of recurring item.	X						X
Recurrence Range Start	Date/Time	N	First date and time of recurring item	X						X
Recurring	Yes/No	N	Whether item is recurring	X						X
Referred By	Text	Y	Name of person who referred contact		X					
Remind Beforehand	Number	Y	Minutes ahead reminder occurs	X						X
Reminder	Yes/No	N	Whether a reminder is set	X						X
Reminder Override Default	Yes/No	N	Yes - use reminder defaults set in Options.	X						X
			No - use values in Reminder Beforehand, Reminder Sound, and Reminder Sound File fields.							
Reminder Sound	Yes/No	N	Whether a sound is played as a reminder	X						X
Reminder Sound File	Text	N	Path of reminder sound file.	X						X
Reminder Time	Date/Time	N	Date and time for reminder	X						X
Reminder Topic	Text	Y	Reminder topic	X						X
Remote Status	Number	N	Remote mail header status:					X	X	
			0 - None							
			1 - Marked							
			2 - Marked for download							
			3 - Marked for copy							
Request Status	Number	N	Assigned task status:							X
			0 - None							
			1 - Not responded							
			2 - Accepted							
			3 - Declined							

PART

IX

APP

C

continues

Field Name	Data Type	Write	Notes	Calendar	Contact	Journal	Note	Post	Task	Document
Required Attendees	Text	Y	Names of required attendees at meeting or appointment (multiple names separated by semicolons)	X						
Retrieval Time	Number	N	Time taken to download a message (in minutes) by Remote Mail.				X	X		
Revision Number	Number	N	Document revision number							X
Role	Text	Y	Contact's role		X					
Schedule+ Priority	Text	N	Priority in Schedule+							X
Sensitivity	Number	N	0 - Normal				X	X		
			1 - Personal							
			2 - Private							
			3 - Confidential							
Sent	Date/Time	N	Date and time message sent to Outbox				X	X		
Show Time As	Number	N	0 - Free	X						
			1 - Tentative							
			2 - Busy							
			3 - Out of office							
Size	Number	N	Bytes occupied by item	X	X	X	X	X	X	X
Slides	Number	N	Number of slides in presentation							X
Spouse	Text	Y	Name of spouse		X					
Start	Date/Time	Y	Item start time	X	X					
Start Date	Date/Time	Y	Start date and time							X
State	Text	Y	Contact's state		X					
Status	Number	N	Task status:							
			0 - Not started							X
			1 - In progress							
			2 - Completed							

Field Name	Data Type	Write	Notes	Calendar	Contact	Journal	Note	Post	Task	Document
			3 - Waiting for someone else							
			4 - Deferred							
Street Address	Text	Y	Contact's street address		X					
Subject	Text	Y	Subject of item. For contact, if Full Name field is empty, value of File As field is used	X	X	X	X	X	X	X
Suffix	Text	Y	Contact's suffix		X					
Team Task	Yes/No	N	Whether team task						X	
Telex	Text	Y	Telex number		X					
Template	Text	N	Document template							X
Title	Text	Y	Contact's title		X					X
To	Text	Y	Names of message recipients					X		
Total Work	Number	Y	Time task is expected to take (saved in minutes)						X	
Tracking Status	Number	N	1 - Delivered					X		
			5 - Read							
			6 - Not read							
TTY/TTD Phone	Text	Y	Contact's TTY/TTD number		X					
User Certificate	Text	N	User certificate		X					
User Field 1	Text	Y	User-defined text		X					
User Field 2	Text	Y	User-defined text		X					
User Field 3	Text	Y	User-defined text		X					
User Field 4	Text	Y	User-defined text		X					
Web Page	Text	Y	URL		X					
Words	Number	N	Number of words in document							X
Zip/Postal Code	Text	Y	Contact's ZIP or postal code		X					

MESSAGE CLASSES

In Outlook, each item is an object that has a message class. The class defines the properties of the object and how that object behaves. One of the most significant properties is the form that's used to display the object.

The Outlook message classes are listed in Table C.5.

TABLE C.5 OUTLOOK MESSAGE CLASSES

Class ID	Item Type
Ipm.Activity	Create journal entry
Ipm.Appointment	Create appointment
Ipm.Contact	Create contact
Ipm.Document	Create document
Ipm.OLE.Class	Create an exception to a recurrence series
Ipm	The specified form cannot be found
Ipm.Note.IMC.Notification	Create a report from the Exchange Server gateway to the Internet
IPM.Note.InetFax	WinFax SE messages (IMO only)
Ipm.Note.Rules.Oof	Show out-of-office templates Template.Microsoft
Ipm.Post	Post note in folder
Ipm.StickyNote	Create note
Ipm.Recall.Report	Create a message recall report
Ipm.Outlook.Recall	Retrieve sent message from recipient inbox
Ipm.Remote	Represent Remote Mail message header
Ipm.Note.Rules	Edit rule reply template ReplyTemplate.Microsoft
Ipm.Report	Report item status
Ipm.Resend	Resend failed message
Ipm.Schedule.Meeting.Canceled	Send meeting cancellation
Ipm.Schedule.Meeting,Request	Create meeting request
IPM.Schedule.Meeting.Resp.Neg	Create decline meeting response
Ipm.Schedule.Meeting.Resp.Pos	Create accept meeting response
Ipm Schedule.Meeting.Resp.Tent	Create tentative meeting response
Ipm.Note.Secure	Send encrypted note
Ipm.Note.Secure.Sign	Send digitally signed note

Class ID	Item Type
Ipm.Task	Create task
Ipm.TaskRequestAccept	Create task request accept response
Ipm.TaskRequestDecline	Create task request decline response
Ipm.TaskRequest	Create task request
Ipm.TaskRequest.Update	Create update to task request

OUTLOOK REGISTRY KEYS

In addition to the files listed previously in this appendix, Outlook saves information in the Windows registry—a database that contains setup information for Windows and applications that run under Windows, as well as information about Windows users.

The registry database is maintained in several files, but you can access the information in those files by using the Registry Editor utility without having to be aware of the files that contain the information. Appendix F, "Working with the Windows Registry," contains information about how you can use the Registry Editor to examine and modify setup information in the registry.

→ To learn more about examining and modifying setup information, **see** "Working with the Windows Registry," **p. 1323**.

When you use the Registry Editor to examine the registry, it looks much like a set of folders and subfolders. Instead of folders and subfolders, however, the structure consists of keys and subkeys. Just as subfolders are referred to as folders in the Windows file system, subkeys in the registry structure as usually referred to as keys.

Table C.6 lists some of the principal registry keys that control Outlook for the current user. A complete list is available in the Office Resource Kit. See the file Regkey.xls.

Note

All the keys in Table C.6 are in the HKEY_CURRENT_USER\Software\Microsoft\ section of the registry. A key listed as Office\9.0\Outlook would have a full path in the registry of HKEY_CURRENT_USER\Software\Microsoft\Office\9.0\Outlook.

TABLE C.6 OUTLOOK KEYS

Key	Outlook Item
At Work Fax	MS Fax (C/W only)
Office\9.0\Outlook	General Outlook key
Office\9.0\Outlook\Appointment	Appointments
Office\9.0\Outlook\Categories	Master Category list

continues

PART

IX

APP

C

TABLE C.6   CONTINUED

Key	Outlook Item
Office\9.0\Outlook\Contact	Contacts folders
Office\9.0\Outlook\Journal	Journal log files
Office\9.0\Outlook\NetFolder	Net Folders log and settings
Office\9.0\Outlook\OLFax\	WinFax SE settings
Office\9.0\Outlook\Options	Outlook Options settings
Office\9.0\Outlook\Preferences	Outlook Preferences settings
Office\9.0\Outlook\Printing	Print settings
Office\9.0\Outlook\Setup	Setup information
Office\9.0\Outlook\Today	Outlook Today settings
Office\Outlook\OMI Account	Account information (IMO Manager only)
Shared Tools\Outlook\Journaling	Settings for applications and items to be Journaled
WAB\Server Properties	Account information for other mail services such as LDAP
WAB\WAB4	Outlook Address Book settings
Windows Messaging Subsystem\Profiles	Information for the Personal Folders files

Note

Additional information relating to Table C.6 is also located in the registry keys and subkeys under HKEY_LOCAL_MACHINE\Software\Microsoft\Exchange.

BACKING UP OUTLOOK

A complete backup of Outlook consists of more than just making a copy of your Personal Folders file. In addition to copying the .PST files that you use, you also need to copy the other files listed previously in this appendix. Copying the recommended files will allow you to retain the customizations that have been done to make Outlook look and work the way you want. Making an export copy of the registry keys listed previously will preserve the Outlook settings and customizations that are not kept in separate files.

To learn more about backing up Outlook, look in the Microsoft Knowledge Base at articles Q168644 and Q181014. These articles were written for earlier versions of Outlook, but the information applies to Outlook 2000. There will also be Knowledge Base articles that will be specifically written for Outlook 2000. More information on backing up Outlook is available at `http://www.slipstick.com/exchange/olbackup.htm`.

Microsoft has indicated that it may make available a utility or Outlook add-in that will back up Outlook. If this utility is created, it will be available at the Office Update Web site.

Outlook's Symbols

In this chapter *by Gordon Padwick*

WHAT ARE SYMBOLS FOR?

Outlook uses symbols to provide information about items. For example, a symbol that looks like a closed envelope indicates a message item is unread, whereas a symbol that looks like an open envelope indicates a message has been read.

The tables in this appendix list the symbols used most frequently with Outlook's items.

SYMBOLS FOR CALENDAR ITEMS

Table D.1 lists the symbols used for Calendar items.

Image	Meaning
TABLE D.1 CALENDAR SYMBOLS	
	Appointment
	Click to see items that don't fit into current view
	Meeting
	Meeting request
	Recurring appointment
	Recurring meeting
	Recurring appointment or meeting
	Reminder for appointment or meeting
	Private appointment or meeting
	Start time for appointment or meeting
	End time for appointment or meeting
	Calendar item has attachment

SYMBOLS FOR CONTACT ITEMS

Table D.2 lists the symbols used for Contact items.

TABLE D.2	CONTACT SYMBOLS
Image	**Meaning**
	Activities for contacts are recorded in journal
	Contact item
	Contact item has attachment
	Contact flagged for follow-up
	Contact follow-up complete
	Distribution list

SYMBOLS FOR MESSAGE ITEMS

Table D.3 lists the symbols used for Message items.

TABLE D.3	MESSAGE SYMBOLS
Image	**Meaning**
	High importance message
	Low importance message
	Read message
	Unread message
	Forwarded message
	Replied to message
	Saved or unsent message
	Encrypted message
	Digitally signed message
	Invalid signed message
	Microsoft Mail 3.x form
	Meeting request

PART

IX

APP

D

continues

TABLE D.3   CONTINUED

Image	Meaning
	Accepted meeting request
	Tentatively accepted meeting request
	Declined meeting request
	Canceled meeting
	Task request
	Accepted task
	Declined task
	Message has attachment
	Message flagged for follow-up
	Message follow-up complete

SYMBOLS FOR JOURNAL ITEMS

Table D.4 lists the symbols used for Journal items.

TABLE D.4   JOURNAL SYMBOLS

Image	Meaning
	Appointment
	Appointment request, appointment response, meeting, meeting request, meeting response
	Meeting canceled
	Conversation
	Document
	E-mail message
	Fax
	Letter
	Microsoft Access database file
	Microsoft Excel workbook file

Image	Meaning
	Microsoft PowerPoint presentation
	Microsoft Word document
	Note
	Phone call
	Task
	Task request, task response
	Remote Session
	Journal item has attachment

SYMBOLS FOR TASK ITEMS

Table D.5 lists the symbols used for Task items.

TABLE D.5	TASK SYMBOLS

Image	Meaning
	Accepted task
	Completed task
	Declined task
	High importance task
	Low importance task
	Recurring task
	Task
	Task assigned to another person
	Task assigned to you
	Task has attachment
	Uncompleted task

PART

IX

APP

D

OUTLOOK RESOURCES

In this appendix   *by Gordon Padwick*

This appendix lists some of the resources I've found useful while working with Outlook.

RESOURCES AVAILABLE ON THE WORLD WIDE WEB

The World Wide Web provides comprehensive resources for information about Outlook and related subjects. Some of the sites I've found useful are listed here. Many of these sites provide links to other related sites. You probably won't have the time to explore these sites in depth, but I suggest you make a preliminary visit to each of them to gain an idea of what's available.

- amazon.com—This is a Web site maintained by the most popular online book store. You can use this site to find books on any subject, including Outlook. The site contains information about, and reviews of, many books. You can, of course, use this site to purchase books.

  `http://www.amazon.com`

- Helen Feddema's Home Page—This Web site contains many useful examples of Visual Basic code that customizes Outlook and also links Outlook to other Office applications.

  `http://www.ulster.net/~hfeddema/`

- Macmillan Computer Publishing—Contains information about books published by Macmillan under all its imprints, including Que. You can download sample chapters of many books, get technical information from resource centers, and much more.

  `http://www.mcp.com`

- Microsoft Office Home Page—You can use this site to find information about any Microsoft Office product, including Outlook. The site has many links that take you to detailed information.

  `http://www.microsoft.com/office/`

- Microsoft Outlook Home Page—This site contains links to Outlook-specific information. One of these links leads you to information about Outlook add-ons available from many sources. If any upgrades for Outlook become available from Microsoft, you'll probably find them on this site.

  `http://www.microsoft.com/outlook/`

- Microsoft Technical Support—This site provides access to Microsoft's Knowledge Base (a collection of some 200,000 technical articles) and other resources.

  `http://support.microsoft.com/support/`

- Outlook Downloads—This site contains Outlook add-ins available from Microsoft for downloading.

  `http://officeupdate.microsoft.com/downloadCatalog/dldoutlook.htm`

- Slipstick Systems Exchange Center—Probably the best and most complete source of information about Outlook and Exchange. The site contains many articles about specific topics together with links to other sources of information.

  `http://www.slipstick.com`

- US East Outlook Developer's Site—Contains an abundance of information about modifying and enhancing Outlook, as well as many practical examples.

  `http://www.outlook.useast.com/outlook/default.htm`

- whatis.com—This site contains an enormous amount of information about computer-related topics in general, including messaging. If you ever want to find out what a word or acronym means, you'll find it here.

  `http://whatis.com`

BOOKS

The following is a list of books that contain detailed information about Outlook and related topics. In addition to the books listed here you can find many more books about Outlook listed by online book stores such as Amazon.

Building Applications with Microsoft Outlook 2000. Randy Byrne Microsoft Press, ISBN: 0-73560-581-5.

Mastering Microsoft Outlook 98. Gini Courter and Annette Marquis. Sybex, ISBN: 0-7821-2276-0.

Microsoft Office 97 Visual Basic Programmer's Guide. Microsoft Press, ISBN: 1-57231-340-4.

Microsoft Exchange User's Guide. Sue Mosher. Duke, ISBN: 1-882419-52-9.

Microsoft Outlook E-mail and Fax Guide. Sue Mosher. Duke, ISBN: 1-882419-82-0.

Programming Microsoft Outlook and Microsoft Exchange. Thomas Rizzo. Microsoft Press. ISBN: 0-73560-509-2.

Special Edition Using Microsoft Internet Explorer 4. Jim O'Donnell and Eric Ladd. Que, ISBN: 0-7897-1046-3.

PART

IX

APP

E

Special Edition Using Microsoft Exchange Server 5.5. Kent Joshi et al. Que, ISBN:0-7897-1503-1.

Special Edition Using Microsoft Outlook 97. Gordon Padwick et al. Que, ISBN: 0-7897-1096-X

Using Outlook 98. Gordon Padwick et al. Que, ISBN: 0-7897-1516-3.

Using the Windows 98 Registry. Jerry Honeycutt. Que, ISBN 0-7897-1658-5.

VBA Developer's Handbook. Ken Getz and Mike Gilbert. Sybex, ISBN 0-7821-1951-4.

Visual Basic for Applications Unleashed. Paul McFedries. SAMS Publishing, ISBN: 0-672-31046-5.

WORKING WITH THE WINDOWS REGISTRY

In this chapter

by Gordon Padwick

WHY WORK WITH THE REGISTRY?

You might wonder why a book about Outlook contains information about the Windows registry. The reason is that Outlook saves a lot of information in the registry. For example, the categories in your personal Master Category List are saved in the registry, as described in Chapter 21, "Using Categories and Entry Types." While you don't need to be concerned with the registry while you use Outlook in your daily work, there are some administrative tasks that can only be done by working with it. If you want to copy a personal Master Category List from one computer to another, you have to copy information from one computer's registry to the other computer's registry.

Quite often, when you consult articles about Outlook in the Microsoft Knowledge Base, or on the TechNet CD-ROM, you'll come across techniques that require you to make changes within the Windows registry.

This appendix provides an introduction to the Windows registry, including the information you need to make changes to the registry when you receive detailed instructions, such as those in various chapters of this book and in information from Microsoft and other software providers.

WHAT IS THE REGISTRY?

The registry is a database that exists in files on your hard disk. Each computer that runs Windows 95, Windows 98, or Windows NT has a registry. The registry contains information about your computer hardware, the operating system, applications (such as Outlook) that run under Windows, and information about computer users.

Although the information in the registry is in several files (*many* files in the case of Windows NT), you don't have to be concerned with how these files are structured. That's because Windows contains various tools for displaying and modifying what's in the registry.

The registries for the three operating systems have similar structures, although some of the contents are different.

BACKING UP AND RESTORING THE REGISTRY

Before you attempt to make any changes to the registry, you should create a backup copy of the registry files. This is because the operation of your computer, when running under Windows, depends on information in the registry. If you inadvertently corrupt your registry, you might not be able to start Windows. It's a very wise precaution, therefore, to create a backup copy of your registry before you begin to make any changes to it.

Having said that, you should also know that Windows automatically keeps a backup of the registry. Rather than relying on that, though, it's much safer to create your own registry backup.

Windows 95 doesn't provide any easy way to access the backup registry files. In Windows 98, though, you can access the registry backup by starting in MS-DOS mode and then entering the command scanreg /restore.

Windows NT also has a means to use the backup registry. Soon after you begin to start Windows NT, a message inviting you to "press spacebar now to invoke hardware profile/last known good menu" appears. You have only a second or so to press the spacebar. Microsoft says that this procedure will restore your registry to its state when you last successfully started your computer.

One way to save a copy of the registry is to export the entire registry to a text file. This method is described in detail in this appendix, in the section "Copying a Registry Key from One Computer to Another." Be aware, though, that if you're using a computer that has Windows profiles for two or more users, this method exports only the registry data associated with the user who is currently logged on.

BACKING UP THE WINDOWS 95 REGISTRY

The Windows 95 registry exists in the two files User.dat and System.dat. The easiest way to back up these files is to use Windows Explorer to copy them.

There are two problems, though. The files may be too big to save on a floppy disk. You can overcome this problem by copying the files to a high-capacity disk (such as a Zip disk). Alternatively, you can use a utility such as PKZip or WinZip to compress the files, which may require several floppy disks.

The other potential problem is that you may find more than one User.dat file and more than one System.dat file on your computer. That occurs when two or more people have separate Windows profiles. If that's the case, make separate copies of each file, keeping a careful note of the folder that each file is in.

BACKING UP THE WINDOWS 98 REGISTRY

Backing up the Windows 98 registry is similar to backing up the Windows 95 registry. The only difference is that Windows 98 may have an additional registry file—Policy.pol. This file exists only if you're using Windows 98 on a network and the network administrator has established some data specific for your network or corporate environment. If there is a Policy.pol file, you should make a backup copy of it.

BACKING UP THE WINDOWS NT REGISTRY

The Windows NT 4.0 registry is contained in too many files to make it practical to save these files individually. The Windows NT Workstation Resource Kit, available from Microsoft, contains a backup utility—regback.exe—that you can use to create a backup of the Windows NT registry.

RESTORING THE REGISTRY

The only time you should need to restore the registry is after it becomes so corrupted that Windows won't start. If that ever happens, I hope you've followed the wise practice of always having an up-to-date Emergency Repair Disk. Use the Emergency Repair Disk to start the computer and subsequently, in the case of Windows 95 or Windows 98, use Windows explorer to copy the backup files into their original location on your hard disk.

In the case of Windows NT, after you've started Windows from the Emergency Repair Disk, you can use Regrest.exe (included in the Windows NT Workstation Resource Kit) to restore your registry.

EXAMINING THE REGISTRY

The Registry Editor utility (Regedit.exe) is automatically installed on your computer when you install Windows. You can use this utility to examine and, if necessary, make changes to the registry.

To open Regedit, choose Start on the Windows Taskbar, then choose Run in the Start menu to display the dialog box shown in Figure F.1.

Figure F.1
Use the Run dialog box to name the utility you want to run.

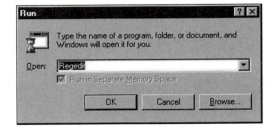

Enter Regedit in the Open box, and then choose OK. The Registry Editor initially opens as shown in Figure F.2.

Figure F.2
The Registry Editor window contains two panes.

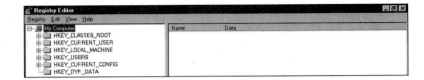

The left pane shows the registry tree with the tree name—My Computer—at the top. Under the tree name are the names of six subtrees. The names of the subtrees are the same for Windows 95, Windows 98, and Windows NT.

Note

A tree consists of subtrees. Subtrees have keys, and keys have subkeys. The word *branch* is used to refer to any level of a tree and all the subordinates of that level.

You can expand a subtree by clicking the small box that contains a plus sign at the left of the subtree name, as shown in Figure F.3.

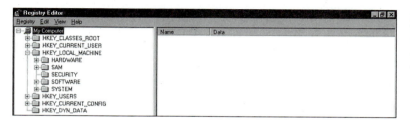

Figure F.3
The HKEY_LOCAL_ MACHINE subtree is expanded here to show the keys it contains.

After you've expanded a subtree, the small square at the left of its name contains a minus sign. You can click that square to compress the list of keys.

The items contained within a subtree are known as keys. Each key may contain a value, or subkeys, or both. A key that contains one or more subkeys has a small square containing a plus sign at the left of its name. The subkeys are revealed when you click that square.

Many keys contain several levels of subkeys. Figure F.4 shows two levels of subkeys under the SOFTWARE key.

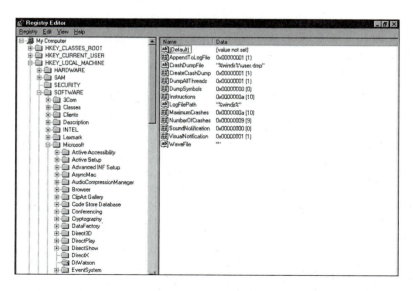

Figure F.4
The DrWatson subkey is selected to show the values it contains.

You can select any key or subkey by clicking it. After you do so, the right pane of the Registry Editor window displays the values contained in that key or subkey, as shown in Figure F.4. Notice also that the status bar at the bottom of the Registry Editor window contains complete information about the path through the tree to get to the selected subkey, much as file path names are defined.

Tip #301 from	You can drag the border between the two panes to make either of them wider.
Gordon Proodle	

The right pane contains two columns. The left column contains the names of various data items; the right column contains the actual value in each data item. You can change the width of the columns by dragging the vertical separator bar at the top of the pane.

Although you can see the values a key or subkey contains, it's rarely clear what these value are for or what would happen if you changed one. To the best of my knowledge, Microsoft hasn't published a definitive list of keys and the values they contain. Neither does any other software provider publish detailed information about the registry entries created when their software is installed. However, in this book and in such resources as Microsoft Knowledge Base articles, when information about making changes to the registry is provided, detailed information about the registry keys and their values is included.

When you've finished examining the registry, choose Registry, Exit to close the Registry Editor.

FINDING INFORMATION IN THE REGISTRY

If you know the path to the subkey you want to see, you can drill down into the registry by expanding the appropriate tree, expanding a key, and successively expanding subkeys. If you don't know the path, you can use the Registry Editor's Find capability.

Using the Find capability, you can search the registry for the names of keys and subkeys, names of values, or actual values. You can search the entire registry, or a key and the subkeys below that key.

You might be interested to search through the entire registry to see if there are Outlook subkeys, which there are. To do this, start by selecting the top of the tree (My Computer), then choose Edit, Find (or press Ctrl+F) to open the dialog box shown in Figure F.5. If you want to search only a part of the registry, such as those keys and subkeys in the HKEY_LOCAL_MACHINE subtree, start by selecting that subtree.

Figure F.5
Use the Find dialog box to define what you want to find in the registry.

Enter the text you want to find in the Find What box. For example, if you want to find keys named Outlook, enter Outlook (you don't have to be concerned about upper- and lower-case). The Find Next button becomes enabled as soon as you enter one character in the box.

You can choose to search key names, value names, or value data, or any combination of these. To search only for key names, check only the Keys check box. Choose Find Next to initiate the search.

After a short delay, the Registry Editor locates the first key or subkey named Outlook, and displays that part of the tree, as shown in Figure F.6.

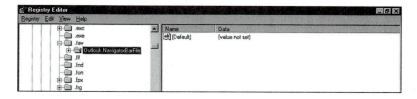

Figure F.6
The tree automatically expands to the level necessary to display the key that's found.

In this case, you know the Outlook subkey contains other subkeys because the square at the left of the subkey name contains a plus sign. You can click the square to see the subkeys within Outlook. Notice also that the status bar at the bottom of the window displays the complete path to the found subkey.

To find the next occurrence of a subkey named Outlook, choose Edit, Find Next (or press F3). If you continue pressing F3, you'll find many subkeys named Outlook and others that have Outlook as part of their names.

ADDING AND DELETING SUBKEYS

Caution

Never add, delete, or change a key or subkey unless you know exactly what you're doing. Even if you do know what you're doing, create a backup of your registry before making any changes.

The procedure for creating a new key is quite simple.

To add a new subkey:

1. Select the key or subkey for which you want to create a new subkey.

2. Choose Edit, move the pointer onto New, and choose Key. The new key appears in the correct position in the tree with a temporary name.

3. Change the temporary name to the appropriate name, then press Enter.

The procedure to delete a key is even simpler.

To delete a subkey:

1. Select the subkey you want to delete.

2. Choose Edit, Delete (or press the Delete key). The Registry Editor asks you to confirm that you want to delete the subkey. Choose Yes to proceed.

CHANGING THE DATA IN A KEY OR SUBKEY VALUE

The most common task is to change the data in one of the values in a key. For example, to change Outlook's default Master Category List, as explained in Chapter 21, you have to change the data in the Default value in the subkey:

`HKEY_LOCAL_MACHINE\SOFTWARE\Microsoft\Office\9.0\Outlook\Categories`

→ For detailed information about changing Outlook's default Master Category List, **see** "Customizing Outlook's Default Master Category List," **p. 613**.

When you select that subkey, you'll see it has a single value named Default, and that the data in that value is the default category names separated by semicolons. To change the default category names, select the value name in the right pane (Default), then choose Edit, Modify to display the Edit String dialog box shown in Figure F.7.

Figure F.7
You can use normal editing techniques to change the category names displayed in the Value Data box. Don't forget to separate category names with semicolons.

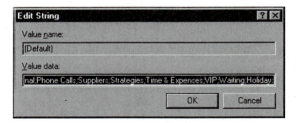

After you've edited the text, choose OK to close the dialog box.

MANAGING VALUES IN A SUBKEY

You can add values to a subkey and you can delete values from a subkey.

ADDING A VALUE TO A SUBKEY

Windows 95 and Windows 98 registry keys can contain the first three types of values listed in Table F.1. Windows NT registry keys can contain the five types of values in the table.

TABLE F.1   TYPES OF VALUES IN A SUBKEY

Value Type	Explanation
String	Alphanumeric text. String values are enclosed by double quotation marks. An empty string value consists of two consecutive double quotation marks.
Binary	Binary data is represented by a series of hexadecimal bytes. A defined value must have at least four bytes.
DWord	A special case of binary data that always consists of four bytes that are displayed in the format 0x00000001(1).
Expandable String	Value that applications can change on-the-fly.
Multiple String	Can contain a list of values.

To add a value to a subkey, start by selecting it. Choose Edit and move the pointer onto New. Choose String Value, Binary Value, or DWord Value. As you're following instructions about adding a value to a subkey, those instructions will tell you which value type to choose. When you choose a value type, the new value appears in the right pane with a temporary name. Change the temporary name to the name you want to use.

After creating a new value, you can change the data in that value using the method described in the previous section, "Changing the Data in a Key or Subkey Value."

DELETING A VALUE IN A KEY OR SUBKEY

To delete a value in a key or subkey, select the name of the value in the right pane. Then choose Edit, Delete (or press the Delete key).

COPYING A REGISTRY KEY FROM ONE COMPUTER TO ANOTHER

You can easily copy a registry key, its subordinate subkeys, and the values in those subkeys to a file, and subsequently copy the information in that file into another computer's registry.

The information given here is based on the assumption that the source and target computers are using the same operating system (such as Windows 98), and the same version of Outlook (such as Outlook 2000). There are differences between the detailed structure of the registry in Windows 95, Windows 98, and Windows NT. Also, there are differences between the directory keys created when you install the various versions of Outlook.

The amount of data in a typical registry key or subkey is usually quite small, and can normally be copied to a floppy disk.

To copy a registry key, its subkeys, and the values in those subkeys to a file:

1. In the Registry Editor, select the registry key you want to copy to a file.

2. Choose <u>R</u>egistry, <u>E</u>xport Registry File to display the dialog box shown in Figure F.8

Figure F.8
Use the Export Registry File dialog box to define what you want to export and the location to which you want to export it.

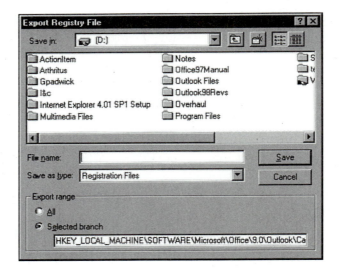

3. Navigate to the folder in which you want to save the file.

4. Enter a name for the exported file in the File <u>N</u>ame box. The Registry Editor automatically provides the extension .reg to exported registry files.

5. By default, the Registry Editor proposes to export only the selected branch of the tree. If you want to export the entire registry, choose <u>A</u>ll in the Export Range section of the dialog box.

6. Choose <u>S</u>ave to save the file.

After saving the file, you can import the file into another computer's registry.

To import a file into the registry:

1. Open the Registry Editor on the target computer.

2. Choose Registry, Import Registry File to display the dialog box shown in Figure F.9.

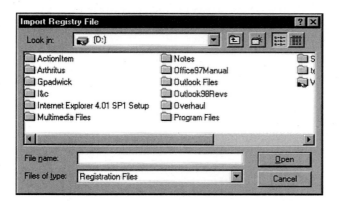

Figure F.9
Use the Import Registry File dialog box to locate the file to be imported.

3. Navigate to find the file you want to import into the registry and select that file.

4. Choose Open to import the file. A message appears telling you that the file has been successfully imported.

APPENDIX **G**

OUTLOOK SHORTCUT KEYS

In this chapter

by Gordon Padwick

SPEED YOUR WORK BY LEARNING SHORTCUTS

Because Outlook has a graphical interface, many people primarily use the mouse (or another pointing device) to control Outlook. It's often faster and more convenient to use a keyboard shortcut. You can speed up your work with Outlook by learning a few of the shortcuts listed in this appendix. For example, if you make frequent use of timelines, using keyboard shortcuts is often much faster than using the mouse.

Note   Many of the shortcuts perform the same, or similar, functions in other Office applications.

This appendix summarizes many of the shortcuts available in Outlook in tables, some of which refer to controls. Here's a reminder: A control is an element on a form or dialog box that displays information or that can be used to input information. Controls include such things as text boxes, drop-down lists, check boxes, groups of option buttons, and command buttons.

WORKING WITH OUTLOOK ITEMS

Table G.1 lists keyboard shortcuts for general use while you're working with Outlook items.

TABLE G.1 GENERAL-USE OUTLOOK ITEM SHORTCUTS	
Task	**Shortcut**
Cancel current operation	Esc
Display ScreenTip for active item	Shift+F1
Expand selected group	+ (numeric keypad)
Collapse selected group	- (numeric keypad)
Select item	Enter
Turn on editing in a field	F2
Move from item to item	Up arrow Down arrow Left arrow Right arrow
Switch to next tab stop	Ctrl+Tab or Ctrl+Page Down
Switch to previous tab stop	Ctrl+Shift+Tab or Ctrl+Page Up
Display address book	Ctrl+Shift+B
Dial	Ctrl+Shift+D
Use Advanced Find	Ctrl+Shift+F
Flag for follow-up	Ctrl+Shift+G
Create new Office document	Ctrl+Shift+H

Task	Shortcut
Next item (with item open)	Ctrl+Shift+>
Previous item (with item open)	Ctrl+Shift+<
Mark as read	Ctrl+Q
Reply to mail message	Ctrl+R
Reply all to mail message	Ctrl+Shift+R
Switch case for selected text in RTF messages	Shift+F3
Switch between panes (folder list, information viewer and preview pane)	F6 or Ctrl+Shift+Tab

Table G.2 lists keyboard shortcuts for adding World Wide Web information to items.

TABLE G.2   WEB SHORTCUTS FOR OUTLOOK ITEMS

Task	Shortcut
Edit a URL within a message	Ctrl+left mouse button
Locate Link Browser	Shift+left mouse button (Specify the browser program that will open URLs)
Insert a hyperlink	Ctrl+K (Word as e-mail editor)

Table G.3 lists keyboard shortcuts for applying formatting to items in Rich Text Format or HTML mail items. In each case, select the text you want to format and then press the shortcut keys.

TABLE G.3   SHORTCUTS FOR APPLYING FORMATTING

Task	Shortcut
Make bold	Ctrl+B
Add bullets	Ctrl+Shift+L
Center	Ctrl+E
Italicize	Ctrl+I
Increase indent	Ctrl+T
Decrease indent	Ctrl+Shift+T
Left align	Ctrl+L
Underline	Ctrl+U
Increase font size	Ctrl+]
Decrease font size	Ctrl+[
Clear formatting	Ctrl+Shift+Z or Ctrl+Spacebar

Table G.4 lists keyboard shortcuts for creating items and files.

TABLE G.4 SHORTCUTS FOR CREATING ITEMS AND FILES	
Task	**Shortcut**
Create an appointment	Ctrl+Shift+A
Create a contact	Ctrl+Shift+C
Create a folder	Ctrl+Shift+E
Create a journal entry	Ctrl+Shift+J
Create a distribution list	Ctrl+Shift+L
Create a message	Ctrl+Shift+M
Create a meeting request	Ctrl+Shift+Q
Create a note	Ctrl+Shift+N
Find people	Ctrl+Shift+P
Create a task	Ctrl+Shift+K
Post in this folder	Ctrl+Shift+S
Create a task request	Ctrl+Shift+U

Table G.5 lists keyboard shortcuts for managing menus. To select any menu command, hold down Alt while you press the underlined character in the menu item name. You can use the same technique to select something on a form or in a dialog box.

TABLE G.5 SOME COMMONLY USED MENU SHORTCUTS	
Task	**Shortcut**
Save	Ctrl+S or Shift+F12
Save and close (contact, appointment, journal and task items)	Alt+S
Send (mail item)	Alt+S
Save as	F12
Go to folder	Ctrl+Y
Go to Inbox folder	Shift+Ctrl+I
Post to a folder	Ctrl+Shift+S
Print	Ctrl+P
Create a new message	Ctrl+N
Cut to the Clipboard	Ctrl+X or Shift+Delete
Copy to the Clipboard	Ctrl+C or Ctrl+Insert

Task	Shortcut
Copy item	Ctrl+Shift+Y
Paste from the Clipboard	Ctrl+V or Shift+Insert
Move item	Ctrl+Shift+V
Check names (in default editor)	Ctrl+K
Check names	Alt+K
Undo	Ctrl+Z or Alt+Backspace
Delete	Ctrl+D
Select all	Ctrl+A
Display context menu	Shift+F10
Display program control menu when menu bar is active	Spacebar
Display program icon menu	Alt+Spacebar
Select next command on menu	DownArrow
Select previous command on menu	UpArrow
Select menu to the left	LeftArrow
Select menu to the right	RightArrow
Select first command on menu	Home
Select last command on menu	End
Make menu bar active	F10
Move between toolbars	Shift+Ctrl+Tab
Advanced Find	F3
Find items (while main Outlook window is active)	Ctrl+Shift+F F4
Find text (while an item is open)	F4
Find next	Shift+F4
Refresh	F5
Check spelling	F7
Display Favorites menu (while main Outlook window is active)	Alt+O
Display format menu (while an item is open)	Alt+O
Close print preview	Alt+C
Accept (within item)	Alt+C
Decline	Alt+D

continues

PART

IX

APP

G

TABLE G.5 CONTINUED

Task	Shortcut
Forward	Ctrl+F
Check for new mail	Ctrl+M F5
Send, post, or invite all (not Word)	Ctrl+Enter
Close menu and submenu (if open)	Alt
Close menu and submenu	Esc
Delete highlighted item in information	Del viewer

Note

The key combination Alt + S will send the mail item using the default account if you are using the Internet Mail Only service option.

Table G.6 lists keyboard shortcuts for moving around in a dialog box. These shortcuts act on the selected control or group within a dialog box. You can select a control by holding down Alt while pressing the underlined character in the control's name.

TABLE G.6 DIALOG BOX SHORTCUTS

Task	Shortcut
Switch to the next tab stop	Ctrl+Tab
Switch to the previous tab stop	Ctrl+Shift+Tab
Move to next option or option group	Tab
Move to previous option or option group	Shift+Tab
Move to next item in drop-down list	DownArrow
Move to previous item in drop-down list	UpArrow
Move to first item in drop-down list	Home
Move to last item in drop-down list	End
Perform action assigned to button	Spacebar
Select or clear check box	Spacebar
Open a drop-down list	Alt+DownArrow
Close a drop-down list	Alt+UpArrow or Esc

Table G.7 lists keyboard shortcuts you can use while working in a text box. The shortcuts are available when you've selected a text box in a form or dialog box. Moving refers to the position of the insertion point within the text box.

TABLE G.7   WEB SHORTCUTS FOR OUTLOOK ITEMS

Task	Shortcut
Move to beginning of text box	Home
Move to end of text box	End
Move one character to left	LeftArrow
Move one character to right	RightArrow
Select from insertion point to beginning	Shift+Home
Select from insertion point to end	Shift+End
Select or unselect one character to left	Shift+LeftArrow
Select or unselect one character to right	Shift+RightArrow
Select or unselect one word to left	Ctrl+Shift+LeftArrow
Select or unselect one word to right	Ctrl+Shift+RightArrow

Table G.8 lists keyboard shortcuts for working with print preview.

TABLE G.8   PRINT PREVIEW SHORTCUTS

Task	Shortcut
Open print preview	Ctrl+F2
Print from print preview	Alt+P
Print preview page setup	Alt+S, then Alt+U
Zoom	Alt+Z
Display next page	PageDown
Display previous page	PageUp
Display first page	Ctrl+UpArrow or Home
Display last page	Ctrl+DownArrow or End

Table G.9 lists keyboard shortcuts for working with windows.

TABLE G.9 WINDOW SHORTCUTS	
Task	**Shortcut**
Switch to next program	Alt+Tab
Switch to previous program	Alt+Shift+Tab
Move to next window	Alt+Shift+Esc
Display Start menu	Ctrl+Esc
End active program	Ctrl+Shift+Delete
Move to next pane	F6
Move to previous pane	Shift+F6
Move to next or previous Outlook window	Shift+Ctrl+F6
Close Outlook window	Alt+F4

Table G.10 lists keyboard shortcuts for working in the Card view of a contact (or other) item. Select a Card view of an Outlook item to use these shortcuts.

TABLE G.10 CARD VIEW SHORTCUTS	
Task	**Shortcut**
Select next card	DownArrow
Select previous card	UpArrow
Select first card	Home
Select last card	End
Select first card on current page	PageUp
Select first card on next page	PageDown
Select closest card in next column	RightArrow
Select closest card in previous column	LeftArrow
Select or unselect active card	Ctrl+Spacebar
Extend selection to next card	Ctrl+Shift+DownArrow
Extend selection to previous card	Ctrl+Shift+UpArrow
Extend selection to next card and unselect previous cards	Shift+DownArrow
Extend selection to previous card and unselect subsequent cards	Shift+UpArrow

Task	Shortcut
Extend selection to last card	Shift+End
Extend selection to first card	Shift+Home
Extend selection to last card on previous page	Shift+PageUp
Extend selection to first card on next page	Shift+PageDown

Table G.11 lists keyboard shortcuts for moving between cards. These shortcuts move to another card without changing which card is selected. Select a card before using these shortcuts.

TABLE G.11   WEB SHORTCUTS FOR OUTLOOK ITEMS

Task	Shortcut
Move to next card	Ctrl+DownArrow
Move to previous card	Ctrl+UpArrow
Move to first card	Ctrl+Home
Move to last card	Ctrl+End
Move to first card on previous page	Ctrl+PageUp
Move to first card next page	Ctrl+PageDown
Move to closest card in previous column	Ctrl+LeftArrow
Move to closest card in next column	Ctrl+RightArrow
Move to field in active card	F2
Move to specific card	Type one or more characters of the name by which cards are sorted

Table G.12 lists keyboard shortcuts for moving between fields in a selected card.

TABLE G.12   SHORTCUTS FOR MOVING BETWEEN FIELDS IN A CARD

Task	Shortcut
Select first or next field in a card	Tab or Enter
Select previous field in a card	Shift+Tab
Add line to multiline field	Enter
Display insertion point in active field	F2

Table G.13 lists general keyboard shortcuts for working with day/week/month views of Calendar items.

TABLE G.13 GENERAL SHORTCUTS FOR CALENDAR ITEMS

Task	Shortcut
View 1–10 days (0 for 10 days)	Alt+<n>
Switch to weeks	Alt+-
Switch to months	Alt+=
Move between Calendar, TaskPad, and folder list	Ctrl+Tab or F6
Select next appointment	Tab
Select previous appointment	Shift+Tab
Go to next day	RightArrow
Go to previous day	LeftArrow
Move selected appointment to next day	Alt+RightArrow
Move selected appointment to previous day	Alt+LeftArrow
Go to same day in next week in daily and Work Week views	Alt+DownArrow
Go to same day in previous week in daily and Work Week views	Alt+UpArrow
Move selected item to same day in next week in monthly view	Alt+DownArrow
Move selected into to same day in previous week in monthly view	Alt+UpArrow
Move from item to item	Tab

Table G.14 lists keyboard shortcuts for working in the Day view.

TABLE G.14 DAY VIEW SHORTCUTS

Task	Shortcut
Select beginning of work day	Home
Select end of work day	End
Select previous block of time	UpArrow
Select next block of time	DownArrow
Select block of time at top of screen	PageUp
Select block of time at bottom of screen	PageDown
Extend selected time	Shift+UpArrow

Task	Shortcut
Reduce selected time	Shift+DownArrow
Move selected appointment back	Alt+UpArrow
Move selected appointment forward	Alt+DownArrow
Move start of selected appointment	Alt+Shift+UpArrow
Move end of selected appointment	Alt+Shift+DownArrow

Table G.15 lists keyboard shortcuts for working in a table.

TABLE G.15 TABLE SHORTCUTS

Task	Shortcut
Select next item	DownArrow
Select previous item	UpArrow
Go to next item without changing selection	Ctrl+DownArrow
Go to previous item with changing selection	Ctrl+UpArrow
Go to first item	Home
Go to last item	End
Go to item at bottom of screen	PageDown
Go to item at top of screen	PageUp
Extend select item(s) by one	Shift+UpArrow
Reduce selected item(s) by one	Shift+DownArrow
Open item	Enter
Select all items	Ctrl+A

Table G.16 lists keyboard shortcuts for working with groups in a table.

TABLE G.16 SHORTCUTS FOR GROUPS IN A TABLE

Task	Shortcut
Expand group	Enter or RightArrow
Collapse group	Enter or LeftArrow
Select previous group	UpArrow
Select next group	DownArrow
Select first group	Home
Select last group	End
Select first item in expanded group	RightArrow

Table G.17 lists keyboard shortcuts for moving around in a timeline when an item is selected.

TABLE G.17	TIMELINE SHORTCUTS WITH ITEM SELECTED
Task	**Shortcut**
Select previous item	LeftArrow
Select next item	RightArrow
Select adjacent previous items	Shift+LeftArrow
Select adjacent subsequent items	Shift+RightArrow
Select non-adjacent previous items	Ctrl+LeftArrow+Spacebar
Select non-adjacent subsequent items	Ctrl+RightArrow+Spacebar
Open selected item	Enter
Display items one screen above	PageUp
Display items one screen below	PageDown
Select first item	Home
Select last item	End
Display first item without selecting	Ctrl+Home
Display last item without selecting	Ctrl+End

Table G.18 lists keyboard shortcuts for moving around in a timeline when a group is selected

TABLE G.18	TIMELINE SHORTCUTS WITH GROUP SELECTED
Task	**Shortcut**
Expand group	Enter or RightArrow
Collapse group	Enter or LeftArrow
Select previous group	UpArrow
Select next group	DownArrow
Select first group	Home
Select last group	End
Select first onscreen item in expanded group	RightArrow
Move back one increment of time	LeftArrow
Move forward one increment of time	RightArrow

Task	Shortcut
Switch from upper to lower time scale	Tab
Switch from lower to upper time scale	Shift+Tab
Select first onscreen item or first group (with lower time scale selected)	Tab

Table G.19 lists keyboard shortcuts for the Date Navigator.

TABLE G.19   DATE NAVIGATOR SHORTCUTS

Task	Shortcut
Go to first day of current week	Alt+Home
Go to last day of current week	Alt+End
Go to same day in previous week	Alt+UpArrow
Go to same day in next week	Alt+DownArrow
Go to first day of current month	Alt+PageUp
Go to last day of current month	Alt+PageDown

Table G.20 lists keyboard shortcuts for moving around in command bars.

TABLE G.20   COMMAND BAR SHORTCUTS

Task	Shortcut
Activate menu bar	F10
Select next toolbar	Ctrl+Tab
Select previous toolbar	Ctrl+Shift+Tab
Select next button or menu	Tab
Select previous button or menu	Shift+Tab
Open selected menu	Enter
Perform action of selected button	Enter
Enter text in selected text box	Enter
Enter text in QuickFind box	F11
Select option from drop-down list or menu	UpArrow or DownArrow, then Enter

Table G.21 lists keyboard shortcuts for the File Open and Insert File dialog boxes.

TABLE G.21 FILE OPEN AND INSERT FILE SHORTCUTS	
Task	**Shortcut**
Return to previously viewed folder	Alt+1
Up one folder level	Alt+2
Search the Web	Alt+3
Delete current selection	Alt+4
Create new folder	Alt+5
Change view	Alt+6
Open Tools menu	Alt+7

Table G.22 lists keyboard shortcuts for the Office Assistant.

TABLE G.22 SHORTCUTS FOR THE OFFICE ASSISTANT	
Task	**Shortcut**
Activate the Office Assistant balloon	Alt+F6
Open Macro Selector	Alt+F8
Open VBA Development Environment	Alt+F11
Select Help topic <n>	Alt+<n>
See more Help topics	Alt+DownArrow
See previous Help topics	Alt+UpArrow
Close Office Assistant message	Esc
Get Help from Office Assistant	F1
Display next tip	Alt+N
Display previous tip	Alt+B
Close tips	Esc

Outlook Fields and Equivalent Properties

by Helen Feddema

TABLE H.1 OUTLOOK FIELDS AND EQUIVALENT PROPERTIES

Name of Field in Outlook Field Chooser	Name of Equivalent Outlook Object Model Property
% Complete	PercentComplete
Account	Account
Actual Work	ActualWork
Address Selected	N/A
Address Selector	N/A
All Day Event	AllDayEvent
Anniversary	Anniversary
Assigned	DelegationState
Assistant's Name	AssistantName
Assistant's Phone	AssistantTelephoneNumber
Attachment	Attachments
Bcc	BCC
Billing Information	BillingInformation
Birthday	Birthday
Business Address	BusinessAddress
Business Address City	BusinessAddressCity
Business Address Country	BusinessAddressCountry
Business Address PO Box	BusinessAddressPostOfficeBox
Business Address Postal Code	BusinessAddressPostalCode
Business Address State	BusinessAddressState
Business Address Street	BusinessAddressStreet
Business Fax	BusinessFaxNumber
Business Home Page	BusinessHomePage
Business Phone	BusinessTelephoneNumber
Business Phone 2	Business2TelephoneNumber
Callback	CallbackTelephoneNumber
Car Phone	CarTelephoneNumber
Categories	Categories
Cc	CC
Changed By	N/A
Children	Children

Name of Field in Outlook Field Chooser	Name of Equivalent Outlook Object Model Property
City	HomeAddressCity
Color	Color
Company	Companies
Company	CompanyName
Company Main Phone	CompanyMainTelephoneNumber
Complete	Complete
Computer Network Name	ComputerNetworkName
Contact	FormDescription.ContactName
Contacts	Links
Content	Body
Conversation	ConversationTopic
Country	HomeAddressCountry
Created	CreationTime
Customer ID	CustomerID
Date Completed	DateCompleted
Defer until	DeferredDeliveryTime
Department	Department
Distribution List Name	DLName
Do Not AutoArchive	NoAging
Download State	N/A
Due By	FlagDueBy
Due Date	DueDate
Duration	Duration
E-mail	Email1Address
E-mail 2	Email2Address
E-mail 3	Email3Address
E-mail Selected	N/A
E-mail Selector	N/A
End	End
Entry Type	Type
Expires	ExpiryTime

continues

TABLE H.1 CONTINUED

Name of Field in Outlook Field Chooser	Name of Equivalent Outlook Object Model Property
File As	FileAs
First Name	FirstName
Flag Status	FlagStatus
Follow-up Flag	FlagRequest
From	SentOnBehalfOfName
FTP Site	FTPSite
Full Name	FullName
Gender	Gender
Government ID Number	GovernmentIDNumber
Have Replies Sent To	ReplyRecipientNames
Hobbies	Hobby
Home Address	HomeAddress
Home Address City	HomeAddressCity
Home Address Country	HomeAddressCountry
Home Address PO Box	HomeAddressPostOfficeBox
Home Address Postal Code	HomeAddressPostalCode
Home Address State	HomeAddressState
Home Address Street	HomeAddressStreet
Home Fax	HomeFaxNumber
Home Phone	HomeTelephoneNumber
Home Phone 2	Home2TelephoneNumber
Icon	FormDescription.Icon
Importance	Importance
In Folder	Parent
Initials	Initials
Internet Free Busy Address	InternetFreeBusyAddress
ISDN	ISDNNumber
Job Title	JobTitle
Journal	Journal
Junk E-Mail Type	N/A
Language	Language

Name of Field in Outlook Field Chooser	Name of Equivalent Outlook Object Model Property
Last Name	LastName
Last Saved Time	N/A
Location	Location
Mailing Address	MailingAddress
Mailing Address Indicator	N/A
Manager's Name	ManagerName
Meeting Status	MeetingStatus
Message	Body
Message Class	MessageClass
Message Flag	FlagStatus
Middle Name	MiddleName
Mileage	Mileage
Mobile Phone	MobileTelephoneNumber
Modified	LastModificationTime
Nickname	NickName
Notes	Body
Office Location	OfficeLocation
Optional Attendees	OptionalAttendees
Organizational ID Number	OrganizationalIDNumber
Organizer	Organizer
Other Address	OtherAddress
Other Address City	OtherAddressCity
Other Address Country	OtherAddressCountry
Other Address PO Box	OtherAddressPostOfficeBox
Other Address Postal Code	OtherAddressPostalCode
Other Address State	OtherAddressState
Other Address Street	OtherAddressStreet
Other Fax	OtherFaxNumber
Other Phone	OtherTelephoneNumber
Outlook Internal Version	OutlookInternalVersion
Outlook Version	OutlookVersion

continues

TABLE H.1   CONTINUED

Name of Field in Outlook Field Chooser	Name of Equivalent Outlook Object Model Property
Owner	Owner
Pager	PagerNumber
Personal Home Page	PersonalHomePage
Phone *n* Selected	N/A
Phone *n* Selector	N/A
PO Box	HomeAddressPostOfficeBox
Primary Phone	PrimaryTelephoneNumber
Priority	Importance
Private	Sensitivity
Profession	Profession
Radio Phone	RadioTelephoneNumber
Read	UnRead
Received	ReceivedTime
Recurrence	RecurrencePattern.RecurrenceType
Recurrence Pattern	N/A
Recurrence Range End	RecurrencePattern.PatternEndDate
Recurrence Range Start	RecurrencePattern.PatternStartDate
Recurring	IsRecurring
Referred By	ReferredBy
Remind Beforehand	ReminderMinutesBeforeStart
Reminder	ReminderSet
Reminder Override Default	ReminderOverrideDefault
Reminder Sound	ReminderPlaySound
Reminder Sound File	ReminderSoundFile
Reminder Time	ReminderTime
Reminder Topic	N/A
Remote Status	RemoteStatus
RequestStatus	N/A
Requested By	N/A
Required Attendess	RequiredAttendees
Resources	Resources

Name of Field in Outlook Field Chooser	Name of Equivalent Outlook Object Model Property
Response Requested	ResponseRequested
Retrieval Time	N/A
Role	Role
Schedule+ Priority	SchedulePlusPriority
Send Plain Text Only	N/A
Sensitivity	Sensitivity
Sent	SentOn
Show Time As	BusyStatus
Size	Size
Spouse	Spouse
Start	Start
Start Date	StartDate
State	HomeAddressState
Status	Status
Street Address	HomeAddressStreet
Subject	Subject
Suffix	Suffix
Team Task	TeamTask
Telex	TelexNumber
Title	Title
To	To
Total Work	TotalWork
Tracking Status	TrackingStatus
TTY/TTDD Phone	TTYTDDTelephoneNumber
User Field 1	User1
User Field 2	User2
User Field 3	User3
User Field 4	User4
Web Page	WebPage
ZIP/Postal Code	HomeAddressPostalCode

PART

IX

APP

H

Glossary

This glossary lists terms and abbreviations you may come across while you're working with Outlook. It doesn't provide broad definitions that necessarily apply in other environments.

Note

The italicized words and phrases within each definition are defined elsewhere within this glossary.

Account   See *User Account*.

Activity   An appointment, event, or meeting. Activities can be one-time or recurring.

Add-In   A software component available from Microsoft that can be added into Outlook to provide extra functionality.

Add-On   A software component available from a third-party that can be added to Outlook to provide extra functionality.

Address Book   A folder that contains names of contacts, together with their addresses and other information.

Administrator   The person who controls a workgroup, LAN, or service (such as Exchange Server).

Age   The length of time since an Outlook item was created or modified.

America Online (AOL)   An organization that offers information and communication facilities to computer users.

American Standard Code for Information Interchange (ASCII)   A code that represents letters, numbers, punctuation marks, and certain other characters by numeric values. Standard ASCII code provides for 128 characters; extended ASCII code provides for 256 characters.

AOL   See *America Online*.

API   See *Applications Programming Interface*.

Applications Programming Interface (API)   A set of functions that may be used by programs running under Windows.

Appointment   A period blocked for a specific purpose in an Outlook user's calendar.

Archive   A file containing Outlook items that are older than a specific age. When Outlook archives items, it moves those items from current folders to an archive folder.

ASCII   See *American Standard Code for Information Interchange*.

ATAPI   See *AT Attachment Protocol Interface*.

AT Attachment Protocol Interface (ATAPI)   The protocol used by AT (and later) computers to communicate with CD-ROM and tape drives. Don't confuse the ATAPI protocol with the TAP and TAPI protocols. See *TAP* and *TAPI*.

Attachment   A file or object that is linked to, or contained in, an Outlook item. Files and objects may be attached to messages, contacts, appointments, tasks, and so on.

AutoAddress   Outlook's capability to separate an address into street, city, state, postal code, and country fields.

AutoArchive   Outlook's capability of moving items of a specific age from the Personal Folders file into an archive file.

AutoCreate   Outlook's capability to automatically convert an item of one type into an item of another type.

AutoDate   Outlook's capability to convert a description of a date into a specific calendar date.

AutoJournal   Outlook's capability to automatically create journal items that record activities involving specific contacts and access to Office files.

AutoName   Outlook's capability to separate a person's full name into first name, middle name, and last name fields.

AutoName Check   Outlook's capability to verify that names entered into To, Cc, and Bcc boxes exist in an Address Book.

AutoPreview   Outlook's capability to display the first three lines of a message without the user having to open the message.

AutoSave   To automatically save data to a file at predetermined intervals.

Balloon   The message box used by the Office Assistant to display information.

Banner   The bar across the top of an Information viewer. The banner contains the name of the folder that contains the items displayed in the viewer.

BASIC   See *Beginners All-Purpose Symbolic Instruction Code.*

Basic Input/Output System (BIOS)   A set of routines, usually in ROM, that support transfer of information between such computer hardware components as the processor, keyboard, disks, memory, and monitor.

BCC   See *Blind Carbon Copy.*

Beginners All-Purpose Symbolic Instruction Code (BASIC)   A high-level programming language initially developed as a means to teach programming. It has subsequently been developed into such programming languages as Visual Basic, Visual Basic for Applications (VBA), and Visual Basic Script (VBS).

BIOS   See *Basic Input/Output System.*

Blind Carbon Copy (BCC)   A copy of a message that is sent without the recipient's name appearing on the copies other people receive. The word "carbon" comes from the carbon paper that was used to make copies on a typewriter.

Boolean Search A database search that uses Boolean operators (usually AND and OR) to combine words or phrases to search for. Searching for "cat AND dog" finds items that contain both "cat" and "dog"; searching for "cat OR dog" finds items that contain either "cat" or "dog," or both words.

Branch The Windows registry has a tree-like structure. Sections of the structure are referred to as branches.

Browser An application that's used to find information on the World Wide Web.

Calendar A component of Outlook in which users plan their activities. See *Activity*. Also, the Outlook Information viewer that displays activities. Outlook saves Calendar items in the Calendar folder.

Carbon Copy (CC) The name of a person to whom an e-mail message is copied. The CC names are included on the messages sent to all recipients. The word "carbon" comes from the carbon paper that was used to make copies on a typewriter.

Card View One of the formats in which Outlook displays or prints Contact information. This view in similar to how information about people appears on a conventional index card.

Category An identifier for an Outlook item. One or more categories may be assigned to each item.

CC See *Carbon Copy*.

Certificate A digital identification used to send secure messages by way of the Internet. See *Key*.

Client A computer, or software running on that computer, that accesses data or services on another computer.

Client/Server A LAN configuration in which one or more computers (servers) provide services to users' computers (clients).

Command Bar A menu bar or toolbar. In Outlook 2000 and other Office 2000 applications, the menu bar is really just a special toolbar.

CompuServe An organization that offers information and communication facilities to computer users. Outlook can send and receive CompuServe e-mail messages.

Contact A person or organization. Outlook maintains a list of contacts in the Contacts folder. Each contact item contains information about one contact.

Contact List The list of contacts maintained by Outlook.

Contacts The Outlook Information viewer that displays information about contacts. Items displayed in this Information viewer are stored in the Contacts folder.

Context Menu A menu displayed when you right-click an object in a window. You can use a context menu to examine and change an item. One of the most useful items in context menus is Properties, which you can use to see and change an object's properties. A context menu is sometimes known as a Shortcut Menu.

Control   An object on a form, used to obtain user input and to display output. Controls available in Outlook are CheckBox, ComboBox, CommandButton, Frame, Image, Label, ListBox, MultiPage, OptionButton, ScrollBar, SpinButton, TabStrip, Textbox, and ToggleButton.

Control Panel   A window in Windows 95 and Windows NT that provides access to the fundamental Window components. To access the Control Panel, choose **Start** in the Windows Taskbar, choose **Settings** in the **Start** menu, and choose **Control Panel**.

Conversation   A sequence of related messages, sometimes known as a thread.

Corporate/Workgroup E-mail Service (C/W)   An Outlook installation that includes capabilities to use various messaging systems, in addition to the Internet, for e-mail, and also provides personal information management capabilities. This e-mail service makes Outlook MAPI-compatible. Compare with *Internet Only E-mail Service*.

Data Link   See *Timex Data Link*.

Date Navigator   The section of the Calendar Information viewer that shows one or more complete months. You can use the Date Navigator to move rapidly to specific dates.

Decrypt   To restore encrypted information to its original intelligible form. See *Encryption*.

Deleted Items   The folder that contains items that have been deleted from other Outlook folders.

Dial-Up Networking (DUN)   Connecting to a network by way of a dialed connection over telephone lines.

Dialog Box   A window displayed by an operating system or application that solicits a response from the user.

Digital Signature   See *Certificate*.

Distribution List   A list of people to whom a message is to be sent.

Directory   A means of locating e-mail addresses. See *Lightweight Directory Access Protocol*. The word *directory* previously referred to a container for files on a disk; the word *folder* is now used for that purpose.

DLL   See *Dynamic-link Library*.

DNS   See *Domain Name Service*.

Document   Something created in an Office application, such as a table created in Access, text created in Word, a workbook created in Excel, or a presentation created in PowerPoint.

Domain   A group of computers on a Windows NT network that shares a directory database.

Domain Name Service (DNS)   A service provided by a DNS server that translates host names into their corresponding IP addresses.

Draft   A version of a message that has been prepared to be sent, but may require revision. Outlook saves draft messages in the Drafts folder.

Drafts   An Outlook folder in which drafts of messages are saved.

Drag and Drop   The capability to select an object created in one Office application and use the mouse to drag that object into another application. Drag and drop can also be used to create one type of Outlook item from another, such as creating a Task item from a Message item (known as *AutoCreate*).

DTMF   See *Dual Tone Multiple-Frequency*.

Dual Tone Multiple-Frequency (DTMF)   An international signaling standard for telephone digits. When you press a button on your telephone, a dual tone is transmitted. The same dual tone is generated when you use your modem to place a call. Numeric pagers decode DTMF signals to display numbers.

DUN   See *Dial-up Networking*.

Dynamic-link Library (DLL)   An operating system capability that allows programs to dynamically exchange and share information and commands.

E-mail   A message sent from one computer user to one or more other users. Most messages consist only of text, but messages may include any type of information that can be created on a computer. Users who interchange e-mail messages may use the same computer, may be part of a workgroup, may be interconnected by way of a *LAN* or *WAN*, or may use a messaging service provider.

Embedded Object   An object included within another object. The included data consists of the object's native data and presentation data.

Encryption   A means of limiting access to data by converting the data into apparently meaningless form. Only people who have the key to the encryption can reverse the process (decryption) to make the data meaningful.

Event   In general, something that happens and is recognized by the computer so an appropriate action can be taken. In Outlook, an event is an activity that occupies one or more days but does not require the user to block time.

Exchange Client   The e-mail client in Windows 95 and Windows NT. Provides messaging capabilities similar to those in Outlook, but does not contain scheduling capabilities. Microsoft now refers to Exchange Client as Windows Messaging.

Exchange Server   An e-mail and collaboration server that runs under Windows NT Server. The Exchange Server information service can be added to a profile so Outlook can use the facilities of Exchange Server.

Fax   An abbreviation of "facsimile." A method of transmitting text and graphics over telephone lines in digital form. Outlook can send and receive fax messages if appropriate *add-ins* or *add-ons* are installed.

Fax Viewer A facility that can display outgoing fax messages.

Favorites A folder that contains shortcuts to items, documents, folders, and Uniform Resource Locators (URLs).

Field An area of memory that contains a specific type of information. Also, a space on a form that displays a specific type of information or in which a user can provide information. Outlook uses a separate field for each type of information it deals with; fields are used for such information as First Name, Middle Name, Last Name, Street Address, City, and so on.

Field Chooser A list of fields that can be used to add fields to a form.

Field Type The type of data a field can contain. Each Outlook field can contain one of the following types of data: combination, currency, date/time, duration, formula, integer, keywords, number, percent, text, and yes/no.

File The basic unit of storage on such media as disks and tape.

File Transfer Protocol (FTP) A common method of sending files from one computer to another by way of the Internet.

Filter An Outlook facility used to access information that satisfies certain specified criteria. The specified criteria refers to contents of fields. Filters can be used to find items that contain certain text in text fields, certain dates (or ranges of dates) in date fields, and certain values (or ranges of values) in numeric fields.

Firewall An application that protects a LAN from unauthorized outside access.

Flag An indication in a message that some follow-up activity is necessary. Messages are indicated as flagged by the flag symbol in the Flag Status column of the message list.

Folder A container for information. Outlook uses a file named Personal Folders as a container for folders. This file contains several folders, one for each type of item. Each folder contains either subfolders or items of a specific type. Users can augment the initial folder structure by adding folders and a hierarchy of subfolders.

Form A window used to display and collect information. Outlook provides forms for such purposes as creating and viewing messages, appointments, and contact information. Some of these forms can be modified to suit custom needs. You can create custom forms.

Forward To send a received message to someone else.

FTP See *File Transfer Protocol*.

Function A unit of program code that can be accessed from other code, performs some operation, and returns a value to the code from which it was accessed.

GAL See *Global Address List*.

Gateway A capability to transmit data from one information system to another. For example, a gateway allows exchange of messages between an Internet message server and the CompuServe messaging system.

Global Address List (GAL)   A list of e-mail and other addresses maintained on a mail server.

GMT   See *Greenwich Mean Time*.

Greenwich Mean Time (GMT)   The current time as it is in Greenwich (London, England). Now known as *Universal Coordinated Time*.

Group   To separate items displayed in a list or timeline into sections, each of which contain items with a common characteristic. For example, a list of contacts can be grouped by category, company, or other characteristics.

HTML   See *Hypertext Markup Language*.

HTTP   See *Hypertext Transport Protocol*.

Hypertext   Text that contains links to other information in the same document or to information in other documents.

Hypertext Markup Language (HTML)   A language used to create hypertext documents for use on the World Wide Web. Outlook includes the ability to send and receive messages created in HTML format. HTML messages can include graphically rich text including images and links. These messages can be read by users who have any HTML-compliant client.

Hypertext Transport Protocol (HTTP)   The protocol used for sending hypertext documents on the Internet.

iCalendar   A format for sending and receiving free/busy information by way of the Internet. Outlook supports iCalendar.

IMAP4   See *Internet Message Access Protocol 4*.

IMO   See *Internet Only E-mail Service*.

Importance   In Outlook and other messaging systems, messages are marked to have high, normal, or low importance.

Inbox   The Outlook Information viewer that displays messages received but not moved to another folder. Items displayed in this Information viewer are stored in the Inbox folder.

Inf   See *Information File*.

Information File (Inf)   A file that defines how an application is to be installed. For example, the Outlbar.inf file defines the default installation of the Outlook Bar.

Information Store   See *Store*.

Information Viewer   The section of an Outlook window that displays a specific type of item. Each Information viewer displays items from a specific folder or subfolder.

Integrated Services Digital Network (ISDN)   A communications system by which many types of information can be transmitted at high speed over telephone lines.

IntelliSense   The capability of the Office Assistant to offer assistance with a user's current task.

Internet   A worldwide, interconnected system of computers that provides information and communication services.

Internet Explorer   An Internet browser available from Microsoft.

Internet Message Access Protocol 4 (IMAP4)   An industry standard protocol used to access remote computers by way of a dial-up connection. This protocol offers more capabilities than the Point-to-Point Protocol and the Serial Line Internet Protocol. Some Internet service providers use this protocol. See *Point-to-Point Protocol (PPP)* and *Serial Line Internet Protocol (SLIP)*. Outlook includes support for this protocol.

Internet Protocol (IP)   The protocol that controls message routing on the Internet.

Internet Read Receipt   An Internet read receipt is created when a recipient reads a message. Outlook supports the Internet read-receipt standard.

Internet Service Provider (ISP)   An organization that provides access to the Internet.

Internet Only E-mail Service   An installation of Outlook that provides Internet and intranet e-mail and personal information management capabilities. Also known as Internet Mail Only (IMO).

Intranet   An Internet-like environment accessible only within an organization.

IP   See *Internet Protocol*.

ISDN   See *Integrated Services Digital Network*.

ISP   See *Internet Service Provider*.

Item   A unit of information in Outlook. E-mail messages, appointments, contacts, tasks, journal entries, and notes are all items.

Journal   The Outlook facility for creating Journal items that automatically record such activities as working with Office files, and sending and receiving e-mail messages. Users can manually record other activities as Journal entry items. Also the Outlook Information viewer that displays Journal items. Items displayed in this Information viewer are stored in the Journal folder.

Key   A digital code used to authenticate and encrypt e-mail messages. Each person who sends a message has access to the recipients' public keys. In order to authenticate a message or decrypt it, recipients use their private keys. A key is also known as a *certificate*.

Also a part of the Windows registry structure that contains information about computer hardware or software settings.

LAN   See *Local Area Network*.

LDAP   See *Lightweight Directory Access Protocol*.

Legacy   Something passed on from the old days. Legacy applications and files are those designed for old computers, but are still used by people with modern computing systems.

Lightweight Directory Access Protocol (LDAP)   A simplified (lightweight) version of the Directory Access Protocol. LDAP is a directory service used by Outlook as well as other e-mail clients to access directories of e-mail addresses. This protocol can be used to find users on the Internet or on a corporate intranet.

Linked Object   An object included within another object. The included data consists of the object's presentation data and a reference to its native data.

Local Access Phone Number   A phone number, usually within your local calling area, that provides free or low-cost access to an Internet service provider.

Local Area Network (LAN)   A computer network limited to a small area, such as one building.

Location   The place where an appointment, event, or meeting is to occur.

Log   A record of specific types of events. For example, Outlook can create an event log that marks the completion of each CompuServe e-mail session.

Mail Client   A computer, or the software running on a computer, that can receive e-mail from, and send e-mail to, a mail server.

Mail Server   A computer, or the software running on a computer, that provides mail services to mail clients. These services include storing messages sent by mail clients until the recipient mail clients retrieve those messages.

Mailbox   The space on a mail server dedicated to storing messages intended for a specific mail user.

Mailing List   See *Distribution List*.

MAPI   See *Messaging Application Programming Interface*.

Master Category List   A list of categories from which a user can choose to assign one or more categories for each item.

Meeting   In Outlook, a period blocked by two or more users for the purpose of a face-to-face or other kind of meeting.

Menu Bar   The row immediately under the title bar in a window that contains menu names. The items in each menu are displayed by choosing the menu name. A Menu bar is a component of *Command Bars*.

Message   Any piece of information sent from one person to one or more other people. A message usually, but not necessarily, originates and is received by a computer. E-mail, voice-mail, and fax are the principal methods of sending messages. Messages may be received by other devices, such as pagers.

Message Class   A field within an Outlook item that specifies the form to be used when the item is displayed.

Message Status   An indication, marked by a flag, of something special about a message.

Messaging   The practice of communicating by means of electronic messages.

Messaging Application Programming Interface (MAPI)   A set of API functions and an OLE interface that Outlook and other messaging clients use to interface with message service providers.

Method   An action defined within an object. Each of Outlook's objects contains certain methods.

MHTML   See *Multilingual Hypertext Markup Language*.

Microsoft Exchange   See Exchange Client and Exchange Server.

Microsoft Fax   A set of API functions Outlook and other Windows applications can use to send and receive fax messages in C/W Outlook.

Microsoft Mail   A set of API functions Outlook and other Windows applications can use to send and receive e-mail messages within a workgroup. Only available in C/W Outlook.

Microsoft Network   A system that offers information and communication facilities to computer users. Outlook can send and receive Microsoft Network e-mail.

Microsoft Outlook   A desktop information manager that includes comprehensive messaging, scheduling, and information management facilities.

Microsoft Outlook Express   An application, provided with Internet Explorer, that provides e-mail facilities and allows access to newsgroups.

Microsoft Outlook Web Access   A Web mail client that can access Exchange Server mailboxes and Public Folders.

Microsoft Project   An application used to plan, control, and track the progress of projects.

Microsoft Team Manager   An application used to allocate tasks among team members and to coordinate the work of those members.

Microsoft Word   A word processor that can be chosen as Outlook's e-mail editor.

MIME   See *Multipurpose Internet Mail Extensions*.

Modem   A device that converts digital information into analog (sound) suitable for transmission over telephone lines, and also converts incoming analog (sound) information into digital form.

Multipurpose Internet Mail Extensions (MIME)   A protocol for e-mail messages that allows those messages to include attachments such as pictures and computer code. See *S/MIME*.

My Computer   An icon on the Windows desktop that provides access to folders on any disk on an Outlook user's computer and to disks that other network users have made available for sharing.

My Documents   A folder that contains a list of documents recently created in, or modified by, an Office or Office-compatible application running under Windows 98. Also see *Personal*.

Native Data   One of the two types of data associated with an OLE object (the other type is Presentation Data). Native data consists of all the data needed by an application to edit the object. See *Presentation Data*.

Navigator   An Internet browser available from Netscape.

Net Folder   A folder that can be shared by way of the Internet, an intranet, or other messaging system.

NetBEUI   See *NetBIOS Extended User Interface*.

NetBIOS   See *Network Basic Input/Output System*.

NetBIOS Extended User Interface   Provides data transport services for communication between computers.

NetMeeting   A Microsoft application that supports communications sessions between two or more Internet users. Also a name used for that communication. During a NetMeeting, users can exchange text, sound, graphics, and video.

Network   Interconnected computers. In a client/server network, a server provides services to clients (individual users). In a peer-to-peer network, any computer can act as a client or a server.

Network Basic Input/Output System (NetBIOS)   Establishes communication between computers in a network

Network Interface Card (NIC)   An electronic assembly that connects a computer to a network. Each computer must have a network interface card to be part of a network.

Network News Transport Protocol (NNTP)   A protocol used to post, distribute, and retrieve messages on the Internet or corporate intranets. Outlook includes an Internet Newsreader that's shared with Internet Explorer.

News Server   A computer on which newsgroup messages are stored. Many news servers are open for anyone to access, but some are private and allow access only to people who are registered and can provide a registered username and password.

Newsgroup   A collection of messages posted on a news server. People who access a newsgroup can access the messages and can post their own messages. All the newsgroups available on the Internet are collectively known as Usenet. See *News Server*.

NIC   See *Network Interface Card*.

NNTP   See *Network News Transport Protocol*.

No E-mail   An installation of Outlook that provides personal information management capabilities, but no capability to send and receive e-mail.

Node   A computer, printer, or other device connected to a network.

Note   A type of Outlook item. A note consists of data that will be subsequently used for any other purpose.

Notes   The Outlook Information viewer that displays notes. Items displayed in this Information viewer are stored in the Notes folder.

Object   An entity that may contain data, and have properties and methods. OLE associates presentation data and native data with objects. Outlook, and other Office applications, contain a hierarchical structure of objects.

Object Linking and Embedding (OLE)   The technology by which objects may be embedded into, or linked to, other objects. Outlook uses OLE to incorporate various kinds of objects into messages and other items.

Office Assistant   The animated icon that may be displayed in an Outlook window to provide help with whatever task a user is attempting.

Offline Store File (OST)   A file on a user's computer that contains a copy of information in that user's Exchange store.

Off Hook   The condition in which a telephone or modem is connected to a telephone line.

On Hook   The condition in which a telephone or modem is not connected to a telephone line.

Organize   In Outlook, the capability to move items into specific folders according to the content of those items.

OST   See *Offline Store File*.

Out of Office Assistant   A facility within Exchange Server that automatically answers or forwards messages. This facility is only available in Outlook when the current profile includes the Exchange Server information service and a network connection to Exchange Server is available.

Outbox   The Outlook Information viewer that displays messages created but not sent. Items displayed in this Information viewer are stored in the Outbox folder.

Outlook   See *Microsoft Outlook*.

Outlook Bar   The bar at the left side of Outlook's Information viewers that contains shortcuts to Information viewers and other folders.

Outlook Express   See *Microsoft Outlook Express*.

Outlook Today   An Outlook window that provides a summary of information relevant to the current day and next few days.

Outlook Web Access (OWA)   The capability of Outlook to access Web pages.

OWA   See *Outlook Web Access*.

Pane   An area within a window that contains related information. See *Preview Pane*.

Password   A private sequence of characters a user types to gain access to a computer, to specific applications running on a computer, and to specific files. In Outlook, information services can be set up so a password is necessary to use them.

Password Authentication   The process by which a server verifies the validity of a user's password.

Peer-to-Peer Network   A network in which each connected computer can be a client and a server.

Permission   A permission allows a user to have access to a shared resource such as a disk drive or a printer. Also see *Right*.

Personal   A folder that contains a list of documents recently created in, or modified by, an Office application running under Windows NT. Also see *My Documents*.

Personal Address Book   An address book that contains an Outlook user's personal list of people's names and information about those people. Available only in C/W Outlook.

Personal Folders File (PST)   A file that contains folders in which Outlook saves items.

Personal Folders   The set of folders in which Outlook stores items. Outlook creates a separate folder for each type of item. Users can add their own hierarchies of folders and subfolders and subsequently move items from one to another.

Personal Information Manager (PIM)   An application used to save and manage personal information including a calendar, an address book, and a to-do list.

PIM   See *Personal Information Manager*.

Point-to-Point Protocol (PPP)   An industry standard protocol used to access remote computers by way of a dial-up connection. Many Internet service providers use this protocol. See *Internet Message Access Protocol 4 (IMAP4)* and *Serial Line Internet Protocol (SLIP)*.

Polling   The process of periodically connecting to a messaging service to ascertain whether messages are waiting and, if so, to move those messages into the Inbox. At the same time, any messages for that service waiting in the Outbox are sent.

POP3   See *Post Office Protocol 3*.

Post   To place a message on a public folder on a server such as Exchange Server, or on a news server.

Post Office Protocol 3 (POP3)   A messaging protocol commonly used by Internet messaging service providers. Messages you receive are transmitted in POP3 format. Outlook includes support for this protocol

Postoffice   A facility on a network that maintains information, including mailbox addresses, about each user and manages the process of sending and receiving messages.

PPP   See *Point-to-Point Protocol*.

Presentation Data   One of the two types of data associated with an OLE object (the other type is Native Data). Presentation data consists of all the data needed by an application to render the object on a display device. See *Native Data*.

Preview Pane   The area within Outlook's Inbox Information viewer that contains previews of received messages.

Private   Items, such as appointments and contacts, that are marked so they are only available to the person who created them.

Profile   A set of information that defines how a specific person uses Outlook. A profile defines the information services to be used and passwords required to access those services. Each profile may be protected by a password.

Project   See *Microsoft Project*.

Property   A characteristic of an icon, form, or an object on a form. Properties include such characteristics as a name, the position of an object on a form, the font used by the object, and various settings.

Protocol   A set of rules that define how computers communicate. A protocol may contain other protocols.

PST   See *Personal Folder File*.

Public Folder   A folder maintained on a server, such as Exchange Server, that can be accessed by users who have access to the server.

RAM   See *Random Access Memory*.

Random Access Memory (RAM)   The memory within a computer in which currently executing programs and information being processed is stored.

RAS   See *Remote Access Service*.

Read Receipt   See *Internet Read Receipt*.

Real-time Clock   The clock within a computer that keeps track of the current date and time.

Recall   The ability to retrieve a message that has been sent. Under some circumstances, Outlook can recall messages that recipients haven't read.

Recipient   A person (mailbox) to whom a message is addressed.

Recurring   An appointment, event, or meeting that occurs regularly.

Registry   Windows files that maintain up-to-date information about a computer's hardware and software configuration, and also about users. Outlook's profiles, Master Category Lists, and other information are maintained in the registry. The registry has a tree-like structure; branches of the tree contain keys, many of which are divided into subkey components.

Reminder   A visual or audible warning Outlook gives a certain time before an item is due. Outlook can provide reminders before appointments, meetings, events, and task due dates.

Remote Access Service (RAS)   In Windows NT, the capability of a client computer to access a server by way of a dialed telephone connection, and the capability of a server to be accessed in this way. Also known as *Dial-up Networking*.

Remote Mail   The facility for working with e-mail at a computer that is not connected permanently to a mail server.

Replication   The process of maintaining up-to-date copies of data in various locations.

Resolve   The process by which Outlook checks message recipient names entered into the Message form by comparing them with names in Address Books, and automatically uses the appropriate e-mail address.

Resource   A facility, such as a conference room, or piece of equipment, such as a projector, that can be scheduled for use at a meeting. In some applications, people are referred to as resources.

Rich Text Format (RTF)   A method of formatting text so documents can be transferred between various applications running on different platforms. Outlook can use RTF.

RichEdit   One of the text editors available within Outlook for creating and editing messages.

Right   A right gives a user access to a domain or a computer. Also see *Permission*.

RPC   See *Remote Procedure Call*.

RTC   See *Real-time Clock*.

RTF   See *Rich Text Format*.

Rule   A directive for how messages are to be handled by Outlook or Exchange Server. In Outlook, the Rules Wizard leads you through the process of creating rules.

S/MIME   See *Secure Multipurpose Internet Mail Extensions*.

Schedule+   A scheduling application provided with Office 95 and now superseded by the scheduling facilities within Outlook. Schedule+ was supplied in some versions of Exchange Server.

Search Engine   An application that searches the Internet to find pages and newsgroups that contain information that matches specific criteria.

Secure Multipurpose Internet Mail Extensions (S/MIME)   An extension of the MIME protocol that incorporates security provisions. The implementation of S/MIME in Outlook includes digital signing and encryption.

Sender   The person who sends a message, or the person on behalf of whom a message is sent.

Sensitivity   In Outlook, a sender can mark a message as having normal, personal, private, or confidential sensitivity. A message recipient cannot change the sensitivity.

Sent Item   A message that has been sent to a mail server. Outlook automatically moves Sent Items from the Outbox subfolder to the Sent Items folder.

Sent Items   The Outlook Information viewer that displays messages that have been sent. Items displayed in this Information viewer are stored in the Sent Items folder.

Serial Line Internet Protocol (SLIP)   An industry standard protocol used to access remote computers by way of a dial-up connection. Some Internet service providers use this protocol. See *Internet Message Access Protocol 4 (IMAP4)* and *Point-to-Point Protocol (PPP)*.

Server   A computer, or the software running on that computer, that provides services to client computers. One server computer may have several server applications; for example a server computer running under Windows NT Server may provide SQL Server and Exchange Server (and other) services.

Service Provider   An organization that provides access to a computer-related service. An Internet service provider (ISP) provides access to the Internet.

Shared Folder   A folder on a server to which several or many users have access so they can share information.

Shortcut   A link to information in a folder or to an application.

Shortcut Menu   See *Context Menu*.

Signature   Text that Outlook can automatically incorporate into all messages you send. Most often used to sign messages.

Simple Mail Transport Protocol (SMTP)   A protocol used by the Internet for transmitting messages. Messages you send are submitted to an e-mail server in SMTP format. Outlook includes support for this protocol.

SLIP   See *Serial Line Internet Protocol*.

SMS   See *System Management Server*.

SMTP   See *Simple Mail Transport Protocol*.

Snail Mail   A slang name for conventional mail delivered by a traditional postal service.

SPX   See *Sequenced Package Exchange*.

Stationery   A pattern or background that Outlook can add to the messages you send.

Status Bar   The row at the bottom of a window that displays certain information about what is displayed in the rest of the window. The status bar at the bottom of Outlook's Information viewers displays the number of items in the displayed viewer.

Status Report   Information about the progress of a task assigned to another person.

STF   See *Setup Table File*.

Store   The location within a server where information is stored.

Subfolder   A component of a folder. In Outlook, a folder may have many subfolders. Each subfolder contains items of a specific type and may contain other subfolders.

Subject   A brief description of an appointment, event, meeting, or message.

Subkey   A component of a Windows registry key.

Subscribe   To become a regular user of a facility. By subscribing to a newsgroup, you can easily find that newsgroup.

Swap   To move data between memory (RAM) and disk. Swapping allows an operating system to have access to much more memory than actually exists as physical RAM. See *RAM*.

Synchronize   To copy data from one folder to another so both folders contain the most recent data.

System Tray   A box at the right end of the Windows Taskbar which may contain the current time and icons that provide access to the battery meter, dial-up networking monitor, fax monitor, mouse properties, PC Card status, volume control, and other facilities. Outlook displays an icon in the system tray when mail is received.

Table   Information arranged in rows and columns. In Outlook, a Table view displays items with one item in each row. Each column contains information in a specific field.

TAP   See *Telelocator Alpha-Paging Protocol*.

TAPI   See *Telephony Application Programming Interface*.

Task   An Outlook item that describes something to be done. A task may have a due date and start date. The person who creates a Task item can assign that task to another person. A person who receives an assigned task can accept or reject the assignment, and can reassign it to someone else.

Taskbar   The bottom row of the Windows Desktop that displays the Start button and buttons representing each active application.

TaskPad   The pane at the bottom-left of the Calendar Information viewer that contains a list of current tasks.

Tasks   The Outlook Information viewer that displays Information about tasks. Items displayed in this Information viewer are stored in the Tasks folder.

TCP   See *Transmission Control Protocol*.

TCP/IP See *Transmission Control Protocol/Internet Protocol*.

Team Manager See *Microsoft Team Manager*.

Telelocator Alpha-Paging Protocol (TAP) A protocol used by alphanumeric pagers. Alphanumeric pagers decode information received in the TAP protocol and display that information on their screens. Don't confuse the TAP protocol with the ATAPI and TAPI protocols. See *AT Attachment Protocol Interface* and *Telelocator Alpha-Paging Protocol*.

Telephony Applications Programming Interface (TAPI) A protocol that controls how Windows applications interact with the telephone system. Don't confuse the TAPI protocol with the ATAPI and TAP protocols. See *ATAPI* and *TAP*.

Template An Outlook item that can be used as the basis for creating other items.

Thread Related messages in a newsgroup. See *Conversation*.

Timex Data Link A protocol for transmitting information to a Timex Data Link watch and to other compatible devices.

Timeline A view of Journal and other items plotted in relation to time.

ToolTip The temporary box that appears under a toolbar button to identify that button.

Toolbar The row (usually under the menu bar) containing buttons that provide quick access to often-used facilities. Toolbars are components of *Command Bars*.

Transmission Control Protocol (TCP) The protocol that controls delivery of sequenced data.

Transmission Control Protocol/Internet Protocol (TCP/IP) A combination of the TCP and IP protocols that controls message routing and delivery.

Tree A term used to describe the structure of the Windows registry.

UCT See *Universal Coordinated Time*.

UNC See *Universal Naming Convention*.

Universal Inbox See *Inbox*.

Universal Naming Convention (UNC) A format for naming files and resources on a network. The format is:

```
\\servername\path\resourcename
```

or

```
\\servername\path\filename
```

Uniform Resource Locator (URL) The address of a resource on the World Wide Web (WWW).

Universal Coordinated Time (UCT) An international, geography-independent way of specifying time. UCT was formally known as Greenwich Mean Time (GMT).

URL   See *Uniform Resource Locator*.

Usenet   See *Newsgroup*.

User   The person using Outlook or another application.

User Account   A person having access to a network is said to have a user account.

UUENCODE   A utility that converts binary information into 7-bit ASCII characters. After conversion, these characters can be transmitted using a text-only e-mail system. At the receiving end, the UUDECODE utility is used to convert the text back into binary format. This system has been mostly replaced by the MIME format. UUENCODE is also used as a name for the format in which converted messages are transmitted. See *MIME*.

VB   See *Visual Basic*.

VBA   See *Visual Basic for Applications*.

VBS   See *Visual Basic Script*.

vCalendar   A format by which meeting request information can be sent and received by way of the Internet. Outlook supports vCalendar.

vCard   A format by which contact information can be sent and received by way of the Internet. Outlook supports vCard.

View   A manner in which Outlook displays information in an Information viewer. A user can select from several standard views and also create custom views. Outlook uses views as formats for printing items.

Visual Basic (VB)   A programming environment (much more than a programming language) based on *BASIC*, that can be used to create Windows applications.

Visual Basic for Applications (VBA)   Dialects of Visual Basic that are tailored for developing applications for Office components (Access, Excel, PowerPoint, and Word).

Visual Basic Scripting Edition (VBS)   A subset of Visual Basic for Applications, originally developed for working with hypertext documents, but now also used for developing extended capabilities in Outlook.

Voting   A capability of Outlook and other MAPI-compatible applications for sending a message in which recipients are asked to reply indicating their choice among two or more answers to a question.

WAN   See *Wide Area Network*.

Web Folder   An Outlook facility that keeps track of information you've accessed on the World Wide Web.

Web Page   A group of related HTML documents, together with associated databases, files, and scripts accessible by way of the World Wide Web.

Wide Area Network (WAN)   A network that covers an area larger than a single building.

Wildcard   A character that represents one or more other characters. "$" used as a wildcard represents any one character; "*" used as a wildcard represents any number of characters.

Window   An area of a display screen that provides access to an operating system or application, and contains information relating to that system or application.

Windows Messaging System (WMS)   A predecessor of Outlook that was also known as Exchange Client.

Wizard   A sequence of windows that helps a user step through what might otherwise be a complex operation.

WMS   See *Windows Messaging System*.

Word   See *Microsoft Word*.

WordMail   A name used to refer to the Word word processor when it is used as the Outlook e-mail editor.

Workgroup   Two or more people using Windows 95 or Windows NT Client whose computers are connected to form a peer-to-peer network.

World Wide Web (WWW)   Hypertext servers interconnected by way of the Internet that give users access to text, graphics, video, and sound files.

WWW   See *Worldwide Web*.

Y2000   The year 2000. Due to the way dates are handled in some operating systems and applications, errors can occur when dates after December 31, 1999 are encountered. Also known as *Y2K*.

Zip Drive   A disk drive that accepts a removable disk capable of storing 100MB or more of information. Zip drives are supplied by Iomega Corporation.

Zipped File   A file compressed in a format introduced by PkWare. Zipped files normally have .zip as the file name extension.

INDEX

D

images. *See* graphics

Imaging for Windows, 260

IMAP4 (Internet Mail Access Protocol 4), 39, 660

Immediate window (VBA), 1197

IMO (Internet Mail Only) Outlook, 17, 51, 53
/select switch, 37
accounts (e-mail), 894-896
advantages, 650
automatically creating Contact items, 854
changing to C/W (Corporate or Workgroup), 1286
closing, 29, 37
configuring, 1286, 1288
Contact form, 302
Contact items, 355
default store (folders), 919-920
dial-up connection, 896
digital signatures, 53
directory services, 352-353
distribution lists, 334
faxing, 53
folder access, 996-999
free/busy information, 396
Internet account, 64-65, 67-69
Internet Mail servers, 999-1001
LDAP directory services, 349-350
MAPI, 53
message formats, 869-870
Net Folders, 53
Other Shortcuts section (Outlook Bar), 23
overview, 51, 53
Personal Folders file, 498-499

reconfiguring mail support, 896
sending and receiving faxes, 128
Tracking Options dialog box, 852
WinFax SE. *See* WinFax SE
workgroups, 649
working remotely, 730-731, 754-755

Import and Export command (File menu), 331, 567, 571, 573, 578, 599

Import and Export Wizard
exporting Outlook items
from/to Windows applications, 576
to Personal Folders file, 571, 573
importing
archived items to original folders, 599-600
data from databases, 578-580
messages from Outlook Express, 567-568
Outlook items from Personal Folders file, 573-575
Outlook items from PIMs, 576
vCards, 331
Outlook items from/to Windows applications, 576

Import button (Internet Accounts dialog box), 277

Import Registry File command (Registry menu), 1333

Import Registry File dialog box (Registry), 1333

Importance drop-down list (Message Options dialog box), 781

importing
archived items, 599-601
contact information, 331, 578-580
data (from/to)
Access databases, 1244-1247
Access tables, 1264-1267
databases, 578-580
Excel worksheets, 581
Excel worksheets tables, 1267-1269
Word letter tables, 1269, 1271-1273
Digital IDs from backup disks, 1008
Internet accounts, 74
messages from Outlook Express, 566, 568
other application information at startup, 566
Outlook items (from)
dBASE, 576
Personal Folders file, 573-575
PIMs, 576
Windows applications, 576
industry-standard file formats, 577
intermediate file format, 577
public keys from Outlook Express, 1020-1021
Registry files, 1333
rules, 639-640
troubleshooting, 602
vCards, 331
Word Mail Merge data files, 329

J

Special Edition Using Microsoft Outlook 2000
by Gordon Padwick

Thank you for purchasing *Special Edition Using Microsoft Outlook 2000* by Gordon Padwick, the most comprehensive book for Microsoft Outlook users. Please help us improve the next edition of *Special Edition Using Microsoft Outlook 2* best fit your needs by taking a few minutes to answer these questions and then returning the survey to us.

You can tear out this form and mail it to the address on the reverse side.

Does your job involve training other users to use Microsoft Outlook or Microsoft Office software, or supporting other users in a help desk setting?
❏　Yes　　　　❏　No

Did you purchase Outlook as part of Microsoft Office or as a standalone product?
❏　Standalone (please skip to question 4)　　　　❏ Part of Office 2000 (please answer question 3)

Which version of Microsoft Office 2000 do you own?
❏　Standard　　　　　　　❏　Professional　　　　　❏　Developer Edition
❏　Small Business Edition　　❏　Premium Edition　　　❏　Not Sure

Do you have Microsoft Outlook for personal use or professional use?
❏　Personal　　　　❏　Professional　　　　❏　Both

Did you buy this book for personal use or professional use?
❏　Personal　　　　❏　Professional　　　　❏　Both

Where did you buy this book?
❏　Bookstore　　　　　❏　Direct from Publisher　　❏　Warehouse Club　　　❏　Internet Site
❏　Computer Store　　　❏　Office Club　　　　　　❏　Department Store　　　❏　Consumer Electronics Store
❏　Mail Order　　　　　❏　Other _____

What operating system do you have on the computer(s) on which you use Outlook 2000?
❏　Windows 95　　　❏　Windows 98　　　❏　Windows NT 4　　　❏　Windows 2000　　　❏　Not Sure

What other Que *Special Edition Using* books about Microsoft Office 2000 applications have you bought or do you plan to buy?

Special Edition Using Microsoft Office 2000
❏　Bought　　　❏　Plan to buy

Special Edition Using Microsoft Word 2000
❏　Bought　　　❏　Plan to buy

Special Edition Using Microsoft Excel 2000
❏　Bought　　　❏　Plan to buy

Special Edition Using Microsoft PowerPoint 2000
❏　Bought　　　❏　Plan to buy

Special Edition Using Microsoft Access 2000
❏　Bought　　　❏　Plan to buy

Special Edition Using Microsoft FrontPage 2000
❏　Bought　　　❏　Plan to buy

Special Edition Using Microsoft Publisher 2000
❏　Bought　　　❏　Plan to buy

Please rate the following factors in making your decision to buy this book:
1 = Very Important　　　2 = Somewhat Important　　　3 = Not Important

Que brand name reputation	1	2	3	*Special Edition Using* brand name reputation	1 2 3
Author reputation	1	2	3	Price of book	1 2 3
Length of book	1	2	3	Description of book on cover	1 2 3
Thorough comparison of coverage versus other books	1	2	3	Contents of CD-ROM with book	1 2 3
Store clerk recommendation	1	2	3	Recommendation of coworker, colleague, or friend	1 2 3
Other _____	1	2	3		

Please rate the quality of the *Signature Tips* in this book:
❏　Excellent　　　❏　Good　　　❏　Fair　　　❏　Poor

...riate box for each application to indicate how often you use the Office 2000 applications and what
...er yourself with each:

| | I use this program... | | | | | I consider my user level for this program. | | |
	daily	1-3 hours daily	A few minutes daily	Less than once a week	Never	Beginner	Intermediate	Expert
	❏	❏	❏	❏	❏	❏	❏	❏
Excel	❏	❏	❏	❏	❏	❏	❏	❏
PowerPoint	❏	❏	❏	❏	❏	❏	❏	❏
Publisher	❏	❏	❏	❏	❏	❏	❏	❏
Access	❏	❏	❏	❏	❏	❏	❏	❏
FrontPage	❏	❏	❏	❏	❏	❏	❏	❏
Outlook	❏	❏	❏	❏	❏	❏	❏	❏
PhotoDraw	❏	❏	❏	❏	❏	❏	❏	❏

11. **Please evaluate the amount and the level of coverage in this book for each Outlook topic:**

| | Amount of coverage | | | Level of coverage | | |
	Not Enough	The right amount	Too much	Too low-level	The right level	Too advanced
Formatting	❏	❏	❏	❏	❏	❏
Formulas	❏	❏	❏	❏	❏	❏
Functions	❏	❏	❏	❏	❏	❏
Charting	❏	❏	❏	❏	❏	❏
Lists and databases	❏	❏	❏	❏	❏	❏
PivotTables	❏	❏	❏	❏	❏	❏
Analysis Tools	❏	❏	❏	❏	❏	❏
Integration with other applications	❏	❏	❏	❏	❏	❏

12. **Please write any additional comments about this book, either positive or negative, here.**

13. **Please write today's date here.** _____

Please print your name and sign here if you give Macmillan Computer Publishing permission to use your comments in marketing, sales, or promotional material related to this book.

_____   _____

Print Name   Signature

FOLD HERE AND TAPE TO MAIL

- -

ı··ıı··ıı···ı·ıı·ıııı····ıı·ı·ıı·ı···ıı·ı·ı·ı

Office 2000 Survey
Macmillan Computer Publishing
201 West 103rd Street
Indianapolis, IN 46290

SPECIAL OFFER

The OfficeReady™ templates you're using are just a selection from the 650 templates offered in the complete version of OfficeReady.

If you're enjoying the time-saving benefits of these professionally designed, ready-to-use templates, just imagine having templates for nearly every task you perform using Microsoft® Office.

It's easy. All of the additional templates are already located on your OfficeReady CD-ROM. You'll immediately be able to use them for all of the work you do using Microsoft Office. Even better, you'll have all 650 templates for only $19.95. That's 50% off the normal retail price!

Ordering is easy. Just call 1-800-385-2155. All of the additional templates are already located on your CD-ROM. You'll be issued a password to unlock the templates.

Designing documents in Microsoft Office can take up hours of your valuable time. Now, for only $19.95, you can save that time, and devote it to something that makes sense – like your business.

Offer subject to availability. Prices subject to change without notice.